VOLUME 1 • REVISED EDITION

The Development of Civilization
A DOCUMENTARY HISTORY OF POLITICS, SOCIETY, AND THOUGHT

VOLUME 1 · REVISED EDITION

The Development of Civilization
A DOCUMENTARY HISTORY OF POLITICS, SOCIETY, AND THOUGHT

HARRY J. CARROLL, JR. *Pomona College*
AINSLIE T. EMBREE *Columbia University*
KNOX MELLON, JR. *Immaculate Heart College*
ARNOLD SCHRIER *University of Cincinnati*
ALASTAIR M. TAYLOR *Queen's University*

SCOTT, FORESMAN AND COMPANY

Library of Congress Catalog Card No. 69-17828.
Copyright © 1961, 1969 by Scott, Foresman and Company, Glenview, Illinois 60025.
Philippines Copyright 1969 by Scott, Foresman and Company.
All Rights Reserved. Printed in the United States of America.
Regional offices of Scott, Foresman and Company are located in Atlanta, Dallas, Glenview, Palo Alto, Oakland, N.J., and London, England.

PREFACE TO THE REVISED EDITION

We are gratified that the first edition of *The Development of Civilization* has been so well received. Its usefulness in survey courses in colleges and universities around the country has encouraged us to bring out a revised edition. The basic organization of this revision remains essentially the same. The principal changes are the addition of new source materials and more recent interpretations in virtually every part.

A major purpose of a textbook recording man's history is to enable the student to approach his present world with an understanding of the institutions and ideas that went to shape it. The purpose of a volume of historical readings is to give a measure of realism and depth to this understanding, as well as to present some of the sources from which historians have evolved their interpretations of the past. No amount of summary can convey the sense of immediacy and reality to events and issues as can the actual words of those who were the active players in the historical drama. Moreover, a variety of source readings, coupled with the varying, sometimes conflicting, interpretations of professional scholars, will help the student to realize that there is no one answer on how to view the past. Our written historical records were penned and transmitted by fallible human beings whose accuracy and viewpoint, despite the best of objective intentions, are open to question. A historian may be defined as a sifter and organizer of these records who tries to arrive at an interpretation of history which seems to him closest to truth. To such detailed efforts the historian brings a trained critical sense. This critical sense in students can be aroused only in modest measure by the study of any single documentary account. But it is an effective way to stimulate the student's interest, to begin to sharpen his historical sense, and to introduce him to the methods of the social sciences and the humanities.

In order to accomplish these aims, we have chosen readings that challenge the student to think about his global heritage, to reflect on and interpret it. He is given original sources, the basic material with which the professional scholar works. He is presented, at clearly indicated intervals, with historical interpretations evolved by scholars from the available evidence of the past. "Great works" and "great men" are liberally represented. We chose them not primarily for their literary worth but rather for the specific arguments that they offer the student in developing critical thinking. It has not been our intention merely to "polish" the student's education with classics or to present him with historical curiosities. The student is being challenged to discriminate between bias and fact, between useful and fallacious generalizations, and to develop a comprehension of historical method. To help guide his reading, the student is provided with a careful framework of introductions and headnotes that go beyond merely identifying specific items; they relate the selections to the broad flow of history and point the way to a discriminate appraisal of the selections.

We editors are also convinced that a critical awareness on the part of the student requires his recognition that his present heritage descends from ideas and institutions gathered from all parts of the globe. The American is indebted not only to his European ancestors and contemporaries but also to the ancient and modern civilizations of the Near East, India, the Orient, and Africa. Several basic survey texts have appeared in the past two decades to meet the growing demand for universality, but until the appearance of *The Development of Civilization* there was no single readings text which attempted to encompass the globe from the early ages of literate society up to our present day.

The general breadth of these volumes will be apparent from an examination of the table of contents. Sources are conceived in their widest sense, everything from diaries to speeches, from inscribed tablets to books, from petitions to laws. The history of the world is a record of changing political entities, but it is also a flow of social, economic, and cultural forces. Within the six parts of each volume we have tried to exhibit a comprehensive range. Selections and editorial comment have been made with an eye to teachability as well as to the general ideas and values underlying a wide span of history. Aware of the varieties of taste and judgment among teachers and the varieties of aptitude among students, we have tried to preserve a balance of coverage and emphasis without trying to accomplish the vain task of pleasing everyone. The organization is topical as well as chronological and editorially provides for continuity or contrast between selections. But flexibility has been sufficiently maintained to allow any rearrangement to suit one's teaching purposes, whether the text be used for world or western history courses, for "civilizations" courses, or for any variety of classes in humanities.

While each of us has generally made his contributions in those fields in which he is most at home, we have collectively been at great pains to make sure that the book has the character of a unified product. We have received advice from one another and have reached what we hope to be a coherence of organization and approach. Harry J. Carroll, Jr., and Knox Mellon, Jr., conceived the original idea of the book. They assumed primary responsibility for the selections and editorial headnotes in Parts Two, Three, and Four of Volume I and the Age of the Enlightenment in Volume II, and supplied as well the first tentative outlines for the other "western" chapters. Arnold Schrier handled the selections and headnotes for Part Five of Volume I and the American and French revolutions and Parts Two, Three, and Five of Volume II. Ainslie T. Embree of Columbia's Committee on Oriental Studies took primary responsibility for all "nonwestern" selections and editorial headnotes. Alastair M. Taylor wrote all part introductions and provided valuable advice at every stage of selection and editing.

We wish to express our gratitude for the contributions of our colleagues and students at Pomona College, Columbia University, Immaculate Heart College, the University of Cincinnati, and Queen's University, who have helped to inform our views of history, the humanities, and of pedagogy, as partially reflected in *The Development of Civilization*. The library staffs of these respective institutions and the editorial personnel of Scott, Foresman and Company gave assistance and guidance for which there is no adequate expression of thanks.

Harry J. Carroll, Jr., Ainslie T. Embree,
Knox Mellon, Jr., Arnold Schrier,
Alastair M. Taylor

CONTENTS

PART ONE
ANCIENT CIVILIZATIONS OF THE NEAR EAST

Introduction 4

EGYPT: THE ACHIEVEMENT OF STABILITY
1. Hymns to the Sun and to the Nile: Life in an Ordered Cosmos 9
2. Hymns to a Pharaoh, Sesostris III: The Role of the King 12
3. The Instruction in Wisdom of the Vizier Ptah-Hotep: The Good Life 14

MESOPOTAMIA: THE SEARCH FOR WORLD ORDER
4. The Creation Epic: The Struggle to Maintain Order Against Chaos 17
5. The Descent of Ishtar into the Underworld:
   The Meaning of the Fertility Cult 20
6. A Sumerian Epic: A Record of Primitive Democracy 23
7. The Code of Hammurabi: The Legal System and Social Custom 24

ISRAEL: THE CONCEPT OF A CHOSEN PEOPLE
8. The Book of the Prophet Isaiah: The Significance of Monotheism 31
9. The Fifth Book of Moses, Called Deuteronomy:
   The Burden of Being Chosen 33
10. The Second Book of Kings: The Nature of History 35
11. The Dead Sea Scrolls: The Community of God's People 38

INTERPRETATIONS OF THE ANCIENT CIVILIZATIONS OF THE NEAR EAST
12. Henri Frankfort, "Myth and Reality":
    The Relation Between Myth and Reality 41
13. V. Gordon Childe, "A Prehistorian's Interpretation of Diffusion":
    The Diffusion of Ancient Cultures 47

PART TWO
CLASSICAL CIVILIZATION: GREECE AND ROME

Introduction 54

"THE GLORY THAT WAS GREECE"

Old and New: The Individual and Society
14. Homer, *Iliad:* The Tradition of Heroic Individualism 59
15. Xenophon, *The Constitution of the Lacedaemonians:*
    The Civic Education of Spartan Youth 65

Greek and Barbarian
16. Herodotus, *History of the Persian Wars:*
    The Greeks in Their Finest Hour 68

Athenian Democracy
17. Sophocles, *Antigone:* A Debate on Law and Individual Obligation 73
18. Thucydides, *History of the Peloponnesian War:*
    Democracy and Power Politics 78
19. The "Old Oligarch," *The Constitution of the Athenians:*
    A Critique of Democracy 83

Interpretations of Athenian Democracy
  20 G. B. Grundy, *Thucydides and the History of His Age:*
      The Paradox of Greek Individualism................................. 86
  21 Alfred Zimmern, *The Greek Commonwealth:* Athens, the Model State....... 89

Alexander and the Hellenistic World
  22 Arrian, *Anabasis of Alexander,* and Plutarch, "On the Fortune or the
      Virtue of Alexander": The World Conqueror in the World State............ 91

Interpretation of the Hellenistic World
  23 Sir William W. Tarn, *Hellenistic Civilisation:*
      A Modern View of Hellenism....................................... 96

The Greek Mind
  24 Hippocrates, "On the Sacred Disease": Rational Medical Inquiry........... 98
  25 Plato, *Apology:* Socrates and Intellectual Integrity........................100
  26 Aristotle, *Politics:* Social Order and Liberal Education....................103

"THE GRANDEUR THAT WAS ROME"

The Republic
  27 Livy, *From the Founding of the City:*
      The Fall of the Tarquins and the Rise of the Republic....................107
  28 Polybius, *Histories:* The Balance of Power in the Roman Republic..........110

The Collapse of the Republic
  29 Cicero, *Laws:* A Conservative's View of Law and the Republic.............114
  30 Brutus, Cassius, Cicero, and Antony, *Letters:* The Legacy of Caesar........118

Interpretations of the Collapse of the Republic
  31 Ronald Syme, *The Roman Revolution:* The Myth of Caesar...............123
  32 Theodor Mommsen, *The History of Rome:* The Hero in History...........129

The Golden Age of Imperial Rome
  33 Augustus, *Res Gestae:* The Accounting of an Emperor....................133
  34 Virgil, *Aeneid* and *Eclogue IV:* Roman Destiny and Christian Prophecy......135

The High Empire
  35 Seneca, "On the God Within Us":
      The Stoic Ideal and the Imperial Aristocracy...........................139
  36 Juvenal, *Satire III:* The Urban Problem.................................141
  37 Pliny the Younger, *Letters:* A Roman Gentleman of the Old School..........143
  38 Tacitus, *Agricola:* A Barbarian's View of Roman Civilization...............145

PART THREE
DECLINE AND RESURGENCE:
CHRISTIANITY, THE TWO EMPIRES, AND ISLAM

Introduction...150

THE RISE OF CHRISTIANITY AND THE FALL OF ROME

The Birth and Growth of Christianity
  39 The Gospel According to Saint Matthew: The Sermon on the Mount.......155
  40 The Epistle of Paul the Apostle to the Romans:
      The Old Law and the New Gospel....................................159
  41 Pliny the Younger and the Emperor Trajan, *Letters:*
      The Christians and Roman Security...................................163
  42 Apuleius, *Metamorphoses:* The Rival Mystery Cults......................165
  43 Minucius Felix, *Octavius:* A Dialogue Between Christian and Pagan........166
  44 Lactantius, *On the Manner in Which the Persecutors Died:*
      Constantine and the Triumph of Christianity..........................169

45 Eusebius, *Life of Constantine the Great*:
    The Arian Controversy and Christian Unity..........................171

The Decline of Rome and the Barbarians

46 The Edict of Diocletian: Legislation for Social and Economic Reform.......176
47 Tacitus, *Germania*: German Tribal Society.............................178
48 Jordanes, *History of the Goths*: The Barbarian Invasions................181

The Age of the Church Fathers

49 *The Rule of St. Benedict*:
    Renunciation of a Troubled World—the Monasteries....................186
50 Venerable Bede, *Ecclesiastical History of the English People*:
    The Conversion of the Heathen......................................190
51 St. Augustine, the *Confessions*: The Conversion of a Church Father.......193

Interpretations of the Rise of Christianity and the Fall of Rome

52 Edward Gibbon, *The Decline and Fall of the Roman Empire*:
    A Rationalist's Appraisal of the Fall of Rome.........................196
53 Michael Rostovtzeff, *Social and Economic History of the Roman Empire*:
    Changing Historical Views of Rome...................................198

THE BYZANTINE EMPIRE

54 Procopius, *History of the Wars* and *Secret Histories*:
    Justinian and the Foundations of the Byzantine Empire.................203
55 Letter of the Second Council of Nicaea to Emperor Constantine VI and
    Empress Irene: The Iconoclastic Controversy and the East-West Schism.....209
56 Michael Psellus, *Chronographia*: The Height of the Byzantine Empire.......212
57 *The Russian Primary Chronicle*:
    The Byzantine Conversion of a Russian Prince.........................216

Interpretation of the Byzantine Empire

58 Peter Charanis, "Economic Factors in the Decline of the
    Byzantine Empire": A Modern Interpretation..........................221

ISLAM

59 *The Koran*: The Faith of Muhammad...................................227
60 Ibn-Said, *Book of the Maghrib*: The Muslims in Politics and War..........232
61 Avicenna, "Autobiography," and Al-Juzjani, "Biography of Avicenna":
    The "Renaissance Man" in the Muslim World..........................236

Interpretation of Islam

62 H. A. R. Gibb, *Mohammedanism*: The Expansion of Islam................241

PART FOUR
THE MIDDLE AGES

Introduction..250

EUROPE'S SEARCH FOR STABILITY

The Quest for Empire

63 Einhard, *Life of Charlemagne*: The Carolingian Empire of the Franks.......256
64 *Anglo-Saxon Chronicle*: William the Conqueror.........................261

Feudalism and the Medieval Economy

65 *Assizes of Romania*: Feudalism.......................................263
66 *Seneschaucie*: Manorialism...268
67 William fitz Stephen, "A Description of the Most Noble City of London":
    The Rise of Town and Trade..271
68 Charter Grants of Emperor Frederick I: Medieval Fairs...................274
69 Statute of Laborers: The Crisis of Medieval Economy....................277
70 Jean Froissart, *Chronicles*: The Wat Tyler Insurrection..................278

Interpretations of Feudalism and the Medieval Economy
- 71 Bryce Lyon, *The Middle Ages in Recent Historical Thought:* New Views on Manorialism and Feudalism..................283
- 72 Henri Pirenne, *Economic and Social History of Medieval Europe:* Origins of the Merchant Class..........................287

Chivalry and the Crusades
- 73 *Song of Roland:* The Ideals of Chivalry..................291
- 74 Decree of the Council of Toulouges: Peace of God and Truce of God.......295
- 75 Ambroise, *Crusade of Richard Lion-Heart*, and Letter of Daimbert, Godfrey, and Raymond to the Pope: The Crusades..................297

THE SPIRIT OF THE CHURCH
- 76 Pope Gregory VII, *Dictatus Papae* and Letter to the German Princes, and Henry IV, Answer to Gregory VII: Papal Supremacy..................303
- 77 St. Bernard of Clairvaux, *De Diligendo Deo* and Epistle: The Cistercian Reformer..................305
- 78 St. Francis of Assisi, *Rule:* The Order of Friars..................308
- 79 Bernard Gui, *Manual of the Inquisitor:* Heresies and the Dominican Inquisition..................311

Interpretation of the Spirit of the Church
- 80 Christopher Dawson, "Church and State in the Middle Ages": The City of God on Earth..................315

STRUGGLES FOR A NATIONAL STATE
- 81 Magna Carta: King Versus Feudal Lords—England..................320
- 82 Jean de Joinville, *Memoirs of the Crusades:* The Rising Power of the King—France..................323
- 83 Charles IV, *Golden Bull:* Constitutional Law for the Holy Roman Empire....326
- 84 Ramon Mutaner, *Chronicle:* In Search of a Christian Kingdom—Spain.......330
- 85 Giovanni Villani, *Chronicle of Florence:* The Italian City-State..................333

THE INTELLECTUAL SYNTHESIS
- 86 St. Thomas Aquinas, *Summa Theologica* and *Summa Contra Gentiles:* Medieval Scholasticism..................337
- 87 Roger Bacon, *Opus Majus:* Medieval Science..................340
- 88 Dante Alighieri, *Divine Comedy:* Literary Synthesis..................343

PART FIVE
RENAISSANCE AND REFORMATION

Introduction..................350

THE QUICKENING OF THE WEST
The Renaissance in Italy
- 89 Francesco Petrarch, Letter to Pulice di Vicenza, May 13, 1353: The Humanistic Revival..................355
- 90 Vespasiano da Bisticci, "Life of Cosimo de' Medici": The Merchant Prince..................357
- 91 Niccolò Machiavelli, *The Prince:* Machiavellian Politics..................362
- 92 Giorgio Vasari, "Leonardo da Vinci, Florentine Painter and Sculptor": The Versatile Renaissance Genius..................364

The Renaissance Beyond Italy
- 93 Desiderius Erasmus, *The Enchiridion:* The Christian Humanist..................368
- 94 Sir Thomas More, *Utopia:* Utopian Protest..................371
- 95 François Rabelais, *Gargantua and Pantagruel:* The Humanist Reformer..................373
- 96 Miguel de Cervantes Saavedra, *The Ingenious Gentleman Don Quixote de la Mancha:* Don Quixote and the Puppets..................379

Interpretations of the Renaissance

97 Jacob Burckhardt, *The Civilization of the Renaissance in Italy:* The Birth of Individualism..................383
98 Charles Homer Haskins, *The Renaissance of the Twelfth Century:* How Unique Was the Renaissance?..................385
99 Wallace K. Ferguson, "The Interpretation of the Renaissance": The Renaissance as the Transition from Medieval to Modern..............387

THE BROADENING HORIZON

New Worlds

100 *Journal of the First Voyage of Vasco da Gama:* Passage to India............392
101 Christopher Columbus, Letter to Lord Raphael Sanchez, March 14, 1493: Discovery of the New World..................395
102 Affonso de Albuquerque, Letter to King Manuel of Portugal, 1510: The Portuguese Invasion of the East..................398
103 Hernando Cortés, Letter to Emperor Charles V, October 1520: The Wonders of Mexico..................400

The Scientific Revolution

104 Nicolas Copernicus, *On the Revolutions of the Heavenly Bodies:* Man and the Universe..................406
105 Sir Francis Bacon, *Instauratio Magna:* The Call for Experimentation........409
106 René Descartes, *Discourse on Method:* The Call for Rational Skepticism.....413

Interpretations of the Broadening Horizon

107 Donald F. Lach, *Asia in the Making of Europe:* Europe and the Century of Discovery..................416
108 Alfred North Whitehead, *Science and the Modern World:* The Significance of the Scientific Revolution..................418

PROTESTANTISM AND REFORMATION

Heresies and Schisms

109 John Wycliffe, Letter to Pope Urban VI, 1384: An Early "Protestant".......420
110 John Hus, *De Ecclesia:* Nationalistic Protest..................422
111 Decrees of *Sacrosancta* and *Frequens:* The Council of Constance...........424

The Age of the Reformation

112 Luther at the Diet of Worms: "Here I Stand"..................426
113 *The Twelve Articles* and Martin Luther's Reply: The Peasant Revolt........432
114 John Calvin, *Institutes of the Christian Religion:* Calvinism...............436
115 *Act for the Exoneration from Exactions Paid to the See of Rome* and *Act of Supremacy:* Henry VIII, Supreme Head of the Church of England.........439
116 St. Ignatius Loyola, *Spiritual Exercises:* The Counter Reformation..........441

Interpretations of Protestantism and Reformation

117 R. H. Tawney, *Religion and the Rise of Capitalism:* Protestantism and Capitalism..................445
118 Hajo Holborn, *A History of Modern Germany:* Historic Results of the Reformation..................449

PART SIX
GREAT CIVILIZATIONS OF THE ORIENT:
ANCIENT AND CLASSICAL PERIODS

Introduction..................454

INDIA

The Vedic Age

119 *Rig-Veda:* The Aryan Attitude Toward Life and War..................459

120 *Upanishads:* The Nature of Reality..................................462

The First Empires and the Rise of Buddhism

121 Buddha, First Sermon on the Four Noble Truths:
     Buddhism, a New Way of Life..464
122 The Edicts of Asoka: The Attempt to Create a Unified Empire............466
123 Kautīlya, *Arthasāstra:* Practical Advice for Statesmen................469

The Hindu Synthesis

124 The Code of Manu: The Organization of Social Life into Four Classes.......473
125 Bhagavad Gitā: The Search for Salvation...............................475
126 Vishnu Purāna: The Worship of God in Many Forms.......................478
127 Rāmāyana: The Ideal of Family Life....................................480

The Coming of the Muslim Conquerors

128 Ziā ud-dīn Barnī, *Tārikh-I-Firūz Shāhī:*
     The Dilemma of the Muslim Ruler in India..............................482

Interpretation of India

129 A. L. Basham, *The Indian Sub-Continent in Historical Perspective:*
     Indian Civilization in Historical Perspective.........................484

CHINA

Concern for the Right Ordering of Society

130 Confucius, *Analects:* Government by Goodness.........................489
131 Mo Tzu: Egalitarianism and Uniformity.................................492
132 Lao Tzu: Mysticism and Anarchy..495
133 Lord Shang: Totalitarianism...496

The Creation of an Imperial Structure

134 Li Ssu, Memorial to the Emperor: The Abolition of Feudalism...........498
135 The Ministers' Memorial: The Concept of Empire........................499
136 Edicts of Kao-Tsu and Hsaio-Wen: The Creation of the Bureaucracy......500
137 Wang Mang, Edicts on Taxation and Monopoly:
     The Imperial Concern for a Sound Economy..............................501

The Flowering of Chinese Civilization

138 Wei Shou: The Ascendancy of Buddhism..................................504
139 Chu Hsi: The Confucian Revival..506
140 Wang An Shih, "Discussion of Current Affairs":
     The Reform of the Bureaucracy...508

Interpretation of China

141 J. K. Fairbank, *The United States and China:*
     The Influence of the Confucian Pattern on Chinese Society.............512

JAPAN

The Foundations of Society

142 Prince Shotoku's Constitution: The Introduction of New Ideals
     of Government...514
143 Document on Buddhism: The Arrival of Buddhism in Japan................517
144 Lady Murasaki, *The Tale of Genji:* The Cult of Beauty................519
145 Kitabatake Chikafusa, *Records of the Legitimate Succession of the Divine
     Sovereigns:* The Position of the Emperor in *Shinto* Thought..........521

Feudalism and the Shogunate

146 The Hojo Code: The Legal and Administrative Ideals of Feudalism.......522
147 Dai-ō and Hōnen: Zen, the Religious Expression of Feudalism, and Amida,
     the Religion of the Masses..526

Interpretations of Japan

148 E. O. Reischauer, *Japan, Past and Present:*
     Growth and Change in Medieval Japan...................................527
149 Sir George Sansom, *Japan, A Short Cultural History:*
     The Nature of Japanese Feudalism......................................529

Part I
Ancient Civilizations of the Near East

The temple at Luxor (opposite page); one of the Dead Sea Scrolls (top left); a seal impression showing a Sumerian trading boat carrying a bull bearing an altar and a priest (bottom left); the top of a stele showing Hammurabi receiving his code from the sun god (right).

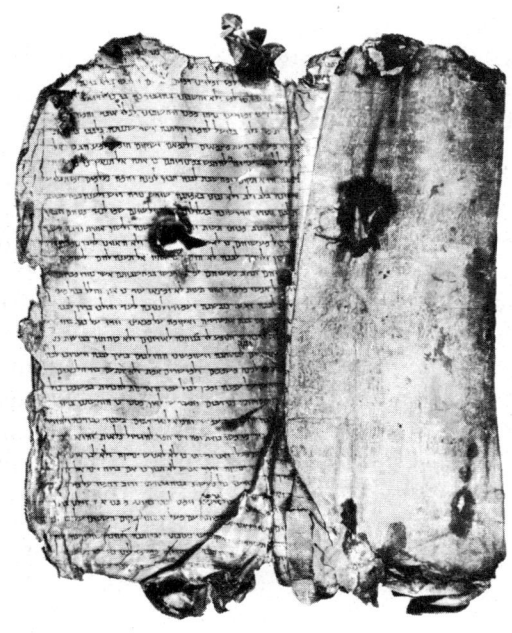

INTRODUCTION

Few words are used more often these days than *civilization*. Thus, we are constantly told that we must defend western civilization against Soviet communism. So we should—but the defense might go better if the term were more clearly understood. One historian, whose international fame rests upon his study of the rise and fall of some twenty or more civilizations, does not tell us what he means by the word. For our part, however, we intend to make the attempt because it is significant to know why, when, and where civilization arose.

Our quest goes back to the beginning of human society. The story of man's biological antecedents is long and complicated, but in any event he is set apart by virtue of his reasoning and imagination and by his ability to fashion tools and to speak, thereby communicating ideas. With his unique biological endowments, man has been no less unique in his relationships with both nature and his fellow man. For more than a million years this tool-maker has been concerned with coming to grips with his environment—and in the process has evolved one culture after another. In our own age of ever-accelerating technological change—wherein each new step but represents the end product of those million years of continuous environmental adaptation and experimentation—it is all too easy to forget how difficult the first steps were for our ancestors. Yet the fact remains that some ninety-nine per cent of man's planetary existence has been devoted to converting stone into weapons and tools for killing, cleaning, and cutting up his daily food supply. During that vast stretch of time, then, man was a savage, living a largely nomadic way of life in company with his family and fellow hunters. This era is known as the Paleolithic, or Old Stone, Age, a term that has both a technological and cultural significance. In the first instance, it refers to the development of various stone implements for the hunt and its aftermath, of which the most important was the all-purpose hand-ax. Secondly, it signifies that stage of cultural evolution when man was still a food gatherer, and therefore subject to environmental conditions almost completely beyond his control.

As the ice age melted away, many types of food animals became extinct because of overspecialization to a cold climate, while other species migrated north. In Europe the receding ice created new coastlines, and around the Baltic and elsewhere men had to adapt themselves to the changed environment by concentrating on fishing, sealing, and gathering shellfish. As a result, they passed into the Mesolithic, or Middle Stone, Age. This was characterized by the invention of more specialized weapons, such as microliths—small flints which, when mounted on shafts of wood or bone, could be used as fish spears and barbed arrows. The Mesolithic was a transitional age; from a cultural standpoint, it enabled man to become sedentary. However, it did not free him as a food collector from continued dependence upon his natural environment.

About eight thousand years ago, a momentous change occurred in human affairs. While Mesolithic communities in Europe were still based on food-gathering economies, various peoples in the Near East began the cultivation of edible plants and the domestication of animals which could be used for food or as beasts of burden. Sometimes described as the "first economic revolution" in history, this development enabled men to move progressively from a food-gathering to a food-producing type of economy. Thus was initiated the Neolithic Age, in which "savagery" was replaced by "barbarism"—a term which, in view of the splendid advances achieved, is one of distinction. Paleolithic and Mesolithic men were exclusively hunters and fishermen; our Neolithic ancestors, on the other hand, were farmers and herdsmen as well.

Characteristically, a food-producing community acquires a fixed habitation. Thus man began to control his environment to the point where he could at last "settle down" and—what is equally important—raise enough foodstuffs to support a larger population than ever before. Let us next look at the sites where the Neolithic Age originated, for they tell a story of direct concern to our quest after the why, when, and where of "civilization." According to the latest scientific dating techniques, the oldest known Neolithic settlements have been found at Jericho in Jordan and at Jarmo and Hassuna in Iraq. A primitive farming economy at Jericho (complete, incidentally, with great walls as described in the Biblical account) was made possible by the existence of a spring which created an oasis. The Iraqi settlements were situated in mountainous uplands where rainfall was greater than on the arid lowlands. In both situations, it should be noted that water—which of course is indispensable to farming—existed in a limited amount only. This limitation was decisive in restricting these Neolithic settlements both in area and in the number of people whom they could sustain. True, these communities would annually set aside some of their harvest to provide seed for the following year's planting, and they might also have enough grain left over to barter for commodities from other groups of people. But too little arable land existed for expansion in area or in population or for full-time support of those members who could specialize in pottery-making, weaving, or any other occupation besides farming. The Neolithic revolution had provided the potential for a new breakthrough in human society—but this potential could be actualized only under different physical conditions, that is, in an environment capable of producing far greater food surpluses.

Such an environment was found in the alluvial valleys of certain great rivers. Three of them lie in a broad steppe and mountain region stretching from North Africa across the Arabian peninsula and the Iranian plateau to the northern areas of the Indian subcontinent. Each of these river systems—the Nile, the Tigris-Euphrates, and the Indus-Ganges—rises in mountainous regions, then flows for hundreds of miles through flat arid stretches, during which journey its current slows and deposits a rich alluvium carried from distant uplands. The result is an immensely rich lower valley, capable of producing more than a hundred times the amount of grain sown. True, the rivers first had to be harnessed to man's needs, by draining marshes, controlling floods, and leading the life-giving waters out into the deserts on either side by means of irrigation ditches. Under man's influence, the river lands could provide food surpluses, enough to support unprecedented numbers of people and make possible the emergence of urban communities. Here specialized groups—such as priests, scribes, potters, basket-weavers, and metal-workers—could develop both the economy and society to a complexity impossible in Neolithic settlements like Jericho and Jarmo.

This is precisely what happened in those three river valleys, beginning with the Tigris-Euphrates system. To its lower valleys came various peoples; some migrated from highlands east of the Tigris, which would indicate that they were acquainted with the Neolithic cultures flourishing in Jarmo and other upland settlements. By about 4000 B.C., the lands where the rivers emptied into the Persian Gulf had evolved a complex way of life which included small city-states. There the temple priests made use of writing—on clay tablets which were afterwards baked—while their scribes in the temple granaries employed arithmetical tables to keep accounts of the city's food supply. The word *civilization* has many meanings, but a good definition must take into account a knowledge of writing and mathematics and, above all, the development of a culture to the point where its communities deserve to be called *cities*—that is, communities that are able to maintain a substantial number of specialists to cope with the religious, political, and economic needs of what has become a relatively complex society, with many levels of activity for its members.

On the basis of these criteria, we may say that the people along the lower reaches of the Tigris-Euphrates had attained civilization by the fifth millennium B.C. It only remains for us to learn what the people themselves were like, and how their society operated.

MESOPOTAMIA—THE "LAND BETWEEN RIVERS"

The fluvial origin of the first great civilization is eloquently attested to by the name which the Greeks gave the area bounded by the Tigris and Euphrates—Mesopotamia, the "land between rivers."

The ancient Egyptians and Greeks left inscriptions that we can decipher despite the ravages of time, because they were carved in stone. There was no stone in the Tigris-Euphrates basin, nor could the Mesopotamians make use of the papyrus reed that grew in the Nile delta, from which the Egyptians made the first paper. The Mesopotamians had to use clay tablets, which were inscribed with wedge-shaped impressions (cuneiform writing) and then baked. A large number of these tablets have come down to us, but the subject matter they contain is fairly narrow; many of them are nothing more than ledger accounts of trading transactions, such as a sale of grain or a purchase of slaves. Admittedly such data has much to tell the economic or social historian, but it sheds little light on the intellectual and religious aspects of Mesopotamian civilization. As with other early societies, we must recognize the role played by oral tradition. The merchants and craftsmen handed down their "trade secrets" by word of mouth to their apprentices, and much of the learning transmitted from scholar to student took the form of verses that could be committed to memory (in ancient India some Brāhmans could recite as many as 100,000 verses). The oral tradition was especially strong in what was regarded as the most important of human activities—religion. The priests believed that their learning was so sacred that to write it down was not worth the risk of its being seen by profane eyes.

Though the evidence is limited, enough has survived to enable us to reconstruct with confidence the structure and character of all the ancient fluvial civilizations. For many years, scholars have been piecing together a cultural jigsaw, from such remaining artifacts as pottery, tools, structural ruins, mortuary remains, and clay tablets, which provides us with a fair picture of the people inhabiting the alluvial plains of the Tigris and Euphrates.

Civilization first emerged in Sumer, the delta of the Tigris-Euphrates system. Once swamps had been drained and the river waters guided into transverse irrigation ditches, the rich alluvial soils gave forth unprecedented yields. The delta was organized into small city-states, chief of which was Erech, or Ur. Each city had its local god to whom honor was paid in a lofty terraced temple known as a ziggurat, where, significantly, the city granary was also kept. The most prosperous period of these Sumerian city-states lasted from about 2900 to 2400 B.C. The subsequent history of Mesopotamia is both complicated and turbulent. Attempts were made periodically to unite the Sumerians, or to compel them to accept the overlordship of Akkad (a region immediately to the north), or to bring them into the empire of the great Hammurabi, who about 1760 B.C. united all of lower Mesopotamia and whose rule centered in the magnificent new capital of Babylon on the Euphrates. Hammurabi's empire was a signal achievement, but his efficient system of administration was destined to be replaced by disunity and struggle within the sprawling river domains. Various factors account for the millennia of conflict and political fragmentation that bedeviled Mesopotamian society. One was the obstacles that hampered navigation the length of the rivers; another was the exposure of the river lands on either side to foreign invasion. A number of warring intruders swept down into the fertile valleys from the mountainous regions that curve in an area from Iran on the east to the high plateaus of Asia Minor in the north. Historically, Mesopotamia and the famous Fertile Crescent served as a cultural melting pot and as a crossroads for the trade and ideas of three continents: Asia, Africa, and Europe.

Throughout the kaleidoscopic Mesopotamian history, one thing remained constant: the life-giving sustenance of the Tigris-Euphrates. For thousands of years, the rhythm of existence kept measure with the annual flooding and ebbing of the river's current and the farmer's cycle of planting and harvesting. An agrarian society like Sumer soon found it essential to keep track of the seasons, so a lunar calendar was devised. The computation of the amount of grain harvested and the wages paid to field hands became vital, so there evolved a system of counting, based on the unit of 60 (which we still use in dividing our hours and minutes). The need to survey and measure the precious river lands led in time to working with simple geometry and algebra, while the questions of ownership and use of these lands stimulated the growth of legal authority and controls.

The river had brought environmental order out of chaos, but the possibility of political anarchy destroying what had been accomplished, resulting in the reversion of irrigated lands to desert, was always imminent. The struggle to maintain order against chaos was never-ending, and consequently became the central problem in one Sumerian epic (see Document 4). Involved too in this struggle of the river against the desert was the question of fertility—a crucial issue in any agrarian society. Fertility cults flourished in Mesopotamia and other major cultures of the ancient Near East. In the beginning these cults were concerned with the best means of propitiating the cosmic forces so as to ensure renewed life each spring in the fields. But soon more than vegetation was involved; human fertility and finally, the renewal of human life beyond the grave became matters of concern for the cults. Here can be perceived the relationship between environment and the growth of basic religious attitudes (see Document 5). Other Mesopotamian writings emphasize the role of environment, especially of the river, in controlling human life. Thus, in the epic *Gilgamesh* we find the story of a devastating flood (which later found its way into Genesis, in the account of Noah and the ark). Interestingly enough, excavations conducted at Ur reveal that a flood of disastrous proportions did occur in that region, and this might well have given rise to the epic story. Written materials which relate to Hammurabi's reign abound in references to his maintenance and construction of canals so as to "gather Sumer and Akkad's scattered folk." In still another way did the great king gather his scattered subjects together. By proclaiming his famous law code (see Document 7), he took vengeance out of private hands and made justice a function of the state—surely a major yardstick of any "civilization."

EGYPT—"GIFT OF THE NILE"

The second fluvial civilization in point of time arose along the banks of the Nile. As in Mesopotamia, environment proved to be a decisive factor in the shaping of ancient Egyptian society. There is strong evidence that during Mesolithic and Neolithic times the lands of northern Africa became increasingly arid, forcing settlers out of the Saharan and Sudanese deserts (where archaeologists have found ruins of ancient settlements). Migrants moved into areas on the Saharan perimeter, including the upper Nile, where primitive settlements began experimenting with barley and wheat cultivation as early as the close of the sixth millennium B.C. Here again, however, the breakthrough from the Neolithic stage to civilization required the utilization of water and land resources on a scale such as only the great Nile could provide.

The characteristics of the ancient Nile culture depend upon many factors. First, the river is extremely predictable in its rise and flooding, so that farmers could plan their planting and harvesting accurately. Second, there is an unbroken stretch of river from the delta to the first cataract, and navigation is further assisted by the fact that while the current runs northward, the prevailing winds blow southward, so that a sailboat can move easily in either direction. Finally, the desert to the west and a ridge of low mountains on the east (between the Nile and the Red Sea) give inhabitants of the valley considerable security from outside attack and immunity from other cultures' influences. At the same time, the land bridge which connects the delta area with the Fertile Crescent region could permit a two-way flow of trade and ideas.

As we might expect from the above, Egyptian society evolved along the banks of the Nile between the delta and the first cataract (at present-day Aswan). At first, two distinct kingdoms arose, one in Lower and the other in Upper Egypt. About 3100 B.C. they were united under a single ruler and capital, and the next thousand years brought a consolidation of the two. The Old Kingdom, as the merger was called, was remarkable for the evolution of religious concepts, including a preoccupation with life after death, the construction of the famous pyramids, and the practice of mummification. Towards the end of the third millennium B.C., Egypt was disrupted by civil wars, but the chaos created by attempts of provincial governors to become independent was ended by the reunification of the country. The resultant Middle Kingdom (2060-1785 B.C.) saw Egypt restored to its former power and its southern borders extended into the Sudan.

In time, however, Egypt was again weakened by civil strife, and its plight was compounded by the invasion of barbarian Hyksos from Asia. The expulsion of the Hyksos heralded the last great period in Egyptian history, the advent of the New Kingdom, or Empire (1580-1085 B.C.). During this time the Egyptians extended their territorial control up the eastern coast of the Mediterranean, conquering Palestine and Syria, and receiving gifts even from the peoples of the Tigris-Euphrates valley. However, these foreign conquests were bought at a heavy price in resources and manpower, and the first millennium B.C. saw Egypt weakened by foreign attack and periodically subjugated—by the Assyrians, the Persians, Alexander the Great and, finally, by the Romans, who made it an imperial province. And after the Romans, the land passed under Muslim control and has remained a major segment of the Islamic world to this day.

The most impressive feature of Egyptian history is its cultural continuity, a feature shared with the fluvial civilizations of the Tigris-Euphrates and of India and China as well. In these long-enduring societies, men achieved harmony with their physical environment. No wonder, then, that Egyptian literature abounds in allusions to the sun and to the Nile, primary sources and unfailing regulators alike of Egyptian society (see Document 1). Like the Mesopotamian rivers, the Nile's risings prompted the invention of a calendar, and the need for measurement of the river lands accurately helped to develop mathematics. Each year's renewal of the Nile's life-giving waters influenced Egyptian religious beliefs; the river came to be associated with a major deity, Osiris. The importance of the sun was reflected in the primacy assigned to Rē, the sun god, among Egyptian deities. "Son of Rē" was one of the pharaoh's titles, for it was believed that the Egyptian ruler was the offspring of the sun god himself. The dominant role of the pharaoh in Egyptian civilization can scarcely be exaggerated, for all power was centralized in him, and from a religious standpoint, he was the god who nourished and sustained the entire Nile Valley.

ISRAEL—"KEEP MY COVENANT"

Situated along the eastern coast of the Mediterranean, on the trade routes that linked the two great fluvial civilizations at either end of the Fertile Crescent, were a cluster of small nations. These included the Phoenicians, a mercantile people whose remarkable trading initiative led them to explore the Mediterranean and to found colonies far to the west. Another Semitic-speaking people, the Hebrews, probably originated in the lower Euphrates and then wandered northwestward to establish a homeland in what is now Palestine. A small nation, periodically subjugated by its powerful neighbors—Egypt, Babylonia, and Assyria—these Hebrews contributed little to the world in the way of art or inventions. Yet they made an ineradicable impact upon the course of human thought. Despite their tribulations and sorrows—begot of enslavement, exile, and mass dispersal—they remained steadfast in their belief that there was but one true God, and that they were His people:

> Now, therefore, if ye will obey my voice indeed, and keep my covenant, then ye shall be a peculiar treasure unto me above all people: for all the earth *is* mine. And ye shall be unto me a kingdom of priests, and a holy nation. These are the words which thou shalt speak unto the children of Israel. (Exodus 19:5-6)

To the Hebrews, God's transcendence and commandments required unswerving fidelity, and the moral and ethical implications of their faith involved a responsibility fraught with promise and punishment alike (see Documents 8 and 9). It was their monotheism which was to sustain the Jewish people in their hours of agony, from their enslavement under the Egyptian pharaohs to their mass slaughter under the Nazis. The monotheism of the Hebrews was also to inspire two other major faiths; Christianity and Islam.

Egypt: The Achievement of Stability

1 HYMNS TO THE SUN AND TO THE NILE: LIFE IN AN ORDERED COSMOS

The surviving monuments of ancient Egypt give an impression of regularity, stability, order—the marks of ancient Egypt's social and political history as well. These characteristics are in some measure reflections of the two natural phenomena that created the particular conditions under which life was lived in the area: the sun and the Nile.

The ancient Egyptians were extraordinarily sensitive to the part played by the sun as a source of life, and they personified it as Rē, chief of the divine powers that governed the universe. The daily journey of the sun was a reënactment of creation; its regularity was a guarantee of victory over chaos and a symbol of immortality. Also associated with the sun was the concept of justice, a concept of considerable social significance, since the king, regarded as the embodiment of the sun (see Document 2), therefore possessed divine authority to dispense justice to his people.

The role of the Nile in providing a background for Egyptian routine and order is fairly obvious, for, like the sun, the Nile contributed to the substratum of life and thought a pattern of cyclical renewal and rebirth. The people were aware that the sharp division between the narrow green valley and the surrounding lifeless desert was due to the seasonal rise and fall of the Nile's waters. They watched the earth turn brown; then unfailingly, the water rose and life returned.

It was the predictable regularity of the sun and the river that made the creation of a high civilization possible, but at the same time, very careful provision had to be made for the control of these natural resources. While the area had great potential fertility, arrangements had to be made for irrigation, protection against floods, and food storage. These needs could best be met by a strong centralized government, and the system that developed gave the area a very long history of stability under a reasonably efficient, although frequently corrupt, bureaucracy. The hymns to the sun and to the Nile printed below show a faith in the endurance of order in the universe, and are not—as prayers addressed to deified natural forces often are—pleas for protection against the malign contingencies of fate. Their mood is rather one of thankfulness for the regulated pattern of life which permitted man to create a civilization whose structures, both institutional and physical, were reflections of a cosmic plan.

In the following selections, in which both the sun and the Nile are addressed as deities, something of the attitude of the people is shown. The dates of these hymns are uncertain; the surviving copies are from the New Kingdom (c. 1500-1200 B.C.), but they probably originated much earlier.

To the Sun.

To the morning sun.
Adoration of Rē, when he ariseth in the eastern horizon of heaven.

Praise to thee, that ariseth in Nun[1] and lighteneth the Two Lands, when he cometh forth.

Thee the whole Ennead praiseth - - - thou goodly, beloved youth—when he ariseth, men live.

Mankind rejoiceth at him; the Souls[2] of Heliopolis shout joyfully to him; the Souls of Buto and Hierakonpolis[3] extol him. The apes[4] adore him; "Praise to thee," say all wild beasts with one consent.

Thy serpent overthroweth thy foes.[5] Thou exultest in thy ship, thy crew is content, and the morning[6] bark receiveth thee.

Thou rejoicest, O lord of gods, over them whom thou hast created, and they praise thee. Nut is blue alongside of thee,[7] and Nun . . . for thee with his rays.

Give me light, that I may see thy beauty.

To the evening sun.
Adoration of Rē-Harakhti, when he setteth in the western horizon of heaven.

Praise to thee, O Rē, when thou settest, Atum, Harakhti! Divine divinity, that came into being of himself, primæval god, that existed at the beginning.

Jubilation to thee that hast fashioned the gods; he that hath raised up the sky to be the pathway (?) for his eyes,[8] that hath fashioned the earth to the extent (?) of his radiance, so that every man may discern the other.

The evening bark is in gladness, and the morning bark exulteth and crieth aloud for joy, when they voyage for thee in peace over Nun. Thy crew is happy, thy serpent hath overthrown thine enemies, and thou hast put an end to the going of Apōphis.

Thou art fair, O Rē, every day; thy mother Nut embraceth thee.

Thou settest beauteous with gladsome heart in the horizon of Manun.[9] The noble dwellers in the West exult. Thou givest light there for the great god Osiris, the ruler of eternity.

The lords of the caverns[10] in their dens, they uplift their hands and praise thee. They address to thee all their prayers, when thou shinest for them.

Text: Adolf Erman (ed.), *The Literature of the Ancient Egyptians*, trans. Aylward M. Blackman (New York: E. P. Dutton & Co., 1927). Reprinted by permission. Pp. 138-39, 146-49.

[1] The celestial ocean.
[2] The gods of the ancient cities are designated "Souls."
[3] The ancient capitals of Lower and Upper Egypt.
[4] The apes, who greet the sun at his rising.
[5] The clouds which threaten the sun, generally conceived of as the snake Apōphis.
[6] The ship which the sun uses by day; at night, in the underworld, he has another; both are manned by gods.
[7] The sky-goddess is here conceived of as a blue ocean over which the sun voyages.
[8] The sun and moon.
[9] A legendary mountain in the West, in which the sun goes down.
[10] The dead.

The lords of the underworld,[11] they are happy when thou bestowest light on the West. Their eyes open when they behold thee. How their hearts rejoice when they behold thee!

Thou hearest the petitions of them that are in the coffin. Thou dispellest their pain and drivest away their evils. Thou givest breath to their nostrils, and they take hold of the rope at the forepart of thy ship[12] in the horizon of Manun.

To the Nile.

Praise to thee, O Nile, that issueth from the earth, and cometh to nourish Egypt. Of hidden nature, a darkness in the daytime - - - -.

That watereth the meadows, he that Rē hath created to nourish all cattle. That giveth drink to the desert places, which are far from water; it is his dew that falleth from heaven.

Beloved of Kēb,[13] director of the corn-god; that maketh to flourish every workshop of Ptah.[14]

Lord of fish, that maketh the water-fowl to go upstream,[15] - - - -.

That maketh barley and createth wheat, so that he may cause the temples to keep festivals.

If he be sluggish, the nostrils are stopped up, and all men are impoverished; the victuals of the gods are diminished, and millions of men perish.

If he be niggardly (?) *the whole land is in* terror *and great and small* lament. - - - - Khnum hath fashioned him. When he riseth, the land is in exultation and every body is in joy. All jaws begin to laugh and every tooth is revealed.

He that bringeth victuals and is rich in food, that createth all that is good. The revered, sweet-smelling - - - -. That createth herbage for the cattle, and giveth sacrifice to every god, be he in the underworld, in heaven, or upon earth - - - -. That filleth the storehouses, and maketh wide the granaries, and giveth things to the poor.

He that maketh trees to grow according to every wish, and men have no lack thereof; the ship is built by his power, for there is no joinery with stones.[16] . . .

---

[11] The dead.
[12] In the underworld, where there is no wind, the boat of the sun is towed along, and this task is undertaken by the grateful dead.
[13] The earth-god.
[14] Ptah, the craftsman, who fashions everything, could effect nothing without the Nile.
[15] To Upper Egypt.
[16] Timber is a rarity in Egypt, stone a common thing.
[17] Sobk has the form of a crocodile and will originally have been a water-god, who rejoices in the inundation.
[18] For hard work, clothes are taken off.
[19] The Nile.
[20] He will henceforth abide in Thebes, where he is so well fêted. His original home knows him no more.

All that is intelligible is: thy young folk and thy children shout for joy over thee, and men hail thee as king. Unchanging of laws, *when he* cometh forth in the presence of Upper and Lower Egypt. Men drink the water - - - -.

He that was in sorrow is become glad, and every heart is joyful. Sobk, the child of Neith,[17] laugheth, and the divine Ennead, that is in thee, is glorious.

Thou that vomitest forth, giving the fields to drink and making strong the people. He that maketh the one rich and loveth the other. *He maketh no distinctions, and boundaries are not made for him.*

Thou light, that cometh from the darkness! Thou fat for his cattle! He is a strong one, that createth . . .

. . . One beholdeth the wealthy as him that is full of care (?), one beholdeth each one with his implements; - - - - None, that (otherwise) goeth clad, is clad,[18] and the children of notables are unadorned - - - -. . . .

Men begin to play to thee on the harp, and men sing to thee with the hand. Thy young folk and thy children shout for joy over thee, and deputations to thee are appointed.

He that cometh with splendid things and adorneth the earth! That causeth the ship to prosper before (?) men; that quickeneth the hearts in them that are with child; that would fain have there be a multitude of all kinds of cattle.

When thou art risen in the city of the sovereign, then men are satisfied with a goodly list. "I would like lotus flowers," saith the little one, "and all manner of things," saith the . . . commander, "and all manner of herbs," say the children. Eating bringeth forgetfulness of him.[19] Good things are scattered over the dwelling - - - -.

When the Nile floodeth, offering is made to thee, cattle are slaughtered for thee, a great oblation is made for thee. Birds are fattened for thee, antelopes are hunted for thee in the desert. Good is recompensed unto thee.

Offering is also made to every other god, even as is done for the Nile, with incense, oxen, cattle, and birds (upon?) the flame. The Nile hath made him his cave in Thebes, and his name shall be known no more in the underworld[20] - - - -.

All ye men, extol the Nine Gods, and stand in awe of the might which his son, the Lord of All, *hath displayed,* even he that maketh green the Two River-banks. Thou art verdant, O Nile, thou art verdant. He that maketh man to live on his cattle, and his cattle on the meadow! Thou art verdant, thou art verdant; O Nile, thou art verdant.

2 HYMNS TO A PHARAOH, SESOSTRIS III: THE ROLE OF THE KING

In answer to his own question "What is the king of Upper and Lower Egypt?" a high official of the Eighteenth Dynasty (1555-1350 B.C.) replied that the king was "a god by whose dealings one lives, the father and mother of all men, alone by himself, without an equal." This definition neatly summarizes the position of the Egyptian king, and underlines his enormous significance. In Egyptian tradition the origin of the institution of kingship was associated with the unification of the country (c. 3000 B.C.). This emphasis on the relation of the king to the creation of the country probably has some historic basis, for the unification of the area under one man apparently coincided with the remarkable birth of cultural achievement—the invention of writing and the use of metal tools, for example—which made possible one of the most brilliant and enduring civilizations.

The uniting of a natural geographic area under one ruler was a common ideal of the ancient world, but the actual achievement was often of short duration, giving rise to an occasional era of memorable greatness. In Egypt, however, unification was the norm, and the failure of a dynasty to maintain control of the whole region was regarded as more than a sign of weakness—it was the indication of a fundamental imbalance between earthly institutions and the cosmic order. The king's function was to maintain the alignment between nature and society; he was able to do this because of his peculiar relationship to both gods and men.

The nature of this relationship and the resultant nature of the king's role in society are suggested by the titles given to the pharaoh in the hymns which follow. The general significance of all these names is that the king was a god. It is important to note that far more was implied in this ascription of divine status than there was in the seventeenth-century European theory of divine-right monarchy or in the belief sometimes held in India that the king was the incarnation of some particular god. The most apt comparison to the Egyptian institution is, perhaps, the Japanese emperor.

One of the king's titles was "Son of Rē," the supreme God. Although it was recognized that the king was born of a human mother, his father was always Rē, who for the purposes of conception, assumed the form of the physical father, the regnant pharaoh. Since, according to mythology, the land of Egypt was the daughter of Rē, the brother-sister marriages of the royal family were a further expression of the king's divine nature. Another title (the one given prominence in the document quoted here) was "Horus," a deity who, like Rē, was called "Lord of Heaven, the Great God."

A title with rather different allusions was that of "King of Upper and Lower Egypt." This is an obvious descriptive statement of the king's control over the two historic geographic divisions of the country—the southern valley area and the northern delta region. The phrase also carries the implication that the natural antipathies of each region's deities would be reconciled in the person of the king who embodied them both.

The king mentioned in the quotation is Sesostris III (or Senusert) who ruled from about 1880 to 1840 B.C. The references are to his conquest of surrounding peoples, notably the Nubians, which gave the Egyptians greater control over the Nile.

Horus, Neter-kheperu, lord of diadems, Neter-mesut, Horus that hath overcome Sēth, Kheper, king of Upper and Lower Egypt, Khakaurē, son of Rē, Sesōstris—he carried off the Two Lands in triumph.

[*First hymn.*]

Praise to thee, Khakaurē! Our Horus, Neter-kheperu!
That protecteth the land and extendeth his boundaries,
That vanquisheth the foreign countries with his crown.
That encloseth the Two Lands in his arms,
And (strangleth?) the foreign lands with his grip;
That slayeth the People of the Bow, without stroke of the club,
Shooting of the arrow, or drawing of the string.
His might hath smitten the Trōglodytes in their land,
And the fear of him hath slain the Nine Bows.
His slaughtering hath made thousands to die

Text: Adolf Erman (ed.), *The Literature of the Ancient Egyptians,* trans. Aylward M. Blackman (New York: E. P. Dutton & Co., 1927). Reprinted by permission. Pp. 134-37.

Of the People of the Bow . . ., that attacked his borders.
He that shooteth the arrow as doth Sekhmet,
When he overthroweth thousands of them that knew not his might.
It is the tongue of his majesty that confineth Nubia,
And it is his utterances that make the Bedouins to flee.
Sole youthful one that fighteth for his boundaries,
And suffereth not his people to wax faint;
That suffereth men to sleep unto daylight,
And his recruits to slumber, for his heart is their defender.
His decrees have made his boundaries,
And his word hath joined in one the Two River-banks.

[*Second hymn.*]

How the gods rejoice: thou hast made their offerings to flourish.
How thy . . . rejoice: thou hast made their boundaries.
How thy (fathers) which were aforetime rejoice: thou hast increased their portions.
How the Egyptians rejoice in thy might: thou hast protected . . .
How the people rejoice in thy designs: thy might hath captured the . . .
How the Two River-banks rejoice in thy strength: thou hast enlarged that which they need.
How thy recruits rejoice in . . . : thou hast caused them to grow.
How thine honoured ones rejoice: thou has renewed their youth.
How the Two Lands rejoice in thy strength: thou hast protected their walls.
Thereafter comes the rubric: Its . . . is: "Horus, that extendeth his boundaries, mayest thou repeat eternity," *doubtless a direction for the singer. It might be a refrain or a specification of the tune.*

[1] That form of the diadem, in which the crown of Upper Egypt is inserted into that of Lower Egypt.
[2] The emblem of Upper Egypt, with which also its king is written, whereas the king of Lower Egypt is denoted in the writing by the bee.
[3] Egyptian and non-Egyptian territory.
[4] A people in the desert between Upper Egypt and the Red Sea, who plundered travellers. The king had just fought against them, as is evident from the following verse.

[*Third hymn.*]

How great is the lord for his city: he alone is a million, little are other men.
How great is the lord for his city: he is like a dyke, that keepeth back the river in its water-floods.
How great is the lord for his city: he is like a cool lodge that letteth a man sleep unto daylight.
[*Two unintelligible verses: the second likens the king to a place of refuge.*]
How great is the lord for his city: he is like a bulwark that delivereth the fearful from his enemy.
How great is the lord for his city: he is like the shade of the season of Overflowing for cooling in summer.
How great is the lord for his city: he is like a corner warm and dry in time of winter.
How great is the lord for his city: he is like a mountain, that keepeth back the storm-blast, at the time when the sky is in riot.
How great is the lord for his city: he is like Sekhmet unto foes that overstep his boundaries.

[*Fourth hymn.*]

He hath come unto us that he may carry away Upper Egypt; the double diadem[1] hath rested on his head.
He hath come unto us and hath united the Two Lands; he hath mingled the reed (?)[2] with the bee.
He hath come unto us and hath brought the Black Land[3] under his sway; he hath apportioned to himself the Red Land.[3]
He hath come unto us and hath taken the Two Lands under his protection; he hath given peace to the Two River-banks.
He hath come unto us and hath made Egypt to live; he hath banished its suffering.
He hath come unto us and hath made the people to live; he hath caused the throat of the subjects to breathe.
He hath come unto us and hath trodden down the foreign countries; he hath smitten the Trōglodytes,[4] that knew not the dread of him.
He hath come unto us and hath (done battle for) his boundaries; he hath delivered them that were robbed . . .

3 THE INSTRUCTION IN WISDOM OF THE VIZIER PTAH-HOTEP: THE GOOD LIFE

In examining an ancient civilization, perhaps the most difficult task of reconstruction comes when an attempt is made to discover how ordinary people thought about their lives, what values they cherished, what goals they sought. Not only is there a lack of materials on which judgments can be based, but there is the realization that in a civilization which covered over two thousand years, as did the Egyptian, value systems must have undergone alteration. There is one interesting group of documents that has come down to us, however, known as "wisdom literature," which gives a clue to men's ordinary aspirations and ambitions. Since these documents were used in the schools as models—the ones that have survived are copies by schoolboys, filled with mistakes—the moral sentiments they embody must have been the accepted standards for a long period. The fluctuations in attitudes expressed by any instructive literature do, of course, mirror changes in social and political structures. Thus the earliest documents (see the selection below) tend to emphasize the attainment of worldly success, with the gods being given only token respect. Later, after the kingdom had been invaded, there was a greater interest in death and in the relation of ethics to the divine.

Ptah-Hotep was the vizier of a Fifth Dynasty king who ruled about 2450 B.C. It was the custom to present literature of instruction as the advice of a wise old man to his son or of an older official to a younger one, so it is possible that the treatise associated with Ptah-Hotep's name was not actually written by him. In any case, it is probably the oldest existing example of a literary genre familiar to all civilizations. Filled with common-sense injunctions for getting on in the world, it nevertheless makes clear that life is lived against a background of order and justice. Keen psychological insight is shown at many points, as in the advice to let a man who wants something express himself fully, even if the request has to be refused, since "a good hearing is a soothing of the heart." And the admonition for the public official to satisfy his clients with what has accrued to him from office suggests that the writer was familiar with the workings of practical politics.

The beginning of the expression of good speech, spoken by the Hereditary Prince and Count, God's Father and God's Beloved, eldest son of the king, of his body, the Mayor and Vizier, Ptah-hotep, in instructing the ignorant about wisdom and about the rules for good speech, as of advantage to him who will hearken and of disadvantage to him who may neglect them.

Then he said to his son:

Let not thy heart be puffed-up because of thy knowledge; be not confident because thou art a wise man. Take counsel with the ignorant as well as the wise. The (full) limits of skill cannot be attained, and there is no skilled man equipped to his (full) advantage. Good speech is more hidden than the emerald, but it may be found with maidservants at the grindstones. . . .

If thou art a leader commanding the affairs of the multitude, seek out for thyself every beneficial deed, until it may be that thy (own) affairs are without wrong. Justice is great, and its appropriateness is lasting; it has not been disturbed since the time of him who made it, (whereas) there is punishment for him who passes over its laws. It is the (right) path before him who knows nothing. Wrongdoing has never brought its undertaking into port. (It may be that) it is fraud that gains riches, (but) the strength of justice is that it lasts, and a man may say: "It is the property of my father." . . .

If thou art one of those sitting at the table of one greater than thyself, take what he may give, when it is set before thy nose. Thou shouldst gaze at what is before thee. Do not pierce him with many stares, (for such) an aggression against him is an abomination to the *ka*.[1] Let thy face be cast down until he addresses thee, and thou shouldst speak (only) when he addresses thee. Laugh after he laughs, and it will be very pleasing to his heart and what thou mayest do will be pleasing to the heart. No one can know what is in the heart.

As for the great man when he is at meals, his purposes conform to the dictates of his *ka*. He will give to the one whom he favors. The great

Text: James B. Pritchard (ed.), *Ancient Near Eastern Texts*, 2nd ed. (Princeton, N.J.: Princeton University Press, 1955), pp. 412-14.

[1] The *ka* was the protecting and guiding vital force of a man, and thus his social mentor.

man gives to *the man whom he can reach,* (but) it is the *ka* that lengthens out his arms. The eating of bread is under the planning of god—it is (only) a fool who would *complain of* it.

If thou art a man of intimacy, whom one great man sends to another, be thoroughly reliable when he sends thee. Carry out the errand for him as he has spoken. Do not be reserved about what is said to thee, and beware of (any) act of forgetfulness. Grasp hold of truth, and do not exceed it. (*Mere*) *gratification is by no means to be repeated.* Struggle against making words worse, (thus) *making one great man hostile to another through vulgar speech.* A great man, a little man—it is the *ka's* abomination. . . .

If thou art a poor fellow, following a man of distinction, one of good standing with the god, know thou not his former insignificance. Thou shouldst not be puffed-up against him because of what thou didst know of him formerly. Show regard for him in conformance with what has accrued to him—property does not come of itself. It is their law for him who wishes them. *As for him who oversteps, he is feared.* It is god who makes (a man's) quality, and he defends him (even) while he is asleep. . . .

If thou art a man of standing and foundest a household and producest a son who is pleasing to god, if he is correct and inclines toward thy ways and listens to thy instruction, while his manners in thy house are fitting, and if he takes care of thy property as it should be, seek out for him every useful action. He is thy son, whom thy *ka* engendered for thee. Thou shouldst not cut thy heart off from him.

(But a man's) seed (often) creates enmity. If he goes astray and transgresses thy plans and does not carry out thy instruction, (so that) his manners in thy household are wretched, and he rebels against all that thou sayest, while his mouth *runs on* in the (most) wretched talk, (quite) *apart from his experience,* while he possesses nothing, THOU SHOULDST CAST HIM OFF: HE IS NOT THY SON AT ALL. He was not really born to thee. (Thus) thou enslavest him entirely according to his (own) speech. . . . He is one whom god has condemned in the (very) womb. . . .

If thou art one to whom petition is made, be calm as thou listenest to the petitioner's speech. Do not rebuff him before he has swept out his body or before he has said that for which he came. A petitioner likes attention to his words better than the fulfilling of that for which he came. He is rejoicing thereat more than any (other) petitioner, (even) before that which has been heard has come to pass. As for him who plays the rebuffer of a petitioner, men say: "Now why is he doing it?" It is not (*necessary*) that everything about which he has petitioned *should* come to pass, (but) a good hearing is a soothing of the heart.

If thou desirest to make friendship last in a home to which thou hast access as master, as a brother, or as a friend, into any place where thou mightest enter, beware of approaching the women. It does not go well with the place where that is done. *The face has no alertness by splitting it.* A thousand men *may be distracted from* their (own) advantage. One is made a fool by limbs of fayence, as she stands (there), become (all) carnelian. A mere trifle, the likeness of a dream—and one attains death through knowing her. . . . Do not do it—it is really an abomination—and thou shalt be free from sickness of heart every day. As for him who escapes from gluttony for it, all affairs will prosper with him. . . .

Do not be covetous at a division. Do not be greedy, unless (it be) for thy (own) portion. Do not be covetous against thy (own) kindred. Greater is the respect for the mild than (for) the strong. He is a mean person who *exposes* his kinsfolk; he is empty of *the fruits of conversation.* It is (only) a little of that for which one is covetous that turns a calm man into a contentious man.

If thou art a man of standing, thou shouldst found thy household and love thy wife at home as is fitting. Fill her belly; clothe her back. Ointment is the prescription for her body. Make her heart glad as long as thou livest. She is a profitable field for her lord. Thou shouldst not contend with her at law, and keep her far from gaining control. . . . Her eye is her stormwind. Let her heart be soothed through what may accrue to thee; it means keeping her long in thy house. . . .

Satisfy thy clients with what has accrued to thee, what accrues to one whom god favors. As for him who evades satisfying his clients, men say: "He is a *ka* of *robbery.* A proper *ka* is a *ka* with which one is satisfied." One does not know what may happen, so that he may understand the morrow. If misfortunes occur among those (now) favored, it is the clients who (still) say: "Welcome!" One does not secure satisfaction from a stranger; one has recourse to a client when there is trouble. . . .

If thou art a man of standing, one sitting in the counsels of his lord, summon thy resources for good. If thou art silent, it is better than *teftef*-plants. If thou speakest, thou shouldst know how thou canst explain (difficulties). It is a (real) craftsman who can speak in counsel, (for) speaking is more difficult than any labor. It is explaining *it that puts it to the stick*. ...

If thou art (now) important after thy (former) unimportance, so that thou mayest do things after a neediness formerly in the town which thou knowest, in contrast to what was thy lot before, do not be miserly with thy wealth, which has accrued to thee as the gift of god. Thou art not behind some other equal of thine to whom the same has happened.

Bow thy back to thy superior, thy overseer from the palace. (Then) thy household will be established in its property, and thy recompense will be as it should be. Opposition to a superior is a painful thing, (for) one lives as long as he is mild. ...

If thou art seeking out the nature of a friend, one whom thou questionest, draw near to him and deal with him alone, until thou art no (longer) troubled about his condition. Reason with him after a while. *Test* his heart with a bit of talk. If what he may have seen should come out of him or he should do something with which thou art displeased, behold, he is still a friend. ... Do not answer in a *state* of turmoil; do not *remove* thyself from him; do not trample him down. His time has never failed to come; he cannot escape from him who predetermined him. ...

If thou hearest this which I have said to thee, thy every project will be (*better*) than (*those of*) *the ancestors*. As for what is left over of their truth, it is their treasure—(*though*) the memory of them *may* escape from the mouth of men— because of the goodness of their sayings. Every word is carried on, without perishing in this land forever. It makes *for expressing well*, the speech of the *very* officials. It is what teaches a man to speak to the future, so that it may hear it, what produces a craftsman, who has heard what is good and who speaks to the future—and it hears it. ...

To hear is of advantage for a son who hearkens. If hearing enters into a hearkener, the hearkener becomes a hearer. (When) hearing is good, speaking is good. Every hearkener (is) an advantage, and hearing is of advantage to the hearkener. To hear is better than anything that is, (and thus) comes the goodly love (of a man). How good it is when a son accepts what his father says! Thereby *maturity* comes to him. He whom god loves is a hearkener, (but) he whom god hates cannot hear. It is the heart which brings up its lord as one who hears or as one who does not hear. The life, prosperity, and health of a man is his heart. ...

If a son accepts what his father says, no project of his miscarries. He whom thou instructest as thy obedient son, who will stand well in the heart of the official, his speech is guided with respect to what has been said to him, one regarded as obedient. ... (But) the *induction* of him who does not hearken miscarries. The wise man rises early in the morning to establish himself, (but) the fool rises early in the morning (only) to *agitate* himself.

As for the fool who does not hearken, he cannot do anything. He regards knowledge as ignorance and profit as loss. He does everything blameworthy, so that one finds fault with him every day. He lives on that through which he should die, and guilt is his food. His character therefrom *is told* as something known to the officials: dying while alive every day. ...

An obedient son is a follower of Horus. It goes well with him when he hears. When he becomes old and reaches a venerable state, he converses in the same way to his children, by renewing the instruction of his father. Every man is *as (well) instructed as he acts*. If he converses with (his) children, then they will speak (to) their children. ...

Mayest thou reach me, with thy body sound, and with the king satisfied with all that has taken place. Mayest thou attain (my) years of life. What I have done on earth is not inconsiderable. I attained one hundred and ten years of life which the king gave me, with favor foremost among the ancestors, through doing right for the king up to the point of veneration.

It has come (to its end, from) its beginning to its end, like that which was found in writing.

Mesopotamia: The Search for World Order

4 THE CREATION EPIC: THE STRUGGLE TO MAINTAIN ORDER AGAINST CHAOS

It has been suggested that the characteristic attribute of Egyptian civilization was a sense of an ordered cosmos, with man in society finding a relationship to this cosmos through various institutions, of which kingship was one of the most vital. This did not mean a static society, or one devoid of tension, but rather the creation of an existence where man's purposes seemed fundamentally at one with those of the gods.

The temper of the great civilizations that arose in Mesopotamia appears to have been curiously different. A reasonable explanation, or at least a useful starting point for one, lies in the difference in the river systems that cradled the two civilizations. The Egyptian area is sharply defined topographically, with a fairly regular flow of controllable water; the Mesopotamian region has no natural boundaries, and its great rivers, the Tigris and Euphrates, far less subject to control than the Nile, did not provide a regulated pattern of life. There was, in contrast to the Egyptian experience, a sense that order was always provisional, that chaos was always imminent. This conflict between order and chaos is the theme of the great creation epic, which in one form or another was familiar to the different peoples who established their rule in Mesopotamia. Another contrast with Egypt may be noted here: while the Nile civilization was mainly the product of one ethnic group which dominated the region throughout the ancient period, the Mesopotamian area was the scene of endless migrations and invasions. A number of great civilizations were created which have taken their names from the predominant groups. Sumeria, Babylonia, and Assyria are the most famous of the great empires that arose between 4000 and 600 B.C. The distinctive contributions made by the Sumerians to the succeeding peoples justify our speaking of a "Mesopotamian" civilization, although the various peoples contributed to the culture of each period.

The form in which the epic appears here probably dates from some time in the second millennium B.C. It was recited at the New Year festival, when, it was believed, creation renewed itself. The performance of the ritual was intended as a dam against chaos. An essential feature of the epic, and the basis for an understanding of the Mesopotamian religion, is the idea that in the beginning there was no one great god nor a clear line of demarcation between the forces of good and evil. In heaven, as on earth, there was no permanent center of authority. Yet, the poem intimates, some kind of authority must be created, even if on a purely arbitrary basis. In the epic, the function of the god Marduk is to create the conditions for an ordered society. He is the warrior-hero, chosen to do battle with Tiamat, the dragon goddess. She is the most ancient of the gods, but also their enemy because she is associated with the chaos out of which the gods have been created. Marduk is triumphant and out of the slain dragon's body creates the heavens, while from the blood of her consort kings he makes man. Although the epic serves thus to explain the creation of man, the legend emphasizes the creation of order in the cosmos. Thus society is possible for both men and gods.

Tablet I
When on high, heaven was not named,
Below, dry land was not named.
Apsu, their first begetter,
Mummu (and) Tiamat, the mother of all of them,
Their waters combined together.
Field was not marked off, sprout had not come forth.

Text: Morris Jastrow, *The Civilization of Babylonia and Assyria* (Philadelphia: J. B. Lippincott Company, 1915), pp. 428-41 *passim*.

When none of the gods had yet come forth,
Had not borne a name,
No destinies had been fixed;
Then gods were created in the midst of heaven.
Lakhmu and Lakhamu came forth
Ages increased . . .
Anshar and Kishar were created.
After many days had passed by there came forth . . .
Anu, their son . . .
Anshar and Anu . . .
Anu . . .

Nudimmud whom his father, his mother, . . .
Of large intelligence, knowing (wise),
Exceeding strong . . .
Without a rival . . .
Then were established. . . .
Then Apsu, the begetter of the great gods,
Cried out, to Mummu, to his messenger, he spoke:
"Oh Mummu, joy of my liver,
Come, unto Tiamat let us go."
They went, and before Tiamat they crouched,
Hatching a plan with regard to the gods . . .
Apsu opened his mouth and spoke,
Unto Tiamat, the splendid one addressed a word:
". . . their course against me
By day I have no rest, at night I cannot lie down, I wish to destroy their course,
So that clamor cease and we may again lie down to sleep."
When Tiamat (heard) this,
She raged and shrieked for (revenge?),
She herself became furiously enraged.
Evil she conceived in her heart.
"All that we have made let us destroy,
That their course may be full of misery so that we may have release."
Mummu answered and counselled Apsu,
Hostile was the counsel of Mummu.
"Come, their course is strong, destroy it!
Then by day thou wilt have rest,
At night thou wilt lie down."
Apsu (hearkened), and his face shone;
Evil he planned against the gods, his sons. . . .
They uttered curses and at the side of Tiamat advanced.
In fury and rage they devised plans ceaselessly night and day.
They rushed to the conflict, raging and furious.
They grouped themselves and ranged the battle array.
Ummu-Khubur, creator of all things,
Gathering invincible weapons, she brought forth huge monsters,
Sharp of tooth and merciless of fang.
With poison instead of blood she filled their bodies.
She clothed with terror the terrible dragons,
Decking them with brilliancy, giving them a lofty stature,
So that whoever beheld them would be overcome with terror.
With their bodies reared up, none could withstand their attack.
She brought forth great serpents, dragons and the Lakhami,
Hurricanes, raging dogs and scorpion men,
Mighty tempests, fish men, and rams,
Bearing cruel weapons, fearless in combat,
Mighty in command, irresistible.
In all eleven monsters of this kind she made.
Among the gods, the first born who formed the assembly,
She exalted Kingu, giving him high rank in their midst;
To march in advance and to direct the host;
To be foremost in arming for the attack,
To direct the fight in supreme control,
To his hand she confided. She decked him out in costly garments:
"I have uttered thy magic formula, in the assembly of the gods I have exalted thee"
The dominion over all the gods was entrusted unto his hands:
"Be thou exalted, my one and only husband;
May the Anunnaki exalt thy name above all the gods!"
She gave him the tablets of fate, to his breast she attached them.
"Oh, thou, thy command will be irresistible!
Firmly established be the utterance of thy mouth!
Now Kingu is exalted, endowed with the power of Anu.
Among the gods, his children, he fixes destinies.
By the word of thy mouth fire will be quenched;
The strong in battle will be increased in strength."

Tablet II

Tiamat finished her work.
(The evil that) she contrived against the gods her offspring,
To avenge Apsu, Tiamat planned evil.
When she had equipped her army, it was revealed to Ea;
Ea heard the words,
And was grievously afflicted, and overwhelmed with grief.
Days passed by and his anger was appeased.
To Anshar, his father, he took the way.
To Father Anshar who begot him he went.
All that Tiamat had planned he repeated to him.
"Tiamat our mother has taken a dislike for us,
She has assembled a host, she rages furiously.
All the gods are gathered to her,
Aye, even those whom thou hast created, march at her side."
[Anshar asks his son Marduk to fight Tiamat]
"Thou art my son of strong courage,
. . . draw nigh to the battle!
. . . at sight of thee there shall be peace."
The Lord rejoiced at the word of his father.
He drew nigh and stood in front of Anshar;
Anshar saw him and his heart was full of joy.
He kissed him on the mouth, and fear departed from him.

"(Oh my father), may the words of thy lips not
  be taken back,
May I go and accomplish the desire of thy heart!"
"Oh, my son, full of all knowledge,
Quiet Tiamat with thy supreme incantation;
Quickly proceed (on thy way)!
Thy blood will not be poured out, thou shalt
  surely return."
The lord rejoiced at the word of his father,
His heart exulted and he spoke to his father.
"Oh Lord of the gods, (who fixes) the fate of
  the great gods,
If I become thy avenger,
Conquering Tiamat, and giving life to thee,
Call an assembly and proclaim the preëminence
  of my lot!
That when in Upshukkinaku thou joyfully seatest
  thyself,
My command in place of thine should fix fates.
What I do should be unaltered,
The word of my lips be never changed or an-
  nulled."

Tablet III

Then they gathered and went,
The great gods, all of them, who fix fates,
Came into the presence of Anshar, they filled
  (the assembly hall),
Embracing one another in the assembly (hall),
They prepared themselves to feast at the banquet.
They ate bread, they mixed the wine,
The sweet mead confused (their senses).
Drunk, their bodies filled with drink,
They shouted aloud, with their spirits exalted,
For Marduk, their avenger, they fixed the destiny.

Tablet IV

They prepared for him a royal chamber,
In the presence of his fathers as ruler he stood.
"Thou art the weightiest among the great gods.
Thy (power of decreeing) fate is unrivalled, thy
  command is (like that of) Anu.
Oh Marduk, thou art mightiest among the great
  gods!
Thy power of decreeing fate unrivalled, thy word
  is like that of Anu!
From now on thy decree will not be altered,
Thine it shall be to raise up and to bring low,
Thy utterance be established, against thy com-
  mand no rebellion!
None among the gods will transgress the limit
  (set by thee).
Abundance is pleasing to the shrines of the gods,
The place of their worship will be established
  as thy place.
Oh Marduk, thou art our avenger!
We give thee kingship over the entire universe,
Take thy seat in the assembly, thy word be
  exalted;
Thy weapon be not overcome, may it crush thy
  enemies.
Oh lord, the life of him who trusts in thee will
  be spared,
But pour out the life of the god who has planned
  evil." . . .
He sent forth the winds which he had created,
  the seven of them;
To trouble the spirit of Tiamat, they followed
  behind him.
Then the lord raised on high the Deluge, his
  mighty weapon.
He mounted the storm chariot, unequalled in
  power,
He harnessed and attached to it four horses,
Merciless, overwhelming, swiftly flying.
(Sharp of) teeth, bearing poison. . . .
Then the lord drew nigh, piercing Tiamat with
  his glance;
He saw the purpose of Kingu, her spouse,
As he (*i.e.*, Marduk) gazed, he (*i.e.*, Kingu)
  tottered in his gait.
His mind was destroyed, his action upset,
And the gods, his helpers, marching at his side,
Saw (the terror of) the hero and leader.
But Tiamat (uttered a cry) and did not turn
  her back,
From her lips there gushed forth rebellious words
. . . "coming to thee as lord of the gods,
As in their own sanctuaries they are gathered
  in thy sanctuary."
Then the lord raised on high the Deluge, the
  great weapon,
And against Tiamat, who was foaming with
  wrath, thus sent forth (his answer).
"Great art thou! Thou hast exalted thyself greatly.
Thy heart hath prompted thee to arrange for
  battle. . . .
Thou hast (exalted) Kingu to be thy husband,
(Thou hast given him power to issue) the de-
  crees of Anu.
(Against the gods, my fathers), thou hast planned
  evil,
Against the gods, my fathers, thou hast planned
  evil.
Let thy army be equipped, thy weapons be girded
  on;
Stand; I and thou, let us join in battle."
When Tiamat heard this,
She was beside herself, she lost her reason.
Tiamat shouted in a paroxysm of fury,
Trembling to the root, shaking in her foundations.
She uttered an incantation, she pronounced a
  magic formula.
The gods of battle, appeal to their weapons.

Then stepped forth Tiamat and the leader of the gods, Marduk.
To the fight they advanced, to the battle they drew nigh.
The lord spread his net and encompassed her,
The evil wind stationed behind him he drove into her face.
Tiamat opened her mouth to its full extent.
He drove in the evil wind before she could close her lips.
The terrible winds filled her belly,
Her heart was seized, and she held her mouth wide open.
He drove in the spear and burst open her belly,
Cutting into her entrails, he slit her heart.
He overcame her and destroyed her life;
He cast down her carcass and stood upon it.
When he had thus subjected Tiamat, the leader,
Her host was scattered, her assembly was dissolved;
And the gods, her helpers, who marched beside her,
In fear and trembling turned about,
Taking to flight to save their lives.
But they were surrounded and could not escape.
He captured them and smashed their weapons,
They were cast into the net, and brought into the snare; . . .
After he (*i.e.*, Marduk) had bound and cast down his enemies,
Had battered down the arrogant foe,
Had completely gained the victory of Anshar over the enemy,
The hero Marduk had attained the aim of Nudimmud,
He strengthened his hold over the captive gods.
To Tiamat, whom he had bound, he came back,
And the lord trampled under foot the foundation of Tiamat.
With his merciless weapon he smashed her skull,
He cut the channels of her blood,
And made the north wind carry them to secret places.
His fathers beheld and rejoiced exceeding glad,
Presents and gifts they brought to him.

Then the lord rested and looked at the carcass.
He divided the flesh of the monster, and created marvellous things.
He split her like a fish flattened into two halves;
One half he took and made it a covering for heaven.
He drew a bolt, he stationed a watchman,
Enjoining that the waters be not permitted to flow out.
He passed over the heavens, inspecting the regions (thereof),
And over against the Apsu, he set the dwelling of Nudimmud.
The lord measured the structure of the Deep.
He established E-sharra as a palace corresponding to it.
The palace E-sharra which he created as heaven,
He caused Anu, Enlil and Ea to inhabit their districts.

Tablet V

He made stations for the great gods,
The stars, their counterparts, the twin stars he fixed.
He fixed the year and divided it into divisions.
For the twelve months he fixed three stars.
Also for the days of the year (he had fashioned) pictures. . . .

Tablet VI

Upon (Marduk's) hearing the word of the gods,
His heart led him to create (marvellous things)
He opened his mouth and (spoke) to Ea
(What) he had conceived in his heart he imparted to him;
"My blood I will take and bone I will (form).
I will set up man that man . . .
I will create man to inhabit (the earth),
That the worship of the gods be fixed, that they may have shrines.
But I will alter the ways of the gods, I will change . . .
They shall be joined in concert, unto evil shall they" . . .
Ea answered him and spoke.

5 THE DESCENT OF ISHTAR INTO THE UNDERWORLD: THE MEANING OF THE FERTILITY CULT

Fertility cults were fundamental to the civilizations of the ancient Near East, and in one form or another they affected almost every aspect of the religious and social lives of the people. The purpose of all fertility rituals was to ensure the continuance of life. Of particular significance were the rites enacted to bring about the renewal of vegetation in the spring, when it seemed that no life existed in the baked brown earth. Closely linked with this concern was the desire to promote human fertility. The central figures in many of the rituals were Inanna (or Ishtar), the queen of heaven and goddess of love, and her consort Tammuz (or Dumuzi), the god of vegetation. The many myths about them followed two general patterns. In one, a version of which is given here, Ishtar goes to the underworld, "the land of no return," and during her absence from earth there is no new creation, either of plants or animals. Why she makes the journey is not clear; it used to be thought she had gone in search of Tammuz, but the text does not bear this out. The stripping of the goddess until she stands naked probably symbolizes the waning of the earth's vegetation. The other form of the myth celebrates the marriage of the goddess of fertility to the god of vegetation. This took place at the New Year festival, which marked the beginning of spring. Apparently, the king sometimes acted the part of Tammuz, the vegetation god—thus the welfare of the state was linked with the victory of life over death, of order over chaos.

To the land of no return, the land of darkness,
Ishtar, the daughter of the Moon-God, directed her thoughts,
Directed her thought, Ishtar, the daughter of Sin,
To the house of shadows, the dwelling of Irkalla,
To the house without exit for him who enters therein,
To the road whence there is no turning,
To the house without light for him who enters therein,
The place where dust is their nourishment, clay their food.
They have no light, in darkness they dwell.
Clothed like birds, with wings as garments,
Over door and bolt, dust has gathered.
Ishtar on arriving at the gate of the land of no return,
To the gate-keeper thus addressed herself:
"Gate-keeper, ho, open thy gate!
Open thy gate that I may enter!
If thou openest not the gate to let me enter,
I will break the door, I will wrench the lock,
I will smash the door-posts, I will force the doors.
I will bring up the dead to eat the living.
(And) the dead will outnumber the living."
The gate-keeper opened his mouth and spoke,
Spoke to the lady Ishtar:
"Desist, O lady, do not destroy it.
I will go and announce thy name to my queen Ereshkigal."
The gate-keeper entered and spoke (to Ereshkigal):
"Ho! here is thy sister, Ishtar . . .
Hostility of the great powers (?) . . ."
When Ereshkigal heard this,
As when one hews down a tamarisk (she trembled?)
As when one cuts a reed, (she shook?):
"What has moved her heart, what has (stirred) her liver?
Ho there, (does) this one (wish to dwell?) with me?
To eat clay as food, to drink (dust?) as wine?
I weep for the men who have left their wives.
I weep for the wives (torn) from the embrace of their husbands;
For the little ones (cut off) before their time.
Go, gate-keeper, open thy gate for her,
Deal with her according to the ancient decree."
The gate-keeper went and opened his gate to her:
"Enter, O lady, let Cuthah greet thee.
Let the palace of the land of no return rejoice at thy presence!"
He bade her enter the first gate which he opened wide, and took the large crown off her head:
"Why, O gate-keeper, dost thou remove the large crown off my head?"
"Enter, O lady, such are the decrees of Ereshkigal."
The second gate he bade her enter, opening it wide and removed her earrings:
"Why, O gate-keeper, dost thou remove my earrings?"
"Enter, O lady, for such are the decrees of Ereshkigal."
The third gate he bade her enter, opened it wide and removed her necklace:
"Why, O gate-keeper, dost thou remove my necklace?"
"Enter, O lady, for such are the decrees of Ereshkigal."
The fourth gate he bade her enter, opened it wide and removed the ornaments of her breast:
"Why, O gate-keeper, dost thou remove the ornaments of my breast?"
"Enter, O lady, for such are the decrees of Ereshkigal."
The fifth gate he bade her enter, opened it wide and removed the girdle of her body studded with birth-stones.
"Why, O gate-keeper, dost thou remove the girdle of my body, studded with birth-stones?"
"Enter, O lady, for such are the decrees of Ereshkigal."

Text: Morris Jastrow, *The Civilization of Babylonia and Assyria* (Philadelphia: J. B. Lippincott Company, 1915), pp. 453–59 *passim.*

The sixth gate, he bade her enter, opened it wide and removed the spangles off her hands and feet.
"Why, O gate-keeper, dost thou remove the spangles off my hands and feet?"
"Enter, O lady, for thus are the decrees of Ereshkigal."
The seventh gate he bade her enter, opened it wide and removed her loin-cloth.
"Why, O gate-keeper, dost thou remove my loin-cloth?"
"Enter, O lady, for such are the decrees of Ereshkigal."
Now when Ishtar had gone down into the land of no return,
Ereshkigal saw her and was angered at her presence.
Ishtar without reflection threw herself at her.
Ereshkigal opened her mouth and spoke,
To Namtar, her messenger, she addressed herself:
"Go Namtar, (imprison her) in my palace.
Send against her sixty diseases, (to punish? Ishtar.)
Eye disease against her eyes,
Disease of the side against her side,
Foot-disease against her foot,
Heart disease against her heart,
Head-disease against her head,
Against her whole being, against (her entire body?)."
After the lady Ishtar had gone down into the land of no return,
The bull did not mount the cow, the ass approached not the she-ass.
To the maid in the street, no man drew near,
The man slept in his apartment,
The maid slept by herself.

The countenance of Papsukal, the messenger of the great gods fell, his face (was troubled).
In mourning garbs he was clothed, in soiled garments clad.
Shamash [the sun-god] went to Sin, his father, weeping,
In the presence of Ea, the king, he went with flowing tears.
"Ishtar has descended into the earth and has not come up.
The bull does not mount the cow, the ass does not approach the she-ass.
The man does not approach the maid in the street,
The man sleeps in his apartment,
The maid sleeps by herself."
Ea in the wisdom of his heart formed a being,
He formed Asu-shu-namir, the eunuch.
"Go, Asu-shu-namir, to the land of no return direct thy face!
The seven gates of the land without return be opened before thee,
May Ereshkigal at sight of thee rejoice!
After her heart has been assuaged, her liver quieted,
Invoke against her the name of the great gods,
Raise thy head, direct (thy) attention to the *khalziku* skin."
"Come, lady, let them give me the *khalziku* skin, that I may drink water out of it."
When Ereshkigal heard this, she struck her side, bit her finger,
"Thou hast expressed a wish that cannot be granted.
Go, Asu-shu-namir, I curse thee with a great curse,
The sweepings of the gutters of the city be thy food,
The drains of the city be thy drink,
The shadow of the wall be thy abode,
The thresholds be thy dwelling-place;
Drunkard and sot strike thy cheek!"
Ereshkigal opened her mouth and spoke,
To Namtar, her messenger, she addressed herself.
"Go, Namtar, knock at the strong palace,
Strike the threshold of precious stones,
Bring out the Anunnaki, seat (them) on golden thrones.
Sprinkle Ishtar with the waters of life and take her out of my presence."
Namtar went, knocked at the strong palace,
Tapped on the threshold of precious stones.
He brought out the Anunnaki and placed them on golden thrones,
He sprinkled Ishtar with the waters of life and took hold of her.
Through the first gate he led her out and returned to her her loin cloth.
Through the second gate he led her out and returned to her the spangles of her hands and feet.
Through the third gate he led her out and returned to her the girdle of her body, studded with birth-stones.
Through the fourth gate he led her out and returned to her the ornaments of her breast.
Through the fifth gate he led her out and returned to her her necklace.
Through the sixth gate he led her out and returned to her her ear-rings.
Through the seventh gate he led her out and returned to her the large crown for her head.

6 A SUMERIAN EPIC: A RECORD OF PRIMITIVE DEMOCRACY

In most of the written records of the ancient Near East, as well as in the great monuments, the power and prestige of the king are emphasized. There are hints here and there, however, that in some stages of Mesopotamian development the king was by no means an absolute ruler, and that there even existed what some scholars have called "primitive democracy." One of the clearest indications of the nature of early government is given in a fragment of a Sumerian epic poem. The events described in the poem probably occurred around 3000 B.C., although the written record was not made until many centuries later.

The poem is concerned with the affairs of Agga, the king of Kish, and Gilgamesh, the king of Erech. At the time, the Mesopotamian area was covered with many small, autonomous city-states, of which Kish and Erech were two. We know from later history that within the city-states power was usually concentrated in the hands of one man. At the same time, each state attempted to expand its power over its neighbors. The end of this process was sometimes the creation of the great centralized empires, ruled over by autocratic monarchs, which came to dominate the whole of the Near East. Our selection is of particular interest because it appears to show the workings of an institution that opposed this overwhelming trend toward autocratic government. This institution was an assembly of the people, made up, one would judge from the text, of two "houses," one composed of the elders, the other of the warriors. The existence of this check on the power of the king down to historic times provides another interesting contrast with Egypt, where the king enters history as a god seated on an earthly throne. While some later Mesopotamian kings did claim divine status, the traditional pattern was simply to exalt the power of the king. He might be "King of Kings and Lord of Lords," but he was not regarded as essentially different from his subjects.

From the epic, it appears that the king of Erech was trying to get the approval of the assembly for a war against his rival, Agga of Kish. The elders wanted peace, even at the price of submission; the warriors were anxious for battle. What the final outcome was, we do not know, although we have learned from other sources that the kings did not always have their own way. Such assemblies as the one pictured here were not unique in the ancient world, but are paralleled elsewhere, notably in India. Few other accounts, however, give such a clear sense of the clash of opposing legislative and kingly wills.

The envoys of Agga, the son of Enmebaraggesi,
Proceeded from Kish to Gilgamesh in Erech.
The Lord Gilgamesh before the elders of his city
Put the matter, seeks out the word:
"Let us not submit to the house of Kish, let us smite it with weapons."

The convened assembly of the elders of his city
Answers Gilgamesh:
"Let us submit to the house of Kish, let us not smite it with weapons."

Gilgamesh, the lord of Kullab,
Who performs heroic deeds for the goddess Inanna,

Text: S. N. Kramer, *From the Tablets of Sumer* (Indian Hills, Colorado: The Falcon's Wing Press, 1956), pp. 29-30. Reprinted by permission of the author.

Took not the words of the elders of his city to heart.

A second time Gilgamesh, the lord of Kullab,
Before the fighting men of his city put the matter, seeks out the word:
"Do not submit to the house of Kish, let us smite it with weapons."

The convened assembly of the fighting men of his city
Answers Gilgamesh:
"Do not submit to the house of Kish, let us smite it with weapons."

Then Gilgamesh, the lord of Kullab,
At the word of the fighting men of his city his heart rejoiced, his spirit brightened.

7 THE CODE OF HAMMURABI: THE LEGAL SYSTEM AND SOCIAL CUSTOM

One of the most famous records of the civilization of the ancient Near East is the law code of Hammurabi, a king of the Old Babylonian Dynasty who reigned from 1728 to 1686 B.C. Written on a block of black stone, it was found in fragments in 1901 by French archaeologists who pieced it together and took it to the Louvre in Paris. The original had 282 articles, but about 1200 B.C. a number of them were erased by an invader. The code includes a long prologue and epilogue, not given here, in which the king reiterates his claim to be "the king of justice," and prays that "in the days to come, for all time, let the king who appears in the land observe the words of justice which I wrote on my stela." Hammurabi's code is not the first of its kind, nor are its ideas original, for its sums up and codifies laws long in existence, but it was of immense importance for the Mesopotamian world because it preserved the experience of a civilized past as a framework for future legal and social systems.

Much of the law code is concerned with a careful regulation of the conditions of trade and commerce, a reminder that the area was the center of a vast urban population whose chief interest was the exchange of goods with all parts of the known world. A conspicuous feature is the detailed discussion of just wages and fees. In cases of injustice, trial by ordeal was common, but many punishments were based on strict reciprocity—an eye for an eye and a tooth for a tooth. There was also a graded system of money fines. A curious feature of the code is that the higher classes were punished more severely for some crimes than were the lower classes; this is a contrast to other cultures, such as ancient India's, where the reverse held true. The death penalty was common, but possibly less practiced than in some parts of seventeenth- and eighteenth-century Europe. Slavery had long been an integral part of the social structure, and laws governing it make up a large section of the code. While slaves seem to have had no rights, the fact that provision was made for the offspring of the marriage of a slave and a free woman suggests a certain freedom in social relations. Marriage contracts were an important part of social life, and women held a fairly high position. The protection given to a divorced wife would be considered generous in many ancient societies. While the father seems to have had almost unrestricted control over the family, the law prevented a child from being disinherited without an acceptable excuse before the courts. On the whole, the code is the product of a mature, orderly society that was certain of its social aims and knew how to achieve them.

The code of Hammurabi also provides a striking illustration of the importance of the invention of writing for the growth and preservation of the great civilizations of the ancient Near East. The first use of standardized symbols to represent either words or parts of words probably developed in Mesopotamia; the practice spread to other areas, and it was carried to its logical conclusion in Egypt, where a true alphabet—a letter to stand for each sound—was inaugurated (though not completed). The development of writing meant that it was possible to transmit the accumulated wisdom and experience of the past to future generations. Such transmission could take place through memorization of sacred texts, but the production of written documents tended to make the material available to more people. The possession of written language gave to a group a greater sense of identity. And as far as trading and commerce were concerned, some form of writing was almost a fundamental necessity. Also, according to the great Egyptologist James Breasted, the widespread use of writing in government, religion, and commerce "created for all time the class distinction between the illiterate and the learned, which is still a problem of modern society."

1. If a man has accused another of laying a *nêrtu* (death spell?) upon him, but has not proved it, he shall be put to death.

2. If a man has accused another of laying a *kišpu* (spell) upon him, but has not proved it, the accused shall go the sacred river, he shall plunge into the sacred river, and if the sacred river shall conquer him, he that accused him shall take possession of his house. If the sacred river shall show his innocence and he is saved,

Text: C. H. W. Johns (ed.), *Babylonian and Assyrian Laws, Contracts and Letters* ("Library of Ancient Inscriptions" [New York: Charles Scribner's Sons, 1904]), pp. 44-67 *passim.*

his accuser shall be put to death. He that plunged into the sacred river shall appropriate the house of him that accused him.

3. If a man has borne false witness in a trial, or has not established the statement that he has made, if that case be a capital trial, that man shall be put to death.

4. If he has borne false witness in a civil law case, he shall pay the damages in that suit.

5. If a judge has given a verdict, rendered a decision, granted a written judgment, and afterward has altered his judgment, that judge shall be prosecuted for altering the judgment he gave and shall pay twelvefold the penalty laid down in that judgment. Further, he shall be publicly expelled from his judgment-seat and shall not return nor take his seat with the judges at a trial.

6. If a man has stolen goods from a temple, or house, he shall be put to death; and he that has received the stolen property from him shall be put to death.

7. If a man has bought or received on deposit from a minor or a slave, either silver, gold, male or female slave, ox, ass, or sheep, or anything else, except by consent of elders, or power of attorney, he shall be put to death for theft.

8. If a patrician has stolen ox, sheep, ass, pig, or ship, whether from a temple, or a house, he shall pay thirtyfold. If he be a plebeian, he shall return tenfold. If the thief cannot pay, he shall be put to death.

9. If a man has lost property and some of it be detected in the possession of another, and the holder has said, "A man sold it to me, I bought it in the presence of witnesses"; and if the claimant has said, "I can bring witnesses who know it to be property lost by me"; then the alleged buyer on his part shall produce the man who sold it to him and the witnesses before whom he bought it; the claimant shall on his part produce the witnesses who know it to be his lost property. The judge shall examine their pleas. The witnesses to the sale and the witnesses who identify the lost property shall state on oath what they know. Such a seller is the thief and shall be put to death. The owner of the lost property shall recover his lost property. The buyer shall recoup himself from the seller's estate.

10. If the alleged buyer on his part has not produced the seller or the witnesses before whom the sale took place, but the owner of the lost property on his part has produced the witnesses who identify it as his, then the [pretended] buyer is the thief; he shall be put to death. The owner of the lost property shall take his lost property.

11. If, on the other hand, the claimant of the lost property has not brought the witnesses that know his lost property, he has been guilty of slander, he has stirred up strife, he shall be put to death.

12. If the seller has in the meantime died, the buyer shall take from his estate fivefold the value sued for.

13. If a man has not his witnesses at hand, the judge shall set him a fixed time not exceeding six months, and if within six months he has not produced his witnesses, the man has lied; he shall bear the penalty of the suit.

14. If a man has stolen a child, he shall be put to death.

15. If a man has induced either a male or female slave from the house of a patrician, or plebeian, to leave the city, he shall be put to death.

16. If a man has harbored in his house a male or female slave from a patrician's or plebeian's house, and has not caused the fugitive to leave on the demand of the officer over the slaves condemned to public forced labor, that householder shall be put to death.

17. If a man has caught either a male or female runaway slave in the open field and has brought him back to his owner, the owner of the slave shall give him two shekels of silver.

18. If such a slave will not name his owner, his captor shall bring him to the palace, where he shall be examined as to his past and returned to his owner.

19. If the captor has secreted that slave in his house and afterward that slave has been caught in his possession, he shall be put to death.

20. If the slave has fled from the hands of his captor, the latter shall swear to the owner of the slave and he shall be free from blame.

21. If a man has broken into a house he shall be killed before the breach and buried there.

22. If a man has committed highway robbery and has been caught, that man shall be put to death.

23. If the highwayman has not been caught, the man that has been robbed shall state on oath what he has lost and the city or district governor in whose territory or district the robbery took place shall restore to him what he has lost.

24. If a life [has been lost], the city or district governor shall pay one mina of silver to the deceased's relatives.

25. If a fire has broken out in a man's house and one who has come to put it out has coveted the property of the householder and appropriated any of it, that man shall be cast into the selfsame fire.

26. If a levy-master, or warrant-officer, who has been detailed on the king's service, has not gone,

or has hired a substitute in his place, that levy-master, or warrant-officer, shall be put to death and the hired substitute shall take his office.

27. If a levy-master, or warrant-officer, has been assigned to garrison duty, and in his absence his field and garden have been given to another who has carried on his duty, when the absentee has returned and regained his city, his field and garden shall be given back to him and he shall resume his duty.

28. If a levy-master, or warrant-officer, has been assigned to garrison duty, and has a son able to carry on his official duty, the field and garden shall be given to him and he shall carry on his father's duty.

29. If the son be a child and is not able to carry on his father's duty, one-third of the field and garden shall be given to his mother to educate him.

30. If such an official has neglected the care of his field, garden, or house, and let them go to waste, and if another has taken his field, garden, or house, in his absence, and carried on the duty for three years, if the absentee has returned and would cultivate his field, garden, or house, it shall not be given him; he who has taken it and carried on the duty connected with it shall continue to do so.

31. If for one year only he has let things go to waste and he has returned, his field, garden, and house shall be given him, and he himself shall carry on his duty.

32. If such an official has been assigned to the king's service (and captured by the enemy) and has been ransomed by a merchant and helped to regain his city, if he has had means in his house to pay his ransom, he himself shall do so. If he has not had means of his own, he shall be ransomed by the temple treasury. If there has not been means in the temple treasury of his city, the state will ransom him. His field, garden, or house shall not be given for his ransom.

33. If either a governor or a prefect has appropriated to his own use the corvée, or has accepted and sent on the king's service a hired substitute in his place, that governor, or prefect, shall be put to death.

34. If either a governor, or a prefect, has appropriated the property of a levy-master, has hired him out, has robbed him by high-handedness at a trial, has taken the salary which the king gave to him, that governor, or prefect, shall be put to death. . . .

40. A votary, merchant, or resident alien may sell his field, garden, or house, and the buyer shall discharge the public service connected with the field, garden, or house that he has bought.

41. If a man has given property in exchange for the field, garden, or house, of a levy-master, warrant-officer, or tributary, such an official shall return to his field, garden, or house, and he shall appropriate the property given in exchange.

42. If a man has hired a field to cultivate and has caused no corn to grow on the field, he shall be held responsible for not doing the work on the field and shall pay an average rent.

43. If he has not cultivated the field and has left it alone, he shall give to the owner of the field an average rent, and the field which he has neglected he shall break up with mattocks and plough it, and shall return it to the owner of the field. . . .

47. If a tenant farmer, because he did not start farming in the early part of the year, has sublet the field, the owner of the field shall not object; his field has been cultivated; at harvest-time he shall take rent, according to his agreement.

48. If a man has incurred a debt and a storm has flooded his field or carried away the crop, or the corn has not grown because of drought, in that year he shall not pay his creditor. Further, he shall post-date his bond and shall not pay interest for that year.

49. If a man has received money from a merchant and has given to the merchant a field, planted with corn, or sesame, and has said to him, "Cultivate the field and reap and take the corn, or sesame, that shall be grown"; if the bailiff has reared corn, or sesame, in the field, at harvest-time the owner of the field shall take what corn, or sesame, has been grown in the field and shall pay corn to the merchant for his money that he took of him and its interest, and for the maintenance of the bailiff. . . .

53, 54. If a man has neglected to strengthen his dike and has not kept his dike strong, and a breach has broken out in his dike, and the waters have flooded the meadow, the man in whose dike the breach has broken out shall restore the corn he has caused to be lost. [54]. If he be not able to restore the corn, he and his goods shall be sold, and the owners of the meadow whose corn the water has carried away shall share the money.

55. If a man has opened his runnel for watering and has left it open, and the water has flooded his neighbor's field, he shall pay him an average crop.

56. If a man has let out the waters and they flood the young plants in his neighbor's field, he shall measure out ten *GUR* of corn for each *GAN* of land.

57. If a shepherd has not agreed with the owner of the field to allow his sheep to eat off the green crop and without consent of the owner

has let his sheep feed off it, the owner of the field shall harvest his crop, but the shepherd who without consent of the owner of the field caused his sheep to eat it shall give to the owner of the field, over and above his crop, twenty GUR of corn for each GAN of land. . . .

Y. [If a man has let a house] and the tenant has paid to the owner of the house the full rent for a term of years, and if the owner of the house has ordered the tenant to leave before his time is up, the owner of the house, because he has ordered his tenant to leave before his time is up, [shall repay a proportionate amount] from what the tenant has paid him.

Z. [If a man has borrowed money of a merchant] and has not corn or money wherewith [to pay], but has goods; whatever is in his hands, he shall give to the merchant, before the elders. The merchant shall not object; he shall receive it.

After the loss of about thirty-five sections the Code resumes:

100. [If an agent has received money of a merchant, he shall write down the amount] and [what is to be] the interest of the money, and when his time is up, he shall settle with his merchant.

101. If he has not had success on his travels, he shall return double what he received to the merchant.

102, 103. If the merchant has given money, as a speculation, to the agent, who during his travels has met with misfortune, he shall return the full sum to the merchant. [103]. If, on his travels, an enemy has forced him to give up some of the goods he was carrying, the agent shall specify the amount on oath and shall be acquitted.

104. If a merchant has given to an agent corn, wool, oil, or any sort of goods, to traffic with, the agent shall write down the money value, and shall return that to the merchant. The agent shall then take a sealed receipt for the money that he has given to the merchant.

105. If the agent forgets and has not taken a sealed receipt for the money he gave to the merchant, money that has not been acknowledged by receipt shall not be put down in the accounts.

106. If an agent has taken money of a merchant, and his principal suspects him, that principal shall prosecute his agent, put him on oath before the elders, as to the money taken; the agent shall pay to the merchant threefold what he misappropriated.

107. If the principal has overcharged the agent and the agent has [really] returned to his principal whatever his principal gave him, and if the principal has disputed what the agent has given him, that agent shall put his principal on oath before the elders, and the merchant, because he has defrauded the agent, shall pay to the agent sixfold what he misappropriated.

108. If the mistress of a beer-shop has not received corn as the price of beer or has demanded silver on an excessive scale, and has made the measure of beer less than the measure of corn, that beer-seller shall be prosecuted and drowned.

109. If the mistress of a beer-shop has assembled seditious slanderers in her house and those seditious persons have not been captured and have not been haled to the palace, that beer-seller shall be put to death.

110. If a votary, who is not living in the convent, open a beer-shop, or enter a beer-shop for drink, that woman shall be put to death. . . .

117. If a man owes a debt, and he has given his wife, his son, or his daughter [as hostage] for the money, or has handed someone over to work it off, the hostage shall do the work of the creditor's house; but in the fourth year he shall set them free.

118. If a debtor has handed over a male or female slave to work off a debt, and the creditor proceeds to sell same, no one can complain.

119. If a man owes a debt, and he has assigned a maid who has borne him children for the money, the owner of the maid shall repay the money which the merchant gave him and shall ransom his maid. . . .

127. If a man has caused the finger to be pointed at a votary, or a man's wife, and has not justified himself, that man shall be brought before the judges, and have his forehead branded.

128. If a man has taken a wife and has not executed a marriage-contract, that woman is not a wife.

129. If a man's wife be caught lying with another, they shall be strangled and cast into the water. If the wife's husband would save his wife, the king can save his servant.

130. If a man has ravished another's betrothed wife, who is a virgin, while still living in her father's house, and has been caught in the act, that man shall be put to death; the woman shall go free.

131. If a man's wife has been accused by her husband, and has not been caught lying with another, she shall swear her innocence, and return to her house.

132. If a man's wife has the finger pointed at her on account of another, but has not been caught lying with him, for her husband's sake she shall plunge into the sacred river.

133. If a man has been taken captive, and there was maintenance in his house, but his wife has left her house and entered into another man's house; because that woman has not preserved her body, and has entered into the house of another, that woman shall be prosecuted and shall be drowned.

134. If a man has been taken captive, but there was not maintenance in his house, and his wife has entered into the house of another, that woman has no blame.

135. If a man has been taken captive, but there was no maintenance in his house for his wife, and she has entered into the house of another, and has borne him children, if in the future her [first] husband shall return and regain his city, that woman shall return to her first husband, but the children shall follow their own father.

136. If a man has left his city and fled, and, after he has gone, his wife has entered into the house of another; if the man return and seize his wife, the wife of the fugitive shall not return to her husband, because he hated his city and fled.

137. If a man has determined to divorce a concubine who has borne him children, or a votary who has granted him children, he shall return to that woman her marriage-portion, and shall give her the usufruct of field, garden, and goods, to bring up her children. After her children have grown up, out of whatever is given to her children, they shall give her one son's share, and the husband of her choice shall marry her.

138. If a man has divorced his wife, who has not borne him children, he shall pay over to her as much money as was given for her bride-price and the marriage-portion which she brought from her father's house, and so shall divorce her.

139. If there was no bride-price, he shall give her one mina of silver, as a price of divorce.

140. If he be a plebeian, he shall give her one-third of a mina of silver.

141. If a man's wife, living in her husband's house, has persisted in going out, has acted the fool, has wasted her house, has belittled her husband, he shall prosecute her. If her husband has said, "I divorce her," she shall go her way; he shall give her nothing as her price of divorce. If her husband has said, "I will not divorce her," he may take another woman to wife; the wife shall live as a slave in her husband's house.

142. If a woman has hated her husband and has said, "You shall not possess me," her past shall be inquired into, as to what she lacks. If she has been discreet, and has no vice, and her husband has gone out, and has greatly belittled her, that woman has no blame, she shall take her marriage-portion and go off to her father's house.

143. If she has not been discreet, has gone out, ruined her house, belittled her husband, she shall be drowned.

144. If a man has married a votary, and that votary has given a maid to her husband, and so caused him to have children, and, if that man is inclined to marry a concubine, that man shall not be allowed to do so, he shall not marry a concubine.

145. If a man has married a votary, and she has not granted him children, and he is determined to marry a concubine, that man shall marry the concubine, and bring her into his house, but the concubine shall not place herself on an equality with the votary.

146. If a man has married a votary, and she has given a maid to her husband, and the maid has borne children, and if afterward that maid has placed herself on an equality with her mistress, because she has borne children, her mistress shall not sell her, she shall place a slave-mark upon her, and reckon her with the slavegirls.

147. If she has not borne children, her mistress shall sell her.

148. If a man has married a wife and a disease has seized her, if he is determined to marry a second wife, he shall marry her. He shall not divorce the wife whom the disease has seized. In the home they made together she shall dwell, and he shall maintain her as long as she lives.

149. If that woman was not pleased to stay in her husband's house, he shall pay over to her the marriage-portion which she brought from her father's house, and she shall go away. . . .

159. If a man, who has presented a gift to the house of his prospective father-in-law and has given the bride-price, has afterward looked upon another woman and has said to his father-in-law, "I will not marry your daughter"; the father of the girl shall keep whatever he has brought as a present.

160. If a man has presented a gift to the house of his prospective father-in-law, and has given the bride-price, but the father of the girl has said, "I will not give you my daughter," the father shall return double all that was presented him.

161. If a man has brought a gift to the house of his prospective father-in-law, and has given the bride-price, but his comrade has slandered him and his father-in-law has said to the suitor, "You shall not marry my daughter," [the father] shall return double all that was presented him. Further, the comrade shall not marry the girl.

162. If a man has married a wife, and she has borne him children, and that woman has gone to her fate, her father shall lay no claim to her marriage-portion. Her marriage-portion is her children's only.

163. If a man has married a wife, and she has not borne him children, and that woman has gone to her fate; if his father-in-law has returned to him the bride-price, which that man brought into the house of his father-in-law, her husband shall have no claim on the marriage-portion of that woman. Her marriage-portion indeed belongs to her father's house.

164. If the father-in-law has not returned the bride-price, the husband shall deduct the amount of her bride-price from her marriage-portion, and shall return her marriage-portion to her father's house.

165. If a man has presented field, garden, or house to his son, the first in his eyes, and has written him a deed of gift; after the father has gone to his fate, when the brothers share, he shall keep the present his father gave him, and over and above shall share equally with them in the goods of his father's estate.

166. If a man has taken wives for the other sons he had, but has not taken a wife for his young son, after the father has gone to his fate, when the brothers share, they shall set aside from the goods of their father's estate money, as a bride-price, for their young brother, who has not married a wife, over and above his share, and they shall cause him to take a wife.

167. If a man has taken a wife, and she has borne him children and that woman has gone to her fate, and he has taken a second wife, and she also has borne children; after the father has gone to his fate, the sons shall not share according to mothers, but each family shall take the marriage-portion of its mother, and all shall share the goods of their father's estate equally.

168. If a man has determined to disinherit his son and has declared before the judge, "I cut off my son," the judge shall inquire into the son's past, and, if the son has not committed a grave misdemeanor such as should cut him off from sonship, the father shall [not] disinherit his son.

169. If he has committed a grave crime against his father, which cuts off from sonship, for the first offence he shall pardon him. If he has committed a grave crime a second time, the father shall cut off his son from sonship.

170. If a man has had children borne to him by his wife, and also by a maid, if the father in his lifetime has said, "My sons," to the children whom his maid bore him, and has reckoned them with the sons of his wife; then after the father has gone to his fate, the children of the wife and of the maid shall share equally. The children of the wife shall apportion the shares and make their own selections.

171. And if the father, in his lifetime, has not said, "My sons," to the children whom the maid bore him, after the father has gone to his fate, the children of the maid shall not share with the children of the wife in the goods of their father's house. The maid and her children, however, shall obtain their freedom. The children of the wife have no claim for service on the children of the maid.

The wife shall take her marriage-portion, and any gift that her husband has given her and for which he has written a deed of gift and she shall dwell in her husband's house; as long as she lives, she shall enjoy it, she shall not sell it. After her death it is indeed her children's.

172. If her husband has not given her a gift, her marriage-portion shall be given her in full, and, from the goods of her husband's estate, she shall take a share equal to that of one son.

If her children have persecuted her in order to have her leave the house, and the judge has inquired into her past, and laid the blame on the children, that woman shall not leave her husband's house. If that woman has determined to leave, she shall relinquish to her children the gift her husband gave her, she shall take the marriage-portion of her father's estate, and the husband of her choice may marry her. . . .

195. If a son has struck his father, his hands shall be cut off.

196. If a man has knocked out the eye of a patrician, his eye shall be knocked out.

197. If he has broken the limb of a patrician, his limb shall be broken.

198. If he has knocked out the eye of a plebeian or has broken the limb of a plebeian, he shall pay one mina of silver.

199. If he has knocked out the eye of a patrician's servant, or broken the limb of a patrician's servant, he shall pay half his value.

200. If a patrician has knocked out the tooth of a man that is his equal, his tooth shall be knocked out.

201. If he has knocked out the tooth of a plebeian, he shall pay one-third of a mina of silver.

202. If a man has smitten the privates of a man, higher in rank than he, he shall be scourged with sixty blows of an ox-hide scourge, in the assembly.

203. If a man has smitten the privates of a patrician of his own rank, he shall pay one mina of silver.

204. If a plebeian has smitten the privates of a plebeian, he shall pay ten shekels of silver.

205. If the slave of anyone has smitten the privates of a free-born man, his ear shall be cut off.

206. If a man has struck another in a quarrel, and caused him a permanent injury, that man shall swear, "I struck him without malice," and shall pay the doctor.

207. If he has died of his blows, [the man] shall swear [similarly], and pay one-half a mina of silver; or,

208. If [the deceased] was a plebeian, he shall pay one-third of a mina of silver.

209. If a man has struck a free woman with child, and has caused her to miscarry, he shall pay ten shekels for her miscarriage.

210. If that woman die, his daughter shall be killed.

211. If it be the daughter of a plebeian, that has miscarried through his blows, he shall pay five shekels of silver.

212. If that woman die, he shall pay half a mina of silver.

213. If he has struck a man's maid and caused her to miscarry, he shall pay two shekels of silver.

214. If that woman die, he shall pay one-third of a mina of silver.

215. If a surgeon has operated with the bronze lancet on a patrician for a serious injury, and has cured him, or has removed with a bronze lancet a cataract for a patrician, and has cured his eye, he shall take ten shekels of silver.

216. If it be [a] plebeian, he shall take five shekels of silver.

217. If it be a man's slave, the owner of the slave shall give two shekels of silver to the surgeon.

218. If a surgeon has operated with the bronze lancet on a patrician for a serious injury, and has caused his death, or has removed a cataract for a patrician, with the bronze lancet, and has made him lose his eye, his hands shall be cut off.

219. If the surgeon has treated a serious injury of a plebeian's slave, with the bronze lancet, and has caused his death, he shall render slave for slave.

220. If he has removed a cataract with the bronze lancet, and made the slave lose his eye, he shall pay half his value.

221. If a surgeon has cured the limb of a patrician, or has doctored a diseased bowel, the patient shall pay five shekels of silver to the surgeon.

222. If he be a plebeian, he shall pay three shekels of silver.

223. If he be a man's slave, the owner of the slave shall give two shekels of silver to the doctor.

224. If a veterinary surgeon has treated an ox, or an ass, for a severe injury, and cured it, the owner of the ox, or the ass, shall pay the surgeon one-sixth of a shekel of silver, as his fee.

225. If he has treated an ox, or an ass, for a severe injury, and caused it to die, he shall pay one-quarter of its value to the owner of the ox, or the ass.

226. If a brander has cut out a mark on a slave, without the consent of his owner, that brander shall have his hands cut off.

227. If someone has deceived the brander, and induced him to cut out a mark on a slave, that man shall be put to death and buried in his house; the brander shall swear, "I did not mark him knowingly," and shall go free.

228. If a builder has built a house for a man, and finished it, he shall pay him a fee of two shekels of silver, for each *SAR* built on.

229. If a builder has built a house for a man, and has not made his work sound, and the house he built has fallen, and caused the death of its owner, that builder shall be put to death.

230. If it is the owner's son that is killed, the builder's son shall be put to death.

231. If it is the slave of the owner that is killed, the builder shall give slave for slave to the owner of the house.

232. If he has caused the loss of goods, he shall render back whatever he has destroyed. Moreover, because he did not make sound the house he built, and it fell, at his own cost he shall rebuild the house that fell.

233. If a builder has built a house for a man, and has not keyed his work, and the wall has fallen, that builder shall make that wall firm at his own expense. . . .

271. If a man has hired oxen, a wagon, and its driver, he shall pay one hundred and sixty *KA* of corn daily.

272. If a man has hired the wagon alone, he shall pay forty *KA* of corn daily.

273. If a man has hired a laborer from the beginning of the year to the fifth month, he shall pay six *ŠE* of silver daily; from the sixth month to the close of the year, he shall pay five *ŠE* of silver daily. . . .

275. If a man has hired a boat, its hire is three *ŠE* of silver daily.

276. If he has hired a fast boat he shall pay two and a half *ŠE* daily.

277. If a man has hired a ship of sixty *GUR* he shall pay one-sixth of a shekel of silver daily for its hire.

278. If a man has bought a male or female slave and the slave has not fulfilled his month,

but the *bennu* disease has fallen upon him, he shall return the slave to the seller and the buyer shall take back the money he paid.

279. If a man has bought a male or female slave and a claim has been raised, the seller shall answer the claim.

280. If a man, in a foreign land, has bought a male, or female, slave of another, and if when he has come home the owner of the male or female slave has recognized his slave, and if the slave be a native of the land, he shall grant him his liberty without money.

281. If the slave was a native of another country, the buyer shall declare on oath the amount of money he paid, and the owner of the slave shall repay the merchant what he paid and keep his slave.

282. If a slave has said to his master, "You are not my master," he shall be brought to account as his slave, and his master shall cut off his ear.

Israel: The Concept of a Chosen People

8 THE BOOK OF THE PROPHET ISAIAH: THE SIGNIFICANCE OF MONOTHEISM

Palestine was a third center of civilization in the ancient Near East, but the measure of its significance is very different from that of either Egypt or the Mesopotamian empires. In cultural achievements—such as the use of writing, technological invention, and artistic skill—and the ability to create a stable political organization it was far inferior to the others. Furthermore, its influence on its contemporaries was negligible. The history of the Hebrew people who settled in Palestine sometime around 1400 B.C.—when the Egyptian and Mesopotamian civilizations were already ancient—is, however, of immense interest for at least two reasons. One reason is that the Hebrews offered intellectual concepts which differed greatly from those of the other ancients; the second is the extraordinary part that these concepts have played in shaping western European civilization and, ultimately, the entire modern world.

While it is wise to guard against ascribing too much originality to the Hebrews—they were profoundly indebted to their neighbors for many of their ideas—it is a fact that their civilization had unique qualities which have given it a special place in the human story. A major factor in making the Hebrews distinctive was their attitude toward their God. In Egyptian and Mesopotamian thought, the aim of those activities we classify as religious had been to create unity between man and the cosmos; divinity was immanent in nature, and there was, in effect, no barrier between the gods and the world. In contrast, Hebrew prophets like Isaiah insisted that their one and all-powerful God was utterly transcendent. "My thoughts are not your thoughts, neither are your ways my ways" (Isaiah 55:8) was a statement typical of this sense of God's isolation and separation from man. He was seen as the creator of the world and all that was in it, but He stood above His handiwork and was not a part of it. This emphasis on God's omnipotence and aloofness had as an inevitable corollary the belief that there could be but one God, the God of Israel, who must also be the God of all the nations.

One result of the belief in God's transcendence and uniqueness was the Hebrew insistence that the mark of a good king, the only measure of his success, was his "faithfulness" to the Lord. For a king to permit the worship of "strange gods," for example, brought down on his head the condemnation of the prophets, no matter how prosperous the nation or how great his conquests. In another direction, and perhaps most important of all the consequences of Hebrew monotheism, the prophets asserted that the demands of God included ethical directives—such requirements as justice toward and compassion for one's fellow men—and that the ritual expression of religion was secondary to righteousness. The implications of ethical monotheism were carried over into Israel's daughter religions, Christianity and Islam, and hence reached to the far corners of the world.

Chapter 45

¹Thus saith the LORD to his
    anointed, to Cyrus,
  whose right hand I have holden,
to subdue nations before him;
  and I will loose the loins of kings,
to open before him the two leaved gates;
  and the gates shall not be shut;
²I will go before thee,
  and make the crooked places straight:
I will break in pieces the gates of brass,
  and cut in sunder the bars of iron:
³And I will give thee the treasures of darkness,
  and hidden riches of secret places,
that thou mayest know that I, the LORD,
  which call *thee* by thy name, *am* the
    God of Israel.
⁴For Jacob my servant's sake,
  and Israel mine elect,
I have even called thee by thy name:
  I have surnamed thee, though thou hast
    not known me.
⁵I *am* the LORD, and *there is* none else,
  there is no God besides me:
  girded thee, though thou hast not
    known me:
⁶That they may know from the rising of the sun,
  and from the west, that *there is*
    none besides me.
I *am* the LORD, and *there is* none else.
⁷I form the light, and create darkness:
  I make peace, and create evil:
  I the LORD do all these *things*.
⁸Drop down, ye heavens, from above,
  and let the skies pour down righteousness:
let the earth open, and let them
  bring forth salvation,
  and let righteousness spring up together;
  I the LORD have created it.
⁹Woe unto him that striveth with his Maker!
Let the potsherd *strive* with the potsherds
  of the earth.
Shall the clay say to him that fashioneth it,
  What makest thou?
  or thy work, He hath no hands?
¹⁰Woe unto him that saith unto *his* father,
  What begettest thou?
  or to the woman, What hast thou
    brought forth?
¹¹Thus saith the LORD,
  the Holy One of Israel, and his Maker,
Ask me of things to come concerning my sons,
  and concerning the work of my
    hands command ye me.
¹²I have made the earth,
  and created man upon it:
I, *even* my hands, have stretched out
    the heavens,
  and all their host have I commanded.
¹³I have raised him up in righteousness,
  and I will direct all his ways:
  he shall build my city,
    and he shall let go my captives,
  not for price nor reward,
    saith the LORD of hosts.
¹⁴Thus saith the LORD,
The labor of Egypt, and merchandise
    of Ethiopia,
  and of the Sabeans, men of stature,
shall come over unto thee, and they shall be thine:
  they shall come after thee;
  in chains they shall come over,
    and they shall fall down unto thee,
  they shall make supplication unto thee, *saying*,
    Surely God *is* in thee; and *there is* none else,
    there is no God.
¹⁵Verily thou *art* a God that hidest thyself,
  O God of Israel, the Saviour.
¹⁶They shall be ashamed, and
    also confounded, all of them:
  they shall go to confusion together *that*
    are makers of idols.
¹⁷*But* Israel shall be saved in the LORD
  with an everlasting salvation:
ye shall not be ashamed nor confounded
    world without end.
¹⁸For thus saith the LORD
that created the heavens;
  God himself
that formed the earth and made it;
  he hath established it,
he created it not in vain,
  he formed it to be inhabited:
I *am* the LORD; and *there is* none else.
¹⁹I have not spoken in secret,
  in a dark place of the earth:
I said not unto the seed of Jacob,
  Seek ye me in vain:
I the LORD speak righteousness,
  I declare things that are right.
²⁰Assemble yourselves and come;
  draw near together,
  ye *that are* escaped of the nations:
they have no knowledge
    that set up the wood of their graven image,
and pray unto a god *that* cannot save.
²¹Tell ye, and bring *them* near; yea,
  let them take counsel together:
who hath declared this from ancient time?
  who hath told it from that time?

Text: Adapted from the Authorized King James Version of the Bible. Verses are indicated by superior numbers.

have not I the LORD?
and *there is* no God else besides me;
a just God and a Saviour;
there is none besides me.
²²Look unto me, and be ye saved,
all the ends of the earth:
for I *am* God, and *there is* none else.
²³I have sworn by myself,
the word is gone out of my mouth *in* righteousness,
and shall not return,
That unto me every knee shall bow,
every tongue shall swear.
²⁴Surely, shall *one* say, in the LORD have I righteousness and strength:
even to him shall *men* come;
and all that are incensed against him shall be ashamed.
²⁵In the LORD shall all the seed of Israel be justified, and shall glory.

9 THE FIFTH BOOK OF MOSES, CALLED DEUTERONOMY: THE BURDEN OF BEING CHOSEN

One of the most pervasive ideas of the Old Testament is the belief that the Hebrews were God's chosen people. In itself this idea is not particularly striking, since most ancient peoples regarded themselves as belonging to their god, but there were overtones to the Hebrew attitude that very early caused them to be referred to as "a people that dwelleth alone and is not reckoned among the nations" (Numbers 23:9). An important aspect of the concept of Israel as a chosen nation was the belief in a covenant made between God and His people; it is this idea that is brought out in the passage which follows. Israel's God, as we have seen, was "wholly other," separated from men by a nature utterly different from theirs. But for a reason never clearly articulated in the Old Testament, except as it is seen as an expression of divine love and grace, He chose a small and unconsidered people and gave them a position in relation to Himself different from all the other nations of the earth, which were, nonetheless, His creation. The belief in being chosen to be God's special people could obviously lead to arrogance and complacency, but this tendency was combated by the prophets' insistence that the covenant relationship did not mean that the Hebrews were God's favorites. On the contrary, the rigorous implications of ethical monotheism were that because much had been given them, much would be expected of them. "You only have I known of all the families of the earth; therefore I will punish you for your iniquities" (Amos 3:2). Ultimately the idea developed that Israel had been chosen, as a late prophet put it, so that "nations shall come to your light" (Isaiah 60:3). Also of primary importance in the covenant relationship was the obligation of the Hebrews toward the Law (as found in the Pentateuch). The demand implicit in the covenant faith was to serve God according to "the Law which was given by Moses." This Law, as interpreted through the centuries, provided its followers with a very difficult but at the same time very precise and understandable guide to everyday living.

Chapter 29

¹These were the terms of the covenant which the LORD commanded Moses to make with the Israelites in the land of Moab, besides the covenant which he had made with them at Horeb.

²Moses then summoned all Israel, and said to them,

"Although you have seen all that the LORD did before your eyes in the land of Egypt to Pharaoh and all his courtiers and all his land, ³the great tests which you saw with your own eyes, the signs, and those great portents, ⁴yet to this day the LORD has not given you a mind to understand, nor eyes to discern, or ears to hear. ⁵For forty years I have led you through the desert, your clothes never getting too worn for you to wear, nor your sandals too worn for your feet, ⁶without bread to eat, or wine or liquor to drink, in order that you might come to know that I, the LORD, am your God. ⁷When you reached this place, Sihon, king of Heshbon, and Og, king of Bashan, came out to engage us in battle; but we defeated them, ⁸and capturing their land, we gave it as a heritage to the Reubenites, Gadites, and half-tribe of Manassites. ⁹Be careful then to observe the terms of this

Text: Reprinted from *The Complete Bible: An American Translation*, Edgar J. Goodspeed (ed.) by permission of The University of Chicago Press. Copyright 1941 by The University of Chicago Press. (Verses indicated by superior numbers.)

covenant, that you may succeed in everything that you undertake.

10"You are all taking your stand today before the Lord your God, the heads of your tribes, your elders, and your officers, even all the men of Israel, 11together with your children, your wives, and the aliens in your employ who are living in your camps, both your wood-gatherers and your water-drawers, 12that you may enter into the covenant of the Lord your God and the solemn compact which the Lord your God is making with you today, 13that he may today make you his own people, and that he may be your God, as he promised you, and as he swore to your fathers, Abraham, Isaac, and Jacob. 14It is not with you alone that I am making this covenant and solemn compact, 15but with those who are here with us today, standing before the Lord our God, and with those who are not here with us today 16(for you yourselves know how we once lived in the land of Egypt, and how we passed through the territory of the nations that you did; 17and so you saw the detestable and horrid things of wood and stone, of silver and gold, that were in their possession), 18lest there should be among you man, woman, family, or tribe, whose heart after all might turn from the Lord our God to go and serve the gods of those nations; lest there should be among you a root bearing poison and wormwood, 19and then upon hearing the terms of this sacred compact he should flatter himself by saying, 'I shall be safe, even though I persist in my stubbornness of mind,' to the destruction of moist and dry alike. 20The Lord would never consent to forgive him, but instead, the anger and resentment of the Lord would burn against such a man; every curse recorded in this book would settle on him; the Lord would blot out his very name from under the heavens; 21and the Lord would single him out from all the tribes of Israel for doom, by all the curses of the covenant recorded in this book of the law. 22Then the next generation, your children who take your place, and the foreigners who come from a distant land, will say, when they see the plagues of that land and the diseases with which the Lord has afflicted it—23all its soil being brimstone and salt, a burning waste, unsown and unproductive, no herbage of any kind growing in it, like the devastation of Sodom and Gomorrah, Admah and Zeboiim, which the Lord devastated in his anger and fury—24indeed all nations will say, 'Why has the Lord done thus to this land? Why this great heat of anger?' 25And the answer will be, 'Because they forsook the covenant, which the Lord, the God of their fathers, made with them, when he brought them out of the land of Egypt, 26and went and served alien gods, and paid homage to them, gods of whom they had no experience, and whom he did not assign to them; 27hence the anger of the Lord blazed against this land, bringing it every curse recorded in this book; 28and the Lord uprooted them from their land in anger, fury, and great wrath, and flung them into an alien land, as at this day.'

29"What is hidden is in the keeping of the Lord our God, but what is revealed concerns us and our children forever, that we should observe all the provisions of this code.

Chapter 30

1"When all these things have befallen you, the blessing as well as the curse which I have put before you, and you call them to mind among all the nations where the Lord your God has driven you, 2if you return to the Lord your God, you and your children, and heed his injunctions, just as I am commanding you today, with all your mind and heart, 3then the Lord your God will restore your fortune, taking pity on you, and gathering you again out of all the peoples where the Lord your God scattered you. 4Even though your outcasts are at the ends of the world, the Lord your God will gather you from there, and take you away. 5The Lord your God will bring you into the land which your fathers occupied, that you may occupy it; and he will prosper you, and make you more numerous than your fathers. 6The Lord your God will circumcise you and your descendants in heart, to love the Lord your God with all your mind and heart, that you may live. 7The Lord your God will inflict all these curses on your enemies and your antagonists who persecuted you; 8but you yourselves shall once more heed the injunctions of the Lord, and observe all his commands which I am giving you today; 9and the Lord your God will give you abounding prosperity in all your labor, in the offspring of your body, the offspring of your cattle, and the produce of your soil; for the Lord will again take delight in prospering you, as he did your fathers; 10for you will be heeding the injunctions of the Lord your God by keeping his commands and statutes, recorded in this book of the law; for you will be returning to the Lord your God with all your mind and heart.

10 THE SECOND BOOK OF THE KINGS: THE NATURE OF HISTORY

Another Hebrew concept of enormous significance involved a special way of interpreting history. Both Egyptians and Mesopotamians tended to think of human history as part of an unchanging drama that was constantly being reënacted. In Egypt, this was symbolized by the myths surrounding the king; in Mesopotamia, by the great New Year festivals with their roots in the fertility cults that served to link man, society, and nature in one whole. Their view of history may be called "cyclical," although it should be borne in mind that the cycle was one related to the processes of nature and not, as in some modern versions of history, simply the idea of recurrent patterns of events. Essentially, however, there was no sense of forward movement, for life was an image of the eternal cosmos, which in Egypt meant a feeling for regularity and order, and in Mesopotamia, a consciousness of conflict between order and chaos. In contrast, the Hebrews had a "linear" concept of history; they believed that man's story does not reflect an eternal state, that it is not the reënactment of a divine drama, but rather that it is the record of God's unfolding purpose being worked out through man's actions. In general terms, this purpose is to get men to obey God's will, not, as in the other great cultures, to achieve an integration of human and divine life.

The Hebrew view of history is succinctly summed up in the account of the great events of Israel's past, given below. The writer was not concerned with what we might call "factual history," an objective report of what happened at a particular time and place. What interested him was the interpretation of events as a revelation of God's will for His people; like his spiritual descendant Oliver Cromwell, he was convinced that "events must *mean* something." Men are instruments of God's purposes, even if they do not know it, and disobedience leads to ruin. Figures from the great contemporary empires appear in the Hebrew chronicles but both they and the history they created are interpreted in the light of the Hebrew writers' religious convictions. Doubtless Sennacherib, one of the greatest of Assyrian conquerors, and Cyrus, the sixth-century Persian who ruled much of the ancient world, would have been vastly amused to have been told that they were the servants of a god unknown to them. Out of this attitude of the Hebrews emerged the possibility of universal history—a history not just of one people but of mankind, with the same divine sovereign governing and controlling all events.

Another vital aspect of the Hebrew view of history was their passionate insistence that righteous living as a nation would lead to reward in terms of prosperity while evil would be punished. Disasters to the nation—and they were very frequent—were seen as punishments for national sin. In other words, history was interpreted in moral terms, and a proposed alliance with Egypt, for example, was judged not in terms of political expediency but as the folly of linking themselves with a sinful, though powerful, nation. In the Book of Deuteronomy the equation of righteous living with prosperity is put forth, but even there doubts arise, and much of the literature of the Hebrews includes variations of the anguished cry, "Why do the righteous suffer, why do the wicked prosper?" When a series of catastrophes ended the political autonomy of the Hebrew people, the prophets were forced to a recognition that the reward of faithfulness to God might be suffering. Nonetheless, their faith in the concept of history as the place where His purposes, however unfathomable, were being fulfilled remained unshaken.

Chapter 18

¹Now in the third year of Hoshea, the son of Elah, king of Israel, Hezekiah, the son of Ahaz, king of Judah, became king. ²He was twenty-five years old when he became king, and he reigned twenty-nine years in Jerusalem; and his mother's name was Abi, the daughter of Zechariah. ³He did that which was right in the sight of the LORD just as David his ancestor had done.

⁴He removed the high places and broke down the sacred pillars and cut down the sacred poles. He also broke in pieces the bronze serpent that Moses had made; for as late as those days the

Text: Reprinted from *The Complete Bible: An American Translation,* Edgar J. Goodspeed (ed.) by permission of The University of Chicago Press. Copyright 1941 by The University of Chicago Press. (Verses indicated by superior numbers.)

Israelites offered sacrifices to it; and they called it Nehushtan. ⁵He trusted in the LORD, the God of Israel; so that after him there was none like him among all the kings of Judah, nor among those who were before him. ⁶For he was loyal to the LORD, he turned not away from following him, but kept his commands which the LORD had commanded Moses.

⁷Moreover the LORD was with him; in all his ventures he prospered, and he rebelled against the king of Assyria, and no longer served him. ⁸He conquered the Philistines as far as Gaza and its territory from the watchtower to the fortified city.

⁹Now in the fourth year of King Hezekiah—that is, the seventh year of Hoshea, the son of Elah—Shalmaneser, king of Assyria, came up against Samaria and besieged it. ¹⁰They took it at the end of three years, in the sixth year of Hezekiah—that is, in the ninth year of Hoshea, king of Israel, was Samaria taken. ¹¹Then the king of Assyria carried Israel away to Assyria and settled them in Halah and on the Habor and the river Gozan, and in the cities of the Medes, ¹²because they did not listen to the voice of the LORD their God, but transgressed his covenant, even all that Moses the servant of the LORD had commanded, and would neither listen nor keep it.

¹³Now in the fourteenth year of King Hezekiah, Sennacherib, king of Assyria, came up against all the fortified cities of Judah and captured them. ¹⁴Then Hezekiah, king of Judah, sent to the king of Assyria to Lachish, saying,

"I have offended; withdraw from me; whatever you lay on me I will bear."

So the king of Assyria made Hezekiah, king of Judah, pay three hundred talents of silver and thirty talents of gold. ¹⁵So Hezekiah gave him all the silver that was found in the house of the LORD, and in the treasuries of the king's house. ¹⁶At that time Hezekiah stripped the doors of the temple of the LORD and the columns, which Hezekiah, king of Judah, had overlaid, and gave the gold to the king of Assyria.

¹⁷Then the king of Assyria sent the commander-in-chief, and the chief of the eunuchs and the field marshal from Lachish with a large army against King Hezekiah at Jerusalem. So they went up, and when they came to Jerusalem, they came and took up their position by the conduit of the upper pool, which is on the highway to the laundrymen's field.

¹⁸Now when they called for the king, Eliakim, the son of Hilkiah, who was the steward of the palace, and Shebna, the scribe, and Joah, the son of Asaph, the recorder, went out to them. ¹⁹Then the field marshal said to them,

"Say now to Hezekiah, 'Thus says the great king, the king of Assyria: "What confidence is this in which you trust? ²⁰Do you think that a mere word of the lips is counsel and strength for war? Now in whom do you trust that you have rebelled against me? ²¹You have put your trust evidently in the staff of this broken reed, Egypt, on which if a man lean, it will run into his hand and pierce it. So is Pharaoh, king of Egypt, to all who trust in him. ²²But if you say to me, 'We trust in the LORD our God,' is not he the one whose high places and altars Hezekiah has taken away, saying to Judah and Jerusalem, 'You shall worship before this altar in Jerusalem?' ²³And now, pray make a wager with my master, the king of Assyria: I will give you two thousand horses, if you are able on your part to set riders upon them. ²⁴How then can you repulse the attack of one of the least of my master's servants? Yet you trust in Egypt for chariots and horsemen. ²⁵Now have I come up against this place to destroy it without the LORD's approval? The LORD himself said to me, 'Go up against this land and destroy it.'"'"

²⁶Then Elkanah, the son of Hilkiah, and Shebna and Joah said to the field marshal,

"Speak now to your servants in Aramaic, for we understand it; but do not speak to us in Judean in the hearing of the people who are on the wall."

²⁷But the field marshal said to them,

"Was it to your master and you that my master sent me to speak these words? Was it not rather to the men who are sitting on the wall, doomed with you to eat their own excrement and drink their own urine?"

²⁸Then the field marshal stood up and cried with a loud voice in Judean and spoke, saying,

"Hear the word of the great king, the king of Assyria! ²⁹Thus says the king: 'Do not let Hezekiah deceive you; for he will not be able to deliver you from his hand. ³⁰Neither let Hezekiah cause you to trust in the LORD by saying, "The LORD will surely deliver us; this city shall not be given into the hand of the king of Assyria." ³¹Do not listen to Hezekiah; for thus says the king of Assyria: "Make peace with me and surrender to me; and eat each of you from his own vine and his own fig tree and drink the water of his own cistern, ³²until I come and take you away to a land like your own, a land of grain and wine, a land of bread and vineyards, a land of olive trees and honey, that you may live and not die." But do not listen to Hezekiah, when he would lure you on by saying, "The LORD will deliver us." ³³Has any of the gods of the nations delivered his land from the hand of the king of Assyria? ³⁴Where are the gods of Hamath and Arpad? Where are the gods of Sepharvaim, Hena, and Ivvah? Where are the gods of Samaria? Did they deliver Samaria from my hand? ³⁵Who were there among all the gods of the lands that delivered their lands from my hand, that the LORD should deliver Jerusalem from my hand?'"

³⁶Then the people were silent and answered him not a word; for the king's command was, "Do not answer him."

³⁷Then Eliakim, the son of Hilkiah, who was steward of the palace, and Shebna, the scribe, and Joah, the son of Asaph, the recorder, came to Hezekiah with their garments torn, and told him the words of the field marshal.

Chapter 19

¹As soon as King Hezekiah heard it, he tore his garments, covered himself with sackcloth, and went into the house of the LORD. ²He also sent Eliakim who was steward of the palace and Shebna, the scribe, and the oldest of the priests, covered with sackcloth, to the prophet Isaiah, the son of Amoz. ³They said to him,

"Thus says Hezekiah: 'This is a day of distress, rebuke, and disgrace; for children have come to the birth, and there is no strength to bear them. ⁴It may be that the LORD your God will hear all the words of the field marshal, whom his master, the king of Assyria, has sent to insult the living God, and will rebuke the words which the LORD your God has heard. Therefore lift up a prayer for the remnant that is left.'"

⁵But when the servants of King Hezekiah came to Isaiah, ⁶Isaiah said to them,

"Thus shall you say to your master: 'Thus says the LORD: "Do not be afraid of the words that you have heard, with which the menials of the king of Assyria have blasphemed me. ⁷Behold, I will put a spirit in him, so that when he hears a certain rumor he shall return to his own land, and I will cause him to fall by the sword in his own land."'"

⁸Then the field marshal returned, and found the king of Assyria warring against Libnah; for he had heard that he had left Lachish. ⁹But when he heard concerning Tirhakah, king of Ethiopia, "Behold, he has come out to fight against you," he sent messengers again to Hezekiah, saying,

¹⁰"Thus shall you say to Hezekiah, king of Judah: 'Do not let your God in whom you trust deceive you, saying, "Jerusalem shall not be given into the hand of the king of Assyria." ¹¹You have surely heard what the kings of Assyria have done to all the lands in completely destroying them, and will you be delivered? ¹²Did the gods of the nations which my fathers destroyed deliver them—Gozan, Haran, Rezeph, and the Edenites who were in Telassar? ¹³Where is the king of Hamath, the king of Arpad, and the king of the city of Sepharvaim, of Hena, and of Ivvah?'"

¹⁴So Hezekiah received the letter from the hand of the messengers and read it. Then Hezekiah went up to the house of the LORD and spread it out before the LORD; ¹⁵and Hezekiah prayed before the LORD and said,

"O LORD, the God of Israel, who art seated upon the cherubim, thou art God, even thou alone, over all the kingdoms of the earth; thou hast made the heavens and the earth. ¹⁶Incline thine ear, O LORD, and hear; open thine eyes, O LORD, and see, and hear all the words of Sennacherib, which he has sent to insult the living God. ¹⁷Of a truth, O LORD, the kings of Assyria have laid waste the nations and their land, ¹⁸and have cast their gods into the fire, for they were no gods, but the work of men's hands, wood and stone; and so they have destroyed them. ¹⁹But now, O LORD our God, deliver us from his hand, that all the kingdoms of the earth may know that thou, O LORD, art God alone."

²⁰Then Isaiah, the son of Amoz, sent to Hezekiah, saying,

"Thus says the LORD, the God of Israel: 'What you have prayed to me concerning Sennacherib, king of Assyria, I have heard.' ²¹This is the word that the LORD has spoken against him: 'She despises you, laughs at you—
the virgin daughter of Zion!
Behind you she wags the head—
the daughter of Jerusalem!
²²Whom have you insulted and blasphemed?
Against whom have you raised your voice,
And lifted up your eyes on high?
against the Holy one of Israel!
²³By the hand of your messengers
you have insulted the Lord and have said,
"With the multitude of my chariots
I ascended the mountain heights,
the recesses of Lebanon;
And I felled its tallest cedars,
its choicest cypresses;
And I entered its remotest retreat,
its densest thicket.
²⁴I dug down,
and drank foreign waters;
And with the soles of my feet I dried up
all the streams of Egypt."
²⁵Have you not heard
how I prepared it long ago,
How I planned it in days of old,
and now have brought it to pass—
That you should turn fortified cities
into ruin heaps,
²⁶While their inhabitants, shorn of their strength,
are dismayed and confounded,

Are become like grass of the field,
   like tender green grass,
Like grass on the housetops,
   blasted before it is grown up.
[27] I know your rising and sitting,
   your going and coming,
   and your raging against me.
[28] Because you have raged against me
   and your arrogance has come up to my ears,
Therefore I will put my hook in your nose
   and my bridle in your lips,
And I will cause you to return by the way
   by which you came.'"

[29] "'And this shall be a sign for you: You shall eat this year that which grows of itself, and in the second year that which springs from the same; but in the third year sow and reap, plant vineyards and eat their fruit. [30] The remnant that survives of the house of Judah shall again take root downward and bear fruit upward; [31] for out of Jerusalem shall go forth a remnant and from Mount Zion an escaped band. The zeal of the LORD shall accomplish this.'

[32] "Therefore thus says the LORD concerning the king of Assyria: 'He shall not enter this city, or shoot an arrow there; neither shall he come before it with shield, or cast up a mound against it. [33] By the way that he came, by the same shall he return; but he shall not enter this city,' is the LORD's oracle. [34] 'For I will defend and save this city for my own sake and for the sake of my servant David.'"

[35] Now that night the angel of the LORD went forth and slew in the camp of the Assyrians one hundred and eighty-five thousand; and when men rose early next morning, they were all dead bodies.

[36] Then Sennacherib, king of Assyria, set out and went and returned, and dwelt at Nineveh.

[37] But as he was worshiping in the temple of Nisroch his god, Adrammelech and Sarezer slew him with the sword, and they escaped into the land of Ararat; and Esarhaddon his son became king in his stead.

11 THE DEAD SEA SCROLLS: THE COMMUNITY OF GOD'S PEOPLE

In the late 1940's and early 1950's a series of remarkable archaeological finds near the Dead Sea in Palestine stirred up lively interest among scholars and laymen alike. The excitement over the discoveries demonstrated the great influence of the ancient Near East on the traditions of the modern western world, for it was widely believed that the discovered manuscripts would reveal the origins of Christianity by showing the Jewish environment in which Jesus may have lived.

The first finds were leather scrolls which a Bedouin boy accidentally discovered in 1947 in one of the caves along a rocky, deserted region beside the Dead Sea. When they finally came into the hands of scholars it was learned that one of the scrolls was a copy of the Book of Isaiah one thousand years older than what had previously been considered the oldest extant Hebrew manuscript of any part of the Old Testament. In the following years, great quantities of scrolls were found in other caves, and when the ruins of a large monastic building were unearthed in a nearby valley known as the Wady Qumran, most scholars assumed that this monastery had been the source of the Dead Sea Scrolls. As the manuscripts were read, a picture unfolded of a group of men who had lived in the Dead Sea area from 125 B.C. to 68 A.D. and who had constituted some kind of sectarian opposition to established Judaism. Prior to the translation of these scrolls, most of our knowledge of the religious life of the time had come either from Christian records or from orthodox Jewish commentary; information from this new source promised to be of great value in reconstructing the period. Two basic questions arose out of this interest in the Qumran materials. One dealt with the nature of the group that had created the community; the other with the significance of the discoveries for the Christian faith.

An answer to the first question is suggested by the Qumran community's "Manual of Discipline," one of the most interesting of the manuscript discoveries. This document lists the rules by which the group lived as well as the ideals that motivated them to exchange the ordinary life of their time for monastic existence in the desolate Dead Sea area. For nearly two hundred years the community was the center of existence for men who were convinced that they were the true remaining descendants of the people whom God had chosen long ago and with whom he had made the covenant (see Documents 9 and 10). Just as Moses had led the children of Israel out of bondage in Egypt and into the desert to find a new life, so the Qumran community called its members from the bondage of the world into the desert to live a life of rigorous discipline. According to Theodor Gaster, one of the leading American authorities on the Dead Sea Scrolls, they sought through their life in the desert to win a victory over the darkness of this world so that they might live "even on earth in a dimension of eternity."

The question of the significance of the Qumran findings for Christian history has been much debated. Since the community flourished during the formative years of Christianity in an area near where John the Baptist and Jesus preached, the possibility of some influence seems great. Furthermore, there are many striking parallels between the practices of the Qumran group and those of the early Christians—the gathering of "saints" who were certain that they were the heirs of God's promises to Israel, expectations of the future coming of God's reign, and the importance of a communal meal. According to some scholars, it is plain that Qumran was the "cradle of Christianity." More cautious scholars find resemblances but insist that the principal value of the recent discoveries is the help they give in understanding the mental and spiritual background of an influential segment of Jewish life in the years when Christianity was established. This is the point made by Gaster when he writes that the Scrolls portray "the environment whose spiritual idiom John and Jesus spoke . . . and they also mirror a form of religious organization many elements of which were adopted by the primitive Church." But, he argues, "there is in them no trace of any of the cardinal theological concepts—the incarnate Godhead, Original Sin, redemption through the Cross, and the like—which made Christianity a distinctive faith."

Of the Commitment

Everyone who wishes to join the community must pledge himself to respect God and man; to live according to the communal rule; to seek God [   ]; to do what is good and upright in His sight, in accordance with what He has commanded through Moses and through His servants the prophets; to love all that He has chosen and hate all that He has rejected; to keep far from all evil and to cling to all good works; to act truthfully and righteously and justly on earth and to walk no more in the stubbornness of a guilty heart and of lustful eyes, doing all manner of evil; to bring into a bond of mutual love all who have declared their willingness to carry out the statutes of God; to join the formal community of God; to walk blamelessly before Him in conformity with His various laws and dispositions; to love all the children of light, each according to his stake in the formal community of God; and to hate all the children of darkness, each according to the measure of his guilt, which God will ultimately requite.

All who declare their willingness to serve God's truth must bring all of their mind, all of their strength, and all of their wealth into the community of God, so that their minds may be purified by the truth of His precepts, their strength controlled by His perfect ways, and their wealth disposed in accordance with His just design. They must not deviate by a single step from carrying out the orders of God at the times appointed for them; they must neither advance the statutory times nor postpone the prescribed seasons. They must not turn aside from the ordinances of God's truth either to the right or to the left.

Of initiation

Moreover, all who would join the ranks of the community must enter into a covenant in the presence of God to do according to all that He has commanded and not to turn away from Him through any fear or terror or through any trial to which they may be subjected through the domination of Belial.

When they enter into that covenant, the priests and the levites are to pronounce a blessing upon the God of salvation and upon all that He does to make known His truth; and all that enter the covenant are to say after them, Amen, amen.

Then the priests are to rehearse the bounteous acts of God as revealed in all His deeds of power, and they are to recite all His tender mercies towards Israel; while the levites are to rehearse the iniquities of the children of Israel and all the guilty transgressions and sins that they have committed through the domination of Belial. And all who enter the covenant are to make confession after them, saying, We have acted perversely, we have transgressed, we have sinned, we have done wickedly, ourselves and our fathers before us, in that we have gone counter to the

Text: Theodor H. Gaster, *The Dead Sea Scriptures.* Copyright © 1956 by Theodor H. Gaster. Reprinted by permission of the publishers, Doubleday & Company, Inc., New York, and Martin Secker & Warburg, Ltd., London. Pp. 39-41, 43-44, 46-47.

truth. God has been right to bring His judgment upon us and upon our fathers. Howbeit, always from ancient times He has also bestowed His mercies upon us, and so will He do for all time to come.

Then the priests are to invoke a blessing on all that have cast their lot with God, that walk blamelessly in all their ways; and they are to say: MAY HE BLESS THEE with all good and KEEP THEE from all evil, and ILLUMINE thy heart with insight into the things of life, and GRACE THEE with knowledge of things eternal, and LIFT UP His gracious COUNTENANCE TOWARDS THEE to grant thee peace everlasting.

The levites, on the other hand, are to invoke a curse on all that have cast their lot with Belial, and to say in response: Cursed art thou for all thy wicked guilty works. May God make thee a thing of abhorrence at the hands of all who would wreak vengeance, and visit thine offspring with destruction at the hands of all who would mete out retribution. Cursed art thou, beyond hope of mercy. Even as thy works are wrought in darkness, so mayest thou be damned in the gloom of the fire eternal. May God show thee no favor when thou callest, neither pardon to forgive thine iniquities. May He lift up an angry countenance towards thee, to wreak vengeance upon thee. May no man wish thee peace of all that truly claim their patrimony.

And all that enter the covenant shall say alike after them that bless and after them that curse, Amen, amen.

Thereupon the priests and the levites shall continue and say: Cursed be every one that hath come to enter this covenant with the taint of idolatry in his heart and who hath set his iniquity as a stumblingblock before him so that thereby he may defect, and who, when he hears the terms of this covenant, blesses himself in his heart, saying, May it go well with me, for I shall go on walking in the stubbornness of my heart! Whether he satisfy his passions or whether he still thirst for their fulfillment, his spirit shall be swept away and receive no pardon. The anger of God and the fury of His judgments shall consume him as by fire unto his eternal extinction, and there shall cleave unto him all the curses threatened in this covenant. God shall set him apart for misfortune, and he shall be cut off from the midst of all the children of light in that through the taint of his idolatry and through the stumblingblock of his iniquity he has defected from God. God will set his lot among those that are accursed for ever! And all who have been admitted to the covenant shall say after them in response, Amen, amen....

Of the two spirits in man

This is for the man who would bring others to the inner vision, so that he may understand and teach to all the children of light the real nature of men, touching the different varieties of their temperaments with the distinguishing traits thereof, touching their actions throughout their generations, and touching the reason why they are now visited with afflictions and now enjoy periods of well-being.

All that is and ever was comes from a God of knowledge. Before things came into existence He determined the plan of them; and when they fill their appointed roles, it is in accordance with His glorious design that they discharge their functions. Nothing can be changed. In His hand lies the government of all things. God it is that sustains them in their needs.

Now, this God created man to rule the world, and appointed for him two spirits after whose direction he was to walk until the final Inquisition. They are the spirits of truth and of perversity.

The origin of truth lies in the Fountain of Light, and that of perversity in the Wellspring of Darkness. All who practice righteousness are under the domination of the Prince of Lights, and walk in ways of light; whereas all who practice perversity are under the domination of the Angel of Darkness and walk in ways of darkness. Through the Angel of Darkness, however, even those who practice righteousness are made liable to error. All their sin and their iniquities, all their guilt and their deeds of transgression are the result of his domination; and this, by God's inscrutable design, will continue until the time appointed by Him. Moreover, all men's afflictions and all their moments of tribulation are due to this being's malevolent sway. All of the spirits that attend upon him are bent on causing the sons of light to stumble. Howbeit, the God of Israel and the Angel of His truth are always there to help the sons of light. It is God that created these spirits of light and darkness and made them the basis of every act, the [instigators] of every deed and the directors of every thought. The one He loves to all eternity, and is ever pleased with its deeds; but any association with the other He abhors, and He hates all its ways to the end of time....

Thus far, the spirits of truth and perversity have been struggling in the heart of man. Men have walked both in wisdom and in folly. If a man casts his portion with truth he does righteously and hates perversity; if he casts it with perversity, he does wickedly and abominates truth. For God has apportioned them in equal measure until the final age, until 'He makes all things new.' He foreknows the effect of their works in every epoch of the world, and He has made men heirs to them that they might know good and evil. But [when the time] of Inquisition [comes], He will determine the fate of every living being in accordance with which of the [two spirits he has chosen to follow].

Of social relations

This is the rule for all the members of the community—that is, for such as have declared their readiness to turn away from all evil and to adhere to all that God in His good pleasure has commanded.

They are to keep apart from the company of the froward.

They are to belong to the community in both a doctrinal and an economic sense.

They are to abide by the decisions of the sons of Zadok, the same being priests that still keep the Covenant, and of the majority of the community that stand firm in it. It is by the vote of such that all matters doctrinal, economic and judicial are to be determined.

They are concertedly and in all their pursuits to practise truth, humility, righteousness, justice, charity and decency, with no one walking in the stubbornness of his own heart or going astray after his heart or his eyes or his fallible human mind.

Furthermore, they are concertedly to remove the impurity of their human mold, and likewise all stiffneckedness.

They are to establish in Israel a solid basis of truth.

They are to unite in a bond indissoluble for ever.

They are to extend forgiveness to all among the priesthood that have freely enlisted in the cause of holiness, and to all among the laity that have done so in the cause of truth, and likewise to all that have associated themselves with them.

They are to make common cause both in the struggle and in the upshot of it.

They are to regard as felons all that transgress the law.

Interpretations of the Ancient Civilizations of the Near East

12 HENRI FRANKFORT, "MYTH AND REALITY": THE RELATION BETWEEN MYTH AND REALITY

In the past century there has been discovered an enormous amount of material bearing on the civilizations of the ancient Near East. Knowledge of the great civilizations whose grandeur was fixed in the memory of modern western man was increased, while others whose existence was not suspected were brought to light. Through the accumulation of written documents and artifacts of all kinds—pottery, tools, monuments—it has been possible to reconstruct, at least in skeletal form, much of the political history of the ancient world. A good deal can also be said with certainty concerning the conditions of social life and the nature of religious belief. But many questions as to the underlying, often unarticulated, assumptions of the civilizations are not directly answered by either documents or artifacts; what is necessary is some re-creation of the thought patterns of ancient men in order to comprehend how they looked at the world around them, how they came to conclusions that often seem preposterous to us.

Henri Frankfort, one of the greatest modern students of the ancient Near East, attempted such a reconstruction. Both an archaeologist and a historian of culture, he drew upon a wide range of material to support his views. In a book appropriately entitled *The Intellectual Adventure of Ancient Man*, he and his colleagues at the University of Chicago examined the records of the past to show how ancient and modern man differ in their understanding of the surrounding world. The difference, Frankfort argued, was that ancient man knew only a "living world," and made no real distinction between animate and inanimate. "Any phenomenon may at any time face him," he wrote, "not as 'It,' but as 'Thou.'" It is this concept he is examining in the following paragraphs.

His argument is that the relation between what we call "myth" and "reality" is the key to the intellectual adventure of civilization.

We are here concerned particularly with thought. It is likely that the ancients recognized certain intellectual problems and asked for the "why" and "how," the "where from" and "where to." Even so, we cannot expect in the ancient Near Eastern documents to find speculation in the predominantly intellectual form with which we are familiar and which presupposes strictly logical procedure even while attempting to transcend it. We have seen that in the ancient Near East, as in present-day primitive society, thought does not operate autonomously. The whole man confronts a living "Thou" in nature; and the whole man—emotional and imaginative as well as intellectual—gives expression to the experience. All experience of "Thou" is highly individual; and early man does, in fact, view happenings as individual events. An account of such events and also their explanation can be conceived only as action and necessarily take the form of a story. In other words, the ancients told myths instead of presenting an analysis or conclusions. We would explain, for instance, that certain atmospheric changes broke a drought and brought about rain. The Babylonians observed the same facts but experienced them as the intervention of the gigantic bird Imdugud which came to their rescue. It covered the sky with the black storm clouds of its wings and devoured the Bull of Heaven, whose hot breath had scorched the crops.

In telling such a myth, the ancients did not intend to provide entertainment. Neither did they seek, in a detached way and without ulterior motives, for intelligible explanations of the natural phenomena. They were recounting events in which they were involved to the extent of their very existence. They experienced, directly, a conflict of powers, one hostile to the harvest upon which they depended, the other frightening but beneficial: the thunderstorm reprieved them in the nick of time by defeating and utterly destroying the drought. The images had already become traditional at the time when we meet them in art and literature, but originally they must have been seen in the revelation which the experience entailed. They are products of imagination, but they are not mere fantasy. It is essential that true myth be distinguished from legend, saga, fable, and fairy tale. All these may retain elements of the myth. And it may also happen that a baroque or frivolous imagination elaborates myths until they become mere stories. But true myth presents its images and its imaginary actors, not with the playfulness of fantasy, but with a compelling authority. It perpetuates the revelation of a "Thou."

The imagery of myth is therefore by no means allegory. It is nothing less than a carefully chosen cloak for abstract thought. The imagery is inseparable from the thought. It represents the form in which the experience has become conscious.

Myth, then, is to be taken seriously, because it reveals a significant, if unverifiable, truth—we might say a metaphysical truth. But myth has not the universality and the lucidity of theoretical statement. It is concrete, though it claims to be inassailable in its validity. It claims recognition by the faithful; it does not pretend to justification before the critical.

The irrational aspect of myth becomes especially clear when we remember that the ancients were not content merely to recount their myths as stories conveying information. They dramatized them, acknowledging in them a special virtue which could be activated by recital.

Of the dramatization of myth, Holy Communion is a well-known example. Another example is found in Babylonia. During each New Year's festival the Babylonians re-enacted the victory which Marduk had won over the powers of chaos on the first New Year's Day, when the world was created. At the annual festival the Epic of Creation was recited. It is clear that the Babylonians did not regard their story of creation as we might accept the theory of Laplace, for instance, as an intellectually satisfying account of how the world came to be as it is. Ancient man had not thought out an answer; an answer had been revealed to him in a reciprocal relationship with nature. If a question had been answered, man shared that answer with the "Thou" which had revealed itself. Hence, it seemed wise that man, each year, at the critical turn of the seasons, should proclaim the knowledge which he shared with the powers, in order to involve them once more in its potent truth.

We may, then, summarize the complex character of myth in the following words: Myth is a form of poetry which transcends poetry in that it proclaims a truth; a form of reasoning which transcends reasoning in that it wants to bring about the truth it proclaims; a form of action, of ritual behavior, which does not find its fulfilment in the act but must proclaim and elaborate a poetic form of truth.

It will now be clear why we said at the beginning of this chapter that our search for spec-

Text: Henri Frankfort, "Myth and Reality," in *The Intellectual Adventure of Ancient Man* by Henri Frankfort et al. Copyright 1946 by The University of Chicago Press and reprinted by their permission. Pp. 6-16, 19-26 *passim*.

ulative thought in the ancient Near East might lead to negative results. The detachment of intellectual inquiry is wanting throughout. And yet, within the framework of mythopoeic thought, speculation may set in. Even early man, entangled in the immediacy of his perceptions, recognized the existence of certain problems which transcend the phenomena. He recognized the problem of origin and the problem of *telos*, of the aim and purpose of being. He recognized the invisible order of justice maintained by his customs, mores, institutions; and he connected this invisible order with the visible order, with its succession of days and nights, seasons and years, obviously maintained by the sun. . . .

We move one step farther if the creation is imagined, not in a purely fantastic manner, but by analogy with human conditions. Creation is then conceived as birth; and the simplest form is the postulate of a primeval couple as the parents of all that exists. It seems that for the Egyptians, as for the Greeks and the Maoris, Earth and Sky were the primeval pair.

The next step, this time one which leads in the direction of speculative thought, is taken when creation is conceived as the action of one of the parents. It may be conceived of as birth by a Great Mother, either a goddess, as in Greece, or a demon, as in Babylonia. Alternatively it is possible to conceive creation as the act of a male. In Egypt, for instance, the god Atum arose unaided from the primeval waters and started the creation of cosmos out of chaos by begetting on himself the first pair of gods. . . .

We also find speculative thought in Babylonia, where chaos is conceived, not as a friendly and co-operative Ogdoad which brings forth the creator, Sun, but as the enemy of life and order. After Ti'amat, the Great Mother, had given birth to countless beings, including the gods, the latter, under the guidance of Marduk, fought a critical battle in which she was overcome and destroyed. And out of her the existing universe was constructed. The Babylonian placed that conflict at the basis of existence.

Throughout the ancient Near East, then, we find speculative thought in the form of myth. We have seen how the attitude of early man toward the phenomena explains his mythopoeic form of thought. But, in order to understand its peculiarities more fully, we should consider the form it takes in somewhat greater detail. . . .

We shall find that if we attempt to define the structure of mythopoeic thought and compare it with that of modern (that is, scientific) thought, the differences will prove to be due rather to emotional attitude and intention than to a so-called prelogical mentality. The basic distinction of modern thought is that between *subjective* and *objective*. On this distinction scientific thought has based a critical and analytical procedure by which it progressively reduces the individual phenomena to typical events subject to universal laws. Thus it creates an increasingly wide gulf between our perception of the phenomena and the conceptions by which we make them comprehensible. We see the sun rise and set, but we think of the earth as moving round the sun. We see colors, but we describe them as wave-lengths. We dream of a dead relative, but we think of that distinct vision as a product of our own subconscious minds. Even if we individually are unable to prove these almost unbelievable scientific views to be true, we accept them, because we know that they can be proved to possess a greater degree of objectivity than our sense-impressions. In the immediacy of primitive experience, however, there is no room for such a critical resolution of perceptions. Primitive man cannot withdraw from the presence of the phenomena because they reveal themselves to him in the manner we have described. Hence the distinction between subjective and objective knowledge is meaningless to him.

Meaningless, also, is our contrast between reality and appearance. Whatever is capable of affecting mind, feeling, or will has thereby established its undoubted reality. There is, for instance, no reason why dreams should be considered less real than impressions received while one is awake. On the contrary, dreams often affect one so much more than the humdrum events of daily life that they appear to be more, and not less, significant than the usual perceptions. The Babylonians, like the Greeks, sought divine guidance by passing the night in a sacred place hoping for a revelation in dreams. And pharaohs, too, have recorded that dreams induced them to undertake certain works. Hallucinations, too, are real. We find in the official annals of Assarhaddon of Assyria a record of fabulous monsters—two-headed serpents and green, winged creatures—which the exhausted troops had seen in the most trying section of their march, the arid Sinai Desert. We may recall that the Greeks saw the Spirit of the Plain of Marathon arisen in the fateful battle against the Persians. As to monsters, the Egyptians of the Middle Kingdom, as much horrified by the desert as are their modern descendants, depicted dragons, griffins, and chimeras among gazelles, foxes, and other desert game, on a footing of perfect equality. . . .

For us there is an essential difference between an act and a ritual or symbolical performance.

But this distinction was meaningless to the ancients. Gudea, a Mesopotamian ruler, describing the founding of a temple, mentions in one breath that he molded a brick in clay, purified the site with fire, and consecrated the platform with oil. When the Egyptians claim that Osiris, and the Babylonians that Oannes, gave them the elements of their culture, they include among those elements the crafts and agriculture as well as ritual usages. These two groups of activities possess the same degree of reality. It would be meaningless to ask a Babylonian whether the success of the harvest depended on the skill of the farmers or on the correct performance of the New Year's festival. Both were essential to success. . . .

We are touching here on the category of *causality*, which is as important for modern thought as the distinction between the subjective and the objective. If science, as we have said before, reduces the chaos of perceptions to an order in which typical events take place according to universal laws, the instrument of this conversion from chaos to order is the postulate of causality. Primitive thought naturally recognized the relationship of cause and effect, but it cannot recognize our view of an impersonal, mechanical, and lawlike functioning of causality. For we have moved far from the world of immediate experience in our search for true causes, that is, causes which will always produce the same effect under the same conditions. We must remember that Newton discovered the concept of gravitation and also its laws by taking into account three groups of phenomena which are entirely unrelated to the merely perceptive observer: freely falling objects, the movements of the planets, and the alternation of the tides. Now the primitive mind cannot withdraw to that extent from perceptual reality. Moreover, it would not be satisfied by our ideas. It looks, not for the "how," but for the "who," when it looks for a cause. Since the phenomenal world is a "Thou" confronting early man, he does not expect to find an impersonal law regulating a process. He looks for a purposeful will committing an act. If the rivers refuse to rise, it is not suggested that the lack of rainfall on distant mountains adequately explains the calamity. When the river does not rise, it has *refused* to rise. The river, or the gods, must be angry with the people who depend on the inundation. At best the river or the gods intend to convey something to the people. Some action, then, is called for. We know that, when the Tigris did not rise, Gudea the king went to sleep in the temple in order to be instructed in a dream as to the meaning of the drought. In Egypt, where annual records of the heights of the Nile flood were kept from the earliest historical times, the pharaoh nevertheless made gifts to the Nile every year about the time when it was due to rise. To these sacrifices, which were thrown into the river, a document was added. It stated, in the form of either an order or a contract, the Nile's obligations.

Our view of causality, then, would not satisfy primitive man because of the impersonal character of its explanations. It would not satisfy him, moreover, because of its generality. We understand phenomena, not by what makes them peculiar, but by what makes them manifestations of general laws. But a general law cannot do justice to the individual character of each event. And the individual character of the event is precisely what early man experiences most strongly. We may explain that certain physiological processes cause a man's death. Primitive man asks: Why should *this* man die *thus* at *this* moment? We can only say that, given these conditions, death will always occur. He wants to find a cause as specific and individual as the event which it must explain. The event is not analyzed intellectually; it is experienced in its complexity and individuality, and these are matched by equally individual causes. Death is *willed*. The question, then, turns once more from the "why" to the "who," not to the "how." . . .

We see, again, that the ancients' conception of a phenomenon differed according to their approach to it. Modern scholars have reproached the Egyptians for their apparent inconsistencies and have doubted their ability to think clearly. Such an attitude is sheer presumption. Once one recognizes the processes of ancient thought, their justification is apparent. After all, religious values are not reducible to rationalistic formulas. Natural phenomena, whether or not they were personified and became gods, confronted ancient man with a living presence, a significant "Thou," which, again, exceeded the scope of conceptual definition. In such cases our flexible thought and language qualify and modify certain concepts so thoroughly as to make them suitable to carry our burden of expression and significance. The mythopoeic mind, tending toward the concrete, expressed the irrational, not in our manner, but by admitting the validity of several avenues of approach at one and the same time. The Babylonians, for instance, worshiped the generative force in nature in several forms: its manifestation in the beneficial rains and thunderstorms was visualized as a lion-headed bird. Seen in the fertility of the earth, it became a snake. Yet in statues, prayers, and cult acts it was represented as a god in human shape. The Egyptians in the earliest times recognized Horus, a god of heaven, as their main deity. He was imagined as a gigantic falcon hovering over the earth with outstretched wings, the colored clouds of sunset and sunrise being his speckled breast and the sun and moon his eyes. Yet this god could also be viewed as a sun-god, since the sun, the most powerful thing in the sky, was naturally considered a manifestation of the god and thus confronted man with the same divine presence which he adored in the falcon spreading its wings over the earth. We should not doubt that mythopoeic thought fully recognizes the unity of each phenomenon which it conceives under so many different guises; the many-sidedness of its images serves to do justice to the complexity of the phenomena. But the procedure of the mythopoeic mind in expressing a phenomenon by manifold images corresponding to unconnected avenues of approach clearly leads away from, rather than toward, our postulate of causality which seeks to discover identical causes for identical effects throughout the phenomenal world.

We observe a similar contrast when we turn from the category of *causality* to that of *space*. Just as modern thought seeks to establish causes as abstract functional relations between phenomena, so it views space as a mere system of relations and functions. Space is postulated by us to be infinite, continuous, and homogeneous—attributes which mere sensual perception does not reveal. But primitive thought cannot abstract a concept "space" from its experience of space. And this experience consists in what we would call qualifying associations. The spatial concepts of the primitive are concrete orientations; they refer to localities which have an emotional color; they may be familiar or alien, hostile or friendly. Beyond the scope of mere individual experience the community is aware of certain cosmic events which invest regions of space with a particular significance. Day and night give to east and west a correlation with life and death. Speculative thought may easily develop in connection with such regions as are outside direct experiences, for instance, the heavens or the nether world. Mesopotamian astrology evolved a very extensive system of correlations between heavenly bodies and events in the sky and earthly localities. Thus mythopoeic thought may succeed no less than modern thought in establishing a co-ordinated spatial system; but the system is determined, not by objective measurements, but by an emotional recognition of values. The extent to which this procedure determines the primitive view of space can best be illustrated by an example. . . .

In Egypt the creator was said to have emerged from the waters of chaos and to have made a mound of dry land upon which he could stand. This primeval hill, from which the creation took its beginning, was traditionally located in the sun temple at Heliopolis, the sun-god being in Egypt most commonly viewed as the creator. However, the Holy of Holies of each temple was equally sacred; each deity was—by the very fact that he was recognized as divine—a source of creative power. Hence each Holy of Holies throughout the land could be identified with the primeval hill. Thus it is said of the temple of Philae, which was founded in the fourth century B.C.: "This [temple] came into being when nothing at all had yet come into being and the earth was still lying in darkness and obscurity." The same claim was made for other temples. The names of the great shrines at Memphis, Thebes, and Hermonthis explicitly stated that they were the "divine emerging primeval island" or used similar expressions. Each sanctuary possessed the essential quality of original holiness; for, when a new temple was founded, it was assumed that the potential sacredness of the site became manifest. The equation with the primeval hill received architectural expression also. One mounted a few steps or followed a ramp at every entrance from court or hall to the Holy of Holies, which was thus situated at a level noticeably higher than the entrance. . . .

To us this view is entirely unacceptable. In our continuous, homogeneous space the place of each locality is unambiguously fixed. We would insist that there must have been one single place where the first mound of dry land actually emerged from the chaotic waters. But the Egyptian would have considered such objections mere quibbles. Since the temples and the royal tombs were as sacred as the primeval hill and showed architectural forms which resembled the hill, they shared essentials. And it would be fatuous to argue whether one of these monuments could be called the primeval hill with more justification than the others.

Similarly, the waters of chaos from which all life emerged were considered to be present in several places, sometimes playing their part in the economy of the country, sometimes necessary to round out the Egyptian image of the universe. The waters of chaos were supposed to subsist in the form of the ocean surrounding the earth, which had emerged from them and now floated upon them. Hence these waters were also present in the subsoil water. In the cenotaph of Seti I at Abydos the coffin was placed upon an island with a double stair imitating the hieroglyph for the primeval hill; this island was surrounded by a channel filled always with subsoil water. Thus the dead king was buried and thought to rise again in the locality of creation. But the waters of chaos, the Nūn, were also the waters of the nether world, which the sun and the dead have to cross. On the other hand, the primeval waters had once contained all the potentialities of life; and they were, therefore, also the waters of the annual inundation of the Nile which renews and revives the fertility of the fields.

The mythopoeic conception of *time* is, like that of space, qualitative and concrete, not quantitative and abstract. Mythopoeic thought does not know time as a uniform duration or as a succession of qualitatively indifferent moments. The concept of time as it is used in our mathematics and physics is as unknown to early man as that which forms the framework of our history. Early man does not abstract a concept of time from the experience of time. . . . Each morning the sun defeats darkness and chaos, as he did on the day of creation and does, every year, on New Year's Day. These three moments coalesce; they are felt to be essentially the same. Each sunrise, and each New Year's Day, repeats the first sunrise on the day of creation; and for the mythopoeic mind each repetition coalesces with—is practically identical with—the original event. . . .

Now this "dramatic conception of nature which sees everywhere a strife between divine and demoniac, cosmic and chaotic powers" (Wensinck), does not leave man a mere spectator. He is too much involved in, his welfare depends too completely upon, the victory of the beneficial powers for him not to feel the need to participate on their side. Thus we find, in Egypt and Babylonia, that man—that is, man in society—accompanies the principal changes in nature with appropriate rituals. Both in Egypt and in Babylonia the New Year, for instance, was an occasion of elaborate celebrations in which the battles of the gods were mimed or in which mock-battles were fought.

We must remember again that such rituals are not merely symbolical; they are part and parcel of the cosmic events; they are man's share in these events. In Babylonia, from the third millennium down to Hellenistic times, we find a New Year's festival which lasted several days. During the celebration the story of creation was recited and a mock-battle was fought in which the king impersonated the victorious god. In Egypt we know mock-battles in several festivals which are concerned with the defeat of death and rebirth or resurrection: one took place at Abydos, during the annual Great Procession of Osiris; one took place on New Year's Eve, at the erection of the Djed pillar; one was fought, at least in the time of Herodotus, at Papremis in the Delta. In these festivals man participated in the life of nature.

Man also arranged his own life, or at least the life of the society to which he belonged, in such a manner that a harmony with nature, a co-ordination of natural and social forces, gave added impetus to his undertakings and increased his chances for success. The whole "science" of omens aims, or course, at this result. But there are also definite instances which illustrate the need of early man to act in unison with nature. In both Egypt and Babylon a king's coronation was postponed until a new beginning in the cycle of nature provided a propitious starting-point for the new reign. In Egypt the time might be in the early summer, when the Nile began to rise, or in the autumn, when the inundation receded and the fertilized fields were ready to receive the seed. In Babylonia the king began his reign on New Year's Day; and the inauguration of a new temple was celebrated only at that time.

This deliberate co-ordination of cosmic and social events shows most clearly that time to early man did not mean a neutral and abstract frame of reference but rather a succession of recurring phases, each charged with a peculiar value and significance. Again, as in dealing with space, we find that there are certain "regions" of time which are withdrawn from direct experience and greatly stimulate speculative thought. They are the distant past and the future. Either of these may become normative and absolute; each then falls beyond the range of time altogether. The absolute past does not recede, nor do we approach the absolute future gradually. The "Kingdom of God" may at any time break into our present. For the Jews the future is normative. For the Egyptians, on the other hand, the past was normative; and no pharaoh could hope to achieve more than the establishment of the conditions "as they were in the time of Rē, in the beginning." . . .

. . . We have attempted to demonstrate how the "logic," the peculiar structure, of mythopoeic thought can be derived from the fact that the intellect does not operate autonomously because it can never do justice to the basic experience of early man, that of confrontation with a significant "Thou." Hence when early man is faced by an intellectual problem within the many-sided complexities of life, emotional and volitional factors are never debarred; and the conclusions reached are not critical judgments but complex images.

Nor can the spheres which these images refer to be neatly kept apart. We have intended . . . to deal successively with speculative thought concerning (1) the nature of the universe; (2) the function of the state; and (3) the values of life. But the reader will have grasped that this, our mild attempt to distinguish the spheres of metaphysics, politics, and ethics, is doomed to remain a convenience without any deep significance. For the life of man and the function of the state are for mythopoeic thought imbedded in nature, and the natural processes are affected by the acts of man no less than man's life depends on his harmonious integration with nature. The experiencing of this unity with the utmost intensity was the greatest good ancient oriental religion could bestow. To conceive this integration in the form of intuitive imagery was the aim of the speculative thought of the ancient Near East.

13 V. GORDON CHILDE, "A PREHISTORIAN'S INTERPRETATION OF DIFFUSION": THE DIFFUSION OF ANCIENT CULTURES

The nature of the relationship between the great centers of civilization in the ancient Near East has been much discussed, and with the increased knowledge we now have of the antiquity of the Indus Valley civilization the problem has become even more complex. On the one hand, the civilizations of the three river systems—the Nile, the Tigris-Euphrates, and the Indus—show many remarkable similarities; on the other hand, their differences both in technological specialization and in fundamental temperament are scarcely less striking.

Two broad theories have been advanced which cover both resemblances and divergences and at the same time take into account such problems as chronology and the reasons for the origin of civilizations at particular times and places. One theory is that civilizations developed independent of each other in various centers, and that institutions and techniques—ranging from kingship through writing to metallurgy—were the result of parallel development and invention. The other theory emphasizes the diffusion of ideas and inventions from one original source to neighboring areas. Neither theory, of course, totally excludes the possibility of both original invention and diffusion working simultaneously; however, each emphasizes the importance of one factor over the other. The problem is understandably complicated, its solution depending upon detailed knowledge of particular cultures as well as an all-encompassing view of many civilizations. In the following selection, V. Gordon Childe, a well-known prehistorian, examines the case for diffusion, taking into consideration such necessary factors as the spatial and temporal proximity of civilizations, the similarity and uniqueness of different cultural manifestations, and the communication problems that would have to be solved before intercultural borrowing could take place.

. . . The archaeologist's attention is focused primarily on man's material culture—the equipment, the extracorporeal organs, that enable human groups to survive and multiply. But within the human species improvement in that equipment takes the place of the hereditary bodily modifications that demarcate genera in the biologist's evolutionary hierarchy. And so such improvement may be taken as a proof of progress in the sense that organic evolution attests a survival of the fittest. But the speed of progress, thus defined, so extraordinarily rapid as compared with organic evolution, seems to be due to the distinctively human capacity of learning from one's neighbor; inventions and devices, created by one society as adjustments to its special environment, can be adopted by another and adapted to its rather different requirements. But that is exactly what I mean by diffusion. To me diffusion means essentially the pooling of ideas, building up from many sides the cultural capital of humanity, or, to use the late Professor Dixon's happy metaphor, diffusion is the process "whereby the achievements of all peoples are distilled into the vessel of Culture."

Now the rigorous proof of diffusion as just defined is essentially a task for archaeology. Until quite recent times, the tradition of historiography,

Text: V. Gordon Childe, "A Prehistorian's Interpretation of Diffusion," in *Independence, Convergence and Borrowing.* Cambridge, Mass.: Harvard University Press, Copyright 1937 by The President and Fellows of Harvard College. Pp. 4-9, 11-20 *passim.*

derived from the slave-owning societies of Greece and Rome, has tended to ignore as mechanic and banausic the very technical processes the improvement of which has constituted the most objective aspect of progress. Even for a process that affected historiography so directly as did printing we have to appeal mainly to archaeological data. Gutenberg's invention had a long line of precursors (sealing, block-printing, and so on) and complex presuppositions (such as ink and paper), ignored by literary historians. In tracing the pedigree of these essential moments in the invention, Carter has had to appeal to documents provided by the archaeologists—to actual European blockprints, to analyses of papers dug up in the Fayum, and to texts preserved by Asian deserts. Yet the invention and diffusion of printing is a recent step in human progress. For earlier periods the archaeologist is called upon to play an exclusive role in the demonstration of diffusion. . . .

Archaeology must renounce all hope of proving myths or of digging up abstractions. But it can establish the reality of intercourse between distinct communities at very remote periods. And the intercourse thus demonstrated proves at least the possibility of that commerce in ideas which constitutes diffusion on the above definition. Admittedly the archaeologist's picture of the prehistoric world from almost the earliest times is a mosaic or rather a kaleidoscope of distinct groups—what are termed in Europe cultures; each owes its archaeological individuality to its peculiar adjustment to its special historical environment, an adjustment imperfectly reflected in the surviving relics of its material culture—its tools and architecture, its dress and art. Admittedly too the groups thus symbolized are at any given time spatially localized and separated from one another by formidable barriers—the seas, mountains and deserts that still exist, the no less formidable tracts of swamp and virgin forest that man himself has gradually reduced. . . .

. . . It is the archaeological exploration of the Near East and the co-operation therein of geology that are providing the most striking and also the earliest proofs of frequent communication over really substantial distances. In the neolithic settlements around the Fayum Lake, perhaps the oldest yet known and dating from 5000 B.C., Caton-Thompson collected shells brought from the Mediterranean and others from the Red Sea, as well as various exotic stones of still uncertain provenance. A little later obsidian was being used for the manufacture of tools by the earliest inhabitants of the Tigris-Euphrates delta and of Assyria as well as by the predynastic Egyptians. Yet supplies of the volcanic glass are geographically very restricted; the Armenian massif or the island of Melos are the most likely sources. The only recorded sources of lapis lazuli are on the Iranian plateau. Yet this stone was being imported into Egypt and Sumer by 4000 B.C. and during the first half of the third millennium was reaching the Indus valley, Baluchistan, Russian Turkestan, and Troy, on the Asiatic shore of the Hellespont. It would be tedious to continue this catalogue, to which each well-conducted expedition adds new items. The transportation of exotic materials over long distances thus attested in prehistoric times only foreshadows that intensive importation of raw materials into Egypt and Sumer to which written records also bear witness as soon as they begin.

Scarcely less conclusive proofs of intercourse are afforded by the distributions of manufactured articles. Of course *ex hypothesi* its "country of origin" is not stamped upon a prehistoric commodity, but it can generally be determined with a high degree of probability. Sometimes the actual factories can be located. At Graig Lwyd, for instance, was found not only the sole deposit of the rock used but also the workshop where the axes, exported to Wiltshire, were fashioned. . . .

And closely related in kind to the argument from the distribution of finished commodities is one that does directly indicate a diffusion of ideas. I refer to the reproduction by distinct groups of arbitrary or specialized types. Archaeologists are apt to define a "specialized type" as one whose peculiarities are not obviously conditioned either by the object's function or by its material and the method of its manufacture. Of course, it could be objected that a subjective element has entered into the above definition. But in practice the selection of types for study is controlled by precisely the same statistical and cartographic methods as are employed in determining the provenance of manufactures: the rarity of the selected type within its class would constitute a rough test of the degree of its specialization. Continuity in its geographical distribution would materially enhance the likelihood that all examples are results of copying. In fact, recent excavations have most satisfactorily filled in gaps in the distributions of types assumed on purely formal grounds to be related, so that the two criteria support each other. . . .

One more archaeological argument deserves to rank as affording valid evidence of intercourse. Exceptionally alien peoples are recognizably portrayed on the figured monuments of ancient civilizations. The Indus cities have yielded many naturalistic figurines of baked clay. Some of these depict persons of distinctly Mongolian type, and anatomical studies of an actual skull from Mohenjo-daro have verified the accuracy of the modeler's delineation. Hence intercourse between the urban civilizations of the Indus valley and Mongolian tribes, presumably already located in Central Asia, is proved for the first half of the third millennium B.C. . . .

On the enlarged and deepened field of history that archaeology is opening up to the judgment of the sociologist, we already receive the impression that the course of man's progress has followed anything but a straight line or a level plain; both temporal and spatial variations in the rate of man's advance towards mastery of his physical environment are perceptible. But the impression is vague not only because of the limitations on archaeology's vision but also because our own standards of valuation are nebulous, and that can be corrected. To this end will you accept as a basis of discussion the restriction on culture to the material plane and the analogy between progress in culture and organic evolution adumbrated earlier? In virtue of that analogy cultural adjustments will be adjudged progressive if they further the multiplication of the species in the long run. There would then be a correlation between population which can ideally be plotted as a graph and progress which by itself is scarcely measurable. The population curve would be a doubtless imperfect reflex of cultural progress; discrepancies between the two curves would cancel out in the vast period surveyed by archaeology. On the strength of this assumed parallelism the curvature in the rate of progress might be asserted more confidently.

Archaeology surveys, say, 250,000 years. For ninety-six per cent of this almost inconceivable time-span, the Old Stone Age, the improvements in man's equipment were relatively slight. And apparently the species *Homo sapiens* or even the genus *Homo* constituted a small and restricted group among competing mammalian genera and species. Food-production—agriculture and mixed farming—represented the first revolutionary advance and was followed by a very marked expansion of the population wherever and whenever the new economy was applied. When the population curve of humanity comes to be plotted over the millennia, it will surely exhibit an upward kink at this point which may accordingly be termed the "Neolithic Revolution." But this "revolution" began so far back, spread so slowly, and was in reality so complex and gradual that it can still only be studied abstractly.

It is succeeded by a second that can be more accurately located in time and space and examined as a concrete process: small villages of self-sufficing peasants are transformed into populous cities wherein manufacture and commerce rank as equals with farming and fishing. The new cities exceed the old neolithic hamlets and chalcolithic townships as much as modern industrial cities exceed medieval burghs and market-towns. The whole scale of human life has been transformed. This Urban Revolution is first discernible in the valleys of the Nile, the Tigris-Euphrates, and the Indus. There it was consummated round about 3000 B.C. Yet on closer inspection the Urban Revolution turns out to be a long and complex process just like the Industrial Revolution to which it may legitimately be compared. Like the latter, it resulted from the application of a variety of distinct but interlocking discovery-complexes. The harnessing by man of non-human motive powers through the sail, the yoke, and the wheel and the metallurgy of copper and bronze take the part of the steam-engine and the power loom, coal and iron, in the modern counterpart. And the recent excavations at Ur and Erech, at Kish and Eshnuna, have revealed explicitly in Mesopotamia preparatory stages of the revolution such as have long been familiar in predynastic Egypt and must still be assumed in India too.

At the same time, as fresh excavations deepen our knowledge of the Egyptian, Sumerian, and Indus civilizations, the distinctness and individuality of each becomes increasingly manifest. The agreements are indeed striking—"the organization of society in cities; the continued but sparing use of stone, side by side with copper and bronze, for the manufacture of weapons, tools and vessels; the use of picture signs for writing; the fashioning of ornaments out of fayence, shell and various kinds of stone" and the other common traits enumerated by Sir John Marshall form an imposing array.

But the agreements are of a very abstract kind. Sumerian cities are obviously organized around temples, Egyptian cities around the court of Pharaoh or of a feudal lord; at Harappa and Mohenjo-daro no such nucleus of capital accumulation is conspicuous at all. The tools, weapons, and vessels have quite different forms in the three regions. The symbols of the scripts differ, and the conventions observed for their use among the Egyptians are not the same as those adopted in Sumer. The most popular types of beads, pendants, and patterns differ as do the parts of the body to be decked and the whole style of dress. In a word, apart from a few interchanged commodities, we are confronted with concrete differences embraced within an abstract identity.

No theory of one-sided diffusion will explain such difference within identity. It would be more preposterous to postulate an Egyptianization of Sumer to account for the agreements between Nilotic and Mesopotamian cultures than to explain similarities between London and Moscow by the phrase "westernization of Russia." The traveler from London to Moscow is indeed struck by similarities of precisely the same order as those subsisting between, say, Abydos and Erech. He can point to "the organization of society in industrial cities; the continued use of horse-drawn carts side by side with trains and automobiles as means of transport; the use of alphabetic signs for printing; the drinking of tea and the paraphernalia for its infusion." But on the one hand closer inspection reveals the superficiality of the agreements: the nucleus of economic power is in the one case a class of private capitalists concretely represented in a luxurious West End, in the other a totalitarian state externally symbolized by a few banners. The printed symbols are different and are not even combined according to the same conventions, since in Russian each character denotes a single sound whereas in English the same letter may stand for as many as four distinct sounds.

On the other hand, research will certainly show that the agreements are in truth results of diffusion—borrowed ideas divergently applied—but that the diffusion has been a most complicated process and the borrowings by no means unilateral.

The revelation of prehistoric intercourse, direct or indirect, between Egypt, Mesopotamia, and even India is indeed by no means the least striking result of recent excavations in the Near East. It is only in the last fifteen years that the prehistory of the Orient has been systematically studied with the same minuteness and with the same cooperation from natural scientists as have been instrumental in establishing the fact of intercourse between the various parts of prehistoric Europe. Yet the earlier Oriental instances already outweigh the European. Before the war the Indus civilization was dreamed of only by a few inspired visionaries. Indeed to the historian the discovery of Harappa and Mohenjo-daro has opened up a world no less new than that uncovered by Columbus to medieval Europe. Archaeology has shown that two thousand years before the earliest hints in cuneiform texts of contact with India, that sub-continent was already sending her manufactures to the lands wherein our own civilization was admittedly cradled. In other words, in the third millennium B.C. India was already in a position to contribute to the building up of the cultural tradition that constitutes our spiritual heritage as she notoriously has done since the time of Alexander. And even since I first wrote these words the excavations of the Oriental Institute near Baghdad have brought to light concrete proofs that the potentiality just envisaged was in truth realized. At Tell Agrab a green steatite vase of typical Sumerian workmanship has been found portraying a humped bull in front of a manger, a characteristic scene of Indus cult. It shows that by 3000 B.C. such a cult was already being practiced in Mesopotamia itself; in other words, that at least a religious idea had been diffused from India to Babylonia.

In general terms then, archaeology demonstrates intercourse between the great riverine centers of population in the period preluding that great acceleration of progress that I termed the Urban Revolution. Surely that intercourse was a factor in promoting the revolution itself. It can hardly be an accident that the earliest evidences of intensive and extensive communications between divergently adjusted human societies are being afforded by the countries of the Ancient East where urban civilization was destined first to blossom. The pooling of ideas for which such communications gave opportunity was perhaps the decisive moment in fomenting the growth of precocious cultures, in the transvaluation of human life.

The environmentalist insisting on soil and climate in his account of the early rise of civilization in the riverine valleys has, as usual, forgotten that the most important element in man's environment is his fellow men. In the case before us it may certainly be conceded that environmental conditions in the Near East—the opportunities for divergent specialization, the dependence of riverine societies on imported raw materials, the desiccation coincident with the melting of the last ice sheets over Europe—were unusually favorable to intercourse precisely during the critical centuries. It suffices here to insist on the proofs of intercourse during the period of urban civilization's gestation. The archaeologist submits this observation to the historian as a critical instance that may be indicative of the significance of diffusion as a factor in promoting progress.

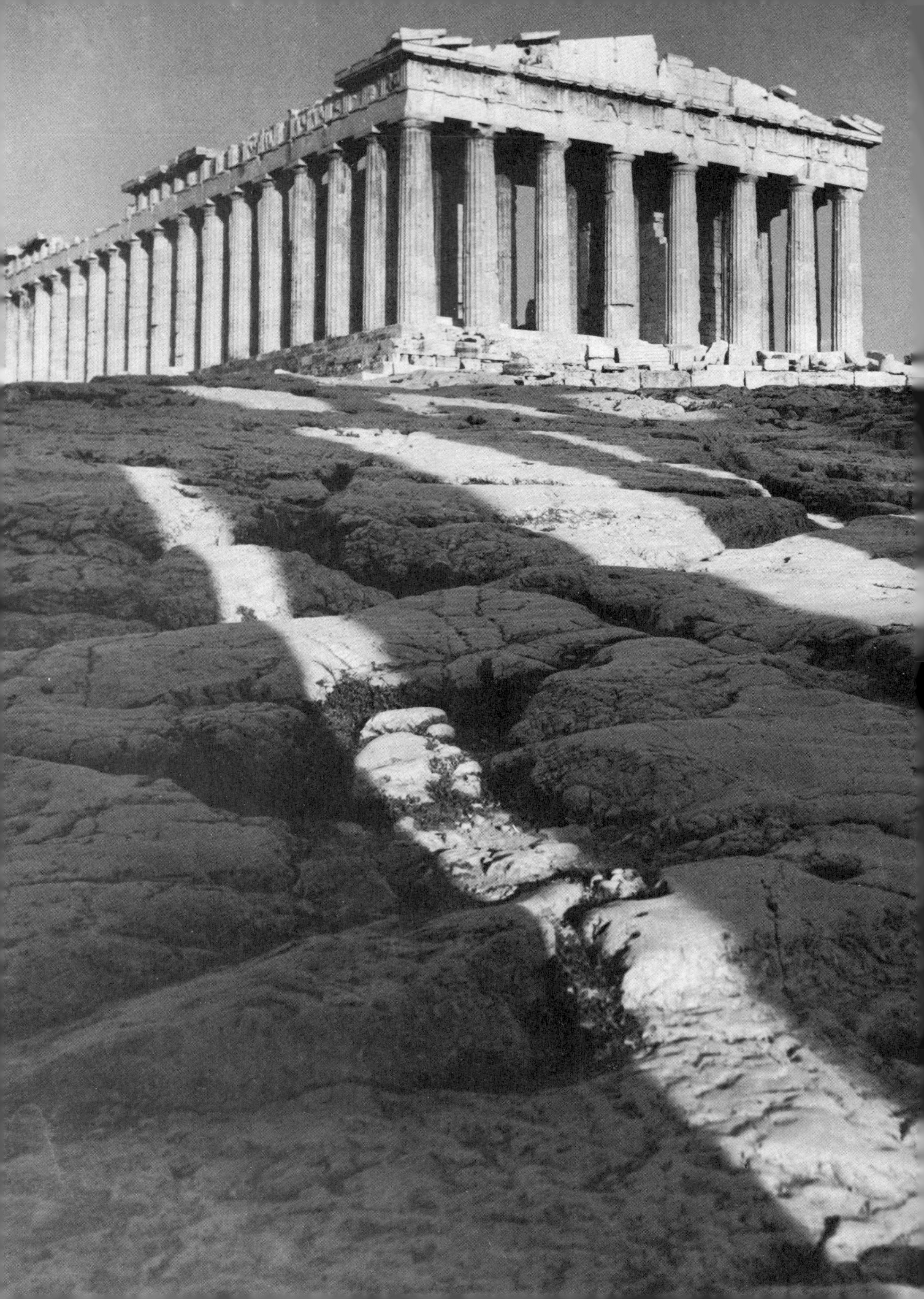

Part II
Classical Civilization: Greece and Rome

A view of the west facade of the Parthenon (opposite page); a painting from a Greek vase showing Achilles binding up a wound on the arm of his friend Patroclus (right); a Roman statue of Marcus Aurelius (below).

INTRODUCTION

That witty British prime minister, Benjamin Disraeli, once said of his wife: "She is an excellent creature, but she never can remember which came first, the Greeks or the Romans." Now quite apart from a genial sympathy for Mrs. Disraeli, we might indeed ask of her husband if *he* knew which actually "came first." True, it is customary to treat the Greeks ahead of the Romans in our textbooks inasmuch as the zenith, and decline, of Hellenic culture was reached first. But in point of fact the two peoples share a common ancestry, and their forebears moved into the Mediterranean region much about the same time. It was this ancestry, together with shared environmental experiences, which went far to differentiate the Greeks and Romans from previous societies in western Asia and North Africa and consequently created the magnificent classical civilization on which our own is in large measure founded.

The Greeks and Romans were offspring of tribes of Indo-Europeans who pushed westward from the grasslands around the Caspian and Black seas during the second millennium B.C. and began to settle along the northern coasts and offshore islands of the Mediterranean. One group of nomads penetrated the peninsula now known as Greece, where they established a center at Mycenae in the Peloponnesus. Subsequently, they occupied islands to the south, and at one stage even conquered Crete, whose inhabitants had already evolved a flourishing culture derived from the Asian mainland and enjoying contacts with Egypt as well. The Mycenaeans, who spoke an early form of Greek, made themselves masters of the Aegean Sea during the fourteenth and thirteenth centuries B.C. and engaged in extensive commercial and cultural interchange with the ancient Semitic cultures of the Near East through the port of Ras Shamra (ancient Ugarit), a Canaanite city of Northern Syria. They in turn fell before the iron weapons of yet other Indo-European invaders, the Dorians, who occupied the Peloponnesus and destroyed Mycenae. Many Mycenaeans fled eastward into Attica, where some settled in Athens, while others crossed over into Asia Minor. There the Ionians, kinsmen of the Athenians, had founded a number of coastal towns, chief of which was Miletus. That there existed a continuity both of language and of culture from Mycenaean times to the rise of Hellenic, or classical, civilization has been proven by the decipherment in recent years of tablets excavated at Mycenae.

To the west, meanwhile, still other Indo-European nomads had been filling up the valleys of the Italian peninsula. Some settled in the fertile lands of the Po, while those called Latins began to farm the lower valley of the Tiber, a region subsequently known as the plain of Latium, where they founded their chief town, Rome. From the Tiber, with its advantageous location in the center of the peninsula, the Latins were in time to fan out and conquer all of Italy.

When they arrived in their peninsular homes, the Greeks and Romans possessed an iron technology, but they were culturally inferior to the great civilizations of Egypt and the Tigris-Euphrates. Thanks, however, to the role of cultural intermediary as played by the inhabitants of Crete, the early Greeks assimilated much of the knowledge originating in older societies, even as the Greeks were later to act as transmitters of culture in turn to the Romans. The Greeks and Romans also differed from the Egyptians and Asians in their fundamental approach to environment. Whereas the latter had developed their societies along the banks of great rivers, to which they always remained oriented no matter how far they pushed into the hinterland, the Greeks and Romans dwelt along the littoral of a great inland sea. Consequently, their political structures and economies alike were oriented to the Mediterranean, while their maritime technology was designed to acquire control over its length and breadth. The Mediterranean, moreover, offered a natural barrier insulating Europe from Africa and Asia.

Consequently, the Greeks and Romans (and the Phoenicians to a much lesser degree) produced the first genuine maritime civilizations in the West. This historic fact had two implications: uniqueness and innovation. The Indo-European communities were well aware of their hereditary and environmental distinctiveness—and indeed they gloried in it. Thus the Greeks revered their earliest literary records, especially the epics of Homer, at once the repository of their most ancient social traditions and the major source of quotations for all Greek statesmen and writers. The *Iliad* and *Odyssey* had another important appeal: the emphasis of these epics upon the heroic, and especially their glorification of the deeds of the individual hero, reflected that strong sense of individualism which marked the Greek *ethos*, or character.

For their part, the Romans were no less eager to remember and glorify the uniqueness of their own origins. The Greeks had fought at Troy and had been immortalized by Homer, but according to myth, a Trojan hero, Aeneas, had in turn been an ancestor of the founders of Rome, and this legend was made the subject of the most popular of Roman epics, Virgil's *Aeneid*. Nor did Livy, the great historian of the Roman Republic, hesitate to attribute either its origins to Aeneas or its greatness to the virtues and manners of the early Romans who had led a simple agrarian existence on the rural hills overlooking the Tiber.

THE GREEK EXPERIENCE

The epic legends surrounding Greek and Roman origins have a significant similarity: both the *Odyssey* and the *Aeneid* relate to seafarers and to their adventures and dangers. In point of fact, the centuries-old histories of both peoples are largely taken up with the challenge of their maritime heritage. The Greeks inhabited a peninsula crisscrossed with mountains, its land rocky, for the most part not arable, and bounded by a deeply indented coastline. These physical factors served to fragment the Greek population into small, relatively isolated settlements, obliged to eke out their meager land resources by turning to the sea. The result was the evolution of city-states, the chief of which were Athens, Sparta, and Corinth. To begin with, the *polis*, or city-state, was organized on a tribal basis, but in time there emerged a collective loyalty which cut across and superseded the original ties of kinship. Civic loyalty and patriotism were strengthened in turn as a result of the Persian invasion of Greece in the early fifth century B.C. (499-479 B.C.) and its repulse by the city-states, spearheaded by Athens. This common threat to their existence underscored the necessity of creating a political framework larger than the traditional city-state. Moreover, by this time the planting of Greek colonies from the Black Sea to the Iberian peninsula and the growth of commerce throughout the Mediterranean had caused the economics of Athens and Corinth to expand to the point where they could no longer be satisfied with the limited home market.

The tragedy of Greek history is found chiefly in the failure of the Hellenes to overcome their parochialism. True, Athens and a number of other city-states did create the Delian League (478 B.C.) to provide a naval shield against the kind of aggression lately suffered at the hands of the Persians. But whereas the League might have provided the nucleus for a comprehensive, and perhaps permanent, Hellenic political structure, it was in fact subverted by the Athenians to further their own imperialistic ambitions. The collective good fell victim to power politics, and the city-states plunged into a fratricidal holocaust—the Peloponnesian War (431-404 B.C.)—from which they emerged shattered as a political force, and were quickly subjugated by Philip of Macedon from the north.

This Macedonian conquest in 338 B.C. brought to a close the Hellenic phase of Greek history—that is, the phase when power and intellectual achievement were centered in the Greek peninsula, particularly in Athens. In its place, Philip's son—Alexander (356-323 B.C.)—ushered in a new era, the Hellenistic, when his Macedonian phalanxes sought by triumph of arms to spread the gospel of Greek culture as far as the Indus River. Alexander's conquests had the effect of shifting the center of gravity of Greek civilization from Athens to Alexandria in Egypt. But his dream of consummating the "marriage of East and West," that is, of uniting the cultures of Europe and Asia within a universal political empire, evaporated with his untimely death. Perhaps Alexander deserves the title "the Great" less for his magnificent military feats than for his conception of a new international order. His vision was at the opposite extreme from the narrow provincialism which had blinded and ultimately destroyed the Hellenes, imprisoned within the narrow loyalties of their respective city-states. Though Hellenistic civilization had some magnificent achievements to its credit, its fortunes as a political force were ephemeral.

THE ROMAN CONQUEST

Meanwhile, how had the Romans met a similar challenge of adapting their political institutions in order to consolidate and retain an expansion of territory in the lands around the Mediterranean? Rome was favored in its situation, not only because it was located in the center of the Italian peninsula but also because the latter was not so geographically fragmented as the Greek peninsula. This factor was to facilitate the political unification of Italy, a process which was inaugurated by the Romans with the aid originally of their kinsmen, the Latin tribes in the vicinity of Rome. When at length war broke out between these allies, the Romans emerged victorious, whereupon they took a step that stood in strong contrast to the kind of policy pursued among the warring Greeks. Instead of subjugating and oppressing the Latins, the Romans granted them a large measure of self-government and eventually bestowed on them the rights of full Roman citizenship. In time the entire Italian peninsula accepted Roman leadership, and its inhabitants joined in bearing the Roman eagle victoriously around the lands of the western basin of the Mediterranean and eventually into the entire eastern basin as well. This process was accompanied and facilitated by various factors. These included: a superb military technology; a willingness on the part of the Romans to respect, and indeed assimilate, the cultures of other peoples, above all, the Greeks; the progressive extension of Roman citizenship to non-Italian regions and the development of a legal system sufficiently comprehensive to be applied to all lands and peoples under Roman sovereignty; and the construction of a magnificent network of roads designed for the efficient movement of legions and merchants. The overall result was one of the most dramatic achievements in history: the creation—by a once insignificant group of settlers on the Tiber—of a multi-racial community extending from Hadrian's Wall in Britain to the lands irrigated by the Nile and the Tigris-Euphrates. For centuries, upwards of a hundred million people lived under the protective shield of the *Pax Romana*.

THE GRAECO-ROMAN MIND

Up to this point, we have dealt largely with the challenge of a maritime environment to the Greeks and Romans and the very different fortunes which they experienced in organizing their respective societies to cope with it. Yet whatever the ultimate consequences of their actions, the Greeks must be credited with the earliest formulation of theories on social organizations. As we have seen, the Hellenes viewed their problem within the framework of the territorially restricted city-state with which they were so familiar. Taking this framework, they proceeded to ask themselves such fundamental questions as: What is the purpose of the state and how best can it be organized? What are the respective rights and obligations of the state and of the individual citizen?

Aristotle (384-322 B.C.) maintained that "man is naturally a political animal" and that "the impulse to political association is innate in all men." Now since the attainment of some good is the object of all associations, the state as the supreme form of political association must consequently have the "supreme good" as its object. This deduction is not unlike the view held by Aristotle's equally famous teacher, Plato (427?-347 B.C.). In the *Republic,* the first systematic treatise on political science, Plato argued that the state must be founded on the idea of justice and have as its function the satisfaction of the common good. The question was how best to organize the state so as to accomplish this object? Athens reached the zenith of its power and creativity in the fifth century B.C., the same time that its democratic institutions flourished. According to the great Athenian leader, Pericles (*c.* 490-429 B.C.), this was no mere coincidence. "For we are lovers of the beautiful, yet simple in our tastes, and we cultivate the mind without loss of manliness. . . . An Athenian citizen does not neglect the state because he takes care of his own household; and even those of us who are engaged in business have a very fair idea of politics." Though not all Athenians shared his belief in the democratic way of life, Athenian democracy in general contrasted sharply with the regimented institutions of Sparta, which today could be described as a police state. The struggle between democracy and totalitarianism was dramatically exemplified by these bitter city-state rivals; we need hardly labor the pertinency of this subject for our own times.

If the question of freedom in the structuring of the state loomed large to the Greeks, they were no less concerned with the accompanying problem of the freedom of the individual within the state and his conduct toward the state. Thus Pericles asked his fellow Athenians to equate their individual interests with their civic obligations to the *polis*. But what is the citizen to do if the dictates of organized society conflict with his own convictions? One of the greatest Greek dramatists, Sophocles, presents this dilemma in its starkest form in his play *Antigone* (see Document 17). This conflict between law and individual convictions is also dramatized by the example of Socrates (469?-399 B.C.)—who resolved the problem by accepting the mortal consequences of an unjust law rather than abandoning his principles, at the same time refusing to seek safety in flight since breaking the law would dishonor his own virtue (see Document 25).

The Romans tended always to be less theoretical than the Greeks in their approach to life; in fact, it may have been the common-sense attitude which they adopted in their relationships first with the nearby Latins and subsequently with other peoples that enabled the city-state on the Tiber to expand into a world empire. At any rate, the republic had reached large proportions before much serious thought was given to Roman political theory. Significantly, it was a Hellenistic Greek, Polybius, who in the second century B.C. made the first serious effort to analyze the reasons for Rome's unprecedented expansion. After examining Aristotle's threefold classifications of government types—monarchy, oligarchy, and democracy—he concluded that the Roman Republic had achieved its success by incorporating features from all three. When the republic was transformed into the empire, many Romans feared that the former checks-and-balances system praised by Polybius would be destroyed by a dominant monarchy, thus paving the way for tyranny. Later, when the empire was at its zenith, many Romans continued to hold divergent views about the role of the state and the place of the individual in it. To Virgil, for example, Rome possessed "imperial arts":

> Let others better mold the running mass
> Of metals, and inform the breathing brass,
> And soften into flesh a marble face;
> Plead better at the bar; describe the skies,
> And when the stars descend, and why they rise,
> But Rome, 'tis thine alone, with awful sway,
> To rule mankind, and make the world obey.

But what of the cost of this imperial mission to peoples who did not want to share the blessings of the *Pax Romana* and who saw in Rome's "sway" only the tyranny of unabashed imperialism? Triumphant Rome found that it is difficult indeed to be powerful and loved at the same time.

Meanwhile, what was happening to the Roman at home? Had peace and prosperity made him soft and indolent? From the first century A.D. on, a substantial number of moralists and satirists deplored the growing laxity in morals and contrasted the self-indulgence of their luxury-seeking contemporaries with the simple life and upright character of the republic's "founding fathers." The problem was compounded by a progressive erosion of traditional religious belief and a growing apprehension about both the future of the state and the freedom of the individual, despite the empire's outward prosperity. Many turned to Stoicism, a philosophy which they considered to be most in keeping with the traditional Roman character; its adherents included many of the finest statesmen and men of letters produced in both the late republic and the empire. Stoicism also possessed ethical and moral qualities which in large measure approximated the religion that was to triumph over all other beliefs in the days of imperial troubles—Christianity.

Finally, how shall we assess these Greeks and Romans? Obviously, the Greeks delighted in reason—often at a cost, for it enabled them to rationalize their inadequacies and, indeed, made them "too clever by half." Still, the Greeks' emphasis on reason encouraged them to "see life and see it whole," to strip away ancient superstitions and to assess objectively both the cosmos and man's place in it. As a result, the Greeks were singularly free of sentimentality; their art is a reasoned approach to truth and beauty—perhaps better described as "fineness," which they prized above all else—while their no less reasoned approach to natural phenomena enabled them to become the founders in the West of science and philosophy alike. "We are all Greeks," rhapsodized the English poet Shelley, an assessment either laudatory or condemnatory, depending on the individual viewpoint of the modern historian. But in any event, we might do worse than apply Churchill's dictum about "so many" owing "so much" to "so few" to our own relationship to the ancient city-states of Greece and, above all, to Athens.

To the eternal credit of the Romans, those practical road- and empire-builders, they both perceived their cultural indebtedness to the Greeks and acknowledged it. In the famous epigram of Horace, *Graecia capta ferum victorem cepit*—"Conquered Greece took captive her fierce conqueror." There is largeness of spirit in such an acknowledgment, but then, the Romans possessed greatness in their own right.

"The Glory That Was Greece"

OLD AND NEW: THE INDIVIDUAL AND SOCIETY

14 HOMER, *ILIAD*: THE TRADITION OF HEROIC INDIVIDUALISM

The occupation of the southernmost reaches of the Balkan peninsula by the Greeks—or Achaeans, as they called themselves—was part of a general westward movement of peoples into Europe toward the end of the third millennium B.C. During the ensuing fifteen hundred years the area of Greek settlement was steadily expanded to the islands of the Aegean, to the western shores of Asia Minor and the Black Sea, to Sicily and southern Italy. As they advanced into the Aegean world, the rude invaders came under the influence of the advanced culture of Minoan Crete, but unlike their cultivated Minoan teachers, the Greeks did not forget their warlike traditions. Ultimately they demolished the luxurious palaces of Crete and built well-fortified citadels which boasted great halls decorated in the Minoan style. At Mycenae on the Greek mainland rose the greatest of these palace-fortresses.

Achaean power did not confine itself to the Greek mainland and to Crete but gradually made itself felt throughout the ancient civilizations of the Near East. Expeditions—partly piratical, partly commercial—touched the coasts of Egypt, Palestine, and Syria. As one of the last acts of their history (c. 1200 B.C.), an Achaean coalition besieged and sacked Troy, an imposing citadel at the mouth of the Hellespont (modern Dardanelles). The importance of Troy to its Achaean conquerors is uncertain, but its location at the entrance to the Black Sea undoubtedly gave it special military or commercial value.

To the Greeks of later centuries, the Achaean warlords were legendary figures, so glorious that they traced their lineage from Zeus and were of special concern to the gods. Material possessions were an indication of high status for the heroes, but the true badge of honor was won in the pursuit of *arete*, or heroic excellence. Excellence meant primarily acts of valor on the battlefield or words of good council in the warrior assembly. As with the warrior aristocracies of medieval Europe and Japan, prestige was maintained by "keeping face" with other heroes, and public opprobrium or "shame" regulated conduct more effectively than did a "guilty conscience." The hero's loyalties were directed less to people, state, or family than to personal prestige. The emphasis on heroic individualism in these early times stood in contrast to the group loyalties which characterized the later Greek city-states, where the ideal of the citizen took precedence over that of the individual hero.

Yet the heroic tradition remained vivid for the Greeks and is the central theme of the *Iliad*, the long epic poem composed by Homer, the first great poet of Greece. Homer's title derives from *Ilion*, a secondary name for Troy, and his subject is the Trojan War. Writing some five hundred years after the event, the poet treats the war in a legendary fashion and confines the action primarily to the ninth year of the war. The climax of the *Iliad* is the duel of Achilles, son of Peleus and the most excellent Achaean hero, with Hector, son of Priam and the Trojan champion. The following selections from the *Iliad*, Books XX-XXII, describe this duel and the slaying of Hector. Seemingly, Homer, writing at the time that the Greek city-state was emerging as a political form, endowed Hector with qualities of civic patriotism, in contrast to the valor of Achilles, who seems somewhat selfish and barbaric. Nevertheless, for Homer and the Greeks thereafter the heroic individualism of Achilles served as a necessary complement to the collective demands of the community. In the interplay and conflict of these two forces, the Greeks found much of the vigor and spirit of their civilization.

Book Twenty

So these now, the Achaians, beside the curved ships were arming around you, son of Peleus, insatiate of battle, while on the other side at the break of the plain the Trojans armed. But Zeus, from the many-folded peak of Olympos, told Themis to summon all the gods into assembly. She went everywhere, and told them to make their way to Zeus' house. There was no river who was not there, except only Ocean, there was

Text: Richmond Lattimore (trans.), *The Iliad of Homer.* Copyright 1951 by The University of Chicago Press and reprinted by their permission. Pp. 404-06, 414-17, 432, 435-46.

not any one of the nymphs who live in the lovely groves, and the springs of rivers and grass of the meadows, who came not. These all assembling into the house of Zeus cloud gathering took places among the smooth-stone cloister walks which Hephaistos had built for Zeus the father by his craftsmanship and contrivance.

So they were assembled within Zeus' house; and the shaker of the earth did not fail to hear the goddess, but came up among them from the sea, and sat in the midst of them, and asked Zeus of his counsel: 'Why, lord of the shining bolt, have you called the gods to assembly once more? Are you deliberating Achaians and Trojans? For the onset of battle is almost broken to flame between them.'

In turn Zeus who gathers the clouds spoke to him in answer: 'You have seen, shaker of the earth, the counsel within me, and why I gathered you. I think of these men though they are dying. Even so, I shall stay here upon the fold of Olympos sitting still, watching, to pleasure my heart. Meanwhile all you others go down, wherever you may go among the Achaians and Trojans and give help to either side, as your own pleasure directs you. For if we leave Achilleus alone to fight with the Trojans they will not even for a little hold off swift-footed Peleion. For even before now they would tremble whenever they saw him, and now, when his heart is grieved and angered for his companion's death, I fear against destiny he may storm their fortress.'

So spoke the son of Kronos and woke the incessant battle, and the gods went down to enter the fighting, with purposes opposed. Hera went to the assembled ships with Pallas Athene and with Poseidon who embraces the earth, and with generous Hermes, who within the heart is armed with astute thoughts. Hephaistos went the way of these in the pride of his great strength limping, and yet his shrunken legs moved lightly beneath him. But Ares of the shining helm went over to the Trojans, and with him Phoibos of the unshorn hair, and the lady of arrows Artemis, and smiling Aphrodite, Leto, and Xanthos.

Now in the time when the gods were still distant from the mortals, so long the Achaians were winning great glory, since now Achilleus showed among them, who had stayed too long from the sorrowful fighting. But the Trojans were taken every man in the knees with trembling and terror, as they looked on the swift-footed son of Peleus shining in all his armour, a man like the murderous war god. But after the Olympians merged in the men's company strong Hatred, defender of peoples, burst out, and Athene bellowed standing now beside the ditch at the wall's outside and now again at the thundering sea's edge gave out her great cry, while on the other side Ares in the likeness of a dark stormcloud bellowed, now from the peak of the citadel urging the Trojans sharply on, now running beside the sweet banks of Simoeis.

So the blessed gods stirring on the opponents drove them together, and broke out among themselves the weight of their quarrel. From high above the father of gods and men made thunder terribly, while Poseidon from deep under them shuddered all the illimitable earth, the sheer heads of the mountains. And all the feet of Ida with her many waters were shaken and all her crests, and the city of Troy, the ships of the Achaians. Aïdoneus, lord of the dead below, was in terror and sprang from his throne and screamed aloud, for fear that above him he who circles the land, Poseidon, might break the earth open and the houses of the dead lie open to men and immortals, ghastly and mouldering, so the very gods shudder before them; such was the crash that sounded as the gods came driving together in wrath. For now over against the lord Poseidon Phoibos Apollo took his stand with his feathered arrows, and against Enyalios the goddess grey-eyed Athene. Against Hera stood the lady of clamour, of the golden distaff, of the showering arrows, Artemis, sister of the far striker. Opposite Leto stood the strong one, generous Hermes, and against Hephaistos stood the great deep-eddying river who is called Xanthos by the gods, but by mortals Skamandros.

Thus gods went on to encounter gods; and meanwhile Achilleus was straining to plunge into the combat opposite Hektor Priam's son, since beyond all others his anger was driving him to glut with his blood Ares the god who fights under the shield's guard. . . . But now Phoibos Apollo stood by Hektor and spoke to him: 'Hektor, do not go out all alone to fight with Achilleus, but wait for him in the multitude and out of the carnage lest he hit you with the spear or the stroke of the sword from close in.'

He spoke, and Hektor plunged back into the swarm of the fighting men, in fear, when he heard the voice of the god speaking. . . .

But now when Hektor saw Polydoros, his own brother, going limp to the ground and catching his bowels in his hands, the mist closed about his eyes also, he could stand no longer to turn there at a distance, but went out to face Achilleus hefting his sharp spear, like a flame, Seeing him Achilleus balanced his spear in turn, and called out to him, and challenged him: 'Here is the man who beyond all others has troubled my anger, who slaughtered my beloved companion.

Let us no longer shrink away from each other along the edgeworks of battle.'

He spoke, and looking darkly at brilliant Hektor spoke to him: 'Come nearer, so that sooner you may reach your appointed destruction.'

But with no fear Hektor of the shining helm answered him: 'Son of Peleus, never hope by words to frighten me as if I were a baby. I myself understand well enough how to speak in vituperation and how to make insults. I know that you are great and that I am far weaker than you are. Still, all this lies upon the knees of the gods; and it may be that weaker as I am I might still strip the life from you with the cast of the spear, since my weapon too has been sharp before this.'

He spoke, and balanced the spear and let it fly. But Athene blew against it and turned it back from renowned Achilleus with an easy blast. It came back again to glorious Hektor and dropped to the ground in front of his feet. Meanwhile Achilleus made a furious charge against him, raging to kill him with a terrible cry, but Phoibos Apollo caught up Hektor easily, since he was a god, and wrapped him in thick mist. Three times swift-footed brilliant Achilleus swept in against him with the brazen spear. Three times his stroke went into the deep mist. But as a fourth time, like something more than a man, he charged in, Achilleus with a terrible cry called in winged words after him: 'Once again now you escaped death, dog. And yet the evil came near you, but now once more Phoibos Apollo has saved you, he to whom you must pray when you go into the thunder of spears thrown. Yet I may win you, if I encounter you ever hereafter, if beside me also there is some god who will help me. Now I must chase whoever I can overtake of the others.' . . .

As inhuman fire sweeps on in fury through the deep angles of a drywood mountain and sets ablaze the depth of the timber and the blustering wind lashes the flame along, so Achilleus swept everywhere with his spear like something more than a mortal harrying them as they died, and the black earth ran blood. Or as when a man yokes male broad-foreheaded oxen to crush white barley on a strong-laid threshing floor, and rapidly the barley is stripped beneath the feet of the bellowing oxen, so before great-hearted Achilleus the single-foot horses trampled alike dead men and shields, and the axle under the chariot was all splashed with blood and the rails which encircled the chariot, struck by flying drops from the feet of the horses, from the running rims of the wheels. The son of Peleus was straining to win glory, his invincible hands spattered with bloody filth. . . .

Book Twenty-one

. . . The aged Priam had taken his place on the god-built bastion, and looked out and saw gigantic Achilleus, where before him the Trojans fled in the speed of their confusion, no war strength left them. He groaned and descended to the ground from the bastion and beside the wall set in motion the glorious guards of the gateway; 'Hold the gates wide open in your hands, so that our people in their flight can get inside the city, for here is Achilleus close by, stampeding them, and I think there will be disaster. But once they are crowded inside the city and get wind again, shut once more the door-leaves closely fitted together. I am afraid this ruinous man may spring into our stronghold.'

He spoke, and they spread open the gates and shoved back the door bars and the gates opening let in daylight. Meanwhile Apollo sprang out to meet them, so that he could fend off destruction from the Trojans, who, straight for the city and the lift of the rampart dusty from the plain and throats rugged with thirst, fled away, and Achilleus followed fiercely with the spear, strong madness forever holding his heart and violent after his glory. . . .

Book Twenty-two

So along the city the Trojans, who had run like fawns, dried the sweat off from their bodies and drank and slaked their thirst, leaning along the magnificent battlements. Meanwhile the Achaians sloping their shields across their shoulders came close to the rampart. But his deadly fate held Hektor shackled, so that he stood fast in front of Ilion and the Skaian gates. Now Phoibos Apollo spoke aloud to Peleion: 'Why, son of Peleus, do you keep after me in the speed of your feet, being mortal while I am an immortal god? Even yet you have not seen that I am a god, but strain after me in your fury. Now hard fighting with the Trojans whom you stampeded means nothing to you. They are crowded in the city, but you bent away here. You will never kill me. I am not one who is fated.'

Deeply vexed Achilleus of the swift feet spoke to him: 'You have balked me, striker from afar, most malignant of all gods, when you turned me here away from the rampart, else many Trojans would have caught the soil in their teeth before they got back into Ilion. Now you have robbed me of great glory, and rescued these people lightly, since you have no retribution to fear hereafter. Else I would punish you, if only the strength were in me.'

He spoke, and stalked away against the city, with high thoughts in mind, and in tearing speed, like a racehorse with his chariot who runs lightly as he pulls the chariot over the flat land. Such was the action of Achilleus in feet and quick knees.

The aged Priam was the first of all whose eyes saw him as he swept across the flat land in full shining, like that star which comes on in the autumn and whose conspicuous brightness far outshines the stars that are numbered in the night's darkening, the star they give the name of Orion's Dog, which is brightest among the stars, and yet is wrought as a sign of evil and brings on the great fever for unfortunate mortals. Such was the flare of the bronze that girt his chest in his running. The old man groaned aloud and with both hands high uplifted beat his head, and groaned amain, and spoke supplicating his beloved son, who there still in front of the gateway stood fast in determined fury to fight with Achilleus. The old man stretching his hands out called pitifully to him: 'Hektor, beloved child, do not wait the attack of this man alone, away from the others. You might encounter your destiny beaten down by Peleion, since he is far stronger than you are. A hard man: I wish he were as beloved of the immortal as loved by me. Soon he would lie dead, and the dogs and the vultures would eat him, and bitter sorrow so be taken from my heart. He has made me desolate of my sons, who were brave and many. He killed them, or sold them away among the far-lying islands. Even now there are two sons, Lykaon and Polydoros, whom I cannot see among the Trojans pent up in the city, sons Laothoë a princess among women bore to me. But if these are alive somewhere in the army, then I can set them free for bronze and gold; it is there inside, since Altes the aged and renowned gave much with his daughter. But if they are dead already and gone down to the house of Hades, it is sorrow to our hearts, who bore them, myself and their mother, but to the rest of the people a sorrow that will be fleeting beside their sorrow for you, if you go down before Achilleus. Come then inside the wall, my child, so that you can rescue the Trojans and the women of Troy, neither win the high glory for Peleus' son, and yourself be robbed of your very life. Oh, take pity on me, the unfortunate still alive, still sentient but ill-starred, whom the father, Kronos' son, on the threshold of old age, will blast the hard fate, after I have looked upon evils and seen my sons destroyed and my daughters dragged away captive and the chambers of marriage wrecked and the innocent children taken and dashed to the ground in the hatefulness of war, and the wives of my sons dragged off by the accursed hands of the Achaians. And myself last of all, my dogs in front of my doorway will rip me raw, after some man with stroke of the sharp bronze spear, or with spearcast, has torn the life out of my body; those dogs I raised in my halls to be at my table, to guard my gates, who will lap my blood in the savagery of their anger and then lie down in my courts. For a young man all is decorous when he is cut down in battle and torn with the sharp bronze, and lies there dead, and though dead still all that shows about him is beautiful; but when an old man is dead and down, and the dogs mutilate the grey head and the grey beard and the parts that are secret, this, for all sad mortality, is the sight most pitiful.'

So the old man spoke, and in his hands seizing the grey hairs tore them from his head, but could not move the spirit in Hektor. And side by side with him his mother in tears was mourning and laid the fold of her bosom bare and with one hand held out a breast, and wept her tears for him and called to him in winged words: 'Hektor, my child, look upon these and obey, and take pity on me, if ever I gave you the breast to quiet your sorrow. Remember all these things dear child, and from inside the wall beat off this grim man. Do not go out as champion against him, o hard one; for if he kills you I can no longer mourn you on the death-bed, sweet branch, o child of my bearing, nor can your generous wife mourn you, but a big way from us beside the ships of the Argives the running dogs will feed on you.'

So these two in tears and with much supplication called out to their dear son, but could not move the spirit in Hektor, but he awaited Achilleus as he came on, gigantic. But as a snake waits for a man by his hole, in the mountains, glutted with evil poisons, and the fell venom has got inside him, and coiled about the hole he stares malignant, so Hektor would not give ground but kept unquenched the fury within him and sloped his shining shield against the jut of the bastion. Deeply troubled he spoke to his own great-hearted spirit: 'Ah me! If I go now inside the wall and the gateway, Poulydamas will be first to put a reproach upon me, to rescue this man or whether to make him, for all his valour, go down under the hands of Achilleus, the son of Peleus.'

Then in answer the goddess grey-eyed Athene spoke to him: 'Father of the shining bolt, dark misted, what is this you said? Do you wish to bring back a man who is mortal, one long since doomed by his destiny, from ill-sounding death and release him? Do it, then; but not all the rest of us gods shall approve you.'

Then Zeus the gatherer of the clouds spoke to her in answer: 'Tritogeneia, dear daughter, do not lose heart; for I say this not in outright anger, and my meaning toward you is kindly. Act as your purpose would have you do, and hold back no longer.'

So he spoke, and stirred on Athene, who was eager before this, and she went in a flash of speed down the pinnacles of Olympos.

But swift Achilleus kept unremittingly after Hektor, chasing him, as a dog in the mountains who has flushed from his covert a deer's fawn follows him through the folding ways and the valleys, and though the fawn crouched down under a bush and be hidden he keeps running and noses him out until he comes on him; so Hektor could not lose himself from swift-footed Peleion. If ever he made a dash right on for the gates of Dardanos to get quickly under the strong-built bastions, endeavouring that they from above with missiles thrown might somehow defend him, each time Achilleus would get in front and force him to turn back into the plain, and himself kept his flying course next the city. As in a dream a man is not able to follow one who runs from him, nor can the runner escape, nor can the other pursue him, so he could not run him down in his speed, nor the other get clear. How then could Hektor have escaped the death spirits, had not Apollo, for this last and uttermost time, stood by him close, and driven strength into him, and made his knees light? But brilliant Achilleus kept shaking his head at his own people and would not let them throw their bitter projectiles at Hektor for fear the thrower might win the glory, and himself come second. But when for the fourth time they had come around to the well springs then the Father balanced his golden scales, and in them he set two fateful portions of death, which lays men prostrate, one for Achilleus, and one for Hektor, breaker of horses, and balanced it by the middle; and Hektor's death-day was heavier and dragged downward toward death, and Phoibos Apollo forsook him. But the goddess grey-eyed Athene came now to Peleion and stood close beside him and addressed him in winged words: 'Beloved of Zeus, shining Achilleus, I am hopeful now that you and I will take back great glory to the ships of the Achaians, after we have killed Hektor, for all his slakeless fury for battle. Now there is no way for him to get clear away from us, not though Apollo who strikes from afar should be willing to undergo much, and wallow before our father Zeus of the aegis. Stand you here then and get your wind again, while I go to this man and persuade him to stand up to you in combat.'

So spoke Athene, and he was glad at heart, and obeyed her, and stopped, and stood leaning on his bronze-barbed ash spear. Meanwhile Athene left him there, and caught up with brilliant Hektor, and likened herself in form and weariless voice to Deïphobos. She came now and stood close to him and addressed him in winged words: 'Dear brother, indeed swift-footed Achilleus is using you roughly and chasing you on swift feet around the city of Priam. Come on, then; let us stand fast against him and beat him back from us.'

Then tall Hektor of the shining helm answered her: 'Deïphobos, before now you were dearest to me by far of my brothers, of all those who were sons of Priam and Hekabe, and now I am minded all the more within my heart to honour you, you who dared for my sake, when your eyes saw me, to come forth from the fortifications, while the others stand fast inside them.'

Then in turn the goddess grey-eyed Athene answered him: 'My brother, it is true our father and the lady our mother, taking my knees in turn, and my companions about me, entreated that I stay within, such was the terror upon all of them. But the heart within me was worn away by hard sorrow for you. But now let us go straight on and fight hard, let there be no sparing of our spears, so that we can find out whether Achilleus will kill us both and carry our bloody war spoils back to the hollow ships, or will himself go down under your spear.'

So Athene spoke and led him on by beguilement. Now as the two in their advance were come close together, first of the two to speak was tall helm-glittering Hektor: 'Son of Peleus, I will no longer run from you, as before this I fled three times around the great city of Priam, and dared not stand to your onfall. But now my spirit in turn has driven me to stand and face you. I must take you now, or I must be taken. Come then, shall we swear before the gods? For these are the highest who shall be witnesses and watch over our agreements. Brutal as you are I will not defile you, if Zeus grants to me that I can wear you out, and take the life from you. But after I have stripped your glorious armour, Achilleus, I will give your corpse back to the Achaians. Do you do likewise.'

Then looking darkly at him swift-footed Achilleus answered: 'Hektor, argue me no agreements. I cannot forgive you. As there are no trustworthy oaths between men and lions, nor wolves and lambs have spirit that can be brought to agreement but forever these hold feelings of hate for each other, so there can be no love between you and me, nor shall there be oaths between us, but one or the other must fall before then to glut with his blood Ares the god who fights under the shield's guard. Remember every valour of yours, for now the need comes hardest upon you to be a spearman and a bold warrior. There shall be no more escape for you, but Pallas Athene will kill you soon by my spear. You will pay in a lump for all those sorrows of my companions you killed in your spear's fury.'

So he spoke, and balanced the spear far shadowed, and threw it; but glorious Hektor kept his eyes on him, and avoided it, for he dropped, watchful, to his knee, and the bronze spear flew over his shoulder and stuck in the ground, but Pallas Athene snatched it, and gave it back to Achilleus, unseen by Hektor shepherd of the people. But now Hektor spoke out to the blameless son of Peleus: 'You missed: and it was not, o Achilleus like the immortals, from Zeus that you knew my destiny; but you thought so; or rather you are someone clever in speech and spoke to swindle me, to make me afraid of you and forget my valour and war strength. You will not stick your spear in my back as I run away from you but drive it into my chest as I storm straight in against you; if the god gives you that; and now look out for my brazen spear. I wish it might be taken full length in your body. And indeed the war would be a lighter thing for the Trojans if you were dead, seeing that you are their greatest affliction.'

So he spoke, and balanced the spear far shadowed, and threw it, and struck the middle of Peleïdes' shield, nor missed it, but the spear was driven far back from the shield, and Hektor was angered because his swift weapon had been loosed from his hand in a vain cast. He stood discouraged, and had no other ash spear; but lifting his voice he called aloud on Deïphobos of the pole shield, and asked him for a long spear, but Deïphobos was not near him. And Hektor knew the truth inside his heart, and spoke aloud: 'No use. Here at last the gods have summoned me deathward. I thought Deïphobos the hero was here close beside me, but he is behind the wall and it was Athene cheating me, and now evil death is close to me, and no longer far away, and there is no way out. So it must long since have been pleasing to Zeus, and Zeus' son who strikes from afar, this way; though before this they defended me gladly. But now my death is upon me. Let me at least not die without a struggle, inglorious, but do some big thing first, that men to come shall know of it.'

So he spoke, and pulling out the sharp sword that was slung at the hollow of his side, huge and heavy, and gathering himself together, he made his swoop, like a high-flown eagle who launches himself out of the murk of the clouds on the flat land to catch away a tender lamb or a shivering hare; so Hektor made his swoop, swinging his sharp sword, and Achilleus charged, the heart within him loaded with savage fury. In front of his chest the beautiful elaborate great shield covered him, and with the glittering helm with four horns he nodded; the lovely golden fringes were shaken about it which Hephaistos had driven close along the horn of the helmet. And as a star moves among stars in the night's darkening, Hesper, who is the fairest star who stands in the sky, such was the shining from the pointed spear Achilleus was shaking in his right hand with evil intention toward brilliant Hektor. He was eyeing Hektor's splendid body, to see where it might best give way, but all the rest of the skin was held in the armour, brazen and splendid, he stripped when he cut down the strength of Patroklos; yet showed where the collar-bones hold the neck from the shoulders, the throat, where death of the soul comes most swiftly; in this place brilliant Achilleus drove the spear as he came on in fury, and clean through the soft part of the neck the spearpoint was driven. Yet the ash spear heavy with bronze did not sever the windpipe, so that Hektor could still make exchange of words spoken. But he dropped in the dust, and brilliant Achilleus vaunted above him: 'Hektor, surely you thought as you killed Patroklos you would be safe, and since I was far away you thought nothing of me, o fool, for an avenger was left, far greater than he was, behind him and away by the hollow ships. And it was I; and I have broken your strength; on you the dogs and the vultures shall feed and foully rip you; the Achaians will bury Patroklos.'

In his weakness Hektor of the shining helm spoke to him: 'I entreat you, by your life, by your knees, by your parents, do not let the dogs feed on me by the ships of the Achaians, but take yourself the bronze and gold that are there in abundance, those gifts that my father and the lady my mother will give you, and give my body to be taken home again, so that the Trojans and the wives of the Trojans may give me in death my rite of burning.'

But looking darkly at him swift-footed Achilleus answered: 'No more entreating of me, you dog, by knees or parents. I wish only that my spirit and fury would drive me to hack your meat away and eat it raw for the things that you have done to me. So there is no one who can hold the dogs off from your head, not if they bring here and set before me ten times and twenty times the ransom, and promise more in addition, not if Priam son of Dardanos should offer to weigh out your bulk in gold; not even so shall the lady your mother who herself bore you lay you on the death-bed and mourn you: no, but the dogs and the birds will have you all for their feasting.'

Then, dying, Hektor of the shining helmet spoke to him: 'I know you well as I look upon you, I know that I could not persuade you, since indeed in your breast is a heart of iron. Be careful now; for I might be made into the gods' curse upon you, on that day when Paris and Phoibos Apollo destroy you in the Skaian gates, for all your valour.'

He spoke, and as he spoke the end of death closed in upon him, and the soul fluttering free of the limbs went down into Death's house mourning her destiny, leaving youth and manhood behind her. Now though he was a dead man brilliant Achilleus spoke to him: 'Die: and I will take my own death at whatever time Zeus and the rest of the immortals choose to accomplish it.'

He spoke, and pulled the brazen spear from the body, and laid it on one side, and stripped away from the shoulders the bloody armour. And the other sons of the Achaians came running about him, and gazed upon the stature and on the imposing beauty of Hektor; and none stood beside him who did not stab him; and thus they would speak one to another, each looking at his neighbour: 'See now, Hektor is much softer to handle than he was when he set the ships ablaze with the burning firebrand.'

So as they stood beside him they would speak, and stab him. But now, when he had despoiled the body, swift-footed brilliant Achilleus stood among the Achaians and addressed them in winged words: 'Friends, who are leaders of the Argives and keep their counsel: since the gods have granted me the killing of this man who has done us much damage, such as not all the others together have done, come, let us go in armour about the city to see if we can find out what purpose is in the Trojans, whether they will abandon their high city, now that this man has fallen, or are minded to stay, though Hektor lives no longer. Yet still, why does the heart within me debate on these things? There is a dead man who lies by the ships, unwept, unburied: Patroklos: and I will not forget him, never so long as I remain among the living and my knees have their spring beneath me. And though the dead forget the dead in the house of Hades, even there I shall still remember my beloved companion. But now, you young men of the Achaians, let us go back, singing a victory song, to our hollow ships; and take this with us. We have won ourselves enormous fame; we have killed the great Hektor whom the Trojans glorified as if he were a god in their city.'

He spoke, and now thought of shameful treatment for glorious Hektor. In both of his feet at the back he made holes by the tendons in the space between ankle and heel, and drew thongs of ox-hide through them, and fastened them to the chariot so as to let the head drag, and mounted the chariot, and lifted the glorious armour inside it, then whipped the horses to a run, and they winged their way unreluctant. A cloud of dust rose where Hektor was dragged, his dark hair was falling about him, and all that head that was once so handsome was tumbled in the dust; since by this time Zeus had given him over to his enemies, to be defiled in the land of his fathers. . . .

15 XENOPHON, *THE CONSTITUTION OF THE LACEDAEMONIANS:* THE CIVIC EDUCATION OF SPARTAN YOUTH

No other Greek city-state, with the exception of Athens, evoked such curiosity among both contemporaries and later generations as Sparta, or, as the inhabitants often called it, Lacedaemon. The Spartans were the descendants of the Dorian invaders who had entered the Greek peninsula at the end of the Bronze Age (1200-1000 B.C.), and during its earlier centuries, Sparta's development paralleled that of the other Greek cities. It knew the civil strife of monarchs against aristocrats, the sacred songs of festival choruses, the enrichment of foreign trade, and the development of a vigorous and artistic ceramic industry. By the eighth century B.C. the quest for new agricultural lands sent the heavy-armed Spartan *hoplites* (foot soldiers) westward into neighboring Messenia, where they reduced the inhabitants to serfdom and divided the rich fields among the Spartan citizens. In the mid-seventh century, the serfs of Messenia, whom the Spartans called *helots,* revolted against their masters and for more than twenty years resisted Spartan efforts to subdue them.

After the Messenian revolt the whole direction of Spartan civilization changed. The difficulties encountered in repressing the uprising convinced the Spartans that domination of the far more numerous *helots* required subordination of all personal interests to the military life. Cultural and artistic pursuits were discarded, and Sparta became an armed camp, suspicious of the outside world but preëminent as the military power.

About this time—according to tradition—Lycurgus (*fl.* 9th century B.C.), the law-giver, appeared in Sparta to exhort the Spartans to effect constitutional reforms aimed at bringing about close coöperative effort and civic patriotism. The idea of dying cheerfully for one's country became the new ideal, and coincided with the emergence of a new political form—the *polis*, or city-state—which insisted that man regard himself not only as an individual but also as a citizen, that is, as a member of a political group with group responsibilities. In Sparta, social responsibilities were to become supreme over personal liberties, and the aim of Spartan life became absolute devotion to the dictates of the state.

Xenophon, an Athenian who lived and wrote at the end of the fifth and beginning of the fourth centuries B.C., witnessed the rise and fall of Spartan leadership in the Greek world. His description of Lacedaemonian institutions is colored slightly by pro-Spartan views, but nevertheless, he remains one of the most important sources for our limited knowledge about the militant people who dwelt along the banks of the Eurotas River in the southern portions of the Peloponnesus.

The selections below from Xenophon's *Constitution of the Lacedaemonians* include an explanation for Sparta's greatness, a description of the rigorous education given Spartan youths, a statement explaining their antipathy toward money-making, and a strong defense of Spartan obedience to the magistrates and the laws. The comments are typical of the idealization of Spartan life and simplicity recorded by many Greek philosophers and historians in the fourth century B.C.

I recall the astonishment with which I first noted the unique position of Sparta among the states of Hellas, the relatively sparse population, and at the same time the extraordinary power and prestige of the community. I was puzzled to account for the fact. It was only when I came to consider the peculiar institutions of the Spartans that my wonderment ceased. Or rather, it is transferred to the legislator who gave them those laws, obedience to which has been the secret of their prosperity. This legislator, Lycurgus, I admire, and hold him to have been one of the wisest of mankind. Certainly he was no servile imitator of other states. It was by a stroke of invention rather, and on a pattern much in opposition to the commonly-accepted one, that he brought his fatherland to this pinnacle of prosperity.

Take for example—and it is well to begin at the beginning—the whole topic of the begetting and rearing of children. Throughout the rest of the world the young girl, who will one day become a mother (and I speak of those who may be held to be well brought up), is nurtured on the plainest food attainable, with the scantiest addition of meat or other condiments; while as to wine they train them either to total abstinence or to take it highly diluted with water. And in imitation, as it were, of the handicraft type, since the majority of artificers are sedentary, we, the rest of the Hellenes, are content that our girls should sit quietly and work wools. That is all we demand of them. But how are we to expect that women nurtured in this fashion should produce a splendid offspring? . . .

. . . Throughout the rest of Hellas the custom on the part of those who claim to educate their sons in the best way is as follows. As soon as the children are of an age to understand what is said to them they are immediately placed under the charge of Paidagogoi (or tutors), who are also attendants, and sent off to the school of some teacher to be taught grammar, music, and the concerns of the palaestra. Besides this they are given shoes to wear which tend to make their feet tender, and their bodies are enervated by various changes of clothing. And as for food, the only measure recognised is that which is fixed by appetite.

But when we turn to Lycurgus, instead of leaving it to each member of the state privately to appoint a slave to be his son's tutor, he set over the young Spartans a public guardian, the Paidonomos, to give him his proper title, with complete authority over them. This guardian was selected from those who filled the highest magistracies. He had authority to hold musters of the boys, and as their overseer, in case of any misbehaviour, to chastise severely. The legislator further provided the pastor with a body of youths in the prime of life, and bearing whips, to inflict punishment when necessary, with this happy result that in Sparta modesty and obedience ever go hand in hand, nor is there lack of either.

Instead of softening their feet with shoe or sandal, his rule was to make them hardy through going barefoot. This habit, if practised, would, as he believed, enable them to scale heights more easily and clamber down precipices with less dan-

Text: Xenophon, *The Constitution of the Lacedaemonians*, trans. Henry G. Dakyns, in *The Greek Historians*, II, ed. Francis R. B. Godolphin. Copyright 1942 by Random House, Inc., and reprinted by their permission. Pp. 658, 660, 661, 666-68.

ger. In fact, with his feet so trained the young Spartan would leap and spring and run faster unshod than another shod in the ordinary way.

Instead of making them effeminate with a variety of clothes, his rule was to habituate them to a single garment the whole year through, thinking that so they would be better prepared to withstand the variations of heat and cold.

Again, as regards food, according to his regulation the perfect, or head of the flock, must see that his messmates gathered to the club meal, with such moderate food as to avoid that heaviness which is engendered by repletion, and yet not to remain altogether unacquainted with the pains of penurious living. His belief was that by such training in boyhood they would be better able when occasion demanded to continue toiling on an empty stomach. They would be all the fitter, if the word of command were given, to remain on the stretch for a long time without extra dieting. The craving for luxuries would be less, the readiness to take any victual set before them greater, and, in general the regime would be found more healthy. Under it he thought the lads would increase in stature and shape into finer men. . . .

Furthermore, and in order that the boys should not want a ruler, even in case the guardian himself were absent, he gave to any citizen who chanced to be present authority to lay upon them injunctions for their good, and to chastise them for any trespass committed. By so doing he created in the boys of Sparta a most rare modesty and reverence. And indeed there is nothing which, whether as boys or men, they respect more highly than the ruler. Lastly, and with the same intention, that the boys must never be reft of a ruler, even if by chance there were no grown man present, he laid down the rule that in such a case the most active of the Leaders or Prefects was to become ruler each of his own division. The conclusion being that under no circumstances whatever are the boys of Sparta destitute of one to rule them. . . .

There are yet other customs in Sparta which Lycurgus instituted in opposition to those of the rest of Hellas, and the following among them. We all know that in the generality of states every one devotes his full energy to the business of making money: one man as a tiller of the soil, another as a mariner, a third as a merchant, whilst others depend on various arts to earn a living. But at Sparta Lycurgus forbade his freeborn citizens to have anything whatsoever to do with the concerns of money-making. As freemen, he enjoined upon them to regard as their concern exclusively those activities upon which the foundations of civic liberty are based.

And indeed, one may well ask, for what reason should wealth be regarded as a matter for serious pursuit in a community where, partly by a system of equal contributions to the necessaries of life, and partly by the maintenance of a common standard of living, the lawgiver placed so effectual a check upon the desire for riches for the sake of luxury? What inducement, for instance, would there be to make money, even for the sake of wearing apparel, in a state where personal adornment is held to lie not in the costliness of the clothes they wear, but in the healthy condition of the body to be clothed? Nor again could there be much inducement to amass wealth, in order to be able to expend it on the members of a common mess, where the legislator had made it seem far more glorious that a man should help his fellows by the labour of his body than by costly outlay. The latter being, as he finely phrased it, the function of wealth, the former an activity of the soul.

He went a step farther, and set up a strong barrier (even in a society such as I have described) against the pursuance of money-making by wrongful means. In the first place, he established a coinage of so extraordinary a sort, that even a single sum of ten minas could not come into a house without attracting the notice, either of the master himself, or of some member of his household. In fact, it would occupy a considerable space, and need a waggon to carry it. Gold and silver themselves, moreover, are liable to search, and in case of detection, the possessor subjected to a penalty. In fact, to repeat the question asked above, for what reason should money-making become an earnest pursuit in a community where the possession of wealth entails more pain than its employment brings satisfaction?

But to proceed. We are all aware that there is no state in the world in which greater obedience is shown to magistrates, and to the laws themselves, than Sparta. But, for my part, I am disposed to think that Lycurgus could never have attempted to establish this healthy condition, until he had first secured the unanimity of the most powerful members of the state. I infer this for the following reasons. In other states the leaders in rank and influence do not even desire to be thought to fear the magistrates. Such a thing they would regard as in itself a symbol of servility. In Sparta, on the contrary, the stronger a man is the more readily does he bow before constituted authority. And indeed, they pride themselves on their humility, and on a prompt obedience, running, or at any rate not crawling with laggard step, at the word of command. Such an example of eager discipline, they are persuaded, set by themselves, will not fail to be followed by the rest. And this is precisely what has taken place. It is reasonable to suppose that it was these same noblest members of the state who combined to lay the foundation of the ephorate, after they had come to the conclusion themselves that of all the blessings which a state, or an army, or a household can enjoy, obedience is the greatest. Since, as they could not but reason, the greater the power with which men fence about authority, the greater the fascination it will exercise upon the mind of the citizen, to the enforcement of obedience.

Accordingly the ephors are competent to punish whomsoever they choose; they have power to exact fines on the spur of the moment; they have power to depose magistrates in mid career, nay, actually to imprison and bring them to trial on the capital charge. Entrusted with these vast powers, they do not, as do the rest of states, allow the magistrates elected to exercise authority as they like, right through the year of office; but, in the style rather of despotic monarchs, or presidents of the games, at the first symptom of an offence against the law they inflict chastisement without warning and without hesitation.

But of all the many beautiful contrivances invented by Lycurgus to kindle a willing obedience to the laws in the hearts of the citizens, none, to my mind, was happier or more excellent than his unwillingness to deliver his code to the people at large, until, attended by the most powerful members of the state, he had betaken himself to Delphi, and there made inquiry of the god whether it were better for Sparta, and conducive to her interests, to obey the laws which he had framed. And not until the divine answer came, "Better will it be in every way." did he deliver them, laying it down as a last ordinance that to refuse obedience to a code which had the sanction of the Pythian god himself was a thing not illegal only, but impious.

GREEK AND BARBARIAN

16   HERODOTUS, *HISTORY OF THE PERSIAN WARS:* THE GREEKS IN THEIR FINEST HOUR

Sometime around the eleventh century B.C., a group of barbaric tribes called Dorians penetrated Greece from the north and laid waste the land. Many inhabitants of the mainland were conquered outright, some fled across the Aegean Sea to settle on the west coast of Asia Minor, while others were deliberately by-passed as the invaders drove southward into the Peloponnesus. The next two hundred years were ones of cultural darkness for Greece in the process of assimilation of institutions and customs between conqueror and conquered.

As the great fifth century approached, it became evident that the emerging Greek city-states were destined to achieve economic, political, and cultural distinction. Most of the necessary ingredients were present: an acquisitive population whose vitality and skill built a successful Greek economy based on trade and industry; a people whose political sensitivity created, at least in many of the city-states, a measure of self-government and representative institutions unknown to other cultures; and finally, a society where intellectual and artistic skills were both admired and encouraged. The one thing that Greece lacked was an ability to achieve permanent political unification.

Shortly after the beginning of the fifth century a great opportunity for unified action presented itself. Persia—which under vigorous rulers like Cyrus the Great (d. 529 B.C.) and Darius I (558?-486? B.C.) had extended into an empire stretching from India to Egypt and Asia Minor—now had begun preparations for the invasion of Europe. The fact that the European Greeks extended aid to Miletus and other Greek cities of Asia Minor in revolt against their Persian masters gave Darius I an excuse for invasion. In the face of his advancing armada, the Greek city-states put aside their petty quarrels and for the first time banded together in common defense.

The two turbulent decades of the Persian War (499-479 B.C.) saw Greeks fighting side by side with Greeks and twice driving the Persians back into Asia. This great struggle has been best recorded by the Greek historian Herodotus (484?-425? B.C.), who based his narrative largely on the accounts of actual participants. When the Greeks emerged victorious from the Persian War, the precedent for political unification was firmly established, but instead, one city-state—Athens—blocked efforts toward successful confederation and sought to create its own empire.

The repulse of the Persians on land and sea becomes in the pages of Herodotus not only a major victory but the climax of a long historical conflict between "barbarians" and Greeks, a conflict which involves not only two peoples but two ways of life. In Herodotus' view, the war is a struggle between East and West, between an autocratic Persian empire and the free communities of Greek city-states, between men who are subjects without human rights' and men who are the legally protected citizens of constitutional republics, between the excessive size, excessive power, excessive wealth of Asia, and the modest, frugal, sometimes poverty-stricken life of Greece.

In the following selections from Herodotus' *History of The Persian Wars*, the first describes a moment in this conflict (490 B.C.) when the Athenians, fighting with the assistance of the Plataeans, repulse the first successful Persian invasion of the Greek mainland. The next deals with the eve of the second invasion (481 B.C.), when King Xerxes (c. 519-465 B.C.), son and heir of Darius, has marshaled the enormous wealth and military might of Persia to wreak revenge on the Greeks. In conversation with Demaratus, an exiled king of Sparta, Xerxes inquires about the military and economic strength of the Greeks. Demaratus gives a ringing defense of the Spartan system, in which the country's modest means are shared by its citizens under a rule of law, as compared with the luxurious but slavish "Persian way." The third selection is Herodotus' tribute to Athens for the vital role she played in the defeat of the Persians.

The Battle of Marathon

And first, before they left the city, the generals sent off to Sparta a herald, one Philippides, who was by birth an Athenian, and by profession and practice a trained runner. This man, according to the account which he gave to the Athenians on his return, when he was near Mount Parthenium, above Tegea, fell in with the god Pan, who called him by his name, and bade him ask the Athenians, "Why they neglected him so entirely, when he was kindly disposed towards them, and had often helped them in times past, and would do so again in time to come?" The Athenians, entirely believing in the truth of this report, as soon as their affairs were once more in good order, set up a temple to Pan under the Acropolis, and, in return for the message which I have recorded, established in his honour yearly sacrifices and a torch-race.

On the occasion of which we speak, when Philippides was sent by the Athenian generals, and, according to his own account, saw Pan on his journey, he reached Sparta on the very next day after quitting the city of Athens. Upon his arrival he went before the rulers, and said:

"Men of Lacedaemon, the Athenians beseech you to hasten to their aid, and not allow that state, which is the most ancient in all Greece, to be enslaved by the barbarians. Eretria is already carried away captive, and Greece weakened by the loss of no mean city."

Thus did Philippides deliver the message committed to him. And the Spartans wished to help

Text: Herodotus, *History of the Persian Wars*, trans. George Rawlinson, in *The Greek Historians*, I, ed. Francis R. B. Godolphin. Copyright 1942 by Random House, Inc., and reprinted by their permission. Pp. 374-76, 421-23, 433.

the Athenians, but were unable to give them any present aid, as they did not like to break their established law. It was the ninth day of the month, and they could not march out of Sparta on the ninth, when the moon had not reached the full. So they waited for the full of the moon.

The barbarians were conducted to Marathon by Hippias, the son of Pisistratus, who the night before had seen a strange vision in his sleep. He seemed to have intercourse with his mother, and conjectured the dream to mean that he would be restored to Athens, recover the power which he had lost, and afterwards live to a good old age in his native country. Such was the sense in which he interpreted the vision. He now proceeded to act as guide to the Persians, and in the first place he landed the prisoners taken from Eretria upon the island that is called Aegileia, belonging to the Styreans, after which he brought the fleet to anchor off Marathon, and marshalled the bands of the barbarians as they disembarked. As he was thus employed it chanced that he sneezed and at the same time coughed with more violence than was his wont. Now as he was a man advanced in years, and the greater number of his teeth were loose, it so happened that one of them was driven out with the force of the cough, and fell down into the sand. Hippias took all the pains he could to find it, but the tooth was nowhere to be seen; whereupon he fetched a deep sigh, and said to the bystanders, "After all the land is not ours, and we shall never be able to bring it under. All my share in it is the portion of which my tooth has possession."

So Hippias believed that this fulfilled his dream.

The Athenians were drawn up in order of battle in a precinct belonging to Heracles, when they were joined by the Plataeans, who came in full force to their aid. Some time before, the Plataeans had put themselves under the rule of the Athenians, and these last had already undertaken many labours on their behalf. The occasion of the surrender was the following. The Plataeans suffered grievous things at the hands of the men of Thebes; so, as it chanced that Cleomenes, the son of Anaxandridas, and the Lacedaemonians were in their neighbourhood, they first of all offered to surrender themselves to them. But the Lacedaemonians refused to receive them, and said, "We dwell too far off from you, and ours would be but cold comfort. You might oftentimes be carried into slavery before one of us heard of it. We counsel you rather to give yourselves up to the Athenians, who are your next neighbours, and well able to shelter you."

This they said, not so much out of good will towards the Plataeans as because they wished to involve the Athenians in trouble by engaging them in wars with the Boeotians. The Plataeans, however, when the Lacedaemonians gave them this counsel, complied at once; and when the sacrifice to the Twelve Gods was being offered at Athens, they came and sat as suppliants about the altar, and gave themselves up to the Athenians. The Thebans no sooner learned what the Plataeans had done than instantly they marched out against them, while the Athenians sent troops to their aid. As the two armies were about to join battle, the Corinthians, who chanced to be at hand, would not allow them to engage; both sides consented to take them for arbitrators, whereupon they made up the quarrel, and fixed the boundary-line between the two states upon this condition: that if any of the Boeotians wished no longer to belong to Boeotia, the Thebans should allow them to follow their own inclinations. The Corinthians, when they had thus decreed, departed to their homes; the Athenians likewise set off on their return, but the Boeotians fell upon them during the march, and a battle was fought wherein they were worsted by the Athenians. Hereupon these last would not be bound by the line which the Corinthians had fixed, but advanced beyond those limits, and made the Asopus the boundary-line between the country of the Thebans and that of the Plataeans and Hysians. Under such circumstances did the Plataeans give themselves up to Athens; and now they were come to Marathon to aid the Athenians.

The Athenian generals were divided in their opinions; and some advised not to risk a battle, because they were too few to engage such a host as that of the Medes; while others were for fighting at once, and among these last was Miltiades. He therefore, seeing that opinions were thus divided, and that the less worthy counsel appeared likely to prevail, resolved to go to the polemarch, and have a conference with him. For the man on whom the lot fell to be polemarch [war magistrate], at Athens was entitled to give his vote with the ten generals, since anciently the Athenians allowed him an equal right of voting with them. The polemarch at this juncture was Callimachus of Aphidnae; to him therefore Miltiades went, and said:

"With you it rests, Callimachus, either to bring Athens to slavery, or, by securing her freedom, to leave behind to all future generations a memory beyond even Harmodius and Aristogeiton. For never since the time that the Athenians became a people were they in so great a danger as now. If they bow their necks beneath the yoke of the Medes, the woes which they will have to suffer when given into the power of Hippias are already determined on; if, on the other hand, they fight and overcome, Athens may rise to be the very first city in Greece. How it comes to pass that these things are likely to happen, and how the determining of them in some sort rests with you, I will now proceed to make clear. We generals are ten in number, and our votes are divided; half of us wish to engage, half to avoid a combat. Now, if we do not fight, I look to see a great disturbance at Athens which will shake men's resolutions, and then I fear they will submit themselves; but if we fight the battle before any unsoundness show itself among our citizens, let the gods but give us fair play, and we are well able to overcome the enemy. On you therefore we depend in this matter, which lies wholly in your own power. You have only to add your vote to my side and your country will be free, and not free only, but the first state in Greece. Or, if you prefer to give your vote to them who would decline the combat, then the reverse will follow."

Miltiades by these words gained Callimachus; and the addition of the polemarch's vote caused the decision to be in favor of fighting. Hereupon all those generals who had been desirous of hazarding a battle, when their turn came to command the army, gave up their right to Miltiades. He however, though he accepted their offers, nevertheless waited, and would not fight, until his own day of command arrived in due course.

Then at length, when his own turn was come, the Athenian battle was set in array, and this was the order of it. Callimachus the polemarch led the right wing, for it was at that time a rule with the Athenians to give the right wing to the polemarch. After this followed the tribes, according as they were numbered, in an unbroken line; while last of all came the Plataeans, forming the left wing. And ever since that day it has been a custom with the Athenians, in the sacrifices and assemblies held each fifth year at Athens, for the Athenian herald to implore the blessing of the gods on the Plataeans conjointly with the Athenians. Now as they marshalled the host upon the field of Marathon, in order that the Athenian front might be of equal length with the Median, the ranks of the centre were diminished, and it became the weakest part of the line, while the wings were both made strong with a depth of many ranks.

So when the battle was set in array, and the victims showed themselves favourable, instantly the Athenians, so soon as they were let go, charged the barbarians at a run. Now the distance between the two armies was little short of a mile. The Persians, therefore, when they saw the Greeks coming on at speed, made ready to receive them, although it seemed to them that the Athenians were bereft of their senses, and bent upon their own destruction; for they saw a mere handful of men coming on at a run without either horsemen or archers. Such was the opinion of the barbarians; but the Athenians in close array fell upon them, and fought in a manner worthy of being recorded. They were the first of the Greeks, so far as I know, who introduced the custom of charging the enemy at a run, and they were likewise the first who dared to look upon the Median garb, and to face men clad in that fashion. Until this time the very name of the Medes had been a terror to the Greeks to hear.

The two armies fought together on the plain of Marathon for a length of time; and in the mid battle, where the Persians themselves and the Sacae had their place, the barbarians were victorious, and broke and pursued the Greeks into the inner country; but on the two wings the Athenians and the Plataeans defeated the enemy. Having so done, they suffered the routed barbarians to fly at their ease, and joining the two wings in one, fell upon those who had broken their own centre, and fought and conquered them. These likewise fled, and now the Athenians hung upon the runaways and cut them down, chasing them all the way to the shore, on reaching which they laid hold of the ships and called aloud for fire.

It was in the struggle here that Callimachus the polemarch, after greatly distinguishing himself, lost his life; Stesilaus too, the son of Thrasilaus, one of the generals, was slain; and Cynaegirus, the son of Euphorion, having seized on a vessel of the enemy's by the ornament at the stern, had his hand cut off by the blow of an axe, and so perished; as likewise did many other Athenians of note and name.

Nevertheless the Athenians secured in this way seven of the vessels, while with the remainder the barbarians pushed off, and taking aboard their Eretrian prisoners from the island where they had left them, doubled Cape Sunium, hoping to reach Athens before the return of the Athenians. The Alcmaeonidae were accused by their countrymen of suggesting this course to them; they had, it was said, an understanding with the Persians, and made a signal to them, by raising a shield, after they were embarked in their ships.

The Persians accordingly sailed round Sunium. But the Athenians with all possible speed marched away to the defence of their city, and succeeded in reaching Athens before the appearance of the barbarians; and as their camp at Marathon had been pitched in a precinct of Heracles, so now they encamped in another precinct of the same god at Cynosarges. The barbarian fleet arrived, and lay to off Phalerum, which was at that time the haven of Athens; but after resting awhile upon their oars, they departed and sailed away to Asia.

There fell in this battle of Marathon, on the side of the barbarians, about 6,400 men; on that of the Athenians, 192. Such was the number of the slain on the one side and the other. A strange prodigy likewise happened at this fight. Epizelus, the son of Cuphagoras, an Athenian, was in the thick of the fray, and behaving himself as a brave man should, when suddenly he was stricken with blindness, without blow of sword or dart, and this blindness continued thenceforth during the whole of his after life. The following is the account which he himself, as I have heard, gave of the matter: he said that a gigantic warrior, with a huge beard, which shaded all his shield, stood over against him, but the ghostly semblance passed him by, and slew the man at his side. Such, as I understand, was the tale which Epizelus told....

Xerxes and Demaratus on the Spartans

Now after Xerxes had sailed down the whole line and was gone ashore, he sent for Demaratus the son of Ariston, who had accompanied him in his march upon Greece, and addressed him thus:

"Demaratus, it is my pleasure at this time to ask you certain things which I wish to know. You are a Greek, and, as I hear from the other Greeks with whom I converse, no less than from your own lips, you are a native of a city which is not the meanest or the weakest in their land. Tell me, therefore, what do you think? Will the Greeks lift a hand against us? My own judgment is, that even if all the Greeks and all the barbarians of the west were gathered together in one place, they would not be able to abide my onset, not being really of one mind. But I would like to know what you think."

Thus Xerxes questioned; and the other replied in his turn, "O king, do you wish me to give you a true answer, or do you wish for a pleasant one?"

Then the king bade him speak the plain truth, and promised that he would not on that account hold him in less favour than heretofore.

So Demaratus, when he heard the promise, spoke as follows, "O king, since you bid me at all risks speak the truth, and not say what will one day prove me to have lied to you, thus I answer. Want has at all times been a fellow-dweller with us in our land, while Valour is an ally whom we have gained by dint of wisdom and strict laws. Her aid enables us to drive out want and escape tyranny. Brave are all the Greeks who dwell in any Dorian land, but what I am about to say does not concern all, but only the Lacedaemonians. First then, come what may, they will never accept your terms, which would reduce Greece to slavery; and further, they are sure to join battle with you, though all the rest of the Greeks should submit to your will. As for their numbers, do not ask how many they are, that their resistance should be a possible thing; for if 1,000 of them should take the field, they will meet you in battle, and so will any number, be it less than this, or be it more."

When Xerxes heard this answer of Demaratus, he laughed and answered, "What wild words, Demaratus! 1,000 men join battle with such an army as this! Come then, will you—who were once, as you say, their king—engage to fight this very day with ten men? I think not. And yet, if all your fellow citizens be indeed such as you say they are, you ought, as their king, by your own country's usages, to be ready to fight with twice the number. If then each one of them be a match for ten of my soldiers, I may well call upon you to be a match for twenty. So would you assure the truth of what you have now said. If, however, you Greeks, who vaunt yourselves so much, are of a truth men like those whom I have seen about my court, as you, Demaratus, and the others with whom I converse, if, I say, you are really men of this sort and size, how is the speech that you have uttered more than a mere empty boast? For, to go to the very verge of likelihood,—how could 1,000 men, or 10,000, or even 50,000, particularly if they were all alike free, and not under one lord, how could such a force, I say, stand against an army like mine? Let them be 5,000, and we shall have more than 1,000 men to each one of theirs. If, indeed, like our troops, they had a single master, their fear of him might make them courageous beyond their natural bent, or they might be urged by lashes against an enemy which far outnumbered them. But left to their own free choice, assuredly they will act differently. For my own part, I believe, that if the Greeks had to contend with the Persians only, and the numbers were equal on both sides, the Greeks would find it hard to stand their ground. We too have among us such men as those of whom you spoke—not many indeed, but still we possess a few. For instance, some of my body-guard would be willing to engage singly with three Greeks. But this you did not know, and therefore it was you talked so foolishly."

Demaratus answered him, "I knew, O king, at the outset, that if I told you the truth, my speech would displease your ears. But as you required me to answer you with all possible truthfulness, I informed you what the Spartans will do. And in this I speak not from any love that I bear them—for you know what my love towards them is likely to be at the present time, when they have robbed me of my rank and my ancestral honours, and made me a homeless exile, whom your father received, bestowing on me both shelter and sustenance. What likelihood is there that a man of understanding should be unthankful for kindness shown him, and not cherish it in his heart? For myself, I pretend not to cope with ten men, or with two, nay, had I the choice, I would rather not fight even with one. But, if need appeared, or if there were any great cause urging me on, I would contend with right good-will against one of those persons who boast themselves a match for any three Greeks. So likewise the Lacedaemonians, when they fight singly, are as good men as any in the world, and when they fight in a body, are the bravest of all. For though they be free men, they are not in all respects free; Law is the master whom they own, and this master they fear more than your subjects fear you. Whatever it commands they do; and its commandment is always the same: it forbids them to flee in battle, whatever the number of their foes, and requires them to stand firm, and either to conquer or die. If in these words, O king, I seem to you to speak foolishly, I am content from this time forward evermore to hold my peace.

I had not now spoken unless compelled by you. But I pray that all may turn out according to your wishes."

Such was the answer of Demaratus, and Xerxes was not angry with him at all, but only laughed, and sent him away with words of kindness. After this interview and after he had made Mascames the son of Megadostes governor of Doriscus, setting aside the governor appointed by Darius, Xerxes started with his army, and marched upon Greece through Thrace. . . .

Herodotus on the Athenians

And here I feel constrained to deliver an opinion, which most men, I know, will dislike, but which, as it seems to me to be true, I am determined not to withhold. Had the Athenians, from fear of the approaching danger, quitted their country, or had they without quitting it submitted to the power of Xerxes, there would certainly have been no attempt to resist the Persians by sea; in which case, the course of events by land would have been the following. Though the Peloponnesians might have carried ever so many breastworks across the Isthmus, yet their allies would have fallen off from the Lacedaemonians, not by voluntary desertion, but because town after town must have been taken by the fleet of the barbarians; and so the Lacedaemonians would at last have stood alone, and, standing alone, would have displayed prodigies of valour, and died nobly. Either they would have done thus, or else, before it came to that extremity, seeing one Greek state after another embrace the cause of the Medes, they would have come to terms with King Xerxes; and thus, either way Greece would have been brought under Persia. For I cannot understand of what possible use the walls across the Isthmus could have been, if the King had had the mastery of the sea. If then a man should now say that the Athenians were the saviours of Greece, he would not exceed the truth. For they truly held the scales, and whichever side they espoused must have carried the day. They too it was who, when they had determined to maintain the freedom of Greece, roused up that portion of the Greek nation which had not gone over to the Medes, and so, next to the gods, they repulsed the invader. Even the terrible oracles which reached them from Delphi, and struck fear into their hearts, failed to persuade them to fly from Greece. They had the courage to remain faithful to their land, and await the coming of the foe.

ATHENIAN DEMOCRACY

17 SOPHOCLES, ANTIGONE: A DEBATE ON LAW AND INDIVIDUAL OBLIGATION

Democracy in Athens was introduced during bitter social conflict and tested by the trials of the Persian War and postwar readjustment. Its most celebrated period ensued during the political leadership of Pericles (461-429 B.C.); at few times in history has the synthesis of politics, literature, art, and everyday life been so harmonious as it was during the Periclean Age.

The male citizens of Athens were the sovereign electoral, legislative, and judicial authority of the democracy. The executive officers—even Pericles—could lead but could neither flaunt nor subvert the ultimate authority of the citizens, or *demos*. The citizen was entitled to the political, the social, and the cultural privileges provided by the democracy and was expected to share in them.

Yet this noble political ideal was in practice narrow. Absence of pay for public service kept the poor from regularly participating in the assembly or the courts. Female citizens were treated with respect but excluded from politics. Naturalization of aliens was almost impossible. The institution of slavery was unquestioned. The postwar defensive alliance formed by the Athenians was made into an Athenian empire, with its revenues subverted to increase the power of Athens over its allies. The justifiable pride of Athens in her achievements threatened to turn into smugness and despotism.

In spite of these limitations, Athens did produce men who represented the Periclean ideal of the citizen raised to the height of genius. One such was Sophocles (496-406 B.C.). Born the son of a businessman, Sophocles early proved his talent as a dancer, an actor, and an author. To Athenians he became the supreme example of the "success story." A good citizen, as well as a poet, he served his city once as a treasurer of the empire and twice as one of the ten generals, the chief executive officers of the democracy. He was regarded by all as an individual of personal warmth and upright character.

In 441 B.C., when the Parthenon was being built and the Athenian empire was at its height, Sophocles presented his play *Antigone*. The legend concerns a quarrel over royal authority. One claimant to the Theban throne, Polyneices, abandons Thebes to his brother Eteocles. In exile, Polyneices raises a host to attack the city. The two brothers kill one another in a duel, and Creon, their uncle and new king of Thebes, decrees that Polyneices was a traitor and therefore is not entitled to proper burial. Antigone, the sister of Polyneices, defies Creon's edict by attempting to inter the body and is arrested. In the following selection, Creon, who is reluctant to put Antigone to death, argues that disregard for the laws shakes the foundations of the civil order and must be severely dealt with. Antigone answers that she is bound by higher laws and blood ties. She is so steadfast that Creon must execute her, whereupon his son, who was Antigone's betrothed, commits suicide. Too late Creon sees the folly of his iron rule, and at the end of the play he is led away a broken man. The great and unresolved debate between Antigone and Creon will remain for all time the classic example of the conflict between individual convictions and the dictates of society.

Sophocles' motivations in writing *Antigone* are impossible to verify. It is not implausible that the playwright hoped that Athenians would see in the character of Creon some warning against arbitrary rule. While *Antigone* was performed, Athenian forces were being marshaled to smash the revolt of its ally Samos. In the audience sat delegates of the various allies who had brought to Athens the annual tribute. Sophocles, unlike the other masters of tragedy, seldom wrote into his plays direct allusions to current political or social issues. Yet the good citizen and friend of Pericles can scarcely have failed to note that his theme could be applied with some urgency to the history of his own time and his own people. By the same token, certain contemporary countries and peoples cannot themselves escape a similar analogy.

Chorus . . . Now here he comes, the king of the land,
Creon, Menoeceus' son,
newly named by the gods' new fate.
What plan that beats about his mind
has made him call this council-session,
sending his summons to all?
Creon My friends, the very gods who shook the state
with mighty surge have set it straight again.
So now I sent for you, chosen from all,
first that I knew you constant in respect
to Laius' royal power; and again
when Oedipus had set the state to rights,
and when he perished, you were faithful still
in mind to the descendants of the dead.
When they two perished by a double fate,
on one day struck and striking and defiled
each by his own hand, now it comes that I
hold all the power and the royal throne
through close connection with the perished men.
You cannot learn of any man the soul,
the mind, and the intent until he shows
his practise of the government and law.
For I believe that who controls the state
and does not hold to the best plans of all,
but locks his tongue up through some kind of fear,
that he is worst of all who are or were.
And he who counts another greater friend
than his own fatherland, I put him nowhere.

So I—may Zeus all-seeing always know it—
could not keep silent as disaster crept
upon the town, destroying hope of safety.
Nor could I count the enemy of the land
friend to myself, not I who know so well
that she it is who saves us, sailing straight,
and only so can we have friends at all.
With such good rules shall I enlarge our state,
And now I have proclaimed their brother-edict.
In the matter of the sons of Oedipus,
citizens, know: Eteocles who died,
defending this our town with champion spear,
is to be covered in the grave and granted
all holy rites we give the noble dead.
But his brother Polyneices whom I name
the exile who came back and sought to burn
his fatherland, the gods who were his kin,
who tried to gorge on blood he shared, and lead
the rest of us slaves—
it is announced that no one in this town
may give him burial or mourn for him.
Leave him unburied, leave his corpse disgraced,
a dinner for the birds and for the dogs.
Such is my mind. Never shall I, myself,
honor the wicked and reject the just.
The man who is well-minded to the state

Text: Sophocles, *Antigone*, trans. Elizabeth Wyckoff, in *Complete Greek Tragedies*, II, ed. David Grene and Richmond Lattimore. Copyright 1960 by The University of Chicago Press and reprinted by their permission. Pp. 164-79.

from me in death and life shall have his honor.
Chorus This resolution, Creon, is your own,
in the matter of the traitor and the true.
For you can make such rulings as you will
about the living and about the dead.
Creon Now you be sentinels of the decree.
Chorus Order some younger man to take this on.
Creon Already there are watchers of the corpse.
Chorus What other order would you give us, then?
Creon Not to take sides with any who disobey.
Chorus No fool is fool as far as loving death.
Creon Death is the price. But often we have known
men to be ruined by the hope of profit.
          (Enter, from the side, a guard.)
Guard Lord, I can't claim that I am out of breath
from rushing here with light and hasty step,
for I had many haltings in my thought
making me double back upon my road.
My mind kept saying many things to me:
"Why go where you will surely pay the price?"
"Fool, are you halting? And if Creon learns
from someone else, how shall you not be hurt?"
Turning this over, on I dilly-dallied.
And so a short trip turns itself to long.
Finally, though, my coming here won out.
If what I say is nothing, still I'll say it.
For I come clutching to one single hope
that I can't suffer what is not my fate.
Creon What is it that brings on this gloom of yours?
Guard I want to tell you first about myself.
I didn't do it, didn't see who did it.
It isn't right for me to get in trouble.
Creon Your aim is good. You fence the fact around.
It's clear you have some shocking news to tell.
Guard Terrible tidings make for long delays.
Creon Speak out the story, and then get away.
Guard I'll tell you. Someone left the corpse just now,
burial all accomplished, thirsty dust
strewn on the flesh, the ritual complete.
Creon What are you saying? What man has dared to do it?
Guard I wouldn't know. There were no marks of picks,
no grubbed-out earth. The ground was dry and hard,
no trace of wheels. The doer left no sign.
When the first fellow on the day-shift showed us,
we all were sick with wonder.
For he was hidden, not inside a tomb,
light dust upon him, enough to turn the curse,
no wild beast's track, nor track of any hound
having been near, nor was the body torn.
We roared bad words about, guard against guard,
and came to blows. No one was there to stop us.
Each man had done it, nobody had done it
so as to prove it on him—we couldn't tell.
We were prepared to hold to red-hot iron,
to walk through fire, to swear before the gods
we hadn't done it, hadn't shared the plan,
when it was plotted or when it was done.
And last, when all our sleuthing came out nowhere,
one fellow spoke, who made our heads to droop
low toward the ground. We couldn't disagree.
We couldn't see a chance of getting off.
He said we had to tell you all about it.
We couldn't hide the fact.
So he won out. The lot chose poor old me
to win the prize. So here I am unwilling,
quite sure you people hardly want to see me.
Nobody likes the bringer of bad news.
Chorus Lord, while he spoke, my mind kept on debating.
Isn't this action possibly a god's?
Creon Stop now, before you fill me up with rage,
or you'll prove yourself insane as well as old.
Unbearable, your saying that the gods
take any kindly forethought for this corpse.
Would it be they had hidden him away,
honoring his good service, his who came
to burn their pillared temples and their wealth,
even their land, and break apart their laws?
Or have you seen them honor wicked men?
It isn't so.
No, from the first there were some men in town
who took the edict hard, and growled against me,
who hid the fact that they were rearing back,
not rightly in the yoke, no way my friends.
These are the people—oh it's clear to me—
who have bribed these men and brought about the deed.
No current custom among men as bad
as silver currency. This destroys the state;
this drives men from their homes; this wicked teacher
drives solid citizens to acts of shame.
It shows men how to practise infamy
and know the deeds of all unholiness.
Every least hireling who helped in this
brought about then the sentence he shall have.
But further, as I still revere great Zeus,
understand this, I tell you under oath,
if you don't find the very man whose hands
buried the corpse, bring him for me to see,
not death alone shall be enough for you
till living, hanging, you make clear the crime.
For any future grabbings you'll have learned
where to get pay, and that it doesn't pay
to squeeze a profit out of every source.
For you'll have felt that more men come to doom

through dirty profits than are kept by them.
Guard May I say something? Or just turn and go?
Creon Aren't you aware your speech is most
unwelcome?
Guard Does it annoy your hearing or your mind?
Creon Why are you out to allocate my pain?
Guard The doer hurts your mind. I hurt your ears.
Creon You are a quibbling rascal through and
through.
Guard But anyhow I never did the deed.
Creon And you the man who sold your mind
for money!
Guard Oh!
How terrible to guess, and guess at lies!
Creon Go pretty up your guesswork. If you don't
show me the doers you will have to say
that wicked payments work their own revenge.
Guard Indeed, I pray he's found, but yes or no,
taken or not as luck may settle it,
you won't see me returning to this place.
Saved when I neither hoped nor thought to be,
I owe the gods a mighty debt of thanks.

(*Creon enters the palace. The Guard
leaves by the way he came.*)

Chorus Many the wonders but nothing walks
stranger than man.
This thing crosses the sea in the winter's storm,
making his path through the roaring waves.
And she, the greatest of gods, the earth—
ageless she is, and unwearied—he wears her away
as the ploughs go up and down from year to year
and his mules turn up the soil.

Gay nations of birds he snares and leads,
wild beast tribes and the salty brood of the sea,
with the twisted mesh of his nets, this clever man.
He controls with craft the beasts of the open air,
walkers on hills. The horse with his shaggy mane
he holds and harnesses, yoked about the neck,
and the strong bull of the mountain.

Language, and thought like the wind
and the feelings that make the town,
he has taught himself, and shelter against the cold,
refuge from rain. He can always help himself.
He faces no future helpless. There's only death
that he cannot find an escape from. He has
contrived
refuge from illnesses once beyond all cure.

Clever beyond all dreams
the inventive craft that he has
which may drive him one time or another to
well or ill.
When he honors the laws of the land and the
gods' sworn right
high indeed is his city; but stateless the man
who dares to dwell with dishonor. Not by my fire,
never to share my thoughts, who does these things.

(*The Guard enters with Antigone.*)

My mind is split at this awful sight.
I know her. I cannot deny
Antigone is here.
Alas, the unhappy girl,
her unhappy father's child.
Oh what is the meaning of this?
It cannot be you that they bring
for breaking the royal law,
caught in open shame.
Guard This is the woman who has done the deed.
We caught her at the burying. Where's the king?

(*Creon enters.*)

Chorus Back from the house again just when he's
needed.
Creon What must I measure up to? What has
happened?
Guard Lord, one should never swear off anything.
Afterthought makes the first resolve a liar.
I could have vowed I wouldn't come back here
after your threats, after the storm I faced.
But joy that comes beyond the wildest hope
is bigger than all other pleasure known.
I'm here, though I swore not to be, and bring
this girl. We caught her burying the dead.
This time we didn't need to shake the lots;
mine was the luck, all mine.
So now, lord, take her, you, and question her
and prove her as you will. But I am free.
And I deserve full clearance on this charge.
Creon Explain the circumstances of the arrest.
Guard She was burying the man. You have it all.
Creon Is this the truth? And do you grasp its
meaning?
Guard I saw her burying the very corpse
you had forbidden. Is this adequate?
Creon How was she caught and taken in the act?
Guard It was like this: when we got back again
struck with those dreadful threatenings of yours,
we swept away the dust that hid the corpse.
We stripped it back to slimy nakedness.
And then we sat to windward on the hill
so as to dodge the smell.
We poked each other up with growling threats
if anyone was careless of his work.
For some time this went on, till it was noon.
The sun was high and hot. Then from the earth
up rose a dusty whirlwind to the sky,
filling the plain, smearing the forest-leaves,
clogging the upper air. We shut our eyes,
sat and endured the plague the gods had sent.
So the storm left us after a long time.
We saw the girl. She cried the sharp and shrill
cry of a bitter bird which sees the nest
bare where the young birds lay.

So this same girl, seeing the body stripped,
cried with great groanings, cried a dreadful curse
upon the people who had done the deed.
Soon in her hands she brought the thirsty dust,
and holding high a pitcher of wrought bronze
she poured the three libations for the dead.
We saw this and surged down. We trapped
  her fast;
and she was calm. We taxed her with the deeds
both past and present. Nothing was denied.
And I was glad, and yet I took it hard.
One's own escape from trouble makes one glad;
but bringing friends to trouble is hard grief.
Still, I care less for all these second thoughts
than for the fact that I myself am safe.
Creon You there, whose head is drooping to
  the ground,
do you admit this, or deny you did it?
Antigone I say I did it and I don't deny it.
Creon (*to the guard*) Take yourself off wherever
  you wish to go
free of a heavy charge.
Creon (*to Antigone*) You—tell me not at length
  but in a word
You knew the order not to do this thing?
Antigone I knew, of course I knew. The word
  was plain.
Creon And still you dared to overstep these laws?
Antigone For me it was not Zeus who made
  that order.
Nor did that Justice who lives with the gods
  below
mark out such laws to hold among mankind.
Nor did I think your orders were so strong
that you, a mortal man, could over-run
the gods' unwritten and unfailing laws.
Not now, not yesterday's, they always live,
and no one knows their origin in time.
So not through fear of any man's proud spirit
would I be likely to neglect these laws,
draw on myself the gods' sure punishment.
I knew that I must die; how could I not?
even without your warning. If I die
before my time, I say it is a gain.
Who lives in sorrows many as are mine
how shall he not be glad to gain his death?
And so, for me to meet this fate, no grief.
But if I left that corpse, my mother's son,
dead and unburied I'd have cause to grieve
as now I grieve not.
And if you think my acts are foolishness
the foolishness may be in a fool's eye.
Chorus The girl is bitter. She's her father's child.
She cannot yield to trouble; nor could he.
Creon These rigid spirits are the first to fall.
The strongest iron, hardened in the fire,
most often ends in scraps and shatterings.

Small curbs bring raging horses back to terms.
Slave to his neighbor, who can think of pride?
This girl was expert in her insolence
when she broke bounds beyond established law.
Once she had done it, insolence the second,
to boast her doing, and to laugh in it.
I am no man and she the man instead
if she can have this conquest without pain.
She is my sister's child, but were she child
of closer kin than any at my hearth,
she and her sister should not so escape
their death and doom. I charge Ismene too.
She shared the planning of this burial.
Call her outside. I saw her in the house,
maddened, no longer mistress of herself.
The sly intent betrays itself sometimes
before the secret plotters work their wrong.
I hate it too when someone caught in crime
then wants to make it seem a lovely thing.
Antigone Do you want more than my arrest and
  death?
Creon No more than that. For that is all I need.
Antigone Why are you waiting? Nothing that
  you say
fits with my thought. I pray it never will.
Nor will you ever like to hear my words.
And yet what greater glory could I find
than giving my own brother funeral?
All these would say that they approved my act
did fear not mute them.
(A king is fortunate in many ways,
and most, that he can act and speak at will.)
Creon None of these others see the case this way.
Antigone They see, and do not say. You have
  them cowed.
Creon And you are not ashamed to think alone?
Antigone No, I am not ashamed. When was it
  shame
to serve the children of my mother's womb?
Creon It was not your brother who died against
  him, then?
Antigone Full brother, on both sides, my parents'
  child.
Creon Your act of grace, in his regard, is crime.
Antigone The corpse below would never say
  it was.
Creon When you honor him and the criminal
  just alike?
Antigone It was a brother, not a slave, who died.
Creon Died to destroy this land the other
  guarded.
Antigone Death yearns for equal law for all the
  dead.
Creon Not that the good and bad draw equal
  shares.
Antigone Who knows that this is holiness below?
Creon Never the enemy, even in death, a friend.

Antigone I cannot share in hatred, but in love.
Creon Then go down there, if you must love, and love
the dead. No woman rules me while I live.
(*Ismene is brought from the palace under guard.*)
Chorus Look there! Ismene is coming out.
She loves her sister and mourns,
with clouded brow and bloodied cheeks,
tears on her lovely face.
Creon You, lurking like a viper in the house,
who sucked me dry. I looked the other way
while twin destruction planned against the throne.
Now tell me, do you say you shared this deed?
Or will you swear you didn't even know?
Ismene I did the deed, if she agrees I did.
I am accessory and share the blame.
Antigone Justice will not allow this. You did not
wish for a part, nor did I give you one.
Ismene You are in trouble, and I'm not ashamed
to sail beside you into suffering.
Antigone Death and the dead, they know whose act it was.
I cannot love a friend whose love is words.
Ismene Sister, I pray, don't fence me out from honor,
from death with you, and honor done the dead.
Antigone Don't die along with me, nor make your own
that which you did not do. My death's enough.
Ismene When you are gone what life can be my friend?
Antigone Love Creon. He's your kinsman and your care.
Ismene Why hurt me, when it does yourself no good?
Antigone I also suffer, when I laugh at you.
Ismene What further service can I do you now?
Antigone To save yourself. I shall not envy you.
Ismene Alas for me. Am I outside your fate?
Antigone Yes. For you chose to live when I chose death.
Ismene At least I was not silent. You were warned.
Antigone Some will have thought you wiser. Some will not.
Ismene And yet the blame is equal for us both.
Antigone Take heart. You live. My life died long ago.
And that has made me fit to help the dead.
Creon One of these girls has shown her lack of sense
just now. The other had it from her birth.
Ismene Yes, lord. When people fall in deep distress
their native sense departs, and will not stay.
Creon You chose your mind's distraction when you chose
to work out wickedness with this wicked girl.
Ismene What life is there for me to live without her?
Creon Don't speak of her. For she is here no more.
Ismene But will you kill your own son's promised bride?
Creon Oh, there are other furrows for his plough.
Ismene But where the closeness that has bound these two?
Creon Not for my sons will I choose wicked wives.
Ismene Dear Haemon, your father robs you of your rights.
Creon You and your marriage trouble me too much.
Ismene You will take away his bride from your own son?
Creon Yes. Death will help me break this marriage off.
Chorus It seems determined that the girl must die.
Creon You helped determine it. Now, no delay!
Slaves, take them in. They must be women now.
No more free running.
Even the bold will fly when they see Death
drawing in close enough to end their life.

18 THUCYDIDES, HISTORY OF THE PELOPONNESIAN WAR: DEMOCRACY AND POWER POLITICS

In the middle decades of the fifth century B.C. the balance of power among the Greek city-states grew increasingly uncertain. For most Greeks Sparta remained an awesome example of political stability and "splendid isolation." Its militarized social order ensured it of a matchless army and general recognition as the major land power of Greece. Under Pericles, Athens had meanwhile steadily expanded its naval armament and its authority throughout the Aegean. The Athenian fleet, supported by the tribute of Athens' allies, was unrivaled throughout the eastern Mediterranean. Its port, the Piraeus, was a focal point of commerce, and its cultural preëminence was unchallenged. The rivalry between the major land power and the major naval power of Greece could not long be denied, particularly when Sparta's allies felt seriously threatened by the commercial and naval supremacy of Athens.

The long and bitter Peloponnesian War which ensued (431-404 B.C.) involved not only Athenians and Spartans but the whole of the Greek world. Fortunes varied throughout the war, but it ended with a crushing defeat for Athens, general exhaustion of the Greek states, and renewed Persian intervention in Greek affairs. The social equilibrium of the Periclean democracy was broken, and bitter class conflicts sapped the energy of Greek society. Brilliant intellectual achievements were yet to be made, but the political vitality of the city-state never quite recovered. As a political form, the city-state was still revered as the traditional Greek "way," but within a few decades Greece surrendered its independence to the Macedonian monarchy.

It was the Athenian Thucydides (c. 460 - c. 400 B.C.) who succeeded in writing the enduring *History of the Peloponnesian War*. To his writing of history Thucydides applied severe standards of historical perspective. Although he could not always acquire exact texts of the speeches which he inserted in his narrative, he endeavored, he said, "as nearly as I could, to give the general purport of what was actually said." Both of the speeches which follow are Thucydidean reconstructions rather than verbatim reports. At the end of the first year of the war, Pericles, who was himself to die of the plague which swept Athens in the following year (429 B.C.), delivered a funeral oration in honor of the Athenian war dead. This unforgettable document pays tribute not only to the power of Athens but to the qualities of her citizens. The democratic citizen is called upon to temper individualism with a firm sense of civic duty. If all citizens cannot provide creative leadership, all are expected to be men of judgment. The speech continually contrasts the cultured Athenian and the militaristic Spartan, although the latter is never directly mentioned. The severely regimented life is contrasted with the freedom of Athens; cultural vacuity with the Athenian love of beauty; propagandized valor with true and natural Athenian courage.

Thucydides also implies that Pericles was the master statesman and that the Athenian war policy after his death was a disastrous reversal of Pericles' cautious strategy. The new leaders of the assembly—"the demagogues"—gave themselves over to reckless daring. Expediency became the order of the day.

In the second selection, the "Melian Dialogue," Thucydides records Athenian expediency at its worst and shows the kind of arrogance which finally lost Athens the sympathy and support of its allies and led to its defeat. The expedition which the Athenians sent against the neutral Melians in 416 B.C. was without moral justification or military significance. The cynical demand of the Athenians that the Melians yield to superior force or perish exemplifies the decay of political morality during the course of the war. Coming as it does on the eve of Athens' disastrous Sicilian expedition, the sack of Melos furnishes a disturbing historical picture of Athenian pride just before its fall.

Pericles' Funeral Oration

36. "My first words shall be for our ancestors; for it is both just to them and seemly that on an occasion such as this our tribute of memory should be paid them. For, dwelling always in this country, generation after generation in unchanging and unbroken succession, they have handed it down to us free by their exertions. So they are worthy of our praises; and still more so are our fathers. For they enlarged the ancestral patrimony by the Empire which we hold to-day and delivered it, not without labour, into the hands of our own generation; while it is we ourselves, those of us who are now in middle life, who consolidated our power throughout the greater part of the Empire and secured the city's complete independence both in war and peace. Of the battles which we and our fathers fought, whether in the winning of our power abroad or in bravely withstanding the warfare of foreigner or Greek at home, I do not wish to say more: they are too familiar to you all. I wish rather to set forth the spirit in which we faced them, and the constitution and manners with which we rose to greatness, and to pass from them to the dead; for I think it not unfitting that these things should be called to mind in to-day's solemnity, and expedient too that the whole gathering of citizens and strangers should listen to them.

37. "For our government is not copied from those of our neighbours: we are an example to them rather than they to us. Our constitution is

Text: From *The History of the Peloponnesian War*, by Thucydides, edited by Sir Richard Livingstone and published by the Oxford University Press. Pp. 111-15, 266-70, 271, 272.

named a democracy, because it is in the hands not of the few but of the many. But our laws secure equal justice for all in their private disputes, and our public opinion welcomes and honours talent in every branch of achievement, not for any sectional reason but on grounds of excellence alone. And as we give free play to all in our public life, so we carry the same spirit into our daily relations with one another. We have no black looks or angry words for our neighbour if he enjoys himself in his own way, and we abstain from the little acts of churlishness which, though they leave no mark, yet cause annoyance to whoso notes them. Open and friendly in our private intercourse, in our public acts we keep strictly within the control of law. We acknowledge the restraint of reverence; we are obedient to whomsoever is set in authority, and to the laws, more especially to those which offer protection to the oppressed and those unwritten ordinances whose transgression brings admitted shame.

38. "Yet ours is no work-a-day city only. No other provides so many recreations for the spirit—contests and sacrifices all the year round, and beauty in our public buildings to cheer the heart and delight the eye day by day. Moreover, the city is so large and powerful that all the wealth of all the world flows in to her, so that our own Attic products seem no more homelike to us than the fruits of the labours of other nations.

39. "Our military training too is different from our opponents'. The gates of our city are flung open to the world. We practise no periodical deportations, nor do we prevent our visitors from observing or discovering what an enemy might usefully apply to his own purposes. For our trust is not in the devices of material equipment, but in our own good spirits for battle.

"So too with education. They toil from early boyhood in a laborious pursuit after courage, while we, free to live and wander as we please, march out none the less to face the self-same dangers. Here is the proof of my words. When the Spartans advance into our country, they do not come alone but with all their allies; but when we invade our neighbours we have little difficulty as a rule, even on foreign soil, in defeating men who are fighting for their own homes. Moreover, no enemy has ever met us in full strength, for we have our navy to attend to, and our soldiers are sent on service to many scattered possessions; but if they chance to encounter some portion of our forces and defeat a few of us, they boast that they have driven back our whole army, or, if they are defeated, that the victors were in full strength. Indeed, if we choose to face danger with an easy mind rather than after a rigorous training, and to trust rather in native manliness than in state-made courage, the advantage lies with us; for we are spared all the weariness of practising for future hardships, and when we find ourselves amongst them we are as brave as our plodding rivals. Here as elsewhere, then, the city sets an example which is deserving of admiration.

40. "We are lovers of beauty without extravagance, and lovers of wisdom without unmanliness. Wealth to us is not mere material for vainglory but an opportunity for achievement; and poverty we think it no disgrace to acknowledge but a real degradation to make no effort to overcome. Our citizens attend both to public and private duties, and do not allow absorption in their own various affairs to interfere with their knowledge of the city's. We differ from other states in regarding the man who holds aloof from public life not as "quiet" but as useless; we decide or debate, carefully and in person, all matters of policy, holding, not that words and deeds go ill together, but that acts are foredoomed to failure when undertaken undiscussed. For we are noted for being at once most adventurous in action and most reflective beforehand. Other men are bold in ignorance, while reflexion will stop their onset. But the bravest are surely those who have the clearest vision of what is before them, glory and danger alike, and yet notwithstanding go out to meet it. In doing good, too, we are the exact opposite of the rest of mankind. We secure our friends not by accepting favours but by doing them. And so we are naturally more firm in our attachments: for we are anxious, as creditors, to cement by kind offices our relation towards our friends. If they do not respond with the same warmness it is because they feel that their services will not be given spontaneously but only as the repayment of a debt. We are alone among mankind in doing men benefits, not on calculations of self-interest, but in the fearless confidence of freedom.

41. "In a word I claim that our city as a whole is an education to Greece, and that her members yield to none, man by man, for independence of spirit, manysidedness of attainment, and complete self-reliance in limbs and brain.

"That this is no vainglorious phrase but actual fact the supremacy which our manners have won us itself bears testimony. No other city of the present day goes out to her ordeal greater than ever men dreamed; no other is so powerful that the invader feels no bitterness when he suffers at her hands, and her subjects no shame at the indignity of their dependence. Great indeed are the symbols and witnesses of our supremacy, at which posterity, as all mankind to-day, will be astonished. We need no Homer or other man of words to praise us; for such give pleasure for a moment, but the truth will put to shame their imaginings of our deeds. For our pioneers have forced a way into every sea and every land, establishing among all mankind, in punishment or beneficence, eternal memorials of their settlement.

42. "Such then is the city for whom, lest they should lose her, the men whom we celebrate died a soldier's death: and it is but natural that all of us, who survive them, should wish to spend ourselves in her service. That, indeed, is why I have spent many words upon the city. I wished to show that we have more at stake than men who have no such inheritance, and to support my praise of the dead by making clear to you what they have done. For if I have chanted the glories of the city it was these men and their like who set hand to array her. With them, as with few among Greeks, words cannot magnify the deeds that they have done. Such an end as we have here seems indeed to show us what a good life is, from its first signs of power to its final consummation. For even where life's previous record showed faults and failures it is just to weigh the last brave hour of devotion against them all. There they wiped out evil with good and did the city more service as soldiers than they did her harm in private life. There no hearts grew faint because they loved riches more than honour; none shirked the issue in the poor man's dreams of wealth. All these they put aside to strike a blow for the city. Counting the quest to avenge her honour as the most glorious of all ventures, and leaving Hope, the uncertain goddess, to send them what she would, they faced the foe as they drew near him in the strength of their own manhood; and when the shock of battle came, they chose rather to suffer the uttermost than to win life by weakness. So their memory has escaped the reproaches of men's lips, but they bore instead on their bodies the marks of men's hands, and in a moment of time, at the climax of their lives, were rapt away from a world filled, for their dying eyes, not with terror but with glory. . . ."

The Melian Dialogue

. . . 84. The next summer the Athenians made an expedition against the isle of Melos. The Melians are a colony of Lacedaemon that would not submit to the Athenians like the other islanders, and at first remained neutral and took no part in the struggle, but afterwards, upon the Athenians using violence and plundering their territory, assumed an attitude of open hostility. The Athenian generals encamped in their territory with their army, and before doing any harm to their land sent envoys to negotiate. These the Melians did not bring before the people, but told them to state the object of their mission to the magistrates and the council; the Athenian envoys then said:

85. *Athenians.*—"As we are not to speak to the people, for fear that if we made a single speech without interruption we might deceive them with attractive arguments to which there was no chance of replying—we realize that this is the meaning of our being brought before your ruling body—we suggest that you who sit here should make security doubly sure. Let us have no long speeches from you either, but deal separately with each point, and take up at once any statement of which you disapprove, and criticize it."

86. *Melians.*—"We have no objection to your reasonable suggestion that we should put our respective points of view quietly to each other, but the military preparations which you have already made seem inconsistent with it. We see that you have come to be yourselves the judges of the debate, and that its natural conclusion for us will be slavery if you convince us, and war if we get the better of the argument and therefore refuse to submit."

87. *Athenians.*—"If you have met us in order to make surmises about the future, or for any other purpose than to look existing facts in the face and to discuss the safety of your city on this basis, we will break off the conversations; otherwise, we are ready to speak."

88. *Melians.*—"In our position it is natural and excusable to explore many ideas and arguments. But the problem that has brought us here is our security, so, if you think fit, let the discussion follow the line you propose."

89. *Athenians.*—"Then we will not make a long and unconvincing speech, full of fine phrases, to prove that our victory over Persia justifies our empire, or that we are now attacking you because you have wronged us, and we ask you not to expect to convince us by saying that you have not injured us, or that, though a colony of Lacedaemon, you did not join her. Let each of us say what we really think and reach a practical agreement. You know and we know, as practical men, that the question of justice arises only between parties equal in strength, and that the strong do what they can, and the weak submit."

90. *Melians.*—"As you ignore justice and have made self-interest the basis of discussion, we must take the same ground, and we say that in our opinion it is in your interest to maintain a principle which is for the good of all—that anyone in danger should have just and equitable treatment and any

advantage, even if not strictly his due, which he can secure by persuasion. This is your interest as much as ours, for your fall would involve you in a crushing punishment that would be a lesson to the world."

91. *Athenians.*—"We have no apprehensions about the fate of our empire, if it did fall; those who rule other peoples, like the Lacedaemonians, are not formidable to a defeated enemy. Nor is it the Lacedaemonians with whom we are now contending: the danger is from subjects who of themselves may attack and conquer their rulers. But leave that danger to us to face. At the moment we shall prove that we have come in the interest of our empire and that in what we shall say we are seeking the safety of your state; for we wish you to become our subjects with least trouble to ourselves, and we would like you to survive in our interests as well as your own."

92. *Melians.*—"It may be your interest to be our masters: how can it be ours to be your slaves?"

93. *Athenians.*—"By submitting you would avoid a terrible fate, and we should gain by not destroying you."

94. *Melians.*—"Would you not agree to an arrangement under which we should keep out of the war, and be your friends instead of your enemies, but neutral?"

95. *Athenians.*—"No: your hostility injures us less than your friendship. That, to our subjects, is an illustration of our weakness, while your hatred exhibits our power."

96. *Melians.*—"Is this the construction which your subjects put on it? Do they not distinguish between states in which you have no concern, and peoples who are most of them your colonies, and some conquered rebels?"

97. *Athenians.*—"They think that one nation has as good rights as another, but that some survive because they are strong and we are afraid to attack them. So, apart from the addition to our empire, your subjection would give us security: the fact that you are islanders (and weaker than others) makes it the more important that you should not get the better of the mistress of the sea."

98. *Melians.*—"But do you see no safety in our neutrality? You debar us from the plea of justice and press us to submit to your interests, so we must expound our own, and try to convince you, if the two happen to coincide. Will you not make enemies of all neutral Powers when they see your conduct and reflect that some day you will attack them? Will not your action strengthen your existing opponents, and induce those who would otherwise never be your enemies to become so against their will?"

99. *Athenians.*—"No. The mainland states, secure in their freedom, will be slow to take defensive measures against us, and we do not consider them so formidable as independent island powers like yourselves, or subjects already smarting under our yoke. These are most likely to take a thoughtless step and bring themselves and us into obvious danger."

100. *Melians.*—"Surely then, if you are ready to risk so much to maintain your empire, and the enslaved peoples so much to escape from it, it would be criminal cowardice in us, who are still free, not to take any and every measure before submitting to slavery?"

101. *Athenians.*—"No, if you reflect calmly: for this is not a competition in heroism between equals, where your honour is at stake, but a question of self-preservation, to save you from a struggle with a far stronger Power."

102. *Melians.*—"Still, we know that in war fortune is more impartial than the disproportion in numbers might lead one to expect. If we submit at once, our position is desperate; if we fight, there is still a hope that we shall stand secure."

103. *Athenians.*—"Hope encourages men to take risks; men in a strong position may follow her without ruin, if not without loss. But when they stake all that they have to the last coin (for she is a spendthrift), she reveals her real self in the hour of failure, and when her nature is known she leaves them without means of self-protection. You are weak, your future hangs on a turn of the scales; avoid the mistake most men make, who might save themselves by human means, and then, when visible hopes desert them, in their extremity turn to the invisible—prophecies and oracles and all those things which delude men with hopes, to their destruction. . . ."

111. *Athenians.*—"Here experience may teach you like others, and you will learn that Athens has never abandoned a siege from fear of another foe. . . . Think it over when we withdraw, and reflect once and again that you have only one country, and that its prosperity or ruin depends on one decision. . . ."

19 THE "OLD OLIGARCH," *THE CONSTITUTION OF THE ATHENIANS:* A CRITIQUE OF DEMOCRACY

That all Athenians did not revere democratic government is evident from a brief tract entitled *The Constitution of the Athenians*, whose unknown author is referred to by modern authorities as the "Old Oligarch." The date of this tract is uncertain, but it was very possibly written in the early years of the Peloponnesian War. Probably it is a work which was circulated among those Athenians who wished to negotiate a peace with Sparta and, with Spartan assistance, establish an oligarchical government at Athens. The arguments of the "Old Oligarch" contrast sharply with Pericles' praise of the democracy and with Thucydides' balanced and incisive weighing of its faults and its virtues. Even the culture of Athens is viewed with contempt: the average citizen of Athens is no longer a man of judgment but a member of a mob. The extreme pettiness of this representative of the oligarchical faction is, perhaps, a minor piece of evidence as to why the Athenian oligarchies established in 411 and 404 were both short-lived and why the Athenians even after the Peloponnesian War preferred to maintain their democratic way of life.

Now, as for the constitution of the Athenians, and the type or manner of constitution which they have chosen, I praise it not, in so far as the very choice involves the welfare of the baser folk as opposed to that of the better class. I repeat, I withhold my praise so far; but, given the fact that this is the type agreed upon, I propose to show that they set about its preservation in the right way; and that those other transactions in connection with it, which are looked upon as blunders by the rest of the Hellenic world, are the reverse.

In the first place, I maintain, it is only just that the poorer classes and the common people of Athens should be better off than the men of birth and wealth, seeing that it is the people who man the fleet, and have brought the city her power. The steersman, the boatswain, the lieutenant, the look-out-man at the prow, the shipwright—these are the people who supply the city with power far rather than her heavy infantry and men of birth and quality. This being the case, it seems only just that offices of state should be thrown open to every one both in the ballot and the show of hands, and that the right of speech should belong to any one who likes, without restriction. For, observe, there are many of these offices which, according as they are in good or in bad hands, are a source of safety or of danger to the People, and in these the People prudently abstains from sharing; as, for instance, it does not think it incumbent on itself to share in the functions of the general or of the commander of cavalry. The commons recognises the fact that in forgoing the personal exercise of these offices, and leaving them to the control of the more powerful citizens, it secures the balance of advantage to itself. It is only those departments of government which bring pay and assist the private estate that the People cares to keep in its own hands.

In the next place, in regard to what some people are puzzled to explain—the fact that everywhere greater consideration is shown to the base, to poor people and to common folk, than to persons of good quality,—so far from being a matter of surprise, this, as can be shown, is the keystone of the preservation of the democracy. It is these poor people, this common folk, this worse element, whose prosperity, combined with the growth of their numbers, enhances the democracy. Whereas, a shifting of fortune to the advantage of the wealthy and the better classes implies the establishment on the part of the commons of a strong power in opposition to itself. In fact, all the world over, the cream of society is in opposition to the democracy. Naturally, since the smallest amount of intemperance and injustice, together with the highest scrupulousness in the pursuit of excellence, is to be found in the ranks of the better class, while within the ranks of the People will be found the greatest amount of ignorance, disorderliness, rascality,—poverty acting as a stronger incentive to base conduct, not to speak of lack of education and ignorance, traceable to the lack of means which afflicts the average of mankind.

The objection may be raised that it was a mis-

Text: "The Old Oligarch," *The Constitution of the Athenians*, trans. Henry G. Dakyns, in *The Greek Historians*, II, ed. Francis R. B. Godolphin. Copyright 1942 by Random House, Inc., and reprinted by their permission. Pp. 633-43 *passim*.

take to allow the universal right of speech and a seat in council. These should have been reserved for the cleverest, the flower of the community. But here, again, it will be found that they are acting with wise deliberation in granting to even the baser sort the right of speech, for supposing only the better people might speak, or sit in council, blessings would fall to the lot of those like themselves, but to the commons the reverse of blessings. Whereas now, any one who likes, any base fellow, may get up and discover something to the advantage of himself and his equals. It may be retorted, "And what sort of advantage either for himself or for the People can such a fellow be expected to hit upon?" The answer to which is, that in their judgment the ignorance and the baseness of this fellow, together with his goodwill, are worth a great deal more to them than your superior person's virtue and wisdom, coupled with animosity. What it comes to, therefore, is that a state founded upon such institutions will not be the best state; but, given a democracy, these are the right means to secure its preservation. The People, it must be borne in mind, does not demand that the city should be well governed and itself a slave. It desires to be free and to be master. As to bad legislation it does not concern itself about that. In fact, what you believe to be bad legislation is the very source of the People's strength and freedom. But if you seek for good legislation, in the first place you will see the cleverest members of the community laying down the laws for the rest. And in the next place, the better class will curb and chastise the lower orders; the better class will deliberate in behalf of the state, and not suffer crack-brained fellows to sit in council, or to speak or vote in the assemblies. No doubt; but under the weight of such blessings the People will in a very short time be reduced to slavery....

The common people put a stop to citizens devoting their time to athletics and to the cultivation of music, disbelieving in the beauty of such training, and recognising the fact that these are things the cultivation of which is beyond its power. On the same principle, in the case of the choregia, the management of athletics, and the command of ships, the fact is recognised that it is the rich man who trains the chorus, and the People for whom the chorus is trained; it is the rich man who is naval commander or superintendent of athletics, and the People that profits by their labours. In fact, what the People looks upon as its right is to pocket the money. To sing and run and dance and man the vessels is well enough, but only in order that the People may be the gainer, while the rich are made poorer. And so in the courts of justice, justice is not more an object of concern to the jurymen than what touches personal advantage.

To speak next of the allies, and in reference to the point that emissaries from Athens come out, and, according to common opinion, calumniate and vent their hatred upon the better sort of people, this is done on the principle that the ruler cannot help being hated by those whom he rules; but that if wealth and respectability are to wield power in the subject cities the empire of the Athenian People has but a short lease of existence. This explains why the better people are punished with infamy, robbed of their money, driven from their homes, and put to death, while the baser sort are promoted to honour. On the other hand, the better Athenians protect the better class in the allied cities. And why? Because they recognise that it is to the interest of their own class at all times to protect the best element in the cities. It may be urged that if it comes to strength and power the real strength of Athens lies in the capacity of her allies to contribute their money quota. But to the democratic mind it appears a higher advantage still for the individual Athenian to get hold of the wealth of the allies, leaving them only enough to live upon and to cultivate their estates, but powerless to harbour treacherous designs.

Again, it is looked upon as a mistaken policy on the part of the Athenian democracy to compel her allies to voyage to Athens in order to have their cases tried. On the other hand, it is easy to reckon up what a number of advantages the Athenian People derives from the practice impugned. In the first place, there is the steady receipt of salaries throughout the year derived from the court fees. Next, it enables them to manage the affairs of the allied states while seated at home without the expense of naval expeditions. Thirdly, they thus preserve the partisans of the democracy, and ruin her opponents in the law courts. Whereas, supposing the several allied states tried their cases at home, being inspired by hostility to Athens, they would destroy those of their own citizens whose friendship to the Athenian People was most marked. But besides all this the democracy derives the following advantages from hearing the cases of her allies in Athens. In the first place, the one per cent levied in Piraeus is increased to the profit of the state; again, the owner of a lodging-house does better, and so, too, the owner of a pair of beasts, or of slaves to be let out on hire; again, heralds and criers are a class of people who fare better owing to the sojourn of foreigners at Athens. Further still, supposing the allies had not to resort to Athens for the hearing of cases, only the official representative of the imperial state would be held in honour, such as the general, or trierarch, or ambassador. Whereas now every single individual among the allies is forced to pay flattery to the People of Athens because he knows that he must betake himself to Athens and win or lose his case at the bar, not of any stray set of judges, but of the sovereign People itself, such being the law and custom at Athens. He is compelled to behave as a suppliant in the courts of justice, and when some juryman comes into court, to grasp his hand. For this reason, therefore, the allies find themselves more and more in the position of slaves to the people of Athens. . . .

Further, states oligarchically governed are forced to ratify their alliances and solemn oaths, and if they fail to abide by their contracts, the offence, by whomsoever committed, lies nominally at the door of the oligarchs who entered upon the contract. But in the case of engagements entered into by a democracy it is open to the People to throw the blame on the single individual who spoke in favour of some measure, or put it to the vote, and to maintain to the rest of the world, "I was not present, nor do I approve of the terms of the agreement." Inquiries are made in a full meeting of the People, and should any of these things be disapproved of, they can at once discover countless excuses to avoid doing whatever they do not wish. And if any mischief should spring out of any resolutions which the People has passed in council, the People can readily shift the blame from its own shoulders. "A handful of oligarchs acting against the interests of the People have ruined us." But if any good result ensue, they the People, at once take the credit of that to themselves.

In the same spirit it is not allowed to caricature on the comic stage or otherwise libel the People, because they do not care to hear themselves ill spoken of. But if any one has a desire to satirise his neighbour he has full leave to do so. And this because they are well aware that, as a general rule, the person caricatured does not belong to the People, or the masses. He is more likely to be some wealthy or well-born person, or man of means and influence. In fact, but few poor people and of the popular stamp incur the comic lash, or if they do they have brought it on themselves by excessive love of meddling or some covetous self-seeking at the expense of the People, so that no particular annoyance is felt at seeing such folk satirised.

What, then, I venture to assert is, that the People of Athens has no difficulty in recognising which of its citizens are of the better sort and which the opposite. And so recognising those who are serviceable and advantageous to itself, even though they be base, the People loves them; but the good folk they are disposed the rather to hate. This virtue of theirs, the People holds, is not engrained in their nature for any good to itself, but rather for its injury. In direct opposition to this, there are some persons who, being born of the People, are yet by natural instinct not commoners. For my part I pardon the People its own democracy, as, indeed, it is pardonable in any one to do good to himself. But the man who, not being himself one of the People, prefers to live in a state democratically governed rather than in an oligarchical state may be said to smooth his own path towards iniquity. He knows that a bad man has a better chance of slipping through the fingers of justice in a democratic than in an oligarchical state. . . .

There is another point in which it is sometimes felt that the Athenians are ill advised, in their adoption, namely, of the less respectable party, in a state divided by faction. But if so, they do it advisedly. If they chose the more respectable, they would be adopting those whose views and interests differ from their own, for there is no state in which the best element is friendly to the people. It is the worst element which in every state favours the democracy—on the principle that like favours like. . . .

INTERPRETATIONS OF ATHENIAN DEMOCRACY

20 G. B. GRUNDY, *THUCYDIDES AND THE HISTORY OF HIS AGE:* THE PARADOX OF GREEK INDIVIDUALISM

Although the names of over two hundred and fifty Greek city-states are known, the history of Greece in the fifth century B.C. remains largely the history of Athens. At the end of the preceding century, under the leadership of Cleisthenes, the Athenians created the most complete set of democratic institutions yet known in Greece or, probably, to any previous civilization. These institutions were successfully defended against the great challenge of the Persian Wars. In the last half of the fifth century, Athens produced or attracted to residence the poets, playwrights, teachers, scientists, and artists who gave her immortality. Athens possessed a record of brilliant, if sometimes erratic, political leadership and vigorous popular sentiment. And yet Athenian history in the fifth century is not all glory, and to ancient and modern historians alike the question has often recurred, "Why did Athens—even under the Periclean democracy—become increasingly tyrannical, feared by rivals and allies alike?"

A balanced and insightful answer to this question appears in the selection below from *Thucydides and the History of His Age* (first published, 1911) by G. B. Grundy, an Honorary Fellow and lecturer in ancient history and geography at the University of Oxford. In his discussion of Periclean democracy and the Athenian empire, Grundy avoids the preoccupation of many historians with the "ideal side of the Periclean creation." He dismisses the tendency, partially derived from Thucydides, to blame Athenian misrule primarily on the political leadership following the death of Pericles. Rather, Grundy sees the development of Athenian imperialism as a natural expression of "a general characteristic of Greek political sentiment" which had always existed—namely, individualism. In terms of the empire, Athens' allies resented encroachments on their independence, and paradoxically, the Athenians were individualists enough to be suspicious of the power of individualism in others and to combat it.

With the semi-revolution brought about by Ephialtes and Perikles begins a new era in Athenian history. A new democracy and a new empire grow up side by side. It is a strange democracy and a strange empire. History does not present any counterpart to either of them. Of the empire we possess considerable knowledge; but the secret of the real inner nature of the democracy died with Perikles. All that can be claimed for this chapter is that it is an attempt to penetrate on economic lines into the mystery of its life story.

It is the ideal side of the Periklean creation which has most attracted the attention of historians; and it must be confessed that the element of idealism within it presents a very fascinating study. But though many of its features are not explicable save on idealistic lines, there are others which are due to some practical necessity which, perhaps, history has not altogether succeeded in elucidating. The disastrous failure of the system after Perikles' death, the intense hatred with which it was regarded by those especially who suffered from its later developments, have led to its story being distorted in contemporary and later evidence. Had it not been for Thucydides and for a few incidental admissions in other authors, it would have come down to us as the vulgar creation of a self-seeking politician who sought to maintain himself in power by yielding to the baser instincts of the ignorant and the idle. Thucydides discloses the fact that it aimed at a high ideal, though he seems well aware that the ideal was too high for average human nature to realise. The incidental admissions of other authors show that those practical elements in it which the later world condemned most severely were designed to meet an urgent practical necessity of the time. It was indeed out of a practical necessity that Perikles sought to create an ideal which should itself obviate such evils as might arise from the measures taken to meet the necessity.

The empire of Athens over her allies was an essential factor in the Periklean design. But there are two phases in the design, that before, and that after, the Peace of 446; and for the later phase the empire is a more important factor than it is for the earlier. Still it is during both periods an essential element in the design.

The process by which the Delian League was converted into an Athenian ἀρχή [*archē*, empire] was partly inevitable, partly deliberate. Severe

---

Text: Reprinted by permission of Basil Blackwell & Mott, Ltd., Oxford, from G. B. Grundy, *Thucydides and the History of His Age*, 2nd ed. (Oxford: Basil Blackwell, 1948), I, 169-75.

as is the condemnation passed upon that process in after time, it would seem that the element of inevitability played in it a greater part than the element of deliberation. In spite of his intense admiration for Perikles, the one man above all others who was responsible for the conversion, Thucydides was no friend of the policy of empire as it presented itself in his day. The language used with respect to the suppression of the revolt of Naxos is so severe that it discloses the opinion of the writer; and, furthermore, it is hard to believe that the supporter of an imperial policy would have deliberately inserted in his history such documents as the speech of Kleon and the Melian dialogue. Yet even Thucydides introduces into his narrative arguments which, taken in conjunction with certain well-known characteristics of Greek political sentiment, go far towards showing that at the outset, at any rate, of the period of Perikles' rule, Athens could not, without great danger to herself, nor indeed without danger to the Hellenic world, have allowed the dissolution of the league. But for its continued maintenance force and constraint were required; and these ultimately spelt empire.

As has been already said, the question is concerned with a general characteristic of Greek political sentiment. Greek public life, whether represented by the individual, by the party, or by the state, was saturated with individualism. Well aware that the individual could not by himself realise his individualism, the Greek sought for the least common measure in life, the smallest form of association in which he could realise it to the fullest extent which was, humanly speaking, possible. He found this in party and in the city state. In any larger form of community the realisation of his own individual interests must necessarily become difficult. He therefore limited his political ideal to the city state. Some writers of Greek history have allowed their admiration for many departments of Greek life to blind them to many of its defects, and have discoursed with much satisfaction on that 'subordination of the individual to the community' in which they profess to discover the most admirable feature of Greek political life at its best. The undeniable state and party individualism of the fourth century they are wont to attribute to that form of the 'social compact' which the Sophists taught in the later half of the fifth. It does not seem to occur to them that this teaching could hardly have borne so large and so terrible a crop of fruit had not its seed been sown on ground adapted by nature to receive it.

Greek individualism, like so many elements in Greek life, is by no means a simple thing, because it was not evolved by a simple race. The Greek was far too keen-witted to fail to see that the individual, in order to gain his individual ends, must combine with others whose aims resemble, though they may not be absolutely identical with, his own. He was keenly anxious to realise as many of those ends as possible. Inasmuch therefore as all forms of combination and association demand the sacrifice of some individual interests, he sought for that form of society which would be sufficiently large to promise the realisation of the ends of the society, and not so large as to sacrifice to the interests of the society the interests on which he set most store. He found this society in the city state, or rather in those associations of party by which the city state could be dominated.

That which above all tends to disguise the individualism of the Greeks is the fact that individualism is peculiarly fearful of itself. It was this fear which introduced into Greek social life an element which contrasts strongly with that which is commonly associated with individualism. In some respects the control of the state over the individual, and the sacrifices which it demanded from him, were greater than in modern states. But the completeness of that control is not necessarily to be attributed to the self-sacrifice of the individual to the community, and furthermore the contrast with the modern state is not emphasised by any peculiar absence of individualism from modern political life. All that this control meant was that the individual recognised that a strong association was necessary in order to keep in check the strong individualism of his fellow Greeks. The individualism of others must always be a danger to the liberty of the individual.

Several well-known and ever-recurrent features of Greek history seem to mark a strong tendency towards individualism, even when it is least apparent, at any rate in the extant records of the time. The Greek would vigorously support the state, when in form and action it promoted what seemed to him to be his own interests. But there his loyalty ended. He was far more attached to party than to the state. His party promoted directly that which he conceived to be his own interest. So did the state, but in a less direct way. If the state promoted his party interests, well and good! But if the interests of party came into conflict with the interests of the state, he sided with his party. Party interest was nearer to individual interest than was the interest of the state; and he was quite determined that his sacrifice to any association with others should be as small as possible. He was quite ready to become a promoter of στάσις [stasis, civil strife] if he thought that the sacrifice demanded by the state was too large. The frequency of στάσις in Greek states is due to the tendency of the political section in power to work the state in its own interests, and to the consequent resentment of those of opposite views to a system under which their special interests must inevitably suffer. But the Greek's consciousness of the individualism of his race, of the strength of this characteristic among his fellow Greeks, and of the danger which it threatened to individual liberty, led him to assent to large sacrifices to the state, the only community which could check the strong individualism of others; that is to say, his individualism reacted upon itself under the influence of fear of the individualism of his fellows. Hence he sought to bring to ruin the commanding individualities which arose among his own race. He had only to look into his own mind to understand the danger of great individualities in great positions. Some of these justified his distrust; some were not given the chance of so doing. Miltiades, Themistokles, Pausanias, Kimon, Alkibiades, and Lysander were sacrificed to the consciousness of the strength of individualism in the Greek race. Herodotus had said that the deity was jealous of great prosperity. He might have attributed the same feeling to his individualistic fellow-countrymen. The Greek race knew itself and feared itself in the personalities of its great men.

The individualism of the Greek seems very paradoxical: but the paradox is more apparent than real. It is shown most markedly in his largest social unit, the city state. In the state he believes himself to have attained to αὐτάρκεια, an independence of that which is external. The state is, therefore, the utmost limit of his sacrifice of individual interest. He is content to make a sacrifice in order that he may have his wants fulfilled. In the state he believes himself to have arrived at that goal. Hence the marked state-individualism which prevailed in the Greek world. It showed itself theoretically in the claim to autonomy on the part of each little city state,—a theoretical claim whose justice was conceded by all the Greek world. It was, indeed, frequently violated, but its violation shocked Greek public opinion.

It was this intense state-individualism which rendered combined action among the Greek states a matter of extreme difficulty. Such action could only be brought about by some form of constraint, exerted either by external danger, or by the *force majeure* [superior force] of some power within the Hellenic world itself. These combinations were never purely voluntary. In the period with which we have to deal they are brought into existence either by the fear of Persian aggression, or by the force exerted by some state more powerful than its neighbors, such as Sparta in Peloponnese or Thebes in Boeotia. But these confederacies had within them from the first the seeds of dissolution. The tendency to break away from the combinations is most marked even in the early stages of their existence. The position of leader of such a union of states was consequently by no means a sinecure, as Athens found before the Delian League had been long in existence. Thucydides shows clearly how powerful were the elements of disruption existing in it from its early years. This tendency had to be met by constraints exercised in the name of the league by Athens, as leading power within it. It was not merely a question of revolt, such as in the cases of Naxos and Thasos. It is evident that this constraint had to be exercised in numerous minor instances of failure to fulfil league obligations. There was no surer way of exciting enmity and hostility in the Hellenic political world; and therefore the words put by Thucydides into the mouth of the Athenian ambassadors at Sparta expressed in all probability the literal truth; 'And, at last, when almost all hated us; when some had already revolted and had been subdued, and when you had ceased to be the friends that once you were, and had become objects of suspicion and dislike, it appeared no longer safe to give up our empire; especially as all who left us would fall to you.'

The critical moment in the history of the league came at the time immediately succeeding the battle of the Eurymedon. Its results had practically dispelled all fear of Persia as a dangerous power in the Aegean, and had guaranteed for the time being, at any rate, the freedom of the continental cities of Asia from Persian control. It may even have been followed by a definite peace; it was, according to the evidence, followed by an agreement excluding the Persian fleet from the Aegean. If ever the time had come for the dissolution of the league, it had come at that moment. Moreover, the Moderate coalition was in control at Athens, a party peculiarly uncommitted to any policy of maintaining the league indefinitely. Yet no steps were taken towards dissolution. There seems to have been a large element of the inevitable in the maintenance of the league and in its evolution into an empire. Thereafter that evolution would proceed rapidly. The majority of the allies may well, before the Eurymedon was fought, have recognised the necessity for the maintenance of the existing combination; but, after that great victory, the continuance of the burdens it entailed, and the loss of state liberty involved in it, must have been felt as peculiarly irksome. The centrifugal force within the league must have become stronger than ever, and have been counteracted by a corresponding increase in the force exerted to resist it: in other words, Athens must have found it necessary to bring into play those methods of rule within the confederacy of which evidence is found in contemporary and later literature and in inscriptions. The use of those methods converted the league into an ἀρχή. At any rate, whether league or empire, the allied states stood ready to hand when Perikles inaugurated his economic policy within the state.

21 ALFRED ZIMMERN, *THE GREEK COMMONWEALTH: ATHENS, THE MODEL STATE*

Like G. B. Grundy (see Document 20), Professor Alfred Zimmern also viewed the empire created by Athens as the culmination of a natural historical process, but with quite different causes and results. In his great work, *The Greek Commonwealth*, Zimmern argues that Athens in the Periclean Age had necessarily become a "model state" which could not avoid imitation by other Greek city-states. Athens' allies gradually became subjects within the empire more because of the attractions of Athenian blessings than because of the imposition of Athenian tyranny. At home and abroad, the fifth-century Athenians were justly acclaimed for their rich culture and their democracy; they were, in Zimmern's view, not only brilliant theorists but also industrious and capable administrators, politicians, businessmen, artists, and craftsmen who got on with their prospects and did not fear making occasional mistakes.

Alfred Zimmern was an outstanding classicist and Montague Burton Professor of International Relations in the University of Oxford. In middle life, he reluctantly put aside his scholarly interests to serve with the League of Nations. His major work of ancient history, *The Greek Commonwealth, Politics and Economics in Fifth Century Athens*, was first published in 1911.

Thus Athens had gradually formed herself, whether her pupils liked it or no, to be 'an education to Greece'. The process was so gradual, and the control so wisely exercised, that the allies could not easily put their hand on any particular cause of complaint. There was plenty of grumbling, especially when the courts were overcrowded with cases and a round of festivals came on to double the arrears. But of practical grievances we hear little or nothing. The Athenian courts did their work well. The advantage of having a sensible code to deal with was too great to be despised. Moreover, surely it was worth the expense to have a fortnight in the capital and to see how the imperial money was being laid out on the Acropolis. So the law courts brought sightseers; the Parthenon and its great Vestibule proved the best of advertisements; and the waggoners and the lodging-house keepers found their own businesses more profitable than sitting still and listening hard for their day's pay in the courts. It is not surprising on the whole, though the fact remains to their credit, that the Athenians were able to boast, without fear of contradiction, before a hostile assembly, of the impartiality of their justice. Indeed they quickly grew accustomed to the judicial mood, and would put on the judge's wig even when it was wholly inappropriate. 'Do remember,' begs a speaker in a difficult debate on policy, 'that you are not sitting in a law court thinking out what sentence these people have deserved, but sitting in Parliament to discover what course is best for yourselves.' Euripides makes a suppliant for Athenian aid put in a similar reminder, when Theseus had given him a long lecture from the Bench. For Athens took her own duties, as she took everything, very seriously, and did her best, in an imperfect world, however complicated the problem, to mete out fair decisions. Nor had the teachers of rhetoric yet appeared to cloud the plain citizen's common sense with their intellectual monkey tricks.

Athens had thus become recognized as a model State; and Greece was in the mood to adopt or imitate her ways in small things as in great. We can see this in the rapid spread of Athenian weights and measures and the Athenian coinage, or of systems arranged so as to work in with them. Athens was standardizing Greek coinage as she was unifying Greek law. She did not, of course

Text: Alfred Zimmern, *The Greek Commonwealth*, 5th ed. (Oxford: The Clarendon Press, 1931), pp. 191-97. Reprinted by permission of The Clarendon Press.

compel her allies to use only Attic money, or money coined on the Attic standard. But she naturally preferred that contributions should be paid in it; and there were indirect ways by which she could encourage it. It was only decent to pay Apollo, and later Athena, in the coinage they preferred to see. And as Athenian coins could always be relied on for good weight, and as the device upon them, the famous owl, was so conveniently uncouth that you could tell it at a glance, there was really no need for a compulsion which would have been against the principle of free exchange. Example was better than precept. Attic silver began to be known and used not only in the Confederacy but all over Greece and among distant barbarians. When Gylippus, after Aegospotami, kept back some of the Spartan State booty, and hid it under his roof tiles, the man who denounced him merely said that there were 'owls in the potters' quarter'. In fact, much as the Spartans hated strangers, and Athenians above all, there were a great many such owls' nests all over their city.

Athenian influence was thus spreading, as Pericles realized, far beyond the Aegean and the confines of the Empire. Her traders were moving East and West, finding their way into every land and every sea, fetching goods, and paying for them in owls or pottery, from the iron mines of Elba or the caravans at Gaza and Cyrene. For this also was part of the imperial mission—to mix freely with all mankind and to give of their best to men and nations. Friendships were knit and alliances made with Greek, and even with barbarian, powers without a thought of the Persians or the original object of the league. For thirty years indeed the Persian War was carried on, in a desultory manner and with varying success. When peace was made in 448 Cyprus was still 'enslaved'. But in the course of a generation freedom had changed its meaning; and Pericles did not feel ashamed to make a convention with the national enemy, or even to receive for the league and put away in its exchequer the contributions of Carians and Lycians. Athens had now become an Empire just like Persia or Assyria, and she did not blush to receive tribute from her inferiors. Indeed she needed it for the fulfilment of the work she had to do: and Pericles, like Darius, was determined to see that she should secure and keep it. Already in 454, when nearly the whole Athenian fleet had been destroyed in Egypt and the Aegean was for a moment exposed to pirates and Phoenicians, it was thought wiser to remove the treasury of the allies from Delos to Athens. Ostensibly this meant no more than a change of banker, Athena taking the place of Apollo. But, practically, the result was to remove it once and for all from the control of the Confederate Parliament, and to make every one see and feel, what they had known in their hearts long ago, that it was the money of Athens, with which she could do what she liked. The world is still blessing her for what she did with it.

When peace was made with Persia in 448 there was indeed a small party of 'Little Athenians' who urged that the alliance should be dissolved and the contributions returned. Athens had no right to spend the money on herself 'as a proud and vain woman decks herself out with jewels'. But their protests passed unheeded, and their leader was sent into exile for his troublesome conscientiousness. Plain facts were too strong. Athens could no more step back than most Englishmen feel they can leave India. She had woken up to find herself an Empire and was resolved to play the part. So Pericles set about the first avowedly imperial piece of organization, and divided the Empire into Provinces for the more convenient collection of tribute. From the year 443 onwards Athena's invoices show the names neatly grouped under five heads—contributions from Ionia, from the Hellespont, from Thrace, from Caria, and from the Islands: those from the Black Sea ports, which were not in the original assessment, are separately classified. This money was what Athens lived on, and still partly lives on. 'It may seem wickedness to have won it; it is quite certainly folly to let it go.'

But this is looking forward. For the men of these two generations of empire-building were not conscious of any wickedness. They were too busy with their work. If they stopped to think at all, as they rested on their oars, it was to reflect on the joy of achievement and how 'all things worked together for good'. For this it is which makes this short half century perhaps the greatest and happiest period in recorded history. The world was moving onwards with extraordinary swiftness, bearing on its bosom, like a strong river in flood, all that lay within its track. And how much that was! 'Freedom, Law, and Progress; Truth and Beauty; Knowledge and Virtue; Humanity and Religion; high things, the conflicts between which have caused most of the disruptions and despondencies of human societies, seemed all to lie in the same direction.' The men who were inspired by these greatest of human watchwords felt as yet no misgivings. They knew their work was right, that it was well and soundly laid, and that posterity would understand it.

For, though the material they worked in was the lives of men and nations, they were still Greeks and still artists; and with the joyousness of the creator, whether in words or institutions, they banished every whisper which could reason them into unhappiness or break up, even for a moment, the harmonious pattern of their life. It was indeed very illogical of Sophocles to hymn eternal justice in his *Oedipus* and yet to take office without a scruple as a misappropriator of imperial funds. It was very illogical of the Sovereign People to entice sister communities into a league of liberty and then to punish them for their withdrawal —as illogical as for Burke, imbued with the spirit of a later Empire, to declare about the American Colonies that 'the more ardently they love liberty the more perfect will be their obedience'. But such contradictions passed unnoticed by all but a few keen-sighted seers, not merely because Athens wished and tried to champion freedom—this alone would not have sufficed to seal the eyes of her citizens—but because, while they were serving her with 'the fighter's daring, the wise man's understanding, and the good man's self-discipline', they felt free within themselves—free and light-hearted and confident and incapable of doing wrong.

They had neither the leisure nor the desire, any more than eighteenth-century Englishmen, to invent an imperial theory of their own. But Thucydides, writing when most of what was mortal in their work had already crumbled into dust, invented one for them. It sounds absurd and vainglorious, as imperial theories always do, to a critical posterity; yet if the dead could rise from the Cerameicus, or if their grave reliefs could find voices, they would bear out, albeit with modesty, the analysis of their historian. 'We are the leaders of civilization, the pioneers of the human race. Our society and intercourse is the highest blessing man can confer. To be within the circle of our influence is not dependence but a privilege. Not all the wealth of the East can repay the riches we bestow. So we can work on cheerfully, using the means and money that flow in to us, confident that, try as they will, we shall still be creditors. For through effort and suffering and on many a stricken field we have found out the secret of human power, which is the secret of happiness. Men have guessed at it under many names; but we alone have learnt to know it and to make it at home in our city. And the name we know it by is Freedom, for it has taught us that to serve is to be free. Do you wonder why it is that "alone among mankind" (will there ever be another nation which can understand what we mean?) "we confer our benefits, not on calculations of self-interest, but in the fearless confidence of Freedom"?'

ALEXANDER AND THE HELLENISTIC WORLD

22 ARRIAN, *ANABASIS OF ALEXANDER*, AND PLUTARCH, "ON THE FORTUNE OR THE VIRTUE OF ALEXANDER": THE WORLD CONQUEROR IN THE WORLD STATE

When Alexander the Great of Macedon died in 323 B.C., he was only thirty-three years of age and had reigned just short of fourteen years, but few historical figures have captured the imagination of their own and future generations more effectively than he. Yet what precisely makes Alexander "the Great" is a matter of conjecture. In his associates' minds he was a man of military skill, fortified by incredible daring and boundless energy. He led the Macedonian army, already battle-hardened by his talented father Philip, the conqueror of Greece, to brilliant victories over the hosts of the Persian Empire. Undaunted by the cautious advice of his generals, he refused to limit his objectives and marched as far east as the Indus Valley and as far north as Turkestan. Only the mutiny of his weary troops prevented him from advancing toward the Ganges, and, if reports are true, he died in the midst of plans for the conquest of Italy and the western Mediterranean.

Few modern historians accept Alexander's greatness upon his military abilities alone, and none, certainly, upon the pomp which he acquired as Lord of Lords of the Persians and as Pharaoh, the god-king of Egypt. More noteworthy to them—as it was to many of his contemporaries—is Alexander's surprising cosmopolitanism. By his colonization, Alexander spread the Greek language, Greek social institutions, and Greek culture from Athens to India. He seems to have envisioned a new culture, rooted in Hellenism but united with the ancient civilizations of the Near East and any other area which might be added to the empire of the future. The narrow distinction which the Greek city-states had drawn between themselves and the "barbarian" world was to be broken down. Each man was now to consider himself a citizen (*polites*) of the universe (*kosmos*) above and beyond his local or national affiliations. The *oiloumene*, the whole of the civilized world, was to be united by bonds of kinship, concord, and affection. To dramatize this goal, Alexander included Persians, Semites, Egyptians, and Bactrians in his civil service. He supported his ideal of cultural diffusion by a mingling of the empire's races by marrying a Bactrian princess and encouraging his soldiers to take foreign wives.

The selections which follow were written by Arrian (*fl.* second century A.D.) and Plutarch (*c.* 46 - *c.* 120 A.D.), Greek authors who wrote some four hundred years after Alexander's death but relied upon sources closer to the time of Alexander. Arrian, especially, is a careful, objective historian who seldom yields to the exaggeration or partisanship which characterized the Hellenistic traditions regarding Alexander's exploits and viewpoints. Both biographers undoubtedly assign to Alexander some ideas which were only fully developed later by the Stoic philosophers. Nevertheless, it seems very likely that it was the world-conqueror Alexander who first sensed the possibility of an international community peacefully bound by the brotherhood of man.

Arrian on Alexander

Alexander now sailed round by sea the distance of the shore of the Persian gulf between the Eulaeus and the Tigris, and then sailed up the Tigris to the camp where Hephaestian had encamped with all his force. Thence again he sailed to Opis, a city built on the Tigris. During this voyage upstream he removed the weirs in the river and made the stream level throughout; these weirs had been made by the Persians to prevent anyone sailing up to their country overmastering it by a naval force. All this had been contrived by the Persians, inexpert as they were in maritime matters; and so these weirs, built up at frequent intervals, made the voyage up the Tigris very difficult. Alexander, however, said that contrivances of this kind belonged to those who had no military supremacy; he therefore regarded these safeguards as of no value to himself, and indeed proved them not worth mention by destroying with ease these labours of the Persians.

On reaching Opis, Alexander summoned his Macedonians and announced that those who from old age or from mutilations were unfit for service he there discharged from the army; and he sent them to their own homes. He promised to give them on departure enough to make them objects of greater envy to those at home, and also stir up the rest of the Macedonians to a zeal for sharing his own dangers and toils. Alexander for his part said this, no doubt, to flatter the Macedonians; they, however, feeling that Alexander rather despised them, by this time, and regarded them as altogether useless for warfare, quite naturally, for their part, were annoyed at his remarks, having been annoyed during this whole campaign with a great deal else, since he caused them indignation frequently by his Persian dress which seemed to point the same way, and the Macedonian equipment of the Oriental "Successors," and the importation of cavalry of foreign tribes into the ranks of the Companions. They did not, then, restrain themselves and keep silence, but called upon him to release them all from the army, and bade him carry on war with the help of his sire (by which title they hinted slightingly at Ammon). When, then, Alexander heard this—for he had grown worse-tempered at that time, and Oriental subservience had rendered him less disposed than before to the Macedonians—he leapt down from the platform with the officers that were about him, and bade them arrest the foremost of those who had disturbed the multitude, himself with his finger pointing out to the guards whom they were to arrest; they were in number thirteen. These he ordered to be marched off to die; but as the others, amazed, remained in dead silence, he remounted the platform and spoke thus.

"I now propose to speak, Macedonians, not with a view to checking your homeward impulse; so far as I am concerned, you may go where you will; but that you may know, if you do so go away, how you have behaved to us, and how we have behaved to you. First then I shall begin my speech with my father Philip, as is right and proper. For Philip found you vagabonds and helpless, most of you clothed with sheepskins, pasturing a few sheep on the mountain sides, and fighting for these, with ill success, against Illyrians and Triballians, and the Thracians on your borders; Philip taught you to wear cloaks, in place of sheepskins, brought you down from the hills to the plains, made you doughty opponents of your neighbouring enemies, so that you trusted now not so much to the natural

Text: Reprinted by permission of the publishers and The Loeb Classical Library from *Arrian,* trans. E. Iliff Robson (Cambridge, Mass.: Harvard University Press, 1933), II, 225-41.

strength of your villages as to your own courage. Nay, he made you dwellers of cities, and civilized you with good laws and customs. Then of those very tribes to whom you submitted, and by whom you and your goods were harried, he made you masters, no longer slaves and subjects; and he added most of Thrace to Macedonia, and seizing the most convenient coast towns, opened up commerce to your country, and enabled you to work your mines in peace. Then he made you overlords of the Thracians, before whom you had long died of terror, and humbling the Phocians, made the high road into Greece broad and easy for you, whereas it had been narrow and difficult. Athens and Thebes, always watching their chance to destroy Macedon, he so completely humbled—ourselves by this time sharing these his labours—that instead of our paying tribute to Athens and obeying Thebes, they had to win from us in turn their right to exist. Then he passed into the Peloponnese, and put all in due order there; and now being declared overlord of all the rest of Greece for the expedition against Persia, he won this new prestige not so much for himself as for all Macedonia.

"All these noble deeds of my father towards you are great indeed, if looked at by themselves, and yet small, if compared with ours. I inherited from my father a few gold and silver cups, and not so much as sixty talents in his treasure; and of debts owed by Philip as much as five hundred talents, and yet having myself borrowed over and above these another eight hundred, I set forth from that country which hardly maintained you in comfort and at once opened to you the strait of the Hellespont, though the Persians were then masters of the sea; then, crushing with my cavalry Dareius' satraps, I added to your empire all Ionia, all Aeolia, Upper and Lower Phrygia, and Lydia; Miletus I took by siege; all else I took by surrender and gave to you to reap the fruits thereof. All good things from Egypt and Cyrene, which I took without striking a blow, come to you; the Syrian Valley and Palestine and Mesopotamia are your own possessions; Babylon is yours, Bactria, and Susa; the wealth of Lydia, the treasures of Persia, the good things of India, the outer ocean, all are yours; you are satraps, you guards, you captains. So what is left for myself from all these toils save the purple and this diadem? I have taken nothing to myself, nor can anyone show treasures of mine, save these possessions of yours, or what is being safeguarded for you. For there is nothing as concerns myself for which I should reserve them, since I eat the same food that you eat, and have such sleep as you have—and yet I hardly think that I do eat the same food as some of you, who live delicately; I know, moreover, that I wake before you, that you may sleep quietly in your beds.

"Yet you may feel that while you were enduring the toils and distresses, I have acquired all this without toil and without distress. But who of you is conscious of having endured more toil for me than I for him? Or see here, let any who carries wounds strip himself and show them; I too will show mine. For I have no part of my body, in front at least, that is left without scars; there is no weapon, used at close quarters, or hurled from afar, of which I do not carry the mark. Nay, I have been wounded by the sword, hand to hand; I have been shot with arrows, I have been struck from a catapult, smitten many a time with stones and clubs, for you, for your glory, for your wealth; I lead you conquerors through every land, every sea, every river, mountain, plain. I married as you married; the children of many of you will be blood-relations of my children. Moreover, if any had debts, I, being no busybody to enquire how they were made, when you were winning so much pay, and acquiring so much plunder, whenever there was plunder after a siege—I have cancelled them all. And further, golden coronals are reminders to the most part of you, both of your bravery and of my high regard—reminders that will never perish. Whosoever has died, his death has been glorious; and splendid has been his burial. To most of them there stand at home brazen statues; their parents are held in esteem, and have been freed from all services and taxes. For while I have led you, not one of you has fallen in flight.

"And now I had in mind to send away those of you who are no longer equal to campaigning, to be the envy of all at home; but since you all wish to go home, depart, all of you; and when you reach home, tell them there that this your King, Alexander, victor over Persians, Medes, Bactrians, Sacaeans, conqueror of Uxians, Arachotians, Drangae, master of Parthyaea, Chorasmia, Hyrcania to the Caspian Sea; who crossed the Caucasus beyond the Caspian gates, who crossed the rivers Oxus and Tanais, yes, and the Indus too, that none but Dionysus had crossed, the Hydaspes, Acesines, Hydraotes; and who would further have crossed the Hyphasis, had not you shrunk back; who broke into the Indian Ocean by both mouths of the Indus; who traversed the Gadrosian desert—where none other had passed with an armed force; who in the line of march captured Carmania and the country of the Oreitans; whom, when his fleet had sailed from India to the Persian Sea, you led back again to Susa—tell them, I say, that you deserted him, that you took yourselves off, leaving him to the care of the wild tribes you had conquered. This, when you declare it, will be, no doubt, glorious among men, and pious in the sight of heaven. Begone!"

When Alexander had finished, he leapt down swiftly from his platform and passed into the palace and paid no attention to his bodily needs, nor was seen by any of the Companions; and, indeed, not even on the day following. But on the third day he summoned within the picked men among the Persians, and divided among them the command of the different brigades; and permitted only those who were now his relatives to give him the customary kiss. The Macedonians, however, were at the time much moved on hearing his speech; and remained in silence there, around the platform; yet no one followed the King when he departed save his personal Companions and the bodyguards; but the mass neither while remaining there had anything to do or say, nor were willing to depart. But when they heard about the Persians and the Medes, and the handing of commands to the Persians, and the Oriental force being drafted into the various ranks, and a Persian squadron called by a Macedonian name, and of Persian "infantry Companions," and others too, and a Persian company of "silver-shields," and "cavalry of the Companions," and a new royal squadron even of this, they could no longer contain, but running all together to the palace they threw their arms before the doors as signs of supplication to the King; they themselves standing shouting before the doors begging to be let in. The instigators of the late disturbance, and those who began the cry, they said they would give up; in fact they would depart from the doors neither day nor night unless Alexander would have some pity on them.

When this was reported to Alexander, he at once came out; and seeing them so humble, and hearing most of the number crying and lamenting, he also shed tears. Then he came forward as if to speak, and they continued beseeching. And one of them, a notable officer of the Companions' cavalry both by age and rank, called Callines, said thus: "This, O King, is what grieves the Macedonians, that you have made Persians your kinsmen and Persians are called 'Alexander's kinsmen,' and they are permitted to kiss you; but no Macedonian has tasted this privilege." On this Alexander broke in: "But all of you I regard as my kinsmen, and so from henceforth I call you." When thus he had spoken, Callines approached and kissed him, and any other who desired to kiss him. And thus they took up their arms again and returned shouting and singing their victory song to the camp. But Alexander in gratitude for this sacrificed to the gods to whom he was wont to sacrifice, and gave a general feast, sitting himself there, and all the Macedonians sitting round him; and then next to them Persians, and next any of the other tribes who had precedence in reputation or any other quality, and he himself and his comrades drank from the same bowl and poured the same libations, while the Greek seers and the Magians began the ceremony. And Alexander prayed for all sorts of blessings, and especially for harmony and fellowship in the empire between Macedonians and Persians. They say that those who shared the feast were nine thousand, and that they all poured the same libation and thereat sang the one song of victory.

Plutarch on Alexander

... [I]f you examine the results of Alexander's instruction, you will see that he educated the Hyrcanians to respect the marriage bond, and taught the Arachosians to till the soil, and persuaded the Sogdians to support their parents, not to kill them, and the Persians to revere their mothers and not to take them in wedlock. O wondrous power of Philosophic Instruction, that brought the Indians to worship Greek gods, and the Seythians to bury their dead, not to devour them! We admire Carneades' power, which made Cleitomachus, formerly called Hasdrubal, and a Carthaginian by birth, adopt Greek ways. We admire the character of Zeno, which persuaded Diogenes the Babylonian to be a philosopher. But when Alexander was civilizing Asia, Homer was commonly read, and the children of the Persians, of the Susianians, and of the Gedrosians learned to chant the tragedies of Sophocles and Euripides. And although Socrates, when tried on the charge of introducing foreign deities, lost his cause to the informers who infested Athens, yet through Alexander Bactria and the Caucasus learned to revere the gods of the Greeks. Plato wrote a book on the One Ideal Constitution, but because of its forbidding character he could not persuade anyone to adopt it; but Alexander established more than seventy cities among savage tribes, and sowed all Asia with Grecian magistracies, and thus overcame its uncivilized and brutish manner of living. Although few of us read Plato's *Laws*, yet hundreds of thousands have made use of Alexander's laws, and continue to use them. Those who were vanquished by Alexander are happier than those who escaped

Text: Reprinted by permission of the publishers and The Loeb Classical Library from *Plutarch's Moralia*, trans. Frank Cole Babbitt (Cambridge, Mass.: Harvard University Press, 1936), pp. 393-405.

his hand; for these had no one to put an end to the wretchedness of their existence, while the victor compelled those others to lead a happy life. Therefore it is even more just to apply Themistocles' saying to the nations conquered by Alexander. For, when Themistocles in exile had obtained great gifts from Artaxerxes, and had received three cities to pay him tribute, one to supply his bread, another his wine, and a third his meat, he exclaimed, "My children, we should be ruined now, had we not been ruined before." Thus Alexander's new subjects would not have been civilized, had they not been vanquished; Egypt would not have its Alexandria, nor Mesopotamia its Seleuceia, nor Sogdiana its Prophthasia, nor India its Bucephalia, nor the Caucasus a Greek city hard by; for by the founding of cities in these places savagery was extinguished and the worse element, gaining familiarity with the better, changed under its influence. If, then, philosophers take the greatest pride in civilizing and rendering adaptable the intractable and untutored elements in human character, and if Alexander has been shown to have changed the savage natures of countless tribes, it is with good reason that he should be regarded as a very great philosopher....

. . . For Alexander did not follow Aristotle's advice to treat the Greeks as if he were their leader, and other peoples as if he were their master; to have regard for the Greeks as for friends and kindred, but to conduct himself toward other peoples as though they were plants or animals; for to do so would have been to cumber his leadership with numerous battles and banishments and festering seditions. But, as he believed that he came as a heaven-sent governor to all, and as a mediator for the whole world, those whom he could not persuade to unite with him, he conquered by force of arms, and he brought together into one body all men everywhere, uniting and mixing in one great loving-cup, as it were, men's lives, their characters, their marriages, their very habits of life. He bade them all consider as their fatherland the whole inhabited earth, as their stronghold and protection his camp, as akin to them all good men, and as foreigners only the wicked; they should not distinguish between Grecian and foreigner by Grecian cloak and targe, or scimitar and jacket; but the distinguishing mark of the Grecian should be seen in virtue, and that of the foreigner in iniquity; clothing and food, marriage and manner of life they should regard as common to all, being blended into one by ties of blood and children.

Now Demaratus the Corinthian, one of Philip's intimate friends, when he had seen Alexander in Susa, exclaimed with tears of joy that all the Greeks who had died before that hour had been deprived of a great joy, since they had not seen Alexander seated on the throne of Darius. But I swear that for my part I feel no envy because of this spectacle toward them that saw it, for it was but the handiwork of Fortune, and the lot of other kings as well. But methinks I would gladly have been a witness of that fair and holy marriage-rite, when he brought together in one golden-canopied tent an hundred Persian brides and an hundred Macedonian and Greek bridegrooms, united at a common hearth and board. He himself, crowned with garlands, was the first to raise the marriage hymn as though he were singing a song of truest friendship over the union of the two greatest and most mighty peoples; for he, of one maid the bridegroom, and at the same time of all the brides the escort, as a father and sponsor united them in the bonds of wedlock. Indeed at this sight I should have cried out for joy, "O dullard Xerxes, stupid fool that spent so much fruitless toil to bridge the Hellespont! This is the way that wise kings join Asia with Europe; it is not by beams nor rafts, nor by lifeless and unfeeling bonds, but by the ties of lawful love and chaste nuptials and mutual joy in children that they join the nations together."

Considering carefully this order of affairs, Alexander did not favour the Median raiment, but preferred the Persian, for it was much more simple than the Median. Since he deprecated the unusual and theatrical varieties of foreign adornment, such as the tiara and the full-sleeved jacket and trousers, he wore a composite dress adapted from both Persian and Macedonian fashion, as Eratosthenes has recorded. As a philosopher what he wore was a matter of indifference, but as sovereign of both nations and benevolent king he strove to acquire the goodwill of the conquered by showing respect for their apparel, so that they might continue constant in loving the Macedonians as rulers, and might not feel hate toward them as enemies.... [T]hey impeach Alexander because, although paying due respect to his own national dress, he did not disdain that of his conquered subjects in establishing the beginnings of a vast empire. For he did not overrun Asia like a robber nor was he minded to tear and rend it, as if it were booty and plunder bestowed by unexpected good fortune, after the manner in which Hannibal later descended upon Italy, or as earlier the Treres descended upon Ionia and the Scythians upon Media. But Alexander desired to render all upon earth subject to one law of reason and one form of government and to reveal all men as one people, and to this purpose he made himself conform. But if the deity that sent down Alexander's soul into this world of ours had not recalled him quickly, one law would govern all mankind, and they all would look toward one rule of justice as though toward a common source of light. But as it is, that part of the world which has not looked upon Alexander has remained without sunlight.

23 INTERPRETATION OF THE HELLENISTIC WORLD

SIR WILLIAM W. TARN, *HELLENISTIC CIVILISATION: A MODERN VIEW OF HELLENISM*

The era between Alexander's death in 323 B.C. and the advent of the Augustan empire of Rome in 30 B.C. is called the Hellenistic Age, an era in which Greek culture was dispersed throughout the ancient Mediterranean world. In the power struggle that followed Alexander's death, three great kingdoms emerged, each ruled by families descended from Alexander's generals: the Seleucid dynasty ruled much of the old Persian empire; the Ptolemys, Egypt; and the Antigonids, Macedonia. One of the greatest present-day Hellenistic historians is Sir Willam W. Tarn, a member of the British Academy, Honorary Fellow of Trinity College, Oxford, and the author of numerous books and articles, many relating to Alexander the Great and the cultural period he initiated. In the passage below, Tarn summarizes the achievements of Hellenistic civilization and draws some timely parallels between that world and our own. He refutes the older view of the period as one of decline and decay, particularly the third century B.C. If there was a decline, he says, it came in the last two centuries B.C. when the Roman Republic overran the eastern Mediterranean and broke the Greek spirit. But as Tarn points out, "Mere subjection by greatly superior force, by whomsoever wielded, naturally has no bearing on the question; it is not the business of history to cheer for the big battalions."

This book aims at giving, in brief outline, a sketch of the civilisation of the three Hellenistic centuries, from the death of Alexander in 323 to the establishment of the Roman empire by Augustus in 30 B.C. These limits are of course conventional, for the germs of certain phenomena of Hellenism begin to appear before Alexander, and in some respects Augustus represents no real break. But they do serve to emphasize two facts: the creative impulses evoked by Alexander's career forbade anything ever to be quite the same again as before, and, after the Hellenistic world had finally gone down in the ruin of the Roman civil wars, with the Empire it began to be built up afresh on different lines, civilisation became Graeco-Roman. Throughout this book Rome and Roman history are taken for granted, and we are concerned simply to see what Hellenism was and what kind of world the Roman Republic found when it came eastward. Unlike the Empire, that Republic, in its contact with Hellenistic civilisation, was purely receptive; the Greece that taught Rome was not the older Greece but contemporary Hellenism, and so far as modern civilisation is based on Greek it is primarily on Hellenism that it is based.

What now does Hellenism mean? To one, it means a new culture compounded of Greek and Oriental elements; to another, the extension of Greek culture to Orientals; to another, the continuation of the pure line of the older Greek civilisation; to yet another, that same civilisation modified by new conditions. All these theories contain a truth, but none represents the whole truth; and all are unworkable the moment one comes down to details, such (for example) as that Hellenistic mathematics were purely Greek, while the sister-science, astronomy, was Graeco-Babylonian. To get a true picture we must look at all the phenomena, and Hellenism is merely a convenient label for the civilisation of the three centuries during which Greek culture radiated far from the homeland; no general definition will cover it all. Moreover, in some respects, these three centuries represent, not one phase of civilisation, but two: the earlier phase creative in science, philosophy, literature, political state-forms, and much else, with an independent Graeco-Macedonian world extending its civilisation to Asia; the later phase distinguished by the exhaustion of the creative impulse and the reaction, both spiritual and material, of the East against the West, while the Graeco-Macedonian

Text: Sir William W. Tarn, *Hellenistic Civilization,* 3rd ed. (New York: St. Martin's Press, Inc. and London: Edward Arnold Ltd., 1952), pp. 1-5. Reprinted by permission of the publishers.

world is caught between that reaction and Rome, until Rome, having destroyed the Hellenistic state-system, is ultimately compelled to take its place as the standard-bearer of Greek culture. The two phases cannot always be definitely separated; but the lines of the evolution of any particular matter are easier to understand if the above broad distinction be kept in mind. There are, however, many respects in which the Hellenistic period does form a connected whole, and as such we may for a moment glance at it.

The world of Hellenism was a changed and enlarged world. Though the particularism of the Greek city-state was to remain vigorous enough in fact, it had broken down in theory; it was being replaced by universalism and its corollary, individualism. The idea emerges of an *oecumene* or " inhabited world" as a whole, the common possession of civilised men; and for its use there grows up the form of Greek known as the *koine*, the "common speech", which was also used by many Asiatics; Greek might take a man from Marseilles to India, from the Caspian to the Cataracts. Nationality falls into the background; common speech and education promote a common culture in every city of the "inhabited world"; literature, learning, above all philosophy, do to some extent envisage a larger world than Greece, and the upper classes in Rome and parts of Asia come to feel that Greek culture is a thing a man must have, at least in externals. Commerce is internationalised. Most of the barriers are down: thought is free as it was not to be again till modern times; race hatred is a thing of the past, except perhaps among some native Egyptians and some Jews; religious persecution on religious grounds is unknown (for Antiochus' attack upon the Jews was a political measure); morality is a matter for science, not for authority. The personality of the individual has free scope. It is an age of specialists, from the scientific worker to the carpenter who makes a door but requires another man to hang it; when Poseidonius tries for the last time to take all learning for his province, as Aristotle had done, his superficiality in certain fields is apparent. And even the creative third century differs from its forerunners in this, that, though the Greek spirit was still of supreme importance, it can no longer be said that every fruitful idea was Greek; for, quite apart from religion and astronomy, the single greatest creation of the age, the Stoic philosophy, originated with one who, whether he had some Greek blood or not, was certainly to his contemporaries a Phoenician.

The resemblance of this world to our own is at first sight almost startling. There was the same complex of states, big and little, with different state-forms, some more advanced than others, working within the bounds of a common civilisation; and, beside some of the phenomena noticed above, there were many others which look very modern. Such are the eternal trouble of prices and wages; Socialism and Communism, the strike and the revolution; the growth of ideas of humanity and brotherhood combined with savage quarrelling; the emancipation of woman and the restriction of population; questions of franchise and (possibly) representation, of emigration and the proletariat; exact learning and crass superstition side by side; a vast literature dealing with every sphere of human activity, often competent, but no longer producing writers equal to the great names of the past; the spread of education, resulting in the manufacture of masses of the half-educated; the more conscious emergence of propaganda; the growth of all the half-worlds that cling to the skirts of science, of history, and of religion. I am not much concerned to draw parallels with the modern world, and have usually left this to the reader. But such parallels must not be drawn too far. Though many things had a certain likeness to the things of to-day, they were seldom the *same;* for example, there is little resemblance between an Egyptian and a modern strike, or between modern and Stoic Communism. And underlying everything were two radical and crucial differences: it was a world empty of machines and full of slaves. This last fact cannot be overemphasised. To see Hellenistic society as it existed, the slave background must never be lost sight of; and such aspirations as freedom and brotherhood—even the very revolutions—too often convey a sense of unreality when it is remembered that a large part of the population was, by most people, excepted from their scope.

The Hellenistic period has often been treated as one of decline, even of decay; but probably few would now care to argue that this was true of the third century. Such terms can only apply, if at all, to what I have called the later phase; and even then it must, I think, largely depend on the point of view. For example, if physical science, or art, be all-important, then the later phase was one of decline; but if the emergence of certain religious instincts and feelings, such as might pave the way for something greater, be at least equally material, then it was one of growth. What we *do* seem to see in the later phase is a mass of contradictions; for example, which really represents the late second century, the slave-market at Delos or the manumissions at Delphi? Are we to argue from the peripatetic magician, or from the Stoic who believed that virtue was its own reward? I myself venture to entertain considerable doubts whether the true Greek, the racial aristocracy of the Aegean, really degenerated. This is not the more usual view; but I have given the facts as they appear to me, and they should enable the reader to form his own conclusions. Much too which at first sight looks like decline can be accounted for by two general considerations. One is the steady diminution in the numbers of the true Greek after *c.* 200, combined with the intrusion, or admixture, of alien stocks, which, whatever their latent capabilities, often had not at the time the intellectual, political, or social energy of the Greek. The other is the behaviour of the Roman Republic, which tended to break the Greek spirit and probably ended by convincing many people beside the kings of Syria and Egypt that efforts doomed beforehand to be fruitless were not worth while. Mere subjection by greatly superior force, by whomsoever wielded, naturally has no bearing on the question; it is not the business of history to cheer for the big battalions.

THE GREEK MIND

24 HIPPOCRATES, "ON THE SACRED DISEASE": RATIONAL MEDICAL INQUIRY

It was the Greek mind, free from religious and other traditional restraints, encouraged to seek beneath surface fact, and curious about cause and logical order, that led the Greeks to develop the scientific approach to knowledge. Archaeological investigation of ancient civilizations, notably the Babylonian and the Egyptian, has revealed a far more extensive fund of astronomical, medical, and mathematical information than was once supposed, but these ancient peoples mixed magic and religious mystery with the results of their observation of the physical world, and they made little critical attempt to formulate general principles. The Egyptians, for example, had some knowledge of medicine and surgery, but superstition restricted any experimentation or theorizing and left them to believe that evil spirits caused disease.

By the sixth and early fifth centuries B.C., the Greeks had succeeded in divorcing science from religion, but they had not yet distinguished between science and philosophy. Both the Ionian Greeks and the "Pythagoreans" of southern Italy and Sicily made advances in astronomy and mathematics—however, much of their concern was the construction of general theories about the nature of the universe. While Pythagoras and his followers, for example, discovered important mathematical principles, they also regarded numbers themselves as being mystical expressions of all things, from the movements of the heavenly bodies to abstract ideas. Limited as they and their contemporaries were, they did make the important advance from mythology and religion to science and philosophy.

By the middle of the fifth century B.C., in the Periclean Age, the systematic investigation of knowledge had progressed beyond the stage of these earlier philosophies, which were really attempts at synthesizing all knowledge. Specialization appeared, so that philosophy was considered to be restricted to such fields as religion, ethics, politics, and metaphysics; and there began the separate study of sciences like physics, mathematics, medicine, biology, and astronomy. Such specialization has characterized science ever since.

Hippocrates of Cos (c. 460-377 B.C.) was a brilliant forerunner in the new tradition. Specializing in one science—medicine—he discarded practices which attributed disease to magical causes or which relegated therapy to incantation and other forms of divine healing. It was also his achievement to repel all speculative philosophers from his field and lay the foundations of scientific method for the physician. Hippocrates founded a medical school which carefully observed and recorded the histories of individual patients, as the forty-two extant case studies reveal. Such studies gave his physicians a basis for predicting the course of the disease in other patients and permitted progress toward a cure. The advanced observation of the Hippocratic school is well represented by the following treatise, "On the Sacred Disease," which describes in detail the symptoms of epilepsy and argues that this disease is not "any more divine or more sacred than other diseases, but has a natural cause." In his discussion, the author does not reject the divine element, any more than do most modern physicians, but like the majority of contemporary practitioners he is firmly convinced that the art of medicine depends primarily on scientific observation and logical analysis. These abilities, not magical rites and incantations, are the true gifts of the gods.

I am about to discuss the disease called "sacred." It is not, in my opinion, any more divine or more sacred than other diseases, but has a natural cause, and its supposed divine origin is due to men's inexperience, and to their wonder at its peculiar character. Now while men continue to believe in its divine origin because they are at a loss to understand it, they really disprove its divinity by the facile method of healing which they adopt, consisting as it does of purifications and incantations. But if it is to be considered divine just because it is wonderful, there will be not one sacred disease but many, for I will show that other diseases are no less wonderful and portentous, and yet nobody considers them sacred. For instance, quotidian fevers, tertians and quartans seem to me to be no less sacred and god-sent than this disease, but nobody wonders at them. Then again one can see men who are mad and delirious from no obvious cause, and committing many strange acts; while in their sleep, to my knowledge, many groan and shriek, others choke, others dart up and rush out of doors, being delirious until they wake, when they become as healthy and rational as they were before, though pale and weak; and this happens not once but many times. Many other instances, of various kinds, could be given, but time does not permit us to speak of each separately.

My own view is that those who first attributed a sacred character to this malady were like the magicians, purifiers, charlatans and quacks of our own day, men who claim great piety and superior knowledge. Being at a loss, and having no treatment which would help, they concealed and sheltered themselves behind superstition, and called this illness sacred, in order that their utter ignorance might not be manifest. They added a plausible story, and established a method of treatment that secured their own position. They used purifications and incantations; they forbade the use of baths, and of many foods that are unsuitable for sick folk—of sea goats. But if to eat or apply these things engenders and increases the disease, while to refrain works a cure, then neither is godhead to blame nor are the purifications beneficial; it is the foods that cure or hurt, and the power of godhead disappears.

Text: Reprinted by permission of the publishers and The Loeb Classical Library from *Hippocrates*, trans. W. H. S. Jones (Cambridge, Mass.: Harvard University Press, 1943), II, 139-51.

Accordingly I hold that those who attempt in this manner to cure these diseases cannot consider them either sacred or divine; for when they are removed by such purifications and by such treatment as this, there is nothing to prevent the production of attacks in men by devices that are similar. If so, something human is to blame, and not godhead. He who by purifications and magic can take away such an affection can also by similar means bring it on, so that by this argument the action of godhead is disproved. By these sayings and devices they claim superior knowledge, and deceive men by prescribing for them purifications and cleansings, most of their talk turning on the intervention of gods and spirits. Yet in my opinion their discussions show, not piety, as they think, but impiety rather, implying that the gods do not exist, and what they call piety and the divine is, as I shall prove, impious and unholy.

For if they profess to know how to bring down the moon, to eclipse the sun, to make storm and sunshine, rain and drought, the sea impassable and the earth barren, and all such wonders, whether it be by rites or by some cunning or practice that they can, according to the adepts, be effected, in any case I am sure that they are impious, and cannot believe that the gods exist or have any strength, and that they would not refrain from the most extreme actions. Wherein surely they are terrible in the eyes of the gods. For if a man by magic and sacrifice will bring the moon down, eclipse the sun, and cause storm and sunshine, I shall not believe that any of these things is divine, but human, seeing that the power of godhead is overcome and enslaved by the cunning of man. But perhaps what they profess is not true, the fact being that men, in need of a livelihood, contrive and devise many fictions of all sorts, about this disease among other things, putting the blame, for each form of the affection, upon a particular god. If the patient imitate a goat, if he roar, or suffer convulsions in the right side, they say that the Mother of the Gods is to blame. If he utter a piercing and loud cry, they liken him to a horse and blame Poseidon. Should he pass some excrement, as often happens under the stress of the disease, the surname Enodia is applied. If it be more frequent and thinner, like that of birds, it is Apollo Nomius. If he foam at the mouth and kick, Ares has the blame. When at night occur fears and terrors, delirium, jumpings from the bed and rushings out of doors, they say that Hecate is attacking or that heroes are assaulting. In making use, too, of purifications and incantations they do what I think is a very unholy and irreligious thing. For the sufferers from the disease they purify with blood and such like, as though they were polluted, blood-guilty, bewitched by men, or had committed some unholy act. All such they ought to have treated in the opposite way; they should have brought them to the sanctuaries, with sacrifices and prayers, in supplication to the gods. As it is, however, they do nothing of the kind, but merely purify them. Of the purifying objects some they hide in the earth, others they throw into the sea, others they carry away to the mountains, where nobody can touch them or tread on them. Yet, if a god is indeed the cause, they ought to have taken them to the sanctuaries and offered them to him. However, I hold that a man's body is not defiled by a god, the one being utterly corrupt the other perfectly holy. Nay, even should it have been defiled or in any way injured through some different agency, a god is more likely to purify and sanctify it than he is to cause defilement. At least it is godhead that purifies, sanctifies and cleanses us from the greatest and most impious of our sins; and we ourselves fix boundaries to the sanctuaries and precincts of the gods, so that nobody may cross them unless he be pure; and when we enter we sprinkle ourselves, not as defiling ourselves thereby, but to wash away any pollution we may have already contracted. Such is my opinion about purifications.

But this disease is in my opinion no more divine than any other; it has the same nature as other diseases, and the cause that gives rise to individual diseases. It is also curable, no less than other illnesses, unless by long lapse of time it be so ingrained as to be more powerful than the remedies that are applied.

25 PLATO, APOLOGY: SOCRATES AND INTELLECTUAL INTEGRITY

Greek philosophy was born among the Ionians of Asia Minor in the sixth century B.C., where religious freedom gave men the opportunity to cultivate a new awareness of the world in which they lived. The earliest philosophers, Thales and Anaximander of Miletus, speculated on the physical character of the universe as it conflicted with the naïve explanations of ancient myth. Shortly after, rival schools of thought emerged in southern Italy, the home of Pythagoras and Empedocles. These pioneers established the Greek tradition of free inquiry, based on their belief that reason (*logos*) could organize and interpret what is perceived by the senses. Henceforth, the decisive questions and answers of western man were couched not in the word pictures of myth, but in abstract concepts.

By the time that Greek philosophy came of age with Socrates and Plato, the scene had shifted to Athens and the emphasis had shifted from the natural philosophy of the pioneers, with their inquiries into the origin and composition of things, to practical questions of ethics, politics, and religion. Socrates (469?-399 B.C.) abandoned what he called "physics" for questions of right and wrong, justice and injustice—questions which continually disturbed democratic Athens in the fifth century B.C. So central to Greek philosophy was Socrates that all philosophers who lived before him are now called "Pre-Socratics." To his fellow citizens, he was an eccentric who spent all his time lounging in the market place or in the homes of friends, asking questions and forcing his hearers to define their terms and concepts accurately, to distinguish between opinion and true knowledge. His conversations sparkled with wit and irony, often at the expense of his listeners, whose views were usually partially unfounded and contradictory. He demanded exact definition of terms like love, temperance, and courage, because he believed that behind them lay absolute ideas. Knowledge of these "ideas" and of the ultimate reality transcending material things was for him the key to virtue.

Since Socrates left no writing, we know him today only through the works of his disciples, Xenophon and particularly Plato (c. 427-347 B.C.), himself a major philosopher. Socrates, we know, was the son of a woodcutter, and he died from drinking hemlock, by command of the public court which convicted him of atheism and the corruption of Athens' youth. The real reason for his condemnation was more political; the oligarchic government set up in Athens after the Peloponnesian War considered his eternal questioning dangerous to the peace of the state. Shortly after Socrates' death, Plato devoted some of his earliest writing to the trial and death of Socrates; in the second of four related works, he abandons his usual dialogue form and writes the

Apology (defense) delivered by Socrates before the law court. Plato's *Apology* is probably not a transcription of the actual speech, but it is a statement representing the integrity of a true "lover of wisdom" who refuses to abandon his convictions in the face of popular pressure and at the risk of his own life.

. . . Men of Athens, I honour and love you; but I shall obey God rather than you, and while I have life and strength I shall never cease from the practice and teaching of philosophy, exhorting any one whom I meet and saying to him after my manner: You, my friend,—a citizen of the great and mighty and wise city of Athens,—are you not ashamed of heaping up the greatest amount of money and honour and reputation, and caring so little about wisdom and truth and the greatest improvement of the soul, which you never regard or heed at all? And if the person with whom I am arguing, says: Yes, but I do care; then I do not leave him or let him go at once; but I proceed to interrogate and examine and cross-examine him, and if I think that he has no virtue in him, but only says that he has, I reproach him with undervaluing the greater, and overvaluing the less. And I shall repeat the same words to every one whom I meet, young and old, citizen and alien, but especially to the citizens, inasmuch as they are my brethren. For know that this is the command of God; and I believe that no greater good has ever happened in the State than my service to the God. For I do nothing but go about persuading you all, old and young alike, not to take thought for your persons or your properties, but first and chiefly to care about the greatest improvement of the soul. I tell you that virtue is not given by money, but that from virtue comes money and every other good of man, public as well as private. This is my teaching, and if this is the doctrine which corrupts the youth, I am a mischievous person. But if any one says that this is not my teaching, he is speaking an untruth. Wherefore, O men of Athens, I say to you, do as Anytus bids or not as Anytus bids, and either acquit me or not; but whichever you do, understand that I shall never alter my ways, not even if I have to die many times.

Men of Athens, do not interrupt, but hear me; there was an understanding between us that you should hear me to the end: I have something more to say, at which you may be inclined to cry out; but I believe that to hear me will be good for you, and therefore I beg that you will not cry out. I would have you know, that if you kill such an one as I am, you will injure yourselves more than you will injure me. Nothing will injure me, not Meletus nor yet Anytus—they cannot, for a bad man is not permitted to injure a better than himself. I do not deny that Anytus may, perhaps, kill him, or drive him into exile, or deprive him of civil rights; and he may imagine, and others may imagine, that he is inflicting a great injury upon him: but there I do not agree. For the evil of doing as he is doing—the evil of unjustly taking away the life of another—is greater far.

And now, Athenians, I am not going to argue for my own sake, as you may think, but for yours, that you may not sin against the God by condemning me, who am his gift to you. For if you kill me you will not easily find a successor to me, who, if I may use such a ludicrous figure of speech, am a sort of gadfly, given to the State by God; and the State is a great and noble steed who is tardy in his motions owing to his very size, and requires to be stirred into life. I am that gadfly which God has attached to the State, and all day long and in all places am always fastening upon you, arousing and persuading and reproaching you. You will not easily find another like me, and therefore I would advise you to spare me. I dare say that you may feel out of temper (like a person who is suddenly awakened from sleep), and you think that you might easily strike me dead as Anytus advises, and then you would sleep on for the remainder of your lives, unless God in his care of you sent you another gadfly. When I say that I am given to you by God, the proof of my mission is this:—if I had been like other men, I should not have neglected all my own concerns or patiently seen the neglect of them during all these years, and have been doing yours, coming to you individually like a father or elder brother, exhorting you to regard virtue; such conduct, I say, would be unlike human nature. If I had gained anything, or if my exhortations had been paid, there would have been some sense in my doing so; but now, as you will perceive, not even the impudence of my accusers dares to say that I have ever exacted or sought pay of any one; of that they have no witness. And I have a sufficient witness to the truth of what I say—my poverty. . . .

Not much time will be gained, O Athenians, in return for the evil name which you will get

Text: Benjamin Jowett (trans.), *The Dialogues of Plato* (Oxford: The Clarendon Press, 1892; New York: Random House, 1947), pp. 413-14, 420-23.

from the detractors of the city, who will say that you killed Socrates, a wise man; for they will call me wise, even although I am not wise, when they want to reproach you. If you had waited a little while, your desire would have been fulfilled in the course of nature. For I am far advanced in years, as you may perceive, and not far from death. I am speaking now not to all of you, but only to those who have condemned me to death. And I have another thing to say to them: You think that I was convicted because I had no words of the sort which would have procured my acquittal—I mean, if I had thought fit to leave nothing undone or unsaid. Not so; the deficiency which led to my conviction was not of words—certainly not. But I had not the boldness or impudence or inclination to address you as you would have liked me to do, weeping and wailing and lamenting, and saying and doing many things which you have been accustomed to hear from others, and which, as I maintain, are unworthy of me. I thought at the time that I ought not to do anything common or mean when in danger: nor do I now repent of the style of my defence; I would rather die having spoken after my manner, than speak in your manner and live. For neither in war nor yet at law ought I or any man to use every way of escaping death. Often in battle there can be no doubt that if a man will throw away his arms, and fall on his knees before his pursuers, he may escape death; and in other dangers there are other ways of escaping death, if a man is willing to say and do anything. The difficulty, my friends, is not to avoid death, but to avoid unrighteousness; for that runs faster than death. I am old and move slowly, and the slower runner has overtaken me, and my accusers are keen and quick, and the faster runner, who is unrighteousness, has overtaken them. And now I depart hence condemned by you to suffer the penalty of death,—they too go their ways condemned by the truth to suffer the penalty of villainy and wrong; and I must abide by my award—let them abide by theirs. I suppose that these things may be regarded as fated,—and I think that they are well.

And now, O men who have condemned me, I would fain prophesy to you; for I am about to die, and in the hour of death men are gifted with prophetic power. And I prophesy to you who are my murderers, that immediately after my departure punishment far heavier than you have inflicted on me will surely await you. Me you have killed because you wanted to escape the accuser, and not to give an account of your lives. But that will not be as you suppose: far otherwise. For I say that there will be more accusers of you than there are now; accusers whom hitherto I have restrained: and as they are younger they will be more inconsiderate with you, and you will be more offended at them. If you think that by killing men you can prevent some one from censuring your evil lives, you are mistaken; that is not a way of escape which is either possible or honourable; the easiest and the noblest way is not to be disabling others, but to be improving yourselves. This is the prophecy which I utter before my departure to the judges who have condemned me.

Friends, who would have acquitted me, I would like also to talk with you about the thing which has come to pass, while the magistrates are busy, and before I go to the place at which I must die. Stay then a little, for we may as well talk with one another while there is time. You are my friends, and I should like to show you the meaning of this event which has happened to me. O my judges—for you I may truly call judges—I should like to tell you of a wonderful circumstance. Hitherto the divine faculty of which the internal oracle is the source has constantly been in the habit of opposing me even about trifles, if I was going to make a slip or error in any matter; and now as you see there has come upon me that which may be thought, and is generally believed to be, the last and worst evil. But the oracle made no sign of opposition, either when I was leaving my house in the morning, or when I was on my way to the court, or while I was speaking, at anything which I was going to say; and yet I have often been stopped in the middle of a speech, but now in nothing I either said or did touching the matter in hand has the oracle opposed me. What do I take to be the explanation of this silence? I will tell you. It is an intimation that what has happened to me is a good, and that those of us who think that death is an evil are in error. For the customary sign would surely have opposed me had I been going to evil and not to good.

Let us reflect in another way, and we shall see that there is great reason to hope that death is a good; for one of two things—either death is a state of nothingness and utter unconsciousness, or, as men say, there is a change and migration of the soul from this world to another. Now, if you suppose that there is no consciousness, but a sleep like the sleep of him who is undisturbed even by dreams, death will be an unspeakable gain. For if a person were to select the night in which his sleep was undisturbed even by dreams, and were to compare with this the other days and nights of his life, and then were to tell us how many days and nights he had passed in the course of his life better and more pleasantly than this one, I think that any man, I will not say a private man, but even the great king will not find many such days or nights, when compared with the others. Now, if death be of such a nature, I say that to die is gain; for eternity is then only a single night. But if death is the journey to another place, and there, as men say, all the dead abide, what good, O my friends and judges, can be greater than this? If, indeed, when the pilgrim arrives in the world below, he is delivered from the professors of justice in this world, and finds the true judges who are said to give judgment there, Minos and Rhadamanthus and Aeacus and Triptolemus, and other sons of God who were righteous in their own life, that pilgrimage will be worth making. What would not a man give if he might converse with Orpheus and Musaeus and Hesiod and Homer? Nay, if this be true, let me die again and again. I myself, too, shall have a wonderful interest in there meeting and conversing with Palamedes, and Ajax the son of Telamon, and any other ancient hero who has suffered death through an unjust judgment; and there will be no small pleasure, as I think, in comparing my own sufferings with theirs. Above all, I shall then be able to continue my search into true and false knowledge; as in this world, so also in the next; and I shall find out who is wise, and who pretends to be wise, and is not. What would not a man give, O judges, to be able to examine the leader of the great Trojan expedition; or Odysseus or Sisyphus, or numberless others, men and women too! What infinite delight would there be in conversing with them and asking them questions! In another world they do not put a man to death for asking questions: assuredly not. For besides being happier than we are, they will be immortal, if what is said is true.

Wherefore, O judges, be of good cheer about death, and know of a certainty, that no evil can happen to a good man, either in life or after death. He and his are not neglected by the gods; nor has my own approaching end happened by mere chance. But I see clearly that the time had arrived when it was better for me to die and be released from trouble: wherefore the oracle gave no sign. For which reason, also, I am not angry with my condemners, or with any accusers; they have done me no harm, although they did not mean to do me any good; and for this I may gently blame them.

Still, I have a favour to ask of them. When my sons are grown up, I would ask you, O my friends, to punish them; and I would have you trouble them, as I have troubled you, if they seem to care about riches, or anything, more than about virtue; or if they pretend to be something when they are really nothing,—then reprove them, as I have reproved you, for not caring about that for which they ought to care, and thinking that they are something when they are really nothing. And if you do this, both I and my sons will have received justice at your hands.

The hour of departure has arrived, and we go our ways—I to die, and you to live. Which is better God only knows.

26 ARISTOTLE, POLITICS: SOCIAL ORDER AND LIBERAL EDUCATION

Plato's famous Academy, which he founded in Athens about 385 B.C. as a center for his teaching, continued for nine centuries as a philosophical institute. Among its noted pupils was Aristotle (384-322 B.C.), who studied there during the last twenty years of Plato's life. While the rumors of friction between the two may have been exaggerated, it is evident from their writings that their interests and outlooks diverged sharply. Plato was a poet and an idealist, given to metaphysical speculation and ethical inquiry which sometimes approached the mystical. Hard-headed, practical Aristotle pursued the particular fact, the concrete object, and the useful application. Unlike his master, his chief interest lay in biological and physical sciences, and he endeavored to be an encyclopedist of the human knowledge of his day, investigating such diverse fields as aesthetics, psychology, physics, mechanics, astronomy, biology, politics, and rhetoric. After the death of Plato he tutored Alexander of Macedon and directed the Lyceum, a rival school to the Academy which he founded in 336 B.C.

The works of Plato and Aristotle have been the most enduring of all ancient philosophy. Through the Neoplatonists of the second and third centuries A.D., the ideas of Plato had a great influence on Christian ethics. In the later Christian era, especially the twelfth and thirteenth centuries, Aristotle was widely read in Latin translation, and medieval philosophers used his natural philosophy, with all its errors, as the foundation of Christian knowledge.

In the following selection from *Politics*, Aristotle attempts to outline the basic characteristics of social and political organization. In his introductory remarks, Aristotle argues that society evolves out of the human penchant for group association and action. This tendency is actualized, he finds, in such social groups as the family and the tribe, and, especially, in the *polis*, or city-state. The greater part of *Politics* is an evaluation of the various forms of government by which the *polis* is ruled and includes lengthy passages which stress the importance of an education in "liberal arts," or those subjects which free the human mind to find a meaningful pattern of conduct in society. It has been noted that, ironically enough, this classic study of the Greek *polis* was written at the very moment when the Greek city-states were being subordinated into a large monarchical empire at the instigation of Aristotle's pupil, Alexander the Great.

Every state is a community of some kind, and every community is established with a view to some good; for mankind always act in order to obtain that which they think good. But, if all communities aim at some good, the state or political community, which is the highest of all, and which embraces all the rest, aims at good in a greater degree than any other, and at the highest good.

Some people think that the qualifications of a statesman, king, householder, and master are the same, and that they differ, not in kind, but only in the number of their subjects. For example, the ruler over a few is called a master; over more, the manager of a household; over a still larger number, a statesman or king, as if there were no difference between a great household and a small state. The distinction which is made between the king and the statesman is as follows: When the government is personal, the ruler is a king; when, according to the rules of the political science, the citizens rule and are ruled in turn, then he is called a statesman.

But all this is a mistake; for governments differ in kind, as will be evident to any one who considers the matter according to the method which has hitherto guided us. As in other departments of science, so in politics, the compound should always be resolved into the simple elements or least parts of the whole. We must therefore look at the elements of which the state is composed, in order that we may see in what the different kinds of rule differ from one another, and whether any scientific result can be attained about each one of them.

He who thus considers things in their first growth and origin, whether a state or anything else, will obtain the clearest view of them. In the first place there must be a union of those who cannot exist without each other; namely, of male and female, that the race may continue (and this is a union which is formed, not of deliberate purpose, but because, in common with other animals and with plants, mankind have a natural desire to leave behind them an image of themselves), and of natural ruler and subject, that both may be preserved. For that which can foresee by the exercise of mind is by nature intended to be lord and master, and that which can with its body give effect to such foresight is a subject, and by nature a slave; hence master and slave have the same interest. Now nature has distinguished between the female and the slave. For she is not niggardly, like the smith who fashions the Delphian knife for many uses; she makes each thing for a single use, and every instrument is best made when intended for one and not for many uses. But among barbarians no distinction is made between women and slaves, because there is no natural ruler among them: they are a community of slaves, male and female. Wherefore the poets say,—

'It is meet that Hellenes should rule over barbarians';

as if they thought that the barbarian and the slave were by nature one.

Out of these two relationships between man and woman, master and slave, the first thing to arise is the family, and Hesiod is right when he says,—

'First house and wife and an ox for the plough';

for the ox is the poor man's slave. The family is the association established by nature for the supply of men's everyday wants, and the members of it are called by Charondas 'companions of the cupboard', and by Epimenides the Cretan, 'companions of the manger'. But when several families are united, and the association aims at something more than the supply of daily needs, the first society to be formed is the village. And the most natural form of the village appears to be that of a colony from the family, composed of the children and grandchildren, who are said to be

Text: Aristotle, *Politica*, trans. Benjamin Jowett, in *The Works of Aristotle*, ed. W. D. Ross (Oxford: The Clarendon Press, 1921), X, 1252-53, 1337-38. Reprinted by permission of The Clarendon Press.

'suckled with the same milk'. And this is the reason why Hellenic states were originally governed by kings; because the Hellenes were under royal rule before they came together, as the barbarians still are. Every family is ruled by the eldest, and therefore in the colonies of the family the kingly form of government prevailed because they were of the same blood. As Homer says:

'Each one gives law to his children and to his wives.'

For they lived dispersedly, as was the manner in ancient times. Wherefore men say that the Gods have a king, because they themselves either are or were in ancient times under the rule of a king. For they imagine, not only the forms of the Gods, but their ways of life to be like their own.

When several villages are united in a single complete community, large enough to be nearly or quite self-sufficing, the state comes into existence, originating in the bare needs of life, and continuing in existence for the sake of a good life. And therefore, if the earlier forms of society are natural, so is the state, for it is the end of them, and the nature of a thing is its end. For what each thing is when fully developed, we call its nature, whether we are speaking of a man, a horse, or a family. Besides, the final cause and end of a thing is the best, and to be self-sufficing is the end and the best.

Hence it is evident that the state is a creation of nature, and that man is by nature a political animal. And he who by nature and not by mere accident is without a state, is either a bad man or above humanity; he is like the

'Tribeless, lawless, hearthless one,'

whom Homer denounces—the natural outcast is forthwith a lover of war; he may be compared to an isolated piece at draughts.

No one will doubt that the legislator should direct his attention above all to the education of youth; for the neglect of education does harm to the constitution. The citizen should be moulded to suit the form of government under which he lives. For each government has a peculiar character which originally formed and which continues to preserve it. The character of democracy creates democracy, and the character of oligarchy creates oligarchy; and always the better the character, the better the government.

Again, for the exercise of any faculty or art a previous training and habituation are required; clearly therefore for the practice of virtue. And since the whole city has one end, it is manifest that education should be one and the same for all, and that it should be public, and not private,—not as at present, when every one looks after his own children separately, and gives them separate instruction of the sort which he thinks best; the training in things which are of common interest should be the same for all. Neither must we suppose that any one of the citizens belongs to himself, for they all belong to the state, and are each of them a part of the state, and the care of each part is inseparable from the care of the whole. In this particular as in some others the Lacedaemonians are to be praised, for they take the greatest pains about their children, and make education the business of the state.

That education should be regulated by law and should be an affair of state is not to be denied, but what should be the character of this public education, and how young persons should be educated, are questions which remain to be considered. As things are, there is disagreement about the subjects. For mankind are by no means agreed about the things to be taught, whether we look to virtue or the best life. Neither is it clear whether education is more concerned with intellectual or with moral virtue. The existing practice is perplexing; no one knows on what principle we should proceed—should the useful in life, or should virtue, or should the higher knowledge, be the aim of our training; all three opinions have been entertained. Again, about the means there is no agreement; for different persons, starting with different ideas about the nature of virtue, naturally disagree about the practice of it. There can be no doubt that children should be taught those useful things which are really necessary, but not all useful things; for occupations are divided into liberal and illiberal; and to young children should be imparted only such kinds of knowledge as will be useful to them without vulgarizing them. And any occupation, art, or science, which makes the body or soul or mind of the freeman less fit for the practice or exercise of virtue, is vulgar; wherefore we call those arts vulgar which tend to deform the body, and likewise all paid employments, for they absorb and degrade the mind. There are also some liberal arts quite proper for a freeman to acquire, but only in a certain degree, and if he attend to them too closely, in order to attain perfection in them, the same evil effects will follow. The object also which a man sets before him makes a great difference; if he does or learns anything for his own sake or for the sake of his friends, or with a view to excellence, the action will not appear illiberal; but if done for the sake of others, the very same action will be thought menial and servile. The received subjects of instruction, as I have already remarked, are partly of a liberal and partly of an illiberal character.

The customary branches of education are in number four; they are—(1) reading and writing, (2) gymnastic exercises, (3) music, to which is sometimes added (4) drawing. Of these, reading and writing and drawing are regarded as useful for the purposes of life in a variety of ways, and gymnastic exercises are thought to infuse courage. Concerning music a doubt may be raised—in our own day most men cultivate it for the sake of pleasure, but originally it was included in education, because nature herself, as has been often said, requires that we should be able, not only to work well, but to use leisure well; for, as I must repeat once again, the first principle of all action is leisure. Both are required, but leisure is better than occupation and is its end; and therefore the question must be asked, what ought we to do when at leisure? Clearly we ought not to be amusing ourselves, for then amusement would be the end of life. But if this is inconceivable, and amusement is needed more amid serious occupations than at other times (for he who is hard at work has need of relaxation, and amusement gives relaxation, whereas occupation is always accompanied with exertion and effort), we should introduce amusements only at suitable times, and they should be our medicines, for the emotion which they create in the soul is a relaxation, and from the pleasure we obtain rest. But leisure of itself gives pleasure and happiness and enjoyment of life, which are experienced, not by the busy man, but by those who have leisure. For he who is occupied has in view some end which he has not attained; but happiness is an end, since all men deem it to be accompanied with pleasure and not with pain. This pleasure, however, is regarded differently by different persons, and varies according to the habit of individuals; the pleasure of the best man is the best, and springs from the noblest sources. It is clear then that there are branches of learning and education which we must study merely with a view to leisure spent in intellectual activity, and these are to be valued for their own sake; whereas those kinds of knowledge which are useful in business are to be deemed necessary, and exist for the sake of other things. And therefore our fathers admitted music into education, not on the ground either of its necessity or utility, for it is not necessary, nor indeed useful in the same manner as reading and writing; which are useful in money-making, in the management of a household, in the acquisition of knowledge and in political life, nor like drawing, useful for a more correct judgement of the works of artists, nor again like gymnastic, which gives health and strength; for neither of these is to be gained from music. There remains, then, the use of music for intellectual enjoyment in leisure; which is in fact evidently the reason of its introduction, this being one of the ways in which it is thought that a freeman should pass his leisure; as Homer says—

'But he who alone should be called to the pleasant feast';

and afterwards he speaks of others whom he describes as inviting

'The bard who would delight them all'.

And in another place Odysseus says there is no better way of passing life than when men's hearts are merry and

'The banqueters in the hall, sitting in order, hear the voice of the minstrel'.

It is evident, then, that there is a sort of education in which parents should train their sons, not as being useful or necessary, but because it is liberal or noble. Whether this is of one kind only, or of more than one, and if so, what they are, and how they are to be imparted, must hereafter be determined. Thus much we are now in a position to say, that the ancients witness to us; for their opinion may be gathered from the fact that music is one of the received and traditional branches of education. Further, it is clear that children should be instructed in some useful things,—for example, in reading and writing,—not only for their usefulness, but also because many other sorts of knowledge are acquired through them. With a like view they may be taught drawing, not to prevent their making mistakes in their own purchases, or in order that they may not be imposed upon in the buying or selling of articles, but perhaps rather because it makes them judges of the beauty of the human form. To be always seeking after the useful does not become free and exalted souls. Now it is clear that in education practice must be used before theory, and the body be trained before the mind; and therefore boys should be handed over to the trainer, who creates in them the proper habit of body, and to the wrestling-master, who teaches them their exercises.

"The Grandeur That Was Rome"

THE REPUBLIC

27 LIVY, FROM *THE FOUNDING OF THE CITY*: THE FALL OF THE TARQUINS AND THE RISE OF THE REPUBLIC

For knowledge of the beginnings of Rome, present-day historians are dependent largely on the evidence of archaeology and inferences from tradition. They know, for example, that the banks of the Tiber were first settled by migrating Indo-Europeans around 1000 B.C., that some two hundred years later the hills of Rome were sites of organized settlements of Latin and Sabine farmers and shepherds, and that in the eighth century B.C. the various villages had coalesced into one city-state, Rome, which was to be ruled by elective kings. Little else than scattered knowledge of early religion, commerce, and art exists.

Roman historians and poets like Ennius, Livy, and Virgil knew even less of early times and depended upon legend and invention to fill in the picture of Rome's past. Legend told how the prince Aeneas escaped from burning Troy and after years of wandering landed in Latium, where he founded the city of Alba Longa, through his son, Ascanius. Later, a descendant, Rhea, gave birth to twins, Romulus and Remus, and one of them, Romulus, founded Rome in 753 B.C. According to tradition, Rome was then ruled by seven kings, beginning with Romulus and terminating with Lucius Tarquinius Superbus (Tarquin the Proud), who was ousted in 509 B.C. to make way for the republic.

Concerning these seven kings, only our evidence of the last Tarquin seems creditable. His family apparently originated in Etruria, a powerful and highly civilized nation to the north of Rome. Tradition places the reign of Tarquin in the latter half of the sixth century B.C., at a time when we know that the Etruscans were making conquests southward as far as the Bay of Naples, but whether the Tarquins captured Rome by force or migrated to Rome and wrested power by political maneuver we do not know. At any rate, the last Etruscan king was eventually ousted and a republican government was formed, with annual elective magistrates (consuls), an advisory body of nobles (the Senate), and an assembly dominated by great property owners.

The combination of history and legend can be found in the work of Titus Livius (59 B.C.-17 A.D.), an early Empire Roman who wrote *From the Founding of the City*, tracing the story of Rome from Aeneas down to Emperor Augustus in 9 A.D. The following excerpt from his history describes the downfall of Tarquin the Proud, an event which was precipitated, according to tradition, by the rape of the Roman noblewoman Lucretia by Tarquin's son, Sextus. Brutus, a cousin of Lucretia's husband, placed himself at the head of the Romans, drove out the Tarquins, and founded the republic. The historian Livy regarded the revolutionists as examples of the stern virtue and legality which was to characterize the Roman Republic. Lucretia, who found death preferable to dishonor, exemplified the courage, purity, and patriotism expected of a Roman woman. In idealizing the early republic, Livy wished to emphasize the virtues which he believed were responsible for the success of Rome.

Now began the reign of Lucius Tarquinius, whose conduct procured him the surname of Superbus, or the Proud. For he denied the rites of sepulture to his own father-in-law, asserting that Romulus had also perished without burial. He put to death the leading senators, whom he believed to have favoured the cause of Servius [the previous king, whom Tarquin caused to be murdered] and, conscious that a precedent for gaining the kingship by crime might be found in his own career and turned against himself, he assumed a body-guard. He had indeed no right to the throne but might, since he was ruling neither by popular decree nor senatorial sanction. Moreover, as he put no trust in the affection of his people, he was compelled to safeguard his authority by fear. To inspire terror therefore in many persons, he adopted the practice of trying capital

Text: Reprinted by permission of the publishers and The Loeb Classical Library from *Livy*, trans. B. O. Foster (Cambridge, Mass.: Harvard University Press, 1957), I, 171-73, 183, 197-209, 219-21.

causes by himself, without advisers; and, under the pretext thus afforded, was able to inflict death, exile, and forfeiture of property, not only upon persons whom he suspected and disliked, but also in cases where he could have nothing to gain but plunder. It was chiefly the senators whose numbers were reduced by this procedure, and Tarquinius determined to make no new appointments to the order, that it might be the more despised for its very paucity, and might chafe less at being ignored in all business of state. For this king was the first to break with the custom handed down by his predecessors, of consulting the senate on all occasions, and governed the nation without other advice than that of his own household. War, peace, treaties, and alliances were entered upon or broken off by the monarch himself, with whatever states he wished, and without the decree of people or senate. The Latin race he strove particularly to make his friends, that his strength abroad might contribute to his security at home. He contracted with their nobles not only relations of hospitality but also matrimonial connections. To Octavius Mamilius of Tusculum, a man by long odds the most important of the Latin name, and descended, if we may believe report, from Ulysses and the goddess Circe, he gave his daughter in marriage, and in this way attached to himself the numerous kinsmen and friends of the man. . . .

But if the king was unjust in peace, yet he was not a bad general in war. Indeed, he would have equalled in this art the kings who had gone before him, if his degeneracy in other things had not also dimmed his glory here. It was he who began the war with the Volsci which was to last more than two hundred years after his time, and took Suessa Pometia from them by storm. There, having sold off the booty and raised forty talents of silver, he conceived the project of a temple of Jupiter so magnificent that it should be worthy of the king of gods and men, the Roman empire, and the majesty of the site itself. The money from the captured city he put aside to build this temple. . . .

. . . Ardea belonged to the Rutuli, who were a nation of commanding wealth, for that place and period. This very fact was the cause of the war, since the Roman king was eager not only to enrich himself, impoverished as he was by the splendour of his public works, but also to appease with booty the feeling of the common people; who, besides the enmity they bore the monarch for other acts of pride, were especially resentful that the king should have kept them employed so long as artisans and doing the work of slaves. An attempt was made to capture Ardea by assault. Having failed in this, the Romans invested the place with intrenchments, and began to beleaguer the enemy. Here in their permanent camp, as is usual with a war not sharp but long drawn out, furlough was rather freely granted, more freely however to the leaders than to the soldiers; the young princes for their part passed their idle hours together at dinners and drinking bouts. It chanced, as they were drinking in the quarters of Sextus Tarquinius, where Tarquinius Collatinus, son of Egerius, was also a guest, that the subject of wives came up. Every man fell to praising his own wife with enthusiasm, and, as their rivalry grew hot, Collatinus said that there was no need to talk about it, for it was in their power to know, in a few hours' time, how far the rest were excelled by his own Lucretia. "Come! If the vigour of youth is in us let us mount our horses and see for ourselves the disposition of our wives. Let every man regard as the surest test what meets his eyes when the woman's husband enters unexpected." They were heated with wine. "Agreed!" they all cried, and clapping spurs to their horses were off for Rome. Arriving there at early dusk, they thence proceeded to Collatia, where Lucretia was discovered very differently employed from the daughters-in-law of the king. These they had seen at a luxurious banquet, whiling away the time with their young friends; but Lucretia, though it was late at night, was busily engaged upon her wool, while her maidens toiled about her in the lamplight as she sat in the hall of her house. The prize of this contest in womanly virtues fell to Lucretia. As Collatinus and the Tarquinii approached, they were graciously received, and the victorious husband courteously invited the young princes to his table. It was there that Sextus Tarquinius was seized with a wicked desire to debauch Lucretia by force; not only her beauty, but her proved chastity as well, provoked him. However, for the present they ended the boyish prank of the night and returned to the camp.

When a few days had gone by, Sextus Tarquinius, without letting Collatinus know, took a single attendant and went to Collatia. Being kindly welcomed, for no one suspected his purpose, he was brought after dinner to a guest-chamber. Burning with passion, he waited till it seemed to him that all about him was secure and everybody fast asleep; then, drawing his sword, he came to the sleeping Lucretia. Holding the woman down with his left hand on her breast, he said, "Be still, Lucretia! I am Sextus Tarquinius. My sword is in my hand. Utter a sound, and you die!" In affright the woman started out of her sleep. No help was in sight, but only imminent death. Then Tarquinius began to declare his love, to plead, to mingle threats with prayers, to bring every resource to bear upon her woman's heart. When he found her obdurate and not to be moved even by fear of death, he went farther and threatened her with disgrace, saying that when she was dead he would kill his slave and lay him naked by her side, that she might be said to have been put to death in adultery with a man of base condition. At this dreadful prospect her resolute modesty was overcome, as if with force, by his victorious lust; and Tarquinius departed, exulting in his conquest of a woman's honour. Lucretia, grieving at her great disaster, dispatched the same message to her father in Rome and to her husband at Ardea: that they should each take a trusty friend and come; that they must do this and do it quickly, for a frightful thing had happened. Spurius Lucretius came with Publius Valerius, Volesus' son. Collatinus brought Lucius Junius Brutus, with whom he chanced to be returning to Rome when he was met by the messenger from his wife. Lucretia they found sitting sadly in her chamber. The entrance of her friends brought the tears to her eyes, and to her husband's question, "Is all well?" she replied, "Far from it; for what can be well with a woman when she has lost her honour? The print of a strange man, Collatinus, is in your bed. Yet my body only has been violated; my heart is guiltless, as death shall be my witness. But pledge your right hands and your words that the adulterer shall not go unpunished. Sextus Tarquinius is he that last night returned hostility for hospitality, and armed with force brought ruin on me, and on himself no less—if you are men—when he worked his pleasure with me." They give their pledges, every man in turn. They seek to comfort her, sick at heart as she is, by diverting the blame from her who was forced to the doer of the wrong. They tell her it is the mind that sins, not the body; and that where purpose has been wanting there is no guilt. "It is for you to determine," she answers, "what is due to him; for my own part, though I acquit myself of the sin, I do not absolve myself from punishment; not in time to come shall ever unchaste woman live through the example of Lucretia." Taking a knife which she had concealed beneath her dress, she plunged it into her heart, and sinking forward upon the wound, died as she fell. The wail for the dead was raised by her husband and her father.

Brutus, while the others were absorbed in grief, drew out the knife from Lucretia's wound and holding it up, dripping with gore, exclaimed, "By this blood, most chaste until a prince wronged it, I swear, and I take you, gods, to witness, that I will pursue Lucius Tarquinius Superbus and his wicked wife and all his children, with sword, with fire, aye with whatsoever violence I may; and that I will suffer neither them nor any other to be king in Rome!" The knife he then passed to Collatinus, and from him to Lucretius and Valerius. They were dumbfounded at this miracle. Whence came this new spirit in the breast of Brutus? As he bade them, so they swore. Grief was swallowed up in anger; and when Brutus summoned them to make war from that very moment on the power of the kings, they followed his lead. They carried out Lucretia's corpse from the house and bore it to the marketplace, where men crowded about them, attracted, as they were bound to be, by the amazing character of the strange event and its heinousness. Every man had his own complaint to make of the prince's crime and his violence. They were moved, not only by the father's sorrow, but by the fact that it was Brutus who chid their tears and idle lamentations and urged them to take up the sword, as befitted men and Romans, against those who had dared to treat them as enemies. The boldest of the young men seized their weapons and offered themselves for service, and the others followed their example. Then, leaving Lucretia's father to guard Collatia, and posting sentinels so that no one might announce the rising to the royal family, the rest, equipped for battle and with Brutus in command, set out for Rome. Once there, wherever their armed band advanced it brought terror and confusion; but again, when people saw that in the van were the chief men of the state, they concluded that whatever it was it could be no meaningless disturbance. And in fact there was no less resentment at Rome when this dreadful story was known than there had been at Collatia. So from every quarter of the City men came running to the Forum. No sooner were they there than a crier summoned the people before the Tribune of the Celeres, which office Brutus then happened to be holding. There he made a speech by no means like what might have been expected of the mind and the spirit which he had feigned up to that day. He spoke of the violence and lust of Sextus Tarquinius, of the shameful defilement of Lucretia and her deplorable death, of the bereavement of Tricipitinus, in whose eyes the death of his daughter was not so outrageous and deplorable as was the cause of her death. He reminded them, besides, of the pride of the king himself and the wretched state of the commons, who were plunged into ditches and sewers and made to clear them out. The men of Rome, he said, the conquerors of all the nations round about, had been transformed from warriors into artisans and stone-cutters. He spoke of the shameful murder of King Tullius, and how his daughter had driven her accursed chariot over her father's body, and he invoked the gods who punish crimes against parents. With these and, I fancy, even fiercer reproaches, such as occur to a man in the very presence of an outrage, but are far from easy for an historian to reproduce, he inflamed the people, and brought them to abrogate the king's authority and to exile Lucius Tarquinius, together with his wife and children. Brutus himself then enrolled the juniors, who voluntarily gave in their names, and arming them set out for the camp at Ardea to arouse the troops against the king. The command at Rome he left with Lucretius, who had been appointed Prefect of the City by the king, some time before. During this confusion Tullia fled from her house, cursed wherever she went by men and women, who called down upon her the furies that avenge the wrongs of kindred.

When the news of these events reached the camp, the king, in alarm at the unexpected danger, set out for Rome to put down the revolt. Brutus, who had perceived the king's approach, made a circuit to avoid meeting him, and at almost the same moment, though by different roads, Brutus reached Ardea and Tarquinius Rome. Against Tarquinius the gates were closed and exile was pronounced. The liberator of the City was received with rejoicings in the camp, and the sons of the king were driven out of it. . . .

The new liberty enjoyed by the Roman people, their achievements in peace and war, annual magistracies, and laws superior in authority to men will henceforth be my theme. This liberty was the more grateful as the last king had been so great a tyrant. For his predecessors so ruled that there is good reason to regard them all as successive founders of parts, at least, of the City, which they added to serve as new homes for the numbers they had themselves recruited. Nor is there any doubt that the same Brutus who earned such honour by expelling the haughty Tarquinius, would have acted in an evil hour for the commonwealth had a premature eagerness for liberty led him to wrest the power from any of the earlier kings. For what would have happened if that rabble of shepherds and vagrants, having deserted their own peoples, and under the protection of inviolable sanctuary having possessed themselves of liberty, or at least impunity, had thrown off their fear of kings only to be stirred by the ruffling storms of tribunician demagogues, breeding quarrels with the senators of a city not their own, before ever the pledges of wife and children and love of the very place and soil (an affection of slow growth) had firmly united their aspirations? The nation would have crumbled away with dissension before it had matured. But it was favoured by the mild restraint of the government, which nursed it up to the point where its ripened powers enabled it to bear good fruit of liberty. Moreover you may reckon the beginning of liberty as proceeding rather from the limitation of the consuls' authority to a year than from any diminution of their power compared with that which the kings had exercised. All the rights of the kings and all their insignia were possessed by the earliest consuls; only one thing was guarded against—that the terror they inspired should not be doubled by permitting both to have the rods. Brutus was the first to have them, with his colleague's consent, and he proved as determined in guarding liberty as he had been in asserting it. To begin with, when the people were still jealous of their new freedom, he obliged them to swear an oath that they would suffer no man to be king in Rome, lest they might later be turned from their purpose by the entreaties or the gifts of princes. In the next place, that the strength of the senate might receive an added augmentation from the numbers of that order, he filled up the list of the Fathers, which had been abridged by the late king's butcheries, drawing upon the foremost men of equestrian rank until he had brought the total up to three hundred. From that time, it is said, was handed down the custom of summoning to the senate the Fathers and the Enrolled, the latter being the designation of the new senators, who were appointed. This measure was wonderfully effective in promoting harmony in the state and attaching the plebs to the Fathers.

28 POLYBIUS, *HISTORIES*: THE BALANCE OF POWER IN THE ROMAN REPUBLIC

The history of the Roman Republic (509-31 B.C.) is a record of the interplay of foreign and domestic policies in the life of a state. The republic began as a nationalist reaction against the tyranny of foreign kings from neighboring Etruria and developed because of Rome's unceasing warfare in the name of conquest. Successful wars require armies of men whose loyalty to the state is unswerving and whose numbers can be increased to correspond with the expansion of the state. To maintain such a militia, Rome's privileged classes were compelled to make increasing concessions to the plebeians, Rome's second-class citizens, and to bestow citizenship on conquered subjects—potential soldiers—to a greater extent than any other city-state had done. The opportunity for citizenship and the gradually acquired equality before the law of all Roman citizens strengthened the patriotism and loyalty of Rome's subjects so that the nation could endure severe defeats and seditions without collapsing. On the other hand, external pressure upon Rome, especially the foreign wars fought with Carthage and the Hellenistic monarchies (264-146 B.C.), required expert leadership, which came from Rome's wealthy families. The relatively few powerful families in the Roman Senate were often forced through necessity to exercise quick, decisive command; they managed for a long time to maintain a political aristocracy which could take such quick action, though all Romans were legally equal. Only in the last century of the republic did the pressures of governing an empire split the aristocracy, stir up class strife, and lead to debilitating civil wars.

By the end of the second century B.C., it was apparent that the city of Rome was to succeed where the Greek cities had failed—in the creation of a unified empire. The reason for Rome's success was of particular concern to Polybius, the most celebrated of Hellenistic historians. Polybius (c. 200-120 B.C.) was a prominent Greek statesman who was seized by the Romans as a political hostage. During his twenty-year enforced stay in Italy, Polybius wrote his *Histories* in forty books (of which the first five and some extracts remain), which covered the events of the Mediterranean world during the period from 220 to 144 B.C. His study of the organization of ancient states led Polybius to conclude that governments rise and fall according to a cyclical and measurable process. Like Aristotle, he argued that there are three basic types of government—kingship, aristocracy, and democracy—but that the three invariably develop into corrupt forms of monarchy, oligarchy, and mob rule, respectively. The first form of government is kingship, which, in Polybius' view, gives rise to its corrupted form, monarchy, which in turn is superseded by aristocracy. Aristocracy then disintegrates into oligarchy, which is then replaced by democracy. For a time democracy is satisfactory, then it turns into mob rule, out of which kingship appears and the cycle begins again. The best government, according to Polybius, is one which incorporates the desirable features of each of the three basic forms, based upon a constitution which includes the attributes of kingship, democracy, and aristocracy in the government. The virtue of a mixed constitution, according to Polybius, lies in a system of checks and balances by which each of the parts is able either to counteract or to cooperate with the others. Should one part become too powerful, the others act to suppress it.

In the passages below, Polybius describes the trifold division of political constitutions and applies the doctrine of balance of power to the Roman Republic's constitution. (See Document 29 for further discussion of the institutions of the Roman Republic.)

Text: Reprinted by permission of the publishers and The Loeb Classical Library from *Histories of Polybius*, trans. W. R. Paton (Cambridge, Mass.: Harvard University Press, 1954), III, 271-77, 295-311.

In the case of those Greek states which have often risen to greatness and have often experienced a complete change of fortune, it is an easy matter both to describe their past and to pronounce as to their future. For there is no difficulty in reporting the known facts, and it is not hard to foretell the future by inference from the past. But about the Roman state it is neither at all easy to explain the present situation owing to the complicated character of the constitution, nor to foretell the future owing to our ignorance of the peculiar features of public and private life at Rome in the past. Particular attention and study are therefore required if one wishes to attain a clear general view of the distinctive qualities of their constitution.

Most of those whose object it has been to instruct us methodically concerning such matters, distinguish three kinds of constitutions, which they call kingship, aristocracy, and democracy. Now we should, I think, be quite justified in asking them to enlighten us as to whether they represent these three to be the sole varieties or rather to be the best; for in either case my opinion is that they are wrong. For it is evident that we must regard as the best constitution a combination of all these three varieties, since we have had proof of this not only theoretically but by actual experience, Lycurgus having been the first to draw up a constitution—that of Sparta—on this principle. Nor on the other hand can we admit that these are the only three varieties; for we have witnessed monarchical and tyrannical governments, which while they differ very widely from kingship, yet bear a certain resemblance to it, this being the reason why monarchs in general falsely assume and use, as far as they can, the regal title. There have also been several oligarchical constitutions which seem to bear some likeness to aristocratic ones, though the divergence is, generally, as wide as possible. The same holds good about democracies. The truth of what I say is evident from the following considerations. It is by no means every monarchy which we can call straight off a kingship, but only that which is voluntarily accepted by the subjects and where they are governed rather by an appeal to their reason than by fear and force. Nor again can we style every oligarchy an aristocracy, but only that where the government is in the hands of a selected body of the justest and wisest men. Similarly that is no true democracy in which the whole crowd of citizens is free to do whatever they wish or purpose, but when, in a community where it is traditional and customary to reverence the gods, to honour our parents, to respect our elders, and to obey the laws, the will of the greater number prevails, this is to be called a democracy. We should therefore assert that there are six kinds of governments, the three above mentioned which are in everyone's mouth and the three which are naturally allied to them, I mean monarchy, oligarchy, and mob-rule. Now the first of these to come into being is monarchy, its growth being natural and unaided; and next arises kingship derived from monarchy by the aid of art and by the correction of defects. Monarchy first changes into its vicious allied form, tyranny; and next, the abolition of both gives birth to aristocracy. Aristocracy by its very nature degenerates into oligarchy; and when the commons inflamed by anger take vengeance on this government for its unjust rule, democracy comes into being; and in due course the licence and lawlessness of this form of government produces mob-rule to complete the series. The truth of what I have just said will be quite clear to anyone who pays due attention to such beginnings, origins, and changes as are in each case natural. For he alone who has seen how each form naturally arises and develops, will be able to see when, how, and where the growth, perfection, change, and end of each are likely to occur again. And it is to the Roman constitution above all that this method, I think,

may be successfully applied, since from the outset its formation and growth have been due to natural causes....

The three kinds of government that I spoke of above all shared in the control of the Roman state. And such fairness and propriety in all respects was shown in the use of these three elements for drawing up the constitution and in its subsequent administration that it was impossible even for a native to pronounce with certainty whether the whole system was aristocratic, democratic, or monarchical. This was indeed only natural. For if one fixed one's eyes on the power of the consuls, the constitution seemed completely monarchical and royal; if on that of the senate it seemed again to be aristocratic; and when one looked at the power of the masses, it seemed clearly to be a democracy. The parts of the state falling under the control of each element were and with a few modifications still are as follows.

The consuls, previous to leading out their legions, exercise authority in Rome over all public affairs, since all the other magistrates except the tribunes are under them and bound to obey them, and it is they who introduce embassies to the senate. Besides this it is they who consult the senate on matters of urgency, they who carry out in detail the provisions of its decrees. Again as concerns all affairs of state administered by the people it is their duty to take these under their charge, to summon assemblies, to introduce measures, and to preside over the execution of the popular decrees. As for preparation for war and the general conduct of operations in the field, here their power is almost uncontrolled; for they are empowered to make what demands they choose on the allies, to appoint military tribunes, to levy soldiers and select those who are fittest for service. They also have the right of inflicting, when on active service, punishment on anyone under their command; and they are authorized to spend any sum they decide upon from the public funds, being accompanied by a quaestor who faithfully executes their instructions. So that if one looks at this part of the administration alone, one may reasonably pronounce the constitution to be a pure monarchy or kingship....

To pass to the senate. In the first place it has the control of the treasury, all revenue and expenditure being regulated by it. For with the exception of payments made to the consuls, the quaestors are not allowed to disburse for any particular object without a decree of the senate. And even the item of expenditure which is far heavier and more important than any other—the outlay every five years by the censors on public works, whether constructions or repairs—is under the control of the senate, which makes a grant to the censors for the purpose. Similarly crimes committed in Italy which require a public investigation, such as treason, conspiracy, poisoning, and assassination, are under the jurisdiction of the senate. Also if any private person or community in Italy is in need of arbitration or indeed claims damages or requires succour or protection, the senate attends to all such matters. It also occupies itself with the dispatch of all embassies sent to countries outside of Italy for the purpose either of settling differences, or of offering friendly advice, or indeed of imposing demands, or of receiving submission, or of declaring war; and in like manner with respect to embassies arriving in Rome it decides what reception and what answer should be given to them. All these matters are in the hands of the senate, nor have the people anything whatever to do with them. So that again to one residing in Rome during the absence of the consuls the constitution appears to be entirely aristocratic; and this is the conviction of many Greek states and many of the kings, as the senate manages all business connected with them.

After this we are naturally inclined to ask what part in the constitution is left for the people, considering that the senate controls all the particular matters I mentioned, and, what is most important, manages all matters of revenue and expenditure, and considering that the consuls again have uncontrolled authority as regards armaments and operations in the field. But nevertheless there is a part and a very important part left for the people. For it is the people which alone has the right to confer honours and inflict punishment, the only bonds by which kingdoms and states and in a word human society in general are held together. For where the distinction between these is overlooked or is observed but ill applied, no affairs can be properly administered. How indeed is this possible when good and evil men are held in equal estimation? It is by the people, then, in many cases that offences punishable by a fine are tried when the accused have held the highest office; and they are the only court which may try on capital charges. As regards the latter they have a practice which is praiseworthy and should be mentioned. Their usage allows those on trial for their lives when found guilty liberty to depart openly, thus inflicting voluntary exile on themselves, if even only one of the tribes that pronounce the verdict has not yet voted. . . . Again it is the people who bestow office on the deserving, the noblest reward of virtue in a state; the people have the power of approving or rejecting laws, and what is most important of all, they deliberate on the question of war and peace. Further in the case of alliances, terms of peace, and treaties, it is the people who ratify all these or the reverse. Thus here again one might plausibly say that the people's share in the government is the greatest, and that the constitution is a democratic one.

Having stated how political power is distributed among the different parts of the state, I will now explain how each of the three parts is enabled, if they wish, to counteract or co-operate with the others. The consul, when he leaves with his army invested with the powers I mentioned, appears indeed to have absolute authority in all matters necessary for carrying out his purpose; but in fact he requires the support of the people and the senate, and is not able to bring his operations to a conclusion without them. For it is obvious that the legions require constant supplies, and without the consent of the senate, neither corn, clothing, nor pay can be provided; so that the commander's plans come to nothing, if the senate chooses to be deliberately negligent and obstructive. It also depends on the senate whether or not a general can carry out completely his conceptions and designs, since it has the right of either superseding him when his year's term of office has expired or of retaining him in command. Again it is in its power to celebrate with pomp and to magnify the successes of a general or on the other hand to obscure and belittle them. For the processions they call triumphs, in which the generals bring the actual spectacle of their achievements before the eyes of their fellow-citizens, cannot be properly organized and sometimes even cannot be held at all, unless the senate consents and provides the requisite funds. As for the people it is most indispensable for the consuls to conciliate them, however far away from home they may be; for, as I said, it is the people which ratifies or annuls terms of peace and treaties, and what is most important, on laying down office the consuls are obliged to account for their actions to the people. So that in no respect is it safe for the consuls to neglect keeping in favour with both the senate and the people.

The senate again, which possesses such great power, is obliged in the first place to pay attention to the commons in public affairs and respect the wishes of the people, and it cannot carry out inquiries into the most grave and important offences against the state, punishable with death, and their correction, unless the *senatus consultum* is confirmed by the people. The same is the case in matters which directly affect the senate itself. For if anyone introduces a law meant to deprive the senate of some of its traditional authority, or to abolish the precedence and other distinctions of the senators or even to curtail them of their private fortunes, it is the people alone which has the power of passing or rejecting any such measure. And what is most important is that if a single one of the tribunes interposes, the senate is unable to decide finally about any matter, and cannot even meet and hold sittings; and here it is to be observed that the tribunes are always obliged to act as the people decree and to pay every attention to their wishes. Therefore for all these reasons the senate is afraid of the masses and must pay due attention to the popular will.

Similarly, again, the people must be submissive to the senate and respect its members both in public and in private. Through the whole of Italy a vast number of contracts, which it would not be easy to enumerate, are given out by the censors for the construction and repair of public buildings, and besides this there are many things which are farmed, such as navigable rivers, harbours, gardens, mines, lands, in fact everything that forms part of the Roman dominion. Now all these matters are undertaken by the people, and one may almost say that everyone is interested in these contracts and the work they involve. For certain people are the actual purchasers from the censors of the contracts, others are the partners of these first, others stand surety for them, others pledge their own fortunes to the state for this purpose. Now in all these matters the senate is supreme. It can grant extension of time; it can relieve the contractor if any accident occurs; and if the work proves to be absolutely impossible to carry out it can liberate him from his contract. There are in fact many ways in which the senate can either benefit or injure those who manage public property, as all these matters are referred to it. What is even more important is that the judges in most civil trials, whether public or private, are appointed from its members, where the action involves large interests. So that all citizens being at the mercy of the senate, and looking forward with alarm to the uncertainty of litigation, are very shy of obstructing or resisting its decisions. Similarly anyone is reluctant to oppose the projects of the consuls as all are generally and individually under their authority when in the field.

Such being the power that each part has of hampering the others or co-operating with them, their union is adequate to all emergencies, so that it is impossible to find a better political system than this. For whenever the menace of some common danger from abroad compels them to act in concord and support each other, so great does the strength of the state become, that nothing which is requisite can be neglected, as all are zealously competing in devising means of meeting the need of the hour, nor can any decision arrived at fail to be executed promptly, as all are co-operating both in public and in private to the accomplishment of the task they have set themselves; and consequently this peculiar form of constitution possesses an irresistible power of attaining every object upon which it is resolved. When again they are freed from external menace, and reap the harvest of good fortune and affluence which is the result of their success, and in the enjoyment of this prosperity are corrupted by flattery and idleness and wax insolent and overbearing, as indeed happens often enough, it is then especially that we see the state providing itself a remedy for the evil from which it suffers. For when one part having grown out of proportion to the others aims at supremacy and tends to become too predominant, it is evident that, as for the reasons above given none of the three is absolute, but the purpose of the one can be counterworked and thwarted by the others, none of them will excessively outgrow the others or treat them with contempt. All in fact remains *in statu quo*, on the one hand, because any aggressive impulse is sure to be checked and from the outset each estate stands in dread of being interfered with by the others. . . .

THE COLLAPSE OF THE REPUBLIC

29 CICERO, *LAWS*: A CONSERVATIVE'S VIEW OF LAW AND THE REPUBLIC

When about the year 509 B.C. the Roman aristocracy overthrew the last Roman monarch, Tarquin the Proud, they imposed upon the state a republic of an oligarchic cast. For an elected king who ruled for life they substituted two consuls appointed for one year only and circumscribed in their power by constitutional checks. The general assembly was dominated by propertied classes. The real master of Rome was the Senate—the permanent advisory body of aristocrats, or "patricians."

The plebeians, or common people, were at first almost powerless. However, as Rome began the creation of an empire in Italy, the plebeians found themselves in possession of a strong asset with which to bargain for concessions from the nobles—their service in the armies. The military coöperation of the masses was indispensable, and it became evident that this coöperation could be won only if the plebeians knew they were gaining political and economic improvements for themselves, not just for the nobility. Moreover, during cycles of economic distress, the poorer plebeians rose to demand political and juridical rights as conditions for their services as laborers.

The first concession which the patricians granted—peacefully if begrudgingly—was the right of the plebeians to maintain their own Tribal Assembly, or "council of plebs." This assembly was given the privilege of electing four (later, ten) annual officers called tribunes, whose duty it was to veto any consular or senatorial acts which were contrary to the interests of the plebeians. About 449 B.C. the plebeians wrested another victory: the laws, which heretofore had been transmitted orally, were written down on Twelve Tables (i.e., tablets). Now the plebeians knew their rights and the rights of others and could quote the law to defend themselves against patrician injustices. About this time, too, the masses secured true legislative power—the right to make laws—in the Tribal Assembly. Later, marriage between plebeians and patricians was allowed, and plebeians were made eligible for the consulship. By about 300 B.C. the old class divisions had largely lost their significance, and by the year 146 B.C. the majority of the "noble families" were not patrician but plebeian; a new aristocracy was formed when the ennobled plebeian families combined with the older patrician families. Now there were two classes: the rich and the poor—the *optimates* and the *populares*.

Henceforth, Rome's domestic history was a tug-of-war between the two factions. The brothers Gracchi as tribunes fought for land reforms in favor of the people but were ultimately destroyed by the *optimates* of the Senate. Marius, demagogue and champion of the popular party, was succeeded by Sulla, the aristocratic dictator who strove for senatorial privileges. Normally, the Senate was supreme because its members included the most talented and experienced men in the republic, making its political and moral influence almost irresistible. Nevertheless, by the middle of the first century B.C., the factional struggles had become so severe, aggravated as they were by economic distress and the pressing responsibilities of empire rule, that the authority of the Senate was greatly strained. Into the power vacuum moved three men—Pompey, Julius Caesar, and Crassus—who formed what became known as the First Triumvirate; the republic was powerless in the hands of these three. When Crassus died in 53 B.C., circumstances put Pompey in league with the Senate, who made common cause against Caesar. Civil war flared, Pompey was defeated, and Caesar became the undisputed master of Rome. (See Document 31.)

It was during these perilous years of the late republic that Marcus Tullius Cicero (106-43 B.C.), the famous Roman orator and statesman, wrote his treatise, the *Laws*. Cicero was the trusted leader of the Italian middle class, a group who disliked popular demagoguery and aristocratic exclusiveness alike, and who preferred the old-fashioned simplicity of life to the cosmopolitan luxury of Rome. With indefatigable energy, Cicero strove to soften the antagonism of the two dominant parties and to reconstruct a solid constitutional party. He advocated the supremacy of the Senate, but the Senate of his ideal was neither an assemblage of oligarchic nobles nor a club whose membership was based on wealth or birth, but rather a ruling body open to all men of virtue, experience, and capability—an assembly of the "natural" aristocracy.

In the *Laws* Cicero presented his conceptions of justice and true Roman constitutional government. Much of his theory of "natural law" was derived from Greek Stoicism, a philosophy of self-discipline and universal brotherhood which appealed to the old Roman sense of duty, piety, and dignity. Cicero's constitutional reforms, given in part below, reflect his earnest desire for a republic of reason, law and order.

... [B]efore we come to the individual laws, let us look at the character and nature of Law,

Text: Reprinted by permission of the publishers and The Loeb Classical Library from Cicero, *De Re Publica De Legibus*, trans. Clinton Walker Keyes (Cambridge, Mass.: Harvard University Press, 1951), pp. 379-89, 463, 465-513 *passim*.

for fear that, though it must be the standard to which we refer everything, we may now and then be led astray by an incorrect use of terms, and forget the rational principles on which our laws must be based. . . .

. . . I find that it has been the opinion of the wisest men that Law is not a product of human thought, nor is it any enactment of peoples, but something eternal which rules the whole universe by its wisdom in command and prohibition. Thus they have been accustomed to say that Law is the primal and ultimate mind of God, whose reason directs all things either by compulsion or restraint. Wherefore that Law which the gods have given to the human race has been justly praised; for it is the reason and mind of a wise lawgiver applied to command and prohibition. . . .

Ever since we were children, . . . we have learned to call, "If one summon another to court," and other rules of the same kind, laws. But we must come to the true understanding of the matter, which is as follows: this and other commands and prohibitions of nations have the power to summon to righteousness and away from wrongdoing; but this power is not merely older than the existence of nations and States, it is coeval with that God who guards and rules heaven and earth. For the divine mind cannot exist without reason, and divine reason cannot but have this power to establish right and wrong. No written law commanded that a man should take his stand on a bridge alone, against the full force of the enemy, and order the bridge broken down behind him; yet we shall not for that reason suppose that the heroic Cocles was not obeying the law of bravery and following its decrees in doing so noble a deed. Even if there was no written law against rape at Rome in the reign of Lucius Tarquinius, we cannot say on that account that Sextus Tarquinius did not break that eternal Law by violating Lucretia, the daughter of Tricipitinus! For reason did exist, derived from the Nature of the universe, urging men to right conduct and diverting them from wrong-doing, and this reason did not first become Law when it was written down, but when it first came into existence; and it came into existence simultaneously with the divine mind. Wherefore the true and primal Law, applied to command and prohibition, is the right reason of supreme Jupiter. . . .

Therefore, just as that divine mind is the supreme Law, so, when [reason] is perfected in man, [that also is Law; and this perfected reason exists] in the mind of the wise man; but those rules which, in varying forms and for the need of the moment, have been formulated for the guidance of nations, bear the title of laws rather by favour than because they are really such. For every law which really deserves that name is truly praiseworthy, as they prove by approximately the following arguments. It is agreed, of course, that laws were invented for the safety of citizens, the preservation of States, and the tranquillity and happiness of human life, and that those who first put statutes of this kind in force convinced their people that it was their intention to write down and put into effect such rules as, once accepted and adopted, would make possible for them an honourable and happy life; and when such rules were drawn up and put in force, it is clear that men called them "laws." From this point of view it can be readily understood that those who formulated wicked and unjust statutes for nations, thereby breaking their promises and agreements, put into effect anything but "laws." It may thus be clear that in the very definition of the term "law" there inheres the idea and principle of choosing what is just and true. . . .

What of the many deadly, the many pestilential statutes which nations put in force? These no more deserve to be called laws than the rules a band of robbers might pass in their assembly. For if ignorant and unskilful men have prescribed deadly poisons instead of healing drugs, these cannot possibly be called physicians' prescriptions; neither in a nation can a statute of any sort be called a law, even though the nation, in spite of its being a ruinous regulation, has accepted it. Therefore Law is the distinction between things just and unjust, made in agreement with that primal and most ancient of all things, Nature; and in conformity to Nature's standard are framed those human laws which inflict punishment upon the wicked but defend and protect the good. . . .

So in the very beginning we must persuade our citizens that the gods are the lords and rulers of all things, and that what is done, is done by their will and authority. . . .

Having established these facts, we shall now proceed to the statement of the laws themselves. . . .

[*The Law Establishing the Tribunes*]

. . . "The tribunes of the plebs have too much power," you say. Who can deny it? But the power of the people themselves is much more cruel, much more violent; and yet this power is sometimes milder in practice because there is a leader to control it than if there were none. For a leader is conscious that he is acting at his own risk, whereas the impulse of the people has no consciousness of any risk to itself. "But," you object, "the tribunes sometimes excite the people." Yes, and they often calm them too. For what college of tribunes could be of so desperate a character that not a single one of the ten retained his sanity? . . .

. . . When the Senate had granted this power to the plebeians, [i.e., representation by the tribunes] conflict ceased, rebellion was at an end, and a measure of compromise was discovered which made the more humble believe that they were accorded equality with the nobility; and such a compromise was the only salvation of the State. "But we have had the two Gracchi," you say. Yes, and you could mention many more besides; for when a college of ten is elected, you will find some tribunes in every period whose activities are harmful, and perhaps more who are irresponsible and without influence for good; but in the meantime the senatorial order is not subject to envy, and the common people make no desperate struggles for their rights. Thus it is clear that either the monarchy ought never to have been abolished, or else that real liberty, not a pretence of it, had to be given to the common people; but this liberty has been granted in such a manner that the people were induced by many excellent provisions to yield to the authority of the nobles. . . .

You say that you cannot fully approve of Pompey in this one matter; but it seems to me that you have hardly given sufficient consideration to this point—that he had to determine, not merely what was ideally best, but also what was practically necessary. For he realized that this office was indispensable in our republic; for when our people had so eagerly sought it before, having had any experience of it, how could they dispense with it now that they had learned what it was? It was the duty of a wise citizen, in dealing with an institution not evil in itself and so dear to the people that it could not be combated, not to leave its defence to a popular leader, which would have had evil consequences. . . .

[*Laws Governing the Senate*]

The law which provides that *the Senate is to consist exclusively of ex-magistrates* is certainly a popular measure, as it ensures that no one shall enter that exalted order except by popular election, the censors being deprived of the right of free choice. But we have provided for a mitigation of this disadvantage, since the authority of the Senate is legally established by our next provision, which is: *Its decrees shall be binding.* For the fact is that if the Senate is recognized as the leader of public policy, and all the other orders defend its decrees, and are willing to allow the highest order to conduct the government by its wisdom, then this compromise, by which supreme power is granted to the people and actual authority to the Senate, will make possible the maintenance of that balanced and harmonious constitution which I have described, especially if our next law is obeyed. It is as follows: *That order* [the Senate] *shall be free from dishonour, and shall be a model for the rest of the citizens.* . . .

. . . If we secure this, we shall have secured everything. For just as the whole State is habitually corrupted by the evil desires and the vices of its prominent men, so is it improved and reformed by self-restraint on their part. The reply made by our common friend, the eminent Lucius Lucullus, to a criticism of the luxury of his villa at Tusculum was considered a very neat one. He said that he had two neighbours, a Roman knight living above him, and a freedman below; as their villas also were most luxurious, he thought that he ought to have the same privilege as members of a lower order. But, Lucullus, do you not see that even their desire for luxury is your own fault? If you had not indulged in it, it would not have been permissible for them to do so. For who could have endured seeing these men's villas crowded with statues and paintings which were partly public property and partly sacred objects belonging to the gods? Who would not put an end to their inordinate desires, if those very men whose duty it was to put an end to them were not guilty of the same passions? For it is not so mischievous that men of high position do evil—though that is bad enough in itself—as it is that these men have so many imitators. For if you will turn your thoughts back to our early history, you will see that the character of our most prominent men has been reproduced in the whole State; whatever change took place in the lives of the prominent men has also taken place in the whole people. And we can be much more confident of the soundness of this theory than of that of our beloved Plato's. For he thought that the characteristics of a nation could be changed by changing the character of its music. But I believe that a transformation takes place in a nation's character when the habits and mode of living of its aristocracy are changed. For that reason men of the upper class who do wrong are especially dangerous to the State, because they not only indulge in vicious practices themselves, but also infect the whole commonwealth with their vices; and not only because they are corrupt, but also because they corrupt others, and do more harm by their bad examples than by their sins. But this law, which applies to the whole senatorial order, could be made even narrower in its application. For a few men—very few, in fact—on account of their high official position and great reputation, have the power either to corrupt the morals of the nation or to reform them.

But I have said enough on this subject, which is treated even more completely in my former work; therefore let us proceed to what follows.

[The Law on Voting]

The next law takes up the subject of votes, which, according to my decree, *shall not be concealed from citizens of high rank, and shall be free to the common people.* . . .

. . . Everyone knows that laws which provide a secret ballot have deprived the aristocracy of all its influence. And such a law was never desired by the people when they were free, but was demanded only when they were tyrannized over by the powerful men in the State. (For this very reason we have records of severer condemnations of powerful men under the oral method of voting than when the ballot was used.) Therefore means should have been found to deprive powerful leaders of the people's undue eagerness to support them with their votes even in the case of bad measures, but the people should not have been provided with a hiding-place, where they could conceal a mischievous vote by means of the ballot, and keep the aristocracy in ignorance of their real opinions. For these reasons no man of high character has ever proposed or supported [such] a measure. . . .

. . . But let me explain . . . that I am granting this freedom to the people in such a way as to ensure that the aristocracy shall have great influence and the opportunity to use it. For the text of my law in regard to votes is as follows: *they shall not be concealed from citizens of high rank, and shall be free to the people.* This law implies the repeal of all the recent laws which ensure the secrecy of the ballot in every possible way, providing as they do that no one shall look at a ballot, and that no one shall question or accost the voters. . . . If such provisions as these are made to interfere with the buying of votes, as they usually are, I do not criticize them; but if laws have never actually prevented bribery, then let the people have their ballots as a safeguard of their liberty, but with the provision that these ballots are to be shown and voluntarily exhibited to any of our best and most eminent citizens, so that the people may enjoy liberty also in this very privilege of honourably winning the favour of the aristocracy. By this means . . . the ballot condemns a smaller number than were condemned by the oral vote, because the people are satisfied with possessing the power; let them but keep that, and in everything else they are governed by influence and favour. And so, to leave out of account the corrupting effect of general donations upon the people's votes, do you not see that if bribery can ever be got rid of, the people, before they vote, will ask the opinion of the aristocracy? Hence our law grants the appearance of liberty, preserves the influence of the aristocracy, and removes the causes of dispute between the classes. . . .

[The Laws of Civil Rights]

Then come two excellent laws taken over from the Twelve Tables, one *prohibiting laws of personal exception,* and the other *forbidding cases in which the penalty is death or loss of citizenship from being tried elsewhere than before the greatest assembly.* For before the tribunes of the plebeians had begun their troublesome existence or had ever been thought of, what admirable measures our ancestors provided for the protection of future generations! They desired that no laws should be proposed which penalized particular individuals, for that is what a law of personal exception is. For nothing could be more unjust than such a law, when the very word "law" implies a decree or command which is binding upon all. They also desired that decisions affecting the fate of individuals should be made only in the Comitia Centuriata; for when the people are divided according to wealth, rank, and age, their decisions are wiser than when they meet without classification in the assembly of the tribes. . . .

30 BRUTUS, CASSIUS, CICERO, AND ANTONY, LETTERS: THE LEGACY OF CAESAR

The "mixed" constitution, which was a major source of Rome's greatness according to Polybius (see Document 28), slipped dangerously out of balance during the last century of the republic (133-31 B.C.). While the popular assemblies remained influential, effective political control was exercised by the Senate and by individual senators who proved strong or daring enough to challenge the authority of that august body. Membership in the Senate was reserved for those elected to the major magistracies, and the candidates for these magistracies came, except in rare cases, from a limited number of aristocratic families. In theory, no individual or his family could become permanently more powerful than his peers in the Senate. In fact, individual senators had to be assigned dominant positions as military commanders in the provinces, for the defense and extension of the Roman Empire. For the ambitious, the temptation to exploit such military authority for personal political ends was great. The Roman Republic, which had subdued mighty foreign adversaries, fell victim to its own leaders, and bitter civil wars ensued.

The end of these wars could come only with the ruin of the Roman state or with the triumph of one commander over his rivals and the submission of the Senate to his authority. The latter alternative seemed at last achieved by Gaius Julius Caesar (102?-44 B.C.), but his mastery of the empire was soon negated by assassins' daggers which struck him down on the Ides of March (March 15), 44 B.C.

The question of who was to end the long period of civil wars and become the new caesar, the first emperor of Rome, was not conclusively decided until the Battle of Actium (31 B.C.), but the true swan song of the republic belongs earlier, to the eighteen months following Caesar's assassination. During this period, the efforts of Brutus and Cicero to restore the Senate's prestige were thwarted. They, along with other major opponents of Caesar's authoritarianism, were eventually eliminated, and the stage was set for the climactic Battle of Actium between Antony and Octavian, the chief claimants to Caesar's succession.

The following selection consists of five letters written while Rome's future was in doubt. Each letter is written by and concerned with the major participants in the contest for empire. None of the writers anticipated publication, and they are prone to express themselves more candidly than they would in public utterance.

Whether for idealistic or opportunistic reasons, Brutus and Cassius had led the conspiracy against Caesar in the name of traditional republican liberty and opposition to a tyrant. Yet popular reaction to the assassination they committed was hostile, especially among Caesar's veterans. Mark Antony, an ambitious adjutant of Caesar and consul in 44 B.C., pretended at first to be conciliatory toward Brutus and Cassius but gradually tried to take advantage of popular sentiments for Caesar. The conspirators saw their hopes for tranquillity and the old order give way to a new threat of civil strife. In Rome, Cicero, the most famous lawyer and humanist of his day (see Document 29), supported the conspirators and denounced Antony in the Senate and Forum. Being somewhat vain, Cicero overestimated his influence as elder statesman of the Senate and hoped that he might moderate the hostile forces and save the Roman Republic. To strengthen his position, he cultivated Octavian, the legal heir to Caesar's property. Although very young, Octavian proved himself extremely adroit and, as the adopted son of Caesar, capitalized upon the sympathies of Caesar's veterans, thus assuring himself of military support. Cicero realized too late that he was merely a temporary convenience for Octavian, who cynically surrendered him to Antony's hatred in late 43 B.C. However, Brutus did not have any misconceptions about Octavian, and wrote frankly and bitterly to Atticus, Cicero's best friend. The bluntness of Brutus has led some scholars to doubt the authenticity of the letter, but most today accept it as a rare revelation of Brutus' inner feelings. Within a few months after the writing of the letter, Cicero was denounced, Cassius and Brutus fell on the battlefield of Pharsalus, and Antony and Octavian, who called themselves allies, made preparations for their future meeting at Actium.

M. Brutus and Cassius, Praetors, to M. Antonius, Consul

Lanuvium, end of May, 44 B.C.

Had we not been convinced of your sincerity and goodwill towards us, we should not have composed this letter to you; and we are assured, such being your habit of mind, that you will put the best possible construction upon it. We are told by letter that a large number of veterans have already assembled at Rome, and that as the Calends of June approach, the number will be much larger. Were we to entertain any doubt or apprehension as regards yourself, we should be untrue to ourselves. But seeing that we have put ourselves at your disposal, and in deference to your advice have dismissed our personal friends from the provincial towns, and have done so not only by edict but by letter as well, we surely deserve that you should admit us into your counsels, especially in a matter which affects ourselves.

And for that reason we beg of you to inform us of your attitude of mind towards us, whether you think we shall be safe amid so great a throng of veteran soldiers, who, we are told, are even thinking of replacing the altar,—a thing we believe that hardly anybody can desire or approve, who desires our own safety and honour.

Text: Reprinted by permission of the publishers and The Loeb Classical Library from *Cicero: The Letters to His Friends* (Cambridge, Mass.: Harvard University Press, 1952), II, 431-37.

That we have from the beginning fixed our eyes on tranquillity, and have sought nothing other than the liberty of the community, is made clear by what has happened. Nobody can play us false but yourself, and that is obviously foreign to your high character and integrity; but nobody else has the means of deceiving us; for it is you, and you alone, that we have trusted and shall continue to trust.

Our friends are terribly alarmed about us; and although they are fully assured of your good faith, still they are obsessed by the reflection that a mass of veterans can be more easily driven in any direction by anybody else than held in check by you. We ask you to reply to us on all points. For the allegation that such an order was issued to veterans because it was your intention to bring forward the question of their interests in the month of June is as frivolous as it is futile. Whom do you suppose to be likely to obstruct your intention, seeing that, as far as we are concerned, it is definitely decided that we shall take no action? Nobody has a right to impute to us an undue love of life, when there is nothing that can befall us unaccompanied by universal ruin and chaos.

Brutus and Cassius, Praetors, Send Greeting to M. Antony, Consul

Naples, August 4, 44 B.C.

Sir,—We have perused your letter, which closely follows the lines of your public proclamation, being insulting, intimidating, and by no means a proper letter for *you* to have addressed to *us*.

On our part, Sir, by no single injurious act have we provoked you, and we never believed that it would cause you surprise if we praetors, or indeed any men holding our position, should have appealed in a public manifesto for some concession from the consul. But if you resent our having ventured so far, permit us at least to regret that so small a favour is being refused by you to a Brutus and a Cassius.

As for your denial that you made any complaint as to the raising of troops, the requisitioning of sums of money, the tampering with the legions, and the sending of despatches across the sea, we indeed credit you with having made that denial in all good faith; at the same time, however, we refuse to acknowledge the truth of a single word of those allegations, and it surprises us that, though you kept silent about all this, you were so little able to control your anger as to reproach us with the death of Caesar.

This much, however, we would have you consider yourself—how far it is to be tolerated that praetors should not be allowed in the interests of harmony and liberty to waive by public announcement some of their own rights without being threatened with armed violence by the Consul. Your reliance on such methods has no terrors for us; for neither is it seemly or suitable for us, on our side, to bow our spirit before any peril, nor is it for Antony to claim lordship over those to whose efforts he owes his freedom. As for ourselves, were we urged by other considerations to wish to fan the flame of civil war, your letter would have no effect whatever; for the man who threatens has no authority among free men. But you are perfectly well aware that we are not to be driven either this way or that, and it is quite likely that the motive of your blustering is to give our prudence the appearance of panic.

Our sentiments are these: we are anxious that you should hold a high and honourable position in any constitution that is free, and we challenge you to no kind of hostility; but, for all that, we attach less value to your friendship than to our own liberty.

Consider again and again what you are undertaking, and what strength you have for it; and be sure you remember, not how long was Caesar's life, but how far from long was his reign. We pray to heaven that your counsels may conduce to the welfare of the State and of yourself; failing that, our prayer is that they may be as little harmful to yourself as is consistent with the welfare and honour of the Republic. Aug. 4th.

Cicero to Brutus

Rome, about April 21, 43 B.C.

Our cause seems in better circumstance; for I know for sure that you have been posted up about our achievements. The consuls have shown up true to their character, as I have often described it to you. But the boy Caesar is marvellously well endowed with manly character. If only I could direct and hold him, now that he is gathering strength from his official position and patronage, as easily as I have held him hitherto! That is altogether a harder task, though I am not losing confidence for all that; for the young man has made up his mind—and it was I who chiefly impressed it upon him—that we owe our safety to his efforts; and to be sure, if he had not drawn Antony away from the city, all would have been lost.

And yet, three or four days before this glorious event the entire citizen body, as if unnerved with fear, was fain to stream out to you with family and all; yet on April 20 they had recovered their nerve and would rather that you should come

Text: Reprinted by permission of the publishers and The Loeb Classical Library from M. Cary (trans.), *The Letters to Brutus*, in *Cicero: The Letters to His Friends* (Cambridge, Mass.: Harvard University Press, 1954), III, 647-49, 675-83.

here than that they should go to you. That was the day on which I gathered the full harvest of my hard toil and frequent vigils, if any substantial harvest can indeed accrue from a well-founded and genuine renown; for the crowd that flocked round me was as vast as our city could contain. I was escorted by it right up to the Capitol and then was made to take my stand on the Rostra amid huge acclamation and applause. I am not at all being vain; there is no justification for that. But all the same, I am deeply impressed by the unanimity of all classes, by their thanksgivings and felicitations, and for this reason, that it is glorious to achieve popularity in the cause of the people's safety. But I would sooner you heard about this from others.

Please spare no pains to keep me informed of your position and your policy, and bear in mind that your generosity must not give an impression of a loss of firm purpose. This is the Senate's, this is the people's conviction, that no enemy ever deserved more richly the utmost rigour of punishment than those citizens who took up arms against their country in this war. These are the men whom I castigate and pursue in all my pronouncements, with the approval of all loyal men. You must judge for yourself how you feel about this; my feeling is that the three brothers are one and all in the same case.

Brutus to Atticus

In camp, early June, 43 B.C.

You write to me that Cicero is surprised that I never refer to any of his activities. In view of your insistence, I shall record my opinions under duress from you. I know that Cicero has always acted with the best intentions; for what could be better approved in my eyes than his high spirit in matters of politics? But I have the impression that this most sagacious of men has acted on some occasions—how shall I put it?—unskilfully, or in his personal interest, seeing that he has not hesitated, "for the state's sake," to incur a feud with Antony when at the height of his power. I know not what to write to you, save just this, that Cicero has inflamed rather than checked the boy's greed and lawlessness and is lavishing upon him so many signs of obsequiousness, that he cannot refrain from making malicious remarks, which recoil upon him in a double sense, in that he has more than one man's blood on his hands and so must own up to murder on his own part, before he can reproach Casca as he does; and again, when he attacks Casca he follows in Bestia's wake. Granted that we do not boast at all hours of the Ides of March, in the same way as he carries the Nones of December on his tongue, does that give Cicero a better warrant to cast abuse on our magnificent deed that Bestia and Clodius possessed when they made a habit of carping at his consulship?

Our Cicero boasts to me, that in civilian garb he bore the brunt of Antony's armed assault. Of what benefit is this to me, if the reward claimed for the overthrow of Antony is to be the reversion to Antony's position, and if he who championed us against that evil has taken the lead in raising up another evil which will be more firmly based and more deeply rooted? Are we to humour him, on the theory that his present doings are inspired by fear of despotism, or of a despot—or of Antony in person? I for my part can feel no obligation to a man who draws the line at serving an *angry* despot, but does not protest against despotism as such. Nay more, a triumph, pay for the army, an incitation in every decree to brazen it out and scramble for the position of the man whose name he has assumed—is that what one expects of a consular or of Cicero?

Since you would not let me remain silent, you will read things which are bound to annoy you. To be sure I also can feel how much it hurts me to write to you in this strain, and I am well aware what are your views about the state, and how desperate too, though not incurable, you consider its condition. And I swear, Atticus, I do not blame you! Your age, your habits, your family dull your spirit; yes, and our friend Flavius too made me realize this!

But to return to Cicero. What is the difference between Salvidienus and him? Why, what more fullsome honours could the former propose? You say, "he fears even now the aftermath of the civil war." Does anyone hold a war that is as good as won in such dread, as not to give a thought to the power of the man who disposes of the victorious army, nor for the adventurousness of the boy, that these give occasion for the utmost alarm? Is this the reason for his particular line of action, that he thinks that everything should be laid at that man's feet, in anticipation of his demands, as a tribute to his greatness? What fools fear makes of men, that your precautions against the object of your dread should actually have the effect of drawing it on and bringing it over you, when there was a chance of steering clear of it! We carry our fear of death and exile and poverty too far. These of course appear to Cicero as the extremes of misfortune, and so long as he can find people who will give him what he wants and will cultivate and compliment him, he does not disdain servitude, so long as it is servitude with honour—if there can be any honour in suffering the deepest and most ignominious affronts.

Let Octavius then call Cicero "father," submit everything to him, compliment him, and express his gratitude, all the same the fact will show through, that his words are belied by his deeds. For what can be so inconsistent with decent human feeling as to treat like a parent a person who does not even count as a free man? Yet this is the object and proceeding of that worthy fellow, this the goal to which he is driving, that Octavius may be gracious to him. For my part I no longer pay any homage to those arts in which I know that Cicero is a virtuoso. For of what use to him are those extremely voluminous writings of his *In Defence of our Country's Freedom, On Dignified Conduct, On Death, On Exile, On Poverty*? Aye, how much surer a touch in those matters has Philippus, seeing that he has given away less to his stepson than Cicero gives away to a stranger. So let him cease positively to pursue us with his boastings and inflame our sores! For what advantage is it to us that Antony has suffered defeat, if his defeat merely serves to put the place which he held at another's disposal?

And yet your letter implies a doubt even now. Very well then! Let Cicero live on as a suppliant and an underling, since he is capable of such things, if he has no respect for his age or high rank or his achievements. For me, I am sure, no terms of servitude will ever be so attractive, but I shall wage war against the real enemy, that is, with monarchy and irregular commands and despotism and a power that presumes to set itself above the laws, no matter how good a man (as you say) Octavius is, though I never took him for that. Nay, our ancestors would not tolerate despotism even in a parent.

If my affection for you were not as great as is Octavius' fondness for Cicero in Cicero's own conviction, I should not have written to you in this tone. I am sorry that your abundant love for your own folk, aye, and for Cicero, is causing you vexation; but assure yourself of this, that my personal goodwill is unabated, though my judgement of him is greatly impaired: for you cannot prevent a man from seeing things in that particular light in which they present themselves to him.

I wish you had informed me of the terms for our dear Attica's betrothal; I should then have been able to give you something of my views. I am not surprised that Porcia's health is causing you anxiety. Finally, I shall be glad to do what you ask me, for your sisters are making the same request. I shall get to know the man and find out his intentions.

M. Antonius to Hirtius and Caesar

The Camp at Mutina, March 43 B.C.

The news of the death of Gaius Trebonius [one of the conspirators in the assassination of Julius Cæsar] caused me as much regret as joy. One cannot help being glad that a wicked wretch has given satisfaction to the ashes and bones of a most illustrious man, and that Divine Providence has manifested its power before the end of one revolving year in the punishment, or immediate prospect of the punishment, of parricide. On the other hand, one cannot repress a sigh that Dolabella [who killed Trebonius] at such a time as this should be adjudged a public enemy for having killed a murderer; and that the Roman people should care more for the son of a mere man-about-town than for Gaius Cæsar. But the most painful thing of all, Aulus Hirtius, is that you who were ennobled by the favours of Cæsar and left by him in a position which surprises yourself—and that you, young sir, who owe everything to his name—are acting in a way to sanction Dolabella's condemnation and to release this pestilent fellow from his state of siege. In order, I suppose, that Brutus and Cassius may be all-powerful! The fact is, you regard the present situation as you did the former, when you used to speak of Pompey's camp as "the senate." You have taken Cicero as your leader, who was beaten then; you are strengthening Macedonia with troops; you have intrusted Africa to Varus, who had been twice made a prisoner; you have sent Cassius to Syria; . . . you have supplied M. Brutus with money sent by Appuleius; you have commended the executions of Petrus and Menedemus, who were presented with the citizenship and were beloved by Cæsar. . . . You have got together an army of soldiers who are either legally mine, or who have served their time, on the pretext of destroying the murderers of Cæsar, and yet have forced them contrary to their expectations to assist in endangering the lives of their own quæstor or commander or fellow soldiers. In fact what have you not consented to or done which Gnæus Pompeius would do, if he could come to life again, or his son if he could regain his home? Lastly, you say that there can be no peace, unless I either allow Decimus Brutus to march out or supply him with corn. Do you mean to tell me that this is the opinion of the veterans who have not yet committed themselves, even though *you* have been corrupted by flattery and insidious gifts to come here? But, you will say, it is besieged soldiers that you are attempting to relieve. Them I have no objection to spare and to allow to go wherever you order them, on the one condition that they give *him* [Brutus] up to the death he has so richly deserved. You say in your letter that mention has been made

Text: Evelyn S. Shuckburgh (trans.), *The Letters of Cicero* (London: G. Bell & Sons, Ltd. 1901), IV, 189-92.

in the senate of a pacification, and that five consulars have been appointed as legates. It is difficult to believe that the men who violently repelled me, though I offered the most equitable terms, and was thinking nevertheless of mitigating even them, should be entertaining any thoughts of moderation or be likely to act with common charity. It is scarcely likely even that men who have declared Dolabella a public enemy for a most righteous act should be capable of sparing us who are at one with him in heart.

Wherefore I would have you consider which of the two courses is in the better taste and the more advantageous to your party—to punish the death of Trebonius or that of Cæsar: and whether it is more right that we should meet as foes and so allow the Pompeian cause so often defeated to revive, or that we should come to terms and so avoid being a laughingstock to our enemies, who will be the gainers whichever of us perishes? Such a spectacle as this Fortune herself as yet has shunned. She has not seen, that is, two armies of the same body politic fighting like gladiators with Cicero for a trainer, who has been so far successful as to deceive you both by the same formal honours by which he has boasted of having deceived Cæsar. For my part I am resolved not to submit to the degradation of myself or my friends, nor to desert the party which Pompey hated, nor to allow the veterans to be turned out of their homes, nor to be dragged off one by one to punishment, nor to break the faith which I pledged to Dolabella, nor to violate my compact with that devoted patriot Lepidus, nor to betray Plancus who is a sharer in my policy.

If the immortal gods, as I hope they will, aid me in my plain and honest course, I shall survive with satisfaction to myself; but if a different fate awaits me, I feel an anticipatory pleasure in the punishment which will befall you. For if the Pompeians are so arrogant in defeat, I would rather you than I should experience what they will be in victory. In fact the upshot of my decision is this: I am ready to put up with the injuries done to my party, if they will either consent to forget that they are Cæsar's assassins, or are prepared to join us in avenging his death. I cannot believe in legates approaching a place which is being at the same time menaced by war. When they have arrived I shall learn their demands.

INTERPRETATIONS OF THE COLLAPSE OF THE REPUBLIC

31 RONALD SYME, *THE ROMAN REVOLUTION*: THE MYTH OF CAESAR

Rome, during most of the first century B.C., was the political battleground between the *populares*, or popular party, and the *optimates*, or senatorial party, both of whom strove for control of the Roman state. In the end neither party won out, for both the popular leaders and the aristocrats became increasingly dependent upon the army, a collection of mercenaries uninterested in politics and quite willing to support whatever leader offered them the fattest rewards.

In order to secure land and booty and thereby retain the allegiance of the army, both parties were forced to wage a series of foreign wars, to the neglect of more pressing domestic needs at Rome. Clearly the army was no instrument for effecting political reform. What emerged in the mid-first century B.C. was neither popular reform nor a return to the older constitutional ways, but instead, a military depotism which only contributed further to the decline of the Roman state.

One of the most gifted and at the same time most controversial Romans in this century-long struggle was the military commander Gaius Julius Caesar (102?-44 B.C.), whose exploits on behalf of the popular party have made his name equal with that of Napoleon or Alexander the Great. In his own day, however, judgments of Caesar varied. As the contemporary Oxford scholar Ronald Syme puts it, "The enemies of Caesar spread rumours to discredit the living Dictator. Caesar dead became a god and a myth, passing from the realm of history into literature and legend, declamation and propaganda."

According to Syme, Caesar was much more than a myth. He was a realist, an opportunist, and a superb politician. He was essentially conservative, and those of his supporters who expected radical social changes after his assumption of power were doomed to disappointment. Syme views the civil strife that was going on in Rome in the middle of the first century as a struggle between oligarchies. There was always, he says, a small group in control, and thus it is a mistake to view the period in terms of a class or constitutional struggle.

In the selection below, from *The Roman Revolution* (1939), Syme examines Caesar's actions in assuming leadership of the Roman state, cautioning the reader that Caesar's acts do not reveal his ultimate designs and that "no statement of unrealized intentions is a safe guide to history."

Sulla was the first Roman to lead an army against Rome. Not of his own choosing—his enemies had won control of the government and deprived him of the command against Mithridates. Again, when he landed in Italy after an absence of nearly five years, force was his only defence against the party that had attacked a proconsul who was fighting the wars of the Republic in the East. Sulla had all the ambition of a Roman noble: but it was not his ambition to seize power through civil strife and hold it, supreme and alone. His work done, the Dictator resigned.

The conquest of Gaul, the war against Pompeius and the establishment of the Dictatorship of Caesar are events that move in a harmony so swift and sure as to appear pre-ordained; and history has sometimes been written as though Caesar set the tune from the beginning, in the knowledge that monarchy was the panacea for the world's ills, and with the design to achieve it by armed force. Such a view is too simple to be historical.

Caesar strove to avert any resort to open war. Both before and after the outbreak of hostilities he sought to negotiate with Pompeius. Had Pompeius listened and consented to an interview, their old *amicitia* [friendship] might have been repaired. With the nominal primacy of Pompeius recognized, Caesar and his adherents would capture the government—and perhaps reform the State. Caesar's enemies were afraid of that—and so was Pompeius. After long wavering Pompeius chose at last to save the oligarchy. Further, the proconsul's proposals as conveyed to the Senate were moderate and may not be dismissed as mere manoeuvres for position or for time to bring up his armies. Caesar knew how small was the party willing to provoke a war. As the artful motion of a Caesarian tribune had revealed, an overwhelming majority in the Senate, nearly four hundred against twenty-two, wished both dynasts to lay down their extraordinary commands. A rash and factious minority prevailed.

The precise legal points at issue in Caesar's claim to stand for the consulate in absence and retain his province until the end of the year 49 B.C. are still matters of controversy. If they were ever clear, debate and misrepresentation soon clouded truth and equity. The nature of the political crisis is less obscure. Caesar and his associates in power had thwarted or suspended the constitution for their own ends many times in the past. Exceptions had been made before in favour of other dynasts; and Caesar asserted both legal and moral rights to preferential treatment. In the last resort his rank, prestige and honour, summed up in the Latin word *dignitas* [political and social standing], were all at stake: to Caesar, as he claimed, 'his *dignitas* had ever been dearer than life itself.' Sooner than surrender it, Caesar appealed to arms. A constitutional pretext was provided by the violence of his adversaries: Caesar stood in defence of the rights of the tribunes and the liberties of the Roman People. But that was not the plea which Caesar himself valued most—it was his personal honour.

His enemies appeared to have triumphed. They had driven a wedge between the two dynasts, winning over to their side the power and prestige of Pompeius. They would be able to deal with Pompeius later. It might not come to open war; and Pompeius was still in their control so long as he was not at the head of an army in the field. Upon Caesar they had thrust the choice between civil war and political extinction. But Caesar refused to join the long roll of Pompeius' victims, to be superseded like Lucullus, to be discarded and disgraced as had been Gabinius, the governor of Syria. If he gave way now, it was the end. Returning to Rome a private citizen, Caesar would at once be prosecuted by his enemies for extortion or treason. They would secure lawyers reputed for eloquence, high principle and patriotism. Cato was waiting for him, rancorous and incorruptible. A jury carefully selected, with moral support from soldiers of Pompeius stationed around the court, would bring in the inevitable verdict. After that, nothing for Caesar but to join the exiled Milo at Massilia and enjoy the red mullet and Hellenic culture of that university city.

Caesar was constrained to appeal to his army for protection. At last the enemies of Caesar had succeeded in ensnaring Pompeius and in working the constitution against the craftiest politician of the day: he was declared a public enemy if he did not lay down his command before a certain day. By invoking constitutional sanctions against Caesar, a small faction misrep-

Text: Ronald Syme, *The Roman Revolution* (Oxford: The Clarendon Press, 1939), pp. 47-60. Reprinted by permission of The Clarendon Press.

resented the true wishes of a vast majority in the Senate, in Rome, and in Italy. They pretended that the issue lay between a rebellious proconsul and legitimate authority. Such venturesome expedients are commonly the work of hot blood and muddled heads. The error was double and damning. Disillusion followed swiftly. Even Cato was dismayed. It had confidently been expected that the solid and respectable classes in the towns of Italy would rally in defence of the authority of the Senate and the liberties of the Roman People, that all the land would rise as one man against the invader. Nothing of the kind happened. Italy was apathetic to the war-cry of the Republic in danger, sceptical about its champions.

The very virtues for which the propertied classes were sedulously praised by politicians at Rome forbade intervention in a struggle which was not their own. Pompeius might stamp with his foot in the land of Italy, as he had rashly boasted. No armed legions rose at his call. Even Picenum, his own barony, went over to the enemy without a blow. No less complete the military miscalculation: the *imperator* did not answer to his repute as a soldier. Insecurity and the feeling of guilt, added to inadequate preparation for war, may have impaired his decision. Yet his plan was no mere makeshift, as it appeared to his allies, but subtle and grandiose—to evacuate Italy, leaving Caesar entrapped between the legions of Spain and the hosts of all the East, and then to return, like Sulla, to victory and to power.

Caesar, it is true, had only a legion to hand: the bulk of his army was still far away. But he swept down the eastern coast of Italy, gathering troops, momentum and confidence as he went. Within two months of the crossing of the Rubicon he was master of Italy. Pompeius made his escape across the Adriatic carrying with him several legions and a large number of senators, a grievous burden of revenge and recrimination. The enemies of Caesar had counted upon capitulation or a short and easy war.

They had lost the first round. Then a second blow, quite beyond calculation: before the summer was out the generals of Pompeius in Spain were outmanœuvred and overcome. Yet even so, until the legions joined battle on the plain of Pharsalus, the odds lay heavily against Caesar. Fortune, the devotion of his veteran legionaries and the divided counsels of his adversaries secured the crowning victory. But three years more of fighting were needed to stamp out the last and bitter resistance of the Pompeian cause in Africa and in Spain.

'They would have it thus,' said Caesar as he gazed upon the Roman dead at Pharsalus, half in patriot grief for the havoc of civil war, half in impatience and resentment. They had cheated Caesar of the true glory of a Roman aristocrat— to contend with his peers for primacy, not to destroy them. His enemies had the laugh of him in death. Even Pharsalus was not the end. His former ally, the great Pompeius, glorious from victories in all quarters of the world, lay unburied on an Egyptian beach, slain by a renegade Roman, the hireling of a foreign king. Dead, too, and killed by Romans, were Caesar's rivals and enemies, many illustrious consulars. Ahenobarbus fought and fell at Pharsalus, and Q. Metellus Scipio ended worthy of his ancestors; while Cato chose to fall by his own hand rather than witness the domination of Caesar and the destruction of the Free State.

That was the nemesis of ambition and glory, to be thwarted in the end. After such wreckage, the task of rebuilding confronted him, stern and thankless. Without the sincere and patriotic cooperation of the governing class, the attempt would be all in vain, the mere creation of arbitrary power, doomed to perish in violence.

It was rational to suspend judgement about the guilt of the Civil War. Pompeius had been little better, if at all, than his younger and more active rival, a spurious and disquieting champion of legitimate authority when men recalled the earlier career and inordinate ambition of the Sullan partisan who had first defied and then destroyed the Senate's rule. Each had sought armed domination. Had Pompeius conquered in battle, the Republic could hardly have survived. A few years, and Pompeius the Dictator would have been assassinated in the Senate by honourable men, at the foot of his own statue.

That was not the point. The cause of Pompeius had become the better cause. Caesar could not compete. Though interest on each side claimed more adherents than principle, interest with the Pompeians usurped the respectable garb of legality. Many of Caesar's partisans were frank adventurers, avid for gain and advancement, some for revolution.

Yet for all that, in the matter of Caesar's party the contrast of disreputable scoundrels on the one side and high-born patriots on the other is as schematic and misleading as the contrast between the aspirant to autocracy and the forces of law and order. Caesar's following was heterogeneous in composition—at its kernel a small group of men paramount in social distinction, not merely *nobiles* [office holders] but patrician; on the outer fringe, many excellent Roman knights, 'the flower of Italy.' The composition of Caesar's party and the character of those adherents with whom he supplemented the Senate and reinforced the oligarchy of government, an important topic, demands separate treatment.

Many senators tried to remain neutral, including several eminent consulars, some of whom Caesar won to sympathy, if not to active support, by his studious moderation. To the survivors of the defeated faction he behaved with public and ostentatious clemency. They were members of his own class: he had not wished to make war upon them or to exterminate the Roman aristocracy. But these proud adversaries did not always leap forward with alacrity to be exhibited as object-lessons of the *clementia* [mercifulness] and *magnitudo animi* [broadmindedness] of Caesar. They took the gift of life and restoration with suppressed resentment: some refused even to ask.

Under these unfavourable auspices, a Sulla but for *clementia*, a Gracchus but lacking a revolutionary programme, Caesar established his Dictatorship. His rule began as the triumph of a faction in civil war: he made it his task to transcend faction, and in so doing wrought his own destruction. A champion of the People, he had to curb the People's rights, as Sulla had done. To rule, he needed the support of the *nobiles*, yet he had to curtail their privileges and repress their dangerous ambitions.

In name and function Caesar's office was to set the State in order again (*rei publicae constituendae*). Despite odious memories of Sulla, the choice of the Dictatorship was recommended by its comprehensive powers and freedom from the tribunician veto. Caesar knew that secret enemies would soon direct that deadly weapon against one who had used it with such dexterity in the past and who more recently claimed to be asserting the rights of the tribunes, the liberty of the Roman People. He was not mistaken. Yet he required special powers: after a civil war the need was patent. The Dictator's task might well demand several years. In 46 B.C. his powers were prolonged to a tenure of ten years, an ominous sign. A gleam of hope that the emergency period would be quite short flickered up for a moment, to wane at once and perish utterly. In January 44 B.C. Caesar was voted the Dictatorship for life. About the same time decrees of the Senate ordained that an oath of allegiance should be taken in his name. Was this the measure of his ordering of the Roman State? Was this a *res publica constituta* [the State restored]?

It was disquieting. Little had been done to repair the ravages of civil war and promote social regeneration. For that there was sore need, as both his adherents and his former adversaries pointed out. From Pompeius, from Cato and from the oligarchy, no hope of reform. But Caesar seemed different: he had consistently advocated the cause of the oppressed, whether Roman, Italian or provincial. He had shown that he was not afraid of vested interests. But Caesar was not a revolutionary. He soon disappointed the rapacity or the idealism of certain of his partisans who had hoped for an assault upon the moneyed classes, a drastic reduction of debts and a programme of revolution that should be radical and genuine. Only the usurers approved of Caesar, so Caelius complained quite early in the Civil War. Not everybody was as outspoken or as radical as Caelius, who passed from words to deeds and perished in an armed rising. Cicero, when lauding the clemency and magnanimity of the Dictator, took the opportunity to sketch a modest programme of moral and social reform. Having written treatises about the Roman Commonwealth some years earlier, he may have expected to be consulted upon these weighty matters. But Cicero's hopes of *res publica constituta* were soon dashed. The Dictator himself expressed alarming opinions about the *res publica*—'it was only a name: Sulla, by resigning supreme power, showed that he was an ignorant fellow'.

Caesar postponed decision about the permanent ordering of the State. It was too difficult. Instead, he would set out for the wars again, to Macedonia and to the eastern frontier of the Empire. At Rome he was hampered: abroad he might enjoy his conscious mastery of men and events, as before in Gaul. Easy victories—but not the urgent needs of the Roman People.

About Caesar's ultimate designs there can be opinion, but no certainty. The acts and projects of his Dictatorship do not reveal them. For the rest, the evidence is partisan—or posthumous. No statement of unrealized intentions is a safe guide to history, for it is unverifiable and therefore the most attractive form of misrepresentation. The enemies of Caesar spread rumours to discredit the living Dictator: Caesar dead became a god and a myth, passing from the realm of history into literature and legend, declamation and propaganda. By Augustus he was exploited in two ways. The avenging of Caesar fell to his adopted son who assumed the title of *Divi filius* [son of a god] as consecration for the ruler of Rome. That was all he affected to inherit from Caesar, the halo. The god was useful, but not the Dictator: Augustus was careful sharply to discriminate between *Dictator* and *Princeps* [leader, chief man]. Under his rule Caesar the Dictator was either suppressed outright or called up from time to time to enhance the contrast between the unscrupulous adventurer who destroyed the Free

State in his ambition and the modest magistrate who restored the Republic. In its treatment of Caesar the inspired literature of the Augustan Principate is consistent and instructive. Though in different words, Virgil, Horace and Livy tell the same tale and point the same moral.

Yet speculation cannot be debarred from playing round the high and momentous theme of the last designs of Caesar the Dictator. It has been supposed and contended that Caesar either desired to establish or had actually inaugurated an institution unheard of in Rome and unimagined there—monarchic rule, despotic and absolute, based upon worship of the ruler, after the pattern of the monarchies of the Hellenistic East. Thus may Caesar be represented as the heir in all things of Alexander the Macedonian and as the anticipator of Caracalla, a king and a god incarnate, levelling class and nation, ruling a subject, united and uniform world by right divine.

This extreme simplification of long and diverse ages of history seems to suggest that Caesar alone of contemporary Roman statesmen possessed either a wide vision of the future or a singular and elementary blindness to the present. But this is only a Caesar of myth or rational construction, a lay-figure set up to point a contrast with Pompeius or Augustus—as though Augustus did not assume a more than human name and found a monarchy, complete with court and hereditary succession; as though Pompeius, the conqueror of the East and of every continent, did not exploit for his own vanity the resemblance to Alexander in warlike fame and even in bodily form. Caesar was a truer Roman than either of them.

The complete synthesis in the person of Caesar of hereditary monarchy and divine worship is difficult to establish on the best of contemporary evidence, the voluminous correspondence of Cicero. Moreover, the whole theme of divine honours is fertile in misunderstandings. After death Caesar was enrolled among the gods of the Roman State by the interested device of the leaders of the Caesarian party. It might appear that subsequent accounts have been guilty of attributing a part at least of the cult of *Divus Julius* [deified Julius] to that very different person, Caesar the Dictator.

The rule of Caesar could well be branded as monarchy on a partisan or conventional estimate. The terms 'rex' [king] and 'regnum' [kingdom] belong to the vocabulary of Roman political invective, applicable alike to the domination of Sulla and the arbitrary power exercised by Cicero during his consulate—for the new man from Arpinum was derided as 'the first foreign king at Rome since the Tarquinii.' It was to silence rumor that Caesar made an ostentatious refusal of the diadem at a public ceremony. 'Caesarem se, non regem esse.' Beyond doubt the Dictator's powers were as considerable as those of a monarch. Caesar would have been the first to admit it: he needed neither the name nor the diadem. But monarchy presupposes hereditary succession, for which no provision was made by Caesar. The heir to Caesar's name, his grand-nephew, attracted little attention at the time of his first appearance in Rome. The young man had to build up a faction for himself and make his own way along the road to power, beginning as a military demagogue.

If Caesar must be judged, it is by facts and not by alleged intentions. As his acts and his writings reveal him, Caesar stands out as a realist and an opportunist. In the short time at his disposal he can hardly have made plans for a long future or laid the foundation of a consistent government. Whatever it might be, it would owe more to the needs of the moment than to alien or theoretical models. More important the business in hand: it was expedited in swift and arbitrary fashion. Caesar made plans and decisions in the company of his intimates and secretaries: the Senate voted but did not deliberate. As the Dictator was on the point of departing in the spring of 44 B.C. for several years of campaigning in the Balkans and the East, he tied up magistracies and provincial commands in advance by placing them, according to the traditional Roman way, in the hands of loyal partisans, or of reconciled Pompeians whose good sense should guarantee peace. For that period, at least, a salutary pause from political activity: with the lapse of time the situation might become clearer in one way or another.

At the moment it was intolerable: the autocrat became impatient, annoyed by covert opposition, petty criticism and laudations of dead Cato. That he was unpopular he well knew. 'For all his genius, Caesar could not see a way out', as one of his friends was subsequently to remark. And there was no going back. To Caesar's clear mind and love of rapid decision, this brought a tragic sense of impotence and frustration—he had been all things and it was no good. He had surpassed the good fortune of Sulla Felix and the glory of Pompeius Magnus. In vain—reckless ambition had ruined the Roman State and baffled itself in the end. Of the melancholy that descended upon Caesar there stands the best of testimony —'my life has been long enough, whether reckoned in years or in renown.' The words were remembered. The most eloquent of his contemporaries did not disdain to plagiarize them.

The question of ultimate intentions becomes irrelevant. Caesar was slain for what he was, not for what he might become. The assumption of a Dictatorship for life seemed to mock and dispel all hope of a return to normal and constitutional government. His rule was far worse than the violent and illegal domination of Pompeius. The present was unbearable, the future hopeless. It was necessary to strike at once—absence, the passage of time and the solid benefits of peace and order might abate men's resentment against Caesar, insensibly disposing their minds to servitude and monarchy. A faction recruited from the most diverse elements planned and carried out the assassination of the Dictator.

That his removal would be no remedy but a source of greater ills to the Commonwealth, the Dictator himself observed. His judgement was vindicated in blood and suffering; and posterity has seen fit to condemn the act of the Liberators, for so they were styled, as worse than a crime—a folly. The verdict is hasty and judges by results. It is all too easy to label the assassins as fanatic adepts of Greek theories about the supreme virtue of tyrannicide, blind to the true nature of political catch-words and the urgent needs of the Roman State. The character and pursuits of Marcus Brutus, the representative figure in the conspiracy, might lend plausible colouring to such a theory. Yet it is in no way evident that the nature of Brutus would have been very different had he never opened a book of Stoic or Academic philosophy. Moreover, the originator of the plot, the dour and military Cassius, was of the Epicurean persuasion and by no means a fanatic. As for the tenets of the Stoics, they could support doctrines quite distasteful to Roman Republicans, namely monarchy or the brotherhood of man. The Stoic teaching, indeed, was nothing more than a corroboration and theoretical defence of certain traditional virtues of the governing class in an aristocratic and republican state. Hellenic culture does not explain Cato, and the *virtus* about which Brutus composed a volume was a Roman quality, not an alien importation.

The word means courage, the ultimate virtue of a free man. With *virtus* go *libertas* [freedom] and *fides* [trust], blending in a proud ideal of character and conduct—constancy in purpose and act, independence of habit, temper and speech, honesty and loyalty. Privilege and station imposed duties, to family, class and equals in the first place, but also towards clients and dependents. No oligarchy could survive if its members refused to abide by the rules, to respect 'liberty and the laws.'

To his contemporaries, Marcus Brutus, firm in spirit, upright and loyal, in manner grave and aloof, seemed to embody that ideal of character, admired by those who did not care to imitate.

His was not a simple personality—but passionate, intense and repressed. Nor was his political conduct wholly to be predicted. Brutus might well have been a Caesarian—neither he nor Caesar were predestined partisans of Pompeius. Servilia reared her son to hate Pompeius, schemed for the Caesarian alliance and designed that Brutus should marry Caesar's daughter. Her plan was annulled by the turn of events in the fatal consulate of Metellus. Caesar was captured by Pompeius: Julia, the bride intended for Brutus, pledged the alliance.

After this the paths of Brutus and of Caesar diverged sharply for eleven years. But Brutus, after Pharsalus, at once gave up a lost cause, receiving pardon from Caesar, high favour, a provincial command and finally the praetorship in 44 B.C. Yet Cato, no sooner dead, asserted the old domination over his nephew more powerfully than ever in life. Brutus came to feel shame for his own disloyalty: he composed a pamphlet in honour of the Republican who died true to his principles and to his class. Then he strengthened the family tie and obligation of vengeance yet further by divorcing his Claudia and marrying his cousin Porcia, Bibulus' widow. No mistake about the meaning of that act; and Servilia disapproved. There were deeper causes still in Brutus' resolve to slay the tyrant—envy of Caesar and the memory of Caesar's amours with Servilia, public and notorious. Above all, to Brutus as to Cato, who stood by the ancient ideals, it seemed that Caesar, avid for splendour, glory and power, ready to use his birth and station to subvert his own class, was an ominous type, the monarchic aristocrat, recalling the kings of Rome and fatal to any Republic.

Brutus and his allies might invoke philosophy or an ancestor who had liberated Rome from the Tarquinii, the first consul of the Republic and founder of *Libertas*. Dubious history—and irrelevant. The Liberators knew what they were about. Honourable men grasped the assassin's dagger to slay a Roman aristocrat, a friend and a benefactor, for better reasons than that. They stood, not merely for the traditions and the institutions of the Free State, but very precisely for the dignity and the interests of their own order. Liberty and the laws are high-sounding words. They will often be rendered, on a cool estimate, as privilege and vested interests.

It is not necessary to believe that Caesar planned to establish at Rome a 'Hellenistic Monarchy', whatever meaning may attach to that phrase. The Dictatorship was enough. The rule of the *nobiles*, he could see, was an anachronism in a world-empire; and so was the power of the Roman plebs when all Italy enjoyed the franchise. Caesar in truth was more conservative and Roman than many have fancied; and no Roman conceived of government save through an oligarchy. But Caesar was being forced into an autocratic position. It meant the lasting domination of one man instead of the rule of the law, the constitution and the Senate; it announced the triumph soon or late of new forces and new ideas, the elevation of the army and the provinces, the depression of the traditional governing class. Caesar's autocracy appeared to be much more than a temporary expedient to liquidate the heritage of the Civil War and reinvigorate the organs of the Roman State. It was going to last—and the Roman aristocracy was not to be permitted to govern and exploit the Empire in its own fashion. The tragedies of history do not arise from the conflict of conventional right and wrong. They are more august and more complex. Caesar and Brutus each had right on his side.

The new party of the Liberators was not homogeneous in origin or in motive. The resentment of pardoned Pompeians, thwarted ambition, personal feuds and personal interest masked by the profession of high principle, family tradition and the primacy of civic over private virtue, all these were in the game. Yet in the forefront of this varied company stood trusted officers of the Dictator, the generals of the Gallic and Civil Wars, rewarded already for service or designated to high office. Their coalition with Pompeians and Republicans calls for explanation.

Without a party a statesman is nothing. He sometimes forgets that awkward fact. If the leader or principal agent of a faction goes beyond the wishes of his allies and emancipates himself from control, he may have to be dropped or suppressed. The reformer Ti. Gracchus was put up by a small group of influential consulars. These prudent men soon refused further support to the rash, self-righteous tribune when he plunged into illegal courses. The political dynast Crassus used Catilina as his agent. Catilina could not, or would not, understand that reform or revolution had no place in the designs of his employer. Crassus drew back, and Catilina went on, to his ruin.

When Caesar took the Dictatorship for life and the sworn allegiance of senators, it seemed clear that he had escaped from the shackles of party to supreme and personal rule. For this reason, certain of the most prominent of his adherents combined with Republicans and Pompeians to remove their leader. The Caesarian party thus split by the assassination of the Dictator none the less survived, joined for a few months with Republicans in a new and precarious front of security and vested interests led by the Dictator's political deputy until a new leader [i.e., Octavian, Augustus Caesar], emerging unexpected, at first tore it in pieces again, but ultimately, after conquering the last of his rivals, converted the old Caesarian party into a national government in a transformed State. . . .

32 THEODOR MOMMSEN, *THE HISTORY OF ROME:* THE HERO IN HISTORY

It is almost an axiom that controversial men breed controversial history. Different historians may have access to identical sources, but the way in which each selects and organizes the sources to give an interpretation to a Caesar, a Cromwell, or a Bismarck largely reflects the historian's political or intellectual presentiments. True, historians cannot distort or invent as long as informed critics are able to correct and challenge, and the writers of histories usually bring to their task a certain professional detachment and the perspective of years or centuries. But nevertheless, their treatment of history is influenced by the temper of their times.

It is thus natural that we should find contrary characterizations of Julius Caesar, a controversial figure in his own and later times. Ronald Syme (see Document 31) is a twentieth-century scholar whose interpretation is calm and scrutinizing and whose prose is dispassionate, as befits an age devoted to scientific probing, reservation, and questioning. On the other hand, Theodor Mommsen, a gifted nineteenth-century German scholar of ancient history, expresses an outlook highly colored by the romanticism of the age in which he wrote—an age marked by a substantial revival of interest in the ancient world and an absorbing concern with great men who "create" history. In the selection below, from his *The History of Rome* (4 vols., 1854-1856), Mommsen sees in Caesar the ideal ruler, the king who never plays the monarch nor is afflicted by the intemperance of the tyrant. "In his character as a man as well as in his place in history," he writes, "Caesar occupies a position where the great contrasts of existence meet and balance each other. Of mighty creative power and yet at the same time of the most penetrating judgment; no longer a youth and not yet an old man; of the highest energy of will and the highest capacity of execution; filled with republican ideals and at the same time born to be a king; a Roman in the deepest essence of his nature, and yet called to reconcile and combine in himself as well as in the outer world the Roman and Hellenic types of culture—Caesar was the entire and perfect man."

If Caesar was not everything that Mommsen thought him to be, he did possess great strength of purpose and rose successfully to meet many of the tribulations he faced. He conquered Gaul, seized Rome, and consolidated his hegemony throughout the eastern edges of the Mediterranean. It would seem too, in retrospect, that Caesar was correct in his perception that Rome was no longer a city-state and could not be governed as one and that a new form of rule had to be adopted. Whether he chose the best means of implementing a new constitution is another question.

Mommsen treats Caesar as the manipulator of events, whereas for Syme, the events were the manipulator of Caesar. It is the old question, does history make the man, or does the man make history?

Caesar was thoroughly a realist and a man of sense; and whatever he undertook and achieved was pervaded and guided by the cool sobriety which constitutes the most marked peculiarity of his genius. To this he owed the power of living energetically in the present, undisturbed either by recollection or by expectation; to this he owed the capacity of acting at any moment with collected vigour, and of applying his whole genius even to the smallest and most incidental enterprise; to this he owed the many-sided power with which he grasped and mastered whatever understanding can comprehend and will can compel; to this he owed the self-possessed ease with which he arranged his periods as well as projected his campaigns; to this he owed the "marvellous serenity" which remained steadily with him through good and evil days; to this he owed the complete independence, which admitted of no control by favourite or by mistress, or even by friend. It resulted, moreover, from this clearness of judgment that Caesar never formed to himself illusions regarding the power of fate and the ability of man; in his case the friendly veil was lifted up, which conceals from man the inadequacy of his working. Prudently as he laid his plans and considered all possibilities, the feeling was never absent from his breast that in all things fortune, that is to say accident, must bestow success; and with this may be connected the circumstance that he so often played a desperate game with destiny, and in particular again and again hazarded his person with daring indifference. As indeed occasionally men of predominant sagacity betake themselves to a pure game of hazard, so there was in Caesar's rationalism a point at which it came in some measure into contact with mysticism.

Gifts such as these could not fail to produce a statesman. From early youth, accordingly, Caesar was a statesman in the deepest sense of the term, and his aim was the highest which man is allowed to propose to himself—the political, military, intellectual, and moral regeneration of his own deeply decayed nation, and of the still more deeply decayed Hellenic nation intimately akin to his own. The hard school of thirty years' experience changed his views as to the means by which this aim was to be reached; his aim itself remained the same in the times of his hopeless humiliation and of his unlimited plenitude of power, in the times when as demagogue and conspirator he stole towards it by paths of darkness, and in those when, as joint possessor of the supreme power and then as monarch, he worked at his task in the full light of day before the eyes of the world. All the measures of a permanent kind that proceeded from him at the most various times assume their appropriate places in the great building-plan. We cannot therefore properly speak of isolated achievements of Caesar; he did nothing isolated. . . .

If the old, in every respect vicious, state of things was to be successfully got rid of and the commonwealth was to be renovated, it was necessary first of all that the country should be practically tranquillized and that the ground should be cleared from the rubbish with which since the recent catastrophe it was everywhere strewn. In this work Caesar set out from the principle of the reconciliation of the hitherto subsisting parties or, to put it more correctly—for, where the antagonistic principles are irreconcilable, we cannot speak of real reconciliation—from the principle that the arena, on which the nobility and

Text: Theodor Mommsen, *The History of Rome*, trans. William Purdie Dickson (London: Macmillan & Co., Ltd., 1913), V, 307-09, 315-19, 415-17, 419-21, 427-28.

the populace had hitherto contended with each other, was to be abandoned by both parties, and that both were to meet together on the ground of the new monarchical constitution. First of all therefore all the older quarrels of the republican past were regarded as done away for ever and irrevocably. While Caesar gave orders that the statues of Sulla which had been thrown down by the mob of the capital on the news of the battle of Pharsalus should be re-erected, and thus recognized the fact that it became history alone to sit in judgment on that great man, he at the same time cancelled the last remaining effects of Sulla's exceptional laws, recalled from exile those who had been banished in the times of the Cinnan and Sertorian troubles, and restored to the children of those outlawed by Sulla their forfeited privilege of eligibility to office. In like manner all those were restored, who in the preliminary stage of the recent catastrophe had lost their seat in the senate or their civil existence through sentence of the censors or political process, especially through the impeachments raised on the basis of the exceptional laws of 702 [52 B.C.]. Those alone who had put to death the proscribed for money remained, as was reasonable, still under attainder; and Milo, the most daring *condottiere* of the senatorial party, was excluded from the general pardon.

Far more difficult than the settlement of these questions which already belonged substantially to the past was the treatment of the parties confronting each other at the moment—on the one hand Caesar's own democratic adherents, on the other hand the overthrown aristocracy. That the former should be, if possible, still less satisfied than the latter with Caesar's conduct after the victory and with his summons to abandon the old standing-ground of party, was to be expected. Caesar himself desired doubtless on the whole the same issue which Gaius Gracchus had contemplated; but the designs of the Caesarians were no longer those of the Gracchans. The Roman popular party had been driven onward in gradual progression from reform to revolution, from revolution to anarchy, from anarchy to a war against property; they celebrated among themselves the memory of the reign of terror and now adorned the tomb of Catilina, as formerly that of the Gracchi, with flowers and garlands; they had placed themselves under Caesar's banner, because they expected him to do for them what Catilina had not been able to accomplish. But as it speedily became plain that Caesar was very far from intending to be the testamentary executor of Catilina, and that the utmost which debtors might expect from him was some alleviations of payment and modifications of procedure, indignation found loud vent in the inquiry, For whom then had the popular party conquered, if not for the people? and the rabble of this description, high and low, out of pure chagrin at the miscarriage of their politico-economic Saturnalia began first to coquet with the Pompeians, and then even during Caesar's absence of nearly two years from Italy (Jan. 706–autumn 707 [48-47 B.C.]) to instigate there a second civil war within the first. . . .

. . . Against a rabble of this sort, which had nothing to do with any political question at all, but solely with a war against property—as against gangs of banditti—the mere existence of a strong government is sufficient; and Caesar was too great and too considerate to busy himself with the apprehensions which the Italian alarmists felt regarding these communists of that day, and thereby unduly to procure a false popularity for his monarchy.

While Caesar thus might leave, and actually left, the late democratic party to the process of decomposition which had already in its case advanced almost to the utmost limit, he had on the other hand, with reference to the former aristocratic party possessing a far greater vitality, not to bring about its dissolution—which time alone could accomplish—but to pave the way for and initiate it by a proper combination of repression and conciliation. Among minor measures, Caesar, even from a natural sense of propriety, avoided exasperating the fallen party by empty sarcasm; he did not triumph over his conquered fellow-burgesses; he mentioned Pompeius often and always with respect, and caused his statue overthrown by the people to be re-erected at the senate-house, when the latter was restored, in its earlier distinguished place. To political prosecutions after the victory Caesar assigned the narrowest possible limits. No investigation was instituted into the various communications which the constitutional party had held even with nominal Caesarians; Caesar threw the piles of papers found in the enemy's headquarters at Pharsalus and Thapsus into the fire unread, and spared himself and the country from political processes against individuals suspected of high treason. Further, all the common soldiers who had followed their Roman or provincial officers into the contest against Caesar came off with impunity. The sole exception made was in the case of those Roman burgesses, who had taken service in the army of the Numidian king Juba; their property was confiscated by way of penalty for their treason. . . .

But this abolition of existing abuses was not the main matter. . . . In the Roman republic, according to the view of the aristocracy and democracy alike, the provinces had been nothing but—what they were frequently called—country-estates of the Roman people, and they were employed and worked out as such. This view had now passed away. The provinces as such were gradually to disappear, in order to prepare for the renovated Helleno-Italic nation a new and more spacious home, of whose several component parts no one existed merely for the sake of another but all for each and each for all; the new existence in the renovated home, the fresher, broader, grander national life, was of itself to overbear the sorrows and wrongs of the nation for which there was no help in the old Italy. These ideas, as is well known, were not new. The emigration from Italy to the provinces that had been regularly going on for centuries had long since, though unconsciously on the part of the emigrants themselves, paved the way for such an extension of Italy. The first who in a systematic way guided the Italians to settle beyond the bounds of Italy was Gaius Gracchus, the creator of the Roman democratic monarchy, the author of the Transalpine conquests, the founder of the colonies of Carthage and Narbo. Then the second statesman of genius produced by the Roman democracy, Quintus Sertorius, began to introduce the barbarous Occidentals to Latin civilization; he gave to the Spanish youth of rank the Roman dress, and urged them to speak Latin and to acquire the higher Italian culture at the training institute founded by him in Osca. When Caesar entered on the government, a large Italian population—though, in great part, lacking stability and concentration—already existed in all the provinces and client-states. To say nothing of the formally Italian towns in Spain and southern Gaul, we need only recall the numerous troops of burgesses raised by Sertorius and Pompeius in Spain, by Caesar in Gaul, by Juba in Numidia, by the constitutional party in Africa, Macedonia, Greece, Asia Minor, and Crete; the Latin lyre—ill-tuned doubtless—on which the town-poets of Corduba as early as the Sertorian war sang the praises of the Roman generals; and the translations of Greek poetry valued on account of their very elegance of language, which the earliest extra-Italian poet of note, the Transalpine Publius Terentius Varro of the Aude, published shortly after Caesar's death.

On the other hand the interpenetration of the Latin and Hellenic character was, we might say, as old as Rome. On occasion of the union of Italy the conquering Latin nation had assimilated to itself all the other conquered nationalities, excepting only the Greek, which was received just as it stood without any attempt at external amalgamation. Wherever the Roman legionary went, the Greek schoolmaster, no less a conqueror in his own way, followed; at an early date we find famous teachers of the Greek language settled on the Guadalquivir, and Greek was as well taught as Latin in the institute of Osca. The higher Roman culture itself was in fact nothing else than the proclamation of the great gospel of Hellenic manners and art in the Italian idiom; against the modest pretension of the civilizing conquerors to proclaim it first of all in their own language to the barbarians of the west the Hellene at least could not loudly protest. Already the Greek everywhere—and, most decidedly, just where the national feeling was purest and strongest, on the frontiers threatened by barbaric denationalization, *e.g.* in Massilia, on the north coast of the Black Sea, and on the Euphrates and Tigris—descried the protector and avenger of Hellenism in Rome; and in fact the foundation of towns by Pompeius in the far east resumed after an interruption of centuries the beneficent work of Alexander.

The idea of an Italo-Hellenic empire with two languages and a single nationality was not new—otherwise it would have been nothing but a blunder; but the development of it from floating projects to a firmly-grasped conception, from scattered initial efforts to the laying of a concentrated foundation, was the work of the third and greatest of the democratic statesmen of Rome.

. . . . The distinctively Italian state of the republic was thus at an end; but the rumour that Caesar was ruining Italy and Rome on purpose to transfer the centre of the empire to the Greek east and to make Ilion or Alexandria its capital, was nothing but a piece of talk—very easy to be accounted for, but also very silly—of the angry nobility. On the contrary in Caesar's organizations the Latin nationality always retained the preponderance; as is indicated in the very fact that he issued all his enactments in Latin, although those destined for the Greek-speaking countries were at the same time issued in Greek. In general he arranged the relations of the two great nations in his monarchy just as his republican predecessors had arranged them in the united Italy; the Hellenic nationality was protected where it existed, the Italian was extended as far as circumstances permitted, and the inheritance of the races to be absorbed was destined for it. This was necessary, because an entire equalizing of the Greek and Latin elements in the state would in all probability have in a very short time occasioned that catastrophe which Byzantinism brought about several centuries later; for the

Greek element was superior to the Roman not merely in all intellectual aspects, but also in the measure of its predominance, and it had within Italy itself in the hosts of Hellenes and half-Hellenes who migrated compulsorily or voluntarily to Italy an endless number of apostles apparently insignificant, but whose influence could not be estimated too highly. To mention only the most conspicuous phenomenon in this respect, the rule of Greek lackeys over the Roman monarchs is as old as the monarchy. The first in the equally long and repulsive list of these personages is the confidential servant of Pompeius, Theophanes of Mytilene, who by his power over his weak master contributed probably more than any one else to the outbreak of the war between Pompeius and Caesar. Not wholly without reason he was after his death treated with divine honours by his countrymen; he commenced, forsooth, the *valet de chambre* government of the imperial period, which in a certain measure was just a dominion of the Hellenes over the Romans. The government had accordingly every reason not to encourage by its fostering action the spread of Hellenism at least in the west. If Sicily was not simply relieved of the pressure of the *decumae* but had its communities invested with Latin rights, which was presumably meant to be followed in due time by full equalization with Italy, it can only have been Caesar's design that this glorious island, which was at that time desolate and had as to management passed for the greater part into Italian hands, but which nature has destined to be not so much a neighbouring land to Italy as rather the finest of its provinces, should become altogether merged in Italy. But otherwise the Greek element, wherever it existed, was preserved and protected. However political crises might suggest to the Imperator the demolition of the strong pillars of Hellenism in the west and in Egypt, Massilia and Alexandria were neither destroyed nor denationalized.

On the other hand the Roman element was promoted by the government through colonization and Latinizing with all vigour and at the most various points of the empire. The principle, which originated no doubt from a bad combination of formal law and brute force, but was inevitably necessary in order to freedom in dealing with the nations destined to destruction—that all the soil in the provinces not ceded by special act of the government to communities or private persons was the property of the state, and the holder of it for the time being had merely an heritable possession on sufferance and revocable at any time—was retained also by Caesar and raised by him from a democratic party-theory to a fundamental principle of monarchical law.

In all these various . . . ordinances—which are traceable at least in plan, if not perhaps all in execution, to Caesar—a definite system is apparent. Italy was converted from the mistress of the subject peoples into the mother of the renovated Italo-Hellenic nation. The Cisalpine province completely equalized with the mother-country was a promise and a guarantee that, in the monarchy of Caesar just as in the healthier times of the republic, every Latinized district might expect to be placed on an equal footing by the side of its elder sisters and of the mother herself. On the threshold of full national and political equalization with Italy stood the adjoining lands, the Greek Sicily and the south of Gaul, which was rapidly becoming Latinized. In a more remote stage of preparation stood the other provinces of the empire, in which, just as hitherto in southern Gaul Narbo had been a Roman colony, the great maritime cities—Emporiae, Gades, Carthage, Corinth, Heraclea in Pontus, Sinope, Berytus, Alexandria—now became Italian or Helleno-Italian communities, the centres of an Italian civilization even in the Greek east, the fundamental pillars of the future national and political levelling of the empire. The rule of the urban community of Rome over the shores of the Mediterranean was at an end; in its stead came the new Mediterranean state. . . .

THE GOLDEN AGE OF IMPERIAL ROME

33 AUGUSTUS, RES GESTAE: THE ACCOUNTING OF AN EMPEROR

The Battle of Actium (31 B.C.) marked not only the end of a century of civil wars but also the survival of Rome as an imperial power and the perpetuation of the authoritarian form of government introduced by Caesar. (See Document 31.) In this battle Octavian defeated his rival, Mark Antony, secured for himself control of the Roman state, and in three more years restored peace throughout the Roman world. In 27 B.C., Octavian appeared before the Senate and offered to surrender his virtually absolute powers in order to restore the republic. The Senate instead voted to confer upon him the military and civil powers necessary for ruling the Roman Empire. Henceforth, he was regularly designated *imperator* (commander) and Augustus, the name by which we now refer to him.

Why the Senate rejected his offer to reëstablish the republic is uncertain. Perhaps the senators, whose numbers had been decimated by wars and proscriptions, doubted Augustus' sincerity and feared reprisals if they accepted his proposal. Perhaps the long wars had shattered any confidence, even among the senators, in their ability to rule. For whatever reason, at this important juncture in their history the Romans chose to keep a strong man at the center of the imperial administration. In the ensuing centuries the emperors grew ever more authoritarian at the expense of the Senate.

The respect for the republic, however, was still strong in the time of Augustus, and the Romans had a profound distrust of *novae res* ("new things"). Augustus, as a good Roman, declared no "New Deal," but a *respublica restituenda* ("the commonwealth restored"). It was in this spirit that at the close of his reign he drew up a long account of his accomplishments, which he ordered inscribed on stone or bronze throughout the empire. In this record he attempted to show that his deeds *(res gestae)* had not been contrary to but in defense of the established traditions of the Roman Republic. Above all, he sought to demonstrate that his new position as *princeps*, or "chief man of state," was not a real departure from tradition. In his favor, it may be said that he, if not his increasingly autocratic successors, attempted to restore republican morality and legal rights, and that the new authoritarian regime established by Augustus was to give the Roman Empire the *Pax Romana*, some two and one-half centuries of peace.

At the age of nineteen, on my own initiative and at my own expense, I raised an army by means of which I restored liberty to the republic, which had been oppressed by the tyranny of a faction. For which service the senate, with complimentary resolutions, enrolled me in its order, in the consulship of Gaius Pansa and Aulus Hirtius, giving me at the same time consular precedence in voting; it also gave me the *imperium*. As propraetor it ordered me, along with the consuls, "to see that the republic suffered no harm." In the same year, moreover, as both consuls had fallen in war, the people elected me consul and a triumvir for settling the constitution.

Those who slew my father I drove into exile, punishing their deed by due process of law, and afterwards when they waged war upon the republic I twice defeated them in battle.

Wars, both civil and foreign, I undertook throughout the world, on sea and land, and when victorious I spared all citizens who sued for pardon. The foreign nations which could with safety be pardoned I preferred to save rather than to destroy. The number of Roman citizens who bound themselves to me by military oath was about 500,000. Of these I settled in colonies or sent back into their own towns, after their term of service, something more than 300,000, and to all I assigned lands, or gave money as a reward for military service. I captured six hundred ships, over and above those which were smaller than triremes.

Twice I triumphed with an ovation, thrice I celebrated curule triumphs, and was saluted as imperator twenty-one times. Although the Senate decreed me additional triumphs I set them aside. When I had performed the vows which I had undertaken in each war I deposited upon the Capitol the laurels which adorned my fasces. For successful operations on land and sea, conducted either by myself or by my lieutenants under my auspices, the senate on fifty-five occasions decreed that thanks should be rendered to the immortal gods. . . .

The dictatorship offered me by the people and the Roman Senate, in my absence and later when present, in the consulship of Marcus Marcellus and Lucius Arruntius I did not accept. I did not decline at a time of the greatest scarcity of grain the charge of the grain-supply, which I so administered that, within a few days, I freed the entire people, at my own expense, from the fear and danger in which they were. . . .

. . . [W]hen the Senate and the Roman people unanimously agreed [that] I should be elected overseer of laws and morals, without a colleague and with the fullest power, I refused to accept any power offered me which was contrary to the traditions of our ancestors. Those things which at that time the senate wished me to administer I carried out by virtue of my tribunician power. And even in this office I five times received from the senate a colleague at my own request. . . .

Text: Reprinted by permission of the publishers and The Loeb Classical Library from Velleius Paterculus, *Res Gestae Divi Augusti*, trans. Frederick W. Shipley (Cambridge, Mass.: Harvard University Press, 1955), pp. 345-57, 385-401 *passim*.

... By order of the people and the senate I increased the number of the patricians. Three times I revised the roll of the senate. In my sixth consulship, with Marcus Agrippa as my colleague, I made a census of the people. I performed the *lustrum* after an interval of forty-one years. In this lustration 4,063,000 Roman citizens were entered on the census roll. A second time, in the consulship of Gaius Censorinus and Gaius Asinius, I again performed the *lustrum* alone, with the consular imperium. In this *lustrum* 4,233,000 Roman citizens were entered on the census roll. ...

After my victory [at Actium in 31 B.C.] I replaced in the temples in all the cities of the province of Asia the ornaments which my antagonist in the war, when he despoiled the temples, had appropriated to his private use. Silver statues of me, on foot, on horseback, and in chariots were erected in the city to the number of about eighty; these I myself removed, and from the money thus obtained I placed in the temple of Apollo golden offerings in my own name and in the name of those who had paid me the honour of a statue.

I freed the sea from pirates. About thirty thousand slaves, captured in that war, who had run away from their masters and had taken up arms against the republic, I delivered to their masters for punishment. The whole of Italy voluntarily took oath of allegiance to me and demanded me as its leader in the war in which I was victorious at Actium. The provinces of the Spains, the Gauls, Africa, Sicily, and Sardinia took the same oath of allegiance. Those who served under my standards at that time included more than 700 senators, and among them eighty-three who had previously or have since been consuls up to the day on which these words were written, and about 170 have been priests.

I extended the boundaries of all the provinces which were bordered by races not yet subject to our empire. The provinces of the Gauls, the Spains, and Germany, bounded by the ocean from Gades to the mouth of the Elbe, I reduced to a state of peace. The Alps, from the region which lies nearest to the Adriatic as far as the Tuscan Sea, I brought to a state of peace without waging on any tribe an unjust war. ...

In my sixth and seventh consulships, when I had extinguished the flames of civil war, after receiving by universal consent the absolute control of affairs, I transferred the republic from my own control to the will of the senate and the Roman people. For this service on my part I was given the title of Augustus by decree of the senate, and the doorposts of my house were covered with laurels by public act, and a civic crown was fixed above my door, and a golden shield was placed in the Curia Julia whose inscription testified that the senate and the Roman people gave me this in recognition of my valour, my clemency, my justice, and my piety. After that time I took precedence of all in rank, but of power I possessed no more than those who were my colleagues in any magistracy.

34 VIRGIL, *AENEID* AND *ECLOGUE IV*: ROMAN DESTINY AND CHRISTIAN PROPHECY

Augustus once boasted that he had found Rome brick and was to leave it marble. Using the wealth of the Egyptian treasury, he built statuary, temples, a theater, and a new senate house in Rome, to which he linked the empire with a network of marvelous roads. The enlightened patronage of Augustus and the prosperity of his reign inspired also the great period of Roman poetry that followed the Ciceronian era of the later republic. The Age of Cicero and the Augustan Age together form Rome's Golden Age (70 B.C.-14 A.D.). It was a period of aristocratic patrons—Maecenas, Messala, the emperor himself—who befriended writers gravitating to the capital for education, profit, or urban amusement. What they produced was not a free literature of independent minds, but a literature in tribute to the fashionable life and—at the emperor's insistence—to the Roman military spirit and the ancient codes of the Roman state. Virgil, Horace, Propertius, and Tibullus all accepted villas and other rewards from rich patrons, and the stamp of patronage is seen in their poetic gratitude and their deference to the glory of empire.

The chief of these new writers and the one who accepted his duty most cheerfully was Publius Vergilius (miswritten Virgilius, hence the English spelling Virgil) Maro (70-19 B.C.), the national poet of Rome. Imperial glorification would seem an unnatural task for this shy, gentle, sensitive man late from the countryside of the Po Valley, but Virgil loved the country life of his youth and identified its stoic virtues with the great spirit of Rome. Thus it was that among the poets approached by Augustus to write a literary epic of Rome, emphasizing the emperor's own role in founding it, only Virgil rose to the occasion. The *Aeneid* was begun in 29 B.C., and remained Virgil's task for the last decade of his life.

Instead of founding his epic on contemporary Rome or on the career of Augustus, Virgil tactfully turned to the Greek and Roman legend of Aeneas, the traditional founder of the Julian line (Augustus' clan). Thereby Virgil could in substance glorify Rome and the present ruler of Rome, while in form follow the great models of Greek epic and reproduce all their sources of interest. The first six books, reminiscent of Homer's *Odyssey*, tell how the Trojan prince Aeneas escaped from burning Troy, and with a small band wandered for years over the Mediterranean, experiencing a series of adventures. The last six books suggest Homer's epic of war, the *Iliad*, with their story of the arrival of Aeneas in Italy and his war for the hand of a beautiful woman, Lavinia. According to tradition, Aeneas then founded Alba Longa, whose Latin citizens were the founders of Rome.

Underlying the entire action of the epic is the idea of the great role played by Rome in the history of the world—a role determined by divine destiny and carried out by the stoic virtue of Rome's sons. This is shown in the following selection from Book IV. At Carthage, the Phoenician city of Africa destined one day to be Rome's greatest enemy, Aeneas faces the danger of love for Dido, the queen of Carthage, who urges Aeneas to stay and share her rule. It is a tribute to the humanity of Virgil that he portrays Dido not as a villainess, but as an intelligent and dignified woman whose love for Aeneas is tragically contrary to the destiny of Rome. A stern sense of duty forces Aeneas to obey the gods and abandon Dido. As he sails from the harbor, the heartbroken queen mounts on a funeral pyre to commit suicide. Before she dies, she curses Aeneas and the Rome to be, calling for continuing enmity between Carthage and Rome and praying for an avenger who will one day ravage Italy. Every Roman reader of the Augustan Age knew that Dido's avenger was Hannibal, who waged a devastating battle on Italian soil for sixteen years in the Second Punic Wars (218-202 B.C.). Dido's curse, which appears below, expresses the finest element of Virgil's poetic art—legend, history, dramatic tension, human passion, and compassion.

The second selection is from the fourth of Virgil's ten little pastorals, the *Eclogues*. It salutes the impending birth of a son in whose lifetime a Golden Age of peace and prosperity would flower. Variously interpreted today as a fulsome tribute to an offspring soon to be born to Virgil's patron, Pollio, or Antony, or even Octavian, it was considered in the Middle Ages to be a prophecy of the coming of Christ the Messiah and accounts in part for Virgil's veneration among Christian writers.

The Aeneid: Book IV

Night fell; weary creatures took quiet slumber all over earth, and woodland and wild waters had sunk to rest; now the stars wheel midway on their gliding path, now all the country is silent, and beasts and gay birds that haunt liquid levels of lake or thorny rustic thicket lay couched asleep under the still night. But not so the distressed Phoenician, nor does she ever sink asleep or take the night upon eyes or breast; her pain redoubles, and her love swells to renewed madness, as she tosses on the strong tide of wrath. Even so she begins, and thus revolves with her heart alone:

'Lo, what do I? Shall I again make trial of mine old wooers that will scorn me? and stoop to sue for a Numidian marriage among those whom already over and over I have disdained for husbands? Then shall I follow the Ilian fleets and the uttermost bidding of the Teucrians? because they are glad to have been once raised up by my succour, or the grace of mine old kindness is fresh in their remembrance? And who will permit me, if I would? or take a hated woman on their proud fleet? art thou ignorant, ah me, even in ruin, and knowest not yet the forsworn race of Laomedon? And then? shall I accompany the triumphant sailors, a lonely fugitive? or plunge forth girt with all my Tyrian train? so hardly severed from Sidon city, shall I again drive them seaward, and bid them spread their sails to the tempest? Nay die thou, as thou deservest, and let the steel end thy pain. With thee it began; overborne by my tears, thou, O my sister, dost load me with this madness and agony, and cast me to the enemy. It was not mine to spend a wild life without stain, far from a bridal chamber, and untouched by this passion. O faith ill kept, that was plighted to Sychaeus' ashes!' Thus her heart broke in long lamentation.

Now Aeneas was fixed to go, and now, with all set duly in order, was taking hasty sleep on

Text: J. W. Mackail (trans.), *Virgil's Works: The Aeneid, Eclogues, Georgics* (New York: The Modern Library, Inc., 1934), pp. 76-81, 274-75.

his high quarterdeck. To him as he slept the god appeared once again in the same fashion of countenance, and thus seemed to renew his warning, in all points like to Mercury, voice and hue and golden hair and limbs gracious in youth. 'Goddess-born, canst thou sleep on in such danger? and seest not the coming perils that hem thee in, madman! nor hearest the breezes blowing fair? She, fixed on death, is revolving craft and crime grimly in her bosom, and swells the changing surge of wrath. Fliest thou not hence headlong, while headlong flight is yet possible? Even now wilt thou see ocean weltering with broken timbers, see the fierce glare of torches and the beach in a riot of flame, if dawn break on thee yet dallying in this land. Up ho! linger no more! Woman is ever a fickle and changing thing.' So spoke he, and melted in the black night.

Then indeed Aeneas, startled by the sudden phantom, leaps out of slumber and bestirs his crew to headlong haste. 'Awake, O men, and sit down to the thwarts; shake out sail speedily. A god sent from high heaven, lo! again spurs us to speed our flight and cut the twisted cables. We follow thee, holy one of heaven, whoso thou art, and again joyfully obey thy command. O be favourable; give gracious aid and bring fair sky and weather.' He spoke, and snatching his sword like lightning from the sheath, strikes at the hawser with the drawn steel. The same zeal catches all at once; rushing and tearing they quit the shore; the sea is hidden under their fleets; strongly they toss up the foam and sweep the blue water.

And now Dawn broke, and, leaving the saffron bed of Tithonus, shed her radiance anew over the world; when the Queen saw from her watch-tower the first light whitening, and the fleet standing out under squared sail, and discerned shore and haven empty of all their oarsmen. Thrice and four times she struck her hand on her lovely breast and rent her yellow hair: 'God!' she cries, 'shall he go? shall an alien make mock of our realm? Will they not issue in armed pursuit from all the city, and some launch ships from the dockyards? Go; bring fire in haste, serve out weapons, ply the oars! What do I talk? or where am I? what mad change is on my purpose? Alas, Dido! now evil deeds touch thee; that had been fitting once, when thou gavest away thy crown. Behold the faith and hand of him! who, they say, carries his household's ancestral gods about with him! who stooped his shoulders to a father outworn with age! Could I not have riven his body in sunder and strewn it on the waves? and slain with the sword his comrades and his dear Ascanius, and served him for the banquet at his father's table? But the chance of battle had been dubious. If it had! whom did I fear in the death-agony? I should have borne firebrands into his camp and filled his decks with flame, blotted out father and son and race together, and flung myself atop of all. Sun, whose fires lighten all the words of the world, and thou, Juno, mediatress and witness of these my distresses, and Hecate, cried on by night in crossways of cities, and you, fatal avenging sisters and gods of dying Elissa, hear me now; bend your just deity to my woes, and listen to our prayers. If it must needs be that the accursed one touch his haven and float up to land, if thus Jove's decrees demand, and this is the appointed term,—yet, distressed in war by an armed and gallant nation, driven homeless from his borders, rent from Iülus' embrace, let him sue for succour and see death on death untimely on his people; nor when he has yielded him to the terms of a harsh peace, may he have joy of his kingdom or the pleasant light; but let him fall before his day and without burial amid its soil. This I pray; this and my blood with it I pour for the last utterance. Then do you, O Tyrians, pursue his seed with your hatred for all ages to come; send this guerdon to our ashes. Let no kindness nor truce be between the nations. Arise, some avenger, out of our dust, to follow the Dardanian settlers with firebrand and steel. Now, then, whensoever strength shall be given, I invoke the enmity of shore to shore, wave to water, sword to sword; let their battles go down to their children's children.'

So speaks she as she kept turning her mind round about, seeking how soonest to break away from the hateful light. Thereon she speaks briefly to Barce, nurse of Sychaeus; for a heap of dusky ashes held her own, in her country of long ago:

'Sweet nurse, bring Anna my sister hither to me. Bid her haste and sprinkle river water over her body, and bring with her the beasts ordained for expiation: so let her come: and thou likewise veil thy brows with a pure chaplet. I would fulfil the rites of Stygian Jove that I have fitly ordered and begun, so to set the limit to my distresses and give over to flame the pyre of the Dardanian chief.'

So speaks she; the old woman went eagerly with quickened pace. But Dido, panting and fierce in her awful purpose, with bloodshot restless gaze, and spots on her quivering cheeks burning through the pallor of imminent death, bursts into the inner courts of the house, and mounts in madness the lofty stairs, and unsheathes the sword of Dardania, a gift sought for other use than this. Then after her eyes fell on the Ilian raiment and the bed she knew, dallying a little with her purpose through her tears, she sank on the pillow and spoke the last words of all:

'Dress he wore, sweet while doom and deity allowed! receive my spirit now, and release me from my distresses. I have lived and fulfilled Fortune's allotted course; and now shall I go a queenly phantom under the earth. I have built a renowned city; I have seen my ramparts rise; by my brother's punishment I have avenged my husband of his enemy; happy, ah me! and over happy, had but the keels of Dardania never touched our shores!' She spoke; and burying her face in the pillow, 'Death it will be,' she cries, 'and unavenged; but death be it. Thus, thus is it good to pass into the dark. Let the pitiless Dardanian's gaze drink in this fire out at sea, and my death be the omen he carries on his way.'

She ceased; and even as she spoke her people see her sunk on the steel, and blood reeking on the sword and spattered on her hands. A cry rises in the high halls; Rumour riots down the quaking city. The house resounds with lamentation and sobbing and bitter crying of women; heaven echoes their loud wails; even as though all Carthage or ancient Tyre went down as the foe poured in, and the flames rolled furious over the roofs of house and temple. Death-stricken her sister heard, and in swift hurrying dismay, with torn face and smitten bosom, darts through them all, and calls the dying woman by her name. 'Was it this, mine own? Was my summons a snare? Was it this thy pyre, ah me, this thine altar fires meant? How shall I begin my desolate moan? Didst thou disdain a sister's company in death? Thou shouldst have called me to share thy doom; in the self-same hour, the self-same pang of steel had been our portion. Did these very hands build it, did my voice call on our father's gods, that with thee lying thus I should be away, O merciless? Thou hast destroyed thyself and me together, O my sister, and the Sidonian lords and people, and this thy city. Give her wounds water: I will bathe them and catch on my lips the last breath that haply yet lingers.' So speaking she had climbed the high steps, and, wailing, clasped and caressed her half-lifeless sister in her bosom, and stanched the dark streams of blood with her gown. She, essaying to lift her heavy eyes, swoons back; the deep-driven wound gurgles in her breast. Thrice she rose, and strained to lift herself on her elbow; thrice she rolled back on the pillow, and with wandering eyes sought the light of high heaven, and moaned as she found it.

Then Juno omnipotent, pitying her long pain and difficult decease, sent Iris down from heaven to unloose the struggling life from the body where it clung. For since neither by fate did she perish, nor as one who had earned her death, but woefully before her day, and fired by sudden madness, not yet had Proserpine taken her tress from the golden head, nor sentenced her to the nether Stygian world. So Iris on dewy saffron pinions flits down through the sky athwart the sun in a trail of a thousand changing dyes, and stopping over her head: 'This lock, sacred to Dis, I take as bidden, and release thee from that body of thine.' So speaks she, and cuts it with her hand. And therewith all the warmth ebbed forth from her, and the life passed away upon the winds.

Eclogue IV

Muses of Sicily, sing we a somewhat ampler strain: not all men's delight is in coppices and lowly tamarisks: if we sing of the woods, let them be woods worthy of a Consul.

Now is come the last age of the Cumaean prophecy: the great cycle of periods is born anew. Now returns the Maid, returns the reign of Saturn: now from high heaven a new generation comes down. Yet do thou at that boy's birth, in whom the iron race shall begin to cease, and the golden to arise over all the world, holy Lucina, be gracious; now thine own Apollo reigns. And in thy consulate, in thine, O Pollio, shall this glorious age enter, and the great months begin their march: under thy rule what traces of our guilt yet remain, vanishing shall free earth for ever from alarm. He shall grow in the life of gods, and shall see gods and heroes mingled, and himself be seen by them, and shall rule the world that his fathers' virtues have set at peace. But on thee, O boy, untilled shall Earth first pour childish gifts, wandering ivytendrils and foxglove, and colocasia mingled with the laughing acanthus: untended shall the she-goats bring home their milk-swoln udders, nor shall huge lions alarm the herds: unbidden thy cradle shall break into wooing blossom. The snake too shall die, and die the treacherous poison-plant: Assyrian spice shall grow all up and down. But when once thou shalt be able now to read the glories of heroes and thy father's deeds, and to know Virtue as she is, slowly the plain shall grow golden with the soft corn-spike, and the reddening grape trail from the wild briar, and hard oaks shall drip dew of honey. Nevertheless there shall linger some few traces of ancient wrong, to bid ships tempt the sea and towns be girt with walls and the earth cloven in furrows. Then shall a second Tiphys be, and a second Argo to sail with chosen heroes: new wars too shall arise, and again a mighty Achilles be sent to Troy. Thereafter, when now strengthening age hath wrought thee into man, the very voyager shall cease out of the sea, nor the sailing pine exchange her merchandise: all lands shall bear all things, the ground shall not suffer the mattock, nor the vine the pruning-hook; now likewise the strong ploughman shall loose his bulls from the yoke. Neither shall wool learn to counterfeit changing hues, but the ram in the meadow himself shall dye his fleece now with soft glowing sea-purple, now with yellow saffron; native scarlet shall clothe the lambs at their pasturage. Run even thus, O ages, said the harmonious Fates to their spindles, by the steadfast ordinance of doom. Draw nigh to thy high honours (even now will the time be come) O dear offspring of gods, mighty germ of Jove! Behold the world swaying her orbed mass, lands and spaces of sea and depth of sky; behold how all things rejoice in the age to come.

Ah many the latter end of a long life then yet be mine, and such breath as shall suffice to tell thy deeds! Not Orpheus of Thrace nor Linus shall surpass me in song, though he have his mother and he his father to aid, Orpheus Calliope, Linus beautiful Apollo. If even Pan before his Arcady contend with me, even Pan before his Arcady shall declare himself conquered. Begin, O little boy, to know and smile upon thy mother, thy mother on whom ten months have brought weary longings. Begin, O little boy: of them who have not smiled on a parent, never was one honoured at a god's board or on a goddess' couch.

THE HIGH EMPIRE

35 SENECA, "ON THE GOD WITHIN US": THE STOIC IDEAL AND THE IMPERIAL ARISTOCRACY

Although Emperor Augustus had made earnest appeals for its revival, traditional Roman morality, the stringent and exacting ideals which were believed to be upheld by the heroic founders of Rome, continued to wane in the century following Augustus' death. The senatorial aristocracy, in particular, experienced a failure of nerve. Deprived of their republican political privileges, many resigned themselves to subordinate careers in the imperial service, while some turned to ostentatious display and gross amusements. A few, whatever their political and social position, felt a need for an inner spirituality which could provide a sense of personal freedom and virtue; for the intellectuals, the philosophy of Stoicism, long popular with the Roman aristocracy, became the source of private consolation lacking in the official pagan cults. Not only did Stoicism encourage detachment from worldly involvements but it required a reliance upon the inner self for high standards of behavior. This emphasis on the self provided a welcome relief from the public pomp and scandals of the imperial court.

A Stoic of the early empire whose ethical views in some respects approached Christianity was Lucius Annaeus Seneca (4 B.C.-65 A.D.). Seneca modified Stoicism by making it more human and more spiritual—more human through his vivid conception of the frailty and misery of men; more spiritual by individualizing the divine as a compassionate Being who helps mortals to live better lives. The early Stoics considered the natural world as part of the divine, but Seneca described the body as a mere husk or temporary prison of man's divine spirit. The flesh he saw as evil, the earth as corrupting. Mortal life was a period of training, during which misfortunes were visited upon man to exercise his powers of self-discipline and to teach him indifference to worldly conditions. Only with the death of the flesh was man's soul released to its true life.

Seneca was a professor of rhetoric who became the tutor and adviser of the young emperor Nero. The teacher's attempt to educate his notorious charge in Stoic principles failed dismally. Indeed, Nero pressured Seneca into committing suicide, an act accomplished with true Stoic resignation. Whatever Seneca's failures as a tutor, he left to posterity a series of moral essays, presumably written for his royal pupil, and numerous *Epistulae Morales*, letters on morals supposedly written to his friend, Lucilius, but in all likelihood prepared for publication. Perhaps his best known letter is the forty-first—"On the God within Us." It is written on so exalted a spiritual plane that early Christians were as impressed with the letter as they were with Virgil's "Messianic" Eclogue (see Document 34). The Stoic Seneca, they said, is *paene noster* ("almost ours").

You are doing an excellent thing, one which will be wholesome for you, if, as you write me, you are persisting in your effort to attain sound understanding; it is foolish to pray for this when you can acquire it from yourself. We do not need to uplift our hands towards heaven, or to beg the keeper of a temple to let us approach his idol's ear, as if in this way our prayers were more likely to be heard. God is near you, he is with you, he is within you. This is what I mean, Lucilius: a holy spirit indwells within us, one who marks our good and bad deeds, and is our guardian. As we treat this spirit, so are we treated by it. Indeed, no man can be good without the help of God. Can one rise superior to fortune unless God helps him to rise? He it is that gives noble and upright counsel. In each good man

A god doth dwell, but what god know we not.

If ever you have come upon a grove that is full of ancient trees which have grown to an unusual height, shutting out a view of the sky by a veil of pleached and intertwining branches, then the loftiness of the forest, the seclusion of the spot, and your marvel at the thick unbroken shade in the midst of the open spaces, will prove to you the presence of deity. Or if a cave, made by the deep crumbling of the rocks, holds up a mountain on its arch, a place not built with hands but hollowed out into such spaciousness by natural causes, your soul will be deeply moved by a certain intimation of the existence of God. We worship the sources of mighty rivers; we erect altars at places where great streams burst suddenly from hidden sources; we adore springs of hot water as divine, and consecrate certain pools because of their dark waters or their immeasurable depth. If you see a man who is unterrified in the midst of dangers, untouched by desires, happy in adversity, peaceful amid the storm, who looks down upon men from a higher plane, and views the gods on a footing of equality, will not a feeling of reverence for him steal over you? Will you not say: "This quality is too great and too lofty to be regarded as resembling this petty body in which it dwells? A divine power has descended upon that man." When a soul rises superior to other souls, when it is under control, when it passes through every experience as if it were of small account, when it smiles at our fears and at our prayers, it is stirred by a force from heaven. A thing like this cannot stand upright unless it be propped by the divine. Therefore, a greater part of it abides in that place from whence it came down to earth. Just as the rays of the sun do indeed touch the earth, but still abide at the source from which they are sent; even so the great and hallowed soul, which has come down in order that we may have a nearer knowledge of divinity, does indeed associate with us, but still cleaves to its origin; on that source it depends, thither it turns its gaze and strives to go, and it concerns itself with our doings only as a being superior to ourselves.

What, then, is such a soul? One which is resplendent with no external good, but only with its own. For what is more foolish than to praise in a man the qualities which come from without? And what is more insane than to marvel at characteristics which may at the next instant be passed on to someone else? A golden bit does not make a better horse. The lion with gilded mane, in process of being trained and forced by weariness to endure the decoration, is sent into the arena in quite a different way from the wild lion whose spirit is unbroken; the latter, indeed, bold in his attack, as nature wished him to be, impressive because of his wild appearance,—and it is his glory that none can look upon him without fear,—is favoured in preference to the other lion, that languid and gilded brute.

No man ought to glory except in that which is his own. We praise a vine if it makes the shoots teem with increase, if by its weight it bends to the ground the very poles which hold its fruit; would any man prefer to this vine one from which golden grapes and golden leaves hand down? In a vine the virtue peculiarly its own is fertility; in man also we should praise that which is his own. Suppose that he has a retinue of comely slaves and a beautiful house, that his farm is large and large his income; none of these things is in the man himself; they are all on the outside. Praise the quality in him which cannot be given or snatched away, that which is the peculiar property of the man. Do you ask what this is? It is soul, and reason brought to perfection in the soul. For man is a reasoning animal. Therefore, man's highest good is attained, if he has fulfilled the good for which nature designed him at birth. And what is it which this reason demands of him? The easiest thing in the world,—to live in accordance with his own nature. But this is turned into a hard task by the general madness of mankind; we push one another into vice. And how can a man be recalled to salvation, when he has none to restrain him, and all mankind to urge him on? Farewell.

Text: Reprinted by permission of the publishers and The Loeb Classical Library from Seneca, *Ad Lucilium Epistulae Morales*, trans. Richard M. Gummere (Cambridge, Mass.: Harvard University Press, 1934), I, 273-79.

36 JUVENAL SATIRE III: THE URBAN PROBLEM

By the end of the first century A.D., the Roman Empire extended from northern England to the Arabian Desert and the second cataract of the Nile. According to recent estimates, it was populated by over seventy million inhabitants, who comprised a cosmopolitan society varying widely in racial and linguistic background, in religion, in social behavior, in political traditions, and in cultural attainments. This vast conglomerate of peoples was united by one thing only—allegiance to Rome. In practicing that allegiance, a degree of internal peace and prosperity, the *Pax Romana* (Roman Peace), was achieved which brought advantages to all. But even those, like the eighteenth-century historian Edward Gibbon, who regard this period as the happiest in human history might have to admit that Rome and her empire suffered from many problems—not the least of which was related to the new mass society, excessive urbanization, affluence, and racial prejudice.

The city of Rome had grown to over one million inhabitants with a vast influx of new Roman subjects, especially from Greece and the Eastern Mediterranean. Although the fortunes of many increased enormously, the problems of poverty, unemployment, and cultural deprivation constantly plagued the city. A class of newly rich came into being, most of whom were foreign emigrants come to Italy to make their way and many of whom were recently freed slaves. Prejudice against the newcomers waxed especially among native Romans who were less successful, or less hard-working, in the affluent society. Life in the metropolis, except for the well-to-do, was hectic. Crowded high-rise apartment buildings rose everywhere, the noise was incessant, the crime rate mounted, and devastating fires were common. The poverty-stricken were never more dependent on *panem et circenses* (bread and circuses), the doles and entertainments provided by the state, and the hand-outs of the affluent.

No Roman more successfully characterized the problems of this new society than Juvenal, a poet of the early second century A.D. Little is known about Juvenal's life except from his poems, and they offer ample evidence that he observed the life of Rome, his own city, in his own time, with a witty and jaundiced eye. The poetic form Juvenal chose was satire, a very popular form of poetry among the Romans, which allowed for biting social criticism. In *Satire III*, Juvenal lampoons his city with rare abandon. The poem begins with the departure from Rome of the narrator, Umbricius, who is moving to a seaside suburb. The selections below present parts of the narrator's description of the agonies of life in the big city, and they are particularly revealing of the prejudices of the old-time Romans against the newcomers—in this case, the Greeks. So biting and universal is much of this satire, that many later poets, including Samuel Johnson, have chosen to parody it in terms of their own times and their own cities.

Against the City of Rome

. . . Umbricius has much on his mind. "Since there's no place in the city,"
He says, "For an honest man, and no reward for his labors,
Since I have less today than yesterday, since by tomorrow
That will have dwindled still more, I have made my decision. I'm going
To the place where, I've heard, Daedalus put off his wings,
While my white hair is still new, my old age in the prime of its straightness,
While my fate spinner still has yarn on her spool, while I'm able

Text: From *Satires of Juvenal*, translated by Rolfe Humphries. Copyright © 1958 by Indiana University Press. Reprinted by permission.

Still to support myself on two good legs, without crutches.
Rome, good-bye! Let the rest stay in town if they want to,
Fellows like A, B, and C, who make black white at their pleasure,
Finding it easy to grab contracts for rivers and harbors,
Putting up temples, or cleaning out sewers, or hauling off corpses,
Or, if it comes to that, auctioning slaves in the market.
Once they used to be hornblowers, working the carneys;
Every wide place in the road knew their puffed-out cheeks and their squealing.
Now they give shows of their own. Thumbs up! Thumbs down! And the killers

Spare or slay, and then go back to concessions for
   private privies.
Nothing they won't take on. Why not?—since the
   kindness of Fortune
(Fortune is out for laughs) has exalted them out of
   the gutter.

"What should I do in Rome? I am no good at lying.
If a book's bad, I can't praise it, or go around or-
   dering copies.
I don't know the stars; I can't hire out as assassin
When some young man wants his father knocked
   off for a price; I have never
Studied the guts of frogs, and plenty of others
   know better
How to convey to a bride the gifts of the first man
   she cheats with.
I am no lookout for thieves, so I cannot expect a
   commission
On some governor's staff. I'm a useless corpse, or
   a cripple.
Who has a pull these days, except your yes men
   and stooges
With blackmail in their hearts, yet smart enough
   to keep silent?
No honest man feels in debt to those he admits to
   his secrets,
But your Verres must love the man who can tattle
   on Verres
Any old time that he wants. Never let the gold of
   the Tagus,
Rolling under its shade, become so important, so
   precious
You have to lie awake, take bribes that you'll have
   to surrender,
Tossing in gloom, a threat to your mighty patron
   forever.

"Now let me speak of the race that our rich men
   dote on most fondly.
These I avoid like the plague, let's have no coy-
   ness about it.
Citizens, I can't stand a Greekized Rome. Yet what
   portion
Of the dregs of our town comes from Achaia only?
Into the Tiber pours the silt, the mud of Orontes,
Bringing its babble and brawl, its dissonant harps
   and its timbrels,
Bringing also the tarts who display their wares at
   the Circus.
Here's the place, if your taste is for hat-wearing
   whores, brightly colored!
What have they come to now, the simple souls
   from the country
Romulus used to know? They put on the *trech-
   edipna*
(That might be called, in our tongue, their run-
   ning-to-dinner outfit),

Pin on their *niketeria* (medals), and smell *ceromatic*
(Attar of wrestler). They come, trooping from
   Samos and Tralles,
Andros, wherever that it is, Azusa and Cucamonga,
Bound for the Esquiline or the hill we have named
   for the vineyard,
Termites into great halls where they hope, some
   day, to be tyrants.
Desperate nerve, quick wit, as ready in speech as
   Isaeus,
Also a lot more long-winded. Look over there! See
   that fellow?
What do you take him for? He can be anybody he
   chooses,
Doctor of science or letters, a vet or a chiropractor,
Orator, painter, masseur, palmologist, tightrope
   walker.
If he is hungry enough, your little Greek stops at
   nothing.
Tell him to fly to the moon, and he runs off for his
   space ship.
Who flew first? Some Moor, some Turk, some
   Croat, or some Slovene?
Not on your life, but a man from the very center
   of Athens.

". . . Agh, what lackeys they are, what sycophants!
   See how they flatter
Some ignoramus's talk, or the looks of some hor-
   rible eyesore,
Saying some Ichabod Crane's long neck reminds
   them of muscles
Hercules strained when he lifted Antaeus aloft on
   his shoulders,
Praising some cackling voice that really sounds like
   a rooster's
When he's pecking a hen. We can praise the same
   objects that they do,
Only, they are believed. . . .

"If you're poor, you're a joke, on each and every
   occasion.
What a laugh, if your cloak is dirty or torn, if your
   toga
Seems a little bit soiled, if your shoe has a crack
   in the leather,
Or if more than one patch attests to more than
   one mending!
Poverty's greatest curse, much worse than the fact
   of it, is that
It makes men objects of mirth, ridiculed, humbled,
   embarrassed.
'Out of the front-row seats!' they cry when you're
   out of money,
Yield your place to the sons of some pimp, the
   spawn of some cathouse,
Some slick auctioneer's brat, or the louts some

trainer has fathered
Or the well-groomed boys whose sire is a gladiator.
Such is the law of place, decreed by the nitwitted Otho:
All the best seats are reserved for the classes who have the most money.
Who can marry a girl if he has less money than she does?
What poor man is an heir, or can hope to be? Which of them ever
Rates a political job, even the meanest and lowest?
Long before now, all poor Roman descendants of Romans
Ought to have marched out of town in one determined migration.
Men do not easily rise whose poverty hinders their merit.
Here it is harder than anywhere else; the lodgings are hovels,
Rents out of sight; your slaves take plenty to fill up their bellies
While you make do with a snack. You're ashamed of your earthenware dishes—
Ah, but that wouldn't be true if you lived content in the country,
Wearing a dark-blue cape, and the hood thrown back on your shoulders. . . .

"Who, in Praeneste's cool, or the wooded Volsinian uplands,
Who, on Tivoli's heights, or a small town like Gabii, say,
Fears the collapse of his house? But Rome is supported on pipestems,
Matchsticks; it's cheaper, so, for the landlord to shore up his ruins,
Patch up the old cracked walls, and notify all the tenants
They can sleep secure, though the beams are in ruins above them.
No, the place to live is out there, where no cry of *Fire!*
Sounds the alarm of the night, with neighbor yelling for water,
Moving his chattels and goods, and the whole third story is smoking.
This you'll never know: for if the ground floor is scared first,
You are the last to burn, up there where the eaves of the attic
Keep off the rain, and the doves are brooding over their nest eggs. . . .

"This is not all you must fear. Shut up your house or your store,
Bolts and padlocks and bars will never keep out all the burglars,
Or a holdup man will do you in with a switch blade.
If the guards are strong over Pontine marshes and pinewoods
Near Volturno, the scum of the swamps and the filth of the forest
Swirl into Rome, the great sewer, their sanctuary, their haven. . . ."

37 PLINY THE YOUNGER, *LETTERS*: A ROMAN GENTLEMAN OF THE OLD SCHOOL

During the years from 98 to 180 A.D. five emperors in turn ruled the Roman Empire—Nerva, Trajan, Hadrian, Antoninus Pius, and Marcus Aurelius. Under the regime of these five "good emperors," the empire prospered and there were none of the disturbances which had troubled the succession in the previous century. For Edward Gibbon, the eighteenth-century historian of *The Decline and Fall of the Roman Empire*, it was the "happiest time in history." In this peaceful and seemingly permanent civilization lived Gaius Plinius Secundus, better known to moderns as Pliny the Younger (62?-c.113). Pliny pursued the legal profession and became a prominent public official, including governor of Bithynia in Asia Minor. His epistles present a rather pleasant view of life in the Roman Empire at its height, and the author emerges as a cultivated aristocrat, with a variety of interests, a warm heart, and an urbane, if slightly superficial, intelligence. Pliny's assured manner, gracious acceptance of his lofty position, enormous wealth, and somewhat too easy adjustment to things as they are might irritate a satirist like Petronius. In the first of the two letters which follow, Pliny is seen as a relaxed senator enjoying a vacation at one of his many Italian villas. In the second, he is the good citizen, the benefactor of Novum Comum, his native town, where he contributed generously to a local school. The tradition of *noblesse oblige* was as much a part of Roman character as was the vulgar ostentation of the newly rich Trimalchio or the Roman mob's appetite for bread and circuses. No more pleasant example of this rather noble breed of Roman can be cited than

Pliny the Younger, whose many failings are somewhat diminished as he pleads the cause of good education to the citizens of his native town.

To Fuscus

You desire to know in what manner I dispose of my day in summer-time at my Tuscan villa.

I rise just when I find myself in the humour, though generally with the sun; often indeed sooner, but seldom later. When I am up, I continue to keep the shutters of my chamber-windows closed. For under the influence of darkness and silence, I find myself wonderfully free and abstracted from those outward objects which dissipate attention, and left to my own thoughts; nor do I suffer my mind to wander with my eyes, but keep my eyes in subjection to my mind, which in the absence of external objects, see those which are present to the mental vision. If I have any composition upon my hands, this is the time I choose to consider it, not only with respect to the general plan, but even the style and expression, which I settle and correct as if I were actually writing. In this manner I compose more or less as the subject is more or less difficult, and I find myself able to retain it. Then I call my secretary, and, opening the shutters, I dictate to him what I have composed, after which I dismiss him for a little while, and then call him in again and again dismiss him.

About ten or eleven of the clock (for I do not observe one fixed hour), according as the weather recommends, I betake myself either to the terrace, or the covered portico, and there I meditate and dictate what remains upon the subject in which I am engaged. From thence I get into my chariot, where I employ myself as before, when I was walking or in my study; and find this changing of the scene preserves and enlivens my attention. At my return home I repose myself a while; then I take a walk; and after that, read aloud and with emphasis some Greek or Latin oration, not so much for the sake of strengthening my elocution as my digestion; though indeed the voice at the same time finds its account in this practice. Then I walk again, am anointed, take my exercises, and go into the bath. At supper, if I have only my wife, or a few friends with me, some author is read to us; and after supper we are entertained either with music, or an interlude. When that is finished, I take my walk with my domestics, in the number of which I am not without some persons of literature. Thus we pass our evenings in various conversation; and the day, even when it is at the longest, is quickly-spent.

Upon some occasions, I change the order in certain of the articles above mentioned. For instance, if I have lain longer or walked more than usual, after my second sleep and reading aloud, instead of using my chariot I get on horseback; by which means I take as much exercise and lose less time. The visits of my friends from the neighbouring towns claim some part of the day; and sometimes by a seasonable interruption, they relieve me, when I am fatigued. I now and then amuse myself with sporting, but always take my tablets into the field, that though I should catch nothing, I may at least bring home something. Part of my time, too (though not so much as they desire), is allotted to my tenants: and I find their rustic complaints give a zest to my studies and engagements of the politer kind. Farewell.

To Cornelius Tacitus

I rejoice that you are safely arrived in Rome; for though I am always desirous to see you, I am more particularly so now. I purpose to continue a few days longer at my Tusculum estate in order to finish a little work which I have upon my hands. For I am afraid, should I put a stop in this design, now that it is so nearly completed, I should find it difficult to resume it. Meanwhile, that I may strike while the iron is hot, I send this letter, like an *avant-courier*, to request a favour of you, which I mean shortly to ask in person. But before I inform you what my request is, I must let you into the occasion of it.

Being lately at my native place, a young lad, son to one of my fellow-townsmen, made me a visit. "Do you go to school?" I asked him. "Yes," said he. "And where?" He told me, "At Milan." "And why not here?" "Because" (said his father, who was present, and had in fact brought the boy with him), "we have no teachers." "How is that?" said I; "surely it nearly concerns you who are fathers" (and very opportunely several of the company were so) "that your sons should receive their education here, rather than any where else. For where can they be placed more agreeably than in their own country, or maintained in more modest habits and at less expense, than at home and under the eye of their parents? Upon what very easy terms might you, by a general contribution, procure teachers, if you would only apply towards raising a salary for them what you now spend on your sons' lodging, journeys,

Text: Reprinted by permission of the publishers and The Loeb Classical Library from Pliny, *Letters*, trans. William Melmoth, rev. W. M. L. Hutchinson (Cambridge, Mass.: Harvard University Press, 1915), II, 259-63; I, 311-15.

and whatever a man has to pay for when abroad (which means, paying for everything). Why, I, who have as yet no children myself, am ready to give a third part of any sum you shall think proper to raise for this purpose, for the benefit of our Commonwealth, whom I regard as a daughter or a parent. I would take upon myself the whole expense, were I not apprehensive that my benefaction might hereafter be abused and perverted to private ends; as I have observed to be the case in several places where teachers are engaged by the local authorities. The single means to prevent this mischief is, to leave the choice of the professors entirely in the breast of the parents, who will be so much the more careful to determine properly, as they shall be obliged to share the expense of maintaining them. For though they may be careless in disposing of another's bounty, they will certainly be cautious how they apply their own; and will see that none but those who deserve it shall receive my money, when they must at the same time receive theirs too. Let my example then encourage you to unite heartily in this design; and be assured the greater the sum my share shall amount to, the more agreeable it will be to me. You can undertake nothing more advantageous to your children, nor more acceptable to your country. They will by this means receive their education where they receive their birth, and be accustomed from their infancy to inhabit and affect their native soil. May you be able to procure professors of such distinguished abilities, that the neighbouring towns shall be glad to draw their learning from hence; and as you now send your children to foreigners for education, may foreigners hereafter flock hither for their instruction."

I thought proper thus to lay open to you the rise of this affair, that you might be the more sensible how agreeable it will be to me, if you undertake the office I request. I entreat you, therefore, with all the earnestness a matter of so much importance deserves, to look out, amongst the great numbers of men of letters which the reputation of your genius brings to you, teachers to whom we may apply for this purpose; but it must be understood that I cannot make a binding agreement with any of them. For I would leave it entirely free to the parents to judge and choose as they shall see proper: all the share I pretend to claim is, that of contributing my care and my money. If therefore any one shall be found who relies upon his own talents, he may repair thither; but under the proviso that the said reliance is all he can count upon, so far as I am concerned. Farewell.

38 TACITUS, *AGRICOLA*: A BARBARIAN'S VIEW OF ROMAN CIVILIZATION

The Roman Empire covered an immense area, at its zenith almost 4,000,000 square miles in extent—diverse in race, language, and culture, in some areas highly civilized and densely populated and in others tribal and solitary. In the East, Rome acquired cultural elements from a far older Hellenistic civilization that united parts of three continents by means of the Greek language of learning and commerce. In the West, Rome was not a pupil but a bearer of civilization. Gaul and Spain quickly became Romanized, ultimately providing Rome with some of its ablest scholars and administrators. An empire embracing a Greek East and a Latin West had not yet divided. The great empire was everywhere pervaded by the *Pax Romana*.

For purposes of administration Augustus and his successors divided the empire into two groups of provinces, those on the frontiers requiring legionary forces and those in the civilized interiors, safe from possible invasion. Commanding these various provinces were governors who were required to render Rome a record of administrative efficiency and honesty. When we add to these military and political safeguards Rome's policies of equitable taxation and justice, one can better understand the otherwise extraordinary fact that Rome required a standing army of only 300,000 men to defend its four million square miles. So efficient was the imperial administration that it weathered the political shake-ups in Rome itself and made most civilized people, with the exception of the Parthians, content to live within the confines of the empire.

At each stage in its expansion, however, Rome met fierce resistance on the part of would-be subjects, particularly as the Roman legions marched north into Dacia, the Germanies, and Britain. The conquest of Britain was begun by Emperor Claudius, who crossed the English Channel in 43 A.D. and within three or four years subdued the lowlands. At that point bloody warfare broke out between the invaders and the wild tribes in the hills and mountains of Wales and Yorkshire, checking further advance.

Not until the decade 70-80 A.D. were Roman generals, among them the famous Agricola, able to achieve the subjugation of Wales and Yorkshire and establish a line of frontier posts in Scotland. In 122 Emperor Hadrian himself came to Britain and built the famous northern rampart bearing his name—a wall to designate, as it were, the limit of the Roman world. Despite occasional outbreaks of rebellion and border raids, Hadrian's Wall remained a protective shield for nearly two hundred years.

In his *Agricola*, the Roman historian Tacitus (54-117 A.D.) recounts the career of his father-in-law, Gnaeus Julius Agricola, a Roman general who successfully promoted the Roman conquest of Britain in 77-85 A.D. Agricola's conquests aroused the jealousy of Emperor Domitian, who recalled him to Rome and forced him into retirement. Tacitus' brief account was written after the death of both Agricola and Domitian, with the express purpose of restoring the reputation of his father-in-law. More important for us, Tacitus supplies considerable information about Britain before and during the Roman conquest. In the following selection, Tacitus puts a scathing denunciation of Roman imperialism into the mouth of a British chieftain, Calgacus, on the eve of the battle of Mount Grampius.

For the Britons, in no wise broken by the issue of the previous battle, and seeing before them vengeance or slavery, and learning at last that a common danger must be repelled by union, had brought into the field, by means of envoys and treaties, the flower of all their states. Already more than thirty thousand armed men were on view, and still the stream flowed in of all who were in their prime and of those whose age was still rude and green, famous warriors wearing their several decorations.

Pre-eminent by character and birth among the many chieftains was one named Calgacus. To the gathered host demanding battle he is reported to have spoken in the following strain:

"As often as I survey the causes of this war and our present straits, my heart beats high that this very day and this unity of ours will be the beginning of liberty for all Britain. We are all of us untouched yet by slavery: there is no other land behind us, and the very sea even is no longer free from alarms, now that the fleet of Rome threatens us. Battle therefore and arms, the strong man's pride, are also the coward's best safety. Former battles in which Rome was resisted left behind them hopes of help in us, because we, the noblest souls in all Britain, the dwellers in its inner shrine, had never seen the shores of slavery and had preserved our very eyes from the desecration and the contamination of tyranny: here at the world's end, on its last inch of liberty, we have lived unmolested to this day, in this sequestered nook of story; for the unknown is ever magnified.

"But to-day the uttermost parts of Britain are laid bare; there are no other tribes to come; nothing but sea and cliffs and these more deadly Romans, whose arrogance you shun in vain by obedience and self-restraint. Harriers of the world, now that earth fails their all-devastating hands, they probe even the sea: if their enemy have wealth, they have greed; if he be poor, they are ambitious; East nor West has glutted them; alone of mankind they behold with the same passion of concupiscence waste alike and want. To plunder, butcher, steal, these things they misname empire: they make a desolation and they call it peace.

"Children and kin are by the law of nature each man's dearest possessions; they are swept away from us by conscription to be slaves in other lands: our wives and sisters, even when thy escape a soldier's lust, are debauched by self-styled friends and guests: our goods and chattels go for tribute; our lands and harvests in requisitions of grain; life and limb themselves are used up in levelling marsh and forest to the accompaniment of gibes and blows. Slaves born to slavery are sold once for all and are fed by their masters free of cost; but Britain pays a daily price for her own enslavement, and feeds the slavers; and as in the slave-gang the new-comer is a mockery even to his fellow-slaves, so in this world-wide, age-old slave-gang, we, the new hands, worth least, are marked out to be made away with: we have no lands or mines or harbours for the working of which we might be set aside.

"Further, courage and high spirit in their subjects displease our masters: our very distance and seclusion, in proportion as they save us, make us more suspected: therefore abandon all hope of pardon, and even at this late hour take courage, whether safety or glory be most prized. A woman could lead the Brigantes to burn a colony, to storm a camp; and had not their success lapsed into listlessness they might have thrown off the yoke; but *we* shall fight as men untamed, men who have never fallen from freedom, not as returning penitents: let us show them at the very first en-

Text: Reprinted by permission of the publishers and The Loeb Classical Library from Tacitus, *Agricola*, trans. Maurice Hutton (Cambridge, Mass.: Harvard University Press, 1946), pp. 219-29.

counter what manner of men Caledonia holds in reserve for her cause in her far places.

"Or do you imagine that the Romans have as much courage in war as wantonness in peace? It is our dissensions and feuds that bring them fame: their enemy's mistake becomes their army's glory. That army, gathered from races widely separate, is held together only by success, and will melt away with defeat: unless you suppose that Gauls and Germans, and even—to their shame be it spoken—many of the tribes of Britain, who lend their blood to an alien tyranny, of which they have been enemies for more years than slaves, are attached to Rome by loyalty and liking. Fear and panic are sorry bonds of love: put these away, and they who have ceased to fear will begin to hate. Every spur to victory makes for *our* victory: there are no wives to inspire the Romans, no parents to reproach the runaway: most of them have no country or another land than this. Few in numbers, uneasy in their novel quarters, all that they see around them, the very sky and sea, strange to their eyes—the gods have delivered them into our hands as though they were caged prisoners. The empty terrors of the eye, the gleam of gold and silver, have neither help in them nor hurt. In the enemy's own battle-line we shall find hands to help us: the Britons will recognise that our cause is theirs: the Gauls will remember their former freedom: the rest of the Germans will desert them, as the Usipi deserted recently; and beyond these there is nothing to fear: empty forts, plantations of veterans, and settlements of low vitality and divided will, made up of ill-affected subjects and unjust rulers. Here you have a general and an army; on the other side lies tribute, labour in the mines, and all the other pangs of slavery. You have it in your power to perpetuate your sufferings for ever or to avenge them to-day upon this field: therefore, before you go into action, think upon your ancestors and upon your children.

They received his speech excitedly, after the manner of barbarians, with singing and shouting and uproar of various kinds: then followed the marshalling of hosts and the glitter of arms, as the bravest came to the front. No sooner was the line of battle in process of formation than Agricola, thinking that his soldiery, though exultant and with difficulty held in leash behind their fortifications, ought to receive yet further inspiration, spoke as follows:

"This is the seventh year, fellow-soldiers, since first your courage, Rome's star, and my care and zeal have been victorious in Britain. In all these campaigns and on these battlefields, whether resolution was required against the enemy or patience and hard work against Nature herself, I have had nothing to regret in my soldiers, or you in your general. Accordingly we have out-distanced, I previous governors, you previous armies: to-day our knowledge of Britain's boundaries rests not on hearsay and report, but on armed occupation: we have both discovered and subdued Britain.

"Often on the march, when swamp, mountain, and river were a weariness, I overheard the exclamations of your bravest, 'When will the enemy be delivered into our hands? When will the battle be?' They are coming: they have been dragged from their coverts; there is nothing now to bar your prayers and prowess. Victory! and the stream is with you. Defeat! and difficulties are everywhere. To have covered so much ground, to have passed the forests, to have forded the estuaries, is honour and glory to an army advancing; but our successes of to-day become the worst of perils in retreat: we have not the same knowledge of locality, we have not the same abundance of supplies; we have but our hands and swords, and therein we have everything. As for myself, I have long ago reached the conviction that retreat is fatal both to army and to general: therefore not only is honourable death always better than life dishonoured, but in our special case safety and honour lie along the same road; nor would it be inglorious to fall at the world's edge and Nature's end.

"If it were unknown tribes and a novel battle-line that confronted you, I would encourage you with the precedents of other armies: as it is, you have only to rehearse your own achievements and question your own eyes. These are the men who last year under cover of night attacked a single legion and were beaten by a shout: these are the most fugitive of the other tribes of Britain, for which reason they have survived so long. When you pierced the thickets and glens, the bravest beasts used to rush to meet you; the timid and spiritless were dislodged by the mere stir of your march. Even so the keenest of the Britons have long since fallen; there is left only the flock of cowards and shirkers. That you have found them at last is not because they have turned; they have been overtaken: desperation and supreme panic have paralysed them here in their lines, for you to win a glorious and spectacular victory. Make an end here of your campaignings: crown fifty years' work with a day of glory: prove to the state that the army has never been to blame if the war has dragged and has given to rebels their opportunity."

Even while Agricola was still speaking the enthusiasm of his men gave voice, and the close of his speech was followed by wild excitement, and they broke up at once to take their place for battle.

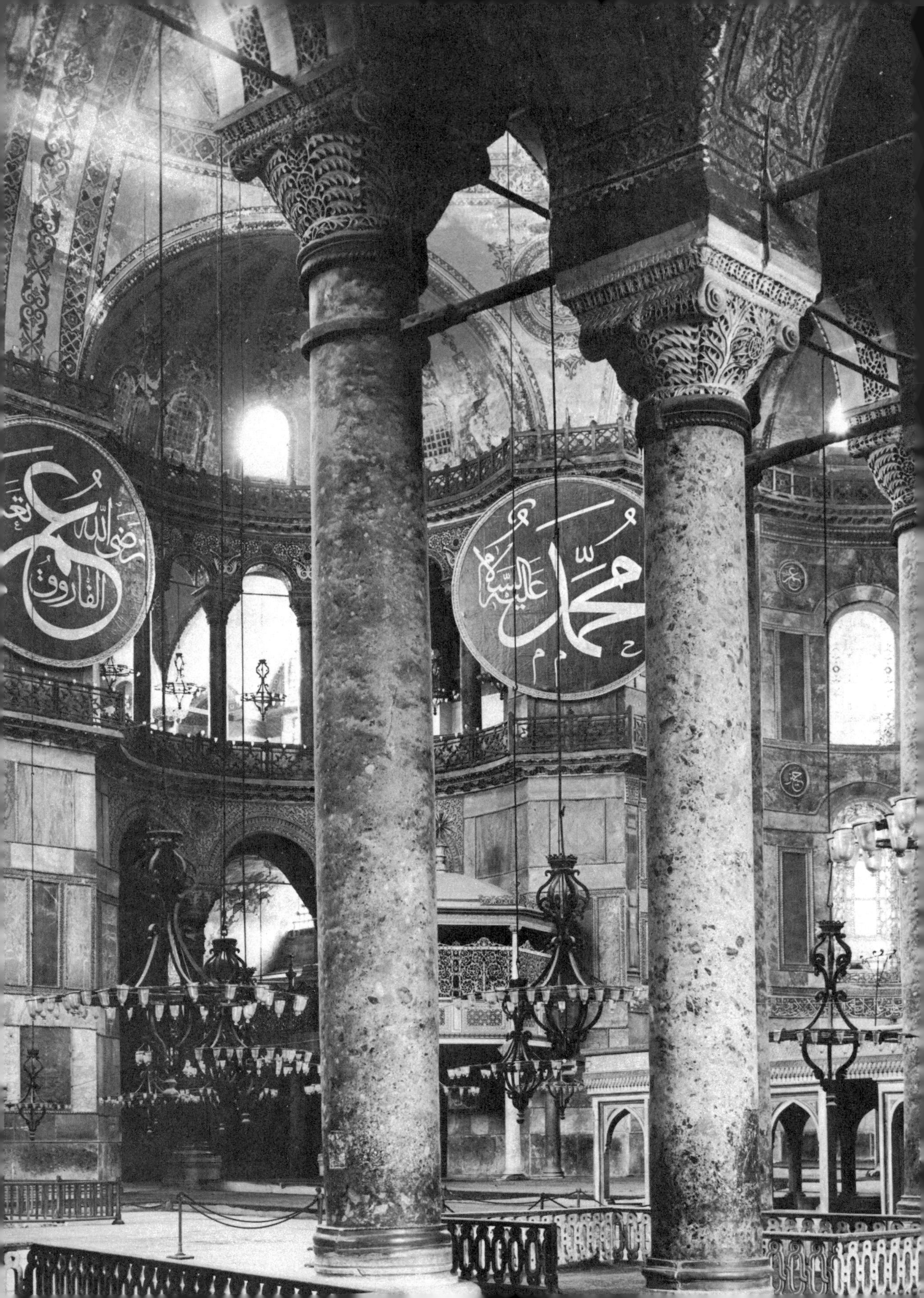
عمر رضى الله الفاروق
محمد عليه السلام

Part III

Decline and Resurgence: Christianity, the Two Empires, and Islam

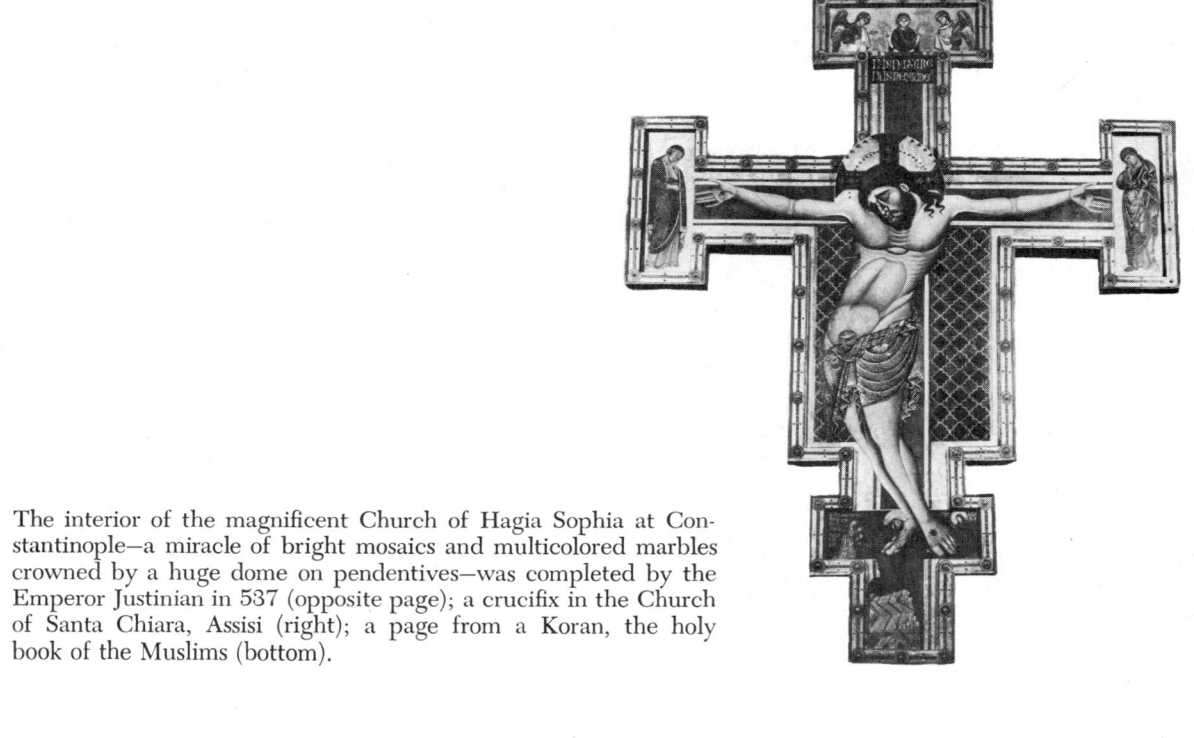

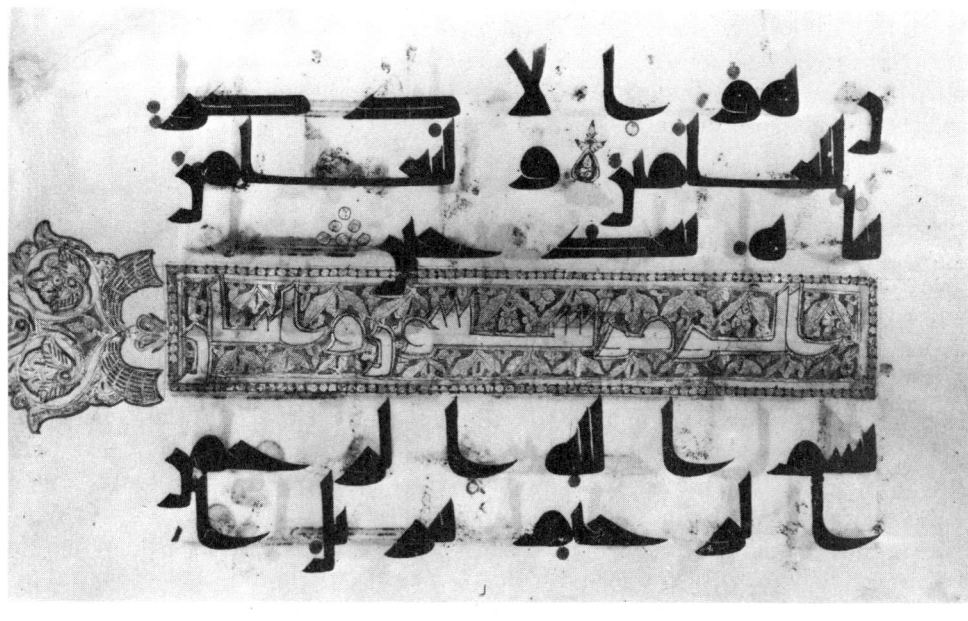

The interior of the magnificent Church of Hagia Sophia at Constantinople—a miracle of bright mosaics and multicolored marbles crowned by a huge dome on pendentives—was completed by the Emperor Justinian in 537 (opposite page); a crucifix in the Church of Santa Chiara, Assisi (right); a page from a Koran, the holy book of the Muslims (bottom).

INTRODUCTION

"The lamp of the world is extinguished, and it is the whole world which has perished in the ruins of this one city." This anguished cry came from St. Jerome in 410 when he learned in Bethlehem that Visigoth barbarians had sacked Rome, "the Eternal City." To Jerome and his contemporaries, this was a final blow in the shattering of both a world-state and a thousand years of civilization. Gone forever was "the immense majesty of the Roman peace"; now the long night of barbarism was descending to engulf the western world. That the *Pax Romana* had in fact possessed "immense majesty" is attested by the endurance of its memory, which has haunted men across the intervening fifteen centuries since its dissolution. Today, we can still recapture the poignancy of Jerome's words, for he foresaw with stark clarity the decline of western civilization into what became known as the "dark ages." What he could not have foreseen was that this period of decline would be followed by a splendid resurgence destined to create a new western world in which were fused the heritage of Greece and Rome and the message of Christianity. Nor could Jerome have perceived in his day that the eastern portion of the Roman Empire would withstand the assaults of barbarians and thereby preserve the classical tradition unbroken until a revitalized West was ready to receive it afresh. And the scholarly saint—who translated the Old and New Testaments into Latin and formed the basis of the version known as the Vulgate—lived two centuries before the birth of another monotheistic religion in the Near East. Jerome, who attacked sharply all whom he considered heretic, would most certainly have denounced both the teachings and the spread of Islam, but the perspective which the intervening centuries have provided enables us to assess its massive contribution to the resurgence of civilization in the lands spreading out from the Mediterranean.

This, then, is the theme of this Part: the decline and resurgence of those lands in the wake of the "fall" of the Roman world-state. So large are the dimensions of this theme in both time and space that to try to condense into a few introductory paragraphs all the events which it contains would be futile. Fortunately, there is a denominator common to the three key societies existing within this great framework, namely, western Europe, the eastern empire, and Islam. It is the vitality of the religious impulse. Classical Greece and Rome had been basically secular in both outlook and motivation. But medieval Europe and Islam owed their dynamic quality to the zeal of religious belief, which permeated and transformed all other aspects of their respective culture patterns. Let us now consider briefly this process at work in the major religious center of each society: Rome, Constantinople, and Mecca.

ROME

Christianity was born in an insignificant province of the Roman world. A narrow maritime rectangle, Palestine had few physical resources to justify the centuries of warfare that had been waged to possess its desert wastes and mountain ridges. At length, however, it had become the homeland of the Jews, whose national pride was inspired by a fiercely held monotheism which at the same time was interpreted to mean that they had entered into a special covenant with Jehovah as His "chosen people." Undeterred by ridicule of their claim to uniqueness and despite exile or conquest by one powerful people after another, the Jews held fast to their belief in ultimate deliverance by a Messiah who would create a new Israel.

Into this emotion-charged environment was born Jesus of Nazareth. When he began teaching, many Jews at first hailed him as the promised Messiah, but their praises turned to insults when they found that the kingdom of which the Nazarene spoke was that of God and not of men. Jesus had no intention of leading a nationalistic revolt against the Roman overlords, nor did his teachings as the new Messiah conform to the orthodox Jewish tradition. His gospel stressed not the uniqueness of the Jews' relationship to God but rather the promise of salvation which God held out to mankind everywhere. At length this derided "King of the Jews" was crucified, and the Roman governor, Pontius Pilate, may well have congratulated himself that swift action had preserved the existing *status quo*.

For so it appeared. A nationalist uprising by the Jews was later sternly quelled by Roman legionaries with the destruction of Jerusalem in 70 A.D. Meanwhile, the name and teachings of Jesus had been all but forgotten except by a few devoted followers. Christianity was apparently to remain only another minor faith among the multitude of creeds and cults to be found throughout the Roman Empire. That it was transformed into a dynamic religion extending far beyond the borders of Palestine was the work primarily of zealous missionaries like "the Apostle of the Gentiles," Paul of Tarsus, a Jewish scholar versed in Greek philosophy, who had been a persecutor of the Christians until his own conversion to the new faith. Subsequently, he worked among the communities of Hellenized Jews in Tarsus, Antioch, and elsewhere. Of even greater importance, perhaps, he preached the universality of Jesus' teachings to the non-Jewish peoples of the Greek-speaking eastern Mediterranean: "For there is no difference between the Jew and the Greek: for the same Lord over all is rich unto all that call upon him" (Romans 10:12). Paul's brilliant missionary efforts among these gentile communities paved the way for the expansion of Christianity into a world religion.

Nevertheless, Christianity's rise was a protracted, bitter struggle. With its diversity of races and cultures, the Roman world-state had tolerated all faiths so long as they accepted the unifying concept of the divinity of the emperors. However, the sternly monotheistic Christians, no less than the Jews, refused to coexist peacefully with other faiths which they considered abhorrent to God—faiths such as Mithraism, a Persian importation popular in the Roman legions, and the cult of Isis. The early Christians were regarded as extremists by the Roman authorities, and to these normally tolerant administrators extremism spelled trouble. When, moreover, Christian noncoöperation included refusal to worship the emperor, it was construed as subversion. As early as the first century popular distrust had been mounting in Rome itself, where the Christians met in such out-of-the-way places as the catacombs, and Nero found it convenient to blame the fire in the capital on the Christian community. While official persecutions were rare, Roman administrators kept a wary eye on Christian activities. We see this attitude clearly shown in the celebrated correspondence between Pliny, Governor of Bithynia near the Black Sea, and Emperor Trajan (see Document 41).

Despite official opposition, Christianity, with its appealing message of personal salvation, continued to win the allegiance of ever growing numbers of people who had lost faith in the established order. Towards the end of the second century, the religion had spread so far throughout the empire as to cause the Church writer Tertullian to tell the pagans: "We have filled your whole world, cities, islands, country towns, even the camps, the tribes, the boards of judges, the palace, the Senate, the bar. We have left you only your temples."

Meanwhile, the capital of the world-state could be expected to become prominent—and indeed dominant—in the organization of the Church. The epistle which Paul addressed to the Christian community at Rome underscores the importance which he attached to that city as a key center for future religious work. Earlier, the apostle Peter had gone to Rome where, according to tradition, he became its first bishop. This was a development of far-reaching importance since the Scriptures taught that Peter had been given the keys of heaven by Christ, and succeeding bishops of Rome could claim in turn to have inherited these powers from Peter. The rise of Rome as the major Christian center in the West coincided with the progressive erosion of its secular power. This was due to the squalid struggles among contenders for imperial power and the throning and dethroning of puppet emperors, the ravaging of the frontiers by restless barbarian peoples and of the home population by plagues, and the decline of the imperial economy, along with bureaucratic inefficiency and crippling taxation. The western half of the empire, moreover, was declining more rapidly than the eastern territories, which possessed more people and greater economic resources.

These two crucial historical movements—on the one hand, the upsurge of Christianity and ecclesiastical Rome and, on the other, the decline of secular Rome and the shift of political power to the East—intersect dramatically in the reign of Constantine the Great (288?-337). Christian persecutions ceased in 313 with his Edict of Milan, which legalized Christianity and put it on a par with all other faiths. Twelve years later, he presided at a great Church council, held in Nicaea, where basic theological dogmas were established and the crucial issue of the Trinitarian nature of God was formally resolved (see Document 48). Then, in 330, Constantine founded a new capital on the Bosporus. An act of far-reaching implications, this meant that Rome's days of temporal supremacy were numbered, for the empire's western defenses were steadily weakening before the combined forces of failing manpower at home and barbarian intrusions on the frontier.

The fourth and fifth centuries were punctuated by hammer blows along the Rhine-Danube borders; terrified Germans seeking refuge against the advance from the east of Hunnish hordes set off a series of wholesale invasions. In 476, the long line of emperors that had begun with Augustus was replaced by outright German control over Italy. But if the Rome of Caesar had fallen, the Rome of the papacy remained. The centuries-old *Pax Romana* now disappeared in the West—however, a new international order had already emerged. During its formative centuries, the Church had developed a highly organized system. Based upon the administrative divisions of the Roman Empire, it provided for a chain of command running all the way from the local parish to the papal palace in Rome. When, therefore, the collapse of the Roman state left a power vacuum in the West, this was progressively filled by an ecclesiastical monarchy whose administrative structure covered all western Europe. At its head stood the Bishop of Rome who as St. Peter's successor could claim to serve as intermediary between heaven and earth. In effect, the leadership of the western world had been transferred from a temporal to a spiritual caesar—a process largely ensured by the forceful Pope Leo the Great (c. 390-461), who is credited with having turned back Attila the Hun from the very gates of Rome. Under later strong pontiffs, the leadership of the papacy—controlling an international administration and vast properties—came to dominate the western world. The barbarians had conquered Rome with the sword, but by conquering the barbarians in turn with the cross, the papacy had restored to Rome its traditional role as capital of the West. And so it remained for most of the Middle Ages.

CONSTANTINOPLE

Rome's tightly knit ecclesiastical organization and control stood in marked contrast to the situation in the "Second Rome" which Constantine had founded in 330 A.D. Situated at the crossroads of Europe and Asia, New Rome—or Constantinople, as it came to be called—was brought into existence to preserve the administration and commerce of lands comprising the eastern, and hence the wealthier and more populous, part of the Roman world. The foresight of Constantine and his imperial successors was justified by events. New Rome withstood all barbarian assaults. Consequently, when Rome on the Tiber fell, the new capital was able to carry on the imperial administration and the massive Graeco-Roman cultural traditions.

True, the ancient empire was both constricted in size and changed in character so that by the seventh century it was sufficiently Hellenized to become known as "Byzantine." But though the Byzantine monarch's title—*Basileus Rhomaion*, "King of the Romans"—was little more than a fiction, the fact remained that the imperial line endured until Constantinople itself fell to the Muslim Turks in 1453. And this fact is salient when we compare the respective ecclesiastical organizations of the two Romes. The Eastern, or Orthodox, Church drew apart from the western Church over differences of theology, ritual, language, and clerical discipline. Most important of all was the issue of ultimate authority. In Rome the pope headed a far-flung international Church and as such regarded himself as supreme in spiritual and secular affairs alike. But in Constantinople lived both the emperor and the patriarch of the Orthodox Church—with the former appointing the latter. In short, the Orthodox Church was a state establishment closely allied with the policies and administration of the Byzantine monarchy. Because of this blending of authority over church and state, the office of the emperor has been described as a form of caesaropapism (combining the functions of a caesar and a pope), an inversion of the situation at Rome where the pope also acted as caesar. Caesaropapism was in turn to be adopted as a fundamental policy by the Russian czars.

For upwards of a millennium the richest trade emporium in the world—so that men in three continents enviously referred to it as "The City"—Constantinople embodied both religious fervor and crass commercialism, the sumptuous and the tawdry alike. Subjected to constant danger as a result of its exposed situation at the eastern boundary of the Graeco-Christian world, the city's atmosphere was charged with free-reigning ideas and emotions, often carried to fanatical extremes. The mass hysteria displayed at the mammoth chariot races might be directed even less at the athletic prowess of the charioteers than at the political prospects of the emperor, remote and aloof in his box high in the Hippodrome. Again, the exaltation of public worship at the cathedral of Santa Sophia contrasted sharply with the fierce theological controversies that split the empire into warring factions (see Document 55). But the extravagances and excesses should not blind us to the massive historical role which Constantinople played—as custodian, as civilizer, and as citadel.

The Byzantines took seriously their inheritance of a splendid cultural legacy. Thus, their custodial efforts were directed to the preservation and study of classical literature and science. Constantinople remained custodian of classical civilization until its demise in 1453, by which time the Graeco-Roman legacy had been safely transmitted to a resurgent West. The Byzantines, moreover, were civilizers in their own right—from the Bosporus eastward into the Black Sea region journeyed missionaries and traders alike, to ascend in turn the rivers that flow through the Steppes of Russia. Kiev, the first important Russian city, owed its initial impetus to the civilizing labors of Byzantium, and the Orthodox Church from its capital in Constantinople carried on evangelical activities among the Slavs, provided them with an alphabet adapted to the Slavic languages, and converted the Russian leaders to Christianity (see Document 57). Meanwhile, for a thousand years Constantinople stood as a citadel against the non-Christian world. Said one modern scholar, "Under the shelter of that defence of the Eastern gateway western Europe could refashion its own life: it is hardly an exaggeration to say that the civilization of western Europe is a by-product of the Byzantine's will to survive."

MECCA

The most dangerous, and indeed ultimately fatal, menace to Constantinople came from the followers of Prophet Muhammad. The Near East had already given birth to two major monotheistic religions in Judaism and Christianity. In the seventh century it produced a third—Islam. Eventually this militant faith was to spread from the Atlantic to the Pacific across a broad band of North Africa and southern Asia. Its origins, however, were in Mecca, and it is still to Mecca that thousands of pious Muslims make long pilgrimages each year.

Pre-Islamic Arabia was largely nomadic, with the Arab Bedouins continually on the move through the desert in search of pastures for their flocks. On the coastal fringes some towns could be found; near the Red Sea was Medina, where a considerable community of Jews had settled, and farther south stood Mecca, a caravan center whose merchants carried on trade with southern Arabia, with Abyssinia across the Red Sea, and with Byzantine lands around the Mediterranean. Mecca was already at this time an important religious center as well, possessing as it did a famous sanctuary known as the Kaaba (cube). This sanctuary contained the sacred Black Stone—according to legend the gift of Gabriel to Abraham and his son Ishmael—together with the images of hundreds of local gods and fetishes. Tribes from all over the peninsula made pilgrimages to the Kaaba.

Muhammad, born in Mecca 570 A.D., was apparently influenced fairly early in life by various monotheistic views then circulating in the Arabian peninsula. His own uncompromising espousal of one God—Allah—served at first only to antagonize most of his fellow townsmen, and in 622 he was forced to flee for safety to Medina. A few years later the Prophet returned with an army, cleansed the Kaaba of its idols, and vigorously spread the tenets of his faith, Islam, throughout Arabia. After Muhammad's death in 632, his monotheistic teachings were compiled in the Koran, at once the holy of holies to all Muslims and the repository of Islamic doctrine and obligations.

Then followed one of the most amazing epochs of religious expansion in history. Muhammad had succeeded in organizing the Arabs into a militant proselytizing force which set about to annex new territories and peoples under the banner of Islam. Within some forty years they had conquered territory extending from Tunisia through Egypt and across the Fertile Crescent to include Iraq and Persia. Within a century of the Prophet's death, Muslims had stormed into the Iberian peninsula and over the Pyrenees, to be turned back only after reaching Tours in central France. While Mecca remained the spiritual capital of Islam, the political center of gravity shifted in accordance with the enlargement of territory and the rise of successive Muslim dynasties. Thus the Umayyad Dynasty ruled from 661 to 750 with Damascus as its capital, but these Arab rulers were in turn overthrown by a non-Arabic dynasty, the Abbasside, which from 750 to 1258 ruled the far-flung Islamic world from a new capital at Baghdad on the Tigris. During the early Abbasside period, Islam reached the zenith of both territorial expansion and commercial and cultural achievement. Straddling as it did three continents, the Muslim world enjoyed a state of prosperity such as post-Roman Europe did not experience until early modern times. Goods shuttled back and forth from China to Spain and from Russia to central Africa. In this cosmopolitan world, the Muslims acted a historic role as middlemen, not only for commerce but for scientific knowledge and technological skills, literature, art, and philosophy as well.

Yet despite these impressive achievements, the Muslims were not able to maintain an integrated empire, so that in time it broke up into smaller Muslim states in Spain and elsewhere. The Muslim world owed its uniqueness to its belief in Islam, in other words to an underlying religious unity. This unity, however, was not due either to the rigid ecclesiastical organization found in western Christendom at this time or to the interlocking relationship found at Constantinople whereby church and state buttressed each other during centuries of stress and storm. It was due rather to a fundamental attitude of social equality. In Muhammad's view there was no need for an ecclesiastical hierarchy which could stand apart from the rest of society. Islam permitted the leading of prayers in the mosque, but there was to be no priesthood acting as intermediaries between God and men. The teachings of the Koran sufficed for the guidance of all true believers, together with the sacred, or canon, law which came to regulate every aspect of Muslim behavior.

The simple theocratic community which Muhammad had envisaged disappeared as Arabs conquered other lands and Islam came to embrace not only diverse races and cultures but also great political dynasties and widespread empires. The geographical distances separating Gibraltar from Indonesia made for political fragmentation—a process hastened by dynastic struggles. Yet underneath all the shifts of fortune to which the Islamic world was subjected for thirteen centuries following the Prophet's death, there endured what was to prove its most dynamic characteristic: the fundamental unity of all true believers, regardless of race, color, or level of cultural attainment. "Know ye," said Muhammad, "that every Muslim is a brother to every other Muslim, and that ye are now one brotherhood." This is the powerful message which a resurgent Islam is carrying to the receptive peoples of awakening northern and equatorial Africa today.

The Rise of Christianity and the Fall of Rome

THE BIRTH AND GROWTH OF CHRISTIANITY

39 THE GOSPEL ACCORDING TO SAINT MATTHEW: THE SERMON ON THE MOUNT

During the imperial reigns of Augustus Caesar and his successor Tiberius, events were taking place in a far-off Roman province which were to influence the entire future of western civilization. Yet to the Roman administration the events in Palestine probably seemed only a minor if time-consuming annoyance in the continuous history of Roman-Jewish animosity. Since 63 B.C. the Romans had dominated the Jews indirectly through client kingdoms ruled by the house of Herod or directly by a Roman procurator of Judea who was responsible to the provincial governor of Syria. In either case, the Jewish people, whose national independence was once again being destroyed, found the will to resist in their national religion, which centered on one God—the God of the Israelites. In their own eyes, the Jews were the "chosen people," the specific object of God's love and His divine instrument on earth. Their hopes foresaw His restoring the kingdom of the Israelites, which would rule supreme over all nations and reëstablish righteousness everywhere on earth. This salvation was for the nation, not for the particular benefit of the individual.

Some Jews associated the restoration of the kingdom with the coming of the Messiah, or "anointed one." Although Jesus of Nazareth (c. 4 B.C.–c. 29 A.D.) was considered by His followers to be this Messiah, the kingdom which He offered was substantially different from that of Jewish tradition. Jesus did not concern Himself with speculative questions about God's relationship to a nation or its future; instead, He emphasized God's continual presence, His fatherly love, His mercy, and His righteousness. Such a gospel of present joy was immediately accessible to every man. Jesus thus developed out of Judaism a certain universality. He taught that man should love God and strive for identity with God's virtue. God loved all men, so each man must likewise love his fellow men. Such religious behavior could become part of practical daily life and was comprehensible to even the unlearned or the child. The religion of Jesus offered a Messianic kingdom, not earthly but spiritual. The kingdom come is the doing of God's will on earth as in heaven.

In the Sermon on the Mount (Matthew, Chapters 5-7), printed in its entirety below, Jesus presented what He considered to be the ideal character of the true disciple. In place of the old Judaic Law, including the Law of Moses or Ten Commandments—which were largely restraints on man's conduct (eight of the Ten Commandments begin, "Thou shalt not")—Jesus taught a new gospel of love. He taught that the test of a good man is not what he has done or not done by overt action but rather what his character and his aspirations are. It is not enough, Jesus says, that "Thou shalt not kill"; a man must not even harbor anger. It is not sufficient that "Thou shalt not commit adultery"; a man must not even lust "in his heart." Jesus thus taught a new set of commandments, summarized in the Beatitudes (beginning "Blessed are the poor in spirit"), which pointed the way to what He considered a higher righteousness and which contained promises appealing to the spiritual aspirations of His followers. In preaching a new mode of life and attempting to reverse tradition—"It was said by them of old time, . . . but I say unto you"—Jesus was in effect challenging the authority of the leaders of the Jewish community. Their answer was condemnation and delivery to the Romans, who executed Him on the Cross.

Jesus believed Himself to be the Messiah, and His personality as much as His teachings drew the devotion of His followers. His Crucifixion may have scattered and temporarily dismayed His followers, but they were inspired with a belief in His eventual reappearance. This renewal of hope and courage became the basis of the Christian Church.

Chapter 5

[1] And seeing the multitudes, he went up into a mountain: and when he was set, his disciples came unto him: [2] And he opened his mouth, and taught them, saying,

[3] Blessed *are* the poor in spirit: for theirs is the kingdom of heaven.

[4] Blessed *are* they that mourn: for they shall be comforted.

[5] Blessed *are* the meek: for they shall inherit the earth.

[6] Blessed *are* they which do hunger and thirst after righteousness: for they shall be filled.

[7] Blessed *are* the merciful: for they shall obtain mercy.

[8] Blessed *are* the pure in heart: for they shall see God.

[9] Blessed *are* the peacemakers: for they shall be called the children of God.

[10] Blessed *are* they which are persecuted for righteousness' sake: for theirs is the kingdom of heaven.

[11] Blessed are ye, when *men* shall revile you, and persecute *you*, and shall say all manner of evil against you falsely, for my sake. [12] Rejoice, and be exceeding glad: for great *is* your reward in heaven: for so persecuted they the prophets which were before you.

[13] Ye are the salt of the earth: but if the salt have lost his savor, wherewith shall it be salted? it is thenceforth good for nothing, but to be cast out, and to be trodden under foot of men.

[14] Ye are the light of the world. A city that is set on a hill cannot be hid. [15] Neither do men light a candle, and put it under a bushel, but on a candlestick; and it giveth light unto all that are in the house. [16] Let your light so shine before men, that they may see your good works, and glorify your Father which is in heaven.

[17] Think not that I am come to destroy the law, or the prophets: I am not come to destroy, but to fulfil. [18] For verily I say unto you, Till heaven and earth pass, one jot or one tittle shall in no wise pass from the law, till all be fulfilled. [19] Whosoever therefore shall break one of these least commandments, and shall teach men so, he shall be called the least in the kingdom

Text: Adapted from the Authorized King James Version of the Bible. Verses are indicated by superior numbers.

of heaven: but whosoever shall do and teach *them,* the same shall be called great in the kingdom of heaven. ²⁰For I say unto you, That except your righteousness shall exceed *the righteousness* of the scribes and Pharisees, ye shall in no case enter into the kingdom of heaven.

²¹Ye have heard that it was said by them of old time, Thou shalt not kill; and whosoever shall kill shall be in danger of the judgment: ²²But I say unto you, That whosoever is angry with his brother without a cause shall be in danger of the judgment: and whosoever shall say to his brother, Raca, shall be in danger of the council: but whosoever shall say, Thou fool, shall be in danger of hell fire. ²³Therefore if thou bring thy gift to the altar, and there rememberest that thy brother hath aught against thee; ²⁴Leave there thy gift before the altar, and go thy way; first be reconciled to thy brother, and then come and offer thy gift. ²⁵Agree with thine adversary quickly, while thou art in the way with him; lest at any time the adversary deliver thee to the judge, and the judge deliver thee to the officer, and thou be cast into prison. ²⁶Verily I say unto thee, Thou shalt by no means come out thence, till thou hast paid the uttermost farthing.

²⁷Ye have heard that it was said by them of old time, Thou shalt not commit adultery: ²⁸But I say unto you, That whosoever looketh on a woman to lust after her hath committed adultery with her already in his heart. ²⁹And if thy right eye offend thee, pluck it out, and cast *it* from thee: for it is profitable for thee that one of thy members should perish, and not *that* thy whole body should be cast into hell. ³⁰And if thy right hand offend thee, cut it off, and cast *it* from thee: for it is profitable for thee that one of thy members should perish, and not *that* thy whole body should be cast into hell.

³¹It hath been said, Whosoever shall put away his wife, let him give her a writing of divorcement: ³²But I say unto you, That whosoever shall put away his wife, saving for the cause of fornication, causeth her to commit adultery: and whosoever shall marry her that is divorced committeth adultery.

³³Again, ye have heard that it hath been said by them of old time, Thou shalt not forswear thyself, but shalt perform unto the Lord thine oaths: ³⁴But I say unto you, Swear not at all; neither by heaven; for it is God's throne: ³⁵Nor by the earth; for it is his footstool: neither by Jerusalem; for it is the city of the great King. ³⁶Neither shalt thou swear by thy head, because thou canst not make one hair white or black. ³⁷But let your communication be, Yea yea; Nay, nay: for whatsoever is more than these cometh of evil.

³⁸Ye have heard that it hath been said, An eye for an eye, and a tooth for a tooth: ³⁹But I say unto you, That ye resist not evil: but whosoever shall smite thee on thy right cheek, turn to him the other also. ⁴⁰And if any man will sue thee at the law, and take away thy coat, let him have *thy* cloak also. ⁴¹And whosoever shall compel thee to go a mile, go with him twain. ⁴²Give to him that asketh thee, and from him that would borrow of thee turn not thou away.

⁴³Ye have heard that it hath been said, Thou shalt love thy neighbor, and hate thine enemy. ⁴⁴But I say unto you, Love your enemies, bless them that curse you, do good to them that hate you, and pray for them which despitefully use you, and persecute you; ⁴⁵That ye may be the children of your Father which is in heaven: for he maketh his sun to rise on the evil and on the good, and sendeth rain on the just and on the unjust. ⁴⁶For if ye love them which love you, what reward have ye? do not even the publicans the same? ⁴⁷And if ye salute your brethren only, what do ye more *than others?* do not even the publicans so? ⁴⁸Be ye therefore perfect, even as your Father which is in heaven is perfect.

Chapter 6

¹Take heed that ye do not your alms before men, to be seen of them: otherwise ye have no reward of your Father which is in heaven.

²Therefore when thou doest *thine* alms, do not sound a trumpet before thee, as the hypocrites do in the synagogues and in the streets, that they may have glory of men. Verily I say unto you, They have their reward. ³But when thou doest alms, let not thy left hand know what thy right hand doeth: ⁴That thine alms may be in secret: and thy Father which seeth in secret himself shall reward thee openly.

⁵And when thou prayest, thou shalt not be as the hypocrites *are:* for they love to pray standing in the synagogues and in the corners of the streets, that they may be seen of men. Verily I say unto you, They have their reward. ⁶But thou, when thou prayest, enter into thy closet, and when thou hast shut thy door, pray to thy Father which is in secret; and thy Father which seeth in secret shall reward thee openly.

⁷But when ye pray, use not vain repetitions, as the heathen *do:* for they think that they shall be heard for their much speaking. ⁸Be not ye therefore like unto them: for your Father knoweth what things ye have need of, before ye ask him. ⁹After this manner therefore pray ye:

Our Father which art in heaven,
Hallowed be thy name.
¹⁰Thy kingdom come.
Thy will be done
    in earth, as *it is* in heaven.
¹¹Give us this day our daily bread.
¹²And forgive us our debts,
    as we forgive our debtors.
¹³And lead us not into temptation,
    but deliver us from evil:
For thine is the kingdom,
    and the power,
    and the glory, for ever. Amen.

¹⁴For if ye forgive men their trespasses, your heavenly Father will also forgive you: ¹⁵But if ye forgive not men their trespasses, neither will your Father forgive your trespasses.

¹⁶Moreover when ye fast, be not, as the hypocrites, of a sad countenance: for they disfigure their faces, that they may appear unto men to fast. Verily I say unto you, They have their reward. ¹⁷But thou, when thou fastest, anoint thine head, and wash thy face; ¹⁸That thou appear not unto men to fast, but unto thy Father which is in secret: and thy Father, which seeth in secret, shall reward thee openly.

¹⁹Lay not up for yourselves treasures upon earth, where moth and rust doth corrupt, and where thieves break through and steal: ²⁰But lay up for yourselves treasures in heaven, where neither moth nor rust doth corrupt, and where thieves do not break through nor steal: ²¹For where your treasure is, there will your heart be also.

²²The light of the body is the eye: if therefore thine eye be single, thy whole body shall be full of light. ²³But if thine eye be evil, thy whole body shall be full of darkness. If therefore the light that is in thee be darkness, how great *is* that darkness!

²⁴No man can serve two masters: for either he will hate the one, and love the other; or else he will hold to the one, and despise the other. Ye cannot serve God and mammon.

²⁵Therefore I say unto you, Take no thought for your life, what ye shall eat, or what ye shall drink; nor yet for your body, what ye shall put on. Is not the life more than meat, and the body than raiment? ²⁶Behold the fowls of the air: for they sow not, neither do they reap, nor gather into barns; yet your heavenly Father feedeth them. Are ye not much better than they? ²⁷Which of you by taking thought can add one cubit unto his stature? ²⁸And why take ye thought for raiment? Consider the lilies of the field, how they grow; they toil not, neither do they spin: ²⁹And yet I say unto you, That even Solomon in all his glory was not arrayed like one of these. ³⁰Wherefore, if God so clothe the grass of the field, which today is, and to-morrow is cast into the oven, *shall he* not much more *clothe* you, O ye of little faith? ³¹Therefore take no thought, saying, What shall we eat? or, What shall we drink? or, Wherewithal shall we be clothed? ³²(For after all these things do the Gentiles seek:) for your heavenly Father knoweth that ye have need of all these things. ³³But seek ye first the kingdom of God, and his righteousness; and all these things shall be added unto you.

³⁴Take therefore no thought for the morrow: for the morrow shall take thought for the things of itself. Sufficient unto the day *is* the evil thereof.

Chapter 7

¹Judge not, that ye be not judged. ²For with what judgment ye judge, ye shall be judged: and with what measure ye mete, it shall be measured to you again. ³And why beholdest thou the mote that is in thy brother's eye, but considerest not the beam that is in thine own eye? ⁴Or how wilt thou say to thy brother, Let me pull out the mote out of thine eye; and, behold, a beam *is* in thine own eye? ⁵Thou hypocrite, first cast out the beam out of thine own eye; and then shalt thou see clearly to cast out the mote out of thy brother's eye.

⁶Give not that which is holy unto the dogs, neither cast ye your pearls before swine, lest they trample them under their feet, and turn again and rend you.

⁷Ask, and it shall be given you; seek, and ye shall find; knock, and it shall be opened unto you: ⁸For every one that asketh receiveth; and he that seeketh findeth; and to him that knocketh it shall be opened. ⁹Or what man is there of you, whom if his son ask bread, will he give him a stone? ¹⁰Or if he ask a fish, will he give him a serpent? ¹¹If ye then, being evil, know how to give good gifts unto your children, how much more shall your Father which is in heaven give good things to them that ask him? ¹²Therefore all things whatsoever ye would that men should do to you, do ye even so to them: for this is the law and the prophets.

¹³Enter ye in at the strait gate: for wide *is* the gate, and broad *is* the way, that leadeth to destruction, and many there be which go in thereat: ¹⁴Because strait *is* the gate, and narrow *is* the way, which leadeth unto life, and few there be that find it.

¹⁵Beware of false prophets, which come to you in sheep's clothing, but inwardly they are ravening wolves. ¹⁶Ye shall know them by their fruits. Do men gather grapes of thorns, or figs of this-

tles? ¹⁷Even so every good tree bringeth forth good fruit; but a corrupt tree bringeth forth evil fruit. ¹⁸A good tree cannot bring forth evil fruit, neither *can* a corrupt tree bring forth good fruit. ¹⁹Every tree that bringeth not forth good fruit is hewn down, and cast into the fire. ²⁰Wherefore by their fruits ye shall know them.

²¹Not every one that saith unto me, Lord, Lord, shall enter into the kingdom of heaven; but he that doest the will of my Father which is in heaven. ²²Many will say to me in that day, Lord, Lord, have we not prophesied in thy name? and in thy name have cast out devils? and in thy name done many wonderful works? ²³And then will I profess unto them, I never knew you: depart from me, ye that work iniquity.

²⁴Therefore whosoever heareth these sayings of mine, and doeth them, I will liken him unto a wise man, which built his house upon a rock: ²⁵And the rain descended, and the floods came, and the winds blew, and beat upon that house; and it fell not: for it was founded upon a rock. ²⁶And every one that heareth these sayings of mine, and doeth them not, shall be likened unto a foolish man, which built his house upon the sand: ²⁷And the rain descended, and the floods came, and the winds blew, and beat upon that house; and it fell: and great was the fall of it.

²⁸And it came to pass, when Jesus had ended these sayings, the people were astonished at his doctrine: ²⁹For he taught them as *one* having authority, and not as the scribes.

40 THE EPISTLE OF PAUL THE APOSTLE TO THE ROMANS: THE OLD LAW AND THE NEW GOSPEL

The Crucifixion of Jesus and the belief in His return from the dead aroused even deeper devotion in His little group of Jewish followers, so much so that His person tended to supplant His gospel as their prime object of faith. He was the Messiah promised by the Jewish prophets, and in a sense He retained this national element in the minds of His earliest disciples. They continued to ask, "Lord, wilt thou at this time restore again the kingdom to Israel?" (Acts 1:6.)

It was Paul, "the Apostle of the Gentiles," who first appreciated the universality of the teachings of Jesus and came to distinguish between Judaism and the gospel of Christ (the Greek translation of Messiah). Paul was born in Tarsus of Jewish origin and in his youth went to Jerusalem. He was at first a vehement persecutor of the Christians, but during a journey to Damascus he was miraculously converted to Christianity and became its most earnest propagator and interpreter. As a missionary he toured Syria, Cyprus, Asia Minor, Macedonia, Greece, and elsewhere, founding churches. His letters, or epistles, to these colonies form a large part of the New Testament. According to Christian tradition he was executed in Rome *circa* 67 A.D.

The Epistle of Paul the Apostle to the Romans, printed in part below, has been called "the first great work of Christian theology." It was probably sent from Corinth, sometime between 56 and 59 A.D., and was written when Paul began to contemplate carrying his missionary work to the west, even to Spain; for this, Rome was a natural base of operations, and before sailing to Rome, he wished to gain the approval and support of its community of Christians. Thus he wrote his epistle to the Romans, defining the fundamental theology of Christianity as he saw it and urging that Christianity was a faith for all men of the Roman world.

Much of the epistle is devoted to Paul's differentiation between the old Judaic Law and the new gospel. Paul himself had been raised in the legalistic religion of later Judaism, which had accrued a body of regulations governing almost every situation conceivable between man and God and between man and man. Complete observance of these rules made a man righteous before God, but from his own experience Paul came to feel that strict observance was impossible. With his conversion to Christianity he came to question what good the Law had served: his answer was that the Law had been temporary, acting as a "schoolmaster" (Galatians 3:24) until the advent of Christ. The Law had exposed man's sinfulness by indicating how far he fell short of perfection; it had also instilled in him a deep sense of sin but had offered him no delivery from it.

In his interpretation of the gospel, Paul granted that man had inherited Adam's original sin, that man was inherently unrighteous—"There is none righteous, no, not one" (Romans 3:10)—but Paul declared that there was a method whereby man could be *justified*, that is, "reckoned to be righteous," even though the Law actually marks him as unrighteous. This method whereby God delivered man from sin was called *grace*, the "free gift" of salvation bestowed by God regardless of a man's merit or desert. This poses two questions, which Paul attempted to answer. First, how did God reveal to man that he could obtain this special favor? Paul asserts that God made the life of Christ the symbol of deliverance through grace: Christ, though sinless Himself, was sent into the world as the bearer of all men's sins; His sacrifice on the Cross came so "that the body of sin might be destroyed" (Romans 6:6); His salvation was signaled in His resurrection. Secondly, how could ordinary man be similarly delivered from the consequences of sin? Human salvation did not automatically result from the sacrificial death of Christ. Paul's answer was that *faith*—complete trust in God's grace as revealed in Christ—must be absorbed by man. If faith is genuine, the love that led to the sacrifice will be imitated; man will have carried out the will of Christ and attained grace. The introduction of faith and love, unrecognized specifically by the Law, established a new relationship between man and God.

Chapter 1

[8]First, I thank my God through Jesus Christ for you all, that your faith is spoken of throughout the whole world. [9]For God is my witness, whom I serve with my spirit in the gospel of his Son, that without ceasing I make mention of you always in my prayers; [10]Making request, if by any means now at length I might have a prosperous journey by the will of God to come unto you. [11]For I long to see you, that I may impart unto you some spiritual gift, to the end ye may be established; [12]That is, that I may be comforted together with you by the mutual faith both of you and me. [13]Now I would not have you ignorant, brethren, that oftentimes I purposed to come unto you, (but was let hitherto,) that I might have some fruit among you also, even as among other Gentiles. [14]I am debtor both to the Greeks, and to the Barbarians; both to the wise, and to the unwise. [15]So, as much as in me is, I am ready to preach the gospel to you that are at Rome also.

[16]For I am not ashamed of the gospel of Christ: for it is the power of God unto salvation to every one that believeth; to the Jew first, and also to the Greek. [17]For therein is the righteousness of God revealed from faith to faith: as it is written, The just shall live by faith.

[18]For the wrath of God is revealed from heaven against all ungodliness and unrighteousness of men, who hold the truth in unrighteousness; [19]Because that which may be known of God is manifest in them; for God hath shewed *it* unto them. [20]For the invisible things of him from the creation of the world are clearly seen, being understood by the things that are made, *even* his eternal power and Godhead; so that they are without excuse: [21]Because that, when they knew God, they glorified *him* not as God, neither were thankful; but became vain in their imaginations, and their foolish heart was darkened. [22]Professing themselves to be wise, they became fools, [23]And changed the glory of the uncorruptible God into an image made like to corruptible man, and to birds, and four-footed beasts, and creeping things.

[24]Wherefore God also gave them up to uncleanness through the lusts of their own hearts, to dishonor their own bodies between themselves: [25]Who changed the truth of God into a lie, and worshipped and served the creature more than the Creator, who is blessed for ever. Amen.

[26]For this cause God gave them up unto vile affections: for even their women did change the natural use into that which is against nature: [27]And likewise also the men, leaving the natural use of the woman, burned in their lust one toward another; men with men working that which is unseemly, and receiving in themselves that recompense of their error which was meet.

[28]And even as they did not like to retain God in *their* knowledge, God gave them over to a reprobate mind, to do those things which are not convenient; [29]Being filled with all unrighteousness, fornication, wickedness, covetousness, maliciousness; full of envy, murder, debate, deceit, malignity; whisperers, [30]Backbiters, haters of God, despiteful, proud, boasters, inventors of evil things, disobedient to parents, [31]Without understanding, covenant-breakers, without natural affection, implacable, unmerciful: [32]Who knowing the judgment of God, that they which commit such things are worthy of death, not only do the same, but have pleasure in them that do them.

Chapter 2

[1]Therefore thou art inexcusable, O man, whosoever thou art that judgest: for wherein thou judgest another, thou condemnest thyself; for thou that judgest doest the same things. [2]But

Text: Adapted from the Authorized King James Version of the Bible. Verses are indicated by superior numbers.

we are sure that the judgment of God is according to truth against them which commit such things. ³And thinkest thou this, O man, that judgest them which do such things, and doest the same, that thou shalt escape the judgment of God? ⁴Or despisest thou the riches of his goodness and forbearance and longsuffering; not knowing that the goodness of God leadeth thee to repentance? ⁵But after thy hardness and impenitent heart treasurest up unto thyself wrath against the day of wrath and revelation of the righteous judgment of God; ⁶Who will render to every man according to his deeds: ⁷To them who by patient continuance in well doing seek for glory and honor and immortality, eternal life: ⁸But unto them that are contentious, and do not obey the truth, but obey unrighteousness, indignation and wrath, ⁹Tribulation and anguish, upon every soul of man that doeth evil, of the Jew first, and also of the Gentile; ¹⁰But glory, honor, and peace, to every man that worketh good, to the Jew first, and also to the Gentile: ¹¹For there is no respect of persons with God.

¹²For as many as have sinned without law shall also perish without law: and as many as have sinned in the law shall be judged by the law; ¹³(For not the hearers of the law *are* just before God, but the doers of the law shall be justified. ¹⁴For when the Gentiles, which have not the law, do by nature the things contained in the law, these, having not the law, are a law unto themselves: ¹⁵Which shew the work of the law written in their hearts, their conscience also bearing witness, and *their* thoughts the mean while accusing or else excusing one another;) ¹⁶In the day when God shall judge the secrets of men by Jesus Christ according to my gospel.

¹⁷Behold, thou art called a Jew, and restest in the law, and makest thy boast of God, ¹⁸And knowest *his* will, and approvest the things that are more excellent, being instructed out of the law; ¹⁹And art confident that thou thyself art a guide of the blind, a light of them which are in darkness, ²⁰An instructor of the foolish, a teacher of babes, which hast the form of knowledge and of the truth in the law. ²¹Thou therefore which teachest another, teachest thou not thyself? thou that preachest a man should not steal, dost thou steal? ²²Thou that sayest a man should not commit adultery, dost thou commit adultery? thou that abhorrest idols, dost thou commit sacrilege? ²³Thou that makest thy boast of the law, through breaking the law dishonorest thou God? ²⁴For the name of God is blasphemed among the Gentiles through you, as it is written.

²⁵For circumcision verily profiteth, if thou keep the law: but if thou be a breaker of the law, thy circumcision is made uncircumcision. ²⁶Therefore if the uncircumcision keep the righteousness of the law, shall not his uncircumcision be counted for circumcision? ²⁷And shall not uncircumcision which is by nature, if it fulfil the law, judge thee, who by the letter and circumcision dost transgress the law? ²⁸For he is not a Jew, which is one outwardly; neither *is that* circumcision, which is outward in the flesh: ²⁹But he *is* a Jew, which is one inwardly; and circumcision *is that* of the heart, in the spirit, *and* not in the letter; whose praise *is* not of men, but of God.

Chapter 3

¹What advantage then hath the Jew? or what profit *is there* of circumcision? ²Much every way: chiefly, because that unto them were committed the oracles of God. ³For what if some did not believe? shall their unbelief make the faith of God without effect? ⁴God forbid: yea, let God be true, but every man a liar; as it is written,

That thou mightest be justified in
    thy sayings,
and mightest overcome when thou art judged.

⁵But if our unrighteousness commend the righteousness of God, what shall we say? *Is* God unrighteous who taketh vengeance? (I speak as a man) ⁶God forbid: for then how shall God judge the world? ⁷For if the truth of God hath more abounded through my lie unto his glory; why yet am I also judged as a sinner? ⁸And not *rather*, (as we be slanderously reported, and as some affirm that we say,) Let us do evil, that good may come? whose damnation is just.

⁹What then? are we better *than they*? No, in no wise: for we have before proved both Jews and Gentiles, that they are all under sin; ¹⁰As it is written,

There is none righteous, no, not one:
¹¹There is none that understandeth, there is
    none that seeketh after God.
¹²They are all gone out of the way, they are
    together become unprofitable,
there is none that doeth good, no, not one.
¹³Their throat *is* an open sepulchre;
with their tongues they have used deceit;
the poison of asps *is* under their
    lips:
¹⁴Whose mouth *is* full of cursing and
    bitterness:
¹⁵Their feet *are* swift to shed blood:
¹⁶Destruction and misery *are* in their ways:
¹⁷And the way of peace have they not
    known:
¹⁸There is no fear of God before
    their eyes.

[19]Now we know that what things soever the law saith, it saith to them who are under the law: that every mouth may be stopped, and all the world may become guilty before God. [20]Therefore by the deeds of the law there shall no flesh be justified in his sight: for by the law *is* the knowledge of sin.

[21]But now the righteousness of God without the law is manifested, being witnessed by the law and the prophets; [22]Even the righteousness of God *which is* by faith of Jesus Christ unto all and upon all them that believe: for there is no difference: [23]For all have sinned, and come short of the glory of God; [24]Being justified freely by his grace through the redemption that is in Christ Jesus: [25]Whom God hath set forth *to be* a propitiation through faith in his blood, to declare his righteousness for the remission of sins that are past, through the forbearance of God; [26]To declare, *I say,* at this time his righteousness: that he might be just, and the justifier of him which believeth in Jesus.

[27]Where *is* boasting then? It is excluded. By what law? of works? Nay: but by the law of faith. [28]Therefore we conclude that a man is justified by faith without the deeds of the law. [29]*Is he* the God of the Jews only? *is he* not also of the Gentiles? Yes, of the Gentiles also: [30]Seeing *it is* one God, which shall justify the circumcision by faith, and uncircumcision through faith. . . .

Chapter 5

[1]Therefore being justified by faith, we have peace with God through our Lord Jesus Christ: [2]By whom also we have access by faith into this grace wherein we stand, and rejoice in hope of the glory of God. [3]And not only *so,* but we glory in tribulations also: knowing that tribulation worketh patience; [4]And patience, experience; and experience, hope: [5]And hope maketh not ashamed; because the love of God is shed abroad in our hearts by the Holy Ghost which is given unto us.

[6]For when we were yet without strength, in due time Christ died for the ungodly. [7]For scarcely for a righteous man will one die: yet peradventure for a good man some would even dare to die. [8]But God commendeth his love toward us, in that, while we were yet sinners, Christ died for us. [9]Much more then, being now justified by his blood, we shall be saved from wrath through him. [10]For if, when we were enemies, we were reconciled to God by the death of his Son, much more, being reconciled, we shall be saved by his life. [11]And not only *so,* but we also joy in God through our Lord Jesus Christ, by whom we have now received the atonement.

[12]Wherefore, as by one man sin entered into the world, and death by sin; and so death passed upon all men, for that all have sinned: [13](For until the law sin was in the world: but sin is not imputed when there is no law. [14]Nevertheless death reigned from Adam to Moses, even over them that had not sinned after the similitude of Adam's transgression, who is the figure of him that was to come.

[15]But not as the offense, so also *is* the free gift. For if through the offense of one many be dead, much more the grace of God, and the gift by grace, *which is* by one man, Jesus Christ, hath abounded unto many. [16]And not as *it was* by one that sinned, *so is* the gift: for the judgment *was* by one to condemnation, but the free gift *is* of many offenses unto justification.

[17]For if by one man's offense death reigned by one; much more they which receive abundance of grace and of the gift of righteousness shall reign in life by one, Jesus Christ.)

[18]Therefore as by the offense of one *judgment came* upon all men to condemnation; even so by the righteousness of one *the free gift came* upon all men unto justification of life. [19]For as by one man's disobedience many were made sinners, so by the obedience of one shall many be made righteous. [20]Moreover the law entered, that the offense might abound. But where sin abounded, grace did much more abound: [21]That as sin hath reigned unto death, even so might grace reign through righteousness unto eternal life by Jesus Christ our Lord.

Chapter 6

[1]What shall we say then? Shall we continue in sin, that grace may abound? [2]God forbid. How shall we, that are dead to sin, live any longer therein? [3]Know ye not, that so many of us as were baptized into Jesus Christ were baptized into his death? [4]Therefore we are buried with him by baptism into death: that like as Christ was raised up from the dead by the glory of the Father, even so we also should walk in newness of life.

[5]For if we have been planted together in the likeness of his death, we shall be also *in the likeness* of *his* resurrection: [6]Knowing this, that our old man is crucified with *him,* that the body of sin might be destroyed, that henceforth we should not serve sin. [7]For he that is dead is freed from sin. [8]Now if we be dead with Christ, we believe that we shall also live with him: [9]Knowing that Christ being raised from the dead dieth no more; death hath no more dominion over him. [10]For in that he died, he died unto sin once: but in that he liveth, he liveth unto God. [11]Likewise

reckon ye also yourselves to be dead indeed unto sin, but alive unto God through Jesus Christ our Lord.

¹²Let not sin therefore reign in your mortal body, that ye should obey it in the lusts thereof. ¹³Neither yield ye your members *as* instruments of unrighteousness unto sin: but yield yourselves unto God, as those that are alive from the dead, and your members *as* instruments of righteousness unto God. ¹⁴For sin shall not have dominion over you: for ye are not under the law, but under grace.

¹⁵What then? shall we sin, because we are not under the law, but under grace? God forbid. ¹⁶Know ye not, that to whom ye yield yourselves servants to obey, his servants ye are to whom ye obey; whether of sin unto death, or of obedience unto righteousness? ¹⁷But God be thanked, that ye were the servants of sin, but ye have obeyed from the heart that form of doctrine which was delivered you. ¹⁸Being then made free from sin, ye became the servants of righteousness. ¹⁹I speak after the manner of men because of the infirmity of your flesh: for as ye have yielded your members servants to uncleanness and to iniquity unto iniquity; even so now yield your members servants to righteousness unto holiness.

²⁰For when ye were the servants of sin, ye were free from righteousness. ²¹What fruit had ye then in those things whereof ye are now ashamed? for the end of those things *is* death. ²²But now being made free from sin, and become servants to God, ye have your fruit unto holiness, and the end everlasting life. ²³For the wages of sin *is* death; but the gift of God *is* eternal life through Jesus Christ our Lord. . . .

Chapter 12

¹I beseech you therefore, brethren, by the mercies of God, that ye present your bodies a living sacrifice, holy, acceptable unto God, *which is* your reasonable service. ²And be not conformed to this world: but be ye transformed by the renewing of your mind, that ye may prove what *is* that good, and acceptable, and perfect, will of God.

³For I say, through the grace given unto me, to every man that is among you, not to think *of himself* more highly than he ought to think; but to think soberly, according as God hath dealt to every man the measure of faith. ⁴For as we have many members in one body, and all members have not the same office: ⁵So we, *being* many, are one body in Christ, and every one members one of another. ⁶Having then gifts differing according to the grace that is given to us, whether prophecy, *let us prophesy* according to the proportion of faith: ⁷Or ministry, *let us wait* on *our* ministering: or he that teacheth, on teaching; ⁸Or he that exhorteth, on exhortation: he that giveth, *let him do it* with simplicity; he that ruleth, with diligence; he that sheweth mercy, with cheerfulness.

⁹*Let* love be without dissimulation. Abhor that which is evil; cleave to that which is good. ¹⁰*Be* kindly affectioned one to another with brotherly love; in honor preferring one another; ¹¹Not slothful in business; fervent in spirit; serving the Lord; ¹²Rejoicing in hope; patient in tribulation; continuing instant in prayer; ¹³Distributing to the necessity of saints; given to hospitality.

¹⁴Bless them which persecute you: bless, and curse not. ¹⁵Rejoice with them that do rejoice, and weep with them that weep. ¹⁶*Be* of the same mind one toward another. Mind not high things, but condescend to men of low estate. Be not wise in your own conceits. ¹⁷Recompense to no man evil for evil. Provide things honest in the sight of all men. ¹⁸If it be possible, as much as lieth in you, live peaceably with all men. ¹⁹Dearly beloved, avenge not yourselves, but *rather* give place unto wrath: for it is written, Vengeance *is* mine; I will repay, saith the Lord. ²⁰Therefore if thine enemy hunger, feed him; if he thirst, give him drink: for in so doing thou shalt heap coals of fire on his head. ²¹Be not overcome of evil, but overcome evil with good.

41 PLINY THE YOUNGER AND THE EMPEROR TRAJAN, LETTERS: THE CHRISTIANS AND ROMAN SECURITY

Although the speed with which Christianity spread in the century following the Crucifixion is less often emphasized than the expansion of Islam six hundred years later, the preaching of the new creed to the gentiles met with phenomenal success. The missionary zeal of Paul, the dispersion of the Jews after the Roman sack of Jerusalem in 70 A.D., the malaise of the pagan religion, and the easy communication which the *Pax Romana* ensured from Britain to the Tigris accelerated the force and spread of the Christian message.

The Roman government itself was generally tolerant toward any religious sect so long as its adherents willingly participated in the official pagan rituals. To take part in these ceremonies, at least upon official request, was considered a demonstration of loyalty to Rome. Since the ceremonies demanded an offering of incense before the images of pagan gods and deified Roman emperors, the Christians, who recognized only their own God and abhorred idolatry, refused to participate. In the Roman view, Christian resistance was less an act of religious impiety than a commission of political treason threatening the security of the empire.

About 111 A.D. Gaius Plinius Caecilius Secundus (62-c. 113), the Roman writer and orator (see Document 37), was appointed governor of Bithynia, a Roman province in Asia Minor. To his amazement Pliny found Christian conversion had emptied the pagan temples and ruined the thriving trade in animals for pagan sacrifices. The resulting exchange of letters between Pliny and his superior, Emperor Trajan, clearly indicates the emerging Roman policy toward "the despised sect." Neither Pliny nor Trajan will seek out Christians for persecution, even though the believers constitute in their view a threat of widespread disloyalty. Yet in ruling capital punishment for Christians who would not renounce Christianity when accused publicly, the enlightened emperor and the enlightened imperial governor created a basic irreconcilability between the pagan Roman state and the Christian Church.

To the Emperor Trajan

It is a rule, Sir, which I inviolably observe, to refer myself to you in all my doubts; for who is more capable of guiding my uncertainty or informing my ignorance? Having never been present at any trials of the Christians, I am unacquainted with the method and limits to be observed either in examining or punishing them. Whether any difference is to be made on account of age, or no distinction allowed between the youngest and the adult; whether repentance admits to a pardon, or if a man has been once a Christian it avails him nothing to recant; whether the mere profession of Christianity, albeit without crimes, or only the crimes associated therewith are punishable—in all these points I am greatly doubtful.

In the meanwhile, the method I have observed towards those who have been denounced to me as Christians is this: I interrogated them whether they were Christians; if they confessed it I repeated the question twice again, adding the threat of capital punishment; if they still persevered, I ordered them to be executed. For whatever the nature of their creed might be, I could at least feel no doubt that contumacy and inflexible obstinacy deserved chastisement. There were others also possessed with the same infatuation, but being citizens of Rome, I directed them to be carried thither.

These accusations spread (as is usually the case) from the mere fact of the matter being investigated and several forms of the mischief came to light. A placard was put up, without any signature, accusing a large number of persons by name. Those who denied they were, or had ever been, Christians, who repeated after me an invocation to the Gods, and offered adoration, with wine and frankincense, to your image, which I had ordered to be brought for that purpose, together with those of the Gods, and who finally cursed Christ—none of which acts, it is said, those who are really Christians can be forced into performing—these I thought it proper to discharge. Others who were named by that informer at first confessed themselves Christians, and then denied it; true, they had been of that persuasion but they had quitted it, some three years, others many years, and a few as much as twenty-five years ago. They all worshipped your statue and the images of the Gods, and cursed Christ.

They affirmed, however, the whole of their guilt, or their error, was, that they were in the habit of meeting on a certain fixed day before it was light, when they sang in alternate verses a hymn to Christ, as to a god, and bound themselves by a solemn oath, not to any wicked deeds, but never to commit any fraud, theft or adultery, never to falsify their word, nor deny a trust when they should be called upon to deliver it up; after which it was their custom to separate, and then reassemble to partake of food—but food of an ordinary and innocent kind. Even this practice, however, they had abandoned after the publication of my edict, by which, according to your orders, I had forbidden political associations. I judged it so much the more necessary to extract the real truth, with the assistance of torture, from two female slaves, who were styled *deaconesses:* but I could discover nothing more than depraved and excessive superstition.

Text: Reprinted by permission of the publishers and The Loeb Classical Library from Pliny, *Letters*, trans. William Melmoth, rev. W. M. L. Hutchinson (Cambridge, Mass.: Harvard University Press, 1947), II, 401-07.

I therefore adjourned the proceedings, and betook myself at once to your counsel. For the matter seemed to me well worth referring to you, —especially considering the numbers endangered. Persons of all ranks and ages, and of both sexes are, and will be, involved in the prosecution. For this contagious superstition is not confined to the cities only, but has spread through the villages and rural districts; it seems possible, however, to check and cure it. 'Tis certain at least that the temples, which had been almost deserted, begin now to be frequented; and the sacred festivals, after a long intermission, are again revived; while there is a general demand for sacrificial animals, which for some time past have met with but few purchasers. From hence it is easy to imagine what multitudes may be reclaimed from this error, if a door be left open to repentance.

Trajan to Pliny

The method you have pursued, my dear Pliny, in sifting the cases of those denounced to you as Christians is extremely proper. It is not possible to lay down any general rule which can be applied as the fixed standard in all cases of this nature. No search should be made for these people; when they are denounced and found guilty they must be punished; with the restriction, however, that when the party denies himself to be a Christian, and shall give proof that he is not (that is, by adoring our Gods) he shall be pardoned on the ground of repentance, even though he may have formerly incurred suspicion. Informations without the accuser's name subscribed must not be admitted in evidence against anyone, as it is introducing a very dangerous precedent, and by no means agreeable to the spirit of the age.

42 APULEIUS, METAMORPHOSES: THE RIVAL MYSTERY CULTS

Opposition to Christianity was not confined to the imperial administration, nor were the violent persecutions the only or perhaps the most dangerous challenges which the early Christian Church encountered. Other philosophies and mystery religions vied for the attention of the Roman world. Stoicism, Neoplatonism, the Dionysian cults, and the Persian-born religions of Manicheism and Mithraism competed with traditional Graeco-Roman paganism and with Christianity. Converts among the army, the merchants, slaves, and even the highest imperial circles spread these diverse doctrines throughout the empire.

One such rival of Christianity was the cult of Isis, a powerful and beneficent feminine deity worshiped in Egypt from ancient times. Like Christianity, the cult of Isis was a "mystery" religion—its rituals were the secret property of initiated members, and conversion to it assured the initiate some form of personal salvation. In the *Metamorphoses*, or *Golden Ass*, a long and romantic fable, Lucius Apuleius (born c. 125 A.D.), a Roman convert to the cult, recounts how a witch turned him into a donkey and how he recovered his human form through the grace of the goddess Isis. The climax is Apuleius' conversion and his consecration as an Isiac priest. The selection below underlines the passionate yearning for personal purification to which the mystery religions appealed and illustrates their concern for secrecy in the initiation ceremony. Reminiscent of Christian belief are the dignity of the ritual, the drama of redemption, and the sanctification of priests.

... I ... learned to be patient, taking part in the daily services of the temple as calmly and quietly as I knew how, intent on pleasing the Goddess. Nor did I have a troublesome and disappointing probation. Soon after this she gave me proof of her grace by a midnight vision in which I was plainly told that the day for which I longed, the day on which my greatest wish would be granted, had come at last. I learned that she had ordered the High Priest Mithras, whose destiny was linked with mine by planetary sympathy, to officiate at my initiation.

These orders and certain others given me at the same time so exhilarated me that I rose before dawn to tell the High Priest about them, and reached his door just as he was coming out. I greeted him and was about to beg him more earnestly than ever to allow me to be initiated, as a privilege that was now mine by right, when he spoke first. "Dear Lucius," he said, "how lucky,

Text: From Apuleius, *The Golden Ass*, trans. Robert Graves (New York: Farrar, Straus & Giroux, Inc., 1951), pp. 251-53. Reprinted by permission of Collins-Knowlton-Wing, Inc. Copyright © 1951 by Robert Graves.

how blessed you are that the Great Goddess has graciously deigned to honour you in this way. There is no time to waste. The day for which you prayed so earnestly has dawned. The many-named Goddess orders me to initiate you into her most holy mysteries."

He took me by the hand and led me courteously to the doors of the vast temple, and when he had opened them in the usual solemn way and performed the morning sacrifice he went to the sanctuary and took out two or three books written in characters unknown to me: some of them animal hieroglyphics, some of them ordinary letters protected against profane prying by having their tops and tails wreathed in knots or rounded like wheels or tangled together in spirals like vine tendrils. From these books he read me out instructions for providing the necessary clothes and accessories for my initiation.

I at once went to my friends the priests and asked them to buy part of what I needed, sparing no expense: the rest I went to buy myself.

In due time the High Priest summoned me and took me to the nearest public baths, attended by a crowd of priests. There, when I had enjoyed my ordinary bath, he himself washed and sprinkled me with holy water, offering up prayers for divine mercy. After this he brought me back to the temple and placed me at the very feet of the Goddess.

It was now early afternoon. He gave me certain orders too holy to be spoken above a whisper, and then commanded me in everyone's hearing to abstain from all but the plainest food for the ten succeeding days, to eat no meat and drink no wine.

I obeyed his instructions in all reverence and at last the day came for taking my vows. As evening approached a crowd of priests came flocking to me from all directions, each one giving me congratulatory gifts, as the ancient custom is. Then the High Priest ordered all uninitiated persons to depart, invested me in a new linen garment and led me by the hand into the inner recesses of the sanctuary itself. I have no doubt, curious reader, that you are eager to know what happened when I entered. If I were allowed to tell you, and you were allowed to be told, you would soon hear everything; but, as it is, my tongue would suffer for its indiscretion and your ears for their inquisitiveness.

However, not wishing to leave you, if you are religiously inclined, in a state of tortured suspense, I will record as much as I may lawfully record for the uninitiated, but only on condition that you believe it. *I approached the very gates of death and set one foot on Proserpine's threshold, yet was permitted to return, rapt through all the elements. At midnight I saw the sun shining as if it were noon; I entered the presence of the gods of the underworld and the gods of the upper-world, stood near and worshipped them.*

Well, now you have heard what happened, but I fear you are still none the wiser.

The solemn rites ended at dawn and I emerged from the sanctuary wearing twelve different stoles, certainly a most sacred costume but one that there can be no harm in my mentioning. Many uninitiated people saw me wearing it when the High Priest ordered me to mount into the wooden pulpit which stood in the centre of the temple, immediately in front of the Goddess's image. I was wearing an outer garment of fine linen embroidered with flowers, and a precious scarf hung down from my shoulders to my ankles with sacred animals worked in colour on every part of it; for instance Indian serpents and Hyperborean griffins, which are winged lions generated in the more distant parts of the world. The priests call this scarf an Olympian stole. I held a lighted torch in my right hand and wore a white palm-tree chaplet with its leaves sticking out all round like rays of light.

The curtains were pulled aside and I was suddenly exposed to the gaze of the crowd, as when a statue is unveiled, dressed like the sun. That day was the happiest of my initiation, and I celebrated it as my birthday with a cheerful banquet at which all my friends were present. Further rites and ceremonies were performed on the third day, including a sacred breakfast, and these ended the proceedings. However, I remained for some days longer in the temple, enjoying the ineffable pleasure of contemplating the Goddess's statue, because I was bound to her by a debt of gratitude so large that I could never hope to pay it.

43 MINUCIUS FELIX, OCTAVIUS: A DIALOGUE BETWEEN CHRISTIAN AND PAGAN

Competition with Christianity during its first three centuries of growth sprang from two sources: those who preached new religions rivaling Christianity (see Document 41) and those who adhered to the traditional paganism of Greece and Rome. To meet the pagan challenge, Christianity had need of men who were literary, well schooled in the pagan philosophies, and therefore capable of producing the Christian apologia—a stout defense to clarify Christian belief and to answer criticism from the pagan intelligentsia. That Christianity found such able men among its ranks refutes the often repeated pagan charge that the new religion was followed by the lowly and ignorant alone.

The *Octavius*, one such Christian apology, was written at some time in the late second century, purportedly by Minucius Felix (*fl.* second and third century A.D.), an eminent Roman lawyer deprived of the right to practice because of his conversion to Christianity. The *Octavius* is written in the pagan philosophical form of the dialogue and introduces two principal speakers: Caecilius, a pagan, and Octavius, a Christian. In the passage below Caecilius in a spirited attack contrasts the secrecy of the Christian service with the openness of the pagan ritual "in temples with altars, victims, ceremonies." To the rites of the Christians he imputes abominable practices. To Christian adherents he ascribes ignorance and criminality even though his Christian friend Octavius is of high social status. His final charge that the pagan gods had produced the Roman Empire, while the Christian God brought nothing but misery and suffering to mankind, was a favorite pagan argument. However, in the concluding sections of the dialogue, Caecilius is defeated in argument by the Christian Octavius and becomes a Christian convert.

"When Protagoras of Abdera, by way of debate rather than of profanity, discussed the godhead, the men of Athens expelled him from their borders, and burned his writings in the market-place. Is it not then deplorable that a gang—excuse my vehemence in using strong language for the cause I advocate—a gang, I say, of discredited and proscribed desperadoes band themselves against the gods? Fellows who gather together illiterates from the dregs of the populace and credulous women with the instability natural to their sex, and so organize a rabble of profane conspirators, leagued together by meetings at night and ritual fasts and unnatural repasts, not for any sacred service but for piacular rites, a secret tribe that shuns the light, silent in the open, but talkative in hid corners; they despise temples as if they were tombs; they spit upon the gods; they jeer at our sacred rites; pitiable themselves, they pity (save the mark) our priests; they despise titles and robes of honour, going themselves half-naked! What a pitch of folly! what wild impertinence! present tortures they despise, yet dread those of an uncertain future; death after death they fear, but death in the present they fear not: for them illusive hope charms away terror with assurances of a life to come.

"Already—for ill weeds grow apace—decay of morals grows from day to day, and throughout the wide world the abominations of this impious confederacy multiply. Root and branch it must be exterminated and accursed. They recognize one another by secret signs and marks; they fall in love almost before they are acquainted; everywhere they introduce a kind of religion of lust, a promiscuous 'brotherhood' and 'sisterhood' by which ordinary fornication, under cover of a hallowed name, is converted to incest. And thus their vain and foolish superstition makes an actual boast of crime. For themselves, were there not some foundation of truth, shrewd rumour would not impute gross and unmentionable forms of vice. I am told that under some idiotic impulse they consecrate and worship the head of an ass, the meanest of all beasts, a religion worthy of the morals which gave it birth. Others say that they actually reverence the private parts of their director and high-priest, and adore his organs as parent of their being. This may be false, but such suspicions naturally attach to their secret and nocturnal rites. To say that a malefactor put to death for his crimes, and wood of the death-dealing cross, are objects of their veneration is to assign fitting altars to abandoned wretches and the kind of worship they deserve. Details of the initiation of neophytes are as revolting as they are notorious. An infant, cased in dough to deceive the unsuspecting, is placed beside the person to be initiated. The novice is thereupon induced to inflict what seem to be harmless blows upon the dough, and unintentionally the infant is killed by his unsuspecting blows; the blood—oh, horrible—they lap up greedily; the limbs they tear to pieces eagerly; and over the victim they make league and covenant, and by complicity in guilt pledge themselves to mutual silence. Such sacred rites are more foul than any sacrilege. Their form of feasting is notorious; it is in everyone's mouth, as testified by the speech of our friend of Cirta. On the day appointed they

Text: Reprinted by permission of the publishers and The Loeb Classical Library from Minucius Felix, *Octavius,* trans. Gerald H. Rendall (Cambridge, Mass.: Harvard University Press, 1931), pp. 335-47.

gather at a banquet with all their children, sisters, and mothers, people of either sex and every age. There, after full feasting, when the blood is heated and drink has inflamed the passions of incestuous lust, a dog which has been tied to a lamp is tempted by a morsel thrown beyond the range of his tether to bound forward with a rush. The tale-telling light is upset and extinguished, and in the shameless dark lustful embraces are indiscriminately exchanged; and all alike, if not in act, yet by complicity, are involved in incest, as anything that occurs by the act of individuals results from the common intention.

"Much I purposely pass over; I have said more than enough of things most or all of which are true, as is shown by the secrecy of this depraved religion. Why make such efforts to obscure and conceal whatever is the object of their worship, when things honourable always rejoice in publicity, while guilt loves secrecy? Why have they no altars, no temples, no recognized images? Why do they never speak in public, never meet in the open, if it be not that the object of their worship and their concealment is either criminal or shameful?

"Whence, who, or where is He, the One and only God, solitary, forlorn, whom no free nation, no kingdom, no superstition known to Rome has knowledge of? The miserable Jewish nationality did indeed worship one God, but even so openly, in temples, with altars, victims, and ceremonies; yet one so strengthless and powerless that he and his dear tribe with him are in captivity to Rome. And yet again what monstrous absurdities these Christians invent about this God of theirs, whom they can neither show nor see! that he searches diligently into the ways and deeds of all men, yea even their words and hidden thoughts, hurrying to and fro, ubiquitously; they make him out a troublesome, restless, shameless and interfering being, who has a hand in everything that is done, interlopes at every turn, and can neither attend to particulars because he is distracted with the whole, nor to the whole because he is engaged with particulars.

"Further, they threaten the whole world and the universe and its stars with destruction by fire, as though the eternal order of nature established by laws divine could be put to confusion, or as though the bonds of all the elements could be broken, the framework of heaven be split in twain, and the containing and surrounding mass be brought down in ruin. Not content with this insane idea, they embellish and embroider it with old wives' tales; say that they are born anew after death from the cinders and the ashes, and with a strange unaccountable confidence believe in one another's lies: you might suppose they had already come to life again. One perversion and folly matches the other. Against heaven and the stars, which we leave even as we found them, they denounce destruction; for themselves when dead and gone, creatures born to perish, the promise of eternity! Hence no doubt their denunciation of funeral pyres and of cremation, just as though the body, even though spared the flame, would not in the course of years and ages be resolved into dust; and just as though it mattered whether it is torn to pieces by wild beasts or drowned in the sea, or buried in the ground, or consumed in the flame; for corpses, if they have sensation, must find all interment painful; while if they have not, speed of dispatch is the best treatment. Under this delusion they promise themselves, as virtuous, a life of never-ending bliss after death; to all others, as evil-doers, everlasting punishment.

"Much might be added on this subject, but my discourse must hasten to its end. That they themselves are evil-doers I need not labour to prove; I have already shown it; though even if I grant their well-doing, guilt or innocence is usually, I know, attributed to destiny. And here we have your agreement; for all action which others ascribe to fate, you ascribe to God; followers of your sect are moved not by their own free-will, but by election; and thus you invent an unjust judge, to punish men for their bad luck, not for their use of will.

"Here I should like to ask whether the resurrection is with bodies or without bodies, and if so, with what bodies, their own or made anew? Without a body? That means, so far as I know, neither mind, nor soul, nor life. With the same body? But that has already gone to pieces. With another body? in that case a new man is born, and not the former man renewed. And yet though time has come and gone, and innumerable ages have flowed on, what single individual has ever returned from the lower regions even with the Protesilaus privilege of a few hours' furlough, so that we might have one example to trust? Your figments of diseased imagination and the futile fairy-tales invented by poets' fancy to give sweetness to their song have been rehashed by your credulity into the service of your God.

"You do not anyhow allow your experiences of the present to undeceive your vain desires of promissory expectation. Let present life, poor fools, be your gauge of what happens after death. See how some part of you, the greater and the better part as you say, suffer want, cold, toil, hunger; and yet your God permits and seems to overlook it; he is unwilling or unable to help his own;

consequently he is either powerless or unjust. You dream of posthumous immortality; when unnerved by danger, when parched with fever, when racked with pain, can you not be sensible of your condition? recognize your feebleness? against your will, poor fool, you are convicted of weakness, and yet will not admit it!

"Things, however, common to all I pass over: but for you there stand in wait punishments, tortures, crosses (crosses not for adoration, but for endurance), yes and the flames which you foretell and fear; where is the God who will succour you in the next life, but in this life cannot? Have not the Romans without your God empire and rule, do they not enjoy the whole world, and lord it over you? Meanwhile in anxious doubt you deny yourselves wholesome pleasures; you do not attend the shows; you take no part in the processions; fight shy of public banquets; abhor the sacred games, meats from the victims, drinks poured in libation on the altars. So frightened are you of the gods whom you deny! You twine no blossoms for the head, grace the body with no perfumes; you reserve your unguents for funerals; refuse garlands even to the graves, pale, trembling creatures, objects for pity—but the pity of our gods! Poor wretches, for whom there is no life hereafter, yet who live not for to-day.

44 LACTANTIUS, ON THE MANNER IN WHICH THE PERSECUTORS DIED: CONSTANTINE AND THE TRIUMPH OF CHRISTIANITY

In the century between the death of Marcus Aurelius and the accession of Diocletian, 180-284 A.D., the Roman Empire was beset by the collapse of constitutional government and the economy throughout the Mediterranean. Mounting barbarian pressures on the German and Persian frontiers stimulated increasingly arbitrary and oppressive government in Rome. The imperial administration became militarized, and the heavy taxes, inflationary policies, and enforced recruiting necessary to support the army and the bureaucracy shattered economic prosperity. Roman citizenship, once highly prized, became a financial and military burden to be abhorred and avoided. The Roman army, which had so long and so successfully defended the frontiers and preserved the *Pax Romana*, involved itself less and less in effective defense measures and more and more in the game of emperor-making. The new emperors, rapidly succeeding one another by assassinations, were often of lowly and barbarian origin, especially of Illyrian stock; their education had usually been acquired in the barracks, and consequently their understanding of Roman traditions was sometimes superficial. Nevertheless, in many cases they proved to be remarkable rulers—the iron men needed for the iron times.

Such a ruler was Diocletian (284-305), who put an end to military anarchy and changed the disordered imperial administration into an efficient organization which survived for a century and a half (see Document 46). The emperor was now a sacrosanct figure, absolute in his authority and surrounded by pomp which was the equivalent of that in an oriental court. Since the empire was so large and its defensive requirements so heavy, the imperial authority was divided between an eastern and a western *augustus*, each with an appointed successor or *caesar* to assist him. Under the new regime, the bureaucracy continued its oppressions, and the state, with increased efficiency, made even severer fiscal and military demands upon its citizens than it had during the military anarchy.

Meanwhile, during the third century, while the Roman Empire had foundered in anarchy, Christianity had been phenomenally successful. It had spread as wide as the empire itself, had evolved a rudimentary theology, and had acquired a considerable ecclesiastical organization. Individual congregations had been brought under the superior authority of bishops and metropolitans, or as they were later called, archbishops; the archbishops and patriarchs of such great cities as Rome, Antioch, and Alexandria had gained special prestige and authority.

However, no period in early Christian history was more fraught with danger to the unity of the Church than the first quarter of the fourth century A.D. In 303, after preliminary restrictions, Emperor Diocletian launched his last and harshest persecutions of Christians by ordering that all Scriptures be surrendered for burning, all churches be destroyed, and all Christian worship be suspended. Not only were Christians stripped of civil rights and political privileges, but they were under constant threat of torture and death. Yet within the next nine years, Constantine, the new emperor, was to triumph in battle under Christian emblems, decree toleration for Christianity, and become a Christian convert. At Nicaea, only thirteen years later, the same emperor sat as chairman at the first ecumenical (world-wide) conference of the Christian Church (325), which convened to deal with the threat to Christian unity posed by the Arian controversy and which wrote the Nicene Creed, the basic document of Christian belief.

The swift reversal of the fortunes of the Christian Church during the reigns of Diocletian and Constantine is described by Lactantius, the tutor of Constantine's sons, in a short, lively essay entitled *On the Manner in which the Persecutors Died*, which Lactantius wrote so "that all who are far away and all who shall be born hereafter, may learn how the Almighty showed his power and omnipotence by overturning and destroying utterly the enemies of his name."

In the selection below, Lactantius describes the great victory of Constantine at the Milvian Bridge of Rome under the emblem of Christ and quotes the edict issued in Milan shortly thereafter (313?) which granted that "the Christians and all others should have liberty to follow that mode of religion which to each of them appeared best." The Edict of Milan strikes an amazing note of toleration in an empire in which persecutions had so recently raged.

And now a civil war broke out between Constantine and Maxentius. Although Maxentius kept himself within Rome, because the soothsayers had foretold that if he went out of it he should perish, yet he conducted the military operations by able generals. In forces he exceeded his adversary; for he had not only his father's army, which deserted from Severus, but also his own, which he had lately drawn together out of Mauritania and Italy. They fought, and the troops of Maxentius prevailed. At length Constantine, with steady courage and a mind prepared for every event, led his whole forces to the neighbourhood of Rome, and encamped them opposite to the Milvian bridge. The anniversary of the reign of Maxentius approached, that is, the sixth of the kalends of November, and the fifth year of his reign was drawing to an end.

Constantine was directed in a dream to cause *the heavenly sign* to be delineated on the shields of his soldiers, and so to proceed to battle. He did as he had been commanded, and he marked on their shields the letter X, with a perpendicular line drawn through it and turned round thus at the top, being the cipher of CHRIST. Having this sign, his troops stood to arms. The enemies advanced, but without their emperor, and they crossed the bridge. The armies met, and fought with the utmost exertions of valour, and firmly maintained their ground. In the meantime a sedition arose at Rome, and Maxentius was reviled as one who had abandoned all concern for the safety of the commonweal; and suddenly, while he exhibited the Circensian games on the anniversary of his reign, the people cried with one voice, "Constantine cannot be overcome!" Dismayed at this, Maxentius burst from the assembly, and having called some senators together, ordered the Sibylline books to be searched. In them it was found that:—

"On the same day the enemy of the Romans should perish."

Led by this response to the hopes of victory, he went to the field. The bridge in his rear was broken down. At sight of that the battle grew hotter. The hand of the Lord prevailed, and the forces of Maxentius were routed. He fled towards the broken bridge; but the multitude pressing on him, he was driven headlong into the Tiber.

This destructive war being ended, Constantine was acknowledged as emperor, with great rejoicings, by the senate and people of Rome. . . .

. . . [O]n the ides of June, while . . . [Licinius] and Constantine were consuls for the third time, he commanded the following edict for the restoration of the Church, directed to the president of the province, to be promulgated:—

"When we, Constantine and Licinius, emperors, had an interview at Milan, and conferred together with respect to the good and security of the commonweal, it seemed to us that, amongst those things that are profitable to mankind in general, the reverence paid to the Divinity merited our first and chief attention, and that it was proper that the Christians and all others should have liberty to follow that mode of religion which to each of them appeared best; so that that God, who is seated in heaven, might be benign and propitious to us, and to every one under our government. And therefore, we judged it a salutary measure, and one highly consonant to right reason, that no man should be denied leave of attaching himself to the rites of the Christians,

Text: Lucius Caelius Lactantius Firmianus, "Of the Manner in Which the Persecutors Died," in *The Ante-Nicene Fathers; Translations of the Writings of the Fathers Down to A.D. 325*, ed. Alexander Roberts, James Donaldson, and A. Cleveland Coxe (New York: Charles Scribner's Sons, 1899), 1st series, VII, 318, 320.

or to whatever other religion his mind directed him, that thus the supreme Divinity, to whose worship we freely devote ourselves, might continue to vouchsafe His favour and beneficence to us. And accordingly we give you to know that, without regard to any provisos in our former orders to you concerning the Christians, all who choose that religion are to be permitted, freely and absolutely, to remain in it, and not to be disturbed any ways, or molested. And we thought fit to be thus special in the things committed to your charge, that you might understand that the indulgence which we have granted in matters of religion to the Christians is ample and unconditional; and perceive at the same time that the open and free exercise of their respective religions is granted to all others, as well as to the Christians. For it befits the well-ordered state and the tranquillity of our times that each individual be allowed, according to his own choice, to worship the Divinity; and we mean not to derogate aught from the honour due to any religion or its votaries. Moreover, with respect to the Christians, we formerly gave certain orders concerning the places appropriated for their religious assemblies; but now we will that all persons who have purchased such places, either from our exchequer or from any one else, do restore them to the Christians, without money demanded or price claimed, and that this be performed peremptorily and unambiguously; and we will also, that they who have obtained any right to such places by form of gift do forthwith restore them to the Christians: reserving always to such persons, who have either purchased for a price, or gratuitously acquired them, to make application to the judge of the district, if they look on themselves as entitled to any equivalent from our beneficence.

"All those places are, by your intervention, to be immediately restored to the Christians. And because it appears that, besides the places appropriated to religious worship, the Christians did possess other places, which belonged not to individuals, but to their society in general, that is, to their churches, we comprehend all such within the regulation aforesaid, and we will that you cause them all to be restored to the society or churches, and *that* without hesitation or controversy: Provided always, that the persons making restitution without a price paid shall be at liberty to seek indemnification from our bounty. In furthering all which things for the behoof of the Christians, you are to use your utmost diligence, to the end that our orders be speedily obeyed, and our gracious purpose in securing the public tranquillity promoted. So shall that divine favour which, in affairs of the mightiest importance, we have already experienced, continue to give success to us, and in our successes make the commonweal happy. And that the tenor of this our gracious ordinance may be made known unto all, we will that you cause it by your authority to be published everywhere."

45 EUSEBIUS, *LIFE OF CONSTANTINE THE GREAT*: THE ARIAN CONTROVERSY AND CHRISTIAN UNITY

Soon after the issuance of Constantine's Edict of Milan (see Document 44) and his conversion to Christianity, a religious controversy broke out in the East which threatened to disrupt the unity of the Christian Church. In 318 an influential presbyter of Alexandria, Arius, publicly denied the doctrine of the Trinity—the doctrine that God the Father, God the Son, and God the Holy Spirit are but a single essence. Defining his own position, Arius affirmed that if the Son (Jesus) were truly a son, there must have been a time when He was not. However far the Son may surpass other created beings, He remains Himself a created being, whom the Father "before all ages" formed "out of nothing." Therefore, Christ in *substance* must be *different* from the Father. The Trinitarians, led by Athanasius, Bishop of Alexandria, vehemently objected: the members of the Trinity, they held, were of the *same substance*, coequal in time, numbering Three and yet at the same time One. To affirm otherwise was to deny the divinity of Christ or, worse, to mark Jesus as a demigod, a thesis which smacked of pagan polytheism.

The intensity of the controversy was such that in 325 Emperor Constantine summoned the bishops of the Church to Nicaea in Asia Minor—to the first ecumenical council in the history of Christianity. At the council a group led by Eusebius of Nicomedia attempted a compromise by proposing the doctrine of "similarity" of substances to replace "difference" or "sameness," but the Trinitarians successfully made their point, and the council finally established the consubstantiality (or "identical substance") of Christ and the Father as the orthodox doctrine. The council also codified other doctrines, and the resultant body of Christian belief became known as the Nicene Creed. Arianism did not die with its condemnation at Nicaea; Arian missionaries succeeded in converting the Goths and Vandals as they invaded the Roman Empire and established their political authority in Italy, southern Gaul, Spain and Africa. In the West, orthodox Christianity was assured of victory only in the sixth century with the conversion of the Franks to the orthodox position and with the counterattack of Emperor Justinian of the East (see Document 54). The Council of Nicaea did, however, set the precedence of holding conferences to arbitrate disputed theological points, thus helping to unify the Church by defining the orthodox view. In the long run, the decisions of the great councils, especially the Nicene, gave the Church the prestige it needed to prevail over its rivals.

A second important outcome of the Council of Nicaea was the precedent it established for the intervention of the emperor in Church affairs. As we see in the following selection from Eusebius' *Life of Constantine*, the council was held under imperial auspices with the active participation of the emperor. Constantine's authority as sole ruler of the Roman Empire and his prestige as a Christian convert perhaps made imperial influence on the Church inevitable, but in any case, caesaropapism remained characteristic of Church-state relations in the Eastern (Byzantine) Empire. According to this theory, the emperor was both secular ruler and titular head of the Christian Church; he was free to intervene in its doctrinal and administrative pursuits. In the West, the popes at Rome steadily resisted this assumption and by the eighth century— with the support of the Franks—they had conclusively secured their independence from the eastern emperors.

. . . But in the midst of his joyful anticipations of the success of this measure, he received tidings of a most serious disturbance which had invaded the peace of the Church. This intelligence he heard with deep concern, and at once endeavored to devise a remedy for the evil. The origin of this disturbance may be thus described. The people of God were in a truly flourishing state, and abounding in the practice of good works. No terror from without assailed them, but a bright and most profound peace, through the favor of God, encompassed his Church on every side. Meantime, however, the spirit of envy was watching to destroy our blessings, which at first crept in unperceived, but soon revelled in the midst of the assemblies of the saints. At length it reached the bishops themselves, and arrayed them in angry hostility against each other, on pretense of a jealous regard for the doctrines of Divine truth. Hence it was that a mighty fire was kindled as it were from a little spark, and which, originating in the first instance in the Alexandrian church, overspread the whole of Egypt and Libya, and the further Thebaid. Eventually it extended its ravages to the other provinces and cities of the empire; so that not only the prelates of the churches might be seen encountering each other in the strife of words, but the people themselves were completely divided, some adhering to one faction and others to another. Nay, so notorious did the scandal of these proceedings become, that the sacred matters of inspired teaching were exposed to the most shameful ridicule in the very theaters of the unbelievers.

Some thus at Alexandria maintained an obstinate conflict on the highest questions. Others throughout Egypt and the Upper Thebaid, were at variance on account of an earlier controversy: so that the churches were everywhere distracted by divisions. The body therefore being thus diseased, the whole of Libya caught the contagion; and the rest of the remoter provinces became affected with the same disorder. For the disputants at Alexandria sent emissaries to the bishops of the several provinces, who accordingly ranged themselves as partisans on either side, and shared in the same spirit of discord.

As soon as the emperor was informed of these facts, which he heard with much sorrow of heart, considering them in the light of a calamity personally affecting himself, he forthwith selected from the Christians in his train one whom he well knew to be approved for the sobriety and genuineness of his faith, and who had before this time distinguished himself by the boldness of his religious profession, and sent him to negotiate peace between the dissentient parties at Alexandria. He also made him the bearer of a most needful and appropriate letter to the original movers of the strife: and this letter, as ex-

Text: Eusebius of Caesarea, "Life of Constantine the Great," in *A Select Library of Nicene and Post-Nicene Fathers of the Christian Church*, ed. Philip Schaff and Henry Wace (New York: Charles Scribner's Sons, 1904), 2nd series, I, 515-18, 521, 523, 525-26.

hibiting a specimen of his watchful care over God's people, it may be well to introduce into this our narrative of his life. Its purport was as follows.

"Victor Constantinus, Maximus Augustus, to Alexander and Arius.

"I call that God to witness, as well I may, who is the helper of my endeavors, and the Preserver of all men, that I had a twofold reason for undertaking that duty which I have now performed.

"My design then was, first, to bring the diverse judgments formed by all nations respecting the Deity to a condition, as it were, of settled uniformity; and, secondly, to restore to health the system of the world, then suffering under the malignant power of a grievous distemper. Keeping these objects in view, I sought to accomplish the one by the secret eye of thought, while the other I tried to rectify by the power of military authority. For I was aware that, if I should succeed in establishing, according to my hopes, a common harmony of sentiment among all the servants of God, the general course of affairs would also experience a change correspondent to the pious desires of them all. . . .

"But, O glorious Providence of God! how deep a wound did not my ears only, but my very heart receive in the report that divisions existed among yourselves more grievous still than those which continued in that country! so that you, through whose aid I had hoped to procure a remedy for the errors of others, are in a state which needs healing even more than theirs. And yet, having made a careful enquiry into the origin and foundation of these differences, I find the cause to be of a truly insignificant character, and quite unworthy of such fierce contention. Feeling myself, therefore, compelled to address you in this letter, and to appeal at the same time to your unanimity and sagacity, I call on Divine Providence to assist me in the task, while I interrupt your dissension in the character of a minister of peace. And with reason: for if I might expect, with the help of a higher Power, to be able without difficulty, by a judicious appeal to the pious feelings of those who heard me, to recall them to a better spirit, even though the occasion of the disagreement were a greater one, how can I refrain from promising myself a far easier and more speedy adjustment of this difference, when the cause which hinders general harmony of sentiment is intrinsically trifling and of little moment?

"I understand, then, that the origin of the present controversy is this. When you, Alexander, demanded of the presbyters what opinion they severally maintained respecting a certain passage in the Divine law, or rather, I should say, that you asked them something connected with an unprofitable question, then you, Arius, inconsiderately insisted on what ought never to have been conceived at all, or if conceived, should have been buried in profound silence. Hence it was that a dissension arose between you, fellowship was withdrawn, and the holy people, rent into diverse parties, no longer preserved the unity of the one body. Now, therefore, do ye both exhibit an equal degree of forbearance, and receive the advice which your fellow-servant righteously gives. What then is this advice? It was wrong in the first instance to propose such questions as these, or to reply to them when propounded. For those points of discussion which are enjoined by the authority of no law, but rather suggested by the contentious spirit which is fostered by misused leisure, even though they may be intended merely as an intellectual exercise, ought certainly to be confined to the region of our own thoughts, and not hastily produced in the popular assemblies, nor unadvisedly intrusted to the general ear. For how very few are there able either accurately to comprehend, or adequately to explain subjects so sublime and abstruse in their nature? Or, granting that one were fully competent for this, how many people will he convince? Or, who, again, in dealing with questions of such subtle nicety as these, can secure himself against a dangerous declension from the truth? It is incumbent therefore on us in these cases to be sparing of our words, lest, in case we ourselves are unable, through the feebleness of our natural faculties, to give a clear explanation of the subject before us, or, on the other hand, in case the slowness of our hearers' understandings disables them from arriving at an accurate apprehension of what we say, from one or other of these causes the people be reduced to the alternative either of blasphemy or schism.

"Let therefore both the unguarded question and the inconsiderate answer receive your mutual forgiveness. For the cause of your difference has not been any of the leading doctrines or precepts of the Divine law, nor has any new heresy respecting the worship of God arisen among you. You are in truth of one and the same judgment: you may therefore well join in communion and fellowship.

"For as long as you continue to contend about these small and very insignificant questions, it is not fitting that so large a portion of God's people should be under the direction of your judgment, since you are thus divided between yourselves. I believe it indeed to be not merely unbecoming, but positively evil, that such should be the case. But I will refresh your minds by a little illustration, as follows. You know that philosophers, though they all adhere to one system, are yet frequently at issue on certain points, and differ, perhaps, in their degree of knowledge: yet they are recalled to harmony of sentiment by the uniting power of their common doctrines. If this be true, is it not far more reasonable that you, who are the ministers of the Supreme God, should be of one mind respecting the profession of the same religion? But let us still more thoughtfully and with closer attention examine what I have said, and see whether it be right that, on the ground of some trifling and foolish verbal difference between ourselves, brethren should assume towards each other the attitude of enemies, and the august meeting of the Synod be rent by profane disunion, because of you who wrangle together on points so trivial and altogether unessential? This is vulgar, and rather characteristic of childish ignorance, than consistent with the wisdom of priests and men of sense. Let us withdraw ourselves with a good will from these temptations of the devil. Our great God and common Saviour of all has granted the same light to us all. Permit me, who am his servant, to bring my task to a successful issue, under the directions of his Providence, that I may be enabled, through my exhortations, and diligence, and earnest admonition, to recall his people to communion and fellowship. For since you have, as I said, but one faith, and one sentiment respecting our religion, and since the Divine commandment in all its parts enjoins on us all the duty of maintaining a spirit of concord, let not the circumstance which has led to a slight difference between you, since it does not affect the validity of the whole, cause any division or schism among you. And this I say without in any way desiring to force you to entire unity of judgment in regard to this truly idle question, whatever its real nature may be. For the dignity of your synod may be preserved, and the communion of your whole body maintained unbroken, however wide a difference may exist among you as to unimportant matters. For we are not all of us like-minded on every subject, nor is there such a thing as one disposition and judgment common to all alike. As far, then, as regards the Divine Providence, let there be one faith, and one understanding among you, one united judgment in reference to God. But as to your subtle disputations on questions of little or no significance, though you may be unable to harmonize in sentiment, such differences should be consigned to the secret custody of your own minds and thoughts. And now, let the preciousness of common affection, let faith in the truth, let the honor due to God and to the observance of his law continue immovably among you. Resume, then, your mutual feelings of friendship, love, and regard; restore to the people their wonted embracings; and do ye yourselves, having purified your souls, as it were, once more acknowledge one another. For it often happens that when a reconciliation is affected by the removal of the causes of enmity, friendship becomes even sweeter than it was before.

"Restore me then my quiet days, and untroubled nights, that the joy of undimmed light, the delight of a tranquil life, may henceforth be my portion. Else must I needs mourn, with constant tears, nor shall I be able to pass the residue of my days in peace. For while the people of God, whose fellow-servant I am, are thus divided amongst themselves by an unreasonable and pernicious spirit of contention, how is it possible that I shall be able to maintain tranquillity of mind? And I will give you a proof how great my sorrow has been on this behalf. Not long since I had visited Nicomedia, and intended forthwith to proceed from that city to the East. It was while I was hastening towards you, and had already accomplished the greater part of the distance, that the news of this matter reversed my plan, that I might not be compelled to see with my own eyes that which I felt myself scarcely able even to hear. Open then for me henceforward by your unity of judgment that road to the regions of the East which your dissensions have closed against me, and permit me speedily to see yourselves and all other peoples rejoicing together, and render due acknowledgment to God in the language of praise and thanksgiving for the restoration of general concord and liberty to all."

In this manner the pious emperor endeavored by means of the foregoing letter to promote the peace of the Church of God. . . . The evil, however, was greater than could be remedied by a single letter, insomuch that the acrimony of the contending parties continually increased, and the effects of the mischief extended to all the Eastern provinces. These things jealousy and some evil spirit who looked with an envious eye on the prosperity of the Church, wrought. . . .

Then as if to bring a divine array against this enemy, he convoked a general council, and invited the speedy attendance of bishops from all quarters, in letters expressive of the honorable estimation in which he held them. Nor was this merely the issuing of a bare command, but the emperor's good will contributed much to its being carried into effect: for he allowed some the use of the public means of conveyance, while he afforded to others an ample supply of horses for their transport. The place, too, selected for the synod, the city Nicæa in Bithynia (named from "*Victory*"), was appropriate to the occasion. As soon then as the imperial injunction was generally made known, all with the utmost willingness hastened thither, as though they would outstrip one another in a race; for they were impelled by the anticipation of a happy result to the conference, by the hope of enjoying present peace, and the desire of beholding something new and strange in the person of so admirable an emperor. Now when they were all assembled, it appeared evident that the proceeding was the work of God, inasmuch as men who had been most widely separated, not merely in sentiment, but also personally, and by difference of country, place, and nation, were here brought together, and comprised within the walls of a single city, forming as it were a vast garland of priests, composed of a variety of the choicest flowers.

In effect, the most distinguished of God's ministers from all the churches which abounded in Europe, Lybia, and Asia were here assembled. And a single house of prayer, as though divinely enlarged, sufficed to contain at once Syrians and Cilicians, Phœnicians and Arabians, delegates from Palestine, and others from Egypt; Thebans and Libyans, with those who came from the region of Mesopotamia. A Persian bishop too was present at this conference, nor was even a Scythian found wanting to the number. Pontus, Galatia, and Pamphylia, Cappadocia, Asia, and Phrygia, furnished their most distinguished prelates; while those who dwelt in the remotest districts of Thrace and Macedonia, of Achaia and Epirus, were notwithstanding in attendance. Even from Spain itself, one whose fame was widely spread took his seat as an individual in the great assembly. The prelate of the imperial city was prevented from attending by extreme old age; but his presbyters were present, and supplied his place. Constantine is the first prince of any age who bound together such a garland as this with the bond of peace, and presented it to his Saviour as a thank-offering for the victories he had obtained over every foe, thus exhibiting in our own times a similitude of the apostolic company.

As soon as the emperor had spoken . . . [to the assembly] in the Latin tongue, which another interpreted, he gave permission to those who presided in the council to deliver their opinions. On this some began to accuse their neighbors, who defended themselves, and recriminated in their turn. In this manner numberless assertions were put forth by each party, and a violent controversy arose at the very commencement. Notwithstanding this, the emperor gave patient audience to all alike, and received every proposition with steadfast attention, and by occasionally assisting the argument of each party in turn, he gradually disposed even the most vehement disputants to a reconciliation. At the same time, by the affability of his address to all, and his use of the Greek language, with which he was not altogether unacquainted, he appeared in a truly attractive and amiable light, persuading some, convincing others by his reasonings, praising those who spoke well, and urging all to unity of sentiment, until at last he succeeded in bringing them to one mind and judgment respecting every disputed question.

The result was that they were not only united as concerning the faith, but that the time for the celebration of the salutary feast of Easter was agreed on by all. Those points also which were sanctioned by the resolution of the whole body were committed to writing, and received the signature of each several member. Then the emperor, believing that he had thus obtained a second victory over the adversary of the Church, proceeded to solemnize a triumphal festival in honor of God. . . .

And now, when the council was on the point of being finally dissolved, he summoned all the bishops to meet him on an appointed day, and on their arrival addressed them in a farewell speech, in which he recommended them to be diligent in the maintenance of peace, to avoid contentious disputations, amongst themselves, and not to be jealous, if any one of their number should appear pre-eminent for wisdom and eloquence, but to esteem the excellence of one a blessing common to all. On the other hand he reminded them that the more gifted should forbear to exalt themselves to the prejudice of their humbler brethren, since it is God's prerogative to judge of real superiority. Rather should they considerately condescend to the weaker, remembering that absolute perfection in any case is a rare quality indeed. Each, then, should be willing to accord indulgence to the other for slight offenses, to regard charitably and pass over mere human weaknesses; holding mutual harmony in the highest honor, that no occasion of mockery might be given by their dissensions to those who are ever ready to blaspheme the word of God: whom indeed we should do all in our power to save, and this cannot be unless our conduct seems to them attractive. But you are well aware of the fact, that testimony is by no means productive of blessing to all, since some who hear are glad to secure the supply of their mere bodily necessities, while others court the patronage of their superiors; some fix their affection on those who treat them with hospitable kindness, others again, being honored with presents, love their benefactors in return; but few are they who really desire the word of testimony, and rare indeed is it to find a friend of truth. Hence the necessity of endeavoring to meet the case of all, and, physician-like, to administer to each that which may tend to the health of the soul, to the end that the saving doctrine may be fully honored by all. Of this kind was the former part of his exhortation; and in conclusion he enjoined them to offer diligent supplications to God on his behalf. Having thus taken leave of them, he gave them all permission to return to their respective countries; and this they did with joy, and thenceforward that unity of judgment at which they had arrived in the emperor's presence continued to prevail, and those who had long been divided were bound together as members of the same body.

THE DECLINE OF ROME AND THE BARBARIANS

46 THE EDICT OF DIOCLETIAN: LEGISLATION FOR SOCIAL AND ECONOMIC REFORM

In the fourth and fifth centuries of the Christian era, two great institutions were undergoing profound transformation. The Roman state, wracked by civil war, barbarian invasion, fiscal irresponsibility, and the almost total absence of civic morality, was in the period of its final fall; while the Roman Church, after its legal recognition by Emperor Constantine, was everywhere on the ascendency and assuming an increasingly important role in the affairs of western Europe.

For almost five hundred years Rome had been dominant in Mediterranean affairs, but now the empire it had created was slipping away in spite of desperate but futile efforts to prevent a final collapse. The Roman economy, especially, was badly in need of reform; inflation and profiteering were rampant, while agricultural and industrial workers, seriously discouraged by high prices, were reluctant to perform their necessary social services. All these factors combined to produce, in the words of Professor Mikhail Rostovtzeff, "an apathy in the rich and discontent amongst the poor." In an effort to stabilize the Roman economy, various emperors put into effect legislation designed to cope with the problems of rising prices and dropping wages.

The selection below is from the introduction to the *Edict of Maximum Prices* issued by the Emperor Diocletian in 301. The decree, operative at least in the eastern provinces, was a comprehensive effort at price control and provided a fixed price for each commodity and each kind of labor or professional service. Violation of the edict was punishable by death. There is little evidence to tell us how effectively later empire laws, such as Diocletian's edict, were enforced or how successful they were in practice. At best, they could do no more than delay a deteriorating social and economic situation from its final collapse.

The Edict of Diocletian.

The Emperor Caesar Gaius Aurelius Valerius Diocletianus, pius, felix, invictus, Augustus, pontifex maximus, Germanicus maximus for the sixth time, Sarmaticus maximus for the fourth time, Persicus maximus for the second time, Brittannicus maximus, Carpicus maximus, Armenicus maximus, Medicus maximus, Adiabenicus maximus, in the eighteenth year of his tribunician power, in his seventh consulship, in the eighteenth year of his imperial power [301 A. D.], pater patriae, proconsul; and the Emperor Caesar Marcus Aurelius Valerius Maximianus, pius, felix, invictus, Augustus, pontifex maximus, Germanicus maximus for the fifth time, Sarmaticus maximus for the fourth time, Persicus maximus for the second time, Brittannicus maximus, Carpicus maximus, Armenicus maximus, Medicus maximus, Adiabenicus maximus, in the seventeenth year of his tribunician power, in his sixth consulship, in the seventeenth year of his imperial power, pater patriae, proconsul; and Flavius Valerius Constantius, Germanicus maximus for the second time, Sarmaticus maximus for the second time, Persicus maximus for the second time, Brittannicus maximus, Carpicus maximus, Armenicus maximus, Medicus maximus, Adiabenicus

Text: Tenney Frank (ed.), *An Economic Survey of Ancient Rome* (Baltimore: The Johns Hopkins Press, 1940), V, 310-17.

maximus, in the ninth year of his tribunician power, in his third consulship, nobilissimus Caesar; and Galerius Valerius Maximianus, Germanicus maximus for the second time, Sarmaticus maximus for the second time, Persicus maximus for the second time, Brittannicus maximus, Carpicus maximus, Armenicus maximus, Medicus maximus, Adiabenicus maximus, in the ninth year of his tribunician power, in his third consulship, nobilissimus Caesar, declare:

That the fortune of our state—to which, after the immortal gods, as we recall the wars which we have successfully fought, we must be grateful for a world that is tranquil and reclining in the embrace of the most profound calm, and for the blessings of a peace that was won with great effort—be faithfully disposed and suitably adorned, is the demand of public opinion and the dignity and majesty of Rome; therefore, we, who by the gracious favor of the gods have repressed the former tide of ravages of barbarian nations by destroying them, must guard by the due defences of justice a peace which was established for eternity. If, indeed, any self-restraint might check the excesses with which limitless and furious avarice rages—avarice which with no thought for mankind hastens to its own gain and increase, not by years or months or days but by hours and even minutes—; or, if the general welfare could endure undisturbed the riotous license by which it, in its misfortune, is from day to day most grievously injured, there would perhaps be left some room for dissimulation and silence, since human forbearance might alleviate the detestable cruelty of a pitiable situation. Since, however, it is the sole desire of unrestrained madness to have no thought for the common need and since it is considered among the unscrupulous and immoderate almost the creed of avarice, swelling and rising with fiery passions, to desist from ravaging the wealth of all through necessity rather than its own wish; and since those whom extremes of need have brought to an appreciation of their most unfortunate situation can no longer close their eyes to it, we—the protectors of the human race—viewing the situation, have agreed that justice should intervene as arbiter, so that the long-hoped-for solution which mankind itself could not supply might, by the remedies of our foresight, be applied to the general betterment of all. Common knowledge recognizes and the facts themselves proclaim how nearly too late our provision for this situation is, while we were laying plans or reserving remedies already devised, in the hope that—as was to be expected through the laws of nature—mankind, apprehended in the most serious offenses, might reform itself, for we think it far better that the stains of intolerable depredation be removed from men's minds by the feeling and decision of the same men whom, as they daily plunged into more and more serious offenses and turned, in their blindness, to crimes against the state, their grievous iniquity had charged with most cruel inhumanity, the enemies of individual and state. We, therefore, hasten to apply the remedies long demanded by the situation, satisfied that there can be no complaints that the intervention of our remedy may be considered untimely or unnecessary, or trivial or unimportant among the unscrupulous who, in spite of perceiving in our silence of so many years a lesson in restraint, have been unwilling to copy it. For who is so insensitive and so devoid of human feeling that he cannot know, or rather, has not perceived, that in the commerce carried on in the markets or involved in the daily life of cities immoderate prices are so widespread that the uncurbed passion for gain is lessened neither by abundant supplies nor by fruitful years; so that without a doubt men who are busied in these affairs constantly plan actually to control the very winds and weather from the movements of the stars, and, evil as they are, they cannot endure the watering of the fertile fields by the rains from above which bring the hope of future harvests, since they reckon it their own loss if abundance comes through the moderation of the weather. And the men whose aim it always is to profit even from the generosity of the gods, to restrain general prosperity, and furthermore to use a poor year to traffic in harvest (?) losses and agents' services—men who, individually abounding in great riches which could completely satisfy whole nations, try to capture smaller fortunes and strive after ruinous percentages—concern for humanity in general persuades us to set a limit, our subjects, to the avarice of such men. But even now we must detail the facts whose urgency after long delay has finally driven our tolerance to action, in order that—although it is difficult for the avarice which rages throughout the whole world to be described by a specific illustration or, rather, fact—nevertheless, the establishment of a remedy may be considered more just when utterly unrestrained men are forced by some sign and token to recognize the untamed desires of their own minds. Who, therefore, does not know that insolence, covertly attacking the public welfare—wherever the public safety demands that our armies be directed, not in villages or towns only, but on every road—comes to the mind of the profiteer to extort prices for merchandise, not fourfold or eightfold, but such that human speech is incapable of describing either the price or the act; and finally that sometimes in a single purchase a soldier is deprived of his bonus and salary, and that the contribution of the whole world to support the armies falls to the abominable profits of thieves, so that our soldiers seem with their own hands to offer the hopes of their service and their completed labors to the profiteers, with the result that the pillagers of the nation constantly seize more than they know how to hold. Aroused justly and rightfully by all the facts which are detailed above, and with mankind itself now appearing to be praying for release, we have decreed that there be established, not the prices of articles for sale—for such an act would be unjust when many provinces occasionally rejoice in the good fortune of wished-for low prices and, so to speak, the privilege of prosperity—, but a maximum, so that when the violence of high prices appears anywhere—may the gods avert such a calamity!—avarice which, as if in immense open areas, could not be restrained, might be checked by the limits of our statute or by the boundaries of a regulatory law. It is our pleasure, therefore, that the prices listed in the subjoined summary be observed in the whole of our empire in such fashion that every man may know that while permission to exceed them has been forbidden him, the blessing of low prices has in no case been restricted in those places where supplies are seen to abound, since special provision is made for these when avarice is definitely quieted. Moreover, among buyers and sellers who customarily visit ports and foreign provinces this universal decree should be a check so that, when they too know that in the time of high prices there is no possibility of transcending the determined prices for commodities, such a reckoning of places, transportation, and the whole business may be made at the time of sale that the justice of our decree forbidding those who transport merchandise to sell anywhere at higher prices may be evident. Since, therefore, it is agreed that even in the time of our ancestors it was customary in passing laws to restrain insolence by attaching a prescribed penalty—since it is indeed rare for a situation tending to the good of humanity to be embraced spontaneously, and since, as a guide, fear is always found the most influential preceptor in the performance of duty—it is our pleasure that anyone who shall have resisted the form of this statute shall for his daring be subject to a capital penalty. And let no one consider the penalty harsh since there is at hand a means of avoiding the danger by the observance of moderation. To the same penalty, moreover, is he subject who in the desire to buy shall have conspired against the statute with the greed of the seller. Nor is he exempt from the same penalty who, although possessing necessities of life and business, believes that subsequent to this regulation he must withdraw them from the general market, since a penalty should be even more severe for him who introduces poverty than for him who harasses it against the law. We, therefore, urge upon the loyalty of all our people that a law constituted for the public good may be observed with willing obedience and due care; especially since in such a statute provision has been made, not for single states and peoples and provinces, but for the whole world, to whose ruin very few are known to have raged excessively, whose avarice neither fullness of time nor the riches for which they strive could lessen or satisfy.

47 TACITUS, *GERMANIA*: GERMAN TRIBAL SOCIETY

The motives of the Germanic invaders who overcame the Roman Empire in the West in the fifth and sixth centuries, the violence of their invasions, and the extent of their numbers are disputed among modern historians. Certainly, it is true that the barbarians did not fall like a bolt from the blue upon the unsuspecting Romans. From the time of Julius Caesar's conquests (57-50 B.C.), interest in the Celts of Gaul and Britain and the Germans beyond the Rhine and the Danube had been lively; wars, trade, and the slave market brought knowledge of the German hinterlands to the imperial city. A Roman society poet reports that even sophisticated Roman matrons bleached their dark Mediterranean tresses in tribute to their savage northern sisters. If not the fashionable, certainly the serious concern for the barbarians is apparent in a short monograph entitled *Germania*, written by the historian Tacitus about 100 A.D. The *Germania* is the first major document of German social history and the principal source of information about the institutions and customs of the German tribes before they had become thoroughly affected by contact with the Roman Empire.

In the passage below, in which Tacitus discusses the military and political organization of the German tribes, some scholars have seen a description of a primitive "democracy." This may be an overstatement, but it is evident that similar political institutions, considered democratic, were carried by Anglo-Saxons from Germany to Britain in the fifth century, and that the Hundreds (the assembly), and the war chieftains who limited the power of kings reappear in the earliest English kingdoms and are a part of traditional Anglo-Saxon law and justice. So, too, the custom which Tacitus calls *comitatus*, or comradeship, is a prototype for the oath of fealty, the basic personal bond of medieval feudalism. The *Germania* offers a vivid picture of the Germans in mid-passage between total barbarity and dominion over the western Roman Empire.

Personally I associate myself with the opinions of those who hold that in the peoples of Germany there has been given to the world a race untainted by intermarriage with other races, a peculiar people and pure, like no one but themselves; whence it comes that their physique, in spite of their vast numbers, is identical: fierce blue eyes, red hair, tall frames, powerful only spasmodically, and impatient at the same time of labour and hard work, and by no means habituated to bearing thirst and heat; to cold and hunger, thanks to the climate and the soil, they are accustomed.

There are some varieties in the appearance of the country, but broadly it is a land of bristling forests and unhealthy marshes; the rainfall is heavier on the side of Gaul; the winds are higher on the side of Noricum and Pannonia.

It is fertile in cereals, but unkindly to fruit-bearing trees; it is rich in flocks and herds, but for the most part they are undersized. Even the cattle lack natural beauty and majestic brows. The pride of the people is rather in the number of their beasts, which constitute the only wealth they welcome.

The gods have denied them gold and silver, whether in mercy or in wrath I find it hard to say; not that I would assert that Germany has no veins bearing gold or silver: for who has explored there? At any rate, they are not affected, like their neighbours, by the use and possession of such things. One may see among them silver vases, given as gifts to their commanders and chieftains, but treated as of no more value than earthenware. Although the border tribes for purposes of traffic treat gold and silver as precious metals, and recognise and collect certain coins of our money, the tribes of the interior practise barter in the simpler and older fashion. The coinage which appeals to them is the old and long-familiar: the denarii with milled edges, showing the two-horsed chariot. They prefer silver to gold: not that they have any feeling in the matter, but because a number of silver pieces is easier to use for people whose purchases consist of cheap objects of general utility.

Even iron is not plentiful among them, as may be gathered from the style of their weapons. Few have swords or the longer kind of lance: they carry short spears, in their language "frameae," with a narrow and small iron head, so sharp and so handy in use that they fight with the same weapon, as circumstances demand, both at close quarters and at a distance. The mounted man is content with a shield and framea: the infantry launch showers of missiles in addition, each man a volley, and hurl these to great distances, for they wear no outer clothing, or at most a light cloak.

There is no bravery of apparel among them: their shields only are picked out with choice colours. Few have breast-plates: scarcely one or two at most have metal or hide helmets. The horses are conspicuous neither for beauty nor speed; but then neither are they trained like our horses to run in shifting circles: they ride them forwards only or to the right, with but one turn from the straight, dressing the line so closely as they wheel that no one is left behind. On a broad view there is more strength in their infantry, and accordingly cavalry and infantry fight in one body, the swift-footed infantryman, whom they pick out of the whole body of warriors and place in front of the line, being well-adapted and suitable for cavalry battles. The number of these men is fixed—one hundred from each canton: and among themselves this, "the Hundred," is the precise name they use; what was once a number only has become a title and a distinction. The battle-line itself is arranged in wedges: to retire, provided you press on again, they treat as a question of tactics, not of cowardice: they carry off their dead and wounded even in drawn battles. To have abandoned one's shield is the height of disgrace; the man so disgraced cannot be present at religious rites, nor attend a council: many survivors of war have ended their infamy with a noose.

Text: Reprinted by permission of the publishers and The Loeb Classical Library from Tacitus, *Germania*, trans. Sir William Peterson (Cambridge, Mass.: Harvard University Press, 1925), pp. 269-83.

They take their kings on the ground of birth, their generals on the basis of courage: the authority of their kings is not unlimited or arbitrary; their generals control them by example rather than command, and by means of the admiration which attends upon energy and a conspicuous place in front of the line. But anything beyond this—capital punishment, imprisonment, even a blow—is permitted only to the priests, and then not as a penalty or under the general's orders, but as an inspiration from the god whom they suppose to accompany them on campaign: certain totems, in fact, and emblems are fetched from groves and carried into battle. The strongest incentive to courage lies in this, that neither chance nor casual grouping makes the squadron or the wedge, but family and kinship: close at hand, too, are their dearest, whence is heard the wailing voice of woman and the child's cry: here are the witnesses who are in each man's eyes most precious; here the praise he covets most: they take their wounds to mother and wife, who do not shrink from counting the hurts and demanding a sight of them: they minister to the combatants food and exhortation.

Tradition relates that some lost or losing battles have been restored by the women, by the incessance of their prayers and by the baring of their breasts; for so is it brought home to the men that the slavery, which they dread much more keenly on their women's account, is close at hand it follows that the loyalty of those tribes is more effectually guaranteed from whom, among other hostages, maids of high birth have been exacted.

Further, they conceive that in woman is a certain uncanny and prophetic sense: they neither scorn to consult them nor slight their answers. In the reign of Vespasian of happy memory we saw Velaeda treated as a deity by many during a long period; but in ancient times also they reverenced Albruna and many other women—in no spirit of flattery, nor for the manufacture of goddesses.

Of the gods, they give a special worship to Mercury, to whom on certain days they count even the sacrifice of human life lawful. Hercules and Mars they appease with such animal life as is permissible. A section of the Suebi sacrifices also to Isis: the cause and origin of this foreign worship I have not succeeded in discovering, except that the emblem itself, which takes the shape of a Liburnian galley, shows that the ritual is imported.

Apart from this they deem it incompatible with the majesty of the heavenly host to confine the gods within walls, or to mould them into any likeness of the human face: they consecrate groves and coppices, and they give the divine names to that mysterious something which is visible only to the eyes of faith.

To divination and the lot they pay as much attention as any one: the method of drawing lots is uniform. A bough is cut from a nut-bearing tree and divided into slips: there are distinguished by certain runes and spread casually and at random over white cloth: afterwards, should the inquiry be official the priest of the state, if private the father of the family in person, after prayers to the gods and with eyes turned to heaven, takes up one slip at a time till he has done this on three separate occasions, and after taking the three interprets them according to the runes which have been already stamped on them: if the message be a prohibition, no inquiry on the same matter is made during the same day; if the message be permissive, further confirmation is required by means of divination; and even among the Germans divination by consultation of the cries and flight of birds is well known, but their special divination is to make trial of the omens and warnings furnished by horses.

In the same groves and coppices are fed certain white horses, never soiled by mortal use: these are yoked to a sacred chariot and accompanied by the priest and king, or other chief of the state, who then observe their neighing or snorting. On no other divination is more reliance placed, not merely by the people but also by their leaders: the priests they regard as the servants of the gods, but the horses are their confidants.

They have another method of taking divinations, by means of which they probe the issue of serious wars. A member of the tribe at war with them is somehow or other captured and pitted against a selected champion of their own countrymen, each in his tribal armour. The victory of one or the other is taken as a presage.

On small matters the chiefs consult; on larger questions the community; but with this limitation, that even the subjects, the decision of which rests with the people, are first handled by the chiefs. They meet, unless there be some unforeseen and sudden emergency, on days set apart—when the moon, that is, is new or at the full: they regard this as the most auspicious herald for the transaction of business. They count not by days as we do, but by nights: their decisions and proclamations are subject to this principle: the night, that is, seems to take precedence of the day.

It is a foible of their freedom that they do not meet at once and when commanded, but a second and a third day is wasted by dilatoriness in assembling: when the mob is pleased to begin, they take their seats carrying arms. Silence is called for by the priests, who thenceforward have power also to coerce: then a king or a chief is listened to, in order of age, birth, glory in war, or eloquence, with the prestige which belongs to their counsel rather than with any prescriptive right to command. If the advice tendered be displeasing, they reject it with groans; if it please them, they clash their spears: the most complimentary expression of assent is this martial approbation.

At this assembly it is also permissible to lay accusations and to bring capital charges. The nature of the death penalty differs according to the offence: traitors and deserters are hung from trees; cowards and poor fighters and notorious evil-livers are plunged in the mud of marshes with a hurdle on their heads: the difference of punishment has regard to the principle that crime should be blazoned abroad by its retribution, but abomination hidden. Lighter offences have also a measured punishment: those convicted are fined in a number of horses and cattle: part of the fine goes to the king or the state; part is paid to the person himself who brings the charge or to his relatives. At the same gatherings are selected chiefs, who administer law through the cantons and villages: each of them has one hundred assessors from the people to be his responsible advisers.

They do no business, public or private, without arms in their hands; yet the custom is that no one take arms until the state has endorsed his competence: then in the assembly itself one of the chiefs or his father or his relatives equip the young man with shield and spear: this corresponds with them to the toga, and is youth's first public distinction: hitherto he seems a member of the household, now a member of the state. Conspicuously high birth, or signal services on the part of ancestors, win the chieftain's approbation even for very young men: they mingle with the others, men of maturer strength and tested by long years, and have no shame to be seen among his retinue. In the retinue itself degrees are observed, depending on the judgment of him whom they follow: there is great rivalry among the retainers to decide who shall have the first place with his chief, and among the chieftains as to who shall have the largest and keenest retinue. This means rank and strength, to be surrounded always with a large band of chosen youths—glory in peace, in war protection: nor is it only so with his own people, but with neighbouring states also it means name and fame for a man that his retinue be conspicuous for number and character: such men are in request for embassies, and are honoured with gifts, and often, by the mere terror of their name, break the back of opposition in war.

48 JORDANES, HISTORY OF THE GOTHS: THE BARBARIAN INVASIONS

When the barbarians drove down from the north to overwhelm the western half of the Roman Empire, they found on their arrival a divided political world and a united Christian community: during the reign of Emperor Theodosius the Great (378-395) an imperial edict had ordered every inhabitant of the empire to accept Christianity, but on the death of Theodosius, his sons formally divided the political empire into independent eastern and western halves, with distinct imperial capitals at Constantinople and Rome.

Sometime after the fourth century A.D., the Roman Empire of the West gradually broke up. Italy and the former provinces of Gaul and Spain were occupied by barbarian tribes from the north and east, who gradually carved out for themselves spheres of influence and settled down in their newly created barbaric kingdoms. In the East, the empire maintained its hegemony, though it too suffered from barbarian pressure, particularly in the late fourth and early fifth centuries, when disgruntled Visigoths rose in revolt against the emperor at Constantinople.

Led by the great warrior Alaric, the Visigoths decided to abandon the eastern empire, and after an expedition through the lower parts of the Balkans, crossed around the top of the Adriatic and finally invaded the Italian peninsula itself. In the selection below, from Jordanes' *History of the Goths*, the famous sacking of Rome (410) is recounted. According to the author, the city was not burned, nor did the Goths permit "serious damage to be done to the holy places." This statement contradicts the Roman claim that the Goths looted indiscriminately.

Jordanes was himself a loyal Goth, who for a time had served as secretary to one of the more important families, and was thoroughly familiar with Gothic institutions and customs. His *History*, written in 551, apparently is an abbreviation of a much longer work (now lost) by the great Roman scholar Cassiodorus.

But after Theodosius, the lover of peace and of the Gothic race, had passed from human cares, his sons began to ruin both empires by their luxurious living and to deprive their Allies, that is to say the Goths, of the customary gifts. The contempt of the Goths for the Romans soon increased, and for fear their valor would be destroyed by long peace, they appointed Alaric king over them. He was of famous stock, and his nobility was second only to that of the Amali, for he came from the family of the Balthi, who because of their daring valor had long ago received among their race the name *Baltha*, that is, The Bold. Now when this Alaric was made king, he took counsel with his men and persuaded them to seek a kingdom by their own exertions rather than serve others in idleness. In the consulship of Stilicho and Aurelian he raised an army and entered Italy, which seemed to be bare of defenders, and came through Pannonia and Sirmium along the right side. Without meeting any resistance, he reached the bridge of the river Candidianus at the third milestone from the royal city of Ravenna.

This city lies amid the streams of the Po between swamps and the sea, and is accessible only on one side. Its ancient inhabitants, as our ancestors relate, were called αἰνετοί, that is, "Laudable." Situated in a corner of the Roman Empire above the Ionian Sea, it is hemmed in like an island by a flood of rushing waters. On the east it has the sea, and one who sails straight to it from the region of Corcyra and those parts of Hellas sweeps with his oars along the right hand coast, first touching Epirus, then Dalmatia, Liburnia and Histria and at last the Venetian Isles. But on the west it has swamps through which a sort of door has been left by a very narrow entrance. To the north is an arm of the Po, called the Fossa Asconis. On the south likewise is the Po itself, which they call the King of the rivers of Italy; and it has also the name Eridanus. This river was turned aside by the Emperor Augustus into a very broad canal which flows through the midst of the city with a seventh part of its stream, affording a pleasant harbor at its mouth. Men believed in ancient times, as Dio relates, that it would hold a fleet of two hundred and fifty vessels in its safe anchorage. Fabius says that this, which was once a harbor, now displays itself like a spacious garden full of trees; but from them hang not sails but apples. The city itself boasts of three names and is happily placed in its threefold location. I mean to say the first is called Ravenna and the most distant part Classis; while midway between the city and the sea is Caesarea, full of luxury. The sand of the beach is fine and suited for riding.

But as I was saying, when the army of the Visigoths had come into the neighborhood of this city, they sent an embassy to the Emperor Honorius, who dwelt within. They said that if he would permit the Goths to settle peaceably in Italy, they would so live with the Roman people that men might believe them both to be of one race; but if not, whoever prevailed in war should drive out the other, and the victor should henceforth rule unmolested. But the Emperor Honorius feared to make either promise. So he took counsel with his senate and considered how he might drive them from the Italian borders. He finally decided that Alaric and his race, if they were able to do so, should be allowed to seize for their own home the provinces farthest away, namely Gaul and Spain. For at this time he had almost lost them, and moreover they had been devasted by the invasion of Gaiseric, king of the Vandals. The grant was confirmed by an imperial rescript, and the Goths, consenting to the arrangement, set out for the country given them.

When they had gone away without doing any harm in Italy, Stilicho, the Patrician and father-in-law of the Emperor Honorius—for the Emperor had married both his daughters, Maria and Thermantia, in succession, but God called both from this world in their virgin purity—this Stilicho, I say, treacherously hurried to Pollentia, a city in the Cottian Alps. There he fell upon the unsuspecting Goths in battle, to the ruin of all Italy and his own disgrace. When the Goths suddenly beheld him, at first they were terrified. Soon regaining their courage and arousing each other by brave shouting, as is their custom, they turned to flight the entire army of Stilicho and almost exterminated it. Then forsaking the journey they had undertaken, the Goths with hearts full of rage returned again to Liguria whence they had set out. When they had plundered and

Text: Charles Christopher Mierow (trans.), *The Gothic History of Jordanes* (Princeton: Princeton University Press, 1915). Copyright 1915 by Charles Christopher Mierow. Pp. 92-103.

spoiled it, they also laid waste Aemilia, and then hastened toward the city of Rome along the Flaminian Way, which runs between Picenum and Tuscia, taking as booty whatever they found on either hand. When they finally entered Rome, by Alaric's express command they merely sacked it and did not set the city on fire, as wild peoples usually do, nor did they permit serious damage to be done to the holy places. Thence they departed to bring like ruin upon Campania and Lucania, and then came to Bruttii. Here they remained a long time and planned to go to Sicily and thence to the countries of Africa.

Now the land of the Bruttii is at the extreme southern bound of Italy, and a corner of it marks the beginning of the Apennine mountains. It stretches out like a tongue into the Adriatic Sea and separates it from the Tyrrhenian waters. It chanced to receive its name in ancient times from a Queen Bruttia. To this place came Alaric, king of the Visigoths, with the wealth of all Italy which he had taken as spoil, and from there, as we have said, he intended to cross over by way of Sicily to the quiet land of Africa. But since man is not free to do anything he wishes without the will of God, that dread strait sunk several of his ships and threw all into confusion. Alaric was cast down by his reverse and, while deliberating what he should do, was suddenly overtaken by an untimely death and departed from human cares. His people mourned for him with the utmost affection. Then turning from its course the river Busentus near the city of Consentia—for this stream flows with its wholesome waters from the foot of a mountain near that city—they led a band of captives into the midst of its bed to dig out a place for his grave. In the depths of this pit they buried Alaric, together with many treasures, and then turned the waters back into their channel. And that none might ever know the place, they put to death all the diggers. They bestowed the kingdom of the Visigoths on Athavulf his kinsman, a man of imposing beauty and great spirit; for though not tall of stature, he was distinguished for beauty of face and form.

When Athavulf became king, he returned again to Rome, and whatever had escaped the first sack his Goths stripped bare like locusts, not merely despoiling Italy of its private wealth, but even of its public resources. The Emperor Honorius was powerless to resist even when his sister Placidia, the daughter of the Emperor Theodosius by his second wife, was led away captive from the city. But Athavulf was attracted by her nobility, beauty and chaste purity, and so he took her to wife in lawful marriage at Forum Julii, a city of Aemilia. When the barbarians learned of this alliance, they were the more effectually terrified, since the Empire and the Goths now seemed to be made one. Then Athavulf set out for Gaul, leaving Honorius Augustus stripped of his wealth, to be sure, yet pleased at heart because he was now a sort of kinsman of his. Upon his arrival the neighboring tribes who had long made cruel raids into Gaul —Franks and Burgundians alike—were terrified and began to keep within their own borders. Now the Vandals and the Alani, as we have said before, had been dwelling in both Pannonias by permission of the Roman Emperors. Yet fearing they would not be safe even here if the Goths should return, they crossed over into Gaul. But no long time after they had taken possession of Gaul they fled thence and shut themselves up in Spain, for they still remembered from the tales of their forefathers what ruin Geberich, king of the Goths, had long ago brought on their race, and how by his valor he had driven them from their native land. And thus it happened that Gaul lay open to Athavulf when he came. Now when the Goth had established his kingdom in Gaul, he began to grieve for the plight of the Spaniards and planned to save them from the attacks of the Vandals. So Athavulf left with a few faithful men at Barcelona his treasures and those who were unfit for war, and entered the interior of Spain. Here he fought frequently with the Vandals and, in the third year after he had subdued Gaul and Spain, fell pierced through the groin by the sword of Euervulf, a man whose short stature he had been wont to mock. After his death Segeric was appointed king, but he too was slain by the treachery of his own men and lost both his kingdom and his life even more quickly than Athavulf.

Then Valia, the fourth from Alaric, was made king, and he was an exceeding stern and prudent man. The Emperor Honorius sent an army against him under Constantius, who was famed for his achievements in war and distinguished in many battles, for he feared that Valia would break the treaty long ago made with Athavulf and that, after driving out the neighboring tribes, he would again plot evil against the Empire. Moreover Honorius was eager to free his sister Placidia from the disgrace of servitude, and made an agreement with Constantius that if by peace or war or any means soever he could bring her back to the kingdom, he should have her in marriage. Pleased with this promise, Constantius set out for Spain with an armed force and in almost royal splendor. Valia, king of the Goths, met him at a pass in the Pyrenees with as great a force. Hereupon embassies were sent by both sides and it was decided to make peace on the following terms, namely that Valia should give up Placidia, the Emperor's sister, and should not refuse to aid the Roman Empire when occasion demanded.

Now at that time a certain Constantine usurped imperial power in Gaul and appointed as Caesar his son Constans, who was formerly a monk. But when he had held for a short time the Empire he had seized, he was himself slain at Arelate and his son at Vienne. Jovinus and Sebastian succeeded them with equal presumption and thought they might seize the imperial power; but they perished by a like fate.

Now in the twelfth year of Valia's reign the Huns were driven out of Pannonia by the Romans and Goths, almost fifty years after they had taken possession of it. Then Valia found that the Vandals had come forth with bold audacity from the interior of Galicia, whither Athavulf had long ago driven them, and were devastating and plundering everywhere in his own territories, namely in the land of Spain. So he made no delay but moved his army against them at once, at about the time when Hierius and Ardabures had become consuls.

But Gaiseric, king of the Vandals, had already been invited into Africa by Boniface, who had fallen into a dispute with the Emperor Valentinian and was able to obtain revenge only by injuring the Empire. So he invited them urgently and brought them across the narrow strait known as the Strait of Gades, scarcely seven miles wide, which divides Africa from Spain and unites the mouth of the Tyrrhenian Sea with the waters of Ocean. Gaiseric, still famous in the City for the disaster of the Romans, was a man of moderate height and lame in consequence of a fall from his horse. He was a man of deep thought and few words, holding luxury in disdain, furious in his anger, greedy for gain, shrewd in winning over the barbarians and skilled in sowing the seeds of dissension to arouse enmity. Such was he who, as we have said, came at the solicitous invitation of Boniface to the country of Africa. There he reigned for a long time, receiving authority, as they say, from God Himself. Before his death he summoned the band of his sons and ordained that there should be no strife among them because of desire for the kingdom, but that each should reign in his own rank and order as he survived the others; that is, the next younger should succeed his elder brother, and he in turn should be followed by his junior. By giving heed to this command they ruled their kingdom in happiness for the space of many years and were not disgraced by civil war, as is usual among other nations; one after the other receiving the kingdom and ruling the people in peace.

Now this is their order of succession: first, Gaiseric who was the father and lord, next Huneric, the third Gunthamund, the fourth Thrasamund, and the fifth Ilderich. He was driven from his throne and slain by Gelimer, who destroyed his race by disregarding his ancestor's advice and setting up a tyranny. But what he had done did not remain unpunished, for soon the vengeance of the Emperor Justinian was manifested against him. With his whole family and that wealth over which he gloated like a robber, he was taken to Constantinople by that most renowned warrior Belisarius, Master of the Soldiery of the East, Ex-Consul Ordinary and Patrician. Here he afforded a great spectacle to the people in the Circus. His repentance, when he beheld himself cast down from his royal state, came too late. He died as a mere subject and in retirement, though he had formerly been unwilling to submit to private life. Thus after a century Africa, which in the division of the earth's surface is regarded as the third part of the world, was delivered from the yoke of the Vandals and brought back to the liberty of the Roman Empire. The country which the hand of the heathen had long ago cut off from the body of the Roman Empire, by reason of the cowardice of emperors and the treachery of generals, was now restored by a wise prince and a faithful leader and to-day is happily flourishing. And though, even after this, it had to deplore the misery of civil war and the treachery of the Moors, yet the triumph of the Emperor Justinian, vouchsafed him by God, brought to a peaceful conclusion what he had begun. But why need we speak of what the subject does not require? Let us return to our theme.

Now Valia, king of the Goths, and his army fought so fiercely against the Vandals that he would have pursued them even into Africa, had not such a misfortune recalled him as befell Alaric when he was setting out for Africa. So when he had won great fame in Spain, he returned after a bloodless victory to Tolosa, turning over to the Roman Empire, as he had promised, a number of provinces which he had rid of his foes. A long time after this he was seized by sickness and departed this life. Just at that time Beremud, the son of Thorismud, whom we have mentioned above in the genealogy of the family of the Amali, departed with his son Veteric from the Ostrogoths, who still submitted to the oppression of the Huns in the land of Scythia, and came to the kingdom of the Visigoths. Well aware of his valor and noble birth, he believed that the kingdom would be the more readily bestowed upon him by his kinsmen, inasmuch as he was known to be the heir of many kings. And who would hesitate to choose one of the Amali, if there were an empty throne? But he was not himself eager to make known who he was, and so upon the death of Valia the Visigoths made Theodorid his successor. Beremud came to him and, with the strength of mind for which he was noted, concealed his noble birth by prudent silence, for he knew that those of royal lineage are always distrusted by kings. So he suffered himself to remain unknown, that he might not bring the established order into confusion. King Theodorid received him and his son with special honor and made him partner in his counsels and a companion at his board; not for his noble birth, which he knew not, but for his brave spirit and strong mind, which Beremud could not conceal.

And what more? Valia (to repeat what we have said) had but little success against the Gauls, but when he died the more fortunate and prosperous Theodorid succeeded to the throne. He was a man of the greatest moderation and notable for vigor of mind and body. In the consulship of Theodosius and Festus the Romans broke the truce and took up arms against him in Gaul, with the Huns as their auxiliaries. For a band of the Gallic Allies, led by Count Gaina, had aroused the Romans by throwing Constantinople into a panic. Now at that time the Patrician Aëtius was in command of the army. He was of the bravest Moesian stock, the son of Gaudentius and born in the city of Durostorum. He was a man fitted to endure the toils of war, born expressly to serve the Roman state; and by inflicting crushing defeats he had compelled the proud Suavi and barbarous Franks to submit to Roman sway. So then, with the Huns as allies under their leader Litorius, the Roman army moved in array against the Goths. When the battle lines of both sides had been standing for a long time opposite each other, both being brave and neither side the weaker, they struck a truce and returned to their ancient alliance. And after the treaty had been confirmed by both and an honest peace was established, they both withdrew.

During this peace Attila was lord over all the Huns and almost the sole earthly ruler of all the tribes of Scythia; a man marvellous for his glorious fame among all nations. The historian Priscus, who was sent to him on an embassy by the younger Theodosius, says this among other things: "Crossing mighty rivers—namely, the Tisia and Tibisia and Dricca—we came to the place where long ago Vidigoia, bravest of the Goths, perished by the guile of the Sarmatians. At no great distance from that place we arrived at the village where King Attila was dwelling, a village, I say, like a great city, in which we found wooden walls made of smooth-shining boards, whose joints so counterfeited solidity that the union of the boards could scarcely be distinguished by close scrutiny. There you might see dining halls of large extent and porticoes planned with great beauty, while the courtyard was bounded by so vast a circuit that its very size showed it was the royal palace." This was the abode of Attila, the king of all the barbarian world; and he preferred this as a dwelling to the cities he captured.

Now this Attila was the son of Mundiuch, and his brothers were Octar and Ruas who are said to have ruled before Attila, though not over quite so many tribes as he. After their death he succeeded to the throne of the Huns, together with his brother Bleda. In order that he might first be equal to the expedition he was preparing, he sought to increase his strength by murder. Thus he proceeded from the destruction of his own kindred to the menace of all others. But though he increased his power by this shameful means, yet by the balance of justice he received the hideous consequences of his own cruelty. Now when his brother Bleda, who ruled over a great part of the Huns, had been slain by his treachery, Attila united all the people under his own rule. Gathering also a host of the other tribes which he then held under his sway, he sought to subdue the foremost nations of the world—the Romans and the Visigoths. His army is said to have numbered five hundred thousand men. He was a man born into the world to shake the nations, the scourge of all lands, who in some way terrified all mankind by the dreadful rumors noised abroad concerning him. He was haughty in his walk, rolling his eyes hither and thither, so that the power of his proud spirit appeared in the movement of his body. He was indeed a lover of war, yet restrained in action, mighty in counsel, gracious to suppliants and lenient to those who were once received into his protection. He was short of stature, with a broad chest and a large head; his eyes were small, his beard thin and sprinkled with gray; and he had a flat nose and a swarthy complexion, showing the evidences of his origin. And though his temper was such that he always had great self-confidence yet his assurance was increased by finding the sword of Mars, always esteemed sacred among the kings of the Scythians. The historian Priscus says it was discovered under the following circumstances:

"When a certain shepherd beheld one heifer of his flock limping and could find no cause for this wound, he anxiously followed the trail of blood and at length came to a sword it had unwittingly trampled while nibbling the grass. He dug it up and took it straight to Attila. He rejoiced at this gift and, being ambitious, thought he had been appointed ruler of the whole world, and that through the sword of Mars supremacy in all wars was assured to him."

THE AGE OF THE CHURCH FATHERS

49 *THE RULE OF ST. BENEDICT:* RENUNCIATION OF A TROUBLED WORLD — THE MONASTERIES

The troubled conditions in the Roman Empire from the fourth century on undoubtedly encouraged the rise of monasticism. Barbarian migrations, economic and political upheavals, decline in social morality—all contributed to an atmosphere of pessimism and despair. Hardship, together with a weariness of vice and luxury, pressed heavily on many early Christians. The logical step for many such persons was withdrawal from worldly temptations and settlement in isolated areas. Since it was easier and more efficient to live as a group, the ascetic ideal of monasticism developed. Religious communities first sprang up in Egypt and Syria, which had always been given to religious contemplation, and from there spread to the West.

In the sixth century A.D. a young Roman nobleman, Benedict of Nursia (480?-543?), turned from a materialistic life to one of contemplation and prayer. He lived alone for a time in the countryside near Rome, but eventually, as more and more followers were attracted to him, he withdrew to Monte Cassino and there in 526 began the most important early monastic order in the West, the Benedictine, which soon flourished throughout Europe. In order to regulate the lives of the monks at Monte Cassino, Benedict drew up his famous *Rule* or constitution for monastic conduct, which called for the three vows of poverty, chastity, and obedience. While a monastery might acquire great wealth, the individual monks were to remain poor; the rule of chastity required that they stay unmarried; and under the rule of obedience they were to submit to the abbot as the central authority of the monastery. The worst sin was idleness; the monks were instructed to engage in physical labor when not actually participating in prayer and meditation. The following selections from Benedict's *Rule* illustrate the three vows, which were taken by all participants in the monastic community.

Despite their desires for a contemplative and ascetic life, the Christian monks of the early Middle Ages were soon bound up in secular activities. To their credit, they provided the principal leadership and institutions for the spread of learning; they helped preserve literacy within the Church, translated classical manuscripts, served as advisers to kings, initiated schools, and established libraries. However, we cannot say that monks and monasteries were always ideal. It is difficult for any such group of men to sustain forever their original fervor, spirit of self-denial, and devotion to a high level of cultural achievement. Inevitably, monasticism experienced cycles of decay and rejuvenation. But history records that most monastic orders periodically underwent reform and that the monastic ideal was approached more often than not.

Prologue. . . . we are about to found . . . a school for the Lord's service; in the organization of which we trust that we shall ordain nothing severe and nothing burdensome. But even if, the demands of justice dictating it, something a little irksome shall be the result, for the purpose of amending vices or preserving charity;— thou shalt not therefore, struck by fear, flee the way of salvation, which can not be entered upon except through a narrow entrance. But as one's way of life and one's faith progresses, the heart becomes broadened, and, with the unutterable sweetness of love, the way of the mandates of the Lord is traversed. Thus, never departing from His guidance, continuing in the monastery in His teaching until death, through patience we are made partakers in Christ's passion, in order that we may merit to be companions in His kingdom. . . .

Text: Ernest F. Henderson (trans. and ed.), *Select Historical Documents of the Middle Ages* (London: G. Bell & Sons, Ltd., 1896), pp. 274-75, 277-79, 283, 284, 289, 297-98, 301, 303-05, 313-14.

What the Abbot should be like. An abbot who is worthy to preside over a monastery ought always to remember what he is called, and carry out with his deeds the name of a Superior. For he is believed to be Christ's representative, since he is called by His name, the apostle saying: "Ye have received the spirit of adoption of sons, whereby we call Abba, Father." . . .

. . . The abbot ought always to remember what he is, to remember what he is called, and to know that from him to whom more is committed, the more is demanded. And let him know what a difficult and arduous thing he has undertaken,—to rule the souls and aid the morals of many. And in one case indeed with blandishments, in another with rebukes, in another with persuasion—according to the quality or intelligence of each one,—he shall so conform and adapt himself to all, that not only shall he not suffer detriment to come to the flock committed to him, but shall rejoice in the increase of a good flock. Above all things, let him not, dissimulating or undervaluing the safety of the souls committed to him, give more heed to transitory and earthly and passing things: but let him always reflect that he has undertaken to rule souls for which he is to render account. And, lest perchance he enter into strife for a lesser matter, let him remember that it is written: "Seek ye first the kingdom of God and His righteousness; and all these things shall be added unto you." And again: "They that fear Him shall lack nothing." And let him know that he who undertakes to rule souls must prepare to render account. And, whatever number of brothers he knows that he has under his care, let him know for certain that at the day of judgment he shall render account to God for all their souls; his own soul without doubt being included. And thus, always fearing the future interrogation of the shepherd concerning the flocks entrusted to him, while keeping free from foreign interests he is rendered careful for his own. And when, by his admonitions, he administers correction to others, he is himself cleansed from his vices.

About calling in the brethren to take council. As often as anything especial is to be done in the monastery, the abbot shall call together the whole congregation, and shall himself explain the question at issue. And, having heard the advice of the brethren, he shall think it over by himself, and shall do what he considers most advantageous. And for this reason, moreover, we have said that all ought to be called to take counsel: because often it is to a younger person that God reveals what is best. The brethren, moreover, with all subjection of humility, ought so to give their advice, that they do not presume boldly to defend what seems good to them; but it should rather depend on the judgment of the abbot; so that whatever he decides to be the more salutary, they should all agree to it. But even as it behoves the disciples to obey the master, so it is fitting that he should providently and justly arrange all matters. In all things, indeed, let all follow the Rule as their guide; and let no one rashly deviate from it. Let no one in the monastery follow the inclination of his own heart; and let no one boldly presume to dispute with his abbot, within or without the monastery. But, if he should so presume, let him be subject to the discipline of the Rule. The abbot, on the other hand, shall do all things fearing the Lord and observing the Rule; knowing that he, without a doubt, shall have to render account to God as to a most impartial judge, for all his decisions. But if any lesser matters for the good of the monastery are to be decided upon, he shall employ the counsel of the elder members alone, since it is written: "Do all things with counsel, and after it is done thou wilt not repent." . . .

Concerning obedience. The first grade of humility is obedience without delay. This becomes those who, on account of the holy service which they have professed, or on account of the fear of hell or the glory of eternal life consider nothing dearer to them than Christ: so that, so soon as anything is commanded by their superior, they may not know how to suffer delay in doing it, even as if it were a divine command. Concerning whom the Lord said: "As soon as he heard of me he obeyed me." And again he said to the learned men: "He who heareth you heareth me." Therefore let all such, straightway leaving their own affairs and giving up their own will, with unoccupied hands and leaving incomplete what they were doing—the foot of obedience being foremost,—follow with their deeds the voice of him who orders. And, as it were, in the same moment, let the aforesaid command of the master and the perfected work of the disciple—both together in the swiftness of the fear of God,—be called into being by those who are possessed with a desire of advancing to eternal life. And therefore let them seize the narrow way of which the Lord says: "Narrow is the way which leadeth unto life." Thus, not living according to their own judgment nor obeying their own desires and pleasures, but walking under another's judgment and command, passing their time in monasteries, let them desire an abbot to rule over them. Without doubt all such live up to that precept of the Lord in which he says: "I am not come to do my own will but the will of him that sent me." . . .

How Divine Service shall be held through the day. As the prophet says: "Seven times in the day do I praise Thee." Which sacred number of seven will thus be fulfilled by us if, at matins, at the first, third, sixth, ninth hours, at vesper time and at "completorium" we perform the duties of our service; for it is of these hours of the day that he said: "Seven times in the day do I praise Thee." For, concerning nocturnal vigils, the same prophet says: "At midnight I arose to confess unto thee." Therefore, at these times, let us give thanks to our Creator concerning the judgments of his righteousness; that is, at matins, etc. . . . , and at night we will rise and confess to him. . . .

Concerning reverence for prayer. If when to powerful men we wish to suggest anything, we do not presume to do it unless with reverence and humility: how much more should we supplicate with all humility, and devotion of purity, God who is the Lord of all. And let us know that we are heard, not for much speaking, but for purity of heart and compunction of tears. And, therefore, prayer ought to be brief and pure; unless perchance it be prolonged by the influence of the inspiration of the divine grace. When assembled together, then, let the prayer be altogether brief; and, the sign being given by the prior, let all rise together. . . .

Whether the monks should have anything of their own. More than any thing else is this special vice to be cut off root and branch from the monastery, that one should presume to give or receive anything without the order of the abbot, or should have anything of his own. He should have absolutely not anything: neither a book, nor tablets, nor a pen—nothing at all.—For indeed it is not allowed to the monks to have their own bodies or wills in their own power. But all things necessary they must expect from the Father of the monastery; nor is it allowable to have anything which the abbot did not give or permit. All things shall be common to all, as it is written: "Let not any man presume or call anything his own." But if any one shall have been discovered delighting in this most evil vice: being warned once and again, if he do not amend, let him be subjected to punishment. . . .

Concerning the daily manual labour. Idleness is the enemy of the soul. And therefore, at fixed times, the brothers ought to be occupied in manual labour; and again, at fixed times, in sacred reading. Therefore we believe that, according to this disposition, both seasons ought to be arranged; so that, from Easter until the Calends of October, going out early, from the first until the fourth hour they shall do what labour may be necessary. Moreover, from the fourth hour until about the sixth, they shall be free for reading. After the meal of the sixth hour, moreover, rising from table, they shall rest in their beds with all silence; or, perchance, he that wishes to read may so read to himself that he do not disturb another. And the nona (the second meal) shall be gone through with more moderately about the middle of the eighth hour; and again they shall work at what is to be done until Vespers. But, if the exigency or poverty of the place demands that they be occupied by themselves in picking fruits, they shall not be dismayed: for then they are truly monks if they live by the labours of their hands; as did also our fathers and the apostles. Let all things be done with moderation, however, on account of the fainthearted. From the Calends of October, moreover, until the beginning of Lent they shall be free for reading until the second full hour. At the second hour the tertia (morning service) shall be held, and all shall labour at the task which is enjoined upon them until the ninth. The first signal, moreover, of the ninth hour having been given, they shall each one leave off his work; and be ready when the second signal strikes. Moreover after the refection they shall be free for their readings or for psalms. But in the days of Lent, from dawn until the third full hour, they shall be free for their readings; and, until the tenth full hour, they shall do the labour that is enjoined on them. In which days of Lent they shall all receive separate books from the library; which they shall read entirely through in order. These books are to be given out on the first day of Lent. Above all there shall certainly be appointed one or two elders, who shall go round the monastery at the hours in which the brothers are engaged in reading, and see to it that no troublesome brother chance to be found who is open to idleness and trifling, and is not intent on his reading; being not only of no use to himself, but also stirring up others. If such a one—may it not happen—be found, he shall be admonished once and a second time. If he do not amend, he shall be subject under the Rule to such punishment that the others may have fear. Nor shall brother join brother at unsuitable hours. Moreover on Sunday all shall engage in reading: excepting those who are deputed to various duties. But if anyone be so negligent and lazy that he will not or can not read, some task shall be imposed upon him which he can do; so that he be not idle. On feeble or delicate brothers such a labour or art is to be imposed, that they shall neither be idle, nor shall they be so oppressed by the violence of labour as to be driven to take flight. Their weakness is to be taken into consideration by the abbot. . . .

Whether a monk should be allowed to receive letters or anything. By no means shall it be allowed to a monk—either from his relatives, or from any man, or from one of his fellows—to receive or to give, without order of the abbot, letters, presents or any gift, however small. But even if, by his relatives, anything has been sent to him: he shall not presume to receive it, unless it have first been shown to the abbot. But if he order it to be received, it shall be in the power of the abbot to give it to whomever he may will. And the brother to whom it happened to have been sent shall not be chagrined; that an opportunity be not given to the devil. Whoever, moreover, presumes otherwise, shall be subject to the discipline of the Rule. . . .

Concerning the manner of receiving brothers. When any new comer applies for conversion, an easy entrance shall not be granted him: but, as the apostle says, "Try the spirits if they be of God." Therefore, if he who comes perseveres in knocking, and is seen after four or five days to patiently endure the insults inflicted upon him, and the difficulty of ingress, and to persist in his demand: entrance shall be allowed him, and he shall remain for a few days in the cell of the guests. After this, moreover, he shall be in the cell of the novices, where he shall meditate and eat and sleep. And an elder shall be detailed off for him who shall be capable of saving souls, who shall altogether intently watch over him, and make it a care to see if he reverently seek God, if he be zealous in the service of God, in obedience, in suffering shame. And all the harshness and roughness of the means through which God is approached shall be told him in advance. If he promise perseverance in his steadfastness, after the lapse of two months this Rule shall be read to him in order, and it shall be said to him: Behold the law under which thou dost wish to serve; if thou canst observe it, enter; but if thou canst not, depart freely. If he have stood firm thus far, then he shall be led into the aforesaid cell of the novices; and again he shall be proven with all patience. And, after the lapse of six months, the Rule shall be read to him; that he may know upon what he is entering. And, if he stand firm thus far, after four months the same Rule shall again be re-read to him. And if, having deliberated with himself, he shall promise to keep everything, and to obey all the commands that are laid upon him: then he shall be received in the congregation; knowing that it is decreed, by the law of the Rule, that from that day he shall not be allowed to depart from the monastery, nor to shake free his neck from the yoke of the Rule, which, after such tardy deliberation, he was at liberty either to refuse or receive. He who is to be received, moreover, shall, in the oratory, in the presence of all, make promise concerning his steadfastness and the change in his manner of life and his obedience to God and to His saints; so that if, at any time, he act contrary, he shall know that he shall be condemned by Him whom he mocks. Concerning which promise he shall make a petition in the name of the saints whose relics are there, and of the abbot who is present. Which petition he shall write with his own hand. Or, if he really be not learned in letters, another, being asked by him, shall write it. And that novice shall make his sign; and with his own hand shall place it (the petition) above the altar. And when he has placed it there, the novice shall straightway commence this verse: "Receive me oh Lord according to thy promise and I shall live, and do not cast me down from my hope." Which verse the whole congregation shall repeat three times, adding: "Glory be to the Father." Then that brother novice shall prostrate himself at the feet of each one, that they may pray for him. And, already, from that day, he shall be considered as in the congregation. If he have any property, he shall either first present it to the poor, or, making a solemn donation, shall confer it on the monastery, keeping nothing at all for himself: as one, forsooth, who from that day, shall know that he shall not have power even over his own body. Straightway, therefore in the oratory, he shall take off his own garments in which he was clad, and shall put on the garments of the monastery. Moreover those garments which he has taken off shall be placed in the vestiary to be preserved; so that if, at any time, the devil persuading him, he shall consent to go forth from the monastery —may it not happen,—then, taking off the garments of the monastery, he may be cast out. That petition of his, nevertheless, which the abbot took from above the altar, he shall not receive again; but it shall be preserved in the monastery. . . .

That they shall be mutually obedient.—The virtue of obedience is not only to be exhibited by all to the abbot, but also the brothers shall be thus mutually obedient to each other; knowing that they shall approach God through this way of obedience. The command therefore of the abbot, or of the provosts who are constituted by him, being given the preference—since we do not allow private commands to have more weight than his,—for the rest, all juniors shall obey their superiors with all charity and solicitude. But if any one is found contentious, he shall be punished. If, moreover, any brother, for any slight cause, be in any way rebuked by the abbot or by any one who is his superior; or if he feel, even lightly, that the mind of some superior is angered or moved against him, however little:—straightway, without delay, he shall so long lie prostrate at his feet, atoning, until, with the benediction, that anger shall be appeased. But if any one scorn to do this, he shall either be subjected to corporal punishment; or, if he be contumacious, he shall be expelled from the monastery.

Concerning the good zeal which the monks ought to have.—As there is an evil zeal of bitterness, which separates from God and leads to Hell; so there is a good zeal, which separates from vice and leads to God and to eternal life. Let the monks therefore exercise this zeal with the most fervent love: that is, let them mutually surpass each other in honour. Let them most patiently tolerate their weaknesses, whether of body or character; let them vie with each other in showing obedience. Let no one pursue what he thinks useful for himself, but rather what he thinks useful for another. Let them love the brotherhood with a chaste love; let them fear God; let them love their abbot with a sincere and humble love; let them prefer nothing whatever to Christ, who leads us alike to eternal life.

Concerning the fact that not every just observance is decreed in this Rule.—We have written out this Rule, indeed, that we may show those observing it in the monasteries how to have some honesty of character, or beginning of conversion. But for those who hasten to the perfection of living, there are the teachings of the holy Fathers: the observance of which leads a man to the heights of perfection. For what page, or what discourse, of Divine authority of the Old or the New Testament is not a most perfect rule for human life? Or what book of the holy Catholic Fathers does not trumpet forth how by the right path we shall come to our Creator? Also the reading aloud of the Fathers, and their decrees, and their lives; also the Rule of our holy Father Basil—what else are they except instruments of virtue for well-living and obedient monks? We, moreover, blush with confusion for the idle, and the evilly living and the negligent. Thou, therefore, whoever doth hasten to the celestial fatherland, perform with Christ's aid this Rule written out as the least of beginnings: and then at length, under God's protection, thou wilt come to the greater things that we have mentioned; to the summits of learning and virtue.

50 VENERABLE BEDE, *ECCLESIASTICAL HISTORY OF THE ENGLISH PEOPLE*: THE CONVERSION OF THE HEATHEN

The last emperor of the western empire was deposed by German mercenaries in 476, the traditional date marking the fall of Rome. Henceforth, the emperor at Constantinople claimed sovereignty over both East and West, but the real power in the West lay in the hands of the barbarians. It should be remembered that, as a rule, the invaders had come not to destroy the Roman Empire—after all, they had been influenced by the Romans for over five hundred years—but to enjoy its advantages. Thus many of the new western kings, though illiterates, encouraged education, adopted elements of Roman law and culture, and received the vestiges of a civilization which had largely abandoned paganism and become Christian.

Such adaptation had important consequences, for as Italy ceased to be the home of emperors and western Europe came to comprise a collection of independent Christian kingdoms, the bishop of Rome became the most widely influential and respected leader in western Europe. The pope in effect succeeded to the primacy of the emperors. This is not to say that the allegiance of the West to the Church of Rome was secured without effort. The invading Germans only gradually abandoned pagan religions, and those who were not heathens were usually Arian Christians—heretics in need of conversion, in the eyes of the orthodox. Moreover, as new waves of barbarians advanced into western Europe, the earlier converts were pushed back into more remote regions and, while preserving their Christianity, tended to be cut off from Rome. The papacy needed the missionary efforts of an ally. It found this pioneer energy in the Benedictine monks, whose consuming interest in expansion and consolidation coincided with that of the popes.

A notable example of the work of this alliance was Pope Gregory the Great's conversion of the Anglo-Saxons in Britain. In 597, from the monastery of St. Andrew in

Rome, he sent St. Augustine[1] and his Benedictine brethren on a mission to England. There Augustine was welcomed by Ethelbert, King of Kent, who, though pagan, was married to a Christian. Ethelbert soon embraced the faith, and at Canterbury, Augustine built Christ Church, the mother church of all England and the base of operations for Roman proselytism throughout the island. Within a century a Roman clergy was well established, and the Benedictines had erected several monasteries. In addition to converting the Anglo-Saxons, the Roman missionaries eventually succeeded in winning the allegiance of the Celts, who had long been Christians but who were isolated in the western and northern reaches of Britain following the Anglo-Saxon invasions of the fifth century.

Our principal knowledge about the triumph of the Roman over the Celtic church and the conversion of the Anglo-Saxons to Latin Christianity comes from the pen of the Venerable Bede (673?-735), a monk who for more than forty years resided at the Northumbrian monastery at Jarrow, where he wrote his *Ecclesiastical History of the English People*. In the passages printed below, Bede tells the story of the conversion of the Britons by St. Augustine.

... I must here relate a story which shows Gregory's deep desire for the salvation of our nation. We are told that one day some merchants who had recently arrived in Rome displayed their many wares in the crowded market-place. Among other merchandise Gregory saw some boys exposed for sale. These had fair complexions, fine-cut features, and fair hair. Looking at them with interest, he enquired what country and race they came from. "They come from Britain," he was told, "where all the people have this appearance." He then asked whether the people were Christians, or whether they were still ignorant heathens. "They are pagans," he was informed. "Alas!" said Gregory with a heartfelt sigh: "how sad that such handsome folk are still in the grasp of the Author of darkness, and that faces of such beauty conceal minds ignorant of God's grace! What is the name of this race?" "They are called Angles," he was told. "That is appropriate," he said, "for they have angelic faces, and it is right that they should become fellow-heirs with the angels in heaven. And what is the name of their Province?" "Deira," was the answer. "Good. They shall indeed be *de ira*—saved from wrath—and called to the mercy of Christ. And what is the name of their king?" he asked. "Aella," he was told. "Then must *Alleluia* be sung to the praise of God our Creator in their land," said Gregory, making play on the name.

Approaching the Pope of the apostolic Roman see —for he was not yet Pope himself—Gregory begged him to send preachers of the word to the English people in Britain to convert them to Christ, and declared his own eagerness to attempt the task should the Pope see fit to direct it. But this permission was not forthcoming, for although the Pope himself was willing, the citizens of Rome would not allow Gregory to go so far away from the city. But directly Gregory succeeded to the Papacy himself, he put in hand this long cherished project and sent other missionaries in his place, assisting their work by his own prayers and encouragement. And I have thought it fitting to include this traditional story in the history of our Church....

In the year of our Lord 582, Maurice, fifty-fourth successor to Augustus, became Emperor, and ruled for twenty-one years. In the tenth year of his reign, Gregory, an eminent scholar and administrator, was elected Pontiff of the apostolic Roman see, and ruled it for thirteen years, six months, and ten days. In the fourteenth year of this Emperor, and about the one hundred and fiftieth year after the coming of the English to Britain, Gregory was inspired by God to send his servant Augustine with several other God-fearing monks to preach the word of God to the English nation. Having undertaken this task at the Pope's command and progressed a short distance on their journey, they became afraid, and began to consider returning home. For they were appalled at the idea of going to a barbarous, fierce, and pagan nation, of whose very language they were ignorant. They unanimously agreed that this was the safest course, and sent back Augustine—who was to be consecrated bishop in the event of their being received by the English—so that he might humbly request the holy Gregory to recall them from so dangerous, arduous, and uncertain a journey. In reply, the Pope wrote them a letter of encouragement, urging them to proceed on their mission to preach God's word, and to trust themselves to his aid. This letter ran as follows:

"GREGORY, Servant of the servants of God, to the

---

[1] St. Augustine of Canterbury (died 604)—not to be confused with St. Augustine of Hippo (354-430), the author of the *City of God* and the *Confessions* (see Document 51).

Text: From *A History of the English Church and People* by Bede, translated by Leo Sherley-Price (London: Penguin Books Ltd., 1955), pp. 66-69 *passim*. Reprinted by permission of the publisher.

servants of God. My very dear sons, it is better never to undertake any high enterprise than to abandon it when once begun. So with the help of God you must carry out this holy task which you have begun. Be constant and zealous in carrying out this enterprise which, under God's guidance, you have undertaken: and be assured that the greater the labour, the greater will be the glory of your eternal reward. When Augustine your leader returns, whom We have appointed your abbot, obey him humbly in all things, remembering that whatever he directs you to do will always be to the good of your souls. May Almighty God protect you with His grace, and grant me to see the result of your labours in our heavenly home. And although my office prevents me from working at your side, yet because I long to do so, I hope to share in your joyful reward. God keep you safe, my dearest sons.

"Dated the twenty-third of July, in the fourteenth year of the reign of our most devout lord Maurice Tiberius Augustus, and the thirteenth year after the Consulship of our said Lord. The fourteenth indiction." . . .

The venerable Pontiff also wrote to Etherius, Archbishop of Arles, asking him to offer a kindly welcome to Augustine on his journey to Britain. This letter reads:

"To his most reverend and holy brother and fellow-bishop Etherius: Gregory, servant of the servants of God.

"Religious men should require no commendation to priests who exhibit the love that is pleasing to God, but since a suitable opportunity to write has arisen, We have written this letter to you, our brother, to certify that its bearer, God's servant Augustine and his companions, of whose zeal we are assured, has been directed by us to proceed to save souls with the help of God. We therefore request Your Lordship to assist them with pastoral care, and to make early provision for their needs." . . .

Reassured by the encouragement of the blessed father Gregory, Augustine and his fellow-servants of Christ resumed their work in the word of God, and arrived in Britain. The King of Kent at this time was the powerful King Ethelbert, whose domains extended northwards to the river Humber, which forms the boundary between the north and south Angles. To the east of Kent lies the large island of Thanet, which by English reckoning is six hundred hides in extent; it is separated from the mainland by a waterway about three furlongs broad called the Wantsum, which joins the sea at either end, and is fordable only in two places. It was here that God's servant Augustine landed with companions, who are said to have been forty in number. At the direction of blessed Pope Gregory, they had brought interpreters from among the Franks, and they sent these to Ethelbert, saying that they came from Rome bearing very glad news, which infallibly assured all who would receive it of eternal joy in heaven, and an everlasting kingdom with the living and true God. On receiving this message, the king ordered them to remain in the island where they had landed, and gave directions that they were to be provided with all necessaries until he should decide what action to take. For he had already heard of the Christian religion, having a Christian wife of the Frankish royal house named Bertha, whom he had received from her parents on condition that she should have freedom to hold and practise her faith unhindered with Bishop Liudhard whom they had sent as her chaplain.

After some days, the king came to the island, and sitting down in the open air, summoned Augustine and his companions to an audience. But he took precautions that they should not approach him in a house, for he held an ancient superstition that if they were practisers of magical arts, they might have opportunity to deceive and master him. But the monks were endowed with power from God, not from the Devil, and approached the king carrying a silver cross as their standard, and the likeness of our Lord and Saviour painted on a board. First of all they offered prayer to God, singing a litany for the eternal salvation both of themselves and of those for whose sake they had come. And when, at the king's command, Augustine had sat down and preached the word of life to the king and his court, the king said: "Your words and promises are fair indeed, but they are new and strange to us, and I cannot accept them and abandon the age-old beliefs of the whole English nation. But since you have travelled far, and I can see that you are sincere in your desire to instruct us in what you believe to be true and excellent, we will not harm you. We will receive you hospitably, and take care to supply you with all that you need; nor will we forbid you to preach and win any people you can to your religion." The king then granted them a dwelling in the city of Canterbury, which was the chief city of all his realm, and in accordance with his promise, he allowed them provisions and did not withdraw their freedom to preach. Tradition says that as they approached the city, bearing the holy cross and the likeness of our great King and Lord Jesus Christ as was their custom, they sang in unison this litany: "We pray Thee, O Lord, in all Thy mercy, that Thy wrath and anger may be turned away from this city and from Thy holy house, for we are sinners. Alleluia." . . .

As soon as they had occupied the house given to them they began to emulate the life of the apostles and the primitive Church. They were constantly at prayer; they fasted and kept vigils; they preached the word of life to whomsoever they could. They regarded worldly things as of little importance, and accepted only necessary food from those they taught. They practised what they preached, and were willing to endure any hardship, and even to die for the Faith which they proclaimed. A number of heathen, admiring the simplicity of their holy lives and the comfort of their heavenly message, believed and were baptized. On the east side of the city stood an old church, built in honour of Saint Martin during the Roman occupation of Britain, where the Christian queen went to pray. Here they first assembled to sing the psalms, to pray, to say Mass, to preach, and to baptize, until the king's own conversion to the Faith enabled them to preach openly, and to build and restore churches everywhere.

At length the king and others, edified by the pure lives of these holy men and their gracious promises, the truth of which they confirmed by many miracles, believed and were baptized. Thenceforward great numbers gathered each day to hear the word of God, forsaking their heathen rites, and entering the unity of Christ's holy Church as believers. While the king was pleased at their faith and conversion, he would not compel anyone to accept Christianity, for he had learned from his instructors and guides to salvation that the service of Christ must be accepted freely and not under compulsion; nevertheless, he showed greater favour to believers, because they were fellow-citizens of the kingdom of heaven. And it was not long before he granted his teachers a property of their own in his capital of Canterbury, and gave them possessions of various kinds to supply their wants. . . .

Meanwhile God's servant Augustine visited Arles, and in accordance with the holy father Gregory's directions, was consecrated archbishop of the English nation by Etherius, archbishop of that city. On his return to Britain, he sent the priest Laurentius and the monk Peter to Rome to inform the blessed Pope Gregory that the English had accepted the Faith of Christ, and that he himself had been consecrated bishop. . . .

51 ST. AUGUSTINE, *THE CONFESSIONS*: THE CONVERSION OF A CHURCH FATHER

During the first four centuries of Christianity, the eastern leaders of the Church dominated Christian theology. The great Church councils, including the first Council of Nicaea (see Document 45), were held in the East and were attended by few westerners. Since Christianity had been born in the East, most of the early Christian literature was written in Greek, which few westerners knew, and the standard version of the Old Testament, still used by the Greek Orthodox Church, was the Greek Septuagint. In the West, the Roman papacy had not yet risen to its eventual level of influence, and relative to the impressive number of great eastern theologians, the West had produced only a few prominent Christian thinkers—the Roman Minucius Felix, Lactantius of Gaul, and Cyprian and Tertullian of Carthage.

By the end of the fourth century, the eclipse of the West had begun to end. The Church of Rome was assuming its primacy and independence and producing theologians of preëminent caliber. One of the Church Fathers, St. Ambrose (340?-397), bishop of Milan, vigorously pitted the authority of the Church against the will of the emperor; he wrote numerous sermons, theological treatises, and hymns, and his inspiring influence won converts like Augustine of Hippo. St. Jerome (340?-420) turned to a monastic and scholarly life and became the most learned Christian of his day; retiring to Palestine late in life, he prepared for the West his Latin translation of the Bible, which is the basis of the Vulgate, the version still used by the Roman Catholic faith. The early churchman who exerted the greatest influence on medieval and modern Christianity was St. Augustine of Hippo (354-430). St. Augustine was born in Numidia, studied at Carthage, and in his late twenties gravitated to Rome. For years he dabbled in philosophy, especially Neoplatonism, and in religions like the oriental Manicheism. Shortly after meeting Bishop Ambrose, however, he was baptized as a Christian (Easter Eve, 387), and the remaining forty-three years of Augustine's life were devoted to the service of the Church. He wrote countless letters, philosophical and theological works, treatises against heresies, and textbooks, most of these as the Bishop of Hippo (modern Bône in Algeria).

The period in which Augustine lived was one not only of political unrest—the barbarians were pressing upon the empire, even sacking Rome itself—but also one in which schism and heresy threatened the unity of the Church. In his theological conflicts, Augustine became convinced that the true Church was characterized by unity and catholicity. Salvation was to be found only within the Church; it alone was the "ark of safety" in which a perishing mankind must seek refuge by submitting to its authority. Augustine finally came to believe in the right even to coerce the unwilling to embrace the Church.

The most famous of Augustine's writings are *The City of God* and the *Confessions*. The former was written to answer the pagan claim that Rome's disasters, particularly the Visigothic sack of Rome in 410, resulted from the desertion of the pagan gods for Christianity. In this work he ascribed human history to a cosmic plan operating under divine providence. Since Adam's fall, he argued, sinful men had been compelled to live in the "earthly city," the series of pagan empires which culminated with the Roman Empire. Yet ever destined in God's ordinance was the heavenly City of God, toward which man aspired. With the coming of Christ, God provided for man a means of salvation from the disasters which according to Augustine had blighted the history of the world.

In his *Confessions*, Augustine left a record of his life from his birth to his conversion and Christian novitiate. He recalled his childish neglect of parental commands, his youthful thefts of fruit, his adolescent indiscretions, and his scholarly arrogance; yet looking back, he saw the providence of God showing him the right way and forgiving his errors. In the following selection from the *Confessions*, Augustine recounts the moment of his conversion—that point in his life separating his earlier restlessness in a career of pagan worldliness from his later peacefulness in the Christian way of life. Augustine's experience was perhaps typical of many in his age who made the transition from sophisticated pagan intellectualism to the simple faith of Christianity.

. . . A garden there was belonging to our lodging, which we had the liberty of, as well as of any other part of the house; for the master of the house, our host, lived not there. Thither had the tempest within my breast now hurried me, where no man might come to non-suit that fiery action which I had entered against myself, until it came to a good issue; but which way, God thou knewest, I did not. Only I was for the time most soberly mad, and dying, to live: sensible enough what piece of misery for the present I now was, but utterly ignorant how good I shortly was to grow. Into that garden went I, and Alypius followed me foot by foot: for I was no less secret when he was near; and how could he forsake me, in such a state? Down we sat us, as far from the house as possibly we could. I fretted in the spirit, angry at myself with a most tempestuous indignation, for that I went not into thy will and covenant, my God, which all my bones cried out upon me to do, extolling it to the very skies. That way we go not in ships, or chariots, or upon our own legs, no not so small a part of the way to it, as I had come from the house into that place, where we were now sitting. For, not to go towards only, but to arrive fully at that place, required no more but the will to go to it, but yet to will it resolutely and thoroughly; not to stagger and tumble down an half wounded will, now on this side, and anon on that side; setting the part advancing itself to struggle with another part that is falling.

Finally, in these vehement passions of my delay, many of those things performed I with my body, which men sometimes would do, but cannot; if either they have not the limbs to do them withal; or if those limbs be bound with cords, weakened with infirmity, or be any other ways hindered. If I tare myself by the hair, beat my forehead, if locking my fingers one within another I beclasped my knee; all this I did because I would. But I might have willed it, and yet not have done it, if so be the motion of my limbs had not been pliable enough to have performed it. So many things therefore I now did, at such time as the will was not all at one with the power; and something on the other side I then did not, which did incomparably more affect me with pleasure, which yet so soon as I had the will to do, I had the power also; because so soon as ever I willed, I willed it thoroughly: for at such a time the power is all one with the will; and the willing is now the doing: and yet was not the thing done, and more easily did my body obey the weakest willing of my mind in the moving of its limbs at her beck, than my mind had obeyed itself in carrying out this great will that could be done in the will alone. . . .

Thus soul-sick I was, and in this manner tormented; accusing myself much more eagerly than

Text: Reprinted by permission of the publishers and The Loeb Classical Library from *St. Augustine's Confessions*, trans. William Watts (Cambridge, Mass.: Harvard University Press, 1946), I, 445-47, 457-67.

I was wont, turning and winding myself in my chain, till that which held me might be utterly broken; which though but little, yet held it me fast enough notwithstanding. And thou, O Lord, pressedst upon me in my inward parts, by a most severe mercy redoubling my lashes of fear and shame, lest I should give way again, and lest that small and tender tie, which now only was left, should not break off but recover strength again, and hamper me again the faster. For I said within myself: Behold, let it be done now, let it be done now. And no sooner had I said the word, but that I began to put on the resolution. Now I even almost did it, yet indeed I did it not: yet notwithstanding, fell I not quite back to my old wont, but stood in the degree next to it, to fetch new breath. Yea, I set upon it again, and I wanted but very little of getting up to it, and within a very little, even by and by obtained I to touch and lay hold of it; and yet could I not get up to it, nor come to touch, or lay full hold of it, still fearing to die unto death, and to live unto life: and the worse which I had been anciently inured unto, prevailed more with me than the better, to which I was unused: yea, the very instant of time wherein I was to become something else, the nearer it approached to me, the greater horror did it strike into me. But for all this did it not strike me utterly back, nor turned me quite off, but kept me in suspense only.

The very toys of all toys, and vanities of vanities, (those ancient favourites of mine) were they which so fast withheld me: they plucked softly at this fleshly garment, and spake softly in mine ears: Canst thou thus part with us? And shall we no more accompany thee from this time for ever? And from this time forth shall it no more be lawful for thee to do this or that for ever? And what were those things which they suggested to me in that phrase this or that, as I said, what were those which they suggested, O my God? Such, as let thy mercy utterly turn away from the soul of thy servant. Oh what impurities, oh what most shameful things did they suggest! And now I much less than half heard them, nor now so freely contradicting me face to face; but muttering as it were softly behind my back, and giving me a privy pluck as I went from them that I might look once more back: yet for all this as I hesitated they did hold me back from snatching away myself, and shaking them off, and leaping from them to the place I was called unto; for violent custom thus rowned me in the ear: Thinkest thou to be ever able to live without all that?

But by this time it spake very faintly. For on that side which I set my face towards, and whither I trembled to go, was that chaste dignity of Continency discovered; cheerful was she, but not dissolutely pleasant, honestly coaxing me to come to her, and doubt nothing: yea stretching forth those devout hands of hers, so full of the multitudes of good examples, both to receive and to embrace me. There were in company with her very many both young men and maidens, a multitude of youth and of all ages: both grave widows and ancient virgins, and Continence herself in every one of them, not barren at all, but a fruitful mother of children, her joys, by thee her husband, O Lord. And she was pleasant with me with a kind of exhorting quip, as if she should have said: Canst not thou perform what these of both sexes have performed? Or can any of these perform thus much of themselves, not rather by the Lord their God? The Lord their God gave me unto them. Why standest thou on thyself, and on thyself standest not? Cast thyself upon him; fear not, he will not slip away and make thee fall. Cast thyself boldly upon him, he will receive thee, and he will heal thee. I blushed all this while to myself very much, for that I yet heard the muttering of those toys, and that I yet hung in suspense. Whereupon she seemed to say again: Stop thine ears against those unclean members of thine, that they may be mortified. They tell thee of delights indeed, but not such as the law of the Lord thy God tells thee of. This was the controversy I felt in my heart, about nothing but myself, against myself. But Alypius sitting by my side, in silence expected the issue of my unaccustomed agitation. . . .

So soon therefore as a deep consideration even from the secret bottom of my soul, had drawn together and laid all my misery upon one heap before the eyes of my heart; there rose up a mighty storm, bringing as mighty a shower of tears with it; which that I might pour forth with such expressions as suited best with them, I rose from Alypius: for I conceived that solitariness was more fit for a business of weeping. So far off then I went, as that even his presence might not be troublesome unto me. Thus disposed was I at that time, and he perceived of it; something I believe I had said before, which discovered the sound of my voice to be big with weeping, and in that case I rose from him. He thereupon stayed alone where we sat together, most extremely astonished. I flung down myself I know not how, under a certain fig tree, giving all liberty to my tears: whereupon the floods of mine eyes gushed out, an acceptable sacrifice to thee, O Lord. And though not perchance in these very words, yet much to this purpose said

I unto thee: And thou, O Lord, how long, how long, Lord, wilt thou be angry, for ever? Remember not our former iniquities: (for I found myself to be still enthralled by them). Yea, I sent up these miserable exclamations, How long? how long still "to-morrow," and "to-morrow"? Why not now? Wherefore even this very hour is there not an end put to my uncleanness?

Thus much I uttered, weeping, in the most bitter contrition of my heart: whenas behold I heard a voice from some neighbour's house, as it had been of a boy or girl, I know not whether, in a singing tune saying, and often repeating: Take up and read, Take up and read. Instantly changing my countenance thereupon, I began very heedfully to bethink myself, whether children were wont in any kind of playing to sing any such words: nor could I remember myself ever to have heard the like. Whereupon refraining the violent torrent of my tears, up I gat me; interpreting it no other way, but that I was from God himself commanded to open the book, and to read that chapter which I should first light upon. For I had heard of Anthony, that by hearing of the Gospel which he once chanced to come in upon, he took himself to be admonished, as if what was read, had purposely been spoken unto him: Go, and sell that thou hast, and give to the poor, and thou shalt have treasure in heaven, and come and follow me: and by such a miracle that he was presently converted unto thee. Hastily therefore went I again to that place where Alypius was sitting; for there had I laid the Apostle's book whenas I rose from thence. I snatched it up, I opened it, and in silence I read that chapter which I had first cast mine eyes upon: Not in rioting and drunkenness, not in chambering and wantonness, not in strife and envying: but put ye on the Lord Jesus Christ; and make not provision for the flesh, to fulfil the lusts thereof. No further would I read; nor needed I. For instantly even with the end of this sentence, by a light as it were of confidence now darted into my heart, all the darkness of doubting vanished away.

Shutting up the book thereupon, and putting my finger between, or I know not what other mark, with a well-quieted countenance I discovered all this unto Alypius. And he again in this manner revealed unto me what also was wrought in his heart, which I verily knew nothing of. He requested to see what I had read: I shewed him the place; and he looked further than I had read, nor knew I what followed. This followed: Him that is weak in faith, receive: which he applied to himself, and shewed it to me. And by this admonition was he strengthened, and unto that good resolution and purpose (which was most agreeable to his disposition, wherein he did always very far differ from me, to the better) without all turbulent delaying did he now apply himself. From thence went we into the house unto my mother: we discover ourselves, she rejoices for it; we declare in order how everything was done; she leaps for joy, and triumpheth, and blessed thee, who art able to do above that which we ask or think; for that she perceived thee to have given her so much more concerning me, than she was wont to beg by her pitiful and most doleful groanings. For so thou convertedst me unto thyself, as that I sought now no more after a wife, nor any other hopes in this world: standing thus upon the same rule of faith, in which thou hadst shewed me unto her in a vision, so many years before. Thus didst thou convert her mourning into rejoicing, and that much more plentifully than she had desired, and with a much dearer and a chaster joy, than she erst required from any grandchildren of my body.

INTERPRETATIONS OF THE RISE OF CHRISTIANITY
AND THE FALL OF ROME

52 EDWARD GIBBON, *THE DECLINE AND FALL OF THE ROMAN EMPIRE*: A RATIONALIST'S APPRAISAL OF THE FALL OF ROME

Edward Gibbon's remarkable history of *The Decline and Fall of the Roman Empire* (five vols., 1776-1788), remains today one of the most significant discourses on the subject. The time span that the work covers is immense; Gibbon (1737-1794) began his history with the second century of the Christian era, when the Roman Empire "comprehended the fairest portion of mankind," and then carried the story of the empire through the withering of its vitality, the collapse of the state, both within and without, first in the West (476) and then the East (1453). The *Decline and Fall* combines both great history and greater literature, despite occasional inaccuracies, due mainly to

later discovery of new materials and to the author's obvious bias against the early Christian Church.

The thought of writing such a history first occurred to Gibbon while on a visit to Rome in 1764. It was, he said, as I sat "musing amidst the ruins of the Capitol, while bare-footed friars were singing vespers in the temple of Jupiter . . . that I first conceived the idea of a work which has amused and exercised nearly twenty years of my life." Gibbon's attacks on Christianity are representative of eighteenth-century humanism, which equated organized religion with political autocracy and intellectual tyranny. In the selection below, Gibbon makes some general observations on the fall of the Roman Empire in the West and in doing so, projects his famous thesis that Christianity was at least partly to blame.

The Greeks, after their country had been reduced into a province, imputed the triumphs of Rome, not to the merit, but to the FORTUNE, of the republic. The inconstant goddess, who so blindly distributes and resumes her favors, had *now* consented (such was the language of envious flattery) to resign her wings, to descend from her globe, and to fix her firm and immutable throne on the banks of the Tiber. A wiser Greek, who has composed, with a philosophic spirit, the memorable history of his own times, deprived his countrymen of this vain and delusive comfort, by opening to their view the deep foundations of the greatness of Rome. The fidelity of the citizens to each other and to the State was confirmed by the habits of education and the prejudices of religion. Honor, as well as virtue, was the principle of the republic; the ambitious citizens labored to deserve the solemn glories of a triumph; and the ardor of the Roman youth was kindled into active emulation as often as they beheld the domestic images of their ancestors. The temperate struggles of the Patricians and Plebeians had finally established the firm and equal balance of the constitution, which united the freedom of popular assemblies with the authority and wisdom of a senate and the executive powers of a regal magistrate. When the consul displayed the standard of the republic, each citizen bound himself, by the obligation of an oath, to draw his sword in the cause of his country till he had discharged the sacred duty by a military service of ten years. This wise institution continually poured into the field the rising generations of freemen and soldiers; and their numbers were reinforced by the warlike and populous states of Italy, who, after a brave resistance, had yielded to the valor and embraced the alliance of the Romans. The sage historian, who excited the virtue of the younger Scipio and beheld the ruin of Carthage, has accurately described their military system; their levies, arms, exercises, subordination, marches, encampments; and the invincible legion, superior in active strength to the Macedonian phalanx of Philip and Alexander. From these institutions of peace and war Polybius has deduced the spirit and success of a people incapable of fear and impatient of repose. The ambitious design of conquest, which might have been defeated by the seasonable conspiracy of mankind, was attempted and achieved; and the perpetual violation of justice was maintained by the political virtues of prudence and courage. The arms of the republic, sometimes vanquished in battle, always victorious in war, advanced with rapid steps to the Euphrates, the Danube, the Rhine, and the Ocean; and the images of gold, or silver, or brass, that might serve to represent the nations and their kings, were successively broken by the *iron* monarchy of Rome.

The rise of a city, which swelled into an empire, may deserve, as a singular prodigy, the reflection of a philosophic mind. But the decline of Rome was the natural and inevitable effect of immoderate greatness. Prosperity ripened the principle of decay; the causes of destruction multiplied with the extent of conquest; and as soon as time or accident had removed the artificial supports, the stupendous fabric yielded to the pressure of its own weight. The story of its ruin is simple and obvious; and instead of inquiring *why* the Roman empire was destroyed, we should rather be surprised that it had subsisted so long. The victorious legions, who, in distant wars, acquired the vices of strangers and mercenaries, first oppressed the freedom of the republic, and afterwards violated the majesty of the purple. The emperors, anxious for their personal safety and the public peace, were reduced to the base expedient of corrupting the discipline which rendered them alike formidable to their sovereign and to the enemy; the vigor of the military government was relaxed and finally dissolved by the partial institutions of Constantine; and the Roman world was overwhelmed by a deluge of barbarians.

Text: Edward Gibbon, *The History of the Decline and Fall of the Roman Empire*, ed. Dean Milman, M. Guizot, and William Smith, "Edition Deluxe" (New York: The Nottingham Society, 1915), IV, 88-92.

The decay of Rome has been frequently ascribed to the translation of the seat of empire; but this history has already shown that the powers of government were *divided* rather than *removed*. The throne of Constantinople was erected in the East; while the West was still possessed by a series of emperors who held their residence in Italy, and claimed their equal inheritance of the legions and provinces. This dangerous novelty impaired the strength and fomented the vices of a double reign: the instruments of an oppressive and arbitrary system were multiplied; and a vain emulation of luxury, not of merit, was introduced and supported between the degenerate successors of Theodosius. Extreme distress, which unites the virtue of a free people, embitters the factions of a declining monarchy. The hostile favorites of Arcadius and Honorius betrayed the republic to its common enemies; and the Byzantine court beheld with indifference, perhaps with pleasure, the disgrace of Rome, the misfortunes of Italy, and the loss of the West. Under the succeeding reigns the alliance of the two empires was restored; but the aid of the Oriental Romans was tardy, doubtful, and ineffectual; and the national schism of the Greeks and Latins was enlarged by the perpetual difference of language and manners, of interests, and even of religion. Yet the salutary event approved in some measure the judgment of Constantine. During a long period of decay his impregnable city repelled the victorious armies of barbarians, protected the wealth of Asia, and commanded, both in peace and war, the important straits which connect the Euxine and Mediterranean seas. The foundation of Constantinople more essentially contributed to the preservation of the East than to the ruin of the West.

As the happiness of a *future* life is the great object of religion, we may hear without surprise or scandal that the introduction, or at least the abuse, of Christianity, had some influence on the decline and fall of the Roman empire. The clergy successfully preached the doctrines of patience and pusillanimity; the active virtues of society were discouraged; and the last remains of military spirit were buried in the cloister: a large portion of public and private wealth was consecrated to the specious demands of charity and devotion; and the soldiers' pay was lavished on the useless multitudes of both sexes who could only plead the merits of abstinence and chastity. Faith, zeal, curiosity, and the more earthly passions of malice and ambition, kindled the flame of theological discord; the Church, and even the State, were distracted by religious factions, whose conflicts were sometimes bloody and always implacable; the attention of the emperors was diverted from camps to synods; the Roman world was oppressed by a new species of tyranny; and the persecuted sects became the secret enemies of their country. Yet party spirit, however pernicious or absurd, is a principle of union as well as of dissension. The bishops, from eighteen hundred pulpits, inculcated the duty of passive obedience to a lawful and orthodox sovereign; their frequent assemblies and perpetual correspondence maintained the communion of distant churches; and the benevolent temper of the Gospel was strengthened, though confined, by the spiritual alliance of the Catholics. The sacred indolence of the monks was devoutly embraced by a servile and effeminate age; but if superstition had not afforded a decent retreat, the same vices would have tempted the unworthy Romans to desert, from baser motives, the standard of the republic. Religious precepts are easily obeyed which indulge and sanctify the natural inclinations of their votaries; but the pure and genuine influence of Christianity may be traced in its beneficial, though imperfect, effects on the barbarian proselytes of the North. If the decline of the Roman empire was hastened by the conversion of Constantine, his victorious religion broke the violence of the fall, and mollified the ferocious temper of the conquerors.

53 MICHAEL ROSTOVTZEFF, SOCIAL AND ECONOMIC HISTORY OF THE ROMAN EMPIRE: CHANGING HISTORICAL VIEWS OF ROME

The reasons for the decline and fall of the Roman Empire have preoccupied men for more than a thousand years, and yet few scholars have written as clearly and forcefully on the subject as Michael I. Rostovtzeff (1870-1952). "The gradual absorption of the educated classes by the masses and the consequent simplification of all functions of political, social and economic life, which we call the barbarization of the ancient world" is, according to Rostovtzeff, "the main phenomenon which underlies the process of Roman decline." In the passage below, taken from his monumental *Social and Economic History of the Roman Empire* (1926), Rostovtzeff examines the accepted contemporary theories for Rome's fall and then discusses his own solution. "Why," he asks, "did such a powerful and brilliant civilization, the growth of ages and apparently destined to last for ages, gradually degenerate?" In other words, why did the creative powers of its makers wax faint—with this result: that mankind slowly reverted to primitive and extremely simple conditions of life and then began to create civilization over again from the very rudiments, reviving the old institutions and studying the old problems?

Every reader of a volume devoted to the Roman Empire will expect the author to express his opinion on what is generally, since Gibbon, called the decline and fall of the Roman Empire, or rather of ancient civilization in general. I shall therefore briefly state my own view on this problem, after defining what I take the problem to be. The decline and fall of the Roman Empire, that is to say, of ancient civilization as a whole, has two aspects: the political, social, and economic on the one hand, and the intellectual and spiritual on the other. In the sphere of politics we witness a gradual barbarization of the Empire from within, especially in the West. The foreign, German, elements play the leading part both in the government and in the army, and settling in masses displace the Roman population, which disappears from the fields. A related phenomenon, which indeed was a necessary consequence of this barbarization from within, was the gradual disintegration of the Western Roman Empire; the ruling classes in the former Roman provinces were replaced first by Germans and Sarmatians, and later by Germans alone, either through peaceful penetration or by conquest. In the East we observe a gradual orientalization of the Byzantine Empire, which leads ultimately to the establishment, on the ruins of the Roman Empire, of strong half-oriental and purely oriental states, the Caliphate of Arabia, and the Persian and Turkish empires. From the social and economic point of view, we mean by decline the gradual relapse of the ancient world to very primitive forms of economic life, into an almost pure 'house-economy'. The cities, which had created and sustained the higher forms of economic life, gradually decayed, and the majority of them practically disappeared from the face of the earth. A few, especially those that had been great centres of commerce and industry, still lingered on. The complicated and refined social system of the ancient Empire follows the same downward path and becomes reduced to its primitive elements: the king, his court and retinue, the big feudal landowners, the clergy, the mass of rural serfs, and small groups of artisans and merchants. Such is the political, social, and economic aspect of the problem. However, we must not generalize too much. The Byzantine Empire cannot be put on a level with the states of Western Europe or with the new Slavonic formations. But one thing is certain: on the ruins of the uniform economic life of the cities there began everywhere a special, locally differentiated, evolution.

From the intellectual and spiritual point of view the main phenomenon is the decline of ancient civilization, of the city civilization of the Greco-Roman world. The Oriental civilizations were more stable: blended with some elements of the Greek city civilization, they persisted and even witnessed a brilliant revival in the Caliphate of Arabia and in Persia, not to speak of India and China. Here again there are two aspects of the evolution. The first is the exhaustion of the creative forces of Greek civilization in the domains where its great triumphs had been achieved, in the exact sciences, in technique, in literature and art. The decline began as early as the second century B.C. There followed a temporary revival of creative forces in the cities of Italy, and later in those of the Eastern and Western provinces of the Empire. The progressive movement stopped almost completely in the second century A.D. and, after a period of stagnation, a steady and rapid decline set in again. Parallel to it, we notice a progressive weakening of the assimilative forces of Greco-Roman civilization. The cities no longer absorb—that is to say, no longer hellenize or romanize—the masses of the country population. The reverse is the case. The barbarism of the country begins to engulf the city population. Only small islands of civilized life are left, the senatorial aristocracy of the late Empire and the clergy; but both, save for a section of the clergy, are gradually swallowed up by the advancing tide of barbarism.

Another aspect of the same phenomenon is the development of a new mentality among the masses of the population. It was the mentality of the lower classes, based exclusively on religion and not only indifferent but hostile to the intellectual achievements of the higher classes.

Text: M. Rostovtzeff, *The Social and Economic History of the Roman Empire*, 2nd ed. (Oxford: The Clarendon Press, 1957), I, 532-41. Reprinted by permission of the Clarendon Press.

This new attitude of mind gradually dominated the upper classes, or at least the larger part of them. It is revealed by the spread among them of the various mystic religions, partly Oriental, partly Greek. The climax was reached in the triumph of Christianity. In this field the creative power of the ancient world was still alive, as is shown by such momentous achievements as the creation of the Christian church, the adaptation of Christian theology to the mental level of the higher classes, the creation of a powerful Christian literature and of a new Christian art. The new intellectual efforts aimed chiefly at influencing the mass of the population and therefore represented a lowering of the high standards of city-civilization, at least from the point of view of literary forms.

We may say, then, that there is one prominent feature in the development of the ancient world during the imperial age, alike in the political, social, and economic and in the intellectual field. It is a gradual absorption of the higher classes by the lower, accompanied by a gradual levelling down of standards. This levelling was accomplished in many ways. There was a slow penetration of the lower classes into the higher, which were unable to assimilate the new elements. There were violent outbreaks of civil strife: the lead was taken by the Greek cities, and there followed the civil war of the first century B.C. which involved the whole civilized world. In these struggles the upper classes and the city-civilization remained victorious on the whole. Two centuries later, a new outbreak of civil war ended in the victory of the lower classes and dealt a mortal blow to the Greco-Roman civilization of the cities. Finally, that civilization was completely engulfed by the inflow of barbarous elements from outside, partly by penetration, partly by conquest, and in its dying condition it was unable to assimilate even a small part of them.

The main problem, therefore, which we have to solve is this. Why was the city civilization of Greece and Italy unable to assimilate the masses, why did it remain a civilization of the *élite*, why was it incapable of creating conditions which should secure for the ancient world a continuous, uninterrupted movement along the same path of urban civilization? In other words: why had modern civilization to be built up laboriously as something new on the ruins of the old, instead of being a direct continuation of it? Various explanations have been suggested, and each of them claims to have finally solved the problem. Let us then review the most important of them. They may be divided into four classes.

(1) The political solution is advocated by many distinguished scholars. For Beloch the decay of ancient civilization was caused by the absorption of the Greek city-states by the Roman Empire, by the formation of a world-state which prevented the creative forces of Greece from developing and consolidating the great achievements of civilized life. There is some truth in this view. It is evident that the creation of the Roman Empire was a step forward in the process of levelling, and that it facilitated the final absorption of the higher classes. We must, however, take into consideration that class war was a common feature of Greek life, and that we have not the least justification for supposing that the Greek city-community would have found a solution of the social and economic problems which produced civil war in the various communities. Further, this view suggests that there was only one creative race in the ancient world, which is notoriously false. Another explanation, tending in the same direction, has been put forward by Kornemann. He regards as the main cause of the decay of the Roman Empire the fact that Augustus reduced the armed forces of the Empire, and that this reduction was maintained by his successors. The suggestion lays the whole emphasis on the military side of the problem, and is therefore a return to the antiquated idea that ancient civilization was destroyed by the barbarian invasions, an idea which should not be resuscitated. Besides, the maintenance of a comparatively small army was imperatively imposed by the economic weakness of the Empire, a fact which was understood by all the emperors. Still less convincing is the idea of Ferrero, that the collapse of the Empire was due to a disastrous event, to an accident which had the gravest consequences. He holds that by transmitting his power to his son Commodus instead of to a man chosen by the senate, M. Aurelius undermined the senate's authority on which the whole fabric of the Roman state rested; that the murder of Commodus led to the usurpation of Septimius and to the civil war of the third century; and that the usurpation and the war destroyed the authority of the senate and deprived the imperial power of its only legitimacy in the eyes of the population which was its main support. Ferrero forgets that legally the power of the emperors in the third century was still derived from the senate and people of Rome, that it was so even in the time of Diocletian, and that the same idea still survived under Constantine and his successors. He also forgets that the subtle formula of Augustus, Vespasian, and the Antonines was incomprehensible to the mass of the people of

the Empire, and was a creation of the upper classes, completely outside the range of popular conceptions. Finally, he fails to understand the true character of the crisis of the third century. The struggle was not between the senate and the emperor, but between the cities and the army —that is to say, the masses of peasants—as is shown by the fact that the lead in the fight was taken not by Rome but by the cities of the province of Africa. A deeper explanation is offered by Heitland. He suggests that the ancient world decayed because it was unable to give the masses a share in the government, and even gradually restricted the numbers of those who participated in the life of the state, ultimately reducing them to the emperor himself, his court, and the imperial bureaucracy. I regard this point as only one aspect of the great phenomenon which I have described above. Have we the right to suppose that the emperors would not have tried the plan of representative government if they had known of it and believed in it? They tried many other plans and failed. If the idea of representative government was foreign to the ancient world (and as a matter of fact it was not), why did the ancient world not evolve the idea, which is not a very difficult one? Moreover, the question arises, Can we be sure that representative government is the cause of the brilliant development of our civilization and not one of its aspects, just as was the Greek city-state? Have we the slightest reason to believe that modern democracy is a guarantee of continuous and uninterrupted progress, and is capable of preventing civil war from breaking out under the fostering influence of hatred and envy? Let us not forget that the most modern political and social theories suggest that democracy is an antiquated institution, that it is rotten and corrupt, being the offspring of capitalism, and that the only just form of government is the dictatorship of the proletariate, which means a complete destruction of civil liberty and imposes on one and all the single ideal of material welfare, and of equalitarianism founded on material welfare.

(2) The economic explanation of the decay of the ancient world must be rejected completely. In speaking of the development of industry in the ancient world, I have dealt with the theory of K. Bücher, accepted with modifications by M. Weber and G. Salvioli. If the theory fails to explain even this minor point, much less will it serve to explain the general phenomenon. Those who defend this theory forget that the ancient world went through many cycles of evolution, and that in these cycles there occur long periods of progress and other long periods of return to more primitive conditions, to the phase of economic life which is generally described as 'house-economy'. It is true that the ancient world never reached the economic stage in which we live. But in the history of the ancient world we have many epochs of high economic development: certain periods in the history of many Oriental monarchies, particularly Egypt, Babylonia, and Persia; the age of the highest development of the city-states, especially the fourth century B.C.; the period of the Hellenistic monarchies, where the climax was reached in the third century B.C.; the period of the late Roman Republic and of the early Roman Empire. All these periods show different aspects of economic life and different aspects of capitalism. In none of them did the forms of house-economy prevail. We may compare the economic aspect of life during these periods to that of many European countries in the time of the Renaissance and later, although in no case would the comparison be perfect, as there is no identity between the economic development of the modern and that of the ancient world. According to the different economic conditions of these several periods in the history of the ancient world, the relations between house-economy and capitalistic economy varied, and they frequently varied not only in the different periods but also in different parts of the ancient world during the same period. The ancient world was in this respect not unlike the modern world. In the industrial countries of Europe, such as England and some parts of Germany and France, economic life nowadays is by no means the same as it is in the agricultural countries, like Russia and the Balkan peninsula and large parts of the Near East. The economic life of the United States of America is not in the least identical with the economic life of Europe or of the various parts of South America, not to speak of China, Japan, and India. So it was in the ancient world. While Egypt and Babylonia had a complex economic life, with a highly developed industry and wide commercial relations, other parts of the Near East lived a quite different and much more primitive life. While Athens, Corinth, Rhodes, Syracuse, Tyre, and Sidon in the fourth century B.C. were centres of a developed commercial capitalism, other Greek cities lived an almost purely agricultural life. In the Hellenistic and Roman periods it was just the same. The main fact which has to be explained is why capitalistic development, which started at many times and in many places, and prevailed in large portions of the ancient world for comparatively long periods, yielded ultimately to more primitive forms of economic life. Even in our own times it has not

completely ousted those forms. It is evident that the problem cannot be solved by affirming that the ancient world lived throughout under the forms of primitive house-economy. The statement is manifestly wrong. We might say exactly the same of large areas of the modern world, and we are not at all sure that a violent catastrophe might not bring the modern capitalistic world back to the primitive phase of house-economy.

To sum up what I have said, the economic simplification of ancient life was not the cause of what we call the decline of the ancient world, but one of the aspects of the more general phenomenon which the theories mentioned above try to explain. Here, just as in the other spheres of human life, the political, social, intellectual, and religious, the more primitive forms of life among the masses were not absorbed by the higher forms but triumphed over them in the end. We may select one of these phenomena and declare it to be the ultimate cause; but it would be an arbitrary assumption which would not convince any one. The problem remains. Why was the victorious advance of capitalism stopped? Why was machinery not invented? Why were the business systems not perfected? Why were the primal forces of primitive economy not overcome? They were gradually disappearing; why did they not disappear completely? To say that they were quantitatively stronger than in our own times does not help us to explain the main phenomenon. That is why many economists, who are aware that the usual explanation only touches the surface and does not probe the problem to the bottom, endeavour to save the economic explanation, and the materialistic conception of historical evolution in general, by producing some potent physical factor as the cause of the weakness of the higher forms of economic life in the ancient world. Such a factor has been found by some scholars in the general exhaustion of the soil all over the ancient world, which reached its climax in the late Roman Empire and ruined the ancient world. I have dealt with this theory above. There are no facts to support it. All the facts about the economic development of the ancient world speak against it. Agriculture decayed in the ancient world just in the same way and from the same causes as the other branches of economic life. As soon as the political and social conditions improved in the various parts of the Empire, the fields and gardens began to yield the same harvests as before. Witness the flourishing state of Gaul in the time of Ausonius and of Sidonius Apollinaris; witness the fact that in Egypt, where the soil is inexhaustible and those parts of it which are not flooded are very easily improved by the most primitive methods, agriculture decayed in the third and fourth centuries, just as in the other provinces. It is plain that the economic explanation does not help us, and that the investigations of the economists reveal, not the cause of the decline of the ancient world, but merely one of its aspects.

(3) The rapid progress of medicine and of biological science has had its influence on the problem of the decay of ancient civilization. A biological solution has been often suggested, and the theories of degeneration and race-suicide have been applied to the ancient world. The biological theory supplies us with an apparently exhaustive explanation of the decline of the assimilative forces of the civilized upper classes. They gradually degenerated and had not the power to assimilate the lower classes but were absorbed by them. According to Seeck, the cause of their degeneration and of their numerical decline was the 'extermination of the best' by foreign and civil wars. Others, like Tenney Frank, think of the contamination of higher races by an admixture of the blood of inferior races. Others, again, regard degeneration as a natural process common to all civilized communities: the best are neither exterminated nor contaminated, but they commit systematic suicide by not reproducing and by letting the inferior type of mankind breed freely. I am not competent to sit in judgement on the problem of degeneration from the biological and physiological point of view. From the historical point of view, I venture to remark against Seeck that in wars and revolutions it is not only the best that are exterminated. On the other hand, revolutions do not always prevent the succeeding period from being a period of great bloom. Against Frank I may suggest that I see no criterion for distinguishing between inferior and superior races. Why are the Greek and Latin races considered the only superior races in the Roman Empire? Some of the races which 'contaminated' the ruling races, for instance, the pre-Indo-European and pre-Semitic race or races of the Mediterranean, had created great civilizations in the past (the Egyptian, the Minoan, the Iberian, the Etruscan, the civilizations of Asia Minor), and the same is true of the Semitic and of the Iranian civilizations. Why did the admixture of the blood of these races contaminate and deteriorate the blood of the Greeks and the Romans? On the other hand, the Celts and the Germans belonged to the same stock as the Greeks and the Romans. The Celts had a high material civilization of their own. The Germans were destined to develop a high civilized life in the

future. Why did the admixture of their blood corrupt and not regenerate their fellow Aryans, the Greeks and the Romans? The theory of a natural decay of civilization by race-suicide states the same general phenomenon of which we have been speaking, the gradual absorption of the upper classes by the lower and the lack of assimilative power shown by the upper. It states the fact, but gives no explanation. The problem this theory has to solve is, Why do the best not reproduce their kind? It may be solved in different ways: we may suggest an economic, or a physiological, or a psychological explanation. But none of these explanations is convincing.

(4) Christianity is very often made responsible for the decay of ancient civilization. This is, of course, a very narrow point of view. Christianity is but one side of the general change in the mentality of the ancient world. Can we say that this change is the ultimate cause of the decay of ancient civilization? It is not easy to discriminate between causes and symptoms, and one of the urgent tasks in the field of ancient history is a further investigation of this change of mentality. The change, no doubt, was one of the most potent factors in the gradual decay of the civilization of the city-state and in the rise of a new conception of the world and of a new civilization. But how are we to explain the change? Is it a problem of individual and mass psychology?

None of the existing theories fully explains the problem of the decay of ancient civilization, if we can apply the word 'decay' to the complex phenomenon which I have endeavoured to describe. Each of them, however, has contributed much to the clearing of the ground, and has helped us to perceive that the main phenomenon which underlies the process of decline is the gradual absorption of the educated classes by the masses and the consequent simplification of all the functions of political, social, economic, and intellectual life, which we call the barbarization of the ancient world.

The evolution of the ancient world has a lesson and a warning for us. Our civilization will not last unless it be a civilization not of one class, but of the masses. The Oriental civilizations were more stable and lasting than the Greco-Roman, because, being chiefly based on religion, they were nearer to the masses. Another lesson is that violent attempts at levelling have never helped to uplift the masses. They have destroyed the upper classes, and resulted in accelerating the process of barbarization. But the ultimate problem remains like a ghost, ever present and unlaid: Is it possible to extend a higher civilization to the lower classes without debasing its standard and diluting its quality to the vanishing point? Is not every civilization bound to decay as soon as it begins to penetrate the masses?

The Byzantine Empire

54 PROCOPIUS, *HISTORY OF THE WARS* AND *SECRET HISTORIES:* JUSTINIAN AND THE FOUNDATIONS OF THE BYZANTINE EMPIRE

Though the empire of the West was dead by the end of the fifth century, the empire of the East remained. Constantinople claimed to be Rome still, its citizens Romans, and its emperor the *Basileus Rhomaian*, or "King of the Romans." However, the East was western in name only: its common language was Greek; its culture Hellenistic; and its court life oriental.

While the rest of the Roman world was being overrun by barbarians, the Byzantine Empire (as it came to be called, after the ancient name for Constantinople—Byzantium) was regarded as the last refuge of civilization. In the ensuing centuries it became the symbol both of eastern Christianity and of rich achievements in the fine arts, and while its lasting contributions to literature and science were small, it served as a repository of the great contributions of ancient Greece and Rome. Industry and trade thrived to produce a splendid, prosperous civilization.

The ability of the eastern empire to survive barbarian attacks and internal strife, to accommodate within its boundaries an infinite variety of peoples, and yet to remain a great power with an impressive cultural history defies total explanation. Possible contributing causes were the traditionally greater populations, older civilizations, and more highly developed commercial and industrial economies of the eastern provinces. The autocratic centralization imposed by Diocletian and Constantine, however bitterly it may have been attacked by contemporaries, remained the basis for the political, fiscal, and military system and ensured in the East a viable administration, which the West lacked. The imperial crown, although often acquired in a welter of conspiracy and civil strife, was worn by enough emperors of strong will and ability to maintain the Byzantine Empire as an independent state for almost a thousand years longer than its western counterpart.

Among the early strong emperors was Justinian (483–565), whose successes and failures parallel the history of the early Byzantine Empire. Justinian sought conscientiously to restore the unity of the Mediterranean world, by creating one Roman Empire and one Christian Church. Yet his immediate military successes in recapturing southern Spain, Italy, and Africa from the German barbarians were long-range failures which exhausted the financial resources of the East. He was a devoted Christian, but his interference in matters of Church doctrine and administration antagonized the papacy at Rome and contributed to the growing alienation of the western and eastern churches. In the name of Christian orthodoxy, he persecuted the Monophysites, a sect who argued that the human nature of Christ was wholly absorbed into the divine nature. As a result, he alienated large numbers of his subjects and made the provinces of Egypt and Syria easy prey for Arab conquerors in the ensuing century. By his command, Roman law and legal interpretation received its final and most complete codification in the famous Justinian Code, yet he ruled—in collaboration with his astute wife, Theodora—as a supreme autocrat and put his stamp of absolutism upon the future of the Byzantine Empire.

The history of the reign of Justinian is recorded by Procopius (c. 490–c. 562), a contemporary who found it politic to present three different viewpoints of the emperor—an adulatory, a balanced, and a highly critical account. The following passage from the *History of the Wars* is a balanced account of Justinian's decision to wage the Vandalic War. Here Justinian appears as a wise, cautious ruler who consults others and sincerely considers national interests. The second selection is from the *Secret Histories*, which was written from a deliberately critical point of view. Nevertheless, it is an excellent source of information on the fiscal and economic policies of Justinian. It also shows the cruel strain which the emperor placed upon his subjects in order to achieve his ambitions.

History of the Wars

Now there was a certain man in the family of Gizeric, Gelimer, the son of Geilaris, the son of Genzon, the son of Gizeric, who was of such age as to be second only to Ilderic [ruler of the Vandal Kingdom of Africa], and for this reason he was expected to come into the kingdom very soon. This man was thought to be the best warrior of his time, but for the rest he was a cunning fellow and base at heart and well versed in undertaking revolutionary enterprises and in laying hold upon the money of others. Now this Gelimer, when he saw the power coming to him, was not able to live in his accustomed way, but assumed to himself the tasks of a king and usurped the rule, though it was not yet due him; and since Ilderic in a spirit of friendliness gave in to him, he was no longer able to restrain his thoughts, but allying with himself all the noblest of the Vandals, he persuaded them to wrest the kingdom from Ilderic, as being an unwarlike king who had been defeated by the Moors, and as betraying the power of the Vandals into the hand of the Emperor Justinus, in order that the kingdom might not come to him, because he was of the other branch of the family; for he asserted slanderously that this was the meaning of Ilderic's embassy to Byzantium, and that he was giving over the empire of the Vandals to Justinus. And they, being persuaded, carried out this plan. Thus Gelimer seized the supreme power [in 530 A.D.], and imprisoned Ilderic, after he had ruled over the Vandals seven years, and also Hoamer and his brother Euagees.

But when Justinian heard these things, having already received the imperial power, he sent envoys to Gelimer in Libya with the following letter: "You are not acting in a holy manner nor worthily of the will of Gizeric, keeping in prison an old man and a kinsman and the king of the Vandals (if the counsels of Gizeric are to be of effect), and robbing him of his office

Text: Reprinted by permission of the publishers and The Loeb Classical Library from Procopius, *History of the Wars*, trans. H. B. Dewing (Cambridge, Mass.: Harvard University Press, 1953), II, 85-99.

by violence, though it would be possible for you to receive it after a short time in a lawful manner. Do you therefore do no further wrong and do not exchange the name of king for the title of tyrant, which comes but a short time earlier. But as for this man, whose death may be expected at any moment, allow him to bear in appearance the form of royal power, while you do all the things which it is proper that a king should do; and wait until you can receive from time and the law of Gizeric, and from them alone, the name which belongs to the position. For if you do this, the attitude of the Almighty will be favourable and at the same time our relations with you will be friendly."

Such was his message. But Gelimer sent the envoys away with nothing accomplished, and he blinded Hoamer and also kept Ilderic and Euagees in closer confinement, charging them with planning flight to Byzantium. And when this too was heard by the Emperor Justinian, he sent envoys a second time and wrote as follows: "We, indeed, supposed that you would never go contrary to our advice when we wrote you the former letter. But since it pleases you to have secured possession of the royal power in the manner in which you have taken and now hold it, get from it whatever Heaven grants. But do you send to us Ilderic, and Hoamer whom you have blinded, and his brother, to receive what comfort they can who have been robbed of a kingdom or of sight; for we shall not let the matter rest if you do not do this. And I speak thus because we are led by the hope which I had based on our friendship. And the treaty with Gizeric will not stand as an obstacle for us. For it is not to make war upon him who has succeeded to the kingdom of Gizeric that we come, but to avenge Gizeric with all our power."

When Gelimer had read this, he replied as follows: "King Gelimer to the Emperor Justinian. Neither have I taken the office by violence nor has anything unholy been done by me to my kinsmen. For Ilderic, while planning a revolution against the house of Gizeric, was dethroned by the nation of the Vandals; and I was called to the kingdom by my years, which gave me the preference, according to the law at least. Now it is well for one to administer the kingly office which belongs to him and not to make the concerns of others his own. Hence for you also, who have a kingdom, meddling in other's affairs is not just; and if you break the treaty and come against us, we shall oppose you with all our power, calling to witness the oaths which were sworn by Zeno, from whom you have received the kingdom which you hold." The Emperor Justinian, upon receiving this letter, having been angry with Gelimer even before then, was still more eager to punish him. And it seemed to him best to put an end to the Persian war as soon as possible and then to make an expedition to Libya; and since he was quick at forming a plan and prompt in carrying out his decisions, Belisarius, the General of the East, was summoned and came to him immediately, no announcement having been made to him nor to anyone else that he was about to lead an army against Libya, but it was given out that he had been removed from the office which he held. And straightway the treaty with Persia was made, as has been told in the preceding narrative.

And when the Emperor Justinian considered that the situation was as favourable as possible, both as to domestic affairs and as to his relations with Persia, he took under consideration the situation in Libya. But when he disclosed to the magistrates that he was gathering an army against the Vandals and Gelimer, the most of them began immediately to show hostility to the plan, and they lamented it as a misfortune, recalling the expedition of the Emperor Leon and the disaster of Basiliscus, and reciting how many soldiers had perished and how much money the state had lost. But the men who were the most sorrowful of all, and who, by reason of their anxiety, felt the keenest regret, were the pretorian prefect, whom the Romans call "praetor," and the administrator of the treasury, and all to whom had been assigned the collection of either public or imperial taxes, for they reasoned that while it would be necessary for them to produce countless sums for the needs of the war, they would be granted neither pardon in case of failure nor extension of time in which to raise these sums. And every one of the generals, supposing that he himself would command the army, was in terror and dread at the greatness of the danger, if it should be necessary for him, if he were preserved from the perils of the sea, to encamp in the enemy's land, and, using his ships as a base, to engage in a struggle against a kingdom both large and formidable. The soldiers, also, having recently returned from a long, hard war, and having not yet tasted to the full the blessings of home, were in despair, both because they were being led into sea-fighting,—a thing which they had not learned even from tradition before then,—and because they were sent from the eastern frontier to the West, in order to risk their lives against Vandals and Moors. But all the rest, as usually happens in a great throng, wished to be spectators of new adventures while others faced the dangers.

But as for saying anything to the emperor to prevent the expedition, no one dared to do this except John the Cappadocian, the pretorian prefect, a man of the greatest daring and the cleverest of all men of his time. For this John, while all the others were bewailing in silence the fortune which was upon them, came before the emperor and spoke as follows: "O Emperor, the good faith which thou dost shew in dealing with thy subjects enables us to speak frankly regarding anything which will be of advantage to thy government, even though what is said and done may not be agreeable to thee. For thus does thy wisdom temper thy authority with justice, in that thou dost not consider that man only as loyal to thy cause who serves thee under any and all conditions, nor art thou angry with the man who speaks against thee, but by weighing all things by pure reason alone, thou hast often shewn that it involves us in no danger to oppose thy purposes. Led by these considerations, O Emperor, I have come to offer this advice, knowing that, though I shall give perhaps offence at the moment, if it so chance, yet in the future the loyalty which I bear you will be made clear, and that for this I shall be able to shew thee as a witness. For if, through not hearkening to my words, thou shalt carry out the war against the Vandals, it will come about, if the struggle is prolonged for thee, that my advice will win renown. For if thou hast confidence that thou wilt conquer the enemy, it is not at all unreasonable that thou shouldst sacrifice the lives of men and expend a vast amount of treasure, and undergo the difficulties of the struggle; for victory, coming at the end, covers up all the calamities of war. But if in reality these things lie on the knees of God, and if it behoves us, taking example from what has happened in the past, to fear the outcome of war, on what grounds is it not better to love a state of quiet rather than the dangers of mortal strife? Thou art purposing to make an expedition against Carthage, to which, if one goes by land, the journey is one of a hundred and forty days, and if one goes by water, he is forced to cross the whole open sea and go to its very end. So that he who brings thee news of what will happen in the camp must needs reach thee a year after the event. And one might add that if thou art victorious over thy enemy, thou couldst not take possession of Libya while Sicily and Italy lie in the hands of others; and at the same time, if any reverse befall thee, O Emperor, the treaty having already been broken by thee, thou wilt bring the danger upon our own land. In fact, putting all in a word, it will not be possible for thee to reap the fruits of victory, and at the same time any reversal of fortune will bring harm to what is well established. It is before an enterprise that wise planning is useful. For when men have failed, repentance is of no avail, but before disaster comes there is no danger in altering plans. Therefore it will be of advantage above all else to make fitting use of the decisive moment."

Thus spoke John; and the Emperor Justinian, hearkening to his words, checked his eager desire for the war. But one of the priests whom they call bishops, who had come from the East, said that he wished to have a word with the emperor. And when he met Justinian, he said that God had visited him in a dream, and bidden him go to the emperor and rebuke him, because, after undertaking the task of protecting the Christians in Libya from tyrants, he had for no good reason become afraid. "And yet," He had said, "I will Myself join with him in waging war and make him lord of Libya." When the emperor heard this, he was no longer able to restrain his purpose, and he began to collect the army and the ships, and to make ready supplies of weapons and of food, and he announced to Belisarius that he should be in readiness, because he was very soon to act as general in Libya. . . .

Secret Histories

. . . Now this Justinian, when his uncle Justinus took over the Empire, did find the Government well supplied with public money. For Anastasius had been both the most provident and the most prudent administrator of all Emperors, and fearing, as actually happened, lest his future successor to the throne, finding himself short of funds, might perhaps take to plundering his subjects—he had filled all the treasuries to overflowing with gold before he completed the term of his life. All this money Justinian dissipated with all speed, partly in senseless buildings on the sea, and partly by his kindness to the barbarians; and yet one would have supposed that even for an Emperor who was going to be extremely prodigal these funds would last for a hundred years. For those who were in charge of all the treasures and treasuries and all the other imperial monies declared that Anastasius, after his reign over the Romans of more than twenty-seven years [A.D. 491–518], left behind him in the Treasury three thousand two hundred centenaria of gold. But during the nine years of the reign of Justinus [A.D. 518–527], while this Jus-

Text: Reprinted by permission of the publishers and The Loeb Classical Library from Procopius, *The Anecdota or Secret History*, trans. H. B. Dewing (Cambridge, Mass.: Harvard University Press, 1954), VI, 227-37, 275-79, 281-85, 289-91.

tinian was inflicting the evils of confusion and disorder upon the Government, they say that four thousand centenaria were brought into the Treasury by illegal means, and that of all this not a morsel was left, but that even while Justinus was still living it had been squandered by this man in the manner described by me in an earlier passage. For as to the amounts which, during all the time he was in power, he succeeded in wrongfully appropriating to himself and then spending, there is no means by which any man could give a reckoning or a calculation or an enumeration of them. For like an everflowing river, while each day he plundered and pillaged his subjects, yet the inflow all streamed straight on to the barbarians, to whom he would make a present of it.

No sooner had he thus disposed of the public wealth than he turned his eyes towards his subjects, and he straightway robbed great numbers of them of their estates, which he seized with high-handed and unjustified violence, haling to court, for crimes that never happened, men both in Byzantium and in every other city who were reputed to be in prosperous circumstances, charging some with belief in polytheism, others with adherence to some perverse sect among the Christians, or with sodomy, or with having amours with holy women, or with other kinds of forbidden intercourse, or with fomenting revolt, or with predilection for the Green Faction, or with insult to himself, or charging crimes of any other name whatsoever, or by his own arbitrary act making himself the heir of deceased persons or, if it should so happen, of the living even, alleging that he had been adopted by them. Such were the most august of his actions. . . .

And he never ceased pouring out great gifts of money to all the barbarians, both those of the East and those of the West and those to the North and to the South, as far as the inhabitants of Britain—in fact all the nations of the inhabited world, even those of whom we had never so much as heard before, but the name of whose race we learned only when we first saw them. For they, of their own accord, on learning the nature of the man, kept streaming from all the earth into Byzantium in order to get to him. And he, with no hesitation, but overjoyed at this situation, and thinking it a stroke of good luck to be bailing out the wealth of the Romans and flinging it to barbarians or, for that matter, to the surging waves of the sea, day by day kept sending them away, one after the other, with bulging purses. In this way the barbarians as a whole came to be altogether the owners of the wealth of the Romans, either by having received the money as a present from the Emperor or by plundering the Roman domain, or by selling back their prisoners of war, or by auctioning off an armistice. . . . However, Justinian succeeded in devising still other ways of exacting booty from his subjects, ways which will be described directly, in so far as I may be able to do so, by which he succeeded completely, not all at once, but little by little, in plundering the property of all men.

First of all, as a general thing he appointed over the people in Byzantium a Prefect, who, while splitting the annual revenue with those who controlled the markets, planned to give them authority to sell their merchandise at whatever price they wanted. And the result for the people of the city was that, although they had to pay a threefold price for the provisions they bought, yet they had no one at all to whom they could protest on account of this. And great harm arose from this business. For since the Treasury received a share of this tax, the official in charge of these matters was eager to use this means of enriching himself. And next, the servants of the official who had undertaken this shameful service, and those who controlled the markets, seizing upon the licence to disregard the law, treated outrageously those who were obliged to buy at that time, not only collecting the prices many times over, as it has been reported, but also contriving certain unheard-of deceptions in the goods offered for sale.

In the second place, he set up a great number of what are called "monopolies," and sold the welfare of his subjects to those who wanted to operate these abominations, and thus he, on the one hand, carried off a price for the transaction, and to those, on the other hand, who had contracted with him he gave the privilege of managing their business as they wished. And he applied this same vicious method, without any concealment, to all the other magistracies. For since the Emperor always derived some small share from the peculations of the magistrates, for this reason these, and also those in charge of each function, kept plundering more fearlessly those who fell into their clutches. . . .

. . . That the cities should be subjected to many damaging exactions at all times and particularly during this period was inevitable; as to the motives that led to their imposition and the manner of their application, I forbear to discuss them on this occasion, lest my treatise become interminable. These assessments were paid by the owners of the lands, each paying an assessed sum in proportion to the tax regularly levied upon him. But the trouble did not stop here; on the contrary, when the plague came, seizing in its grip the whole civilized world and especially the Roman Empire, and wiping out most of the farmers, and when for this reason the lands, as one might expect, had become deserted, the Emperor shewed no mercy to the owners of these lands. For he never relaxed his exaction of the annual tax, not merely as he imposed it upon each separate person, but also exacting the share which fell to his deceased neighbours. And in addition they also had to stand all the other exactions . . . falling upon those who were cursed with the ownership of farms, and over and above all these things, they had to house the soldiers, in the best and most expensive of their rooms and to wait upon them, while they themselves throughout this whole time lived in the meanest and the most dilapidated of their outhouses.

All these evils kept constantly afflicting the people during the reign of Justinian and Theodora, for it so happened that neither war nor any other of the greatest calamities subsided during this time. And since we have made mention of rooms for billeting, we must not pass over the fact that the owners of the houses in Byzantium, having to turn over their dwellings there as lodgings for barbarians to the number of about seventy thousand, not only could derive no benefit from their own property, but were also afflicted by these other disagreeable conditions.

Nor assuredly is his treatment of the soldiers to be consigned to silence; for over them he put in authority the most villainous of all men, bidding them collect from this source as much as they could, and these officers were well aware that the twelfth part of what they should thus procure would fall to them. And he gave them the title of "Logothetes."

. . . Later on also some of the Palace Guards were sent out through the whole Roman Empire, and ostensibly they were in search of any among the armies who were quite unsuitable for active service; and they dared to strip the belts from some of these as being unfit or too old, and these thereafter had to beg their bread from the pious in the public square of the market-place, so that they became a constant cause for tears and lamentation on the part of all who met them; and from the rest they exacted great sums of money, to the end that they might not suffer the same fate, so that the soldiers, broken in manifold ways, had become the poorest of all men and had not the slightest zest for warfare. It was for just this reason that the Roman power came to be destroyed in Italy. Indeed, when Alexander the Logothete was sent thither, he had the effrontery to lay these charges without compunction upon the soldiers, and he tried to exact money from the Italians, alleging that he was punishing them for their behaviour during the reign of Theoderic and the Goths. And it was not alone the soldiers who were oppressed by destitution and poverty through the conduct of the Logothetes, but also the subordinates who served all the generals, formerly a numerous and highly esteemed group, laboured under the burden of starvation and dire poverty. For they had not the means wherewith to provide themselves with their customary necessities.

And I shall add one further item to those I have mentioned, since the subject of the soldiers leads me thereto. The Roman Emperors in earlier times stationed a very great multitude of soldiers at all points of the Empire's frontier in order to guard the boundaries of the Roman domain, particularly in the eastern portion, thus checking the inroads of the Persians and the Saracens; these troops they used to call *limitanei*. These the Emperor Justinian at first treated so casually and so meanly that their paymasters were four or five years behind in their payments to them, and whenever peace was made between the Romans and the Persians, these wretches were compelled, on the supposition that they too would profit by the blessings of peace, to make a present to the Treasury of the pay which was owing to them for a specified period. And later on, for no good reason, he took away from them the very name of regular troops. Thereafter the frontiers of the Roman Empire remained destitute of guards and the soldiers suddenly found themselves obliged to look to the hands of those accustomed to works of piety. . . .

And I shall pass on to explain still another of his methods of plundering his subjects. Those who mount guard or handle dispatches for the Emperor and the officials in Byzantium, or who perform any other service whatsoever, are assigned at first to the lowest ranks, and as time goes on they advance steadily to fill the places of those who have died or retired, and each of them keeps moving up from the rank he has held until such time as he mounts the topmost step and attains to the highest attainable point of this career. For those who have achieved this high rank a salary has been assigned from of old, so huge that each year they gather in more than one hundred centenaria of gold, and it has come about that not only they themselves are cared for in old age but that many others also share with them, as a general thing, the assistance derived from this source, and the affairs of the State have in this way advanced to a high point of prosperity. But this Emperor, by depriving them of practically all these revenues, has brought woes upon them and the rest of mankind. For poverty laid hold upon them first and then passed on through the rest who previously had had some share of their benefit. And if anyone should calculate the loss which fell upon them from this source over a period of thirty-two years, he would arrive at the measure of the amount of which it was their misfortune to be deprived.

Thus were the men in service mishandled by this tyrant. . . .

55 LETTER OF THE SECOND COUNCIL OF NICAEA TO EMPEROR CONSTANTINE VI AND EMPRESS IRENE: THE ICONOCLASTIC CONTROVERSY AND THE EAST-WEST SCHISM

Few nations have survived harder times than did the Byzantine Empire in the three centuries between the death of Justinian (565) and the beginning of the Macedonian Dynasty (867). The serious threat of the Persians on the eastern flank of the empire was replaced by the inspired armies of the Muslim conquest; within thirty years after the death of Muhammad (632), Egypt, Palestine, Syria, and eastern Asia Minor were under Arab sway. Shortly thereafter, North Africa fell, at the same time that Muslim armies were pressing upon the gates of Constantinople. Meanwhile, Slavs and Bulgars were flooding into the Balkan provinces to the north. The Arab and Slavic incursions constricted the frontiers of the empire and brought about the gradual militarization of the entire administration.

Internal quarrels also afflicted the empire. In the reign of Leo III (717-741), there erupted in Constantinople a religious crisis over the use of icons—statues or pictures of Christ, the Virgin, or the saints—on the ground that they were imitative of pagan idolatry and polytheism. At first, the iconoclasts (image-breakers) were actively supported by the emperors (including Leo III) in their campaign to remove the images from the churches and to destroy them. The Roman pope, however, steadily refused to credit the position of the iconoclasts and pronounced them heretics. Only a shift in the attitude of Emperor Constantine VI and his Empress Mother Irene prevented in the late eighth century a schism of the western and the eastern churches; iconoclasm was formally condemned at the seventh ecumenical council held at Nicaea near Constantinople in 787. The condemnation appears below in the letter from the council to Emperor Constantine VI. Although its viewpoint is identical with that of the papacy, the letter indicates the caesaropapism of the emperor in ecclesiastical questions by listing him and his mother before the patriarch of Constantinople.

Almost all texts favorable to the iconoclasts were condemned and destroyed; the few remaining fragments of their doctrine appear usually in quotations in the tracts of their opponents. The origins of iconoclasm are obscure, but it seems to have won support especially from Syrian elements within the empire, who may have been influenced by the strong objections of the Jews and Muslims to holy images. Certainly, the emperors used iconoclasm to fight the growing power and wealth of the eastern monasteries, where images and relics were especially venerated. While iconoclasm was rejected in the East, and open schism avoided, relations between the eastern empire and the pope at Rome were permanently affected by the controversy. The pope turned henceforth for temporal support to the Frankish monarchy of the West, an action further alienating the Latin West from the Greek East.

The Letter of the Synod to the Emperor and Empress

To our most religious and most serene princes, Constantine and Irene his mother. Tarasius, the unworthy bishop of your God-protected royal city, new Rome, and all the holy Council which met at the good pleasure of God and upon the command of your Christ-loving majesty in the renowned metropolis of Nice, the second council to assemble in this city.

Christ our God (who is the head of the Church) was glorified, most noble princes, when your heart, which he holds in his hands, gave forth

Text: "The Letter of the Synod to the Emperor and Empress," in *A Select Library of Nicene and Post-Nicene Fathers of the Christian Church,* ed. Philip Schaff and Henry Wace (New York: Charles Scribner's Sons, 1900), 2nd series, XIV, 571-74.

that good word bidding us to assemble in his name, in order that we might strengthen our hold on the sure, immovable, and God-given truth contained in the Church's dogmas. As your heads were crowned with gold and most brilliant stones, so likewise were your minds adorned with the precepts of the Gospel and the teachings of the Fathers. And being the disciples and companions, as it were, of those whose sounds went forth into all the earth, ye became the leaders in the way of piety of all who bore the name of Christ, setting forth clearly the word of truth, and giving a brilliant example of orthodoxy and piety; so that ye were to the faithful as so many burning lamps. The Church which was ready to fall, ye upheld with your hands, strengthening it with sound doctrine, and bringing into the unity of a right judgment those who were at variance. We may therefore well say with boldness that it was through you that the good pleasure of God brought about the triumph of godliness, and filled our mouth with joy and our tongue with gladness. And these things our lips utter with a formal decree. For what is more glorious than to maintain the Church's interests; and what else is more calculated to provoke our gladness?

Certain men rose up, having the form of godliness, inasmuch as they were clothed with the dignity of the priesthood, but denying the power thereof; and thus deserving for themselves the charge of being but priests of Babylon. Of such the word of prophecy had before declared that "lawlessness went forth from the priests of Babylon." Nay more, they banded themselves together in a sanhedrim, like to that which Caiaphas held, and became the propagators of ungodly doctrines. And having a mouth full of cursing and bitterness, they thought to win the mastery by means of abusive words. With a slanderous tongue and a pen of a like character, and objecting to the very terms used by God himself, they devised marvellous tales, and then proceeded to stigmatise as idolaters the royal priesthood and the holy nation, even those who had put on Christ, and by his grace had been kept safe from the folly of idols. And having a mind set upon evil, they took in hand unlawful deeds, thinking to suppress altogether the depicting of the venerable images. Accordingly, as many icons as were set in mosaic work they dug out, and those which were in painted waxwork, they scraped away; thus turning the comely beauty of the sacred temples into complete disorder. Among doings of this sort, it is to be specially noted that the pictures set up on tablets in memory of Christ our God and of his Saints, they gave over to the flames. Finally, in a word, having desecrated our churches, they reduced them to utter confusion. Then some bishops became the leaders of this heresy and where before was peace, they fomented strife among the people; and instead of wheat sowed tares in the Church's fields. They mingled wine with water, and gave the foul draught to those about them. Although but Arabian wolves, they hid themselves under sheeps' clothing, and by specious reasoning against the truth sought to commend their lie. But all the while "they hatched asps' eggs and wove a spider's web," as says the prophet; and "he that would eat of their eggs, having crushed one, found it to be addled, with a basilisk within it," and giving forth a deadly stench.

In such a state of affairs, with a lie busy destroying the truth, ye, most gracious and most noble princes, did not idly allow so grave a plague, and such soul-destroying error long to continue in your day. But moved by the divine Spirit which abideth in you, ye set yourselves with all your strength utterly to exterminate it, and thus preserve the stability of the Church's government, and likewise concord among your subjects; so that your whole empire might be established in peace agreeably with the name [Irene] you bear. Ye rightly reasoned, that it was not to be patiently endured, that while in other matters we could be of one mind and live in concord, yet in what ought to be the chief concern of our life, the peace of the Churches, there was amongst us strife and division. And that too, when Christ being our head, we ought to be members one of another, and one body, by our mutual agreement and faith. Accordingly, ye commanded our holy and numerously-attended council to assemble in the metropolis of Nice, in order that after having rid the Church of division, we might restore to unity the separated members, and might be careful to rend and utterly destroy the coarse cloak of false doctrine, which they had woven of thorn fibre, and unfold again the fair robe of orthodoxy.

And now having carefully traced the traditions of the Apostles and Fathers, we are bold to speak. Having but one mind by the inbreathing of the most Holy Spirit, and being all knit together in one, and understanding the harmonious tradition of the Catholic Church, we are in perfect harmony with the symphonies set forth by the six, holy and ecumenical councils; and accordingly we have anathematised the madness of Arius, the frenzy of Macedonius, the senseless understanding of Appolinarius, the man-worship of Nestorius, the irreverent mingling of the natures devised by Eutyches and Dioscorus, and the many-headed hydra which is their companion. We have also anathematised the idle tales of Origen, Didymus, and Evagrius; and the doctrine of one will held by Sergius, Honorius, Cyrus, and Pyrrhus, or rather, we have anathematised their own evil will. Finally, taught by the Spirit, from whom we have drawn pure water, we have with one accord and one soul, altogether wiped out with the sponge of the divine dogmas the newly devised heresy, well-worthy to be classed with those just mentioned, which springing up after them, uttered such empty nonsense about the sacred icons. And the contrivers of this vain, but revolutionary babbling we have cast forth far from the Church's precincts.

And as the hands and feet are moved in accordance with the directions of the mind, so likewise, we, having received the grace and strength of the Spirit, and having also the assistance and co-operation of your royal authority, have with one voice declared as piety and proclaimed as truth: that the sacred icons of our Lord Jesus Christ are to be had and retained, inasmuch as he was very man; also those which set forth what is historically narrated in the Gospels; and those which represent our undefiled Lady, the holy Mother of God; and likewise those of the Holy Angels (for they have manifested themselves in human form to those who were counted worthy of the vision of them), or of any of the Saints. [We have also decreed] that the brave deeds of the Saints be pourtrayed on tablets and on the walls, and upon the sacred vessels and vestments, as hath been the custom of the holy Catholic Church of God from ancient times; which custom was regarded as having the force of law in the teaching both of those holy leaders who lived in the first ages of the Church, and also of their successors our reverend Fathers. [We have likewise decreed] that these images are to be reverenced ($\pi\rho o\sigma\kappa\upsilon\nu\epsilon\hat{\iota}\nu$), that is, salutations are to be offered to them. The reason for using the word is, that it has a two-fold signification. For $\kappa\upsilon\nu\epsilon\iota\nu$ in the old Greek tongue signifies both "to salute" and "to kiss." And the preposition $\pi\rho o s$ [toward] gives to it the additional idea of strong desire towards the object; as for example, we have $\phi\acute{\epsilon}\rho\omega$ [bring] and $\pi\rho o\sigma\phi\acute{\epsilon}\rho\omega$ [offer], $\kappa\upsilon\rho\hat{\omega}$ [to attain] and $\pi\rho o\sigma\kappa\upsilon\rho\omega$ [to reach], and so also we have $\kappa\upsilon\nu\acute{\epsilon}\omega$ [kiss, greet] and $\pi\rho o\sigma\kappa\upsilon\nu\acute{\epsilon}\omega$ [worship]. Which last word implies salutation and strong love; for that which one loves he also reverences and what he reverences that he greatly loves, as the everyday custom, which we observe towards those we love, bears witness, and in which both ideas are practically illustrated when two friends meet together. The word is not only made use of by us, but we also find it set down in the Divine Scriptures by the ancients. For it is written in the histories of the Kings, "And David rose up and fell upon his face and did reverence to Jonathan three times and kissed him" (1 Kings xx., 41). And what is it that the Lord in the Gospel says concerning the Pharisees? "They love the uppermost rooms at feasts and greetings in the markets." It is evident that by "greetings" here, he means reverence for the Pharisees being very high-minded and thinking themselves to be righteous were eager to be reverenced by all, but not [merely] to be kissed. For to receive salutations of this latter sort savoured too much of lowly humility, and this was not to the Pharisees' liking. We have also the example of Paul the divine Apostle, as Luke in the Acts of the Apostles relates: "When we were come to Jerusalem, the brethren received us gladly, and the day following Paul went in with us unto James, and all the presbyters were present. And when he had saluted them, he declared particularly what things God had wrought among the Gentiles by his ministry" (Acts xxi., 17, 18, 19). By the salutation here mentioned, the Apostle evidently intended to render that reverence of honour which we shew to one another, and of which he speaks when he says concerning Jacob, that "he reverenced the top of his staff" (Heb. xi., 21). With these examples agrees what Gregory surnamed Theologus says: "Honour Bethlehem, and reverence the manger."

Now who of those rightly and sincerely understanding the Divine Scriptures, has ever supposed that these examples which we have cited speak of the worship in spirit? [Certainly no one has ever thought so] except perhaps some persons utterly bereft of sense and ignorant of all knowledge of the Scriptures and of the teaching of the Fathers. Surely Jacob did not adore the top of his staff; and surely Gregory Theologus does not bid us to adore the manger? By no means. Again, when offering salutations to the life-giving Cross, we together sing: "We reverence thy cross, O Lord, and we also reverence the spear which opened the life-giving side of thy goodness." This is clearly but a salutation, and is so called, and its character is evinced by our touching the things mentioned with our lips. We grant that the word $\pi\rho o\sigma\kappa\acute{\upsilon}\nu\eta\sigma\iota s$ [worship] is frequently found in the Divine Scriptures and in the writings of our learned and holy Fathers for the worship in spirit, since, being a word of many significations, it may be used to express that kind of reverence which is service. As there is also the veneration of honour, love and fear. In this sense it is, that we venerate your glorious and most noble majesty. So also there is another veneration which comes of fear alone, thus Jacob venerated Esau. Then there is the veneration of gratitude, as Abraham reverenced the sons of Heth, for the field which he received from them for a burying place for Sarah his wife. And finally, those looking to obtain some gift, venerate those who are above them, as Jacob venerated Pharaoh. Therefore because this term has these many significations, the Divine Scriptures teaching us, "Thou shalt venerate the Lord thy God, and him only shalt thou serve," says simply that veneration is to be given to God, but does not add the word "only;" for veneration being a word of wide meaning is an ambiguous term; but it goes on to say "thou shalt serve him *only*," for to God alone do we render latria.

The things which we have decreed, being thus well supported, it is confessedly and beyond all question acceptable and well-pleasing before God, that the images of our Lord Jesus Christ as man, and those of the undefiled Mother of God, the ever-virgin Mary, and of the honourable Angels and of all Saints, should be venerated and saluted. And if anyone does not so believe, but undertakes to debate the matter further and is evil affected with regard to the veneration due the sacred images, such an one our holy ecumenical council (fortified by the inward working of the Spirit of God, and by the traditions of the Fathers and of the Church) anathematises. Now anathema is nothing less than complete separation from God. For if any are quarrelsome and will not obediently accept what has now been decreed, they but kick against the pricks, and injure their own souls in their fighting against Christ. And in taking pleasure at the insults which are offered to the Church, they clearly shew themselves to be of those who madly make war upon piety, and are therefore to be regarded as in the same category with the heretics of old times, and their companions and brethren in ungodliness.

We have sent our brethren and fellow priests, God-beloved Bishops, together with certain of the Hegumenoi and clergy, that they may give a full report of our proceedings to your godly-hearing ears. In proof and confirmation of what we have decreed, and also for the assurance of your most religious majesty, we have submitted proofs from the Fathers, a few of the many we have gathered together in illustration of the brightly shining truth.

And now may the Saviour of us all, who reigns with you and who was pleased to vouchsafe his peace to the Churches through you, preserve your kingdom for many years, and also your council, princes, and faithful army, and the whole estate of the empire; and may he also give you victory over all your enemies. For he it is, who says: "As I live, saith the Lord, they that glorify me, I will glorify." He it is also who hath girded you with strength, and will smite all your enemies, and make your people to rejoice.

And do thou, O city, the new Sion, rejoice and be glad; thou that art the wonder of the whole world. For although David hath not reigned in thee, nevertheless thy pious princes here preside over thy affairs as David would have done. The Lord is in the midst of thee; may his name be blessed forever and ever. Amen.

56

MICHAEL PSELLUS, CHRONOGRAPHIA: THE HEIGHT OF THE BYZANTINE EMPIRE

The conclusion of the iconoclastic controversy (see Document 55) did not spare the Byzantine Empire a multitude of internal and external problems. On the southern and eastern frontiers Muslim pressure continued. By the tenth century the western Arabs had conquered Sicily and their pirate fleets were terrorizing the Mediterranean. To the north, the Bulgars, although converted to eastern Christianity, controlled a powerful and often hostile kingdom. Meanwhile, unresolved differences between the eastern and western churches constituted not only a religious but a political and diplomatic hazard for the Byzantine Empire, since the Roman popes, in order to protect themselves from Byzantine caesaropapism, turned for protection to the Frankish Empire of Charlemagne and subsequently to its German successor which they sanctified as "Holy" and "Roman." (See Document 83.) At home, the eastern emperors were beset by severe economic and social difficulties as there developed, in spite of imperial resistance, a powerful landholding aristocracy which threatened to ruin the free peasantry and to challenge the autocratic position of the emperors themselves.

Faced with such heavy pressures and an imperial succession which was often determined by assassination, military revolt, coup d'état, or dynastic marriage, the Byzantine Empire not only survived but flourished for two golden centuries under the Macedonian

Dynasty (867-1081). The history of this dynasty defies the popular idea that the empire by this time was a weak and fossilized institution. The background of the emperors themselves testifies to the amazing social mobility and adaptability of Byzantine politics and society. These "Macedonians" were Greek by language and culture and were probably Slavic and Armenian by origin. Under their rule, the feudal aristocracy was temporarily restrained and the march of Islam was momentarily checked and slightly abated. The Bulgarian Kingdom was destroyed, and new barbarians from the north were repulsed. Byzantine government flourished with new legislation and jurisprudence to adapt Justinian's code to changing conditions; provincial government was reorganized and improved. Byzantine monasticism flourished, especially on Mt. Athos, and Byzantine missionaries converted the pagan Rus (see Document 57).

The great failure of the Macedonian Dynasty was in the West. The quarrel with the western Roman Church ultimately became a permanent schism (1054). Less than a half century before the crusades, western and eastern Christianity were at odds, with dire consequences for the future of the Byzantine Empire, which was caught between the warring crusaders and Muslims.

For Michael Psellus, a titled official and an illustrious savant of the latter years of the Macedonian Dynasty, the coming crisis was not yet apparent. Although he freely inserts personal history into his narrative and evaluates emperors by personal opinion rather than record, his *Chronographia* (History) is a valuable source of eleventh-century history, the latter half of the Macedonian period. His description of the reign of Basil II (976-1025) barely touches on that emperor's major achievement—the ruthless destruction of the Bulgarian Kingdom, for which he earned the title *Bulgaroktonos* (Bulgarian Slayer). Nevertheless, Basil emerges as the successful autocrat that he apparently was, who humbled his aristocratic rivals, defended the frontier, commanded the army, legislated vigorously, and patronized the flourishing culture of the Byzantine Empire at its height.

Once invested with supreme power over the Romans, Basil was loath to share his designs with anyone else or to accept advice on the conduct of public affairs. On the other hand, having had no previous experience of military matters or of good civil administration, he discovered that he was unable to rely on his own judgment alone, and he was therefore compelled to turn for assistance to the *parakoimomenus* [Lord Chamberlain] Basil. Now this man happened to be at that time the most remarkable person in the Roman Empire, both for the depth of his intellect and for his bodily stature and regal appearance.... It was to him that the civilian population looked, to him that the army turned, and he was responsible, indeed solely responsible, for the administration of public finance and the direction of government. In this task he was constantly assisted by the emperor, both in word and deed, for Basil not only backed up his minister's measures, but even confirmed them in writing.

To most men of our generation who saw the emperor Basil he seemed austere and abrupt in manner, an irascible man who did not quickly change his mind, sober in his daily habits and averse to all effeminacy, but if I am to believe the historians of that period who wrote about him, he was not at all like that when his reign began. A change took place in his character after he acceded to the throne, and instead of leading his former dissolute, voluptuous sort of life, he became a man of great energy. It was the pressure of events that brought about this complete alteration in the course of his life. His character stiffened, so to speak. Feebleness gave way to strength and the old slackness disappeared before a new fixity of purpose. In his early days he used to feast quite openly, and frequently indulged in the pleasures of love. His main concern was with his banqueting and his life was spent in the gay, indolent atmosphere of the court. The combination of youth and unlimited power gave him opportunities for self-indulgence, and he enjoyed them to the full. The complete change in his mode of living dates from the attempted revolutions of the notorious Sclerus and of Phocas. Sclerus twice raised the standard of revolt and there were other aspirants to the throne, with two parties in opposition to the emperor....

The emperor Basil was well aware of disloyalty among the Romans, but not long before this a picked band of Scythians had come to help him from the Taurus, and a fine body of men they were. He had these men trained in a separate

Text: Michael Psellus, *Chronographia*, trans. E. R. A. Sewter New Haven: Yale University Press, 1953), pp. 12-13, 17, 19-21, 22-26, 27, 28. (Revised edition entitled *Fourteen Byzantine Rulers*, Penguin Books Ltd., 1966.)

corps, combined with them another mercenary force, divided by companies, and sent them out to fight the rebels. . . .

Basil personally took part in these operations with the Roman army. He had just begun to grow a beard and was learning the art of war from experience in actual combat. Even his brother Constantine took his place in the battleline, armed with breastplate and long spear. . . .

The complete change in the emperor's character dates from that time. While he rejoiced at the death of his enemy, he was no less grieved by the sad condition of his own affairs, with the result that he became suspicious of everyone, a haughty and secretive man, ill-tempered, and irate with those who failed to carry out his wishes.

Far from allowing the *parakoimomenus* Basil to continue in his general supervision of the government, the emperor, from now on, decided to supervise himself. Further, he proceeded to pursue his minister with a relentless hatred, which he showed in all manner of ways, and refused to see him. Although the *parakoimomenus* was a relative, although the emperor was greatly indebted to him and the minister had done good service, at no little inconvenience to himself, and despite the very high office in the state that he held, Basil regarded him as an enemy. Nothing on earth would persuade him to change this attitude. The truth is, it offended his pride to think that he, the emperor and a full-grown man, should be allowed only a share in the government, as if he were an ordinary citizen. One would imagine he had never ascended the throne, but shared authority on equal terms with another man, or held inferior rank in the government. He gave the subject considerable thought, and it was only after much vacillation that he finally made up his mind. Once the decision was taken, however, he dismissed the *parakoimomenus* and deposed him at one blow. What made it worse was the fact that this change in the latter's fortunes was not softened by any sign of respect: in fact, the emperor's action was incredibly cruel, for he shipped him off into exile.

Nor did this disgrace prove to be the end of Basil's troubles. Rather was it the prelude to further misfortunes, for the emperor next proceeded to review the events of his reign ever since he acceded to the throne and the *parakoimomenus* began to govern the Empire. He examined the various measures that had been taken during all that period. Whatever happened to contribute to his own (the emperor's) welfare, or to the good of the state, was allowed to remain on the statutes. All those decrees, on the other hand, which referred to the granting of favours or positions of dignity, were now rescinded. The former, the emperor contended, had been approved by himself: of the latter he knew nothing. . . .

. . . Now that he observed the diverse character of his dominions, and saw that it was no easy matter to wield such tremendous power, Basil abjured all self-indulgence. He even went so far as to scorn bodily ornaments. His neck was unadorned by collars, his head by diadems. He refused to make himself conspicuous in purple-coloured cloaks. He put away superfluous rings, even clothes of different colours. On the other hand, he took great pains to ensure that the various departments of the government should be centralized in himself, and that they should work without friction. He adopted a supercilious manner, not only in his dealings with other men, but even towards his brother. To Constantine he allotted a mere handful of guards, as though he grudged him protection of a more dignified or imposing character. Having first straitened himself, so to speak, and having cheerfully stripped off the proud contraptions of monarchy in his own case, he now dealt with his brother and gradually decreased his authority too. He left him to enjoy the beauties of the country, the delights of bathing and hunting, his special hobbies, while he himself went out to the frontiers, where his armies were being hard pressed. His ambition, in fact, was to purge the Empire completely of all the barbarians who encircle us and lay siege to our borders, both in the east and in the west.

This project, however, had to be postponed to the future, for Sclerus kept the emperor occupied with . . . revolt, and the intended expedition against the barbarians became impossible, at least for the moment. . . .

The rebellion began in the summer and dragged on into the autumn. A whole year passed by, and the intrigue was still not crushed. As a matter of fact, this evil troubled the state for many years to come. The truth was, the men who had enrolled in Sclerus's army were no longer divided in their loyalties: every one of them was a declared rebel. Their leader inspired them with his own resolute determination and bound them into one coherent body. By favours he won their loyalty, by his kindliness he earned their devotion. He reconciled their differences, ate at the same table as his men, drank from the same cup, called them by name, and by his flattery bound them to his allegiance.

The emperor tried all his wiles and tricks to frustrate him, but Sclerus evaded all these attempts with the greatest of ease. Like a good general, he answered his opponent's schemes and plans with stratagems of his own. So Basil, seeing that his enemy could never be caught, sent an embassy to him with the suggestion that terms should be arranged, and that Sclerus should abandon the revolt. If he accepted the emperor's proposals, he was to occupy rank second only to Basil himself. At first, the pretender did not respond to these overtures with any great alacrity, but later, when he had given the matter deep thought and compared his present position with the past, guessing what the future might hold for him in comparison with the present; when he considered his personal prospects thus (he was already an old man), the proffered negotiations were not unattractive. So he assembled the whole of his army, to support him at the reception of the imperial envoys, and made peace with Basil on the following terms: he (Sclerus) was to resign his crown and give up wearing the purple, but to take precedence immediately after the emperor; the generals and other ranks who had revolted with him were to retain their present positions, and to enjoy as long as they lived whatever privileges he had conferred upon them; they would be deprived neither of property formerly in their possession, nor of any thereafter acquired through Sclerus, nor would they be stripped of any other advantages which had fallen to their lot.

Agreement was reached on these conditions, and the emperor set out from the capital to one of his most magnificent estates, there to receive the rebel and ratify the treaty. Basil seated himself in the royal tent. Sclerus, some distance away, was introduced by the guards. . . .

. . . Basil proceeded to question him, as a man accustomed to command, about his Empire, how it could be preserved free from dissension. Sclerus had an answer to this, although it was not the sort of advice one would expect from a general; in fact, it sounded more like a diabolical plot. 'Cut down,' he said, 'the governors who become overproud. Let no generals on campaign have too many resources. Exhaust them with unjust exactions, to keep them busied with their own affairs. Admit no woman to the imperial councils. Be accessible to no one. Share with few your most intimate plans.'

On this note their conversation came to an end. Sclerus went off to the country estate which had been apportioned him, and soon afterwards he died. We will leave him and return to the emperor. In his dealings with his subjects, Basil behaved with extraordinary circumspection. It is perfectly true that the great reputation he built up as a ruler was founded rather on terror than on loyalty. As he grew older and became more experienced he relied less on the judgment of men wiser than himself. He alone introduced new measures, he alone disposed his military forces. As for the civil administration, he governed, not in accordance with the written laws, but following the unwritten dictates of his own intuition, which was most excellently equipped by nature for the purpose. Consequently he paid no attention to men of learning: on the contrary, he affected utter scorn—towards the learned folk, I mean. It seems to me a wonderful thing, therefore, that while the emperor so despised literary culture, no small crop of philosophers and orators sprang up in those times. . . .

However, we must return to the emperor. Having purged the Empire of the barbarians, he dealt with his own subjects and completely subjugated them too—I think 'subjugate' is the right word to describe it. He decided to abandon his former policy, and after the great families had been humiliated and put on an equal footing with the rest, Basil found himself playing the game of power-politics with considerable success. He surrounded himself with favourites who were neither remarkable for brilliance of intellect, nor of noble lineage, nor too learned. To them were entrusted the imperial rescripts, and with them he was accustomed to share the secrets of state. However, since at that time the emperor's comments on memoranda or requests for favour were never varied, but only plain, straightforward statements (for Basil, whether writing or speaking, eschewed all elegance of composition) he used to dictate to his secretaries just as the words came to his tongue, stringing them all together, one after the other. There was no subtlety, nothing superfluous, in his speech.

By humbling the pride or jealousy of his people, Basil made his own road to power an easy one. He was careful, moreover, to close the exit-doors on the monies contributed to the treasury. So a huge sum of money was built up, partly by the exercise of strict economy, partly by fresh additions from abroad. Actually, the sum accumulated in the imperial treasury reached the grand total of 200,000 talents. As for the rest of his gains, it would indeed be hard to find words adequately to describe them. All the treasures amassed in Iberia and Arabia, all the riches found among the Celts or contained in the land of the Scyths—in brief, all the wealth of the barbarians who surround our borders—all were gathered together in one place and deposited in the emperor's coffers. . . . As he spent the greater part of his reign serving as a soldier on guard at our frontiers and keeping the barbarians from raiding our territories, not only did he draw nothing from his reserves of wealth, but even multiplied his riches many times over.

On his expedition against the barbarians, Basil did not follow the customary procedure of other emperors, setting out at the middle of spring and returning home at the end of summer. For him the time to return was when the task in hand was accomplished. He endured the rigours of winter and the heat of summer with equal indifference. He disciplined himself against thirst. In fact, all his natural desires were kept under stern control, and the man was as hard as steel. He had an accurate knowledge of the details of army life, and by that I do not mean the general acquaintance with the composition of his army, the relative functions of individual units in the whole body, or the various groupings and deployments suited to the different formations. His experience of army matters went further than that: the duties of the *protostate*, the duties of the *hemilochites*, the tasks proper to the rank immediately junior to them—all these were no mysteries to Basil, and the knowledge stood him in good stead in his wars. Accordingly, jobs appropriate to these ranks were not devolved on others, and the emperor, being personally conversant with the character and combat duties of each individual, knowing to what each man was fitted either by temperament or by training, used him in this capacity and made him serve there. . . .

Basil's character was two-fold, for he readily adapted himself no less to the crises of war than to the calm of peace. Really, if the truth be told, he was more of a villain in wartime, more of an emperor in time of peace. Outbursts of wrath he controlled, and like the proverbial 'fire under the ashes', kept anger hid in his heart, but if his orders were disobeyed in war, on his return to the palace he would kindle his wrath and reveal it. Terrible then was the vengeance he took on the miscreant. Generally, he persisted in his opinions, but there were occasions when he did change his mind. In many cases, too, he traced crimes back to their original causes, and the final links in the chain were exonerated. So most defaulters obtained forgiveness, either through his sympathetic understanding, or because he showed some other interest in their affairs. He was slow to adopt any course of action, but never would he willingly alter the decision, once it was taken. Consequently, his attitude to friends was unvaried, unless perchance he was compelled by necessity to revise his opinion of them. Similarly, where he had burst out in anger against someone, he did not quickly moderate his wrath. Whatever estimate he formed, indeed, was to him an irrevocable and divinely-inspired judgment. . . .

The emperor seems to have lived a very long time, more than all the other sovereigns, for from birth up to his twentieth year he shared imperial power with his father and Phocas Nicephorus, and later with John Tzimisces, the latter's successor. During this period he occupied a subordinate position, but for the next fifty-two years he ruled supreme. He was therefore in his seventy-second year when he died.

57 THE RUSSIAN PRIMARY CHRONICLE: THE BYZANTINE CONVERSION OF A RUSSIAN PRINCE

Far to the north of the Roman Empire, the Slavs at the beginning of the Christian era had settled along the upper reaches of the Vistula River and in the adjoining wooded marshlands to the east. By the sixth and seventh centuries A.D. they had expanded throughout most of European Russia and central Europe. Following in the path of the Goths, migrating Slavs moved southward to attack Byzantine possessions in the Balkan peninsula and to settle there in large enough numbers to become the dominant racial and linguistic element. With the Slavs came also the Bulgars, a people of Hunnish origin, who eventually established themselves on the western shores of the Black Sea.

After spreading throughout the vast Russian expanses, the Slavs were soon threatened by new invaders. These were small aggressive bands of Scandinavians who were committed to adventure, piracy, and commerce and who were related to the Northmen or Vikings concurrently pillaging the European coasts and sailing the north Atlantic. In the East the Northmen were generally called Varangians, and in specific areas they referred to themselves as Rus, a name which was ultimately applied to the whole land of Russia. The permanent settlement of the Rus along the Dnieper River gave Russia her first significant political organization with a capital at Kiev and a ruling dynasty which soon mixed Slavic blood with Scandinavian. Using the great chain of lakes and rivers which links northern Russia with the Black Sea, the Rus established profitable trade relations with the Arabs of central Asia and with the Byzantine Empire. Their fleets became the terror of the Black Sea and occasionally even threatened Constantinople.

For the Byzantine Empire, already assailed by the Muslim Arabs, the threat of the Bulgars and the Slavs was ominous. This threat the Byzantine emperors met not only with armaments and diplomacy but also with the energetic missionary effort on the part of the Eastern Church, which was carried on sometimes in competition with equally energetic missionaries of the Roman papacy.

The supreme triumph of Byzantine efforts was the conversion of Vladimir, the grand prince of Kiev (c. 956-1015), who became the first Russian saint. Vladimir's conversion and marriage to a Byzantine princess assured the eastern empire of long-lasting peaceful and friendly relations, including extensive trade. For Russia, conversion to the eastern rite and the resulting influence of Byzantine autocracy, administration, and culture had enormous import in shaping her future political, religious, and cultural history.

Vladimir's conversion is recounted below in selections from *The Russian Primary Chronicle* of the Kievan Rus, which was apparently compiled by monks of the Crypt Monastery in Kiev in the late eleventh and twelfth centuries. The account of the conversions compounds two traditions. The first tradition is probably apocryphal and has Vladimir converted by a Greek monk against the competition of Jewish, Muslim, and Roman Catholic missionaries. The second version relates the conversion to Vladimir's marriage to Princess Anna of Byzantium and makes it a product of international diplomacy as well as of missionary zeal.

Vladimir had appointed his uncle Dobrỹnya to rule over Novgorod. When Dobrỹnya came to Novgorod, he set up an idol beside the river Volkhov, and the people of Novgorod offered sacrifice to it as if to God himself. Now Vladimir was overcome by lust for women. His lawful wife was Rogned, whom he settled on the Lybed', where the village of Predslavino now stands. By her he had four sons: Izyaslav, Mstislav, Yaroslav, and Vsevolod, and two daughters. The Greek woman bore him Svyatopolk; by one Czech he had a son Vÿsheslav; by another, Svyatoslav and Mstislav; and by a Bulgarian woman, Boris and Gleb. He had three hundred concubines at Vÿshgorod, three hundred at Belgorod, and two hundred at Berestovo in a village still called Berestovoe. He was insatiable in vice. He even seduced married women and violated young girls, for he was a libertine like Solomon. For it is said that Solomon had seven hundred wives and three hundred concubines. He was wise, yet in the end he came to ruin. But Vladimir, though at first deluded, eventually found salvation. Great is the Lord, and great is his power, and of his wisdom there is no end. . . .

For at this time the Russes were ignorant pagans. The devil rejoiced thereat, for he did not know that his ruin was approaching. He was so eager to destroy the Christian people, yet he was expelled by the true cross even from these very lands. The accursed one thought to himself, "This is my habitation, a land where the apostles have not taught nor the prophets prophesied." He knew not that the Prophet had said, "I will call those my people who are not my people" (*Hosea*, ii, 23). Likewise it is written of the Apostles, "Their message has gone out into all the earth and their words to the end of the world" (*Ps.*, xix, 5). Though the Apostles have not been there in person, their teachings resound like trumpets in the churches throughout the world. Through their instruction we overcome the hostile adversary, and trample him under our feet. For likewise did the Holy Fathers trample upon him, and they have received the heavenly crown in company with the holy martyrs and the just.

Vladimir was visited by Bulgars of Mohammedan faith, who said, "Though you are a wise and prudent prince, you have no religion. Adopt our faith, and revere Mahomet." Vladimir inquired what was the nature of their religion. They replied that they believed in God, and that Mahomet instructed them to practice circumcision, to eat no pork, to drink no wine, and, after death, promised them complete fulfillment of their carnal desires. "Mahomet," they asserted, "will give each man seventy fair women. He may choose one fair one, and upon that woman will Mahomet confer the charms of them all, and she shall be his wife. Mahomet promises that one may then satisfy every desire, but whoever is poor in this world will be no different in the next." They also spoke other false things

Text: Samuel H. Cross and Olgerd P. Sherbowitz-Wetzor (trans. and ed.), *The Russian Primary Chronicle* (Cambridge: The Mediaeval Academy of America, 1953), pp. 94, 96-98, 110-13, 116-17.

which out of modesty may not be written down. Vladimir listened to them, for he was fond of women and indulgence, regarding which he heard with pleasure. But circumcision and abstinence from pork and wine were disagreeable to him. "Drinking," said he, "is the joy of the Russes. We cannot exist without that pleasure."

Then came the Germans, asserting that they were come as emissaries of the Pope. They added, "Thus says the Pope: 'Your country is like our country, but your faith is not as ours. For our faith is the light. We worship God, who has made heaven and earth, the stars, the moon, and every creature, while your gods are only wood.'" Vladimir inquired what their teaching was. They replied, "Fasting according to one's strength. But whatever one eats or drinks is all to the glory of God, as our teacher Paul has said." Then Vladimir answered, "Depart hence; our fathers accepted no such principle."

The Jewish Khazars heard of these missions, and came themselves saying, "We have learned that Bulgars and Christians came hither to instruct you in their faiths. The Christians believe in him whom we crucified, but we believe in the one God of Abraham, Isaac, and Jacob." Then Vladimir inquired what their religion was. They replied that its tenets included circumcision, not eating pork or hare, and observing the Sabbath. The Prince then asked where their native land was, and they replied that it was in Jerusalem. When Vladimir inquired where that was, they made answer, "God was angry at our forefathers, and scattered us among the gentiles on account of our sins. Our land was then given to the Christians." The Prince then demanded, "How can you hope to teach others while you yourselves are cast out and scattered abroad by the hand of God? If God loved you and your faith, you would not be thus dispersed in foreign lands. Do you expect us to accept that fate also?"

Then the Greeks sent to Vladimir a scholar, who spoke thus: "We have heard that the Bulgarians came and urged you to adopt their faith, which pollutes heaven and earth. They are accursed above all men, like Sodom and Gomorrah, upon which the Lord let fall burning stones, and which he buried and submerged. The day of destruction likewise awaits these men, on which the Lord will come to judge the earth, and to destroy all those who do evil and abomination. For they moisten their excrement, and pour the water into their mouths, and anoint their beards with it, remembering Mahomet. The women also perform this same abomination, and even worse ones." Vladimir, upon hearing their statements, spat upon the earth, saying, "This is a vile thing."

Then the scholar said, "We have likewise heard how men came from Rome to convert you to their faith. It differs but little from ours, for they commune with wafers, called *oplatki*, which God did not give them, for he ordained that we should commune with bread. For when he had taken bread, the Lord gave it to his disciples, saying, 'This is my body broken for you.' Likewise he took the cup, and said, 'This is my blood of the New Testament.' They do not so act, for they have modified the faith." Then Vladimir remarked that the Jews had come into his presence and had stated that the Germans and the Greeks believed in him whom they crucified. To this the scholar replied, "Of a truth we believe in him. For some of the prophets foretold that God should be incarnate, and others that he should be crucified and buried, but arise on the third day and ascend into heaven. "For the Jews killed the prophets, and still others they persecuted. When their prophecy was fulfilled, our Lord came down to earth, was crucified, arose again, and ascended into heaven. He awaited their repentance for forty-six years, but they did not repent, so that the Lord let loose the Romans upon them. Their cities were destroyed, and they were scattered among the gentiles, under whom they are now in servitude." . . .

As he spoke thus, he exhibited to Vladimir a canvas on which was depicted the Judgment Day of the Lord, and showed him, on the right, the righteous going to their bliss in Paradise, and on the left, the sinners on their way to torment. Then Vladimir sighed and said, "Happy are they upon the right, but woe to those upon the left!" The scholar replied, "If you desire to take your place upon the right with the just, then accept baptism!" Vladimir took this counsel to heart, saying, "I shall wait yet a little longer," for he wished to inquire about all the faiths. Vladimir then gave the scholar many gifts, and dismissed him with great honor.

Vladimir summoned together his boyars and the city-elders, and said to them, "Behold, the Bulgars came before me urging me to accept their religion. Then came the Germans and praised their own faith; and after them came the Jews. Finally the Greeks appeared, criticizing all other faiths but commending their own. . . . Their words were artful, and it was wondrous to listen and pleasant to hear them. They preach the existence of another world. 'Whoever adopts our religion and then dies shall arise and live forever. But whosoever embraces another faith, shall be consumed with fire in the next world.' What is your opinion on this subject, and what do you answer?" The boyars and the elders replied,

"You know, oh Prince, that no man condemns his own possessions, but praises them instead. If you desire to make certain, you have servants at your disposal. Send them to inquire about the ritual of each and how he worships God."

Their counsel pleased the prince and all the people, so that they chose good and wise men to the number of ten, and directed them to go first among the Bulgars and inspect their faith. The emissaries went their way, and when they arrived at their destination they beheld the disgraceful actions of the Bulgars and their worship in the mosque; then they returned to their country. Vladimir then instructed them to go likewise among the Germans, and examine their faith, and finally to visit the Greeks. They thus went into Germany, and after viewing the German ceremonial, they proceeded to Tsar'grad, where they appeared before the Emperor. He inquired on what mission they had come, and they reported to him all that had occurred. When the Emperor heard their words, he rejoiced, and did them great honor on that very day.

On the morrow, the Emperor sent a message to the Patriarch to inform him that a Russian delegation had arrived to examine the Greek faith, and directed him to prepare the church and the clergy, and to array himself in his sacerdotal robes, so that the Russes might behold the glory of the God of the Greeks. When the Patriarch received these commands, he bade the clergy assemble, and they performed the customary rites. They burned incense, and the choirs sang hymns. The Emperor accompanied the Russes to the church, and placed them in a wide space, calling their attention to the beauty of the edifice, the chanting, and the pontifical services and the ministry of the deacons, while he explained to them the worship of his God. The Russes were astonished, and in their wonder praised the Greek ceremonial. Then the Emperors Basil and Constantine invited the envoys to their presence, and said, "Go hence to your native country," and dismissed them with valuable presents and great honor.

Thus they returned to their own country, and the Prince called together his boyars and the elders. Vladimir then announced the return of the envoys who had been sent out, and suggested that their report be heard. He thus commanded them to speak out before his retinue. The envoys reported, "When we journeyed among the Bulgars, we beheld how they worship in their temple, called a mosque, while they stand ungirt. The Bulgar bows, sits down, looks hither and thither like one possessed, and there is no happiness among them, but instead only sorrow and a dreadful stench. Their religion is not good. Then we went among the Germans, and saw them performing many ceremonies in their temples; but we beheld no glory there. Then we went to Greece, and the Greeks led us to the edifices where they worship their God, and we knew not whether we were in heaven or on earth. For on earth there is no such splendor or such beauty, and we are at a loss how to describe it. We only know that God dwells there among men, and their service is fairer than the ceremonies of other nations. For we cannot forget that beauty. Every man, after tasting something sweet, is afterward unwilling to accept that which is bitter, and therefore we cannot dwell longer here." Then the boyars spoke and said, "If the Greek faith were evil, it would not have been adopted by your grandmother Olga who was wiser than all other men." Vladimir then inquired where they should all accept baptism, and they replied that the decision rested with him.

After a year had passed, in 6496 (988), Vladimir proceeded with an armed force against Kherson, a Greek city, and the people of Kherson barricaded themselves therein. Vladimir halted at the farther side of the city beside the harbor, a bowshot from the town, and the inhabitants resisted energetically while Vladimir besieged the town. Eventually, however, they became exhausted, and Vladimir warned them that if they did not surrender, he would remain on the spot for three years. When they failed to heed this threat, Vladimir marshalled his troops and ordered the construction of an earthwork in the direction of the city. While this work was under construction, the inhabitants dug a tunnel under the city-wall, stole the heaped-up earth, and carried it into the city, where they piled it up in the center of the town. But the soldiers kept on building, and Vladimir persisted. Then a man of Kherson, Anastasius by name, shot into the Russ camp an arrow on which he had written, "There are springs behind you to the east, from which water flows in pipes. Dig down and cut them off." When Vladimir received this information, he raised his eyes to heaven and vowed that if this hope was realized, he would be baptized. He gave orders straightway to dig down above the pipes, and the water-supply was thus cut off. The inhabitants were accordingly overcome by thirst, and surrendered.

Vladimir and his retinue entered the city, and he sent messages to the Emperors Basil and Constantine, saying, "Behold, I have captured your glorious city. I have also heard that you have an unwedded sister. Unless you give her to me to wife, I shall deal with your own city as I have with Kherson." When the Emperors heard this message they were troubled, and replied, "It is not meet for Christians to give in marriage to pagans. If you are baptized, you shall have her to wife, inherit the kingdom of God, and be our companion in the faith. Unless you do so, however, we cannot give you our sister in marriage." When Vladimir learned their response, he directed the envoys of the Emperors to report to the latter that he was willing to accept baptism, having already given some study to their religion, and that the Greek faith and ritual, as described by the emissaries sent to examine it, had pleased him well. When the Emperors heard this report, they rejoiced, and persuaded their sister Anna to consent to the match. They then requested Vladimir to submit to baptism before they should send their sister to him, but Vladimir desired that the Princess should herself bring priests to baptize him. The Emperors complied with his request, and sent forth their sister, accompanied by some dignitaries and priests. Anna, however, departed with reluctance. "It is as if I were setting out into captivity," she lamented; "better were it for me to die at home." But her brothers protested, "Through your agency God turns the land of Rus' to repentance, and you will relieve Greece from the danger of grievous war. Do you not see how much harm the Russes have already brought upon the Greeks? If you do not set out, they may bring on us the same misfortunes." It was thus that they overcame her hesitation only with great difficulty. The Princess embarked upon a ship, and after tearfully embracing her kinfolk, she set forth across the sea and arrived at Kherson. The natives came forth to greet her, and conducted her into the city, where they settled her in the palace.

By divine agency, Vladimir was suffering at that moment from a disease of the eyes, and could see nothing, being in great distress. The Princess declared to him that if he desired to be relieved of this disease, he should be baptized with all speed, otherwise it could not be cured. When Vladimir heard her message, he said, "If this proves true, then of a surety is the God of the Christians great," and gave order that he should be baptized. The Bishop of Kherson, together with the Princess's priests, after announcing the tidings, baptized Vladimir, and as the Bishop laid his hand upon him, he straightway received his sight. Upon experiencing this miraculous cure, Vladimir glorified God, saying, "I have now perceived the one true God." When his followers beheld this miracle, many of them were also baptized.

Vladimir was baptized in the Church of St. Basil, which stands at Kherson upon a square in the center of the city, where the Khersonians trade. The palace of Vladimir stands beside this church to this day, and the palace of the Princess is behind the altar. After his baptism, Vladimir took the Princess in marriage. Those who do not know the truth say he was baptized in Kiev, while others assert this event took place in Vasil'ev, while still others mention other places. . . .

When the Prince arrived at his capital [Kiev], he directed that the idols should be overthrown, and that some should be cut to pieces and others burned with fire. . . .

Thereafter Vladimir sent heralds throughout the whole city to proclaim that if any inhabitants, rich or poor, did not betake himself to the river, he would risk the Prince's displeasure. When the people heard these words, they wept for joy, and exclaimed in their enthusiasm, "If this were not good, the Prince and his boyars would not have accepted it." On the morrow, the Prince went forth to the Dnieper with the priests of the Princess and those from Kherson, and a countless multitude assembled. They all went into the water: some stood up to their necks, others to their breasts, and the younger near the bank, some of them holding children in their arms, while the adults waded farther out. The priests stood by and offered prayers. . . .

When the people were baptized, they returned each to his own abode. Vladimir, rejoicing that he and his subjects now knew God himself, looked up to heaven and said, "Oh God, who has created heaven and earth, look down, I beseech thee, on this thy new people, and grant them, oh Lord, to know thee as the true God, even as the other Christian nations have known thee. Confirm in them the true and inalterable faith, and aid me, oh Lord, against the hostile adversary, so that, hoping in thee and in thy might, I may overcome his malice." Having spoken thus, he ordained that wooden churches should be built and established where pagan idols had previously stood. He thus founded the Church of St. Basil on the hill where the idol of Perun and the other images had been set, and where the Prince and the people had offered their sacrifices. He began to found churches and to assign priests throughout the cities, and to invite the people to accept baptism in all the cities and towns.

He took the children of the best families, and sent them for instruction in book-learning. The mothers of these children wept bitterly over them, for they were not yet strong in faith, but mourned as for the dead. When these children were assigned for study, there was fulfilled in the land of Rus' the prophecy which says, "In those days, the deaf shall hear words of Scripture, and the voice of the stammerers shall be made plain" (*Is.*, xxix, 18). . . .

INTERPRETATION OF THE BYZANTINE EMPIRE

58 PETER CHARANIS, "ECONOMIC FACTORS IN THE DECLINE OF THE BYZANTINE EMPIRE": A MODERN INTERPRETATION

Although Byzantine civilization continued to produce important statesmen, military commanders, scholars, and artists, the nearly four centuries between the fall of the Macedonian Dynasty (1081) and the conquest of Constantinople by the Ottoman Turks (1453) was a period of decline and humiliation for the Byzantine Empire. The successful military policies of the Macedonian emperors were shortly negated by disastrous defeats at the hands of the Muslim Turks, who constituted an expansive new power in the Muslim world from the eleventh century on. The appeal of the embattled eastern emperors to western Christendom opened the era of the crusades, but in no lasting sense could the Greek and Latin churches or their armies create a united front against Islam. Suspicion and hostility grew steadily until the Fourth Crusade (1202-1204), when Latin crusaders disregarded the Holy Land to besiege and capture Christian Constantinople. The Latin Empire established on Byzantine soil was a short-lived victory for the papacy over the Eastern Church, though it yielded commercial advantages for the aggressive Italian city-states of Venice and Genoa. Within sixty years the Greeks were able to expel the crusaders, restore the Byzantine crown, and reëstablish the eastern religious rite, but the Byzantine Empire never again recovered its position as a great power. Gradually it was engulfed by Muslim advances and long before Constantinople fell the city had been bypassed and isolated by Turkish invaders of Europe. In 1453, the city's walls were finally breached by Turkish cannon, the last "Roman" emperor fell in the fighting, and imperial Constantinople became the capital of the new Muslim empire of the Ottoman Turks.

The reasons for the decline and fall of the eastern Roman Empire are as complex as, and in some respects similar to, those for the collapse of the western empire one thousand years earlier (see Document 53). In the selection following, Peter Charanis, a modern Byzantine scholar of eminence, analyzes social and economic factors which contributed to the decline. Of central importance is the gradual elimination of the free peasantry, who were the source of Byzantine military power. Coincident with the suppression of the free peasants is the growth of a land-holding aristocracy which frequently came into conflict with the highly centralized and autocratic Byzantine administration. The efforts of the emperors to control the aristocracy by disarming it only further weakened the empire's powers of resistance. The borders of the Byzantine Empire were further constricted as her military establishment declined and her once remarkable ability to resist numerous external enemies gave way to weakness and inertia on the part of her latter-day emperors, governors, and military officials.

Economic Factors in the Decline of the Byzantine Empire

It is now five hundred years since the Byzantine empire was brought to an end by the Ottoman Turks. Scholars today quite justly reject Gibbon's assumption that the Byzantine empire was, throughout its entire existence, in a state of decline. They have come to rank it, instead, as one of the great empires in history. And this for good reasons. It endured for over a thousand

Text: Peter Charanis, "Economic Factors in the Decline of the Byzantine Empire," in *The Journal of Economic History*, XIII (1953), 412-24.

years. Down to about the middle of the eleventh century it was the center of civilization in Christendom. It preserved the thought and literature of antiquity; it developed new forms of art; it held back the barbarians. It produced great statesmen, soldiers, and diplomats as well as reformers and renowned scholars. Its missionaries, aided by its diplomats and sometimes by its armies, spread the gospel among the pagan tribes, especially the Slavs, which dwelt along its frontiers and beyond. As a Czech historian has put it, Byzantium "molded the undisciplined tribes of Serbs, Bulgars, Russians, Croats even, and made nations out of them; it gave to them its religion and institutions, taught their princes how to govern, transmitted to them the very principles of civilization—writing and literature." Byzantium was a great power and a great civilizing force.

Yet in a sense Gibbon was right. For the Byzantine empire did not come to an end as the result of a single blow as, for instance, the battle of Nineveh of 612 B.C. is said to have brought to an end the mighty Assyrian empire. The empire which Mohammed II destroyed on May 29, 1453, had been wasting away for over three hundred years, although part of this time, notably during the period of the Comneni, it was not an insignificant force. By the time of the fall of Constantinople, however, the Morea, one or two islands in the Aegean, and Constantinople were all that had been left of its once widely extensive territories. Constantinople itself, which in the tenth century had a population of perhaps one million people, had been reduced to probably not more than 75,000 inhabitants. As a center of commerce it had long been eclipsed by Galata, the Genoese colony on the opposite side of the Golden Horn. The Byzantine emperors became puppets in the hands of the Italian commercial republics, notably Genoa and Venice, served the Ottoman sultans as vassals, or miserably toured the West begging for help in return for which they were ready to sacrifice the religious traditions of their people. What a far cry from the august position of their predecessors of the tenth century who challenged East and West and challenged them not without success! "I shall conquer your lands," wrote Nicephorus Phocas to the Caliph of Bagdad, "and I shall go as far as Mecca. . . . I shall conquer all the Orient and the Occident and I shall spread everywhere the religion of the cross." The same emperor declared to the ambassador of the German emperor, Otto I: "Do you want a greater scandal than that [Otto] should call himself emperor and claim for himself provinces belonging to our empire? Both these things are intolerable; and if both are unsupportable, that especially is not to be borne, nay, not to be heard of that he calls himself emperor." What brought the empire from this pinnacle of power down to the abject position in which we find it in the fourteenth and fifteenth centuries is one of the most interesting problems in history.

In the history of the Byzantine empire, war and religion were the two principal factors that molded the society of the empire and determined its external position. War was the normal state of things throughout its long existence. The external crisis, however, that particularly affected the evolution of its society was that of the seventh century.

The advances of the Saracens and the incursions of the Slavs and Bulgars reduced virtually the whole empire to a frontier province. To cope with this situation the emperors of the seventh century reorganized the provincial administration of the empire, introducing what is known as the *theme* system, the essence of which was the subordination of civil to military authority exercised in each province by the commander of the army corps stationed there. But with the establishment of the *theme* system is connected the establishment of another institution, the system of military estates. These military estates, small in size and granted to individuals in return for military service, became the opening wedge in the formation of a new class of free peasant proprietors. The soldiers themselves constituted the nucleus of this class, but others gradually were added. For while the eldest son of a soldier inherited his father's plot together with the obligation of military service, the rest of the family were free to reclaim and cultivate the land that was vacant. The free peasants, cultivating their own land, paying the taxes, and, if necessary, serving in the army, came to constitute the dominant element in the agrarian society of Byzantium. They became a bulwark of the state, lent to it new vigor, and enabled it eventually to recover its position in the Orient. By the end of the tenth century, Byzantium had become the most powerful state throughout the Christian-Moslem world.

The situation changed in the eleventh century. During the second half of that century the empire suffered a series of military reverses from which it never fully recovered. The most serious of these was the disastrous defeat at Manzikert (1071). The battle of Manzikert decided the fate of Asia Minor and conditioned the subsequent history of the Byzantine empire. But Manzikert was only a battle, and battles had been lost before without the serious consequences that followed Manzikert. What explains the decline that set in after it and that would lead eventually to the disappearance of the empire were the conditions which came to prevail in the social and economic life of the empire in the eleventh century and later. Manzikert itself was the result of these conditions.

The dominant fact in the social and economic life of the empire in the eleventh century is the triumph of the landed military aristocracy and the decline of the soldiery-peasantry which had for centuries served as the bulwark of the state. From the very beginning of its history the large estate had been a feature of Byzantine society. The complicated and burdensome fiscal administration affected by the reorganization of the empire following the political and economic crisis of the third century worked in such a way as to give impetus to the growth of the large estates. The society revealed by the papyri and the great legislative monuments of the fifth and the sixth centuries is a society dominated by these estates. *Coloni*, reduced to serfs, composed the vast majority of the agrarian population, although the free peasant proprietors did not disappear completely. The development of the soldiery-peasantry in the seventh century lessened the extent of the large estates, but did not eliminate them. By the end of the ninth century they had become larger and more numerous. Those who possessed them occupied important positions in the administration and used these positions to increase their holdings. This they did by absorbing, often through dubious means, the properties of the small peasants. Thus the small, free peasant proprietors began to disappear.

The great emperors of the tenth century realized the dangerous social and political implications of this development and tried to check it. Every major emperor from Romanus Lecapenus to and including Basil II, with the exception of John Tzimeskes, issued more than one novel [constitutional law] for this purpose. These emperors sought to preserve the free peasantry because they considered it an essential element for the health of the state. As Romanus Lecapenus put it in one of his novels:

> It is not through hatred and envy of the rich that we take these measures, but for the protection of the small and the safety of the empire as a whole. . . . The extension of the power of the strong . . . will bring about the irreparable loss of the public good, if the present law does not bring a check to it. For it is the many, settled on the land, who provide for the general needs, who pay the taxes and furnish the army with its recruits. Everything falls when the many are wanting.

The strictest among the measures taken for the protection of the free peasantry was that issued by Basil II concerning the *allelengyon*, a measure which required the landed aristocracy to pay the tax arrears of peasants too poor to meet their own obligations. But with the death of Basil (1025) the effort to stop the growth of the large estates came to an end. His law concerning the *allelengyon* was repealed and the other measures, although kept in the books, were not enforced. The fate of the free peasantry was definitely decided.

Meanwhile, a similar fate befell the class of the enrolled soldiers, holders of the military estates. For the aristocracy, which, by one means or another, absorbed the estates of the small peasants, absorbed also those of the soldiers. The protection of the interests of these soldiers had been one of the deepest concerns of the emperors of the tenth century. Wrote Constantine Porphyrogenitus in the novel that he issued for the protection of the estates of the soldiers: "The army is to the state what the head is to the body. . . . He who neglects it neglects the safety of the state. . . . Therefore in promulgating our Constitution [on the military estates], we feel we are working for the welfare of all." But in this as in the case of the small peasants the measures taken by the emperors of the tenth century were of no avail. It proved impossible to stop the aristocracy from absorbing the properties of the small, whether the latter were soldiers or not.

What consummated the depression of the enrolled soldiers, however, was the anti-military policy which some of the emperors of the eleventh century followed in order to reduce the power of the military magnates in the administration of the empire. Those who occupied the high military posts in the empire were also great landholders. Their wealth, plus the powers which they exercised as military commanders, made them extremely dangerous to the central government. This danger, indeed, was one of the principal reasons why Basil II issued the novel concerning the *allelengyon* to which reference has already been made. He had faced two formidable revolts, both headed by members of the powerful aristocracy, and it was only with difficulty that he survived. When, after 987, Basil was reconciled with Bardas Skleros, one of the powerful rebels, the latter advised him that, if he wished to preserve the imperial authority, he should permit no one of the aristocracy to prosper and should exhaust their means by heavy taxes. Hence, the various measures he took, including that of the *allelengyon*, were designed not only to protect the poor peasants but also to crush the aristocracy. But on both the question of land and that of taxation the aristocracy triumphed.

One of the important reasons for the triumph of the aristocracy was the very strong hold that it had upon the military organization of the empire. If it could be shaken from this hold, it would lose in power and influence and would become more amenable to the wishes of the imperial government. And this is precisely what certain emperors of the eleventh century, notably Constantine IX Monomachos (1042-1055), Michael VI (1056-1057), and Constantine X Dukas (1059-1067), tried to do. The means of attack which they employed was to weaken the military organization by reducing the size of the army, thus depriving the aristocracy of its military commands. The great military triumphs of the tenth century, the crushing of the Saracens and the Bulgarians and the pushing of the frontiers to the Euphrates and the Tigris in the east and to the Danube in the Balkans, created a sense of security and the feeling that the maintenance of a powerful army was no longer necessary. With Constantine IX, peace became the keynote of the imperial foreign policy, and there began a systematic elimination of the aristocracy from the army while at the same time the development of a civil bureaucracy was promoted. But the aristocracy fought back, and a new struggle ensued, this time between the aristocracy as a military class and a new party of civil officials who came to dominate the imperial court.

The struggle plunged the empire into a series of civil wars that squandered its resources and manpower at a time when new and formidable enemies were making their appearance, both in the East and in the West. But the most serious result of the imperial policy was the deterioration of the army and the depression of the enrolled soldiers. By the time of Constantine X Dukas the profession of the soldier had lost much of its attraction and so, as a Byzantine historian puts it, "the soldiers put aside their arms and became lawyers or jurists." The same author, writing of the army that took the field in one of the expeditions against the Seljuks, states:

> The Army was composed of Macedonians and Bulgarians and Varangians and other barbarians who happened to be about. There were gathered also those who were in Phrygia [the *theme* Anatolikon]. And what one saw in them [the enrolled soldiers of the *theme* Anatolikon] was something incredible. The renowned champions of the Romans who had reduced into subjection all of the east and the west now numbered only a few and these were bowed down by poverty and ill treatment. They lacked in weapons, swords, and other arms, such as javelins and scythes. . . . They lacked also in cavalry and other equipment, for the emperor had not taken the field for a long time. For this reason they were regarded as useless and unnecessary and their wages and maintenance were reduced.

The enrolled soldiers, depressed and forgotten, became more and more a minor element in the Byzantine army. The bulk of this army, in the eleventh century and later, came to be composed almost entirely of foreign mercenaries —Russians, Turks, Alans, English, Normans, Germans, Patzinaks, Bulgarians, and others. These mercenaries were swayed more by their own interests than by those of the empire.

Meanwhile, the development of two institutions, the *pronoia* and the *exkuseia*, added further to the wealth and power of the landed aristocracy, both lay and ecclesiastic. The *pronoia* was the principal means that the emperors of the second half of the eleventh century, but especially later, adopted to recuperate much of the deserted land, to reconstitute the class of soldiers with landed interests, and to reward many of their partisans. A *pronoia* was granted to an individual for a specific period of years, usually his lifetime, in return for military or other services rendered or to be rendered. It was never hereditary, unless it was specifically declared so by a special measure. It consisted usually of land, but it could be a river or a fishery. Some of the *pronoiae* were very extensive, others less so, but the general effect of all was to increase the power and influence of the aristocracy and to lessen the hold of the central government over the agrarian population. For the holder of a *pronoia* exercised over those who inhabited it important financial and judicial powers which were granted to him along with the land. He was expected to serve in the army and also to furnish troops according to the size of his *pronoia*. But when we first meet with the *pronoia* in the second half of the eleventh century, it was not primarily a military grant; it became so during the reign of Alexius Comnenus and those of his successors. The *pronoia* differed from the old military estate in that it was held by persons high in the social order, whereas the recipients of the latter were peasant soldiers. In a study which I devoted to the aristocracy of Byzantium in the thirteenth century I showed that many of the holders of *pronoiae* belonged to the great families of the empire, families that were related to each other and to the ruling dynasty. The extensive use of the *pronoia* contributed not only to the increase, relatively speaking, of the power and wealth of the aristocracy but also to the development of the appanage system and thus weakened the central administration.

The central administration was weakened also by the development of the *exkuseia*. The term, which derives no doubt from the Latin *excusatio* (*excusare*), refers to the fiscal and judicial immunities that the imperial government often granted, especially to monasteries. It was formerly thought that the *exkuseia* first appeared in the eleventh century, but it is now known to be older than that, and may have developed out of the various privileges granted to the Christian clergy in the fourth century. Its use on a wide scale, however, is associated with the eleventh century and later. As the monastic properties during this period were very extensive, the revenue that the imperial government lost by the grant of *exkuseiae* must have been considerable. At the same time the *exkuseia* contributed to increasing the wealth of members of the lay aristocracy, for the emperors of the second half of the eleventh century and later often rewarded their partisans by granting to them the revenues of monasteries, such grants being then known as *kharistikia*. And monasteries whose revenues were thus granted often enjoyed the privilege of *exkuseia*.

Thus the failure to enforce the measures that had been issued for the protection of the soldiery-peasantry and the various grants of privileges made to the aristocracy had made the large estates, by the eleventh century, the dominant features of the agrarian landscape of Byzantium. These estates were worked by tenant peasants, the *paroikoi* of the Byzantine texts, people who were personally free, but who were tied to certain obligations and corvées that curtailed their movement. Some free peasant proprietors continued to exist, but they had become hardly distinguishable from the *paroikoi*. Besides working for the lord, the *paroikoi* had allotments of their own for which they paid rent and performed various obligations and from which, after the passage of a number of years, they could not be evicted. These allotments were transmissible from father to son. These tenant peasants, weighed down by the heavy burden of taxation and numerous corvées, lost all feeling for the welfare of the state as a whole. It is well known that the peasantry of the interior of Asia Minor offered no resistance to the Seljuk Turks, whose establishment in Asia Minor after Manzikert started the empire on the road to general decline. In the twelfth century the Comneni, by utilizing every resource at their disposal, succeeded in bringing about a partial recovery of the political power of the state, but neither they nor their successors tried to check the economic decay of the agrarian population. In the fourteenth century the deplorable economic conditions of the population were a big factor in the social and political strife that shook the empire and opened the way for the rise of the Ottoman Turks. In the tenth century, as we have pointed out above, Romanus Lecapenus had declared in one of his novels designed to protect the free peasantry that the extension of the power of the strong and the depression of the many would "bring about the irreparable loss of the public good." His prediction had come true. The disappearance of the free peasantry, the increase in the wealth, privileges, and power of the aristocracy, and the consequent depression of the agrarian population constitute, I think, some of the principal factors in the decline of the Byzantine empire.

But the society of the Byzantine empire was not purely agrarian. Included in the empire were a number of cities—Constantinople and Thessalonica immediately come to mind—whose role in the economic life of the empire was by no means insignificant. The penury of the sources makes impossible a detailed analysis of the urban economy of Byzantium, but that it was comparatively highly developed there can be no doubt.

What characterized the urban economy of Byzantium during the great days of the empire was its strict regulation by the state. This regulation consisted of two elements: the strict control over foreign commerce and the organization of the domestic trades and professions into private and public guilds supervised by the government. The object of this regulation was both political and economic: political in that the government sought to assure for itself arms and an ample supply of manufactured goods—in the main, luxuries—not only for the imperial household but also for the use of its diplomacy in the form of presents to barbarian chieftains and other princes; economic in that the government sought to keep the great cities well provisioned with the necessities of life, assure the quality of goods, and prevent exorbitant prices. The urban economy was also an important source of revenue. All imports and exports were subject to a 10 per cent duty, and the professions and trades, besides being liable for certain taxes, also performed various liturgies. The precise amount of this revenue, because of the fragmentary nature of the sources, cannot be determined, but it must have been considerable.

The regulation of urban economy was relaxed beginning with the last quarter of the eleventh century. The significant step in this development was taken in 1082 when Alexius Comnenus granted to the Venetians, in return for their alliance against the Normans of Sicily, various privileges among which the most important was that of trading freely, without the payment of any duty, in virtually all the cities of the empire, including the capital. These privileges, renewed by the emperors of the twelfth century, although not without reluctance, rendered the Venetians virtual masters of the commercial life of the empire. In the thirteenth century, in an effort to lessen the influence of the Venetians, similar privileges were granted to the Genoese (the treaty of Nymphaeum, 1261), but that was the substitution of one exploiter for another. The Italian merchants, whether Genoese or Venetians, became so entrenched in Constantinople that they controlled the economy of that city and determined the price of even the daily necessities. According to the patriarch Athanasius (end of the thirteenth century), the fate of the Romans had completely passed into the hands of the Latins, "who," he complained bitterly to the emperor Andronicus II, "make fun of us and scorn us to the point that, full of overweening conceit, they take the wives of our compatriots as security for the wheat which they deliver to us."

Meanwhile, the guild organization which was such a strong feature of the urban organization of the tenth century had virtually ceased to exist by the end of the thirteenth century. This at least is the impression created by the letters of the patriarch Athanasius which, although not yet published, have been analyzed by two different scholars. The patriarch complained to the emperor that false weights were used, that the wheat was hoarded, was often mixed with chaff or wheat that had rotted, and was sold at exorbitant prices. He urged the emperor to appoint a commissioner to supervise everything that concerned the provisioning of the capital. The emperor (Andronicus II) took cognizance of the complaints and ordered an investigation. He was especially anxious to determine who were those who exercised the trade of baker, how many of them there were, and under what conditions were the ships, which brought the food supplies to Constantinople, sold and bought. Thus, at the end of the thirteenth century it was not officially known who were the bakers in Constantinople and how many of them there were. Nor were they supervised with the view of assuring the quality of and a fair price for their produce. Contrast this with what the *Book of the Prefect* says about the bakers as they functioned in the tenth century:

The bakers shall make their profits according to the amount of grain purchased at the order of the Prefect. They shall purchase the proper amount of grain by the nomisma from their assessor. When they have ground it and leavened it, they shall calculate their profit at a keration and two miliarisia on the nomisma. The keration will be pure profit, while the two miliarisia will go for the support of their workmen, the food of their mill animals, the fuel for the ovens, and the lighting. . . .

Whenever there is an increase or decrease in the supply of grain, the bakers shall go to the Prefect to have the weights of their loaves fixed by the assessor in accordance with the purchase price of grain.

Obviously by the end of the thirteenth century the bakers' guild had completely broken down; there was not even a semblance of governmental control over the baker's trade. And what was true of this trade was probably also true of the others. The only indication of a trade organization in the fourteenth century was that of the mariners of Thessalonica. It has been suggested that this guild was organized by the mariners themselves in order to protect their interests, but more probably it was a continuation of an older organization which became more or less autonomous as the power of the central government declined in the fourteenth century. The guild of the mariners took the leadership in the terrible social upheaval that shook Thessalonica in 1345 and resulted in the slaughter of about one hundred members of the aristocracy.

It has been said that "Byzantium's weakness, which led to her fatal decline in the course of the eleventh century" was "her rigid, defensive attitude toward the outside world . . . embodied in the cultural and economic barriers she raised against all outsiders." The economic barriers spoken of in this statement refer no doubt to the strict controls that Byzantium had exercised over commerce and industry. It is extremely doubtful if this indeed was Byzantium's weakness. The simple observation that the period during which these controls were most rigidly enforced is the period of the greatness of the empire suggests the opposite, and this suggestion is reinforced by the further observation that the period of decline coincides with the breakdown of these controls. The power of a state and as a consequence its ability to maintain its position in the world is commensurate with its financial resources, the principal source of which is taxation. In Byzantium this source, seriously compromised by the disappearance of the free peasantry and the increase in the wealth, privileges, and power of the aristocracy was reduced almost to the vanishing point by the commercial privileges granted to the Italian republics and the consequent loss by Byzantium of control over its urban economy. This was Byzantium's weakness that brought about its decline and final fall.

Islam

59 THE KORAN: THE FAITH OF MUHAMMAD

No sooner had Christianity introduced civilization to the barbarians of the West and eastern emperors consolidated the Byzantine Empire than other invaders came into the Mediterranean world to disrupt the new-found stability—this time, the Arabs.

For countless ages the Arabian peninsula—the desert expanse midway between the fertile lands of the Nile and the Tigris-Euphrates valleys—had been the home of Semitic tribes, mostly nomads, camel drivers, and caravan traders. They had few cities; Mecca was one of the few—an ancient holy place of sacred idols and sacred stone. In this city about the year 570 A.D. a boy named Muhammad was born to parents who were among the guardians of the temple. When they died soon after, the young Muhammad struggled for his livelihood, first as a shepherd, then as a camel driver, meanwhile receiving only the barest education. He had great ambition, however, and eventually gained a wealthy wife and a lucrative career as a merchant. At the age of forty, his life was suddenly transformed by revelations that he believed were entrusted to him by the one great God, Allah. Allah commanded him to recite these revealed truths and to go among the Arabs to preach the new religion called Islam. His fundamental message was, "There is no God but Allah, and Muhammad is his prophet."

Muhammad's monotheism and proselytizing drew the anger of the heathen priests of Mecca, who denounced him and roused the citizens against him. Muhammad and a small group of disciples fled to the neighboring city of Yathrib, which came to be called Medina, the "city of the Prophet." This escape is known as the Hegira or the "flight of the Prophet." Its date, 622 A.D., marks the year one of Muslim chronology.

What Muhammad did not win immediately by the word, he won eventually by the sword. At Medina he gathered more and more followers, ultimately raising a host that was to vanquish neighboring Arab tribes and conquer Mecca itself (630). The conquests which Muhammad had begun were continued even more zealously after his death in 632; within a decade the Arab Muslims, though few in number, had wrested Syria and Palestine from the Byzantine Empire and had overrun Egypt and the Persian Empire; within less than a century they had conquered the African shores of the Mediterranean and Spain. These amazing conquests were not accomplished without civil wars, minor setbacks, and the coöperation of many Christians who preferred Arab masters to Byzantine autocracy and orthodoxy, but the Arab achievement in relation to their previously minor history is one of the most striking historical examples of the force of religion.

The Koran (Arabic Qur'ān, or "recitation") is the bible of Islam. It is regarded by Muslims as the word of Allah, and except in the first sura—which is a prayer to Allah—and a few passages in which Muhammad or the angels speak, the speaker throughout is Allah. God's word was first delivered orally by Muhammad, and not until some twenty years after his death were the 114 suras, or chapters, organized into a standard version of the Koran. In the selections below, we can perceive Islam's relation to Judaism and Christianity; according to the faithful, God had revealed Himself to man through the prophets, to some of whom He gave a scripture—to Moses the law, or Torah; to Jesus, the gospel; to Muhammad, the Koran. Muhammad, however, was "the seal of the prophets," that is, the last and greatest of the prophets. He was the "messenger" through whose guidance Islam would ultimately triumph and "prevail over all religions." The passages below contain several key beliefs of Islam: the importance of the prophets; the unity of God (Allah) and the parallel rejection of the Christian doctrine of the Trinity; and the nature of the final judgment.

The Exordium

In the Name of Allah, the Compassionate, the Merciful.

Text: From *The Koran*, trans. N. J. Dawood (London: Penguin Books Ltd., 1968), pp. 15, 52-53, 270-73, 376-78, 382-87 *passim*. Reprinted by permission of the publisher.

Praise be to Allah, Lord of the Creation,
The Compassionate, the Merciful,
King of Judgement-day!
You alone we worship, and to You alone we pray for help.
Guide us to the straight path.

The path of those whom You have favoured,
Not of those who have incurred Your wrath.
Nor of those who have gone astray.

The Tidings

In the Name of Allah, the Compassionate, the Merciful.

About what are they asking?

About the fateful tidings—the theme of their disputes.

But they shall know the truth; before long they shall know it.

Did We not spread the earth like a bed and raise the mountains like pillars?

We created you in pairs and gave you rest in sleep. We made the night a mantle, and ordained the day for work. We built above you seven mighty heavens and placed in them a shining lamp. We sent down abundant water from the clouds, bringing forth grain and varied plants, and gardens thick with foliage.

Fixed is the Day of Judgement. On that day the Trumpet shall be sounded and you shall come in multitudes. The gates of heaven shall swing open and the mountains shall pass away and become like vapour.

Hell will lie in ambush, a home for the transgressors. There they shall abide long ages; there they shall taste neither refreshment nor any drink, save boiling water and decaying filth: a fitting recompense.

They disbelieved in Our reckoning and roundly denied Our revelations. But We counted all their doings and wrote them down. We shall say: 'Taste this: you shall have nothing but mounting torment!'

As for the righteous, they shall surely triumph. Theirs shall be gardens and vineyards, and high-bosomed maidens for companions: a truly overflowing cup.

There they shall hear no idle talk nor any falsehood. Such is the recompense of your Lord—a gift that will suffice them: the Lord of the heavens and the earth and all that lies between them; the Merciful, with whom no one can speak.

On the day when the Spirit and the angels stand up in their ranks, they shall not speak; except him who shall receive the sanction of the Merciful and declare what is right.

That day is sure to come. Let him who will, seek a way back to his Lord. We have forewarned you of an imminent scourge: the day when man will look upon his works and the unbeliever cry: 'Would that I were dust!'

Victory

In the Name of Allah, the Compassionate, the Merciful.

We have given you a glorious victory,[1] so that Allah may forgive your past and future sins, and perfect His goodness to you; that He may guide you to the right path and bestow on you His mighty help.

It was He who sent down tranquillity[2] into the hearts of the faithful so that their faith might grow stronger. His are the legions of the heavens and the earth. Allah is wise and all-knowing.

He has caused you to do as you have done that He may bring the believers, both men and women, into gardens watered by running streams, there to abide for ever; that He may forgive them their sins (this, in Allah's sight, is a glorious triumph); and that He may punish the hypocrites and the idolaters, men and women, who think evil thoughts about Him. A turn of evil shall befall them, for Allah is angry with them. He has laid on them His curse and prepared for them the fire of Hell: an evil fate.

His are the legions of the heavens and the earth. Allah is mighty and wise.

We have sent you[3] forth as a witness and as a bearer of news and warnings, so that you[4] may have faith in Allah and His apostle and that you may assist him, honour him, and praise Him morning and evening.

Those that swear fealty to you swear fealty to Allah Himself. The Hand of Allah is above their hands. He that breaks his oath breaks it at his own peril, but he that keeps his pledge to Allah shall be richly rewarded.

The desert Arabs who stayed behind[5] will say to you: 'We were occupied with our goods and families. Implore Allah to pardon us.' They will say with their tongues what they do not mean in their hearts.

Say: 'Who can prevent Allah from punishing you or being gracious to you, if He is pleased to do either? Allah is cognizant of all your actions.'

No, You[6] thought the Apostle and the believers would never return to their people; and with this fancy your hearts were delighted. You harboured evil thoughts and thus incurred damnation.

For those that disbelieve in Allah and His apostle We have prepared a blazing Fire. Allah's is the kingdom of the heavens and the earth. He pardons whom He will and punishes whom He pleases. Allah is forgiving and merciful.

[1] The taking of Mecca, A.D. 630, or of Khaybar a year earlier.
[2] This is the meaning of the Arabic word *sakeenah*, which, however, could well be in this context an echo of the Hebrew word *shekheenah* (the Holy Presence).
[3] Mohammed.
[4] The Meccans.
[5] Away from the war.
[6] The desert Arabs.

When you set forth to take the spoils those that stayed away will say: 'Let us come with you.'

They seek to change the word of Allah. Say: 'You shall not come with us. So Allah has said beforehand.'

They will reply: 'You are jealous of us.' But how little they understand!

Say to the desert Arabs who stayed behind: 'You shall be called upon to fight a mighty nation, unless they embrace Islam. If you prove obedient you shall receive a good reward from Allah. But if you run away, as you have done before this, He will inflict on you a stern chastisement.'

It shall be no offence for the blind, the lame, and the sick to stay behind. He that obeys Allah and His apostle shall be admitted to gardens watered by running streams; but he that turns and flees shall be sternly punished.

Allah was well pleased with the faithful when they swore allegiance to you under the tree. He knew what was in their hearts. Therefore He sent down tranquillity upon them and rewarded them with a speedy victory and with the many spoils which they have taken. Mighty is Allah and wise.

Allah has promised you rich booty and has given you this[7] with all promptness. He has protected you from your enemies, so that He may make your victory a sign to true believers and guide you along a straight path.

And Allah knows of other spoils which you have not yet taken. Allah has power over all things.

If the unbelievers join battle with you, they shall be put to flight. They shall find none to protect or help them.

Such were the ways of Allah in days gone by: and you shall find that they remain unchanged.

It was He who made peace between you in the Valley of Mecca[8] after He had given you victory over them. Allah was watching over all your actions.

Those were the unbelievers who debarred you from the Sacred Mosque and prevented your offerings from reaching their destination. But for the fear that you might have trampled under foot believing men and women unknown to you and thus incurred unwitting guilt on their account, Allah would have commanded you to fight it out with them; but He ordained it thus that He might bring whom He will into His mercy. Had the faithful stood apart from them, We would have sternly punished the unbelievers.

And while bigotry—the bigotry of ignorance—was holding its reign in the hearts of the unbelievers, Allah sent down His tranquillity on His apostle and the faithful and made the word of piety binding on them, for they were most worthy and deserving of it. Allah has knowledge of all things.

Allah has in all truth fulfilled His apostle's vision, in which He had said: 'If Allah will, you shall enter the Sacred Mosque secure and fearless, with hair cropped or shaven.' He knew what you did not know; and what is more, He granted you a speedy victory.

It is He that has sent forth His apostle with guidance and the true faith, so that he may exalt it above all religions. Allah is the all-sufficient Witness.

Mohammed is Allah's apostle. Those who follow him are ruthless to the unbelievers but merciful to one another. You see them adoring on their knees, seeking the grace of Allah and His good will. Their marks[9] are on their faces, the traces of their prostrations. Thus they are described in the Torah and in the Gospel: they are like the seed which puts forth its root and strengthens it, so that it rises stout and firm upon its stalk, delighting the sowers. Through them Allah seeks to enrage the unbelievers. Yet to those of them who will embrace the Faith and do good works He has promised forgiveness and a rich reward.

The Table

In the Name of Allah, the Compassionate, the Merciful.

Believers, be true to your obligations. It is lawful for you to eat the flesh of all beasts other than that which is hereby announced to you. Game is forbidden while you are on pilgrimage. Allah decrees what He will.

Believers, do not violate the rites of Allah, or the sacred month, or the offerings or their ornaments, or those that repair to the Sacred House seeking Allah's grace and pleasure. Once your pilgrimage is ended, you shall be free to go hunting.

Do not allow your hatred for those who would debar you from the Holy Mosque to lead you into sin. Help one another in what is good and pious, not in what is wicked and sinful. Have fear of Allah, for He is stern in retribution.

You are forbidden the flesh of animals that die a natural death, blood, and pig's meat; also any flesh dedicated to any other than Allah. You are forbidden the flesh of strangled animals and of those beaten or gored to death; of those killed by a fall or mangled by beasts of prey (unless you make it clean by giving the death-stroke yourselves); also of animals sacrificed to idols.

You are forbidden to settle disputes by consulting the Arrows. That is a vicious practice.

The unbelievers have this day abandoned all

---

[7] The spoils taken at Khaybar.

[8] The allusion is probably to the peace of Hudaybiyah, A.D. 628.

[9] Dust.

hope of vanquishing your religion. Have no fear of them: fear Me.

This day I have perfected your religion for you and completed My favour to you. I have chosen Islam to be your faith.

He that is constrained by hunger to eat of what is forbidden, not intending to commit sin, will find Allah forgiving and merciful.

They ask you what is lawful to them. Say: 'All good things are lawful to you, as well as that which you have taught the birds and beasts of prey to catch, training them as Allah has taught you. Eat of what they catch for you, pronouncing upon it the name of Allah. And have fear of Allah: swift is Allah's reckoning.'

All good things have this day been made lawful to you. The food of those to whom the Scriptures were given[10] is lawful to you, and yours to them.

Lawful to you are the believing women and the free women from among those who were given the Scriptures before you, provided that you give them their dowries and live in honour with them, neither committing fornication nor taking them as mistresses.

He that denies the faith shall gain nothing from his labours. In the world to come he shall have much to lose.

Believers, when you rise to pray wash your faces and your hands as far as the elbow, and wipe your heads and your feet to the ankle. If you are polluted cleanse yourselves. But if you are sick or travelling the road; or if, when you have just relieved yourselves or had intercourse with women, you can find no water, take some clean sand and rub your hands and faces with it. Allah does not wish to burden you; He seeks only to purify you and to perfect His favour to you, so that you may give thanks.

Remember the favours which Allah has bestowed upon you, and the covenant with which He bound you when you said: 'We hear and obey.' Have fear of Allah. He knows your inmost thoughts.

Believers, fulfil your duties to Allah and bear true witness. Do not allow your hatred for other men to turn you away from justice. Deal justly; justice is nearer to true piety. Have fear of Allah; He is cognizant of all your actions.

Allah has promised those that have faith and do good works forgiveness and a rich reward. As for those who disbelieve and deny Our revelations, they shall become the heirs of Hell.

Believers, remember the favour which Allah bestowed upon you when He restrained the hands of those who sought to harm you. Have fear of Allah. In Allah let the faithful put their trust.

Allah made a covenant with the Israelites and raised among them twelve chieftains. He said: 'I shall be with you. If you attend to your prayers and pay the alms-tax; if you believe in My apostles and assist them and give Allah a generous loan, I shall forgive you your sins and admit you to gardens watered by running streams. But he that hereafter denies Me shall stray from the right path.'

But because they broke their covenant We laid on them Our curse and hardened their hearts. They have perverted the words of the Scriptures and forgotten much of what they were enjoined. You will ever find them deceitful, except for a few of them. But pardon them and bear with them. Allah loves the righteous.

With those who said they were Christians We made a covenant also, but they too have forgotten much of what they were enjoined. Therefore We stirred among them enmity and hatred, which shall endure till the Day of Resurrection, when Allah will declare to them all that they have done.

People of the Book! Our apostle has come to reveal to you much of what you have hidden of the Scriptures, and to forgive you much. A light has come to you from Allah and a glorious Book. . . .

Believers, take neither Jews nor Christians for your friends. They are friends with one another. Whoever of you seeks their friendship shall become one of their number. Allah does not guide the wrongdoers. . . .

We made a convenant with the Israelites and sent forth apostles among them. But whenever an apostle came to them with a message that did not suit their fancies they either rejected him or slew him. They thought no harm would come to them; they were blind and deaf. Allah turned to them in mercy, but many of them again became blind and deaf. Allah is ever watching over their actions.

Unbelievers are those that say: 'Allah is the Messiah, the son of Mary.' For the Messiah himself said: 'Children of Israel, serve Allah, my Lord and your Lord.' He that worships other gods besides Allah shall be forbidden Paradise and shall be cast into the fire of Hell. None shall help the evil-doers.

Unbelievers are those that say: 'Allah is one of three.' There is but one God. If they do not desist from so saying, those of them that disbelieve shall be sternly punished.

Will they not turn to Allah in repentance and seek forgiveness of Him? He is forgiving and merciful.

The Messiah, the son of Mary, was no more than an apostle: other apostles passed away before him. His mother was a saintly woman. They both ate earthly food.

See how We make plain to them Our revelations. See how they ignore the truth.

Say: 'Will you serve instead of Allah that which

---

[10] The Jews (but not the Christians).

can neither harm nor help you? Allah hears all and knows all.'

Say: 'People of the Book! Do not transgress the bounds of truth in your religion. Do not yield to the desires of those who have already erred; who have led many astray and have themselves strayed from the even path.'

Those of the Israelites who disbelieved were cursed by David and Jesus, the son of Mary: they cursed them because they rebelled and committed evil and never restrained one another from wrongdoing. Evil were their deeds.

You see many of them making friends with unbelievers. Evil is that to which their souls prompt them. They have incurred the wrath of Allah and shall endure eternal torment. Had they believed in Allah and the Prophet and that which is revealed to him they would not have befriended them. But many of them are evil-doers.

You will find that the most implacable of men in their enmity to the faithful are the Jews and the pagans, and that the nearest in affection to them are those who say: 'We are Christians.' That is because there are priests and monks among them; and because they are free from pride.

When they listen to that which was revealed to the Apostle, you will see their eyes fill with tears as they recognize its truth. They say: 'Lord, we believe. Count us among Your witnesses. Why should we not believe in Allah and in the truth that has come down to us? Why should we not hope for admission among the righteous?' And for their words Allah has rewarded them with gardens watered by running streams, where they shall dwell for ever. Such is the recompense of the righteous. But those that disbelieve and deny Our revelations shall be the heirs of Hell.

Believers, do not forbid the wholesome things which Allah has made lawful to you. Do not transgress; Allah does not love the transgressors. Eat of the lawful and wholesome things which Allah has given you. Have fear of Allah, in whom you believe.

Allah will not punish you for that which is inadvertent in your oaths. But He will take you to task for the oaths which you solemnly swear. The penalty for a broken oath is the feeding of ten needy men with such food as you normally offer to your own people; or the clothing of ten needy men; or the freeing of one slave. He that cannot afford any of these must fast three days. In this way you shall expiate your broken oaths. Therefore be true to that which you have sworn. Thus Allah makes plain to you His revelations, so that you may give thanks.

Believers, wine and games of chance, idols and divining arrows, are abominations devised by Satan. Avoid them, so that you may prosper. Satan seeks to stir up enmity and hatred among you by means of wine and gambling, and to keep you from the remembrance of Allah and from your prayers. Will you not abstain from them?

Obey Allah, and obey the Apostle. Beware; if you give no heed, know that Our apostle's duty is only to give plain warning.

No blame shall be attached to those that have embraced the faith and done good works in regard to any food they may have eaten, so long as they fear Allah and believe in Him and do good works; so long as they fear Allah and believe in Him; so long as they fear Allah and do good works. Allah loves the charitable. . . .

60

IBN-SAID, *BOOK OF THE MAGHRIB*:
THE MUSLIMS IN POLITICS AND WAR

In 661 A.D. the Umayyad leader Moawiyah seized control of the Islamic Empire, was proclaimed caliph, and established his capital in the Syrian city of Damascus. For the next nine decades the Umayyad Dynasty expanded the territorial limits of Islam, until by the mid-eighth century the Mediterranean could be said to be Muslim-dominated. The only area to succeed in resisting the Islamic conquest was the Byzantine Empire, despite the almost overwhelming pressure exerted against it by Caliph Sulayman, whose armies penetrated to the gates of Constantinople itself (717-718).

Muslim armies pushed eastward as far as India, and in the West they drove steadily along the North African coast, seizing Carthage, Algeria, and Morocco. Finally, in 711, a mixed force of Arabs and Berbers under the Berber general, Tariq, swept across the Strait of Gibraltar and into the Christian lands of western Europe. The lack of Spanish opposition encouraged the Muslims to settle permanently in the Iberian peninsula. After a time, raiding expeditions even seeped across the Pyrenees into southern France, but these skirmishes were largely unproductive. The Muslims withdrew to Spain and there laid the foundation for a flourishing Islamic civilization.

In 750 the Umayyads of Damascus were overthrown and their place taken by the Abbasside Caliphate (750–c. 1100). The internal strife stirred up by this dynastic struggle resulted in serious divisions within the Muslim Empire and the emergence of a number of independent Islamic states. The first to secede was Spain, where the Umayyad fugitive Abdarrahman in 756 seized control, proclaimed himself emir, and founded a Moorish state with a capital at Cordova. For the next several centuries this new reign continued, and Muslim Spain developed independent of political control from the Abbasside capital at Baghdad.

The selection below comprises excerpts from the *Book of the Maghrib* by ibn-Said (1208?-1274?), a North African philologist and historian. It describes the early successes and achievements of the Moors in Spain and then warns of the difficulties into which the caliphate has fallen and of the Christian threat to continuing Islamic rule. "Instead of defending the common cause, the cause of religion and truth," says ibn-Said, the Spanish Muslims confederate and ally against one another. The Christians, meanwhile, "advance farther and farther until they subdue the whole of that country exposed to their inroads, where once established and fortified, they will direct their attacks to another part of the Moslem territories, and carry on the same war of havoc and destruction."

The pomp and magnificence of the caliphs at Cordova is alluded to by ibn-Said, although he points out that during the periods of threat to Islamic hegemony, the Muslim people in Spain looked with increased displeasure at such extravagance.

Andalus [the Iberian peninsula], which was conquered in the year 92 of the Hijra, continued for many years to be a dependency of the Eastern Khalifate, until it was snatched away from their hands by one of the surviving members of the family of Umeyyah [Umayyad], who, crossing over from Barbary, subdued the country, and formed therein an independent kingdom, which he transmitted to his posterity. During three centuries and a half, Andalus, governed by the princes of this dynasty, reached the utmost degree of power and prosperity, until civil war breaking out among its inhabitants, the Moslems, weakened by internal discord, became every where the prey of the artful Christians, and the territory of Islám was considerably reduced, so much so that at the present moment the worshippers of the crucified hold the greatest part of Andalus in their hands, and their country is divided into various powerful kingdoms, whose rulers assist each other whenever the Moslems attack their territories. This brings to my recollection the words of an eastern geographer who visited Andalus in the fourth century of the Hijra [tenth century A.D.], and during the prosperous times of the Cordovan Khalifate, I mean Ibnu Haukal Annassíbí, who, describing Andalus, speaks in very unfavourable terms of its inhabitants. As

Text: Ahmed ibn Mohammed al-Makkari, *The History of the Mohammedan Dynasties in Spain*, trans. Pascual de Gayangos (London: Oriental Translation Fund, 1840), I, 95-102.

his words require refutation I shall transcribe here the whole of the passage. "Andalus," he says, "is an extensive island, a little less than a month's march in length, and twenty and odd days in width. It abounds in rivers and springs, is covered with trees and plants of every description, and is amply provided with every article which adds to the comforts of life; slaves are very fine, and may be procured for a small price on account of their abundance; owing, too, to the fertility of the land, which yields all sorts of grain, vegetables, and fruit, as well as to the number and goodness of its pastures in which innumerable flocks of cattle graze, food is exceedingly abundant and cheap, and the inhabitants are thereby plunged into indolence and sloth, letting mechanics and men of the lowest ranks of society overpower them and conduct their affairs. Owing to this it is really astonishing how the Island [*i.e.*, peninsula] of Andalus still remains in the hands of the Moslems, being, as they are, people of vicious habits and low inclinations, narrow-minded, and entirely devoid of fortitude, courage, and the military accomplishments necessary to meet face to face the formidable nations of Christians who surround them on every side, and by whom they are continually assailed."

Such are the words of Ibnu Haukal; but, if truth be told, I am at a loss to guess to whom they are applied. To my countrymen they certainly are not; or, if so, it is a horrible calumny, for if any people on the earth are famous for their courage, their noble qualities, and good habits, it is the Moslems of Andalus; and indeed their readiness to fight the common enemy, their constancy in upholding the holy tenets of their religion, and their endurance of the hardships and privations of war, have become almost proverbial. So, as far as this goes, Ibnu Haukal is decidedly in error, for as the proverb says, "the tongue of stammering is at times more eloquent than the tongue of eloquence." As to the other imputation, namely, their being devoid of all sense, wisdom, and talent, either in the field or in administration, would to God that the author's judgment were correct, for then the ambition of the chiefs would not have been raised, and the Moslems would not have turned against each other's breasts and dipped in each other's blood those very weapons which God Almighty put into their hands for the destruction and annihilation of the infidel Christian. But, as it is, we ask—were those Sultáns and Khalifs wanting in prudence and talents who governed this country for upwards of five hundred years, and who administered its affairs in the midst of foreign war and civil discord? Were those fearless warriors deficient in courage and military science who withstood on the frontiers of the Moslem empire the frightful shock of the innumerable infidel nations who dwell within and out of Andalus, whose extensive territories cover a surface of three months' march, and all of whom ran to arms at a moment's notice to defend the religion of the crucified? And if it be true that at the moment I write the Moslems have been visited by the wrath of heaven, and that the Almighty has sent down defeat and shame to their arms, are we to wonder at it at a time when the Christians, proud of their success, have carried their arms as far as Syria and Mesopotamia, have invaded the districts contiguous to the country which is the meeting-place of the Moslems, and the cupola of Islám, committed all sorts of ravages and depredations, conquered the city of Haleb (Aleppo) and its environs, and done other deeds which are sufficiently declared in the histories of the time? No, it is by no means to be wondered at, especially when proper attention is paid to the manner in which the Andalusian Moslems have come to their present state of weakness and degradation. The process is this: the Christians will rush down from their mountains, or across the plain, and make an incursion into the Moslem territory; there they will pounce upon a castle and seize it; they will ravage the neighbouring country, take the inhabitants captive, and then retire to their country with all the plunder they have collected, leaving, nevertheless, strong garrisons in the castles and towers captured by them. In the meanwhile the Moslem king in whose dominions the inroad has been made, instead of attending to his own interests and stopping the disease by applying cauterization, will be waging war against his neighbours of the Moslems; and these, instead of defending the common cause, the cause of religion and truth,—instead of assisting their brother, will confederate and ally to deprive him of whatever dominions still remain in his hands. So, from a trifling evil at first, it will grow into an irreparable calamity, and the Christians will advance farther and farther until they subdue the whole of that country exposed to their inroads, where, once established and fortified, they will direct their attacks to another part of the Moslem territories, and carry on the same war of havoc and destruction. Nothing of this, however, existed at the time when Ibnu Haukal visited Andalus; for although we are told by Ibnu Hayyán and other writers that the Christians began as early as the reign of 'Abdu-r-rahmán III. [912-961] to grow powerful, and to annoy the

Moslems on the frontiers, yet it is evident that until the breaking out of the civil wars, which raged with uncommon violence throughout Andalus, the encroachments of the barbarians on the extensive and unprotected frontiers of the Moslem empire were but of little consequence.

But to return to our subject. During the first years after the conquest the government of Andalus was vested in the hands of military commanders appointed by the Viceroys of Africa, who were themselves named by the Khalifs of Damascus. These governors united in their hands the command of the armies and the civil power, but, being either removed as soon as named, or deposed by military insurrections, much confusion and disorder reigned at all times in the state, and the establishment and consolidation of the Moslem power in Andalus were thwarted in their progress at the very onset. It was not until the arrival of the Bení Umeyyah in Andalus that the fabric of Islám may be said to have rested on a solid foundation. When 'Abdu-r-rahmán Ibn Mu'awiyeh had conquered the country, when every rebel had submitted to him, when all his opponents had sworn allegiance to him, and his authority had been universally acknowledged, then his importance increased, his ambition spread wider, and both he and his successors displayed the greatest magnificence in their court, and about their persons and retinue, as likewise in the number of officers and great functionaries of the state. At first they contented themselves with the title of *Benú-l-khaláyif* (sons of the Khalifs), but in process of time, when the limits of their empire had been considerably extended by their conquests on the opposite land of Africa, they took the appellation of Khalifs and *Omará-l-múmenín* (Princes of the believers). It is generally known that the strength and solidity of their empire consisted principally in the policy pursued by these princes, the magnificence and splendour with which they surrounded their court, the reverential awe with which they inspired their subjects, the inexorable rigour with which they chastised every aggression on their rights, the impartiality of their judgments, their anxious solicitude in the observance of the civil law, their regard and attention to the learned, whose opinions they respected and followed, calling them to their sittings and admitting them to their councils, and many other brilliant qualities; in proof of which frequent anecdotes occur in the works of Ibnu Hayyán and other writers; as, for instance, that whenever a judge summoned the Khalif, his son, or any of his most beloved favourites, to appear in his presence as a witness in a judicial case, whoever was the individual summoned would attend in person—if the Khalif, out of respect for the law—and if a subject, for fear of incurring his master's displeasure.

But when this salutary awe and impartial justice had vanished, the decay of their empire began, and it was followed by a complete ruin. I have already observed that the princes of that dynasty were formerly styled *Omará-bná-l-kholafá* (Amírs, sons of the Khalifs), but that in latter times they assumed the title of *Omará-l-númenín* (Princes of the believers). This continued until the disastrous times of the civil war, when the surviving members of the royal family hated each other, and when those who had neither the nobility nor the qualities required to honour the Khalifate pretended to it and wished for it; when the governors of provinces and the generals of armies declared themselves independent and rose every where in their governments, taking the title of *Molúku-t-tawáyif* (Kings of small estates), and when confusion and disorder were at their highest pitch. These petty sovereigns, of whom some read the *khotbah* for the Khalifs of the house of Merwán—in whose hands no power whatsoever remained—while others proclaimed the Abbasside Sultáns, and acknowledged their Imám, all began to exercise the powers and to use the appendages of royalty, assuming even the titles and names of former Khalifs, and imitating in every thing the bearing and splendour of the most powerful sovereigns,—a thing which they were enabled to accomplish from the great resources of the countries over which they ruled, —for although Andalus was divided into sundry petty kingdoms, yet such was the fertility of the land, and the amount of taxes collected from it, that the chief of a limited state could at times display at his court a greater magnificence than the ruler of extensive dominions. However, the greatest among them did not hesitate to assume, as I have already observed, the names and titles of the most famous Eastern Khalifs; for instance, Ibnu Rashík Al-kairwání says that 'Abbád Ibn Mohammed Ibn 'Abbád took the surname of Al-mu'atadhed, and imitated in all things the mode of life and bearing of the Abbasside Khalif Al-mu'atadhed-billah; his son, Mohammed Ibn 'Abbád, was styled Al-mu'atamed; both reigned in Seville, to which kingdom they in process of time added Cordova and other extensive territories in the southern and western parts of Andalus, as will hereafter be shown.

As long as the dynasty of Umeyyah occupied the throne of Cordova, the successors of 'Abdu-r-rahmán contrived to inspire their subjects with love of their persons, mixed with reverential awe; this they accomplished by surrounding their courts with splendour, by displaying the greatest magnificence whenever they appeared in public, and by employing other means which I have already hinted at, and deem it not necessary to repeat: they continued thus until the times of the civil war, when, having lost the affections of the people, their subjects began to look with an evil eye at their prodigal expense, and the extravagant pomp with which they surrounded their persons. Then came the Bení Hamúd, the descendants of Idrís, of the progeny of 'Alí Ibn Abí Tálib, who, having snatched the Khalifate from the hands of the Bení Merwán, ruled for some time over the greatest part of Andalus. These princes showed also great ostentation, and, assuming the same titles that the Abbasside Khalifs had borne, they followed their steps in every thing concerning the arrangements of their courts and persons; for instance, whenever a *munshid* wanted to extemporize some verses in praise of his sovereign, or any subject wished to address him on particular business, the poet or the petitioner was introduced to the presence of the Khalif, who sat behind a curtain and spoke without showing himself, the *Hájib* or curtain-drawer standing all the time by his side to communicate to the party the words or intentions of the Khalif. So when Ibnu Mokéná Al-lishbóní (from Lisbon), the poet, appeared in presence of the Hájib of Idrís Ibn Yahya Al-hamúdí, who was proclaimed Khalif at Malaga, to recite that *kassídah* of his which is so well known and rhymes in *min*, when he came to that part which runs thus—

The countenance of Idrís, son of Yahya, son of Alí, son of Hamúd, prince of the believers, is like a rising sun; it dazzles the eyes of those who look at it—

Let us see it, let us seize the rays of yonder light, for it is the light of the master of the worlds—

the Sultán himself drew the curtain which concealed him, and said to the poet—"Look, then," and showed great affability to Ibn Mokéná, and rewarded him very handsomely.

But when, through the civil war, the country was broken up into sundry petty sovereignties, the new monarchs followed quite a different line of politics; for, wishing to become popular, they treated their subjects with greater familiarity, and had a more frequent intercourse with all classes of society; they often reviewed their troops, and visited their provinces; they invited to their presence the doctors and poets, and wished to be held from the beginning of their reign as the patrons of science and literature: but even this contributed to the depression of the royal authority, which thus became every day less dreaded; besides, the arms of the Moslems being employed during the long civil wars against one another, the inhabitants of the different provinces began to look on each other with an evil eye; the ties by which they were united became loose, and a number of independent states were formed, the government of which passed from father to son, in the same manner as the empire of Cordova had been transmitted to the sons and heirs of the Khalifs. Thus separated from each other, the Moslems began to consider themselves as members of different nations, and it became every day more difficult for them to unite in the common cause; and owing to their divisions, and to their mutual enmity, as well as to the sordid interest and extravagant ambition of some of their kings, the Christians were enabled to attack them in detail, and subdue them one after the other. However, by the arrival of the Bení 'Abdu-l-múmen all those little states were again blended into one, and the whole of Andalus acknowledged their sway, and continued for many years to be ruled by their successors, until, civil war breaking out again, Ibn Húd, surnamed Al-mutawákel, revolted, and finding the people of Andalus ill-disposed against the Almohades, and anxious to shake off their yoke, he easily made himself master of the country. Ibn Húd, however, followed the policy of his predecessors (the kings of the small states); he even surpassed them in folly and ignorance of the rules of good government, for he used to walk about the streets and markets, conversing and laughing with the lowest people, asking them questions, and doing acts unsuitable to his high station, and which no subject ever saw a Sultán do before, so much so that it was said, not without foundation, that he looked more like a performer of legerdemain than a king. Fools, and the ignorant vulgar seemed, it is true, to gaze with astonishment and pleasure at this familiarity, but as the poet has said—

These are things to make the fools laugh, but the consequences of which prudent people are taught to fear.

These symptoms went on increasing until populous cities and extensive districts became the prey of the Christians, and whole kingdoms were snatched from the hands of the Moslems. Another very aggravating circumstance added its weight to the general calamity, namely, the facility with which the power changed hands. Whoever has read attentively what we have just said about the mode of attaining and using the royal power in Andalus, must be convinced that nothing was so easy, especially in latter times, as to arrive at it. The process is this: whenever a knight is known to surpass his countrymen in courage, generosity, or any of those qualities which make a man dear to the vulgar, the people cling to him, follow his party, and soon after proclaim him their king, without paying the least regard to his ascendancy, or stopping to consider whether he is of royal blood or not. The new king then transmits the state as an inheritance to his son or nearest relative, and thus a new dynasty is formed. I may, in proof of this, quote a case which has just taken place among us: a certain captain made himself famous by his exploits, and the victories he won over the enemy, as likewise by his generous and liberal disposition towards the citizens and the army; all of a sudden his friends and partisans resolved to raise him to the throne, and regardless of their own safety, as well as that of their families, friends, and clients residing at court, and whose lives were by their imprudence put in great jeopardy, they rose in a castle, and proclaimed him king; and they never ceased toiling, calling people to their ranks, and fighting their opponents, until their object was accomplished, and their friend solidly established on his throne. Now Eastern people are more cautious about altering the succession, and changing the reigning dynasty; they will on the contrary avoid it by all possible means, and do their best to leave the power in the hands of the reigning family, rather than let discord and civil dissensions sap the foundations of the state, and introduce dissolution and corruption into the social body.

Among us the change of dynasty is a thing of frequent occurrence, and the present ruler of Andalus, Ibnu-l-ahmar, is another instance of what I have advanced. He was a good soldier, and had been very successful in some expeditions against the Christians, whose territories he was continually invading, sallying out at the head of his followers from a castle called *Hisn-Arjónah* (Arjona), where he generally resided. Being a shrewd man, and versed in all the stratagems of war, he seldom went out on an expedition without returning victorious, and laden with plunder, owing to which he amassed great riches, and the number of his partisans and followers were considerably increased. At last, being prompted by ambition to aspire to the royal power, he at first caused his troops to proclaim him king; then sallying out of his stronghold he got possession of Cordova, marched against Seville, took it, and killed its king Al-bájí. After this he subdued Jaen, the strongest and most important city in all Andalus, owing to its walls and the position it occupies, conquered likewise Malaga, Granada, and their districts, and assumed the title of *Amíru-l-moslemín* (Prince of the Moslems); and at the moment I write he is obeyed all over Andalus, and every one looks to him for advice and protection.

61 AVICENNA, "AUTOBIOGRAPHY," AND AL-JUZJANI, "BIOGRAPHY OF AVICENNA": THE "RENAISSANCE MAN" IN THE MUSLIM WORLD

Along with spreading a new religious faith and the Arab language, Islam synthesized the best elements of the cultures with which it came into contact, thus encouraging intellectual vigor in the eastern world. The cosmopolitan spirit that pervaded the cultural capitals of Damascus, Baghdad, and, later, Cordova allowed the utmost diversity of ideas; and the translation into Arabic of Hellenic, Persian, Indian, and Chinese philosophy and science provided a strong foundation of knowledge upon which the Muslims could build their own great achievements.

Part of the Arabic achievement was the transmission and development of earlier accumulations of knowledge. The Arabs adopted the Chinese process of papermaking, using pulpwood or rags. From India the Muslims passed on the rudiments of a numerical system which we call "Arabic." Hindu and Persian science inaugurated the Arabic study of astronomy; Greek and Alexandrian learning furthered the Arabic practice of medicine, as it did the study of algebra, geometry, and trigonometry. It was with such Muslim philosophers as Averroës (1126-1198) of Spain that the glorification of Aristotle began, and from them the belief that in Aristotle human reason had reached its summit passed to the medieval European Scholastics (see Document 86).

The debt of the western world to the *original* contributions of the Muslims, however, is far greater than many people realize. The Arabs founded the science of optics (earlier work was not systematic), forwarding our knowledge of the velocity and refraction of light. Their chemists originated certain methods of sublimation and filtration and discovered basic substances like alum, borax, sodium carbonate, silver nitrate, nitric acid, sulphuric acid, and niter. Arab physicians like Rhazes (c. 860–925) and Avicenna (980-1037) made the first accurate descriptions of smallpox, measles, and pleurisy and discovered principles of infection and contagion. The architecture of the Muslims—the arabesque designs, the traceried windows, and the cusped arches—provided inspirations for many Gothic architects in Europe. Not only in science and art but also in commerce were the Arabs noteworthy innovators; it was Muslim merchants who developed modern tools of business like checks, letters of credit, and joint-stock companies. In sum, the vast Arab achievements from the eighth to the twelfth centuries A.D. are one of the cultural marvels of history.

If the Muslim world produced no single individual of infinite variety like Leonardo da Vinci (see Document 92), it did have many men of extremely broad interests. Such a versatile genius was ibn-Sina, or Avicenna, as he is more commonly known. As a physician, philosopher, mathematician, philologist, theologian, and astronomer, Avicenna wrote over one hundred treatises. No science was unknown to him. His fame as a physician was great in medieval Europe; his *Canon of Medicine*, a compendium of Graeco-Arabic knowledge, was first translated into Latin in the twelfth century and remained the standard textbook of medicine as late as the seventeenth century. In the following excerpts from Avicenna's autobiography and the supplementary biography of Al-Juzjani something of his dedication to learning and his breadth of interest is indicated.

Autobiography of Avicenna.

My father was a man of Balkh, and he moved from there to Bukhara during the days of Nūḥ ibn Mansūr; in his reign he was employed in the administration, being governor of a village-centre in the outlying district of Bukhara called Kharmaithan. Near by is a village named Afshana, and there my father married my mother and took up his residence; I was also born there, and after me my brother. Later we moved to Bukhara, where I was put under teachers of the Koran and of letters. By the time I was ten I had mastered the Koran and a great deal of literature, so that I was marvelled at for my aptitude.

Now my father was one of those who had responded to the Egyptian propagandist (who was an Ismaili); he, and my brother too, had listened to what they had to say about the Spirit and the Intellect, after the fashion in which they preach and understand the matter. They would therefore discuss these things together, while I listened and comprehended all that they said; but my spirit would not assent to their argument. Presently they began to invite me to join the movement, rolling on their tongues talk about philosophy, geometry, Indian arithmetic; and my father sent me to a certain vegetable-seller who used the Indian arithmetic, so that I might learn it from him. Then there came to Bukhara a man called Abū 'Abd Allāh al-Nātilī who claimed to be a philosopher; my father invited him to stay in our house, hoping that I would learn from him also. Before his advent I had already occupied myself wth Muslim jurisprudence, attending Ismā'īl the Ascetic; so I was an excellent enquirer, having become familiar with the methods of postulation and the techniques of rebuttal according to the usages of the canon lawyers. I now commenced reading the *Isagoge* (of Porphyry) with al-Nātilī: when he mentioned to me the definition of *genus* as a term applied to a number of things of different species in answer to the question "What is it?" I set about verifying this definition in a manner such as he had never heard. He marvelled at me exceedingly, and warned my father that I should not engage in any other occupation but learning; whatever problem he stated to me, I showed a better mental conception of it than he. So I continued until I had read all the straightforward parts of Logic with him; as for the subtler points, he had no acquaintance with them.

From then onward I took to reading texts of myself; I studied the commentaries, until I had completely mastered the science of Logic. Similarly with Euclid I read the first five or six figures with him, and thereafter undertook on my own account to solve the entire remainder of the book. Next I moved on to the *Almagest* (of Ptolemy); when I had finished the prolegomena and reached the geometrical figures, al-Nātilī told me to go on reading and to solve the problems by myself; I should merely revise what I read with him, so that he might indicate to me what was right and what was wrong. The truth is that he did not really teach this book; I began to solve the work, and many were the

Text: Arthur J. Arberry, *Avicenna on Theology* ("Wisdom of the East" series [London: John Murray, Ltd., 1951]), pp. 9-24.

complicated figures of which he had no knowledge until I presented them to him, and made him understand them. Then al-Nātilī took leave of me, setting out for Gurganj.

I now occupied myself with mastering the various texts and commentaries on natural science and metaphysics, until all the gates of knowledge were open to me. Next I desired to study medicine, and proceeded to read all the books that have been written on this subject. Medicine is not a difficult science, and naturally I excelled in it in a very short time, so that qualified physicians began to read medicine with me. I also undertook to treat the sick, and methods of treatment derived from practical experience revealed themselves to me such as baffle description. At the same time I continued between whiles to study and dispute on law, being now sixteen years of age.

The next eighteen months I devoted entirely to reading; I studied Logic once again, and all the parts of philosophy. During all this time I did not sleep one night through, nor devoted my attention to any other matter by day. I prepared a set of files; with each proof I examined, I set down the syllogistic premises and put them in order in the files, then I examined what deductions might be drawn from them. I observed methodically the conditions of the premises, and proceeded until the truth of each particular problem was confirmed for me. Whenever I found myself perplexed by a problem, or could not find the middle term in any syllogism, I would repair to the mosque and pray, adoring the All-Creator, until my puzzle was resolved and my difficulty made easy. At night I would return home, set the lamp before me, and busy myself with reading and writing; whenever sleep overcame me or I was conscious of some weakness, I turned aside to drink a glass of wine until my strength returned to me; then I went back to my reading. If ever the least slumber overtook me, I would dream of the precise problem which I was considering as I fell asleep; in that way many problems revealed themselves to me while sleeping. So I continued until I had made myself master of all the sciences; I now comprehended them to the limits of human possibility. All that I learned during that time is exactly as I know it now; I have added nothing more to my knowledge to this day.

I was now a master of Logic, natural sciences and mathematics. I therefore returned to metaphysics; I read the *Metaphysica* (of Aristotle), but did not understand its contents and was baffled by the author's intention; I read it over forty times, until I had the text by heart. Even then I did not understand it or what the author meant, and I despaired within myself, saying, "This is a book which there is no way of understanding." But one day at noon I chanced to be in the booksellers' quarter, and a broker was there with a volume in his hand which he was calling for sale. He offered it to me, but I returned it to him impatiently, believing that there was no use in this particular science. However he said to me, "Buy this book from me: it is cheap, and I will sell it to you for four dirhams. The owner is in need of the money." So I bought it, and found that it was a book by Abū Naṣr al-Fārābī *On the Objects of the Metaphysica*. I returned home and hastened to read it; and at once the objects of that book became clear to me, for I had it all by heart. I rejoiced at this, and upon the next day distributed much in alms to the poor in gratitude to Almighty God.

Now the Sultan of Bukhara at that time was Nūḥ ibn Manṣūr, and it happened that he fell sick of a malady which baffled all the physicians. My name was famous among them because of the breadth of my reading; they therefore mentioned me in his presence, and begged him to summon me. I attended the sick-room, and collaborated with them in treating the royal patient. So I came to be enrolled in his service. One day I asked his leave to enter their library, to examine the contents and read the books on medicine; he granted my request, and I entered a mansion with many chambers, each chamber having chests of books piled one upon another. In one apartment were books on language and poetry, in another law, and so on; each apartment was set aside for books on a single science. I glanced through the catalogue of the works of the ancient Greeks, and asked for those which I required; and I saw books whose very names are as yet unknown to many—works which I had never seen before and have not seen since. I read these books, taking notes of their contents; I came to realize the place each man occupied in his particular science.

So by the time I reached my eighteenth year I had exhausted all these sciences. My memory for learning was at that period of my life better than it is now, but to-day I am more mature; apart from this my knowledge is exactly the same, nothing further having been added to my store since then.

There lived near me in those days a man called Abu 'l-Ḥasan the Prosodist; he requested me to compose a comprehensive work on this science, and I wrote for him the *Majmūʿ* ("Compendium") which I named after him, including in it all the branches of knowledge except mathematics. At that time I was twenty-one. Another man lived in my neighbourhood called Abū Bakr al-Barqī, a Khwarizmian by birth; he was a lawyer at heart, his interests being focused on jurisprudence, exegesis and asceticism, to which subjects he was extremely inclined. He asked me to comment on his books, and I wrote for him *al-Ḥāṣil wa'l-maḥṣūl* ("The Import and the Substance") in about twenty volumes, as well as a work on ethics called *al-Birr wa'l-ithm* ("Good Works and Sin"); these two books are only to be found in his library, and are unknown to anyone else, so that they have never been copied.

Then my father died, and my circumstances changed. I accepted a post in the Sultan's employment, and was obliged to move from Bukhara to Gurganj, where Abu 'l-Ḥusain al-Sahlī was a minister, being a man devoted to these sciences. I was introduced to the Amir, 'Alī ibn al-Ma'mūn, being at that time dressed in the garb of lawyers, with scarf and chinwrap; they fixed a handsome salary for me, amply sufficient for the like of me. Then I was constrained to move to Nasa, and from there to Baward, and thence successively to Tus, Shaqqan, Samanqan, Jajarm the frontier-post of Khurasan, and Jurjan. My entire purpose was to come to the Amir Qābūs; but it happened meanwhile that Qābūs was taken and imprisoned in a fortress, where he died.

After this I went to Dihistan, where I fell very ill. I returned to Jurjan, and there made friends with Abū 'Ubaid al-Jūzjānī.

Biography of Avicenna.

From this point I mention those episodes of the Master's life of which I was myself a witness during my association with him, up to the time of his death.

There was at Jurjan a man called Abū Muḥammad al-Shīrāzī, who loved these sciences; he had bought for the Master a house near where he lived, and lodged him there. I used to visit him every day, reading the *Almagest* and listening to him lecturing on Logic; he dictated to me *al-Mukhtaṣar al-ausaṭ* ("The Middle Summary") on that subject. For Abū Muḥammad al-Shīrāzī he composed *al-Mabda' wa'l-ma'ād* ("The Origin and the Return") and *al-Arṣād al-kullīya* ("The General Observations"). He wrote many books there, such as the first part of *al-Qānūn* ("The Canon"), the *Mukhtaṣar al-Majisṭī* ("Summary of Almagest") and many essays. Then he composed in the Jebel country the rest of his books.

After this the master removed to Raiy, where he joined the service of al-Saiyida and her son Majd al-Daula; they knew of him because of the many letters he brought with him containing appreciations of his worth. At that time Majd al-Daula was overcome by melancholy, and the Master applied himself to treating him. At Raiy he composed the *Kitāb al-Ma'ād* ("Book of the Return"), staying there until Shams al-Daula attacked the city following the slaying of Hilāl ibn Badr ibn Hasanawaih and the rout of the Baghdad army. Thereafter circumstances conspired to oblige him to leave Raiy for Qazwin, and from Qazwin he proceeded to Hamadhan, where he entered the service of Kadhbānūya in order to investigate her finances. Shams al-Daula then became acquainted with him, and summoned him to his court because of an attack of colic which had afflicted him; he treated him, until God cured him of the sickness, and he departed from his palace loaded with many costly robes. So he returned home, having passed forty days and nights at the palace and become one of the Amir's intimates.

Now it came to pass that the Amir went up to Qarmisin, to make war on 'Anāz, the Master accompanying him; but he was routed, and returned to Hamadhan. They then asked him [Avicenna] to take the office of vizier, and he accepted; but the army conspired against him, fearing for themselves on his account; they surrounded his house, haled him off to prison, pillaged his belongings, and took all that he possessed. They even demanded of the Amir that he should put him to death, but this he refused, though he was agreeable to banishing him from the State, being anxious to conciliate them. The Master concealed himself for forty days in the house of Abū Sa'd ibn Dakhdūk; at the end of which time Shams al-Daula was again attacked by colic, and sent for him. He came to court, and the Amir apologized to him profoundly; so the Master applied himself to treating him. As a result he continued in honour and high consideration at court, and was appointed vizier a second time.

Then it was that I asked him to write a commentary on the works of Aristotle; but he remarked that he had not the leisure at that time, adding, "If you will be satisfied for me to compose a book setting forth the parts of those sciences which I believe to be sound, not disputing therein with any opponents nor troubling to reply to their arguments, I will gladly do so." This offer I accepted, and he began work on the physical sections of the *Kitāb al-Shifā'* ("Book of the Remedy"). He had already composed the first book of the *Qānūn;* and every night students gathered in his house, and by turns I would read the *Shifā'* and another the *Qānūn*. When we had finished the allotted portion the various musicians would enter; vessels were brought out for a drinking party; and so we occupied ourselves. The studying was done by night because during the day his attendance upon the Amir left him no spare time.

We continued after this fashion for some while. Then the Amir set out for Tarm, to fight the prince of that place. Upon this expedition the colic again visited the Amir near Tarm; the attack was severe, and was aggravated by complications brought on by his irregular habits and his disinclination to follow the Master's advice. The army feared he would die, and at once returned towards Hamadhan carrying him in a cradle, but he died on the way. Shams al-Daula's son was thereupon sworn in as Amir, and the army now requested that the Master should be appointed vizier, but this he declined; he corresponded in secret with 'Alā' al-Daula, seeking to come to his court and join his service. . . .

So some time elapsed. . . . Then it seemed good to the Master to betake himself to Isfahan; he went forth in disguise, accompanied by myself, his brother and two slaves, in the habit of Sufis, and so we reached Tabaran at the gate of Isfahan, having suffered great hardships on the way. Friends of the Master, and courtiers of 'Alā' al-Daula came out to welcome him; robes were brought, and fine equipages, and he was lodged in a quarter called Gun-Gunbadh at the house of 'Abd Allāh b. Bābā; his apartment was furnished and carpeted in the most ample manner. At court he was received with the respect and consideration which he so richly merited; and 'Alā' al-Daula appointed every Friday night a meeting for learned discussion before him, to be attended by all the scholars according to their various degrees, the Master Abū 'Alī among them; in these gatherings he proved himself quite supreme and unrivalled in every branch of learning.

At Isfahan he set about completing the *Shifā'*; he finished the logic and the *Almagest*, and had already epitomized Euclid, the arithmetic and the music. In each book of the mathematical section he introduced supplementary materials as he thought to be necessary; in the *Almagest* he brought up ten new figures on various points of speculation, and in the astonomical section at the end of that work he added things which had never been discovered before. In the same way he introduced some new examples into Euclid, enlarged the arithmetic with a number of excellent refinements, and discussed problems on music which the ancient Greeks had wholly neglected. So he finished the *Shifā'*, all but the botany and zoology which he composed in the year when 'Alā' al-Daula marched to Sabur-Khwast; these parts he wrote *en route*, as well as the *Kitāb al-Najāt* ("Book of Deliverance").

The Master had now become one of the intimate courtiers of 'Alā' al-Daula. When the latter determined to attack Hamadhan, the Master accompanied him; and one night a discussion took place in the Amir's presence concerning the imperfections that occur in the astronomical tables according to the observations of the ancients. The Amir commanded the Master to undertake observations of the stars, supplying him with all the funds he might require; so he began this new work, deputing me to select the instruments and engage the skilled assistants needed. So many old problems were elucidated, it being found that the imperfections in the former observations were due to their being conducted in the course of many journeys, with all the impediments resulting therefrom.

At Isfahan the Master also wrote the *'Alā'ī* (an encyclopaedia named after 'Alā' al-Daula). Now one of the remarkable things about the Master was, that during the twenty-five years I accompanied and served him I never saw him take a new book and read it right through; he looked always for the difficult passages and complicated problems and examined what the author had said on these, so as to discover what his degree of learning and level of understanding might be.

One day the Master was seated before the Amir, and Abū Manṣūr al-Jabbān was also present. A philological problem came up for discussion; the Master gave his views as they occurred to him, whereupon Abū Manṣūr turned to him and remarked, "You are a philosopher and a wise man; but you have never studied philology to such an extent that we should be pleased to hear you discourse on the subject." The Master was stung by this rebuke, and devoted the next three years to studying books on philology; he even sent for the *Tahdhīb al-lugha* of Abū Manṣūr al-Azharī from Khurasan. So he achieved a knowledge of philology but rarely attained. He composed three odes full of rare expressions, as well as three letters—one in the style of Ibn al-'Amīd, one after the fashion of al-Ṣāḥib, and the third imitating al-Ṣābī; then he ordered these to be bound, and the binding to be rubbed. So he suggested to the Amir that he should show this volume to Abū Manṣūr al-Jabbān, remarking that "we found this volume in the desert while hunting, and you must look it through and tell us what it contains". Abū Manṣūr examined the book, and was baffled by many passages occurring in it. The Master suggested to him that "all you are ignorant of in this book you can find mentioned in such-and-such a context in the works on philology", naming books well known in that science; for he had memorized these phrases from them. Abū Manṣūr merely conjectured as to the words which the Master introduced, without any real certainty as to their meaning; then he realized that the letters had really been composed by the Master, and that he had been induced to do so by the affront he had offered him that day; he therefore extracted himself from the situation by apologizing to the Master. The latter then composed a work on philology which he entitled *Lisān al-ʿArab* ("The Arab Language"), the like of which was never composed; he did not transcribe it into a fair copy, so that at his death it was still in the rough draft and no man could discover a way to put it in order. . . .

While engaged upon his astronomical observations the Master invented instruments the like of which had never been seen before; he also composed a treatise on the subject. I remained eight years engaged upon this work, my object being to verify the observations which Ptolemy reported on his own account, and in fact some part of these were confirmed for me. The Master also composed the *Kitāb al-Inṣāf* ("Book of Rectification"), but on the day when Sultan Masʿūd came to Isfahan his army plundered the Master's luggage; this book was part of it, and was never seen again.

The Master was powerful in all his faculties, and he was especially strong sexually; this indeed was a prevailing passion with him, and he indulged it to such an extent that his constitution was affected; yet he relied upon his powerful constitution to pull him through. At last in the year when ʿAlāʾ al-Daula fought Tāsh Farrāsh at the gates of al-Karkh, the Master was attacked by the colic; because of his eagerness to cure himself—being afraid the Amir might suffer defeat, in which case his sickness would not allow him to travel back—he injected himself eight times in a single day, so that his intestines were ulcerated and the abrasion showed on him. Yet he must needs accompany ʿAlāʾ al-Daula; so they made haste towards Idhaj, where the epilepsy which sometimes follows colic manifested itself. Despite this he continued to treat himself, taking injections for the abrasion and the rest of the colic. One day he ordered the mixing of two *dangs* of celery-seed in the injection, desiring to break the wind of the colic; one of the physicians attending him put in five *dirhams* of celery seed—I know not whether purposely or in error, for I was not with him—and the sharpness of the celery aggravated the abrasion. He also took *mithradatum* for the epilepsy; but one of his slaves went and threw in a great quantity of opium, and he consumed the mixture; this being because they had robbed him of much money from his treasury, and they desired to do away with him so that they might escape the penalty of their actions.

In this state the Master was brought to Isfahan, where he continued to look after himself, though he was now so weak that he could no longer stand; nevertheless he went on treating himself, until he was able to walk. He once more attended the court of ʿAlāʾ al-Daula; however, he was incautious and indulged his sexual appetite too far, so that he was never wholly cured, suffering repeated relapses. Then ʿAlāʾ al-Daula marched towards Hamadhan, and the Master went with him; the same malady revisited him upon the way, and when he finally reached Hamadhan he knew that his strength was exhausted and no longer adequate to repel the disease. He therefore gave up treating himself, and took to saying, "The manager who used to manage me is incapable of managing me any more; so it is no use trying to cure my sickness."

So he continued some days, and was then transported to the Presence of his Lord. He was buried at Hamadhan, being 58 years old; his death occurred in the year 428.

INTERPRETATION OF ISLAM

62 H. A. R. GIBB, *MOHAMMEDANISM: THE EXPANSION OF ISLAM*

Most writers, says Hamilton A. R. Gibb, the distinguished Arabic scholar, "approach the subject of Mohammedanism from one or other of two opposed points of view, neither of which is free from conscious prejudgment." On the one hand, there are the practicing Muslims, determined to defend their faith from outside attack, and on the other, those who look upon Islam as a distinctly inferior religion—this latter view has been particularly noticeable in the writings of Christian missionaries. His own interpretation, says Gibb, is influenced by two beliefs, "that Islam is an autonomous expression of thought and experience which must be viewed in and through itself and its own principles and standards," and that, "while the practice of every religion to some extent falls short of its highest ideals, the exposition of an outside observer should lay more stress upon the ideals which it strives to realize than upon the failings of our own common humanity." This is the approach which Professor Gibb takes in his provocative monograph *Mohammedanism*, a selection from which appears below. In the essay Gibb traces the development of Islam in western Asia and the spread of Islamic ideas throughout the Mediterranean world and at the same time examines some of the processes by which its institutions were given their uniquely Islamic character.

Dr. Gibb, who is currently at Harvard University, was for many years Professor of Oriental Studies at Oxford. He is considered one of the outstanding living authorities on the Islamic world.

But still more astonishing than the speed of the [Muhammadan] conquests was their orderly character. Some destruction there must have been during the years of warfare, but by and large the Arabs, so far from leaving a trail of ruin, led the way to a new integration of peoples and cultures. The structure of law and government which Mohammed had bequeathed to his successors, the Caliphs, proved its value in controlling these Bedouin armies. Islam emerged into the civilized outer world, not as the crude superstition of marauding hordes, but as a moral force that commanded respect and a coherent doctrine that could challenge on their own ground the Christianity of East Rome and the Zoroastrianism of Persia. It is true that the tribal instincts and traditions of the Bedouin broke out from time to time in revolts and civil wars; but in the end they served only to affirm more effectively the strength and the will to order of the new imperial power.

To the peoples of the conquered countries the Arab supremacy signified at first little more than a change of masters. There was no breach in the continuity of their life and social institutions, no persecution, no forced conversion. But little by little Islam began to modify the old social structure of Western Asia and Egypt, and Arab elements to penetrate the old Hellenistic and Persian cultures. The Arab colonies planted in the newly won territories were not merely garrison towns and headquarters of armies; they were also centres from which the new religion was propagated. Enriched by the wealth drawn from the subject provinces and swelled by the constant influx of converts, they became the matrices of the new Islamic civilization.

Already in 660 the capital of the Arab Empire had shifted to Damascus, the seat of the new dynasty of Caliphs of the Umayyad House. While Medina remained the centre of Muslim religious learning, the government and public life of the Empire were influenced by the Hellenistic tradition of East Rome. This first stage of interaction with the older civilizations is symbolized by the two exquisite monuments of the Umayyad age, the Great Mosque of Damascus and the Dome of the Rock at Jerusalem, as well as by the sudden profusion of sects and heresies in the 'new provinces'. But the ultimate consequence was a cleavage between the religious and secular institutions of the Muslim community, which sapped the foundations of the Umayyad Caliphate and, reinforced by the grievances of the non-Arab subjects and the outbreak of a civil war between the Arab tribes, brought about their downfall in A.D. 750.

Such a conflict, however, demonstrates that in the century that had elapsed since the death of Mohammed the religious culture of Islam had itself undergone a considerable development and consolidation in its Medinian homeland. A great religious teacher on the one hand represents the culmination of a spiritual process. He sums up its essentials and so vitalizes them by his personality and his insight that they come to his fellow-men as a revelation of new truth. On the other hand, he stands at the beginning of a new spiritual process, whose width and depth are determined not so much by his own vision as by the spiritual insight of his followers and their capacity to develop his teaching. Still more is this the case when the original teaching expands over wide areas outside its original home, and in contact with other deep-rooted cultures and civilizations is subjected to those interactions and pressures to which all living organisms are exposed.

The new tensions which were created in and by Islam and the new spiritual standards and

Text: Hamilton A. R. Gibb, *Mohammedanism: An Historical Survey*, 2nd ed. (London: Oxford University Press, 1953), pp. 4-22 *passim*.

ideals which it set up will be analysed in their proper place. Here we are concerned only to note the immediate release of intellectual energies which paralleled the expansion of the Arabs into the outer world. The vitality of the imprint made by Mohammed on the minds of his followers is shown by the cultural stimulus which it gave—in the first instance, of course, within the field of the religious movement itself. In assimilating and expanding the new teaching, system and method were introduced into the intellectual life of the Arabs. New sciences were founded: the study of the Prophetic Tradition, philology, history, and above all law. The transformation is amazing when one looks back at the intellectual poverty and isolation of Medina a bare hundred years before, still more when it is remembered that this was in the main the work of Arabs themselves, building upon the foundations laid by Mohammed, self-evolved with none but the most meagre external influences.

This was the fundamental and decisive contribution of the Arabs to the new Muslim culture. To its material civilization they contributed little. That began its brilliant career when the dynasty of Abbasid Caliphs succeeded to the Umayyads and founded their new capital of Baghdad in 762. The first age of external conquest was over, and to it succeeded an age of internal expansion. The ninth and tenth centuries witnessed the climax of Islamic civilization in breadth and creative effort. Industry, commerce, architecture, and the minor arts flourished with immense vitality as Persia, Mesopotamia, Syria, and Egypt brought their contribution to the common stock.

These new energies found an outlet in intellectual life as well. While the Medinian sciences continued to develop in a score of new centres strung out from Samarqand to North Africa and Spain, literature and thought, drawing upon Greek, Persian, and even Indian sources, broke out in new directions, often independent of the Muslim tradition and more or less in revolt against the narrowness of the orthodox system. Under the stimulus of the widening physical and intellectual horizons the material and the spiritual were interacting at the highest pressure.

It is difficult to indicate in a few words the many-sided intellectual activities of this age. The older 'Muslim sciences' of history and philology broadened out to embrace secular history and belles-lettres. Greek medical and mathematical science were made accessible in a library of translations and were developed by Persian and Arab scholars, especially in algebra, trigonometry, and optics. Geography—perhaps the most sensitive barometer of culture—flowered in all its branches, political, organic, mathematical, astronomical, natural science, and travel, and reached out to embrace the lands and civilizations of far-distant peoples.

While these new sciences touched only the fringes of the religious culture, the inroads of Greek logic and philosophy inevitably produced a sharp and bitter conflict, which came to a head in the third Islamic century. The leaders of Islam saw its spiritual foundations endangered by the subtle infidelities of pure rationalism, and although they ultimately triumphed over the Hellenizing school, philosophy always remained an object of suspicion in their eyes, even when it came to be studied merely as an apologetic tool. More serious still, however, were the further consequences of their victory—the growth in theological circles of a kind of jealousy of any intellectual pursuit which was purely secular or ventured beyond the range of their control.

Such a deliberate narrowing-down of intellectual interests had one peculiar effect. The Medinian sciences rested on a foundation of Arabic philology, and Arabic philology was based upon the old pre-Islamic poetry. Just as the learning of Western Christianity in the Middle Ages was based exclusively upon Latin, and thus preserved in uneasy partnership with the Christian tradition the poetry, mythology, and social heritage of Rome, so the Muslim scholar steeped himself in the literary and social heritage of the ancient Arabs. Their virtues were idealized, their proverbs supplied the staple of popular ethics. That the whole of Muslim literature in its first four formative centuries was written in Arabic, and that it was pervaded at all points by this Arab tradition, are the factors chiefly responsible for the enduring Arabian impress upon Islamic culture.

The struggle to subordinate all intellectual life to the authority of religion went on for many centuries in successive regions of the Muslim world. Where no fresh stimulus arose to prolong and revive flagging energies, the religious culture caught all other intellectual activities on the rebound, and by minor concessions held them and converted them into its own instruments. Those which it could not use, such as medicine and mathematics, stagnated or ultimately died away. But from time to time fresh outbursts of creative activity, like that in Muslim Spain in the eleventh and twelfth centuries, bore witness to the continuing absorptive and expansive power of the Islamic civilization.

Yet again, the assertion of the supremacy of the religious culture could not have succeeded had that culture not offered within itself enough scope for the active exercise of the intellectual faculties. The study which in some sense took the place of the discarded sciences was not, however, theology. The master science of the Muslim world was Law. Law, indeed, might be said to embrace all things, human and divine, and both for its comprehensiveness and for the ardour with which its study was pursued it would be hard to find a parallel elsewhere, except in Judaism.

But apart altogether from its intellectual pre-eminence and scholastic function, Islamic Law was the most far-reaching and effective agent in moulding the social order and the community life of the Muslim peoples. By its very comprehensiveness it exerted a steady pressure upon all private and social activities, setting a standard to which they conformed more and more closely as time went on, in spite of the resistance of ancient habits and time-honoured customs, especially amongst the more independent nomadic and mountain tribes. Moreover, Islamic Law gave practical expression to the characteristic Muslim quest for unity. In all essentials it was uniform, although the various schools differed in points of detail. To its operation was due the striking convergence of social ideals and ways of life throughout the medieval Muslim world. It went far deeper than Roman law; by reason of its religious bases and its theocratic sanctions it was the spiritual regulator, the conscience, of the Muslim community in all its parts and activities.

This function of law acquired still greater significance as political life in the Muslim world swung ever further away from the theocratic ideal of Mohammed and his successors. The decline of the Abbasid Caliphate in the tenth and eleventh centuries opened the door to political disintegration, the usurpation of royal authority by local princes and military governors, the rise and fall of ephemeral dynasties, and repeated outbreaks of civil war. But however seriously the political and military strength of the vast Empire might be weakened, the moral authority of the Law was but the more enhanced and held the social fabric of Islam compact and secure through all the fluctuations of political fortune.

At the end of the tenth century, the geographical area of Islam was but little wider than it had been in 750. But a great civilization had been built up, brilliant in intellectual life, wealthy and enterprising in economic life, powerfully cemented by an authoritative Law—the whole a visible embodiment of the temporal and spiritual might of Islam. As its military strength declined, it, like the Roman Empire six centuries before, fell gradually under the domination of the barbarians from beyond its frontiers, but also, like the Roman Empire, imposed upon the barbarians its religion, its law, and respect for its civilization.

These barbarians were Turkish tribesmen from Central Asia. The same westward pressure that had carried the Bulgars, Magyars, Comans, and Patzinaks into Southern Russia and Eastern Europe carried other tribes into Persia and westward into Iraq and Anatolia. The work of conversion to Islam had begun while they were still in their Central Asian homelands; consequently, the establishment of Turkish Sultanates in Western Asia made at first little outward difference to the domestic life of the Muslim community. The first result was a fresh military expansion; south-eastwards into Northern India, north-westwards into Asia Minor. Simultaneously, in the far West, nomadic Berber tribesmen were carrying Islam into the fringes of Negro Africa in the Senegal and Niger basins, while nomadic Arab tribesmen, no longer controlled by the religious authority of the early Caliphs, were destroying by pillage and neglect the centres of civilization that their Arab predecessors had built on the debris of Roman and Byzantine Africa.

The resurgence of the nomadic elements in all parts of the Muslim world confronted the Muslim community with a problem which has close analogies with the problem of the Christian Church confronted by the Germanic kingdoms. Islam had grown up within the framework of an urban civilization. Its social background was the settled life of the centralized State, and so strong had this tradition become that, as the example just mentioned shows, its influence amongst even the Bedouin Arabs had dwindled away. It was now faced with the task of making the religious order and culture effective within a social structure in which tribalism predominated. The old solution (dating back to Mohammed himself), to force or beguile the tribesmen into settled life, could now be applied at most only to the small group of ruling tribes who formed the retinue and officers of the Sultan in the new capital cities. Although the Sultans themselves were often enthusiastic Muslims, and their governments within two or three generations conformed to the normal patterns of the settled communities into which they had come, they were seldom able to maintain complete control over their nomadic or semi-nomadic followers.

This task of preventing the social and cultural disintegration of Islam and of bringing the tribesmen within the radius of its civilizing and cohesive forces was met by a new instrument which had been forged among the urban populations during the preceding centuries. By this time the pressure of Muslim doctrine and practice had mastered most of the resistances that had, at an earlier time, sought an outlet in heterodox and subversive movements. But this did not lead to stagnation. On the contrary, the devotional feeling of the townsmen, grinding a channel of its own, burst the bonds of orthodox disciplines and found a new freedom in the ranges of mysticism. From the eleventh century onwards mysticism enlisted in its service a large proportion of the vital spiritual energies of the Muslim community, and created within Islam a fount of self-renewal which maintained its spiritual vigour through all the later centuries of political and economic decay.

The growth and development of Sūfism (to give this movement its proper name) display many of the characteristic features of Islamic culture. It welled up from below, by the spontaneous action of individual citizens, mostly of the urban artisan classes. No formal authorization or recognition was asked for or received—at first, indeed, there was much opposition from the learned and some persecution. It remained autonomous and personal and only after some centuries of growth began to organize itself in institutional forms. Above all, in the tension between the element of rigidity represented by the Sacred Law and the element of flexibility arising out of the spiritual intuition of the individual, it conformed to the pattern which runs through all the spiritual and cultural manifestations of Islam.

The mystics, whether as individual missionaries or (later on) as members of organized brotherhoods, were the leaders in the task of conversion among the pagans and the superficially Islamized tribes. The most successful missions were often those of co-nationals of the tribesmen, uncouth, illiterate, and crude though many of them were. They laid the foundations upon which in later generations the refining influences of orthodox law and theology could be brought to bear. It was mainly due to them that through successive centuries the religious frontiers of Islam were steadily extended in Africa, in India and Indonesia, across Central Asia into Turkestan and China, and in parts of South-eastern Europe.

All this activity offers a close parallel to the work of the monastic organizations in Northern and Central Europe. But Muslim missionary activity was always peculiarly individual and unregulated. The Sūfi movement was never fully co-ordinated with the orthodox scholastic organization, but jealously maintained independence of, and even some degree of antagonism towards it. There was no orthodox central authority to bring them together and to assume the control and direction of Sūfi activities. True, there was at one time the Caliphate. But the Caliphate was not a Papacy, and from Umayyad times on the theologians and legists had resolutely refused to concede to it any spiritual authority. The Caliphs were the religious as well as secular heads of the Islamic community, in that they embodied the supremacy of the Faith and the Sacred Law. But an attempt by three Caliphs in the ninth century to define orthodox dogma was decisively defeated, and the attempt was never repeated.

Furthermore, independent rulers, while outwardly acknowledging the religious authority of the Caliphs, were quick to resent and to suppress interference in the affairs of their kingdoms. Not infrequently they held their Sūfi spiritual directors in higher esteem than the orthodox scholars and legists, who for their part also found themselves in a somewhat ambiguous relationship to the secular power.

Since the tenth century the State had gradually diverged more and more from the path traced out by the Muslim theorists. It elaborated an ethic of its own, whose values were derived from the old imperial traditions of Asia and very far removed from the Islamic values. Against this inverted culture the Muslim legists waged an unceasing struggle, in the effort to reconvert the State into an embodiment of the principles of the Sacred Law. Later on, indeed, Muslim political theorists, accommodating themselves to the changed situation, began to distinguish Caliphate from Kingship, applying the former term in a new sense to denote any government which recognized and enforced the Sacred Law, as against a secular despotism which governed by arbitrary or natural law.

But while the conflict to maintain the Muslim ideals preserved the spiritual and intellectual life of Islam from stagnation, the legists were fighting on the whole a losing battle. The fault lay partly in themselves, that the more scrupulous were loth to hold any religious office under the Sultans and, in rejecting public service, left the field to their more time-serving and less scrupulous brethren. While the purity of their motives may be respected, their withdrawal weakened their power to combat effectively the vices which were taking firm root amongst the governing classes in every province of the Muslim world. The middle classes in general, on the other hand, accepted—if they did not always live up to—the Islamic ideal, and as time went on both they and the theologian-legists were more and more permeated by Sūfi influences. Thus one may say, with some little exaggeration, that in the Muslim world, concealed by common outward profession of Islam, there were two distinct societies living side by side and interacting to some extent but in their basic principles opposed to one another.

The evolution sketched above was greatly accelerated by the disasters which followed one another in Western Asia in the thirteenth and fourteenth centuries. A first invasion of heathen Mongols devastated the north-eastern provinces between 1220 and 1225. The second wave occupied Persia and Iraq, put an end to the historic Caliphate of Baghdad in 1256, and made the whole eastern Muslim world, except Egypt, Arabia, and Syria, tributary to the vast Mongol Empire. The remnants were saved by the military caste of Turkish and Circassian 'slaves', the Mamlūks, who had seized the political power in Egypt. Under Mamlūk rule the old Arabic Muslim civilization continued for some two and a half centuries to flourish in the material arts (especially in architecture and metalwork), but with a gradual decay of spiritual and intellectual vigour.

Meanwhile, a revived and in some respects brilliant Persian Muslim civilization grew up in the Mongol dominions. It too excelled in architecture and the fine arts, including the art of miniature painting; spiritually it was rooted in Sūfism. In spite of two virulent 'Black Deaths' and the destructive campaigns of Timur (Tamerlane) in the fourteenth century, which reduced Persia itself to a state of extreme physical exhaustion, Persian culture moulded the intellectual life of the new Islamic empires that were growing up on either side—in Anatolia and the Balkans, and in India.

The expansion of the Ottoman Empire in Asia and North Africa and the establishment of the Mughal Empire in India in the sixteenth century brought the greater part of the Muslim world once more under the government of powerful and highly centralized civil States. A marked feature of both Empires was the strong emphasis laid on Muslim orthodoxy and the Sacred Law; Church and State were not indeed unified, since the military and higher civil polity was constructed on independent non-Islamic lines, but buttressed one another by a sort of concordat that endured into the nineteenth century.

Yet of the two channels of Muslim religious life the mystical was the broader and deeper. The seventeenth and early eighteenth centuries saw the apogee of the Sūfi brotherhoods. The greater orders spread a network of congregations from end to end of the Islamic world, while smaller local orders and sub-orders grouped the members of different classes and occupations into compact communities. . . .

The net result of this expansion over thirteen centuries is that Islam is to-day the dominant religion in a wide belt of territory which extends across North Africa and Western Asia up to the Pamirs and thence eastwards through Central Asia into China proper. In India it is professed by several large and many smaller communities, then becomes predominant again in the Malay Peninsula and through the chain of the East Indies till it tapers away in the Philippines. On the western coast of the Indian Ocean it extends down a narrow strip of the African coast to Zanzibar and Tanganyika, with discontinuous groups continuing into the Union of South Africa. In Europe Muslim communities exist in most of the Balkan countries and in Southern Russia, and it is represented in both North and South America by small groups of immigrants from the Middle East.

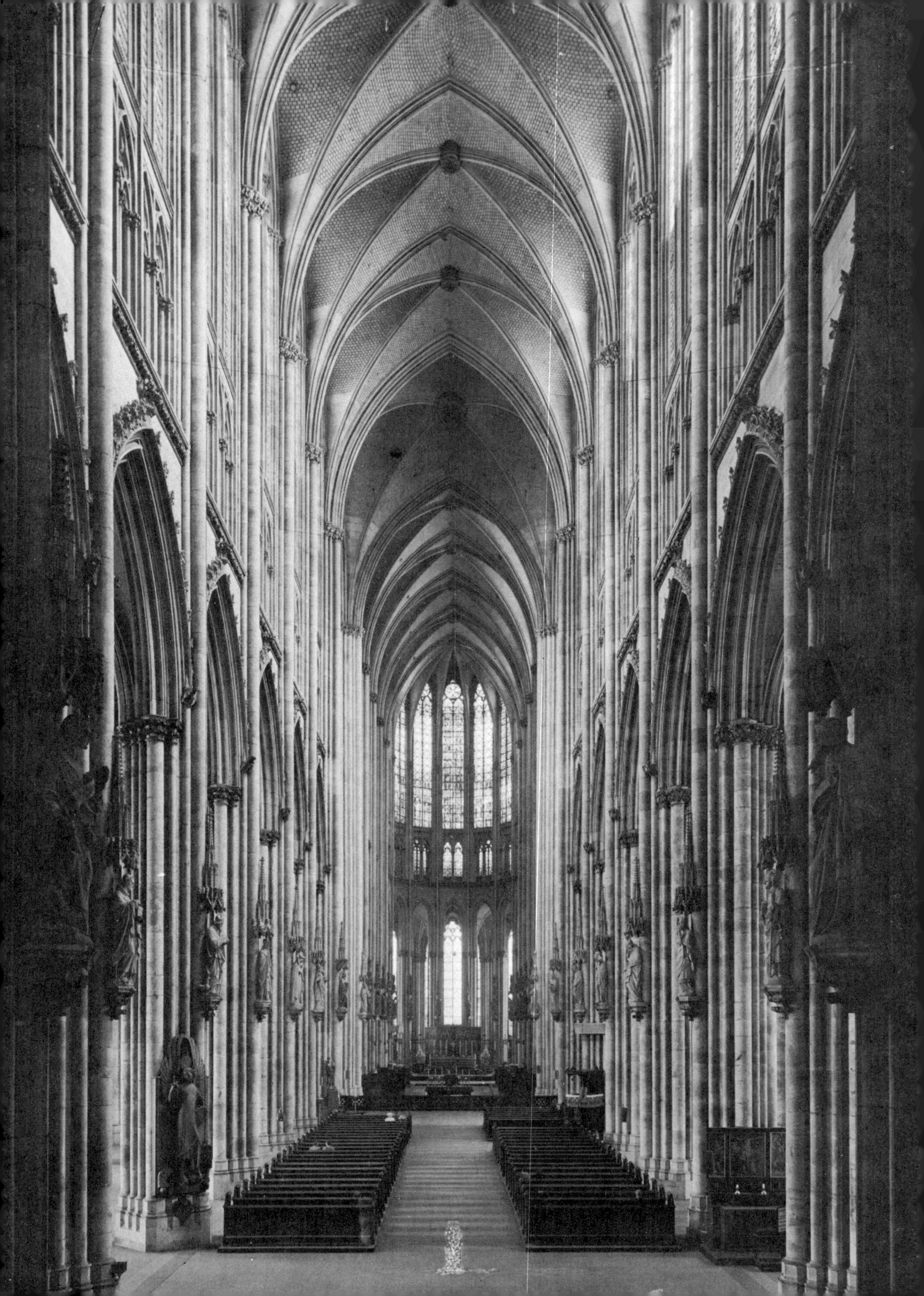

Part IV
The Middle Ages

The interior of the cathedral at Cologne (opposite page); an argricultural scene from a Flemish manuscript of 1482 (top); Harlech Castle in Wales, built in the late thirteenth century (bottom).

INTRODUCTION

How men come to grips with their environment is reflected in the changes they bring about in the landscape. Evidence of Roman power is still seen in the ruins of massive public buildings and triumphal arches in a hundred cities and of aqueducts, bridges, and roads in the surrounding countryside. The medieval landscape in western Europe was no less significant for the way of life it portrayed. The great Roman roads, along which had posted imperial couriers and marched Roman legions guarding far-flung frontiers, had fallen into disuse to be overgrown with brambles. For where once all roads had led ultimately to Rome, in medieval Europe there was "no place to go" in the former, compelling sense. With the overthrow of the imperial structure and economy, the cities of western Europe had contracted, commerce had withered, and life had decelerated to the subsistence level. Cities call for highways, but now villages took root in woodland clearings—western Europe was still heavily forested in the Middle Ages—and along natural routes by land and water, such as near fording places or within bowshot of sites that could be readily defended. In place of imperial highways there proliferated a network of narrow, winding farm roads leading to the fields and of woodland trackways linking scattered villages. Here, then, is a typical profile of the medieval rural landscape: a clearing near a stream with a cluster of cottages at one end of a small bridge; above the roof line the tower of the parish church; and above the tree line, on a nearby eminence, the rounded tower of a baronial keep. Let us examine the three main elements of this picture—the castle, the village, and the church—and their significance for medieval life.

THE CASTLE

The *castra* spaced along the Rhine and Danube had constituted part of a vast Roman fortifications system that guarded the sprawling perimeter of the empire. But with the crumbling of these defenses, the interior lands never recovered the stability which the barbarian invasions had destroyed. True, Charlemagne (742-814) had attempted to restore the empire in the West, but despite his lifelong efforts to achieve and retain political control over a relatively small part of it—an effort that kept him almost constantly on horseback—after his death the territory was quickly fragmentized. In 847, when the Carolingian Empire was breaking up, all freemen were ordered to place themselves under lords who could protect them, an admission of the government's incapacity to do so. Having gained immunity from royal interference, the landed aristocracy became virtually independent. The rank of the noble was generally an indication of the amount of land his tenants farmed, the number of mounted retainers—or knights—he could muster to his banner, and the size and splendor of his castle, at once his military stronghold, his administrative center, and his social capital. Consequently, the castle symbolized the emergence of feudalism, in which the possession of land—the physical foundation of the entire system—was carefully controlled by a rigidly enforced caste structure involving personal obligations between lords and their vassals.

In effect feudalism, which became the dominant social system of Europe by 900, was man's answer to the political disintegration and geographical fragmentation that followed the collapse of the Carolingian Empire. In retrospect, feudalism seems a crude and static system, but it ensured survival and stabilized society at a critical time in western history. Feudalism, moreover, upheld the rule of law. The interdependence of rights and duties between noble and vassal, the responsibilities entailed in tenure and use of land—these were the concerns of the medieval courts of justice. In an age of local loyalties, warfare was well-nigh universal, yet even here the Church attempted to bring it under the rule of law by subjecting to spiritual punishment those who desecrated churches and other holy places, who fought during Lent, or who injured noncombatants. Finally, by its insistence upon the sanctity of human contracts, however often these might be violated in practice, feudalism made its contribution to the founding of modern democratic concepts.

The castle was also the center and arbiter of social behavior. In the highly stratified feudal society, strict rules of conduct governed the lives of the castle's "gentle born" who took their places at the banqueting table "above the salt" as well as the lives of the commoners who sat at the lower end. Formalized into what is known as chivalry, the feudal code of behavior and deportment placed supreme value upon fidelity to the Church and one's lord and vows, and stressed the protection of women, children, and the infirm. However restrictive in practice— for a peasant's daughter could not expect the same courtesy or security of person as a duke's daughter despite their similarity of sex—chivalry proved a useful, indeed necessary, antidote to the crudities and violence of a society that had retrogressed to civilization's lower level. The chivalric code, moreover, did inspire deeds of courage and generosity among some of the most renowned figures in medieval society and acted as a constant source of inspiration to the poets and troubadours who entertained the isolated inhabitants of the castle, where life tended otherwise to be as drab and monotonous as the forbidding expanse of gray stone.

VILLAGE AND MANOR

Meanwhile, the food and fuel consumed in the castle were being supplied by the labor of the nearby villagers. Much of the land cultivated in Roman times had reverted to woodland in the early Middle Ages; between the sixth and tenth centuries the amount of land reclaimed for cultivation was probably offset by areas which were lost to farming as a result of political disorder and the ravages of the Norsemen and the Angles, Saxons, and Jutes along the riverine lands of western Europe. After 1000 A.D., however, the clearing and cultivation of forest and marshy areas was accelerated, and this in turn enabled medieval Europe to support a larger population. This development was accompanied by significant improvements in farming methods, such as the introduction of the three-field system of planting, which resulted in larger plantings and harvests, and the invention of improved harnesses and collars, which relieved the pressure on draft animals' windpipes, so that they could pull loads up to four times as heavy as formerly.

The freemen and serfs who tilled the land lived in compact villages—cottages lining a single street. There might be some fifty families in a typical village, with each receiving an annual allotment of strips of land for cultivation. Much of the land was shared by all, such as the woods and the "common" where the animals were pastured. This village estate, which if large might encompass 5000 acres, belonged to the local noble and was known as his manor. Part of the manor was called the demesne, and this section of the best farming land was worked by serfs for the direct use of the lord's own household. The manor together with its village was thus the basic unit of the feudal economy, and its administration was composed of representatives of both "management" and "labor." If the lord possessed a number of manors, he had a "steward" who administered all of them, while his representative on a particular manor was the "bailiff," who collected rents and dues and inspected the peasants' work. Chosen by villagers to protect their interests were the reeves, one of whom was described by Chaucer in the following lines:

Well could he keep a garner and a bin,
There was no auditor could do him in.
And he could estimate by drought and rain
What he would get from seed, and how much grain. . . .
No bailiff, herd or hind but he could tell
Their shifts and trickeries—he knew them well;
These fellows feared him as they feared the death.[1]

To Chaucer we can also turn for "profiles" of other types to be found on the manor. He gives us a sympathetic description of the Ploughman:

[He] in his time had carted many a load
Of dung; true toiler and a good was he,
Living in peace and perfect charity.
And always for the poor he loved to labor,
And he would thresh and ditch and dyke, and take
Nothing for pay, but do it for Christ's sake.
Fairly he paid his tithes when they were due,
Upon his goods and on his produce, too.

Much less attractive was the "thick-shouldered, knotty, broad, and tough" Miller who could unhinge a door by ramming it with his head:

Broad gaped his mouth as some great furnace door.
He would go babbling boastfully, or roar
Jests full of sin and vile scurrility.
He stole, and multiplied his toll by three.

One of Chaucer's most appealing characters is the Parson, or parish priest, and the lengthy description given to him is appropriate in view of the prominence of the village church in both the rural landscape and the lives of its inhabitants. In a very real sense, the church was the center of manorial existence. Situated in the heart of the village, it was in the church's interior that the villagers were baptized, confirmed, and married, and in its sanctified grounds their remains were laid to rest. The castle on the hill enforced the temporal order of the day; the church was no less the landmark of a spiritual order that permeated every aspect of the lives of our medieval ancestors—and, importantly, cut across the social barriers that stood between the lord in his castle and the peasants toiling on his manor. For of the parish priest:

To tempt folk unto heaven by high endeavor
And good example was his purpose ever.
But any person who was obstinate,
Whoever he was, of high or low estate,
Him on occasion would he sharply chide.

THE TOWN

Although post-Roman Europe was largely agrarian, we should not imagine either that the country estates were completely self-sufficient or that towns had

---

[1] The excerpts here and following are reprinted from The Prologue to Geoffrey Chaucer's *The Canterbury Tales*, trans. Frank Ernest Hill, by permission of the publishers, Longmans, Green & Co., Inc.

ceased to exist. Wool, hides, and wine were produced for outside markets, and even in the so-called "Dark Ages" considerable trading in such goods took place in fairs and town markets. A number of urban centers, moreover, were sustained by the activities of the Church. Its administration called for the siting of bishoprics in strategically placed towns, while the larger cities were often favored by the location of the archbishops' palaces. Thus, while the civil nobility was land-centered, the ecclesiastical hierarchy was town-centered. From early medieval times, the town was largely made up of clerics from the cathedral and other local churches, the teachers and students of ecclesiastical schools, monks and other regular clergy, and artisans and servitors employed by these various clerical bodies.

Consequently, spires were a familiar part of the skyline of the medieval town, which, however, owed its striking appearance largely to the walls and battlements that surrounded it. In the last days of the Roman Empire towns had been enclosed with walls as protection against the barbarians, and they remained centers both of defense and of political control. Thus, after William conquered England in 1066, he set about constructing royal castles in or alongside the towns to make his power felt and respected. The most famous example was the Tower of London, but thirty-four other castles were also built during the Conqueror's reign. By his time town life throughout western Europe was being revitalized as a result of the revival of commerce. Various factors accounted for this development: the growth of population, the re-opening of the Mediterranean to trade following the defeat of the Muslims on the sea, and an increase both in traffic across the Alps and in the numbers of pilgrims to Italy and the Holy Land. Certain areas in particular reflected this renewal of trade and town life. In northern Italy, Venice and Genoa prospered as Europe's greatest ports with their own merchant fleets, while Florence produced fine cloth and later evolved into a major banking center. The most important cloth center in the north was Flanders, which supported one of the most densely populated areas in western Europe. In the thirteenth century a group of north German cities, including Hamburg, Lübeck, and Danzig, formed a wealthy trading association, the Hanseatic League, which largely controlled fisheries and commerce in the Baltic and North seas and distributed goods throughout northern Europe. In addition, commerce was stimulated by the establishment of great fairs, to which merchants came from all over Europe to buy and sell produce. Leipzig and Frankfurt were famous for their fairs, as were Ypres and Lille in the Low Countries, but the most famous were held in Champagne in northeastern France. Important to medieval life as a clearing house for goods and ideas alike, the fair was also instrumental in stimulating the use of a money economy, rather than the old system based on barter, and such mercantile innovations as bills of exchange and letters of credit.

By Chaucer's day (the end of the fourteenth century), the revival of town life was in full swing, and this is reflected in the appearance in his *Canterbury Tales* of various urban craftsmen and tradesmen. Thus the craft guilds are represented by

> A Haberdasher, a Dyer, a Carpenter,
> A Weaver and a Carpet-maker
> Were with us too, clad all in livery
> Of one illustrious great fraternity. . . .
> Each of them seemed a burgess proud, and fit
> In guildhall on a dais high to sit.

And of course a member of the most prosperous of the guilds was to be found among the Canterbury retinue, namely the Merchant:

> High on his horse he sat,
> Upon his head a Flanders beaver hat;
> His boots were buckled fair and modishly.
> He spoke his words with great solemnity,
> Having in mind his gain in pounds and pence.
> He wished the sea, regardless of expense,
> Kept safe from Middleburg to Orëwell.
> Cunningly could he buy French crowns, or sell,
> And great sagacity in all ways showed;
> No man could tell of any debt he owed.

THE LORDS SPIRITUAL

Whether we turn to the rural or to the urban medieval landscape, we find two great coexistent orders—the spiritual and the temporal—each with its own ranks and powers. For the most part, the two orders coöperated and together created a medieval way of life that sought to bring order into all human activities. In a society based upon hierarchies of groups and officials, this bringing about of order was entrusted to the "law of divinity" that had as its purpose "to lead the lowest through the intermediate to the highest things." Princes and prelates alike could accept these words of Pope Boniface VIII as enunciated in his famous bull, *Unam Sanctam,* in 1302. But trouble arose over a fundamental conflict separating the two orders: when for any reason they disagreed, which possessed supreme authority? According to Boniface, there could be but one answer:

> Both swords, the spiritual and the material . . . are in the power of the Church; the one indeed, to be wielded for the Church, the other by the Church; the one by the hand of the priest, the other by the hand of kings and knights, but at the will and sufferance of the priest. One sword, moreover, ought to be under the other, and the temporal authority to be subjected to the spiritual.

Though princes challenged this papal claim in Boniface's own day, the ecclesiastical hierarchy succeeded in dominating the earlier centuries of the Middle Ages. In post-Roman Europe the Church was the only universal institution, and though Charlemagne succeeded in bringing about a measure of temporal unity, the Church could always claim that it had placed the crown upon his head at Rome and invested him with imperial powers. After his death, moreover, when the empire was fragmentized and feudal loyalties emerged, the temporal power of the Church seemed great indeed. This ascendancy is dramatized in the eleventh century in the quarrel between Pope Gregory VII and Emperor Henry IV, the result of which was that the latter was forced to stand barefoot in the Alpine snows at Canossa and beg forgiveness from the pope. That the papacy was bent on wielding both the spiritual and temporal "swords" is attested by the initiative taken later that same century on the part of Urban II, who proclaimed the First Crusade for recovery of the Holy Land from the Muslims.

At its zenith the medieval papacy undertook still other activities in keeping with this interpretation of its office and responsibilities. In order to extirpate heresy, Innocent III instituted a crusade against the Albigensians, a move in which religious and political motives were inextricably bound together. The initiation of the Inquisition in the thirteenth century was yet another means of giving the spiritual sword an effective temporal cutting edge. At the same time, the papacy was no less interested in correcting errors within the Church itself. In the twelfth century, the forces of reform and otherworldliness were greatly strengthened by the efforts of Bernard of Clairvaux, who militantly inveighed against the luxury and corruption that had crept into what had become the most powerful and wealthy institution in Europe. The following century saw the tempo of European life accelerate with the growth of commerce and towns and the rise of new national states. More reforming zeal was forthcoming from clerics such as Dominic and Francis of Assisi, who founded new orders specifically organized to preach the Church's message throughout the countryside and in all the towns. Such a new impetus was required, for the preëminence of the spiritual authority was now being effectively challenged.

THE LORDS TEMPORAL

> And, inasmuch as the kingdom, together with the empire, is ours by the election of the princes from God alone, who, by the passion of His Son Christ subjected the world to the rule of the two necessary swords; and since the apostle Peter informed the world with this teaching, "Fear God, honour the king": whoever shall say that we received the imperial crown as a benefice from the lord pope, contradicts the divine institutions and the teaching of Peter, and shall be guilty of a lie.

With these trenchant words, Frederick Barbarossa (c. 1123-1190), emperor of the Holy Roman Empire and companion of Richard the Lion-Hearted on the Third Crusade, rejected the papal attempt to subordinate the temporal to the spiritual sword. Though this challenge by Frederick was in keeping with his strong nature, it was no isolated assertion of the independence of temporal authority. Previously, William the Conqueror had bluntly rejected the demand of Pope Gregory VII (of Canossa fame) to take an oath of fealty, and the English king had also denied the Church the right to appeal cases to the high courts at Rome without royal approval.

Earlier, we mentioned William's construction of royal castles in or alongside strategically placed towns in order to consolidate his administration on a national basis. These activities ran counter to feudalism which, as we saw, was local in both environmental control and in loyalties and was basically agrarian in its structure. In a fragmented, feudal society, the Church had been at once spiritual and temporal ruler since its power alone transcended the patchwork of local fiefs. But from William's reign on, a new order began to emerge in England—a phenomenon duplicated in France and other countries. It was no coincidence that towns, trade, and new national states all grew together. All of them required a network of roads, the efficient administration of law and order, and systems of currency and taxation on a national, rather than a local, level. Inevitably, however, the temporal princes found themselves in opposition not only to the feudal lords but equally to the spiritual princes, whose political and legal authority they now challenged. But the new nation-makers could rely upon a powerful ally. This was the rising middle class in the towns, who looked to the kings for protection against the landed gentry and for expansion in foreign commerce and who in return provided the monarch with money in taxes to pay for the royal armies. So if the earlier Middle Ages belonged to the spiritual lords, the later Middle Ages—a period of nation-making in western Europe—came progressively to belong to the temporal lords.

TO THE GREATER GLORY OF GOD

Despite the political struggles in which the two "swords" periodically clashed, we must not lose sight of one cardinal concept, namely, that to our medieval ancestors both were sustained by the power of God. In other words, human existence had no meaning except insofar as it comprised a synthesis of the spiritual and temporal orders which governed the world. It was this synthesis which the greatest philosopher of the epoch, Thomas Aquinas, sought to achieve by a reconciliation of reason and faith, of Aristotle and scripture. A similar synthesis between religion and natural science was attempted by Roger Bacon, who shared the view that theology was the queen of the sciences; but this belief did not prevent him from pleading strongly for making use of empirical, rational methods in scientific investigation. And in Dante's supreme poetic masterpiece, the *Divine Comedy*, again we see man's creative powers dedicated to the principle that human existence becomes intelligible only through a reconciliation of the temporal with the timeless, of man with God.

Seen in this perspective, the medieval world-order depended upon a divinely ordained unity, but it was a unity that permitted almost endless diversity so as to embrace every facet of human existence. Thus the Gothic cathedral, which has been described as a unique synthesis of faith, Scholasticism, and architectural innovation, made use of a wealth of symbolic sculptural detail to carry out its central theme of man-in-communion-with-God. Indeed, the subject matter and treatment of the innumerable details making up a Gothic cathedral—such as the famous gargoyles of Notre Dame de Paris or the statues of devils blowing lustily on bagpipes—undoubtedly struck some later generations as an apparently blasphemous intrusion of irreverent, if not downright carnal, images into the pantheon of angels and saints. But to our medieval forebears, the ridiculous as well as the sublime, the earthly—and earthy!—no less than the transcendental, were part and parcel of human existence, and had to be accorded their place in its architectural expression. Only in this way could men construct, and live, to the greater glory of God.

Europe's Search for Stability

THE QUEST FOR EMPIRE

63

**EINHARD, *LIFE OF CHARLEMAGNE*:
THE CAROLINGIAN EMPIRE OF THE FRANKS**

In the years from the fourth to the sixth centuries A.D., barbaric tribes overran the thinly guarded Roman frontiers and established independent kingdoms within the western confines of the empire (see Documents 47-48). This great transitional period, which involved the decline of the ancient world and the beginning of the medieval, also saw a virtual cessation of intellectual progress in western Europe. Everywhere there was a movement toward simpler and more primitive ways of life. By the eighth century, however, a new dynasty emerged within the Frankish Kingdom in Gaul, led by Pepin of Héristal. Fifty years later (771) his great-grandson, Charles the Great, or Charlemagne (742-814), assumed the imperial throne.

It was during this period that a revival of learning took place. At his court at Aix-la-Chapelle (German Aachen), Charlemagne gathered around him the leading scholars of Europe, whose cultural efforts led to our historical designation of the period as the Carolingian Renaissance, although its relatively small cumulative effects somewhat belie that proud description, since there was a return to the intellectual doldrums in the next century.

The most intimate and best picture of Charlemagne is provided by Einhard, a monk who served at the emperor's court and knew him well. In the selection below from his *Life of Charlemagne*, Einhard first describes how Charlemagne extended the Frankish boundaries and refurbished his capital and other cities; he then gives a moving account of the private life and character of the emperor. The humility, piety, and devotion to learning that characterized Charlemagne are impressive in an age in which fierce martial values, fanatical prejudice, or savage cunning are more usually reported as the qualities of the mighty.

These, then, are the wars this mighty King waged during the course of forty-seven years—for his reign extended over that period—in different parts of the world with the utmost skill and success. By these wars he so nobly increased the kingdom of the Franks, which was great and strong when he inherited it from his father Pippin, that the additions he made almost doubled it. For before his time the power of the Frankish kingdom extended only over that part of Gaul which is bounded by the Rhine, the Loire, and the Balearic Sea; and that part of Germany which is inhabited by the so-called eastern Franks and which is bounded by Saxony, the Danube, the Rhine, and the river Saal, which stream separates the Thuringians and the Sorabs; and, further, over the Alamanni and the Bavarians. But Charles, by the wars that have been mentioned, conquered and made tributary the following countries:—First, Aquitania and Gascony, and the whole Pyrenean range, and the country of Spain as far as the Ebro, which rising in Navarre and passing through the most fertile territory of Spain, falls into the Balearic Sea, beneath the walls of the city of Tortosa; next, all Italy from Augusta Praetoria as far as lower Calabria, where are the frontiers of the Greeks and Beneventans, a thousand miles and more in length; next, Saxony, which is a considerable portion of Germany, and is reckoned to be twice as broad and about as long as that part of Germany which is inhabited by the Franks; then both provinces of Pannonia and Dacia, on one side of the river Danube, and Histria and Liburnia and Dalmatia, with the exception of the maritime cities which he left to the Emperor of Constantinople on account of their friendship and the treaty made between them; lastly, all the barbarous and fierce nations lying between the Rhine, the Vistula, the Ocean, and the Danube, who speak much the same language, but in character and dress are very unlike. The chief of these last are the Welatabi, the Sorabi, the Abodriti, and the Bohemians; against these he waged war, but the others, and by far the larger number, surrendered without a struggle.

The friendship, too, which he established with certain kings and peoples increased the glory of his reign.

Aldefonsus, King of Gallaecia and Asturica, was joined in so close an alliance with him that whenever he sent letters or ambassadors to Charles he gave instructions that he should be called "the man" of the Frankish King.

Further, his rich gifts had so attached the kings of the Scots to his favour that they always called him their lord and themselves his submissive servants. Letters are still in existence sent by them to Charles in which those feelings towards him are clearly shown.

With Aaron, the King of the Persians, who ruled over all the East, with the exception of India, he entertained so harmonious a friendship that the Persian King valued his favour before the friendship of all the kings and princes in the world, and held that it alone deserved to be cultivated with presents and titles. When, therefore, the ambassadors of Charles, whom he had sent with offerings to the most holy sepulchre of our Lord and Saviour and to the place of His resurrection, came to the Persian King and proclaimed the kindly feelings of their master, he not only granted them all they asked but also allowed that sacred place of our salvation to be reckoned as part of the possessions of the Frankish King. He further sent ambassadors of his own along with those of Charles upon the return journey, and forwarded immense presents to Charles—robes and spices, and the other rich products of the East—and a few years earlier he had sent him at his request an elephant, which was then the only one he had.

The Emperors of Constantinople, Nicephorus, Michael, and Leo, too, made overtures of friendship and alliance with him, and sent many ambassadors. At first Charles was regarded with

Text: A. J. Grant, ed., *Early Lives of Charlemagne by Eginhard and the Monk of St. Gall* ("The King's Classics") [London: Alexander Moring, Ltd., The De La More Press, 1905]), pp. 26-33, 34-35, 36-37, 40-45, 46-48.

much suspicion by them, because he had taken the imperial title, and thus seemed to aim at taking from them their empire; but in the end a very definite treaty was made between them, and every occasion of quarrel on either side thereby avoided. For the Romans and the Greeks always suspected the Frankish power; hence, there is a well-known Greek proverb: "The Frank is a good friend but a bad neighbour."

Though he was so successful in widening the boundaries of his kingdom and subduing the foreign nations he, nevertheless, put on foot many works for the decoration and convenience of his kingdom, and carried some to completion. The great church dedicated to Mary, the holy Mother of God, at Aix, and the bridge, five hundred feet in length, over the great river Rhine near Mainz, may fairly be regarded as the chief of his works. But the bridge was burnt down a year before his death, and though he had determined to rebuild it of stone instead of wood it was not restored, because his death so speedily followed. He began also to build palaces of splendid workmanship—one not far from the city of Mainz, near a town called Ingelheim; another at Nimeguen, on the river Waal, which flows along the south of the Batavian island. And he gave special orders to the bishops and priests who had charge of sacred buildings that any throughout his realm, which had fallen into ruin through age should be restored, and he instructed his agents to see that his orders were carried out.

He built a fleet, too, for the war against the Northmen, constructing ships for this purpose near those rivers which flow out of Gaul and Germany into the northern ocean. And because the Northmen laid waste the coasts of Gaul and Germany by their constant attacks he planted forts and garrisons in all harbours and at the mouths of all navigable rivers, and prevented in this way the passage of the enemy. He took the same measures in the South, on the shore of Narbonne and Septimania, and also along all the coasts of Italy as far as Rome, to hold in check the Moors, who had lately begun to make piratical excursions. And by reason of these precautions Italy suffered no serious harm from the Moors, nor Gaul and Germany from the Northmen, in the days of Charles; except that Centumcellae, a city of Etruria, was betrayed into the hands of the Moors and plundered, and in Frisia certain islands lying close to Germany were ravaged by the Northmen.

I have shown, then, how Charles protected and expanded his kingdom and also what splendour he gave to it. I shall now go on to speak of his mental endowments, of his steadiness of purpose under whatever circumstances of prosperity or adversity, and of all that concerns his private and domestic life.

As long as, after the death of his father, he shared the kingdom with his brother he bore so patiently the quarrelling and restlessness of the latter as never even to be provoked to wrath by him. Then, having married at his mother's bidding the daughter of Desiderius, King of the Lombards, he divorced her, for some unknown reason, a year later. He took in marriage Hildigard, of the Suabian race, a woman of the highest nobility, and by her he had three sons—viz., Charles and Pippin and Ludovicus, and three daughters—Hrotrud and Bertha and Gisla. He had also three other daughters—Theoderada and Hiltrud and Hruodhaid. Two of these were the children of his wife Fastrada, a woman of the eastern Franks or Germans; the third was the daughter of a concubine, whose name has escaped my memory. On the death of Fastrada he married Liutgard, of the Alemannic race, by whom he had no children. After her death he had four concubines—namely, Madelgarda, who bore him a daughter of the name of Ruothild; Gersuinda, of Saxon origin, by whom he had a daughter of the name of Adolthrud; Regina, who bore him Drogot and Hugo; and Adallinda, who was the mother of Theoderic. . . .

In educating his children he determined to train them, both sons and daughters, in those liberal studies to which he himself paid great attention. Further, he made his sons, as soon as their age permitted it, learn to ride like true Franks, and practise the use of arms and hunting. He ordered his daughters to learn wool work and devote attention to the spindle and distaff, for the avoidance of idleness and lethargy, and to be trained to the adoption of high principles.

He lost two sons and one daughter before his death—namely, Charles, his eldest; Pippin, whom he made King of Italy; and Hruotrud, his eldest daughter, who had been betrothed to Constantine, the Emperor of the Greeks. Pippin left one son, Bernard, and five daughters—Adalheid, Atula, Gundrada, Berthaid, and Theoderada. In his treatment of them Charles gave the strongest proof of his family affection, for upon the death of his son he appointed his grandson Bernard to succeed him, and had his granddaughters brought up with his own daughters.

He bore the deaths of his two sons and of his daughter with less patience than might have been expected from his usual stoutness of heart, for his domestic affection, a quality for which he was as remarkable as for courage, forced him to shed tears. Moreover, when the death of Hadrian, the Roman Pontiff, whom he reckoned as the chief of his friends, was announced to him, he wept for him as though he had lost a brother or a very dear son. For he showed a very fine disposition in his friendships: he embraced them readily and maintained them faithfully, and he treated with the utmost respect all whom he had admitted into the circle of his friends. . . .

He had by a concubine a son called Pippin—whom I purposely did not mention along with the others—handsome, indeed, but deformed. When Charles, after the beginning of the war against the Huns, was wintering in Bavaria, this Pippin pretended illness, and formed a conspiracy against his father with some of the leaders of the Franks, who had seduced him by a vain promise of the kingdom. When the design had been detected and the conspirators punished Pippin was tonsured and sent to the monastery of Prumia, there to practise the religious life, to which in the end he was of his own will inclined.

Another dangerous conspiracy had been formed against him in Germany at an earlier date. The plotters were some of them blinded and some of them maimed, and all subsequently transported into exile. Not more than three lost their lives, and these resisted capture with drawn swords, and in defending themselves killed some of their opponents. Hence, as they could not be restrained in any other way, they were cut down.

The cruelty of Queen Fastrada is believed to be the cause and origin of these conspiracies. Both were caused by the belief that, upon the persuasion of his cruel wife, he had swerved widely from his natural kindness and customary leniency. Otherwise his whole life long he so won the love and favour of all men both at home and abroad that never was the slightest charge of unjust severity brought against him by anyone.

He had a great love for foreigners, and took such pains to entertain them that their numbers were justly reckoned to be a burden not only to the palace but to the kingdom at large. But, with his usual loftiness of spirit, he took little note of such charges, for he found in the reputation of generosity and in the good fame that followed such actions a compensation even for grave inconveniences. . . .

In speech he was fluent and ready, and could express with the greatest clearness whatever he wished. He was not merely content with his native tongue but took the trouble to learn foreign languages. He learnt Latin so well that he could speak it as well as his native tongue; but he could understand Greek better than he could speak it. His fluency of speech was so great that he even seemed sometimes a little garrulous.

He paid the greatest attention to the liberal arts, and showed the greatest respect and bestowed high honours upon those who taught them. For his lessons in grammar he listened to the instruction of Deacon Peter of Pisa, an old man; but for all other subjects Albinus, called Alcuin, also a deacon, was his teacher—a man from Britain, of the Saxon race, and the most learned man of his time. Charles spent much time and labour in learning rhetoric and dialectic, and especially astronomy, from Alcuin. He learnt, too, the art of reckoning, and with close application scrutinised most carefully the course of the stars. He tried also to learn to write, and for this purpose used to carry with him and keep under the pillow of his couch tablets and writing-sheets that he might in spare moments accustom himself to the formation of letters. But he made little advance in this strange task, which was begun too late in life.

He paid the most devout and pious regard to the Christian religion, in which he had been brought up from infancy. And, therefore, he built the great and most beautiful church at Aix, and decorated it with gold and silver and candelabras and with wicket-gates and doors of solid brass. And, since he could not procure marble columns elsewhere for the building of it, he had them brought from Rome and Ravenna. As long as his health permitted it he used diligently to attend the church both in the morning and evening, and during the night, and at the time of the Sacrifice. He took the greatest care to have all the services of the church performed with the utmost dignity, and constantly warned the keepers of the building not to allow anything improper or dirty either to be brought into or to remain in the building. He provided so great a quantity of gold and silver vessels, and so large a supply of priestly vestments, that at the religious services not even the door-keepers, who form the lowest ecclesiastical order, had to officiate in their ordinary dress. He carefully reformed the manner of reading and singing; for he was thoroughly instructed in both, though he never read publicly himself, nor sang except in a low voice and with the rest of the congregation.

He was most devout in relieving the poor and in those free gifts which the Greeks call alms. For he gave it his attention not only in his own country and in his own kingdom, but he also used to send money across the sea to Syria, to Egypt, to Africa—to Jerusalem, Alexandria, and Carthage—in compassion for the poverty of any

Christians whose miserable condition in those countries came to his ears. It was for this reason chiefly that he cultivated the friendship of kings beyond the sea, hoping thereby to win for the Christians living beneath their sway some succour and relief.

Beyond all other sacred and venerable places he loved the church of the holy Apostle Peter at Rome, and he poured into its treasury great wealth in silver and gold and precious stones. He sent innumerable gifts to the Pope; and during the whole course of his reign he strove with all his might (and, indeed, no object was nearer to his heart than this) to restore to the city of Rome her ancient authority, and not merely to defend the church of Saint Peter but to decorate and enrich it out of his resources above all other churches. But although he valued Rome so much, still, during all the forty-seven years that he reigned, he only went there four times to pay his vows and offer up his prayers.

But such were not the only objects of his last visit; for the Romans had grievously outraged Pope Leo, had torn out his eyes and cut off his tongue, and thus forced him to throw himself upon the protection of the King. He, therefore, came to Rome to restore the condition of the church, which was terribly disturbed, and spent the whole of the winter there. It was then that he received the title of Emperor and Augustus, which he so disliked at first that he affirmed that he would not have entered the church on that day—though it was the chief festival of the church—if he could have foreseen the design of the Pope. But when he had taken the title he bore very quietly the hostility that it caused and the indignation of the Roman emperors. He conquered their ill-feeling by his magnanimity, in which, doubtless, he far excelled them, and sent frequent embassies to them, and called them his brothers.

When he had taken the imperial title he noticed many defects in the legal systems of his people; for the Franks have two legal systems differing in many points very widely from one another, and he, therefore, determined to add what was lacking, to reconcile the differences, and to amend anything that was wrong or wrongly expressed. He completed nothing of all his designs beyond adding a few capitularies, and those unfinished. But he gave orders that the laws and rules of all nations comprised within his dominions which were not already written out should be collected and committed to writing....

At the very end of his life, when already he was feeling the pressure of old age and sickness, he summoned his own son Lewis, King of Aquitania, the only surviving son of Hildigard, and then solemnly called together the Frankish nobles of his whole kingdom; and then, with the consent of all, made Lewis partner in the whole kingdom and heir to the imperial title. After that, putting the diadem on his head, he ordered them to salute him "Imperator" and Augustus. This decision of his was received by all present with the greatest favour, for it seemed to them a divine inspiration for the welfare of the realm. It added to his dignity at home and increased the terror of his name abroad.

He then sent his son back to Aquitania, and himself, though broken with old age, proceeded to hunt, as his custom was, not far from the palace of Aix, and after spending the rest of the autumn in this pursuit he came back to Aix about the beginning of November. Whilst he was spending the winter there he was attacked by a sharp fever, and took to his bed. Then, following his usual habit, he determined to abstain from food, thinking that by such self-discipline he would be able either to cure or alleviate the disease. But the fever was complicated by a pain in the side which the Greeks call pleurisy; and, as Charles still persisted in fasting, and only very rarely drank something to sustain his strength, seven days after he had taken to his bed he received holy communion, and died, in the seventy-second year of his life and in the forty-seventh year of his reign, on the fifth day before the Kalends of February, at the third hour of the day.

His body was washed and treated with the usual ceremonies, and then, amidst the greatest grief of the whole people, taken to the church and buried. At first there was some doubt as to where he should rest, since he had given no instructions during his lifetime. But at length all were agreed that he could be buried nowhere more honourably than in the great church which he had built at his own expense in the same town, for the love of our Lord God Jesus Christ and the honour of His holy and ever-virgin Mother. There he was buried on the same day on which he died. A gilded arch was raised above the tomb, with his statue, and an inscription. The inscription ran as follows:—

"Beneath this tomb lies the body of Charles, the great and orthodox Emperor, who nobly expanded the kingdom of the Franks and reigned prosperously for forty-seven years. He departed this life, more than seventy years of age, in the eight hundred and fourteenth year of our lord, in the seventh indiction, on the fifth day before the Kalends of February."

64 ANGLO-SAXON CHRONICLE: WILLIAM THE CONQUEROR

The death of Charlemagne in 814 brought on the disintegration of his western European empire. Such efficiency as the Carolingian government possessed was due more to the personality of Charlemagne than to any lasting institutions. Centralized authority broke down, and in its place arose a number of small feudal states continually embroiled in petty dynastic quarrels. Adding to the confusion were repeated raids by the Norsemen, who annually swept up the rivers from the Atlantic and the North seas to loot Frankish abbeys and towns. By the end of the ninth century, the Norse attacks had intensified; the Frankish kings were powerless to resist and submitted to a treaty in 912, granting the Norse leader Rollo a dukedom at the mouth of the Seine River. During the next two decades Duke Rollo extended Norse hegemony over the areas of northwestern France, and his successors molded Normandy into the most powerful and the best governed of all feudal states in the West, with a culture which fused the best elements of the Norse and Frankish traditions, expressing itself in the developing French language.

In the year 1066, William, then Duke of Normandy, (c. 1028-1087) claimed the English crown and crossed the channel with an invasion army. On October 14 at the Battle of Hastings he defeated Harold, the Saxon pretender, and seized the throne of England. The Norman conquest established in England a new aristocracy with a strong monarchy; the organization of Norman society had been a feudal one, based on feudal military organization, land tenure, and private justice, but it was a feudalism held in check by a dominant king, and this same administrative system was now introduced into England.

The selection below contains an excellent description of the latter years of William's reign, derived from the *Anglo-Saxon Chronicle*, perhaps the most important document written in the English language before the twelfth century. The *Chronicle* is not one continuous work, but rather a series of accounts of events in England, written by scribes in the various monasteries and covering the period from the end of the ninth until the middle of the twelfth centuries.

Dated 1086 is an entry recording the famous "Domesday" survey which William initiated in order to ascertain the real value of property within his English Kingdom and thus to determine a feasible basis for taxation and administration. This was the first time in English history that such a royal inquest was used.

[1085]. The king spent Christmas with his councillors at Gloucester, and held his court there for five days, which was followed by a three-day synod held by the archbishop and the clergy. At this synod Maurice was elected bishop of London and William bishop of Norfolk and Robert bishop of Cheshire: they were all chaplains of the king.

After this the king had important deliberations and exhaustive discussions with his council about this land and how it was peopled, and with what sort of men. Then he sent his men all over England into every shire to ascertain how many hundreds of 'hides' of land there were in each shire, and how much land and live-stock the king himself owned in the country, and what annual dues were lawfully his from each shire. He also had it recorded how much land his archbishops had, and his diocesan bishops, his abbots and his earls, and—though I may be going into too great detail—and what or how much each man who was a landholder here in England had in land or in live-stock, and how much money it was worth. So very thoroughly did he have the inquiry carried out that there was not a single 'hide,' not one virgate of land, not even—it is shameful to record it, but it did not seem shameful for him to do—not even one ox, nor one cow, nor one pig which escaped notice in his survey. And all the surveys [known collectively as the Domesday Book] were subsequently brought to him.

[1086]. In this year the king wore his crown and held his court in Winchester at Easter; and journeyed so that by Whit Sunday he was at Westminster, and there he dubbed his son Henry knight. Thereafter he journeyed around the country so that he came to Salisbury by Lammas,

Text: Reprinted by permission of the publishers from G. N. Garmonsway (trans.), *The Anglo-Saxon Chronicle*, "Everyman's Library" (New York: E. P. Dutton & Co., Inc.; London: J. M. Dent & Sons, Ltd., 1953), pp. 216-21.

where he was met by his council and all the landholders who were of any account throughout England, no matter whose vassals they might be. All did him homage and became his men, and swore him oaths of allegiance that they would be faithful to him against all other men. From thence he journeyed to the Isle of Wight because he purposed to go to Normandy, and so he did thereafter. First, however, he did as he was wont, he levied very heavy taxes on his subjects, upon any pretext, whether justly or unjustly. He journeyed thereafter into Normandy, and prince Edgar, the kinsman of king Edward, then left his court because he had had little honour from him: but may the Almighty God give him honour in the life to come. Christina, the prince's sister, retired into the nunnery at Romsey and took the veil.

And this same year was very disastrous, and a very vexatious and anxious year throughout England, because of a pestilence among livestock; and corn and fruits were at a standstill. It is difficult for anyone to realize what great misfortune was caused by the weather: so violent was the thunder and lightning that many were killed. Things steadily went from bad to worse for everybody. May God Almighty remedy it when it shall be His will!

[1087]. One thousand and eighty-seven years after the nativity of our Lord Jesus Christ, in the twenty-first year of William's rule and reign over England, as God had granted to him, there was a very disastrous and pestilential year in this land. Such a malady fell upon men that very nearly every other person was in the sorriest plight and down with fever: it was so malignant that many died from the disease. Thereafter, in consequence of the great storms which came as we have already told, there came a great famine over all England, so that many hundreds died miserable deaths because of it. Alas! how wretched and how unhappy the times were then! So fever-stricken lay the unhappy people in those days that they were never far from death's door, until the pangs of hunger finished them off.

Who can fail to be moved to compassion by days such as these? Or who is so hard-hearted that he cannot bewail such misfortune? But such things come to pass because of a nation's sins, because its people will not love God and righteousness. So was it then in those days, when no righteousness was to be found in this land in any man's heart, but only amongst the monks where they lived virtuously. The king and the leading men were fond, yea, too fond, of avarice: they coveted gold and silver, and did not care how sinfully it was obtained, as long as it came to them. The king granted his land on the hardest terms and at the highest possible price. If another buyer came and offered more than the first had given, the king would let it go to the man who offered him more. If a third came and offered still more, the king would make it over to the man who offered him most of all. He did not care at all how very wrongfully the reeves got possession of it from wretched men, nor how many illegal acts they did; but the louder the talk of law and justice, the greater the injustices committed. Unjust tolls were levied and many other unlawful acts were committed which are distressing to relate.

Also, in the same year, before autumn, the holy church of St. Paul, the episcopal see of London, was burnt down, as well as many other churches and the largest and fairest part of the whole city. Likewise too, at the same time, almost every important town in the whole of England was burnt down. Alas! a miserable and lamentable time was it in that year, which brought forth so many misfortunes.

Also, in the same year, before the Assumption of St. Mary [15 August], king William went from Normandy into France with levies, and made war against his own lord, Philip the king, and slew a great number of his men, and burnt down the town of Mantes and all the holy churches inside the town. Two holy men who served God living in an anchorite's cell were there burnt to death.

After these events, king William returned again to Normandy. A cruel deed he had done, but a crueller fate befell him. How crueller? He fell sick and suffered terribly.

What can I say? That bitter death that spares neither high nor low seized him. He died in Normandy on the day following the Nativity of St. Mary [9 September], and was buried at Caen in the abbey of St. Stephen, which he had formerly built and afterwards endowed in various ways.

Alas! how deceitful and transitory is the prosperity of this world. He who was once a mighty king, and lord of many a land, was left of all the land with nothing save seven feet of ground: and he who was once decked with gold and jewels, lay then covered over with earth.

He left behind him three sons. The eldest was called Robert, who became duke of Normandy after him. The second was called William, who wore the royal crown in England after him. The third was called Henry, to whom his father bequeathed treasures innumerable.

If anyone desires to know what kind of man he was or in what honour he was held or how many lands he was lord over, then shall we write of him as we have known him, who have ourselves seen him and at one time dwelt in his court. King William, of whom we speak, was a man of great wisdom and power, and surpassed in honour and in strength all those who had gone before him. Though stern beyond measure to those who opposed his will, he was kind to those good men who loved God. On the very spot where God granted him the conquest of England he caused a great abbey to be built; and settled monks in it and richly endowed it. During his reign was built the great cathedral at Canterbury, and many another throughout all England. This land too was filled with monks living their lives after the rule of St. Benedict. Such was the state of religion in his time that every man who wished to, whatever considerations there might be with regard to his rank, could follow the profession of a monk.

Moreover he kept great state. He wore his royal crown three times a year as often as he was in England: at Easter at Winchester, at Whitsuntide at Westminster, at Christmas at Gloucester. On these occasions, all the great men of England were assembled about him: archbishops, bishops, abbots, earls, thanes, and knights. He was so stern and relentless a man that no one dared do aught against his will. Earls who resisted his will he held in bondage. Bishops he deprived of their sees and abbots of their abbacies, while rebellious thanes he cast into prison, and finally his own brother he did not spare. His name was Odo. He was a powerful bishop in Normandy, and Bayeux was his episcopal see; he was the foremost man after the king. He had an earldom in England, and was master of the land when the king was in Normandy. William put him in prison. Among other things we must not forget the good order he kept in the land, so that a man of any substance could travel unmolested throughout the country with his bosom full of gold. No man dared to slay another, no matter what evil the other might have done him. If a man lay with a woman against her will, he was forthwith condemned to forfeit those members with which he had disported himself.

He ruled over England, and by his foresight it was surveyed so carefully that there was not a 'hide' of land in England of which he did not know who held it and how much it was worth; and these particulars he set down in his survey. Wales was in his domain, in which country he built castles and so kept its people in subjection. Scotland also he reduced to subjection by his great strength. Normandy was his by right of birth, while he also ruled over the county called Maine. If he had lived only two years more he would have conquered Ireland by his astuteness and without any display of force. Assuredly in his time men suffered grievous oppression and manifold injuries.

He caused castles to be built
Which were a sore burden to the poor.
A hard man was the king
And took from his subjects many marks
In gold and many more hundreds of pounds in silver.
These sums he took by weight from his people,
Most unjustly and for little need.
He was sunk in greed
And utterly given up to avarice.
He set apart a vast deer preserve and imposed laws concerning it.
Whoever slew a hart or a hind
Was to be blinded.
He forbade the killing of boars
Even as the killing of harts.
For he loved the stags as dearly
As though he had been their father.
Hares, also, he decreed should go unmolested.
The rich complained and the poor lamented.
But he was too relentless to care though all might hate him,
And they were compelled, if they wanted
To keep their lives and their lands
And their goods and the favour of the king,
To submit themselves wholly to his will.
Alas! that any man should bear himself so proudly
And deem himself exalted above all other men!
May Almighty God shew mercy to his soul
And pardon him his sins.

We have set down these things about him, both the good and the evil, so that men may cherish the good and utterly eschew the evil, and follow the path that leads us to the Kingdom of Heaven.

FEUDALISM AND THE MEDIEVAL ECONOMY

65 ASSIZES OF ROMANIA: FEUDALISM

The two centuries following the death of Charlemagne witnessed not only the destruction of his empire but also the evolution of a political and social substitute for it.

With him died in western Europe the last vestige of any central government able to provide direct protection for individuals. Riot and disorder ensued, with robbers, lawless bands, and Norsemen marauding at will. No man's family or possessions were safe. The ninth and tenth centuries, therefore, saw local landowners trying desperately to resurrect some semblance of law and order, military defense, and economic stability in the regions they inhabited. Certain powerful landowners assumed primacy among their neighbors, either through usurpation of power or by delegation of power from weak kings who helplessly acknowledged the disintegration of their own authority. The lesser landowners themselves encouraged this atomization of government. For their own survival during terrifying confusion, they voluntarily placed themselves and their property under the protection and control of these powerful landowners. Lesser nobles gave allegiance to higher, whereby the inferior noble became a "vassal" in homage to the higher "lord." Usually a noble was both a lord over lesser vassals and also a vassal himself, sworn to the service of a higher lord, perhaps to the king at the top. As thousands upon thousands of these lord-and-vassal relationships were established, society in western Europe gradually began to fall into a pattern, with a complex hierarchy of social classes—from kings, princes, dukes, counts, and marquises down to the lowest vassals, the knights.

This new pattern of government, which we call feudalism, was more than a type of private defense. It was a combined political and social order. The vassal, in giving up ownership of his land (or fief) to the lord, still retained a kind of permanent lease on it, for which he paid in goods and services. Economically, each lord's domain became self-sufficient, what with the almost total absence of trade and money as a medium of exchange during those unstable times. Moreover, the vassal was obligated to assist in judicial proceedings and to furnish soldiers for his lord's private wars. It might especially be noted that the vassal's oath of loyalty to his lord was personal; loyalty in feudalism was a matter not between an individual and a state but between individuals.

It must be remembered, however, that feudalism in the Middle Ages was never regimented into any fixed *system*. Feudal customs varied from region to region and from century to century according to local circumstances. In reality, Europe was a collection of various institutions—feudal states, city-states, papal states, dukedoms, kingdoms, and various other forms of socio-political order. In viewing medieval western Europe as a whole, we can say only that the tendencies were toward the feudalism we have described.

By the time of the crusades (eleventh to thirteenth centuries), nevertheless, the *basic* institutions of feudalism were largely acknowledged, if only tacitly. So when the Latin crusaders conquered portions of the Holy Land and the old Byzantine Empire, they founded states—short-lived though they proved to be—whose governments were based on the feudal customs with which the crusaders were acquainted. Among the most important of these states was the principality of Morea (or Achaia), which in geographical extent comprised roughly the Peloponnesian peninsula in Greece. Unlike in the West, where feudal states slowly evolved unguided by any preconceived formulas, the principality of Morea sometime in the thirteenth century was given a written code of law. The *Assizes of Romania*, to give this Morean document its familiar name, shares with the *Assizes of Jerusalem* (for the Latin Kingdom of Jerusalem) the distinction of being one of the two most complete feudal codes extant. These documents drawn up for the East comprise perhaps one of our best sources of knowledge about western conceptions of feudal government.

The *Assizes of Romania*, printed in part below, is a code of 219 articles which admirably suggest the character of the feudal society of Morea's French conquerors and their descendants. The barons were the overlords, from among whom a prince was designated to rule as first among equals (this prince of Morea—or Achaia—in turn owed homage to the Latin emperor of Constantinople). These barons, along with the lesser lords temporal and spiritual, formed a privileged aristocratic class, sharply distinguished from the lower vassals and serfs.

A distinction is made in the *Assizes* between a vassal of liege homage (a liegeman) and a vassal of simple homage. The two categories resulted from the fact that a man usually held fiefs—hereditary grants of land—from several lords, to each of whom he was sworn to render homage and services. If, however, as was often the case, two of his lords were enemies, how could the vassal be loyal to both? From this conflict of interests there arose the practice of a vassal giving liege homage to one lord—to this liege lord the vassal was theoretically bound in all cases to give first priority of loyalty.

And to the other lords he merely gave an oath of simple homage, which really amounted merely to an acknowledgment of tenure of land. In practice, the distinction was not useful; self-interest determined the vassal's choice of a liege lord and he could switch choices when the advantages seemed greater than the risks. Complications such as this indicate the great instability of the feudal structure in practice—the ease of breaking personal vows and the continual existence on the brink of anarchy—that expressed itself in constant feudal warfare.

Prologue

When the holy city of Jerusalem was conquered by the Christians and by the faith of Christ, and by the exhortation and preaching of Peter the Hermit, in the year of the incarnation of our Lord Jesus Christ 1104 [1099], the princes and the barons who had conquered it chose as King of the said Realm of Jerusalem Duke Godfrey of Bouillon. And when he received the lordship, he did not wish to be consecrated or named King of the said Realm, nor further did he wish to wear the crown of gold, there where the King of Kings, the Son of God, our Lord Jesus Christ, had worn the crown of thorns on the day of His Holy Passion; at first he desired to be crowned with a crown of straw. And thus the said Duke Godfrey, wishing to put the said Realm into such good state and good condition that all manner of men going and coming and remaining in the said Realm should be governed and protected and maintained by justice, right, and reason, took counsel with the patriarch of the said city of Jerusalem and with the other barons, princes, lords, and wise men who were there from various lands and divers countries; and having asked of each of them the usages and customs of his province and country, he ordered put into writing everything that each one said and that could be well understood. And then in his own presence and before his lordship the patriarch and all of the other princes and barons who took part in the said conquest he caused the document to be read and examined; and with the counsel of all it was made and constituted the usages and assizes which were to be maintained and held and kept in the said Realm of Jerusalem. Then Duke Godfrey established in the said Realm two secular courts: one was called the High Court and the other the Low Court, that is, the Court of the Bourgeois, to which he appointed a man to be governor and justiciar in his place who was called Viscount. And he appointed as judges of the High Court his barons and knights and vassals, whom he held enfeoffed to himself through the homage or oath which they had made. And to the Low Court, that is, that of the Bourgeois, he summoned the most loyal and the wisest burgesses whom he could find in the city, and had them swear the oath of the bourgeoisie as is provided in the Great Book of the Court of the Bourgeois. And the said king ordained that the knights and vassals be brought into and judged by the High Court while the other people, whom he did not wish to be taken into the High Court, be brought into and judged by the Court of the Bourgeois. And this was accomplished by the common accord of the lord and his barons. And after the said usages and assizes had been established, as was said above, they were mentioned and many times were amended by the other kings and lords who succeeded in the said Realm; for those things which they saw and recognized to be good they added thereto....

1. THIS IS THE BEGINNING OF THE USAGES OF THE EMPIRE OF ROMANIA. HOW THE PRINCE MUST DO HOMAGE TO THE EMPEROR. In the first place, by the aforementioned Usages, the Prince of Achaia, the present as well as the future one, must do liege homage and fealty to the above-said Emperor of Constantinople, and must swear an oath in the presence of his barons, his faithful liegemen and his other subjects, that he shall protect and defend and to the full extent of his power shall secure the maintenance and defense by his officials of all the franchises and usages of the Empire of Romania.

2. And after the Prince has taken the oath to his barons, as is stated above, the said barons and liegemen are required to do homage, ligeance and fealty to the said Prince. And the others who hold fiefs must do homage; and the other subjects must take an oath of fealty. But if the Prince wishes that the said oath be taken through his procurator or procurators, or if he should not be in the Principality, then none of his subjects need do him homage or take an oath.

3. THE MANNNER IN WHICH A VASSAL SHOULD ACT WHEN HE BECOMES A LIEGEMAN OF HIS LORD. When a vassal becomes the liegeman of his lord, he should say: "Sire, I become your liegeman for this fief" (and he names the fief for which he is doing homage); "and I promise to keep and

Text: Peter W. Topping (trans.), *Feudal Institutions as Revealed in the Assizes of Romania* (Philadelphia: University of Pennsylvania Press, 1949), pp. 17-26, 30-34, 62, 76-82, 92.

protect you as my lord against all persons, and against everything which can live and die." And the lord should reply: "And I receive you in the faith of God and in mine." And he should kiss him on the mouth in sign of faith. But if he or she who does homage, as is above said, to the chief lord, has previously performed liege homage to another lord or lady, who may or may not be a vassal of the chief lord, he must save him in doing homage. And the reason is that no one who is another's man can afterward do homage to somebody else, if he does not first save his first lord, or unless he does it with his leave and consent; otherwise, he would be false in the fealty to him whose man he was first. And he who performs homage to another than the chief lord for anything which is in his land must do it in the above-described manner. For one cannot do homage except to one lord, since a man cannot perform more than one ligeance without great wrong-doing. And a man who does homage to another than the one of whom he is a liegeman is bound to his lord by the fealty which he pays him and by the homage which he does to him, to protect and guard him against all persons, and against everything which can live and die: and this does he promise him in doing homage. And from this it appears that he is bound never to raise his hand against the body or the person [of his lord], nor, in so far as he is able, may he consent or suffer that another should do it; nor is he to take or cause to be taken anything from his lord or from him whose liegeman he is. Nor should any man or woman act as counsel against his lord, unless the lord has appointed him counsel; nor should a man or woman speak words in court [against the lord], unless it is as his counsel; for if he does so, he places himself in the mediate or final judgment [of the court] with respect to things which are against the lord. Nor should he bear arms against his lord, to whom he is bound in fealty. Nor should he to his knowledge bring about the shame or damage of his lord nor within his power allow or consent that another may do so. Neither should he violate the body of the lady or daughter of his lord nor lie with them in carnal intercourse unless it be in marriage, nor with the lord's sister so long as she is a maiden in the house of his lord; nor should he suffer anyone else to do so. And he should loyally give counsel to his lord in that in which he shall ask counsel.

Neither should the lord raise his hand nor cause another hand to be raised against the person of his vassal or against his fief unless it is done by the mediate or final judgment of his court. And the lord is bound to his liegeman by the fealty which exists between them in all things heretofore said by which the man is bound to his lord and the lord to him; because between the lord and his man there is fealty, and fealty should be common to both in respect of all the things said above. And each one must preserve his fealty to the other firmly and completely. And the vassal is so much the more bound to his lord in that he must enter into hostageship in order to release his lord from prison, if he is requested to do so by his lord or through his messages. And every man is held, by his fealty to his lord, if he finds him in need of arms, on foot, in the midst of his enemies, or in any place wherein he stands in danger of death, to use all his power to place him on a horse and rescue him from that peril. And if otherwise he is not able to do so, he must give him his own horse or whatever other [mount he has], if the lord requires it, and help him to mount. And whoever fails to do any of these things for his lord fails in his fealty to him. And if the lord can prove this by the record of the court, he can do to him and to his possessions as he should to a man who has failed in his fealty. But if he takes care to do any of these things for his lord, the lord is bound by his fealty through his loyal power to free him or those who have been made hostages for his liberation. In addition the man is bound to his lord to serve as a pledge for him to the full value of his fief. And he who fails his lord in this I believe should lose his fief as long as he shall live. And if a case should arise where the man serving as hostage or pledge for his lord should receive any damage through the said service, the lord is bound to make good to him every loss, and this through the fealty by which he is bound to him.

4. HOW THE PRINCE CANNOT PUNISH ANY BARON OR VASSAL OF HIS WITHOUT THE CONSENT OF HIS LIEGEMEN. The Prince cannot punish any baron or vassal of his, either in civil or criminal action, nor injure him, nor place a penalty on him, without the counsel and consent of his liegemen or of the major part of them; nor render a decision concerning someone's fief or commission others to decide his actions at law; but he must render a decision through his liegemen. And the said lord or his officials cannot have any jurisdiction; but, in petty actions, like the matter of the vineyard of a fief or [the disposition] of a serf, the lord can entrust the judgment to his liegemen if the parties agree. And the lord cannot by force place any liegeman in any office against his will, nor punish him, nor retain his

fief, unless it is with the judgment of his other liegemen.

5. HOW NO LIEGEMAN CAN BE HELD BY HIS LORD EXCEPT FOR TWO CAUSES. It has been ordered in the said Usages that no liegeman of the Principality can be detained in person by his lord for any reason except these two, to wit: for the causes of homicide and treason. And it is thus because his fief provides his security.

6. WHAT SHOULD BE DONE IF A LIEGEMAN COMMITS HOMICIDE OR TREASON? If it should happen that a liegeman has committed homicide or treason, what should be done? To this the answer is, that according to the customs and usages aforesaid the lord cannot punish or detain him unless the homicide or treason has first been proved and unless the judgment has been made in the case of the said liegeman by the other liegemen of the Principality. The lord can neither detain nor seize nor take his goods except by the judgment of the liegemen of the Principality....

22. The Prince cannot separate the liegeman from his vassals in the performance of service, unless the liegeman consents to it (and rightly, because he can and ought to have more confidence in his own men than in strangers). And the lord cannot order a baron or liegeman to serve in any place if he does not send him accompanied with a reasonable company and in accordance with the needs and necessities of the place to which he is sending him. (And this is quite a reasonable thing.)

23. By the Usage and Custom of the Empire of Romania, the Prince cannot place upon his vassals or freemen, or even on their serfs, any tallages [i.e., taxes] or collections on any condition or under any name whatever, or anything, for the utility of the country, without the counsel and consent as well of the liegemen and vassals as of the other freemen. And in this case, those who consent are under obligation, and those who do not consent are under none. But in truth, if he wishes to marry his daughter or ransom himself from his enemies when he has been taken by them, in this case he can levy a collection on the men of simple homage. Moreover, the lord should take care that no vassal, baron, or soldier allows straw, poultry, or any other thing to be taken by force from the serfs of his subjects....

25. HOW ONLY THE PRINCE CAN MAINTAIN AND MAKE FREE A SERF. Only the Seignior, that is the Prince, can maintain and make free his serf or that of another, with the consent of the lord of the serf. And the Seignior can give a fief to the Church or part of a fief, or even a serf. But if the donation is made by someone else, it shall be valid only during the lifetime of the donor....

28. WHEN THE PRINCE MAKES WAR ON ONE OF HIS BARONS, WHAT SHOULD THE VASSALS OF THIS BARON DO? If the Prince makes war on one of his barons or vassals, the vassals of that baron or vassal are held to defend their lord if the Prince has unjustly begun the war. Further, the said baron or vassal is bound to request the lord once, twice, or three times that he must abstain from this molestation; and he should do this in the presence of his barons and of his liegemen, if he can have a sufficient number of these; if he cannot have them, then before and in the presence of other men worthy of faith. And if he [the Prince] is not willing to abstain, the vassals are bound to defend their lord, and they can do so without penalty. But if he began the war justly, the sub-vassals are not bound to defend their lord against the higher lord if they have done homage, reserving their fealty to the superior; otherwise, they are bound to defend him until by judgment of court he shall be disinherited.

30. HOW THE LIEGEMAN, OR THE LIEGEWOMAN, CAN GRANT A THIRD OF THE FIEF. It is also contained in the Usages of the Empire that a liegeman or liegewoman can freely grant a third of his or her fief or fiefs to him or to those whom they wish, with the service due for that land. But he cannot sell it without the consent of his lord. A man of simple homage cannot grant either a third or fourth part, nor a serf nor any land without permission of his lord, from whom he holds the land.

And the lord cannot constrain any liegeman to accept an office against his will....

32. HOW FIEFS AND BARONIES ARE INHERITED BY PRIMOGENITURE. In truth, in a fief, a barony, or in the Principality the first-born succeeds the father or the mother and if there is no son or daughter, the nearest relative who appears in the Principality succeeds, if he is of the line from which the paternal or maternal fief proceeds. And if a fief dates from the conquest of the Principality, the nearest relative, however remote, succeeds, provided always that he is of the paternal or maternal family....

107. HOW A LIEGEMAN CAN GIVE A PERSON ONE OR TWO SERFS FOR A RETURN. A liegeman can give one or two serfs or more to a person for some return, provided that he does not exceed the value of a fifth part of his fief or fiefs. And such a vassal is not obliged to take an oath of fealty or homage, but the investiture of his lord is sufficient....

151. IF A LIEGEMAN KILLS A SERF, WHAT SHOULD BE DONE? If it happens that a liegeman should

kill a serf by misadventure, he is required to give the latter's lord another serf worth as much as the victim. But if he acted on premeditation, he shall submit to the sentence of the liegemen of the lord at the place where the homicide was committed, if the lord of the place has jurisdiction in criminal matters. . . .

153. HOW, IF THERE IS LITIGATION FOR A VACANT FIEF, THAT FIEF SHOULD BE SEQUESTERED. If it happens that a fief or part of a fief becomes vacant and a dispute arises between two persons, in this case it is just that the fief or the part thereof be sequestered by the lord and handed over to someone worthy of trust until the aforementioned dispute is settled. But what shall happen if the dispute is between the lord and those who ask for the fief? The answer is that the fief shall remain in the hands of the lord while the dispute is being adjudged. . . .

157. WHEN ONE WISHES TO DO BATTLE WITH ANOTHER, HE MUST GIVE THE WAGER OF BATTLE. If somebody wishes to do battle with another person, according to the Custom of the Empire of Romania, he can do so by giving the wager of battle. . . .

161. HOW IN KILLING SOMEONE IN SELF-DEFENSE, ONE DOES NOT MERIT A PENALTY. The vassal, or whoever it may be, [who] in defending himself will kill someone, does not for this merit any penalty. . . .

167. When a person deserts his lord in battle and flees before the battle has been lost, he deserves to be disinherited of his land by judgment of the court of his lord. And if a man kills another man and is taken, and is punished with death by the court, he does not lose his [movable] goods but can freely dispose of his goods by will, unless he is a traitor. . . .

197. HOW THE LORD CAN TAKE ALL OF THE MOVABLE GOODS OF HIS SERF. In accordance with the custom of the above-mentioned Principality the lord can take all of the movable goods of his male or female serf, if he wishes, and can take further his or her *staxia* and give it to another of his serfs. But he must leave to the deprived serf his sustenance, so that the fief to which the serf belongs is not diminished.

198. A Greek serf cannot be a witness against a liegeman in a criminal case involving life or limb. . . .

66 SENESCHAUCIE: MANORIALISM

During the early Middle Ages, while western Europe was almost completely rural in complexion and town life was unimportant, the power and wealth of the nobility depended heavily on the economic support of the peasants who worked their landed estates. The leisured classes could hunt, fight, and have castles and churches because the peasants were there to labor for the everyday necessities of life. They tilled the fields and tended the livestock, made clothing, furniture, and armor, and built roads, bridges, and castles for the lords. Yet, while the peasants comprised about ninety-five per cent of the total population in the early Middle Ages and were economically indispensable to the feudal system, they were entirely outside of the political and social hierarchy of feudalism. Only the nobles held the reins of privilege and government.

To admit that the nobles exacted heavy toil and heavy taxes from the peasantry, however, is not to say that the peasants failed to reap benefits from the feudal system. The lords and their military retinue gave the peasants life-saving protection from plunderers and invaders and afforded them access to manorial courts for what there existed of civil and criminal justice.

The character of a typical manorial village—the local unit of feudal government and economy—has been described in the general introduction, pages 251-52. Suffice it here to add that before the eleventh century about ninety per cent of western Europeans lived all their lives in such an environment. They were born, grew up, raised families, worked, and died in these rural communities—which may have varied locally in custom and organization but comprised the same general features. Few knew anything of the world beyond the limited horizons of their village.

In the following extract from an anonymous treatise entitled *Seneschaucie* (probably written no later than the thirteenth century in England) we are given instructions on how the lord and his servants should ideally perform their assigned roles in life. (The seneschal, from whom the treatise draws its name, was usually the chief officer in the house of a medieval English lord; he handled the administration of justice and had entire control of the domestic arrangements of the manor.) In reading this selection, one should remember that the employments and titles of manorial officers varied considerably throughout western Europe, depending on local needs and traditions. This selection presents merely one example of manorial organization.

Here begins the book of the office of seneschal.

The seneschal of lands ought to be prudent and faithful and profitable, and he ought to know the law of the realm, to protect his lord's business and to instruct and give assurance to the bailiffs who are beneath him in their difficulties. He ought two or three times a year to make his rounds and visit the manors of his stewardship, and then he ought to inquire about the rents, services, and customs, hidden or withdrawn, and about franchises of courts, lands, woods, meadows, pastures, waters, mills, and other things which belong to the manor and are done away with without warrant, by whom, and how: and if he be able let him amend these things in the right way without doing wrong to any, and if he be not, let him show it to his lord, that he may deal with it if he wish to maintain his right.

The seneschal ought, at his first coming to the manors, to cause all the demesne lands of each to be measured by true men, and he ought to know by the perch of the country how many acres there are in each field, and thereby he can know how much wheat, rye, barley, oats, peas, beans, and dredge one ought by right to sow in each acre, and thereby can one see if the provost or the hayward account for more seed than is right, and thereby can he see how many ploughs are required on the manor . . . And if there be any cheating in the sowing, or ploughing, or reaping, he shall easily see it. And he must cause all the meadows and several pastures to be measured by acres, and thereby can one know the cost, and how much hay is necessary every year for the sustenance of the manor, and how much stock can be kept on the several pasture, and how much on the common.

The seneschal has no power to remove a bailiff or servant who is with the lord, and clothed and kept by him, without the special order of the lord, for so he would make of the head the tail; but if the bailiff be less capable or less profitable than he ought to be, or if he have committed trespass or offence in his office, let it be shown to the lord and to his council, and he shall do as he shall think good.

The seneschal should not have power to sell wardship, or marriage, or escheat, nor to dower any lady or woman, nor to take homage or suit, nor to sell or make free a vilein without special warrant from his lord. And the seneschal ought not to be chief accountant for the things of his office, for he ought on the account of each manor to answer for his doings and commands and improvements, and for fines and amerciaments of the courts where he has held pleas as another, because no man can or ought to be judge or justice of his own doings.

The seneschal ought, on his coming to each manor, to see and inquire how they are tilled, and in what crops they are, and how the cart-horses and avers, oxen, cows, sheep, and swine are kept and improved. And if there be loss or damage from want of guard, he ought to take fines from those who are to blame, so that the lord may not lose. . . .

The seneschal ought, on his coming to the manors, to inquire how the bailiff bears himself within and without, what care he takes, what improvement he makes, and what increase and profit there is in the manor in his office, because of his being there. And also of the provost, and hayward, and keeper of cattle, and all other offices, how each bears himself towards him, and thereby he can be more sure who makes profit and who harm. Also he ought to provide that there should be no waste or destruction on any manor, or overcharge of anything belonging to the manor. He ought to remove all those that are not necessary for the lord, and all the servants who do nothing, and all overcharge in the dairy, and other profitless and unreasonable offices which are called wrong outlays, without profit.

The seneschal ought, on his coming to the manors, to inquire about wrong-doings and trespasses done in parks, ponds, warrens, conygarths, and dove-houses, and of all other things which are done to the loss of the lord in his office.

The office of bailiff.

The bailiff ought to be faithful and profitable, and a good husbandman, and also prudent, that he need not send to his lord or superior seneschal to have advice and instruction about everything connected with his baillie, unless it be an extraordinary matter, or of great danger; for a bailiff is worth little in time of need who knows nothing, and has nothing in himself without the instruction of another. The bailiff ought to rise every morning and survey the woods, corn, meadows, and pastures, and see what damage may have

Text: Elizabeth Lamond (trans. and ed.), *Walter of Henley's Husbandry, Together with an Anonymous Husbandry, Seneschaucie, and Robert Grosseteste's Rules* (London: Longmans, Green & Co., 1890), pp. 85-91, 93, 95-101, 105-07.

been done. And he ought to see that the ploughs are yoked in the morning, and unyoked at the right time, so that they may do their proper ploughing every day, as much as they can and ought to do by the measured perch. And he must cause the land to be marled, folded, manured, improved, and amended as his knowledge may approve, for the good and bettering of the manor. . . .

And the bailiff ought to oversee the ploughs and the tillage, and see that the lands are well ploughed with small furrows, and properly cropped, and well sown with good and pure seed, and cleanly harrowed; and all the winter seed may be bought by warrant of the writ of the lord or seneschal, for this is a point that must have warrant; and all the spring seed may be sown from his own store, if cheapness does not prevent him by the order from a writ.

Let nothing on the manors which ought to be sold be taken by the people, but let it be sent to fairs and markets at several places, and be inspected and bargained for, and whoever will give the most shall have it; for it is not chattel of death, or of war, or sold from the king's pinfold.

No seneschal or bailiff, or servant, or provost, or bedel, or hayward, should take for money, or through any sale, anything from the manors of which he is keeper; for they ought not, by right, to buy the things or take for price what they themselves ought to make profitable and sell. . . .

The bailiff ought, in August, to see and command throughout the manors that the corn be well gathered and reaped evenly, and that the cocks and sheaves be small, so will the corn dry the quicker; and one can load, stack, and thresh the small sheaf best, for there is greater loss in the large sheaf than in the small. . . .

The office of provost.

The provost ought to be elected and presented by the common consent of the township, as the best husbandman and the best approver among them. And he must see that all the servants of the court rise in the morning to do their work, and that the ploughs be yoked in time, and the lands well ploughed and cropped, and turned over, and sown with good and clean seed, as much as they can stand. And he ought to see that there be a good fold of wooden hurdles on the demesne, strewed within every night to improve the land. . . .

. . . And the provost ought often to see that all the beasts are well provided with forage and kept as they ought to be, and that they have enough pasture without overcharge of the other beasts, and he ought to see that the keepers of all kinds of beasts do not go to fairs, or markets, or wrestling-matches, or taverns, by which the beasts aforesaid may go astray without guard, or do harm to the lord or another, but they must ask leave, and put keepers in their places that no harm may happen; and if harm or loss do come about, let the amend be taken from the keepers and the damage made good. Let no provost have power to hold pleas involving penalty or amerciament, but he or the hayward or the bedel may receive the plaints and make the attachments and deliver them to the bailiff. And no provost ought to permit or suffer any man to have his allowance if he be not deserving, nor ought he to allow any overcharge of underdairywomen in the dairy, nor shall they carry from the dairy cheese, butter, milk, or curds, to the impoverishment of the dairy, and the decrease of cheese. Let no provost remain over a year as provost, if he be not proved most profitable and faithful in his doings, and a good husbandman. Each provost ought every year to account with his bailiff, and tally the works and customs commuted in the manor, whereby he can surely answer in money for the surplus in the account, for the money for customs is worth as much as rent. . . .

The office of the lord.

The lord ought to love God and justice, and be faithful and true in his sayings and doings, and he ought to hate sin and injustice, and evildoing. The lord ought not to take counsel with young men full of young blood, and ready courage, who know little or nothing of business, nor of any juggler, flatterer, or idle talker, nor of such as bear witness by present, but he ought to take counsel with worthy and faithful men, ripe in years, who have seen much, and know much, and who are known to be of good fame, and who never were caught or convicted for treachery or any wrong-doing; nor for love, nor for hate, nor for fear, nor for menace, nor for gain, nor for loss, will turn aside from truth, and knowingly counsel their lord to do him harm.

The lord ought to command and ordain that the accounts be heard every year, but not in one place but on all the manors, for so can one quickly know everything, and understand the profit and loss. And he ought to command and ordain that no bailiff have his food in the manors except at a fixed price in money, so that he take nothing from the manors but hay, firewood, and straw; and that no friend, stranger, nor anyone from the lord's hostel or elsewhere be received at the manors at the lord's expense, nor shall anything be given or delivered to them without warrant of writ, unless the bailiff or provost wish to acquit it from their own purses for the great expense one is unnecessarily put to, as can be seen above in another chapter.

The lord ought to inquire by his own men and others on his manors as many as there are, about his seneschal and his doings, and the approvements he has made since his coming; in the same way he ought to inquire about profits and losses from the bailiff and provost, and how much he will have to seek from both. He ought to ask for his auditors and rolls of account, then he ought to see who has done well and who not, and who has made improvement and who not, and who has made profit and who not, but loss, and those he has then found good and faithful and profitable, let him keep on this account. And if anyone be found who has done harm and is by no means profitable, let him answer for his doing and take farewell. And if the lord observe these said forms, then will each lord live a good man and honestly, and be as he will rich and powerful without sin, and will do injustice to no one.

67 WILLIAM FITZ STEPHEN, "A DESCRIPTION OF THE MOST NOBLE CITY OF LONDON": THE RISE OF TOWN AND TRADE

The emergence of more ordered governments, the steadying influence of the Church, a reduction in the number of Norse invaders, and a substantial population increase, all contributed to a resurgence of western European economic development in the eleventh and twelfth centuries. The expansion of European trade and commerce occurred first in the Mediterranean and later along the North and Baltic seas. But as commerce spread to the hinterland, manufacturing grew, new industries were created, towns sprang up, populations rose, and everywhere merchants found increased demands for a variety of products. By the end of the eleventh century commercial centers like London, Bruges, Ghent, Ypres, and Arras were bustling with activity. The growth of cities had a profound effect upon the feudal society of the Middle Ages. As one of the great medieval historians, Henri Pirenne (1862-1935), put it:

The rigid confines of the demesnial (manorial) system, which up to now had hemmed in all economic activity, were broken down and the whole social order was patterned along more flexible, more active and more varied lines. As in antiquity, the country oriented itself afresh on the city. Under the influence of trade the old Roman cities took on new life and were repopulated, or mercantile groups formed round about the military burgs and established themselves along the sea coasts, on river banks, at confluences, at the junction points of the natural routes of communication. Each of them constituted a market which exercised an attraction, proportionate to its importance, on the surrounding country or made itself felt afar.

Closely associated with the rise of towns and the growth of trade, is the emergence of the influential middle class, or bourgeoisie. These were shopkeepers and merchants who, by virtue of their wealth, often banded together and purchased town charters from hard pressed lords, thus gaining a substantial amount of local independence. The rise of a middle class altered the older social relationships that had existed between serfs and nobles in the early Middle Ages. The new bourgeoisie was ambitious and possessed money. Its members did not accept political or social discrimination without making efforts to improve their material lot, and as money became increasingly important, their goals were realized. By the end of the Middle Ages the bourgeoisie had begun to supersede the aristocracy as the dominant social force in western Europe.

The selection below is a late twelfth-century description of London. The author, William fitz Stephen, colorfully depicts the increasing urbanization of the inhabitants and institutions, and one sees readily the rising influence of the middle class.

Among the noble and celebrated cities of the world that of London, the capital of the kingdom of the English, is one which extends its glory farther than all the others and sends its wealth and merchandise more widely into distant lands. Higher than all the rest does it lift its head. It is happy in the healthiness of its air; in its observance of Christian practice; in the strength of its fortifications; in its natural situation; in the

Text: David C. Douglas and George W. Greenaway (eds.), *English Historical Documents 1042-1189* (New York: Oxford University Press; London: Eyre & Spottiswoode, Ltd., 1953), II, 956-61. Reprinted by permission of the publishers.

honour of its citizens; and in the modesty of its matrons. It is cheerful in its sports, and the fruitful mother of noble men. Let us look into these things in turn.

If the mildness of the climate of this place softens the character of its inhabitants, it does not make them corrupt in following Venus, but rather prevents them from being fierce and bestial, making them liberal and kind.

In the church of St. Paul there is the episcopal seat. Once it was metropolitan, and some think it will again become so, if the citizens return to the island, unless perhaps the archiepiscopal title of the blessed martyr, Thomas, and the presence of his body preserves that dignity for ever at Canterbury where it is at present. But as St. Thomas has made both cities illustrious, London by his rising and Canterbury by his setting, each can claim advantage of the other with justice in respect of that saint. As regards the practice of Christian worship, there are in London and its suburbs thirteen greater conventual churches and, besides these, one hundred and twenty-six lesser parish churches.

It has on the east the Palatine castle [Tower of London], very great and strong: the keep and walls rise from very deep foundations and are fixed with a mortar tempered by the blood of animals. On the west there are two castles very strongly fortified, and from these there runs a high and massive wall with seven double gates and with towers along the north at regular intervals. London was once also walled and turreted on the south, but the mighty Thames, so full of fish, has with the sea's ebb and flow washed against, loosened, and thrown down those walls in the course of time. Upstream to the west there is the royal palace [Westminster] which is conspicuous above the river, a building incomparable in its ramparts and bulwarks. It is about two miles from the city and joined thereto by a populous suburb.

Everywhere outside the houses of those living in the suburbs, and adjacent to them, are the spacious and beautiful gardens of the citizens, and these are planted with trees. Also there are on the north side pastures and pleasant meadow lands through which flow streams wherein the turning of mill-wheels makes a cheerful sound. Very near lies a great forest with woodland pastures in which there are the lairs of wild animals: stags, fallow deer, wild boars and bulls. The tilled lands of the city are not of barren gravel, but fat Asian plains that yield luxuriant crops and fill the tillers' barns with the sheaves of Ceres.

There are also outside London on the north side excellent suburban wells with sweet, wholesome and clear water that flows rippling over the bright stones. Among these are Holywell, Clerkenwell and St. Clement's Well, which are all famous. These are frequented by great numbers and much visited by the students from the schools and by the young men of the city, when they go out for fresh air on summer evenings. Good indeed is this city when it has a good lord! . . . St. Paul, the church of the Holy Trinity, and the church of St. Martin) have famous schools by special privilege and by virtue of their ancient dignity. But through the favour of some magnate, or through the presence of teachers who are notable or famous in philosophy, there are also other schools. On feast-days the masters hold meetings for their pupils in the church whose festival it is. The scholars dispute, some with oratory and some with argument; some recite enthymemes; others excel in using perfect syllogisms. Some dispute for ostentation like wrestlers with opponent; others argue in order to establish the truth in its perfection. Sophists who speak paradoxes are praised for their torrent of words, whilst others seek to overthrow their opponents by using fallacious arguments. Now and then orators use rhetoric for persuasion, being careful to omit nothing essential to their art. Boys of different schools strive against each other in verses, or contend about the principles of grammar and the rules governing past and future tenses. Others use epigrams, rhythm and metre in the old trival banter; they pull their comrades to pieces with "Fescennine Licence": mentioning no names, they dart abuse and gibes, and mock the faults of their comrades and sometimes even those of their elders, using Socratic salt and biting harder even than the tooth of Theon in daring dithyrambics. Their hearers, ready to enjoy the joke, wrinkle up their noses as they guffaw in applause.

Those engaged in business of various kinds, sellers of merchandise, hirers of labour, are distributed every morning into their several localities according to their trade. Besides, there is in London on the river bank among the wines for sale in ships and in the cellars of the vintners a public cook-shop. There daily you may find food according to the season, dishes of meat, roast, fried and boiled, large and small fish, coarser meats for the poor and more delicate for the rich, such as venison and big and small birds. If any of the citizens should unexpectedly receive visitors, weary from their journey, who would fain not wait until fresh food is bought and cooked, or until the servants have brought bread or water for washing, they hasten to the river bank and there find all they need. However great the multitude of soldiers and travellers entering the city, or preparing to go out of it, at any hour of the day or night—that these may not fast too long, and those may not go out supperless—they turn aside thither, if they please, where every man can refresh himself in his own way. Those who would cater for themselves fastidiously need not search to find sturgeon or the bird of Africa or the Ionian godwit. For this is a public kitchen, very convenient to the city, and part of its amenities. Hence the dictum in the Gorgias of Plato that the art of cookery is an imitation of medicine and flatters a quarter of civic life.

Immediately outside one of the gates there is a field [Smithfield] which is smooth both in fact and in name. On every sixth day of the week, unless it be a major feast-day, there takes place there a famous exhibition of fine horses for sale. Earls, barons and knights, who are in the town, and many citizens come out to see or to buy. It is pleasant to see the high-stepping palfreys with their gleaming coats, as they go through their paces, putting down their feet alternately on one side together. Next, one can see the horses suitable for esquires, moving faster though less smoothly, lifting and setting down, as it were, the opposite fore and hind feet: here are colts of fine breed, but not yet accustomed to the bit, stepping high with jaunty tread; there are the sumpter-horses, powerful and spirited; and after them there are the war-horses, costly, elegant of form, noble of stature, with ears quickly tremulous, necks raised and large haunches. As these show their paces, the buyers first try those of gentler gait, then those of quicker pace whereby the fore and hind feet move in pairs together. . . .

By themselves in another part of the field stand the goods of the countryfolk: implements of husbandry, swine with long flanks, cows with full udders, oxen of immense size, and woolly sheep. There also stand the mares fit for plough, some big with foal, and others with brisk young colts closely following them.

To this city from every nation under heaven merchants delight to bring their trade by sea. The Arabian sends gold; the Sabaean spice and incense. The Scythian brings arms, and from the rich, fat lands of Babylon comes oil of palms. The Nile sends precious stones; the men of Norway and Russia, furs and sables; nor is China absent with purple silk. The Gauls come with their wines.

London, as historians have shown, is a much older city than Rome, for though it derives from the same Trojan ancestors, it was founded by Brutus before Rome was founded by Romulus and Remus. Wherefore they still have the same laws from their common origin. This city is like Rome divided into wards; it has annual sheriffs instead of consuls; it has its senatorial order and lower magistrates; it has drains and aqueducts in its streets; it has its appointed place for the hearing of cases deliberative, demonstrative and judicial; it has its several courts, and its separate assemblies on appointed days.

I do not think there is a city with a better record for church-going, doing honour to God's ordinances, keeping feast-days, giving alms and hospitality to strangers, confirming betrothals, contracting marriages, celebrating weddings, providing feasts, entertaining guests, and also, it may be added, in care for funerals and for the burial of the dead. The only plagues of London are the immoderate drinking of fools and the frequency of fires.

To this it may be added that almost all the bishops, abbots and magnates of England are in a sense citizens and freemen of London, having their own splendid town-houses. In them they live, and spend largely, when they are summoned to great councils by the king or by their metropolitan, or drawn thither by their private affairs.

We now come to speak of the sports of the city, for it is not fitting that a city should be merely useful and serious-minded, unless it be also pleasant and cheerful. For this cause on the seals of the supreme pontiff, down to the time of the last Pope Leo, on one side of the lead was engraved the figure of Peter the fisherman and above him a key, as it were, held out to him from heaven by the hand of God, and around it was inscribed the verse, "For me didst thou leave the ship, receive now the key." And on the other side was engraved a city with the inscription "Golden Rome". Moreover, it was said in honour of Augustus Caesar and Rome, "It rains all night, games usher in the day; Caesar, thou dost divide dominion with Jove." Instead of shows in the theatre and stage-plays, London provides plays of a more sacred character, wherein are presented the miracles worked by saintly confessors or the sufferings which made illustrious the constancy of martyrs. Furthermore, every year on the day called Carnival—to begin with the sports of boys (for we were all boys once)— scholars from the different schools bring fighting-cocks to their masters, and the whole morning is set apart to watch their cocks do battle in the schools, for the boys are given a holiday that day. After dinner all the young men of the town go out into the fields in the suburbs to play ball. The scholars of the various schools have their own ball, and almost all the followers of each occupation have theirs also. The seniors and the fathers and the wealthy magnates of the city come on horseback to watch the contests of the younger generation, and in their turn recover their lost youth: the motions of their natural heat seem to be stirred in them at the mere sight of such strenuous activity and by their participation in the joys of unbridled youth.

On feast-days throughout the summer the young men indulge in the sports of archery, running, jumping, wrestling, slinging the stone, hurling the javelin beyond a mark and fighting with sword and buckler. Cytherea leads the dance of maidens, and until the moon rises, the earth is shaken with flying feet.

In winter on almost every feast-day before dinner either foaming boars, armed with lightning tusks, fight for their lives "to save their bacon", or stout bulls with butting horns, or huge bears do battle with the hounds let loose upon them. When the great marsh that washes the north wall of the city is frozen over, swarms of young men issue forth to play games on the ice. Some, gaining speed in their run, with feet set well apart, slide sideways over a vast expanse of ice. Others make seats out of a large lump of ice, and whilst one sits thereon, others with linked hands run before and drag him along behind them. So swift is their sliding motion that sometimes their feet slip, and they all fall on their faces. Others, more skilled at winter sports, put on their feet the shin-bones of animals, binding them firmly round their ankles, and, holding poles shod with iron in their hands, which they strike from time to time against the ice, they are propelled swift as a bird in flight or a bolt shot from an engine of war. Sometimes, by mutual consent, two of them run against each other in this way from a great distance, and, lifting their poles, each tilts against the other. Either one or both fall, not without some bodily injury, for, as they fall, they are carried along a great way beyond each other by the impetus of their run, and wherever the ice comes in contact with their heads, it scrapes off the skin utterly. Often a leg or an arm is broken, if the victim falls with it underneath him; but theirs is an age greedy of glory, youth yearns for victory, and exercises itself in mock combats in order to carry itself more bravely in real battles.

Many of the citizens take pleasure in sporting with birds of the air, with hawks, falcons and such-like, and with hounds that hunt their prey in the woods. The citizens have the rights of the chase in Middlesex, Hertfordshire, all the Chiltern country, and in Kent as far as the river Cray. The Londoners, who were then known as Trinobantes, drove back Julius Caesar, whose delight it was to wade through paths steeped in blood. Whence Lucan writes: "To the Britons whom he had sought he turned his back in flight."

68 CHARTER GRANTS OF EMPEROR FREDERICK I: MEDIEVAL FAIRS

The return of trade to the European economy in the Middle Ages involved regularizing the contact between town and country, so that the merchants' products of specialized industry could be exchanged for the food and raw materials of the manor. This link between town and country was the market, which was usually held once a week at the center of a town or on the approaches to a manorial castle or abbey. Supervision of the market and its arrangements were in the hands of local magistrates or merchant guilds.

The annual fair was the weekly market on a grander scale. It served a wider territory, attracted merchants from all over Europe, and usually lasted from one to six weeks. While the bulk of retail trade took place in the weekly local markets, the fairs served as centers for wholesaling, principally in goods not obtainable locally—woolens from Flanders and Italy, linens from Champagne and the Rhine, iron and leather from Germany and Spain, furs from Russia, Scandinavia, and Africa, wines from France and Spain, spices and silks from the Orient. The charter to hold a fair, usually granted by a king, was eagerly sought by feudal lords because of the great profits and fees that gave prosperity to their regions. To ensure the success of a fair, the charter grant offered attending merchants special privileges—freedom of trade, guarantees of fair dealing, speedy justice at law, immunities from certain taxes and tolls, and similar inducements.

The fairs of Champagne in France were the most celebrated of the countless fairs held all over Europe in the twelfth and thirteenth centuries—elsewhere in France at

Lyons and St. Denis near Paris; in England at St. Giles, St. Ives, Stourbridge, and Bartholomew; in Flanders at Thourout, Bruges, Ypres, and Lille; in Germany at Aix-la-Chapelle, Cologne, Frankfurt, and Augsburg; in Russia at Novgorod; in Switzerland at Geneva; and in Sweden at Uppsala—to name a few of the greatest fairs. Eventually, as the merchants established an annual round from fair to fair, they began to function not only as buyers and sellers of goods but also as incipient bankers—establishing monetary exchange rates, transferring debts, and providing credits and loans at traditional locations in Italy, France, the Low Countries, and Germany. These merchants were providing an impetus for the breakdown of the old feudal isolation by introducing money as a medium of international economy and bringing about the exchange of the ideas as well as the goods of nations.

The first selection below is a charter granted in 1166 by Frederick Barbarossa, Holy Roman Emperor, for the conduct of a fair at Aix-la-Chapelle, which was such an important crossroads that fairs were held there twice a year. To be noted are the personal legal protection afforded to the merchants and also the precise regulations regarding coinage and monetary exchange. The second selection is a sequel to the first—a charter issued by Frederick in 1173 to provide a fair site at Duisburg for sea merchants, to supplement the fair at Aix-la-Chapelle for merchants coming by land. Again the merchant is induced to come by guarantees of legal protection and assurances of monetary stability.

I

In the name of the Holy and Indivisible Trinity, Frederick, by favor of divine clemency, Emperor Augustus of the Romans. Since the royal palace of Aix-la-Chapelle excels all provinces and cities in dignity and honor, both for the praise given there to the body of the most blessed Emperor Charlemagne, which that city alone is known to have, and because it is a royal seat at which the Emperors of the Romans were first crowned, it is fitting and reasonable that we, following the example of the holy lord Charlemagne and of other predecessors of ours, should fortify that same place, which is a pillar of support to the empire, with lavish gifts of liberty and privileges, as if with walls and towers. We have therefore decreed that there should be held twice a year the solemn and universal fairs of Aix-la-Chapelle. And this we have done on the advice of the merchants. Moreover, we have preserved the rights of neighboring cities, so that these fairs may not only not be a hindrance to their fairs but may rather increase their profits. And so, on the advice of our nobles, we have given, out of respect for the most holy lord, the Emperor Charlemagne, this liberty to all merchants—that they may be quit and free of all toll throughout the year at these fairs in this royal place, and they may buy and sell goods freely just as they wish. No merchant, nor any other person, may take a merchant to court for the payment of any debt during these fairs, nor take him there for any business that was conducted before the fairs began; but if anything be done amiss during the fairs, let it be made good according to justice during the fairs. Moreover, the first fair shall begin on Quadragesima Sunday, which is six weeks before Easter, and it shall last for fifteen days. The second fair shall begin eight days before the feast of St. Michael and shall continue for eight days after that feast. And all people coming to, staying at, or going from the fairs shall have peace for their persons and goods. And lest the frequent changing of coins, which are sometimes light and sometimes heavy, should redound to the hurt of so glorious a place at any time in the future, on the advice of our court, we have ordered money to be struck there of the same purity, weight, and form, and in the same quantity, and to be kept to the same standard. Twenty-four solidi shall be struck from a mark, always having the value of twelve solidi of Cologne, so that twelve Cologne solidi may always be made from twenty-four of these solidi, just as twenty-four solidi may always be struck from twelve solidi of Cologne. The form of the coins will be such that on one side will be the image of St. Charles the Great and his superscription, and on the obverse our own image with the superscription of our own name. And a certain abuse has prevailed for a long time in the courts of Aix-la-Chapelle so that if he, who was impleaded for calumny or for any other thing, could not offer satisfaction by compensation for his offense, except he flee from the country at once, he incurred the full penalty of composition; therefore, we, condemning this bad law forever, have decreed that any one may offer in this our royal town of Aix-la-Chapelle, for any cause for which he has

Text: Roy C. Cave and Herbert H. Coulson (eds.), *A Source Book for Medieval Economic History* (Milwaukee: Bruce Publishing Company, 1936), pp. 120-24.

been impleaded, compensation by whatever small thing he is able to take off with his hands while standing upright, without bending his body, such thing as a cloak, tunic, hat, shirt, or other garment. And because the taking and exchanging of money, other than the money of Aix-la-Chapelle, has been condemned by an unjust law, we have decreed to the contrary, that all money shall be current in our city according to its quality, and it shall be accepted by everyone according to what it has been declared to be worth. Moreover, we grant and confirm to the merchants of that city that they may have a mint and a house for exchanging their silver and money whenever they decide to go away on business. Whoever out of boldness decides to oppose our decree, or by temerity to break it, shall be in our mercy and will pay a hundred pounds of gold to our court. And in order that all the things we have decreed may be accepted as genuine and be faithfully observed we have ordered this charter to be written and to be sealed by the impression of our seal.

II

Frederick, by the grace of God, Emperor Augustus of the Romans. We make known to the faithful of our empire that, on the petition of our beloved Count Philip of Flanders, we have decreed four fairs for the merchants of Flanders. Two of these are to be held for merchants by land at stated times at Aix-la-Chapelle, and two for merchants by sea at Duisburg. The beginning of one fair will be on the feast of St. Bartholomew at Duisburg and it will last for fourteen days; the beginning of another will be on Mid-Lent Sunday and will last through the whole of Lent. The beginning of one fair at Aix will be on Quadragesima Sunday and it will last for fourteen days, the other will begin on the feast of St. Michael and will last for the same length of time. When each fortnight is over the men of Flanders and other merchants shall afterwards remain quietly for another fourteen days, refraining from selling any of their cloth, but at the end of that time they may sell freely, paying such toll at Duisburg as they are accustomed to pay at Cologne, and they shall pay the toll by weight. In order that there might be greater convenience for the merchants we have ordered new money to be struck in denarii at Duisburg and in oboles at Aix, a mark of which will equal one denarius of the money of Cologne. And the Count of Flanders has ordered those coins to be accepted throughout all the land.

Whatever merchants, whether Flemish or foreign, pledge their goods to any one, let them do it in the presence of a judge and assessors who can produce evidence of the pledging afterwards; and on the testimony of the judge and assessors the merchants so doing will receive the goods pledged; but if he has not had the testimony of the judge and assessors about the goods pledged he, from whom the goods are demanded, shall purge himself with an oath that he is not the debtor. A merchant of any country, who cannot regain goods pledged on the testimony of a judge and assessors, shall demand and seek justice from the judge and assessors of that place which his debtor inhabits, and then the debtor shall be sent with him to the judge and assessors who were present at the pledging, and in their presence he should show the debtor to be guilty. If he does not obtain the justice he seeks, a pledge may be taken from the merchants of that place where justice was denied him until justice be done. Let him not molest the merchants of another place for this cause. If any one have followed a merchant from the greater to the lesser place alleging some evil to have been done, if he wish to lodge a complaint, let him return with that merchant to the place where the wrong was done and let him obtain justice before a judge. But, before he returns, let him who is seeking justice give a pledge to the merchant that he does not wish to prosecute his case in the greater place. If he does not accompany but deserts the merchant, let him make satisfaction in reconciliation according to the pledge he has made. But if he has not made such a pledge he shall not annoy the merchant, but shall depart in peace. If any merchant feel that he has been wronged, contrary to justice, he may have permission to appeal from the smaller to the greater place from which the lesser takes its laws. Let no one provoke a Flemish merchant to a duel, but if any one has anything to say against him, let him take his oath. Merchants shall have the right to ascend or go down the Rhine under our protection for their persons and goods, and on other waters in other parts of our empire. If anyone presumes to use force against them or to injure them, he will be deprived of our favor forever. In order that these rules may be safe and secure we have ordered our seal with that of Count Philip of Flanders to be put to this charter. Done in the year of the Incarnation of the Lord 1173, at Fulda, on the twenty-ninth of May. Amen.

69 STATUTE OF LABORERS: THE CRISIS OF MEDIEVAL ECONOMY

The Black Death, which plagued all of Europe in the years 1347-1350 and nearly halved the population, accelerated the disruption of the medieval order. The static economy of the almost self-sufficient manor had already been severely shaken by the revival of trade, the growth of towns, the influx of gold and creation of monetary exchange systems, and the emergence of urban classes who were relatively free of feudal bonds—the bourgeoisie, the artisans, and the day laborers. The freedoms exercised by townsmen as well as the bourgeois power arising to challenge the old authority of the landed nobility aroused the jealousy of the agricultural population, still restricted by feudal law. Class distinctions based on mercantile wealth or noble lineage were also becoming more objectionable to the lower orders, as the opportunities for freedoms became more apparent. Thus rumbles of discontent had long been heard throughout Europe when the decimations of the Black Death suddenly created in both town and country a severe labor shortage, thereby causing what modern economists call a sellers' market in labor. Workers who "sold" their labor were wooed for their services by both bourgeoisie and manorial lords; the workers were in an ideal position to demand concessions such as higher wages in the town and freedman status in the rural economy.

In an effort to check this economic revolution, governmental authority sometimes intervened to preserve the old order. In England—the best governed and probably the most prosperous of the fourteenth-century states—King Edward III issued a "Statute of Laborers" (printed below) designed to fix wages and prices and to compel laborers to accept work when offered. But just as Diocletian's "Edict of Prices" failed to legislate an economic crisis out of existence (see Document 46), so did Edward's royal ordinance fail to arrest the emancipation of serfs or calm the social and economic storm. Landowners began to enclose for sheep-raising, which required fewer laborers, and inflation created new fortunes to upset the political and social hegemony of the old aristocracy.

Edward by the grace of God etc. to the reverend father in Christ William, by the same grace archbishop of Canterbury, Primate of all England, greeting. Because a great part of the people and especially of the workmen and servants has now died in that pestilence, some, seeing the straights of the masters and the scarcity of servants, are not willing to serve unless they receive excessive wages, and others, rather than through labour to gain their living, prefer to beg in idleness: We, considering the grave inconveniences which might come from the lack especially of ploughmen and such labourers, have held deliberation and treaty concerning this with the prelates and nobles and other learned men sitting by us; by whose consentient counsel we have seen fit to ordain: that every man and woman of our kingdom of England, of whatever condition, whether bond or free, who is able bodied and below the age of sixty years, not living from trade nor carrying on a fixed craft, nor having of his own the means of living, or land of his own with regard to the cultivation of which he might occupy himself, and not serving another, —if he, considering his station, be sought after to serve in a suitable service, he shall be bound to serve him who has seen fit so to seek after him; and he shall take only the wages, liveries, meed or salary which, in the places where he sought to serve, were accustomed to be paid in the twentieth year of our reign of England, or the five or six common years next preceding. Provided, that in thus retaining their service, the lords are preferred before others of their bondsmen or their land tenants: so, nevertheless that such lords thus retain as many as shall be necessary and not more; and if any man or woman, being thus sought after in service, will not do this, the fact being proven by two faithful men before the sheriffs or the bailiffs of our lord the king, or the constables of the town where this happens to be done,—straightway through them, or some one of them, he shall be taken and sent to the next jail, and there he shall remain in strict custody until he shall find surety for serving in the aforesaid form.

And if a reaper or mower, or other workman or servant, of whatever standing or condition

Text: Ernest F. Henderson (trans. and ed.), *Select Historical Documents of the Middle Ages* (London: G. Bell & Sons, Ltd., 1896), pp. 165-68.

he be, who is retained in the service of any one, do depart from the said service before the end of the term agreed, without permission or reasonable cause, he shall undergo the penalty of imprisonment, and let no one, under the same penalty, presume to receive or retain such a one in his service. Let no one, moreover, pay or permit to be paid to any one more wages, livery, meed or salary than was customary as has been said; nor let any one in any other manner exact or receive them, under penalty of paying to him who feels himself aggrieved from this, double the sum that has thus been paid or promised, exacted or received; and if such person be not willing to prosecute, then it (the sum) is to be given to any one of the people who shall prosecute in this matter; and such prosecution shall take place in the court of the lord of the place where such case shall happen. And if the lords of the towns or manors presume of themselves or through their servants in any way to act contrary to this our present ordinance, then in the Counties, Wapentakes and Trithings suit shall be brought against them in the aforesaid form for the triple penalty (of the sum) thus promised or paid by them or their servants; and if perchance, prior to the present ordinance any one shall have covenanted with any one thus to serve for more wages, he shall not be bound by reason of the said covenant to pay more than at another time was wont to be paid to such person; nay, under the aforesaid penalty he shall not presume to pay more.

Likewise saddlers, skinners, white-tawers, cordwainers, tailors, smiths, carpenters, masons, tilers, shipwrights, carters and all other artisans and labourers shall not take for their labour and handiwork more than what, in the places where they happen to labour, was customarily paid to such persons in the said twentieth year and in the other common years preceding, as has been said; and if any man take more, he shall be committed to the nearest jail in the manner aforesaid.

Likewise let butchers, fishmongers, hostlers, brewers, bakers, pulters and all other vendors of any victuals, be bound to sell such victuals for a reasonable price, having regard for the price at which such victuals are sold in the adjoining places: so that such vendors may have moderate gains, not excessive, according as the distance of the places from which such victuals are carried may seem reasonably to require; and if any one sell such victuals in another manner, and be convicted of it in the aforesaid way, he shall pay the double of that which he received to the party injured, or in default of him, to another who shall be willing to prosecute in this behalf; and the mayor and bailiffs of the cities and burroughs, merchant towns and others, and of the maritime ports and places shall have power to enquire concerning each and every one who shall in any way err against this, and to levy the aforesaid penalty for the benefit of those at whose suit such delinquents shall have been convicted; and in case that the same mayor and bailiffs shall neglect to carry out the aforesaid, and shall be convicted of this before justices to be assigned by us, then the same mayor and bailiffs shall be compelled through the same justices, to pay to such wronged person or to another prosecuting in his place, the treble of the thing thus sold, and nevertheless, on our part too, they shall be grievously punished.

And because many sound beggars do refuse to labour so long as they can live from begging alms, giving themselves up to idleness and sins, and, at times, to robbery and other crimes—let no one, under the aforesaid pain of imprisonment presume, under colour of piety or alms to give anything to such as can very well labour, or to cherish them in their sloth,—so that thus they may be compelled to labour for the necessaries of life.

70 JEAN FROISSART, CHRONICLES: THE WAT TYLER INSURRECTION

By the late fourteenth century, England, France, and most of the other nations of Europe were faced with agrarian and artisan discontent so severe that it threatened to break out into social revolution. The climax of this feeling in England came during the reign of Richard II in Wat Tyler's "Insurrection" of 1381—a march on London of discontented agricultural workers and laborers demanding a redress of wrongs. The peasants were fearful of efforts to restore serfdom, and the artisans were worried about increased foreign competition. The Statute of Laborers (Document 69) and other restrictive labor legislation continued to be a source of discontent. The complaints of the participants in the march were directed primarily against the feudal nobility and the royal officials. The person of the king, however, was highly respected, and the marchers expected him to concur with their demands and in effect to rule as a compliant "king of commons." The reforms the marchers requested were long in coming, and it is clear that the majority of the peasants had only a vague idea of what constitutes political rebellion and were seeking only an improvement of their difficult situation.

The selection below is the classic description of the Wat Tyler insurrection by Jean Froissart (1339-1410), a French chronicler of the Hundred Years' War who spent many years in England and may have been an eyewitness to these events. One of the finest medieval chroniclers, Froissart summarizes the demands of the insurrectionists, the grievances they sought to relieve, the violent antinoble and anticlerical character of the revolt, and its inept leadership, which failed to disrupt the power of the nobility or to provide a successful program of social reform. The revolt itself was ephemeral; the workers secured no significant gains, the concessions that had been made were revoked, and afterward life everywhere settled back to the old routine.

... While these conferences were going forward there happened great commotions among the lower orders in England, by which that country was nearly ruined. In order that this disastrous rebellion may serve as an example to mankind, I will speak of all that was done from the information I had at the time. It is customary in England, as well as in several other countries, for the nobility to have great privileges over the commonalty; that is to say, the lower orders are bound by law to plough the lands of the gentry, to harvest their grain, to carry it home to the barn, to thrash and winnow it; they are also bound to harvest and carry home the hay. All these services the prelates and gentlemen exact of their inferiors; and in the counties of Kent, Essex, Sussex, and Bedford, these services are more oppressive than in other parts of the kingdom. In consequence of this the evil disposed in these districts began to murmur, saying, that in the beginning of the world there were no slaves, and that no one ought to be treated as such, unless he had committed treason against his lord, as Lucifer had done against God; but they had done no such thing, for they were neither angels nor spirits, but men formed after the same likeness as these lords who treated them as beasts. This they would bear no longer; they were determined to be free, and if they laboured or did any work, they would be paid for it. A crazy priest in the county of Kent, called John Ball, who for his absurd preaching had thrice been confined in prison by the Archbishop of Canterbury, was greatly instrumental in exciting these rebellious ideas. Every Sunday after mass, as the people were coming out of church, this John Ball was accustomed to assemble a crowd around him in the marketplace and preach to them. On such occasions he would say, "My good friends, matters cannot go on well in England until all things shall be in common; when there shall be neither vassals nor lords; when the lords shall be no more masters than ourselves. How ill they behave to us! for what reason do they thus hold us in bondage? Are we not all descended from the same parents, Adam and Eve? And what can they show, or what reason can they give, why they should be more masters than ourselves? They are clothed in velvet and rich stuffs, ornamented with ermine and other furs, while we are forced to wear poor clothing. They have wines, spices, and fine bread, while we have only rye and the refuse of the straw; and when we drink, it must be water. They have handsome seats and manors, while we must brave the wind and rain in our labours in the field; and it is by our labour they have wherewith to support their pomp. We are called slaves, and if we do not perform our service we are beaten, and we have no sovereign to whom we can complain or who would be willing to hear us. Let us go to the king and remonstrate with him; he is young, and from him we may obtain a favourable answer, and if not we must ourselves seek to amend our condition." With such language as this did John Ball harangue the people of his village every Sunday after mass. The archbishop, on being informed of it, had him arrested and imprisoned for two or three months by way of punishment; but the moment he was out of prison, he returned to his former course. Many in the city of London envious of the rich and noble, having heard of John Ball's preaching, said among themselves that the country was badly governed, and that the nobility had seized upon all the gold and silver. These wicked Londoners, therefore, began to assemble in parties, and to show signs of rebellion; they also invited all those who held like opinions in the adjoining counties to come to London; telling them that they would find the town open to them and the commonalty of the same way of thinking as themselves, and that they would so press the king, that there should no longer be a slave in England.

Text: From the book *The Chronicles of England, France and Spain* by Sir John Froissart. H. P. Dunster's condensation of the Thomas Johnes translation. Dutton Paperback Edition (1961). Reprinted by permission of E. P. Dutton & Co., Inc. and J. M. Dent & Sons Ltd.

By this means the men of Kent, Essex, Sussex, Bedford, and the adjoining counties, in number about 60,000, were brought to London, under command of Wat Tyler, Jack Straw, and John Ball. This Wat Tyler, who was chief of the three, had been a tiler of houses—a bad man and a great enemy to the nobility. . . .

. . . When the rebels had done all they wanted at Rochester, they left that city and came to Dartford, continuing to destroy all the houses of lawyers and proctors on the right and left of the road; from Dartford they came to Blackheath, where they took up their quarters, saying, that they were armed for the king and commons of England. When the principal citizens of London found that the rebels were quartered so near them, they caused the gates of London-bridge to be closed, and placed guards there, by order of Sir William Walworth, Mayor of London; . . . .

. . . But to return to the commonalty of England: on Corpus Christi day King Richard heard mass in the Tower of London, after which he entered his barge, attended by the Earls of Salisbury, Warwick, and Suffolk, and some other knights, and rowed down the Thames towards Rotherhithe, a royal manor, where upwards of 10,000 of the insurgents had assembled. As soon as the mob perceived the royal barge approaching, they began shouting and crying as if all the spirits of the nether world had been in the company. . . .

When the king and his lords saw this crowd of people, and the wildness of their manner, the boldest of the party felt alarm, and the king was advised not to land, but to have his barge rowed up and down the river. "What do you wish for?" he demanded of the multitude; "I am come hither to hear what you have to say." Those near him cried out, "We wish you to land, and then we will tell you what our wants are." Upon this the Earl of Salisbury cried out, "Gentlemen, you are not properly dressed, nor are you in a fit condition for a king to talk with." Nothing more was said on either side, for the king was prevailed upon at once to return to the Tower. The people seeing this were in a great passion, and returned to Blackheath to inform their companions how the king had served them; upon hearing which, they all cried out, "Let us instantly march to London." Accordingly they set out at once, and on the road thither destroyed all the houses of lawyers and courtiers, and all the monasteries they met with. In the suburbs of London, which are very handsome and extensive, they pulled down many fine houses; they demolished also the king's prison, called the Marshalsea, and set at liberty all who were confined in it; moreover, they threatened the Londoners at the entrance of the bridge for having shut the gates of it, declaring that they would take the city by storm, and afterwards burn and destroy it.

With regard to the common people of London, numbers entertained these rebellious opinions, and on assembling at the bridge asked of the guards, "Why will you refuse admittance to these honest men? they are our friends, and what they are doing is for our good." So urgent were they, that it was found necessary to open the gates, when crowds rushed in and took possession of those shops which seemed best stocked with provisions; indeed, wherever they went, meat and drink were placed before them, and nothing was refused in the hope of appeasing them. Their leaders, John Ball, Jack Straw, and Wat Tyler, then marched through London, attended by more than 20,000 men, to the palace of the Savoy, which is a handsome building belonging to the Duke of Lancaster, situated on the banks of the Thames on the road to Westminster: here they immediately killed the porters, pushed into the house, and set it on fire. Not content with this outrage, they went to the house of the Knight-hospitalers of Rhodes, dedicated to St. John of Mount Carmel, which they burnt together with their church and hospital.

After this they paraded the streets, and killed every Fleming they could find, whether in house, church, or hospital; they broke open several houses of the Lombards, taking whatever money they could lay their hands upon. They murdered a rich citizen, by name Richard Lyon, to whom Wat Tyler had formerly been servant in France, but having once beaten him, the varlet had never forgotten it; and when he had carried his men to his house, he ordered his head to be cut off, placed upon a pike, and carried through the streets of London. Thus did these wicked people act, and on this Thursday they did much damage to the city of London. Towards evening they fixed their quarters in a square, called St. Catherine's, before the Tower, declaring that they would not depart until they had obtained from the king everything they wanted—until the Chancellor of England had accounted to them, and shown how the great sums which were raised had been expended. Considering the mischief which the mob had already done, you may easily imagine how miserable, at this time, was the situation of the king and those who were with him. . . . On Friday morning the rebels, who lodged in the square of St. Catherine's, before the Tower, began to make themselves ready. They shouted much and said, that if the king would not come out to them, they would attack the Tower, storm it, and slay all who were within. The king, alarmed at these menaces, resolved to speak with the rabble; he therefore sent orders for them to retire to a handsome meadow at Mile-end, where, in the summertime, people go to amuse themselves, at the same time signifying that he would meet them there and grant their demands. Proclamation to this effect was made in the king's name, and thither, accordingly, the commonalty of the different villages began to march; many, however, did not care to go, but stayed behind in London, being more desirous of the riches of the nobles and the plunder of the city. Indeed, covetousness and the desire of plunder was the principal cause of these disturbances, as the rebels showed very plainly. . . .

. . . While the king was on his way to Mile-end, his two brothers, the Earl of Kent and Sir John Holland, stole away from his company, not daring to show themselves to the populace. The king himself, however, showed great courage, and on his arrival at the appointed spot instantly advanced into the midst of the assembled multitude, saying in a most pleasing manner, "My good people, I am your king and your lord, what is it you want? What do you wish to say to me?" Those who heard him made answer, "We wish you to make us free for ever. We wish to be no longer called slaves, nor held in bondage." The king replied, "I grant your wish; now therefore return to your homes, and let two or three from each village be left behind, to whom I will order letters to be given with my seal, fully granting every demand you have made: and in order that you may be the more satisfied, I will direct that my banners be sent to every stewardship, castlewick, and corporation."

These words greatly appeased the more moderate of the multitude, who said, "It is well: we wish for nothing more." The king, however, added yet further, "You, my good people of Kent, shall have one of my banners; and you also of Essex, Sussex, Bedford, Suffolk, Cambridge, Stafford, and Lincoln, shall each have one; I pardon you all for what you have hitherto done, but you must follow my banners and now return home on the terms I have mentioned," which they unanimously consented to do. Thus did this great assembly break up. The king instantly employed upwards of thirty secretaries, who drew up the letters as fast as they could, and when they were sealed and delivered to them, the people departed to their own counties. The principal mischief, however, remained behind: I mean Wat Tyler, Jack Straw, and John Ball, who declared, that though the people were satisfied, they were by no means so, and with them were about 30,000 also of the same mind. These all continued in the city without any wish to receive the letters or the king's seal, but did all they could to throw the town into such confusion, that the lords and rich citizens might be murdered and their houses pillaged and destroyed. . . .

On Saturday morning the king left the Wardrobe and went to Westminster, when he and his lords heard mass in the abbey. In this church there is a statue of our Lady, in which the kings of England have much faith. To this on the present occasion King Richard and his nobles paid their devotions and made their offerings; they then rode in company along the causeway to London; but when they had proceeded a short distance, King Richard, with a few attendants, turned up a road on the left to go away from the city.

This day all the rabble again assembled under Wat Tyler, Jack Straw, and John Ball, at a place called Smithfield, where every Friday the horsemarket is kept. There were present about 20,000, and many more were in the city, breakfasting, and drinking Rhenish wine and Malmsey Madeira in the taverns and in the houses of the Lombards, without paying for anything; and happy was he who could give them good cheer to satisfy them. Those who collected in Smithfield had with them the king's banner, which had been given to them the preceding evening; and the wretches, notwithstanding this, wanted to pillage the city, their leaders saying, that hitherto they had done nothing. "The pardon which the king has granted will be of no use to us; but if we be of the same mind, we shall pillage this rich and powerful town of London before those from Essex, Suffolk, Cambridge, Bedford, Warwick, Reading, Lancashire, Arundel, Guildford, Coventry, Lynne, Lincoln, York, and Durham shall arrive; for they are on their road, and we know for certain that Vaquier and Lister will conduct them hither. Let us, then, be beforehand in plundering the wealth of the city; for if we wait for their arrival, they will wrest it from us." To this opinion all had agreed, when the king, attended by 60 horses, appeared in sight; he was at the time not thinking of the rabble, but had intended to continue his ride, without coming into London; however, when he arrived before the abbey of St. Bartholomew, which is in Smithfield, and saw the crowd of people, he stopped, saying that he would ascertain what they wanted, and endeavour to appease them. Wat Tyler, seeing the king and his party, said to his men, "Here is the king, I will go and speak with him; do you not stir until I give you a signal." He then made a motion with his hand, and added, "When you shall see me make this signal, then step forward, and kill every one except the king; but hurt him not, for he is young, and we can do what we please with him; carrying him with us through England, we shall be lords of the whole country, without any opposition." On saying which he spurred his horse and galloped up to the king, whom he approached so near that his horse's head touched the crupper of the king's horse.

His first words were these: "King, dost thou see

all these men here?" "Yes," replied the king; "why dost thou ask?" "Because they are all under my command, and have sworn by their faith and loyalty to do whatsoever I shall order." "Very well," said the king: "I have no objection to it." Tyler, who was only desirous of a riot, made answer: "And thou thinkest, king, that these people, and as many more in the city, also under my command, ought to depart without having thy letters? No, indeed, we will carry them with us." "Why," replied the king, "it has been so ordered, and the letters will be delivered out one after another; but, friend, return to thy companions, and tell them to depart from London; be peaceable and careful of yourselves; for it is our determination that you shall all have the letters by towns and villages according to our agreement." As the king finished speaking, Wat Tyler, casting his eyes round, spied a squire attached to the king's person bearing a sword. This squire Tyler mortally hated, and on seeing him, cried out, "What hast thou there? give me thy dagger." "I will not," said the squire: "why should I give it thee?" The king upon this said, "Give it to him; give it to him"; which the squire did, though much against his will. When Tyler took the dagger, he began to play with it in his hand, and again addressing the squire, said, "Give me that sword." "I will not," replied the squire, "for it is the king's sword, and thou being but a mechanic art not worthy to bear it; and if only thou and I were together, thou wouldst not have dared to say what thou hast, for a heap of gold as large as this church." "By my troth," answered Tyler, "I will not eat this day before I have thy head." At these words the Mayor of London, with about twelve men, rode forward, armed under their robes, and seeing Tyler's manner of behaving, said, "Scoundrel, how dare you to behave thus in the king's presence?" The king, also enraged at the fellow's impudence, said to the mayor, "Lay hands on him." Whilst King Richard was giving this order, Tyler still kept up the conversation, saying to the mayor: "What have you to do with it; does what I have said concern you?" "It does," replied the mayor, who found himself supported by the king, and then added: "I will not live a day unless you pay for your insolence." Upon saying which, he drew a kind of scimitar, and struck Tyler such a blow on the head as felled him to his horse's feet. As soon as the rebel was down, he was surrounded on all sides, in order that his own men might not see him; and one of the king's squires, by name John Standwich, immediately leaped from his horse, and drawing his sword, thrust it into his belly, so that he died.

When the rebels found that their leader was dead, they drew up in a sort of battle array, each man having his bow bent before him. The king at this time certainly hazarded much, though it turned out most fortunately for him; for as soon as Tyler was on the ground, he left his attendants, giving orders that no one should follow him, and riding up to the rebels, who were advancing to revenge their leader's death, said, "Gentlemen, what are you about: you shall have me for your captain: I am your king, remain peaceable." The greater part, on hearing these words, were quite ashamed, and those among them who were inclined for peace began to slip away; the riotous ones, however, kept their ground. The king returned to his lords, and consulted with them what next should be done. Their advice was to make for the fields; but the mayor said, that to retreat would be of no avail. "It is quite proper to act as we have done; and I reckon we shall very soon receive assistance from our good friends in London."

While things were in this state, several persons ran to London, crying out, "They are killing the king and our mayor;" upon which alarm, all those of the king's party sallied out towards Smithfield, in number about seven or eight thousand. Among the first came Sir Robert Knolles and Sir Perducas d'Albret, well attended; then several aldermen, with upwards of 600 men-at-arms, and a powerful man of the city, by name Nicholas Bramber, the king's draper, bringing with him a large force on foot. These all drew up opposite to the rebels, who had with them the king's banner, and showed as if they intended to maintain their ground by offering combat.

The king created at this time three knights: Sir William Walworth, Sir John Standwich, and Sir Nicholas Bramber. As soon as Sir Robert Knolles arrived at Smithfield, his advice was immediately to fall upon the insurgents, and slay them; but King Richard would not consent to this. "You shall first go to them," he said, "and demand my banner; we shall then see how they will behave; for I am determined to have this by fair means or foul." The new knights were accordingly sent forward, and on approaching the rebels made signs to them not to shoot, as they wished to speak with them; and when within hearing, said, "Now attend; the king orders you to send back his banners; and if you do so, we trust he will have mercy upon you." The banners, upon this, were given up directly, and brought to the king. It was then ordered, under pain of death, that all those who had obtained the king's letters should deliver them up. Some did so, but not all; and the king on receiving them had them torn in pieces in their presence. You must know that from the time the king's banners were surrendered, these fellows kept no order; but the greater part, throwing their bows upon the ground, took to their heels and returned to London. Sir

Robert Knolles was very angry that the rebels were not attacked at once and all slain; however, the king would not consent to it, saying, that he would have ample revenge without doing so. . . .

This whole day the king passed with his mother, and a proclamation was made through all the streets, that every person who was not an inhabitant of London, and who had not resided there for a whole year, should instantly depart; for if any of a contrary description were found in the city on Sunday morning at sunrise, they would be arrested as traitors to the king, and have their heads cut off. This proclamation no one dared to infringe, but all instantly departed to their homes quite discomfited.

John Ball and Jack Straw were found hidden in an old ruin, where they had secreted themselves, thinking to steal away when things were quiet; but this they were prevented doing, for their own men betrayed them. With this capture the king and his barons were much pleased, and had their heads cut off, as was that of Tyler's, and fixed on London-bridge, in the room of those whom these wretches themselves had placed there.

News of this total defeat of the rebels in London was sent throughout the neighbouring counties, in order that all those who were on their way to London might hear of it; and as soon as they did so, they instantly returned to their homes, without daring to advance further. . . .

INTERPRETATIONS OF FEUDALISM AND THE MEDIEVAL ECONOMY

71 BRYCE LYON, *THE MIDDLE AGES IN RECENT HISTORICAL THOUGHT: NEW VIEWS ON MANORIALISM AND FEUDALISM*

Feudalism and manorialism in the Middle Ages were two distinct, though mutually sustaining, systems. Feudalism involved a contractual relationship between two free men of nobility, whereby the one—the lord—guaranteed land and protection to the other—the vassal—in return for specific services, most commonly of a juridical or military nature. What the vassal acquired was rights over a piece of land, or fief, which usually came equipped with a manor and peasants. Manorialism, on the other hand, involved a relationship between men of two socially different classes, one free—the lord—and the other bound to the lord's land and to his service—the peasant-serf. The serf was scarcely to be differentiated from a slave: he could, in theory, own no property, and he could be sold. The law did give him a personality by allowing him to appear in court against another serf, but he could not bring charges against any freeman, not to mention his lord. Moreover, his freedom of movement was legally curtailed; this is to say that the ordinary serf was virtually bound to the land he tilled. The function of the vassal was political and military, that of the serf, economic.

After these things are taken into account, the fact remains that such definitions of medieval society are merely generalizations. And in recent decades the historiography of the period has come more and more to emphasize the diversity of political, economic, and cultural forms during the Middle Ages and to regard the concept of a regularized, unified Christendom as at best an ideal of the philosophers. Social institutions varied not only from place to place but from century to century.

The following extracts from a monograph by Professor Bryce Lyon exemplify some of the current restudy of the Middle Ages. Mr. Lyon is a member of the history faculty of the University of California at Berkeley and has written widely on the Middle Ages; among his works are *From Fief to Indenture: The Transition from Feudal to Non-Feudal Contract in Western Europe* (1957) and *Constitutional and Legal History of Medieval England* (1960).

The Meaning of Manorialism

Manorialism (often referred to as seignorialism) has always occupied a prominent place in any history of the Middle Ages. This is justified because manorialism was the economic system by which western Europe lived for centuries. But one must take issue with the cavalier and old-fashioned manner in which much of the material is presented. A reading of most secondary texts leads to the conclusion that many teachers are still explaining

Text: Bryce Lyon, *The Middle Ages in Recent Historical Thought* (Washington, D. C.: Service Center for Teachers of History, American Historical Association, 1959), pp. 7-17 *passim.*

manorialism upon the basis of what was known and said around the middle of the nineteenth century. The classic and now trite description of the peasant village with its three-field system is all too familiar. What is not familiar to enough teachers is the new picture of manorialism that has been emerging during the past half century. From the utilization of new records, from an increased knowledge of medieval technology, from intensive topographical and cartographical study, from aerial photography, from agronomy, from place-name study, and from the application of sociological and anthropological methods, has arisen a new concept of manorialism.

As to the chronological span of manorialism, historians generally agree that it took root in western Europe during the third century and existed in full vigor down to the twelfth century. Before the onslaught of the money economy it then began to disappear in some areas and to decline with varying tempo in others. By the end of the Middle Ages only vestiges of the manorial system remained in western Europe. Historians also agree that the decline of the money economy in the late Roman Empire gave rise to manorialism and that the revival of a money economy caused its demise. What talk there still is about agrarian communities of free farmers in the early Middle Ages who controlled their economic, social, and legal affairs is, according to consensus of opinion, adduced from slim evidence. What seems tenable is that under the manorial system a landed aristocracy controlled most of the land along with the economic, political, and legal perquisites that came with such authority. The mass of the inhabitants of early medieval Europe were unfree peasants, tightly bound to the soil and to their lord's will. Though students of manorialism have long been careful to make a distinction between manorialism and feudalism, the systems are often confused and are lumped together under the term feudalism. Feudalism, in spite of being termed an economic system of exploitation by Marx, was the political and military system which came into prominence some four centuries after manorialism and which was superimposed upon it. All the men involved in feudalism were free and were generally aristocrats bound to each other by highly honorable and mutual obligations. The men involved in manorialism were unfree peasants bound to lords by unhonorable obligations. The feudal knight followed the honorable profession of fighting; the peasant followed the unhonorable occupation of working the soil so that his master could eat.

The feature of manorialism still so inadequately explained and understood by many teachers is its heterogeneous organization. Rather than a simple and uniform system which continued unchanged for centuries, it was a complicated and highly dissimilar system, one upon which no expert in the field cares to generalize. The remark of Elizabeth Levett that "in the history of land problems there is no sin like the sin of generalization" is especially applicable to manorialism. Instead of talking about typical and classical manors, scholars now speak of manorial diversity.

The arrangement of an agrarian village and the arable fields is the best example of manorial diversity. Generalization is dangerous beyond saying that the three-field system prevailed in northern Europe and the two-field system in southern Europe. Scholars in England, France, Germany, and Belgium have amassed such a wealth of detail from regional studies that we now know village and field arrangements differed within a country and even within a small area. Before broaching these complications, we should note the most common arrangements. The system prevailing in much of northern Europe consisted of a nucleated village (a concentration of huts for the peasants) encircled by the arable fields in which were scattered the strips of the peasants. Another arrangement found in the poorer parts of France, England, and the Mediterranean area was the hamlet system. This consisted of a compact farm cultivated by one peasant and his family who customarily lived in an isolated house on the land. When the land became exhausted, other land was appropriated and cultivated; this agrarian technique is known as "in-field" and "out-field" exploitation. . . .

. . . Chiefly responsible for the new picture of medieval agriculture are the disciplines and techniques noted at the beginning of this discussion; we may be certain that they will continue to be applied to field systems and will keep our knowledge of them in a state of flux for many years to come. The same disciplines and the utilization of new records have also increased knowledge about many other manorial problems as, for example, the problems of the origin and decline of manorialism. No longer can we confidently assert that the manorial system was derived principally from late Roman imperial estate organization. Marc Bloch and others have by means of far-extended and comparative studies shown that the Germans as well as the people of Africa and Asia Minor were familiar with an agrarian system like that of the late Empire. With great ingenuity Marc Bloch has suggested that the principal features of a co-operative and communal agrarian system date much earlier than the Romans who probably borrowed their system from a more primitive one. His argument hinges around the evidence that primitive agrarian societies were organized upon the family and clan and, being highly patriarchal, found co-operative and communal organization a natural and practical way of deriving their living from the soil. Though subsequent economic developments, particularly in the third, fourth, and fifth centuries, contributed much to the formation of the manorial system, we can no longer confidently assert that manorialism was derived from a late imperial institution to which were fused German agrarian practices.

Research is still needed on the decline of manorialism. In the last twenty-five years, however, our understanding of this phenomenon has been modified and greatly illuminated. No longer do we teach the old stories that most peasants secured their freedom by charters of emancipation emanating from lords, or by running away from the manor to the towns. The emancipation of the peasant, which caused the disintegration of manorialism, did not happen so simply. A complexity of causes explains the emancipation of the peasantry of western Europe, an emancipation that came gradually and informally. Intense work in England and France has proven that a large part of the peasantry was freed through the commutation of labor services. And the commutation of labor services is not explained simply by the mutual economic interest of lord and peasant; we are now aware of the interdependence of the commutation of labor services with other contemporary economic developments. The towns which, as islands of freedom, offered an avenue of escape and a better life, competed with the surrounding manors and forced the lords to commute labor services in order to hold their peasants and to keep the land under cultivation. An even greater stimulus to the commutation of labor services was the vast land reclamation movement that characterized Europe between the eleventh and fourteenth centuries. To supply the towns and the growing population with food, new land was opened to cultivation; land was reclaimed from the sea, marshes were drained, and forests were cleared. Lords interested in such reclamation got their labor forces from the peasants who were lured into this pioneer work by grants of land and freedom. These projects formed large escape valves throughout Europe and the peasants eagerly took advantage of them. If the old manors hoped to keep their tenants they had to free them. The process of emancipation was thus quickened but it was still gradual and informal, accomplished without charter or law. The emancipation of agrarian communities led to their acquiring economic, legal, and political liberties comparable to those of the great towns. Beside an urban commune might stand a small rural commune with almost the same privileges. No longer can we contrast the liberty of the town with the unfreedom of the agrarian village. At least since the twelfth century a free peasant often had the status of an urban bourgeois.

To generalize from this brief survey of the organization, the origin, and the decline of manorialism is dangerous; it is safer to emphasize the heterogeneity of medieval manorialism. One can still justifiably teach that Europe was characterized by the three- and two-field systems with field rotation and co-operative labor, that fields were open, and that the classic nucleated village prevailed in northwestern Europe. But within the framework of this generalization one must acknowledge the large number of field variations and the untypical villages and hamlets. Agrarian life was little more uniform in the Middle Ages than it is in modern America where methods, crops, and markets are constantly being developed and changed. It must also be remembered that manorialism, though necessitated by the disintegration of the Roman Empire in the West, was an agrarian system not peculiarly Roman but characteristic of numerous primitive agrarian societies such as the German. Finally, the decline of manorialism must not be oversimplified. To see the return of a money economy to western Europe as the basic cause for the demise of manorialism is also to admit that money provided a variety of ways by which the peasant unlocked his tenurial bonds and attained freedom.

The Significance of Feudalism

In the discussion of manorialism the point was made that medievalists now generally consider it an economic system distinct from feudalism which was a military and political system. When feudalism is thus understood as a unique military and political system that dominated western Europe for hundreds of years, it is possible to inquire into its significance. The feudalism discussed here, it must be emphasized, was a system peculiar to western Europe and was not found elsewhere except in a few regions of the Mediterranean and the Middle East where it was introduced for a time by the Crusaders. This does not mean that there were not feudal systems in other areas of the world, but that western feudalism was quite different from Byzantine, Moslem, Japanese, and Chinese feudalism. These feudal systems existed during different periods of world history, were organized on different principles, and were developed to meet demands peculiar to the regions in which they arose. As a result of especially careful research on western feudalism and feudal systems throughout the world and of comparative studies of these different feudal systems, teachers of history should no longer labor under the misconception that having mastered western feudalism they can understand all feudal systems.

As any reader of the vast historical literature on feudalism knows, there has been a long and bitter debate over the origin of western feudalism. One group of historians, of which there are still some, has derived feudalism from practices that arose in the late Roman Empire and in the Merovingian period. They argue that the origin of feudalism is found in a system of clientage whereby a powerful military and political person or a great landlord attached to himself clients. Generally the powerful individuals granted pieces of land called *precaria* or *beneficia* to men in return for military, political, or economic service. The great lord secured loyal service and, in turn, extended his protection to men sorely in need of security when central law and order were not to be found. This view has some merit but its adherents have not been able to prove that the relations and services were honorable like those of medieval feudalism. Another school of historians has taken a critical view of Roman origins and regarded feudalism as coming primarily from the German *comitatus*, the war band organization in which German military leaders surrounded themselves with warriors who fought loyally unto death for honor, for booty and plunder, and for adventure. This, it is contended, was a highly honorable relation between aristocratic warriors. But this school of historians has had difficulty in finding the grants of land that always characterized feudalism. Other historians such as Heinrich Brunner, Ferdinand Lot, and Carl Stephenson have modified this view somewhat by suggesting that vassalage was derived from the *comitatus* but that the land—the fief—did not come into existence until granted out by the Carolingians in the eighth century to military vassals in return for their service against the Magyars and Arabs. These historians believed that real feudalism began only in the eighth century when vassalage and fief-holding were fused. A few more eclectic historians such as F. L. Ganshof find the origin of feudalism in both German and Roman antecedents and regard feudalism as developing gradually from the late imperial period onward. The Roman and German practices and customs of personal loyalty, service, and grants of land fused, culminating in the feudal system of the eighth and ninth centuries. Though the debate will continue, it would seem from available evidence that the institution of vassalage was German and that the granting of land in return for service was a Roman practice. The two seem to have meshed into a "system" during the eighth century. . . .

Though all these works do an excellent job of explaining feudal principles, it is those of Stephenson and Painter that best describe how feudalism provided a form of government for western Europe. Using the monographs devoted to the feudal history and institutions of the principal states, they have shown feudalism as a useful and constructive political system. They believe that feudalism, rather than being a destructive political force breeding particularism and anarchy, was a constructive and unifying system that made possible the political rehabilitation of western Europe in the eleventh and twelfth centuries and that provided the conditions necessary for the formation of the strong centralized states that were England, France, Normandy, and Flanders. Feudalism was the only military and political system possible in the eighth century. It provided the Carolingian rulers and their successors with the essential military and political services and was not responsible, as many historians have asserted, for the morseling of the Carolingian Empire. That uncertain structure was doomed to failure by its size; it could not survive, based as it was, upon a primitive agrarian economy. Feudalism could operate effectively only within a small area. In a county like Flanders or in a compact kingdom like England the feudal rulers could make feudalism work. They could maintain the personal bond of loyalty inherent in vassalage and could force their vassals to perform feudal obligations. Upon the foundation of feudalism these rulers built the successful states that we find by the twelfth century. Scholarly opinion, it should be noted, now supports this thesis, that feudalism was a constructive and unifying political force. It is inaccurate to teach feudalism as an anarchical political system that contributed to the darkness of the early Middle Ages.

The other revision of feudalism in the last quarter century relates to its decline. Traditionally historians have equated the end of the Middle Ages and the beginning of the modern world with the death of feudalism in the fifteenth century. We have often been told that the strong rulers of the early sixteenth century put feudal particularism and the feudal aristocracy to rout and then proceeded to construct the national state. This is but partially true. In the first place there was little feudalism left in the fifteenth and sixteenth centuries to rout. Most of what we call feudalism had declined in the thirteenth century; there were only vestiges in the following two centuries. F. M. Stenton has made a good case for feudalism beginning its decline in England during the later twelfth century. And scholars such as Henri Pirenne and Robert Fawtier have come to similar conclusions for the Continent. It was during the thirteenth century that feudalism lost its *raison d'être* and became a vestigial organ.

But feudalism was not yet dead. Men had so long been habituated to doing things in a feudal manner and thinking in feudal terms that they could not abruptly scrap the feudal mentality. Simply because the money economy rendered obsolete fiefs of land and the service performed, was no reason that men should forget about homage and fiefs. They merely superimposed feudal custom upon money. They granted annual incomes of money—money fiefs—to men in return for homage and service, be it military, political, or diplomatic. A new feudalism of money partially succeeded the old feudalism of land; it remained prominent down to the middle of the fifteenth century when it was replaced by another system closely associated with feudalism.

We now know that since the late thirteenth century rulers and great lords had been securing military and political service by means of the indenture system. A lord would conclude a contract (indenture) with a man that would entail some sort of military or political service. Each swore to be loyal to the other and a yearly fee was customarily paid by the lord to his indentured retainer. These agreements could be for life, for a term of years, or for a very limited period. The indenture system supplemented, and eventually replaced, the feudal system and was used by the English kings and by continental lords to raise a large part of their armies in the fourteenth and fifteenth centuries. It was also used to build up political gangs or parties that enabled lords to control local politics and to gain enough influence in national politics so as to pack parliament with their men. How effective the indenture system was in constructing political parties on the national level is still being debated by such scholars as K. B. McFarlane, J. S. Roskell, and W. H. Dunham, Jr.

Obviously modeled upon feudalism—especially upon the new feudalism of money—the indenture system was so close to being a feudal system that some historians have called it "bastard feudalism." It was a "bastard" system but was it a form of feudalism? In that homage was not involved, that the fee was non-feudal and non-heritable, and that the feudal aids and incidents did not apply, some historians contend that the indenture system was non-feudal. The only nexus between the contracting parties was cash and mutual respect. Others, on the contrary, hold that the indenture system was a form of feudalism because it involved a contractual relationship, mutual obligations, and good lordship. But such differences over the nature of the indenture system are technical. Without attempting to resolve them, we may say that both the new feudalism of money and the indenture system prove how strong a hold feudal thinking still had over men in the fourteenth and fifteenth centuries.

In summary it may be said that the traditional system of feudalism declined in the thirteenth century and was of slight importance in the fourteenth and fifteenth centuries. Feudal thinking and behavior, however, remained strong and account for the feudalism of money and the indenture system, both prominent in the fourteenth and fifteenth centuries. When speaking of the decline of feudalism, we must evade the pitfall of keeping the traditional feudalism around until the end of the Middle Ages and must speak instead of a feudalism of money and of an indenture system that nourished variant forms of feudalism down to the sixteenth century.

72 HENRI PIRENNE, ECONOMIC AND SOCIAL HISTORY OF MEDIEVAL EUROPE: ORIGINS OF THE MERCHANT CLASS

If a first place can ever be awarded to one scholar over his fellows, in the field of medieval studies perhaps that man would be the Belgian historian, Henri Pirenne (1862-1935). While for many years historians had been qualifying and modifying the traditional conceptions of medieval history, it remained for Pirenne to offer comprehensive theories which completely revolutionized historical discussion. His first book to appear in translation was the seven-volume *History of Belgium* (1900, 1932). This was followed by *Belgian Democracy: Its Early History* (1909), *Medieval Cities: Their Origins and the Revival of Trade* (1927), *Economic and Social History of Medieval Europe* (1933), and *Mohammed and Charlemagne* (published posthumously, 1939).

While many of Pirenne's theories have been challenged by later historians—particularly his thesis that the ancient world gave way to the Middle Ages not with the barbarian onslaught but with the Arab seizure of the Mediterranean Sea in the seventh and eighth centuries—his work has formed the basis for much of the subsequent discussion of such problems. In the following selections from his *Economic and Social History of Medieval Europe*, some of the problems inherent in a shift from a manorial subsistence economy to an economy based on cities and trade are examined. His ideas about the origins of the bourgeois class should be compared with the later interpretations of the decline of manorialism noted by Professor Bryce Lyon (see Document 71).

The Merchants and the Bourgeoisie

The essential difference between the merchants and artisans of the nascent towns and the agricultural society in the midst of which they appeared, was that their kind of life was no longer determined by their relations with the land. In this respect they formed, in every sense of the word, a class of *déracinés* [the uprooted]. Commerce and industry, which up till then had been merely the adventitious or intermittent occupations of manorial agents, whose existence was assured by the great landowners who employed them, now became independent professions. Those who practised them were incontestably "new men." Attempts have often been made to derive them from the servile personnel attached to the domestic workshops of the manor, or the serfs who were charged with feeding the household in times of scarcity and in time of plenty disposed of their surplus production outside. But such an evolution is neither supported by the sources nor probable. There is no doubt that territorial lords here and there preserved economic prerogatives in the nascent towns for a fairly long time, such prerogatives for instance, as the obligation of the burgesses to use the lord's oven and mill, the monopoly of sale enjoyed by his wine for several days after the vintage, or even certain dues levied from the craft gilds. But the local survival of these rights is no proof of the manorial origin of urban economy. On the contrary, what we note everywhere is that from the moment that it appears, it appears in a condition of freedom.

But the question immediately occurs, how are we to explain the formation of a class of free merchants and artisans in the midst of an exclusively rural society, where serfdom was the normal condition of the people? Scarcity of information prevents us from replying with that precision which the importance of the problem demands, but it is at least possible to indicate the chief factors. First, it is incontestable that commerce and industry were originally recruited from among landless men, who lived, so to speak, on the margin of a society where land alone was the basis of existence. Now these men were very numerous. Apart altogether from those, who in times of famine or war left their native soil to seek a livelihood elsewhere and returned no more, we have to remember all the individuals whom the manorial organisation itself was unable to support. The peasants' holdings were of such a size as to secure the regular payment of the dues assessed upon them. Thus the younger sons of a man overburdened with children were often forced to leave their father in order to enable him to make his payments to the lord. Thenceforth they swelled the crowd of vagabonds who roamed through the country, going from abbey to abbey taking their share of alms reserved for the poor, hiring themselves out to the peasants at harvest time or at the vintage, and enlisting as mercenaries in the feudal troops in times of war.

These men were quick to profit by the new means of livelihood offered them by the arrival of ships and merchants along the coasts and in the river estuaries. Many of the more adventurous certainly hired themselves to the Venetian and Scandinavian boats as sailors; others joined the merchant caravans which took their way more and more frequently to the "ports." With luck, the best among them could not fail to seize the many opportunities of making a fortune, which commercial life offered to the vagabonds and adventurers who threw themselves into it with energy and intelligence. . . .

. . . The new kind of life which offered itself to the roving masses of landless men had an irresistible attraction for them, by reason of the promise of gain which it offered. The result was a real emigration from the country to the nascent towns. Soon, it was not only vagabonds . . . who bent their steps thither. The temptation was too great not to cause a number of serfs to run away from the manors where they were born and settle in the towns, either as artisans or as employees of the rich merchants whose reputation spread through the land. The lords pursued them and brought them back to their holdings, when they succeeded in laying hands on them. But many eluded their search, and as the city population increased, it became dangerous to try to seize the fugitives under its protection. . . . The foundation of large

Text: Henri Pirenne, *Economic and Social History of Medieval Europe*, trans. I. E. Clegg. Reprinted by permission of the publishers, Harcourt, Brace & World, Inc. Pp. 45-56 *passim*.

fortunes was certainly at this period a common phenomenon in all centres where an export trade was developing. Just as landowners had in the past showered gifts of land on the monasteries, so now merchants used their fortunes . . . to spend themselves in religious or charitable works for the benefit of their fellow-citizens and the good of their own souls. Indeed, religion may well have spurred many of them on to win a fortune, which they intended to dedicate to the service of God. It should not be forgotten that Peter Waldo, the founder in 1173 of the Poor Men of Lyons, which shortly gave rise to the sect of the Waldenses, was a merchant and that, almost at the same date, St. Francis was born at Assisi in the house of another merchant. Other *nouveaux riches*, more bitten with worldly ambition, sought to raise themselves in the social hierarchy by giving their daughters in marriage to knights; and their fortune must have been very large to have stifled the aristocratic reluctance of the latter.

These great merchants, or rather *nouveaux riches*, were naturally the leaders of the bourgeoisie, since the bourgeoisie itself was a creation of the commercial revival and in the beginning the words *mercator* and *burgensis* were synonymous. But while it developed as a social class this bourgeoisie was also forming itself into a legal class of a highly original nature, which we must now consider.

Urban Institutions and Law

The needs and tendencies of the bourgeoisie were so incompatible with the traditional organisation of Western Europe that they immediately aroused violent opposition. They ran counter to all the interests and ideas of a society dominated materially by the owners of large landed property and spiritually by the Church, whose aversion to trade was unconquerable. It would be unfair to attribute to "feudal tyranny" or "sacerdotal arrogance" an opposition which explains itself, although the attribution has often been made. As always, those who were the beneficiaries of the established order defended it obstinately, not only because it guaranteed their interests, but because it seemed to them indispensable to the preservation of society. Moreover, the bourgeois themselves were far from taking up a revolutionary attitude towards this society. They took for granted the authority of the territorial princes, the privileges of the nobility and, above all, those of the Church. They even professed an ascetic morality, which was plainly contradicted by their mode of life. They merely desired a place in the sun, and their claims were confined to their most indispensable needs.

Of the latter, the most indispensable was personal liberty. Without liberty, that is to say, without the power to come and go, to do business, to sell goods, a power not enjoyed by serfdom, trade would be impossible. Thus they claimed it, simply for the advantages which it conferred, and nothing was further from the mind of the bourgeoisie than any idea of freedom as a natural right; in their eyes it was merely a useful one. Besides, many of them possessed it *de facto;* they were immigrants, who had come from too far off for their lord to be traced and who, since their serfdom could not be presumed, necessarily passed for free, although born of unfree parents. But the fact had to be transformed into a right. It was essential that the villeins, who came to settle in the towns to seek a new livelihood, should feel safe and should not have to fear being taken back by force to the manors from which they had escaped. They must be delivered from labour services and from all the hated dues by which the servile population was burdened, such as the obligation to marry only a woman of their own class and to leave to the lord part of their inheritance. Willy-nilly, in the course of the twelfth century these claims, backed up as they often were by dangerous revolts, had to be granted. The most obstinate conservatives, such as Guibert de Nogent, in 1115, were reduced to a wordy revenge, speaking of those "detestable communes" which the serfs had set up to escape from their lord's authority and to do away with his most lawful rights. Freedom became the legal status of the bourgeoisie, so much so that it was no longer a personal privilege only, but a territorial one, inherent in urban soil just as serfdom was in manorial soil. In order to obtain it, it was enough to have resided for a year and a day within the walls of the town. "City air makes a man free" (*Stadtluft macht frei*), says the German proverb.

But if liberty was the first need of the burgess, there were many others besides. Traditional law with its narrow, formal procedure, its ordeals, its judicial duels, its judges recruited from among the rural population, and knowing no other custom than that which had been gradually elaborated to regulate the relations of men living by the cultivation or the ownership of the land, was inadequate for a population whose existence was based on commerce and industry. A more expeditious law was necessary, means of proof more rapid and more independent of chance, and judges who were themselves acquainted with the professional occupations of those who came under their jurisdiction, and could cut short their arguments by a knowledge of the case at issue. Very early, and at latest at the beginning of the eleventh century, the pressure of circumstances led to the creation of a *jus mercatorum,* i.e., an embryonic commercial code. It was a collection of usages born of business experience, a sort of international custom, which the merchants used among themselves in their transactions. Devoid of all legal validity, it was impossible to invoke it in the existing law courts, so the merchants agreed to choose among themselves arbitrators who had the necessary competence to understand their disputes and to settle them promptly. It is here undoubtedly that we must seek the origin of those law courts, which in England received the picturesque name of courts of *piepowder* (*pied poudré*), because the feet of the merchants who resorted to them were still dusty from the roads. Soon this *ad hoc* jurisdiction became permanent and was recognised by public authority. At Ypres, in 1116, the Count of Flanders abolished the judicial duel, and it is certain that about the same date he instituted in most of his towns local courts of *échevins,* chosen from among the burgesses and alone competent to judge them. Sooner or later the same thing happened in all countries. In Italy, France, Germany and England the towns obtained judicial autonomy, which made them islands of independent jurisdiction, lying outside the territorial custom.

This jurisdictional autonomy was accompanied by administrative autonomy. The formation of urban agglomerations entailed a number of arrangements for convenience of defence, which they had to provide for themselves in the absence of the traditional authorities, who had neither the means nor the wish to help them. It is a strong testimony to the energy and the initiative of the bourgeoisie that it succeeded by its own efforts in setting on foot the municipal organisation, of which the first outlines appear in the eleventh century, and which was already in possession of all its essential organs in the twelfth. The work thus accomplished is all the more admirable because it was an original creation. There was nothing in the existing order of things to serve it as a model, since the needs it was designed to meet were new.

The most pressing was the need for defence. The merchants and their merchandise were, indeed, such a tempting prey that it was essential to protect them from pillagers by a strong wall. The construction of ramparts was thus the first public work undertaken by the towns and one which, down to the end of the Middle Ages, was their heaviest financial burden. Indeed, it may be truly said to have been the starting-point of their financial organisation, whence, for example, the name of *firmitas,* by which the communal tax was always known at Liège, and the appropriation in a number of cities *ad opus castri* (i.e., for the improvement of the fortifications) of a part of the fines imposed by the borough court. The fact that to-day municipal coats of arms are surrounded by a walled crown shows the importance accorded to the ramparts. There were no unfortified towns in the Middle Ages.

Money had to be raised to provide for the expenses occasioned by the permanent need for fortifications, and it could be raised most easily from the burgesses themselves. All were interested in the common defence and all were obliged to meet the cost. The quota payable by each was calculated on the basis of his fortune. This was a great innovation. For the arbitrary seigneurial tallage, collected in the sole interest of the lord, it substituted a payment proportionate to the means of the taxpayer and set apart for an object of general utility. Thus taxation recovered its public character, which had disappeared during the feudal era. To assess and collect this tax, as well as to provide for the ordinary necessities whose numbers grew with the constant increase of the town population, the establishment of quays and markets, the building of bridges and parish churches, the regulation of crafts and the supervision of food supplies, it soon became necessary to elect or allow the setting up of a council of magistrates, consuls in Italy and Provence, *jurés* in France and aldermen in England. In the eleventh century they appeared in the Lombard cities, where the consuls of Lucca are mentioned as early as 1080. In the following century, they became everywhere an institution ratified by public authority and inherent in every municipal constitution. In many towns, as in those of the Low Countries, the *échevins* were at once the judges and administrators of the townsfolk.

The lay princes soon discovered how advantageous the growth of the cities was to themselves. For in proportion as their trade grew on road and river and their increasing business transactions required a corresponding increase of currency, the revenues from every kind of toll and from the mints likewise flowed in increasing quantities into the lord's treasury. Thus it is not surprising that the lords assumed on the whole a benevolent attitude towards the townsfolk. Moreover, living as a rule in their country castles, they did not come in contact with the town population and thus many causes of conflict were avoided. It was quite otherwise with the ecclesiastical princes. Almost to a man they offered a resistance to the municipal movement, which at times developed into an open struggle. The fact that the bishops were obliged to reside in their cities, the centres of diocesan administration, necessarily impelled them to preserve their authority and to oppose the ambitions of the bourgeoisie all the more resolutely because they were roused and directed by the merchants, ever suspect in the eyes of the Church. In the second half of the eleventh century the quarrel of the Empire and the Papacy gave the city populations of Lombardy a chance to rise against their simoniacal prelates. Thence the movement spread through the Rhine valley to Cologne. In 1077, the town of Cambrai rose in revolt against Bishop Gerard II and formed the oldest of the "communes" that we meet with north of the Alps. In the diocese of Liège the same thing happened. In 1066 Bishop Théoduin was forced to grant the burgesses of Huy a charter of liberties which is several years earlier than those whose text has been preserved in the rest of the Empire. In France, municipal insurrections are mentioned at Beauvais about 1099, at Noyon in 1108-9, and at Laon in 1115.

Thus, by fair means or foul, the towns gained peaceably or by force, some at the beginning, others in the course of the twelfth century, municipal constitutions suitable to the life of their inhabitants. Originating in the "new burgs," in the *portus,* where the merchants and artisans were grouped, they were soon developed to include the population of the "old burgs" and the "cities," whose ancient walls, surrounded on all sides by the new quarters, were falling into ruin like the old law itself. Henceforth, all who resided within the city wall, with the sole exception of the clergy, shared the privileges of the burgesses.

The essential characteristic of the bourgeoisie was, indeed, the fact that it formed a privileged class in the midst of the rest of the population. From this point of view the medieval town offers a striking contrast both to the ancient town and to the town of to-day, which are differentiated only by the density of their population and their complex administration; apart from this, neither in public nor in private law do their inhabitants occupy a peculiar position in the State. The medieval burgess, on the contrary, was a different kind of person from all who lived outside the town walls. Once outside the gates and the moat we are in another world, or more exactly, in the domain of another law. The acquisition of citizenship brought with it results analogous to those which followed when a man was dubbed knight or a clerk tonsured, in the sense that they conferred a peculiar legal status. Like the clerk or the noble, the burgess escaped from the common law; like them, he belonged to a particular estate (*status*), which was later to be known as the "third estate."

The territory of the town was as privileged as its inhabitants. It was a sanctuary, an "immunity," which protected the man who took refuge there from exterior authority, as if he had sought sanctuary in a church. In short, the bourgeoisie was in every sense an exceptional class. Each town formed, so to speak, a little state to itself, jealous of its prerogatives and hostile to all its neighbours. Very rarely was a common danger or a common end able to impose on its municipal particularism the need for alliances or leagues such, for example, as the German Hanse. In general, urban politics were determined by the same sacred egoism which was later to inspire State politics. For the burgesses the country population existed only to be exploited. Far from allowing it to enjoy their franchises, they always obstinately refused it all share in them. Nothing could be further removed from the spirit of modern democracy than the exclusiveness with which the medieval towns continued to defend their privileges, even, and indeed above all, in those periods when they were governed by the crafts.

CHIVALRY AND THE CRUSADES

73 SONG OF ROLAND: THE IDEALS OF CHIVALRY

The knight of the early Middle Ages had to live with the anarchy of nascent feudalism and at the same time defend himself against the barbarian inroads of Norsemen, Magyars, and Saracens. In this age of warriors he fought ruthlessly to survive, to gather land, to found a family. But eventually, as feudal knights bound themselves together by ties of vassalage, settled permanently on lands, and passed their titles and offices on to their heirs generation after generation, they acquired the attributes of an aristocratic and exclusive class. A code of behavior slowly grew up defining the role of a noble knight, which to a great extent was that of a vassal to his lord, encompassing bravery, fidelity, and loyalty. The demeanor of the knight continued to be crude, and the ideal of knightly honor appeared relatively late, but by the twelfth century, during a time of crusades and intense interest in religious matters, chivalry more closely approached the Christian standard.

During the twelfth century and later, chivalry was also profoundly influenced by a new literary tradition: the popular romances of Arthur, Charlemagne, and other famous heroes. These historical figures assumed heroic proportions in the songs of medieval troubadours and poets, and their legends achieved amazing popularity throughout western Europe for the rest of the Middle Ages. The songs sung in the new vernacular languages (French, German, Italian, English) instead of the language of the Church (Latin) set the standards for knightly honor and bravery which became the code of the noble classes. Aristocratic manners became less brutal, and a spirit of knight-errantry grew up. It became the knight's duty to render chivalrous service to his lady according to the code of "courtly love." Foremost, it became his mission to defend Christianity, to protect the Church, and to battle against the infidel.

The selection below is derived from the *Chanson de Roland (Song of Roland),* the major poem of the Charlemagne cycle of medieval romances. The four-thousand-line poem, written in old French, deals with the ambush of the emperor's nephew, Roland, by the Moors at Roncesvalles in the Pyrenees. Because the ambush resulted from the treason at Ganelon, a Frankish courtier, the themes of heroic courage, of friendship and its betrayal, are prominent. These excerpts deal first with the moments before the battle when Roland, his friend Olivier, and other Franks encourage their troops, and second with the death of Roland, who summons Charlemagne's aid too late. The ideal of honorable death in preference to cowardly life and the contrast between Roland's loyalty and Ganelon's treachery are typical chivalric themes.

In tales such as the *Song of Roland,* people of the Middle Ages found examples and ideals for their own conduct. If these ideals were not always followed, at least they set a standard which helped in some degree to soften and make more charitable the rough and sometimes brutal conventions which had grown out of the long centuries of barbarity and insecurity preceding the age of chivalry.

Roland is daring and Olivier wise,
Both of marvellous high emprise;
On their chargers mounted, and girt in mail,
To the death in battle they will not quail.
Brave are the counts, and their words are high,
And the Pagans are fiercely riding nigh.
"See, Roland, see them, how close they are,
The Saracen foemen, and Karl how far!
Thou didst disdain on thy horn to blow.
Were the king but here we were spared this woe.
Look up through Aspra's dread defile,
Where standeth our doomed rear-guard the while;
They will do their last brave feat this day,
No more to mingle in mortal fray."
"Hush!" said Roland, "the craven tale—
Foul fall who carries a heart so pale;
Foot to foot shall we hold the place,
And rain our buffets and blows apace."

When Roland felt that the battle came,
Lion or leopard to him were tame;
He shouted aloud to his Franks, and then
Called to his gentle compeer agen.
"My friend, my comrade, my Olivier,
The Emperor left us his bravest here;
Twice ten thousand he set apart,
And he knew among them no dastard heart.
For his lord the vassal must bear the stress
Of the winter's cold and the sun's excess—
Peril his flesh and his blood thereby:
Strike thou with thy good lance-point and I,
With Durindana, the matchless glaive

Which the king himself to my keeping gave,
That he who wears it when I lie cold
May say 't was the sword of a vassal bold."

Archbishop Turpin, above the rest,
Spurred his steed to a jutting crest.
His sermon thus to the Frank's he spake:—
"Lords, we are here for our monarch's sake;
Hold we for him, though our death should come;
Fight for the succor of Christendom.
The battle approaches—ye know it well,
For ye see the ranks of the infidel.
Cry *mea culpa,* and lowly kneel;
I will assoil you, your souls to heal.
In death ye are holy martyrs crowned."
The Franks alighted, and knelt on ground;
In God's high name the host he blessed,
And for penance gave them—to smite their best.

The Franks arose from bended knee,
Assoiled, and from their sins set free;
The archbishop blessed them fervently:
Then each one sprange on his bounding barb,
Armed and laced in knightly garb,
Apparelled all for the battle line.
At last said Roland, "Companion mine,
Too well the treason is now displayed,
How Ganelon hath our band betrayed.

Text: *The Song of Roland,* in *Epic and Saga,* "The Harvard Classics," ed. Charles W. Eliot (New York: P. F. Collier & Son, 1910), pp. 136-38, 178-84.

To him the gifts and the treasures fell;
But our Emperor will avenge us well.
King Marsil deemeth us bought and sold;
The price shall be with our good swords told."

Roland rideth the passes through,
On Veillantif, his charger true;
Girt in his harness that shone full fair,
And baron-like his lance he bare.
The steel erect in the sunshine gleamed,
With the snow-white pennon that from it
  streamed;
The golden fringes beat on his hand.
Joyous of visage was he, and bland,
Exceeding beautiful of frame;
And his warriors hailed him with glad acclaim.
Proudly he looked on the heathen ranks,
Humbly and sweetly upon his Franks.
Courteously spake he, in words of grace—
"Ride, my barons, at gentle pace.
The Saracens here to their slaughter toil:
Reap we, to-day, a glorious spoil,
Never fell to Monarch of France the like."
At his word, the hosts are in act to strike.

Said Olivier, "Idle is speech, I trow;
Thou didst disdain on thy horn to blow.
Succor of Karl is far apart;
Our strait he knows not, the noble heart:
Not to him nor his host be blame;
Therefore, barons, in God's good name,
Press ye onward, and strike your best,
Make your stand on this field to rest;
Think but of blows, both to give and take,
Never the watchword of Karl forsake."
Then from the Franks resounded high—
"*Montjoie!*" Whoever had heard that cry
Would hold remembrance of chivalry.
Then ride they—how proudly, O God, they ride!—
With rowels dashed in their coursers' side.
Fearless, too, are their paynim foes.
Frank and Saracen, thus they close.

. . . .

Alone seeks Roland the field of fight,
He searcheth vale, he searcheth height.
Ivon and Ivor he found, laid low,
And the Gascon Engelier of Bordeaux,
Gerein and his fellow in arms, Gerier;
Otho he found, and Berengier;
Samson the duke, and Anseis bold,
Gerard of Roussillon, the old.
Their bodies, one after one, he bore,
And laid them Turpin's feet before.
The archbishop saw them stretched arow,
Nor can he hinder the tears that flow;
In benediction his hands he spread:

"Alas! for your doom, my lords," he said,
"That God in mercy your souls may give,
On the flowers of Paradise to live;
Mine own death comes, with anguish sore
That I see mine Emperor never more."

Once more to the field doth Roland wend,
Till he findeth Olivier his friend;
The lifeless form to his heart he strained,
Bore him back with what strength remained,
On a buckler laid him, beside the rest,
The archbishop assoiled them all, and blessed.
Their dole and pity anew find vent,
And Roland maketh his fond lament:
"My Olivier, my chosen one,
Thou wert the noble Duke Renier's son,
Lord of the March unto Rivier vale.
To shiver lance and shatter mail,
The brave in council to guide and cheer,
To smite the miscreant foe with fear,—
Was never on earth such cavalier."

Dead around him his peers to see,
And the man he loved so tenderly,
Fast the tears of Count Roland ran,
His visage discolored became, and wan,
He swooned for sorrow beyond control.
"Alas," said Turpin, "how great thy dole!"

To look on Roland swooning there,
Surpassed all sorrow he ever bare;
He stretched his hand, the horn he took,—
Through Roncesvailes there flowed a brook,—
A draught to Roland he thought to bring;
But his steps were feeble and tottering,
Spent his strength, from waste of blood,—
He struggled on for scarce a rood,
When sank his heart, and drooped his frame,
And his mortal anguish on him came.

Roland revived from his swoon again;
On his feet he rose, but in deadly pain;
He looked on high, and he looked below,
Till, a space his other companions fro,
He beheld the baron, stretched on sward,
The archbishop, vicar of God our Lord.
Mea Culpa was Turpin's cry,
While he raised his hands to heaven on high,
Imploring Paradise to gain.
So died the soldier of Carlemaine,—
With word or weapon, to preach or fight,
A champion ever of Christian right,
And a deadly foe of the infidel.
God's benediction within him dwell!
When Roland saw him stark on earth
(His very vitals were bursting forth,
And his brain was oozing from out his head),

He took the fair white hands outspread,
Crossed and clasped them upon his breast,
And thus his plaint to the dead addressed,—
So did his country's law ordain:—
"Ah, gentleman of noble strain,
I trust thee unto God the True,
Whose service never man shall do
With more devoted heart and mind:
To guard the faith, to win mankind,
From the apostles' days till now,
Such prophet never rose as thou.
Nor pain or torment thy soul await,
But of Paradise the open gate."

Roland feeleth his death is near,
His brain is oozing by either ear.
For his peers he prayed—God keep them well;
Invoked the angel Gabriel.
That none reproach him, his horn he clasped;
His other hand Durindana grasped;
Then, far as quarrel from crossbow sent,
Across the march of Spain he went,
Where, on a mound, two trees between,
Four flights of marble steps were seen;
Backward he fell, on the field to lie;
And he swooned anon, for the end was nigh.

High were the mountains and high the trees,
Bright shone the marble terraces;
On the green grass Roland hath swooned away.
A Saracen spied him where he lay:
Stretched with the rest he had feigned him dead,
His face and body with blood bespread.
To his feet he sprang, and in haste he hied,—
He was fair and strong and of courage tried,
In pride and wrath he was overbold,—
And on Roland, body and arms, laid hold.
"The nephew of Karl is overthrown!
To Araby bear I this sword, mine own."
He stooped to grasp it, but as he drew,
Roland returned to his sense anew.

He saw the Saracen seize his sword;
His eyes he oped, and he spake one word—
"Thou art not one of our band, I trow,"
And he clutched the horn he would ne'er forego;
On the golden crest he smote him full,
Shattering steel and bone and skull,
Forth from his head his eyes he beat,
And cast him lifeless before his feet.
"Miscreant, makest thou then so free,
As, right or wrong, to lay hold on me?
Who hears it will deem there a madman born;
Behold the mouth of mine ivory horn
Broken for thee, and the gems and gold
Around its rim to earth are rolled."

Roland feeleth his eyesight reft,
Yet he stands erect with what strength is left:
From his bloodless cheek is the hue dispelled,
But his Durindana all bare he held.
In front a dark brown rock arose—
He smote upon it ten grievous blows.
Grated the steel as it struck the flint,
Yet it brake not, nor bore its edge one dint.
"Mary, Mother, be thou mine aid!
Ah, Durindana, my ill-starred blade,
I may no longer thy guardian be!
What fields of battle I won with thee!
What realms and regions 't was ours to gain,
Now the lordship of Carlemaine!
Never shalt thou possessor know
Who would turn from face of mortal foe;
A gallant vassal so long thee bore,
Such as France the free shall know no more."

He smote anew on the marble stair.
It grated, but breach nor notch was there.
When Roland found that it would not break,
Thus began he his plaint to make.
"Ah, Durindana, how fair and bright
Thou sparklest, flaming against the light!
When Karl in Maurienne valley lay,
God sent his angel from heaven to say—
'This sword shall a valorous captain's be,'
And he girt it, the gentle king, on me.
With it I vanquished Poitou and Maine,
Provence I conquered and Aquitaine;
I conquered Normandy the free,
Anjou, and the marches of Brittany;
Romagna I won, and Lombardy,
Bavaria, Flanders from side to side,
And Burgundy, and Poland wide;
Constantinople affiance vowed,
And the Saxon soil to his bidding bowed;
Scotia, and Wales, and Ireland's plain,
Of England made he his own domain.
What mighty regions I won of old,
For the hoary-headed Karl to hold!
But there presses on me a grievous pain,
Lest thou in heathen hands remain.
O God our Father, keep France from stain!"

His strokes once more on the brown rock fell,
And the steel was bent past words to tell;
Yet it brake not, nor was notched the grain,
Erect it leaped to the sky again.
When he failed at the last to break his blade,
His lamentation he inly made.
"Oh, fair and holy, my peerless sword,
What relics lie in thy pommel stored!
Tooth of Saint Peter, Saint Basil's blood,
Hair of Saint Denis beside them strewed,
Fragment of holy Mary's vest.

'Twere shame that thou with the heathen rest;
Thee should the hand of a Christian serve
One who would never in battle swerve.
What regions won I with thee of yore,
The empire now of Karl the hoar!
Rich and mighty is he therefore."

That death was on him he knew full well;
Down from his head to his heart it fell.
On the grass beneath a pine tree's shade,
With face to earth, his form he laid,
Beneath him placed he his horn and sword,
And turned his face to the heathen horde.
Thus hath he done the sooth to show,
That Karl and his warriors all may know,
That the gentle count a conqueror died.
Mea Culpa full oft he cried;
And, for all his sins, unto God above,
In sign of penance, he raised his glove.

Roland feeleth his hour at hand;
On a knoll he lies towards the Spanish land.
With one hand beats he upon his breast:
"In thy sight, O God, be my sins confessed.
From my hour of birth, both the great and small,
Down to this day, I repent of all."
As his glove he raises to God on high,
Angels of heaven descend him nigh.

Beneath a pine was his resting-place,
To the land of Spain hath he turned his face,
On his memory rose full many a thought—
Of the lands he won and the fields he fought;
Of his gentle France, of his kin and line;
Of his nursing father, King Karl benign;—
He may not the tear and sob control,
Nor yet forgets he his parting soul.
To God's compassion he makes his cry:
"O Father true, who canst not lie,
Who didst Lazarus raise unto life agen,
And Daniel shield in the lions' den;
Shield my soul from its peril, due
For the sins I sinned my lifetime through."
He did his right-hand glove uplift—
Saint Gabriel took from his hand the gift;
Then drooped his head upon his breast,
And with claspèd hands he went to rest.
God from on high sent down to him
One of his angel Cherubim—
Saint Michael of Peril of the sea,
Saint Gabriel in company—
From heaven they came for that soul of price,
And they bore it with them to Paradise.

74 DECREE OF THE COUNCIL OF TOULOUGES: PEACE OF GOD AND TRUCE OF GOD

The ideals of chivalry expressed in medieval romance were ideals, not realities. If the knight of the later Middle Ages became less gruff and brutal, he was still far from being the polished and gallant gentleman pictured by the troubadours. The ideals of warfare—the knightly quests in the name of noble causes—often vanished in the face of expediency or private interest. War was usually a matter of business, a means of defending or augmenting one's lands or titles or even merely a means of profit, as a chronicler of the battle of Aljubarrota callously reveals: "Lo, behold the great evil adventure that fell that Saturday. For they slew as many good prisoners as would well have been worth, one with another, 400,000 francs."

Whatever his motives, however, the feudal knight was through necessity endowed with a strong fighting instinct. Feudalism had evolved to reduce the chances of anarchy by establishing rights and obligations among lords and vassals, but these feudal controls often failed to restrain an ambitious noble or save a weak one. There was no central government strong enough to suppress local wars. The problem thus was to find other controls, which would either curb the knight's bellicosity or release it into socially acceptable channels. It was here that the Church intervened, appealing to the spiritual side of the knight's nature—particularly his ardent desire for perfect salvation and forgiveness of sins. The Church itself had a personal interest, for its bishops, as great lords and vassals controlling lands and peasantry, were involved in the chronic conflict.

The ecclesiastical movement for peace began as early as the tenth century in southern France, with the proclamation by local synods of the Peace of God *(Pax Dei)*. This was an attempt to curb warfare or at least to prevent unreasonable oppression, by excluding women, peasants, merchants, and the clergy from attacks of violence on pain of excommunication for the violator. This attempt to *exempt certain members of the population* from violence, however, was at best only partially successful, and in the early eleventh century the Church tried a new idea. The Truce of God *(Truga Dei)* attempted to *limit the period of time* that nobles could fight one another. On threat of excommunication it forbade private war on certain days, originally only on Sundays and certain Church holidays, but later the period of time was increased to include some 240 days each year. The constant reënactment of such measures throughout western Europe and their reiteration at such important gatherings as the Council of Clermont (1095), where the Peace and Truce of God were proclaimed along with the First Crusade, indicate that they were not so effective as the Church might have wished them. Nevertheless, they provided a constant pressure with which nobles had to reckon.

The following decree of the Council of Toulouges, issued in 1041, or, as some authorities believe, in 1065, is typical of the decrees combining the features of both the Peace and the Truce.

This Peace has been confirmed by the bishops, by the abbots, by the counts and viscounts and the other God-fearing nobles in this bishopric, to the effect that in the future, beginning with this day, no man may commit an act of violence in a church, or in the space which surrounds it and which is covered by its privileges, or in the burying-ground, or in the dwelling-houses which are, or may be, within thirty paces of it.

We do not include in this measure the churches which have been, or which shall be, fortified as châteaux, or those in which plunderers and thieves are accustomed to store their ill-gotten booty, or which give them a place of refuge. Nevertheless we desire that such churches be under this protection until complaint of them shall be made to the bishop, or to the chapter. If the bishop or chapter act upon such information and lay hold of the malefactors, and if the latter refuse to give themselves up to the justice of the bishop or chapter, the malefactors and all their possessions shall not be immune, even within the church. A man who breaks into a church, or into the space within thirty paces around it, must pay a fine for sacrilege, and double this amount to the person wronged.

Furthermore, it is forbidden that any one attack the clergy, who do not bear arms, or the monks and religious persons, or do them any wrong; likewise it is forbidden to despoil or pillage the communities of canons, monks, and religious persons, the ecclesiastical lands which are under the protection of the Church, or the clergy, who do not bear arms; and if any one shall do such a thing, let him pay a double composition.

Let no one burn or destroy the dwellings of the peasants and the clergy, the dove-cotes and the granaries. Let no man dare to kill, to beat, or to wound a peasant or serf, or the wife of either, or to seize them and carry them off, except for misdemeanors which they may have committed; but it is not forbidden to lay hold of them in order to bring them to justice, and it is allowable to do this even before they shall have been summoned to appear. Let not the raiment of the peasants be stolen; let not their ploughs, or their hoes, or their olive-fields be burned.

. . . Let any one who has broken the peace, and has not paid his fines within a fortnight, make amends to him whom he has injured by paying a double amount, which shall go to the bishop and to the count who shall have had charge of the case.

The bishops of whom we have spoken have solemnly confirmed the Truce of God, which has been enjoined upon all Christians from the setting of the sun of the fourth day of the week, that is to say, Wednesday, until the rising of the sun on Monday, the second day. . . . If any one during the Truce shall violate it, let him pay a double composition and subsequently undergo the ordeal of cold water. When any one during the Truce shall kill a man, it has been ordained, with the approval of all Christians, that if the crime was committed intentionally the murderer shall be condemned to perpetual exile, but if it occurred by accident the slayer shall be banished for a period of time to be fixed by the bishops and the canons. If any one during the Truce shall attempt to seize a man or to carry him off from his château, and does not succeed in his purpose, let him pay a fine to the bishop and to the chapter, just as if he had succeeded. It is likewise forbidden during the Truce, in Advent and Lent, to build any château or fortification, unless it was begun a fortnight before the time of the Truce. It has been ordained also that at all times disputes and suits on the subject of the Peace and Truce of God shall be settled before the bishop and his chapter, and likewise for the peace of the churches which have before been enumerated. When the bishop

Text: Frederic Austin Ogg (ed.), *A Source Book of Mediaeval History* (New York: American Book Company, 1907), pp. 230-32.

and the chapter shall have pronounced sentences to recall men to the observance of the Peace and the Truce of God, the sureties and hostages who show themselves hostile to the bishop and the chapter shall be excommunicated by the chapter and the bishop, with their protectors and partisans, as guilty of violating the Peace and the Truce of the Lord; they and their possessions shall be excluded from the Peace and the Truce of the Lord.

75 AMBROISE, *CRUSADE OF RICHARD LION-HEART*, AND LETTER OF DAIMBERT, GODFREY, AND RAYMOND TO THE POPE: THE CRUSADES

Since the close of the tenth century the Church had tried to purify the feudal instinct for private war—most notably through the Peace and Truce of God (see Document 74). But it was an easier thing to consecrate the bellicose instinct than to curb it, and the crusades represent such a clerical consecration for ideal ends and noble purposes. Seen as the climax of a religious revival that had spread through medieval Europe, the crusades were a series of campaigns—seven major ones and countless others—undertaken by the Christians of western Europe from 1096 to 1291 for the recovery of the Holy Land from the Muslims. The knight who joined the crusades might thus still indulge the fighting side of his nature, under the aegis of the Cross, and in doing so he would also attain what the spiritual side of his genius fervently desired—the Church's remission of his sins.

Piety was not the sole motive for the crusades, however. The spirit of adventure ran high in medieval Europe; the riches of the East attracted the ambitions of secular kings and nobles and ultimately engaged the commercial interests of the Italian city-states. But by the end of the crusading era many of the highest religious and secular expectations had been disappointed—the eastern Mediterranean remained under Muslim domination (the Christian conquest of the Holy Land proved to be only temporary); the Byzantine Empire, a bastion against Islam, was seriously weakened (and ultimately fell to the Turks in 1453); and Frankish knighthood had been decimated in futile military ventures. Nevertheless, although present-day historians are reluctant to mark the crusades as the primary cause of the enlightenment of the later Middle Ages, most will still agree that the crusades were a valuable factor in the revival of trade from Venice, Genoa, and Pisa and that the intellectual and commercial horizons of medieval Europe were expanded by contact with the most advanced Byzantine and Arabic cultures.

The first selection below is a letter written by three leaders of the First Crusade (1095-1099) from Laodicea in Asia Minor to Pope Urban II in Rome. The letter summarizes the main events of the expedition from the moment it crossed into Asia at Nicaea to the conquest of Jerusalem. Notable are the exaggerated estimates of Muslim numbers, the quarreling among the leaders, and the bloodthirsty fanaticism which marred the capture of Jerusalem. Nevertheless, a sublime confidence in the righteousness of their cause is evident in the attitude of the crusaders.

The second selection below is an excerpt from *The Crusade of Richard the Lion-Heart*, written about a century later by the Norman French poet Ambroise. The Third Crusade (1189-1192), which it describes, was probably the most celebrated because of its heroes: Philip Augustus of France, Frederick Barbarossa of the Holy Roman Empire, and Richard I of England, who were opposed by the Muslim sultan Saladin. This crusade, after winning an initial success at Acre in Syria, failed to recover Jerusalem. Richard, Saladin, and Saladin's brother, Sapladin, emerge as heroes of chivalry.

DAIMBERT, GODFREY AND RAYMOND, TO THE POPE.

Laodicea, September, 1099.

To lord Paschal, pope of the Roman church, to all the bishops, and to the whole Christian people, from the archbishop of Pisa, duke Godfrey, now, by the grace of God, defender of the church of the Holy Sepulchre, Raymond, count of St. Gilles, and the whole army of God, which is in the land of Israel, greeting.

Multiply your supplications and prayers in the sight of God with joy and thanksgiving, since God has manifested His mercy in fulfilling by our hands

Text: *Translations and Reprints from the Original Sources of European History* (Philadelphia: University of Pennsylvania Press, 1897), Vol. I, no. 4, pp. 8-12.

what He had promised in ancient times. For after the capture of Nicaea, the whole army, made up of more than three hundred thousand soldiers, departed thence. And, although this army was so great that it could have in a single day covered all Romania and drunk up all the rivers and eaten up all the growing things, yet the Lord conducted them amid so great abundance that a ram was sold for a penny and an ox for twelve pennies or less. Moreover, although the princes and kings of the Saracens rose up against us, yet, by God's will, they were easily conquered and overcome. Because, indeed, some were puffed up by these successes, God opposed to us Antioch, impregnable to human strength. And there He detained us for nine months and so humbled us in the siege that there were scarcely a hundred good horses in our whole army. God opened to us the abundance of His blessing and mercy and led us into the city, and delivered the Turks and all of their possessions into our power.

Inasmuch as we thought that these had been acquired by our own strength and did not worthily magnify God who had done this, we were beset by so great a multitude of Turks that no one dared to venture forth at any point from the city. Moreover, hunger so weakened us that some could scarcely refrain from eating human flesh. It would be tedious to narrate all the miseries which we suffered in that city. But God looked down upon His people whom He had so long chastised and mercifully consoled them. Therefore, He at first revealed to us, as a recompense for our tribulation and as a pledge of victory, His lance which had lain hidden since the days of the apostles. Next, He so fortified the hearts of the men, that they who from sickness or hunger had been unable to walk, now were endued with strength to seize their weapons and manfully to fight against the enemy.

After we had triumphed over the enemy, as our army was wasting away at Antioch from sickness and weariness and was especially hindered by the dissensions among the leaders, we proceeded into Syria, stormed Barra and Marra, cities of the Saracens, and captured the fortresses in that country. And while we were delaying there, there was so great a famine in the army that the Christian people now ate the putrid bodies of the Saracens. Finally, by the divine admonition, we entered into the interior of Hispania, and the most bountiful, merciful and victorious hand of the omnipotent Father was with us. For the cities and fortresses of the country through which we were proceeding sent ambassadors to us with many gifts and offered to aid us and to surrender their walled places. But because our army was not large and it was the unanimous wish to hasten to Jerusalem, we accepted their pledges and made them tributaries. One of the cities forsooth, which was on the seacoast, had more men than there were in our whole army. And when those at Antioch and Laodicea and Archas heard how the hand of the Lord was with us, many from the army who had remained in those cities followed us to Tyre. Therefore, with the Lord's companionship and aid, we proceeded thus as far as Jerusalem.

And after the army had suffered greatly in the siege, especially on account of the lack of water, a council was held and the bishops and princes ordered that all with bare feet should march around the walls of the city, in order that He who entered it humbly in our behalf might be moved by our humility to open it to us and to exercise judgment upon His enemies. God was appeased by this humility and on the eighth day after the humiliation He delivered the city and His enemies to us. It was the day indeed on which the primitive church was driven thence, and on which the festival of the dispersion of the apostles is celebrated. And if you desire to know what was done with the enemy who were found there, know that in Solomon's Porch and in his temple our men rode in the blood of the Saracens up to the knees of their horses.

Then, when we were considering who ought to hold the city, and some moved by love for their country and kinsmen wished to return home, it was announced to us that the king of Babylon had come to Ascalon with an innumerable multitude of soldiers. His purpose was, as he said, to lead the Franks, who were in Jerusalem, into captivity, and to take Antioch by storm. But God had determined otherwise in regard to us.

Therefore, when we learned that the army of the Babylonians was at Ascalon, we went down to meet them, leaving our baggage and the sick in Jerusalem with a garrison. When our army was in sight of the enemy, upon our knees we invoked the aid of the Lord, that He who in our other adversities had strengthened the Christian faith, might in the present battle break the strength of the Saracens and of the devil and extend the kingdom of the church of Christ from sea to sea, over the whole world. There was no delay; God was present when we cried for His aid, and furnished us with so great boldness, that one who saw us rush upon the enemy would have taken us for a herd of deer hastening to quench their thirst in running water. It was wonderful, indeed, since there were in our army not more than 5,000 horsemen and 15,000 foot-soldiers, and there were probably in the enemy's army 100,000 horsemen and

400,000 foot-soldiers. Then God appeared wonderful to His servants. For before we engaged in fighting, by our very onset alone, He turned this multitude in flight and scattered all their weapons, so that if they wished afterwards to attack us, they did not have the weapons in which they trusted. There can be no question how great the spoils were, since the treasures of the king of Babylon were captured. More than 100,000 Moors perished there by the sword. Moreover, their panic was so great that about 2,000 were suffocated at the gate of the city. Those who perished in the sea were innumerable. Many were entangled in the thickets. The whole world was certainly fighting for us, and if many of ours had not been detained in plundering the camp, few of the great multitude of the enemy would have been able to escape from the battle.

And although it may be tedious, the following must not be omitted: On the day preceding the battle the army captured many thousands of camels, oxen and sheep. By the command of the princes these were divided among the people. When we advanced to battle, wonderful to relate, the camels formed in many squadrons and the sheep and oxen did the same. Moreover, these animals accompanied us, halting when we halted, advancing when we advanced, and charging when we charged. The clouds protected us from the heat of the sun and cooled us.

Accordingly, after celebrating the victory, the army returned to Jerusalem. Duke Godfrey remained there; the count of St. Gilles, Robert, count of Normandy, and Robert, count of Flanders, returned to Laodicea. There they found the fleet belonging to the Pisans and to Bohemond. After the archbishop of Pisa had established peace between Bohemond and our leaders, Raymond prepared to return to Jerusalem for the sake of God and his brethren.

Therefore, we call upon you of the catholic church of Christ and of the whole Latin church to exult in the so admirable bravery and devotion of your brethren, in the so glorious and very desirable retribution of the omnipotent God, and in the so devoutedly hoped-for remission of all our sins through the grace of God. And we pray that He may make you—namely, all bishops, clerks and monks who are leading devout lives, and all the laity—to sit down at the right hand of God, who liveth and reigneth God for ever and ever. And we ask and beseech you in the name of our Lord Jesus, who has ever been with us and aided us and freed us from all our tribulations, to be mindful of your brethren who return to you, by doing them kindnesses and by paying their debts, in order that God may recompense you and absolve you from all your sins and grant you a share in all the blessings which either we or they have deserved in the sight of the Lord. Amen.

Text: Ambroise, *The Crusade of Richard Lion-Heart*, trans. Merton Jerome Hubert (New York: Columbia University Press, 1941), pp. 235-36, 240-53, 260-61, 269-71.

THE CRUSADE OF RICHARD LION-HEART.

The Crusader Host

Aug. 23, 1191

'Twas Friday when the Christian host,
Whose story I am telling, crossed
The stream; the morrow was a feast,
When every man his labor ceased;
'Twas of our Lord's disciple, who
Is known as Saint Bartholomew.
The Monday following this day
Was just two years since the array
Of Christians came here and assailed
Acre, where at last their force prevailed.
On Sunday, then, the host set out   Aug. 25
In God's name, Who doth guide throughout
All things. The chiefs arose at dawn
And drew up each battalion.
There had ye seen fair chivalry,
The bravest young nobility,
The noblest and best chosen men
E'er seen before or seen since then;
So many tried men in fair fettle,
And armor of such sturdy metal;
So many sergeants firm and bold,
For valor worthily extolled;
Ye had seen so many pennants streaming,
So many lance blades brightly gleaming;
Ye had seen so many floating banners
Broidered and worked in divers manners;
So many hauberks and fair helms,
Their like was not in full five realms;
Ye had seen an army drawn up here
Well fitted to inspire fear.
Now in the fore guard went the king,
With men who feared not anything.
It was the Norman knights who bore
The standard, as ofttimes before.
The duke, leading the proud French nation,
Within the rear guard took his station. . . .
The Christian army moved away
From the stream; but went not far that day.
'Neath Caïphas they camped, and so
Awaited those whose pace was slow.

Where They Rest

'Neath Caïphas along the coast
Was camped the proud and valiant host.
Divided in two parts were we
Between the tower and the sea.

Two days we sojourned, to repair
Our armor and supplies with care,
Abandoning all that useless seemed
And keeping that which we esteemed;
For the foot soldiers, those of less
Importance, suffered great distress,
Being burdened in such painful wise
With weight of weapons and supplies
That many, who could not abide
The heat and thirst, perished and died.

Conditions of the March

When that the host of God at length
At Caïphas had gathered strength,
On Tuesday they took up their way   Aug. 27
Marching in orderly array.
The Temple were the *avant-garde;*
At the rear the Hospital kept ward.
All those who saw the ranks move forth
Could judge that these were men of worth;
The host was led with skill—far more
Than it had had the time before—
And they must needs complete a long
Day's march, being rested and made strong.
But they found all along the bank
Thick briers, herbage dense and rank,
Which struck the footmen's faces, making
Most difficult their undertaking.
The land was all one desert place;
There had ye witnessed many a chase,
For all along the shore they found
Wild game in plenty. From the ground
It rose up at their very feet,
And they took much of it for meat. . . .
Each eve, when they had shelter got,
Before the army slumber sought,
There was a man who would cry out,
Cheering the whole host with his shout,
For his voice sounded far and wide;
"Help, Holy Sepulcher!" he cried.
And all would echo his loud cry,
Lifting their hands toward the sky,
Tears flowing from their eyes. And then
The man would cry out once again,
Till three times he had raised his voice
And all the army would rejoice. . . .

The Fleet Brings Provisions

At the casal where it had stayed
The host its preparations made
To fight its hated foes and quell
The onslaughts of the infidel.
The place where they had stopped was wide,
And the king made the host to bide
Two full days in inaction   Aug. 28-29
While waiting for provision.
Then came the fleet, and with them were
Galleys and ships with provender;
They had followed close along the coast
Carrying victual for the host.
To the casal our troops returned.
At the Merle, where the king sojourned,   Aug. 30
He had arranged all things, decided
The marching order, and provided
That he would take the fore guard, thus
Making the van secure for us,
And that the Templars should take care
Of the rear guard and keep watch there;
Because the Saracens close by
Harassed the army constantly.

. . . .

After they had two days reposed   Sept. 1-2
Beside the stream, the gallant host
Set out. Slowly and without haste
They crossed a land barren and waste.   Sept. 3
This day into the hills they bore
Their course, because they found the shore
So cumbered and inimical
That they could not pass through at all.
Likewise they kept more close array
Than they had any other day. . . .
So through the wood they came at last
And by the Mount of Arsur passed,
Emerging into the champaign,
Where they camped in an open plain
Beside the River Rochetaillée,
Despite the circumcised array
Who had gathered in such mighty force
That one who saw the vast concourse
And gazed upon it with his eyes,
Striving to estimate its size,
Judged them three hundred thousand strong
And thought his judgment not far wrong.
While our host Christian numbered then
Only a hundred thousand men.
Beside the River Rochetaillée
The Lord's own faithful army lay.
'Twas Thursday when their camp
  they made   Sept. 5
And all day Friday there they stayed.   Sept. 6

Richard Disposes His Troops for Battle

On Saturday, when it was dawn,   Sept. 7
Ye had seen each and every one
Make ready to defend his head;
For to them plainly had been said
That till in battle they had met
These dogs, no farther they could get.
The foe, in many an ordered band,
Drew nigh the host on every hand,
And, seeing this, the Christian host
Against them in such wise disposed
Itself that naught had to be changed
Nor any squadrons rearranged.

Richard, the king of England, who
So well the art of warfare knew,
Ordered in his way who should man
The rear guard, who should take the van.
He made twelve great divisions
And ordered the battalions,
Composed of valiant men whose worth
Had no superior on earth,
And whose hearts were intent to serve
Their God, nor ever flinch nor swerve.
The vanguard was by Templars manned;
In the rear the Hospital took stand.
Methinks Bretons and Angevins
Followed the van; then came the prince,
King Guy, with soldiers from Poitou
(I am assured that this is true);
The Normans and the Englishmen,
Who bore the dragon, followed; then,
Following these, the Hospital
In the rear guard rode last of all.
The rear guard that day was composed
Of noble barons, and they closed
Their ranks in serried companies,
Riding together in such wise
That were an apple 'mongst them cast
It could not but strike man or beast.
And it extended from the host
Of Saracens down to the coast.
There had ye seen fair banners wave
And men with countenances brave. . . .

The Saracens, Many and Fierce

Thus did the army with its freight
Slowly and at an easy gait
Move forward, marching steadily;
The king, the duke of Burgundy,
With gentlemen honored and tried
In front and rear and on each side,
To right and left, marched with the host
To view the Turks, see how disposed
They were, and guide the host aright.
They fell into a grievous plight,
Because, an hour before tierce,
They were assaulted by a fierce
Onslaught and hemmed in by their foemen,
Who had more than two thousand bowmen.
Following these a black race came—
Noirets is their most common name,
Or Saracens of the *berrue*—
Loathesome, and black as soot in hue,
Foot soldiers swift and agile, armed
With bows and with light shields. They swarmed
Upon the host, and closely pressed
The assault, with neither cease nor rest.
Ye had seen great bands of Turks, who ride
In squadrons through the countryside,
With numerous rich pennons streaming

And flags and banners of fair seeming;
And thirty thousand Turkish troops
And more, ranged in well-ordered groups,
Garbed and accoutered splendidly
Dashed on the host impetuously.
Like lightning sped their horses fleet,
And dust rose thick before their feet!
Moving ahead of the emirs
There came a band of trumpeteers,
And other men with drums and tabors
There were, who had no other labors
Except upon their drums to hammer,
And hoot, and shriek, and make great clamor.
So loud their tabors did discord
They had drowned the thunder of the Lord.
And thus the infidel dogs closed
Tumultuously upon the host;
For two leagues round there was no scrap
Of earth as big as my own lap
That was not filled with them, no place
Unoccupied by their foul race. . . .

Routs the Enemy

The king, seeing his men break away
From line and charge into the fray,
At once drove spurs into his steed
And forced him to his swiftest speed:
Charging without delay, he made
All haste to lend these first troops aid.
Swifter than crossbow bolt doth fly
He rode, with his bold company
Toward the right, where with fierce hand
He fell upon a pagan band
With such impetuous attack
That they were mazed and taken back
And from their saddles hurled and thrown,
So that like sheaves of grain thick strewn
Ye had seen them lying on the earth;
And England's king, of valiant worth,
Took after them and close pursued
Them, with such skill and fortitude
That round him all the road was filled
With Saracens who had been killed.
Both fore and aft, both sides, they lay
In heaps. Others fled or gave way.
For nigh a half a league of space
The trail of corpses marked his trace.
Down crashed full many a Turk accursed;
Ye had seen Saracens unhorsed,
And ye had seen thick dust clouds fly.
Our men were greatly harmed thereby,
Because, so thick the dust did smother,
They could not recognize each other
When they came forth from out the press,
The which redoubled their distress.
They smote to left and smote to right:
Then were the Turks in sorry plight.

Ye had seen men of valor wield
Their arms, men bloody leave the field;
Ye had seen many a rich-hued flag
Droop down into the dust, and drag;
Many a good sword had ye seen
And many a javelin sharp and keen;
Ye might have picked up on the place
Arrow and quiver, bow and mace,
Quarrels and bolts and shafts and darts
Enough to fill a score of carts.
Ye had seen bearded Turks lie slain,
As thick and close as sheaves of grain.
While those of them who still held out
Against us, fiercely laid about;
And others still who had been tossed
From out their saddles and had lost
Their mounts fled midst the bushes. These
Sought refuge, climbing into trees:
They were pulled down therefrom, and filled
The air with shrieks when they were killed.
And some gave up their mounts to flee
As best they could toward the sea,
And flung them from the cliff tops steep
Full ten ells down into the deep.
They suffered a most fearsome rout,
So that for two leagues all about
Fugitives filled the countryside,
Who once were boastful in their pride. . . .

Saladin Jeers at His Men

After the army of the Turk
Was vanquished, after this day's work
Was known to Saladin, who still
Kept to his quarters on the hill,
After he learned that his élite,
His finest troops, had met defeat,
In wrath and fury manifest
His chosen emirs he addressed:
"Where is my household, that was wont
So pridefully to boast and vaunt?
Now at their will the Christians ride
Throughout the Syrian countryside
With none to hinder them or stay,
And I meanwhile know not what way
To turn. Where are those threatening words,
Those blows of maces and of swords,
Which, blustering, ye said would be
Dealt when ye met the enemy?
Where is the fulsome talk and prattle
Of rich conquest and mighty battle?
Where are the great disasters told
In scriptures written down of old—
So runneth the narration—
Which our forefathers wrought upon
The might of Christian insolence?
Badly doth this affair commence,
For the world holds our valor light
In warfare, battle, or in fight.
Our ancestors, who gave us birth,
Were valiant; we are nothing worth."

Who Pay Tribute to Richard's Valor

Now did the Saracen emirs
Hearken to these, Saladin's jeers,
Reproaching them for their disgrace,
And not one lifted up his face
Save one, Sanguin d'Aleppo, who
Upon his steed sat straight and true.
And said: "Sultan of justice, hear
Me now. With bitter and severe
Reproach you hold us up to shame.
But wherefore cast on us the blame
Without knowing the reason why?
You do not look with reason's eye.
We did not fail for any lack
Of bravery in our attack.
We launched, with fearless hearts and leal,
Upon the Franks iron and steel;
Before their blows we did not quail,
But naught against them can prevail,
For they are safely girt about
With armor strong, secure, and stout,
Which guards them from our weapons' shock,
As firm and solid as a rock,
Impervious to all our blows.
Who has to deal with men like those,
How shall he gird him to fulfill
His task? And more astounding still
Is one Frank of their company
Who slays our people terribly.
Such man we never saw indeed:
At all times he is in the lead.
At every point he wields his might
Like a well-tried and stalwart knight.
It is before him that we fall
In sheaves: Melek Richard they call
Him. Such a melek should hold land,
Win wealth, and spend it with free hand."

76
The Spirit of the Church

POPE GREGORY VII, *DICTATUS PAPAE* AND LETTER TO THE GERMAN PRINCES, AND HENRY IV, *ANSWER TO GREGORY VII:* PAPAL SUPREMACY

By the end of the tenth century a religious revival aimed at restoring the purity and regularity of spiritual life in the Roman Church was arising in various areas throughout western Europe. Efforts were made to improve discipline, eliminate corruption, restore moral standards, and in general elevate the spiritual life of man. A prime mover in this reformist spirit was the monastic order begun at Cluny in southern Burgundy, which, because of the rapid growth of daughter houses, soon raised the standards of the regular clergy to conform with the new ideals, and, because of the increased number of bishops appointed from the order, influenced the secular clergy as well. The authority of the Roman Church spread rapidly in the eleventh century. Denmark, Norway, Iceland, and Sicily all adopted Christianity and, significantly, the religious enthusiasm which had been a part of the movement was now directed toward the papacy. As one medievalist put it, "the same sort of loyalty to Christ, which had inspired men's souls, was now confounded with loyalty to the Pope."

The papacy itself was undergoing a transformation. Pope Leo IX (1049-1054) helped restore papal influence and prestige by attacking simony, pluralism, moral laxity, and other abuses. His efforts were continued by Nicholas II (1058-1061), who instituted the College of Cardinals in 1059, thereby insuring Church jurisdiction over the selection of new popes and eliminating interference by secular monarchs. The desire to free the clergy of secular control reached a height after the Italian monk Hildebrand was raised to the papal throne in 1073. This remarkable man, who took the title of Gregory VII (1073-1085), became one of the most celebrated of all medieval popes.

Gregory whole-heartedly embraced the cause of religious reform. During the early years of his pontificate, he vigorously attacked the old problems of simony, clerical marriage, and corruption. Opposed in these reforms by some German bishops who were profiting by such irregularities, Gregory replied by removing those who were most stubborn. Then in 1075 he precipitated a break with Holy Roman Emperor Henry IV (1056-1106) by prohibiting lay investitures. He formally forbade secular rulers to invest bishops with the symbols of their spiritual offices. Excommunication was threatened against any layman or ecclesiastic who disobeyed. This edict struck at an old imperial tradition upon which was based the emperor's power in Germany. Henry refused to adhere to Gregory's edict on investiture and, when threatened with excommunication, gathered the German bishops to his side and denounced Gregory, declaring him "unfit to occupy the Holy See" and calling him a "false monk." The pope responded by excommunicating and deposing Henry, thereby releasing his subjects from allegiance and producing political and ecclesiastical chaos in Germany. The German nobility, who had long suffered under Henry's absolutism, welcomed the opportunity to revolt and in 1076 officially deposed the emperor. The way was now open for the legal election of a new king and Gregory prepared for the journey to Augsburg to assist in the elections. Henry, on the verge of losing his throne, hurried to meet Gregory and come to terms. The famous encounter occurred at Canossa in northern Italy on January 21, 1077. According to reports the emperor, barefooted and clad in coarse wool, appeared outside the castle in which the pope was staying. There he remained three days until Gregory finally received the penitent and granted him forgiveness.

The question that has continued to bother historians is who won in this struggle. Henry was forced to humiliate himself and in doing so agreed to accept the Church's position on investitures. However, by receiving absolution Henry retained his imperial title and gained vitally needed time to rebuild his authority. The controversy between emperor and pope broke out again but was finally settled, at least on the surface, by the Concordat of Worms in 1122. This whole struggle was part of the papal thrust for power which began in the eleventh century and reached its culmination during the pontificate of Innocent III in the thirteenth century. The first passage below is an expression by Gregory of his superiority and an assertion of the papal right to exert absolute rule over the Church; the second is a reply to Gregory by Henry; and the third is Gregory's description of the famous scene at Canossa.

The Dictate of the Pope

That the Roman church was founded by God alone,

That the Roman pontiff alone can with right be called universal.

That he alone can depose or reinstate bishops.

That, in a council, his legate, even if a lower grade, is above all bishops, and can pass sentence of deposition against them.

That the pope may depose the absent.

That, among other things, we ought not to remain in the same house with those excommunicated by him.

That for him alone is it lawful, according to the needs of the time, to make new laws, to assemble together new congregations, to make an abbey of a canonry; and, on the other hand, to divide a rich bishopric and unite the poor ones.

That he alone may use the imperial insignia.

That of the pope alone all princes shall kiss the feet.

That his name alone shall be spoken in the churches.

That this is the only name in the world.

That it may be permitted to him to depose emperors.

That he may be permitted to transfer bishops if need be.

That he has power to ordain a clerk of any church he may wish.

That he who is ordained by him may *preside* over another church, but may not hold a subordinate position; and that such a one may not receive a higher grade from any bishop.

That no synod shall be called a general one without his order.

That no chapter and no book shall be considered canonical without his authority.

That a sentence passed by him may be retracted by no one; and that he himself, alone of all, may retract it.

That he himself may be judged by no one.

That no one shall dare to condemn one who appeals to the apostolic chair.

That to the latter should be referred the more important cases of every church.

That the Roman church has never erred; nor will it err to all eternity, the Scripture bearing witness.

That the Roman pontiff, if he have been canonically ordained, is undoubtedly made a saint by the merits of St. Peter; . . .

Henry IV's Answer to Gregory VII, Jan. 24, 1076

Henry, king not through usurpation but through the holy ordination of God, to Hildebrand, at present not pope but false monk. Such greeting as this hast thou merited through thy disturbances, inasmuch as there is no grade in the church which thou hast omitted to make a partaker not of honour but of confusion, not of benediction but of malediction. For, to mention few and especial cases out of many, not only hast thou not feared to lay hands upon the rulers of the holy church, the anointed of the Lord—the archbishops, namely, bishops and priests—but thou hast trodden them under foot like slaves ignorant of what their master is doing. Thou hast won favour from the common herd by crushing them; thou hast looked upon all of them as knowing nothing, upon thy sole self, moreover, as knowing all things. This knowledge, however, thou hast used not for edification but for destruction; . . . And we, indeed, have endured all this, being eager to guard the honour of the apostolic see; thou, however, hast understood our humility to be fear, and hast not, accordingly, shunned to rise up against the royal power conferred upon us by God, daring to threaten to divest us of it. As if we had received our kingdom from thee! As if the kingdom and the empire were in thine and not in God's hand! And this although our Lord Jesus Christ did call us to the kingdom, did not, however, call thee to the priesthood. For thou hast ascended by the following steps. By wiles, namely, which the profession of monk abhors, thou hast achieved money; by money, favour; by the sword, the throne of peace. And from the throne of peace thou has disturbed peace, inasmuch as thou hast armed subjects against those in authority over them; inasmuch as thou, who wert not called, hast taught that our bishops called of God are to be despised; inasmuch as thou hast usurped for laymen the ministry over their priests, allowing them to depose or condemn those whom they themselves had received as teachers from the hand of God through the laying on of hands of the bishops. On me also who, although unworthy to be among the anointed, have nevertheless been anointed to the kingdom, thou hast lain thy hand; me who—as the tradition of the holy Fathers teaches, declaring that I am not to be deposed for any crime unless, which God forbid, I should have strayed from the faith—am subject to the judgment of God alone. . . . For he says: "If any one, either I or an angel from Heaven, should preach a gospel other than that which has been preached to you, he shall be damned." Thou, therefore, damned by this curse and by the judgment of all our bishops and by our own, descend and relinquish the apostolic chair which thou hast usurped. Let another ascend

Text: Ernest F. Henderson (trans. and ed.), *Select Historical Documents of the Middle Ages* (London: G. Bell & Sons, Ltd., 1896), pp. 366-67, 372-73, 385-87.

the throne of St. Peter, who shall not practise violence under the cloak of religion, but shall teach the sound doctrine of St. Peter. I Henry, king by the grace of God, do say unto thee, together with all our bishops: Descend, descend, to be damned throughout the ages.

Gregory VII's Letter to the German Princes Concerning the Penance of Henry IV at Canossa

. . . We learned for certain that the king was approaching. He also, before entering Italy, sent on to us suppliant legates, offering in all things to render satisfaction to God, to St. Peter and to us. And he renewed his promise that, besides amending his life, he would observe all obedience if only he might merit to obtain from us the favour of absolution and the apostolic benediction. When, after long deferring this and holding frequent consultations, we had, through all the envoys who passed, severely taken him to task for his excesses: he came at length of his own accord, with a few followers, showing nothing of hostility or boldness, to the town of Canossa where we were tarrying. And there, having laid aside all the belongings of royalty, wretchedly, with bare feet and clad in wool, he continued for three days to stand before the gate of the castle. Nor did he desist from imploring with many tears the aid and consolation of the apostolic mercy until he had moved all of those who were present there, and whom the report of it reached, to such pity and depth of compassion that, interceding for him with many prayers and tears, all wondered indeed at the unaccustomed hardness of our heart, while some actually cried out that we were exercising, not the gravity of apostolic severity, but the cruelty, as it were, of a tyrannical ferocity.

Finally, conquered by the persistency of his compunction and by the constant supplications of all those who were present, we loosed the chain of the anathema and at length received him into the favour of communion and into the lap of the holy mother church, those being accepted as sponsors for him whose names are written below. And of this transaction we also received a confirmation at the hands of the abbot of Cluny, of our daughters Matilda and the countess Adelaide, and of such princes, episcopal and lay, as seemed to us useful for this purpose.

77 ST. BERNARD OF CLAIRVAUX, *DE DILIGENDO DEO* AND EPISTLE: THE CISTERCIAN REFORMER

It is almost an historical axiom that all great institutions have sustained their vigor and usefulness only as long as they have been able and willing to reform and progress. The supremacy of the medieval Church between 1000 and 1300 can be largely attributed to this capability, just as the loss of this drive in the succeeding two centuries contributed to its decline.

Church reform advanced on several fronts from the eleventh to the thirteenth centuries. It established the absolute spiritual authority of the Church under powerful popes like Gregory VII, who humbled Emperor Henry IV at Canossa in 1077 (see Document 76), and Innocent III, who triumphed over John of England in 1213. It acted vigorously to root out heretical movements threatening its existence (see Document 79). And it founded new religious orders aimed at purifying the Church and meeting new problems of society. Thus, in the tenth and eleventh centuries the Benedictine Abbey at Cluny in southeastern France sought—by an example of piety, enthusiasm, and a highly centralized organization—to bring about reform in the monastic orders; unhappily, in time the Cluniacs too became worldly and luxurious, and the need for additional reform resulted in the founding of the Cistercian order (1098) by St. Robert, a former Benedictine abbot. The man responsible for the successful reformations made by the Cistercians, however, was St. Bernard of Clairvaux.

St. Bernard (1091-1153) was the preëminent ecclesiastic of his age. His ascetic life, theological studies, and stirring eloquence made him the oracle of Christendom. Although a mystic in theology, he had a profoundly practical mind. He was consulted by princes upon politics of state and exerted enormous influence on the popes of his day. He reportedly drew up the rule for the Knights Templar, as well as dictated the stringent rules by which the Cistercians reformed the Benedictines. He took great interest in the Christian occupation of the Holy Land and preached the Second Crusade (1147-1149), arousing religious fervor throughout Germany and France. His powerful influence effectively threw down an antipope in 1137 and healed a serious schism in the Church. He took issue with leading school theologians, with whom he had little sympathy, and was the chief agent in securing in Rome the condemnation of Abélard, whose rational inquiries into religious matters questioned the very principle of Bernard's unquestioning faith. His beliefs upheld tradition and embodied the ideal of his age—medieval monasticism, of which he was an enthusiastic advocate.

Over 790 separate writings of Bernard—epistles, treatises, and hymns—are extant. Below are printed selections denoting two sides of his nature. *De Diligendo Deo (Of Loving God)* reveals Bernard as an inspired monk, dedicated to the life of contemplation. For him, love is the object of contemplation for it pervades human and divine affairs, and its mystical powers, working through the agency of Jesus Christ, make man's salvation and union with God possible. Bernard's "Letter of 1138 to Louis VII, King of France" reveals his clerical statecraft and is an example of his voluminous correspondence with the papacy and the churches of Western Christendom on practical matters of discipline and administration. The Bishop of Langres had been replaced by Pope Innocent II with a candidate from the monastery of Clairvaux. Bernard's letter persuades the king—very diplomatically—to countermand his previous orders and to invest the newly installed bishop with the feudal properties for which the See of Langres owed homage to the crown of France.

De Diligendo Deo

Love is a natural affection, one of the four [love, fear, joy, sorrow]. As it exists by nature, it should diligently serve the Author of nature first of all. But as nature is frail and weak, love is compelled by necessity first to serve itself. This is carnal love, whereby, above everything, man loves himself for his own sake. It is not set forth by precept, but is rooted in nature; for who hates his own flesh? As love becomes more ready and profuse, it is not content with the channel of necessity, but will pour forth and overspread the broad fields of pleasure. At once the overflow is bridled by the command, "Thou shalt love thy neighbour as thyself." This is just and needful, lest what is part of nature should have no part in grace. A man may concede to himself what he will, so long as he is mindful to provide the same for his neighbour. The bridle of temperance is imposed on thee, O man, out of the law of life and discipline, in order that thou shouldst not follow thy desires, nor with the good things of nature serve the enemy of the soul, which is lust. If thou wilt turn away from thy pleasures, and be content with food and raiment, little by little it will not so burden thee to keep thy love from carnal desires, which war against the soul. Thy love will be temperate and righteous when what is withdrawn from its own pleasures is not denied to its brother's needs. Thus carnal love becomes social when extended to one's kind.

Yet in order that perfect justice should exist in the love of neighbour, God must be regarded (*Deum in causa haberi necesse est*). How can one love his neighbour purely who does not love in God? God makes Himself loved, He who makes all things good. He who founded nature so made it that it should always need to be sustained by Him. In order that no creature might be ignorant of this, and arrogate for himself the good deeds of the Creator, the Founder wisely decreed that man should be tried in tribulations. By this means, when he shall have failed and God have aided, God shall be honoured by him whom He has delivered. The result is that man, animal and carnal, who knew not how to love any one beside himself, begins for his own sake to love God; because he has found out that in God he can accomplish everything profitable, and without Him can do nothing.

So now for his own interest, he loves God—love's second grade; but does not yet love God for God's sake. If, however, tribulation keeps assailing him, and he continually turns to God for aid, and God delivers him, will not the man so oft delivered, though he have a breast of iron and a heart of stone, be drawn to cherish his deliverer, and love Him not only for His aid but for Himself? Frequent necessities compel man to come to God incessantly; repeatedly he tastes and, by tasting, proves how sweet is the Lord. At length God's sweetness, rather than human need, draws the man to love Him. Thereafter it will not be hard for the man to fulfil the command to love his neighbour. Truly loving God, he loves for this reason those who are God's. He loves chastely, and is not oppressed through obeying the chaste command; he loves justly, and willingly embraces the just command. That is the third grade of love, when God is loved for Himself.

Happy is he who attains to the fourth grade, where man loves himself only on account of God.

Text: Henry Osborn Taylor, *The Mediaeval Mind*, 4th ed. (Cambridge, Mass.: Harvard University Press), I, 423-25.

Thy righteousness, O God, is as the mountain of God; love is that mountain, that high mountain of God. Who shall ascend into the mountain of the Lord? Who will give me the wings of a dove and I will fly away and be at rest. Alas! for my long-drawn sojourning! When shall I gain that habitation in Zion, and my soul become one spirit with God? Blessed and holy will I call him to whom in this mortal life such has been given though but once. For to be lost to self and not to feel thyself, and to be emptied of thyself and almost to be made nothing, that pertains to heavenly intercourse, not to human affection. And if any one among mortals here gain admission for an instant, at once the wicked world is envious, the day's evil disturbs, the body of death drags down, fleshly necessity solicits, corruption's debility does not sustain, and, fiercest of all, brotherly love calls back! Alas! he is dragged back to himself, and forced to cry: "O Lord, I suffer violence, answer thou for me" (Isa. xxxviii. 14); 'Who will deliver me from the body of this death?' (Rom. vii. 24).

Yet Scripture says that God made all things for His own sake; that will come to pass when the creation is in full accord with its Author. Therefore we must sometime pass into that state wherein we do not wish to be ourselves or anything else, except for His sake and by reason of His will, not ours. Then not our need or happiness, but His will, will be fulfilled in us. O holy love and chaste! O sweet affection! O pure and purged intention of the will, in which nothing of its own is mingled! This is it to be made God (*deificari*). As the drop of water is diffused in a jar of wine, taking its taste and colour, and as molten iron becomes like to fire and casts off its form, and as the air transfused with sunlight is transformed into that same brightness of light, so that it seems not illumined, but itself to be the light, thus in the saints every human affection must in some ineffable mode be liquefied of itself and transfused into the will of God. How could God be all in all if in man anything of man remained? A certain substance will remain, but in another form, another glory, another power.

Letter to Louis the Younger, King of France

Though all the world were to combine in making me attempt something against your royal Majesty, yet I would fear God and not dare to oppose the king whom he had ordained. I know where it is written, 'He that resisteth the power, resisteth the ordinance of God'. But I shall speak the truth to you because I also know how wrong it is for any Christian to lie, especially for one of my profession. What happened at Langres concerning my prior happened contrary to all my expectations, and contrary to the intentions of the bishops and myself. But there is one who is able to secure the assent of unwilling men and compel them to serve the purpose he wishes, even against their wills. Never have I feared a danger for myself that I have not also feared just as much for him whom I love as myself. Never have I not shrunk from the company of those who would bind heavy burdens on the backs of men, and not lift a finger to move them. But what has been done, is done; against you nothing, against myself a lot. The support of my weakness has been taken from me, the light of my eyes has been snatched away, my right hand has been cut off. All these great storms and high waves have passed over me; wrath has come upon me and there is no way of escape open to me. By flying from burdens I have brought them upon myself, unwelcome and unwanted. I find it hard to kick against the pricks. Perhaps it would have been more tolerable had I willingly accepted the burden instead of kicking against it and refusing it. For if there is any strength in me, would it not be easier for me to carry it on my own shoulders rather than in the person of another?

But I submit to one who has disposed otherwise. To rebel against him, either in judgement or in action, would not be safe or even possible for me, nor would it be for you, because he is feared amongst all the kings of the earth. It were an awful thing to fall into the hands of the living God, awful even for you, O king. How sorry I am to hear things of you so contrary to the fair promise of your beginnings. But how much more bitter would be the sorrow of the Church if, after having tasted such fair joys from you, she were to be deprived (which God forbid) of the glad hope of having a shield in your good dispositions, such as she has had hitherto. Alas the virgin, the church of Rheims, has fallen, and there is none to lift her up! And the church of Langres has also fallen, and there is no one to hold out a hand to her. May the goodness of God take from your heart any intention of adding to our grief, of piling up sorrow upon sorrow for us! I would rather die than see a king of such a fair reputation and of even better hopes, attempt to oppose the will of God and stir up against himself the wrath of the supreme Judge, bathe the feet of the Father of orphans in the tears of the afflicted, cause the portals of heaven to

Text: Bruno Scott James (trans.), *The Letters of St. Bernard of Clairvaux* (Chicago: Henry Regnery Company; London: Burns & Oates, Ltd., 1953), pp. 257-59.

resound with the cries of the poor, the prayers of the saints, and the just complaints of the chaste bride of Christ who is the Church of the living God. May God forbid such a thing! We hope for better things, we expect more joyful things of you. God will not forget to be merciful, nor will his wrath set bounds to his pity. He will not permit his Church to be saddened through him and on account of him by whom he has already given her such joy on so many occasions. And if you think otherwise, this also he will reveal to you, schooling your heart in wisdom. This is our wish and our prayer day and night. Believe this of me, and believe it of my brethren. This truth will never be denied by us, and the honour of our king and the welfare of his realm will never be diminished by us.

We render thanks to your goodness for the kind answer you deigned to send us. But nevertheless this delay terrifies us who see the land given up to pillage and plunder. It is your land; and in this we clearly see and deplore a disgrace to your kingdom, that you should have commanded us to forgo our rights, because there is none to defend them. What else has been done that can be rightly said to have diminished your royal dignity? The election was duly held and the elected is faithful. But he would not be faithful if he wished to hold your lands otherwise than by you. He has not stretched forth his hand to your lands, he has not entered your city, and he certainly has not put himself forward in any matter although strongly urged to do so by the clergy and people, by the sufferings of the downtrodden, and by the wishes of all good men. The state of affairs being what it is, you will see that you should take speedy counsel in the matter, as much for your own sake as for ours. Unless your Highness can answer this petition by the messengers who bring it according to the wishes of the expectant people, your people, the hearts of many religious men who are now devoted to you will be troubled, which would be most unfortunate; and I fear too that your very *regalia*, which appertains to the church, will suffer not a little damage.

78 ST. FRANCIS OF ASSISI, *RULE:* THE ORDER OF FRIARS

The Benedictines, Cistercians, and other monastic orders possessed as their ideal the renunciation of society and the retreat to a life of religious asceticism. In spite of the public vigor of some monks like St. Bernard of Clairvaux (see Document 77), the monastic reforming zeal was largely effective only in purifying the internal affairs of the Church—in restoring devout habits of clerics, improving administrative efficiency, and upholding traditional doctrine. In the twelfth and thirteenth centuries, however, the rise of commercial towns—the focal points of new ideas, skepticism, and materialism—presented the Church with a great problem requiring the efforts of clerics dedicated to intimate involvement with the affairs of the people.

A new kind of Christian order thus arose which lived by a rule but which, unlike the monastic orders, devoted all its efforts to the service of mankind. The first order of friars, as these men were called, was founded by St. Francis of Assisi (c. 1181-1226), a rich merchant's son who, at the age of twenty-four and after much meditation, abandoned a career of luxury, embraced a life of utter poverty, and soon dedicated himself to preaching the gospel and caring for the poor and outcast. His object was to lead a life as closely modeled after Christ's as possible. When his example produced followers, he drew up a rule, which was approved by Pope Innocent III. The Franciscan order grew rapidly in numbers, spreading to every region of Europe, for in the eyes of ordinary men and women these brown-robed friars exemplified in their conduct a higher idealism and Christlike quality than any of the Benedictine houses; historically, they offered a simple, democratic faith well suited to a society in transition. The Franciscans were highly successful in caring for the spiritual needs of the poor and did their best work in the towns. Their faithful attendance is verified by the fact that 124,000 Franciscans fell victims to their zeal for the care of the sick and for the spiritual ministration to the dying during the devastating Black Death of the following century.

The selection below comprises an early version of the Franciscan Rule, which explains clearly some of the ideals of St. Francis, particularly his call for a greater participation in the worldly affairs of this life, an injunction which set him apart from other monastic founders.

The Franciscan Rule

This is the rule and life of the Minor Brothers, namely, to observe the holy gospel of our Lord Jesus Christ by living in obedience, in poverty, and in chastity. Brother Francis promises obedience and reverence to pope Honorius and to his successors who shall be canonically elected, and to the Roman Church. The other brothers are bound to obey brother Francis, and his successors.

If any, wishing to adopt this life, come to our brothers [to ask admission], they shall be sent to the provincial ministers, who alone have the right to receive others into the order. The provincial ministers shall carefully examine them in the catholic faith and the sacraments of the church. And if they believe all these and faithfully confess them and promise to observe them to the end of life, and if they have no wives, or if they have wives, and the wives have either already entered a monastery, or have received permission to do so, and they have already taken the vow of chastity with the permission of the bishop of the diocese [in which they live], and their wives are of such an age that no suspicion can rise against them, let the provincial ministers repeat to them the word of the holy gospel, to go and sell all their goods and give to the poor [Matt. 19:21]. But if they are not able to do so, their good will is sufficient for them. And the brothers and provincial ministers shall not be solicitous about the temporal possessions of those who wish to enter the order; but let them do with their possessions whatever the Lord may put into their minds to do. Nevertheless, if they ask the advice of the brothers, the provincial ministers may send them to God-fearing men, at whose advice they may give their possessions to the poor. Then the ministers shall give them the dress of a novice, namely: two robes without a hood, a girdle, trousers, a hood with a cape reaching to the girdle. But the ministers may add to these if they think it necessary. After the year of probation is ended they shall be received into obedience [that is, into the order], by promising to observe this rule and life forever. And according to the command of the pope they shall never be permitted to leave the order and give up this life and form of religion. For according to the holy gospel no one who puts his hand to the plough and looks back is fit for the kingdom of God [Luke 9:62]. And after they have promised obedience, those who wish may have one robe with a hood and one without a hood. Those who must may wear shoes, and all the brothers shall wear common clothes, and they shall have God's blessing if they patch them with coarse cloth and pieces of other kinds of cloth. But I warn and exhort them not to despise nor judge other men who wear fine and gay clothing, and have delicious foods and drinks. But rather let each one judge and despise himself.

The clerical brothers shall perform the divine office according to the rite of the holy Roman church, except the psalter, from which they may have breviaries. The lay brothers shall say 24 Paternosters at matins, 5 at lauds, 7 each at primes, terces, sexts, and nones, 12 at vespers, 7 at completorium, and prayers for the dead. And they shall fast from All Saints' day [November 1] to Christmas. They may observe or not, as they choose, the holy Lent which begins at epiphany [January 6] and lasts for 40 days, and which our Lord consecrated by his holy fasts. Those who keep it shall be blessed of the Lord, but those who do not wish to keep it are not bound to do so. But they shall all observe the other Lent [that is, from Ash-Wednesday to Easter]. The rest of the time the brothers are bound to fast only on Fridays. But in times of manifest necessity they shall not fast. But I counsel, warn, and exhort my brothers in the Lord Jesus Christ that when they go out into the world they shall not be quarrelsome or contentious, nor judge others. But they shall be gentle, peaceable, and kind, mild and humble, and virtuous in speech, as is becoming to all. They shall not ride on horseback unless compelled by manifest necessity or infirmity to do so. When they enter a house they shall say, "Peace be to this house." According to the holy gospel, they may eat of whatever food is set before them.

I strictly forbid all the brothers to accept money or property either in person or through another. Nevertheless, for the needs of the sick, and for clothing the other brothers, the ministers and guardians may, as they see that necessity requires, provide through spiritual friends, according to the locality, season, and the degree of cold which may be expected in the region where they live. But, as has been said, they shall never receive money or property.

Those brothers to whom the Lord has given the ability to work shall work faithfully and devotedly, so that idleness, which is the enemy of the soul, may be excluded and not extinguish the spirit of prayer and devotion to which all temporal things should be subservient. As the price of their labors they may receive things that are necessary for themselves and the brothers, but not money or property. And they shall humbly receive what is given them, as is becoming to the

Text: Oliver J. Thatcher and Edgar H. McNeal, *A Source Book for Mediaeval History* (New York: Charles Scribner's Sons, 1905), pp. 499-504.

servants of God and to those who practise the most holy poverty.

The brothers shall have nothing of their own, neither house, nor land, nor anything, but as pilgrims and strangers in this world, serving the Lord in poverty and humility, let them confidently go asking alms. Nor let them be ashamed of this, for the Lord made himself poor for us in this world. This is that highest pitch of poverty which has made you, my dearest brothers, heirs and kings of the kingdom of heaven, which has made you poor in goods, and exalted you in virtues. Let this be your portion, which leads into the land of the living. Cling wholly to this, my most beloved brothers, and you shall wish to have in this world nothing else than the name of the Lord Jesus Christ. And wherever they are, if they find brothers, let them show themselves to be of the same household, and each one may securely make known to the other his need. For if a mother loves and nourishes her child, how much more diligently should one nourish and love one's spiritual brother? And if any of them fall ill, the other brothers should serve them as they would wish to be served.

If any brother is tempted by the devil and commits a mortal sin, he should go as quickly as possible to the provincial minister, as the brothers have determined that recourse shall be had to the provincial ministers for such sins. If the provincial minister is a priest, he shall mercifully prescribe the penance for him. If he is not a priest, he shall, as may seem best to him, have some priest of the order prescribe the penance. And they shall guard against being angry or irritated about it, because anger and irritation hinder love in themselves and in others.

All the brothers must have one of their number as their general minister and servant of the whole brotherhood, and they must obey him. At his death the provincial ministers and guardians shall elect his successor at the chapter held at Pentecost, at which time all the provincial ministers must always come together at whatever place the general minister may order. And this chapter must be held once every three years, or more or less frequently, as the general minister may think best. And if at any time it shall be clear to the provincial ministers and guardians that the general minister is not able to perform the duties of his office and does not serve the best interests of the brothers, the aforesaid brothers, to whom the right of election is given, must, in the name of the Lord, elect another as general minister. After the chapter at Pentecost, the provincial ministers and guardians may, each in his own province, if it seems best to them, once in the same year, convoke the brothers to a provincial chapter.

If a bishop forbids the brothers to preach in his diocese, they shall obey him. And no brother shall preach to the people unless the general minister of the brotherhood has examined and approved him and given him the right to preach. I also warn the brothers that in their sermons their words shall be chaste and well chosen for the profit and edification of the people. They shall speak to them of vices and virtues, punishment and glory, with brevity of speech, because the Lord made the word shortened over the earth [Rom. 9:28].

The ministers and servants shall visit and admonish their brothers and humbly and lovingly correct them. They shall not put any command upon them that would be against their soul and this rule. And the brothers who are subject must remember that for God's sake they have given up their own wills. Wherefore I command them to obey their ministers in all the things which they have promised the Lord to observe and which shall not be contrary to their souls and this rule. And whenever brothers know and recognize that they cannot observe this rule, let them go to their ministers, and the ministers shall lovingly and kindly receive them and treat them in such a way that the brothers may speak to them freely and treat them as lords speak to, and treat, their servants. For the ministers ought to be the servants of all the brothers. I warn and exhort the brothers in the Lord Jesus Christ to guard against all arrogance, pride, envy, avarice, care, and solicitude for this world, detraction, and murmuring. And those who cannot read need not be anxious to learn. But above all things let them desire to have the spirit of the Lord and his holy works, to pray always to God with a pure heart, and to have humility, and patience in persecution and in infirmity, and to love those who persecute us and reproach us and blame us. For the Lord says, "Love your enemies, and pray for those who persecute and speak evil of you" [cf. Matt. 5:44]. "Blessed are they who suffer persecution for righteousness' sake, for theirs is the kingdom of heaven" [Matt. 5:10]. "He that endureth to the end shall be saved" [Matt. 10:22].

I strictly forbid all the brothers to have any association or conversation with women that may cause suspicion. And let them not enter nunneries, except those which the pope has given them special permission to enter. Let them not be intimate friends of men or women, lest on this account scandal arise among the brothers or about brothers.

If any of the brothers shall be divinely inspired to go among Saracens and other infidels they must get the permission to go from their provincial minister, who shall give his consent only to those who he sees are suitable to be sent. In addition, I command the ministers to ask the pope to assign them a cardinal of the holy Roman church, who shall be the guide, protector, and corrector of the brotherhood, in order that, being always in subjection and at the feet of the holy church, and steadfast in the catholic faith, they may observe poverty, humility, and the holy gospel of our Lord Jesus Christ, as we have firmly promised to do. Let no man dare act contrary to this confirmation. If anyone should, etc.

79 BERNARD GUI, *MANUAL OF THE INQUISITOR:* HERESIES AND THE DOMINICAN INQUISITION

The rise of towns with their new social, economic, and political requirements created a wave of discontent against the old restrictions of feudalism (see Document 65). Such discontent often found its expression in revolt against ecclesiastical authority, for in their struggles for emancipation from feudal rule, the towns often ran afoul of the Church itself. As a great landowner and feudal lord the Church often opposed movements for local self-government in the towns under its jurisdiction. Moreover, the urban, commercial atmosphere provoked new ideas and criticisms—a new spirit of independence—which tended to conflict with the traditional authority of the Church. The crusades, sponsored by the Church itself, encouraged the trend towards skepticism; the constant contact for two centuries with the more advanced Byzantine and Muslim cultures taught the crusaders a respect for eastern civilization and dispelled many old prejudices. Some crusaders even became Muhammadans; a few became freethinkers.

The heresies of the Middle Ages thus were not matters of doctrine only (however important) but were symptoms of social and intellectual movements common to people of many lands. The heretics encouraged a popular feeling of discontent towards a religious institution that over the ages had become rich and powerful and therefore rigorously attached to the old order of things. First the heretical sects attacked the Church's sore points—the materialism of the clergy and the secular ambitions of high church dignitaries—and in this they had the support not only of the mass of people but also of the secular lords jealous of the rule of the Church. The heretics, in addition, usually practiced a faith of ascetic simplicity which won them wide sympathy.

Most famous of the heretical sects were the Albigensians, who flourished in large numbers in Provence in southern France, probably the most urban and cultured area of western Europe at the beginning of the thirteenth century. The popular appeal of the Albigensians, whose doctrine seems to have been a variety of Manicheism (see Document 42), was so great that Pope Innocent III, after abortive attempts at peaceful conversion, ordered a crusade against them; the wars which followed ultimately destroyed the Provençal civilization.

After the violence and bloodshed of the Albigensian Crusade, the Church relied largely upon the Office of the Holy Inquisition, established in 1233, to combat heresy. Especially important in this role were the Dominicans, an order of friars organized by a Spanish cleric Dominic (1170-1221) with the original purpose of converting the Albigensians. Since the orders of friars had been founded in reaction to the wealth and exclusiveness of the monasteries and since they made a vocation of popular preaching, they were effective in opposing the heretics. In addition to their activities in the Inquisition the Dominicans figured prominently in intellectual activities and contributed greatly to scholarship and learning.

The Inquisition, which was administered from a central papal office, consisted of local boards of judges, normally friars, who were charged with discovering and extirpating heresy and punishing heretics within their jurisdiction. It was within their power to acquit or convict those charged with heresy and to assign penalties against which the condemned had no appeal. The penalties varied from simple penance to imprisonment, and for those heretics who would not recant or relapsed after recanting, there was the consuming fire of the stake.

The Inquisitorial procedures and penalties were often severe and arbitrary, and in many respects the Inquisition damaged the prestige of the Church more than it strengthened orthodoxy. But it should be remembered that the majority of the Inquisitors were men of sincerity and extreme religious fervor who believed that a heretic was doomed to damnation unless he was detected and forced to recant. The seriousness with which they approached their task and the efforts they made to follow an orderly procedure are evident in the selections following from a *Manual of the Inquisitor* written by Bernard Gui (c. 1261-1331), a conscientious Dominican inquisitor in southeastern France, who in seventeen years judged 613 heretics, of whom 45 were committed to the stake.

General Instructions

. . . If a person spoke openly and clearly against the faith, offering the arguments and authorities upon which heretics usually rely, it would be very easy for the faithful learned of the Church to convict him of heresy, since he would be deemed a heretic by the very fact that he tried to defend error. But since present day heretics attempt and seek to conceal their errors rather than to avow them openly, men trained in the learning of the Scriptures cannot convict them, because they escape in verbal trickery and wily thinking. Learned men are even apt to be confounded by them, and the heretics congratulate themselves and are all the stronger therefore, seeing that they can thus delude the learned to the point of escaping artfully by the twists and turns of their crafty, cheating and underhanded replies.

It is, indeed, all too difficult to bring heretics to reveal themselves when, instead of frankly avowing their error they conceal it, or when there is not sure and sufficient testimony against them. Under these circumstances difficulties rise on all sides for the investigator. On the one hand his conscience will torment him if he punishes without having obtained a confession or conviction of heresy; on the other hand, all that repeated experience has taught him of the falseness, guile and malice of such people will cause him still greater anguish. If they escape punishment owing to their fox-like craftiness it is to the great harm of the faith, for they become even stronger, more numerous and more wily than before. Moreover, lay persons devoted to the faith find it scandalous that an inquisitorial case, once begun, should be abandoned more or less for lack of method. Seeing that the learned are fooled by common, base people, they are thereby weakened in their faith to a certain degree, for they believe that we always have at our disposal convincing and clear arguments against which no one can contend, without our immediately being able to convince him, and in such a way that the laity themselves would clearly understand these arguments. Thus, under such circumstances it is inexpedient, in the presence of laity, to discuss the faith with heretics who are so guileful.

Just as a simple remedy is not suitable to all diseases, and medication varies according to the particular case, so one cannot use for all the heretics of the different sects the same method of questioning, investigation and examination, but should employ a method particular and appropriate to each case or group. Therefore the inquisitor, as a wise doctor of souls, will proceed with caution in the investigation and questioning, according to the persons he is questioning or in whose company he is conducting the investigation, taking into account their rank, condition, status, malady and with due regard for local conditions. . . .

Of the Sect of the Waldenses and First of Its Origins and Beginnings

The sect or heresy of the Waldenses or the Poor of Lyon came into being about the year of the Lord 1170. The man responsible for its creation was an inhabitant of Lyon, Waldes or Waldo, whence the name of its devotees. He was wealthy, but, after giving up all his property, determined to practice poverty and evangelic perfection in the manner of the apostles. He had had the Gospels and several other books of the Bible translated into vulgar tongue for his use, as well as several maxims of Saints Augustine, Jerome, Ambrose and Gregory, grouped under titles, which he and his followers called sentences. They read them very often, although they hardly understood them; nevertheless, infatuated with themselves, although they had little learning, they usurped the role of the apostles and dared to preach the Gospel in the streets and public squares. The said Waldes or Waldo drew into this presumption numerous accomplices of both sexes whom he sent out preaching as disciples.

These people, although stupid and unlearned, traveled through the villages, men and women, and entered homes, and, preaching in the squares and even in the churches, the men especially, spread about them a mass of errors.

Summoned by the Archbishop of Lyon, the lord Jean aux Blanches-Mains, who forbade them such a presumption, they refused obedience, declaring, in order to excuse their madness, that one

Text: Bernard Gui, *Manual of the Inquisitor*, in *Introduction to Contemporary Civilization in the West*, ed. Contemporary Civilization Staff of Columbia College, Columbia University, 3rd ed. (New York: Columbia University Press, 1960), I, 197-202, 204-05.

should obey God rather than man. God ordered the apostles to preach the Gospel to all beings, they said, applying to themselves that which had been said of the apostles, whose followers and successors they boldly declared themselves to be, by a false profession of poverty and by masquerading under an appearance of holiness. Indeed they despised the prelates and clergy because, they said, they owned great wealth and lived in pleasures.

Owing to this arrogant usurpation of the function of preaching, they became teachers of error. Summoned to renounce preaching, they disobeyed and were declared in contempt, and consequently excommunicated and banished from their town and country. Finally, as they persisted, a council held at Rome before the Lateran Council [reference is to fourth Lateran Council, 1215] declared them schismatic and condemned them as heretics. Thus multiplied upon the earth they scattered through the provinces, into neighboring regions and unto the borders of Lombardy. Separated and cut off from the Church, and joining, on the other hand, with other heretics and drinking in their errors, they blended with their own concoctions the errors and heresies of earlier heretics.

The Errors of the Present Waldenses
(They Previously Held Several Others)

Disdain for ecclesiastical authority was and still is the prime heresy of the Waldenses. Excommunicated for this reason and delivered over to Satan, they have fallen into innumerable errors, and have blended the errors of earlier heretics with their own concoctions.

The misled believers and sacrilegious masters of this sect hold and teach that they are in no way subject to the lord Pope or Roman Pontiff, or to the other prelates of the Roman Church, and that the latter persecute and condemn them unjustly and improperly. Moreover, they declare that they cannot be excommunicated by this Roman Pontiff and these prelates, and that obedience is owed to none of them when they order and summon the followers and masters of the said sect to abandon or abjure this sect, although this sect be condemned as heretical by the Roman Church. . . .

Moreover, the sect does not accept canonical authority, or the decretals or constitutions of the Sovereign Pontiffs, any more than the regulations concerning fasts and the observance of the feasts or the decrees of the Fathers. Straying from the straight road, they recognize no authority therein, scorn them, reject and condemn them.

Moreover, the followers of the sect are even more perniciously mistaken concerning the sacrament of penance and the power of the keys. They declare they have received—this is their doctrine and their teaching—from God and none other, like the apostles who held it of Christ, the power of hearing the confessions of men and women who desire to confess to them, of granting them absolution and of prescribing penance. Thus they hear confessions, grant absolution and prescribe penance, although they have not been ordained as priests or clerics by a bishop of the Roman Church and although they are just laymen. They in no way claim to hold this power from the Roman Church, on the contrary, they deny it; and in fact, they hold it neither from God nor from His Church, since they have been cast out from the Church by this very Church, outside which there is neither true penance nor salvation.

Moreover, this same sect hold up to ridicule the indulgences established and granted by the prelates of the Church, saying they are worthless.

Moreover, they are in error with respect to the sacrament of the Eucharist. They claim, not publicly but secretly, that in the sacrament of the altar the bread and wine do not become body and blood of Christ when the priest who celebrates or consecrates is a sinner; and by sinner they mean any man who does not belong to their sect. Moreover, they claim, on the contrary, that any upright man, even a layman, without having received priestly ordination from the hands of a Catholic bishop, may consecrate the body and blood of Christ, provided he be of their sect. They believe that women too can do this, subject to the same condition. Thus they hold that any holy man is a priest.

Of the False and Crafty Replies in Which They Hide

It is very difficult to question and examine the Waldenses; to such an extent do they hide in duplicity and tricks of words, in order not to be discovered, that one cannot draw from them the truth about their errors. Thus it is necessary at this point to say a few words about their deceit and guile.

They act in the following manner. When one of them is arrested for investigation, he usually presents himself fearlessly, as if his conscience were tranquil and without remorse. Ask him if he knows the cause of his arrest, and he will answer softly and with a smile: "My lord, I would be happy to learn it from your lips." Asked about his faith and beliefs: "I believe all that a good Christian believes," he declares. Try to learn what he means by a good Christian: "He who believes what is taught by the Holy Church." What does he call the Holy Church: "My lord," he replies, "what you yourself say and believe to be the Holy Church." If you say, "I believe it is the Roman Church ruled by the Pope and the other prelates under his authority," he replies: "And I too believe it," meaning "I am convinced that that is indeed your belief.". . .

Instructions Concerning the Procedure To Be Followed with Persons Who Have Confessed the Truth in Court and with Those Who Have Been Charged and Are Suspect Who Refuse To Do So

If having stated in court the truth concerning the infractions committed by himself or by another person, having adjured all heresy and been reconciled with the unity of the Church, an accused shows repentance that seems sincere; and if, moreover, there is no fear that he may flee, be corrupted or relapse, and if there are no other objections, he shall be released with another person as bond for him until the time of the general sermon in the course of which penance for his crimes will be imposed on him, among others.

On the other hand, when a person who is suspected of, denounced or reported for or accused of the crime of heresy has been charged and refuses to confess, he shall be held in prison until the truth comes to light; the status and station of the person, as well as the nature of the suspicion and of the crime should, however, be taken into account. He may be released with another person as bond for him, especially when proof of his guilt is not conclusive, when the accusation was not direct but incidental and when suspicion was not clearcut, until such time as a new charge shall be raised against him. Nevertheless, those who benefit from this leniency shall, instead of imprisonment, take a position before the door of the home of the inquisitor each day until the midday meal, and after this meal until the supper hour, and shall not depart therefrom without permission of the inquisitor.

Stationing in this fashion, it should be noted, has sometimes proved more harmful than beneficial, especially when there were several such persons together and they advised each other and, this has been observed and proved, were confirmed in their errors.

When an accused is strongly suspect and in all likelihood and probability guilty, and when the inquisitor is thoroughly convinced thereof; in such a case, when the person is obdurate in his testimony and persists in his denials, as I have observed time and time again, he should not be released for any reason whatever, but should be held for a number of years, in order that his trials may open his mind. Many have I seen who, thus subjected for a number of years to this regime of vexations and confinement, and by admitting not only recent but even long-standing and old crimes, going back thirty and forty years or more. . . .

The Manner of Acting Toward Heretics Who Repent at the Moment of Execution

Should it happen, as it already has on several occasions, that a condemned person abandoned and handed over to the secular arm, taken by said court and brought to the place of execution, should bespeak and affirm a desire to repent and renounce the said errors, he should be spared and returned to the inquisitors. And they should receive him, unless he had perhaps already relapsed into heresy, for here equity is to be preferred to severity, and that shock to the weak should be avoided that comes when the Church refuses the sacrament of penance to him who requests it. The office of the Inquisition formerly acted in this fashion at times.

In such a case, the inquisitors should take all necessary precautions, for those who are converted in such an extremity are rightfully suspect of acting in fear of punishment, and the inquisitors should carefully consider whether the conversion is genuine or feigned. Let them test the convert to see if he walks in the shadows or in the light, lest he be a wolf beneath a lamb's appearance.

And this may be brought out in several ways and according to several signs: if, for example, he promptly and spontaneously reveals and denounces all his accomplices to the inquisitors; if he attacks his sect in gesture, words and deeds; if he admits his former errors humbly and one by one; if he detests and abjures them; and all of these things can be known with certainty through the questioning he will undergo and the confession he will sign.

When he has thus been readmitted to trial and has therein confessed, he should then retract and detest, with his own lips, all his old errors, publicly and legally abjure these same errors in particular and all heresy in general, confess the Catholic faith, and promise and swear all other things usually required of those who abjure. And then will he be subjected to life imprisonment, there to do penance, the right to commute the penalty being reserved, as is the custom.

As has already been said, this clemency and admission to penance after pronouncement of sentence is not, in truth in common law; but the office of the Inquisition, holding very broad powers, has introduced this procedure in many cases of this kind. And since what it has in view and seeks above all is the salvation of souls and purity of the faith, it admits to penance, the first time, heretics who wish to be converted and return to the unity of the Church. Moreover, the confessions of these converts frequently lead to the discovery of accomplices and of errors: the truth is brought to light, falsehood is uncloaked, and the office benefits thereby.

Once a conversion of this type appears to the inquisitors probably to be feigned and simulated, everything is brought to a halt and the sentence is carried out.

INTERPRETATION OF THE SPIRIT OF THE CHURCH

80 CHRISTOPHER DAWSON, "CHURCH AND STATE IN THE MIDDLE AGES": THE CITY OF GOD ON EARTH

The nature of the relationship between the Roman Church and the various states of medieval Christendom has encouraged much controversy among modern scholars. According to Christopher Dawson, an eminent English medievalist of Oxford University, it is an error to deal with this problem under the influence of the modern conception of Church and state as separate organizations. The unitary idea of the Middle Ages regarded both as different aspects of a single Christian society. Not only the Church but the states and their anointed king were sacred—this viewpoint made it relatively easy for a Byzantine emperor or a Charlemagne to raise claims to authority over spiritual affairs. At the same time, the Church became deeply involved in the feudal system and many churchmen held positions of authority in the temporal governments of medieval monarchies.

The Church's tendency to become too deeply submerged in the structure of the territorial state was stoutly resisted by the great Church reform movements, culminating in the Investiture struggle of the eleventh century (see Document 76). An important aim of the reformers was the achievement of a more efficient Church organization. The reformers were indebted to the Church legalists, who developed the study of Canon Law, in reaching a clear definition of this organization and also of ecclesiastical jurisdiction. Canon Law was the Roman law of the Justinian Code and Digest, revised and applied in principle to the government of the Church. Such jurisprudence was centered at the Italian university of Bologna and reached its pinnacle of expression with Gratian's *Decretum* (c. 1141), at once a code and a treatise on Canon Law.

The climax of the reform movements and the development of Canon Law occurred during the pontificate of Innocent III (1198-1216), who was a profound believer in the right of papal power to guide the Church and exercise ultimate authority over the temporal monarchies. Not only did Innocent force Philip Augustus of France to forgo a divorce but he required John of England to cede his kingdom to the papacy and to receive it back in fief, thus establishing momentarily the principle that temporal monarchs were vassals of the papacy. At the height of the medieval papacy's strength, Innocent called the Fourth Lateran Council at Rome (1216), which legislated numerous improvements in Church administration. Afterwards, although the Church made imposing claims, it was never able to exercise the widespread authority which it did for a brief moment under Innocent III.

It is impossible to understand the history of the medieval Church, and its relations with the State and to social life in general, if we treat it in the analogy of modern conditions. The Church was not only a far more universal and far-reaching society than the medieval State, it possessed many of the functions that we regard as essentially political. As F. W. Maitland used to insist, it is difficult to find any definition of a State which would not include the medieval Church, while the State under feudal conditions often lacked prerogatives and functions without which we can hardly conceive a State existing.

In the modern world the Church is regarded as essentially a voluntary society of limited membership and limited functions, while the State is the fundamental fact that dominates every aspect of social life and leaves little room for any independent activity. The chief problem for us is how to safeguard that minimum of social auton-

Text: Reprinted by permission of the author and The Society of Authors from *Medieval Essays* by Christopher Dawson (London: Sheed and Ward, Ltd., 1953), pp. 75-78, 80-86, 88-94 *passim.*

omy without which neither the spiritual society of the Church nor natural social organisms like the family can fulfil their functions. In the early Middle Ages, however, the State had neither the physical power nor the moral prestige to make such universal claims. It was sufficiently occupied with the problems of bare existence. It occupied a precarious position between the universal society of the Church, which possessed a monopoly of the higher culture, and the lesser territorial units which possessed so large a measure of local autonomy as to leave few political prerogatives in the hands of the nominal sovereign. Accordingly, in the Middle Ages the ultimate social reality was not the national kingdom, but the common unity of the Christian people of which the State itself was but the temporal organ and the king the divinely appointed guardian and defender.

Thus to the medieval mind the distinction was not between Church and State as two perfect and independent societies, but rather between the two different authorities and hierarchies which respectively administered the spiritual and temporal affairs of this one society. . . .

It is, however, important to remember that these two aspects of medieval society are not to be identified simply with the ecclesiastical and political categories in the narrower sense. The medieval king was not merely the representative of the old barbarian national monarchies; he was also an officer in the Christian society, who stood in a peculiarly close relationship to the Church and was consecrated by religious rites. However much the reforming canonists might insist on the essential distinction between the royal and the sacerdotal unctions, the medieval monarchy possessed a sacred and quasi-sacerdotal character which it never entirely lost until the end of the old regime at the close of the eighteenth century.

This religious conception of the State and the royal office found its most complete expression in the Carolingian Empire, which had so vast an influence on the subsequent development of medieval culture. The Carolingian Empire was the most complete political expression of these unitary and universalist tendencies of which we have spoken. It was regarded by Charlemagne and his successors and their ecclesiastical advisers not merely as a Frankish imperial State, nor even as the revival of the Roman Empire in the West, but as the political organ and counterpart of the Catholic Church. In the words of Charlemagne's letter to Leo III, the emperor is "the representative of God who has to protect and govern all the members of God"; he is Lord and Father, King and Priest, Leader and Guide of all Christians.

This unitary conception of Christian society naturally tended under a strong emperor to result in a kind of Cæsaropapism like that of the Byzantine Church. The emperor was regarded as the apex of the pyramid of Christian society, the culminating point at which the ecclesiastical and civil hierarchies converged. The Carolingian Empire, however, unlike the Christian Empire of the East, possessed no trained bureaucracy or class of lawyers and was consequently far more dependent on the assistance of ecclesiastics in the task of civil administration than was the Byzantine State. Alike in the Carolingian Empire and its Germanic successor, the bishops were the mainstay of the government, and the ecclesiastics of the royal *capella* under the archchaplain formed the imperial chancery and the central organ of administration. Thus, on the one hand, the emperor was continually interfering in purely ecclesiastical matters in virtue of his general prerogative as defender of the faith and overseer of ecclesiastical order, while, on the other hand, the clergy took a leading part in the secular administration of the Empire. Under such conditions the distinction between Church and State tended to become blurred and effaced. . . .

The history of the medieval Church consists largely of a series of attempts to remedy this state of affairs and to emancipate the spiritual power from lay control and exploitation by a return to the traditional principles of canonical order. . . .

. . . [T]he essential principle of the reforming movement was the same as that which has inspired the whole development of canon law in medieval and modern times—that is to say, the constitution of the Church as a free and universal spiritual society under the sovereignty of the Apostolic See, with its own code of laws and its own independent legislative and judicial system. But owing to the special circumstances of medieval society it was impossible to maintain this principle without at the same time claiming a large measure of control and responsibility in regard to the temporal power. Given the unitary conception of Christian society, the programme of the reformers involved the substitution of the Pope for Emperor as *de facto* head of Christendom and leader and judge of the Christian people. From the modern point of view there is an immense gulf between these two sides of the reforming programme, but the reformers themselves were hardly conscious of it and we find in their writings the claim to spiritual freedom and the claim to supremacy over the temporal power treated as inseparable parts of a single whole. Thus, in the famous propositions, known as the *Dic-*

tatus Papae, which seem to have been drafted by Gregory VII himself in 1075, we find claims like that of the right of the Pope to use the imperial insignia, to depose Emperors and to release subjects from their oath of allegiance to unjust rulers asserted at the same time and, as it were, in the same breath with strictly canonical principles like the supreme authority of the Holy See, the irreformability of papal decrees, and the power of the Pope to depose or absolve bishops.

In the same way the imperialist writers do not restrict themselves to defending the purely political prerogatives of the temporal power, to rejecting the right of the Pope to depose rulers or to use the temporal sword against their opponents. They in their turn claim for the Emperor the right to interfere in purely ecclesiastical matters, not merely in the appointment of bishops, but even in the affairs of the Papacy, so that the Emperor was the ultimate arbiter in the government of the Church, and had the right to control the election of the Pope and to depose him if he was unworthy, as in the famous example of the Synod of Sutri [1046] when Henry III [Holy Roman Emperor] deposed the three claimants to the Papacy and substituted his own nominee.

Thus the struggle between the Empire and the Papacy concerning the investitures was involved in an almost inextricable confusion which renders it very difficult for the modern student to judge both parties fairly. It is a profound mistake to read into the history of the early Middle Ages that opposition between the claims of the national monarchy and the universal jurisdiction of the Papacy which was characteristic of the age of the Renaissance and the Reformation. It was not the new political State with its ideals of centralized administration and its strongly developed national consciousness that was the enemy which Gregory VII and his successors had to combat, but rather the old Carolingian and Ottonian tradition of the Christian Empire with its universal claims and its theocratic ideal. It was not until the Church had asserted her claim to freedom from secular control that the State became conscious of its proper mission and was able to vindicate its political autonomy. The revival of Roman law which played so great a part in the medieval political renaissance and the development of the European State was itself the sequel and consequence of the revival of canon law which accompanied the reforming movement. The revival of Roman law was never regarded as a danger by the Roman Church. On the contrary, it was the Papacy that was the first to assimilate the principles of the legal renaissance and it found in them an invaluable instrument for carrying out its task of legal reorganization and centralization. Civilians and canonists were not enemies or even rivals; they were allies in the task of rationalizing and clarifying the complex tangle of political and ecclesiastical relations that constituted medieval society. Indeed the creators of the new State and the new law were themselves for the most part churchmen, as, for example, Roger of Salisbury, Hubert Walter and Henry of Bracton in England.

Thus it was the Papacy and not the Empire which first applied the revived science of law to the task of government. The development of canon law on scientific principles by Gratian and his successors gave the whole system of ecclesiastical government a rational legal basis such as the medieval State did not as yet possess. While the latter was still feebly groping after the rudiments of an administrative order, the Church was already constituted as an organized international society, complete with a centralized government, a written code of laws and an elaborate system of appellate jurisdiction and representative and legislative assemblies.

The result of this development was to make the Papacy an effective power in the public life of Europe and to give it an international prestige which far outweighed that of the empire or any of the feudal kingdoms. Even in its greatest days under Charlemagne or Otto I or Henry III the power of the Empire had rested in the last resort on its military strength and it was incapable of exerting its influence effectively in Italy, for example, without repeated military expeditions which had much of the character of a barbarian invasion. The superiority of the Papacy, on the other hand, was both moral and intellectual, and even the powers which fought against it were incapable of resisting its spiritual prestige.

While the Holy Roman Empire gradually lost its old position as the representative of the unity of Christendom and became an unwieldy and disorganized mass of feudal territories, the Papacy became the head of Christendom in every sense of the word and exercised an effective superpolitical authority over the peoples of Western Europe. This authority was not confined to the ecclesiastical sphere: it extended to every side of social life and human activity. It judged the affairs of kingdoms, it organized crusades against the infidel and the heretic, and excommunicated and deposed rulers who had offended against the common law of Christendom. In fact, the medieval Papacy combined two distinct but related functions. It was the ruler of the Church in the strict sense, the representative of Peter and the head of the ecclesiastical hierarchy, but it was also the leader and judge of Christian society in the widest sense—the president of a kind of European league of nations and the supreme authority in international law.

This twofold aspect of the medieval Papacy finds its most complete expression in the pontificate of Innocent III, who is often regarded as the greatest of the medieval popes. On the one hand, he completed the organization of the medieval Church according to the principles of the new canon law, and the great Lateran Council of 1215 marks the final triumph of the programme of ecclesiastical reform that had been initiated under Leo IX and his successors. But, on the other hand, he was the head and ruler of Christendom, who realized the ideal of the unity of Christian civilization under a single head far more completely and effectively than Charlemagne or Otto the Great.

In the words of the Bible which he took as the text of his sermon on the day of his consecration, he was "set over the nations and over the kingdoms to pluck up and to break down, to destroy and to overthrow, to build and to plant. . . ." He judged between nation and nation, between kings and peoples, between the rival claimants to the Empire, between the King of France and the King of England and between the latter and his rebellious subjects. These two aspects of the papal authority were not, however, distinguished by Innocent III himself as different in kind or principle. Both of them were derived from the claim of the Pope to be Vicar of God on earth. In the words of Innocent, the Pope was the judge of the world, "set in the midst between God and Man, below God and above Man"; he is "the representative of Him to whom the earth belongs with all that it contains and all its inhabitants"; he is a priest after the order of Melchizedek, at once priest and king who unites in his person the fullness of all power and authority.

It is obvious that so wide a claim to universal authority leaves little room for the modern distinction between the two autonomous orders and societies of Church and State. But I have already pointed out the medieval conception of Christian society was essentially a unitary one. State and Church were not two independent organisms but different orders or functions in a single society of which the Pope was the head. Yet at the same time this did not mean that the two orders were confused or identified with one another. The prince had his own proper function in Christian society and his own rights within the sphere of its exercise. The authority of the Pope was a super-political one, which transcended that of the king without destroying it.

This is what the Pope means when he replies to Philip II's protest against his intervention in the quarrel with King John that he is not judging about the fief but about sin. In other words, he intervenes in a political quarrel because moral issues are at stake of which he is the divinely appointed guardian. . . .

The fact is that throughout the earlier part of the Middle Ages and down to the emergence of Thomism there was an inevitable confusion between the temporal and the spiritual orders which led to tragic misunderstanding and conflicts. The struggle between the Papacy and the Empire was not a struggle between the Church and the secular State such as we know today. It was a conflict between two parallel forms of the same ideal, between the ideal of a theocratic empire and that of a theocratic church, each of which was inspired by the same vision of an all-embracing Christian society—the City of God on earth.

It is needless to point out how vast was the gulf between this grandiose vision of a universal order and the semibarbaric anarchy of feudal Europe. And the tragic irony of the contrast was heightened by the fact that these conflicting idealisms were so often used to serve the ends of selfish ambition. . . .

. . . [T]he rise of the new Christian philosophy of St. Thomas at last provided a solid intellectual foundation for the ideal of an autonomous State which does not transcend its proper sphere by theocratic claims. . . . It was left for St. Thomas to define clearly and exhaustively the idea of an autonomous natural order and a natural law and to lay down the principle that "the divine right, which is of grace, does not destroy the human right which is of human reason" (*S.T.*, II-IIæ, Q. x, art. 10). Elsewhere in the commentary on the Sentences he seems to draw the obvious political corollary of this principle when he states that "in matters of civil good, it is better to obey the secular power than the spiritual." Nevertheless, it was centuries before this principle was worked out in detail and made the basis of the classical Catholic doctrine of the two *societates perfectæ*. St. Thomas himself, in the passage to which I have just referred, qualifies his principle by adding: "Unless perchance the secular power is conjoined with the spiritual as in the Pope who holds the summit of both the spiritual and secular power alike, by the ordering of Him who is both Priest and King." Thus, too, we find that the most eminent disciple of St. Thomas in the following generation, Aegidius Romanus, is at the same time the most uncompromising advocate of the theocratic claims of the Papacy in their most totalitarian form. Although he admits that the two powers are distinct, at least in theory, he makes them both alike dependent on the Pope as their ultimate source. For since God is the source of all authority and since there is neither law nor justice save in obedience to Him, it follows that all rights whether political or economic, are ultimately dependent on the authority of God's vicar on earth, and the prince who rebels against the Pope thereby destroys the basis of his own derived and delegated power. And thus the unitary conception of society is no longer restricted to its historic basis, the actual society of Western Christendom, but is extended to the world in general and to humanity as a whole. The kingdoms of the heathen are nothing more than organized robberies with no higher sanction than the reign of force, for outside the Church there is no justice and without justice there is no legitimate authority, whether spiritual or temporal.

Thus the first effect of the new philosophy was to accentuate the universalist tendencies in medieval social doctrine, and we see the same thing on the imperialist side in the case of Dante, that other disciple of St. Thomas. Never, in fact, did the vision of unity that haunted the memory and inspired the imagination of the medieval world receive fuller and nobler expression than in the work of the great Ghibelline poet. But though Dante was profoundly Christian and Catholic it is no longer to the Church that he looks for his ideal of unity as the thinkers of the earlier Middle Ages had done, imperialists no less than papalists. For Dante, the ideal unity was not that of the Church but of humanity, and the Roman Empire was its divinely predestined servant and instrument. Thus the claims of the Empire are based not on its ministerial office towards the spiritual power, but, as he puts it, "on the necessity of human civilization," which cannot realize its essential and natural ends without the peace and order which only political unity can give. . . .

This exaltation of the State as such, with its idealization of ancient Rome and its intense Latin patriotism, is almost unique in medieval literature and is much farther removed from the main tradition of medieval thought than the theocratic totalitarianism of Aegidius Romanus and his successors, though it is even more dependent on Thomism in its philosophical presuppositions. Nevertheless, though it had no direct influence on the main current of medieval thought, it is profoundly significant from the historical point of view, since it embodies in an individual synthesis the diverging tendencies of medieval thought and Western culture. While, on the one hand, it looks back to the medieval ideal of a universal society and to the tradition of Charlemagne and the Holy Roman Empire; on the other, it looks forward to the Renaissance, to the national monarchy and to the new humanist culture. Looked at superficially, Dante's thesis may seem to differ little from the old theocratic imperialism. There is much in Dante's *De Monarchia* which recalls Jordan of Osnabrück's apologia for the Empire, even to the latter's extreme conclusion "that as the Roman Church is the Church of God so the Roman Empire is the kingdom of God." Yet when we look deeper we see that with Dante the whole character of the imperialist theory is changed by being brought into relation with the Thomist doctrine of natural law and the Aristotelian social theory, on the one hand, and with the new political consciousness and lay culture of the Italian city state, on the other. It marks a definite break with the unitary theory of society which had dominated the previous five centuries, though the revolutionary character of the change was obscured by the fact that Dante's political hopes were still fixed on the universal Empire of the past and not on the national monarchy of the future. By an unfortunate fatality the country of St. Thomas and Dante, the one country of medieval Europe which was far enough advanced in culture to acquire complete political self-consciousness, lacked the historical conditions for national self-determination, and consequently Dante's intense Italian patriotism was forced to ally itself incongruously with its natural enemy, the alien power of Germanic imperialism. On the other hand, where historical conditions were favourable to the rise of the national monarchy, as in France and England, the state of culture was not sufficiently advanced for the Church to disentangle herself from her political commitments and for the State to fulfil its own proper functions without the Church's help. Consequently in northern Europe the relations between Church and State were still dominated by the old unitary conception of society, which now tended to find national forms of expression, a state of things which prepared the way for the ultimate dissolution of religious unity and the rise of the national Churches in the sixteenth century.

Struggles for a National State

81 MAGNA CARTA: KING VERSUS FEUDAL LORDS — ENGLAND

During much of the early Middle Ages, western Europe suffered from devastating raids by Norse tribes who swept southward almost annually to loot and plunder towns and villages. Neither Carolingian monarchs nor English kings were able to halt the ravages, piracy, and general chaos that often prevailed. In addition, Muslim domination of the Mediterranean cut off the major supply of eastern goods, and by the tenth century trade and commerce in the West had been sharply curtailed. Most of Europe reverted to a self-sufficient agricultural economy; towns and urban life declined, and in this unsettled atmosphere people sought security above all else. Out of this background emerged the feudal relationship; with the breakdown in central political authority, a period began in which governmental functions had to be both delegated and localized and in which private individuals usurped public responsibilities.

In 1215 in England a revolt of the barons, intent upon protecting their localized feudal privileges, inadvertently laid the basis for modern English constitutional government. King John of England (1199-1216), engaged in a struggle with the French monarch, Philip Augustus, had attempted to force the barons to assist him in his foreign campaigns, and had resorted to arbitrary and, in the eyes of the barons, illegal methods. He raised taxes, demanded extraordinary services, made use of foreign troops against any Englishmen who resisted him, extorted money, and generally violated English feudal law and custom. A solution was finally achieved on June 14, 1215, near Runnymede, when John reluctantly accepted the demands set forth by the rebellious barons in the document known as the *Magna Carta* (Great Charter). Although by the terms of the Magna Carta John promised that he and his heirs would cease in the abuses listed by the barons, these were, by and large, violations of his role as feudal lord. Far more important were two principles embodied in the document: first, that there existed a body of law in the nation which belonged to the subjects and which the king was obliged to respect; second, that if the monarch failed in his obligation, the subjects might take action to enforce compliance. In short, the Magna Carta declared that the king was not above the law, that he did not possess unlimited powers. Whereas the Great Charter was essentially a feudal document and was directed toward releasing aristocratic vassals from infringements by an arbitrary monarch, its provisions were stated so generally that the principles would centuries later be applied to larger segments of the English population, and the Magna Carta would become the bedrock of English constitutional development.

The rise of an urban economy and the accompanying growth of cities in the thirteenth and fourteenth centuries contributed to the decline of feudalism. Laborers were no longer inevitably bound to the soil—a new type of citizen emerged, the free laborer, the skilled workingman, and in time the employer of skilled workingmen, the middle class. Both the Holy Roman Empire and the papacy declined in influence, while the development of strong national states with centralized monarchies in England and France made public functions once again the responsibility of national governments. The old feudal relationships were thus altered and the way prepared for substantial changes in the political and social institutions of western Europe. As a feudal document designed to block the resurgence of monarchal power, the Magna Carta thus was ultimately doomed to failure. But with its resuscitation by parliamentarians and common-law lawyers in the seventeenth century, it was reinterpreted as a guarantee of the basic rights of all Englishmen.

John, by the grace of God king of England, lord of Ireland, duke of Normandy and Aquitaine, count of Anjou: to the archbishops, bishops, abbots, earls, barons, justices, foresters, sheriffs, prevosts, serving men, and to all his bailiffs and faithful subjects, greeting. Know that we, by the will of God and for the safety of our soul, and of the souls of all our predecessors and our heirs, to the honour of God and for the exalting

Text: Ernest F. Henderson (trans. and ed.), *Select Historical Documents of the Middle Ages* (London: G. Bell & Sons, Ltd., 1896), pp. 135-36, 138-44, 146-48.

of the holy church and the bettering of our realm. . . .

1. First of all have granted to God, and, for us and for our heirs forever, have confirmed, by this our present charter, that the English church shall be free and shall have its rights intact and its liberties uninfringed upon. And thus we will that it be observed. As is apparent from the fact that we, spontaneously and of our own free will, before discord broke out between ourselves and our barons, did grant and by our charter confirm—and did cause the lord pope Innocent III. to confirm—freedom of elections, which is considered most important and most necessary to the church of England. Which charter both we ourselves shall observe, and we will that it be observed with good faith by our heirs forever. We have also granted to all free men of our realm, on the part of ourselves and our heirs forever, all the subjoined liberties, to have and to hold, to them and to their heirs, from us and from our heirs. . . .

9. Neither we nor our bailiffs shall seize any revenue for any debt, so long as the chattels of the debtor suffice to pay the debt; nor shall the sponsors of that debtor be distrained so long as that chief debtor has enough to pay the debt. But if the chief debtor fail in paying the debt, not having the wherewithal to pay it, the sponsors shall answer for the debt. And, if they shall wish, they may have the lands and revenues of the debtor until satisfaction shall have been given them for the debt previously paid for him; unless the chief debtor shall show that he is quit in that respect towards those same sponsors. . . .

12. No scutage or aid shall be imposed in our realm unless by the common counsel of our realm; except for redeeming our body, and knighting our eldest son, and marrying once our eldest daughter. And for these purposes there shall only be given a reasonable aid. In like manner shall be done concerning the aids of the city of London.

13. And the city of London shall have all its old liberties and free customs as well by land as by water. Moreover we will and grant that all other cities and burroughs, and towns and ports, shall have all their liberties and free customs.

14. And, in order to have the common counsel of the realm in the matter of assessing an aid otherwise than in the aforesaid cases, or of assessing a scutage,—we shall cause, under seal through our letters, the archbishops, bishops, abbots, earls, and greater barons to be summoned for a fixed day—for a term, namely, at least forty days distant,—and for a fixed place. And, moreover, we shall cause to be summoned in general, through our sheriffs and bailiffs, all those who hold of us in chief. And in all those letters of summons we shall express the cause of the summons. And when a summons has thus been made, the business shall be proceeded with on the day appointed according to the counsel of those who shall be present, even though not all shall come who were summoned. . . .

17. Common pleas shall not follow our court but shall be held in a certain fixed place. . . .

20. A freeman shall only be amerced for a small offence according to the measure of that offence. And for a great offence he shall be amerced according to the magnitude of the offence, saving his contenement; and a merchant, in the same way, saving his merchandize. And a villein, in the same way, if he fall under our mercy, shall be amerced saving his wainnage. And none of the aforesaid fines shall be imposed save upon oath of upright men from the neighbourhood.

21. Earls and barons shall not be amerced save through their peers, and only according to the measure of the offence.

22. No clerk shall be amerced for his lay tenement except according to the manner of the other persons aforesaid; and not according to the amount of his ecclesiastical benefice.

23. Neither a town nor a man shall be forced to make bridges over the rivers, with the exception of those who, from of old and of right ought to do it. . . .

28. No constable or other bailiff of ours shall take the corn or other chattels of any one except he straightway give money for them, or can be allowed a respite in that regard by the will of the seller. . . .

32. We shall not hold the lands of those convicted of felony longer than a year and a day; and then the lands shall be restored to the lords of the fiefs. . . .

39. No freeman shall be taken, or imprisoned, or disseized, or outlawed, or exiled, or in any way harmed—nor will we go upon or send upon him—save by the lawful judgment of his peers or by the law of the land.

40. To none will we sell, to none deny or delay, right or justice.

41. All merchants may safely and securely go out of England, and come into England, and delay and pass through England, as well by land as by water, for the purpose of buying and selling, free from all evil taxes, subject to the ancient and right customs—save in time of war, and if they are of the land at war against us. And if such be found in our land at the beginning of the war, they shall be held, without harm to their

bodies and goods, until it shall be known to us or our chief justice how the merchants of our land are to be treated who shall, at that time, be found in the land at war against us. And if ours shall be safe there, the others shall be safe in our land.

42. Henceforth any person, saving fealty to us, may go out of our realm and return to it, safely and securely, by land and by water, except perhaps for a brief period in time of war, for the common good of the realm. But prisoners and outlaws are excepted according to the law of the realm; also people of a land at war against us, and the merchants, with regard to whom shall be done as we have said. . . .

49. We shall straightway return all hostages and charters which were delivered to us by Englishmen as a surety for peace or faithful service. . . .

51. And straightway after peace is restored we shall remove from the realm all the foreign soldiers, crossbowmen, servants, hirelings, who may have come with horses and arms to the harm of the realm.

52. If any one shall have been disseized by us, or removed, without a legal sentence of his peers, from his lands, castles, liberties or lawful right, we shall straightway restore them to him. And if a dispute shall arise concerning this matter it shall be settled according to the judgment of the twenty five barons who are mentioned below as sureties for the peace. But with regard to all those things of which any one was, by king Henry our father or king Richard our brother, disseized or dispossessed without legal judgment of his peers, which we have in our hand or which others hold, and for which we ought to give a guarantee: we shall have respite until the common term for crusaders. Except with regard to those concerning which a plea was moved, or an inquest made by our order, before we took the cross. But when we return from our pilgrimage, or if, by chance, we desist from our pilgrimage, we shall straightway then show full justice regarding them. . . .

55. All fines imposed by us unjustly and contrary to the law of the land, and all amerciaments made unjustly and contrary to the law of the land, shall be altogether remitted, or it shall be done with regard to them according to the judgment of the twenty five barons mentioned below as sureties for the peace, or according to the judgment of the majority of them together with the aforesaid Stephen archbishop of Canterbury, if he can be present, and with others whom he may wish to associate with himself for this purpose. . . .

60. Moreover all the subjects of our realm, clergy as well as laity, shall, as far as pertains to them, observe, with regard to their vassals, all these aforesaid customs and liberties which we have decreed shall, as far as pertains to us, be observed in our realm with regard to our own.

61. Inasmuch as, for the sake of God, and for the bettering of our realm, and for the more ready healing of the discord which has arisen between us and our barons, we have made all these aforesaid concessions,—wishing them to enjoy for ever entire and firm stability, we make and grant to them the following security: that the barons, namely, may elect at their pleasure twenty five barons from the realm, who ought, with all their strength, to observe, maintain and cause to be observed, the peace and privileges which we have granted to them and confirmed by this our present charter. In such wise, namely, that if we, or our justice, or our bailiffs, or any one of our servants shall have transgressed against any one in any respect, or shall have broken some one of the articles of peace or security, and our transgression shall have been shown to four barons of the aforesaid twenty five: those four barons shall come to us, or, if we are abroad, to our justice, showing to us our error; and they shall ask us to cause that error to be amended without delay. And if we do not amend that error, or, we being abroad, if our justice do not amend it within a term of forty days from the time when it was shown to us or, we being abroad, to our justice: the aforesaid four barons shall refer the matter to the remainder of the twenty five barons, and those twenty five barons, with the whole land in common, shall distrain and oppress us in every way in their power,—namely, by taking our castles, lands and possessions, and in every other way that they can, until amends shall have been made according to their judgment. Saving the persons of ourselves, our queen and our children. And when amends shall have been made they shall be in accord with us as they had been previously. And whoever of the land wishes to do so, shall swear that in carrying out all the aforesaid measures he will obey the mandates of the aforesaid twenty five barons, and that, with them, he will oppress us to the extent of his power. And, to any one who wishes to do so, we publicly and freely give permission to swear; and we will never prevent any one from swearing. Moreover, all those in the land who shall be unwilling, themselves and of their own accord, to swear to the twenty five barons as to distraining and oppressing us with them: such ones we shall make to swear by our mandate, as has been said. . . .

62. And we have fully remitted to all, and pardoned, all the ill-will, anger and rancour which

have arisen between us and our subjects, clergy and laity, from the time of the struggle. Moreover we have fully remitted to all, clergy and laity, and—as far as pertains to us—have pardoned fully all the transgressions committed, on the occasion of that same struggle, from Easter of the sixteenth year of our reign until the reestablishment of peace. In witness of which, moreover, we have caused to be drawn up for them letters patent of lord Stephen, archbishop of Canterbury, lord Henry, archbishop of Dublin, and the aforesaid bishops and master Pandulf, regarding that surety and the aforesaid concessions.

63. Wherefore we will and firmly decree that the English church shall be free, and that the subjects of our realm shall have and hold all the aforesaid liberties, rights and concessions, duly and in peace, freely and quietly, fully and entirely, for themselves and their heirs, from us and our heirs, in all matters and in all places, forever, as has been said. Moreover it has been sworn, on our part as well as on the part of the barons, that all these above mentioned provisions shall be observed with good faith and without evil intent. The witnesses being the above mentioned and many others. Given through our hand, in the plain called Runnimede between Windsor and Stanes, on the fifteenth day of June, in the seventeenth year of our reign.

82 JEAN DE JOINVILLE, *MEMOIRS OF THE CRUSADES:* THE RISING POWER OF THE KING—FRANCE

The emergence of French civilization, French nationalism, and French royal absolutism absorbs a deservedly large part of medieval history. In the high Middle Ages (1100-1400), French culture was the most cosmopolitan and the most admired throughout Europe for its chivalry, for the art of its troubadours, and for the majesty of its Gothic architecture. Not only was Paris a wealthy metropolis and capital, but its university was the most respected center of Scholastic philosophy and theology in Christendom.

By comparison with its brilliant social and intellectual history, the development of a centralized French monarchy and a unified French nation seems slow. Yet in spite of some desperate military defeats and diplomatic disasters, the French monarchy established itself as a medieval power of the first magnitude and laid political foundations significant for the future history of the French state.

Among medieval French kings of the royal line established by Hugh Capet, two of outstanding merit are Philip II (1180-1223) and Louis IX (1226-1270). It was Philip who, by a firm insistence on his feudal superiority, by skillful exploitation of political opportunities, and by military force, so enlarged the domain and material resources of the French crown that he won for himself the honorific *Augustus* ("the increaser"). His longest, though ultimately triumphant, contest was with the contemporary English kings, who, through inheritance and marriage held feudal claims over Normandy, Aquitaine, and Anjou.

The triumphs of Philip Augustus were the inheritance of his grandson, Louis IX, who came to the throne as a child and reigned to become the ideal medieval monarch and a Christian saint. For Louis IX, the medieval political ideal—"the most Christian king"—was embodied in a life of simplicity, moderation, faith, and love for his subjects, for the salvation of whose souls the state bore a responsibility as well as the Church. In this capacity the king was a relentless persecutor of heresy and an overzealous crusader who led disastrous expeditions against the Muslims of Egypt and Tunis.

Louis' extreme pietism, however, did not inhibit his remarkable executive abilities and his ability as a temporal ruler. The increased royal domain so painstakingly acquired by his grandfather was protected and extended by the king and his ministers, and royal prerogatives guarded against feudal encroachment. The *curia regis* or advisory council of the kings grew increasingly specialized, especially in its legal functions which were handled by a department called *parlement*, a term originally reserved for any assembly. The local officials on the royal domain, named *baillis* in the north and seneschals in the south, were increasingly chosen from among the bourgeoisie of the towns, who tended to ally themselves with the crown against the feudal nobility.

In the following selection the moral and religious principles by which Louis IX lived and ruled are described by Jean de Joinville (c. 1224-c. 1319), the king's friend and confidant. The king's remarkable combination of administrative efficiency and Christian virtue is seen in Joinville's report of the royal reform of his subjects' offices of *baillis* and provost, the chief royal official of Paris. Not only is the king sensitive to royal prerogative, but he also carefully protects his people against local tyrannies by his own officials.

Habits and Customs of St. Louis—He Refuses the Unjust Demands of His Bishops

... Of his wisdom will I now speak to you. There were times when people bore witness that no one of his council was as wise as he. And this appeared in that when people spoke to him of any matter, he did not say: "I will take advice thereon;" but if he saw the right clearly and evidently he answered without appeal to his councillors, and at once. In this wise I heard that he gave answer to all the prelates of the kingdom of France regarding a petition they made to him in the following case.

The Bishop Guy of Auxerre spake to him for all of them, and said: "Sire, these archbishops and bishops here present have charged me to tell you that Christendom decays and melts in your hands, and that it will decay still further unless you give thought thereto, because no man stands in fear of excommunication. We require you therefore to command your bailiffs and your sergeants to compel all excommunicate persons who have been under sentence for a year and a day, to make satisfaction to the Church." And the king replied, without taking any advice, that he would willingly order his bailiffs and sergeants to constrain excommunicate persons in the manner desired, provided full cognisance of the sentence were given to him in each case, so that he might judge whether the sentence were righteous or not.

And they consulted together, and answered the king that they would not give him such cognisance, because the matters involved were spiritual. And the king replied in turn that he would not give them cognisance of such matters as pertained to him, nor order his sergeants to constrain excommunicate persons to obtain absolution, whether such excommunication were rightful or wrongful. "For if I did so," said the king, "I should be acting contrary to God and against right. And I will give you an example, which is this: that the bishops of Brittany held the Count of Brittany for seven years under sentence of excommunication; and then the count obtained absolution from the court of Rome; and if I had constrained him at the end of the first year, I should have constrained him wrongfully." ...

St. Louis' Love of Peace

Now it happened that the saintly king laboured so effectually that the King of England [Henry III], his wife, and his children, came to France to treat of a peace between them and him. To this peace his council were strongly opposed, and they spoke to him thus: "Sire, we marvel greatly that you are minded to give to the King of England a great portion of the land which you and your predecessors have won from him, and which he has forfeited by misfeasance. Now it seems to us that if you believe you have no right to the land, you are not making full restitution unless you restore all the conquests that you and your predecessors have made; while if you believe that you have a right to the land, it seems to us that whatever you restore is restored to your loss."

To this the saintly king replied after the following manner: "Lords, I am convinced that the King of England's predecessors were rightfully dispossessed of all the conquered land that I hold; and the land that I am giving him I do not give as a thing that I am bound to give either to himself or to his heirs; but I give it so that there may be love between my children and his, who are cousins-german. And meseems that what I give him is given to good purpose, since he has not hitherto been my liegeman, but will now have to do me homage."

No man in the world laboured more to maintain peace among his subjects, and specially among the great men who were neighbours, and the princes of the realm; as, for instance, between the Count of Chalon, uncle of the Lord of Joinville, and his son the Count of Burgundy, who were at war when we came back from overseas. And in order to make peace between the father and the son he sent men of his council, at his own charges, into Burgundy; and by his efforts peace was established between the father and the son.

There was at that time war between King Thibaut the Second, of Champagne, and Count John of Chalon, and the Count of Burgundy, his son, regarding the abbey of Luxeuil. To appease this war my lord the king sent Gervais of Escraines, who was then master of the meats in France; and by his efforts he reconciled them. ...

As to the foreigners whom the king had reconciled, there were some of his council who said

Text: From Villehardouin and De Joinville, *Memoirs of the Crusades,* trans. Sir Frank T. Marzials, "Everyman's Library," 1908. Reprinted by permission of the publishers, E. P. Dutton & Co., Inc., New York, and J. M. Dent & Sons, Ltd., London. Pp. 304-05, 307-09, 311-16.

he would have done better to let them fight; for if he suffered them to impoverish themselves, they would attack him less readily than if they were rich. And to this the king made answer, and said that they spoke unwisely. "For if the neighbouring princes saw that I let them fight together, they might consult and say: 'It is from malice that he lets us fight together thus.' And so, perchance, out of hatred, they would come and fall upon me, which might be greatly to my loss, to say nothing of the enmity of God that I should incur, who has said: 'Blessed are the peacemakers.'"

Whence it also came that the people of Burgundy and Lorraine, whom he had pacified, loved and obeyed him so well that I have seen them come and plead their suits before him at his courts of Rheims, Paris and Orléans. . . .

How the King Reformed His Bailiffs, Provosts, and Mayors— and How He Instituted New Ordinances—and How Stephen Boileau Was His Provost of Paris

After King Louis had returned to France from overseas, he bore himself very devoutly towards our Saviour, and very justly towards his subjects; wherefore he considered and thought it would be a fair thing, and a good, to reform the realm of France. First he established a general ordinance for all his subjects throughout the realm of France, in the manner following:—

We, Louis, by the grace of God King of France, ordain that Our bailiffs, viscounts, provosts, mayors, and all others, in whatever matter it may be, and whatever office they may hold, shall make oath that, so long as they hold the said office, or perform the functions of bailiffs, they shall do justice to all, without acceptation of persons, as well to the poor as to the rich, and to strangers as to those who are native-born; and that they shall observe such uses and customs as are good and have been approved.

And if it happens that the bailiffs, or viscounts, or others, as the sergeants or foresters, do aught contrary to their oaths, and are convicted thereof, we order that they be punished in their goods, or in their persons, if the misfeasance so require; and the bailiffs shall be punished by Ourselves, and others by the bailiffs.

Henceforward the other provosts, the bailiffs and the sergeants shall make oath to loyally keep and uphold Our rents and Our rights, and not to suffer Our rights to lapse or to be suppressed or diminished; and with this they shall swear not to take or receive, by themselves or through others, gold, nor silver, nor any indirect benefit, nor any other thing, save fruit, or bread, or wine, or other present, to the value of ten *sous*, the said sum not being exceeded.

And besides this, they shall make oath not to take, or cause to be taken, any gift, of whatever kind, through their wives, or their children, or their brothers, or their sisters, or any other persons connected with them; and so soon as they have knowledge that any such gifts have been received, they will cause them to be returned as soon as may be possible. And, besides this, they shall make oath not to receive any gift, of whatever kind, from any man belonging to their bailiwicks, nor from any others who have a suit or may plead before them.

Henceforth they shall make oath not to bestow any gift upon any men who are of Our council, nor upon their wives, or children, or any person belonging to them; nor upon those who shall receive the said officers' accounts on Our behalf, nor to any persons whom we may send to their bailiwicks, or to their provostships, to enquire into their doings. And with this they shall swear to take no profit out of any sale that may be made of Our rents, Our bailiwicks, Our coinage, or aught else to Us belonging.

And they shall swear and promise, that if they have knowledge of any official, sergeant, or provost, serving under them, who is unfaithful, given to robbery and usury, or addicted to other vices whereby he ought to vacate Our service, then they will not uphold him for any gift, or promise, or private affection, or any other cause, but punish and judge him in all good faith.

Henceforward Our provosts, Our viscounts, Our mayors, Our foresters, and Our other sergeants, mounted and dismounted, shall make oath not to bestow any gift upon their superiors, nor upon their superiors' wives, nor children, nor upon any one belonging to them. . . .

We will and ordain that all Our provosts and bailiffs abstain from saying any word that would bring into contempt God, or our Lady, or the saints; and also that they abstain from the game of dice and keep away from taverns. We ordain that the making of dice be forbidden throughout Our realm, and that lewd women be turned out of every house; and whosoever shall rent a house to a lewd woman shall forfeit to the provost, or the bailiff, the rent of the said house for a year.

Moreover, We forbid Our bailiffs to purchase wrongfully, or to cause to be purchased, either directly, or through others, any possession or lands that may be in their bailiwick, or in any other, so long as they remain in Our service, and without Our express permission; and if any such purchases are made, We ordain that the lands in question be, and remain, in Our hands. . . .

And We ordain that those who hold the office of provost viscount, or any other office, do not sell such office to others without Our consent; and if several persons buy jointly any of the said offices, We order that one of the purchasers shall perform the duties of the office for all the rest, and alone enjoy such of its privileges in respect of journeyings, taxes, and common charges, as have been customary aforetime.

And We forbid that they sell the said offices to their brothers, nephews, or cousins, after they have bought them from Us; and that they claim any debts that may be due to themselves, save such debts as appertain to their office. As regards their own personal debts, they will recover them by authority of the bailiff, just as if they were not in Our service. . . .

From henceforth we command that Our provosts and bailiffs dispossess no man from the seisin which he holds, without full enquiry, or Our own especial order; and that they impose upon Our people no new exactions, taxes and imposts; and that they compel no one to come forth to do service in arms, for the purpose of exacting money from him; for We order that none who owes Us service in arms shall be summoned to join the host without sufficient cause, and that those who would desire to come to the host in person should not be compelled to purchase exemption by money payment. . . .

By these ordinances the king did much to improve the conditions of the kingdom.

Reform of the Provostship of Paris

The provostship of Paris was at that time sold to the citizens of Paris, or indeed to any one; and those who bought the office upheld their children and nephews in wrongdoing; and the young folk relied in their misdoings on those who occupied the provostship. For which reason the mean people were greatly downtrodden; nor could they obtain justice against the rich, because of the great presents and gifts that the latter made to the provosts.

Whenever at that time any one spoke the truth before the provost, and wished to keep his oath, refusing to perjure himself regarding any debt, or other matter on which he was bound to give evidence, then the provost levied a fine upon that person, and he was punished. And because of the great injustice that was done, and the great robberies perpetrated in the provostship, the mean people did not dare to sojourn in the king's land, but went and sojourned in other provostships and other lordships. And the king's land was so deserted that when the provost held his court, no more than ten or twelve people came thereto.

With all this there were so many malefactors and thieves in Paris and the country adjoining that all the land was full of them. The king, who was very diligent to enquire how the mean people were governed and protected, soon knew the truth of this matter. So he forbade that the office of provost in Paris should be sold; and he gave great and good wages to those who henceforward should hold the said office. And he abolished all the evil customs harmful to the people; and he caused enquiry to be made throughout the kingdom to find men who would execute good and strict justice, and not spare the rich any more than the poor.

Then was brought to his notice Stephen Boileau, who so maintained and upheld the office of provost that no malefactor, nor thief, nor murderer dared to remain in Paris, seeing that if he did, he was soon hung or exterminated: neither parentage, nor lineage, nor gold, nor silver could save him. So the king's land began to amend, and people resorted thither for the good justice that prevailed. And the people so multiplied, and things so amended, that sales, seisines, purchases, and other matters were doubled in value, as compared with what the king had received aforetime.

"In all these matters which We have ordained for the advantage of Our subjects, and of Our realm, we reserve to Ourselves the right to elucidate, amend, adjust, or diminish, according as We may determine."

By this ordinance also the king did much to reform the kingdom of France, as many wise and ancient persons bear witness. . . .

83 CHARLES IV, GOLDEN BULL: CONSTITUTIONAL LAW FOR THE HOLY ROMAN EMPIRE

Many historians have repeated Voltaire's jibe that the Holy Roman Empire was neither holy, nor Roman, nor an empire. Perhaps it could be more fairly claimed that it was at once an exalted political ideal and a monumental political failure. In theory, it was the "universal state" of medieval Europe, based on what were conceived to be the traditions of the Roman and the Carolingian empires. By historical record, it was a confusion of shifting German and Italian principalities and communes which quarreled and warred with one another as endlessly and as disastrously as had the Greek city-states. In theory, the universal empire was the "second sword" of the Christian Church, and its emperor, who was crowned at Rome by the pope, was the supreme secular defender of the faith. In practice, pope and emperor, Church and empire, were in almost continual conflict throughout the Middle Ages. The tendencies in England and France toward powerful royal administrations and judiciaries were generally lacking in the empire, where the imperial office remained elective and fiercely contested among the great feudal houses of Germany. Only a few of the emperors, such as Frederick I (1152-1190)—called "Barbarossa" (red-beard) by his Italian subjects—made a serious effort to transform the imperial ideal into a political reality and in each case they failed.

Although the struggle between empire and papacy was of continuing importance in the late Middle Ages, the center of interest in the Holy Roman Empire's history shifted north of the Alps. Here, in the late thirteenth and the fourteenth centuries, at least three political and social tendencies predominated: (1) the concentration of power and territory in the hands of great princely houses, such as the Hapsburgs and the Luxemburgs; (2) a countermovement toward a multitude of very small and quarrelsome principalities which were to characterize a disunited Germany until the nineteenth century; and (3) the development of a thriving commerce, both foreign and domestic, which coincided with an appreciable revival of towns, a vigorous new class of urban dwellers, and the development of communal government.

In an effort to introduce some kind of stabilizing force in this period of upheaval, Holy Roman Emperor Charles IV of Luxembourg issued his famous edict, the *Golden Bull* (1356), intended as a fundamental statute for the government of the Holy Roman Empire. The chief purpose of the Bull, as stated in its preface, was to eliminate as far as possible the civil and private wars which were sapping the strength of the German states. A major source of these conflicts—the rivalry between great feudal houses for the imperial crown—was to be done away with by regulating the imperial elections: the seven legally constituted electors were specifically designated; time limits were set for assemblying in Frankfort on the Main and accomplishing the elections; and the principle of majority decision was decreed. In carefully protecting the rights, privileges, territories, and revenues of the electors in perpetuity, Charles IV hoped that the electors might function as a kind of imperial advisory board for assuring peace and stability in Germany. However, the regulations governing private wars proved ineffectual, as is indicated by the widespread incidence of private war and the inability of the emperor to check it quickly. Nonetheless, the electoral procedure which the *Golden Bull* established remained in practice, with slight modifications, until the end of the Empire in 1806, and the peaceful intents of Emperor Charles IV, if by no means realized, were at least kept as an aim of the imperial administration. In effect, the *Golden Bull* recognized that Germany was not a united state but indicated a hope that the coöperation of its great magnates, the electors, would ensure its peace and prosperity. Throughout the document no mention was made of the pope, although the heirs of the electors were to be instructed "from their seventh years" in Italian as well as in Czech and German. This certainly implied a decline of imperial interest in Italy and the exhausting struggle with the pope. Implicit also was the decay of the medieval ideal that a revived Roman Empire should direct the political destinies of the Christian world. Within a century and a half the concomitant ideal of one Catholic Church unifying Christianity was also to be lost.

Inasmuch as we [Charles IV], through the office by which we possess the imperial dignity, are doubly—both as emperor and by the electoral right which we enjoy—bound to put an end to future danger of discords among the electors themselves, to whose number we, as king of Bohemia are known to belong: we have promulgated, decreed and recommended for ratification, the subjoined laws for the purpose of cherishing unity among the electors, and of bringing about a unanimous election, and of closing all approach to the aforesaid detestable discord and to the various dangers which arise from it. This we have done in our solemn court at Nurem-

Text: Ernest F. Henderson (trans. and ed.), *Select Historical Documents of the Middle Ages* (London: G. Bell & Sons, Ltd., 1896), pp. 221-23, 229-31, 242-44.

berg, in session with all the electoral princes, ecclesiastical and secular, and amid a numerous multitude of other princes, counts, barons, magnates, nobles and citizens; after mature deliberation, from the fulness of our imperial power; sitting on the throne of our imperial majesty, adorned with the imperial bands, insignia and diadem; in the year of our Lord 1356, in the 9th Indiction, on the 4th day before the Ides of January, in the 10th year of our reign as king, the 1st as emperor.

What sort of escort the electors should have, and by whom furnished.

We decree, and, by the present imperial and ever valid edict, do sanction of certain knowledge and from the plenitude of the imperial power: that whenever, and so often as in future, necessity or occasion shall arise for the election of a king of the Romans and prospective emperor, and the prince electors, according to ancient and laudable custom, are obliged to journey to such election, —each prince elector, if, and whenever, he is called upon to do this, shall be bound to escort any of his fellow prince electors or the envoys whom they shall send to this election, through his lands, territories and districts, and even as much beyond them as he shall be able; and to lend them escort without guile on their way to the city in which such election is to be held, and also in returning from it. This he shall do under pain of perjury and the loss, for that time only, of the vote which he was about to have in such election; which penalty, indeed, we decree that he or they who shall prove rebellious or negligent in furnishing the aforesaid escort shall, by the very act, incur.

We furthermore decree, and we command all other princes holding fiefs from the holy Roman empire, whatever the service they have to perform,—also all counts, barons, knights, noble and common followers, citizens and communities of castles, cities and districts of the holy empire: that at this same time—when, namely, an election is to take place of king of the Romans and prospective emperor—they shall, without guile, in the manner aforesaid, escort through their territories and as far beyond as they can, any prince elector demanding from them, or any one of them, help of this kind, or the envoys whom, as has been explained before, he shall have sent to that election. But if any persons shall presume to run counter to this our decree they shall, by the act itself, incur the following penalties: all princes and counts, barons, noble knights and followers, and all nobles acting counter to it, shall be considered guilty of perjury and deprived of all the fiefs which they hold of the holy Roman empire and of any lords whatever, and also of all their possessions no matter from whom they hold them. All cities and guilds, moreover, presuming to act counter to the foregoing, shall similarly be considered guilty of perjury, and likewise shall be altogether deprived of all their rights, liberties, privileges and favours obtained from the holy empire, and both in their persons and in all their possessions shall incur the imperial bann and proscription. . . .

Concerning the election of a king of the Romans.

After, moreover, the oft-mentioned electors or their envoys shall have entered the city of Frankfort, they shall, straightway on the following day at dawn, in the church of St. Bartholomew the apostle, in the presence of all of them, cause a mass to be sung to the Holy Spirit, that the Holy Spirit himself may illumine their hearts and infuse the light of his virtue into their senses; so that they, armed with his protection, may be able to elect a just, good and useful man as king of the Romans and future emperor, and as a safeguard for the people of Christ. After such mass has been performed all those electors or their envoys shall approach the altar on which that mass has been celebrated, and there the ecclesiastical prince electors, before the gospel of St. John: "In the beginning was the word," which must there be placed before them, shall place their hands with reverence upon their breasts. But the secular prince electors shall actually touch the said gospel with their hands. And all of them, with all their followers, shall stand there unarmed. And the archbishop of Mainz shall give to them the form of the oath, and he together with them, and they, or the envoys of the absent ones, together with him, shall take the oath in common. . . .

Such oath having been taken by the electors or their envoys in the aforesaid form and manner, they shall then proceed to the election. And from now on they shall not disperse from the said city of Frankfort until the majority of them shall have elected a temporal head for the world and for the Christian people; a king, namely, of the Romans and prospective emperor. But if they shall fail to do this within thirty days, counting continuously from the day when they took the aforesaid oath: when those thirty days are over, from that time on they shall live on bread and water, and by no means leave the aforesaid city unless first through them, or the majority of them, a ruler or temporal head of the faithful shall have been elected, as was said before.

Moreover after they, or the majority of them, shall have made their choice in that place, such election shall in future be considered and looked upon as if it had been unanimously carried through by all of them, no one dissenting. And if any one of the electors or their aforesaid envoys should happen for a time to be detained and to be absent or late, provided he arrive before the said election has been consummated, we decree that he shall be admitted to the election in the stage at which it was at the actual time of his coming. And since by ancient approved and laudable custom what follows has always been observed inviolately, therefore we also do establish and decree by the plenitude of the imperial power that he who shall have, in the aforesaid manner, been elected king of the Romans, shall, directly after such election shall have been held, and before he shall attend to any other cases or matters by virtue of his imperial office, without delay or contradiction, confirm and approve, by his letters and seals, to each and all of the elector princes, ecclesiastical and secular, who are known to be the nearer members of the holy empire, all their privileges, charters, rights, liberties, ancient customs, and also their dignities and whatever they shall have obtained and possessed from the empire before the day of the election. And he shall renew to them all the above after he shall have been crowned with the imperial adornments. Moreover, the elected king shall make such confirmation to each prince elector in particular, first as king, then, renewing it, under his title as emperor; and, in these matters, he shall be bound by no means to impede either those same princes in general or any one of them in particular, but rather to promote them with his favour and without guile. . . .

Concerning the revocation of privileges.

Moreover we establish, and by this perpetual imperial edict do decree, that no privileges or charters concerning any rights, favours, immunities, customs or other things, conceded, of our own accord or otherwise, under any form of words, by us or our predecessors of blessed memory the divine emperors or kings of the Romans, or about to be conceded in future by us or our successors the Roman emperors and kings, to any persons of whatever standing, pre-eminence or dignity, or to the corporation of cities, towns, or any places: shall or may, in any way at all, derogate from the liberties, jurisdictions, rights, honours or dominions of the ecclesiastical and secular prince electors; even if in such privileges and charters of any persons, whatever their pre-eminence, dignity or standing, as has been said, or of corporations of this kind, it shall have been, or shall be in future, expressly cautioned that they shall not be revokable unless, concerning these very points and the whole tenor included in them, special mention word for word and in due order shall be made in such revocation. For such privileges and charters, if, and in as far as, they are considered to derogate in any way from the liberties, jurisdictions, rights, honours or dominions of the said prince electors, or any one of them, in so far we revoke them of certain knowledge and cancel them, and decree, from the plenitude of our imperial power, that they shall be considered and held to be revoked.

Concerning those from whom, as being unworthy, their feudal possessions are taken away.

In very many places the vassals and feudatories of lords unseasonably renounce or resign, verbally and fraudulently, fiefs or benefices which they hold from those same lords. And, having made such resignation, they maliciously challenge those same lords, and declare enmity against them, subsequently inflicting grave harm upon them. And, under pretext of war or hostility, they again invade and occupy benefices and fiefs which they had thus renounced, and hold possession of them. Therefore we establish, by the present ever-to-be-valid decree, that such renunciation or resignation shall be considered as not having taken place, unless it shall have been freely and actually made by them in such way that possession of such benefices and fiefs shall be personally and actually given over to those same lords so fully that, at no future time, shall they, either through themselves or through others, by sending challenges, trouble those same lords as to the goods, fiefs or benefices resigned; nor shall they lend counsel, aid or favour to this end. He who acts otherwise, and in any way invades his lords as to benefices and fiefs, resigned or not resigned, or disturbs them, or brings harm upon them, or furnishes counsel, aid or favour to those doing this: shall, by the act itself, lose such fiefs and benefices, shall be dishonoured and shall underlie the bann of the empire; and no approach or return to such fiefs or benefices shall be open to him at any time in future, nor may the same be granted to him anew under any conditions; and a concession of them, or an investiture which takes place contrary to this, shall have no force. Finally, by virtue of this present edict, we decree that he or they who, not having made such resignation as we have described, acting fraudulently against his or their lords, shall knowingly invade them—whether a challenge has previously been sent or has been omitted,—shall, by the act itself, incur all the aforesaid punishments.

84 RAMON MUTANER, *CHRONICLE:* IN SEARCH OF A CHRISTIAN KINGDOM—SPAIN

Medieval Spain and Portugal were subject to three major political stresses. The first was the struggle for national identity, which was waged under the leadership of Christian monarchs who were constantly embroiled with powerful and rebellious feudal lords and beset by dynastic conflicts. Such difficulties were common to the other emergent national states of western Europe, but the Spanish peoples labored under a second and unique burden. For centuries they were absorbed in a continual crusade aimed at breaking the power of the Moors on the Iberian peninsula and expelling, along with the Moors, the faith of Islam. Both national identity and Christian triumph were endangered by a third condition; the several independent kingdoms which constituted medieval Christian Spain were almost as willing to war with one another as with the Muslims.

After a swift conquest of almost the whole of the Iberian peninsula, the Moors—a mixture of Arabs and North African Berbers—had remained the chief military and cultural force in Spain for more than three centuries (711-1031). Christian Spain had been compressed into the mountainous north and west and divided politically into the principalities of Catalonia, Navarre, Leon, Castile, Aragon, and Portugal. Under these circumstances, the Christian counteroffensive against the Moors came about as a surprising reversal of history, dependent partly upon a breakdown of Muslim unity in Spain and the assistance of the papacy. However, its success was owed chiefly to the vigorous encouragement of the Spanish Church, the tenacity of the Spanish kings, and the valor of Spanish chivalry.

As the Christian frontier was pushed southward, new kingdoms were instated—such as Majorca, Valencia, and Murcia—but they were almost immediately dominated by Aragon, Castile, or Portugal, three European states of rising importance in the thirteenth century. Their rulers were autocrats, whose authority was nevertheless occasionally checked by their various *cortés*, that is, assemblies of clergy, nobles, and burgers, comparable to the medieval English Parliament or French Estates-General. Aragon became so powerful—thanks to the fleet of its dependency, Catalonia—that Aragonese King Pedro III (1236-1285) was able to enforce his claims to the crown of Sicily against French and papal objections in 1282.

The exploits of Pedro's son, James (or Jaime) II (c. 1260-1327) are recounted below in selections from the *Chronicle* of Muntaner, a courtier of the Aragonese king. After brief remarks which suggest the influential position of Aragon in Italian affairs and the power of its fleet, the selection deals with internal affairs in Spain and supplies ample evidence of the bickerings, the warfare, and the intrigues among Castile, Aragon, the other Christian kingdoms, and the Moors of the Kingdom of Granada. In the romanticized reports of fighting, particularly in the duel between the Aragonese prince *(Infante)* and the Moorish prince, we find the spirit of chivalry and martial valor which characterizes the history and legend of medieval Spain.

Spain was not finally unified until the marriage of Ferdinand of Aragon and Isabella of Castile in 1479, and Granada, the last Moorish stronghold, was not surrendered until 1492. At this propitious moment the peoples of Spain and Portugal, whose national identities had been forged in the *Reconquista* (reconquest), had solved three great medieval problems and were prepared to turn to the new Age of Discovery.

When the Lord King of Aragon [James II] saw that he was at peace with all the world, he . . . went, a first time, to see the Pope in Rome, after peace had been made. And the Pope and the cardinals and all the Romans showed him much honour, and also much honour was shown him at Genoa and at Pisa. But, at this visit, he did not obtain peace between King Charles [of Naples] and the King [Fadrique] of Sicily. He returned to Catalonia and took my Lady the Queen with him, as I have told you already.

And then, some time later, the Lord King of Aragon sent a message to the admiral in Sicily, to come to Catalonia, and the admiral came to him at once. And then not much time passed

Text: Lady Goodenough (trans.), *The Chronicle of Muntaner* (London: The Hakluyt Society, 1921), II, 448-51, 453-55, 587-93. Reprinted by permission of Cambridge University Press, New York.

before the Lord King, with a great fleet, departed from Catalonia, to go to the Pope, to treat fully of the peace between King Fadrique and King Charles. . . .

And the Lord King went and laboured in this journey, yet he could never arrange a peace between King Charles, his father-in-law, and King Fadrique, his brother, before he returned to Catalonia. His people were greatly pleased that God had sent him back safe and sound, and my Lady the Queen likewise.

And so I must cease to speak to you of the affairs in Sicily and must turn to speak to you of King En Fernando of Castile [i.e., Ferdinand IV] who, being ill-advised, defied the Lord King of Aragon, not long after peace was made with King Charles. . . .

And when the Lord King of Aragon considered in his heart the challenge the King of Castile had sent him, he felt it a great insult and said it was necessary to make him repent of it. And he commanded the Lord Infante En Pedro to get ready with a thousand armed horse and fifty thousand almugavars, and to invade Castile through Aragon, and he would, likewise, invade the Kingdom of Murcia with a great force. Should I tell you much about it? As the Lord King had dictated, so it was accomplished. The Lord Infante En Pedro invaded Castile with full a thousand Catalan and Aragonese horse and full fifty thousand men afoot. And he entered full nine journeys into Castile, so that he besieged the city of Leon and discharged catapults against it.

And so I must let the Lord Infante En Pedro be, who holds besieged the city of Leon which is well within Castile, eight journeys from Aragon, and must turn again to speak to you of the Lord King of Aragon who is invading the Kingdom of Murcia and enters it by land and by sea.

And the first place in the Kingdom of Murcia to which he came was Alicante and he attacked the town and took it. . . .

Then, when the Lord King had settled Alicante, he went to Elche and besieged it and discharged catapults against it. And during the time he was holding Elche besieged, he took all the valley of Elda and Novelda and of Nompot and Aspe and Petrel and la Mola; and he took Crevillente of which place the alcaide came to him and became his man and vassal. And then he took Abanilla and Callosa and Guardarmar. What shall I tell you? He held Elche besieged so long that he took it; it surrendered to him. And then he took Orihuela and the castle thereof, which Pedro Ruiz de Sent Sabria, who was alcaide there, surrendered to him when he saw that he had taken the town of Orihuela. And it was good that he surrendered the castle without a blow and without cost, for it is one of the strongest and most royal castles of Spain. And so you can imagine that this knight did a very worthy and courteous thing in thus surrendering the castle to the Lord King. And he took the castle of Montagut and the city of Murcia and Cartagena and Lorca and Molina and many other places which, in truth, for the greater part, it was fit should belong to the Lord King by good right, according to what you have already heard of the conquest of Murcia. And when the Lord King had taken the city of Murcia and the greater part of the Kingdom, he garrisoned the land and left as procurator the noble En Jaime Pedro, his brother, with much good chivalry which he left there with him.

And, when he had returned to the Kingdom of Valencia, news came to him that the Infante En Pedro, his brother, had died of illness at the siege of Leon, and also En Ramon de Anglesola. . . .

And the host departed from Leon with the bodies of the Lord Infante and of En Ramon de Anglesola and returned to Aragon, with banners unfurled. And when they were in Aragon and the Lord King heard the news, he was much displeased at the death of the Lord Infante, and had all done that was due to him, as a good lord should for a dear and virtuous brother. The Lord Infante was much regretted. God, in His mercy, keep his soul, as He should keep that of a good and just and upright lord. . . .

When the Lord King of Aragon had taken the Kingdom of Murcia from King En Fernando of Castile and had devastated much of his territory, the Lord Infante En Pedro of Castile and others of Castile saw that the war with Aragon did them no good and they, and in particular Don Enrique who was very old and wise, negotiated a peace with the Lord King of Aragon; so that peace was made in this manner; that the eldest son of the King of Aragon, called the Infante En Jaime, was to take to wife the daughter of King En Fernando as soon as she was old enough; and they delivered her at once to the Lord King of Aragon, who had her brought up in Aragon. And the Lord King of Aragon gave up the Kingdom of Murcia to King Don Fernando, except what was of his conquest. . . .

And when he had signed the peace, the Lord King of Aragon thought that, as he was at peace with all peoples, he would attack the Saracens, namely the King of Granada, who had broken the truce when the King of Castile had left him; therefore he wished to take a complete revenge for this.

And he arranged with the King of Castile that they should march resolutely against the King of Granada in this manner, that the King of Castile, with all his power, should go and besiege Algeciras de Alhadra, and the Lord King of Aragon should go and besiege the city of Almeria. And so it was ordained and promised by both Kings, that this should be done on a fixed day, and that neither should abandon the war nor his siege without the leave of the other. And this was wisely ordained in order that the King of Granada should be obliged to divide his followers in two parts. And so it was done; the King of Castile went to besiege Algeciras and the Lord King of Aragon, Almeria, which is a very fine city. And the siege lasted full nine months; the Lord King conducted it with catapults and with mangonels and with all the apparel belonging to a siege. The Lord King of Aragon came to it very powerfully apparelled, with many Catalan and Aragonese richs homens and barons. And amongst others came the Lord Infante En Ferrando, son of the Lord King of Mallorca, very richly apparelled with a hundred armed horse and with many men afoot and with galleys and lenys which brought the horses and victuals and companies and catapults. For the Lord King of Mallorca wished him to come to the assistance of the Lord King of Aragon well arrayed at all points, as one who was himself one of the most accomplished knights of the world. And this was well apparent in all the feats which fell to his share in the siege, for, amongst other affairs, he had three times encounters with the Moors and he carried off the palm of chivalry from all men.

It happened one day, on the eve of Saint Bartholomew, that the Moors had all got ready, all there were in the Kingdom of Granada, against the Lord King of Aragon, through the fault of the King of Castile, who raised the siege he was conducting without letting the Lord King of Aragon know anything about it. And it was a great crime of the King of Castile not to let the Lord King of Aragon know that he was raising the siege, for it put the Lord King of Aragon into great hazard; he was surprised by so many people who came upon him, a thing he had not expected. And so all the power of Granada came, on the eve of Saint Bartholomew, upon the host of the Lord King of Aragon. And he, when he saw this great power, marvelled much; but he was nothing dismayed by it, but ordained that the Lord Infante En Ferrando should stay with his company near the city, at a place called the esperonte of Almeria, in order that if anyone should attempt to issue from the city to attack the besiegers whilst he was fighting with the Saracens, the Lord Infante should prevent it. And I wish you to know that it was the most threatened point there was, and therefore the Lord Infante chose it, otherwise he would not have remained there. What shall I tell you? When the Lord King was ready with all his host to attack the host of the Saracens, there came out of Almeria by the esperonte, a son of the King of Guadix with full three hundred horsemen and many afoot, wading through the sea, with water up to the horses' girths. And the cry of alarm arose in the tents of the Lord Infante. And he, very handsomely arrayed, with his company, issued forth with all his chivalry in very good order. And when the Moors had passed the esperonte, this son of the Moorish King, who was an expert knight and one of the handsomest of the world, came on first with a javelin in his hand, crying:—"Ani be ha Soltan!" No other words issued from his mouth. And the Lord Infante asked "What is he saying?" And the interpreters who were near him said:—"My Lord, he says that he is a King's son." Said the Lord Infante:—"He is a King's son, and so, too, am I." And the Lord Infante rushed towards him and before he could get near him, he had killed more than six knights with his own hand and had broken his lance; and then he seized his sword and, sword in hand, made room for himself, until he came to him who was shouting that he was a King's son. And he, seeing him come and knowing that he was the Infante, came towards him and gave him such a blow with his sword that the last quarter of the Infante's shield fell to the ground (and it was a most marvellous blow) and he cried:— "Ani be ha Soltan!" But the Lord Infante gave him such a blow with his sword on the head that he cut it open to the teeth, and he fell dead to the ground. And at once the Saracens were discomfited and those who could return by the esperonte saved their lives, but the others all died and so the Lord Infante overcame those of the city.

And whilst this clamour at the esperonte was going on, the Moors of the host were preparing to attack, and the Lord King wished to attack, but En Guillem de Anglesola and En Asberto de Mediona dismounted and seizing the King's bridle said:—"My Lord, what is this? On no account do this; there are those already in the van who will attack and do it well." The Lord King was so desirous of attacking that his heart was nearly broken. And I tell you that if he had not had those richs homens and other honourable men to hold him back, he would not have refrained, but he could not help himself. And so the van attacked amongst the Moors and vanquished them; and, assuredly, the Moors would have lost all their chivalry on that day, had it not been that the pursuit had to stop, for fear that others might come and attack the besiegers from another side. Nevertheless innumerable Moors died that day, horse and foot; it was the greatest feat ever done and the greatest victory. From that day the Moors so feared the Christians that they dared not resist them. What shall I tell you? The Lord King returned with all his followers, with great joy and gladness, to the tents where they found that the Lord Infante En Ferrando had performed as many feats of arms as Roland could have done, had he been there. And on the following day they celebrated worthily the feast of the blessed Saint Bartholomew, apostle.

And when the King of Granada saw the marvellous deed performed by the Lord King of Aragon and his followers, he held himself for lost, for he had not thought at all that there was so much strenuousness and so much valour in them. And so he chose his messengers, whom he sent to the Lord King of Aragon to tell him that he begged him to raise the siege, for winter was coming upon him; and that he might see well that he was working for people in whom he would find no merit; that the Castilians had raised the siege of Algeciras in order that the King of Aragon and his followers should be killed; that this conquest was not worthy of him; and so he begged him to be pleased to make a truce with him. And he offered always to support him in war against all the men in the world, and again that, for love of him, he would liberate all the Christian captives he had, which was a considerable matter.

And when the Lord King had heard the message, he called his council together and put before them what the King of Granada had sent to tell him. And in the end the advice was that, for three reasons especially, he should return to his country. The first reason was that winter was coming upon him; the other was the great ingratitude the Castilians had shown him; and the third was the surrendering of the Christian captives, which was a greater thing than if he had taken two cities of Almeria. And so it was agreed and the truce confirmed.

And so the Lord King had all his followers collected with all their property. And when they were collected the Lord King, with all his followers and all their property, returned, some by sea and some by land to the Kingdom of Valencia. And so you may understand whether the Lord King of Aragon is desirous of increasing and multiplying the Holy Catholic faith, when he went to conduct a siege in a conquest which was none of his. You may all be certain that, if the Kingdom of Granada had been of his conquest, it would long ago have belonged to the Christians.

And when this was done the Lord King of Aragon returned to Valencia and the Lord Infante En Ferrando, with his galleys and his followers, returned to Roussillon, to the Lord King his father, who had great joy in seeing him, and especially as he had so well performed his tasks.

85 GIOVANNI VILLANI, *CHRONICLE OF FLORENCE:* THE ITALIAN CITY-STATE

The town as a center of industry, commerce, and local self-government was, by the late Middle Ages, a well-known phenomenon throughout Europe. The greatest urban centers of the north, such as Paris, London, the Flemish communes, and the Baltic ports of the Hansa, were focal points in a powerful network of trade routes capable of surviving the ravages of war, famine, and plague.

However, for the northern merchant princes the Mediterranean remained the foyer of an international trade with the Muslim Near East and, through it, the Orient. This trade, stimulated by the crusades, grew even more extensive and lucrative. The central role which the Mediterranean played in the commercial history of Europe assured the towns of northern Italy of a virtual monopoly in European export and import until the age of exploration. Since they were favored by their geographical location, their ancient Roman traditions, their close association with the Byzantine Empire and the crusader kingdoms, it is not surprising that the Italian cities were leaders in the revival of trade, industry, and municipal government.

The sea-born commerce and war fleets of Genoa and Venice made these cities not only wealthy but also politically strong enough to dominate the shattered Byzantine Empire throughout the last century of its history. Milan and its neighbors dominated the carrying trade over the Alpine passes, and Florence early became the industrial center of Italy and a major European metropolis. Florentine bankers along with other Italian financial houses ignored the medieval Church's restrictions against usury and created new instruments of international credit and exchange to serve the quickening commercial climate.

The intense economic life of the Italian cities was matched and often darkened by the violence of their political history. Almost from the beginning, Italian municipal governments, which depended originally upon an oligarchical union of the landed nobility and the rich merchant guilds, were rent by family and party feuds which erupted into riots and vicious street fighting. These conflicts were intensified by class conflicts, as the lesser guilds of tradesmen and the general populace began to make their force felt in local politics. The bloody internal dissensions were aggravated by constant wars between the various cities on the Italian landscape and by their involvement in the conflict between the Holy Roman Empire and the papacy. By the thirteenth century there developed throughout Italy factions called Guelphs, who in general supported the papacy, and Ghibellines, who in general supported the empire. The splintering of these factions produced further political divisions such as the "Whites" and "Blacks" of Florence in the time of Dante.

The intense political and social life of the Italian city-states is recorded in Villani's *Chronicle of Florence*, a history of the city from its Roman beginnings to the fourteenth century. Although the conflicts which he describes are all too typical of northern Italian affairs, it is well to remember that they coincide with a vigorous revival of intellectual and artistic genius which foretells the coming of the Italian Renaissance, a period which also included political violence and class warfare.

How the parties of the Guelfs and Ghibellines arose in Florence.

In the year of Christ 1215, M. Gherardo Orlandi being Podestà in Florence, one M. Bondelmonte dei Bondelmonti, a noble citizen of Florence, had promised to take to wife a maiden of the house of the Amidei, honourable and noble citizens; and afterwards as the said M. Bondelmonte, who was very charming and a good horseman, was riding through the city, a lady of the house of the Donati called to him, reproaching him as to the lady to whom he was betrothed, that she was not beautiful or worthy of him, and saying: "I have kept this my daughter for you;" whom she showed to him, and she was most beautiful; and immediately by the inspiration of the devil he was so taken by her, that he was betrothed and wedded to her, for which thing the kinsfolk of the first betrothed lady, being assembled together, and grieving over the shame which M. Bondelmonte had done to them, were filled with the accursed indignation, whereby the city of Florence was destroyed and divided. For many houses of the nobles swore together to bring shame upon the said M. Bondelmonte, in revenge for these wrongs. And being in council among themselves, after what fashion they should punish him, whether by beating or killing, Mosca de' Lamberti said the evil word: 'Thing done has an end'; to wit, that he should be slain; and so it was done; for on the morning of Easter of the Resurrection the Amidei of San Stefano assembled in their house, and the said M. Bondelmonte coming from Oltrarno, nobly arrayed in new white apparel, and upon a white palfrey, arriving at the foot of the Ponte Vecchio on this side, just at the foot of the pillar where was the statue of Mars, the said M. Bondelmonte was dragged from his horse by Schiatta degli Uberti, and by Mosca Lamberti and Lambertuccio degli Amidei assaulted and smitten, and by Oderigo Fifanti his veins were opened and he was brought to his end; and there was with them one of the counts of Gangalandi. For the which thing the city rose in arms and tumult; and this death of M. Bondelmonte was the cause and beginning of the accursed parties of Guelfs and Ghibellines in Florence, albeit long before there were factions among the noble citizens and the said parties existed by reason of the strifes and questions between the Church and the Empire; but by reason of the death of the said M. Bondelmonte all the families of the nobles and the other citizens of Florence were divided, and some held with the Bondelmonti, who took the side of the Guelfs, and were its leaders, and some with the Uberti, who were the leaders of the Ghibellines, whence followed much evil and disaster to our city, as hereafter shall be told; and it is believed that it will never have an end, if God do not cut it short. And surely it shows that the enemy of the human race, for the sins of the Florentines, had power in that idol of Mars, which the pagan Florentines of old were wont to worship, that at the foot of his statue such a murder was

Text: Rose E. Selfe (trans.), *Villani's Chronicle*, ed. Philip H. Wicksteed (London: Archibald Constable & Co., Ltd., 1906), pp. 121-25, 140-46, 149-50, 152-54.

committed, whence so much evil followed to the city of Florence. The accursed names of the Guelf and Ghibelline parties are said to have arisen first in Germany by reason that two great barons of that country were at war together, and had each a strong castle the one over against the other, and the one had the name of Guelf, and the other of Ghibelline, and the war lasted so long, that all the Germans were divided, and one held to one side, and the other to the other; and the strife even came as far as to the court of Rome, and all the court took part in it, and the one side was called that of Guelf, and the other that of Ghibelline; and so the said names continued in Italy. . . .

. . . And many . . . families of honourable citizens and popolani held some with one side, and some with the other, and they changed with the times in mind and in party, which would be too long a matter to relate. And for the said cause the accursed parties first began in Florence, albeit before that there had been a division secretly among the noble citizens, whereof some loved the rule of the Church [i.e., the Guelphs] and some that of the Empire [i.e., the Ghibellines]; nevertheless they were all agreed as to the state and well-being of the commonwealth. . . .

How the Guelf party was first driven from Florence by the Ghibellines and the forces of the Emperor Frederick.

In the said times when Frederick [II of the Holy Roman Empire] was in Lombardy, having been deposed from the title of Emperor by Pope Innocent, as we have said, in so far as he could he sought to destroy in Tuscany and in Lombardy the faithful followers of Holy Church, in all the cities where he had power. And first he began to demand hostages from all the cities of Tuscany, and took them from both Ghibellines and Guelfs, and sent them to Samminiato del Tedesco; but when this was done, he released the Ghibellines and retained the Guelfs, which were afterwards abandoned as poor prisoners, and abode long time in Samminiato as beggars. And forasmuch as our city of Florence in those times was not among the least notable and powerful of Italy, he desired especially to vent his spleen against it, and to increase the accursed parties of the Guelfs and Ghibellines, which had begun long time before through the death of M. Bondelmonte, and before, as we have already shown. But albeit ever since this the said parties had continued among the nobles of Florence (who were also ever and again at war among themselves by reason of their private enmities), and albeit they were divided into the said parties, each holding with his own, they which were called the Guelfs loving the side of the Pope and of Holy Church, and they which were called the Ghibellines loving and favouring the Emperor and his allies, nevertheless, the people and commonwealth had been maintained in unity to the well-being and honour, and good estate of the republic. But now the said Emperor sent ambassadors and letters to the family of the Uberti, which were heads of his party, and their allies which were called Ghibellines, inviting them to drive their enemies, which were called Guelfs, from the city, and offering them aid of his horsemen; and this caused the Uberti to begin dissension and civil strife in Florence, whence the city began to be disordered, and the nobles and all the people to be divided, some holding to one party, and some to the other; and in divers parts of the city there was fighting long time. Among the other places, the chief was at the houses of the Uberti, which were where the great palace of the people now is. They gathered there with their allies, and fought against the Guelfs of the sesto of San Piero Scheraggio, whereof were leaders the family dal Bagno, called Bagnesi, and the Pulci, and the Guidalotti, and all the allies of the Guelfs of that sesto; and also the Guelfs of Oltrarno passing over the mill-dams, came to succour them when they were attacked by the Uberti. . . . Thus it came to pass that the said frays endured long time, and there was fighting at barricades from street to street, and from one tower to another (for there were many in Florence in these times, 100 cubits and more in height), and with mangonels and other engines they fought together by day and by night. And in the midst of this strife and fighting the Emperor Frederick sent into Florence King Frederick, his bastard son, with 1,600 horsemen of his German followers. When the Ghibellines heard that they were nigh unto Florence, they took courage fighting with more force and boldness against the Guelfs, which had no allies, nor were expecting any succour, forasmuch as the Church was at Lyons on the Rhone beyond the mountains, and the power of Frederick was beyond measure great in all parts of Italy. And on this occasion the Ghibellines used a device of war; for at the house of the Uberti the greater part of the Ghibelline forces assembled, and when the fight began at the places of battle set forth above, they went in a mass to oppose the Guelfs, and in this wise they overcame them well-nigh in every part of the city, save in their own neighbourhood against the barricades of the Guidalotti and the Bagnesi, which endured more stoutly; and to that place the Guelfs repaired, and all the forces of the Ghibellines against them. At last, the Guelfs saw themselves to be hard pressed, and heard that Frederick's knights were already in Florence (King Frederick having already entered with his followers on Sunday morning), yet they held out until the following Wednesday. Then, not being able longer to resist the forces of the Ghibellines, they abandoned the defence, and departed from the city on the night of S. Mary Candlemas in the year of Christ 1248. When the Guelf party were driven from Florence, the nobles of that party withdrew, some of them to the fortress of Montevarchi in Valdarno, and some to the fortress of Capraia; and Pelago, and Ristonchio, and Magnale, up to Cascia, were held by the Guelfs, and were called the League; and therein they made war against the city and the territory around Florence. Other popolani of that party repaired to their farms and to their friends in the country. The Ghibellines which remained masters in Florence, with the forces and the horsemen of the Emperor Frederick, changed the ruling of the city after their mind, and caused thirty-six fortresses of the Guelfs to be destroyed, palaces and great towers, among the which the most noble was that of the Tosinghi upon the Mercato Vecchio, called the Palace. . . . And note, that since the city of Florence had been rebuilt, not one house had been destroyed, and the said accursed destruction thereof was then begun by the Ghibellines. And they ordained that of the Emperor Frederick's followers there should remain 1,800 German horsemen in their pay, whereof Count Giordano was captain. It came to pass that in the same year when the Guelfs were driven from Florence, they which were at Montevarchi were attacked by the German troops which were in garrison in the fortress of Gangareta in the market place of the said Montevarchi, and there was a fierce battle of but few people, as far as the Arno, between the Guelf refugees from Florence, and the Germans. In the end the Germans were discomfited, and a great part thereof slain and taken prisoners, and this was in the year of Christ 1248. . . .

How the Primo Popolo was formed in Florence to be a defence against the violence and attacks of the Ghibellines.

. . . [In 1250 in] Florence there was great contention amongst the citizens, inasmuch as the Ghibellines, who ruled the land, crushed the people with insupportable burdens, taxes, and imposts; and with little to show for it, for the Guelfs were already established up and down in the territory of Florence, holding many fortresses and making war upon the city. And besides all this, they of the house of the Uberti and all the other Ghibelline nobles tyrannized over the people with ruthless extortion and violence and outrage. Wherefore the good citizens of Florence, tumultuously gathering together, assembled themselves at the church of San Firenze; but not daring to remain there, because of the power of the Uberti, they went and took their stand at the church of the Minor Friars at Santa Croce, and remaining there under arms they dared not to return to their homes, lest when they had laid down their arms they should be broken by the Uberti and the other nobles and condemned by the magistrates. So they went under arms to the houses of the Anchioni of San Lorenzo, which were very strong, and there, still under arms, they forcibly elected thirty-six corporals of the people, and took away the rule from the Podestà, which was then in Florence, and removed all the officials. And this done, with no further conflict they ordained and created a popular government with certain new ordinances and statutes. They elected captain of the people M. Uberto da Lucca, and he was the first captain of Florence, and they elected twelve Ancients of the people, two for each sesto, to guide the people and counsel the said captain, and they were to meet in the houses of the Badia over the gate which goes to Santa Margherita, and to return to their own homes to eat and sleep; and this was done on the twentieth day of October, the year of Christ 1250. And on this day the said captain distributed twenty standards amongst the people, giving them to certain corporals divided according to companies of arms and districts, including sundry parishes, in order that when need were every man should arm himself and draw to the standard of his company, and then with the said standards draw to the said captain of the people. And they had a bell made which the said captain kept in the Lion's Tower. And the chief standard of the people, which was the captain's, was dimidiated white and red. . . .

How the Popolo of Florence peaceably restored the Guelfs to Florence.

The same night that the Emperor Frederick [II] died [1250], the Podestà who ruled for him in Florence, died also, who was named Messer Rinieri di Montemerlo; for, as he slept in his bed, there fell upon him of the vaulting from the roof of the chamber, which was in the house of the Abati. And this was a sure sign that in the city of Florence his lordship was to be ended, and this came to pass very soon; for the common people having risen in Florence against the violence and outrages of the Ghibelline nobles, as we have said, and tidings coming to Florence of the death of the said Frederick, a few days after, the people of Florence recalled and restored to Florence the party of the Guelfs who had been banished thence, causing them to make peace with the Ghibellines, and this was the seventh day of January, the year of Christ 1250.

How at the time of the said Popolo the Florentines discomfited the men of Pistoia, and afterwards banished certain families of the Ghibellines from Florence.

Greatly did the party for the Church and the Guelf party rejoice throughout all Italy at the death of the Emperor; and the party for the Empire, and the Ghibellines were brought low, inasmuch as Pope Innocent returned from beyond the mountains with his court to Rome, bringing aid to the faithful followers of the Church. It came to pass that in the month of July, in the year of Christ 1251, the people and commonwealth of Florence gathered a host against the city of Pistoia, which had rebelled against them, and fought with the said inhabitants of Pistoia, and discomfited them at Mount Robolini with great loss in slain and prisoners of the men of Pistoia. And at that time Messer Uberto da Mandella of Milan was Podestà of Florence. And because the government of the Popolo was not pleasing to the greater part of the Ghibelline families in Florence, forasmuch as it seemed to them that they favoured the Guelfs more than was pleasing to them, and as in past times they were used to do violence, and to be tyrannical, relying on the Emperor, therefore they were even now unwilling to follow the people and the commonwealth on the said expedition against Pistoia, rather did they both in word and in deed oppose it through factious hatred; forasmuch as Pistoia was ruled in those days by the Ghibelline party; whereby was caused so great mistrust, that when the host returned victorious from Pistoia, the said Ghibelline families in Florence were banished and sent forth from the city by the people of Florence, the said month of July, 1251. And the heads of the Ghibellines in Florence being banished, the people and the Guelfs who remained in the lordship of Florence, changed the arms of the commonwealth of Florence; and whereas of old they bore the field red and the lily white, they now made on the contrary the field white and the lily red; and the Ghibellines retained the former standard, but the ancient standard of the commonwealth dimidiated white and red, to wit, the standard that went with the host upon the carroccio, never was changed. . . .

The Intellectual Synthesis

86 ST. THOMAS AQUINAS, *SUMMA THEOLOGICA* AND *SUMMA CONTRA GENTILES*: MEDIEVAL SCHOLASTICISM

The term "Middle Ages" originated in the seventeenth century, when literary men first used it to note the period between the fall of Roman civilization and the era of immense artistic and intellectual activity known as the Renaissance. To these men medieval times connoted a dark age of superstition and barbarism. Such popular conceptions are historically inaccurate. Our ancestors were not barbarians struggling blindly forward, unguided by civilization, but were enterprising, intelligent, civilized people who were repeatedly stimulated by highly sophisticated influences. Throughout the medieval era the Church served as a stabilizing force; from the Carolingian period onward the progress of art and learning was impelled successively by the revival of Latin classics and the writings of the Latin Church Fathers, by the new translations of the Greek philosophers, and by the introduction of Arabic science into Christian Europe. The scholarly influences filtering in from Moorish Spain and the Near East further broadened the intellectual horizon. Medieval Europe contained a forward-moving, dynamic culture which by the end of the thirteenth century had surpassed the level of Graeco-Roman civilization.

The task of accommodating the newly introduced pagan learning to the theology of Christian tradition fell to a brilliant line of medieval scholars—notably Pierre Abélard (1079-1142), Albertus Magnus (1193?-1280), St. Thomas Aquinas (1225?-1274), St. Bonaventure (1221-1274), and Duns Scotus (c. 1265-c. 1308)—whose intellectual discipline came to be known as *Scholasticism.* Unlike the modern scholar who confines himself to a limited field of study, the medieval Scholastic took all knowledge as his province and attempted to reconcile apparent contradictions between knowledge based on reason (in the Greek sense) and knowledge based on Christian faith. At the outset of the Scholastic era, pagan philosophy was absolutely subordinate to theology: either a scholar refused to endorse any Aristotelian tenet which was contrary to faith, or, in the words of Abélard, restricted himself to "analyzing the basis of our faith through illustrations based on human understanding." Then arrived the high point of medieval Scholasticism in the thirteenth century, when the old Christianity and the new secular learning were allied. From the pen of the greatest Scholastic of them all, St. Thomas Aquinas, came a theology harmonizing the truth of reason and the truth of revelation: reason, according to St. Thomas, starts from sense-data and gives up knowledge of the existence, unity, goodness, and "reasonableness" of God and His creation; faith rests on revelation and Scriptural authority and attains to a knowledge of God as a purely spiritual Being (e.g., the doctrine of the Trinity, though rationally incomprehensible, must be accepted on faith). Thus, in the systems of the great schoolmen the rights of reason are fully established and acknowledged.

Unknowingly, however, St. Thomas and his contemporaries were exposing the breach between reason and faith. The harmony of the two eventually proved debatable, and a reaction set in; more and more fields of knowledge were withdrawn from the test of reason. Scriptural authority was stringently reimposed, setting the stage for the Protestant Revolt and the open conflict between religion and science which followed it.

Below are printed selections from St. Thomas Aquinas' major works, *Summa Theologica* and *Summa Contra Gentiles*. In the first, St. Thomas turns to the question of whether the existence of God can be rationally proved; he finds that both reason and faith have a role in the search for truth. In the selection from *Summa Contra Gentiles* he asserts that happiness is imperfect if one's knowledge of God depends on faith alone or upon reason alone. True happiness comes only with the unity of intellectual and spiritual knowledge.

St. Thomas Aquinas was born in the village of Aquino in the Kingdom of Naples, was educated at the University of Naples, joined the Dominican order of friars, and became a major figure at the University of Paris, then the greatest school of theology and philosophy.

Summa Theologica

The existence of God and other like truths about God, which can be known by natural reason, are not articles of faith, but are preambles to the articles; for faith presupposes natural knowledge, even as grace presupposes nature and perfection the perfectible. Nevertheless, there is nothing to prevent a man, who cannot grasp a proof, from accepting, as a matter of faith, something which in itself is capable of being scientifically known and demonstrated. . . .

Whether God Exists? . . .

Objection 1. It seems that God does not exist; because if one of two contraries be infinite, the other would be altogether destroyed. But the name *God* means that He is infinite goodness. If, therefore, God existed, there would be no evil discoverable; but there is evil in the world. Therefore God does not exist.

Obj. 2. Further, it is superfluous to suppose that what can be accounted for by a few principles has been produced by many. But it seems that everything we see in the world can be accounted for by other principles, supposing God did not exist. For all natural things can be reduced to one principle, which is nature; and all voluntary things can be reduced to one principle, which is human reason, or will. Therefore there is no need to suppose God's existence.

On the contrary, It is said in the person of God: *I am Who am* (*Exod.* iii. 14).

I answer that, The existence of God can be proved in five ways.

The first and more manifest way is the argument from motion. It is certain, and evident to our senses, that in the world some things are in motion. Now whatever is moved is moved by another, for nothing can be moved except it is in potentiality to that towards which it is moved; whereas a thing moves inasmuch as it is in act. For motion is nothing else than the reduction of something from potentiality to actuality. But nothing can be reduced from potentiality to actuality, except by something in a state of actuality. Thus that which is actually hot, as fire, makes wood, which is potentially hot, to be actually hot, and thereby moves and changes it.

Text: Anton C. Pegis (ed.), *Introduction to Saint Thomas Aquinas* (New York: The Modern Library; London: Burns & Oates, Ltd.). Copyright 1945 by Random House, Inc. Pp. 24-27, 453-54.

Now it is not possible that the same thing should be at once in actuality and potentiality in the same respect, but only in different respects. For what is actually hot cannot simultaneously be potentially hot; but it is simultaneously potentially cold. It is therefore impossible that in the same respect and in the same way a thing should be both mover and moved, *i.e.*, that it should move itself. Therefore, whatever is moved must be moved by another. If that by which it is moved be itself moved, then this also must needs be moved by another, and that by another again. But this cannot go on to infinity, because then there would be no first mover, and, consequently, no other mover, seeing that subsequent movers move only inasmuch as they are moved by the first mover; as the staff moves only because it is moved by the hand. Therefore it is necessary to arrive at a first mover, moved by no other; and this everyone understands to be God.

The second way is from the nature of efficient cause. In the world of sensible things we find there is an order of efficient causes. There is no case known (neither is it, indeed, possible) in which a thing is found to be the efficient cause of itself; for so it would be prior to itself, which is impossible. Now in efficient causes it is not possible to go on to infinity, because in all efficient causes following in order, the first is the cause of the intermediate cause, and the intermediate is the cause of the ultimate cause, whether the intermediate cause be several, or one only. Now to take away the cause is to take away the effect. Therefore, if there be no first cause among efficient causes, there will be no ultimate, nor any intermediate, cause. But if in efficient causes it is possible to go on to infinity, there will be no first efficient cause, neither will there be an ultimate effect, nor any intermediate efficient causes; all of which is plainly false. Therefore it is necessary to admit a first efficient cause, to which everyone gives the name of God.

The third way is taken from possibility and necessity, and runs thus. We find in nature things that are possible to be and not to be, since they are found to be generated, and to be corrupted, and consequently, it is possible for them to be and not to be. But it is impossible for these always to exist, for that which can not-be at some time is not. Therefore, if everything can not-be, then at one time there was nothing in existence. Now if this were true, even now there would be nothing in existence, because that which does not exist begins to exist only through something already existing. Therefore, if at one time nothing was in existence, it would have been impossible for anything to have begun to exist; and thus even now nothing would be in existence—which is absurd. Therefore, not all beings are merely possible, but there must exist something the existence of which is necessary. But every necessary thing either has its necessity caused by another, or not. Now it is impossible to go on to infinity in necessary things which have their necessity caused by another, as has been already proved in regard to efficient causes. Therefore we cannot but admit the existence of some being having of itself its own necessity, and not receiving it from another, but rather causing in others their necessity. This all men speak of as God.

The fourth way is taken from the gradation to be found in things. Among beings there are some more and some less good, true, noble, and the like. But *more* and *less* are predicated of different things according as they resemble in their different ways something which is the maximum, as a thing is said to be hotter according as it more nearly resembles that which is hottest; so that there is something which is truest, something best, something noblest, and, consequently, something which is most being, for those things that are greatest in truth are greatest in being, as it is written in *Metaph.* ii. Now the maximum in any genus is the cause of all in that genus, as fire, which is the maximum of heat, is the cause of all hot things, as is said in the same book. Therefore there must also be something which is to all beings the cause of their being, goodness, and every other perfection; and this we call God.

The fifth way is taken from the governance of the world. We see that things which lack knowledge, such as natural bodies, act for an end, and this is evident from their acting always, or nearly always, in the same way, so as to obtain the best result. Hence it is plain that they achieve their end, not fortuitously, but designedly. Now whatever lacks knowledge cannot move towards an end, unless it be directed by some being endowed with knowledge and intelligence; as the arrow is directed by the archer. Therefore some intelligent being exists by whom all natural things are directed to their end; and this being we call God.

Reply Obj. 1. As Augustine says: *Since God is the highest good, He would not allow any evil to exist in His works, unless His omnipotence and goodness were such as to bring good even out of evil.* This is part of the infinite goodness of God, that He should allow evil to exist, and out of it produce good.

Reply Obj. 2. Since nature works for a determinate end under the direction of a higher agent, whatever is done by nature must be traced back to God as to its first cause. So likewise whatever is done voluntarily must be traced back to some higher cause other than human reason and will, since these can change and fail; for all things that are changeable and capable of defect must be traced back to an immovable and self-necessary first principle, as has been shown.

Summa Contra Gentiles

. . . [I]f man's ultimate happiness does not consist in external things, which are called goods of fortune; nor in goods of the body; nor in goods of the soul, as regards the sensitive part; nor as regards the intellectual part, in terms of the life of moral virtue; nor in terms of the intellectual virtues which are concerned with action, namely, art and prudence:—it remains for us to conclude that man's ultimate happiness consists in the contemplation of truth.

For this operation alone is proper to man, and it is in it that none of the other animals communicates.

Again. This is not directed to anything further as to its end, since the contemplation of the truth is sought for its own sake.

Again. By this operation man is united to beings above him, by becoming like them; because of all human actions this alone is both in God and in the separate substances. Also, by this operation man comes into contact with those higher beings, through knowing them in any way whatever.

Besides, man is more self-sufficing for this operation, seeing that he stands in little need of the help of external things in order to perform it.

Further. All other human operations seem to be ordered to this as to their end. For perfect contemplation requires that the body should be disencumbered, and to this effect are directed all the products of art that are necessary for life. Moreover, it requires freedom from the disturbance caused by the passions, which is achieved by means of the moral virtues and of prudence; and freedom from external disturbance, to which the whole governance of the civil life is directed. So that, if we consider the matter rightly, we shall see that all human occupations appear to serve those who contemplate the truth.

Now, it is not possible that man's ultimate happiness consist in contemplation based on the understanding of first principles; for this is most imperfect, as being most universal, containing potentially the knowledge of things. Moreover, it is the beginning and not the end of human inquiry, and comes to us from nature, and not through the pursuit of the truth. Nor does it consist in contemplation based on the sciences that have the lowest things for their object, since happiness must consist in an operation of the intellect in relation to the most noble intelligible objects. It follows then that man's ultimate happiness consists in wisdom, based on the consideration of divine things.

It is therefore evident also by way of induction that man's ultimate happiness consists solely in the contemplation of God, which conclusion was proved above by arguments.

87 ROGER BACON, *OPUS MAJUS*: MEDIEVAL SCIENCE

Toward the end of the eleventh century western Europe was invigorated by the recovery of some classical contributions to science and particularly by the introduction of the science of the East through Latin translation of Arabic works. These latter, during the next few centuries, came largely from Spain, a lustrous center of Muslim art and learning, and also from Sicily and Syria. The scientific movement in medieval Christendom was largely one of absorption of earlier knowledge; if there were some advances, notes the English scientific historian Charles Singer, "they hardly justify a revision of the standard view that modern science arose in the 15th and 16th centuries."

Neither experimentation nor scientific observation, though often recommended and occasionally practiced, was truly compatible with the medieval reverence for written authority. Medieval man found his science more in the library than in the laboratory. Scientific authority rested primarily on the Aristotelian treatise *Parts of Animals* and other minor works of ancient science, which contained along with some very accurate observations some very foolish ones—as for example that a heavy body falls faster than a light one. Since knowledge of Greek was almost lost in the West, the Church tended to put its stamp of approval on such digests without inquiring too much into their contents and without consulting some of the best works of the ancient scientists.

To admit shortcomings, however, is not to deny a debt to the Middle Ages for reviving an interest in natural lore, especially for having pointed the way to scientific progress. Several medieval scholars made scientific learning their special preoccupation: notably Adelard of Bath (c. 1116-c. 1142), Vincent of Beauvais (1190-1264), and Robert Grosseteste (c. 1175-1253). Most famous of the harbingers of modern science was Roger Bacon (c. 1214-1294), an English Franciscan friar whose studies at Oxford and Paris won him the title of "Wonderful Doctor." During an era when Aristotle's influence was almost overpowering, Bacon turned away from Scholastic philosophy to science and mathematics. Of contemporary scholars he was severely scornful, accusing them of pedantry; he criticized Thomas Aquinas, along with innumerable others, calling him a "teacher yet unschooled" and one whose works were full of "puerile vanity and voluminous superfluity." Bacon pleaded for a new experimental method to replace the "stumbling blocks . . . of frail and unworthy authority." "For there are," he said, "two modes of acquiring knowledge, namely, by reasoning and experience. Reasoning draws a conclusion and makes us grant the conclusion, but does not make the conclusion certain, nor does it remove doubt so that the mind may rest on the intuition of truth, unless the mind discovers it by the path of experience. . . ."

We know that Bacon was not the first medieval scholar to advocate the need for experimentation. And although many inventions and discoveries have been credited to him—notably in optics and astronomy—some of them were undoubtedly derived from study of Arabian scientists. He knew, for example, that the combination and ignition of sulphur, niter, and charcoal produced a lightning explosion—in other words, a gunpowder blast—but its previous use by Arabs has since been proven. Nevertheless, Bacon was consciously laying the foundations of the coming age of modern science by describing and popularizing scientific knowledge. Some have since called him a martyr to his cause, for near the end of his life he was condemned and imprisoned twelve years for suspected "novelties" in his teaching, although never did he question the validity of Christian faith or the authority of the Scriptures or of the Church.

Having laid down fundamental principles of the wisdom of the Latins so far as they are found in language, mathematics, and optics, I now wish to unfold the principles of experimental science, since without experience nothing can be sufficiently known. For there are two modes of acquiring knowledge, namely, by reasoning and experience. Reasoning draws a conclusion and makes us grant the conclusion, but does not make the conclusion certain, nor does it remove doubt so that the mind may rest on the intuition of truth, unless the mind discovers it by the path of experience; since many have the arguments relating to what can be known, but because they lack experience they neglect the arguments, and neither avoid what is harmful nor follow what is good. For if a man who has never seen fire should prove by adequate reasoning that fire burns and injures things and destroys them, his mind would not be satisfied thereby, nor would he avoid fire, until he placed his hand or some combustible substance in the fire, so that he might prove by experience that which reasoning taught. But when he has had actual experience of combustion his mind is made certain and rests in the full light of truth. Therefore reasoning does not suffice, but experience does.

This is also evident in mathematics, where proof is most convincing. But the mind of one who has the most convincing proof in regard to the equilateral triangle will never cleave to the conclusion without experience, nor will he heed it, but will disregard it until experience is offered him by the intersection of two circles, from either intersection of which two lines may be drawn to the extremities of the given line; but then the man accepts the conclusion without any question. Aristotle's statement, then, that proof is reasoning that causes us to know is to be understood with the proviso that the proof is accompanied by its appropriate experience, and is not to be understood of the bare proof. His statement also in the first book of the Metaphysics that those who understand the reason and the cause are wiser than those who have empiric knowledge of a fact, is spoken of such as know only the bare truth without the cause. But I am here speaking of the man who knows the reason and the cause through experience. These men are perfect in their wisdom, as Aristotle maintains in the sixth book of the Ethics, whose simple statements must be accepted as if they offered proof, as he states in the same place.

He therefore who wishes to rejoice without doubt in regard to the truths underlying phenomena must know how to devote himself to experiment. For authors write many statements, and people believe them through reasoning which they formulate without experience. Their reasoning is wholly false. For it is generally believed

Text: Robert Belle Burke (trans.), *The Opus Majus of Roger Bacon* (Philadelphia: University of Pennsylvania Press, 1928), II, 583-87.

that the diamond cannot be broken except by goat's blood, and philosophers and theologians misuse this idea. But fracture by means of blood of this kind has never been verified, although the effort has been made; and without that blood it can be broken easily. For I have seen this with my own eyes, and this is necessary, because gems cannot be carved except by fragments of this stone. Similarly it is generally believed that the castors employed by physicians are the testicles of the male animal. But this is not true, because the beaver has these under its breast, and both the male and female produce testicles of this kind. Besides these castors the male beaver has its testicles in their natural place; and therefore what is subjoined is a dreadful lie, namely, that when the hunters pursue the beaver, he himself knowing what they are seeking cuts out with his teeth these glands. Moreover, it is generally believed that hot water freezes more quickly than cold water in vessels, and the argument in support of this is advanced that contrary is excited by contrary, just like enemies meeting each other. But it is certain that cold water freezes more quickly for any one who makes the experiment. People attribute this to Aristotle in the second book of the Meteorologics; but he certainly does not make this statement, but he does make one like it, by which they have been deceived, namely, that if cold water and hot water are poured on a cold place, as upon ice, the hot water freezes more quickly, and this is true. But if hot water and cold are placed in two vessels, the cold will freeze more quickly. Therefore all things must be verified by experience.

But experience is of two kinds; one is gained through our external senses, and in this way we gain our experience of those things that are in the heavens by instruments made for this purpose, and of those things here below by means attested by our vision. Things that do not belong in our part of the world we know through other scientists who have had experience of them. As, for example, Aristotle on the authority of Alexander sent two thousand men through different parts of the world to gain experimental knowledge of all things that are on the surface of the earth, as Pliny bears witness in his Natural History. This experience is both human and philosophical, as far as man can act in accordance with the grace given him; but this experience does not suffice him, because it does not give full attestation in regard to things corporeal owing to its difficulty, and does not touch at all on things spiritual. It is necessary, therefore, that the intellect of man should be otherwise aided, and for this reason the holy patriarchs and prophets, who first gave sciences to the world, received illumination within and were not dependent on sense alone. The same is true of many believers since the time of Christ. For the grace of faith illuminates greatly, as also do divine inspirations, not only in things spiritual, but in things corporeal and in the sciences of philosophy; as Ptolemy states in the Centilogium, namely, that there are two roads by which we arrive at the knowledge of facts, one through the experience of philosophy, the other through divine inspiration, which is far the better way, as he says.

Moreoever, there are seven stages of this internal knowledge, the first of which is reached through illuminations relating purely to the sciences. The second consists in the virtues. For the evil man is ignorant, as Aristotle says in the second book of the Ethics. Moreover, Algazel says in his Logic that the soul disfigured by sins is like a rusty mirror, in which the species of objects cannot be seen clearly; but the soul adorned with virtues is like a well-polished mirror, in which the forms of objects are clearly seen. For this reason true philosophers have labored more in morals for the honor of virtue, concluding in their own case that they cannot perceive the causes of things unless they have souls free from sins. Such is the statement of Augustine in regard to Socrates in the eighth book of the City of God, chapter III. Wherefore the Scripture says, "in a malevolent soul, etc." For it is not possible that the soul should rest in the light of truth while it is stained with sins, but like a parrot or magpie it will repeat the words of another which it has learned by long practice. The proof of this is that the beauty of truth known in its splendor attracts men to the love of it, but the proof of love is the display of a work of love. Therefore he who acts contrary to the truth must necessarily be ignorant of it, although he may know how to compose very elegant phrases, and quote the opinions of other people, like an animal that imitates the words of human beings, and like an ape that relies on the aid of men to perform its part, although it does not understand their reason. Virtue, therefore, clarifies the mind, so that a man comprehends more easily not only moral but scientific truths. I have proved this carefully in the case of many pure young men, who because of innocency of soul have attained greater proficiency than can be stated, when they have had sane advice in regard to their study. Of this number is the bearer of this present treatise, whose fundamental knowledge very few of the Latins have acquired. For since he is quite young, about twenty years of age, and very poor, nor has he been able to have teachers, nor has he spent one year in learning his great store of knowledge, nor is he a man of great genius nor of a very retentive memory, there can be no other cause except the grace of God, which owing to the purity of his soul has granted to him those things that it has as a rule refused to show to all other students. For as a spotless virgin he has departed from me, nor have I found in him any kind of mortal sin, although I have examined him carefully, and he has, therefore, a soul so bright and clear that with very little instruction he has learned more than can be estimated. And I have striven to aid in bringing it about that these two young men should be useful vessels in God's Church, to the end that they may reform by the grace of God the whole course of study of the Latins.

The third stage consists in the seven gifts of the Holy Spirit, which Isaiah enumerates. The fourth consists in the beatitudes, which the Lord defines in the Gospels. The fifth consists in the spiritual senses. The sixth consists in fruits, of which is the peace of God which passes all understanding. The seventh consists in raptures and their states according to the different ways in which people are caught up to see many things of which it is not lawful for a man to speak. And he who has had diligent training in these experiences or in several of them is able to assure himself and others not only in regard to things spiritual, but also in regard to all human sciences. Therefore since all the divisions of speculative philosophy proceed by arguments, which are either based on a point from authority or on the other points of argumentation except this division which I am now examining, we find necessary the science that is called experimental. . . .

88 DANTE ALIGHIERI, *DIVINE COMEDY:* LITERARY SYNTHESIS

By the middle of the thirteenth century the city-states of northern Italy, with a favorable position midway between northwestern Europe and Byzantine and Muslim East and with the stimulus of the crusades, had become important commercial and financial centers. Although their increasing prosperity contributed to their brilliant patronage of the arts, their external and internal relations of state were violently rent by the key question of Italian politics—whether to support the claims of the pope or of the emperor to suzerainty over Italy. During this period, the party of the Guelphs, which adhered to the papal position and was more attractive to the merchants and artisans, was in ascendancy over the Ghibellines, the supporters of the imperial cause, which was usually defended by the feudal aristocracy. In 1265, the power of the Ghibellines was finally broken in Florence, a city destined for cultural glory and political squabbling unmatched by any European city with the possible exception of ancient Athens. In the same year was born Dante Alighieri, one of the earliest of Florence's many sons of genius.

In his early adulthood, Dante was active in the political life of his city, as a moderate Guelph who hoped for a delicate balance of power among pope, emperor, and the free Italian communes. In 1302, because of his outspoken criticisms of the extravagant and autocratic claims of Pope Boniface VIII, he was banished from Florence and until his death at Ravenna in 1321 he was a wanderer, sometimes poverty-stricken and always dependent upon the patronage of political sympathizers in the Italian cities. Yet it was during this period that he established himself as a competent political theorist and as one of the greatest philosophical poets of all times.

If Florentine politics are one vital part of Dante's background, classical literature, Provençal love poetry, and the philosophy of St. Thomas Aquinas are equally important. In the Scholastic tradition, Dante regarded questions of theology, politics, morality, and art as ultimately interrelated and insisted that knowledge was God's gift to man for understanding the relationships. For him, as for Aquinas, the ultimate happiness for man was union with God, and though this happiness was unattainable in life, it could be prepared for by seeking to understand God's creation to the limit of one's human ability.

Dante's major work was the *Divine Comedy*, a long poem containing a rich blend of theological, political, moral, and literary traditions. Comprising three books, the poem recounts a pilgrimage by Dante through hell (the *Inferno*), purgatory (the *Purgatorio*), and heaven (the *Paradiso*). From classical literature comes the poet

Virgil to lead Dante through the first two realms. From Provençal literary traditions of romantic love comes Beatrice, a lady to whom Dante was sublimely devoted in real life, to lead him through the planetary spheres of paradise. The first passage below is from the *Inferno* and deals with the ninth or lowest circle of hell, where frozen in ice lie various types of traitors: there is Count Ugolino, a contemporary of Dante who tells a horrible story of political betrayal and counterbetrayal; there is Satan himself, condemned to chewing upon the archtraitors with his three mouths. For a Christian it comes as no surprise that Judas Iscariot, the betrayer of Jesus, holds the central place in hell, but to understand why Brutus and Cassius, the assassins of Julius Caesar, are second only to Judas in infamy, requires a knowledge of Dante's political belief, namely that a revived Roman Empire, symbolized by Caesar, was a necessary partner of the Roman Church in the longed-for unity of the Christian world. In the second passage below, near the end of the *Purgatorio*, Dante is greeted by a heavenly procession announcing the coming of Beatrice, who will guide him through paradise. In mixed terms of the poetry of courtly love and the Roman epic, Dante greets the object of his almost religious devotion. There, the unity which Dante so devoutly sought but never found in the papal and imperial politics of his time is captured by Dante's true poetical genius.

Inferno

. . . Leaving him then, I saw two souls together
  in a single hole, and so pinched in by the ice
  that one head made a helmet for the other.
As a famished man chews crusts—so the one sinner
  sank his teeth into the other's nape
    at the base of the skull, gnawing his loathsome dinner.
Tydeus in his final raging hour
  gnawed Menalippus' head with no more fury
  than this one gnawed at skull and dripping gore.
"You there," I said, "who show so odiously
  your hatred for that other, tell me why
  on this condition: that if in what you tell me
you seem to have a reasonable complaint
  against him you devour with such foul relish,
  I, knowing who you are, and his soul's taint,
may speak your cause to living memory,
  God willing the power of speech be left to me." . . .
The sinner raised his mouth from his grim repast
  and wiped it on the hair of the bloody head
  whose nape he had all but eaten away. At last
he began to speak: "You ask me to renew
  a grief so desperate that the very thought
  of speaking of it tears my heart in two.
But if my words may be a seed that bears
  the fruit of infamy for him I gnaw,
  I shall weep, but tell my story through my tears.
Who you may be, and by what powers you reach
  into this underworld, I cannot guess,
  but you seem to me a Florentine by your speech.
I was Count Ugolino, I must explain;
  this reverend grace is the Archbishop Ruggieri:
  now I will tell you why I gnaw his brain.
That I, who trusted him, had to undergo
  imprisonment and death through his treachery,
  you will know already. What you cannot know—
that is, the lingering inhumanity
  of the death I suffered—you shall hear in full:
  then judge for yourself if he has injured me.

A narrow window in that coop of stone
  now called the Tower of Hunger for my sake
  (within which others yet must pace alone)
had shown me several waning moons already
  between its bars, when I slept the evil sleep
  in which the veil of the future parted for me.
This beast appeared as master of a hunt
  chasing the wolf and his whelps across the mountain
  that hides Lucca from Pisa. Out in front
of the starved and shrewd and avid pack he had placed
  Gualandi and Sismondi and Lanfranchi
  to point his prey. The father and sons had raced
a brief course only when they failed of breath
  and seemed to weaken; then I thought I saw
  their flanks ripped open by the hounds' fierce teeth.
Before the dawn, the dream still in my head,
  I woke and heard my sons, who were there with me,
  cry from their troubled sleep, asking for bread.
You are cruelty itself if you can keep
  your tears back at the thought of what foreboding
  stirred in my heart; and if you do not weep,
at what are you used to weeping?—The hour when food
  used to be brought, drew near. They were now awake,
  and each was anxious from his dream's dark mood.
And from the base of that horrible tower I heard
  the sound of hammers nailing up the gates:
  I stared at my sons' faces without a word.
I did not weep: I had turned stone inside.

Text: From *The Inferno* by Dante Alighieri, translated by John Ciardi. Copyright, 1954, by John Ciardi. Reprinted by permission of The New American Library, Inc., New York.

They wept. 'What ails you, Father, you look so
    strange,'
  my little Anselm, youngest of them, cried.
But I did not speak a word nor shed a tear:
  not all that day nor all that endless night,
    until I saw another sun appear.
When a tiny ray leaked into that dark prison
  and I saw staring back from their four faces
    the terror and the wasting of my own,
I bit my hands in helpless grief. And they,
  thinking I chewed myself for hunger, rose
    suddenly together. I heard them say:
'Father, it would give us much less pain
  if you ate us: it was you who put upon us
    this sorry flesh; now strip it off again.'
I calmed myself to spare them. Ah! hard earth,
  why did you not yawn open? All that day
    and the next we sat in silence. On the fourth,
Gaddo, the eldest, fell before me and cried,
  stretched at my feet upon that prison floor:
    'Father, why don't you help me?' There he died.
And just as you see me, I saw them fall
  one by one on the fifth day and the sixth.
    Then, already blind, I began to crawl
from body to body shaking them frantically.
  Two days I called their names, and they were
    dead.
    Then fasting overcame my grief and me."
His eyes narrowed to slits when he was done,
  and he seized the skull again between his teeth
    grinding it as a mastiff grinds a bone.
Ah, Pisa! foulest blemish on the land
  where "si" sounds sweet and clear, since those
    nearby you
  are slow to blast the ground on which you stand,
may Caprara and Gorgona drift from place
  and dam the flooding Arno at its mouth
    until it drowns the last of your foul race!
For if to Ugolino falls the censure
  for having betrayed your castles, you for your
    part
  should not have put his sons to such a torture:
you modern Thebes! those tender lives you spilt—
  Brigata, Uguccione, and the others
    I mentioned earlier—were too young for guilt! . . .
"On march the banners of the King of Hell,"
  my Master said. "Toward us. Look straight ahead:
    can you make him out at the core of the frozen
      shell?"
Like a whirling windmill seen afar at twilight,
  or when a mist has risen from the ground—
    just such an engine rose upon my sight
stirring up such a wild and bitter wind
  I cowered for shelter at my Master's back,
    there being no other windbreak I could find.
I stood now where the souls of the last class
  (with fear my verses tell it) were covered wholly;
    they shone below the ice like straws in glass.
Some lie stretched out; others are fixed in place
  upright, some on their heads, some on their soles;
    another, like a bow, bends foot to face.
When we had gone so far across the ice
  that it pleased my Guide to show me the foul
    creature
  which once had worn the grace of Paradise,
he made me stop, and, stepping aside, he said:
  "Now see the face of Dis! This is the place
    where you must arm your soul against all dread."
Do not ask, Reader, how my blood ran cold
  and my voice choked up with fear. I cannot
    write it:
  this is a terror that cannot be told.
I did not die, and yet I lost life's breath:
  imagine for yourself what I became,
    deprived at once of both my life and death.
The Emperor of the Universe of Pain
  jutted his upper chest above the ice;
    and I am closer in size to the great mountain
the Titans make around the central pit,
  than they to his arms. Now, starting from this
    part,
  imagine the whole that corresponds to it!
If he was once as beautiful as now
  he is hideous, and still turned on his Maker,
    well may he be the source of every woe!
With what a sense of awe I saw his head
  towering above me! for it had three faces:
    one was in front, and it was fiery red;
the other two, as weirdly wonderful,
  merged with it from the middle of each shoulder
    to the point where all converged at the top of
      the skull;
the right was something between white and bile;
  the left was about the color that one finds
    on those who live along the banks of the Nile.
Under each head two wings rose terribly,
  their span proportioned to so gross a bird:
    I never saw such sails upon the sea.
They were not feathers—their texture and their
    form
  were like a bat's wings—and he beat them so
    that three winds blew from him in one great
      storm:
it is these winds that freeze all Cocytus.
  He wept from his six eyes, and down three chins
    the tears ran mixed with bloody froth and pus.
In every mouth he worked a broken sinner
  between his rake-like teeth. Thus he kept three
    in eternal pain at his eternal dinner.
For the one in front the biting seemed to play
  no part at all compared to the ripping: at times
    the whole skin of his back was flayed away.
"That soul that suffers most," explained my Guide,
  "is Judas Iscariot, he who kicks his legs

on the fiery chin and has his head inside.
Of the other two, who have their heads thrust forward,
   the one who dangles down from the black face
is Brutus: note how he writhes without a word.
And there, with the huge and sinewy arms, is the soul
   of Cassius.—But the night is coming on
and we must go, for we have seen the whole." . . .
He first, I second, without thought of rest
   we climbed the dark until we reached the point
   where a round opening brought in sight the blest
and beauteous shining of the Heavenly cars.
And we walked out once more beneath the Stars.

Purgatorio

My soul hung tranced in joy beyond all measure
   and yearning for yet more, as I moved on
   through those first fruits of the eternal pleasure;
when, under the green boughs that spread before us
   the air became a blaze, and the sweet sound
   we had been hearing grew into a chorus. . . .
Above the gold array flamed seven times seven
   candles more lucent than the mid-month moon
   at midnight in the calm of clearest heaven.
I turned about, amazed at what I saw,
   to my good Virgil, and he answered me
   in silence, with a look of equal awe. . . .
And there, advancing two by two beneath
   that seven-striped sky came four-and-twenty elders,
   each crowned in glory with a lily-wreath.
And all sang with one voice, triumphantly:
   "Blessèd art thou among the daughters of Adam!
   Blessèd thy beauty to eternity!"
And when those souls elect, as in a dream,
   had left behind the flowers and the new grass
   that shone before me, there across the stream,
as star follows on star in the serene
   of heaven's height, there came on at their backs
   four beasts, and these wore wreaths of living green.
Each had three pairs of wings, and every pair
   was full of eyes. Were Argus living yet,
   his eyes would be most like what I saw there.
I cannot spend my rhymes as liberally
   as I should like to in describing them,
   for, reader, other needs are pressing me:
but read Ezekiel where he sets forth
   how they appeared to him in a great storm
   of wind and cloud and fire out of the North;
and such as he recounts, such did I see;
   except that in the number of their wings
   John differs with him, and agrees with me.
Within the space they guarded there came on
   a burnished two-wheeled chariot in triumph,
   and harnessed to the neck of a great Griffon
whose wings, upraised into the bands of light,
   inclosed the middle one so perfectly
   they cut no part of those to left or right.
Higher than sight its wing-tips soared away.
   Its bird-like parts were gold; and white the rest
   with blood-red markings. Will it serve to say
Rome never saw such a caparison,
   no, not for Africanus, nor yet Augustus?
   The Sun's own would seem shabby by comparison;
yes, even the Sun's own chariot, which strayed
   and was destroyed in fire by Jove's dark justice
   that day the frightened Earth devoutly prayed.
Beside the right wheel, dancing in a gyre,
   three maidens came. The first one was so red
   she would be barely visible in fire.
The second looked as if both flesh and bone
   were made of flawless emerald. The third
   seemed a new snow no slightest wind has blown.
And now the white one led the dance, and now
   the red: and from the song the red one sang
   the others took their measure, fast or slow.
Beside the left wheel, dancing in a flame
   of purple robes, and led by one who had
   three eyes within her head, four glad nymphs came. . . .
And when the chariot had reached the place
   across from me, I heard a thunderclap
   that seemed a signal to those souls in grace,
for there, in unison with the exalted
first flaming standards, all that pageant halted. . . .
Time and again at daybreak I have seen
   the eastern sky glow with a wash of rose
   while all the rest hung limpid and serene,
and the Sun's face rise tempered from its rest
   so veiled by vapors that the naked eye
   could look at it for minutes undistressed.
Exactly so, within a cloud of flowers
   that rose like fountains from the angels' hands
   and fell about the chariot in showers,
a lady came in view: an olive crown
   wreathed her immaculate veil, her cloak was green,
   the colors of live flame played on her gown.
My soul—such years had passed since last it saw
   that lady and stood trembling in her presence,
   stupefied by the power of holy awe—
now, by some power that shone from her above
   the reach and witness of my mortal eyes,
   felt the full mastery of enduring love.
The instant I was smitten by the force,

Text: From *The Purgatorio* by Dante Alighieri, translated by John Ciardi. Copyright © 1957, 1959, 1960, 1961 by John Ciardi. Reprinted by permission of The New American Library, Inc., New York.

which had already once transfixed my soul
  before my boyhood years had run their course,
I turned left with the same assured belief
  that makes a child run to its mother's arms
  when it is frightened or has come to grief,
to say to Virgil: "There is not within me
  one drop of blood unstirred. I recognize
  the tokens of the ancient flame." But he,
he had taken his light from us. He had gone.
  Virgil had gone. Virgil, the gentle Father
  to whom I gave my soul for its salvation!
Not all that sight of Eden lost to view
  by our First Mother could hold back the tears
  that stained my cheeks so lately washed with dew.
"Dante, do not weep yet, though Virgil goes.
  Do not weep yet, for soon another wound
  shall make you weep far hotter tears than those!"
As an admiral takes his place at stern or bow
  to observe the handling of his other ships
  and spur all hands to do their best—so now,
on the chariot's left side, I saw appear
  when I turned at the sound of my own name
  (which, necessarily, is recorded here),
that lady who had been half-veiled from view
  by the flowers of the angel-revels. Now her eyes
  fixed me across the stream, piercing me through.
And though the veil she still wore, held in place
  by the wreathed flowers of wise Minerva's leaves,
  let me see only glimpses of her face,
her stern and regal bearing made me dread
  her next words, for she spoke as one who saves
  the heaviest charge till all the rest are read.
"Look at me well. I am she. I am Beatrice.
  How dared you make your way to this high mountain?
  Did you not know that here man lives in bliss?"
I lowered my head and looked down at the stream.
  But when I saw myself reflected there,
  I fixed my eyes upon the grass for shame.
I shrank as a wayward child in his distress
  shrinks from his mother's sternness, for the taste
  of love grown wrathful is a bitterness:
She paused. At once the angel chorus sang
  the blessed psalm: *"In te, Domine, speravi."*
  As far as *"pedes meos"* their voices rang.
As on the spine of Italy the snow
  lies frozen hard among the living rafters
  in winter when the northeast tempests blow;
then, melting if so much as a breath stir
  from the land of shadowless noon, flows through itself
  like hot wax trickling down a lighted taper—
just so I froze, too cold for sighs or tears
  until I heard that choir whose notes are tuned
  to the eternal music of the spheres.
But when I heard the voice of their compassion
  plead for me more than if they had cried out:
  "Lady, why do you treat him in this fashion?";
the ice, which hard about my heart had pressed,
  turned into breath and water, and flowed out
  through eyes and throat in anguish from my breast.
Still standing at the chariot's left side,
  she turned to those compassionate essences
  whose song had sought to move her, and replied:
"You keep your vigil in the Eternal Day
  where neither night nor sleep obscures from you
  a single step the world takes on its way;
but I must speak with greater care that he
  who weeps on that far bank may understand
  and feel a grief to match his guilt. Not only
by the workings of the spheres that bring each seed
  to its fit end according to the stars
  that ride above it, but by gifts decreed
in the largesse of overflowing Grace,
  whose rain has such high vapors for its source
  our eyes cannot mount to their dwelling place;
this man, potentially, was so endowed
  from early youth that marvelous increase
  should have come forth from every good he sowed.
But richest soil the soonest will grow wild
  with bad seed and neglect. For a while I stayed him
  with glimpses of my face. Turning my mild
and youthful eyes into his very soul,
  I let him see their shining, and I led him
  by the straight way, his face to the right goal.
The instant I had come upon the sill
  of my second age, and crossed and changed my life,
  he left me and let others shape his will.
When I rose from the flesh into the spirit,
  to greater beauty and to greater virtue,
  he found less pleasure in me and less merit.
He turned his steps aside from the True Way,
  pursuing the false images of good
  that promise what they never wholly pay.
Not all the inspiration I won by prayer
  and brought to him in dreams and meditations
  could call him back, so little did he care.
He fell so far from every hope of bliss
  that every means of saving him had failed
  except to let him see the damned. For this
I visited the portals of the dead
  and poured my tears and prayers before that spirit
  by whom his steps have, up to now, been led.
The seal Almighty God's decree has placed
  on the rounds of His creation would be broken
  were he to come past Lethe and to taste
the water that wipes out the guilty years
without some scot of penitential tears!"

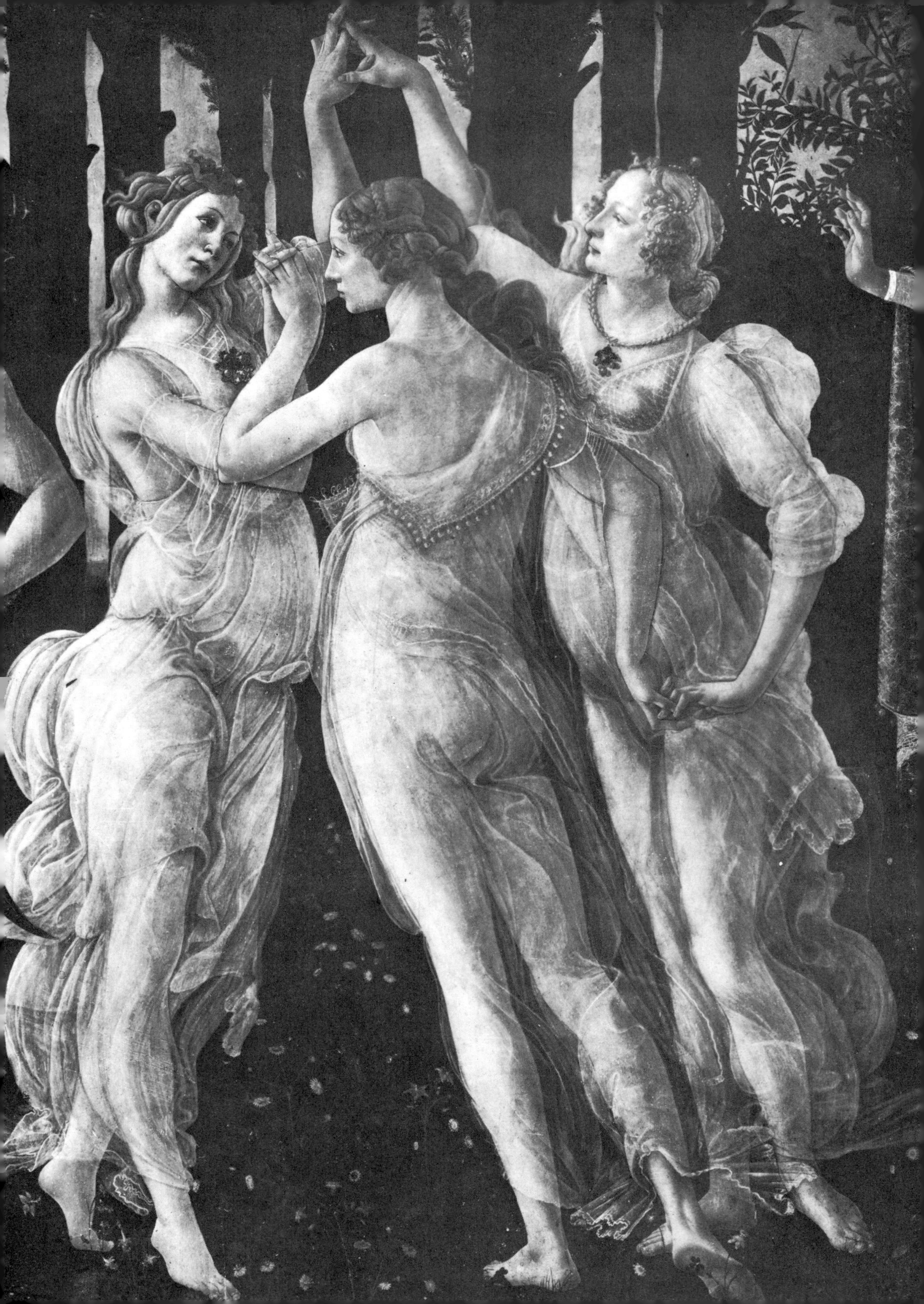

Part V
Renaissance and Reformation

A detail from Botticelli's painting, *Primavera* (opposite page); statue of Moses by Michelangelo (left); a sketch of a human embryo by Leonardo da Vinci (top right); the frontispiece for the Book of Genesis from Luther's translation of the Bible, published in 1534 (bottom right).

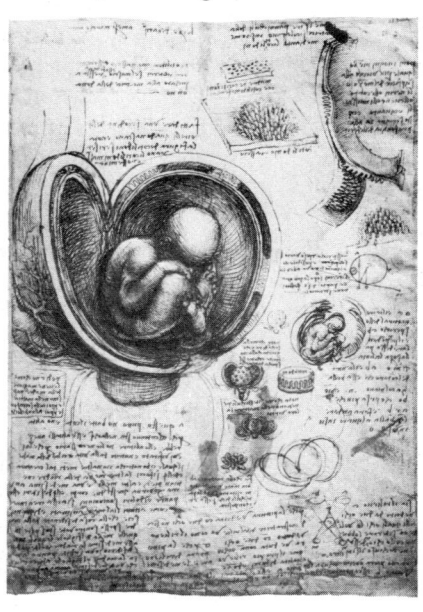

INTRODUCTION

Change is inherent in all human activities. In history, change often takes the form of a gradual, evolutionary process—as in the development of English common law or the progressive refinement of the steam engine. Or it may be precedent-breaking and abrupt—as was the advent of the French Revolution or the first detonation of the atomic bomb. This second category of change is spectacular and so obviously revolutionary that the historian may regard it as the opening of a new epoch in human experience. However, the historian is seldom presented with such ready-made historical demarcations. For example, from the outset of Augustus' rule, the Roman Empire began undergoing changes, at once political, economic, and social. Five centuries later the empire in the West "fell"—the question is, when precisely did the "decline" begin? At what stage, if any, did the accumulation of progressive stresses result in a really fundamental change which in turn brought about a final, rapid collapse of the political structure?

These are questions much easier to ask than to answer, but we have a reason for asking them. For many years historians have been arguing the question of when the Renaissance began—or indeed if there ever was a "Renaissance" at all. Why? To begin with, whereas the storming of the Bastille in Paris on July 14, 1789, touched off the French Revolution, we have no such concrete event to inaugurate the Renaissance. Since nothing of a revolutionary character took place that suddenly initiated a distinctive new political and social epoch, should we therefore agree with those historians who argue that the Renaissance represents no miraculous "rebirth" but only a logical continuation of developments already to be found in the Middle Ages? To do so would seem to be in keeping with their emphasis upon the evolutionary processes in society and upon the basic continuity of both historical phenomena and human nature itself.

Yet by taking this approach, are we still able to account for a complex of factors—social, political, intellectual, and esthetic—which taken together give to Italian society in the fifteenth century a character, or *ethos,* distinguishable from previous societies—or indeed contemporary societies elsewhere? What we are asking is this: does not the Renaissance represent an accumulation of differences to the point where a new social order has evolved with a unique *ethos?*

"I HAVE SET YOU IN THE CENTER OF THE WORLD"

The Renaissance perhaps *is* a meaningful historical concept precisely because a fundamental shift of ideas took place in man's assessment of his own role in the universe. As we saw earlier, medieval man looked upon himself as part of a world order that was God-centered—even as the medieval maps placed Jerusalem in the center of the world because it was there that the great drama of God-made-man had taken place. In the medieval scheme of things, in which the spiritual "sword" could claim to direct the temporal, God and His commandments were accepted implicitly as a divine yardstick for measuring human activities. In the Renaissance, on the other hand, though the primacy of God was not disputed, men came increasingly to judge events and problems in terms of human yardsticks. In other words, there was an acceptance of the old Greek maxim—first enunciated by Protagoras—that "man is the measure of all things."

This shift of emphasis was due to various causes. One was a reaction in Italy against the ideals of asceticism, mortification of the flesh, and otherworldliness so long prevalent in the medieval culture pattern. Another was the rediscovery of classical learning and, with it, the attitudes of the pagan Greeks and their frank embrace of the joys of this world. As a corollary, too, there was the understandable desire of various Renaissance philosophers to reconcile the basic dogmas of a God-centered Church with the man-orientated outlook of the classical world.

Hence the emergence in fifteenth-century Florence of a flourishing school of Christian Platonism—one of whose outstanding members was Giovanni Pico della Mirandola (1463-1494). In his Neoplatonic doctrine, Pico assigns man to a central place in the creation of God, to Whom he attributes these words:

> The other creatures have a defined nature which is fixed within limits prescribed by me. You, unhampered, may determine your own limits according to your own will, in whose power I have placed you. I have set you in the center of the world; from there you can better see whatever is in the world. I have made you neither heavenly nor terrestrial, neither mortal nor immortal, in order that, like a free and sovereign artificer, you can fashion your own form out of your own substance.

A century before Pico, the first step in moving man from the wings to the center of the world stage had been taken by Francesco Petrarch (1304-1374). Known as the "father of humanism" (humanism was to stimulate the study of both the rediscovered classics and the natural world itself), Petrarch exemplified in his own life the transition from medieval to Renaissance ideals. The product of an essentially medieval world outlook, Petrarch always carried with him a copy of St. Augustine's *Confessions,* while at the same time he was seldom without a volume of the works of his beloved master, the pagan Cicero.

In the words of Pico, Petrarch's successors in Italy gladly set about unhampered to determine their own limits according to their own will. A group of strong personalities concerned themselves with the role of the individual—how he should organize and rule society; how to conduct himself in it; how, as patron, to stimulate the arts or, as artist, to depict the new ideational and esthetic currents swirling about him. The fifteenth and sixteenth centuries in Italy were turbulent and admirably suited to experiment of all kinds. As in an earlier and no less individualistic society—Greece—northern Italian society was based upon small city-states, often ruled by banking or merchant princes. Conditioned by bourgeois practices of the town market place instead of by the feudal political system or the chivalric code of conduct of their less sophisticated contemporaries elsewhere, these acquisitive princes sought power and fame. Both objectives were attained by the remarkable Medici, who ruled Florence for decades (see Document 90). With the Medici in mind, the most incisive and candid political theorist of his age, Niccolò Machiavelli (1469-1527), set forth the techniques by which a strong individual could grasp political control and exploit it effectively, a process which today is called power politics (see Document 91).

Machiavelli advocated strong medicine—too strong for the English statesman and humanist, Sir Thomas More (1478-1535). For his part, he blueprinted an idealistic type of society in which coöperation and peace were preferred to autocracy and war (see Document 94). Whatever the precise formula, there was no dearth of energetic minds anxious to promote remedies for the reform of society. To the voluble satirist François Rabelais (1490?-1553), it seemed most necessary to get rid of the mountains of humbug—both ecclesiastic and secular—with which the age had been saddled by traditional institutions (see Document 95). In the eyes of the Spanish humanist Miguel de Cervantes Saavedra (1547-1616), the creator of the immortal Don Quixote, the ideals of the Middle Ages were nothing but dangerous and futile illusions for the men of the Renaissance (see Document 96).

In the world of art, too, creative minds were coming to grips with the dynamics of individualism. The medieval painter had filled his canvases almost exclusively with religious subjects, paying little or no attention to such worldly concerns as the laws of perspective. But once man *per se* was "set . . . in the center of the world," it became essential to place him accurately in the three-dimensional framework in which he functions. The development and application of techniques of perspective was a major achievement of Renaissance artists.

"I CANNOT AND I WILL NOT RECANT ANYTHING"

The same spirit of inquiry that put the basic assumptions of so many traditions to the test was bound also to challenge the doctrines and authority of the central institution of the Middle Ages, namely, the Church. As we have seen, the medieval culture pattern, with its emphasis upon various collectivities, had been dominated by the all-encompassing Church, which regulated the lives of princes and peasants alike. The passing of the medieval world order had seen the emancipation of the serf from the suzerain, the businessman from the guild, and the national state and its king from the dictates of a universal papacy and from the restrictions of local feudalism. Everywhere, then, the individual had asserted himself in the temporal sphere. It would have been strange indeed had he omitted to challenge the authority of the spiritual order as well.

As early as the fourteenth century, in fact, this challenge had been taking form. This was a period when the new national monarchies were disputing the political claims of the papacy—an undertaking in which they were not alone. Within the Church itself, reformers had attempted to curb papal power by making it answerable to clerical councils. This Conciliar Movement sought also to end various financial and moral abuses that had taken root in the ecclesiastical structure. The office of the pope suffered a critical blow at this time by the incumbent's embroilment in French national politics, as a result of which the papal court was removed from Rome to Avignon, where it remained under French influence from 1309 to 1376. This Babylonian Captivity, as it was called, further stimulated an already widespread outcry for papal reform and an end to worldliness in high places.

Among the reformers was John Wycliffe (1320?-1384) of Oxford, who not only assailed Church abuses, but went so far as to challenge its doctrines. Because he maintained that the Church should be subordinate to the State and that salvation was basically an individual matter between man and God, Wycliffe has been called the dawn-star of the Reformation. Wycliffe's views, judged heretical by the Church, nevertheless had a wide influence on the Continent, especially on the Bohemian preacher, John Huss (1369?-1415).

Bad as it was, the Babylonian Captivity had an even more disastrous aftermath—the Great Schism, with two rival popes reigning simultaneously, one at Avignon and the other at Rome. To bring this intolerable state of affairs to an end was the objective of the Council of Pisa (1409), but the attempt misfired—with the result that the papal throne acquired three claimants. Another council, this time held in Constance (1414-1417), ended the Great Schism, but the Conciliar Movement failed to reform other serious abuses. And the papacy, having forbidden the calling of further councils, proceeded to immerse itself in Italian politics and to play the role of patron to a brilliant coterie of artists who dazzled the eye with one masterpiece after another. It was all very exciting, but the abuses against which Wycliffe and Huss had stormed remained uncorrected. And now another Wycliffe arose—in the person of a German monk named Martin Luther (1483-1546).

The Renaissance has no dramatic beginning, but the Reformation has. The catalyst that was to sunder Christendom into irreconcilable theological camps and eventually compound the split with bloodshed—surely the most terrible of sins when committed in the name of the Prince of Peace—consisted of a simple act performed at noon on October 31, 1517, at the door of a church in Wittenberg. For then and there Luther posted his famous ninety-five theses, in which he challenged the prevailing views on indulgences. Thus began a course of action that soon led the theologian-monk to reject the infallibility of the pope in favor of the infallibility of the Scriptures and to assert that a man's salvation depended upon faith alone. Excommunicated by Pope Leo X and summoned by Emperor Charles V to the Diet at Worms to account for his heretical behavior, Luther reaffirmed his stand:

> Unless I am convicted by Scripture and plain reason—I do not accept the authority of popes and councils, for they have contradicted each other—my conscience is captive to the Word of God, I cannot and will not recant anything, for to go against conscience is neither right nor safe. God help me. Amen.

Uncompromising words—and they brought in their train the Protestant Revolt. They are no less than the application of Renaissance individualism to the religious sphere—man's insistence on being his own priest and mediator and approaching God directly by faith. Other dissenters followed Luther's lead: Ulrich Zwingli in Zurich, John Calvin in Geneva. Even the English King Henry VIII, though he detested Luther and had no wish to deviate from the main body of Catholic doctrine, at length supplanted the pope with his own royal person as head of the Church of England. In the case of Henry VIII it may be said that conscience was supplanted by expediency, but against the others that charge cannot be fairly made. With Zwingli and Calvin, as with John Knox in Scotland, "conscience is captive to the word of God."

But conscience was not monopolized by the Protestants; it was no less sincere among those who continued to uphold papal authority. For decades prior to Luther's advent there had been reformers within the Church who sought to restore it to its original purity and vigor. Some of the most enlightened contemporaries of Luther—including Sir Thomas More and the "scholar of Europe," Desiderius Erasmus—held that reforms could best be effected within the existing ecclesiastical framework, not by shattering the unity of western Christendom. Now with the split having taken place, the pressures within the Church to institute a Catholic Reformation became so strong that the previously defeated Conciliar Movement gained fresh life.

A general council was held at Trent (1545-1563), where over a period of nearly twenty years Catholic doctrine was carefully enunciated. Papal supremacy was reaffirmed, as were the validity of the sacramental system and the Church's claim to be the only true repository of the living faith. On the other hand, such corrupt practices as simony, nepotism, and clerical laxity were strictly forbidden. After decades of being on the defensive, a revitalized Church now passed to a counter-offensive against Lutheranism in Germany and elsewhere. In its proselytizing labors it was aided by a number of new Catholic orders, the most militant and effective being the Society of Jesus, or Jesuits, founded by Ignatius Loyola (1491-1556).

By its very nature, individualism tends to fragment and atomize, and the Reformation represents at once the triumph of Renaissance individualism and the atomization of western Christendom. Thus, the aftermath of the labors of Luther and other Protestant leaders saw a proliferation of new sects, each claiming the right to determine its own set of beliefs. But as so often happens when individualism is carried to extremes, the overzealous emphasis on the right of self-determination led to a narrow determinism which forbade to others the same freedom of belief which was claimed for one's self. And so in both major camps—Protestant and Catholic alike—intolerance grew. On each side this led to the persecution of minorities and, in extreme cases, to death by burning or hanging; between the camps there developed religious wars, whose fanaticism and cruelty were exacerbated by the crass political motives that got injected. The flames of passion and bigotry eventually died down in the seventeenth century, but only because by that time religion was ceasing to be the dominant motivation in western society.

"THE WORLD ENCOMPASSED"

The Renaissance not only heightened man's awareness of himself and his relationship to God; it also increased his perception of the physical world about him and stimulated his interest in science.

The same curiosity which had prompted Petrarch and other humanists to seek out the intellectual treasures of the classical world in turn propelled Columbus and a band of like-minded explorers to seek out the riches of the unknown world that dipped ever beyond the horizon's receding rim. The quest led them around the southernmost tip of Africa, across the North Atlantic to the Caribbean and the coasts of the Americas, and eventually westward across the Pacific's seemingly endless expanse until the whole world had been encompassed. Europe stood on the threshold of planetary dominion.

In this breath-taking epoch of geographical exploration and overseas settlement, men were once again aided by that unusual combination of backward-looking and forward-thrusting factors which comprise the Renaissance. They rediscovered not only the ancient maps of Ptolemy and other classical geographers but, perhaps even more important, the cartographical techniques which those ancients had employed. The use of a grid system of lines of latitude and longitude (on which the modern science of cartography is based) enabled them to plot positions and distances with increasing accuracy. To these classical techniques they added the empirical knowledge gained from their close observation of natural phenomena, gleaned during their voyages of discovery. From this happy marriage of past theory and contemporary experimentation emerged the outlines of a recognizable map, and with it a chart or guide which was to carry men into early modern times.

The mapping of the world was presently accompanied by an ambition to map the heavens as well. Was the earth the center of the universe, as medieval theology taught, or was it part of a cosmic order held together by natural laws, as some of the ancients had believed? Put simply, did the sun rotate around the earth—as the physical senses appeared to confirm—or did the earth circle the sun? A Polish astronomer addressed himself to this question. Nicolas Copernicus (1473-1543) was near-sighted and possessed no telescope, yet long observation of the movements of Mars convinced him that the sun and not the earth was the center of our planetary system. His treatise on the subject (see Document 104) was subsequently condemned by Catholic and Protestant theologians alike, who feared that it both contradicted Scripture and robbed the earth of its central place in God's creation. Copernicus' death in 1543 seemed to leave his opponents in undisputed possession of the field—if not the heavens—but in fact a mighty revolution had begun. By the early seventeenth century two other astronomers, the German Kepler and the Italian Galileo, had been able to verify the heliocentric theory and to explain the mechanics of planetary motion.

The work of these three men had done even more than establish the scientific foundations of modern astronomy; they had also demonstrated the truth held by ancient Greeks but forgotten, or rejected, by medieval philosophers: that the universe is governed by immutable, mechanical laws which can be mathematically determined. Once more the Renaissance's mating of classical theory with contemporary empirical evidence had resulted in a revolution—in this instance a revolution fully as great in magnitude as the geographical discoveries which had earlier refashioned a man's knowledge about the surface of his planet. Already the world had been encompassed, and it in turn had been placed in its proper sphere within the all-encompassing heavens. What more might not be accomplished if men would only establish new methods of inquiry in order to harness science to the proper service of mankind? The English scientist and philosopher, Francis Bacon (1561-1626), provided a major portion of the answer when he advocated the inductive method; while a younger French contemporary, René Descartes (1596-1650), supplied much of the remainder in championing the deductive, or mathematical, method. Their techniques paved the way for the magnificent scientific advancements of which we today are the opulent, but also overwhelmed, beneficiaries.

The Quickening of the West

THE RENAISSANCE IN ITALY

89 FRANCESCO PETRARCH, LETTER TO PULICE DI VICENZA, MAY 13, 1353: THE HUMANISTIC REVIVAL

The humanistic tradition is so much a part of our modern climate of opinion that it is generally taken for granted. It was not always so. The thousand years of the Middle Ages were characterized by an attitude of supernaturalism and otherworldliness; it was an era when creation was thought to be related to man's struggle for salvation. By contrast, humanism emphasizes an interest in man and nature for their own sakes. The gradual transition from a medieval to a more modern world-view took place during the Renaissance, and its most characteristic feature was the revival of humanism. Humanism as an intellectual movement began in the fourteenth and fifteenth centuries and was, said Ferdinand Schevill in his *History of Florence*, "a movement of the human mind which began when, following the rise of the towns, the urban intelligentsia slowly turned away from the transcendental values imposed by religion to the more immediately perceptible values of Nature and of man."

As a literary movement humanism expressed itself in a rediscovery of the classics of ancient Greece and Rome—not surprisingly, for the ancient writers' primary interests lay in the problems of man and nature. The geographical center and origin of humanism was to be found in Italy, particularly in the burgeoning town life of the north. We may pinpoint it further and say that the revival of interest in the classics was largely associated with the life and popularity of one man, Francesco Petrarch (1304-1374). Petrarch believed that anything great must necessarily come from Greece and Rome, and he spent a lifetime collecting and translating the classics of antiquity. In an era when printing was still unknown in Europe, Petrarch wrote hundreds of letters to correspondents throughout the Continent, letters in which he poured forth his views on a great variety of human affairs and his fervor for the classics. So contagious was his enthusiasm that he may be credited with having begun a new intellectual age.

Here, in one of the many letters written by Petrarch, we have a discussion about Cicero, the early humanists' great hero; it is worth noting that Petrarch attempted to take a more balanced view of Cicero, and that he still considered himself a Christian.

To Pulice di Vicenza.

On my way I stopped overnight in one of Vicenza's suburbs, and there I found something new to write about. It happened that I had left Padua not much before noon, and so did not reach the outskirts of your city until the sun was getting low. I tried to make up my mind whether I had better put up there or push on a little farther; for I was in a hurry, and the days are long now, and it would be light for a good while yet. I was still hesitating, when lo!—for who can remain hidden from the friends who love him?—all my doubts were happily resolved by your arrival, in company with several other men of mark, such as that little city has always produced in great abundance. My mind was tossing this way and that, but you and your companions, with your pleasant varied talk, furnished the cable that bound it fast. I planned to go, but still stayed on; and did not realise that the daylight was slipping away from me until night was actually at hand. So I discovered once again what I had observed often before, that there is nothing that filches time away from us, without our perceiving it, like converse with our friends. They are the greatest of all thieves of time. And yet we ought to deem no time less truly stolen from us, less truly lost out of our lives, than such as is expended (next to God) upon them.

Well, not to review the story at too great length, you remember that some one made mention of Cicero, as will very often happen among men of literary tastes. This name at once brought our desultory conversation to an end. We all turned our thoughts toward him. Nothing but Cicero was discussed after that. As we sat and feasted together we vied with one another in singing his praises. Still, there is nothing in this world that is absolutely perfect; never has the man existed in whom the critic, were he ever so lenient, would see nothing at all to reprehend. So it chanced that while I expressed admiration for Cicero, almost without reservation, as a man whom I loved and honoured above all others, and amazement too at his golden eloquence and his heavenly genius, I found at the same time a little fault with his fickleness and inconsistency, traits that are revealed everywhere in his life and works. At once I saw that all who were present were astonished at so unusual an opinion, and one among them especially so. I refer to the old man, your fellow-citizen, whose name has gone from me, although his image is fresh in my memory, and I revere him, both for his years and for his scholarship.

Well, the circumstances seemed to demand that I fetch the manuscript of my correspondence with my friends, which I had with me in my chest. It was brought in, and added fuel to the flame. For among the letters that were written to my contemporaries there are a few, inserted with an eye to variety and for the sake of a little diversion in the midst of my more serious labours, that are addressed to some of the more illustrious men of ancient times. A reader who was not forewarned would be amazed at these, finding names so old and of such renown mingled with those of our own day. Two of them are to Cicero himself; one criticising his character, the other praising his genius. These two you read, while the others listened; and then the strife of words grew warmer. Some approved of what I had written, admitting that Cicero deserved my censure. But the old man stood his ground, more stubbornly even than before. He was so blinded by love of his hero and by the brightness of his name that he preferred to praise him even when he was in the wrong; to embrace faults and virtues together, rather than make any exceptions. He would not be thought to condemn anything at all in so great a man. So instead of answering our arguments he rang the changes again and again upon the splendour of Cicero's fame, letting authority usurp the place of reason. He would stretch out his hand and say imploringly, "Gently, I beg of you, gently with my Cicero." And when we asked him if he found it impossible to believe that Cicero had made mistakes, he would close his eyes and turn his face away and exclaim with a groan, as if he had been smitten, "Alas! alas! Is my beloved Cicero accused of doing wrong?" just as if we were speaking not of a man but of some god. I asked him, accordingly, whether in his opinion Tullius was a god, or a man like others. "A god," he replied; and then, realising what he had said, he added, "a god of eloquence." "Oh, very well!" I answered; "if he is a god, he certainly could not have erred. However, I never heard him styled so before. And yet, if Cicero calls Plato his god, why should not you in turn speak of Cicero as yours?—except that it is not in harmony with our religious beliefs for men to fashion gods for themselves as they may fancy." "I am only jesting," said he; "I know that Tullius was a man, but he was a man of godlike genius." "That is better," I responded; "for when Quintilian called him heavenly he spoke no more than the truth. But then, if you admit that he was a man,

Text: Reprinted by permission of the publishers and The Loeb Classical Library from *Petrarch, The First Modern Scholar and Man of Letters,* trans. and ed. James Harvey Robinson and Henry Winchester Rolfe (Cambridge, Mass.: Harvard University Press, 1909), pp. 243-49.

it follows necessarily that he could make mistakes, and did so." As I spoke these words he shuddered and turned away, as if they were aimed not at another man's reputation but at his own life. What could I say, I who am myself so great an admirer of Cicero's genius? I felt that the old scholar was to be envied for his ardour and devotion, which had something of the Pythagorean savour. I was rejoiced at finding such reverence for even one great man; such almost religious regard, so fervent that to suspect any touch of human weakness in its object seemed like sacrilege. I was amazed, too, at having discovered a person who cherished a love greater than mine for the man whom I always had loved beyond all others; a person who in old age still held, deeply rooted in his heart, the opinions concerning him which I remember to have entertained in my boyhood; and who, notwithstanding his advanced years, was incapable of arguing that if Cicero was a man it followed that in some cases, in many indeed, he must have erred, a conclusion that I have been forced, by common sense and by knowledge of his life, to accept at this earlier stage of my development,—although this conviction does not alter the fact that the beauty of his work delights me still, beyond that of any other writer. Why, Tullius himself, the very man of whom we are speaking, took this view, for he often bewailed his errors, bitterly. If, in our eagerness to praise him, we deny that he thus understood himself, we deprive him of a large part of his renown as a philosopher, the praise, namely, that is due to self-knowledge and modesty.

To return, however, to that day; after a long discussion we were compelled by the lateness of the hour to desist, and separated with the question still unsettled. But as we parted you asked me to send you from my first resting-place, inasmuch as the shortness of the time would not let me attend to it just then, a copy of each of these letters of mine, in order that you might look into the matter a little more carefully, and be in a position to act as a mediator between the parties, or, possibly, as a champion of Cicero's steadfastness and consistency. I approve of your intention, and send the copies herewith. I do so, strange to say, with a fear that I may be victorious, and a hope that I may be vanquished. And one thing more: I must tell you that if you do prove the victor you have a larger task on your hands than you now imagine. For Annæus Seneca, whom I criticise in my very next letter in a similar way, insists that you act as his champion too.

I have dealt familiarly with these great geniuses, and perhaps boldly, but lovingly, but sorrowfully, but truthfully, I think; with somewhat more of truthfulness, in fact, than I myself relish. There are many things in both of them that delight me, only a few that trouble me. Of these few I felt constrained to write; perhaps to-day I should feel otherwise. For, although I have grouped these letters together at the end, it is only because their subject-matter is so unlike the others; they came from the anvil long ago.

The fact is, I still grieve over the fate of these great men; but I do not lament their faults any the less because of that. Furthermore, I beg you to note that I say nothing against Seneca's private life, nor against Cicero's attitude toward the state. Do not confuse the two cases. It is Cicero alone whom we are discussing now; and I am not forgetting that he as consul was vigilant and patriotic, and cured the disease from which the republic was suffering; nor that as a private citizen he always loved his country faithfully. But what of his fickleness in friendship; and his bitter quarrels upon slight provocation,—quarrels that brought ruin upon himself and good to no one; and his inability to understand his own position and the condition of the republic, so unlike his usual acumen; and, finally, the spectacle of a philosopher, in his old age, childishly fond of useless wrangling? These things I cannot praise. And remember that they are things concerning which no unbiased judgment can be formed, by you or anyone else, without a careful reading of the entire correspondence of Cicero, which suggested this controversy.

90 VESPASIANO DA BISTICCI, "LIFE OF COSIMO DE' MEDICI": THE MERCHANT PRINCE

With commerce centered in the Mediterranean during the fifteenth century, the towns of Italy became the biggest and busiest in all Europe. Many merchant families made fortunes in trade, and the more enterprising among them expanded into banking, thus building up even greater riches. Rivalry was the order of the day—family competed with family, guild with guild, city with city, each seeking greater power, position, and prestige. While this contributed to a lively urban climate, it also fostered an agitated political life which kept Italy divided into independent, fiercely competitive city-states.

Here was an environment where men of energy and resourcefulness could develop their talents and where remarkable individuals could push their way to fame and fortune. For to accumulate great wealth, to obtain high office, to carry on affairs of state, to make and unmake alliances—in short, to outwit rivals, whether political or commercial, domestic or foreign, required a high order of personal confidence and competence. However, making money and seeking power were not the sole activities of the fifteenth-century Italian merchant princes. They were also men of taste who were well versed in classical literature, patronized the arts, built libraries, and constructed public buildings. They were men who appreciated things of beauty and sought satisfaction in their creation.

Among the most illustrious families of fifteenth-century Italy was the Medici of Florence. The man who established the immense fortune of this family was Giovanni (1360-1429), a merchant and banker. Upon his death, the inheritance passed to his two sons, the elder of whom was Cosimo (1389-1464), then forty years old. It was Cosimo's grandson who brightened history as Lorenzo the Magnificent (1449-1492), the famous poet, connoisseur, and patron of art and learning. Two of his descendants became popes, and two Medici women became queens of France.

Lorenzo was the most famous of the Medici, but Cosimo was the more astute as a financier and statesman. To the day he died, Cosimo was devoted to business. Through friendly relations with the papacy he greatly enlarged the wealth of his family. So great was his power that he was able to become absolute ruler of the Florentine Republic without holding any fixed office; for the last thirty years of his life he was the dominant figure in Florence. Cosimo, though not a poet like Lorenzo, was no less ardent in promoting the arts. Besides constructing noble villas and a palace, he built and enlarged several churches, purchased many Greek and Latin manuscripts, founded libraries, and became the patron of the outstanding sculptors and architects of his day. He died at the age of seventy-five while listening to one of Plato's dialogues.

The following description of Cosimo was written by one of his contemporaries, Vespasiano da Bisticci. As a bookseller and bibliophile he collected many books for Cosimo's library and came to know him well. While his account can hardly be called impartial, it does give us a good first-hand picture of the qualities and characteristics of a prominent Renaissance figure who typified the spirit of his times.

Cosimo di Giovanni de' Medici was of most honourable descent, a very prominent citizen and one of great weight in the republic. He was well versed in Latin letters, both sacred and secular, of capable judgment in all matters and able to argue thereupon. His teacher was Roberto dei Rossi, a good Greek and Latin scholar and of excellent carriage. At this time many other youths of good station were his fellow-pupils: Domenico di Lionardo Buoninsegni, Bartolo Tebaldi, Luca di Messer Maso degli Albizzi, Messer Alessandro degli Alessandri and many others who came together regularly for instruction. Roberto lived in his own house, unmarried, and when he went out he was usually accompanied by the above-named, who were held in much esteem both for their good conduct and learning: moreover, Roberto would often entertain his pupils at table. He made a most excellent will which divided his large library of books written by his own hand—and he was one of the finest of scribes —amongst his pupils.

Returning to Cosimo, he had a knowledge of Latin which would scarcely have been looked for in one occupying the station of a leading citizen engrossed with affairs. He was grave in temperament, prone to associate with men of high station who disliked frivolity, and averse from all buffoons and actors and those who spent time unprofitably. He had a great liking for men of letters and sought their society, chiefly conversing with the Fra Ambrogio degli Agnoli, Messer Lionardo d' Arezzo, Nicolao Nicoli, Messer Carlo d' Arezzo and Messer Poggio. His natural bent was to discuss matters of importance; and, although at this time the city was full of men of distinction, his worth was recognized on account of his praiseworthy qualities, and he began to find employment in affairs of every kind. By his twenty-fifth year he had gained great reputation in the city, and, as it was recognised that he was aiming at a high position, feeling ran strong against him, and the report of those who knew roused a fear that he would win success. The Council of Constance, gathered from all parts of the world, was

Text: Vespasiano da Bisticci, *The Vespasiano Memoirs*, trans. William George and Emily Waters (New York: The Dial Press, 1926), pp. 213-18, 221-25, 231.

then sitting; and Cosimo, who was well acquainted with foreign affairs as well as those of the city, went thither with two objects: one to allay the ill-feeling against him, and the other to see the Council which had in hand the reform of the Church, now greatly vexed by divisions. After staying some time at Constance, and witnessing the procedure of the Council, he visited almost all parts of Germany and France, spending some two years in travel. He hoped thus to let cool the ill-feeling against him which had greatly increased. He understood his own disposition which made him discontented with low estate, and made him seek to rise out of the crowd of men of small account. Many people remarked this tendency, and warned him that it might lead him into danger of death or exile. By way of lessening this resentment he began to absent himself from the palace, and to consort with men of low estate without either money or position, all by way of temporising; but his foes took this in bad part, affirming that what he did was a mere pretence to abate the suspicions of others. . . .

On the eighth day of September, 1433, they sent to bid Cosimo come at once to the Signoria. On his way thither he met at Or San Michele his kinsman and friend Alamanno Salviati, who bade him not go, or he would lose his life; whereupon Cosimo answered, "However that may be, I must obey the Signori," not suspecting their attitude towards him. When he arrived at the palace, without further parley, he was taken into a prison in the bell tower called the Berghettina; the Signori were still bent on making an end of him, believing that by no other means could they hold the government, so great was his power, within the city and without. While he was thus imprisoned, he learned the intention of his foes and feared greatly for his life, so he refused to eat any of the food that was brought to him, in order that they should not poison him. While things were in suspense, some of Cosimo's friends tried to induce the gonfaloniere to spare his life and banish him, and they promised five hundred ducats if he would do this. The heads of the faction who had elected the gonfaloniere clamoured for the execution of Cosimo, pointing out that, if through kindness he should be spared, he would soon be recalled from exile and would prove their ruin; but the gonfaloniere prevailed with his associates to spare Cosimo's life, and let him be exiled to Venice. Thus it came about that Cosimo and Lorenzo withdrew to Venice. . . . While Cosimo tarried at Venice, he was greatly esteemed by all the Venetians, who determined to despatch an ambassador to encourage the Signoria and those in power to recall him from exile. They began to favour him in divers ways, secretly, and to arrange for his return; and as many in Florence were on his side, before a year had passed they made a plan to procure his recall by the help of the Priorato which was friendly to him. At the end of the year his adversaries took up arms, being suspicious as to what might be the results of his return, whereupon Pope Eugenius, like a good pastor, appeared as a mediator to arrange a peace between the two parties of citizens. Those of the government of 1433, who had taken up arms, laid them down and submitted themselves to the good faith of the Pope. But though they were under the Papal guarantee, they were exiled after Cosimo's return. In this matter Pope Eugenius was deceived, for he believed that good faith would be kept on both sides and the city pacified.

Cosimo having come back to Florence, to the great satisfaction of the citizens and of his own party, his friends procured the banishment of divers of those who had opposed his recall, and of those who were neutral; at the same time bringing forward new people. He rewarded those who had brought him back, lending to one a good sum of money, and making a gift to another to help marry his daughter or buy lands, while great numbers were banished as rebels. He and his party took every step to strengthen their own position, following the example of those of the government of 1433. In Florence there were many citizens who were men of weight in the state; and, as they were friendly to Cosimo and had helped to recall him, they retained their influence. Cosimo found that he must be careful to keep their support by temporising and making believe that he was fain they should enjoy power equal to his own. Meantime he kept concealed the source of his influence in the city as well as he could. I have no wish to set down here everything that I could tell, for what I write is only by way of memorandum. I leave the rest to anyone who may write his life. But I say that anyone who may be fain to bring new forms into the state, that those who wrought the changes in 1433, brought ruin to themselves and to the state also. Many leading citizens, men of weight, never wished for these changes, declaring they had no wish to dig their own graves.

Cosimo, after he had settled the government, called for a Balia which banished many citizens. At this time Duke Francesco was in command of the allied forces of Florence and Venice near Lucca; the two republics having agreed to share the cost of the soldiers' pay, but now the Venetians refused to contribute their part. Whereupon, after several letters had been sent in vain, Cosimo, as one highly esteemed in Venice, was sent to request the Venetians to hold to their promise and to pay the sum due to Duke Francesco.

On Cosimo's arrival all the citizens deemed that the Signory should take a new line and observe the promise they had made. Cosimo pressed his claims with the strongest arguments, but the Venetians kept obstinately to their view, for they were determined that the Florentines should not get Lucca without pay for it. When Cosimo perceived that they were set on this policy, and that they declined to recognize the benefits they had received, he grew to hate them on account of their bad faith; so he wrote to Florence asking leave to withdraw and return by way of Ferrara, where Pope Eugenius had gone with all his court. When he arrived, he waited upon the Pope according to his commission and made complaint of the ingratitude of the Venetians. But Eugenius made light of this, knowing their character, and the College of Cardinals was of the same mind. From the way in which the Venetians bore themselves towards the Pope, they greatly roused his anger, as it appeared from what happened later. Cosimo went on several embassies and brought back great honour to the city. . . .

He next considered how he might best gather together in these lodgings a company of worthy and learned men. First, he determined to collect a suitable lot of books, and one day, when I was with him, he said: "What plan can you suggest for the formation of this library?" I replied that if the books were to be bought, it would be impossible, for the reason that they could not be found. Then he went on, "Then tell me what you would do in the matter." I said it would be necessary to have the books transcribed, whereupon he wanted to know whether I would undertake the task. I said that I would, whereupon he replied that I might begin when I liked, that he left everything to me, and that, as for the money for daily costs, he would order Don Archangelo, the prior, to present the cheques at the bank where they would be duly paid. He was anxious I should use all possible despatch, and, after the library was begun, as there was no lack of money, I engaged forty-five scribes and completed two hundred volumes in twenty-two months, taking as a model the library of Pope Nicolas and following directions written by his own hand, which Pope Nicolas had given to Cosimo.

First came the Bibles and Concordances with comments ancient and modern. The first of the commentators was Origen, who showed the way to all his followers. He wrote in Greek, and a portion of his work, "On the five books of Moses," was translated by S. Jerome. There were the works of S. Ignatius the martyr, who also wrote in Greek, and was a pupil of S. John the Evangelist, most zealous for Christianity as a writer and as a preacher; those of S. Basil of Cappadocia, a Greek; those of S. Gregory Nazianzen, of Gregory of Nice his brother, of S. John Chrysostom, of S. Athanasius of Alexandria, of S. Ephrem the monk, of Giovanni Climaco, a Greek, and of all the Greek doctors which are translated into Latin, and after these came all the sacred works of the Latin doctors beginning with Lactantius.

As soon as the library was finished he provided the church with fitting books for the choir, and a fine psalter in many volumes. He gave hangings, missals, and chalices for the sacristy and all necessary utensils. The whole cost from what I have heard was seventy thousand ducats. At S. Croce he built the Noviciate with a chapel and a choir close to the sacristy at a cost of eight thousand florins or more, and he built his palace in the city from the foundations, spending sixty thousand ducats. At Careggi he built the greater part of what we now see and the same at Cafaggiuolo in Mugello at a cost of fifteen thousand ducats. These works maintained many poor men who laboured thereon. There was not a year when he did not expend on building from fifteen to eighteen thousand florins, all of which went to the state. He was most particular as to his payment. He gave the contract for the building of Careggi to a master surveyor; and, by the time it was half done, Cosimo saw that before it should be finished the man would lose several thousand florins. So he said to the contractor, "Lorenzo, you have taken this work in hand, and I know that in the end you will be a loser of several thousands of florins. That was never my intention, but rather that you should make a profit. Go on with your work. You shall not lose, and whatever may be right I will give you." And he did what he had promised. Most men would have held that after the master surveyor had made the contract he should have kept it, but Cosimo with rare liberality thought otherwise. In all his dealings he never wished that those who worked for him should lose, but that they should be paid for their trouble.

I once heard Cosimo say that the great mistake of his life was that he did not begin to spend his wealth ten years earlier; because, knowing well the disposition of his fellow-citizens, he was sure that, in the lapse of fifty years, no memory would remain of his personality or of his house save the few fabrics he might have built. He went on, "I know that after my death my children will be in worse case than those of any other Florentine who has died for many years past; moreover, I know I shall not wear the crown of laurel more than any other citizen." He spake thus because he knew the difficulty of ruling a state as he had ruled Florence, through the opposition of influential citizens who had rated themselves his equals in former times. He acted privately with the greatest discretion in order to safeguard himself, and whenever he sought to attain an object he contrived to let it appear that the matter had been set in motion by someone other than himself and thus he escaped envy and unpopularity. His manner was admirable; he never spoke ill of anyone, and it angered him greatly to hear slander spoken by others. He was kind and patient to all who sought speech with him: he was more a man of deeds than of words: he alway performed what he promised, and when this had been done he sent to let the petitioner know that his wishes had been granted. His replies were brief and sometimes obscure, so that they might be made to bear a double sense.

He had a very long memory which retained everything. One evening at home, when he wished for the love of God to give some more books to S. Marco—which books had lain for a long time in a press—he recalled all the books by name, and noted especially one of them, the *Digesto vecchio*, and said: "Make a note mentally that there is thereon the singular name of a certain German who formerly possessed it," remembering thus both the name of the book and of the German. When he came upon it he said, "I once owned it forty years ago and I have never seen it since." So great was his knowledge of all things, that he could find some matter of discussion with men of all sorts; he would talk literature with a man of letters and theology with a theologian, being well versed therein through his natural liking, and for the reading of the Holy Scripture. With philosophy it was just the same, also with astrology, of which he had complete knowledge from having practised it with Maestro Pagolo and other astrologers. Indeed, he put faith in it, and always made use of it in his affairs. He took kindly notice of all musicians, and delighted greatly in their art. He had dealings with painters and sculptors and had in his house works of divers masters. He was especially inclined towards sculpture and showed great favour to all worthy craftsmen, being a good friend to Donatello and all sculptors and painters; and because in his time the sculptors found scanty employment, Cosimo, in order that Donatello's chisel might not be idle, commissioned him to make the pulpits of bronze in S. Lorenzo and the doors of the sacristy. He ordered the bank to pay every week enough money to Donatello for his work and for that of his four assistants. And because Donatello was wont to go clad in a fashion not to Cosimo's taste, Cosimo gave him a red mantle and a cowl, with a cloak to go under the mantle, all new, and one festal day in the morning he sent them in order that Donatello might wear them. After a day or two of wear he put them aside, saying that he would not wear them again as they were too fine for him. Cosimo was thus liberal to all men of worth through his great liking for them. He had good knowledge of architecture, as may be seen from the buildings he left, none of which were built without consulting him; moreover, all those who were about to build would go to him for advice.

Of agriculture he had the most intimate knowledge, and he would discourse thereupon as if he had never followed any other calling. At S. Marco the garden, which was a most beautiful one, was laid out after his instructions. Hitherto it had been a vacant field belonging to some friars who had held it before the reformation of the order by Pope Eugenius. In all his possessions there were few farming operations which were not directed by him. He did much fruit planting and grafting; and, wonderful as it may seem, he knew about every graft that was made on his estates; moreover, when the peasants came into Florence, he would ask them about the fruit trees and where they were planted. He loved to do grafting and lopping with his own hand. One day I had some talk with him when, being then a young man, he had gone from Florence—where there was sickness—to Careggi. It was then February, when they prune the vines, and I found him engaged in two most excellent tasks. One was to prune the vines every morning for two hours as soon as he rose (in this he imitated Pope Boniface IX, who would prune certain vines in the vineyard of the papal palace at Rome every year in due season. Moreover, at Naples they have preserved till this day his pruning-knife with two silver rings, in memory of Pope Boniface). Cosimo's other employment, when he had done with pruning, was to read the *Moralia* of S. Gregory, an excellent work in thirty-five books, which task occupied him for six months. Both at his villa and in Florence he spent his time well; taking pleasure in no game, save chess, of which he would occasionally play a game or two after supper by way of pastime. He knew Magnolino, who was the best chess player of his age. . . .

In his time lived many men of mark, both lay and cleric, and in literature of all sorts. They were to be met, not only in Florence, but in every part of Italy and foreign lands. First of all in his day lived Pope Martin, who reformed the Church of God which had long been vexed by schism and discord. Then came Pope Eugenius, and Pope Nicolas not inferior to either of these two. Outside Italy reigned the Emperor Sigismond, who held, besides the imperial dominion, the kingdom of Hungary, a valiant foe of the impious Turk, as is plainly manifest, because in his reign they were kept within their own limits and not suffered to oppress Christian people as in former days. Then there was King Alfonso, the paragon of the rulers of his time through the noble qualities which graced him, and Duke Filippo of Milan, who, though certain faults were blended with his undoubted merits, wielded such power that, when he was engaged with the Florentines and the Venetians at the same time, he gave them plenty to think about. To him succeeded Duke Francesco, a master of the art of war, who by his own strength made himself master of Milan. The Doge of Venice was Francesco Foscari, by whose valour and skilful policy the Venetians acquired almost all their territories on the mainland. Cosimo de' Medici was inferior to no one of these distinguished men in his remarkable qualities and outstanding merits.

91 NICCOLÒ MACHIAVELLI, *THE PRINCE:* MACHIAVELLIAN POLITICS

Some men have so great an impact on history that their very names become part of the everyday language of future generations. Such a man was Niccolò Machiavelli. Rightly or wrongly, the term *Machiavellian* has come to signify something opportunistic and cynical, if not downright evil. It would not be an exaggeration to say that no other writings on the art of politics have led to so much controversy as have those of Machiavelli—to some he has appeared as the wicked adviser of tyrants; to others he has seemed to be the noble herald of Italian patriotism. A final judgment will probably never be made, for each generation continues to interpret his thought in the light of its own problems and experiences. In all fairness to Machiavelli, however, it behooves us to view him in the light of his own times.

Machiavelli's lifetime, stretching as it did from 1469 to 1527, spanned a period that represented the culmination of the Italian Renaissance. He grew up while the Medici family was master of Florence, when Lorenzo the Magnificent was carving out for Florence a strategic position in Italian politics. After Lorenzo's death (1492), the Italian peninsula became something of an international football, kicked about by the rival monarchs of France, Spain, and the Holy Roman Empire. During the last thirty-three years of his life Machiavelli saw Italy devastated by French, Spanish, and German invasions. He witnessed the rise and fall of governments; he saw great powers band together to destroy smaller powers; he observed that some states succeeded despite— or rather because of—the duplicity they practiced. The fashioning of some means for reëstablishing a sense of security, of finding some method for re-creating at least the minimum conditions of civil order in his beloved Italy became Machiavelli's great goal.

What we must remember, then, is that Machiavelli lived at a time when Renaissance politics were at their most ruthless and chaotic. That is why he had so little to say about normal government in ordinary happy times: in his day it did not exist. Instead, living in a period of perpetual crises, he offered his advice to the adventurer, the self-made man who ruled, or tried to rule, under emergency conditions. In a world where thrones were shaky, where every state felt its neighbor a threat, where even the great Italian states suffered repeated topplings of government, it was natural that Machiavelli's political formulae should embrace the clever, the crafty, and the violent. It is therefore not surprising that *The Prince*, Machiavelli's most famous political treatise, should be a handbook of maxims specially tailored to a tyrant's purposes, although it is precisely because of this that he has been criticized by later generations.

The selections below are fairly representative of the general tenor of *The Prince*. One may well compare his attitudes toward the violent seizure of power and the cruelty of rulers with those of twentieth-century tyrants.

Of the Things for Which Men, and Especially Princes, Are Praised or Blamed.

It now remains to be seen what are the methods and rules for a prince as regards his subjects and friends. And as I know that many have written of this, I fear that my writing about it may be deemed presumptuous, differing as I do, especially in this matter, from the opinions of others. But my intention being to write something of use to those who understand, it appears to me more proper to go to the real truth of the matter than to its imagination; and many have imagined republics and principalities which have never been seen or known to exist in reality; for how we live is so far removed from how we ought to live, that he who abandons what is done for what ought to be done, will rather learn to bring about his own ruin than his preservation. A man who wishes to make a profession of goodness in everything must necessarily come to grief among so many who are not good. Therefore it is necessary for a prince, who wishes to maintain himself, to learn how not to be good, and to use this knowledge and not use it, according to the necessity of the case.

Leaving on one side, then, those things which concern only an imaginary prince, and speaking of those that are real, I state that all men, and especially princes, who are placed at a greater height, are reputed for certain qualities which bring them either praise or blame. Thus one is considered liberal, another *misero* or miserly (using a Tuscan term, seeing that *avaro* with us still means one who is rapaciously acquisitive and *misero* one who makes grudging use of his own); one a free giver, another rapacious; one cruel, another merciful; one a breaker of his word, another trustworthy; one effeminate and pusillanimous, another fierce and high-spirited; one humane, another haughty; one lascivious, another chaste; one frank, another astute; one hard, another easy; one serious, another frivolous; one religious, another an unbeliever, and so on. I know that every one will admit that it would be highly praiseworthy in a prince to possess all the above-named qualities that are reputed good, but as they cannot all be possessed or observed, human conditions not permitting of it, it is necessary that he should be prudent enough to avoid the scandal of those vices which would lose him the state, and guard himself if possible against those which will not lose it him, but if not able to, he can indulge them with less scruple. And yet he must not mind incurring the scandal of those vices, without which it would be difficult to save the state, for if one considers well, it will be found that some things which seem virtues would, if followed, lead to one's ruin, and some others which appear vices result in one's greater security and wellbeing....

How Much Fortune Can Do in Human Affairs and How It May Be Opposed.

It is not unknown to me how many have been and are of opinion that worldly events are so governed by fortune and by God, that men cannot by their prudence change them, and that on the contrary there is no remedy whatever, and for this they may judge it to be useless to toil much about them, but let things be ruled by chance. This opinion has been more held in our day, from the great changes that have been seen, and are daily seen, beyond every human conjecture. When I think about them, at times I am partly inclined to share this opinion. Nevertheless, that our free will may not be altogether extinguished, I think it may be true that fortune is the ruler of half our actions, but that she allows the other half or thereabouts to be governed by us. I would compare her to an impetuous river that, when turbulent, inundates the plains, casts down trees and buildings, removes earth from this side and places it on the other; every one flees before it, and everything yields to its fury without being able to oppose it; and yet though it is of such a kind, still when it is quiet, men can make provisions against it by dykes and banks, so that when it rises it will either go into a canal or its rush will not be so wild and dangerous. So it is with fortune, which shows her power where no measures have been taken to resist her, and directs her fury where she knows that no dykes or barriers have been made to hold her. And if you regard Italy, which has been the seat of these changes, and which has given the impulse to them, you will see her to be a country without dykes or banks of any kind. If she had been protected by proper measures, like Germany, Spain, and France, this inundation would not have caused the great changes that it has, or would not have happened at all.

This must suffice as regards opposition to fortune in general. But limiting myself more to particular cases, I would point out how one sees a certain prince to-day fortunate and to-morrow ruined, without seeing that he has changed in character or otherwise. I believe this arises in the first place from the causes that we have already discussed at length; that is to say, because the prince who bases himself entirely on

---

Text: Niccolò Machiavelli, *The Prince*, trans. N. H. Thomson, "The Harvard Classics," ed. Charles W. Eliot (New York: P. F. Collier & Son Company, 1910), Vol. 36, pp. 92-93, 131-34.

fortune is ruined when fortune changes. I also believe that he is happy whose mode of procedure accords with the needs of the times, and similarly he is unfortunate whose mode of procedure is opposed to the times. For one sees that men in those things which lead them to the aim that each one has in view, namely, glory and riches, proceed in various ways; one with circumspection, another with impetuosity, one by violence, another by cunning, one with patience, another with the reverse; and each by these diverse ways may arrive at his aim. One sees also two cautious men, one of whom succeeds in his designs, and the other not, and in the same way two men succeed equally by different methods, one being cautious, the other impetuous, which arises only from the nature of the times, which does or does not conform to their method of procedure. From this it results, as I have said, that two men, acting differently, attain the same effect, and of two others acting in the same way, one attains his goal and not the other. On this depend also the changes in prosperity, for if it happens that time and circumstances are favourable to one who acts with caution and prudence he will be successful, but if time and circumstances change he will be ruined, because he does not change his mode of procedure. No man is found so prudent as to be able to adapt himself to this, either because he cannot deviate from that to which his nature disposes him, or else because having always prospered by walking in one path, he cannot persuade himself that it is well to leave it; and therefore the cautious man, when it is time to act suddenly, does not know how to do so and is consequently ruined; for it one could change one's nature with time and circumstances, fortune would never change.

Pope Julius II acted impetuously in everything he did and found the times and conditions so in conformity with that mode of procedure, that he always obtained a good result. Consider the first war that he made against Bologna while Messer Giovanni Bentivogli was still living. The Venetians were not pleased with it, neither was the King of Spain, France was conferring with him over the enterprise, notwithstanding which, owing to his fierce and impetuous disposition, he engaged personally in the expedition. This move caused both Spain and the Venetians to halt and hesitate, the latter through fear, the former through the desire to recover the entire kingdom of Naples. On the other hand, he engaged with him the King of France, because seeing him make this move and desiring his friendship in order to put down the Venetians, that king judged that he could not refuse him his troops without manifest injury. Thus Julius by his impetuous move achieved what no other pontiff with the utmost human prudence would have succeeded in doing, because, if he had waited till all arrangements had been made and everything settled before leaving Rome, as any other pontiff would have done, it would never have succeeded. For the king of France would have found a thousand excuses, and the others would have inspired him with a thousand fears. I will omit his other actions, which were all of this kind and which all succeeded well, and the shortness of his life did not suffer him to experience the contrary, for had times followed in which it was necessary to act with caution, his ruin would have resulted, for he would never have deviated from these methods to which his nature disposed him.

I conclude then that fortune varying and men remaining fixed in their ways, they are successful so long as these ways conform to circumstances, but when they are opposed then they are unsuccessful. I certainly think that it is better to be impetuous than cautious, for fortune is a woman, and it is necessary, if you wish to master her, to conquer her by force; and it can be seen that she lets herself be overcome by the bold rather than by those who proceed coldly. And therefore, like a woman, she is always a friend to the young, because they are less cautious, fiercer, and master her with greater audacity.

92 GIORGIO VASARI, "LEONARDO DA VINCI, FLORENTINE PAINTER AND SCULPTOR": THE VERSATILE RENAISSANCE GENIUS

The Renaissance ideal of greatness was the universal man, the man of genius in all fields. One of the few who actually achieved this ideal was Leonardo da Vinci (1452-1519). The mere enumeration of his accomplishments displays the staggering array of his talents—he was at once a painter, sculptor, architect, musician, mechanic, engineer, inventor, and natural philosopher, and was proficient as well in geology, botany, physiology, anatomy, mathematics, and poetry. Little wonder that for generations Leonardo da Vinci has stood as a symbol of the highest aspirations of the Renaissance.

Despite the universality of his genius, in his own day Leonardo achieved fame chiefly as a painter and sculptor. This in itself illustrates two important features of the Renaissance. One is that the Renaissance was not a popular movement; it was confined to the elite of society. Art and artists flourished because they were supported by kings, popes, and wealthy merchant princes; only the rich and the wellborn had the wherewithal to subsidize men of talent for long periods of time while they labored to produce their masterpieces. Renaissance artists did not live in garrets, awaiting the time when the products of their genius would attract attention at a public exhibition; no artist could sustain himself by producing for the "public." Instead they were commissioned by their patrons to execute specific works of art. Thus the existence of an affluent class of patrons—including princes, prelates, and businessmen, whose cultural tastes inclined them to support the artists of their day—helps explain why art flourished during the Renaissance. Had Leonardo lived at a time and in a place where this type of social class did not exist, it is doubtful that the world would have been enriched by his genius to the degree that it was.

The second characteristic of the Renaissance illustrated by Leonardo's career is the distance between the soaring imagination of an artist like Leonardo and the technical level or even the scientific interest of his era. Into his notebooks he crammed descriptions and sketches of a multitude of machines—from machines for grinding needles to machines for flying. But in an age that cared less for science than for the enhancement of personality and the perpetuation of beauty and that in any case did not command the mechanical energy that was needed to operate something like a flying machine, many of Leonardo's inventions were unrealizable. This, and the fact that they were written in such a way that they could be read only with a mirror, explains why the 5000 pages of notes and sketches he left behind lay unread for 250 years.

The following sketch of Leonardo was published in 1550, only thirty-one years after his death, by Giorgio Vasari (1511-1574), himself an architect and painter. Spiced with amusing anecdotes, it presents a wonderful picture of the many-faceted genius who was not above playing weirdly clever practical jokes on his friends. Notice how differently Vasari, a typical man of the Renaissance, reacts to Leonardo as painter and Leonardo as engineer.

The most heavenly gifts seem to be showered on certain human beings. Sometimes supernaturally, marvelously, they all congregate in one individual. Beauty, grace, and talent are combined in such bounty that in whatever that man undertakes, he outdistances all other men and proves himself to be specially endowed by the hand of God. He owes his pre-eminence not to human teaching or human power. This was seen and acknowledged by all men in the case of Leonardo da Vinci, who had, besides the beauty of his person (which was such that it has never been sufficiently extolled), an indescribable grace in every effortless act and deed. His talent was so rare that he mastered any subject to which he turned his attention. Extraordinary strength and remarkable facility were here combined. He had a mind of regal boldness and magnanimous daring. His gifts were such that his celebrity was worldwide, not only in his own day, but even more after his death, and so will continue until the end of time.

Text: Giorgio Vasari, "Leonardo da Vinci, Florentine Painter and Sculptor," in *Vasari's Lives of the Artists*, ed. Betty Burroughs. Copyright, 1946, by Betty Burroughs. Reprinted by permission of the publishers, Simon and Schuster, Inc., New York, and George Allen & Unwin, Ltd., London. Pp. 187-89, 191-93, 195-97.

Truly admirable, indeed, and divinely endowed was Leonardo da Vinci, the son of Ser Piero da Vinci. He might have been a scientist if he had not been so versatile. But the instability of his character caused him to take up and abandon many things. In arithmetic, for example, he made such rapid progress during the short time he studied it that he often confounded his teacher by his questions. He also began the study of music and resolved to learn to play the lute, and as he was by nature of exalted imagination, and full of the most graceful vivacity, he sang and accompanied himself most divinely, improvising at once both verses and music.

Though he divided his attention among pursuits so varied, Leonardo never abandoned his drawing, and also continued to model in relief, occupations which attracted him more than any others. His father, Ser Piero, observing this and taking into account the extraordinary character of his son's genius, took some of Leonardo's drawings to Andrea del Verrocchio, his intimate friend. He begged Andrea to tell him whether the boy showed promise. Verrocchio was amazed at these early efforts of Leonardo's and advised Ser Piero to see to it that his son become a painter. Leonardo was therefore sent to study in the shop of Andrea, whither he went most willingly. He studied not one branch of art only, but all. Admirably intelligent, and an excellent geometrician besides, Leonardo not only worked in sculpture—certain terra-cotta heads of smiling women and others of children done in early boyhood seem to be the work of a master—but, as an architect, designed ground plans and entire buildings; and, as an engineer, was the one who first suggested making a canal from Florence to Pisa by altering the river Arno. Leonardo also designed mills and water-driven machines. But, as he had resolved to make painting his profession, he spent most of his time drawing from life. He sometimes modeled clay figures on which he draped soft cloth dipped in plaster, and from these he made careful drawings on fine linen. He drew on paper also with so much care and so perfectly that no one has equaled him. Leonardo, imbued with power and grace, was endowed with so marvelous a facility, and his mind, his memory, and his hand were so efficient in the service of his intellect, that he confounded every antagonist.

Leonardo was frequently occupied in the preparation of plans to remove mountains or to pierce them with tunnels from plain to plain. By means of levers, cranes, and screws, he showed how to lift or move great weights. Designing dredging machines and inventing the means of drawing water from the greatest depths were among the speculations from which he never rested. Many drawings of these projects exist which are cherished by those who practice our arts. Besides all this, he wasted not a little time designing curiously intertwined cords made into a circle. A very curiously complicated and exceedingly difficult specimen of these coils may be seen engraved about the words *Leonardus Vinci Academia.* Among Leonardo's models and drawings is one by means of which he sought to prove to the ruling citizens of Florence, many of them men of great discernment, that the church of San Giovanni could be raised and mounted upon a flight of steps without injury to the building. He was so persuasive that it seemed feasible while he spoke, although every one of his hearers, when he was gone, could see for himself that such a thing was impossible. Indeed, he was so pleasing in conversation that he won all hearts.

Though his patrimony was a mere pittance, and though he worked very little, Leonardo kept many servants and horses, taking extraordinary delight in the latter. He was fond of all animals, and it is told that he used to buy caged birds only to set them free. Leonardo, in mind and spirit, gave evidence of such admirable power and perfection that whatever he did bore an impress of harmony, truthfulness, goodness, sweetness, and grace, beyond all other men.

Leonardo, with his profound comprehension of art, began many things that he never completed, because it seemed to him that perfection must elude him. He frequently formed in his imagination enterprises so difficult and so subtle that they could not be entirely realized and worthily executed by human hands. His conceptions were varied to infinity. In natural philosophy, among other things, he examined plants and observed the stars—the movements of the planets, the variations of the moon, and the course of the sun. . . .

When Ludovico Sforza became duke of Milan in 1493, he invited Leonardo most ceremoniously to come and play the lute before him. Leonardo took an instrument he had himself constructed of silver in the shape of a horse's head, a form calculated to render the tone louder and more sonorous. Leonardo was one of the best *improvisatori* in verse of his time. He surpassed all the musicians who had assembled to perform and so charmed the duke by his varied gifts that the nobleman delighted beyond measure in his society. The duke prevailed on him to paint a Nativity for an altarpiece to be sent as a present to the Emperor [Maximilian I]. For the Dominican monks of Santa Maria delle Grazie at Milan, Leonardo painted the *Last Supper.* This is a most beautiful and admirable work. The master gave so much beauty and majesty to the heads of the Apostles that he was constrained to leave the Christ unfinished, convinced as he was that he could not render the divinity of the Redeemer. Even so, this work has always been held in the highest estimation by the Milanese and by foreigners as well. Leonardo rendered to perfection the doubts and anxieties of the Apostles, their desire to know by whom their Master is to be betrayed. All their faces show their love, terror, anger, grief, or bewilderment, unable as they are to fathom the meaning of the Lord. The spectator is also struck by the determination, hatred, and treachery of Judas. The whole is executed with the most minute exactitude. The texture of the tablecloth seems actually made of linen.

The story goes that the prior was in a great hurry to see the picture done. He could not understand why Leonardo should sometimes remain before his work half a day together, absorbed in thought. He would have him work away, as he compelled the laborers to do who were digging in his garden, and never put the pencil down. Not content with seeking to hurry

Leonardo, the prior even complained to the duke, and tormented him so much that at length, he sent for Leonardo and courteously entreated him to finish the work. Leonardo, knowing the duke to be an intelligent man, explained himself as he had never bothered to do to the prior. He made it clear that men of genius are sometimes producing most when they seem least to labor, for their minds are then occupied in the shaping of those conceptions to which they afterward give form. He told the duke that two heads were yet to be done: that of the Saviour, the likeness of which he could not hope to find on earth and had not yet been able to create in his imagination in perfection of celestial grace; and the other, of Judas. He said he wanted to find features fit to render the appearance of a man so depraved as to betray his benefactor, his Lord, and the Creator of the world. He said he would still search but as a last resort he could always use the head of that troublesome and impertinent prior. This made the duke laugh with all his heart. The prior was utterly confounded and went away to speed the digging in his garden. Leonardo was left in peace.

The head of Judas, as we see it finished, is indeed the image of treachery and wickedness. The nobility of this painting, in composition and in high finish, made the king of France [Francis I] wish to remove it to his own kingdom. He attempted to find architects to frame it in wood that it might be transported without injury. He was not deterred by any consideration of cost, but as the painting was on the wall, he had to forgo his desire, and the Milanese kept their picture. . . .

Leonardo afterward gave his attention to human anatomy, in company with Messer Marcantonio della Torre, an eminent philosopher. Messer Marcantonio was then lecturing in Pavia and writing on anatomy, a subject which had, until that time, been lost in the darkness of ignorance. Leonardo filled Marcantonio's book with drawings in red crayon outlined with the pen. These were drawn with the utmost care from bodies dissected by his own hand. He set forth the structure, arrangement, and disposition of the bones. Later he added the nerves in their due order, and then the muscles. He wrote an explanation, left-handed and backward, that can be read only with a mirror. . . . It seems almost incredible that this sublime genius could discourse, as he had done, of art, and of the muscles, nerves, veins, and every other part of the frame. There are besides, other writings of Leonardo's, also written with the left hand. They treat of painting and design in general and his theory of color. . . .

When Leo X became pope, Leonardo went to Rome with Duke Giuliano de' Medici. The pontiff was interested in philosophical inquiry and especially in alchemy. Leonardo made some fanciful figures of animals out of wax paste, hollow and very light, which floated in the air when they were inflated, but fell to the ground as the air escaped. A gardener of the Belvedere one day brought in a curious lizard for which Leonardo made wings from the skins of other lizards. In these wings he put quicksilver, so that, when the animal walked, the wings moved with a tremulous motion. He then made eyes, horns, and a beard for the creature, which he tamed and kept in a cage. He showed it to his visitors, and all who saw it ran away terrified. More than once, he had the intestines of a sheep cleaned and scraped until they were so fine that they could be held in the hollow of the hand. Then he fastened one end to a pair of bellows in another room and blew them up so that they filled the whole room, which was a very large one. Anyone who was there had to take refuge in a corner. He made numbers of these follies and occupied himself with mirrors and optical instruments. He also made experiments in oils and varnishes for painting. Leonardo received a commission for a picture from Pope Leo and immediately began to distill oils and herbs for the varnish, whereupon the pontiff remarked, "Alas! this man will do nothing at all, since he is thinking of the end before he has made a beginning."

There was constant discord between Michelangelo Buonarroti and Leonardo. Michelangelo even left Florence because of it, and Duke Giuliano excused him by saying that the pope had summoned him to Rome. When Leonardo heard of this, he departed for France to the court of the king [Francis I] who already owned several of his works and wished him to paint the cartoon of Saint Anne. Leonardo kept him waiting, according to his custom, a long time. Finally, being old, he lay sick for many months. When he found himself near death he made every effort to acquaint himself with the doctrine of the Catholic ritual. Then he confessed himself with great penitence and devoutly received the sacrament, sustained, because he could not stand, by his servants and friends. The King, who used to visit him often, came immediately afterward to his room. Leonardo was lamenting to him his fear that he had offended God and man, since he had not labored in art as he should have done, when he was seized with a violent paroxysm, the forerunner of death. The king rose and supported his head to assist him, in the hope of alleviating his pain, and Leonardo departed this life in the arms of the monarch.

The death of Leonardo caused great sorrow to all who had known him. Nor was there ever an artist who did more to honor the art of painting. The radiance of his countenance, which was splendidly beautiful, brought cheer to the most melancholy. He was most persuasive and could make a man say "yes" or "no" as he desired. He was physically so strong that he could bend a horseshoe as if it were lead. His generous liberality offered hospitality to rich or poor, provided only that his guest was distinguished by talent or excellence. The poorest or most insignificant abode was adorned by his presence, and as the city of Florence was blessed by his birth, it suffered grievously by his death. To the art of painting he contributed a mode of deepening the shadows which the moderns have used to give force and relief to their figures. His ability in sculpture is proved by three figures in bronze over the north door of San Giovanni. These were cast by Giovan Francesco Rustici, but under the direction of Leonardo, and are, without doubt, most beautiful in design and finish. We are indebted to Leonardo for a work on the anatomy of the horse and for a still more valuable one on human anatomy. For his many admirable qualities, with which he was so richly endowed, although he talked of more things than he actually accomplished, his fame can never be extinguished. Messer Giovan Battista Strozzi wrote this in his praise:—"He alone vanquished all others: he surpassed Phidias, surpassed Apelles and all their proud followers."

THE RENAISSANCE BEYOND ITALY

93 DESIDERIUS ERASMUS, *THE ENCHIRIDION:* THE CHRISTIAN HUMANIST

Outside of Italy the Renaissance took on a different form, or at least a different spirit. Less boisterous and amoral in tone, the humanists of Germany, France, Spain, the Low Countries, and England were motivated by a deeper religious sense. All humanists were profoundly interested in the classics, but while the Italian humanists studied the ancient Greeks and Romans for what they could learn of man and nature, those beyond Italy studied the Hebrew, Greek, and Latin texts of the Bible and the Church Fathers in order to restore the moral vitality of Christianity. For the latter, universities were still centers of scholastic learning, and among them there was much less consciousness of any sudden break with the Middle Ages than there was among the Italian humanists. In Germany alone, fourteen universities were founded between 1386 and 1506, all concentrating upon theology, medicine, or law; none of the fourteen gave much encouragement to experimental science or to the study of literature. Significantly, a new university was established in 1502 at Wittenberg—the very place from which Martin Luther was to launch the Protestant Reformation fifteen years later.

Not only did humanistic scholarship take on a profounder religious tone beyond Italy, but the religious impulse was also manifested in lay religious movements. In earlier days people strongly motivated by religion were inclined to take holy orders; now people more often preferred to remain laymen. This was an ominous development for the Church, as the religiously inclined humanists and laymen were separating themselves from and becoming progressively more critical of the clergy and its worldliness. Nowhere was this lay religion more active than in the Netherlands. By 1400 a group known as the Brothers of the Common Life had come into being. While not opposed to the organized church, they were never officially recognized by it. The Brothers of the Common Life opened many schools which taught, in addition to the elementary subjects of reading and writing, a Christian ideal of character and conduct. At the end of the fifteenth century there were thousands of laymen in the Lowlands and Rhenish Germany who had been pupils of the Brothers.

This was the environment within which the greatest of all humanists grew up—Desiderius Erasmus (1466?-1536) of Rotterdam. For the first two decades of the sixteenth century this man dominated the cultivated European world. Concerned about the abuses of the Church—he was a contemporary of the most notorious of the worldly Renaissance popes—Erasmus as the scholar and man of letters put his faith in education. He hoped that people would gain a better understanding of Christian teaching through reading the new Greek and Latin editions of the New Testament that he had prepared. Erasmus felt that Christianity should be an expression of broad and tolerant values, just as he was a man of reasonableness and restraint. Hating all worldly pretensions and ambitions, he was convinced that a man might meaningfully engage in the affairs of this world and still remain a devout Christian.

In the following selection, Erasmus writes to a courtier friend to explain how a man of affairs, a courtier and warrior, may defend himself against the temptations of vice and sin. It is interesting to note that Erasmus, as both humanist and Christian, urges his friend to read the classics as well as the Scriptures, and that he tries to reconcile the two. And note, too, how Erasmus' mixture of Christianity and humanism is neatly exemplified by the two weapons he considers most powerful against the seven capital sins.

Of the Weapons of the Christian Warfare.

I think that principle which among the first pertains to the discipline of this military service is that you give especial thought and consideration to what kind of arms is most powerful for the sort of enemies you must encounter, then that you have them always in readiness lest at any time that wiliest of schemers may crush you unarmed and unaware. In your earthly wars it is quite common for you to pause either while the enemy is in winter quarters or when there is a period of truce. For us while as yet we fight in this body it is not permitted to be separated even a finger's breadth (as they say) from our arms. Never should we fail to stand in the battle line, never should we cease to keep watch, because our enemy never ceases in his attacks. Verily, when he is peaceful, when he pretends flight or a truce, then he is most of all preparing traps; nor ought we ever more cautiously to stand watch than when he shows the appearance of peace; never ought we to be less frightened by him than when he rises against us in open war. Therefore let the first care be that the mind be not unarmed. . . .

But we will speak about Christian armor in detail in its proper place. Meanwhile, to speak summarily, two weapons should especially be prepared for him who must fight those seven nations, the Canaanites, the Hittites, the Amorites, the Perizzites, the Girgashites, the Hivites, the Jebusites, that is, against the whole troop of vices, of which the seven capital sins are numbered most powerful. These two weapons are prayer and knowledge. Paul always expresses the desire that men be so armed, for he commands them to pray without ceasing. Pure prayer directed to heaven subdues passion, for it is a citadel inaccessible to the enemy. Knowledge furnishes the intellect with salutary opinions so that nothing else may be lacking.

Text: From *Advocates of Reform, From Wyclif to Erasmus*, LCC, Vol. XIV, edited by Matthew Spinka. Published in the U.S.A. by The Westminster Press, 1953. Used by permission.

"So truly does each claim the other's aid,
 and make with it a friendly league."

The former implores, but the latter suggests what should be prayed for, that you should pray eagerly, and, according to James, "nothing wavering." Faith and hope prove that you should seek the things of salvation in Jesus' name; knowledge shows you how to do this. The sons of Zebedee heard from Christ these words: "You do not know what you seek." But prayer is indeed more powerful, making it possible to converse with God, yet knowledge is no less necessary. . . .

But hear what Christ teaches us in Matthew's Gospel: "When you pray, do not talk much as the heathen do, for they think they shall be heard for their much speaking. Be not therefore like them, for your Father knows what your need is before you ask him." And Paul contemns ten thousand words spoken in the spirit, that is, with the lips, in favor of five put forth in the understanding. . . . Then, therefore, you should familiarize yourself with this fact: when the enemy attacks and the remaining vices molest you, you should immediately with sure faith arouse your mind toward heaven, whence comes your help. But also raise your hands to heaven. It is safest to be occupied with the duties of piety, that your works may be concerned, not with earthly studies, but with Christ.

But lest you contemn the support of knowledge, consider this. . . . Believe me, dearest beloved brother, there is no attack of the enemy so violent, that is, no temptation so formidable, that an eager study of the Scriptures will not easily beat it off; there is no adversity so sad that it does not render it bearable. . . . For all Holy Scripture was divinely inspired and perfected by God its Author. What is small is the lowliness of the Word, hiding under almost sordid words the greatest mysteries. What is dazzling is no doctrine of mortals, for it is not blemished by any blot of error; the doctrine of Christ alone is wholly snow-white, wholly dazzling, wholly pure. What is inflexible and rough expresses the mystery clothed in the letter. If anyone touches the surface, the pod, what is harder and harsher? They did not taste the manna without the husk who spoke, "This is a hard saying, and who can hear it?" Pluck out the spiritual sense: now nothing is sweeter, nothing more succulent. The word *manna* sounds to the Hebrews like, "What is this?" This agrees beautifully in divine Scripture, which contains nothing idle, nor one tittle . . . not worthy of these words, "What is this?" . . . For what is the water concealed in the veins of the earth but the mystical meaning imprisoned in the letter? What is this same water when it is made to gush forth but the mystical meaning drawn out and explained? Because it is spread far and wide for the edification of the hearers, what prevents its being called a river?

Therefore if you will dedicate yourself wholly to the study of the Scriptures, if you will meditate on the law of the Lord day and night, you will not be afraid of the terror of the night or of the day, but you will be fortified and trained against every onslaught of enemies. Nor would I, for my part, disapprove your taking your preliminary training for military service in the writings of the pagan poets and philosophers, but gradually, at the proper age, . . . and cursorily—not tarrying, as it were, to perish on the sirens' rocks. Saint Basil also calls the young to these studies to establish them in Christian morals and recall them to the muses. Our Augustine was his pupil. Nor is Jerome displeased by the well-beloved captive. Cyprian is praised because he adorned the temple of the Lord with the spoils of Egypt, but I do not want you to imbibe the morals of the Gentiles along with their letters. And yet you will find out very many things there conducing to right living. Nor ought you to despise pagan authors, for they too are often good moral teachers. Moses did not despise the advice of his father-in-law Jethro. Those letters shape and nourish the child's nature and wonderfully prepare one for the understanding of divine Scriptures, to break in upon which with unwashed feet and hands is almost a sacrilege. Jerome belabors the impudence of those who, advanced in secular studies, dare to treat the divine Scriptures, yet how much more shamelessly do they act who not even having tasted Scripture dare so to do!

But as divine Scripture does not bear much fruit if you persist in and cling to the letter, so is the poetry of Homer or Virgil quite useful if you remember the whole of it to be allegorical. That is something no one will deny who finds the learning of the ancients supremely to his taste. I will not at all insist that you undertake the study of obscene poets—certainly not to look into them more deeply—unless perhaps you learn rather to abhor the vices described and by the contention of wicked things more strongly to love honest ones. Among the philosophers I would prefer you to follow the Platonists, for the reason that in very many of their opinions and in their way of speaking they approach as closely as possible the prophetic and Gospel pattern. . . . Therefore as soon as you feel nausea, you ought to hasten as fast as possible to the manna of heavenly wisdom, which will abundantly nourish and revive you, until as victor you reach those palms of promised reward which will never be lacking. . . .

The first requirement is that you feel worthy sentiments concerning Scripture. Consider these oracles as genuine and sprung from the presence of divine mind. You will feel yourself breathed upon by divine will, affected, seized, transfigured in an ineffable manner, if you approach Scripture religiously, with veneration, humbly. You will see the delights of the blessed Bridegroom; you will see the riches of the richest man, Solomon; you will see the hidden treasures of eternal wisdom. But beware lest you wickedly break into the chamber. The doorway is low. Watch out lest you dash your head against it and be thrown back. Hence believe none of those things which you see with your own eyes and handle with your own hands to be as true as what you read there. It is certain from the divine words that heaven and earth will pass away, but not one jot or tittle of the law is going to pass away before all things are fulfilled. Although men lie and err, the truth of God neither deceives nor is deceived.

From the interpreters of Holy Scripture choose those especially who depart as much as possible from the literal sense. Of this sort, after Paul, among the first are Origen, Ambrose, Jerome, Augustine. For I see the modern theologians too freely and with a certain captious subtlety drinking in the letter, rather than plucking out the mysteries and giving their attention (as if Paul had not spoken the truth) to the fact that our law is spiritual. I have heard some who are to such an extent pleased with these little human comments that they contemn the interpretations of the ancients almost as if they were dreams. To such an extent has Duns Scotus brought confidence to them that, without ever having read the Holy Scriptures, they nevertheless think themselves to be absolute theologians. Even if they say the acutest things, it is for others to judge whether their words are worthy of the Holy Spirit. If you prefer to be more animated in spirit than trained in contention, if you seek the feasting of the soul rather than the itching of natural inclination, read especially the ancients, whose piety is more tried and tested, whose learning richer, and whose prayer is neither poor nor sordid, and whose interpretation of the sacred mysteries more appropriate. Nor will I say that I contemn the moderns, but that I prefer teachings more useful and more conducive to what you have proposed.

94 SIR THOMAS MORE, *UTOPIA*: UTOPIAN PROTEST

As Machiavelli's name added to the English language an adjective connoting the cynicism of power politics, Sir Thomas More's *Utopia* added a word of diametrically opposite meaning. While to be "Machiavellian" is to be brutally realistic, to be "utopian" has come to mean being idealistic and visionary. And yet, as opposed to one another as *The Prince* and *Utopia* seem to be, they have this much in common—they were both attempts to deal with the problems of their age, and they were both written by men who were at once statesmen and humanists. But here the parallel must stop; for More, the most significant figure among English humanists, was far closer to the ideals of his good friend Erasmus than he was to those of Niccolò Machiavelli.

Like Erasmus, Thomas More (1478-1535) was a reformer, and his *Utopia* represented a bitter protest against what he considered to be the great evil of his day, the acquisitiveness of west European and particularly English society. This was the age of Henry VIII and the new statesmanship, when warring princes sought to become the autocratic rulers of centralized states. This was also the era of the new economics, when rising commercial capitalists and great landlords enclosed the common lands and peasant villages to convert them into more profitable sheep pastures for large-scale sheep farming, which became the basis for the English textile economy. From Thomas More's time until the eighteenth century, woolen cloth was to be England's main staple of export. But More, consistently medieval in his viewpoint, was deeply distressed by the emergence of this new economy, based as it was on the free use of capital. He spoke out against the landlords who sacrificed their tenants to economic progress and to the law of supply and demand in the wool market. To Thomas More it seemed that the love of money was indeed the root of all evil.

Utopia was therefore a general indictment of the English society of 1515, the year in which it appeared. It lashed out at the dynastic wars, the abuse of power, the greed of the wealthy, the poverty of the working classes, the cruelties of the criminal law, and the evils resulting from the enclosure movement. The satire behind the portrayal of a mythical island where men lived in peace, harmony, and useful labor was so obvious that the book could not be published in England. Under the editorship of Erasmus it was printed in Latin in Louvain and the first English version did not appear until 1551, sixteen years after More's death.

More himself was a tragic victim of the changing times. Besides being an accomplished scholar of Greek and Latin, he was a successful lawyer and rose to be Lord Chancellor of England under Henry VIII. But his steadfast fidelity to the Church, after Henry's break with the papacy, led to his beheading in 1535. He was a man caught in the currents of the age, for while he had agreed to serve the new state, he had insisted on retaining his old loyalties. The consequence was his own destruction.

Now I have declared and described unto you, as truly as I could the form and order of that commonwealth, which verily in my judgment is not only the best, but also that which alone of good right may claim and take upon it the name of a commonwealth or public weal. For in other places they speak still of the commonwealth, but every man procureth his own private wealth. Here where nothing is private, the common affairs be earnestly looked upon. And truly on both parts they have good cause so to do as they do. For in other countries who knoweth not that he shall starve for hunger, unless he make some several provision for himself, though the commonwealth flourish never so much in riches? And therefore he is compelled even of very necessity to have regard to himself, rather than to the people, that is to say, to other. Contrariwise, there where all things be common to every man, it is not to be doubted that any man shall lack anything necessary for his private uses, so

Text: Sir Thomas More, *Utopia*, "The Harvard Classics," ed. Charles W. Eliot (New York: P. F. Collier & Son Company, 1910), Vol. 36, pp. 250-54.

that the common storehouses and barns be sufficiently stored. For there nothing is distributed after a niggish sort, neither there is any poor man or beggar. And though no man have anything, yet every man is rich. For what can be more rich, than to live joyfully and merrily, without all grief and pensiveness; not caring for his own living, nor vexed or troubled with his wife's importunate complaints, not dreading poverty to his son, nor sorrowing for his daughter's dowry? Yea they take no care at all for the living and wealth of themselves and all theirs, of their wives, their children, their nephews, their children's children, and all the succession that ever shall follow in their posterity. And yet besides this there is no less provision for them that were once labourers and be now weak and impotent, than for them that do now labour and take pain. Here now would I see, if any man dare be so bold as to compare with this equity, the justice of other nations; among whom, I forsake God, if I can find any sign or token of equity and justice. For what justice is this, that a rich goldsmith, or an usurer, or to be short, any of them which either do nothing at all, or else that which they do is such that it is not very necessary to the commonwealth, should have a pleasant and a wealthy living, either by idleness, or by unnecessary business; when in the meantime poor labourers, carters, ironsmiths, carpenters and ploughmen, by so great and continual toil, as drawing and bearing beasts be scant able to sustain, and again so necessary toil, that without it no commonwealth were able to continue and endure one year, do yet get so hard and poor a living, and live so wretched and miserable a life, that the state and condition of the labouring beasts may seem much better and wealthier? For they be not put to so continual labour, nor their living is not much worse, yea to them much pleasanter, taking no thought in the mean season for the time to come. But these silly poor wretches be presently tormented with barren and unfruitful labour. And the remembrance of their poor indigent and beggarly old age killeth them up. For their daily wages is so little, that it will not suffice for the same day, much less it yieldeth any overplus, that may daily be laid up for the relief of old age. Is not this an unjust and an unkind public weal, which giveth great fees and rewards to gentlemen, as they call them, and to goldsmiths, and to such other, which be either idle persons, or else only flatterers, and devisers of vain pleasures; and of the contrary part maketh no gentle provision for poor ploughmen, colliers, labourers, carters, ironsmiths, and carpenters: without whom no commonwealth can continue. But when it hath abused the labours of their lusty and flowering age, at the last when they be oppressed with old age and sickness, being needy, poor, and indigent of all things, then forgetting their so many painful watchings, not remembering their so many and so great benefits, recompenseth and acquitteth them most unkindly with miserable death. And yet besides this the rich men not only by private fraud, but also by common laws, do every day pluck and snatch away from the poor some part of their daily living. So whereas it seemed before unjust to recompense with unkindness their pains that have been beneficial to the public weal, now they have to this their wrong and unjust dealing (which is yet a much worse point) given the name of justice, yea and that by force of a law. Therefore when I consider and weigh in my mind all these commonwealths, which nowadays anywhere do flourish, so God help me, I can perceive nothing but a certain conspiracy of rich men procuring their own commodities under the name and title of the commonwealth. They invent and devise all means and crafts, first how to keep safely, without fear of losing, that they have unjustly gathered together, and next how to hire and abuse the work and labour of the poor for as little money as may be. These devices, when the rich men have decreed to be kept and observed for the commonwealth's sake, that is to say for the wealth also of the poor people, then they be made laws. But these most wicked and vicious men, when they have by their insatiable covetousness divided among themselves all those things, which would have sufficed all men, yet how far be they from the wealth and felicity of the Utopian commonwealth? Out of the which, in that all the desire of money with the use thereof is utterly secluded and banished, how great a heap of cares is cut away! How great an occasion of wickedness and mischief is plucked up by the roots! For who knoweth not, that fraud, theft, ravine, brawling, quarreling, brabling, strife, chiding, contention, murder, treason, poisoning, which by daily punishments are rather revenged than refrained, do die when money dieth? And also that fear, grief, care, labours and watchings do perish even the very same moment that money perisheth? Yea poverty itself, which only seemd to lack money, if money were gone, it also would decrease and vanish away. And that you may perceive this more plainly, consider with yourselves some barren and unfruitful year, wherein many thousands of people have starved for hunger. I dare be bold to say, that in the end of that penury so much corn or grain might have been found in the rich men's barns, if they had been searched, as being divided among them whom famine and pestilence have killed, no man at all should have felt that plague and penury. So easily might men get their living, if that same worthy princess, lady money, did not alone stop up the way between us and our living, which a God's name was very excellently devised and invented, that by her the way thereto should be opened. I am sure the rich men perceive this, nor they be not ignorant how much better it were to lack no necessary thing, than to abound with overmuch superfluity; to be rid out of innumerable cares and troubles, than to be besieged with great riches. And I doubt not that either the respect of every man's private commodity, or else the authority of our saviour Christ (which for his great wisdom could not but know what were best, and for his inestimable goodness could not but counsel to that which he knew to be best) would have brought all the world long ago into the laws of this weal public, if it were not that one only beast, the princess and mother of all mischief, pride, doth withstand and let it. She measureth not wealth and prosperity by her own commodities, but by the miseries and incommodities of other: she would not by her good will be made a goddess, if there were no wretches left, whom she might be lady over to mock and scorn; over whose miseries her felicity might shine, whose poverty she might vex, torment and increase by gorgeously setting forth her riches. This hell-hound creepeth into men's hearts, and plucketh them back from entering the right path of life, and is so deeply rooted in men's breasts, that she cannot be plucked out. This form and fashion of a weal public, which I would gladly wish unto all nations, I am glad yet that it hath chanced to the Utopians, which have followed those institutions of life, whereby they have laid such foundations of their commonwealth, as shall continue and last not only wealthily, but also, as far as man's wit may judge and conjecture, shall endure for ever. For seeing the chief causes of ambition and sedition with other vices be plucked up by the roots and abandoned at home, there can be no jeopardy of domestical dissension, which alone hath cast under foot and brought to nought the well fortified and strongly-defenced wealth and riches of many cities. But forasmuch as perfect concord remaineth, and wholesome laws be executed at home the envy of all foreign princes be not able to shake or move the empire, though they have many times long ago gone about to do it, being evermore driven back.

Thus when Raphael had made an end of his tale, though many things came to my mind, which in the manners and laws of that people seemed to be instituted and founded of no good reason, not only in the fashion of their chivalry, and in their sacrifices and religions, and in other of their laws, but also, yea and chiefly, in that which is the principal foundation of all their ordinances, that is to say, in the community of their life and living, without any occupying of money, by the which thing only all nobility, magnificence, worship, honour and majesty, the true ornaments and honours, as the common opinion is, of a commonwealth, utterly be overthrown and destroyed; yet because I knew that he was weary of talking, and was not sure whether he could abide that anything should be said against his mind; specially because I remembered that he had reprehended this fault in other, which be afraid lest they should seem not to be wise enough, unless they could find some fault in other men's inventions; therefore I praising both their institutions and his communication, took him by the hand, and led him in to supper; saying that we would choose another time to weigh and examine the same matters, and to talk with him more at large therein. Which would to God it might once come to pass. In the meantime, as I cannot agree and consent to all things that he said, being else without doubt a man singularly well learned, and also in all worldly matters exactly and profoundly experienced, so must I needs confess and grant that many things be in the Utopian weal public, which in our cities I may rather wish for, than hope after.

Thus endeth the afternoon's talk of Raphael Hythloday concerning the laws and institutions of the Island of Utopia.

95 FRANÇOIS RABELAIS, GARGANTUA AND PANTAGRUEL: THE HUMANIST REFORMER

The reformist spirit of the Renaissance outside Italy assumed many guises. To the Christian humanism of Erasmus and the utopian protest of Thomas More was added the mocking ridicule of François Rabelais (1495-1553), the outstanding humanist in France. Although he was known to his contemporaries primarily as a skillful physician and as a man whose profound scholarship ranged widely over the whole field of classical learning, he is best known to history as the author of *Gargantua and Pantagruel* (1533-1552), one of the most uproarious social satires ever written. Unlike either Erasmus or More, Rabelais was fired with a tremendous enthusiasm for life in all its phases and thus represented the secular spirit of the Renaissance. In the striking image of John Herman Randall, he was "Great, sprawling, multitudinous Rabelais, monk and wise physician, grasping with both hands the overflowing fulness of all life from the gutter to the stars, his crammed belly ever shaking with peals of wholesouled laughter."

There is much of extravagant buffoonery in *Gargantua and Pantagruel*. But there are also sections of it that reveal Rabelais as a humanist reformer, aspiring for social and political improvement and discussing seriously important questions of education, ethics, government, justice, law, international relations, and the relations between Church and State. Rabelais lived at a time when Francis I of France was the would-be conqueror of Italy, when the Holy Roman Emperor Charles V was constantly trying to enlarge his power, and when for nearly a century no peace lasted for more than six years. His response was to contrast noble and pacific kings with hasty and ambitious monarchs, and to paint in vivid colors the folly and absurdity of wars of conquest. Aware of the abuses, the delays, and the venality of the law courts, he ridiculed them mercilessly with his picture of the old judge who, after listening to a long recitation of evidence, decided cases with a throw of the dice—and "judged no worse than other judges."

Equally telling were his attacks on the old medieval system of education which had persisted into the Renaissance. Despising the narrow logic-chopping which the universities perpetuated, he wanted a system where all arts, all languages, all sciences, and all sports would be taught. In short, he upheld the Renaissance ideal of universality and humanism as opposed to the scholasticism of the Middle Ages. Nevertheless, in his educational scheme he made room for the reading of the Bible in Hebrew and Greek so that the gospel might be studied in its purest simplicity.

He reserved his sharpest attacks for what he considered to be abuses within the Church. As a monk, he knew and hated the debased form of monasticism as it then existed in some quarters. He fiercely satirized the ignorance, apathy, dirt, idleness, drunkenness, gluttony, and vice that he found among some of his confreres. Nowhere, however, did he speak with disrespect of the fundamental doctrines of Christianity. In an age when the Protestant Revolt had shattered the unity of western Christendom and had led to the growth of extreme intolerance, Rabelais advocated free thought and free worship. Even so, he placed his major hope on reform within the Catholic Church.

Rabelais, too, tried his hand at utopia-building and like Thomas More, made it serve as a critique of his own society. But there is an important difference, for unlike More's *Utopia*, Rabelais' Abbey of Thélème sprang from the mind of a man who heartily relished the worldliness of his Renaissance environment. Rabelais the critic-reformer and Rabelais the secularist are both revealed in the passage below.

How Gargantua Had the Abbey of Thélème Built for the Monk.

There remained the monk to provide for. Gargantua wanted to make him Abbot of Seuilly, but the friar refused. He wanted to give him the Abbey of Bourgueil or that of Saint-Florent, whichever might suit him best, or both, if he had a fancy for them. But the monk gave a peremptory reply to the effect that he would not take upon himself any office involving the government of others.

"For how," he demanded, "could I govern others, who cannot even govern myself? If you are of the opinion that I have done you, or may be able to do you in the future, any worthy service, give me leave to found an abbey according to my own plan."

This request pleased Gargantua, and the latter offered his whole province of Thélème, lying along the River Loire, at a distance of two leagues from the great Forest of Port-Huault. The monk then asked that he be permitted to found a convent that should be exactly the opposite of all other institutions of the sort.

"In the first place, then," said Gargantua, "you don't want to build any walls around it; for all the other abbeys have plenty of those."

"Right you are," said the monk, "for where there is a wall (*mur*) in front and behind there is bound to be a lot of *murmur*—ing, jealousy and plotting on the inside."

Text: From *All the Extant Works of Francois Rabelais,* translated by Samuel Putnam. © 1929 by Covici Friede, Inc. Used by permission of Crown Publishers, Inc.

Moreover, in view of the fact that in certain convents in this world there is a custom, if any woman (by which, I mean any modest or respectable one) enters the place, to clean up thoroughly after her wherever she has been—in view of this fact, a regulation was drawn up to the effect that if any monk or nun should happen to enter this new convent, all the places they had set foot in were to be thoroughly scoured and scrubbed. And since, in other convents, everything is run, ruled, and fixed by hours, it was decreed that in this one there should not be any clock or dial of any sort, but that whatever work there was should be done whenever occasion offered. For, as Gargantua remarked, the greatest loss of time he knew was to watch the hands of the clock. What good came of it? It was the greatest foolishness in the world to regulate one's conduct by the tinkling of a time-piece, instead of by intelligence and good common sense.

Another feature: Since in those days women were not put into convents unless they were blind in one eye, lame, hunchbacked, ugly, misshapen, crazy, silly, deformed, and generally of no account, and since men did not enter a monastery unless they were snotty-nosed, underbred, dunces, and trouble-makers at home—

"Speaking of that," said the monk, "of what use is a woman who is neither good nor good to look at?"

"Put her in a convent," said Gargantua.

"Yes," said the monk, "and set her to making shirts."

And so, it was decided that in this convent they would receive only the pretty ones, the ones with good figures and sunny dispositions, and only the handsome, well set-up, good-natured men.

Item: Since in the convents of women, men never entered, except under-handedly and by stealth, it was provided that, in this one, there should be no women unless there were men also, and no men unless there were also women.

Item: Inasmuch as many men, as well as women, once received into a convent were forced and compelled, after a year of probation, to remain there all the rest of their natural lives—in view of this, it was provided that, here, both men and women should be absolutely free to pick up and leave whenever they happened to feel like it.

Item: Whereas, ordinarily, the religious take three vows, namely, those of chastity, poverty and obedience, it was provided that, in this abbey, one might honorably marry, that each one should be rich, and that all should live in utter freedom.

With regard to the lawful age for entering, the women should be received from the age of ten to fifteen years, and men from the age of twelve to eighteen.

How the Abbey of the Thelemites Was Built and Endowed....

This building was a hundred times more magnificent than the one at Bonivet, at Chambord, or at Chantilly; for in it there were nine-thousand-three-hundred-thirty-two rooms, each equipped with a dressing-room, a study, a wardrobe, and a chapel, and each opening into a large hall. Between the towers, in the center of the main building, was a winding-stair, the steps of which were partly of porphyry, partly of Numidian stone, and partly of serpentine marble, each step being twenty-two feet long and three fingers thick, with an even dozen between each pair of landings. On each landing were two fine antique arches, admitting the daylight, while through these arches, one entered a loggia of the width of the stair, the stair itself running all the way to the roof and ending in a pavilion. From this stair one could enter, from either side, a large hall, and from this hall the rooms.

From the tower known as Arctic to the one called Cryere, there were fine large libraries, in Greek, Latin, Hebrew, French, Tuscan, and Spanish, separated from each other according to the different languages. In the middle of the building was another and marvelous stairway, the entrance to which was from outside the house, by way of an arch thirty-six feet wide. This stair was so symmetrical and capacious that six men-at-arms, their lances at rest, could ride up abreast, all the way to the roof. From the tower Anatole to Mesembrine, there were large and splendid galleries, all containing paintings representative of deeds of ancient prowess, along with historical and geographical scenes. In the center of this elevation was still another gateway and stair, like the one on the river-side. Over this gate, there was inscribed, in large old-fashioned letters, the following poem:

Inscription Over the Great Portal of Thélème.

You hypocrites and two-faced, please stay out:
Grinning old apes, potbellied snivelbeaks,
Stiffnecks and blockheads, worse than Goths, no doubt,
Magogs and Ostrogoths we read about;
You hairshirt whiners and you slippered sneaks;
You fur-lined beggars and you nervy freaks;
You bloated dunces, trouble-makers all;
Go somewhere else to open up your stall.

  Your cursed ways
  Would fill my peaceful days

With nasty strife;
With your lying life,
You'd spoil my roundelays—
With your cursed ways.

Stay out, you lawyers, with your endless guts,
You clerks and barristers, you public pests,
You Scribes and Pharisees, with your "if's" and "but's,"
You hoary judges (Lord, how each one struts!):
You feed, like dogs, on squabbles and bequests;
You'll find your salary in the hangman's nests;
Go there and bray, for here there is no guile
That you can take to court, to start a trial.

No trials or jangles
Or legal wrangles:
We're here to be amused.
If your jaws must be used,
You've bags full of tangles,
Trials and jangles.

Stay out, you usurers and misers all,
Gluttons for gold, and how you hoard the stuff!
Greedy windjammers, with a world of gall,
Hunchbacked, snubnosed, your money-jars full, you bawl
For more and more; you never have enough;
Your stomachs never turn, for they are tough,
As you heap your piles, each miser-faced poltroon:
I hope Old Death effaces you, right soon!

That inhuman mug
Makes us shrug:
Take it to another shop,
And please don't stop,
But elsewhere lug
That inhuman mug!

Stay out of here, at morning, noon and night,
Jealous old curs, dotards that whine and moan,
All trouble-makers, full of stubborn spite,
Phantom avengers of a Husband's plight,
Whether Greek or Latin, worst wolves ever known;
You syphilitics, mangy to the bone,
Go take your wolfish sores, and let them feed at ease—
Those cakey crusts, signs of a foul disease.

Honor, praise, delight
Rule here, day and night;
We're gay, and we agree;
We're healthy, bodily;
And so, we have a right
To honor, praise, delight.

But welcome here, and very welcome be,
And doubly welcome, all noble gentlemen.
This is the place where taxes all are free,
And incomes plenty, to live merrily,
However fast you come—I shan't "say when":
Then, be my cronies in this charming den;
Be spruce and jolly, gay and always mellow,
Each one of us a very pleasant fellow.

Companions clean,
Refined, serene,
Free from avarice;
For civilized bliss,
See, the tools are keen,
Companions clean.

And enter here, all you who preach and teach
The living Gospel, though the heathen raves:
You'll find a refuge here beyond their reach,
Against the hostile error you impeach,
Which through the world spreads poison, and depraves;
Come in, for here we found a faith that saves;
By voice and letter, let's confound the herd
Of enemies of God's own Holy Word.

The word of grace
We'll not efface
From this holy place;
Let each embrace,
And himself enlace
With the word of grace.

Enter, also, ladies of high degree!
Feel free to enter and be happy here,
Each face with beauty flowering heavenly,
With upright carriage, pleasing modesty:
This is the house where honor's held most dear,
Gift of a noble lord whom we revere,
Our patron, who's established it for you,
And given us his gold, to see it through.

Gold given by gift
Gives golden shrift—
To the giver a gift,
And very fine thrift,
A wise man's shift,
Is gold given by gift.

What Kind of Dwelling the Thelemites Had.

In the middle of the lower court was a magnificent fountain of beautiful alabaster, above which were the three Graces with cornucopias, casting out water through their breasts, mouths, ears, eyes, and the other openings of their bodies.

The interior of the portion of the dwelling that opened upon this court rested upon great pillars of chalcedony and of porphyry, fashioned with the finest of antique workmanship. Above were splendid galleries, long and wide, adorned with paintings, with the horns of deer, unicorns, rhinoceroses, and hippopotamuses, as well as with elephants' teeth and other objects interesting to look upon.

The ladies' quarters extended from the tower Arctic to the Mesembrine gate. The men occupied the rest of the house. In front of the ladies' quarters, in order that the occupants might have something to amuse them, there had been set up, between the first two outside towers, the lists, the hippodrome, the theatre, and the swimming-pools, with wonderful triple-stage baths, well provided with all necessary equipment and plentifully supplied with water of myrrh.

Next the river was a fine pleasure-garden, in the center of which was a handsome labyrinth. Between the towers were the tennis courts and the ball-grounds. On the side by the tower Cryere was the orchard, full of all sorts of fruit-trees, all of them set out in the form of quincunxes. Beyond was the large park, filled with every sort of savage beast. Between the third pair of towers were the targets for arquebus, archery, and crossbow practice. The servants' quarters were outside the tower Hesperia and consisted of one floor only, and beyond these quarters were the stables. In front of the latter stood the falcon-house, looked after by falconers most expert in their art. It was furnished annually by the Candians, the Venetians, and the Sarmatians, with all kinds of out-of-the-ordinary birds: eagles, gerfalcons, goshawks, sakers, lanners, falcons, sparrow-hawks, merlins, and others, all so well trained and domesticated that, when these birds set out from the castle for a little sport in the fields, they would take everything that came in their way. The hunting-kennels were a little farther off, down toward the park.

All the halls, rooms and closets were tapestried in various manners, according to the season of the year. The whole floor was covered with green cloth. The bedding was of embroidered work. In each dressing-room was a crystal mirror, with chasings of fine gold, the edges being trimmed with pearls; and this mirror was of such a size that—it is the truth I am telling you—it was possible to see the whole figure in it at once. As one came out of the halls into the ladies' quarters, he at once encountered the perfumers and the hair-dressers, through whose hands the gentlemen passed when they came to visit the ladies. These functionaries each morning supplied the women's chambers with rose, orange, and "angel" water; and in each room a precious incense-dish was vaporous with all sorts of aromatic drugs.

How the Monks and Nuns of Thélème Were Clad.

The ladies, when the abbey was first founded, dressed themselves according to their own fancy and good judgment. Later they of their own free will introduced a reform. In accordance with this revised rule, they went clad as follows:

They wore scarlet or kermes-colored stockings, and these extended above their knees for a distance of three inches, to be precise, the borders being of certain fine embroideries and pinkings. Their garters were of the same color as their bracelets, and clasped the leg above and below the knee. Their shoes, pumps, and slippers were of brilliant-colored velvet, red or violet, shaped in the form of a lobster's barbel.

Above the chemise, they wore a fine bodice, of a certain silk-camlet material, and a taffeta petticoat, white, red, tan, gray, etc. Over this went a skirt of silver taffeta, made with embroideries of fine gold or elaborate needlework, or, as the wearer's fancy might dictate, and depending upon the weather, of satin, of damask, or of velvet, being orange, tan, green, ash-gray, blue, bright yellow, brilliant red, or white in color, and being made of cloth-of-gold, silver tissue, thread-work, or embroidery, according to the feast-days. Their gowns, which were in keeping with the season, were of gold tissue or silver crisping, and were made of red satin, covered with gold needle-work, or of white, blue, black, or tan taffeta, silk serge, silk-camlet, velvet, silver-cloth, silver-tissue, or of velvet or satin with gold facings of varying design.

In summer, on certain days, in place of gowns they wore cloaks of the above-mentioned materials, or sleeveless jackets, cut in the Moorish fashion and made of violet-colored velvet, with crispings of gold over silver needlework, or with gold knots, set off at the seams with little Indian pearls. And they always had a fine plume, matching the color of their sleeves and well trimmed with golden spangles.

In winter, they wore taffeta gowns of the colors mentioned, trimmed with the fur of lynxes, black-spotted weasels, Calabrian or Siberian sables, and other precious skins. Their chaplets, rings, gold-chains, and goldwork-necklaces contained fine stones: carbuncles, rubies, balas rubies, diamonds, sapphires, emeralds, turquoises, garnets, agates, beryls, and pearls great and small.

Their head-dress, likewise, depended upon the weather. In winter, it was after the French fashion; in spring, after the Spanish style; in summer, after the Tuscan. That is, excepting feast-days and Sundays, when they wore the French coiffure, for the reason that it is more respectable and better in keeping with matronly modesty.

The men dressed after a fashion of their own. Their stockings were of broadcloth or of serge, and were scarlet, kermes-hued, white, or black in color. Their hose were of velvet and of the same colors, or very nearly the same, being embroidered and cut to suit the fancy. Their doublets were of cloth-of-gold, silver-cloth, velvet, satin, damask, or taffeta, of the same shades, all being cut, embroidered, and fitted in a most excellent fashion. Their girdles were of the same-colored silk, the buckles being of well enameled gold. Their jackets and vests were of cloth-of-gold, gold-tissue, silver-cloth, or velvet. Their robes were as precious as the ladies' gowns, the girdles being of silk, of the same color as the doublet. Each one carried a fine sword at his side, with a gilded handle, the scabbard being of velvet, of the same shade as the stockings, while the tip was of gold or goldsmith-work, with a dagger to match. Their bonnets were of black velvet, trimmed with a great many berry-like ornaments and gold buttons, and the white plume was most prettily divided by golden spangles, from the ends of which dangled handsome rubies, emeralds, etc.

Such a sympathy existed between the men and the women that each day they were similarly dressed; and in order that they might not fail on this point, there were certain gentlemen whose duty it was to inform the men each morning what livery the ladies proposed to wear that day, for everything depended upon the will of the fair ones. In connection with all these handsome garments and rich adornments you are not to think that either sex lost any time whatsoever, for the masters of the wardrobe had the clothing all laid out each morning, and the ladies of the chamber were so well trained that in no time at all their mistresses were dressed and their toilets completed from head to foot.

In order to provide the more conveniently for these habiliments, there was, near the wood of Thélème, a large group of houses extending for half a league, houses that were well lighted and well equipped, in which dwelt the goldsmiths, lapidaries, embroiderers, tailors, gold-thread-workers, velvet-makers, tapestry-makers, and upholsterers; and there each one labored at his trade and the whole product went for the monks and nuns of the abbey. These workmen were supplied with material by my Lord Nausicletus, who every year sent them seven ships from the Pearl and Cannibal Islands, laden with gold-nuggets, raw silk, pearls, and precious stones. And if certain pearls showed signs of aging and of losing their native luster, the workmen by their art would renew these, by feeding them to handsome cocks, in the same manner in which one gives a purge to falcons.

How the Thelemites Were Governed in Their Mode of Living.

Their whole life was spent, not in accordance with laws, statutes, or rules, but according to their own will and free judgment. They rose from bed when they felt like it and drank, ate, worked, and slept when the desire came to them. No one woke them, no one forced them to drink or eat or do any other thing. For this was the system that Gargantua had established. In the rule of their order there was but this one clause:

Do what thou wouldst

for the reason that those who are free born and well born, well brought up, and used to decent society possess, by nature, a certain instinct and spur, which always impels them to virtuous deeds and restrains them from vice, an instinct which is the thing called honor. These same ones, when, through vile subjection and constraint, they are repressed and held down, proceed to employ that same noble inclination to virtue in throwing off and breaking the yoke of servitude, for we always want to come to forbidden things; and we always desire that which is denied us.

In the enjoyment of their liberty, the Thelemites entered into a laudable emulation in doing, all of them, anything which they thought would be pleasing to one of their number. If anyone, male or female, remarked: "Let us drink," they all drank. If anyone said: "Let us play," they all played. If anyone suggested: "Let us go find some sport in the fields," they all went there. If it was hawking or hunting, the ladies went mounted upon pretty and easy-paced nags or proud-stepping palfreys, each of them bearing upon her daintily gloved wrist a sparrow-hawk, a lanneret, or a merlin. The men carried the other birds.

They were all so nobly educated that there was not, in their whole number, a single one, man or woman, who was not able to read, write, sing, play musical instruments, and speak five or six languages, composing in these languages both poetry and prose.

In short, there never were seen knights so bold, so gallant, so clever on horse and on foot, more vigorous, or more adept at handling all kinds of weapons than were they. There never were seen ladies so well groomed, so pretty, less boring, or more skilled at hand and needlework and in every respectable feminine activity. For this reason, when the time came that any member of this abbey, either at the request of his relatives or from some other cause, wished to leave, he always took with him one of the ladies, the one who had taken him for her devoted follower, and the two of them were then married. And if they had lived at Thélème in devotion and friendship, they found even more of both after their marriage, and remained as ardent lovers at the end of their days, as they had been on the first day of their honeymoon.

96   MIGUEL DE CERVANTES SAAVEDRA, *THE INGENIOUS GENTLEMAN DON QUIXOTE DE LA MANCHA:* DON QUIXOTE AND THE PUPPETS

In Spain the full tide of the Renaissance was reached by the mid-sixteenth century and blossomed forth in the dazzling, century-long Golden Age of Spanish culture. The first of the great writers of this Golden Age was Miguel de Cervantes Saavedra (1547-1616), born at a time when the Spanish Empire was at its height and when Spanish power was the most feared in all of Europe. The magnificent mineral wealth of Mexico and Peru, the rich spice cargoes and sacks of pearls and emeralds from the East, the rare plants and fruits and animals—all of this poured into Spain in vast profusion. The king of Spain, Philip II (1556-1598), who was also King of Hungary, Dalmatia, the Two Sicilies, the Canary Islands, the Oriental and Occidental Indies, and the islands of the Ocean, Archduke of Austria, Count of Flanders, Count of the Tyrol, Duke of Burgundy, and Duke of Athens, was the wealthiest and most powerful monarch in the western world.

Along with its wealth and power, Spain claimed recognition as a great cultural center. New palaces, new churches, and twenty new universities shed splendor on Spanish cities. Even in Erasmus' day Spanish letters were a model for the rest of Europe. Foreign scholars, artists, and travelers came to Spain in increasing numbers and the Spanish language was spoken in most countries of Europe.

By the end of the sixteenth century, however, the decline of Spain had begun. The treasury was empty and taxes were a heavy burden. There was a general restlessness—the countryside was full of lazy poor, the roads swarmed with tramps and brigands, and in the cities sloth, idleness, greed, and soft living were paramount. The corruption of the law courts, the growth of materialism, and the shirking of hard work all made a profound impression on Cervantes.

It was an age, too, when there was a great vogue for chivalric romances. These popular novels were the escapist literature of their day; their heroes achieved the impossible with such ease that the value of all achievement was degraded and chivalry was made a mockery. If that was chivalry, Cervantes wanted none of it, and became determined to destroy the vogue for those romances. That determination became the serious purpose behind his writing of *Don Quixote*, the most famous novel ever written.

A comic yet pathetic character, Don Quixote set out into the world to restore true chivalry as the defender of women and the champion of the weak, the poor, and the oppressed. It was a futile effort—not because the high ideals which inspired him were wrongheaded, but because the means at hand were inadequate. Don Quixote was the first active utopian, the do-gooder who failed because he attempted too much, a man of noble intent who ruined himself and others because he innocently believed in the goodness of human nature. Cervantes did not laugh away the chivalry of Spain, but he condemned the misuse of chivalry, just as he condemned the misuse of religion, science, poetry, truth, and justice. In short, he condemned the gulf between sham and substance, between illusion and reality. In Don Quixote's amusing encounter with the puppets, Cervantes lays bare this eternal problem while preserving the comic character of the noble knight whose good intentions somehow went awry.

. . . Don Quixote and Sancho did as they had been requested and went to the place where the puppet theater had been set up. It was uncovered and surrounded on all sides by lighted wax tapers, which made it look very bright and gay. Since he was the one who had to manipulate the puppets, Master Pedro took his place in the rear, while out in front, to act as interpreter, stood a lad who was his servant. It was the interpreter's business to explain the mysteries of the performance, and he had a rod with which he pointed to the figures as they came out. When

Text: From *The Ingenious Gentleman Don Quixote de la Mancha,* translated and edited by Samuel Putnam. Copyright 1949 by The Viking Press, Inc. Reprinted by permission of The Viking Press, InI. Pp. 679-87.

all those in the house had taken their places in front of the stage, some of them standing, and with Don Quixote, Sancho, the page, and the cousin in the best seats, the interpreter began speaking. . . .

The Tyrians and Trojans were silent all,

by which I mean to say that all those watching the show were hanging on the lips of the one who announced its marvels, when of a sudden, from behind the scene, there came the sound of drums and trumpets with much artillery firing. This lasted but a short while, and then the lad raised his voice and spoke.

"This true story," he said, "which your Worships are about to witness, is taken word for word from the French chronicles and Spanish ballads that you hear in the mouths of people everywhere, even the young ones in the street. It tells how Señor Don Gaiferos freed his wife, Melisendra, who was held captive by the Moors in Spain, in the city of Sañsuena, for that was the name then given to what is now known as Saragossa. Here your Worships may see Don Gaiferos playing at backgammon, as in the song:

At backgammon playing is Don Gaiferos,
Melisendra's already forgotten now.

And that personage whom you see there, with a crown on his head and a scepter in his hand, is the Emperor Charlemagne, Melisendra's supposed father, who, angered by his son-in-law's idleness and unconcern, comes to chide him. Observe how vehemently and earnestly he does it. You would think he was going to give him half a dozen raps with his scepter, and there are some authors who say that he did let him have it, and properly.

"After making a long speech on how his son-in-law is imperiling his honor by not endeavoring to procure his wife's release, Charlemagne, according to the ballad, addresses these words to him:

Enough I have said; see to it.

Your Worships will observe how the emperor turns his back on Don Gaiferos and leaves him fretting and fuming. Impatiently and in a towering rage, Gaiferos flings the draughtboard far from him; he hastily asks for his armor and begs his cousin, Don Orlando, to lend him his sword, Durindana. Orlando refuses to do this but offers his company in the difficult undertaking. The valiant Gaiferos, however, in his anger will not accept it, saying that he is well able to save his wife singlehanded though she were hidden away at the center of the earth. He then goes to don his armor and set out on his journey.

"Notice, your Worships, the eyes on the bull you see there, which is supposed to be one of those of the palace at Saragossa, today known as the Aljafería. That lady who appears upon the balcony, dressed in the Moorish fashion, is the peerless Melisendra, who from that vantage point often gazes out upon the road that leads from France, for this is the way she consoles herself in her captivity, by thinking of Paris and of her husband. Note, also, the strange thing that is about to happen now, the like of which has never been seen before, it may be. Behold that Moor who silently and stealthily, a finger on his mouth, creeps up behind her. Next, he gives her a kiss full on the lips, and she cannot wait to spit it out as she wipes her mouth with the white sleeve of her smock. Hear her moans; watch her as she tears her hair, as if it were to blame for the wrong that has been done her.

"That stately looking Moor you see in that corridor is King Marsilio of Sansueña. He has witnessed the other Moor's insolence, and although the man is a kinsman and a great favorite of his, he has him arrested at once and orders that he be given two hundred lashes as he is borne through the streets in accordance with the custom of the city.

with criers in front
and rods of justice behind.

You will note how quickly they carry out the sentence, though the offense has barely been committed; for with the Moors there are no indictments, warrants, and similar processes as there are with us."

"Child, child," said Don Quixote in a loud voice at this point, "keep to the straight line of your story and do not go off on curves and tangents; for a great deal of proof is required in such cases."

From behind the scenes Master Pedro also spoke up. "Boy," he said, "don't try any flourishes but do as this gentleman says, that is the safest way. Stick to your plain song and don't try any counterpoint melodies, for they are likely to break down from being overfine."

"I will do so," replied the lad; and then he went on, "This figure on horseback, wearing a Gascon cloak, is Don Gaiferos himself, and this is his wife, who has now been avenged for the enamored Moor's bold affront. With calmer mien she has taken her place on the balcony of the tower, from which she speaks to her husband, believing him to be some traveler, and holds a long conversation with him:

> If to France you go, Sir Knight,
> Ask for Gaiferos.

as the ballad has it. I will not repeat it all, since prolixity begets disgust. It is enough for you to observe how Don Gaiferos makes himself known, and how Melisendra by her happy manner shows that she has recognized him. We now see her lowering herself from the balcony to take her place upon the crupper of her worthy consort's steed—but ah! the unfortunate one! The edge of her petticoat has caught on one of the iron railings and she is left hanging in the air, unable to reach the ground.

"But see how merciful Heaven sends aid when it is needed most. Don Gaiferos now comes up and, without minding whether or not he tears the rich petticoat, he brings her down by main force and then in a trice lifts her onto his horse, seating her astride like a man and bidding her put her arms around him so that she will not fall, for the Señora Melisendra is not used to riding in that manner. See, too, how the steed neighs, as a sign that he is proud to bear such a burden of valor and beauty in the persons of his master and mistress. See how they wheel and leave the city behind them and joyfully take the road for Paris. Go in peace, O true and peerless lovers; may you find safety in your beloved fatherland, and may fortune place no obstacle in the way of your happy journey. May the eyes of your friends and kinsfolk rest upon you as you spend in peace and tranquillity the remaining days of your life—and let them be as many as those of Nestor!"

Here, once again, Master Pedro raised his voice. "Speak plainly, lad, and don't indulge in any flights. All affectation is bad."

The interpreter made no reply to this, but continued as follows:

"There was no want of idle eyes of the kind that see everything; and, seeing Melisendra descend from the balcony and mount her husband's horse, these persons notified King Marsilio, who at once ordered the call to arms to be sounded. Observe with what haste they go about it. The entire city is now drowned in the sound of bells, pealing from the towers of all the mosques."

At this point Don Quixote interrupted him. "No," he said, "that won't do. In this matter of the bells Master Pedro is far from accurate, for bells are not in use among the Moors; instead, they employ kettledrums and a kind of flute somewhat like our flageolet. So, you can see that this business of bells ringing in Sansueña is beyond a doubt a great piece of nonsense."

Hearing this, Master Pedro stopped ringing the bells. "Don't be looking for trifles, Señor Don Quixote," he said, "or expect things to be impossibly perfect. Are not a thousand comedies performed almost every day that are full of inaccuracies and absurdities, yet they run their course and are received not only with applause but with admiration and all the rest? Go on, boy, and let him talk; for so long as I fill my wallet, it makes no difference if there are as many inaccuracies in my show as there are motes in the sun."

"You have spoken the truth," was Don Quixote's reply.

With this, the lad resumed his commentary. "And now, just see the glittering cavalcade that is leaving the city in pursuit of the Catholic lovers; listen to all the trumpets and flutes, the drums and tabors. I fear me they are going to overtake them and bring them back tied to the tail of their own horse, which would be a dreadful sight to behold."

Upon seeing such a lot of Moors and hearing such a din, Don Quixote thought that it would be a good thing for him to aid the fugitives; and, rising to his feet, he cried out, "Never as long as I live and in my presence will I permit such violence to be done to so famous a knight and so bold a lover as Don Gaiferos. Halt, lowborn rabble; cease your pursuit and persecution, or otherwise ye shall do battle with me!"

With these words he drew his sword, and in one bound was beside the stage; and then with accelerated and unheard-of fury he began slashing at the Moorish puppets, knocking some of them over, beheading others, crippling this one, mangling that one. Among the many blows he dealt was one downward stroke that, if Master Pedro had not ducked and crouched, would have sliced off his head more easily than if it had been made of almond paste.

"Stop, Señor Don Quixote!" cried Master Pedro. "Those are not real Moors that your Grace is knocking over, maiming, and killing, but pasteboard figures. Sinner that I am, if you haven't destroyed and ruined all the property I own!"

But this was not sufficient to halt the rain of cuts and slashes, down-strokes, back-strokes, and doublehanded blows that Don Quixote was dealing. The short of the matter is, in less time than it takes to say two Credos he had knocked the entire theater to the ground and had slashed to bits all its fixtures and its puppets, King Marsilio being badly wounded while the Emperor Charlemagne had both his head and his crown split in two. The audience, meanwhile, had been thrown into confusion; the ape fled over the roof of the inn, the cousin was frightened, the page was intimidated, and even Sancho Panza was terrified, for, as he swore upon his word when the tempest was over, he had never seen his master in such a towering passion.

When the destruction of the theater had been completed, Don Quixote calmed down a bit. "I only wish," he said, "that I had here before me right now those who do not or will not see how useful knights-errant are to the world. Just think, if I had not been present, what would have become of the worthy Don Gaiferos and the beauteous Melisendra? You may be sure that those dogs would have overtaken them by this time and would have committed some outrage upon them. And so I say to you: Long live knight-errantry over all living things on the face of this earth!"

"Let it live, and welcome," said Master Pedro in a sickly voice, "and let me die, since I am so unfortunate that I can say with the king, Don Rodrigo:

> Yesterday I was lord of Spain,
> And today I do not have a tower left
> That I can call my own.

Not half an hour ago, nay, not half a minute ago, I was lord of kings and emperors; my stables were filled with countless horses and my trunks and bags with any number of gala costumes; and now I am but a poor beggar, ruined and destitute. Above all, I have lost my ape; for I give you my word, my teeth will sweat before I get him back, and all owing to the ill-advised wrath of this Sir Knight. I have heard it said of him that he protects orphans, sets wrongs to right, and performs other acts of charity; but in my case alone he has failed to manifest his generous intentions, blessed be the highest heavens! I can well believe that he is the Knight of the Mournful Countenance, seeing he has so disfigured mine!"

Sancho Panza was quite touched by the puppet master's words. "Don't cry, Master Pedro," he begged him; "don't carry on like that, you break my heart. For I can tell you that my master, Don Quixote, is so Catholic and scrupulous a Christian that if he can be brought to see he has done you any wrong, he will own up to it, and what's more, he will want to pay you for all the damage he has caused you and a good deal over and above it."

"If Señor Don Quixote," replied the puppet master, "will but pay me for some small part of my fixtures which he has destroyed, I will be satisfied and his Grace will have a clear conscience; for one cannot be saved who holds the property of another against its owner's will without making restitution."

"That is true enough," said Don Quixote, "but up to now I am not aware that I hold anything of yours, Master Pedro."

"How is that?" replied the showman. "Those remains lying there on the hard and barren ground, what was it scattered and annihilated them if not the invincible strength of that mighty arm? Whose puppets were those if not mine? And how else did I make my living?"

"I am now coming to believe," said Don Quixote, "that I was right in thinking, as I often have, that the enchanters who persecute me merely place figures like these in front of my eyes and then change and transform them as they like. In all earnestness, gentlemen, I can assure you that everything that took place here seemed to me very real indeed, and Melisendra, Don Gaiferos, Marsilio, and Charlemagne were all their flesh-and-blood selves. That was why I became so angry. In order to fulfill the duties of my profession as knight-errant, I wished to aid and favor the fugitives, and with this in mind I did what you saw me do. If it came out wrong, it is not my fault but that of my wicked persecutors; but, nevertheless, I willingly sentence myself to pay the costs of my error, even though it did not proceed from malice. Reckon up what I owe you, Master Pedro, for those figures I have destroyed, and I will reimburse you in good Castilian currency."

Master Pedro bowed. "I expected no less," he said, "of so rare a Christian as the valiant Don Quixote de la Mancha, the true friend and protector of all needy vagabonds. Mine host here and the great Sancho shall act as arbiters between your Grace and me and they shall appraise the value, or likely value, of the properties destroyed."

Both the landlord and Sancho agreed to act in this capacity, and Master Pedro then picked up off the ground King Marsilio of Saragossa, minus his head.

"You can see," he said, "how impossible it is to restore this king to his former state; and so, it seems to me, saving your better judgment, that for his death, demise, and final end I should have four and a half reales."

"Proceed," said Don Quixote.

"As for this one who is split open from top to bottom," Master Pedro went on, taking in his hands the late Emperor Charlemagne, "it would not be too much if I were to ask five reales and a quarter."

"That's no small sum," said Sancho.

"Nor is it very much," replied the innkeeper.

"Give him the whole five and a quarter," said Don Quixote. "The sum total of this memorable disaster does not hang on a quarter more or less. And please be quick about it, Master Pedro, for it is suppertime and I feel the stirrings of hunger."

"This figure," continued Master Pedro, "without a nose and with one eye missing, is that of the beauteous Melisendra; and for it I ask, and I think I am right in doing so, two reales and twelve maravedis."

"The devil," said Don Quixote, "must have a hand in it if Melisendra and her husband have not reached the French border, at the very least, by this time, for the horse they rode on seemed to me to fly rather than gallop; and so there is no need to try to sell me the cat for the hare by showing me here a Melisendra without any nose when she is now, if things went right, stretched out at her ease and enjoying herself with her husband in France. God help everyone to his own, Master Pedro. Let us deal plainly and with honest intent. You may continue."

Master Pedro perceived that Don Quixote's wits were wandering and that he was beginning to harp on the old chord again, but he was not disposed to let him off so easily.

"This cannot be Melisendra after all," he said; "it must be one of the damsels that waited upon her; and if you will give me sixty maravedis for her, I will consider myself well paid."

In this manner he went on putting a price on each of the puppets that had been destroyed, and after these estimates had been adjusted by the two arbiters to the satisfaction of both parties, it was found that the total came to forty reales and three quarters, and Sancho promptly handed over this sum; whereupon Master Pedro asked for two reales more for the trouble of catching the ape.

"Give them to him, Sancho," said Don Quixote, "not for catching the ape, but for getting the she-ape by the tail. And I would further give two hundred right now to anyone who could assure me that Melisendra and Don Gaiferos are safe in France with their own people."

"No one can tell you that better than my ape," said Master Pedro, "but there's no devil that could catch him now, although I fancy lonesomeness and hunger will force him to come looking for me tonight, and God will bring another day, and we shall see what we shall see."

The storm centering around the puppet theater having finally subsided, they all sat down to eat their supper in peace and good companionship, and all at Don Quixote's expense, for he was extremely generous.

INTERPRETATIONS OF THE RENAISSANCE

97 JACOB BURCKHARDT, *THE CIVILIZATION OF THE RENAISSANCE IN ITALY:* THE BIRTH OF INDIVIDUALISM

Our modern conception of the Renaissance has been very largely shaped by a Swiss historian named Jacob Burckhardt (1818-1897). In 1860 he brought out his *Civilization of the Renaissance in Italy*, a masterpiece of historical synthesis which has since become one of the classics in historical literature. For more than fifty years this work was accepted unquestioningly by the majority of historians, one of whom went so far as to call it "the most penetrating and subtle treatise on the history of civilization that exists in literature." Today it is the center of a spirited historical controversy.

As a cultural historian, Burckhardt meant his masterpiece to be an investigation of what he called the inner spirit of the Italian Renaissance, rather than a comprehensive history. To achieve this, he abandoned the technique of straight narrative history in favor of a topical and analytical approach. The result was a beautifully coherent but static picture of Italian civilization from the beginning of the fourteenth to the beginning of the sixteenth century. The central point of Burckhardt's interpretation was that individualism, the dominant trait of modern civilization, first made its appearance during the Renaissance in Italy. Hence it was in Renaissance Italy that the modern world was born. Burckhardt further insisted that while the revival of classicism colored the Renaissance, it alone did not sum up the whole period. The essential quality of the Renaissance—the consciousness of character—might have been the same without the revival of antiquity. For him, individualism remained the key to the interpretation of the Renaissance.

Now that this point in our historical view of Italian civilization has been reached, it is time to speak of the influence of antiquity, the 'new birth' of which has been one-sidedly chosen as the name to sum up the whole period. The conditions which have been hitherto described would have sufficed, apart from antiquity, to upturn and to mature the national mind; and most of the intellectual tendencies which yet remain to be noticed would be conceivable without it. But both what has gone before and what we have still to discuss are coloured in a thousand ways by the influence of the ancient world; and though the essence of the phenomena might still have been the same without the classical revival, it is only with and through this revival that they are actually manifested to us. The Renaissance would not have been the process of world-wide significance which it is, if its elements could be so easily separated from one another. We must insist upon it, as one of the chief propositions of this book, that it was not the revival of antiquity alone, but its union with the genius of the Italian people, which achieved the conquest of the western world. The amount of independence which the national spirit maintained in this union varied according to circumstances. In the modern Latin literature of the period, it is very small, while in the visual arts, as well as in other spheres, it is remarkably great; and hence the alliance between two distant epochs in the civilization of the same people, because concluded on equal terms, proved justifiable and fruitful. The rest of Europe was free either to repel or else partly or wholly to accept the mighty impulse which came forth from Italy. Where the latter was the case we may as well be spared the complaints over the early decay of mediæval faith and civilization. Had these been strong enough to hold their ground, they would be alive to this day. If those elegiac natures which long to see them return could pass but one hour in the midst of them, they would gasp to be back in modern air. That in a great historical process of this kind flowers of exquisite beauty may perish, without being made immortal in poetry or tradition, is undoubtedly true; nevertheless, we cannot wish the process undone. The general result of it consists in this—that by the side of the Church which had hitherto held the countries of the West together (though it was unable to do so much longer) there arose a new spiritual influence which, spreading itself abroad from Italy, became the breath of life for all the more instructed minds in Europe. The worst that can be said of the movement is, that it was antipopular, that through it Europe became for the first time sharply divided into the cultivated and uncultivated classes. The reproach will appear groundless when we reflect that even now the fact, though clearly recognized, cannot be altered. The separation, too, is by no means so cruel and absolute in Italy as elsewhere. The most artistic of her poets, Tasso, is in the hands of even the poorest.

The civilization of Greece and Rome, which, ever since the fourteenth century, obtained so powerful a hold on Italian life, as the source and basis of culture, as the object and ideal of existence, partly also as an avowed reaction against preceding tendencies—this civilization had long been exerting a partial influence on mediæval Europe, even beyond the boundaries of Italy. The culture of which Charlemagne was a representative was, in face of the barbarism of the seventh and eighth centuries, essentially a Renaissance, and could appear under no other form. Just as in the Romanesque architecture of the North, beside the general outlines inherited from antiquity, remarkable direct imitations of the antique also occur, so too monastic scholarship had not only gradually absorbed an immense mass of materials from Roman writers, but the style of it, from the days of Einhard onwards, shows traces of conscious imitation.

But the resuscitation of antiquity took a different form in Italy from that which it assumed in the North. The wave of barbarism had scarcely gone by before the people, in whom the former life was but half effaced, showed a consciousness of its past and a wish to reproduce it. Elsewhere in Europe men deliberately and with reflection borrowed this or the other element of classical civilization; in Italy the sympathies both of the learned and of the people were naturally engaged on the side of antiquity as a whole, which stood to them as a symbol of past greatness. The Latin language, too, was easy to an Italian, and the numerous monuments and documents in which the country abounded facilitated a return to the past. With this tendency other elements—the popular character which time had now greatly modified, the political institutions imported by the Lombards from Germany, chivalry and other northern forms of civilization, and the influence of religion and the Church—combined to produce the modern Italian spirit, which was destined to serve as the model and ideal for the whole western world.

How antiquity influenced the visual arts, as soon as the flood of barbarism had subsided, is

Text: From *The Civilization of the Renaissance in Italy* by Jacob Burckhardt (London: Phaidon Press Ltd. and George Allen & Unwin Ltd., 1944), pp. 128-32. Reprinted by permission of the publishers.

clearly shown in the Tuscan buildings of the twelfth and in the sculptures of the thirteenth centuries. In poetry, too, there will appear no want of similar analogies to those who hold that the greatest Latin poet of the twelfth century, the writer who struck the keynote of a whole class of Latin poems, was an Italian. We mean the author of the best pieces in the so-called 'Carmina Burana.' A frank enjoyment of life and its pleasures, as whose patrons the gods of heathendom are invoked, while Catos and Scipios hold the place of the saints and heroes of Christianity, flows in full current through the rhymed verses. Reading them through at a stretch, we can scarcely help coming to the conclusion that an Italian, probably a Lombard, is speaking; in fact, there are positive grounds for thinking so. To a certain degree these Latin poems of the 'Clerici vagantes' of the twelfth century, with all their remarkable frivolity, are, doubtless, a product in which the whole of Europe had a share; but the writer of the song 'De Phyllide et Flora' and the 'Aestuans Interius' can have been a northerner as little as the polished Epicurean observer to whom we owe 'Dum Dianæ vitrea sero lampas oritur.' Here, in truth, is a reproduction of the whole ancient view of life, which is all the more striking from the mediæval form of the verse in which it is set forth. There are many works of this and the following centuries, in which a careful imitation of the antique appears both in the hexameter and pentameter of the metre and in the classical, often mythological, character of the subject, and which yet have not anything like the same spirit of antiquity about them. In the hexametric chronicles and other works of Guglielmus Apuliensis and his successors (from about 1100), we find frequent traces of a diligent study of Virgil, Ovid, Lucan, Statius, and Claudian; but this classical form is, after all, a mere matter of archæology, as is the classical subject in compilers like Vincent of Beauvais, or in the mythological and allegorical writer, Alanus ab Insulis. The Renaissance, however, is not a fragmentary imitation or compilation, but a new birth; and the signs of this are visible in the poems of the unknown 'Clericus' of the twelfth century.

But the great and general enthusiasm of the Italians for classical antiquity did not display itself before the fourteenth century. For this a development of civic life was required, which took place only in Italy, and there not till then. It was needful that noble and burgher should first learn to dwell together on equal terms, and that a social world should arise which felt the want of culture, and had the leisure and the means to obtain it. But culture, as soon as it freed itself from the fantastic bonds of the Middle Ages, could not at once and without help find its way to the understanding of the physical and intellectual world. It needed a guide, and found one in the ancient civilization, with its wealth of truth and knowledge in every spiritual interest. Both the form and the substance of this civilization were adopted with admiring gratitude; it became the chief part of the culture of the age. The general condition of the country was favourable to this transformation. The mediæval empire, since the fall of the Hohenstaufen, had either renounced, or was unable to make good, its claims on Italy. The Popes had migrated to Avignon. Most of the political powers actually existing owed their origin to violent and illegitimate means. The spirit of the people, now awakened to self-consciousness, sought for some new and stable ideal on which to rest. And thus the vision of the world-wide empire of Italy and Rome so possessed the popular mind that Cola di Rienzi could actually attempt to put it in practice. The conception he formed of his task, particularly when tribune for the first time, could only end in some extravagant comedy; nevertheless, the memory of ancient Rome was no slight support to the national sentiment. Armed afresh with its culture, the Italian soon felt himself in truth citizen of the most advanced nation in the world.

98 CHARLES HOMER HASKINS, *THE RENAISSANCE OF THE TWELFTH CENTURY*: HOW UNIQUE WAS THE RENAISSANCE?

Brilliant as it was, Burckhardt's great essay (see Document 97) had serious shortcomings. For one thing, it exaggerated the individualism of the Renaissance. For another, it too sharply contrasted the Italian Renaissance with the preceding Middle Ages. The result was that Burckhardt tended to minimize the continuity of history and the gradual flowing of one period into another. It has taken generations of revisionist scholarship to illuminate these and other faults of the Burckhardt interpretation.

The vanguard of the revisionists has been led by the twentieth-century medievalists who were determined to prove that there was less of a contrast between the Middle Ages and the Renaissance than Burckhardt had supposed. To this cause Charles Homer Haskins (1870-1937), for many years the dean of American medieval historians, contributed his *The Renaissance of the Twelfth Century* (1927). A great teacher and inspired scholar, Haskins did much to further the growth of medieval studies in the United States. His book was one of the most widely read works of its kind and had a significant influence upon historical thought.

Haskins firmly rejected the notion that medieval men neither knew nor cared about the ancient classics. He demonstrated that the twelfth century saw a great revival of Latin learning and literature, as well as Greek science and philosophy. His work—in which the subject was given a broad cultural treatment—was tantamount to a general intellectual history of the high Middle Ages. But being a man of sober and judicious temperament, he did not completely cast out the idea of an Italian Renaissance—as some of his more immoderate colleagues have done. Nevertheless there is little doubt that he was on the side of the medievalists.

The title of this book will appear to many to contain a flagrant contradiction. A renaissance in the twelfth century! Do not the Middle Ages, that epoch of ignorance, stagnation, and gloom, stand in the sharpest contrast to the light and progress and freedom of the Italian Renaissance which followed? How could there be a renaissance in the Middle Ages, when men had no eye for the joy of beauty and knowledge of this passing world; their gaze ever fixed on the terrors of the world to come? Is not this whole period summed up in Symonds' picture of St. Bernard, blind to the beauties of Lake Leman as he bends "a thought-burdened forehead over the neck of his mule," typical of an age when "humanity had passed, a careful pilgrim, intent on the terrors of sin, death, and judgment, along the highways of the world, and had scarcely known that they were sightworthy, or that life is a blessing"?

The answer is that the continuity of history rejects such sharp and violent contrasts between successive periods, and that modern research shows us the Middle Ages less dark and less static, the Renaissance less bright and less sudden, than was once supposed. The Middle Ages exhibit life and color and change, much eager search after knowledge and beauty, much creative accomplishment in art, in literature, in institutions. The Italian Renaissance was preceded by similar, if less wide-reaching movements; indeed it came out of the Middle Ages so gradually that historians are not agreed when it began, and some would go so far as to abolish the name, and perhaps even the fact, of a renaissance in the Quattrocento.

To the most important of these earlier revivals the present volume is devoted, the Renaissance of the Twelfth Century which is often called the Mediaeval Renaissance. This century, the very century of St. Bernard and his mule, was in many respects an age of fresh and vigorous life. The epoch of the Crusades, of the rise of towns, and of the earliest bureaucratic states of the West, it saw the culmination of Romanesque art and the beginnings of Gothic; the emergence of the vernacular literatures; the revival of the Latin classics and of Latin poetry and Roman law; the recovery of Greek science, with its Arabic additions, and of much of Greek philosophy; and the origin of the first European universities. The twelfth century left its signature on higher education, on the scholastic philosophy, on European systems of law, on architecture and sculpture, on the liturgical drama, on Latin and vernacular poetry. . . .

The European Middle Ages form a complex and varied as well as a very considerable period of human history. Within their thousand years of time they include a large variety of peoples, institutions, and types of culture, illustrating many processes of historical development and containing the origins of many phases of modern civilization. Contrasts of East and West, of the North and the Mediterranean, of old and new, sacred and profane, ideal and actual, give life and color and movement to this period, while its close relations alike to antiquity and to the modern world assure it a place in the continuous history of human development. Both continuity and change are characteristic of the Middle Ages, as indeed of all great epochs of history.

This conception runs counter to ideas widely prevalent not only among the unlearned but among many who ought to know better. To these the Middle Ages are synonymous with all that is

Text: Reprinted by permission of the publishers from Charles Homer Haskins, *The Renaissance of the Twelfth Century* (Cambridge, Mass.: Harvard University Press). Copyright 1927 by The President and Fellows of Harvard College, 1955 by Clare Allen Haskins. Pp. vii-viii, 3-6.

uniform, static, and unprogressive; 'mediaeval' is applied to anything outgrown, until, as Bernard Shaw reminds us, even the fashion plates of the preceding generation are pronounced 'mediaeval.' The barbarism of Goths and Vandals is thus spread out over the following centuries, even to that 'Gothic' architecture which is one of the crowning achievements of the constructive genius of the race; the ignorance and superstition of this age are contrasted with the enlightenment of the Renaissance, in strange disregard of the alchemy and demonology which flourished throughout this succeeding period; and the phrase 'Dark Ages' is extended to cover all that came between, let us say, 476 and 1453. Even those who realize that the Middle Ages are not 'dark' often think of them as uniform, at least during the central period from *ca.* 800 to *ca.* 1300, distinguished by the great mediaeval institutions of feudalism, ecclesiasticism, and scholasticism, and preceded and followed by epochs of more rapid transformation. Such a view ignores the unequal development of different parts of Europe, the great economic changes within this epoch, the influx of the new learning of the East, the shifting currents in the stream of mediaeval life and thought. On the intellectual side, in particular, it neglects the mediaeval revival of the Latin classics and of jurisprudence, the extension of knowledge by the absorption of ancient learning and by observation, and the creative work of these centuries in poetry and in art. In many ways the differences between the Europe of 800 and that of 1300 are greater than the resemblances. Similar contrasts, though on a smaller scale, can be made between the culture of the eighth and the ninth centuries, between conditions *ca.* 1100 and those *ca.* 1200, between the preceding age and the new intellectual currents of the thirteenth and fourteenth centuries.

For convenience' sake it has become common to designate certain of these movements as the Carolingian Renaissance, the Ottonian Renaissance, the Renaissance of the Twelfth Century, after the fashion of the phrase once reserved exclusively for the Italian Renaissance of the fifteenth century. Some, it is true, would give up the word renaissance altogether, as conveying false impressions of a sudden change and an original and distinct culture in the fifteenth century, and, in general, as implying that there ever can be a real revival of something past; Mr. Henry Osborn Taylor prides himself on writing two volumes on *Thought and Expression in the Sixteenth Century* without once using this forbidden term. Nevertheless, it may be doubted whether such a term is more open to misinterpretation than others, like the Quattrocento or the sixteenth century, and it is so convenient and so well established that, like Austria, if it had not existed we should have to invent it. There was an Italian Renaissance, whatever we choose to call it, and nothing is gained by the process which ascribes the Homeric poems to another poet of the same name. But—thus much we must grant—the great Renaissance was not so unique or so decisive as has been supposed. The contrast of culture was not nearly so sharp as it seemed to the humanists and their modern followers, while within the Middle Ages there were intellectual revivals whose influence was not lost to succeeding times, and which partook of the same character as the better known movement of the fifteenth century. To one of these this volume is devoted, the Renaissance of the Twelfth Century, which is also known as the Mediaeval Renaissance.

99 WALLACE K. FERGUSON, "THE INTERPRETATION OF THE RENAISSANCE": THE RENAISSANCE AS THE TRANSITION FROM MEDIEVAL TO MODERN

There can be no final solutions in historical interpretation. But so varied have been the scholars' criticisms of the Burckhardt thesis in the century since it first appeared, so ardent have been the defenders of that thesis, and so numerous have been the specialized studies of both Renaissance and medieval historians, that one might think it time for a new interpretation, in the form of a synthesis, to replace Burckhardt. How would one approach so formidable an undertaking? A possible answer has been provided by Wallace K. Ferguson, Professor of History at the University of Western Ontario. Widely known for his writings on the Renaissance, his most significant work to date is *The Renaissance in Historical Thought: Five Centuries of Interpretation* (1948), now an indispensable guide. Neither denying the arguments of the medievalists, nor yet rejecting the Burckhardt school, Professor Ferguson contends that the Renaissance should be regarded as a distinctive period of transition, as a kind of unique bridge in historical time which leads from the medieval to the modern world.

Much of this chronological confusion arose, it seems to me, from constructing the concept of the Renaissance upon too narrow a foundation. If we take into consideration the total complex of European civilization, it will become evident, I think, that all the countries of Western Europe entered upon a period of decisive change about the beginning of the fourteenth century. The character as well as the rate of change varied from country to country, and from one type of culture, or institution, or form of activity, to another. But wherever we look, the typically medieval forms begin to disintegrate, while new and recognizably modern forms appear, if only in embryo. At the same time the centre of gravity shifts noticeably from the social and cultural factors that had been dominant in the Middle Ages to those minority phenomena that were to assume a leading role in the modern period. To define the Renaissance in a sentence seems rather like rushing in where not only angels but even fools would fear to tread. To avoid doing so at this point, however, would savor of moral cowardice. Viewing the Renaissance as an age in the history of Western Europe, then, I would define it as the age of transition from medieval to modern civilization, a period characterized primarily by the gradual shift from one fairly well coordinated and clearly defined type of civilization to another, yet, at the same time, possessing in its own right certain distinctive traits and a high degree of cultural vitality. And on the basis of this concept or hypothesis, I would set the arbitrary dates—1300 to 1600—as its chronological boundaries. To invest the definition with any significant content, however, and to pin down the weasel words, it is necessary, first of all, to indicate what may be considered the prevailing elements of both medieval and modern civilization, and then to trace the main lines of development within the transitional period.

In the broadest terms, then: the two dominant institutions of the Middle Ages were the feudal system and the universal church. Between them, they determined both the social structure and the ideological content of medieval civilization. And both, in their institutional aspects, were founded upon an agrarian, land-holding economy. Feudalism, indeed, took shape in the early Middle Ages very largely because it was the only possible means of maintaining social and political organization in a moneyless economy—an economy in which the land and its produce were almost the sole form of wealth—commerce, industry and normal city life having virtually disappeared. Lacking financial resources in fluid form, central government was unable to maintain effective political or judicial authority, and was forced to relinquish these into the hands of the great landholders. Lay society was divided into two hereditary classes of widely divergent status: the land-holding nobility, whose duty it was to fight and govern; and the peasants, more or less servile, whose duty it was to work the land. Only one other class had a useful service to perform: the clergy, whose duty it was to pray and to care for the souls of men. Having no other means of support, the clergy necessarily became a landholding class, and, as land-holders, the officers of the church became feudal lords. On the material side, then, the church was deeply involved in the feudal system. At the same time, the church had inherited from its origins in the Roman Empire a principle of universality and a centralized, hierarchical government, which it never lost. But this universal authority was of too large a sort to come into direct conflict with the highly localized government of the feudal nobles. Feudalism and the universal church, indeed, could live more or less harmoniously together as *concordantia oppositorum*.

Into this agrarian, feudal society the commercial revival of the eleventh and twelfth centuries introduced the new and alien elements of commerce and skilled industry, with the resulting growth of cities and the expansion of money economy. This was followed by a notable increase in the prosperity and the fluid wealth of the land-holding classes. It was also accompanied by a great quickening of cultural activity, by that full development of clerical and feudal culture that made the twelfth and thirteenth centuries the classic period of medieval civilization. The economic stimulus which spread from the growing cities, together with the heightened tempo of intercommunication along the lines of trade, was, I think, the material factor that made possible the immense cultural vitality of these two centuries. But the content and spirit of that culture did not emanate from the urban classes. Learning remained the exclusive monopoly of the clergy. Art and music served the church. And vernacular literature expressed the ideals of feudalism and chivalry. Exceptions to these broad statements will, of course, leap to mind immediately. It is my contention, merely, that the elements of medieval civilization which I have mentioned were the most general, and the most characteristic.

When we turn to the modern age, say by the beginning of the seventeenth century, the general complex of European civilization has changed so

Text: Wallace K. Ferguson, "The Interpretation of the Renaissance," *Journal of the History of Ideas*, XII, No. 4 (October 1951), pp. 486-94.

radically that it amounts to a change in kind rather than in degree. The economic balance has shifted from agriculture to commerce and industry. Money economy has become almost universal, and capitalism has replaced all but the vestigial remnants of medieval economic organization. On the political side, the national states with centralized government have taken the place of feudal particularism, while at the same time the unity of Christendom has been decisively broken. Beside the Catholic Church stand the Protestant churches and sects, in their infinite variety. The social balance has shifted, so that the urban classes are no longer a minor element in society, but are prepared to assume political and cultural leadership. The clerical monopoly of learning has been broken, and laymen have replaced the clergy as the most numerous and influential group, both as patrons and creators of the higher forms of culture. The secular elements in literature, learning, and general *Weltanschauung* now decisively outweigh the transcendental; and the natural sciences have replaced theology as the dominant form of knowledge.

Compared with the revolutionary changes in the character of Western European civilization between the years 1300 and 1600, the changes in the following three centuries are changes in degree rather than in kind. Despite the increasingly rapid tempo of development, the evolution of modern civilization has followed, or did follow at least until our generation, lines already clearly established by the beginning of the seventeenth century. It is my contention, then, that medieval and modern civilization, despite the common elements that have remained constant in the Western world for the past two thousand years or more, are in effect, two different types of civilization, and that the change from the one to the other occurred during the three centuries of the Renaissance.

But, in thus asserting the transitional character of the Renaissance, I have done no more than lay the ground work for an interpretation of the age itself. The mere characterization of the types of civilization that preceded and followed it suggests the lines of change within the transitional age, but does nothing to indicate how or why the changes took place. Here we must face the fundamental problem of causation. What were the dynamic forces that disintegrated the medieval social structure, and as a result altered medieval ways of thinking, gradually at first, but in the long run so profoundly as to create a new type of culture? In thus framing the question, I am, of course, implying a partial answer to the problem of causation, for there is implied in the question the assumption that the fundamental causes of change in the forms of culture are to be found in antecedent changes in economic and political institutions and in the whole structure of society. This is an assumption that many scholars, notably those imbued with the traditions of Hegelian or Thomist idealism, would be loath to accept. Yet it seems to me that, if we regard the whole complex of European civilization in this period, social change everywhere precedes cultural change, and that what is new in Renaissance culture, including novel adaptations of inherited traditions, can most readily be explained as the product of a changed social milieu.

Let me repeat my earlier generalization—that medieval culture was predominantly feudal and ecclesiastical, the product of a society founded upon an agrarian, land-holding economy. By the beginning of the fourteenth century that society had already been replaced in Italy by an urban society, constructed upon an economic foundation of large-scale commerce and industry, and with rapidly developing capitalist institutions. In the northern countries the expansion of money economy worked more slowly, but by 1300 it was already disintegrating the land-holding basis of feudal society, and had at the same time made possible the effective exercise of central government in the great national or territorial states. Both politically and economically, the feudal nobles were losing ground to the rising forces of monarchy and the bourgeoisie. Meanwhile the church was also entering upon a period of profound crisis when, with its moral prestige sapped by a monetary fiscal policy, it was forced into a losing battle with the newly arisen political power of the national states. Though it survived as a universal church for about a century after the Council of Constance, it never recovered the prestige and authority lost during the period of the Babylonian Captivity and the Great Schism.

The changes in the social structure and in the balance of the social classes, which resulted from these economic and political developments, were not reflected immediately or in equal degree everywhere by changes in the forms of higher culture. But, with due allowance for a normal cultural lag, it seems to me that as the economic, political, and social balance shifted, the leadership in all forms of intellectual and aesthetic activity also shifted in the same directions: from the clergy to the laity, from the feudal classes to the urban, and from the isolation of monastic foundations and baronial castles to the concentrated society of cities and of royal or princely courts.

One of the ways in which the influence of economic and political change worked most directly upon Renaissance culture was through the spread of lay education and lay patronage of art, learning, and letters. And this, I think, was clearly the result of the massing of population in cities, of the growth of large private fortunes, and of the concentration of both fluid wealth and political power in the hands of kings and princes. Under the conditions of feudal life, the noble classes made no pretence to intellectual eminence or scholarship sublime, and as Professor Pollard once remarked, even today a little thinking goes a long way in rural England. Not only did ideas circulate more rapidly in an urban atmosphere, but capitalist enterprise necessitated a general literacy among the middle and upper classes of the cities, while at the same time it furnished the most prosperous of the urban patriciate with the means for liberal patronage. In similar fashion, the growth of centralized state governments, supported by taxation, opened up careers to laymen trained in law and administration, and also created new centres of lay patronage. The princely courts of Italy all became active centres of lay culture, and had also, incidentally, broken completely with the feudal traditions that had inspired the greater part of lay culture in the Middle Ages. The royal courts of the North, and semi-royal courts like that of the Dukes of Burgundy, retained the forms of a feudal and chivalrous society, but the literary reflections of these forms had by the fifteenth century lost the vitality that had inspired the feudal literature of the twelfth and thirteenth centuries. The forms of feudalism and chivalry no longer bore a close relation to social reality. Economic and political pressure combined to transform the semi-independent baron of the Middle Ages into the Renaissance courtier. The ranks of the nobility were being infiltrated by the *nouveau riche*, and beside the remnants of the old *noblesse d'épée* now stood the wealthy and highly cultured members of the *noblesse de la robe*. To maintain their position at court, scions of the old nobility were being forced to don a veneer of education and cultured taste, and to extend their intellectual interests beyond the spheres of courtly love and refined homicide which had been the principal themes of medieval feudal literature. The spread of lay education among the upper ranks of both the bourgeoisie and the nobility thus served not only to break the ecclesiastical monopoly of learning and the patronage of art, but also to modify radically the feudal and chivalrous spirit of vernacular literature. As higher education was adapted increasingly to the needs of a lay society, even the clergy were exposed more than ever before to secular learning, so that their contribution to Renaissance culture was in many instances indistinguishable from that of the educated layman.

The increasing laicization of education and of learning, literature, art and music was accompanied, almost inevitably, by an expansion of their secular content, and frequently by the introduction of a more secular tone. By this I do not mean to imply that the men of the Renaissance were, in general, less religious than those of the Middle Ages. There has been enough nonsense written about the pagan spirit of the Renaissance without my adding to it. On the other hand, it seems to me equally nonsensical to seize upon every evidence of religious feeling or belief in the Renaissance as proof that its culture was still basically medieval. Christianity was not a medieval invention. The Christian tradition certainly continued from the Middle Ages through the Renaissance—and beyond—but it did not continue unaltered, nor did it in the same degree dominate the culture of the age. In the first place, the greatly increased participation of laymen introduced into learning, literature and art whole areas of secular knowledge and subjects of general human interest which, if not wholly lacking in the Middle Ages, were yet inadequately represented. In the second place, the writer or artist, who worked for a predominantly lay audience or for lay patrons, had to meet the demands and satisfy the taste of men not trained in theology nor bound by clerical traditions. Even the religious art of the Renaissance gives frequent evidence of consideration for the taste of lay patrons. Finally, religion itself was in some degree laicized. This is evident, in the fourteenth and fifteenth centuries, in the growth of anti-clerical sentiment, and in revolts against the hierarchical authority of the church and the sacramental-sacerdotal aspects of medieval religion. The Wycliffite and Hussite heresies are extreme cases. But even within the bounds of orthodoxy, such movements of popular mysticism as the *Devotio Moderna* in the Netherlands show a tendency toward the development of a peculiarly lay piety. The religious writing of the Christian humanists offers further examples of an increasingly independent participation of laymen in the shaping of religious thought. These men were deeply pious, but they had little in common with Thomas Aquinas or Innocent III. The Protestant Reformation itself was in part a revolt against the sacerdotal domination of religion. In proclaiming the priesthood of all believers, Luther placed the believing layman on an even footing with the cleric. The whole problem of the relation of the Reformation to both medieval and Renaissance culture is, however, too complex to be discussed here. For the present, I can do no more than assert the opinion that it can be fully understood only if it is considered in relation to the changes that had altered the whole structure of European society and the character of European culture since the beginning of the fourteenth century. In short, I think that the Reformation must be interpreted as one aspect of Renaissance civilization rather than as something running counter to it.

The emphasis I have placed upon social and cultural change, upon the decline of medieval and the rise of modern elements, is in accordance with my conception of the Renaissance as a transitional age. But, as I defined it, the Renaissance was also an age which possessed, aside from the uneasy co-existence within it of medieval and modern characteristics, certain distinctive traits and a high degree of cultural vitality. Here I can do no more than suggest answers to a few of the innumerable questions posed by this latter aspect of the problem. In the first place, whence came the cultural vitality of the Renaissance? Having no time for any but the briefest and most dogmatic of statements, I would say that it was made possible by unprecedented wealth and by the participation of an unprecedented variety of social types. I would say, further, that it drew its positive inspiration from the intellectual excitement caused by the challenge of new conditions of life, of new potentialities in every field of culture, and, in general, of a sense of breaking new ground and of scanning ever-widening horizons. Within the civilization of the Renaissance there were, of course, innumerable crosscurrents, inconsistencies, and apparent reactions. These, I think, were the natural results of the conflict, more intense in this age than in any other since the dawn of Christianity, between inherited traditions and a changing society. The Renaissance was an age of moral, religious, intellectual and aesthetic crisis. This has been recognized often enough. What has not always been so clearly recognized in this connection is that it was also an age of acute crisis in economic, political and social life.

In the second place, was the Renaissance an age marked to a peculiar degree by the spirit of individualism? This is a difficult question to answer, for individualism is a perilously protean concept. It is also more than a little shop-worn, and it bears the marks of much careless handling. In any case, I find it difficult to think in terms of *the spirit* of the Renaissance, just as I find it impossible to envisage *the Renaissance man*. Such a complex and vital age must have had many spirits, good and bad, though probably few indifferent. Nevertheless, it does seem to me that there was in this transitional age a growing awareness of personality and a keener sense of individual autonomy than had been possible in the social and cultural conditions of the Middle Ages; and it may be that this trait was more strongly marked, more aggressive, in the Renaissance than in later ages, when the individual's right to self-determination was more easily taken for granted. To individualism, thus defined, many factors contributed, in addition to those mentioned by Burckhardt; for there were more changes in the heaven and earth of Renaissance men than were dreamed of in Burckhardt's philosophy—for example the growth of a lay piety that stressed the individual man's direct communion with God, and, at the other end of the moral spectrum, the development of a capitalist spirit that stressed the individual man's direct communion with Mammon. With the dislocation of European society that accompanied the breaking up of medieval institutions, men were left more dependent than before upon their own personal qualities, while the increasing complexity of social organization opened up a wider choice of careers, and more varied opportunities for the development of personal tastes and interests.

Finally, what is the rôle in the Renaissance of the revival of antiquity? That I have left discussion of the classical revival to the last does not mean that I regard it as unimportant. Rather the reverse. But I do think that its causative force, great though it was, was of a secondary character; that, indeed, the enthusiasm with which classical literature and learning were seized upon was itself caused by antecedent changes in the social structure, which became effective first in Italy, and later in the North. That men should love the classics, once exposed to them, has always seemed to classicists an obvious fact needing no explanation. Yet I think that the intense, almost excessive enthusiasm for classical culture, which was peculiar to the Renaissance, can be explained only by the fact that it was perfectly designed to meet the needs of educated, urban laymen, of a society that had ceased to be predominantly either feudal or ecclesiastical, yet had in its own immediate past nothing to draw upon for inspiration but the feudal and ecclesiastical traditions of the Middle Ages. I am not forgetting that the twelfth century also had its clerical humanists, notably John of Salisbury, but their humanism was of a different sort, and between them and Petrarch fell the shadow of scholasticism. The humanism of the Renaissance was not a clerical humanism, though there were clerical humanists—and it was certainly not feudal. It cut across the most characteristic of medieval traditions. When the mania for antiquity had passed its peak, and the writers of the sixteenth century were laying the foundations for the modern national literatures, they wrote not only for one class but for all cultured people.

The Broadening Horizon

NEW WORLDS

100 JOURNAL OF THE FIRST VOYAGE OF VASCO DA GAMA: PASSAGE TO INDIA

One aspect of Renaissance man's quest for greater knowledge of himself and his world was manifested in a surge of discoveries and voyages that began in the fifteenth century. Within the space of a generation, intrepid seafarers had crossed the fearsome Atlantic to find a new world, had pushed steadily southward until Africa was rounded and a new route to India was opened, and had circumnavigated the globe to prove conclusively that the earth was round. In the long run these exploits were to have a revolutionizing effect on the course of European development. In the sixteenth century the Atlantic was already emerging as Europe's new highway to fortune, power, and empire, and European civilization, which for so long had been centered on the Mediterranean, began its momentous shift to the west and north.

There were several reasons for the number of voyages and discoveries at this particular time. In the fifteenth century important improvements were made in shipbuilding and the art of sailing; together with the adoption of the mariner's compass and the astrolabe (for calculating latitude), it became possible to sail into the open sea out of sight of land. There was also the urgent desire to find some direct route to the Indies, the fabled source of spices, in order to break the Italian monopoly on the spice trade. In an age which had no refrigeration, spices were essential for the preservation of meat. The finding of such a route would bring untold profits to its discoverers.

In the course of things it was Portugal that led the way, largely because its royal house was the first willing to sponsor and encourage exploration. Prince Henry (1394-1460), known to history as "the Navigator," was the man who launched Portugal into the era of discovery and exploration. Although he was partially motivated by a desire to continue the crusade against the Moors and find the legendary kingdom of Prester John, he was primarily interested in expanding Portuguese commerce. By the time of his death, Prince Henry's sea captains had sailed some two thousand miles down the African coast and discovered the mouths of the Senegal and Gambia rivers. After a lapse of some twenty years, Henry's work was continued by his grand nephew King John II (1481-1495). John guessed that Africa could be rounded by sea and, gambling on its feasibility, he outfitted several expeditions. In 1488 Bartholomew Diaz rounded the Cape of Good Hope and proved his king was right. Diaz, on royal orders, then set to work supervising the building of more seaworthy ships for the journey to India.

In 1497 these ships, four in all, were placed under the command of a little-known member of the Portuguese nobility. Unlettered, brutal, and violent, he was nevertheless a man of iron physique and absolute fearlessness; Vasco da Gama (1460-1524) was made to order for the job that lay ahead—to lead his men and ships on a long, dangerous voyage that would take two years to complete. In May 1498 he succeeded in reaching India. His voyage thereby became one of the landmarks of world history, opening for the first time direct sea communications between Europe and the East.

The perils of that first voyage, the qualities of its commander, the lure of riches as well as of Prester John, are all evident in the following passages taken from a journal kept by one of the members of the da Gama expedition.

Mozambique

On Friday morning [March 2], Nicolau Coelho, when attempting to enter the bay, mistook the channel and came upon a bank. When putting about ship toward the other ships which followed in his wake, Coelho perceived some sailing boats approaching from a village on this island, in order to welcome the Captain Major and his brother. As for ourselves, we continued in the direction of our proposed anchorage, these boats following us all the while and making signs for us to stop.

When he had cast anchor in the roadstead of the island from which these boats had come, there approached seven or eight of them, including almadias, the people in them playing upon *anafils* [trumpets]. They invited us to proceed farther into the bay, offering to take us into port if we desired it. Those among them who boarded our ships ate and drank what we did, and went their way when they were satisfied.

The Captain thought that we should enter this bay in order that we might find out what sort of people we had to deal with; that Nicolau Coelho should go first in his vessel, to take soundings at the entrance; and that, if found practicable, we should follow him. As Coelho prepared to enter he struck the point of the island and broke his helm, but he immediately disengaged himself and regained deep water. I was with him at the time. When we were again in deep water, we struck our sails and cast anchor at a distance of two bowshots from the village.

The people of this country are of a ruddy complexion and well made. They are Mohammedans and their language is the same as that of the Moors [Arabic]. Their dresses are of fine linen or cotton stuffs, with variously colored stripes, and of rich and elaborate workmanship. They all wear *touca*s with borders of silk embroidered in gold. They are merchants, and have transactions with white Moors, four of whose vessels were at the time in port, laden with gold, silver, cloves, pepper, ginger, and silver rings, as also with quantities of pearls, jewels and rubies, all of which articles are used by the people....

We understood them to say that all these things, with the exception of the gold, were brought thither by these Moors; that farther on, where we were going to, they abounded, and that precious stones, pearls, and spices were so plentiful that there was no need to purchase them, as they could be collected in baskets. All this we learned through a sailor the Captain Major had with him and who, having formerly been a prisoner among the Moors, understood their language.

These Moors, moreover, told us that along the route which we were about to follow we should meet with numerous shoals; that there were many cities along the coast, and also an island one half the population of which consisted of Moors and the other half of Christians, who were at war with each other. This island was said to be very wealthy.

We were told, moreover, that Prester John resided not far from this place, that he held many cities along the coast, and that the inhabitants of those cities were great merchants and owned big ships. The residence of Prester John was said to be far in the interior, and could be reached only on the back of camels. These Moors had also brought hither two Christian captives from India. This information, and many other things which we heard, rendered us so happy that we cried with joy, and prayed God to grant us health, so that we might behold what we so much desired.

In this place and island of Moncobiquy [Mozambique] there resided a chief [*senhor*] who had the title of Sultan, and was like a viceroy. He often came aboard our ships attended by some of his people. The Captain Major gave him many good things to eat, and made him a present of hats, *marlotas* [Persian-type dresses], corals, and many other articles. He was, however, so proud that he treated all we gave him with contempt, and asked for scarlet cloth, of which we had none. We give him, however, of all the things we had.

One day the Captain Major invited him to a repast, when there was an abundance of figs and comfits, and begged him for two pilots to go with us. He at once granted this request, subject to our coming to terms with them. The Captain Major gave each of them 30 mitkals [coins reckoned at about $3] in gold and two *marlotas*, on condition that from the day on which they received this payment one of them should always remain on board if the other desired to go on land. With these terms they were well satisfied.

On Saturday, March 10, we set sail and anchored one league out at sea close to an island, where mass was said on Sunday, when those who wished to do so confessed and joined in the communion.

One of our pilots lived on the island, and when we had anchored we armed two boats to go in search of him. The Captain Major went in one boat and Nicolau Coelho in the other. They were met by five or six boats (*barcas*) coming from the island, and crowded with people

Text: Reprinted from *Great Adventures and Explorations*, ed. Vilhjalmur Stefansson. Copyright 1947 by The Dial Press and used with their permission. Pp. 174-77, 181-83.

armed with bows and long arrows and bucklers, who gave them to understand by signs that they were to return to the town. When the Captain saw this he secured the pilot, whom he had taken with him, and ordered the bombards to fire upon the boats.

Paulo da Gama, who had remained with the ships so as to be prepared to render succor in case of need, no sooner heard the reports of the bombards than he started in the *Berrio*. The Moors, who were already flying, fled still faster, and gained the land before the *Berrio* was able to come up with them. We then returned to our anchorage.

The vessels of this country are of good size and decked. There are no nails, and the planks are held together by cords, as are also those of their boats (*barcos*). The sails are made of palm matting. Their mariners have Genoese needles, by which they steer, quadrants, and navigating charts.

The palms of this country yield a fruit as large as a melon, of which the kernel is eaten [coconut]. It has a nutty flavor. There also grow in abundance melons and cucumbers, which were brought to us for barter.

On the day in which Nicolau Coelho entered the port, the lord of the place came on board with a numerous suite. He was received well, and Coelho presented him a red hood, in return for which the lord handed him a black rosary which he made use of when saying his prayers, to be held as a pledge. He then begged Nicolau Coelho for the use of his boat to take him ashore. This was granted. And after he had landed he invited those who had accompanied him to his house, where he gave them to eat. He then dismissed them, giving them a jar of bruised dates made into a preserve with cloves and cumin, as a present for Nicolau Coelho. Subsequently he sent many things to the Captain Major.

All this happened at the time when he took us for Turks or for Moors from some foreign land, for in case we came from Turkey he begged to be shown the bows of our country and our books of the Law. But when they learned that we were Christians, they arranged to seize and kill us by treachery. The pilot, whom we took with us, subsequently revealed to us all they intended to do, if they were able. . . .

Mombasa

On Saturday [April 7], we cast anchor off Mombasa, but did not enter the port. No sooner had we been perceived than a *zavra* [small open vessel] manned by Moors came out to us. In front of the city there lay numerous vessels all dressed in flags. And we, anxious not to be outdone, also dressed our ships, and we actually surpassed their show, for we wanted in nothing but men, even the few whom we had being very ill, [with scurvy]. We anchored here with much pleasure, for we confidently hoped that on the following day we might go on land and hear mass jointly with the Christians reported to live there under their own alcaide in a quarter separate from that of the Moors.

The pilots who had come with us told us there resided both Moors and Christians in this city; that these latter lived apart under their own lords; and that on our arrival they would receive us with much honor and take us to their houses. But they said this for a purpose of their own, for it was not true.

At midnight there approached us a *zavra* with about a hundred men, all armed with cutlasses (*tarsados*) and bucklers. When they came to the vessel of the Captain Major, they attempted to board her, armed as they were, but this was not permitted, only four or five of the most distinguished men among them being allowed on board. They remained about a couple of hours, and it seemed to us that they paid us this visit merely to find out whether they might not capture one or the other of our vessels.

On Palm Sunday [April 8], the King of Mombasa sent the Captain Major a sheep and large quantities of oranges, lemons, and sugar cane, together with a ring as a pledge of safety, letting him know that in case of his entering the port he would be supplied with all he stood in need of. This present was conveyed to us by two men, almost white, who said they were Christians, which appeared to be the fact.

The Captain Major sent the King a string of coral beads as a return present, and let him know that he purposed entering the port on the following day. On the same day the Captain Major's vessel was visited by four Moors of distinction.

Two men were sent by the Captain Major to the King, still further to confirm these peaceful assurances. When these landed, they were followed by a crowd as far as the gates of the palace. Before reaching the King they passed through four doors, each guarded by a doorkeeper with a drawn cutlass.

The King received them hospitably, and ordered that they should be shown over the city. They stopped on their way at the house of two Christian merchants, who showed them a paper (*carta*), an object of their adoration, on which was a sketch of the Holy Ghost. When they had seen all, the King sent them back with samples of cloves, pepper, and corn, with which articles he would allow us to load our ships.

On Tuesday [April 10], when weighing anchor to enter the port, the Captain Major's vessel would not pay off, and struck the vessel which followed astern. We therefore again cast anchor. When the Moors who were in our ship saw that we did not go on, they scrambled into a *zavra* attached to our stern, while the two pilots whom we had brought from Mozambique jumped into the water and were picked up by the men in the *zavra*.

At night the Captain Major questioned two Moors [from Mozambique] whom we had on board, by dropping boiling oil upon their skin, so that they might confess any treachery intended against us. They said that orders had been given to capture us as soon as we entered the port, and thus to avenge what we had done at Mozambique. And when this torture was being applied a second time, one of the Moors, although his hands were tied, threw himself into the sea, while the other did so during the morning watch.

About midnight two almadias with many men in them approached. The almadias stood off while the men entered the water, some swimming in the direction of the *Berrio*, others in that of the *Raphael*. Those who swam to the *Berrio* began to cut the cable. The men on watch thought at first that they were tunny fish, but when they perceived their mistake, they shouted to the other vessels. The other swimmers had already got hold of the rigging of the mizzenmast. Seeing themselves discovered, they silently slipped down and fled. These and other wicked tricks were practiced upon us by these dogs, but Our Lord did not allow them to succeed, because they were unbelievers.

101 CHRISTOPHER COLUMBUS, LETTER TO LORD RAPHAEL SANCHEZ, MARCH 14, 1493: DISCOVERY OF THE NEW WORLD

Even before the Portuguese da Gama set sail on his epoch-making voyage (see Document 100), Spain had become a serious competitor in the quest for new routes to the Indies. In 1492 a Genoese flying the colors of Spain had sailed westward across the Atlantic in search of such a route and in the process discovered the lands of the Western Hemisphere. Christopher Columbus (1451-1506) had no inkling that his achievement would alter the whole current of world affairs, for to the day he died he never realized that he had opened to Europe a vast new continent.

Although Columbus believed that the earth was round and that land could be found by sailing west, neither of these ideas was original with him; virtually all educated people of the Renaissance believed the earth to be spherical, and many others besides Columbus believed that there was land at the western end of the Atlantic. Of greater significance was the fact that Columbus underestimated the circumference of the earth, and by doing so he grossly exaggerated the size of Asia and the extent to which that continent projected eastward. On the basis of these miscalculations he was convinced that the distance between the west coast of Europe and the east coast of Asia was much shorter than is actually the case. He was also familiar with Marco Polo's famous book and was particularly interested in the description of Cipangu (Japan), which Polo claimed was fabulously rich, although he had never visited it. And since Polo erred in placing Japan too far east of China, Columbus was certain that only a short voyage across the Atlantic would bring him to the fabulous wealth of Cipangu and Cathay.

It seemed natural to approach the leading patron of exploration, King John II of Portugal, to secure backing for his scheme. But the Portuguese king turned him down; for while Columbus talked well and impressively, he came of a poor family and had little formal education. Furthermore, John felt that the price Columbus asked for his services—demands for rewards and titles—was too high. Undaunted, Columbus in 1485 turned to Spain, at the same time sending his brother to France and England in a vain attempt to interest Charles VIII and Henry VII. In Spain, despite the support of Queen Isabella, he had to endure seven long years of tedious negotiations before approval was finally given. Spain was simply too engrossed in the problems of unifying the country, subduing rebellious nobles, and expelling the Moors. It was, says Samuel Eliot Morison, Columbus' biographer, as if a polar explorer had tried to interest Abraham Lincoln in the conquest of the Antarctic about the time of the Battle of Gettysburg. In any case, by January 1492 Moorish Granada was conquered, and shortly thereafter the Spanish monarchs agreed to outfit a westward expedition to Cathay.

In August 1492 Columbus sailed out of Palos with the *Niña*, the *Pinta* and the *Santa María*. After stopping at the Canary Islands for repairs, finally, on September 6, 1492, the three caravels headed due west across the trackless wastes of the Atlantic on what was to be the most important single voyage on record. With excellent weather and a favorable wind, the expedition enjoyed very fast sailing. Five weeks later, at two in the morning on October 12, Rodrigo da Triana, on lookout on the *Pinta's* forecastle, shouted "Tierra! Tierra!" San Salvador in the Bahamas had been discovered. Sailing southward through the Bahamas, Columbus reached Cuba, which he assumed was part of Cathay. Then turning eastward he found Haiti and mistakenly thinking that island to be part of the Indies, he called the natives Indians. The letter below, written by Columbus in Lisbon on March 14, 1493, ten days after his return, describes what he discovered on that first historical voyage and clearly reveals his misconceptions. Note, too, his zealous crusading for the cause of Christianity.

A Letter addressed to the noble Lord Raphael Sanchez, Treasurer to their most invincible Majesties, Ferdinand and Isabella, King and Queen of Spain, by Christopher Columbus, to whom our age is greatly indebted, treating of the islands of India recently discovered beyond the Ganges, to explore which he had been sent eight months before under the auspices and at the expense of their said Majesties.

Knowing that it will afford you pleasure to learn that I have brought my undertaking to a successful termination, I have decided upon writing you this letter to acquaint you with all the events which have occurred in my voyage, and the discoveries which have resulted from it. Thirty-three days after my departure from Cadiz I reached the Indian sea, where I discovered many islands, thickly peopled, of which I took possession without resistance in the name of our most illustrious Monarch, by public proclamation and with unfurled banners. To the first of these islands, which is called by the Indians Guanahani, I gave the name of the blessed Saviour (San Salvador), relying upon whose protection I had reached this as well as the other islands; to each of these I also gave a name, ordering that one should be called Santa Maria de la Concepcion, another Fernandina, the third Isabella, the fourth Juana, and so with all the rest respectively. As soon as we arrived at that, which as I have said was named Juana, I proceeded along its coast a short distance westward, and found it to be so large and apparently without termination, that I could not suppose it to be an island, but the continental province of Cathay. Seeing, however, no towns or populous places on the sea coast, but only a few detached houses and cottages, with whose inhabitants I was unable to communicate, because they fled as soon as they saw us, I went further on, thinkng that in my progress I should certainly find some city or village. At length, after proceeding a great way and finding that nothing new presented itself, and that the line of coast was leading us northwards (which I wished to avoid, because it was winter, and it was my intention to move southwards; and because moreover the winds were contrary), I resolved not to attempt any further progress, but rather to turn back and retrace my course to a certain bay that I had observed, and from which I afterwards dispatched two of our men to ascertain whether there were a king or any cities in that province. These men reconnoitred the country for three days, and found a most numerous population, and great numbers of houses, though small, and built without any regard to order; with which information they returned to us. In the mean time I had learned from some Indians whom I had seized, that that country was certainly an island: and therefore I sailed towards the east, coasting to the distance of three hundred and twenty-two miles, which brought us to the extremity of it; from this point I saw lying eastwards another island, fifty-four miles distant from Juana, to which I gave the name of Española: I went thither, and steered my course eastward as I had done at Juana, even to the distance of five hundred and sixty-four miles along the north coast. This said island of Juana is exceedingly fertile, as indeed are all the others; it is surrounded with many bays, spacious, very secure, and surpassing any that I have ever seen; numerous large and healthful rivers intersect it, and it also contains many very lofty mountains. All these islands are very beautiful, and distinguished by a diversity of scenery; they are filled with a great variety of trees of immense height, and which I believe to retain their foliage in all seasons; for when I saw them they were as verdant and luxuriant as they usually are in Spain in the month of May,— some of them were blossoming, some bearing fruit, and all flourishing in the greatest perfec-

Text: R. H. Major (trans. and ed.), *Select Letters of Christopher Columbus, with Other Original Documents Relating to His Four Voyages to the New World* (London: Hakluyt Society, 1847), pp. 1-8, 15-17.

tion, according to their respective stages of growth, and the nature and quality of each: yet the islands are not so thickly wooded as to be impassable. The nightingale and various birds were singing in countless numbers, and that in November, the month in which I arrived there. There are besides in the same island of Juana seven or eight kinds of palm trees, which, like all the other trees, herbs, and fruits, considerably surpass ours in height and beauty. The pines also are very handsome, and there are very extensive fields and meadows, a variety of birds, different kinds of honey, and many sorts of metals, but no iron. In that island also which I have before said we named Española, there are mountains of very great size and beauty, vast plains, groves, and very fruitful fields, admirably adapted for tillage, pasture, and habitation. The convenience and excellence of the harbours in this island, and the abundance of the rivers, so indispensable to the health of man, surpass anything that would be believed by one who had not seen it. The trees, herbage, and fruits of Española are very different from those of Juana, and moreover it abounds in various kinds of spices, gold, and other metals. The inhabitants of both sexes in this island, and in all the others which I have seen, or of which I have received information, go always naked as they were born, with the exception of some of the women, who use the covering of a leaf, or small bough, or an apron of cotton which they prepare for that purpose. None of them, as I have already said, are possessed of any iron, neither have they weapons, being unacquainted with, and indeed incompetent to use them, not from any deformity of body (for they are well-formed), but because they are timid and full of fear. They carry however in lieu of arms, canes dried in the sun, on the ends of which they fix heads of dried wood sharpened to a point, and even these they dare not use habitually; for it has often occurred when I have sent two or three of my men to any of the villages to speak with the natives, that they have come out in disorderly troop, and have fled in such haste at the approach of our men, that the fathers forsook their children and the children their fathers. This timidity did not arise from any loss or injury that they had received from us; for, on the contrary, I gave to all I approached whatever articles I had about me, such as cloth and many other things, taking nothing of theirs in return: but they are naturally timid and fearful. As soon however as they see that they are safe, and have laid aside all fear, they are very simple and honest, and exceedingly liberal with all they have; none of them refusing any thing he may possess when he is asked for it, but on the contrary inviting us to ask them. They exhibit great love towards all others in preference to themselves: they also give objects of great value for trifles, and content themselves with very little or nothing in return. I however forbad that these trifles and articles of no value (such as pieces of dishes, plates, and glass, keys, and leather straps) should be given to them, although if they could obtain them, they imagined themselves to be possessed of the most beautiful trinkets in the world. It even happened that a sailor received for a leather strap as much gold as was worth three golden nobles, and for things of more trifling value offered by our men, especially-newly coined blancas, or any gold coins, the Indians would give whatever the seller required; as, for instance, an ounce and a half or two ounces of gold, or thirty or forty pounds of cotton, with which commodity they were already acquainted. Thus they bartered, like idiots, cotton and gold for fragments of bows, glasses, bottles, and jars; which I forbad as being unjust, and myself gave them many beautiful and acceptable articles which I had brought with me, taking nothing from them in return; I did this in order that I might the more easily conciliate them, that they might be led to become Christians, and be inclined to entertain a regard for the King and Queen, our Princes and all Spaniards, and that I might induce them to take an interest in seeking out, and collecting, and delivering to us such things as they possessed in abundance, but which we greatly needed. . . .

. . . They assure me that there is another island larger than Española, whose inhabitants have no hair, and which abounds in gold more than any of the rest. I bring with me individuals of this island and of the others that I have seen, who are proofs of the facts which I state. Finally, to compress into few words the entire summary of my voyage and speedy return, and of the advantages derivable therefrom, I promise, that with a little assistance afforded me by our most invincible sovereigns, I will procure them as much gold as they need, as great a quantity of spices, of cotton, and of mastic (which is only found in Chios), and as many men for the service of the navy as their Majesties may require. I promise also rhubarb and other sorts of drugs, which I am persuaded the men whom I have left in the aforesaid fortress have found already and will continue to find; for I myself have tarried no where longer than I was compelled to do by the winds, except in the city of Navidad, while I provided for the building of the fortress, and took the necessary precautions for the perfect security of the men I left there. Although all I have related may appear to be wonderful and unheard of, yet the results of my voyage would have been more astonishing if I had had at my disposal such ships as I required. But these great and marvellous results are not to be attributed to any merit of mine, but to the holy Christian faith, and to the piety and religion of our Sovereigns; for that which the unaided intellect of man could not compass, the spirit of God has granted to human exertions, for God is wont to hear the prayers of his servants who love his precepts even to the performance of apparent impossibilites. Thus it has happened to me in the present instance, who have accomplished a task to which the powers of mortal men had never hitherto attained; for if there have been those who have anywhere written or spoken of these islands, they have done so with doubts and conjectures, and no one has ever asserted that he has seen them, on which account their writings have been looked upon as little else than fables. Therefore let the king and queen, our princes and their most happy kingdoms, and all the other provinces of Christendom, render thanks to our Lord and Saviour Jesus Christ, who has granted us so great a victory and such prosperity. Let processions be made, and sacred feasts be held, and the temples be adorned with festive boughs. Let Christ rejoice on earth, as he rejoices in heaven in the prospect of the salvation of the souls of so many nations hitherto lost. Let us also rejoice, as well on account of the exaltation of our faith, as on account of the increase of our temporal prosperity, of which not only Spain, but all Christendom will be partakers.

Such are the events which I have briefly described. Farewell.

Lisbon, the 14th of March.

Christopher Columbus,
Admiral of the Fleet of the Ocean

102 AFFONSO DE ALBUQUERQUE, LETTER TO KING MANUEL OF PORTUGAL, 1510: THE PORTUGUESE INVASION OF THE EAST

When Vasco da Gama reached Calicut, India, in May 1498 (see Document 100), he had sailed into a world long dominated by Muslim merchants and traders, some of whom were Arabs and some Persians. Intensely jealous of any interloper who might encroach upon their monopoly, they recognized the threat that da Gama, a European and a Christian, represented to their commercial position. After narrowly escaping an assassination plot against him, it became clear to da Gama that no satisfactory trade could be established by the Portuguese so long as the Muslim merchants remained in control.

Da Gama returned to Portugal, and a significant decision was reached. The Portuguese, only dimly aware of the magnitude of the problem before them, decided to destroy the Muslim trade monopoly in the Indian Ocean. At that time (the end of the fifteenth century), the well-organized Muslim-dominated commerce stretched from the Red Sea in the west to China in the east. At the western terminal Venetian merchants waited to carry the spices and silks to an eager Europe. Everyone along the line profited handsomely, from the Muslim merchants, to the sultans of Egypt and Turkey, to the Doge of Venice. All concerned were vitally interested in preserving so lucrative a system. This was what little Portugal now proposed to destroy, not realizing that it would require nothing less than gaining control of the entire Indian Ocean.

In the decade following da Gama's voyage, the Portuguese sent out ever larger fleets to tap the wealth of the Orient and to establish their primacy in the Indian Ocean. By 1507 they had captured Mozambique, along with three important ports in East Africa, and empire-building was begun. The Venetians, aware of the danger to their own position and anxious to stop the Portuguese before it was too late, lent their support to the Sultan of Egypt, who assembled a great fleet with which to annihilate the intruders. The climax came in February 1509. Sighting the mighty Egyptian armada off Diu on the west coast of India, the Portuguese boldly attacked, and although heavily outnumbered, they succeeded in completely destroying the Muslim navy. It was a turning point of the first magnitude in the struggle to dominate the Indian Ocean.

There now appeared on the scene Affonso de Albuquerque (1453-1515), who was destined to become Portugal's greatest hero and empire-builder in the East. In 1509, fifty-six years old, he was battle-hardened through long years of service in European wars, and ruthless to the point of brutality. He so dominated the Indian Ocean in the short six years (1509-1515) that he governed for his king that four and a half centuries later his reputation still lives on. The genius of Albuquerque lay in his ability to perceive that if Portuguese sea power in the East was to be solidly established, it had to be built on a few key land bases so strategically located that with them a small but determined European nation could control the whole vast perimeter of the Indian Ocean. Only four such bases were necessary: one in the east (Malacca), two in the west (Hormuz and Aden), and one in the center (Gôa). To his everlasting fame, he came within an ace of completing his grandiose scheme, failing only to capture Aden permanently. In effect he had established for Portugal, a nation of less than two million people, a sprawling commercial empire in the East. Albuquerque, in creating the first European empire overseas, anticipated, or initiated the expansion of Europe that was to proceed unabated for the next four hundred years.

In the letter below, written to the King of Portugal to explain and defend the capture of Gôa (1510), Albuquerque lays bare the basis of his naval strategy in the Indian Ocean and indicates how crucial a factor the conquest of Gôa was for Portuguese prestige and power.

. . . Sire, I captured Goa, because Your Highness ordered me to do so, and the Marshal had orders to take it in his instruction, I took it also because it was the headquarters of the league which was set on foot in order to cast us out of India, and if the fleet which the Turks had prepared in Goa river (with a large force of men, artillery, and arms, specially assembled for this object) had pushed forward, and the fleet of the Rumes had come at this juncture, as they had expected, without doubt I should have been utterly discomfited; yea, even if ever so great a fleet had come from Portugal they would not have allowed it to make good its arrival in the country. But when once Goa was conquered, everything else was at our command without any further trouble, and when Goa was taken, that one victory alone did more for the advancement of Your Highness' *prestige* than all the fleets which have come to India during the last fifteen years. And if Your Highness, in deference to the opinions of those who have written this advice to you, thinks it possible to secure your dominions in these parts by means of the fortresses of Cochim and Cananor, it is impossible; for, if once Portugal should suffer a reverse at sea, your Indian possessions have not power to hold out a day longer than the kings of the land choose to suffer it; for if one of our men take anything by force from a native, immediately they raise the drawbridge and shut the gates of the fortress; and this causes Your Highness not to be Lord of the Land, as of Goa, for in this territory the injury which is done to Moors or to Portuguese does not reach beyond the Captain of the Fortress. Justice is yours, and yours the arm, yours the sword, and in the hand of your Captain-General reposes the punishment, and before him lies the remedy for the complaint of every one; and if today there be any improvement in regard to the obedience shown by the natives of the land, it is plainly to be referred to the fact that the taking of Goa keeps India in repose and quiet; and the fact that the island has so frequently been attacked by the Turks, as those who wrote to Your Highness assert, and so valiantly defended by the Portuguese, enhances the credit which the progress of affairs in these parts deserves. And I have so completely disheartened the members of the league against us, that the King of Cambaya, powerful prince as he is, lost no time in sending to me his Ambassadors, and restoring to me all the Cavaliers and *Fidalgoes* who were shipwrecked with D. Afonso de Noronha, my nephew, on their voyage from Cacotora, without my sending to ask this of him, and even offered me permission to build a fortress in Diu, a matter of such immense importance that even now I can hardly believe it; and I am now importuned by the Camorim of Calicut, who desires to grant me a site to build a fortress in his city, and is willing to pay a yearly tribute to the Crown. All this is the result of our holding Goa, without my waging war upon any of these princes.

And I hold it to be free from doubt, that if fortresses be built in Diu and Calicut (as I trust in Our Lord they will be)—when once they have been well fortified, if a thousand of the Sultan's ships were to make their way to India, not one of these places could be brought again under his dominion. But if those of your council understood Indian affairs as I do, they would not fail to be aware that Your Highness cannot be lord over so extensive a territory as India by placing all your power and strength in your marine only (a policy at once doubtful and full of serious inconveniences); for this, and not to

Text: Walter De Gray Birch (trans. and ed.), *The Commentaries of the Great Afonso Dalboquerque* (London: Hakluyt Society, 1880), III, 258-63.

build fortresses, is the very thing which the Moors of these lands wish you to do, for they know well that a dominion founded on a navy alone cannot last, and they desire to live on their estates and property, and to carry their spiceries to the ancient and customary markets which they maintain, but they are unwilling to be subject to Your Highness, neither will they trade or be on friendly terms with you. And if they will not have any of these things, how is it likely that they will be pleased to see us establishing ourselves in this city of Goa, and strengthening its defences, and Your Highness lord of so important a port and bar as this is, and not labour with all their might to hinder us from accomplishing our intentions? And if it seems a hard matter to those who have written about this to Your Highness that the recovery of Goa should have been so many times attempted, how much harder must it have been to gain the country from so powerful a king as the Hidalcão, lord of so many armies, who is not likely to refrain from straining every nerve to recover the possession of it and striking a decisive blow at our *prestige,* if he could do so? And whenever any one of his captains shall come up against this city, are we to surrender it immediately without first of all measuring our forces against him? If this be so, Your Highness may as well leave India to the Moors, and seek to maintain your position therein with such extraordinary outlays and expenses on the navy, in ships as rotten as cork, only kept afloat by four pumps in each of them.

As for the extraordinary expenses connected with the maintenance of Goa, of which these idle fellows write to Your Highness, the mere dross of India is so great, that if the Portuguese possessions be properly farmed by your officers, the revenue from them alone would suffice to repay a great part of these expenses to which we are put, and if they say that the reason why I desire to keep possession of Goa is because it was I who took it, Your Lordship may rest assured that if I were a Portuguese of such a character as they are, I would be the first, if you ordered me to destroy it, to put the pickaxe into the walls, and to fire the barrel of gunpowder under the keep, if only for the pleasure of seeing the cards of the game of India shuffled for a new deal; but as long as I live, and while it remains my duty to send an account to Your Highness of Indian affairs, Goa must not be dismantled, for I would not that my enemies should exult in the contemplation of any serious disaster in this estate; and I must sustain it at my own cost, until they get their wishes and another Governor be sent to rule over it.

If this that I say does not agree with the ideas of some of those who are half-hearted about this matter of Goa, Your Highness may know for certain that as yet there is one man who is governing it: and old and weak as I am, I will accept the government of this conquered territory at Your Highness's hands, if it may be permitted me to confer the lands of the Moors upon the Cavaliers and *Fidalgoes* who have assisted me to gain them. But do not require of me every year an account of what I am doing as if I were a taxgatherer, because four ill-mannered fellows, who sit at home like idols in their pagodas, have born false witness against me; but honour me, and thank me, for I shall be happy to complete this enterprise, and spend what little I have upon it: and, in conclusion, all that I have to say is, that if Your Highness either now or at any other time surrender[s] Goa to the Turks, then plainly Our Lord desires that the Portuguese dominion in India should come to an end; and, as for me, Your Highness may be sure that, so long as I am Governor, although I be put to much trouble, I shall not at any rate send you painted pictures of fictitious places, but rather kingdoms taken by force of arms from their masters, and fortified by me in such a manner that they may give a good account of themselves in all time.

This is my opinion concerning this question of Goa, which Your Highness commanded me to discuss with its captains and officers.

103 HERNANDO CORTÉS, LETTER TO EMPEROR CHARLES V, OCTOBER 1520: THE WONDERS OF MEXICO

Columbus' return in 1493 with news of his discoveries immediately set in motion a bitter rivalry between Spain and Portugal for the control of the overseas territories and trade routes. The problem was finally settled in 1494 by the Treaty of Tordesillas, which divided the world between the two Iberian nations. Portugal received all rights of trade in Asia and the East Indies with the exception of the Philippines, which Magellan had discovered for Spain; Spain received all of America with the exception of Brazil, which the Portuguese Cabral had discovered in 1500. For the next hundred years, while the other major nations of Europe were engrossed in the internal problems of political unification and wracked by the religious wars of the Reformation, Spain and Portugal were left free to exploit their respective hemispheres. Not until the seventeenth century were the British, French, and Dutch in a position to embark upon sustained overseas ventures.

The Spanish and Portuguese pursued divergent imperial policies. Portugal was content to wax wealthy on the eastern trade monopoly secured by Albuquerque. With so small a population, and in contact everywhere with populations and civilizations at least equal to their own, the Portuguese made no serious attempt at colonization. Theirs remained an empire based on trade and supremacy of the seas—and that proved to be its chief weakness. Later, when stronger maritime powers such as the Dutch Republic and England made their appearance, Portugal's empire in the East disintegrated.

The story of Spain in the New World was far different. Unlike the Portuguese, the Spanish set out to conquer and to colonize the lands they discovered. As early as 1494 Columbus' brother, Bartholomew, established the settlement of Santo Domingo on the south coast of the island of Haiti (then called Hispaniola). Now the capital of the Dominican Republic, it is the oldest town of European origin in the Western Hemisphere. In 1510 Columbus' son, Diego, was sent out as Viceroy of the West and it was clear that a new age had begun in America. By then settlements had already been made on Puerto Rico, Cuba, and Jamaica. These islands contained little mineral wealth but the Spaniards brought with them sugar cane and swine, and these two commodities constituted the basis of a highly profitable agricultural system.

The most astonishing phase of Spanish activity, however, still lay ahead. Thus far, very few settlements had been made on the mainland itself, even though there were persistent rumors of fabulously wealthy cities far inland. These tales excited the imagination—and the cupidity—of a group of restless, ambitious adventurers eager to make their fame and fortune. Known to history as the *conquistadores*, they were calloused veterans of Spain's European wars drawn to America in search of easy wealth. As remarkable for their excesses as for their exploits, no easy judgment of them is possible. In the words of Boies Penrose, "Their courage was peerless, their cruelty revolting; their endurance was heroic, their lust for riches despicable; their devotion to their leaders was often the personification of fidelity, but the treachery of the leaders to one another was often beneath contempt."

The achievement of the *conquistadores* was nothing less than the subjugation of the American continent from Mexico to Peru. Gold, of course, was their principal goal, and the great riches of the Aztecs and Incas surpassed the wildest fantasies of even the most avaricious *conquistador*. Once the accumulated treasure had been drained off to Spain, with profound consequences for all of Europe, the Spanish remained to colonize and impose upon the natives their own civilization. Long before the first Englishmen landed at Jamestown (1607), the American continent from Mexico southward was already being "Europeanized."

Greatest of all the *conquistadores* was Hernando Cortés, conqueror of Mexico. In October 1520 he penned the first account ever written of the wonders of Mexico in a letter addressed to the Holy Roman Emperor Charles V (King of Spain). In the selections below, taken from that letter, we catch a glimpse not only of the magnificence of Mexican civilization, but of Cortés' shrewdness in dealing with the Aztecs and his determination to impose Christianity upon them.

... The following day I mounted the pass between the two mountains of which I have spoken, and, descending it, we beheld one of the provinces, of the country of the said Montezuma, called Chalco, where, about two leagues before we reached the town, I found a very good dwelling place, which had been recently built, and was so large that all my company and myself were very commodiously lodged in it; this although I had with me more than four thousand Indians, of these provinces of Tascaltecal, Guasucingo, Churultecal, and Cempoal, for whom there were ample provisions of food. Here great fires of plenty of wood were burned in all the rooms, for the cold was very bitter, as we were surrounded by two mountains both covered with snow.

Text: Reprinted by permission of the Arthur H. Clark Company, publishers, from Francis Augustus MacNutt (trans. and ed.), *Hernando Cortés, His Five Letters of Relation to the Emperor Charles V*. Copyright 1908 by Francis Augustus MacNutt. Vol. I, pp. 226-27, 229-36, 253-55, 259-62.

Certain persons came to speak to me here who seemed to be chiefs, amongst whom was one who, I was told, was brother to Montezuma. He brought me about three thousand dollars of gold, and told me in Montezuma's name that the latter sent that to me, and prayed me to go back, and not insist on coming to his city, as the country was scarce of food, and the roads leading there were bad; and, as it was all on the water, I could enter it only in canoes. He also enumerated many other inconveniences to prevent me going. They said I had only to say what I wanted, for Montezuma their sovereign would order it to be given to me, and would likewise agree to give me annually *certum quid*, which would be taken to the coast, or wherever I wished. I received them very well and gave them some Spanish articles, such as they esteem very much, especially to him who was said to be a brother of Montezuma's. I replied to his embassy, that, if it was in my hands to return, I would do so in order to please Montezuma, but that I had come to this country by order of Your Majesty, and that the principal thing, of which you had ordered me to give an account, was Montezuma, and his great city, of whom, and of which, Your Majesty had possessed information since a long time. I said also that they should tell him from me, that I prayed him to approve my going to see him, because no injury would result from it to his person and country, but rather that he should receive good; and if after I had seen him he did not wish to have me in his company, then I would return; and that we could better decide between ourselves, how he should serve Your Highness, than through third persons, even were they those in whom we had full confidence. With this answer they departed. . . .

I departed immediately after them, accompanied by many people who seemed to be of much importance, as it afterwards appeared, and I continued along the road by the shore of that great lake. A league from my last stopping place, I saw in this lake, two musket-shots distant from the shore, a small city which might have had one or two thousand inhabitants, and which was all afloat on the water; having many towers as it seemed but no entrance. About a league from there, we reached a great causeway, as broad as a horseman's lance, extending within the lake about two-thirds of a league. This led to the city, which though small, was the most beautiful we had yet seen, not only on account of the well decorated houses and towers, but also because of the excellent construction of its foundations in the water.

In this city, which has about two thousand inhabitants, we were very well received, and they gave us excellent food. The lord and chiefs of it came to speak with me, and prayed me to remain, and sleep there; however, Montezuma's messengers who were with me told me not to stop, but to go on to another city, called Iztapalapan, about three leagues distant, belonging to a brother of Montezuma; so I did this. The exit from the said city where we dined, whose name at present does not occur to my memory, is by another causeway, a long league in length, which extends to the mainland.

Having arrived at this city of Iztapalapan, the chief of it came out to receive me, as well as one from another great city, called Calnaalcan, which is near, being perhaps three leagues distant, and these were accompanied by many other chiefs who were waiting for me; and they gave me three or four thousand *castellanos*, some female slaves, and wearing apparel, receiving me very well. This city of Iztapalapan has some twelve or fifteen thousand households, and stands on the shore of a great salt lake, half of it in the water, and the other half on land. Its chief has some new houses, which, though still unfinished, are as good as the best in Spain; I say as large and well constructed, not only in the stone work, but also in the wood work, and all arrangements for every kind of household service, all except the relief work, and other rich details, which are used in Spanish houses, but are not found here. There are both upper and lower rooms, and very refreshing gardens, with many trees and sweet scented flowers, bathing places of fresh water, well constructed, with steps leading down to the bottom. He has also a large garden round his house, in which there is a terrace with many beautiful corridors and rooms, and, within the garden, is a great pool of fresh water, very well built with sides of handsome masonry, around which runs an open walk with well laid tile pavements, so broad that four persons can walk abreast on it, and four hundred paces square, making, in all, sixteen hundred paces. On the other side of this promenade, towards the wall of the garden, it is all surrounded by a lattice work of canes, behind which are arbours, planted with fragrant shrubs. The pool contains many fish, and water fowl, such as ducks, cranes, and other kinds of water birds, in such numbers that the water is covered with them.

The next day after I had arrived in this city, I left, and having gone half a league, I reached another causeway, leading out into the lake a distance of two leagues to the great city of Temixtitan, which stands in the midst of the said lake. This causeway is two lances broad, and so well built that eight horsemen can ride abreast; and, within these two leagues, there are three cities, on one and the other side of the said highway, one called Mesicalsingo, founded for the greater part within the said lake, and the other two, called Niciaca, and Huchilohuchico, on the other shore of it, with many of their houses on the water.

The first of these cities may have three thousand families, the second more than six thousand, and the third four or five thousand. In all of them, there are very good edifices, of houses and towers, especially the residences of the lords and chief persons, and the mosques or oratories, where they keep their idols. These cities have a great trade in salt, which they make from the water of the lake, and from the crust of the land which is bathed by the lake, and which they boil in a certain manner, making loaves of salt, which they sell to the inhabitants in the neighbourhood.

I followed the said causeway for about half a league before I came to the city proper of Temixtitan. I found at the junction of another causeway, which joins this one from the mainland, another strong fortification, with two towers, surrounded by walls, twelve feet high with castellated tops. This commands the two roads, and has only two gates, by one of which they enter, and from the other they come out. About one thousand of the principal citizens came out to meet me, and speak to me, all richly dressed alike according to their fashion; and when they had come, each one in approaching me, and before speaking, would use a ceremony which is very common amongst them, putting his hand on the ground, and afterwards kissing it, so that I was kept waiting almost an hour, until each had performed his ceremony. There is a wooden bridge, ten paces broad, in the very outskirts of the city, across an opening in the causeway, where the water may flow in and out as it rises and falls. This bridge is also for defence, for they remove and replace the long broad wooden beams, of which the bridge is made, whenever they wish; and there are many of these bridges in the city, as Your Highness will see in the account which I shall make of its affairs.

Having passed this bridge, we were received by that lord, Montezuma, with about two hundred chiefs, all barefooted, and dressed in a kind of livery, very rich, according to their custom, and some more so than others. They approached in two processions near the walls of the street, which is very broad, and straight, and beautiful, and very uniform from one end to the other, being about two thirds of a league long, and having, on both sides, very large houses, both dwelling places, and mosques. Montezuma came in the middle of the street, with two lords, one on the right side, and the other on the left, one of whom was the same great lord, who, as I said, came in that litter to speak with me, and the other was the brother of Montezuma, lord of that city Iztapalapan, whence I had come that day. All were dressed in the same manner, except that Montezuma was shod, and the other lords were barefooted. Each supported him below his arms, and as we approached each other, I descended from my horse, and was about to embrace him, but the two lords in attendance prevented me, with their hands, that I might not touch him, and they, and he also, made the ceremony of kissing the ground. This done, he ordered his brother who came with him, to remain with me, and take me by the arm, and the other attendant walked a little ahead of us. After he had spoken to me, all the other lords, who formed the two processions, also saluted me, one after the other, and then returned to the procession. When I approached to speak to Montezuma, I took off a collar of pearls and glass diamonds, that I wore, and put it on his neck, and, after we had gone through some of the streets, one of his servants came with two collars, wrapped in a cloth, which were made of coloured shells. These they esteem very much; and from each of the collars hung eight golden shrimps executed with great perfection and a span long. When he received them, he turned towards me, and put them on my neck, and again went on through the streets, as I have already indicated, until we came to a large and handsome house, which he had prepared for our reception. There he took me by the hand, and led me into a spacious room, in front of the court where we had entered, where he made me sit on a very rich platform, which had been ordered to be made for him, and told me to wait there; and then he went away.

After a little while, when all the people of my company were distributed to their quarters, he returned with many valuables of gold and silver work, and five or six thousand pieces of rich cotton stuffs, woven, and embroidered in diverse ways. After he had given them to me, he sat down on another platform, which they immediately prepared near the one where I was seated, and being seated he spoke in the following manner:

"We have known for a long time, from the chronicles of our forefathers, that neither I, nor those who inhabit this country, are descendants from the aborigines of it, but from strangers who came to it from very distant parts; and we also hold, that our race was brought to these parts by a lord, whose vassals they all were, and who returned to his native country. After a long time he came back, but it was so long, that those who remained here were married with the native women of the country, and had many descendants, and had built towns where they were living; when, therefore, he wished to take them away with him, they would not go, nor still less receive him as their ruler, so he departed. And we have always held that those who descended from him would come to subjugate this country and us, as his vassals; and according to the direction from which you say you come, which is where the run rises, and from what you tell us of your great lord, or king, who has sent you here, we believe, and hold for certain, that he is our rightful sovereign, especially as you tell us that since many days he has had news of us. Hence you may be sure, that we shall obey you, and hold you as the representative of this great lord of whom you speak, and that in this there will be no lack or deception; and throughout the whole country you may command at your will (I speak of what I possess in my dominions), because you will be obeyed, and recognized, and all we possess is at your disposal.

"Since you are in your rightful place, and in your own homes, rejoice and rest, free from all the trouble of the journey, and wars which you have had, for I am well aware of all that has happened to you, between Puntunchan and here, and I know very well, that the people of Cempoal, and Tascaltecal, have told you many evil things respecting me. Do not believe more than you see with your own eyes, especially from those who are my enemies, and were my vassals, yet rebelled against me on your coming (as they say), in order to help you. I know they have told you also that I have houses, with walls of gold, and that the furniture of my halls, and other things of my service, were also of gold, and that I am, or make myself, a god, and many other things. The houses you have seen are of lime and stone and earth." And then he held up his robes, and showing me his body he said to me, "Look at me, and see that I am flesh and bones, the same as you, and everybody, and that I am mortal and tangible." And touching his arms and body with his hands, "Look how they have lied to you! It is true indeed that I have some things of gold, which have been left to me by my forefathers. All that I possess, you may have whenever you wish.

"I shall now go to other houses where I live; but you will be provided here with everything necessary for you and your people, and you shall suffer no annoyance, for you are in your own house and country."

I answered to all he said, certifying that which seemed to be suitable, especially in confirming his belief that it was Your Majesty whom they were expecting. After this, he took his leave, and, when he had gone, we were well provided with chickens, and bread, and fruits, and other necessities, especially such as were required for the service of our quarters. Thus I passed six days well provided with everything necessary, and visited by many of the lords. . . .

This decision and offer of the said lords, for the royal service of Your Majesty having been completed, I spoke to Montezuma one day, and told him that Your Highness was in need of gold, on account of certain works ordered to be made, and I besought him to send some of his people, and I would also send some Spaniards, to the provinces and houses of those lords who had there submitted themselves, to pray them to assist Your Majesty with some part of what they had. Besides Your Highness's need, this would testify that they began to render service, and Your Highness would the more esteem their good will towards your service; and I told him that he also should give me from his treasures, as I wished to send them to Your Majesty, as I had done with the other things. He asked me afterwards to choose the Spaniards whom I wished to send, and two by two, and five by five, he distributed them through many provinces and cities, whose names I do not remember, as the papers have been lost, and also because they were many and divers; and moreover some of them were at eighty and one hundred leagues from the said great city of Temixtitan. He sent some of his people with them ordering them to go to the lords of those provinces and cities, and tell them that I had commanded each one of them to contribute a certain measure of gold which he gave them. Thus it was done, and all those lords to whom he sent gave very compliantly, as had been asked, not only in valuables, but also in bars and sheets of gold, besides all the jewels of gold, and silver, and the featherwork, and the stones, and the many other things of value which I assigned and allotted to Your Sacred Majesty, amounting to the sum of one hundred thousand *ducats,* and more. These, besides their value, are such, and so marvellous, that for the sake of their novelty and strangeness they have no price, nor is it probable that all the princes ever heard of in the world, possess such treasures. Let not what I say appear fabulous to Your Majesty, because, in truth, all the things created on land, as well as in the sea, of which Montezuma had ever heard, were imitated in gold, most naturally, as well as in silver, and in precious stones, and featherwork, with such perfection that they seemed almost real. He gave me a large number of these for Your Highness, besides others, he ordered to be made in gold, for which I furnished him the designs, such as images, crucifixes, medals, jewelry of small value, and many other of our things which I made them copy. In the same manner, Your Highness obtained, as the one-fifth of the silver which was received, one hundred and odd *marks,* which I made the natives cast in large and small plates, porringers, cups, and spoons, which they executed as perfectly as we could make them comprehend.

Besides these, Montezuma gave me a large quantity of stuffs, which considering it was cotton, and not silk, was such that there could not be woven anything similar in the whole world, for texture, colours, and handiwork. Amongst these, were many marvellous dresses for men and women, bed clothing, with which that made of silk could not be compared, and other stuffs such as tapestry, suitable for drawing-rooms and churches. There were also blankets and rugs, for beds both of featherwork, and of cotton in divers colours, also very marvellous, and many other things so curious and numerous I do not know how to specify them to Your Majesty. He also gave me a dozen *cerbatanas,* with which he shoots, and of their perfection I likewise know not what to say to Your Highness; for they were decorated with very excellent paintings of perfect hues, in which there were figures of many different kinds of birds, animals, flowers, and divers other objects, and the mouthpieces and extremities were bordered with gold, a span deep, as was also the middle, all beautifully worked. He gave me a pouch of gold network for the balls, which he told me he would give me also of gold. He gave me also some turquoises [*sic*] of gold, and many other things, whose number is almost infinite. . . .

This great city contains many mosques, or houses for idols, very beautiful edifices situated in the different precincts of it; in the principal ones of which are the religious orders of their sect, for whom, besides the houses in which they keep their idols, there are very good habitations provided. All these priests dress in black, and never cut or comb their hair from the time they enter the religious order until they leave it; and the sons of all the principal families, both of chiefs as well as noble citizens, are in these religious orders and habits from the age of seven or eight years till they are taken away for the purpose of marriage. This happens more frequently with the first-born, who inherit the property, than with the others. They have no access to women, nor are any allowed to enter the religious houses; they abstain from eating certain dishes, and more so at certain times of the year than at others.

Amongst these mosques, there is one principal one, and no human tongue is able to describe its greatness and details, because it is so large that within its circuit, which is surrounded by a high wall, a village of five hundred houses could easily be built. Within, and all around it, are very handsome buildings, in which there are large rooms and galleries, where the religious who live there are lodged. There are as many as forty very high and well-built towers, the largest having fifty steps to reach the top; the principal one is higher than the tower of the chief church in Seville. They are so well built, both in their masonry, and their wood work, that they could not be better made nor constructed anywhere; for all the masonry inside the chapels, where they keep their idols, is carved with figures, and the wood work is all wrought with designs of monsters, and other shapes. All these towers are places of burial for the chiefs, and each one of their chapels is dedicated to the idol to which they have a particular devotion. Within this great mosque, there are three halls wherein stand the principal idols of marvellous grandeur in size, and much decorated with carved figures, both of stone and wood; and within these halls there are other chapels, entered by very small doors, and which have no light, and nobody but the religious are admitted to them. Within these are the images and figures of the idols, although, as I have said, there are many outside.

The principal idols in which they have the most faith and belief I overturned from their seats, and rolled down the stairs, and I had those chapels, where they kept them, cleansed, for they were full of blood from the sacrifices; and I set up images of Our Lady, and other Saints in them, which grieved Montezuma, and the natives not a little. At first they told me not to do it, for, if it became known throughout the town, the people would rise against me, as they believed that these idols gave them all their temporal goods, and, in allowing them to be ill-treated, they would be angered, and give nothing, and would take away all the fruits of the soil, and cause the people to die of want. I made them understand by the interpreters how deceived they were in putting their hope in idols, made of unclean things by their own hands, and I told them that they should know there was but one God, the Universal Lord of all, who had created the heavens, and earth, and all things else, and them, and us, who was without beginning, and immortal; that they should adore, and believe in Him, and not in any creature, or thing. I told them all I knew of these matters, so as to win them from their idolatries, and bring them to a knowledge of God, Our Lord; and all of them, especially Montezuma, answered that they had already told me they were not natives of this country, and that it was a long time since their forefathers had come to it, therefore they might err in some points of their belief, as it was so long since they left their native land, whilst I, who had recently arrived, should know better than they what they should believe, and hold; and if I would tell them, and explain to them, they would do what I told them, as being for the best. Montezuma and many chiefs of the city remained with me until the idols were taken away and the chapels cleansed, and the images put up, and they all wore happy faces. I forbade them to sacrifice human beings to the idols, as they were accustomed to do, for besides its being very hateful to God, Your Majesty had also prohibited it by your laws, and commanded that those who killed should be put to death. Henceforth they abolished it, and, in all the time I remained in the city, never again were they seen to sacrifice any human creature.

THE SCIENTIFIC REVOLUTION

104 NICOLAS COPERNICUS, ON *THE REVOLUTIONS OF THE HEAVENLY BODIES*: MAN AND THE UNIVERSE

No one who reads a newspaper in the twentieth century can remain unaware of the role that science plays in the modern world. Its most obvious manifestation, of course, is technology, which, with its plethora of machines and gadgets, gives contemporary civilization its look. But this is hardly the most important result of the growth of modern science. The truly significant fact is that modern man thinks differently about his world and himself than did the man of the Middle Ages. It is this difference in thinking, not the development of automobiles, television, or rockets, that most sharply defines the modernity of our age and sets it apart from anything that preceded it. A Thomas Aquinas would have little difficulty in understanding the operation of an internal combustion engine, but he would find completely incomprehensible our conception of the universe and man's place in it. Thus the real origin of the modern world is to be found in the intellectual revolution wrought by modern science. The recognition of this fact has led distinguished historians such as Herbert Butterfield to declare that the scientific revolution "outshines everything since the rise of Christianity and reduces the Renaissance and Reformation to the rank of mere episodes."

To medieval man it seemed natural that he should be the focal point for the entire universe and that all of nature should exist for his purposes. He firmly believed that rain, floods, earthquakes, and the like occurred primarily for his benefit or for his chastisement, as God willed. It was inconceivable to him that such phenomena were quite independent of and indifferent to man's purposes. Moreover, if all of nature concentrated on man, it followed that the earth, upon which man lived, must be the center of the universe around which all else revolved. The universe seemed to be a small, finite place; its center, the earth, was thought to be solid and motionless while the starry heavens, not very far off, were a light, airy sphere which moved easily around the earthly center. Medieval man was convinced that all this existed exclusively for him to know and enjoy, and that man existed so that he might "know God and enjoy him forever." In sum, the whole natural world was part of one great divine drama, with the earth as the central stage and man as the principal actor.

The first decisive break with this medieval view came with the scientific revolution, which began in the sixteenth century. In 1543, Nicolas Copernicus (1473-1543), a canon of the Catholic Church in Poland, published a book entitled *On the Revolutions of the Heavenly Bodies*. It was one of the most momentous works of science the world has ever seen, for it presented a new conception of the universe. The sun, said Copernicus, not the earth, was the center of the universe; furthermore, the earth was not stationary—it revolved around the sun and turned on its own axis as well. Afraid of the unsettling impact that so revolutionary a theory might have upon attitudes which had prevailed for over a millennium, Copernicus withheld the publication of his book for twenty years. Its first appearance, in 1543, came only six weeks before his death.

It is evident in the "Dedication" from this work (printed below) that the man who helped launch the modern scientific revolution was, ironically, neither a revolutionary by nature nor a scientist in the modern sense of the word. First and foremost, Nicolas Copernicus was a speculative mathematician—a philosopher—who was disturbed by the complexities and illogicalities of the Ptolemaic system. His belief—that God, the grand architect of all things, designed the universe with greater consistency than was then apparent—was no less medieval than the belief that inspired Thomas Aquinas. But Copernicus was also a product of his times, a Renaissance humanist. The first thing he did in quest of a new theory was to search the writings of the ancients, the Greeks and Romans. Also significant was the fact that unlike a modern scientist, what he offered was not a hypothesis based on new data but one based on mathematical speculation. In his mind, the best recommendation for his theory was its simplicity and symmetry, its ability to satisfy the demand for order and regularity in the universe.

I can easily conceive, most Holy Father, that as soon as some people learn that in this book which I have written concerning the revolutions of the heavenly bodies, I ascribe certain motions to the Earth, they will cry out at once that I and my theory should be rejected. For I am not so much in love with my conclusions as not to weigh what others will think about them, and although I know that the meditations of a philosopher are far removed from the judgment of the laity, because his endeavor is to seek out the truth in all things, so far as this is permitted by God to the human reason, I still believe that one must avoid theories altogether foreign to orthodoxy. Accordingly, when I considered in my own mind how absurd a performance it must seem to those who know that the judgment of many centuries has approved the view that the Earth remains fixed as center in the midst of the heavens, if I should, on the contrary, assert that the Earth moves; I was for a long time at a loss to know whether I should publish the commentaries which I have written in proof of its motion, or whether it were not better to follow the example of the Pythagoreans and of some others, who were accustomed to transmit the secrets of Philosophy not in writing but orally, and only to their relatives and friends, as the letter from Lysis to Hipparchus bears witness. They did this, it seems to me, not as some think, because of a certain selfish reluctance to give their views to the world, but in order that the noblest truths, worked out by the careful study of great men, should not be despised by those who are vexed at the idea of taking great pains with any forms of literature except such as would be profitable, or by those who, if they are driven to the study of Philosophy for its own sake by the admonitions and the example of others, nevertheless, on account of their stupidity, hold

a place among philosophers similar to that of drones among bees. Therefore, when I considered this carefully, the contempt which I had to fear because of the novelty and apparent absurdity of my view, nearly induced me to abandon utterly the work I had begun.

My friends, however, in spite of long delay and even resistance on my part, withheld me from this decision. First among these was Nicolaus Schonberg, Cardinal of Capua, distinguished in all branches of learning. Next to him comes my very dear friend, Tidemann Giese, Bishop of Culm, a most earnest student, as he is, of sacred and, indeed, of all good learning. The latter has often urged me, at times even spurring me on with reproaches, to publish and at last bring to light the book which had lain in my study not nine years merely, but already going on four times nine. Not a few other very eminent and scholarly men made the same request, urging that I should no longer through fear refuse to give out my work for the common benefit of students of Mathematics. They said I should find that the more absurd most men now thought this theory of mine concerning the motion of the Earth, the more admiration and gratitude it would command after they saw in the publication of my commentaries the mist of absurdity cleared away by most transparent proofs. So, influenced by these advisors and this hope, I have at length allowed my friends to publish the work, as they had long besought me to do.

But perhaps Your Holiness will not so much wonder that I have ventured to publish these studies of mine, after having taken such pains in elaborating them that I have not hesitated to commit to writing my views of the motion of the Earth, as you will be curious to hear how it occurred to me to venture, contrary to the accepted view of mathematicians, and well-nigh contrary to common sense, to form a conception of any terrestrial motion whatsoever. Therefore I would not have it unknown to Your Holiness, that the only thing which induced me to look for another way of reckoning the movements of the heavenly

---

Text: Nicolas Copernicus, "Dedication of *The Revolutions of the Heavenly Bodies*," trans. E. J. Spedding, in *Prefaces and Prologues to Famous Books* (Vol. 39 of "The Harvard Classics" [New York: P. F. Collier & Son Company, 1910]), pp. 55-60.

bodies was that I knew that mathematicians by no means agree in their investigations thereof. For, in the first place, they are so much in doubt concerning the motion of the sun and the moon, that they can not even demonstrate and prove by observation the constant length of a complete year; and in the second place, in determining the motions both of these and of the five other planets, they fail to employ consistently one set of first principles and hypotheses, but use methods of proof based only upon the apparent revolutions and motions. For some employ concentric circles only; others, eccentric circles and epicycles; and even by these means they do not completely attain the desired end. For, although those who have depended upon concentric circles have shown that certain divers motions can be deduced from these, yet they have not succeeded thereby in laying down any sure principle, corresponding indisputably to the phenomena. These, on the other hand, who have devised systems of eccentric circles, although they seem in great part to have solved the apparent movements by calculations which by these eccentrics are made to fit, have nevertheless introduced many things which seem to contradict the first principles of the uniformity of motion. Nor have they been able to discover or calculate from these the main point, which is the shape of the world and the fixed symmetry of its parts; but their procedure has been as if someone were to collect hands, feet, a head, and other members from various places, all very fine in themselves, but not proportionate to one body, and no single one corresponding in its turn to the others, so that a monster rather than a man would be formed from them. Thus in their process of demonstration which they term a "method," they are found to have omitted something essential, or to have included something foreign and not pertaining to the matter in hand. This certainly would never have happened to them if they had followed fixed principles; for if the hypotheses they assumed were not false, all that resulted therefrom would be verified indubitably. Those things which I am saying now may be obscure, yet they will be made clearer in their proper place.

Therefore, having turned over in my mind for a long time this uncertainty of the traditional mathematical methods of calculating the motions of the celestial bodies, I began to grow disgusted that no more consistent scheme of the movements of the mechanism of the universe, set up for our benefit by that best and most law abiding Architect of all things, was agreed upon by philosophers who otherwise investigate so carefully the most minute details of this world. Wherefore I undertook the task of rereading the books of all the philosophers I could get access to, to see whether any one ever was of the opinion that the motions of the celestial bodies were other than those postulated by the men who taught mathematics in the schools. And I found first, indeed, in Cicero, that Niceta perceived that the Earth moved; and afterward in Plutarch I found that some others were of this opinion, whose words I have seen fit to quote here, that they may be accessible to all:—

"Some maintain that the Earth is stationary, but Philolaus the Pythagorean says that it revolves in a circle about the fire of the ecliptic, like the sun and moon. Heraklides of Pontus and Ekphantus the Pythagorean make the Earth move, not changing its position, however, confined in its falling and rising around its own center in the manner of a wheel."

Taking this as a starting point, I began to consider the mobility of the Earth; and although the idea seemed absurd, yet because I knew that the liberty had been granted to others before me to postulate all sorts of little circles for explaining the phenomena of the stars, I thought I also might easily be permitted to try whether by postulating some motion of the Earth, more reliable conclusions could be reached regarding the revolution of the heavenly bodies, than those of my predecessors.

And so, after postulating movements, which, farther on in the book, I ascribe to the Earth, I have found by many and long observations that if the movements of the other planets are assumed for the circular motion of the Earth and are substituted for the revolution of each star, not only do their phenomena follow logically therefrom, but the relative positions and magnitudes both of the stars and all their orbits, and of the heavens themselves, become so closely related that in none of its parts can anything be changed without causing confusion in the other parts and in the whole universe. Therefore, in the course of the work I have followed this plan: I describe in the first book all the positions of the orbits together with the movements which I ascribe to the Earth, in order that this book might contain, as it were, the general scheme of the universe. Thereafter in the remaining books, I set forth the motions of the other stars and of all their orbits together with the movement of the Earth, in order that one may see from this to what extent the movements and appearances of the other stars and their orbits can be saved, if they are transferred to the movement of the Earth. Nor do I doubt that ingenious and learned mathematicians will sustain me, if they are willing to recognize and weigh, not superficially, but with that thoroughness which Philosophy demands above all things, those matters which have been adduced by me in this work to demonstrate these theories. In order, however, that both the learned and the unlearned equally may see that I do not avoid anyone's judgment, I have preferred to dedicate these lucubrations of mine to Your Holiness rather than to any other, because, even in this remote corner of the world where I live, you are considered to be the most eminent man in dignity of rank and in love of all learning and even of mathematics, so that by your authority and judgment you can easily suppress the bites of slanderers, albeit the proverb hath it that there is no remedy for the bite of a sycophant. If perchance there shall be idle talkers, who, though they are ignorant of all mathematical sciences, nevertheless assume the right to pass judgment on these things, and if they should dare to criticise and attack this theory of mine because of some passage of scripture which they have falsely distorted for their own purpose, I care not at all; I will even despise their judgment as foolish. For it is not unknown that Lactantius, otherwise a famous writer but a poor mathematician, speaks most childishly of the shape of the Earth when he makes fun of those who said that the Earth has the form of a sphere. It should not seem strange then to zealous students, if some such people shall ridicule us also. Mathematics are written for mathematicians, to whom, if my opinion does not deceive me, our labors will seem to contribute something to the ecclesiastical state whose chief office Your Holiness now occupies; for when not so very long ago, under Leo X, in the Lateran Council the question of revising the ecclesiastical calendar was discussed, it then remained unsettled, simply because the length of the years and months, and the motions of the sun and moon were held to have been not yet sufficiently determined. Since that time, I have given my attention to observing these more accurately, urged on by a very distinguished man, Paul, Bishop of Fossombrone, who at that time had charge of the matter. But what I may have accomplished herein I leave to the judgment of Your Holiness in particular, and to that of all other learned mathematicians; and lest I seem to Your Holiness to promise more regarding the usefulness of the work than I can perform, I now pass to the work itself.

105 SIR FRANCIS BACON, *INSTAURATIO MAGNA*: THE CALL FOR EXPERIMENTATION

The scientific revolution was compounded of several elements. One was the impact of Copernicus (see Document 104), whose new system of astronomy changed the whole picture of man in the universe. A second was the influence of René Descartes (1596-1650), the French mathematician and philosopher who insisted that instead of looking for purposes in nature we should look for laws. (See Document 106.) A third element was the work of the English philosopher Francis Bacon (1561-1626), whose basic point was that man must learn as much as possible about nature in order to master and make use of it. In Bacon's view, the true ends of knowledge were "for the benefit and use of life." This quest for useful knowledge has since become the prime motivation of all modern science.

Looked at from another angle, modern science may be thought of as a composite of two things, an ever-growing body of factual data and a particular method of investigation. Copernicus and his successors are largely associated with the first, Bacon and Descartes with the second. By the early seventeenth century the question of method began to occupy the attention of many general thinkers and philosophers as well as of practicing scientists. To be sure, there were men in the late Middle Ages who had learned to be careful observers of nature. But more often than not they tended to compile encyclopedias of purely descriptive matter. If something had to be explained they did not, as do modern scientists, derive their theories from the observations themselves; instead, they relied upon the explanations provided by the ancients. Bacon was distressed by this divorce between observation and explanation and he was determined to show how explanation must arise out of observation.

Living in an age still dominated by religion and annoyed that science was being impeded by the prejudice and conservatism of the theologians, Bacon argued that science and religion should be separated. There are two kinds of truth, he said, the truth of religion and the truth of science. They are not the same, and to confuse the two would work only to the detriment of science. Therefore, "give to faith that which is faith's" and let not the scientist become entangled in a search for final causes. Most important of all, Bacon felt that existing interpretations of nature had too narrow a foundation in experiment. He firmly believed that if men wanted to achieve anything new in the world, they had to recognize that the adoption of new practices and policies would be necessary. What this boiled down to was a need for more experiments and especially for directed experiments. He exhorted his contemporaries to abandon the hollow abstractions of Aristotelian science which dominated his times and to concentrate instead upon increasing the store of available facts through experimentation. For, he argued, only when all the information about a particular phenomenon had been collected could any general conclusions or hypotheses be formulated. Such generalizations in turn would point the way to further experiments. In this way the process would be perpetuated, and man's knowledge would be increased.

Ironically, Bacon made very few experiments of his own, for he was primarily a philosopher rather than a scientist. His historical importance lies in the fact that through his writings he helped popularize science, especially in England, and had an important influence in stimulating research. The selection below, taken from the preface to Bacon's *Instauratio Magna* (1620), illustrates how an early seventeenth-century philosopher-propagandist went about the task of arousing his countrymen to a greater interest in science and instructing them in the proper methods of scientific investigation.

That the state of knowledge is not prosperous nor greatly advancing; and that a way must be opened for the human understanding entirely different from any hitherto known, and other helps provided, in order that the mind may exercise over the nature of things the authority which properly belongs to it.

It seems to me that men do not rightly understand either their store or their strength, but overrate the one and underrate the other. Hence it follows, that either from an extravagant estimate of the value of the arts which they possess, they seek no further; or else from too mean an estimate of their own powers, they spend their strength in small matters and never put it fairly to the trial in those which go to the main. These are as the pillars of fate set in the path of knowledge; for men have neither desire nor hope to encourage them to penetrate further. And since opinion of store is one of the chief causes of want, and satisfaction with the present induces neglect of provision for the future, it becomes a thing not only useful, but absolutely necessary, that the excess of honour and admiration with which our existing stock of inventions is regarded be in the very entrance and threshold of the work, and that frankly and without circumlocution, stripped off, and men be duly warned not to exaggerate or make too much of them. For let a man look carefully into all that variety of books with which the arts and sciences abound, he will find everywhere endless repetitions of the same thing, varying in the method of treatment, but not new in substance, insomuch that the whole stock, numerous as it appears at first view, proves on examination to be but scanty. And for its value and utility it must be plainly avowed that that wisdom which we have derived principally from the Greeks is but like the boyhood of knowledge, and has the characteristic property of boys: it can talk, but it cannot generate; for it is fruitful of controversies but barren of works. So that the state of learning as it now is appears to be represented to the life in the old fable of Scylla, who had the head and face of a virgin, but her womb was hung round with barking monsters, from which she could not be delivered. For in like manner the sciences to which we are accustomed have certain general positions which are specious and flattering; but as soon as they come to particulars, which are as the parts of generation, when they should produce fruit and works, then arise contentions and barking disputations, which are the end of the matter and all the issue they can yield. Observe also, that if sciences of this kind had any life in them, that could never have come to pass which has been the case now for many ages—that they stand almost at a stay, without receiving any augmentations worthy of the human race; insomuch that many times not only what was asserted once is asserted still, but what was a question once is a question still, and instead of being resolved by discussion is only fixed and fed; and all the tradition and succession of schools is still a succession of masters and scholars, not of inventors and those who bring to further perfection the things invented. In the mechanical arts we do not find it so; they, on the contrary, as having in them some breath of life, are continually growing and becoming more per-

Text: Sir Francis Bacon, "Preface to the *Instauratio Magna,*" in *Prefaces and Prologues to Famous Books* (Vol. 39 of "The Harvard Classics" [New York: P. F. Collier & Son Company, 1910]), pp. 127-35 *passim.*

fect. As originally invented they are commonly rude, clumsy, and shapeless: afterwards they acquire new powers and more commodious arrangements and constructions; in so far that men shall sooner leave the study and pursuit of them and turn to something else, than they arrive at the ultimate perfection of which they are capable. Philosophy and the intellectual sciences, on the contrary, stand like statues, worshiped and celebrated, but not moved or advanced. Nay, they sometimes flourish most in the hands of the first author, and afterwards degenerate. For when men have once made over their judgments to others' keeping, and (like those senators whom they called *Pedarii*) have agreed to support some one person's opinion, from that time they make no enlargement of the sciences themselves, but fall to the servile office of embellishing certain individual authors and increasing their retinue. And let it not be said that the sciences have been growing gradually till they have at last reached their full stature, and so (their course being completed) have settled in the works of a few writers; and that there being now no room for the invention of better, all that remains is to embellish and cultivate those things which have been invented already. Would it were so! But the truth is that this appropriating of the sciences has its origin in nothing better than the confidence of a few persons and the sloth and indolence of the rest. For after the sciences have been in several parts perhaps cultivated and handled diligently, there has risen up some man of bold disposition, and famous for methods and short ways which people like, who has in appearance reduced them to an art, while he has in fact only spoiled all that the others had done. And yet this is what posterity like, because it makes the work short and easy, and saves further inquiry, of which they are weary and impatient. . . .

. . . And if there be any who have determined to make trial for themselves, and put their own strength to the work of advancing the boundaries of the sciences, yet have they not ventured to cast themselves completely loose from received opinions or to seek their knowledge at the fountain; but they think they have done some great thing if they do but add and introduce into the existing sum of science something of their own; prudently considering with themselves that by making the addition they can assert their liberty, while they retain the credit of modesty by assenting to the rest. But these mediocrities and middle ways so much praised, in deferring to opinions and customs, turn to the great detriment of the sciences. For it is hardly possible at once to admire an author and to go beyond him; knowledge being as water, which will not rise above the level from which it fell. Men of this kind, therefore, amend some things, but advance little; and improve the condition of knowledge, but do not extend its range. Some, indeed, there have been who have gone more boldly to work, and taking it all for an open matter and giving their genius full play, have made a passage for themselves and their own opinions by pulling down and demolishing former ones; and yet all their stir has but little advanced the matter; since their aim has been not to extend philosophy and the arts in substance and value, but only to change doctrines and transfer the kingdom of opinions to themselves; whereby little has indeed been gained, for though the error be the opposite of the other, the causes of erring are the same in both. And if there have been any who, not binding themselves either to other men's opinions or to their own, but loving liberty, have desired to engage others along with themselves in search, these, though honest in intention, have been weak in endeavour. For they have been content to follow probable reasons, and are carried round in a whirl of arguments, and in the promiscuous liberty of search have relaxed the severity of inquiry. There is none who has dwelt upon experience and the facts of nature as long as is necessary. . . . [A]ll industry in experimenting has begun with proposing to itself certain definite works to be accomplished, and has pursued them with premature and unseasonable eagerness; it has sought, I say, experiments of Fruit, not experiments of Light; not imitating the divine procedure, which in its first day's work created light only and assigned to it one entire day; on which day it produced no material work, but proceeded to that on the days following. . . .

Upon the whole therefore, it seems that men have not been happy hitherto either in the trust which they have placed in others or in their own industry with regard to the sciences; especially as neither the demonstrations nor the experiments as yet known are much to be relied upon. But the universe to the eye of the human understanding is framed like a labyrinth; presenting as it does on every side so many ambiguities of way, such deceitful resemblances of objects and signs, natures so irregular in their lines, and so knotted and entangled. And then the way is still to be made by the uncertain light of the sense, sometimes shining out, sometimes clouded over, through the woods of experience and particulars; while those who offer themselves for guides are (as was said) themselves also puzzled, and increase the number of errors and wanderers. In circumstances so difficult neither the natural force of man's judgment nor even any accidental felicity offers any chance of success. No excellence of wit, no repetition of chance experiments, can overcome such difficulties as these. Our steps must be guided by a clue, and the whole way from the very first perception of the senses must be laid out upon a sure plan. Not that I would be understood to mean that nothing whatever has been done in so many ages by so great labours. We have no reason to be ashamed of the discoveries which have been made, and no doubt the ancients proved themselves in everything that turns on wit and abstract meditation, wonderful men. But as in former ages when men sailed only by observation of the stars, they could indeed coast along the shores of the old continent or cross a few small and mediterranean seas; but before the ocean could be traversed and the new world discovered, the use of the mariner's needle, as a more faithful and certain guide, had to be found out; in like manner the discoveries which have been hitherto made in the arts and sciences are such as might be made by practice, meditation, observation, argumentation,—for they lay near to the senses, and immediately beneath common notions; but before we can reach the remoter and more hidden parts of nature, it is necessary that a more perfect use and application of the human mind and intellect be introduced.

For my own part at least, in obedience to the everlasting love of truth, I have committed myself to the uncertainties and difficulties and solitudes of the ways, and relying on the divine assistance have upheld my mind both against the shocks and embattled ranks of opinion, and against my own private and inward hesitations and scruples, and against the fogs and clouds of nature, and the phantoms flitting about on every side; in the hope of providing at last for the present and future generations guidance more faithful and secure. Wherein if I have made any progress, the way has been opened to me by no other means than the true and legitimate humiliation of the human spirit. For all those who before me have applied themselves to the invention of arts have but cast a glance or two upon facts and examples and experience, and straightway proceeded, as if invention were nothing more than an exercise of thought, to invoke their own spirits to give them oracles. I, on the contrary, dwelling purely and constantly among the facts of nature, withdraw my intellect from them no further than may suffice to let the images and rays of natural objects meet in a point, as they do in the sense of vision; whence it follows that the strength and excellency of the wit has but little to do in the matter. And the same humility which I use in inventing I employ likewise in teaching. For I do not endeavour either by triumphs of confutation, or pleadings of antiquity, or assumption of authority, or even by the veil of obscurity, to invest these inventions of mine with any majesty; which might easily be done by one who sought to give lustre to his own name rather than light to other men's minds. I have not sought (I say) nor do I seek either to force or ensnare men's judgments, but I lead them to things themselves and the concordances of things, that they may see for themselves what they have, what they can dispute, what they can add and contribute to the common stock. And for myself, if in anything I have been either too credulous or too little awake and attentive, or if I have fallen off by the way and left the inquiry incomplete, nevertheless I so present these things naked and open, that my errors can be marked and set aside before the mass of knowledge be further infected by them; and it will be easy also for others to continue and carry on my labours. And by these means I suppose that I have established for ever a true and lawful marriage between the empirical and the rational faculty, the unkind and ill-starred divorce and separation of which has thrown into confusion all the affairs of the human family.

Wherefore, seeing that these things do not depend upon myself, at the outset of the work I most humbly and fervently pray to God the Father, God the Son, and God the Holy Ghost, that remembering the sorrows of mankind and the pilgrimage of this our life wherein we wear out days few and evil, they will vouchsafe through my hands to endow the human family with new mercies. This likewise I humbly pray, that things human may not interfere with things divine, and that from the opening of the ways of sense and the increase of natural light there may arise in our minds no incredulity or darkness with regard to the divine mysteries; but rather that the understanding being thereby purified and purged of fancies and vanity, and yet not the less subject and entirely submissive to the divine oracles, may give to faith that which is faith's. Lastly, that knowledge being now discharged of that venom which the serpent infused into it, and which makes the mind of man to swell, we may not be wise above measure and sobriety, but cultivate truth in charity.

And now having said my prayers I turn to men; to whom I have certain salutary admonitions to offer and certain fair requests to make. My first admonition (which was also my prayer) is that men confine the sense within the limits of duty in respect to things divine: for the sense is like the sun, which reveals the face of earth, but seals and shuts up the face of heaven. My next, that in flying from this evil they fall not into the opposite error, which they will surely do if they think that the inquisition of nature is in any part interdicted or forbidden. For it was not that pure and uncorrupted natural knowledge whereby Adam gave names to the creatures according to their propriety, which gave occasion to the fall. It was the ambitious and proud desire of moral knowledge to judge of good and evil, to the end that man may revolt from God and give laws to himself, which was the form and manner of the temptation. Whereas of the sciences which regard nature, the divine philosopher declares that "it is the glory of God to conceal a thing, but it is the glory of the King to find a thing out." Even as though the divine nature took pleasure in the innocent and kindly sport of children playing at hide and seek, and vouchsafed of his kindness and goodness to admit the human spirit for his play-fellow at that game. Lastly, I would address one general admonition to all; that they consider what are the true ends of knowledge, and that they seek it not either for pleasure of the mind, or for contention, or for superiority to others, or for profit, or fame, or power, or any of these inferior things; but for the benefit and use of life; and that they perfect and govern it in charity. For it was from lust of power that the angels fell, from lust of knowledge that man fell; but of charity there can be no excess, neither did angel or man ever come in danger by it.

The requests I have to make are these. Of myself I say nothing; but in behalf of the business which is in hand I entreat men to believe that it is not an opinion to be held, but a work to be done; and to be well assured that I am labouring to lay the foundation, not of any sect or doctrine, but of human utility and power. . . .

106 RENÉ DESCARTES, DISCOURSE ON METHOD: THE CALL FOR RATIONAL SKEPTICISM

The seventeenth century saw an increasing preoccupation on the part of thinkers, led by Francis Bacon (1561-1626) and his younger contemporary, René Descartes (1596-1650), with the problem of scientific method. Both men were primarily concerned with the same question: how do we discover truth? Bacon's answer (as we saw in Document 105) was that knowledge or truth may be discovered through orderly experimentation, and he urged the experimental method upon his countrymen. Descartes, on the other hand, emphasized the need for methods based upon mathematics and systematic skepticism. These two ideas became Descartes' outstanding contributions to the history of scientific thought. The answers of Bacon and Descartes, though differing in emphasis, are not mutually exclusive. Modern science today rests firmly on a combination of both methods—the empiricism of Bacon and the rationalism of Descartes.

In his quest for truth Descartes ultimately persuaded himself that there was only one infallible way that he could attain it—he rejected all that he had ever been taught and rethought everything from the very beginning. He subjected all opinions, beliefs, and even sense impressions to a rigorous and complete skepticism; he accepted nothing as true until it was established beyond doubt, as far as that was possible. Descartes, however, did not propose a system of doubt for doubting's sake; doubt was merely a means for finding a surer basis for certainty. A pattern of intensive analysis, if followed carefully, would lead to the discovery of fundamental truths. Once in possession of such truths, one could reconstruct a more perfect picture of the world.

The starting point for Descartes was the consciousness of his own existence. This was so self-evident that he could not doubt it, for he could not deny his own existence. The next step was the realization that consciousness of existence implies thinking; from this Descartes deduced a fundamental axiom—"*Cogito, ergo sum*" ("I think, therefore I am"), one of the most famous sentences in philosophy. On the basis of his axiom Descartes believed he could construct a sound body of universal philosophy. He used the geometry method because he was convinced that only mathematicians could reason with any degree of accuracy or precision. Using the language of mathematics, he set out to describe the universe on the basis of his propositions. He emerged with a vision of the universe as a perfectly ordered mechanism and of science as a single, universal system. In the words of Herbert Butterfield, this vision was "perhaps one of [Descartes'] most remarkable contributions to the scientific revolution."

In the selection below one sees the rational process of a philosophic genius at work, as Descartes reasons his way through the rejection of all previous knowledge, the establishment of his method, and the discovery of his famous axiom.

... I thought that the sciences found in books —in those at least whose reasonings are only probable and which have no demonstrations, composed as they are of the gradually accumulated opinions of many different individuals—do not approach so near to the truth as the simple reasoning which a man of common sense can quite naturally carry out respecting the things which come immediately before him. Again I thought that since we have all been children before being men, and since it has for long fallen to us to be governed by our appetites and by our teachers (who often enough contradicted one another, and none of whom perhaps counselled us always for the best), it is almost impossible that our judgments should be so excellent or solid as they should have been had we had complete use of our reason since our birth, and had we been guided by its means alone. . . .

But as regards all the opinions which up to this time I had embraced, I thought I could not do better than endeavour once for all to sweep them completely away, so that they might later on be replaced, either by others which were better, or by the same, when I had made them confirm to the uniformity of a rational scheme. And I firmly believed that by this means I should succeed in directing my life much better than if I had only built on old foundations, and relied on principles of which I allowed myself to be in youth persuaded without having inquired into their truth. . . . My design has never extended beyond trying to reform my own opinion and to build on a foundation which is entirely my own. If my work has given me a certain satisfaction, so that I here present to you a draft of it, I do not so do because I wish to advise anybody to imitate it. . . . The simple resolve to strip oneself of all opinions and beliefs formerly received is not to be regarded as an example that each man should follow. . . .

But I had been taught, even in my College days, that there is nothing imaginable so strange or so little credible that it has not been maintained by one philosopher or other, and I further recognised in the course of my travels that all those whose sentiments are very contrary to ours are yet not necessarily barbarians or savages, but may be possessed of reason in as great or even a greater degree than ourselves. I also considered how very different the self-same man, identical in mind and spirit, may become, according as he is brought up from childhood amongst the French or Germans, or has passed his whole life amongst Chinese or cannibals. I likewise noticed how even in the fashions of one's clothing the same thing that pleased us ten years ago, and which will perhaps please us once again before ten years are passed, seems at the present time extravagant and ridiculous. I thus concluded that it is much more custom and example that persuade us than any certain knowledge, and yet in spite of this the voice of the majority does not afford a proof of any value in truths a little difficult to discover, because such truths are much more likely to have been discovered by one man than by a nation. I could not, however, put my finger on a single person whose opinions seemed preferable to those of others, and I found that I was, so to speak, constrained myself to undertake the direction of my procedure.

But like one who walks alone and in the twilight I resolved to go so slowly, and to use so much circumspection in all things, that if my advance was but very small, at least I guarded myself well from falling. I did not wish to set about the final rejection of any single opinion which might formerly have crept into my beliefs without having been introduced there by means of Reason, until I had first of all employed sufficient time in planning out the task which I had undertaken, and in seeking the true Method of arriving at a knowledge of all the things of which my mind was capable.

Among the different branches of Philosophy, I had in my younger days to a certain extent studied Logic; and in those of Mathematics, Geometrical Analysis and Algebra—three arts or sciences which seemed as though they ought to contribute something to the design I had in view. But in examining them I observed in respect to Logic that the syllogisms and the greater part of the other teaching served better in explaining to others those things that one knows (or like the art of Lully, in enabling one to speak without judgment of those things of which one is ignorant) than in learning what is new. And although in reality Logic contains many precepts which are very true and very good, there are at the same time mingled with them so many others which are hurtful or superfluous, that it

Text: E. S. Haldane and G. R. T. Ross (trans. and ed.), *The Philosophical Works of Descartes* (New York: Cambridge University Press, 1911), pp. 88-92, 100-02 *passim.*

is almost as difficult to separate the two as to draw a Diana or a Minerva out of a block of marble which is not yet roughly hewn. And as to the Analysis of the ancients and the Algebra of the moderns, besides the fact that they embrace only matters the most abstract, such as appear to have no actual use, the former is always so restricted to the consideration of symbols that it cannot exercise the Understanding without greatly fatiguing the Imagination; and in the latter one is so subjected to certain rules and formulas that the result is the construction of an art which is confused and obscure, and which embarrasses the mind, instead of a science which contributes to its cultivation. This made me feel that some other Method must be found, which, comprising the advantages of the three, is yet exempt from their faults. And as a multiplicity of laws often furnishes excuses for evil-doing, and as a State is hence much better ruled when, having but very few laws, these are most strictly observed; so, instead of the great number of precepts of which Logic is composed, I believed that I should find the four which I shall state quite sufficient, provided that I adhered to a firm and constant resolve never on any single occasion to fail in their observance.

The first of these was to accept nothing as true which I did not clearly recognise to be so: that is to say, carefully to avoid precipitation and prejudice in judgments, and to accept in them nothing more than what was presented to my mind so clearly and distinctly that I could have no occasion to doubt it.

The second was to divide up each of the difficulties which I examined into as many parts as possible, and as seemed requisite in order that it might be resolved in the best manner possible.

The third was to carry on my reflections in due order, commencing with objects that were the most simple and easy to understand, in order to rise little by little, or by degrees, to knowledge of the most complex, assuming an order, even if a fictitious one, among those which do not follow a natural sequence relatively to one another.

The last was in all cases to make enumerations so complete and reviews so general that I should be certain of having omitted nothing.

Those long chains of reasoning, simple and easy as they are, of which geometricians make use in order to arrive at the most difficult demonstrations, had caused me to imagine that all those things which fall under the cognisance of man might very likely be mutually related in the same fashion; and that, provided only that we abstain from receiving anything as true which is not so, and always retain the order which is necessary in order to deduce the one conclusion from the other, there can be nothing so remote that we cannot reach to it, nor so recondite that we cannot discover it. . . .

Because I wished to give myself entirely to the search after Truth, I thought that it was necessary for me to take an apparently opposite course, and to reject as absolutely false everything as to which I could imagine the least ground of doubt, in order to see if afterwards there remained anything in my belief that was entirely certain. Thus, because our senses sometimes deceive us, I wished to suppose that nothing is just as they cause us to imagine it to be; and because there are men who deceive themselves in their reasoning and fall into paralogisms, even concerning the simplest matters of geometry, and judging that I was as subject to error as was any other, I rejected as false all the reasons formerly accepted by me as demonstrations. And since all the same thoughts and conceptions which we have while awake may also come to us in sleep, without any of them being at that time true, I resolved to assume that everything that ever entered into my mind was no more true than the illusions of my dreams. But immediately afterwards I noticed that whilst I thus wished to think all things false, it was absolutely essential that the 'I' who thought this should be somewhat, and remarking that this truth *I think, therefore I am* was so certain and so assured that all the most extravagant suppositions brought forward by the sceptics were incapable of shaking it, I came to the conclusion that I could receive it without scruple as the first principle of the Philosophy for which I was seeking.

And then, examining attentively that which I was, I saw that I could conceive that I had no body, and that there was no world nor place where I might be; but yet that I could not for all that conceive that I was not. On the contrary, I saw from the very fact that I thought of doubting the truth of other things, it very evidently and certainly followed that I was; on the other hand if I had only ceased from thinking, even if all the rest of what I had ever imagined had really existed, I should have no reason for thinking that I had existed. From that I knew that I was a substance the whole essence or nature of which is to think, and that for its existence there is no need of any place, nor does it depend on any material thing; so that this 'me,' that is to say, the soul by which I am what I am, is entirely distinct from body, and is even more easy to know than is the latter; and even if body were not, the soul would not cease to be what it is.

After this I considered generally what in a proposition is requisite in order to be true and certain; for since I had just discovered one which I knew to be such, I thought that I ought also to know in what this certainty consisted. And having remarked that there was nothing at all in the statement '*I think, therefore I am*' which assures me of having thereby made a true assertion, excepting that I see very clearly that to think it is necessary to be, I came to the conclusion that I might assume, as a general rule, that the things which we conceive very clearly and distinctly are all true—remembering, however, that there is some difficulty in ascertaining which are those that we distinctly conceive.

INTERPRETATIONS OF THE BROADENING HORIZON

107 DONALD F. LACH, *ASIA IN THE MAKING OF EUROPE: EUROPE AND THE CENTURY OF DISCOVERY*

The age of exploration was the dramatic opening phase of an era of unparalleled European expansion. Ultimately that expansion resulted in Europe's hegemony over not only the tribes and civilizations of the Americas and Africa but over the great cultures of Asia as well. No one could have predicted this in the sixteenth century. Yet to think solely in terms of Europe's eventual supremacy is to lose sight of two important facts. One is that the cultures of Asia were as great as, if not greater than, that of Europe in the sixteenth century; the other is that the discovery of Asia had a profound and lasting impact on the western world. In the selection below from a significant new study, Professor Donald Lach of the University of Chicago demonstrates that the awakening of Europe to the existence of Asia occurred at a time when Asia and Europe were close rivals in brilliance and mutual influence.

What were the drives which first impelled the men of the Renaissance to push out into the unknown worlds beyond the sea frontiers of Europe? How did the expansion of Europe maintain its momentum for four centuries until there were no more continents left to conquer on this earth? Historians, fascinated and impressed by the uniqueness in world history of the European expansion movement, have spent a great deal of time trying to analyze and explain the cultural dynamism which lay behind the thrust into the overseas world. While unanimously hailing the discoveries as a triumph of European enterprise and ingenuity, many modern scholars have been bitterly divided along national and religious lines in their assessments and evaluations of the forces which motivated the overseas pioneers. Others, less concerned with causation, have produced extended narratives and analytical monographs devoted to describing the voyages, reconstructing the administrative structure of overseas trade, and probing the colonizing techniques of the empire-builders. Researchers of mission history have traced in meticulous detail the attempt to transplant Christian institutions and ideas to the pagan world. But very few students of European expansion have sought to investigate the significance of the discoveries for the development of Western civilization itself.

The expansion and resulting rise to world predominance of the European nations meant the obscuring of the ancient and brilliant cultures of the East by the newer and more dynamic civilizations of the West. Historians have usually attributed this eclipse of the East to the rapid industrial growth of the West and the failure of the East to keep pace with it. None of the great centers of Asian civilization, they point out, was able to mount an industrial revolution of its own comparable to that which transformed Europe after 1800 and gave to the West its decisive technical and military superiority.

Students in both Europe and Asia, in their preoccupation with the period and problems of Europe's world predominance, have all too often given the impression that the entire history of the intercourse between East and West is simply the story of how the Westerners got to the East, how they maintained themselves there, and how they contributed to the modernization, Westernization, and transformation of Asia's traditional cultures and modes of life. As a consequence these scholars

Text: Reprinted from *Asia in the Making of Europe* by Donald F. Lach by permission of The University of Chicago Press. Copyright © 1965 by The University of Chicago Press. Pp. xi-xii, 833-35.

have neglected to point out that an eclipse is never permanent, that this one was never total, and that there was a period in early modern times when Asia and Europe were close rivals in the brilliance of their civilizations.

From 1500 to 1800 relations between East and West were ordinarily conducted within a framework and on terms established by the Asian nations. Except for those who lived in a few colonial footholds, the Europeans in the East were all there on sufferance. This was related to the obvious but often overlooked fact that, while Europeans dispatched trading, diplomatic, and religious missions to Asia, Asian countries never sent similar missions to Europe on their own initiative. Although the Europeans traveled with seeming ease along the maritime routes of Asia, they penetrated the main continental states infrequently and with difficulty. And, in the sixteenth century, they were never in a position to force their will upon the imperial rulers of India or China; the great political and cultural capitals of the Asiatic continent in no way felt threatened by their arms. Still, it is surprising how much a handful of enterprising Europeans was able to do toward making East and West conscious of each other. . . .

While the Europeans in the field bemused themselves with hopes of conquest, their fellows collected weird bits of fact and fiction about Asian customs and traditions. Some of these stories are reportorial and true; others are myths, some of which are still current in Asia; and still others are probably distorted or imaginary. The dog-headed Indians and the gold-digging ants of antiquity have disappeared, but Asia has not lost any of its exoticism. For example, Javans and Malabars run amuck as a form of protest or revenge. Self-torture or self-destruction is proof of sincerity. In Malacca nobody may wear yellow colors without royal permission. The Burmans have a temple guarded by tame fish which can be called to the surface by a particular spoken word. Neither a Javan nor a Malay will permit anything to be above his shoulders or head. The king of Arakan selects his harem by submitting his prospective brides to a smell test. Strangers are called upon in Tenasserim to deflower a virgin before her marriage. In Pegu merchants may legally contract temporary alliances with native women. Burmese and Cantonese will eat anything no matter how distasteful it appears to others. A vast lake stands high in the mountains of central Asia from which all the continental rivers descend. Eclipses are traditionally believed in Siam to be caused by a huge snake which has swallowed the moon. Horses are unable to reproduce in India, hence the scarcity of them there. Hogs are ceremonially killed in the Bisayan Islands and their flesh is reserved for old women to eat. White elephants are sacred in Siam and Burma, and wars begin over their possession. In Siam the nobles of the land delight in washing in the urine of the white elephant. Malabars worship for the day the first thing they meet each morning. Foot-binding was introduced into China by the men to keep their women at home and at work. These and a multitude of other curious stories added immeasurably to the repertory of the imaginative, and soon became a part of the stockpile of exotic items from which artists and poets still draw examples.

European characterizations of the national or regional qualities of various Asian people are likewise a mixture of the factual and fanciful, and, not surprisingly, resemble many of the beliefs still popular in the West. All the islanders are fantastic swimmers and divers. The Sinhalese are effeminate and weak. Natives of Tana are brutish and self-centered. Malabars are dirty, superstitious, belligerent, and unperceptive. Bengalis are wary and treacherous but clever. Peguans are industrious, honest, peaceful, and timid. Provincialism, temperance, and peace are the fundamental qualities of the Siamese. Malays are frivolous poetasters who are more afraid of work than war. Moluccans are stupid and lazy. Cebuans love peace, ease, and quiet. The proud Japanese are overly sensitive, intellectually curious, self-controlled, and warlike. The wise Chinese exhibit rational, just, and frivolous sides to their nature, are clever and industrious in the peaceful arts, and timid about fighting. Notice from the above how inferior the "blacks" of Asia are held to be in contrast to the "whites."

This stark picture of Asia with its shortage of grays and other shadings was transmitted to Europe over the entire sixteenth century through various channels. Pieced together from pamphlets, books, maps, and marketplace gossip, such an adumbration was reinforced and given reality in Europe by the influx in a steady stream of Asian products, works of art and craftsmanship, and peoples. More than two hundred different spices and drugs from all parts of the East filled the shops of Europe. Ship-builders in Portugal soon learned to use coir from India and tung oil from China to calk and varnish their ships. Persons interested in sailing heard about keeled and unkeeled vessels without nails, Javan ships with four masts, Chinese junks with ingenious pumps, and sailing chariots for use on land. The nautically minded also added new types of ships and names to their vocabularies: *cuttar* (from which "cutter" may possibly derive), sampans, houseboats, barangays, and praus. Those interested in the arts could find fancy textiles and embroideries, oriental rugs, finely wrought jewelry, swords inlaid with precious stones, lacquered screens and beds, printed books published in China, manuscript books written in Gujarati, and Jesuit-printed books in Tamil, Chinese, and Japanese. Curiosa collectors might cherish plumages of the Bird of Paradise, poisoned arrows and darts, cowrie shells, bamboo furniture, costumes, carnelians, strange sexual devices, new plants, seeds, and fruits as well as live and stuffed animals from the East. Others interested in language could find sample words and terms from Malayālam, Kanarese, Konkani, Marāthi, Tamil, Sanskrit, Pali, Mon, Talaing, Thai, Cambodian, Malay, Tagalog, Bisayan, Chinese, and Japanese. Sample characters from Chinese and Japanese were available in printed and manuscript writings. Of Asian persons in Europe we have references and sometimes considerable detail on the activities of Arab and Malay pilots, Malabar students, Chinese merchants, Gujarati translators, Japanese emissaries, and a Filipino convert.

While concrete samples from Asia's life and cultures certainly testified to its existence as a civilized, rich, and variegated part of an expanding world, what were the products, institutions, and ideas which stimulated the Europeans most and which ones most caused them to speculate about their own? On a realistic level they were especially fascinated by the mere existence of new places, by exotic varieties of flora and fauna, and by the crafts of silk production, rice cultivation, book-making, weaponry, and ship-building. Of the innumerable artistic products of Asia the Europeans are rapturous in their admiration for monuments, sculptures, porcelains, lacquers, and embroideries. They also evince profound interest in statistics on Asian populations, products, armies, exports, and imports. On a more abstract plane the Europeans were impressed by mass warfare techniques, the widespread existence of the lunar calendar, and the use of Malay as the *lingua franca* of Asian commerce. While merchants and missionaries used various Asian languages in their work, a few speculative minds began to concern themselves with the relationship of the Asian tongues to one another and of the possible relationships between the ideographic languages of the Far East and the hieroglyphics of Egypt and the Indian languages of America. Considerable scholarly interest also appeared with respect to the pre-European history of Asia, the oral and written sources for Asian history, the relative reliability of European and Asian chronologies and methods of dating, and the correlation or disparity between Europe's pre-discovery and post-discovery knowledge of Asia.

The nations of Asia were also billed as exemplars. China, the model state, was quickly recognized to be the possessor of unique and effective governmental and educational institutions: examinations for public office; state-supported schools; social services; and courier systems; and the law of avoidance or the requirement that provincial governors should never be natives of their jurisdictions. The West also had lessons to learn from Japan, particularly in physical and mental discipline. But perhaps what is most significant of all is the dawning realization in the West that not all truth and virtue were contained within its own cultural and religious traditions. The century of the great discoveries, viewed from the perspective of the present, can be taken as the date from which Westerners began self-consciously to question their own cultural premises, to weigh them in a balance against the presuppositions and accomplishments of other high cultures, and to initiate fundamental revisions in their own views of the world, man, and the future.

108 ALFRED NORTH WHITEHEAD, *SCIENCE AND THE MODERN WORLD*: THE SIGNIFICANCE OF THE SCIENTIFIC REVOLUTION

Few people have been able to grasp so well the essential meaning of the revolution wrought by modern science as has Alfred North Whitehead (1861-1947). One of the great philosophers of our time, he began his career as a mathematician at Cambridge University. At the age of sixty-three, when most men are preparing for retirement, Whitehead packed his books and moved to Harvard University to begin an extraordinary second career. He remained there for more than two decades to inspire and stimulate another generation of students with his lectures and writings.

Probably the most widely read of all his philosophic works is *Science and the Modern World*, originally delivered as a series of Lowell Lectures at Harvard in 1925. John Dewey called it "The most significant restatement for the general reader of the present relations of science, philosophy, and the issues of life which has yet appeared." Convinced that the attitude or mentality of an age springs from the world outlook which is dominant among its educated elements, Whitehead, in this book, examined how in the past three hundred years science has influenced western culture. While he admitted that men's attitudes are also shaped by such things as aesthetics, ethics, and religion, he insisted that for the past three centuries "the cosmology derived from science has been asserting itself at the expense of older points of view." It is the emergence of this new science-oriented frame of mind that represents the true significance of the intellectual revolution set in motion by Copernicus and his successors. Moreover, as Whitehead points out in the passage below, it was a phenomenon with the quality of universality, for while "modern science was born in Europe, . . . its home is the whole world." In an age of nuclear neuroses, Whitehead's observations take on a profounder—and graver—meaning.

The progress of civilisation is not wholly a uniform drift towards better things. It may perhaps wear this aspect if we map it on a scale which is large enough. But such broad views obscure the details on which rests our whole understanding of the process. New epochs emerge with comparative suddenness, if we have regard to the scores of thousands of years throughout which the complete history extends. Secluded races suddenly take their places in the main stream of events: technological discoveries transform the mechanism of human life: a primitive art quickly flowers into full satisfaction of some aesthetic craving: great religions in their crusading youth spread through the nations the peace of Heaven and the sword of the Lord.

The sixteenth century of our era saw the disruption of Western Christianity and the rise of modern science. It was an age of ferment. Nothing was settled, though much was opened—new worlds and new ideas. In science, Copernicus and Vesalius may be chosen as representative figures: they typify the new cosmology and the scientific emphasis on direct observation. Giordano Bruno was the martyr: though the cause for which he suffered was not that of science, but that of free imaginative speculation. His death in the year 1600 ushered in the first century of modern science in the strict sense of the term. In his execution there was an unconscious symbolism: for the subsequent tone of scientific thought has contained distrust of his type of general speculativeness. The Reformation, for all its importance, may be considered as a domestic affair of the European races. Even the Christianity of the East viewed it with profound disengagement. Furthermore, such disruptions are no new phenomena in the history of Christianity or of other religions. When we project this great revolution upon the whole history of the Christian Church, we cannot look upon it as introducing a new principle into human life. For good or for evil, it was a great transformation of religion; but it was not the coming of religion. It did not itself claim to be so. Reformers maintained that they were only restoring what had been forgotten.

It is quite otherwise with the rise of modern science. In every way it contrasts with the contemporary religious movement. The Reformation was a popular uprising, and for a century and a half drenched Europe in blood. The beginnings of the scientific movement were confined to a minority among the intellectual élite. In a generation which saw the Thirty Years' War and remembered Alva in the Netherlands, the worst that happened to men of science was that Galileo suffered an honourable detention and a mild reproof, before dying peacefully in his bed. The way in which the persecution of Galileo has been remembered is a tribute to the quiet commencement of the most intimate change in outlook which the human race had yet encountered. Since a babe was born in a manger, it may be doubted whether so great a thing has happened with so little stir.

The thesis which these lectures will illustrate is that this quiet growth of science has practically recoloured our mentality so that modes of thought which in former times were exceptional are now broadly spread through the educated world. This new colouring of ways of thought had been proceeding slowly for many ages in the European peoples. At last it issued in the rapid development of science, and has thereby strengthened itself by its most obvious application. The new mentality is more important even than the new science and the new technology. It has altered the metaphysical presuppositions and the imaginative contents of our minds; so that now the old stimuli provoke a new response. Perhaps my metaphor of a new colour is too strong. What I mean is just that slightest change of tone which yet makes all the difference. This is exactly illustrated by a sentence from a published letter of that adorable genius, William James. When he was finishing his great treatise on the

Text: From *Science and the Modern World* by Alfred North Whitehead. Copyright 1925 by The Macmillan Company and reprinted by their permission. Pp. 1-4.

Principles of Psychology, he wrote to his brother Henry James, "I have to forge every sentence in the teeth of irreducible and stubborn facts."

This new tinge to modern minds is a vehement and passionate interest in the relation of general principles to irreducible and stubborn facts. All the world over and at all times there have been practical men, absorbed in "irreducible and stubborn facts": all the world over and at all times there have been men of philosophic temperament who have been absorbed in the weaving of general principles. It is this union of passionate interest in the detailed facts with equal devotion to abstract generalisation which forms the novelty in our present society. Previously it had appeared sporadically and as if by chance. This balance of mind has now become part of the tradition which infects cultivated thought. It is the salt which keeps life sweet. The main business of universities is to transmit this tradition as a widespread inheritance from generation to generation.

Another contrast which singles out science from among the European movements of the sixteenth and seventeenth centuries is its universality. Modern science was born in Europe, but its home is the whole world. In the last two centuries there has been a long and confused impact of Western modes upon the civilisation of Asia. The wise men of the East have been puzzling, and are puzzling, as to what may be the regulative secret of life which can be passed from West to East without the wanton destruction of their own inheritance which they so rightly prize. More and more it is becoming evident that what the West can most readily give to the East is its science and its scientific outlook. This is transferable from country to country, and from race to race, wherever there is a rational society.

Protestantism and Reformation

HERESIES AND SCHISMS

109 JOHN WYCLIFFE, LETTER TO POPE URBAN VI, 1384: AN EARLY "PROTESTANT"

In the sixteenth century the greatest shock to the settled habits of European society at large came neither from the discovery of new lands and trade routes nor from the gradual reshaping of man's concept of the universe. It came rather from a profound religious upheaval which resulted in the permanent sundering of medieval Europe's most characteristic institution—the western Christian Church.

There is no easy explanation for the Reformation. At the end of the thirteenth century the Church, centered around the papacy, stood at the height of its power. It was a vast international organization run by hundreds of thousands of people: bishops, canons, priests, chaplains, vicars, curates, monks, friars, and nuns. The Church also held great amounts of land in various countries in Europe and derived a large income from rents, dues, and fees. It was this highly organized institution that declined in power after the thirteenth century. In part the decline was due to the growing self-absorption of the papacy in the maintenance of its own wealth and grandeur, the inability to bring about needed reforms, and the refusal to allow reforms to be made by others. In part, too, the decline was caused by the emergence after 1300 of strong, assertive forces outside the Church—the new national monarchies and the urban commercial classes, which ever more frequently clashed with the clergy and resisted the demands of the international Church.

In the fourteenth century the prestige of the papacy was badly undermined when, under pressure from the King of France, the pope moved his residence from the historic city of Rome to the city of Avignon in southern France. Thus began the seventy-year-long Babylonian Captivity (1309-1376), and throughout Europe the popes at Avignon came to be looked upon as tools of France. Matters were made worse in 1378 when the College of Cardinals, split into French and anti-French factions, elected two popes. For forty years (1378-1417) Europe was confronted by the scandalous spectacle of the Great Schism: two popes, one at Avignon backed by France and one at Rome backed by Germany and England, each claiming to be the one true source of authority.

How could a pious Christian be certain where to seek salvation? While the papal courts at Avignon and Rome tried to outdo one another in splendor and sumptuousness, a sense of religious insecurity settled over Europe. In a society that was still essentially religious, this created a feeling of "unutterable uneasiness and dread," to use the phrase of Professor Robert Palmer.

Unsettled social conditions in the fourteenth century further aggravated the problem. The growth of a money economy was converting guild journeymen into wage-earners who saw no future for themselves, and in the countryside it led to discontent and even open rebellion among the peasants. To be sure, the rebellious peasants were ruthlessly suppressed by the upper classes, but the restlessness remained. Nor was there any compensating political stability. Royal governments were still weak, and feudal wars with their accompanying civil turmoil were rampant. Then, beginning in 1347 a bubonic plague, the terrifying Black Death, swept over Europe from east to west. For fifty years the plague kept reappearing, striking wantonly wherever it might, suddenly wiping out half the population in some areas. It seemed to the people as if the wrath of God had descended from the heavens. Society became somewhat unhinged, and a kind of mass neurosis spread through Europe.

It was in such circumstances that reformers arose, insisting that the Church must be reformed and purified. One of the most notable of these early reformers was John Wycliffe (1320-1384), a preacher and writer who was considered the greatest intellectual in England during his time. Wycliffe condemned the great wealth of the Church and declared it contrary to true Christian poverty. To back up his argument, he provided his countrymen with an English translation of the Bible so that they could see for themselves the differences between the simplicity of early Christianity and the present power and wealth of the Church. He also supported the English kings who wished to withhold funds from Rome by insisting that the Church had no right to interfere in government. The pope's only authority, he claimed, was that given in Scriptures, and in any case the Bible took precedence over the pope in all matters of religion. He defined the Church as being much broader than the ecclesiastical organization; the true Church, he said, was made up of all believing Christians. Long before Martin Luther, Wycliffe had given a "Protestant" definition of the Church.

The Church promptly branded Wycliffe a heretic and summoned him to Rome. In the letter below Wycliffe refuses the pope's summons, and in doing so he clearly sets forth his heretical views.

I have joy fully to tell what I hold, to all true men that believe and especially to the Pope; for I suppose that if my faith be rightful and given of God, the Pope will gladly confirm it; and if my faith be error, the Pope will wisely amend it.

I suppose over this that the gospel of Christ be heart of the corps of God's law; for I believe that Jesus Christ, that gave in his own person this gospel, is very God and very man, and by his heart passes all other laws.

I suppose over this that the Pope be most obliged to the keeping of the gospel among all men that live here; for the Pope is highest vicar that Christ has here in earth. For moreness of Christ's vicar is not measured by worldly moreness, but by this, that this vicar follows more Christ by virtuous living; for thus teacheth the gospel, that this is the sentence of Christ.

And of this gospel I take as believe, that Christ for time that he walked here, was most poor man of all, both in spirit and in having; for Christ says that he had nought for to rest his head on. And Paul says that he was made needy for our love. And more poor might no man be, neither bodily nor in spirit. And thus Christ put from him all manner of worldly lordship. For the gospel of John telleth that when they would have made Christ king, he fled and hid him from them, for he would none such worldly highness.

And over this I take it as believe, that no man should follow the Pope, nor no saint that now is in heaven, but in as much as he follows Christ. For John and James erred when they coveted worldly highness; and Peter and Paul sinned also when they denied and blasphemed in Christ; but men should not follow them in this, for then they went from Jesus Christ. And this I take as wholesome counsel, that the Pope leave his worldly lordship to worldly lords, as Christ gave them,—and move speedily all his clerks to do so. For thus did Christ, and taught thus his disciples, till the fiend had blinded this world. And it seems to some men that clerks that dwell lastingly in this error against God's law, and flee to

Text: Translations and Reprints from the Original Sources of European History (Philadelphia: University of Pennsylvania Press. 1902), II, 13-14.

follows Christ in this, been open heretics, and their fautors been partners.

And if I err in this sentence, I will meekly be amended, yea, by the death, if it be skilful, for that I hope were good to me. And if I might travel in mine own person, I would with good will go to the Pope. But God has needed me to the contrary, and taught me more obedience to God than to men. And I suppose of our Pope that he will not be Antichrist, and reverse Christ in this working, to the contrary of Christ's will; for if he summon against reason, by him or by any of his, and pursue this unskilful summoning, he is an open Antichrist. And merciful intent excused not Peter, that Christ should not clepe him Satan; so blind intent and wicked counsel excuses not the Pope here; but if he ask of true priests that they travel more than they may, he is not excused by reason of God, that he should not be Antichrist. For our belief teaches us that our blessed God suffers us not to be tempted more than we may; how should a man ask such service? And therefore pray we to God for our pope Urban the sixth, that his old holy intent be not quenched by his enemies. And Christ, that may not lie, says that the enemies of a man been especially his home family; and this is sooth of men and fiends.

110 JOHN HUS, *DE ECCLESIA*: NATIONALISTIC PROTEST

The followers of John Wycliffe were called Lollards. Lollardry was finally exterminated in England fifty years after Wycliffe's death, but by then his doctrines had spread to central Europe. In Bohemia they fused with social and political demands to develop into a Czech nationalistic movement. This combination of forces foreshadowed by a century the general conditions that were to bring about the Lutheran revolt.

The Holy Roman Empire, of which Bohemia was a part, was a sprawling conglomeration of principalities, feudal enclaves, bishoprics, and city-states that stretched from the Dutch Lowlands to the borders of Poland and from Italy to the borders of Denmark. It possessed neither unity nor strength. Ambitious princes, feuding nobles, powerful church prelates, and wealthy city-states, each intensely jealous of its own prerogatives, were determined to prevent any increase in the emperor's power. Attempts on the part of various emperors to establish effective royal institutions of government were repeatedly frustrated. The rulers failed to create either a centralized imperial administration or a strong territorial state; the Holy Roman Empire continued to remain divided into more than three hundred political units with varying degrees of autonomy. Since the emperorship was an elective office, the man chosen was usually the weakest candidate available—the consequence was that during the fifteenth century the empire degenerated into a state of feudal anarchy. Long before the Reformation, princes began to gain control over religious affairs within their principalities. In Bohemia, the nobles extended their authority and increased their wealth at the expense of both the crown and the Church.

In this situation the views of John Wycliffe found an eloquent disciple in John Hus (1369?-1415), an ordained priest who rose to be dean of the faculty of philosophy at the University of Prague. Serving also as a preacher in the Bethlehem Chapel in Prague, Hus aroused his Czech countrymen to a high pitch of nationalistic opposition to the Church. Like Wycliffe before him, he stressed the universal priesthood of all believers and insisted that the sole head of the Church was Christ, not the pope. In 1410 the Church excommunicated him as a heretic. Five years later Hus accepted in good faith the promise of a safe-conduct pass so that he might appear before the Council of Constance to defend his views. Despite the safe-conduct pass, he was seized and burned at the stake in a meadow outside the city of Constance in the summer of 1415. Heretics, argued the Church, had no civil rights which had to be respected. The burning of Hus transformed him into a martyr for Czech nationalism. For decades in the early fifteenth century Hussite wars ravaged central Europe, and the papacy never succeeded in ending the Bohemian heresy. There emerged in Bohemia an independent church which was basically Protestant in doctrine and practice. Known as the New Unity of the Brotherhood, it confiscated the property of the Catholic Church and monasteries. The doctrines of Hus and the new church were eventually merged with those of Lutheranism and Calvinism in the sixteenth century. It is worth noting that although Bohemia was eventually reconverted to Catholicism during the Thirty Years' War, the execution of Hus has remained a Czech national holiday down to the present day.

Hus' most important work was his *De Ecclesia*, from which the following selection is taken. In defining his conception of the true Christian Church, Hus takes occasion to condemn the worldliness of the Renaissance papacy and prelates. It is obvious that from the Catholic Church's point of view, doctrines such as those propounded below could scarcely be allowed to go unchallenged if the Church wished to maintain itself as an authoritative institution.

... And, if it be objected that a layman is expected and bound to believe of his prelates that they are the heads of the church and parts of the church either by virtue of predestination or present righteousness, it is to be said in reply that a layman is not expected to believe anything of his superior except what is true. It is clear that no one is held to believe anything which he is not moved by God to believe. But God does not move a man to believe what is false. Howbeit good may come by a false faith under certain circumstances, and howbeit God moves to the essence of an act, nevertheless, God does not so move a man that the man is deceived. Therefore, if a layman believes about his prelate that he is a holy member of the church while in fact he is not, his faith or his believing will be false. Therefore, a pastor is expected, by giving instruction in works that are more virtuous, to influence those under him to believe that he is such. Hence, if an inferior does not discern the works of his superior to be virtuous, he is not bound to believe that he is a member of the church by the law of present righteousness, or to believe with godly fear and conditionally that he is such genuinely, *simpliciter*, namely by virtue of predestination. And, if he certainly knows his sin, then he ought to conclude from his works that at that time he is not righteous but an enemy of Jesus Christ. And so it is clear that the third conclusion is false. For there is no confusion in the church militant, by reason of the fact that without revelation we do not know certainly who are members of Christ's mystical body on earth.

... Therefore, better would the doctors have said that Christ is the head of the holy Roman church, and each of the predestinate a member and that all together are the body, which is the church, than to have said that the pope is the head of the Roman church and the college of cardinals the body, for in this case they would have agreed with the apostles and with the saints quoted in Chapter I, especially with St. Augustine, *de doct. christ.* III [*Nic. Fathers*, 2 : 569], who says: "For, in truth, that is not the Lord's body which will not remain with him through eternity." If, therefore, the college of cardinals will not remain through eternity, a thing which is hidden from me, how is it the body of the holy Roman church or of Christ? In a similar way, how is the pope with the aforesaid college the holy Roman church against which the gates of hell cannot prevail?

Therefore, we will speak more safely with St. Augustine who, *Commentary on Psalms*, 80 : 1 [*Nic. Fathers*, 7 : 386], says: "Finally by this testimony, the confession is made both of Christ and the vine that is the head and the body, king and people, shepherd and flock, and the whole mystery of all Christians, Christ and the church." See, how the doctor of holy church shows us another holy church with its head than the one defined of the [eight] doctors who, without support of Scripture, say that the body of the holy Roman church is the college of cardinals, for which college it were well if its parts were members of the holy church of Jesus Christ. And we ought to think how St. Augustine himself feared to call Christ Lord-man, for the reason that this sense does not appear in Scripture; therefore much more ought we to fear to call any Christian head of the holy church militant, lest Christ perhaps be blasphemed, to whom this name is reserved by the Nicene council, *Trinitatis concilio*, as proper to him. How, then, do the doctors, without any Scripture proof, teach that the pope is head of holy church and the college its body? Since it is enough for the faithful Christian with inwrought faith and perseverance to believe the article of faith concerning the catholic church that it is the one totality of all the predestinate faithful who are to be saved by virtue of the merit of Christ—who is the head of the catholic church—it is not permissible for us expressly to descend to any particular vicar whom the Christian might recognize as the chief —*capitalis*. For many have been saved in Judea, Asia and Ethiopia who have believed in Christ, following the teaching of the apostles, and who did not expressly recognize Peter, nay, or expressly believe what concerns Peter, just as they did not hear anything about him.

The third point is this: the pope is the manifest and true successor of the prince of the

Text: Reprinted with the permission of Charles Scribner's Sons from John Huss, *The Church*, trans. David S. Schaff (New York: Charles Scribner's Sons, 1915), pp. 49-50, 138-41, 143-44.

apostles, and about this I have treated in Chapter VII near the close. It is, however, to be said again that the doctors do not prove this point. And, as the vicar ought to occupy the place of his superior from whom he has received vicarial power, therefore, occupying his place, he ought more directly to be conformed to him in his works or otherwise the power would be frustrated in him. From this, then, the argument is constructed: a man is the vicar of the person whose place he fills and from whom, in a legitimate way, he receives procuratorial power [delegated as with the Roman procurators]. But no one truly occupies the place of Christ, or Peter, unless he follows him in his life, for no other kind of following is more fitting; nor does any one otherwise receive procuratorial power. The requirements, therefore, of the vicarial office are conformity of life and authority from him who appoints. If, therefore, the pope is a most humble man, depending little upon mundane honors and the gain of this world, if he is a shepherd deriving his name from the pasturage of God's Word, of which pasturage the Lord said to Peter, "Pasture my sheep," John 21 : 17, if he pasture the sheep by the Word and the example of his virtues being made ensample [example] of the flock with his whole heart, as Peter says, I Peter 5 : 3, if he is meek, patient, chaste, laboring anxiously and solicitously in the service of the church, esteeming all temporal things as dung —then, without doubt, is he the true vicar of Jesus Christ, manifest to God and men, so far as the judgment of the outward senses can determine. But, if he lives at discord with these virtues—for there is "no communion between Christ and Belial," II Cor. 6 : 15, and, as Christ himself said, "He that is not with me is against," Matt. 12 : 30—how can he be the true and manifest vicar of Christ or of Peter and not rather the vicar of antichrist, seeing he resists Christ in morals and in life?

. . . Likewise, Augustine, Com. on John, also *Decretum*, 8 : 1 [*Nic. Fathers*, 7 : 446, Friedberg, I : 596], pointing out who are not true shepherds, but mercenaries, says: "There are some superiors in the church about whom the apostle Paul says: 'they seek their own things and not the things of Christ.' What is it, therefore, 'to seek one's own things'? Not to love Christ freely, not to seek God for His own sake, to follow after temporal comforts, to heap up riches, to hanker after honors from men. When these are loved by the superior, and when God is served for such things, whoever he may be that serves, he is a mercenary and he does not count himself among the children."

. . . From these and other sayings it is evident that no pope is the manifest and true successor of Peter, the prince of the apostles, if in morals he lives at variance with the principles of Peter; and, if he is avaricious, then is he the vicar of Judas, who loved the reward of iniquity and sold Jesus Christ. And by the same kind of proof the cardinals are not the manifest and true successors of the college of Christ's other apostles unless the cardinals live after the manner of the apostles and keep the commands and counsels of our Lord Jesus Christ. For, if they climb up by another way than by the door of our Lord Jesus Christ, then are they thieves and robbers, just as the Saviour himself declared when of all such he said: "All that came before me are thieves and robbers," John 10 : 8. Whosoever, therefore, say that they are Christ's true and manifest vicars, knowing that they are living in sin, lie.

. . . Hence, if the cardinals heap up to themselves ecclesiastical livings and barter with them and take money for their sale either themselves or through others, and so devour and consume in luxurious living the goods of the poor, and if they do not do miracles or preach the Word of God to the people or pray sincerely or fill the place of deacons—whom the apostles appointed, Acts 6—by not performing their duties or living their lives—in how far, I ask, are they the vicars of the apostles? In this that they heap up livings or, like Gehazi, seize upon gifts, or because very early in the morning they come into the pope's presence clad in the most splendid apparel, and attended with the most sumptuous retinue of horsemen—thus attended, not on account of the distance of place or difficulty of the journey but to show their magnificence to the world and their contrariety to Christ and his apostles, who went about among the towns, cities, and castles clad in humble garb, on foot, preaching—*evangelizando*—the kingdom of God.

111 DECREES OF SACROSANCTA AND, FREQUENS: THE COUNCIL OF CONSTANCE

With heresy assuming serious proportions and with a divided papacy indifferent to the growing demand for reforms, thoughtful men, both clerical and lay, began to argue that only a general European council of the Church could reëstablish unity, suppress heresy, and reform the Church "in head and members." The argument ran that a general Church council would represent the will of the entire Church, and therefore the popes as well as the whole ecclesiastical hierarchy would be duty bound to obey all such decisions. The popes, recognizing the threat to their own authority, refused to summon any general council. Taking matters into their own hands, the cardinals convened a council at Pisa in 1409 with delegates from all the Latin West. The major order of business was to terminate the disgraceful schism—the two reigning popes were declared deposed and a new pope elected. But the Council of Pisa had acted too precipitously, for the first two popes refused to resign and Europe found itself with three popes.

Five years later an even greater council was called at the insistence of Holy Roman Emperor Sigismund. The Council of Constance, which met from 1414 to 1418, had three avowed aims: to end the papal schism, to wipe out heresy, and to reform the Church. Proceeding more cautiously than had its predecessor, it finally compelled or persuaded all three popes to resign and restored unity to the Church by electing a new pope. To deal with the problem of heresy, it ordered John Hus burned at the stake, although in the long run this did not prove to be a final solution (see Document 110). On the question of reforms the council was a conspicuous failure. No sooner had the new pope, Martin V, been elected than he reasserted the authority of the papacy. In 1418 he dissolved the Council of Constance and for the next thirty years western Christendom witnessed an unceasing struggle for supremacy between the papacy and the councils. Not until the middle of the fifteenth century was the prestige of the papacy at last restored. In the meantime the cause of reform had been virtually abandoned in the heat of the bitter jurisdictional battle.

The height of the Conciliar Movement was reached at the Council of Constance, which was notable for the issuance of two revolutionary decrees. One, called *Sacrosancta* (1415), declared that a general council was superior to the pope. The other, called *Frequens* (1417), decreed that general councils should meet regularly every ten years. Both decrees, reproduced below, were repudiated by Pope Martin V. However, it should be remembered that while the Conciliar Movement was unsuccessful, the reformist zeal which inspired it persisted for decades afterward.

Decree Sacrosancta

In the name of the Holy and indivisible Trinity; of the Father, Son, and Holy Ghost. Amen.

This holy synod of Constance, forming a general council for the extirpation of the present schism and the union and reformation, in head and members, of the Church of God, legitimately assembled in the Holy Ghost, to the praise of Omnipotent God, in order that it may the more easily, safely, effectively and freely bring about the union and reformation of the church of God, hereby determines, decrees, ordains and declares what follows:—

It first declares that this same council, legitimately assembled in the Holy Ghost, forming a general council and representing the Catholic Church militant, has its power immediately from Christ, and every one, whatever his state or position, even if it be the Papal dignity itself, is bound to obey it in all those things which pertain to the faith and the healing of the said schism, and to the general reformation of the Church of God, in head and members.

Text: *Translations and Reprints from the Original Sources of European History* (Philadelphia: University of Pennsylvania Press, 1907), III, 31-32.

It further declares that any one, whatever his condition, station or rank, even if it be the Papal, who shall contumaciously refuse to obey the mandates, decrees, ordinances or instructions which have been, or shall be issued by this holy council, or by any other general council, legitimately summoned, which concern, or in any way relate to the above mentioned objects, shall, unless he repudiate his conduct, be subject to condign penance and be suitably punished, having recourse, if necessary, to the other resources of the law.

Decree Frequens

A frequent celebration of general councils is an especial means for cultivating the field of the Lord and effecting the destruction of briars, thorns, and thistles, to wit, heresies, errors and schism, and of bringing forth a most abundant harvest. The neglect to summon councils, fosters and develops all these evils, as may be plainly seen from a recollection of the past and consideration of existing conditions. Therefore, by a perpetual edict, we sanction, decree, establish and ordain that general councils shall be celebrated in the following manner, so that the next one shall follow the close of this present council at the end of five years. The second shall follow the close of that, at the end of seven years and councils shall thereafter be celebrated every ten years in such places as the Pope shall be required to designate and assign, with the consent and approbation of the council, one month before the close of the council in question, or which, in his absence, the council itself shall designate. Thus, with a certain continuity, a council will always be either in session, or be expected at the expiration of a definite time. This term may, however, be shortened on account of emergencies, by the Supreme Pontiff, with the counsel of his brothers, the cardinals of the Holy Roman Church, but it may not be hereafter lengthened. The place, moreover, designated for the future council may not be altered without evident necessity. If, however, some complication shall arise, in view of which such a change shall seem necessary, as, for example, a state of siege, a war, a pest, or other obstacles, it shall be permissible for the Supreme Pontiff, with the consent and subscription of his said brethren or two-thirds of them (*duarum partium*) to select another appropriate place near one determined upon, which must be within the same country, unless such obstacles, or similar ones, shall exist throughout the whole nation. In that case, the council may be summoned to some appropriate neighboring place, within the bounds of another nation. To this the prelates, and others, who are wont to be summoned to a council, must betake themselves, as if that place had been designated from the first. Such change of place, or shortening of the period, the Supreme Pontiff is required legitimately and solemnly to publish and announce one year before the expiration of the term fixed, that the said persons may be able to come together for the celebration of the council within the term specified.

THE AGE OF THE REFORMATION

112 LUTHER AT THE DIET OF WORMS: "HERE I STAND"

It is no accident of history that the Reformation, which profoundly affected all of Europe, broke out first in Germany, or more correctly, the Holy Roman Empire. Anywhere else Martin Luther's protests might have been easily squelched; in Germany, because of internal political and social conditions, they assumed the proportions of a national outburst.

The history of the Holy Roman Empire throughout the fifteenth century was one of dissension, debility, and disintegration. As territorial princes reasserted their authority and consolidated their power, the position of the emperor correspondingly declined. While strong national monarchies were emerging in France, England, and Spain, each intent on reducing papal control in their own countries, no comparable unified central government capable of resisting the papacy developed in Germany. Hence, as papal revenues from France and England declined, the Church sought to make up the deficiency by drawing more heavily on Germany. A favorite way of obtaining additional money was through the sale of indulgences (remission of temporal punishments for sins). Although hardly tolerated in other countries, it became a general practice in Germany. So long as the Church allowed the petty princes a share of the profits, it could easily obtain permission from them to issue indulgences in princely territories. People in Germany came to feel they were being mulcted to support the corruption and immorality of the papacy, and resentment was deep and widespread. An incipient German national consciousness manifested itself in mounting criticism of the priesthood and condemnation of its power and privileges. The sumptuous papal court came to be looked upon as a foreign power which oppressed and exploited the Germans, and Rome was regarded as the chief enemy of the nation.

Martin Luther (1483-1546) was a monk and professor of theology at the University of Wittenberg with a local reputation as an outstanding preacher in the city church. Convinced that indulgences were deluding the people and distressed at their continual sale, he decided to make an issue of this particular abuse—his intention was not to arouse the public but rather to warn the Church of the dangers of continuing to sell indulgences. The method he chose was typically academic. At noon on October 31, 1517, he nailed his ninety-five theses to the door of the castle church. The church door served as a kind of bulletin board and Luther was simply posting a notice offering his theses as a basis for theological debate. If Luther intended this to remain a purely academic matter, he was greatly mistaken. The theses, though written in Latin, were soon translated into German, given to a printer, and rapidly distributed throughout the country. His criticisms expressed the keenly felt sentiments of more Germans than he knew and in a short time Luther's name became a household word in Germany.

Events then moved swiftly. At first Luther appealed to the pope to reform the abuse of indulgences. When the pope refused, Luther called for a general Church council, and was again refused. To rally public opinion behind him, Luther published a series of revolutionary pamphlets in 1519 and 1520. In them he forcefully stated his doctrines of "justification by faith" and the "universal priesthood of all believers," and called upon German princes to reform the Church. The papacy countered by branding Luther a heretic and excommunicating him. To the twenty-year-old emperor, Charles V, this rebellion against the Church seemed especially dangerous because it could lead to rebellion against the state. Yet he could not ignore the aroused spirit of the German people nor the demands of the German electors who were pressing for reforms. At the urging of Prince Frederick the Wise of Saxony, Luther's protector, Charles V finally consented to give Luther a hearing at the imperial diet scheduled to meet at Worms early in 1521. He granted Luther a safe-conduct pass to and from Worms, and on April 18, 1521, Luther appeared before the emperor at the imperial diet. It was the most dramatic public event of Luther's career. The attention of all of Germany was focused upon him, for the religious and political significance of the occasion was apparent to all his contemporaries. The drama of that event, Luther's unwavering stand, his audacity in insisting that it was the Church's responsibility to prove him wrong, are all recaptured in the description of the encounter given below. Note, too, how Luther censured the Council of Constance for condemning John Hus on a proposition which was at the very core of Luther's own doctrines.

The Speech of Dr. Martin Luther before the Emperor Charles and Princes at Worms on the Fifth Day after Misericordias Domini [April 18] In the Name of Jesus

"Most serene emperor, most illustrious princes, most clement lords, obedient to the time set for me yesterday evening, I appear before you, beseeching you, by the mercy of God, that your most serene majesty and your most illustrious lordships may deign to listen graciously to this my cause—which is, as I hope, a cause of justice and of truth. If through my inexperience I have either not given the proper titles to some, or have offended in some manner against court customs and etiquette, I beseech you to kindly pardon me, as a man accustomed not to courts but to the cells of monks. I can bear no other witness about myself but that I have taught and written up to this time with simplicity of heart, as I had in view only the glory of God and the sound instruction of Christ's faithful.

"Most serene emperor, most illustrious princes, concerning those questions proposed to me yesterday on behalf of your serene majesty, whether I acknowledged as mine the books enumerated and published in my name and whether I wished to persevere in their defense or to retract them, I have given to the first question my full and complete answer, in which I still persist and shall persist forever. These books are mine and they have been published in my name by me, unless in the meantime, either through the craft or the mistaken wisdom of my emulators, something in them has been changed or wrongly cut out. For plainly I cannot acknowledge anything except what is mine alone and what has been written by me alone, to the exclusion of all interpretations of anyone at all.

"In replying to the second question, I ask that your most serene majesty and your lordships may deign to note that my books are not all of the same kind.

"For there are some in which I have discussed religious faith and morals simply and evangelically, so that even my enemies themselves are compelled to admit that these are useful, harmless, and clearly worthy to be read by Christians. Even the bull [the papal bull, *Exsurge Domine*, issued in Rome June 15, 1520], although harsh and cruel, admits that some of my books are inoffensive, and yet allows these also to be condemned with a judgment which is utterly monstrous. Thus, if I should begin to disavow them, I ask you, what would I be doing? Would not I, alone of all men, be condemning the very truth upon which friends and enemies equally agree, striving alone against the harmonious confession of all?

"Another group of my books attacks the papacy and the affairs of the papists as those who both by their doctrines and very wicked examples have laid waste the Christian world with evil that af-

Text: Martin Luther, *Works,* ed. Helmut T. Lehmann and George W. Forell (Philadelphia: Muhlenberg Press, 1958), XXXII, 105, 108-17, 120-23. Reprinted by permission of the Fortress Press.

fects the spirit and the body. For no one can deny or conceal this fact, when the experience of all and the complaints of everyone witness that through the decrees of the pope and the doctrines of men the consciences of the faithful have been most miserably entangled, tortured, and torn to pieces. Also, property and possessions, especially in this illustrious nation of Germany, have been devoured by an unbelievable tyranny and are being devoured to this time without let-up and by unworthy means. [Yet the papists] by their own decrees . . . warn that the papal laws and doctrines which are contrary to the gospel or the opinions of the fathers are to be regarded as erroneous and reprehensible. If, therefore, I should have retracted these writings, I should have done nothing other than to have added strength to this [papal] tyranny and I should have opened not only windows but doors to such great godlessness. It would rage farther and more freely than ever it has dared up to this time. Yes, from the proof of such a revocation on my part, their wholly lawless and unrestrained kingdom of wickedness would become still more intolerable for the already wretched people; and their rule would be further strengthened and established, especially if it should be reported that this evil deed had been done by me by virtue of the authority of your most serene majesty and of the whole Roman Empire. Good God! What a cover for wickedness and tyranny I should have then become.

"I have written a third sort of book against some private and (as they say) distinguished individuals—those, namely, who strive to preserve the Roman tyranny and to destroy the godliness taught by me. Against these I confess I have been more violent than my religion or profession demands. But then, I do not set myself up as a saint; neither am I disputing about my life, but about the teaching of Christ. It is not proper for me to retract these works, because by this retraction it would again happen that tyranny and godlessness would, with my patronage, rule and rage among the people of God more violently than ever before.

"However, because I am a man and not God, I am not able to shield my books with any other protection than that which my Lord Jesus Christ himself offered for his teaching. When questioned before Annas about his teaching and struck by a servant, he said: 'If I have spoken wrongly, bear witness to the wrong' [John 18:19-23]. If the Lord himself, who knew that he could not err, did not refuse to hear testimony against his teaching, even from the lowliest servant, how much more ought I, who am the lowest scum and able to do nothing except err, desire and expect that somebody should want to offer testimony against my teaching! Therefore, I ask by the mercy of God, may your most serene majesty, most illustrious lordships, or anyone at all who is able, either high or low, bear witness, expose my errors, overthrowing them by the writings of the prophets and the evangelists. Once I have been taught I shall be quite ready to renounce every error, and I shall be the first to cast my books into the fire.

"From these remarks I think it is clear that I have sufficiently considered and weighed the hazards and dangers, as well as the excitement and dissensions aroused in the world as a result of my teachings, things about which I was gravely and forcefully warned yesterday. To see excitement and dissension arise because of the Word of God is to me clearly the most joyful aspect of all in these matters. For this is the way, the opportunity, and the result of the Word of God, just as He [Christ] said, 'I have not come to bring peace, but a sword. For I have come to set a man against his father, etc.' [Matt. 10:34-35]. Therefore, we ought to think how marvelous and terrible is our God in his counsels, lest by chance what is attempted for settling strife grows rather into an intolerable deluge of evils, if we begin by condemning the Word of God. And concern must be shown lest the reign of this most noble youth, Prince Charles (in whom after God is our great hope), become unhappy and inauspicious. I could illustrate this with abundant examples from Scripture—like Pharaoh, the king of Babylon, and the kings of Israel who, when they endeavored to pacify and strengthen their kingdoms by the wisest counsels, most surely destroyed themselves. For it is He who takes the wise in their own craftiness [Job 5:13] and overturns mountains before they know it [Job 9:5]. Therefore we must fear God. I do not say these things because there is a need of either my teachings or my warnings for such leaders as you, but because I must not withhold the allegiance which I owe my Germany. With these words I commend myself to your most serene majesty and to your lordships, humbly asking that I not be allowed through the agitation of my enemies, without cause, to be made hateful to you. I have finished."

When I had finished, the speaker for the emperor said, as if in reproach, that I had not answered the question, that I ought not call into question those things which had been condemned and defined in councils; therefore what was sought from me was not a horned response, but a simple one, whether or not I wished to retract.

Here I answered:

"Since then your serene majesty and your lordships seek a simple answer, I will give it in this manner, neither horned nor toothed: Unless I am convinced by the testimony of the Scriptures or by clear reason (for I do not trust either in the pope or in councils alone, since it is well known that they have often erred and contradicted themselves), I am bound by the Scriptures I have quoted and my conscience is captive to the Word of God. I cannot and I will not retract anything, since it is neither safe nor right to go against conscience.

"I cannot do otherwise, here I stand, may God help me, Amen."

The princes deliberated about this speech of Dr. Martin. When they had examined it the secretary of Trier began to tear it apart in this fashion: "Martin, you have answered more impudently than befits your person, and not to the point either. You have made various distinctions among your books, but in such a way that none of them contributes anything to this investigation. If you had recanted those which contain a large portion of your errors, no doubt his imperial majesty, in his innate clemency, would not have tolerated a persecution of the rest which are good. But now you revive those [errors] which the general Council of Constance, composed of the whole German nation, has condemned, and you wish to be refuted by means of Scripture. In this you are completely mad. For what purpose does it serve to raise a new dispute about matters condemned through so many centuries by church and council? Unless perhaps a reason must be given to just anyone about anything whatsoever. But if it were granted that whoever contradicts the councils and the common understanding of the church must be overcome by Scripture passages, we will have nothing in Christianity that is certain or decided. And for this reason his imperial majesty seeks from you an answer, simple and straightforward, either a no or a yes: Do you wish to regard all your works as catholic? Or do you wish to retract anything from them?"

But Dr. Martin nevertheless asked that his imperial majesty not allow him to be compelled to retract contrary to his conscience, captive to and bound by holy Scripture, without the clear arguments of those who spoke against him. If they sought an answer which was unambiguous, simple, and true, he had none other than what he had uttered before: Unless his adversaries by sufficient arguments would extricate his conscience, which was captured by those errors (as they called them), he would not be able to get out of the nets in which he was entangled. Whatever the councils agreed upon was not immediately true; further, the councils have erred and have often contradicted themselves. Moreover, the arguments of his contradictors were not convincing. He was able to show that the councils had erred: he was not able to retract that which the Scripture zealously proclaimed. He added at this place an exclamation, "God help me!"

To these words there was no reply from the secretary except a very few words to the effect that it could not be shown that the councils had erred. Martin said that he was truly able and willing to do that.

However, since darkness had by then come over the whole audience hall, each one departed to his home. As he departed from his imperial majesty and the tribunal, a large group of Spaniards followed Luther, the man of God, with jeers, derisive gestures, and much loud noise.

On the sixth day after Misericordias Domini [April 19], when the princes, electors, dukes, and the nobles of every rank who were ordinarily present at the assemblies, had met, the emperor sent this message, which he had written with his own hand to this council.

"Our ancestors who were also Christian princes, were nevertheless obedient to the Roman church which Dr. Martin now attacks. And because he is determined to move not even a hair's breadth from his errors, we are not able with propriety to depart from the example of our ancestors in defending the ancient faith, and giving aid to the Roman see. Therefore, we shall pursue Martin himself and his adherents with excommunication, and use other methods available for their liquidation."

However, because he did not wish to violate the agreement which had been granted and signed, he would therefore do his best that Luther might return safely from where he was summoned.

The electoral princes, dukes, and the imperial orders debated this judgment of Charles on the sixth day throughout the whole afternoon, and even on the whole of the Saturday which followed, and during this time Dr. Martin received no word from his imperial majesty.

Meanwhile, he was seen and visited by many princes, counts, barons, knights, nobles, and priests, both religious and secular, not to mention a number of the common people. These constantly besieged the residence, and their desire to see was never satisfied. . . .

On the Feast of St. George [April 23], after dinner, [a messenger] returned at the command of his prince, the archbishop of Trier, saying that on the next day at the hour recently designated, Luther should be present at the lodging of his lordship.

On Wednesday, the day after the Feast of St. George [April 24], obedient to the command, Dr. Martin entered the lodging of the archbishop of Trier, accompanied by the latter's chaplain and the imperial herald and followed by those who had accompanied him here from Saxony and Thuringia, and some other very good friends. When he was before the archbishop of Trier, Margrave Joachim of Brandenburg, Duke George of Saxony, the bishops of Augsburg [Christopher von Stadion] and of Brandenburg [Jerome Scultetus], the master of the Teutonic Order [Dietrich von Cleen], Count George of Wertheim, Dr. Bock of Strassburg, and Dr. Peutinger, Dr. Vehus, chancellor of Baden, began to speak and declared: He [Luther] had not been called to this meeting to enter upon an argument or debate, but only out of Christian charity and clemency had the princes sought permission from his imperial majesty to exhort him kindly and fraternally. Next, although the councils had set forth varying views, they did not contradict one another. But even if the councils had erred greatly, they had certainly not thereby destroyed their authority to such a degree that anyone should wish to rely on his own interpretation in opposition to them. Adding many things concerning the centurion [Matt. 8:5-13] and Zacchaeus [Luke 19:2-10] about human institutions, ceremonies, and decrees, and affirming that all these things were sanctioned for the repression of vice according to the temper and vicissitudes of the times, he said that the church was not able to exist without human institutions. The tree is known by its fruit [Matt. 12:33]. Moreover, it is said that many good things are the result of laws. And St. Martin, St. Nicholas, and many other saints had taken part in councils. Further he said that his [Luther's] books would excite great disturbances and unbelievable confusion. The common people were using his book, *The Freedom of a Christian,* to throw off the yoke, and to strengthen disobedience. Now we are far from the time when those who believed were of one heart and soul [Acts 4:32]. Therefore, laws are necessary. Moreover, it must be considered that although he [Luther] had written many good things, and without doubt with a fine spirit, such as *Of Threefold Justice* and others, the devil was using this fact and working through secret snares, so that all his works might be condemned in perpetuity. He would be judged from these he had written last, just as a tree is known not by its flower but by its fruit. There he [Vehus] added the quotation about the destruction that wastes at noonday and the pestilence that stalks in darkness and the arrow that flies [Ps. 91:5-6]. The whole oration was an exhortation, full of rhetorical commonplaces about the usefulness and wholesomeness of laws, and, on the other hand, the dangers to conscience and safety, both public and private. As in the beginning, so in the middle and the end, he asserted the same thing, that this admonition was the result of the most kind attitude and singular mercy of the princes. In closing he added threats in a final speech, saying that if [Luther] persevered in his position, the emperor would proceed against him, exiling him from the empire and condemning his works, and he reminded him again that he should think about these things and weigh them.

Dr. Martin answered:

"Most clement and illustrious princes and lords, for that most clement and kind will of yours from which this admonition proceeded, I thank you as humbly as I am able. For I know that I am by far too lowly a man to be warned by such great princes. I have not censured all councils, but only that of Constance because of the most powerful reason that it condemned the Word of God, which is shown in its condemnation of this proposition of John Huss: 'The church of Christ is the community of the elect.' This statement the council at Constance condemned and thus the article of faith: 'I believe in the holy catholic church.' "

He [Luther] did not refuse to pay with his life and blood, provided he were not reduced to the point where he might be compelled to retract the clear Word of God. For in its defense it is necessary to obey God rather than man [Acts 5:29]. Moreover, there are two kinds of offenses, one involving charity and the other faith. Offenses against charity depend upon morals and life; those involving faith or doctrine depend on the Word of God and cannot be avoided. For it is not in his [Luther's] power, that Christ should not become a "stumbling-stone" [Isa. 8:14-15; Rom. 9:32-33; I Pet. 2:8]. If the faith were truly preached and magistrates were good, one law, informed by the spirit of the gospel, would be sufficient and human laws useless. He knew that magistrates and men in power must be obeyed, even those who live evil and unjust lives. He knew also that private opinions should give way, for that is also taught in his writings. If only he would not be forced to deny the Word of God he would show himself in all other things most obedient. . . .

In the forenoon on Thursday, the Feast of St. Mark [April 25], Peutinger and [Vehus of] Baden attempted to persuade Dr. Martin that he should leave the judgment of his books simply and absolutely to the emperor and the empire. He answered that he would do and endure everything if only they supported themselves by the authority of holy Scripture, for he would trust in nothing less. For God had once spoken through the prophet, "Put not your trust in princes, in the sons of men, in whom there is no help" [Ps. 146:3]. And again, "Cursed is the man who trusts in man" [Jer. 17:5]. And when they pressed him harder he answered that nothing ought less to be entrusted to the judgment of men than the Word of God. Thus they left him, asking him to think over a better answer, and saying that they would come back after luncheon.

After luncheon they returned and attempted in vain the same thing as in the morning. They pleaded with him to at least submit his case to the judgment of some future council. And he granted this, but on the condition that they show him the parts excerpted from his books for submission to the council, and that they judge them by the testimony of Scripture and the divine Word. Upon leaving Dr. Martin they told the archbishop of Trier that he had promised to submit some parts of his works to a council and that meanwhile he would be silent about them. But Dr. Martin had never even considered this, as he had always up to this time refused to either deny or to cast aside whatever concerned the Word of God.

Therefore it came about, through the work of God, that [the archbishop of] Trier summoned Dr. Martin to hear him personally....

To [the archbishop of] Trier, who asked what he would do if some articles were selected for the purpose of submitting them to a council, Luther answered that he would accept, provided that they were not those which the Council of Constance had condemned. [The archbishop of] Trier said that he feared that those would be the very ones. Then Luther said, "About these, I am unable and unwilling to keep silent, for I am certain that by those decrees the Word of God was condemned and I would rather lose my life and head than desert the clear Word of God."

When [the archbishop of] Trier saw that Dr. Martin would never submit the Word of God to the judgment of men, he dismissed him in a kindly manner, and when asked [by Luther] if he would obtain permission from his imperial majesty to leave, he answered that he would properly care for the matter and would report back.

Not long afterward, the secretary of [the archbishop of] Trier, in the presence of the chancellor of Austria and Maximilian, the imperial secretary, read to Dr. Martin in his lodging the emperor's decree:

"Because, although he has so often been warned in vain by the emperor, the electors, the princes, and the estates, he is unwilling to return to the heart and unity of the catholic faith, it remains for the emperor as defender of the catholic faith to act. Therefore, it is the command of the emperor that within twenty-one days from this time, he return to his home under a safe-conduct passage and with his liberty secured, and that on the journey he not stir up the people either by preaching or writing."

The most Christian father, answering very modestly, began thus:

"As it has pleased the Lord so it has happened. Blessed be the name of the Lord [Job 1:21]. First of all to his most serene majesty, to the prince electors, the princes, and the rest of the imperial estates, I give most humble thanks for a favorable and kind audience and for the safe-conduct which has been kept and is to be kept. For I have desired nothing in all this except a reformation according to holy Scripture, and this I have urgently demanded. Otherwise I will endure all things for his imperial majesty and the empire: life and death, fame and infamy, reserving nothing at all for myself except only the right to confess and testify to the Word of the Lord. I most humbly commend myself and subject myself to his imperial majesty and the whole empire."

Therefore, on the next day, that is, the sixth day after Jubilate [April 26], after he had paid his respects to his supporters and friends who had visited him frequently, he left after breakfast, at about ten in the morning, accompanied both by those with whom he had traveled there and by Dr. Jerome Schurff, the lawyer of Wittenberg. Caspar Sturm, the herald, after a few hours followed him and found him at Oppenheim and accompanied him according to the verbal order of Emperor Charles.

113. THE TWELVE ARTICLES AND MARTIN LUTHER'S REPLY: THE PEASANT REVOLT

As his doctrines swept over Germany in the early 1520's, Luther was looked to as spokesman by all manner of discontented groups with long-standing grievances. His notion of Christian liberty, which Luther conceived of as the inner spiritual freedom that came to a true believer of the gospels, was quickly interpreted by the masses as the freedom to judge what was right in political, economic, and social matters. Unforeseen and unintended, Luther's religious revolution was being transformed into a social and political revolution bent on a vast national upheaval.

The peasants of Germany were particularly receptive to the idea of Christian freedom, for they saw in it a justification of their demands for reform. All during the latter part of the fifteenth century their position became progressively worse. Since it was a time of inflation and rising costs, many landlords proceeded to revive old feudal dues in an effort to meet their mounting financial needs. After 1500 the territorial princes added to the burden by imposing new taxes. The peasants, convinced of the injustice of such feudal payments and taxes, grew increasingly restive. Even before Luther appeared on the scene, there were instances of peasant outbreaks in southern Germany; his evangelical movement simply added fuel to the flames.

The Peasant Revolt broke out in full force in June 1524, and by early 1525 it had spread through a third of Germany. Acting on the assumption that what they were doing was in accordance with the gospel proclaimed by Luther, the peasants set forth their demands for reforms in twelve articles. On the face of it the demands did not seem excessive, but as the movement spread it became more violent and more revolutionary—in a short while the entire countryside was aroused.

Luther's reaction to the violence of the peasants was one of horrified revulsion. The peasants, he thundered, had misinterpreted and betrayed the gospels; no true Christian had the right to take justice into his own hands. He therefore urged the princes to suppress the revolt with all the severity at their command, and to show no mercy to the peasants, who, he maintained, should be treated like "mad dogs." The princes needed no further urging and crushed the uprising with great brutality.

The peasant uprising and Luther's stand resulted in two important consequences. For one thing, Luther from this time forward strongly distrusted the peasants and relied heavily on established authority to maintain peace and order. Ultimately, he came to accept the divine-right theory of government. The second consequence was that Luther's movement lost a good deal of its popular support. After 1525 many peasants turned to the more radical forms of Protestantism, such as Anabaptism.

The Twelve Articles

The First Article: First, it is our humble petition and desire, as also our will and resolution, that in the future we should have power and authority so that each community should choose and appoint a pastor, and that we should have the right to depose him should he conduct himself improperly. The pastor thus chosen should teach us the Gospel pure and simple, without any addition, doctrine or ordinance of man. For to teach us continually the true faith will lead us to pray God that through his grace this faith may increase within us and become a part of us. For if his grace work not within us we remain flesh and blood, which availeth nothing; since the Scripture clearly teaches that only through true faith can we come to God. Only through his mercy can we become holy. Hence such a guide and pastor is necessary, and in this fashion grounded upon the Scriptures.

The Second Article: According as the just tithe is established by the Old Testament and fulfilled in the New, we are ready and willing to pay the fair tithe of grain. The word of God plainly provides that in giving according to right to God and distributing to his people the services of a pastor are required. We will that for the future our church provost, whomsoever the community may appoint, shall gather and receive this tithe. From this he shall give to the pastor, elected by the whole community, a decent and sufficient maintenance for him and his [*im und den seynen*], as shall seem right to the whole

Text: Translations and Reprints From the Original Sources of European History (Philadelphia: University of Pennsylvania Press, 1902), II, 314-17.

community (or, with the knowledge of the community). What remains over shall be given to the poor of the place, as the circumstances and the general opinion demand. Should anything farther remain, let it be kept, lest anyone should have to leave the country from poverty. Provision should also be made from this surplus to avoid laying any land tax on the poor. In case one or more villages have themselves sold their tithes on account of want, and the village has taken action as a whole, the buyer should not suffer loss, but we will that some proper agreement be reached with him for the repayment of the sum by the village with due interest. But those who have tithes which they have not purchased from a village, but which were appropriated by their ancestors, should not, and ought not, to be paid anything farther by the village, which shall apply its tithes to the support of the pastors elected as above indicated, or to solace the poor, as is taught by the Scriptures. The small tithes, whether ecclesiastical or lay, we will not pay at all, for the Lord God created cattle for the free use of man. We will not, therefore, pay farther an unseemly tithe which is of man's invention.

The Third Article: It has been the custom hitherto for men to hold us as their own property, which is pitiable enough, considering that Christ has delivered and redeemed us all, without exception by the shedding of his precious blood, the lowly as well as the great. Accordingly, it is consistent with Scripture that we should be free and wish to be so. Not that we would wish to be absolutely free and under no authority. God does not teach us that we should lead a disorderly life in the lusts of the flesh, but that we should love the Lord our God and our neighbor. We would gladly observe all this as God has commanded us in the celebration of the communion. He has not commanded us not to obey the authorities, but rather that we should be humble, not only towards those in authority, but towards everyone. We are thus ready to yield obedience according to God's law to our elected and regular authorities in all proper things becoming to a Christian. We, therefore, take it for granted that you will release us from serfdom, as true Christians, unless it should be shown us from the Gospel that we are serfs.

The Fourth Article: In the fourth place it has been the custom heretofore, that no poor man should be allowed to touch venison or wild fowl, or fish in flowing water, which seems to us quite unseemly and unbrotherly, as well as selfish, and not agreeable to the word of God. In some places the authorities preserve the game to our great annoyance and loss, recklessly permitting the unreasoning animals to destroy to no purpose our crops, which God suffers to grow for the use of man, and yet we must remain quiet. This is neither godly nor neighborly. For when God created man he gave him dominion over all the animals, over the birds of the air and over the fish in the water. Accordingly it is our desire if a man holds possession of waters that he should prove from satisfactory documents that his right has been unwittingly acquired by purchase. We do not wish to take it from him by force, but his rights should be exercised in a Christian and brotherly fashion. But whosoever cannot produce such evidence should surrender his claim with good grace.

The Fifth Article: In the fifth place we are aggrieved in the matter of woodcutting, for the noble folk have appropriated all the woods to themselves alone. If a poor man requires wood he must pay double for it, [or perhaps, two pieces of money]. It is our opinion in regard to a wood which has fallen into the hands of a lord, whether spiritual or temporal, that unless it was duly purchased it should revert again to the community. It should, moreover, be free to every member of the community to help himself to such firewood as he needs in his own home. Also, if a man requires wood for carpenter's purposes he should have it free, but with the knowledge of a person appointed by the community for that purpose. Should, however, no such forest be at the disposal of the community, let that which has been duly bought be administered in a brotherly and Christian manner. If the forest, although unfairly appropriated in the first instance, was later duly sold, let the matter be adjusted in a friendly spirit and according to the Scriptures.

The Sixth Article: Our sixth complaint is in regard to the excessive services demanded of us, which are increased from day to day. We ask that this matter be properly looked into so that we shall not continue to be oppressed in this way, and that some gracious consideration be given us, since our forefathers were required only to serve according to the word of God.

The Seventh Article: Seventh, we will not hereafter allow ourselves to be farther oppressed by our lords, but will let them demand only what is just and proper according to the word of the agreement between the lord and the peasant. The lord should no longer try to force more services or other dues from the peasant without payment, but permit the peasant to enjoy his holding in peace and quiet. The peasant should, however, help the lord when it is necessary, and at proper times, when it will not be disadvantageous to the peasant, and for a suitable payment.

The Eighth Article: In the eighth place, we are greatly burdened by holdings which cannot support the rent exacted from them. The peasants suffer loss in this way and are ruined; and we ask that the lords may appoint persons of honor to inspect these holdings, and fix a rent in accordance with justice, so that the peasant shall not work for nothing, since the laborer is worthy of his hire.

The Ninth Article: In the ninth place, we are burdened with a great evil in the constant making of new laws. We are not judged according to the offence, but sometimes with great ill will, and sometimes much too leniently. In our opinion we should be judged according to the old written law, so that the case shall be decided according to its merits, and not with partiality.

The Tenth Article: In the tenth place, we are aggrieved by the appropriation by individuals of meadows and fields which at one time belonged to a community. These we will take again into our own hands. It may, however, happen that the land was rightfully purchased, but when the land has unfortunately been purchased in this way, some brotherly arrangement should be made according to circumstances.

The Eleventh Article: In the eleventh place we will entirely abolish the due called *Todfall* [i.e., heriot], and will no longer endure it, nor allow widows and orphans to be thus shamefully robbed against God's will, and in violation of justice and right, as has been done in many places, and by those who should shield and protect them. These have disgraced and despoiled us, and although they had little authority they assumed it. God will suffer this no more, but it shall be wholly done away with, and for the future no man shall be bound to give little or much.

Conclusion: In the twelfth place it is our conclusion and final resolution, that if one or more of the articles here set forth should not be in agreement with the word of God, as we think they are, such article we will willingly recede from, when it is proved really to be against the word of God by a clear explanation of the Scripture. Or if articles should now be conceded to us that are hereafter discovered to be unjust, from that hour they shall be dead and null and without force. Likewise, if more complaints should be discovered which are based upon truth and the Scriptures, and relate to offences against God and our neighbor, we have determined to reserve the right to present these also, and to exercise ourselves in all Christian teaching. For this we shall pray God, since he can grant this, and he alone. The peace of Christ abide with us all.

Martin Luther's Reply

You invoke the name of God, and you say that you will act according to his Word; forget not, before all things, that God punishes him who takes his name in vain. Dear friends, keep the fear of his anger ever before you. What are you, and what is this world? do you forget that He is the all-powerful and terrible God, the God of the deluge, the God who destroyed Sodom in his wrath? Now, it is easy to see that by your present conduct you do not honour to his name. Has not God said: *They that take the sword shall perish with the sword?* and Saint Paul: *Render, therefore, honour to whom honour is due.* How can you, after reading these precepts, still pretend that you are acting according to the gospel? Beware, beware, least a terrible judgment fall upon you!

But say you, authority is wicked, cruel, intolerable; it will not allow us the gospel, it overwhelms us with burdens beyond all reason or endurance; it ruins us, soul and body. To this I reply, that the wickedness and injustice of authority are no warrant for revolt, seeing that it befits not all men indiscriminately to take upon themselves the punishment of wickedness. Besides which, the natural law says that no man shall be the judge in his own cause, nor revenge his own quarrel. The divine law teaches us the same lesson: *Vengeance is mine, saith the Lord, I will repay.* Your enterprise, therefore, is not only wrong according to Bible and gospel law, but it is opposed also to natural law and to equity; and you cannot properly persevere in it, unless you prove that you are called to it by a new commandment of God, especially directed to you, and confirmed by miracles.

You see the mote in the eye of authority, but you see not the beam in your own. Authority is unjust, in that it interdicts the Gospel, and oppresses you with burdens; but you are still more in the wrong even than authority, you who, not content with interdicting the Word of God, trample it under foot, and arrogate to yourselves the power reserved to God alone. . . .

Do you not perceive, my friends, that if your doctrine were tenable, there would remain upon the earth neither authority, nor order, nor any species of justice. Every man would act entirely as his own judge, his own vindicator, and nought would be seen but murder, rapine, and desolation.

What would you do, if, of your own body, each member insisted upon his independence of the

Text: M. Michelet (ed.), *The Life of Luther Written by Himself*, trans. William Hazlitt, 2nd ed. (London: George Bell & Sons, 1884), pp. 171-76, 178-79.

rest, administered his own justice, revenged his own quarrel? Would you permit this? Would you not say that it was for the leaders, for the superiors to judge of the matter? . . .

To take an example in the very times wherein we live: How, I ask you, has it happened that neither the emperor nor the pope has been able to effect anything against me? that the more strenuous the efforts they have made to arrest the progress of the gospel, and to destroy it, the more has the gospel gained ground and force. I have never drawn the sword; I have never taken a step towards revolt; I have always preached, always inculcated obedience to authority, even to the authority which was bitterly persecuting me; I always relied wholly upon God; I placed everything in his hands. It is for this reason, that, in despite of the pope and of the other tyrants, he has not only preserved my life, which is in itself a miracle, but he has also more and more advanced and spread my gospel; it is you yourselves, who, while you think you are serving the gospel, are in reality impeding it; you are giving it a terrible blow, you are destroying its effect in the minds of men, you are crushing it by your perverse and insane enterprise.

I say all this unto you, my dear friends, that you may see to what an extent you are profaning the name of Christ and of his holy law; however just your demands may be, it befits not a Christian to draw the sword, or to employ violence; you should rather suffer yourselves to be defrauded, according to the law which has been given unto you (1 Corinthians, vi.). At all events, if you persist in carrying out the dictates of a perverse will, desecrate not the name of Christ, nor impiously make use of it as a pretext and cloak for your unrighteous conduct. I will not permit you to do so; I will not excuse it; I will wrest that name from you by any effort of which I am capable, sacrificing, if necessary, the last drop of blood in my veins. . . .

The demands you have drawn up, are not in themselves contrary to natural law and to equity, but they are rendered so by the violence with which you seek to force them from the hands of authority; so, too, he who prepared them is not a pious and sincere man; he has cited a great number of chapters of the gospel, without giving the verses themselves, which he has done for the purpose of seducing you, and involving you in danger by specious appearances, without enabling you from the text itself to confute him.

For I will tell you that when we come to read the chapters he has indicated, so far from their telling in favour of your enterprise, they are, on the contrary, against you; for they inculcate that all men should live and act as becomes Christians. He who has thus essayed to attack the gospel by your means, is assuredly a prophet of sedition and of murder; but God will resist him, and preserve you from him.

In the first place, you glorify yourselves in your preface, for that you only ask to live according to the gospel. But do you not yourselves admit that you are in revolt? How then, I ask you, can you have the audacity to cloak such conduct under the holy name of the gospel? . . .

Nor is it true that your articles do, as you announce in your preface, teach the gospel; nor is it true that they are conformable with it. Is there any one of the twelve founded upon evangelical doctrine? On the contrary, is not the sole object of them all the temporal emancipation of your persons and your property? Have they not all reference to temporal things? You covet power, and the goods of the earth; you are unwilling to endure any wrong. The gospel, on the contrary, has no heed to these things, and constitutes the external life of Christians of suffering, of enduring injustice, of submitting to be defrauded, of bearing the cross, of patience, of contempt of life and of all the things of this world.

It is absolutely essential, then, that you should either abandon your enterprise, and consent to endure the wrongs that men may do unto you, if you desire still to bear the name of Christians; or else, if you persist in your resolutions, that you should throw aside that name, and assume some other. Choose one or the other of these alternatives: there is no medium. . . .

I am filled with anguish and pity when I reflect upon two inevitable calamities that are about to befal both parties; would to God I could avert them, by the sacrifice of my own life! In the first place, seeing that you both fight in an unrighteous cause, it is perfectly certain that all of you who shall perish in the struggle will be eternally lost, body and soul, for you will die in your sins, without repentance, without the succour of divine grace. The other calamity I foresee, with tearful eyes and bursting heart is, that Germany will become a prey to devastation; for once such a carnage as is now threatened shall begin, it can hardly terminate until all parties are involved in the destruction. It is very easy to begin the battle, but it will not be in our power to put a stop to it, when once begun. Madmen! What have the old men, the women, and children, whom you will drag down with you into destruction—what have they done to you, that you should fill the country with blood and rapine, that you should make so many widows and orphans?

Oh, this is a glorious, a joyful sight for the enemy of man! Satan must shout aloud with self-gratulation when he sees God thus terribly angry with us, thus menacing to overwhelm us with his wrath. Take heed, take heed, dear friends! you are all involved in the danger. I cannot think that, upon reflection, you will persist in damning yourselves eternally, and leaving behind you, in this world, a bleeding and burning country.

114 JOHN CALVIN, *INSTITUTES OF THE CHRISTIAN RELIGION*: CALVINISM

For a quarter of a century after the suppression of the Peasant Revolt (see Document 113) the cause of Lutheranism became closely allied with the cause of the German territorial princes struggling for power against the emperor. When the Schmalkaldic League of Lutheran princes and free cities, supported by Francis I of France, the rival of Emperor Charles V, finally went to war against the emperor in 1546, Germany sank into an anarchy of civil war between Lutheran and Catholic states. After nine years the conflict ended with the Peace of Augsburg in 1555. It was a great victory for Protestantism—by the terms of the peace treaty, each state of the empire had the right to choose either Lutheranism or Catholicism. Moreover, as each separate state went its own way—the northern ones becoming Lutheran and the southern remaining Catholic—the Peace of Augsburg also represented a step toward Germany's political disintegration.

The Peace of Augsburg made no mention of another important group of religious revolutionaries—the Calvinists. John Calvin (1509-1564), a Frenchman by birth and a lawyer by training, was Martin Luther's most brilliant pupil and the second greatest figure in the Protestant Reformation. More thorough and more logical than Lutheranism, Calvinism became the principal force for the international Protestant movement. Luther's appeal was largely confined to Germany and Scandinavia, for his writings served either as a policy guide for the action of German princes or as a program of opposition for German national feeling against Rome. By contrast, Calvin's writings contained universal arguments that could be applied in any area where people were dissatisfied with the Roman Church. The result was that outside of Germany—in France, in the Netherlands, in Britain, and ultimately in the American colonies—the Reformation was molded in Calvin's image, not in Luther's.

In a doctrinal sense Calvin accepted most of Luther's basic religious ideas, particularly justification by faith and the priesthood of all believers. However, Calvin placed much greater emphasis on the idea of predestination than did Luther. God, he said, knew all beforehand and had already decided who was to be saved and who damned. There was no positive way of knowing God's decision, but if a person lived a moral life and exerted himself always to resist temptation, it was a sign that he was in God's grace. As interpreted by Calvin, predestination thus became a challenge to unrelenting effort and unremitting toil. It was an uncompromising doctrine, but believers were fortified by the knowledge that they were doing battle for the Lord. Calvinists became resolute perfectionists; in England and later in America they were called Puritans.

The second major difference between Luther and Calvin lay in their attitude toward society and the state. Luther made religion subservient to the state; the good Christian, he said, owed perfect obedience to established authority. Calvin reversed this relationship by insisting that true Christians should Christianize the state and remake society into a religious community. In such a society all members, from the rulers on down, must live stern, saintly, disciplined lives. Calvin had an opportunity to put his ideas into practice in Geneva, and reformers from all over Europe flocked to that city to observe the model theocratic community. Geneva became the great international center of reformed doctrine, a kind of Protestant Rome.

Calvin's most important writing was the *Institutes of the Christian Religion*, originally published in 1536 when he was only twenty-seven. A work of enormous labor, well reasoned and well written, it represents a summing up of the whole of Protestant Christian doctrine and practice. In the selections below, Calvin presents the two chief ideas which characterize his theological system, the doctrine of providence (God's omniscience) and the doctrine of predestination. Especially significant is his statement that he regards "calling as the evidence of election"; it was the foundation upon which was later built the "Weber thesis" (see Document 117).

The Knowledge of God and of Ourselves Mutually Connected.—Nature of the Connection.

Our wisdom, in so far as it ought to be deemed true and solid wisdom, consists almost entirely of two parts: the knowledge of God and of ourselves. But as these are connected together by many ties, it is not easy to determine which of the two precedes, and gives birth to the other. For, in the first place, no man can survey himself without forthwith turning his thoughts towards the God in whom he lives and moves; because it is perfectly obvious, that the endowments which we possess cannot possibly be from ourselves; nay, that our very being is nothing else than subsistence in God alone. In the second place, those blessings which unceasingly distil to us from heaven, are like streams conducting us to the fountain. Here, again, the infinitude of good which resides in God becomes more apparent from our poverty. In particular, the miserable ruin into which the revolt of the first man has plunged us, compels us to turn our eyes upwards; not only that while hungry and famishing we may thence ask what we want, but being aroused by fear may learn humility. For as there exists in man something like a world of misery, and ever since we were stript of the divine attire our naked shame discloses an immense series of disgraceful properties, every man, being stung by the consciousness of his own unhappiness, in this way necessarily obtains at least some knowledge of God. Thus, our feeling of ignorance, vanity, want, weakness, in short, depravity and corruption, reminds us (see Calvin on John iv. 10) that in the Lord, and none but He, dwell the true light of wisdom, solid virtue, exuberant goodness. We are accordingly urged by our own evil things to consider the good things of God; and, indeed, we cannot aspire to Him in earnest until we have begun to be displeased with ourselves. For what man is not disposed to rest in himself? Who, in fact, does not thus rest, so long as he is unknown to himself; that is, so long as he is contented with his own endowments, and unconscious or unmindful of his misery? Every person, therefore, on coming to the knowledge of himself, is not only urged to seek God, but is also led as by the hand to find him.

On the other hand, it is evident that man never attains to a true self-knowledge until he have previously contemplated the face of God, and come down after such contemplation to look into himself. For (such is our innate pride) we always seem to ourselves just, and upright, and wise, and holy, until we are convinced, by clear evidence, of our injustice, vileness, folly, and impurity. Convinced, however, we are not, if we look to ourselves only, and not to the Lord also —He being the only standard by the application of which this conviction can be produced. For, since we are all naturally prone to hypocrisy, any empty semblance of righteousness is quite enough to satisfy us instead of righteousness itself. And since nothing appears within us or around us that is not tainted with very great impurity, so long as we keep our mind within the confines of human pollution, anything which is in some small degree less defiled, delights us as if it were most pure: just as an eye, to which nothing but black had been previously presented, deems an object of a whitish, or even of a brownish hue, to be perfectly white. Nay, the bodily sense may furnish a still stronger illustration of the extent to which we are deluded in estimating the powers of the mind. If, at mid-day, we either look down to the ground, or on the surrounding objects which lie open to our view, we think ourselves endued with a very strong and piercing eyesight; but when we look up to the sun, and gaze at it unveiled, the sight which did excellently well for the earth, is instantly so dazzled and confounded by the refulgence, as to oblige us to confess that our acuteness in discerning terrestrial objects is mere dimness when applied to the sun. Thus, too, it happens in estimating our spiritual qualities. So long as we do not look beyond the earth, we are quite pleased with our own righteousness, wisdom, and virtue; we address ourselves in the most flattering terms, and seem only less than demigods. But should we once begin to raise our thoughts to God, and reflect what kind of Being he is, and how absolute the perfection of that righteousness, and wisdom, and virtue, to which, as a standard, we are bound to be conformed, what formerly delighted us by its false show of righteousness, will become polluted with the greatest iniquity; what strangely imposed upon us under the name of wisdom, will disgust by its extreme folly; and what presented the appearance of virtuous energy, will be condemned as the most miserable impotence. So far are those qualities in us, which seem most perfect, from corresponding to the divine purity. . . .

Of the Eternal Election, by Which God Has Predestined Some to Salvation, and Others to Destruction.

The covenant of life is not preached equally to all, and among those to whom it is preached, does not always meet with the same reception. This diversity displays the unsearchable depth

Text: John Calvin, *Institutes of the Christian Religion*, trans. Henry Beveridge (Grand Rapids: Wm. B. Eerdmans Publishing Co., 1957), I, 37-39; II, 202-04, 206-07, 210-11.

of the divine judgment, and is without doubt subordinate to God's purpose of eternal election. But if it is plainly owing to the mere pleasure of God that salvation is spontaneously offered to some, while others have no access to it, great and difficult questions immediately arise, questions which are inexplicable, when just views are not entertained concerning election and predestination. To many this seems a perplexing subject, because they deem it most incongruous that of the great body of mankind some should be predestinated to salvation, and others to destruction. How causelessly they entangle themselves will appear as we proceed. We may add, that in the very obscurity which deters them, we may see not only the utility of this doctrine, but also its most pleasant fruits. We shall never feel persuaded as we ought that our salvation flows from the free mercy of God as its fountain, until we are made acquainted with his eternal election, the grace of God being illustrated by the contrast—viz. that he does not adopt promiscuously to the hope of salvation, but gives to some what he denies to others. It is plain how greatly ignorance of this principle detracts from the glory of God, and impairs true humility. But though thus necessary to be known, Paul declares that it cannot be known unless God, throwing works entirely out of view, elect those whom he has predestined. His words are, "Even so then at this present time also, there is a remnant according to the election of grace. And if by grace, then it is no more of works: otherwise grace is no more grace. But if it be of works, then it is no more grace: otherwise work is no more work" (Rom. xi. 6). If to make it appear that our salvation flows entirely from the good mercy of God, we must be carried back to the origin of election, then those who would extinguish it, wickedly do as much as in them lies to obscure what they ought most loudly to extol, and pluck up humility by the very roots. Paul clearly declares that it is only when the salvation of a remnant is ascribed to gratuitous election, we arrive at the knowledge that God saves whom he wills of his mere good pleasure, and does not pay a debt, a debt which never can be due. Those who preclude access, and would not have any one to obtain a taste of this doctrine, are equally unjust to God and men, there being no other means of humbling us as we ought, or making us feel how much we are bound to him. Nor, indeed, have we elsewhere any sure ground of confidence. This we say on the authority of Christ, who, to deliver us from all fear, and render us invincible amid our many dangers, snares, and mortal conflicts, promises safety to all that the Father hath taken under his protection (John x. 26). From this we infer, that all who know not that they are the peculiar people of God, must be wretched from perpetual trepidation, and that those, therefore, who, by overlooking the three advantages which we have noted, would destroy the very foundation of our safety, consult ill for themselves and for all the faithful. What? Do we not here find the very origin of the Church, which, as Bernard rightly teaches (Serm. in Cantic.), could not be found or recognised among the creatures, because it lies hid (in both cases wondrously) within the lap of blessed predestination, and the mass of wretched condemnation?

But before I enter on the subject, I have some remarks to address to two classes of men. The subject of predestination, which in itself is attended with considerable difficulty, is rendered very perplexed, and hence perilous by human curiosity, which cannot be restrained from wandering into forbidden paths, and climbing to the clouds, determined if it can that none of the secret things of God shall remain unexplored. When we see many, some of them in other respects not bad men, everywhere rushing into this audacity and wickedness, it is necessary to remind them of the course of duty in this matter. First, then, when they inquire into predestination, let them remember that they are penetrating into the recesses of the divine wisdom, where he who rushes forward securely and confidently instead of satisfying his curiosity will enter an inextricable labyrinth. For it is not right that man should with impunity pry into things which the Lord has been pleased to conceal within himself, and scan that sublime eternal wisdom which it is his pleasure that we should not apprehend but adore, that therein also his perfections may appear. Those secrets of his will, which he has seen it meet to manifest, are revealed in his word—revealed in so far as he knew to be conducive to our interest and welfare. . . .

The predestination by which God adopts some of the hope of life, and adjudges others to eternal death, no man who would be thought pious ventures simply to deny; but it is greatly cavilled at, especially by those who make prescience its cause. We, indeed, ascribe both prescience and predestination to God; but we say that it is absurd to make the latter subordinate to the former (see chap. xxii. sec. 1). When we attribute prescience to God, we mean that all things always were, and ever continue, under his eye; that to his knowledge there is no past or future, but all things are present, and indeed so present, that it is not merely the idea of them that is before him (as those objects are which we retain in our memory), but that he truly sees and contemplates them as actually under his immediate inspection. This prescience extends to the whole circuit of the world, and to all creatures. By predestination we mean the eternal decree of God, by which he determined with himself whatever he wished to happen with regard to every man. All are not created on equal terms, but some are preordained to eternal life, others to eternal damnation; and, accordingly, as each has been created for one or other of these ends, we say that he has been predestined to life or to death. This God has testified, not only in the case of single individuals; he has also given a specimen of it in the whole posterity of Abraham, to make it plain that the future condition of each nation was entirely at his disposal. . . .

. . . We say, then, that Scripture clearly proves this much, that God by his eternal and immutable counsel determined once for all those whom it was his pleasure one day to admit to salvation, and those whom, on the other hand, it was his pleasure to doom to destruction. We maintain that this counsel, as regards the elect, is founded on his free mercy, without any respect to human worth, while those whom he dooms to destruction are excluded from access to life by a just and blameless, but at the same time incomprehensible judgment. In regard to the elect, we regard calling as the evidence of election, and justification as another symbol of its manifestation, until it is fully accomplished by the attainment of glory. But as the Lord seals his elect by calling and justification, so by excluding the reprobate either from the knowledge of his name or the sanctification of his Spirit, he by these marks in a manner discloses the judgment which awaits them. I will here omit many of the fictions which foolish men have devised to overthrow predestination. There is no need of refuting objections which the moment they are produced abundantly betray their hollowness. I will dwell only on those points which either form the subject of dispute among the learned, or may occasion any difficulty to the simple, or may be employed by impiety as specious pretexts for assailing the justice of God.

115 ACT FOR THE EXONERATION FROM EXACTIONS PAID TO THE SEE OF ROME AND ACT OF SUPREMACY: HENRY VIII, SUPREME HEAD OF THE CHURCH OF ENGLAND

The Reformation spread to Scotland when John Knox introduced Calvinism there in the 1550's and established the Presbyterian Church. In the remainder of Britain, however, the Reformation developed in a uniquely English fashion. Henry VIII (1491-1547) had no desire to change Catholic doctrine. Indeed, when he learned that Lutheran ideas were being bruited about in England, he promptly wrote a *Defense of the Sacraments* (1520), for which the grateful pope bestowed upon him the title "Defender of the Faith." Proud of his religious orthodoxy, Henry's chief concern was political and dynastic: he was worried because his wife had produced no male heir through whom the Tudor monarchy could be perpetuated. Fundamentally it was this desire for a son that led to his break with the papacy.

Normally the pope would have granted Henry's request for an annulment of his marriage to Catherine of Aragon so that he might remarry. The difficulty lay in the fact that Catherine's nephew was the Emperor Charles V, who at that very moment was besieging Rome. The pope tried desperately to stall for time, wishing to offend neither Charles nor Henry. Henry, impatient and impetuous, decided to take matters into his own hands. By posing as a victim of papal policy, he was able to capitalize on the rising tide of antipapalism and anticlericalism to increase his own popularity. His first tactic was to use intimidation; he allowed Parliament to attack clerical abuses in England and to pass a law which permitted the king to suspend the payment of annates to the papacy. When this failed to persuade the pope, Henry appointed a new archbishop of Canterbury. The archbishop was head of the highest ecclesiastical court in the country and to this court Henry submitted his request for annulment. In May 1533 the court ruled in favor of the king; a few days later Henry was excommunicated by the pope.

Henry wanted to have the break with Rome legalized. The following year, 1534, Parliament stopped all payments of the English clergy to the papacy, gave the king the power to confirm ecclesiastical appointments, and forbade the payment of Peter's pence (an annual tribute by every householder) to the papal curia. Most important of all, it passed the Act of Supremacy declaring the king to be "the supreme head of the Church of England." By these acts Parliament greatly enhanced the power of the king and placed the English Church under the complete control of the state. When Sir Thomas More, the former Lord Chancellor, refused to take an oath in support of the act, he was beheaded. (See Document 94.) Since Henry had no desire to introduce doctrinal innovations and wanted only to be head of the English Catholic Church, no major changes in principles or practice were made during his reign. The Anglican Church in its "protestantized" form emerged during the reign of his daughter, Elizabeth I (1558-1603). Henry, however, did take advantage of the clauses in the Act of Supremacy which entitled him to all "preëminences, jurisdictions, privileges and profits" pertaining to the clergy by closing all monasteries and confiscating their extensive land holdings. These lands, which comprised about a tenth of the national wealth, Henry distributed to his many followers. He thus created a new landed gentry that remained loyal to both the Tudor monarchy and the Anglican Church, regardless of what its doctrines might be.

An Act for the Exoneration from exactions paid to the See of Rome.

Most humble beseeching your most Royal Majesty your obedient and faithful subjects the Commons of this your present Parliament assembled by your most dread commandment; That where your subjects of this your Realm, and of other countries and dominions being under your obeisance, by many years past have been and yet be greatly decayed and impoverished by such intolerable exactions of great sums of money as have been claimed and taken and yet continually be claimed to be taken out of this your Realm and other your said countries and dominions, by the Bishop of Rome called the Pope and the See of Rome, as well in pensions, censes, Peter's pence, procurations, fruits, suits, for provisions and expeditions, of bulls for archbishoprics and bishoprics, and for delegacies and rescripts in causes of contentions and appeals, jurisdictions legatine, and also for dispensations, licenses, faculties, grants, relaxations, writs called *perinde valere*, rehabilitations, abolitions, and other infinite sorts of bulls, breves, and instruments of sundry natures, names, and kinds in great numbers heretofore practiced and obtained otherwise than by the laws, laudable uses, and customs of this Realm should be permitted, the specialities whereof been over long large in number and tedious here particularly to be inserted; wherein the Bishop of Rome aforesaid hath not been only to be blamed for his usurpation in the premises but also for his abusing and beguiling your subjects, pretending and persuading to them that he hath full power to dispense with all humane laws, uses, and customs of all Realms in all causes which he called spiritual, which matter hath been usurped and practiced by him and his predecessors by many years in great derogation of your imperial crown and authority royal contrary to right and conscience; For where this your Grace's Realm, recognizing no superior under God but only your Grace, hath been and is free from subjection to any man's laws, but only to such as have been devised, made, and ordained within this Realm for the wealth of the same, or to such other as by sufferance of your Grace and your progenitors the people of this your Realm have taken at their free liberty by their own consent to be used among them, and have bound themselves by long use and custom to the observance of the same, not as to the observance of the laws of any foreign prince, potentate, or prelate, but as to the accustomed and ancient laws of this Realm originally established as laws of the same by the said sufferance, consents, and custom, and none otherwise: It standeth therefore with natural equity and good reason that in all and every such laws humane, made within this Realm or induced into this Realm by the said sufferance, consents, and customs, your Royal Majesty and your Lords Spiritual and Temporal and Commons, representing the whole state of your Realm in this your most high Court of Parliament, have full power and authority not only to dispense but also to authorize some elected person or persons to dispense with those and all other humane laws of this your Realm and with every one of them, as the quality of the persons and matter shall require; And also the said laws and every of them to abrogate, annul, amplify, or diminish as it shall be seen unto your Majesty and the nobles and Commons of your Realm present in your Parliament meet and convenient for the wealth of your Realm, as by divers good and wholesome acts of Parliament's made and established as well in your time as in the time of your most noble progenitors it may plainly and evi-

Text: The Statutes of the Realm; Printed by Command of His Majesty George the Third (London, 1817), III, 464-71, 492 *passim*. The spelling has been modernized.

dently appear; And by cause that it is now in these days present seen that the state, dignity, superiority, reputation, and authority of the said imperial Crown of this Realm by the long sufferance of the said unreasonable and uncharitable usurpations and exactions practiced in the times of your most noble progenitors is much and sore decayed and diminished, and the people of this Realm thereby impoverished and so or worse be like to continue if remedy be not therefore shortly provided:

It may therefore please your most noble Majesty for the honour of Almighty God and for the tender love, zeal, and affection that ye bear and always have borne to the wealth of this your Realm and subjects of the same, for as much as your Majesty is supreme head of the Church of England as the prelates and clergy of your Realm representing the said church in their synods and convocations have recognized, in whom consisteth full power and authority upon all such laws as have been made and used within this Realm, to ordain and enact by the assent of your Lords Spiritual and Temporal and the Commons in this your present Parliament assembled and by authority of the same, that no person or persons of this your Realm or of any other your Dominions shall from henceforth pay any pensions, censes, portions, Peter's pence, or any other impositions to the use of the said Bishop or of the See of Rome, like as heretofore they have used by usurpation of the said Bishop of Rome and his predecessors and sufferance of your Highness and your most noble progenitors to do; but that all such pensions, censes, portions and Peter's pence, which the said Bishop of Rome otherwise called the Pope hath heretofore taken and perceived or caused to be taken and perceived to his use and his chambers which he calleth Apostolic by usurpation and sufferance as is above said within this your Realm or any other your dominions, shall from henceforth clearly surcease and never more be levied, taken, perceived, nor paid to any person or persons in any manner of wise; any constitution, use, prescription, or custom to the contrary thereof notwithstanding. . . .

Act of Supremacy

Albeit the King's Majesty justly and rightfully is and oweth to be the supreme head of the Church of England, and so is recognized by the clergy of this Realm in their convocations; yet nevertheless for corroboration and confirmation thereof, and for increase of virtue in Christ's religion within this Realm of England, and to repress and extirpate all errours, heresies, and other enormities and abuses heretofore used in the same, Be it enacted by authority of this present Parliament that the King our Sovereign Lord, his heirs, and successours, kings of this Realm, shall be taken, accepted, and reputed the only supreme head in earth of the Church of England called *Anglicana Ecclesia*, and shall have and enjoy, annexed and united to the Imperial Crown of this Realm as well the title and style thereof, as all honours, dignities, preëminences, jurisdictions, privileges, authorities, immunities, profits, and commodities to the said dignity of supreme head of the same Church belonging and appertaining: And that our said Sovereign Lord, his heirs, and successours, kings of this Realm shall have full power and authority from time to time to visit, repress, redress, reform, order, correct, restrain, and amend all such errours, heresies, abuses, offences, contempts, and enormities whatsoever they be, which by any manner spiritual authority or jurisdiction ought or may lawfully be reformed, repressed, ordered, redressed, corrected, restrained, or amended, most to the pleasure of Almighty God the increase of virtue in Christ's religion and for the conservation of the peace, unity, and tranquility of this Realm: any usage, customs, foreign laws, foreign authority, prescription, or any other thing or things to the contrary hereof notwithstanding.

116 ST. IGNATIUS LOYOLA, *SPIRITUAL EXERCISES*: THE COUNTER REFORMATION

The Catholic Church did not stand idly by as the tide of Protestantism mounted ever higher. Motivated in part by a genuine desire to correct existing abuses and in part by a need to meet the specific Protestant challenge, the Church developed within itself a number of instruments with which to conduct a Catholic or Counter Reformation. The most important of these new instruments were not initiated directly by the papacy but sprang from the collective efforts of clergy and laymen alike, although those efforts were organized within the institutional framework of the ecclesiastical apparatus. A case in point was the demand for a general Church council to reform abuses. Although the Conciliar Movement had been defeated by the popes around 1450, pressure for a new council revived after 1500. Despite continued resistance from the popes, who feared the political complications and dangers of such a council, the demand became too insistent to be refused. In 1545 the pope relented and convened a general council at the city of Trent. The Council of Trent met over a period of nearly twenty years (1545-1563), and its historic decisions set the course for all modern Catholicism. By reaffirming the principle of papal supremacy it warded off the threat of dissolution into national churches and preserved the papacy as a center of unity for the Catholic Church. Refusing to make concessions to the Protestants, it restated Catholic doctrine and practice in clear, authoritative terms. The council also decreed a series of reforms, particularly for monastic orders, thereby strengthening the structure of ecclesiastical administration.

The deliberations and decisions of the Council of Trent were given added strength by the resurgence of a profound spirit of religious piety. This new Catholic religious feeling manifested itself in the appearance of a number of men imbued with a strong moral fervor. By the mid-sixteenth century, for example, a group of reforming popes began to dominate the Vatican and provided the leadership for powerful constructive forces astir within the Catholic world. The most vigorous of these forces expressed itself in a revival of reformist monasticism, notably in Spain and Italy, where monastic orders developed in great profusion. Probably the most famous of the new monastic orders was the Society of Jesus, founded by Ignatius Loyola (1491-1556), a Spanish nobleman and ex-soldier. During a long convalescence from a battle wound, Loyola experienced a religious conversion and resolved to devote the rest of his life to a militant crusade for the Church and the papacy. The society he created, which was authorized by the pope in 1540, was a new type of monastic order. The Jesuits were governed by an iron discipline and dedicated themselves to preaching and teaching; they placed the greatest emphasis upon educating the young, and so successful did they become in this field that for two hundred years they were the chief schoolmasters of Catholic Europe. As preachers the Jesuits became an effective international missionary force and won back to Catholicism large numbers of people in France, Germany, Bohemia, Poland, and Hungary. The Society of Jesus was, in fact, the single most important instrument of the Catholic Reformation.

Every Jesuit had to undergo an exacting training which Loyola set forth in his *Spiritual Exercises*. In addition to inculcating absolute obedience to superior authority and the infallibility of the Catholic Church, the *Exercises* required of each candidate a rigorous, mystical training. The consequence was that only men of proven intellectual force and strength of character were admitted to the order. The rigor of that mysticism is revealed in the selection below, which comprises the first two exercises. One should note the basic principle and foundation upon which the whole *Spiritual Exercises* is predicated. Would Luther and Calvin have accepted that principle? In what way did the new emphasis on science represent a challenge to this proposition?

The First Exercise Is a Meditation with the Three Powers upon the First, Second, and Third Sin. It Contains in Itself, after One Preparatory Prayer and Two Preludes, Three Principal Points and a Colloquy.

Prayer. The preparatory prayer is to ask grace of God our Lord that all my intentions, actions and operations may be ordered purely to the service and praise of His Divine Majesty.

First Prelude. The first prelude is a composition, seeing the place. Here it is to be noticed that in a contemplation, or visible meditation, such as contemplating Christ our Lord, who is visible, the composition will be to see with the sight of the imagination the corporeal place where is found the object that I wish to contemplate. I say the corporeal place, such as a temple or mountain where is found Jesus Christ or Our Lady, according to what I wish to contemplate.

In the invisible, such as is here of the sins, the composition will be to see with the imaginative sight, and to consider my soul to be imprisoned in this corruptible body, and the whole substance to be in this valley, as though exiled among brute animals. I say the whole substance, soul and body.

Second Prelude. The second is to ask of God our Lord what I want and desire. The petition must be according to the subject-matter: that is to say, if the contemplation is of the resurrection, to ask for joy with Christ rejoicing: if it is of the Passion, to ask for pain, tears, and torment with Christ tormented. Here it will be to ask for shame and confusion at myself, seeing how many

Text: The Rev. C. Lattey, S.J. (ed.), *The Spiritual Exercises of St. Ignatius* (St. Louis: B. Herder Book Company, 1928), pp. 25-31, 159-63.

have been marred through a single mortal sin, and how often I have deserved to be condemned for ever for my so many sins.

Note. Before all contemplations or meditations, there should always be made the preparatory prayer without any change, and the two preludes already mentioned, changing them sometimes according to the subject-matter.

First Point. The first point will be to take the memory over the first sin, which was that of the angels, and then the understanding over the same, reasoning, and then the will, wishing to remember and understand all this in order to shame and confound myself the more, bringing into comparison with a single sin of the angels my so many sins: and whereas they, for one sin, went to hell, how many times I have deserved it for so many. I say, to call to mind the sin of the angels, how they were created in grace, and not being willing to assist themselves with their liberty to pay reverence and obedience to their Creator and Lord, coming to pride, were changed from grace to malice, and cast down from heaven to hell: and thereupon in this way to discourse more in detail with the understanding, and thereupon to move the affections more by the will.

Second Point. The second: to do the same again, that is to say, to take the three powers over the sin of Adam and Eve, bringing to the memory how for that sin they did penance for so long a time, and how much corruption came into the human race, so many people going to hell. I say, to call to mind the second sin, that of our parents: how, after Adam had been created in the plain of Damascus and placed in the terrestrial paradise, and after Eve had been created from his rib, being forbidden to eat of the tree of knowledge, they ate and thereby sinned, and afterwards, clothed in tunics of skins and cast out from Paradise, lived without the original justice, which they had lost, all their life in many labours and much penance. And thereupon to discourse with the understanding more in detail, using the will as has been said.

Third Point. The third: in the same manner, to do as much again upon the third sin, the particular sin of each person who for one mortal sin has gone to hell, and many others without number have done so for less sins than I have committed. I say, to do as much again upon the third, the particular sin, calling to mind the gravity and malice of the sin against his Creator and Lord: and to discourse with the understanding, considering how, for sinning and acting against the Infinite Goodness, he has justly been condemned for ever: and to conclude with the will as has been said.

Colloquy. Imagining Christ our Lord present and placed upon the cross, to make a colloquy, considering how from Creator He came to make Himself man, and from eternal life came to temporal death, and thus to die for my sins. In like manner, looking at myself, to consider what I have done for Christ: what I am doing for Christ: what I ought to do for Christ. And then, seeing Him such as He is, and thus hanging on the cross, to discourse of what may offer itself.

The colloquy is made, properly speaking, just as one friend talks to another, or a servant to his master, now asking for some favour, now blaming himself for some ill deed, now disclosing his affairs and seeking counsel in them. And a *Pater noster* is said.

The Second Exercise Is Meditation on One's Sins, and Contains in Itself after the Preparatory Prayer and Two Preludes, Five Points and a Colloquy.

Prayer. Let the preparatory prayer be the same.

The First Prelude. The first prelude will be the same composition.

The Second Prelude. The second is to ask what I want: here it will be to beg for ever-growing and intense sorrow and tears for my sins.

First Point. The first point is the review of one's sins, that is to say, to call to mind all the sins of one's life, looking at it year by year or period by period; for which three things are useful. The first, to observe the place and house in which I have dwelt: the second, the intercourse I have held with others: the third, the calling in which I have lived.

Second Point. The second: to weigh the sins, considering the foulness and malice which every mortal sin committed contains in itself, even if it were not forbidden.

Third Point. The third: to consider who I am, belittling myself by examples: first, what I am in comparison with all mankind: secondly, what are men in comparison with all the angels and saints of Paradise: thirdly, to consider what is all that is created in comparison with God: I alone, then, what can I be? Fourthly, to look at all my corruption and bodily filth: fifthly, to look upon myself as a wound and ulcer whence have come forth so many sins and so many iniquities, and poison so utterly foul.

Fourth Point. The fourth: to consider who God is against whom I have sinned, according to His attributes, comparing them with their contraries in myself: His wisdom with my ignorance: His omnipotence with my weakness: His justice with my iniquity: His goodness with my malice.

Fifth Point. The fifth: an exclamation of wonder with ever-growing emotion, passing in review all creatures, how they have left me in life and preserved me in it: the angels, though they are the sword of the divine justice, how they have borne with me and protected and prayed for me: the saints, how they have been interceding and praying for me: and the heavens, sun, moon, stars and elements, fruits, birds, fish, and animals: and the earth, how it has not opened itself to swallow me up, creating new hells that I might suffer for ever in them.

Colloquy. To end with a colloquy of mercy, reflecting and giving thanks to God our Lord because He has given me life until now, proposing amendment by His grace in future. *Pater noster.*

For the True Feeling Which in the Church Militant We Ought to Have, Let the Following Rules Be Kept.

First Rule. The first: laying aside all judgment, we ought to keep a mind prepared and prompt to obey in everything the true Spouse of Christ our Lord, which is our Holy Mother the Hierarchical Church.

Second Rule. The second: to praise confession to a priest, and the receiving of the Most Holy Sacrament once in the year, and much more in every month, and much better from week to week, with the conditions required and due.

Third Rule. The third: to praise the hearing Mass often, likewise chants, psalms, and long prayers in the church and outside of it; likewise the hours arranged at appointed times for every divine office, and for all prayer and all canonical hours.

Fourth Rule. The fourth: to praise much religious orders, virginity and continence, and not so much matrimony as any of these.

Fifth Rule. The fifth: to praise vows of religion, of obedience, of poverty, of chastity, and of other perfections of supererogation; and it is to be noticed that since a vow regards things which approach to evangelical perfection, in the things which depart from it a vow ought not to be made, such as to be a merchant, or to be married, *etc.*

Sixth Rule. To praise relics of saints, showing veneration to the former, and praying to the latter: praising stations, pilgrimages, indulgences, jubilees, *bullae cruciatae,* and candles lit in the churches. .

Seventh Rule. To praise constitutions regarding fasts and abstinences, such as of Lent, Ember Days, vigils, Friday and Saturday; likewise penances, not only interior but also exterior.

Eighth Rule. To praise adornments and buildings of churches; likewise images, and to venerate them according to what they represent.

Ninth Rule. Finally, to praise all precepts of the Church, holding the mind ready to seek reasons in her defence, and in no way for attacking her.

Tenth Rule. We ought to be more ready to approve and to praise both ordinances, recommendations and behavior of our superiors; for although some of these may not be, or may not have been, praiseworthy, yet to speak against them, whether in public preaching, or in talking before the common people, would beget more murmuring and scandal than profit; and thus the people would become indignant against their superiors, whether temporal or spiritual. Nevertheless, as it does harm to speak evil of superiors in their absence to the common people, so it may profit to speak of their evil behaviour to the persons themselves who can remedy them.

Eleventh Rule. To praise the positive and scholastic doctrine; for as it is more peculiar to the positive Doctors, such as Saint Jerome, Saint Augustine and Saint Gregory, *etc.*, to move the feelings to love and to serve God our Lord in everything; so it is more peculiar to the scholastics, such as Saint Thomas, Saint Bonaventure and the Master of the Sentences, *etc.*, to define or to explain for our own times the things necessary for eternal salvation, and which better assail and expose all errors and all fallacies. For the scholastic doctors, as they are more modern, not only profit by the right understanding of the Holy Scripture and of the positive and holy doctors; but further, being themselves illuminated and enlightened by the divine power, they assist themselves by the councils, canons and constitutions of our holy Mother Church.

Twelfth Rule. We ought to be careful about making comparisons between those who are alive with us and the blessed departed; for no small mistake is made in this, that is to say, in saying, "This man knows more than Saint Augustine," "he is another or greater Saint Francis," "he is another Saint Paul in goodness, sanctity, *etc.*"

Thirteenth Rule. We ought always to hold, in order to be right in every way, that the white which I see, I believe to be black, if the Hierarchical Church so determines it; believing that between Christ our Lord the Bridegroom and the Church His bride is the same Spirit which governs and directs us for the salvation of our souls; for by the same Spirit and our Lord who gave the ten commandments, is directed and governed our Holy Mother Church.

Fourteenth. Although it is very true' that no one can be saved without being predestined, and without possessing faith and grace, much attention must be given to the manner of speaking and treating of all these matters.

Fifteenth. We ought not to speak much of predestination by way of custom; but if in some manner and sometimes one should speak of it, one should so speak that the common people may not come to any error, as sometimes they are wont to, saying, "Whether I am to be saved or condemned is already decided, and cannot now be otherwise on account of any well or ill doing of mine." And being rendered torpid by this, they neglect the works which conduce to the salvation and spiritual profit of their souls.

Sixteenth. In the same way care must be taken lest by speaking much of faith with great stress, without any distinction and explanation, occasion be given to the people to become torpid and slothful in works, whether before faith is informed with charity or afterwards.

Seventeenth. Likewise we ought not to speak at such length, and with such insistence, about grace, that poison may be engendered, whereby liberty may be taken away. So that of faith and grace one may speak, as far as it may be possible by means of the divine help, for the greater praise of His Divine Majesty; but not in such sort nor by such methods, especially in our so dangerous times, that works and free will receive any detriment or be accounted as nothing.

Eighteenth. Although to serve our Lord much for pure love is above all to be esteemed, yet we ought also to praise much the fear of His Divine Majesty; because not only filial fear is a thing pious and most holy, but even servile fear, where a man does not attain to anything better or more profitable, helps much towards coming forth from mortal sin; and having come forth, he easily comes to the filial fear, which is wholly acceptable and pleasing to God our Lord, because it is in union with the divine Love.

INTERPRETATIONS OF PROTESTANTISM AND REFORMATION

117 R. H. TAWNEY, *RELIGION AND THE RISE OF CAPITALISM:* PROTESTANTISM AND CAPITALISM

On the face of it there would appear to be little or no connection between two such diverse movements as Protestantism and capitalism. In 1904-1905, however, a German sociologist named Max Weber published a study entitled "The Protestant Ethic and the Spirit of Capitalism." Ever since then, scholars throughout the western world have argued about the "Weber thesis." The idea of a "spirit of capitalism" was not original with Weber; he had borrowed it from the German economist Werner Sombart. Indeed, he agreed with Sombart that this "spirit of capitalism" was one of the crucial factors in the development of our modern capitalistic economy. Unlike Sombart, however, Weber was curious about the source or origin of this capitalistic "spirit" and speculated that the answer might be found in religion. More specifically he suggested that it was the religious tenets and social effects of Calvinism that gave rise to the "spirit of capitalism."

Among those who accepted the Weber thesis in its major outlines was R. H. Tawney (1880-   ), a noted English economist and economic historian. In 1926 he published a work entitled *Religion and the Rise of Capitalism*, a book that has been even more widely read in the English-speaking world than Weber's original essays. Tawney, however, viewed the problem in far broader perspective than did Weber. "The capitalist spirit," he pointed out, "is as old as history, and was not . . . the offspring of Puritanism. But it found in certain aspects of later Puritanism a tonic which braced its energies and fortified its already vigorous temper." In effect, Tawney rejected Weber's emphasis on the unique role of Calvinism as inadequate to explain the overall relationship between Protestantism and capitalism. One had to consider the Protestant movement as a whole and also take into account general political, social, and economic conditions during the sixteenth and seventeenth centuries. As Tawney makes clear in the passage below, Calvinism was an urban movement and sought to moralize a type of life "in which the main features of a commercial civilization are taken for granted." Thus, while the spirit of capitalism existed long before Calvinism, the significance of Calvinism was that it transformed that spirit into a positive moral virtue and, incidentally, made it one of the prime movers of western society.

The most characteristic and influential form of Protestantism in the two centuries following the Reformation is that which descends, by one path or another, from the teaching of Calvin. Unlike the Lutheranism from which it sprang, Calvinism, assuming different shapes in different countries, became an international movement, which brought, not peace, but a sword, and the path of which was strewn with revolutions. Where Lutheranism had been socially conservative, deferential to established political authorities, the exponent of a personal, almost a quietistic, piety, Calvinism was an active and radical force. It was a creed which sought, not merely to purify the individual, but to reconstruct Church and State, and to renew society by penetrating every department of life, public as well as private, with the influence of religion.

Upon the immense political reactions of Calvinism, this is not the place to enlarge. As a way of life and a theory of society, it possessed from the beginning one characteristic which was both novel and important. It assumed an economic organization which was relatively advanced, and expounded its social ethics on the basis of it. In this respect the teaching of the Puritan moralists who derive most directly from Calvin is in marked contrast with that both of medieval theologians and of Luther. The difference is not merely one of the conclusions reached, but of the plane on which the discussion is conducted. The background, not only of most medieval theory, but also of Luther and his English contemporaries, is the traditional stratification of rural society. It is a natural, rather than a money, economy, consisting of the petty dealings of peasants and craftsmen in the small market town, where industry is carried on for the subsistence of the household and the consumption of wealth follows hard upon the production of it, and where commerce and finance are occasional incidents, rather than the forces which keep the whole system in motion. When they criticize economic abuses, it is precisely against departures from that natural state of things—against the enterprise, the greed of gain, the restless competition, which disturb the stability of the existing order with clamorous economic appetites—that their criticism is directed.

These ideas were the traditional retort to the evils of unscrupulous commercialism, and they left some trace on the writings of the Swiss reformers. Zwingli, for example, who, in his outlook on society, stood midway between Luther and Calvin, insists on the oft-repeated thesis that private property originates in sin; warns the rich that they can hardly enter the Kingdom of Heaven; denounces the Councils of Constance and Basel—"assembled, forsooth, at the bidding of the Holy Ghost"—for showing indulgence to the mortgaging of land on the security of crops; and, while emphasizing that interest must be paid when the State sanctions it, condemns it in itself as contrary to the law of God. Of the attempts made at Zürich and Geneva to repress extortion something is said below. But these full-blooded denunciations of capitalism were not intended by their authors to supply a rule of practical life, since it was the duty of the individual to comply with the secular legislation by which interest was permitted, and already, when they were uttered, they had ceased to represent the conclusion of the left wing of the Reformed Churches.

For Calvin, and still more his later interpreters, began their voyage lower down the stream. Unlike Luther, who saw economic life with the eyes of a peasant and a mystic, they approached it as men of affairs, disposed neither to idealize the patriarchal virtues of the peasant community, nor to regard with suspicion the mere fact of capitalist enterprise in commerce and finance. Like early Christianity and modern socialism, Calvinism was largely an urban movement; like them, in its earlier days, it was carried from country to country partly by emigrant traders and workmen; and its stronghold was precisely in those social groups to which the traditional scheme of social ethics, with its treatment of economic interests as a quite minor aspect of human affairs, must have seemed irrelevant or artificial. As was to be expected in the exponents of a faith which had its headquarters at Geneva, and later its most influential adherents in great business centers, like Antwerp, with its industrial hinterland, London, and Amsterdam, its leaders addressed their teaching, not of course exclusively, but none the less primarily, to the classes engaged in trade and industry, who formed the most modern and progressive elements in the life of the age.

In doing so they naturally started from a frank recognition of the necessity of capital, credit and banking, large-scale commerce and finance, and the other practical facts of business life. They thus broke with the tradition which, regarding a preoccupation with economic interests "beyond what is necessary for subsistence" as reprehensible, had stigmatized the middleman as a parasite and the usurer as a thief. They set the profits of trade and finance, which to the medieval writer,

Text: Reprinted by permission of the publishers from R. H. Tawney, *Religion and the Rise of Capitalism.* Copyright 1926 by Harcourt, Brace & World, Inc.; renewed 1954 by R. H. Tawney. Pp. 102-10.

as to Luther, only with difficulty escaped censure as *turpe lucrum,* on the same level of respectability as the earnings of the laborer and the rents of the landlord. "What reason is there," wrote Calvin to a correspondent, "why the income from business should not be larger than that from land-owning? Whence do the merchant's profits come, except from his own diligence and industry?" It was quite in accordance with the spirit of those words that Bucer, even while denouncing the frauds and avarice of merchants, should urge the English Government to undertake the development of the woollen industry on mercantilist lines.

Since it is the environment of the industrial and commercial classes which is foremost in the thoughts of Calvin and his followers, they have to make terms with its practical necessities. It is not that they abandon the claim of religion to moralize economic life, but that the life which they are concerned to moralize is one in which the main features of a commercial civilization are taken for granted, and that it is for application to such conditions that their teaching is designed. Early Calvinism, as we shall see, has its own rule, and a rigorous rule, for the conduct of economic affairs. But it no longer suspects the whole world of economic motives as alien to the life of the spirit, or distrusts the capitalist as one who has necessarily grown rich on the misfortunes of his neighbor, or regards poverty as in itself meritorious, and it is perhaps the first systematic body of religious teaching which can be said to recognize and applaud the economic virtues. Its enemy is not the accumulation of riches, but their misuse for purposes of self-indulgence or ostentation. Its ideal is a society which seeks wealth with the sober gravity of men who are conscious at once of disciplining their own characters by patient labor, and of devoting themselves to a service acceptable to God.

It is in the light of that change of social perspective that the doctrine of usury associated with the name of Calvin is to be interpreted. Its significance consisted, not in the phase which it marked in the technique of economic analysis, but in its admission to a new position of respectability of a powerful and growing body of social interests, which, however irrepressible in practice, had hitherto been regarded by religious theory as, at best, of dubious propriety, and, at worst, as frankly immoral. Strictly construed, the famous pronouncement strikes the modern reader rather by its rigor than by its indulgence. "Calvin," wrote an English divine a generation after his death, "deals with usurie as the apothecarie doth with poyson." The apologetic was just, for neither his letter to Oecolampadius, nor his sermon on the same subject, reveal any excessive tolerance for the trade of the financier. That interest is lawful, provided that it does not exceed an official maximum, that, even when a maximum is fixed, loans must be made *gratis* to the poor, that the borrower must reap as much advantage as the lender, that excessive security must not be exacted, that what is venial as an occasional expedient is reprehensible when carried on as a regular occupation, that no man may snatch economic gain for himself to the injury of his neighbor—a condonation of usury protected by such embarrassing entanglements can have offered but tepid consolation to the devout moneylender.

Contemporaries interpreted Calvin to mean that the debtor might properly be asked to concede some small part of his profits to the creditor with whose capital they had been earned, but that the exaction of interest was wrong if it meant that "the creditor becomes rich by the sweat of the debtor, and the debtor does not reap the reward of his labor." There have been ages in which such doctrines would have been regarded as an attack on financial enterprise rather than as a defense of it. Nor were Calvin's specific contributions to the theory of usury strikingly original. As a hard-headed lawyer, he was free both from the incoherence and from the idealism of Luther, and his doctrine was probably regarded by himself merely as one additional step in the long series of developments through which ecclesiastical jurisprudence on the subject had already gone. In emphasizing the difference between the interest wrung from the necessities of the poor and the interest which a prosperous merchant could earn with borrowed capital, he had been anticipated by Major; in his sanction of a moderate rate on loans to the rich, his position was the same as that already assumed, though with some hesitation, by Melanchthon. The picture of Calvin, the organizer and disciplinarian, as the parent of laxity in social ethics, is a legend. Like the author of another revolution in economic theory, he might have turned on his popularizers with the protest: "I am not a Calvinist."

Legends are apt, however, to be as right in substance as they are wrong in detail, and both its critics and its defenders were correct in regarding Calvin's treatment of capital as watershed. What he did was to change the plane on which the discussion was conducted, by treating the ethics of money-lending, not as a matter to be decided by an appeal to a special body of doctrine on the subject of usury, but as a particular case of the general problem of the social relations of a Christian community, which must be solved in the light of existing circumstances. The significant feature in his discussion of the subject is that he assumes credit to be a normal and inevitable incident in the life of society. He therefore dismisses the oft-quoted passages from the Old Testament and the Fathers as irrelevant, because designed for conditions which no longer exist, argues that the payment of interest for capital is as reasonable as the payment of rent for land, and throws on the conscience of the individual the obligation of seeing that it does not exceed the amount dictated by natural justice and the golden rule. He makes, in short, a fresh start, argues that what is permanent is, not the rule *"non fœnerabis,"* but *"l'équité et la droiture,"* and appeals from Christian tradition to commercial common sense, which he is sanguine enough to hope will be Christian. On such a view all extortion is to be avoided by Christians. But capital and credit are indispensable; the financier is not a pariah, but a useful member of society; and lending at interest, provided that the rate is reasonable and that loans are made freely to the poor, is not *per se* more extortionate than any other of the economic transactions without which human affairs cannot be carried on. That acceptance of the realities of commercial practice as a starting-point was of momentous importance. It meant that Calvinism and its offshoots took their stand on the side of the activities which were to be most characteristic of the future, and insisted that it was not by renouncing them, but by untiring concentration on the task of using for the glory of God the opportunities which they offered, that the Christian life could and must be lived.

It was on this practical basis of urban industry and commercial enterprise that the structure of Calvinistic social ethics was erected. Upon their theological background it would be audacious to enter. But even an amateur may be pardoned, if he feels that there have been few systems in which the practical conclusions flow by so inevitable a logic from the theological premises. "God not only foresaw," Calvin wrote, "the fall of the first man, . . . but also arranged all by the determination of his own will." Certain individuals he chose as his elect, predestined to salvation from eternity by "his gratuitous mercy, totally irrespective of human merit"; the remainder have been consigned to eternal damnation, "by a just and irreprehensible, but incomprehensible, judgment." Deliverance, in short, is the work, not of man himself, who can contribute nothing to it, but of an objective Power. Human effort, social institutions, the world of culture, are at best irrelevant to salvation, and at worst mischievous. They distract man from the true aim of his existence and encourage reliance upon broken reeds.

That aim is not personal salvation, but the glorification of God, to be sought, not by prayer only, but by action—the sanctification of the world by strife and labor. For Calvinism, with all its repudiation of personal merit, is intensely practical. Good works are not a way of attaining salvation, but they are indispensable as a proof that salvation has been attained. The central paradox of religious ethics—that only those are nerved with the courage needed to turn the world upside down, who are convinced that already, in a higher sense, it is disposed for the best by a Power of which they are the humble instruments—finds in it a special exemplification. For the Calvinist the world is ordained to show forth the majesty of God, and the duty of the Christian is to live for that end. His task is at once to discipline his individual life, and to create a sanctified society. The Church, the State, the community in which he lives, must not merely be a means of personal salvation, or minister to his temporal needs. It must be a "Kingdom of Christ," in which individual duties are performed by men conscious that they are "ever in their great Taskmaster's eye," and the whole fabric is preserved from corruption by a stringent and all-embracing discipline.

The impetus to reform or revolution springs in every age from the realization of the contrast between the external order of society and the moral standards recognized as valid by the conscience or reason of the individual. And naturally it is in periods of swift material progress, such as the sixteenth and eighteenth centuries, that such a contrast is most acutely felt. The men who made the Reformation had seen the Middle Ages close in the golden autumn which, amid all the corruption and tyranny of the time, still glows in the pictures of Nürnberg and Frankfurt drawn by Aeneas Silvius and in the woodcuts of Dürer. And already a new dawn of economic prosperity was unfolding. Its promise was splendid, but it had been accompanied by a cynical materialism which seemed a denial of all that had been meant by the Christian virtues, and which was the more horrifying because it was in the capital of the Christian Church that it reached its height. Shocked by the gulf between theory and practice, men turned this way and that to find some solution of the tension which racked them. The German reformers followed one road and preached a return to primitive simplicity. But who could obliterate the achievements of two centuries, or blot out the new worlds which science had revealed? The Humanists took another, which should lead to the gradual regeneration of mankind by the victory of reason over superstition and brutality and avarice. But who could wait for so distant a consummation? Might there not be a third? Was it not possible that, purified and disciplined, the very qualities which economic success demanded—thrift, diligence, sobriety, frugality—were themselves, after all, the foundation, at least, of the Christian virtues? Was it not conceivable that the gulf which yawned between a luxurious world and the life of the spirit could be bridged, not by eschewing material interests as the kingdom of darkness, but by dedicating them to the service of God?

118 HAJO HOLBORN, A HISTORY OF MODERN GERMANY: HISTORIC RESULTS OF THE REFORMATION

Hajo Holborn (1902-   ) is widely recognized as one of the most distinguished living American scholars of modern European history. Born and educated in Germany, he emigrated to the United States in 1933 when the Nazis forbade him to teach because of his outspokenly liberal views. He joined the faculty at Yale University, where he is now Sterling Professor of History. In addition to a multitude of articles, Professor Holborn has written many books in German and English. Perhaps his best known works in this country are *Ulrich von Hutten and the German Reformation* (1937), *American Military Government: Its Organization and Policies* (1947), and *The Political Collapse of Europe* (1951).

The following selection is taken from Professor Holborn's *A History of Modern Germany—The Reformation* (1959), which is the first of a two-volume study of German history down to the end of the Second World War. The work as a whole is an attempt at a fresh reappraisal of the last five centuries of German history. As we have seen, Germany for a century and a half was the focal center of the Reformation movement (see Documents 110-113). Professor Holborn goes further; in this first volume he takes the position that the age of the Reformation was "the historic period in which Germany exercised her greatest influence on the rest of Europe"; he therefore treats the problem within a broad European setting. That breadth of view is fully evident in the passage below where Professor Holborn thoughtfully assesses the political implications of the Reformation era not merely for Germany but for all of Europe.

Historic Results of the Age.

With the Peace of Westphalia all attempts to reconstruct a strong central government of the Empire that had broken down in the thirteenth century came to an end. Often the religious division has been held responsible for this outcome, but the problems are actually far more complex than such an explanation would imply. Even if Protestantism had never come into being, Charles V would not have found support for a German monarchy, nor could he have subdued the German princes. The part played by the Catholic princes in depriving Charles V of his victory over the Schmalkaldic princes in the years after 1547 and the dramatic break between Maximilian of Bavaria and Emperor Ferdinand II at the height of their victories over heresy and local autonomy in 1629 are ample proof that a common faith could not have submerged the basic antagonism of German politics.

On the other hand, assuming for a moment that all of Germany had become Protestant by 1580, the Empire would then have become a very loose federation of princes with a merely titular emperor as its head. Maybe this federation might have assumed greater coherence if a defense of its religious faith against strong foreign threats had become necessary. But this is mere speculation, and the actual conduct of the Protestant princes in the gravest political crises of German Protestantism does not lend any substance to such conjectures. It could as well be argued that if Catholicism had vanished from Germany, the Protestant princes might have gone to war among themselves over the booty or the ecclesiastical territories, or fallen apart into various camps of differing Protestant faiths.

The adoption of Lutheranism by the German princes was undoubtedly helped by their feeling that it would strengthen their local and territorial interests. This is not to deny the honest religious

Text: Reprinted from Hajo Holborn, *A History of Modern Germany—The Reformation,* by permission of Alfred A. Knopf, Inc. Copyright 1959 by Hajo Holborn. Pp. 371-74.

motives of a good many of them nor the unholy appetite for possessions of the Church in others. But none of them had national aspirations. It is true that the Lutheran movement started as a popular movement and for a while assumed strong national trends. Yet the territorial authorities remained unmoved and used the social revolutionary outbreaks of the knights' revolt and the peasants' revolution to suppress such unpalatable tendencies. The religious policy of the majority of the German princes choosing Protestantism as the protective shield of traditional local life found its parallels in the nobility of the Austrian territories and in the Huguenot noblemen of France. In England and Scandinavia Protestantism from the beginning was connected with the strong national tendencies that pressed to the surface in that age. No doubt the geographical position of these countries, which had allowed them to weaken the control of Rome long before, was an important element in their particular ecclesiastical history. In the Netherlands Protestantism started as a movement of the estates, but the rise of the Dutch burghers to commercial eminence in Europe made Protestantism here an agent in the birth of a nation. The Dutch revolt contributed to the survival of German Protestantism by keeping a major part of Spain's power occupied. But without the intervention of Sweden which gave the Protestant cause in Germany at a historic juncture an effective European leadership, such as had never been provided by the German princes, German Protestantism would have been doomed.

Yet German Protestantism owed its survival even more to the decline of universalism in the Catholic world. The papacy failed to give Charles V or Ferdinand II unreserved support. On the contrary, both in 1547 and 1629 the policy of the Vatican helped to ruin the triumphs of the emperors. The motives of papal policy were manifold. Leaving aside the considerations stemming from the desire to make the Church states secure, two aims were particularly pressing. The first was the determination not to allow the emperors an overwhelming power that would have made them also the actual rulers of the Catholic Church; the second was the wish to keep the Church above all nations and not to alienate some of them by the exclusive support of the Habsburgs. But such an attitude did not secure the leadership of the Church in European politics any longer. Not even in the face of the rising Protestantism could the solidarity of the Catholic nations be restored. The French monarchy adhered to religious orthodoxy and uniformity but conducted a foreign policy in accordance with national political interests. Richelieu, who ended the Huguenot wars, allied himself with the German Protestant princes and Sweden to defeat the Roman Catholic cause in Germany. The Church of Rome ceased to have a determining influence on international politics. When Pope Innocent X solemnly protested against the Peace of Westphalia, the lack of any response laid bare the impotence of the Church to regulate relations between states.

The Modern State.

At the end of the age of the Reformation the states emerged as sovereign agencies in foreign affairs. At the same time their internal sovereignty had grown immensely. Nowhere had the popular forces been allowed to organize their own ecclesiastical life by themselves, and under the conditions of the age few groups would have been capable of doing so. The defense of the old Church, reformations, and counter-reformations were always directed by the political governments. The religious struggle permitted the states to extend their control over the Churches far beyond the level that it had reached before the Reformation. The direction of Church affairs by the state never went so far in the Catholic as in the Protestant world. The establishment of a firm canon of faith and discipline by the Council of Trent served as a unifying bond of the Catholic Church beyond political frontiers. Moreover, the personal life of the faithful was enriched by the religious strength dispensed from Rome through the orders, among which the Jesuits were the most prominent. But in the following century the trend was distinctly toward the growth of independent indigenous forces, and religious as well as political causes were eventually to lead to the suspension of the Jesuit order. On the Protestant side, state control usually comprised the whole external administration of the Church, although there was not even a sure protection against interference with matters of doctrine and internal discipline. The territorial Churches of Protestant Germany were, more than any Protestant Church, in the hands of political powers.

As from the beginning political problems largely determined the course of European and German events in the age of the Reformation, it was the state that emerged in the end tremendously strengthened by new powers gained. Yet it was not the pagan state that the Italian Renaissance had seemed to usher in. In spite of all the abuse of religion and of all the violence and crime committed in the name of religion during the Reformation, the political rulers of the age had to admit that the government of men was more than a ruthless technique, and that it had to embody the highest spiritual principles of law and morality. The epoch which followed the Reformation saw absolute rulers almost everywhere on the Continent, but it was not an epoch of unashamed tyranny. Whatever the personal moral capacity of these princes may have been, the existence of laws and customs derived from transcendental absolutes was never questioned in these hereditary monarchies. The secularization of the state which began in the period of enlightened despotism and was completed in the French Revolution had to meet the same standards. We can see today the damage which politics inflicted upon the religious ideas of the age of the Reformation. But by making power *and* law, instead of mere power, the essence of the state, this age regained and preserved one of the mainsprings of Western civilization.

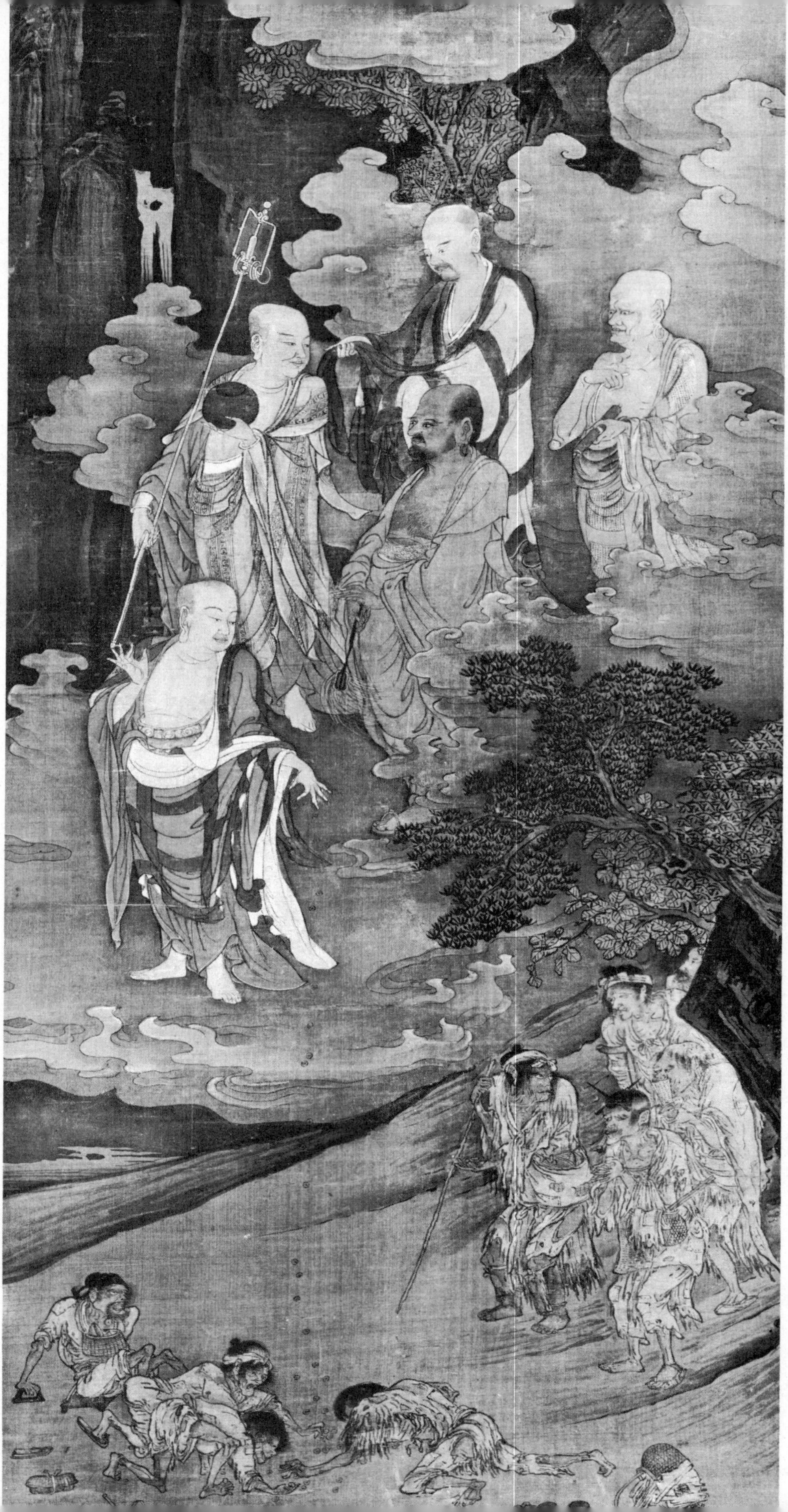

Part VI

Great Civilizations of the Orient: Ancient and Classical Periods

Arhats Bestowing Alms Upon Beggars, a Chinese painting of the Sung period (opposite page), Courtesy, Museum of Fine Arts, Boston; Phoenix Hall in Uji, Japan (below); a statue of Siva from India (right), Courtesy, Museum of Fine Arts, Boston, Beardsell Collection, Marianne Brimmer Fund.

INTRODUCTION

Half the world's population of some three billions today is concentrated on one of the six continents—Asia. And of this vast aggregation, fully a billion inhabit China and India. To understand the reason for this extraordinary concentration of planetary population, we need only look at a map. Both countries occupy subcontinental stretches, drained by mighty river systems—the Hwang Ho and Yangtze in China, the Indus and Ganges in India. Since recorded time, fluvial societies have populated the fertile lands that stretch for thousands of miles along these vast waterways and their myriad tributaries. As a result, India and China can each boast a continuous civilization that has flourished for some five thousand years, and indeed their cultures extend beyond that point of time back through Neolithic antecedents into the dim recesses of early Paleolithic communities. This is evidenced in the case of China, for example, by the unearthed remains of Peking Man (a somewhat younger offshoot of Java's *Pithecanthropus erectus*), who inhabited caves in the vicinity of China's present-day capital.

The mid twentieth century has seen a resurgence of the peoples of Asia and Africa, a movement of decisive significance since it represents a redress of the balance between East and West that was disturbed in the West's favor when Europe embarked five centuries ago upon a career of global discovery and expansion. Their insistence upon both economic and political parity springs from a highly developed awareness of their cultural antiquity, uniqueness, and worth and, consequently, from their resolve to play a role in world affairs commensurate with their past contributions to human advancement.

INDIA: UNITY IN DIVERSITY

Contrary to popular belief, neither India nor China evolved in isolation. In the case of India, many scholars have come to regard the Tigris-Euphrates region as part of a "Greater Near East" that extended beyond the Fertile Crescent through Iran and Baluchistan to the Indus Valley. By investigating this larger western Asia setting, archaeologists are discovering significant cultural relationships between Mesopotamia, Iran, and preliterate India. It would appear that agriculture was first introduced into Baluchistan and Sind from western Asia, one of the earliest farming regions being the Quetta Valley in the now semi-arid upland region of Baluchistan. Here and elsewhere in western India there developed pottery- and bronze-making communities which shared various cultural features: the people adhered to a fertility cult and worshiped a mother goddess—practices common also to farming communities elsewhere in the Greater Near East.

But like Jericho and Jarmo (see p. 5), these primitive agricultural centers in Sind and Baluchistan did not possess the physical resources—and above all, the water—necessary for effecting a breakthrough onto the high socioeconomic platform of "civilization." This step was taken, however, to the east in the not distant Indus Valley. According to most recent estimates, the Indus civilization arose about 2200 B.C. and lasted almost a millennium. It extended some thousand miles along the Indus Valley, from the Himalayan foothills in the north to the coastal lands of the Arabian Sea, and embraced an area about twice the size of the Old Kingdom in Egypt. A noteworthy feature of the Indus civilization was its possession of two capitals, some 350 miles apart—Harappa and Mohenjo-Daro. Despite this distance, the Indus River made possible an economy and administration so uniform that the houses of the two cities were built of bricks of the same dimensions, and the inhabitants everywhere employed a standard system of weights and used an identical script (which has not yet been deciphered). The layout of the capitals strongly indicates that the people were highly practical and austere in their tastes. Like the Quetta Valley inhabitants, they worshiped a mother goddess and, in addition, a three-faced male god who may well have been the prototype of Shiva, the Hindu deity of destruction.

About 1300 B.C. this massive civilization came to a sudden end. The heaped-up skeletons found at Mohenjo-Daro attest to some sudden disaster—it may have been a plague or flood or an attack from outside the valley. By this time invaders had begun to swarm through the Khyber Pass and settle in the upper Indus Valley. Members of the Indo-European family of peoples whose descendants still speak related languages—and which included the Greeks, Romans, and Persians—these newcomers called themselves Aryans. A tall people with fair skins, they lived in tribes headed by rajahs and contemptuously referred to the darker-skinned natives whom they subjugated in India as *Dasyu*, or slaves, though in many respects, the *Dasyu* were the more advanced. The Indo-Aryans from the northwest eventually conquered the entire subcontinent, but the culture which emerged was a synthesis of the two peoples' cultures.

Next followed some 2000 years of political and social consolidation, during which time the country acquired that distinctive culture pattern which we know today as Indian—that is, primarily Hindu. The great triangular area was sufficiently homogeneous in topography to permit the process of consolidation to proceed progressively. At the same time, while fairly well insulated from massive external interference, the land permitted entrance from the northwest; as a result, these two millennia saw periodic military incursions and also an influx of new ideas and esthetic concepts from beyond the mountain passes and across the seas which wash two sides of the subcontinent. In the fourth century B.C., the ambitious Alexander the Great marched to the banks of the Indus before his weary Macedonian troops forced him to abandon his dream of striking still farther to the east. In the wake of this brief visitation there eventually arose a Hellenistic outpost in Afghanistan called Bactria, so that for a time there flourished an eastern culture that contained a mixture of Greek and Indian elements.

Shortly after Alexander's march there also arose the first great Indian empire. Founded by the Maurya Dynasty, it lasted from 321 to about 185 B.C. and controlled all of northern India, since by then the Indo-Aryans had extended their holdings to include the Ganges drainage basin to the east. After the death of the outstanding monarch, Asoka, there occurred a period of upheaval, followed in turn by another famous empire, the Gupta (320-*c.* 535 A.D.). The political zenith of the Guptas in the fifth century A.D. was accompanied by brilliant scientific, literary, and esthetic achievements. Then came another of those all too familiar periods of political fragmentation and weakening of Indian society, leaving the country divided and open to large-scale invasion. This time the invaders were Muslims, who by the twelfth century had conquered all northern India. Fiercely monotheistic, the Muslims often treated their apparently polytheistic Hindu enemies with unrelenting ruthlessness. In time, Muslim sultanates gained control over the Deccan to the south, but Islamic tenets and culture acquired permanent roots only in the Punjab and around the delta of the Ganges—regions which today comprise West and East Pakistan.

With its austerity and uncompromising character, Islam has been called a product of the desert, while Hinduism, ever proliferating its beliefs, deities, and ceremonies, has been likened to the foliage of the jungle. Whatever the merits of this analogy, it is true that the culture patterns evolving around these faiths were so antithetical that the subcontinent was broken into two distinct political segments after World War II. Elsewhere, we have examined the tenets of Islam (see pp. 227-247 and Documents 59-62). Here it is necessary to speak about the antecedents of Hinduism, for they lie at the heart of present-day India.

These antecedents begin in the *Vedas*, the oldest Sanskrit literature and the source of Indo-Aryan views on religion, philosophy, and magic. Of this Vedic literature, the oldest is the *Rig-Veda* (see Document 119), a collection of over a thousand sacred psalms or hymns. The *Vedas* show the evolution of Indian religion from a simple belief in many gods toward a pantheistic conception of the universe and everything in it as a manifestation of a world soul. The deep metaphysical probing of which the ancient Indo-Aryans were capable is shown in a "creation hymn" which questions life's origin. The pantheistic concept was subsequently expounded with more elaboration and greater subtlety in the *Upanishads*, theological works which became the metaphysical foundation for later Hinduism. In them one finds the most fundamental questions of existence—such as the nature of reality, the relationship of man to that cosmic reality, and the conduct which should emerge from this relationship. From these philosophical tenets developed the great religious synthesis known as Hinduism.

Then, in the sixth century B.C., there arose in northern India one of the world's most influential religious reformers, Gautama Buddha. Ignoring the priestly structure of Hinduism, its sacred texts, and the social caste system it incorporated, Buddha called for a return to the core of Upanishadic philosophy. He taught that one could win deliverance from earthly illusion and pain only by living the true philosophy, which he summed up in his Four Noble Truths and Eight-Fold Way. Before Buddhism found its permanent home in the lands around the subcontinent, it gave to India its greatest ruler, the enlightened Asoka.

CHINA: LAND OF THE HAN AND T'ANG

China's more than three million square miles are drained by various river systems: in the north, the Hwang Ho, or Yellow River; in the central area, the Yangtze; and in the south, lesser rivers which converge on the modern city of Canton. Providing rich alluvial soil, copious water for irrigation and ready access into the hinterland, these rivers stimulated the rise of the early fluvial communities out of which a splendid civilization evolved. The mountain ranges and desert wastes sprawling to the west permitted this civilization to develop in comparative seclusion during its formative period; its peoples were fused into a homogeneous society which possessed a distinctive culture pattern.

Peking man's artifacts attest to the existence of ancient Paleolithic cultures in China, and in recent years many Neolithic communities have been excavated over a wide area. Some of the most important of these communities were situated near the confluence of the Hwang Ho and its tributary, the Wei. From these Neolithic cultures, apparently, sprang the earliest stage of Chinese civilization (about 1500 B.C.), which was associated with the period of the Shang Dynasty. Elements which became important in later Chinese life can be discerned in these early societies: fertility and ancestor rites connected with agrarian existence; the development of writing upon which subsequent Chinese script was built; and the creation of splendid bronze vessels, the style of which has continued down to our times.

In the eleventh century B.C. the Shang was replaced by another dynasty, the Chou, whose nearly eight centuries (*c*. 1000-256 B.C.) upon the throne is unrivaled in Chinese history. Much of this period, however, was rendered chaotic by a weakening of the central government and incessant warfare among rival princedoms. This era of feudal fragmentation was brought to an end in 221 B.C. by the victorious rule of Ch'in, who defeated the last of his rivals and reunited the country. Assuming the title of "First Emperor," he created the Chinese Empire which was to endure under various dynasties for over two thousand years—until 1912.

Certain of these dynasties became illustrious. Thus, during the four centuries of Han rule (202 B.C.-220 A.D.), China's frontiers were extended into central Asia, as well as into part of Korea, and the region about Canton. Han science devised an accurate solar calendar, while its technology introduced paper. This was the period, too, when Buddhism appeared in China and consequently proved a decisive influence upon Chinese thought and art alike. In proud memory of this epoch, the Chinese like to refer to themselves as the "Sons of Han." That they are also known as the "Men of T'ang" is a tribute to the next outstanding dynasty. Founded in 618 A.D., the T'ang Empire came to extend from Korea and Manchuria through Tibet and central Asia to the borders of India and Persia. In addition to the administrative efficiency and economic expansion that marked the earlier decades, the T'ang period was remarkable for scholarship, the invention of printing, and the finest flowering of poetry in all Chinese history. All in all, the T'ang (618-907) is remembered as *the* golden age in China, no less resplendent that the Gupta period in India.

As in the case of India, the history of China was replete with the rise and fall of dynasties, the amassing of political and intellectual achievements which were unfortunately dissipated just when a creative zenith had been attained. In both civilizations we find an underlying cultural continuity despite an ebb and flow of dynastic fortunes, yet more than once this continuity was threatened by massive attacks from without. Thus, the political disintegration following the demise of the T'ang Dynasty in the early tenth century was compounded by the seizure of regions in the north by Mongolian invaders. By the twelfth century Chinese control had ceased to exist beyond the natural divide separating the Hwang Ho and Yangtze valleys. China's continued independence had been made possible by the rivalries among the nomadic Mongols, but this state of affairs came to an abrupt end when the redoubtable leader, Genghis Khan (1162-1227), united the Mongols and swiftly subjugated all of China. For the first time in its history, China had been conquered by foreigners. Nevertheless, it did not lose its cultural independence; Genghis' successors became more and more Sinicized, that is, Chinese in character and outlook, as time went on. One of the outstanding Mongol emperors was Kublai Khan (1216?-1294), who wisely recognized the cultural superiority of his subject people. We are indebted to Marco Polo, the author of what is probably the world's most famous travelog, for a vivid first-hand account of China's magnificence in the thirteenth century. Despite Kublai Khan's efforts to maintain Mongol rule, the resurgence of the overwhelmingly more populous and culturally stronger Chinese could not be prevented, so that in 1368 a new dynasty established itself in Peking. The Ming Dynasty ruled until the middle of the seventeenth century and was replaced in turn by what proved to be the final dynasty in imperial China—the Manchu.

While it is risky to generalize, it can at least be suggested that whereas India throughout its history has sought to fashion a cultural synthesis out of the variegated elements that have found their way into the subcontinent, China has taken a different tack. Perhaps because of the strong clannishness created by thousands of years of virtual seclusion in east Asia, the Chinese people have consistently dominated all intruding elements and made them conform to the established pattern of existence. It has been said that the Chinese dragon ends by devouring each new conqueror. This was true of the Mongols in the Middle Ages and the Japanese in recent decades. But now a new and unprecedented factor has been imposed upon the Chinese culture pattern—Marxism, from the Occident. We are presented with a familiar question: will Marxism permanently communize China, or will China eventually Sinicize Marxism?

The political and social stresses to which Chinese society has been peculiarly subjected have long challenged its thinkers to work out rules of conduct for both the individual and the group. Chinese philosophy developed during the chaotic centuries of the Chou Dynasty (c. 1000-256 B.C.). The most influential of all Chinese philosophers, Confucius, lived during this period. Seeing the problem primarily in moral and ethical terms, Confucius stressed the necessity of achieving proper relationships among individuals and between ruler and ruled (see Document 130). The great influence of Confucianism upon the course of Chinese society was due in no small measure to its humanistic emphasis (in contrast to the metaphysical values of Indian thought), which has always been a mark of Chinese life. The cultivation of man's earthy lot is regarded as an end in itself.

On the other hand, Confucius advocated a system that emphasized both traditionalism and a complex system of social checks and balances. In his view, this system depended for its justification upon the practice of virtue. In the minds of totalitarian-minded Chinese thinkers, however, a better principle to employ was that of naked force or, again, the centralization of all administrative functions and the standardization not only of weights and measures but of men's ideas as well.

Meanwhile, another significant strand of Chinese thought had been fashioned in opposition to the rationalistic approach advocated by Confucius and his followers. This second school—known as Taoism—was created by Lao Tzu, who sought an intuitive and mystical understanding of life (see Document 132). With its belief in the silent, ceaseless flow of nature in every atom and its return to the absolute as the supreme goal, Taoism has much in common with Indian metaphysics.

The essentially practical bent of the Chinese mind is shown by the creation of an administrative system that endured for thousands of years and made possible a continuity of ordered existence, despite dynastic upheavals. Chinese thinking was also concerned to a marked degree with problems of statecraft which are far from unfamiliar to us today—inflation, fiscal reform, and aid to the farmer who, then as now, had difficulties in marketing his crops and in obtaining a fair return. Today, as never before, the West needs to know and understand more about China's ancient society—an immemorial way of life upon which some 650 million Chinese today are building and against which at the same time they are consciously rebelling.

JAPAN: A THALASSIC CIVILIZATION

The Japanese archipelago today supports a population of over eighty million. However, the land is mountainous (only 17 per cent of it being arable), foodstuffs have to be imported, the country is deficient in iron, coal, and oil, and it is prone to recurring earthquakes and typhoons. Despite these grave drawbacks, the Japanese are passionately fond of their islands, for geography has greatly influenced their society. To begin with, the sea has separated them from other peoples and fostered unity. It has made them a thalassic, or sea-oriented, society; from earliest days, Japanese fishermen have been venturesome and outgoing, as attested today by their large merchant fleet, prosperous export trade, and world's largest ship-building industry. But if their island location succeeded—up to 1945—in preventing any large-scale invasion of peoples, it did not hinder invasions of ideas and cultures. Proximity to the Asian mainland permitted new racial groups, religions, and art forms to cross over to the archipelago freely; once there, they were modified to become an integral part of a distinctly Japanese culture pattern.

In ancient times, the mountainous topography of the islands led to the growth of numerous small tribal states. Eventually, however, one tribal group, the Yamato—occupying a fertile area in Honshu, the principal island—became dominant and established an imperial family which today boasts the oldest unbroken dynastic line in the world. Throughout its history, Japan's rise to civilization was aided also by important contributions from the mainland. These included a script for writing the language, the works of Confucius, and the teachings of Buddhism. A strong advocate of Buddhist and Confucian thought was Prince Shotoku, whose admiration of Chinese statecraft led him in 604 to reorganize the Japanese government. As a result, there evolved the concept of an absolute monarch exercising his authority through a group of well-born officials chosen by competitive civil service examinations.

In time Prince Shotoku's centralized state was torn by strife, as powerful noble families sought to control the emperors, who were reduced to little more than puppet rulers. Lawlessness increased in the provinces, and the provincial lords hired bands of professional soldiers to protect their estates. In this way feudal society began to develop, so that in the twelfth century power shifted from a civil aristocracy to a military nobility. Japanese society was feudalistic until the nineteenth century. The *samurai*, or warrior nobility, lived according to the tenets of Zen Buddhism and practiced the unwritten code of chivalry known as *Bushido*. Despite the political fragmentation that invariably accompanies feudalism, nominal allegiance to the imperial ruler on the part of the *samurai* never faltered. The warriors coupled their unquestioning obeisance with a fanatical belief in militarism and sense of national duty. When, in the nineteenth century, the emperor was once again invested with real authority, he had at his command a military caste and tradition which, once western technology had been acquired, would make Japan the foremost Asian power and the force that was to spearhead Asia's reëmergence in the world arena of power politics.

India

THE VEDIC AGE

119 RIG-VEDA: THE ARYAN ATTITUDE TOWARD LIFE AND WAR

In the millennium following 2500 B.C., when great civilizations flourished in the valleys of the Nile and the Tigris-Euphrates (see Part One), the Indus River system in northwest India was the center of a culture that contained large, well-planned cities, carried on an extensive trade, and evidently possessed an extremely efficent form of government. Unlike the other civilizations, however, we know very little of the Indus culture; indeed, no one even knew of its existence until 1922, when the remains of its buildings were accidentally uncovered. Indus writing has not yet been deciphered, so our knowledge of the culture is based entirely upon the ruins of buildings and various artifacts.

Previous to the sensational discovery of the Indus civilization, it was assumed that the first civilized people in India were the Aryans, the name given to the peoples of an ethnic stock that had spread throughout much of Europe—the ancestors of the Greeks, Latins, Teutons, and other races speaking "Indo-European" languages. The Aryans drifted slowly into India from their original homeland, located somewhere on the great steppe that stretches from Poland to central Asia. They found in India a land already inhabited by civilized people living in walled cities; and the ruins of Harappa and Mohenjo-Daro have suggested that the Aryan invaders sacked and destroyed the great city civilization. This may be true, but there is evidence that the great cities had already been weakened by floods and other natural disasters, and they had probably already lost control of the Indus plain.

The Vedic literature, as the works composed by the Aryans in their first thousand years in India are called, is regarded by Hindus as scripture, and provides the basis for subsequent developments in Indian religious and philosophical speculation. The oldest part of the literature is the *Rig-Veda*, a vast collection of over a thousand hymns. The culture shown in the *Rig-Veda* is by no means primitive, for the people possessed a highly developed and elaborate religious system, but it was based on an economy that centered on the raising of cattle and had no use for the kind of cities the Indus people had built. The Aryans, as the following hymns from the *Rig-Veda* show, were above all a warlike people, glorying in their swift horses and chariots, proud of their skill with their great bows. Their gods personified the forces of nature—rain, thunder, dawn, fire, wind, and earth. Their chief god was Indra, the god of the thunderstorm, the great warrior who brought about the destruction of the *Dasyu*, the dark-skinned inhabitants of the Indian cities and countryside. Like Marduk of Mesopotamia, slayer of Tiamat (see Document 4), Indra had conquered the dragon Vritra, symbol of chaos, or opposition to the Aryans. Indra's character reflects the values upheld by the Aryan people. Violent and sensual, fond of getting drunk and brawling with the other gods, greatly addicted to gambling, he was nevertheless generous to those who worshiped him. Varuna, the second most popular figure among the gods, was the upholder of the moral order of the universe. He was a far less colorful figure than Indra, but in the long run the concepts he embodied had a greater impact on Indian thought.

Hymn XII.

Indra.

He who, just born, chief God of lofty spirit by power and might became the Gods' protector,
Before whose breath through greatness of his valour the two worlds trembled, He, O men, is Indra.
He who fixed fast and firm the earth that staggered, and set at rest the agitated mountains,
Who measured out the air's wide middle region and gave the heaven support, He, men, is Indra.
Who slew the Dragon, freed the Seven Rivers, and drove the kine forth from the cave of Vala,
Begat the fire between two stones, the spoiler in warrior's battle, He, O men, is Indra.
By whom this universe was made to tremble, who chased away the humbled brood of demons,
Who, like a gambler gathering his winnings, seized the foe's riches, He, O men, is Indra.
Of whom, the Terrible they ask, Where is He? or verily they say of him, He is not.
He sweeps away, like birds, the foe's possessions. Have faith in him, for He, O men, is Indra.
Stirrer to action of the poor and lowly, of priest, of suppliant who sings his praises;
Who, fair-faced, favours him who presses Soma with stones made ready, He, O men, is Indra.
He under whose supreme control are horses, all chariots, and the villages, and cattle;
He who gave being to the Sun and Morning, who leads the waters, He, O men, is Indra.
To whom two armies cry in close encounter, both enemies, the stronger and the weaker;
Whom two invoke upon one chariot mounted, each for himself, He, O ye men, is Indra.
Without whose help our people never conquer; whom, battling, they invoke to give them succour;
He of whom all this world is but the copy, who shakes things moveless, He, O men, is Indra.

Text: Ralph T. H. Griffith (trans.), *The Hymns of the Rig Veda*, 3rd ed. (Benares: E. J. Lazarus and Company, 1920), I, 272-73, 294-95, 645-47.

He who hath smitten, ere they knew their danger, with his hurled weapon many grievous sinners;
Who pardons not his boldness who provokes him, who slays the Dasyu, He, O men, is Indra. . . .

Hymn XXVIII.

Varuna.

This laud of the self-radiant wise Aditya shall be supreme o'er all that is in greatness.
I beg renown of Varuna the Mighty, the God exceeding kind to him who worships.
Having extolled thee, Varuna, with thoughtful care may we have high fortune in thy service.
Singing thy praises like the fires at coming, day after day, of mornings rich in cattle.
May we be in thy keeping, O thou Leader, wide ruling Varuna, Lord of many heroes.
O Sons of Aditi, for ever faithful, pardon us, Gods, admit us to your friendship.
He made them flow, the Aditya, the Sustainer: the rivers run by Varuna's commandment.
These feel no weariness, nor cease from flowing: swift have they flown like birds in air around us.
Loose me from sin as from a band that binds me: may we swell, Varuna, thy spring of Order.
Let not my thread, while I weave song, be severed, nor my work's sum, before the time be shattered.
Far from me, Varuna, remove all danger: accept me graciously, thou holy Sovran.
Cast off, like cords that hold a calf, my troubles: I am not even mine eyelid's lord without thee.
Strike us not, Varuna, within those dread weapons which, Asura, at thy bidding wound the sinner.
Let us not pass away from light to exile. Scatter, that we may live, the men who hate us.
O mighty Varuna, now and hereafter, even as of old, will we speak forth our worship.
For in thyself, invincible God, thy statutes ne'er to be moved are fixed as on a mountain.
Move far from me what sins I have committed: let me not suffer, King, for guilt of others.
Full many a morn remains to dawn upon us: in these, O Varuna, while we live direct us.
O King, whoever, be he friend or kinsman, hath threatened me affrighted in my slumber—
If any wolf or robber fain would harm us, therefrom, O Varuna, give thou us protection.
May I not live, O Varuna, to witness my wealthy, liberal, dear friend's destitution.
King, may I never lack well-ordered riches. Loud may we speak with heroes, in assembly.

Hymn LXXV.

Weapons of War.

The Warrior's look is like a thunderous raincloud's when, armed with mail, he seeks the lap of battle.
Be thou victorious with unwounded body; so let the thickness of thy mail protect thee. With bow let us win kine, with bow the battle, with bow be victor in our hot encounters.
The Bow brings grief and sorrow to the foeman: armed with the Bow may we subdue all regions.
Close to his ear, as fain to speak, She presses, holding her well-loved Friend in her embraces.
Strained on the Bow, She whispers like a woman— this Bow-string that preserves us in the combat.
These, meeting like a woman and her lover, bear, mother-like their child upon their bosom.
May the two Bow-ends, starting swift asunder, scatter, in unison, the foes who hate us.
With many a son, father of many daughters, He clangs and clashes as he goes to battle.
Slung on the back, pouring his brood, the Quiver vanquishes all opposing bands and armies.
Upstanding in the Car the skilful Charioteer guides his strong Horses on whithersoe'er he will.
See and admire the strength of those controlling Reins which from behind declare the will of him who drives.
Horses whose hoofs rain dust are neighing loudly, yoked to the Chariots, showing forth their vigour.
With their forefeet descending on the foemen, they, never flinching, trample and destroy them.
Car-bearer is the name of his oblation, whereon are laid his Weapons and his Armour.
So let us here, each day that passes, honour the helpful Car with hearts exceeding joyful.
In sweet association lived the fathers who gave us life, profound and strong in trouble.
Unwearied, armed with shafts and wondrous weapons, free, real heroes, conquerors of armies.
The Brâhmans, and the Fathers meet for Somadraughts, and, graciously inclined, unequalled Heaven and Earth.
Guard us from evil, Pûshan, guard us strengtheners of Law: let not the evil-wisher master us.
Her tooth a deer, dressed in an eagle's feathers, bound with cow-hide, launched forth, She flieth onward.
There where the heroes speed hither and thither, there may the Arrows shelter and protect us.
Avoid us thou whose flight is straight, and let our bodies be as stone.
May Soma kindly speak to us, and Aditi protect us well.
He lays his blows upon their backs, he deals his blows upon their thighs.
Thou, Whip, who urgest horses, drive sagacious horses in the fray.

It compasses the arm with serpent windings, fend-
away the friction of the bowstring:
So may the Brace, well-skilled in all its duties,
guard manfully the man from every quarter.
Now to the Shaft with venom smeared, tipped
with deer-horn, with iron mouth,

Celestial, of Parjany's seed, be this great adoration paid.
Loosed from the Bowstring fly away, thou Arrow, sharpened by our prayer.
Go to the foemen, strike them home, and let not one be left alive.

120 UPANISHADS: THE NATURE OF REALITY

The literature of ancient India leaves unanswered many of the questions we are inclined to ask concerning the nature of the political organizations under which the people lived, the economic structure of society, or the extent of trade with other people. What the literature does give us, however, to a degree perhaps unparalleled in any other ancient culture, is a knowledge of how people thought, what intellectual problems faced them, and what assumptions colored man's life in society. Preoccupation with these issues is most evident in the *Upanishads*, the product of thinkers who lived around 600 B.C. This century brought changes everywhere in the ancient world—in Greece, China, Palestine, and Persia. Unfortunately, the reasons for changes perceptible in the Indian culture of this time are less discoverable than those that were at work elsewhere. What is clear is that the Indian people had adopted ways of looking at life that were quite different from any attitudes found in the *Rig-Veda*. The newer concepts came to dominate human existence not only in India but to some extent throughout the vast regions of the East which Indian thought had penetrated.

The most pervasive of these ideas are the doctrines of *karma* and reincarnation. *Karma*, a word that means "action," is best used in its untranslated form. It implies that every act man performs must inevitably produce some result. Closely bound up with *karma* is the belief in reincarnation, the other ruling assumption of the Indian tradition. If an action cannot find fruition within the span of one human life, then it will in another. This means that one's actions and motivations determine future births, just as past deeds have determined one's present existence. The system is one of perfect justice; within the Indian tradition there is no need to ask with the Hebrew psalmist, "Why do good men suffer, why do the wicked prosper?" What we are is because of what we have been. This does not mean, as has often been suggested, a fatalistic attitude toward life. On the contrary, it can be the basis for optimism, since the doctrines of *karma* and reincarnation mean that man is responsible for his future and can control it by his actions. That Indian culture may be seen as pessimistic in its orientation and "life-negating" in its values is the result of another aspect of *karma*. Looking at the endless transmigration of the human soul, thoughtful men asked, "How is it possible to bring this interminable cycle of births and rebirths to an end?" Many answers were given, but the one that pervades Indian thought is the belief that "salvation" comes through true knowledge of what constitutes ultimate reality. For this reason, philosophical speculation in India has the intensely practical end of defining what reality is and how it may be known.

The selections given here are from one of the greatest of the *Upanishads*; the first part deals with the idea of *karma*, the second with reincarnation, and the third with the nature of reality and how it is to be known. It contains the most famous phrase in Indian thought—the equation, "That art thou," meaning that true knowledge comes with the realization that reality in this world is identical with the human soul.

The Doctrine of Karma

... Now as a caterpillar, when it has come to the end of a blade of grass, in taking the next step draws itself together towards it, just so this soul in taking the next step strikes down this body, dispels its ignorance, and draws itself together [for making the transition].

As a goldsmith, taking a piece of gold, reduces it to another newer and more beautiful form, just so this soul, striking down this body and dispelling

Text: From *The Thirteen Principal Upanishads*, translated by Robert Ernest Hume, published by the Oxford University Press, India.

its ignorance, makes for itself another newer and more beautiful form like that either of the fathers, or of the Gandharvas, or of the gods, or of Prajāpati, or of Brahma, or of other beings.

Verily, this soul is Brahma, made of knowledge, of mind, of breath, of seeing, of hearing, of earth, of water, of wind, of space, of energy and of non-energy, of desire and of non-desire, of anger and of non-anger, of virtuousness and of non-virtuousness. It is made of everything. This is what is meant by the saying "made of this, made of that."

According as one acts, according as one conducts himself, so does he become. The doer of good becomes good. The doer of evil becomes evil. One becomes virtuous by virtuous action, bad by bad action.

But people say: "A person is made [not of acts, but] of desires only." [In reply to this I say:] As is his desire, such is his resolve; as is his resolve, such the action he performs; what action (*karma*) he performs, that he procures for himself.

On this point there is this verse:—
Where one's mind is attached—the inner self
Goes thereto with action, being attached to it alone.
   Obtaining the end of his action,
   Whatever he does in this world,
   He comes again from that world
   To this world of action.
—So the man who desires.

REINCARNATION

. . . Accordingly, those who are of pleasant conduct here—the prospect is, indeed, that they will enter a pleasant womb, either the womb of a Brahman, or the womb of a Kshatriya, or the womb of a Vaiśya. But those who are of stinking conduct here—the prospect is, indeed, that they will enter a stinking womb, either the womb of a dog, or the womb of a swine, or the womb of an outcast (*caṇḍāla*).

REALITY: CONVERSATION BETWEEN ŚVETAKETU AND HIS FATHER

First Khaṇḍa

The threefold development of the elements and of man from the primary unitary Being.

1. *Om!* Now, there was Śvetaketu Āruṇeya. To him his father said: "Live the life of a student of sacred knowledge. Verily, my dear, from our family there is no one unlearned [in the Vedas] (*an-ūcya*), a Brahman by connection (*brahma-bandhu*), as it were."

2. He then, having become a pupil at the age of twelve, having studied all the Vedas, returned at the age of twenty-four, conceited, thinking himself learned, proud.

3. Then his father said to him: "Śvetaketu, my dear, since now you are conceited, think yourself learned, and are proud, did you also ask for that teaching whereby what has not been heard of becomes heard of, what has not been thought of becomes thought of, what has not been understood becomes understood?"

4. "How, pray, sir, is that teaching?"

(4) "Just as, my dear, by one piece of clay everything made of clay may be known—the modification is merely a verbal distinction, a name; the reality is just 'clay'—

5. Just as, my dear, by one copper ornament everything made of copper may be known—the modification is merely a verbal distinction, a name: the reality is just 'copper'—

6. Just as, my dear, by one nail-scissors everything made of iron may be known—the modification is merely a verbal distinction, a name; the reality is just 'iron'—so, my dear, is that teaching."

7. "Verily, those honored men did not know this; for, if they had known it, why would they not have told me? But do you, sir, tell me it."

"So be it, my dear," said he.

Ninth Khaṇḍa

The unitary World-Soul, the immanent reality of all things and of man.

1. "As the bees, my dear, prepare honey by collecting the essences of different trees and reducing the essence to a unity, [2] as they are not able to discriminate 'I am the essence of this tree,' 'I am the essence of that tree'—even so, indeed, my dear, all creatures here, though they reach Being, know not 'We have reached Being.'

3. Whatever they are in this world, whether tiger, or lion, or wolf, or boar, or worm, or fly, or gnat, or mosquito, that they become.

4. That which is the finest essence—this whole world has that as its soul. That is Reality. That is Ātman (Soul). That art thou, Śvetaketu."

"Do you, sir, cause me to understand even more."

"So be it, my dear," said he.

Tenth Khaṇḍa

1. "These rivers, my dear, flow, the eastern toward the east, the western toward the west. They go just from the ocean to the ocean. They become the ocean itself. As there they know not 'I am this one,' 'I am that one'—even so, indeed, my dear, all creatures here, though they have come forth from Being, know not 'We have come forth from Being.' Whatever they are in this world, whether tiger, or lion, or wolf, or boar, or worm, or fly, or gnat, or mosquito, that they become.

3. That which is the finest essence—this whole world has that as its soul. That is Reality. That is Ātman (Soul). That art thou, Śvetaketu."

"Do you, sir, cause me to understand even more."
"So be it, my dear," said he.

Twelfth Khanda

[The father said to Śvetaketu:]
1. "Bring hither a fig from there."
"Here it is, sir."
"Divide it."
"It is divided, sir."
"What do you see there?"
"These rather *(iva)* fine seeds, sir."
"Of these, please *(aṅga)*, divide one."
"It is divided, sir."
"What do you see there?"
"Nothing at all, sir."
2. Then [his father] said to him: "Verily, my dear, that finest essence which you do not perceive —verily, my dear, from that finest essence this great Nyagrodha (sacred fig) tree thus arises.
3. Believe me, my dear," said he, "that which is the finest essence—this whole world has that as its soul. That is Reality. That is Ātman (Soul). That art thou, Śvetaketu."
"Do you, sir, cause me to understand even more."
"So be it, my dear," said he.

Thirteenth Khanda

1. "Place this salt in the water. In the morning come unto me."
Then [Śvetaketu] did so.
Then [his father] said to him: "That salt you placed in the water last evening—please bring it hither."
Then he grasped for it, but did not find it, as it was completely dissolved.
2. "Please take a sip of it from this end," said he. "How is it?"
"Salt."
"Take a sip from the middle," said he. "How is it?"
"Salt."
"Take a sip from that end," said he. "How is it?"
"Salt."
"Set it aside. Then come unto me."
He did so, saying, "It is always the same."
Then [his father] said to him: "Verily, indeed, my dear, you do not perceive Being here. Verily, indeed, it is here.
3. That which is the finest essence—this whole world has that as its soul. That is Reality. That is Ātman (Soul). That art thou, Śvetaketu."
"Do you, sir, cause me to understand even more."
"So be it, my dear," said he.

Fourteenth Khanda

1. "Just as, my dear, one might lead away from the Gandhāras a person with his eyes bandaged, and then abandon him in an uninhabited place; as there he might be blown forth either to the east, to the north, or to the south, since he had been led off with his eyes bandaged and deserted with his eyes bandaged; as, if one released his bandage and told him, 'In that direction are the Gandhāras; go in that direction!' he would, if he were a sensible man, by asking [his way] from village to village, and being informed, arrive home at the Gandhāras —even so here on earth one who has a teacher knows: 'I shall remain here only so long as I shall not be released [from the bonds of ignorance]. Then I shall arrive home.'
3. That which is the finest essence—this whole world has that as its soul. That is Reality. That is Ātman (Soul). That art thou, Śvetaketu."

THE FIRST EMPIRES AND THE RISE OF BUDDHISM

121 BUDDHA, FIRST SERMON ON THE FOUR NOBLE TRUTHS: BUDDHISM, A NEW WAY OF LIFE

One of the manifestations of the ferment of religious and intellectual thought that was taking place in India in the sixth century B.C. was the rise of Buddhism. "Buddha," meaning "The Enlightened One," is the title given to Siddhartha, the young prince who grew dissatisfied with his comfortable life and left his palace to search for a more meaningful way of life. The traditional story is that, distressed by the sight of old age, sickness, and death, he sought to find an explanation for the pain of human existence. The answers he discovered are summed up in the Four Noble Truths and the Eight-Fold Way. The four truths of human life that he taught are these:

1. The facing of the fact that life is sorrowful;
2. The realization that sorrow is caused by craving and desire;
3. The knowledge that the cycle of existence can be ended by the stopping of desire;

4. The willingness to overcome desire by a disciplined existence—the Eight-Fold Way—which culminates in monasticism.

These teachings accept the common Indian belief in *karma* and rebirth, but they differ radically in completely ignoring the whole structure of priestly religion as well as the sacred texts of the tradition. It should also be noted that there is no mention of any deity, no calling upon divine help of any kind.

For two centuries Buddhism spread very slowly in northern India, but eventually it gained a number of adherents, and, most important for its consequent power, it received the support of great kings. Buddhism ultimately died out in the land of its birth, but long before that it spread to India's neighbors, such as Ceylon, as well as to China, Japan, and the whole of southeast Asia. The simple teachings of Buddha were greatly changed, but the Four Noble Truths and the Eight-Fold Way remained at the heart of Buddhism.

The five monks of the Bhadra-group, Ajñátakaundinya, Aśvaki, Bhadraka, Vāshpa, Mahānāman were dwelling in the Rishipatana. The Lord having gone out of Benares after collecting his alms and finishing his meal went to the Rishipatana. The five saw the Lord. On seeing him coming from afar they decided on their behaviour. "This ascetic Gautama is coming, he is slack, he lives in abundance, and has given up striving. No one ought to get up." The Lord came, and they did not remain in their places. Just as birds in their nests or on a bough fly up when fire from below heats them, even so the five monks, as he came from afar, finding no pleasure in their seats, rose up and went to meet the Lord. "Come, friend Gautama, welcome, friend Gautama, greeting to friend Gautama." The Lord said, "you have broken your agreement, monks. Do not, monks, greet the Tathāgata with the word 'friend'." Then when the Lord addressed them with the word 'pupil', all their marks as brahmin students, their dress and behaviour, at once disappeared, and they appeared in the three robes with shining bowls, with hair arranged naturally, and their gait was as if they were monks of a hundred years standing. This was the ordination of leaving the world of the five monks. [The narrative is broken here, and the First Sermon follows as it would appear in its place in the Canon.]

Thus have I heard: at one time the Lord was dwelling at Benares, at Rishivadana in the deerpark. Then the Lord addressed the five elders: "Monks." "Lord," the monks replied to the Lord. The Lord said to them: There are these two extremes, monks, for one who has left the world. What are the two? The one, devotion to lusts and pleasures, vulgar, belonging to the common people, ignoble and purposeless, does not tend to a completely religious life, to disgust, absence of passion, to the state of ascetic, to enlightenment, to Nirvāna; and the other, devoted to self-mortification, painful, ignoble, purposeless. These, monks, are the two extremes of one who has left the world, and the Tathāgata by avoiding both these extremes has through enlightenment in the noble Doctrine and Discipline attained the Middle Path, which produces insight, tends to calm, and leads to disgust, absence of passion, cessation, to the state of ascetic, to enlightenment, to Nirvāna. And what, monks, is the Middle Path . . . won by the Tathāgata? It is the Noble Eightfold Path, namely, right view, right resolve, right effort, right action, right livelihood, right speech, right mindfulness, right concentration. This, monks, is the Middle Path in the noble doctrine and discipline won through enlightenment by the Tathāgata, which produces insight, tends to calm, and leads to disgust, absence of passion, cessation, to the state of ascetic, to enlightenment, to Nirvāna.

Now, monks, there are these four Noble Truths. What are the four? The Noble Truth of pain, the Noble Truth of the cause of pain, the Noble Truth of the cessation of pain, and the Noble Truth of the Path that leads to the cessation of pain.

Herein, monks, what is the Noble Truth of pain? It is, birth is pain, old age is pain, sickness is pain, death is pain, union with unpleasant things is pain, separation from pleasant things is pain, not getting what one wishes and pursues is pain; the body is pain, feeling is pain, perception is pain, the mental elements are pain, consciousness is pain, in short, the five groups of grasping are pain. This, monks, is the Noble Truth of pain.

Herein, what is the Noble Truth of the cause of pain? It is craving, tending to rebirth, combined with delight and passion, and finding delight here and there. This, monks, is the Noble Truth of the cause of pain.

Text: E. J. Thomas (ed.), *The Quest of Enlightenment* ("Wisdom of the East" series [London: John Murray, Ltd., 1950]), pp. 34-37.

Herein, what is the Noble Truth of the cessation of pain? It is the complete and trackless destruction, cessation, abandonment, relinquishment, and rejection of that craving which tends to rebirth and finds delight here and there. This, monks, is the Noble Truth of the cessation of pain.

Herein, what is the Noble Truth of the Path that leads to the cessation of pain? It is the Noble Eightfold Way, namely, right view, right resolve, right effort, right action, right livelihood, right speech, right mindfulness, right concentration. This, monks, is the Noble Truth of the Path that leads to the cessation of pain.

This is pain: as I reflected, monks, on doctrines unheard before, knowledge arose, insight arose, intelligence arose, wisdom arose, light appeared.

This is the cause of pain: as I reflected . . . wisdom arose, light appeared.

This is the cessation of pain: as I reflected . . . wisdom arose, light appeared.

And this is the Path that leads to the destruction of pain: as I reflected . . . wisdom arose, light appeared.

Again, I must comprehend the Noble Truth of pain.

As I reflected . . . wisdom arose, light appeared.

Again, the Noble Truth of the cause of pain must be abandoned: as I reflected . . . wisdom arose, light appeared.

Again, the Noble Truth of the cessation of pain must be realized: as I reflected . . . wisdom arose, light appeared.

Again, the Noble Truth of the Path leading to the cessation of pain must be practised: as I reflected . . . wisdom arose, light appeared.

As long, monks, as I did not with due wisdom truly comprehend these four Noble Truths with the three sections and twelve divisions, so long I did not understand with full enlightenment, nor did knowledge arise in me, nor was my steady release of mind realized. But when, monks, with due wisdom I truly comprehended these four Noble Truths with the three sections and twelve divisions then I understood that I was enlightened with full enlightenment, knowledge arose in me, and my steady release of mind and release of wisdom was realized.

122 THE EDICTS OF ASOKA: THE ATTEMPT TO CREATE A UNIFIED EMPIRE

In the fourth century B.C. the powerful Maurya Dynasty created the first great empire in Indian history. Long before this, however, there had been an awareness on the part of kings and priests that all the people of India had something in common and that there was a distinction between them and "foreigners." The great symbol of this sense of unity was the grandest of the ancient rituals, the horse sacrifice, in which a horse was allowed to wander throughout as many kingdoms as he could and was then sacrificed. On one level, the ritual act can be seen as a device for a king to set in motion a policy of territorial expansion, but it also served to express the idea of the universal sovereign, the ruler of all the land. From very early times this impulse worked toward what may be called national unity; however, the forces working against the ideal obscured it for long periods as a practical aim of statesmanship. The existence of many independent kings, a multitude of languages, a wide variety of religious customs, vast distances, internal geographic boundaries—all these have stood as obstacles to unification. It is a measure of the political skill and military might of the Mauryas that they were able to hold together a vast empire for over a hundred years. The empire created by Chandragupta (c. 322-298 B.C.) reached its zenith of power and prosperity under his grandson, Asoka (c. 269-232 B.C.), the most famous of Indian rulers. No other ruler until Aurangzeb, who was in power at the end of the seventeenth century, was to control so much of India as did Asoka.

The only major territorial conquest that Asoka is known to have made was that of Kalinga, but this campaign had a profound effect on him. The devastating slaughter of the conquered people by the victorious Mauryans caused Asoka to reject war and accept Buddhism with its condemnation of violence and its compassion for all living creatures. This was one of the fateful decisions of history; through Asoka's patronage, Buddhism was established throughout India and eventually made its way to the rest of Asia. It has been suggested that Asoka's conversion came at a convenient time, since the conquest of Kalinga rounded out his vast empire, and that, furthermore, he may have foreseen Buddhism's becoming a force for unification. The temptation to compare his motives with those of Constantine in adopting Christianity is great. No doubt he was attracted to the possibilities of Buddhism as a unifying ideology for a country torn by disruptive elements. In any case, Asoka attempted to create what has been called "a theocracy without God," by making India a land governed by righteousness and truth as interpreted in Buddhist teachings.

The record of Asoka's endeavors is given in a large number of edicts which he had carved in rock throughout his kingdom. Most of the edicts are general maxims exhorting the people and the officials to live righteously. They quite clearly aimed at using the power of the monarchy to enforce the moral virtues that Asoka believed in as ultimate truths and as agencies promoting a well-ordered commonwealth. In accordance with a sentiment already widespread in India, he campaigned against the eating of meat and the killing of animals for sacrifice. It seemed probable that his efforts have had a considerable part in giving Indian society its bias against animal foods. Asoka was not a pacifist, however; he still maintained armies to defend his borders and he did not abolish the death penalty. But in general his edicts evidence a just and humane government and are a monument to one of the world's greatest rulers.

True Conquest.

The Kalingas were conquered by His Sacred and Gracious Majesty the King when he had been consecrated eight years. One hundred and fifty thousand persons were thence carried away captive, one hundred thousand were there slain, and many times that number perished.

Directly after the annexation of the Kalingas, began His Sacred Majesty's zealous protection of the Law of Piety, his love of that Law, and his giving instruction in that Law (dharma). Thus arose His Sacred Majesty's remorse for having conquered the Kalingas, because the conquest of a country previously unconquered involves the slaughter, death, and carrying away captive of the people. That is a matter of profound sorrow and regret to His Sacred Majesty.

There is, however, another reason for His Sacred Majesty feeling still more regret, inasmuch as in such a country dwell Brahmans or ascetics, or men of various denominations, or householders, upon whom is laid this duty of hearkening to superiors, hearkening to father and mother, hearkening to teachers, and proper treatment of friends, acquaintances, comrades, relatives, slaves, and servants, with fidelity of attachment. To such people in such a country befalls violence, or slaughter, or separation from their loved ones. Or misfortune befalls the friends, acquaintances, comrades, and relatives of those who are themselves well protected, while their affection is undiminished. Thus for them also that is a mode of violence. All these several happenings to men are matter of regret to His Sacred Majesty; because it is never the case that people have not faith in some one denomination or other.

Thus of all the people who were then slain, done to death, or carried away captive in the Kalingas, if the hundredth or the thousandth part were to suffer the same fate, it would now be matter of regret to His Sacred Majesty. Moreover, should any one do him wrong that too must be borne with by His Sacred Majesty, if it can possibly be borne with. Even upon the forest folk in his dominions His Sacred Majesty looks kindly and he seeks their conversion, for (if he did not) repentance would come upon His Sacred Majesty. They are bidden to turn from evil ways that they be not chastised. For His Sacred Majesty desires that all animate beings should have security, self-control, peace of mind, and joyousness.

And this is the chiefest conquest in the opinion of His Sacred Majesty—the conquest by the Law of Piety—this it is that is won by His Sacred Majesty both in his own dominions and in all the neighbouring realms as far as six hundred leagues—where the Greek King named Antiochus dwells, and north of that Antiochus to where dwell the four kings severally named Ptolemy, Antigonus, Magas and Alexander [identified as rulers of Syria, Egypt, Macedonia, Cyrene, and Epirus in about 258 B.C.]; and in the south the realms of the Cholas and the Pandyas, with Ceylon likewise—and here, too, in the King's dominions, . . . everywhere men follow His Sacred Majesty's instruction in the Law of Piety. Even where the envoys of His Sacred Majesty do not penetrate, there too, men hearing His Sacred Majesty's ordinance . . . practise and will practise the Law.

And, again, the conquest thereby won everywhere is everywhere a conquest of delight. Delight is found in the conquests made by the law. That delight, however, is only a small matter. His Sacred Majesty regards as bearing much fruit only that which concerns the other world.

And for this purpose has this pious edict been written in order that my sons and grandsons, who may be, should not regard it as their duty to con-

Text: Vincent A. Smith (trans. and ed.), *The Edicts of Asoka* (Broad Campden, England: Essex House Press, 1909), pp. 8-13, 16-17, 18-19, 24-25.

quer a new conquest. If, perchance, they become engaged in conquest by arms, they should take pleasure in patience and gentleness, and regard as [the only true] conquest the conquest won by piety. That avails for both this world and the next. Let all joy be in [moral] effort, because that avails for both this world and the next.

The Quinquennial Circuit.

"Thus saith His Sacred and Gracious Majesty the King:—When I had been consecrated twelve years I issued this command:—

Everywhere in my dominions the (subordinate) officials, and the Commissioners, and the District officers every five years must proceed on circuit, as well for their other duties, as for this special purpose, namely, to proclaim the Law of Piety, to wit, 'A meritorious thing is the hearkening to father and mother; a meritorious thing is liberality to friends, acquaintances, relatives, Brahmans, and ascetics; a meritorious thing it is to abstain from slaughter of living creatures; a meritorious thing it is to spend little and store little.'

Let the (monastic) communities also appoint officials for the reckoning with regard to both the objects and the accounts (or, 'in accordance with reason and specific instructions')."

Rock Edict IV.

The Practice of Piety.

"For a long time past, even for many hundred years, the slaughter of living creatures, cruelty to animate beings, disrespect to relatives, and disrespect to Brahmans and ascetics have grown.

But now, by reason of the practice of piety by His Sacred and Gracious Majesty the King, instead of the sound of the war-drum the sound of the drum of piety is heard, while heavenly spectacles of processional cars, elephants, illuminations, and the like are displayed to the people.

As for many hundred years past has not happened, at this present, by reason of the proclamation of the Law of Piety by His Sacred and Gracious Majesty the King, the cessation of slaughter of living creatures, the prevention of cruelty to animate beings, respect to relatives, respect to Brahmans and ascetics, hearkening to father and mother, and hearkening to elders are growing.

Thus, and in many other ways, the practice of piety is growing, and His Sacred and Gracious Majesty the King will cause that practice of piety to grow still more.

The sons, grandsons, and great-grandsons of His Sacred and Gracious Majesty the King will promote the growth of that practice until the end of the cycle, and, abiding in piety and morality, will proclaim the Law of Piety. For this is the best of all deeds, the proclamation of the Law of Piety, and the practice of piety is not for the immoral man.

In this matter growth is meritorious, and not to decrease is meritorious.

For this very purpose has this writing been made, in order that men in this matter may strive for growth and not suffer decrease.

This has been written by command of His Sacred and Gracious Majesty the King after he had been consecrated twelve years."

Rock Edict V.

Censors of the Law of Piety.

"Thus saith His Sacred and Gracious Majesty the King:—A good deed is a difficult thing. Now by me many good deeds have been done. He who performs a good deed does a difficult thing. Should my sons, grandsons, and my descendants after them until the end of the cycle follow in this path, they will do well; but in this matter, should a man neglect the commandment, he will do ill, because sin is an easy thing.

Now in all the long ages past, officers known as Censors of the Law of Piety never had been appointed, whereas by me, after I had been consecrated thirteen years, Censors of the Law of Piety were made.

Among people of all denominations they are engaged in promoting the establishment of piety, the progress of piety, and the welfare and happiness of the lieges, as well as of the Yonas, Kambojas, Gandhāras, Rāshtrikas, Pitenikas, and other nations on my borders.

They are engaged in promoting the welfare and happiness of servants and masters, of Brahmans and the rich, of the poor, and of the aged, as well as in removing hindrances from the path of the lieges. They are engaged in the prevention of wrongful imprisonment or chastisement, in the work of removing hindrances and of deliverance, considering cases where a man has a large family, has been smitten by calamity, or is advanced in years.

Here, at Pātaliputra, and in all the provincial towns they are everywhere engaged in supervising the female establishments of my brothers and sisters and other relatives.

Everywhere in my loyal empire these Censors of the Law of Piety are engaged with those among my lieges who are devoted to piety, established in piety, or addicted to almsgiving.

For this purpose has this pious edict been written, that it may endure for long, and that my subjects may act accordingly."

The Prompt Dispatch of Business.

"Thus saith His Sacred and Gracious Majesty the King:—During long ages past business has not been disposed of, nor have reports been received at all hours. Now by me this arrangement has been made that at all hours and in all places —whether I am dining, or in the ladies' apartments, or in my bedroom, or in my closet, or in my carriage, or in the palace-gardens—the official reporters should report to me on the people's business. At all places I am ready to dispose of the people's business.

And if, perchance, I personally by word of mouth command that a gift be made or order executed, or anything urgent is entrusted to the officials, and in that business a dispute arises or fraud occurs among the communities, I have commanded that immediate report be made to me at any hour and at any place, for I am never fully satisfied with my efforts and my dispatch of business.

Work I must for the welfare of all, and the root of the matter is in effort and the dispatch of business, for nothing is more efficacious to secure the welfare of all. And for what do I toil? For no other end than this, that I may discharge my debt to animate beings, and that while I make some happy here, they may in the next world gain heaven.

For this purpose have I caused this pious edict to be written, that it may long endure, and that my sons, grandsons, and great-grandsons may strive for the welfare of all. That, however, is a difficult thing, save by the utmost exertion.

Rock Edict VII.

Imperfect Fulfilment of the Law.

"His Sacred and Gracious Majesty the King desires that in all places men of every denomination may abide, for they all desire mastery over the senses and purity of mind.

Man, however, is various in his wishes, and various in his likings.

Some of the denominations will perform the whole, others will perform but one part of the commandment. Even for a person to whom lavish liberality is impossible, the virtues of mastery over the senses, purity of mind, gratitude, and steadfastness are altogether indispensable."

True Almsgiving.

"Thus saith his Sacred and Gracious Majesty the King:

There is no such almsgiving as is the almsgiving of the Law of Piety—friendship in piety, the distribution of piety, kinship in piety. Herein does it consist—in proper treatment of slaves and servants, hearkening to father and mother, giving to friends, comrades, relations, ascetics, and Brahmans, and sparing of living creatures. Therefore a father, son, brother, master, friend, comrade, nay, even a neighbour, ought to say, 'This is meritorious, this ought to be done.'

He who acts thus both gains this world and in the other world begets infinite virtue, by means of this very almsgiving of piety."

Toleraton.

"His Sacred and Gracious Majesty the King does reverence to men of all sects whether ascetics or householders, by gifts and various forms of reverence.

His Sacred Majesty, however, cares not so much for gifts or external reverence as that there should be a growth of the essence of the matter in all sects. The growth of the essence of the matter assumes various forms, but the root of it is restraint of speech, to wit, a man must not do reverence to his own sect or disparage that of another man without reason. Depreciation should be for specific reasons only, because the sects of other people all deserve reverence for one reason or another.

By thus acting, a man exalts his own sect, and at the same time does service to the sects of other people.

By acting contrariwise, a man hurts his own sect, and does disservice to the sects of other people. For he who does reverence to his own sect while disparaging the sects of others wholly from attachment to his own, with intent to enhance the splendour of his own sect, in reality by such conduct inflicts the severest injury on his own sect.

Concord, therefore, is meritorious, to wit, hearkening and hearkening willingly to the Law of Piety as accepted by other people. For this is the desire of His Sacred Majesty that all sects should hear much teaching and hold sound doctrine."

123 KAUTĪLYA, ARTHASĀSTRA: PRACTICAL ADVICE FOR STATESMEN

The edicts of Asoka (see Document 122), with their emphasis on tolerance and righteousness, must be seen against the background of a political structure which had been created and sustained by very different political methods and ideals than those urged by the great king. The clearest expression of the prevailing views of political practice in ancient India is found in a remarkable treatise, the *Arthasāstra*, supposed to have been written by Kautilya, chief minister of King Chandragupta Maurya. Even if the *Arthasāstra* originated considerably later, as many scholars argue, it is reasonably certain that the spirit that informs it represents the thinking and practice of many rulers. Asoka's "law of righteousness" can thus be seen as a reaction against popular views, although it seems unlikely that Asoka went so far as to abolish such features of the general system as the control of subordinates through a network of spies.

The ideal put forth in the *Arthasāstra* is a tightly organized bureaucratic state, with every detail of the economic and political life of the people controlled by government regulations. Wages and conditions of work were to be fixed; every conceivable article was to be taxed; anyone who practiced a profession, from physician to dancer, was to be licensed by the state. Forms of torture for obtaining information were carefully outlined. Punishments were severe, but the legal protection offered to slaves, women, and minors was of a high order. Spies were the eyes of the king and were to be found everywhere—barbers and musicians being especially valuable since they had free access to homes. The use of *agents provocateurs* are recommended by the *Arthasāstra* as useful in stirring up trouble in a neighboring kingdom, thus giving an excuse for intervention. All this was justified on the grounds that the king was always in danger, with the only law being "the law of the fish"—the bigger eats the smaller. Since foreign affairs were a major concern of any king, much attention was given to the conduct of interstate relations. The *Arthasāstra* advises attacking when strong and using guile when weak, while always assuming that one's immediate neighbor is an enemy while a state on the neighbor's further border is a natural ally.

The starkly realistic statecraft enjoined by the *Arthasāstra* refutes some misconceptions concerning the nature of Indian life. The picture of a people engrossed in "spiritual" concerns, caring nothing for the things of this world, receives decisive contradiction from an examination of ancient India's political philosophy. In general, the guiding maxim of rulers seems to have been the words of the great epic poem, the *Mahābhārata:* "might makes right, right proceeds from might."

The Duties of a King

If a king is energetic, his subjects will be equally energetic. If he is reckless, they will not only be reckless likewise, but also eat into his works. Besides, a reckless king will easily fall into the hands of his enemies. Hence the king shall ever be wakeful.

He shall divide both the day and the night into eight nālikās (1½ hours), or according to the length of the shadow (cast by a gnomon standing in the sun): the shadow of three purushas (36 aṅgulās or ¾ inches), of one purusha (12 inches), of four aṅgulās (3 inches), and absence of shadow denoting midday are the four one-eighth divisions of the forenoon; like divisions (in the reverse order) in the afternoon.

Of these divisions, during the first one-eighth part of the day, he shall post watchmen and attend to the accounts of receipts and expenditure; during the second part, he shall look to the affairs of both citizens and country people; during the third, he shall not only bathe and dine, but also study; during the fourth, he shall not only receive revenue in gold but also attend to the appointments of superintendents; during the fifth, he shall correspond in writs with the assembly of his ministers, and receive the secret information gathered by his spies; during the sixth, he may engage himself in his favourite amusements or in self-deliberation; during the seventh, he shall superintend elephants, horses, chariots, and infantry; and during the eighth part, he shall consider various plans of military operations with his commander-in-chief.

At the close of the day, he shall observe the evening prayer.

During the first one-eighth part of the night, he shall receive secret emissaries; during the second, he shall attend to bathing and supper and study; during the third, he shall enter the bedchamber amid the sound of trumpets and enjoy sleep during the fourth and fifth parts; having been awakened by the sound of trumpets during the sixth part, he shall recall to his mind the injunctions of sciences as well as the day's duties; during the seventh, he shall sit considering administrative measures and send out spies; and during the eighth division of the night, he shall receive benedictions from sacrificial priests, teachers and the high priest, and having seen his physician, chief cook and astrol-

Text: R. Shamasastry (trans.), *Kautilya's Arthasastra*, 4th ed. (Mysore: Sri Raghuveer Press, 1951), pp. 36-39, 68-69, 256-57. Sanskrit words in parentheses have been deleted throughout.

oger, and having saluted both a cow with its calf and a bull by circumambulating round them, he shall get into his court.

Or in conformity to his capacity, he may alter the time-table and attend to his duties.

When in the court, he shall never cause his petitioners to wait at the door, for when a king makes himself inaccessible to his people and entrusts his work to his immediate officers, he may be sure to engender confusion in business, and to cause thereby public disaffection, and himself a prey to his enemies.

He shall, therefore, personally attend to the business of gods, of heretics, of Brāhmans learned in the Vēdas, of cattle, of sacred places, of minors, the aged, the afflicted, and the helpless, and of women;—all this in order (of enumeration) or according to the urgency or pressure of those works.

All urgent calls he shall hear at once, but never put off; for when postponed, they will prove too hard or impossible to accomplish.

Having seated himself in the room where the sacred fire has been kept, he shall attend to the business of physicians and ascetics practising austerities; and that in company with his high priest and teacher and after preliminary salutation (to the petitioners).

Accompanied by persons proficient in the three sciences but not alone lest the petitioners be offended, he shall look to the business of those who are practising austerities, as well as of those who are experts in witchcraft and Yoga.

Of a king, the religious vow is his readiness to action; satisfactory discharge of duties is his performance of sacrifice; equal attention to all is the offer of fees and ablution towards consecration.

In the happiness of his subjects lies his happiness; in their welfare his welfare; whatever pleases himself he shall not consider as good, but whatever pleases his subjects he shall consider as good.

Hence the king shall ever be active and discharge his duties; the root of wealth is activity, and of evil its reverse.

In the absence of activity acquisitions present and to come will perish; by activity he can achieve both his desired ends and abundance of wealth.

Chapter VIII.

... When a government servant has been proved to be guilty of having misappropriated part of a large sum in question, he shall be answerable for the whole.

Any informant who supplies information about embezzlement just under perpetration shall, if he succeeds in proving it, get as reward one-sixth of the amount in question; if he happens to be a government servant, he shall get for the same act one-twelfth of the amount.

If an informant succeeds in proving only a part of a big embezzlement, he shall, nevertheless, get the prescribed share of the part of the embezzled amount proved.

An informant who fails to prove (his assertion) shall be liable to monetary or corporal punishment, and shall never be acquitted.

When the charge is proved, the informant may impute the tale bearing to someone else or clear himself in any other way from the blame. Any informant who withdraws his assertion prevailed upon by the insinuations of the accused shall be condemned to death.

Chapter IX.

Those who are possessed of ministerial qualifications shall, in accordance with their individual capacity, be appointed as superintendents of government departments. While engaged in work, they shall be daily examined; for men are naturally fickleminded, and, like horses at work, exhibit constant change in their temper. Hence the agency and tools which they make use of, the place and time of the work they are engaged in, as well as the precise form of the work, the outlay, and the results shall always be ascertained.

Without dissension and without any concert among themselves, they shall carry on their work as ordered.

When in concert, they eat up (the revenue).

When in disunion, they mar the work.

Without bringing to the knowledge of their master, they shall undertake nothing except remedial measures against imminent dangers.

A fine of twice the amount of their daily pay and of the expenditure (incurred by them) shall be fixed for any inadvertence on their part.

Whoever of the superintendents makes as much as, or more than, the amount of fixed revenue shall be honoured with promotion and rewards.

(My) teacher holds that that officer who spends too much and brings in little revenue eats it up; while he who improves the revenue (*i.e.*, brings in more than he spends) as well as the officer who brings in as much as he spends does not eat up the revenue.

But Kautilya holds that cases of embezzlement or no embezzlement can be ascertained through spies alone.

Whoever lessens the revenue eats the king's wealth. If owing to inadvertence he causes diminution in revenue, he shall be compelled to make good the loss.

Whoever doubles the revenue eats into the vitality of the country. If he brings in double the amount to the king, he shall, if the offence is small, be warned not to repeat the same; but if the offence be grave he shall proportionally be punished.

Whoever spends the revenue (without bringing in any profit) eats up the labour of workmen. Such an officer shall be punished in proportion to the value of the work done, the number of days taken, the amount of capital spent, and the amount of daily wages paid.

Hence the chief officer of each department shall thoroughly scrutinise the real amount of the work done, the receipts realised from, and the expenditure incurred in, that departmental work both in detail and in the aggregate.

He shall also check prodigal, spendthrift and niggardly persons.

Whoever unjustly eats up the property left by his father and grandfather is a prodigal person.

Whoever eats all that he earns is a spendthrift.

Death with or without Torture

When a man murders another in a quarrel, he shall be tortured to death. When a person wounded in a fight dies within seven nights, he who caused the wound shall be put to instantaneous death. If the wounded man dies within a fortnight, the offender shall be punished with the highest amercement. If the wounded man dies within a month, the offender shall be compelled to pay not only a fine of 500 panas, but also an adequate compensation (to the bereaved).

When a man hurts another with a weapon, he shall pay the highest amercement; when he does so under intoxication, his hand shall be cut off; and when he causes instantaneous death, he shall be put to death.

When a person causes abortion in pregnancy by striking, or with medicine, or by annoyance, the highest, middlemost, and first amercements shall be imposed respectively.

Those who cause violent death either to men or women, or those who are in the habit of often going to meet prostitutes, those who inflict unjust punishment upon others, those who spread false or contemptuous rumours, who assault or obstruct travellers on their way, who commit house-breaking, or who steal or cause hurt to royal elephants, horses, or carriages, shall be hanged.

Whoever burns or carries away the corpses of the above offenders shall meet with similar punishment or pay the highest amercement.

When a person supplies murderers or thieves with food, dress, any requisites, fire, information, any plan, or assistance in any way, he shall be punished with the highest amercement. When he does so under ignorance, he shall be censured.

Sons or wives of murderers or of thieves shall, if they are found not in concert, be acquitted; but they shall be seized if found to have been in concert.

Any person who aims at the kingdom, who forces entrance into the king's harem, who instigates wild tribes or enemies (against the king), or who creates disaffection in forts, country parts, or in the army, shall be burnt alive from head to foot.

If a Brāhman does similar acts, he shall be drowned.

Any person who murders his father, mother, son, brother, teacher, or an ascetic, shall be put to death by burning both his head and skin; if he insults any of the above persons, his tongue shall be cut off; if he bites any limb of these persons, he shall be deprived of the corresponding limb.

When a man wantonly murders another, or steals a herd of cattle, he shall be beheaded.

A herd of cattle shall be considered to consist of not more than ten heads.

When a person breaks the dam of a tank full of water, he shall be drowned in the very tank; of a tank without water, he shall be punished with the highest amercement; and of a tank which is in ruins owing to neglect, he shall be punished with the middlemost amercement.

Any man who poisons another and any woman who murders a man shall be drowned.

Any woman who murders her husband, preceptor, or offspring, sets fire to another's property, poisons a man, or cuts off any of the bodily joints of another shall be torn off by bulls, no matter whether or not she is big with a child, or has not passed a month after giving birth to a child.

Any person who sets fire to pasture lands, fields, yards prepared for threshing out grains, houses, forests of timber, or of elephants shall be thrown into fire.

Any person who insults the king, betrays the king's council, makes evil attempts (against the king), or disregards the sanctity of the kitchens of Brāhmans shall have his tongue cut off.

THE HINDU SYNTHESIS

124 THE CODE OF MANU: THE ORGANIZATION OF SOCIAL LIFE INTO FOUR CLASSES

By the third century A.D. the diverse ethnic and cultural streams of India had coalesced to create what is often referred to as "the Hindu synthesis." One of the most important features of the synthesis is the existence of a unique social organization that differentiates Indian civilization from all others. The class structure of India is extraordinarily complex, and there is a widespread disagreement as to its origin and inner nature, but in very general terms it is based on the assumption that there are fundamental, inborn differences between one man and another. The concept appears in very ancient times—as early as the *Rig-Veda*—dividing mankind into four classes. The Brāhmans were the priests and learned men; the Kshatriyas were the warriors; the Vaishyas were merchants and farmers; and the Shudras (in the text below, written as "Çūdras") were the menials. Outside this hierarchical structure were the groups later known as the "untouchables," peoples who, for a variety of reasons, would not fit into the class system. Membership in the classes was determined by birth. Of greatest significance were the duties and functions assigned to the classes; these duties are comprised in the word *dharma*, which carries with it a sense of obligation but is far more than a "moral imperative." Everyone has an appropriate *dharma*; each is obligated to carry this out in the way laid down by the sanctions of his class.

The concept of *dharma* is responsible for more aspects of Indian society than the class structure itself. It has meant that there was no single norm to which all men subscribed, and ethical behavior was understood largely in terms of fulfilling the regulations of one's class. In ancient India—and to some extent in modern India—seeing that no class transgressed on the duties of another became a principal function of the king. This idea is expressed in one of the codes of law, that of Gautama, in the saying that on the king depends "the prevention of the confusion of the classes and the sacred law."

The fourfold division of society given in the law books was the statement of an ideal rather than the description of reality. The ideal of the *dharma* of class had to be fitted in with the existing pattern of relationships as embodied in the word *caste*. The caste system grew up alongside the traditional four classes, but is not identical with it. There are literally thousands of castes in modern India, all of which developed from sources other than the classical division of society and should not be confused with it.

The passages given here are from the code of Manu, one of the most famous of the books concerned with defining the *dharma* of the different classes. The author was obviously anxious to maintain the prerogatives of his own Brāhman class, and the injunctions are to be understood as an expression of the desires of a zealous partisan rather than as laws actually put into practice. One of the errors made by Europeans in their first contacts with India was to assume that the code of Manu describes the legal system of the Hindus, when it generally states pious aspirations rather than "laws" in the western sense. Its emphasis on the distinction between the "twice-born" (the three upper classes), and the "once-born" (the shudras), is extremely important, however, for it provided the central concept around which the society was organized.

... Now, for the sake of preserving all this creation, the most glorious Being ordained separate duties for those who sprang from His mouth, arm, thigh, and feet.

For Brahmans he ordered teaching, study, sacrifice, and sacrificing as priests for others, also giving and receiving gifts.

Defense of the people, giving alms, sacrifice, also study, and absence of attachment to objects of sense, in short, for a Kshatriya.

Tending of cattle, giving alms, sacrifice, study, trade, usury, and also agriculture for a Vaishya.

One duty the Lord assigned to a Shudra—service to those before-mentioned classes, without grudging.

Text: Arthur Coke Burnell and Edward W. Hopkins (trans. and ed.), *The Ordinances of Manu* (London: Trübner and Co., 1884), pp. 12-13, 221-23.

Man is declared purer above the navel; therefore the purest part of him is said by the Self-Existent to be his mouth.

Since he sprang from the most excellent part, since he was the first-born, and since he holds the Vedas, the Brahman is, by right, the lord of all this creation.

Him the Self-Existent, after having performed penance, created in the beginning from his own mouth, for presentation of oblations to the gods and offerings to the manes, and for the preservation of all this world.

What being is then superior to him, by whose mouth the gods eat oblations and the manes offerings?

Of beings, the most excellent are said to be the animated; of the animated, those which subsist by intelligence; of the intelligent, men; of men, the Brahmans.

But of the Brahmans, the learned are most excellent; of the learned, those who know their duty; of those who know it, such as do it; and of those who do it, those who know the Vedas.

The birth of a Brahman is a perpetual incarnation of *dharma;* for he exists for the sake of *dharma,* and is for the existence of the Vedas.

When a Brahman is born, he is born above the world, the chief of all creatures, to guard the treasury of *dharma.*

Thus, whatever exists in the universe is all the property of the Brahman; for the Brahman is entitled to it all by his superiority and eminence of birth.

The Brahman eats his own alone, wears his own, and gives away his own; through the benevolence of the Brahman, indeed, the other people enjoy all they have.

For the ascertainment of his duties and those of the other castes in order, the prudent Manu Svāyambhuva composed this treatise.

This treatise must be strenuously perused by a learned Brahman and explained rightly to the pupil, but not by any other person. . . .

A Kshatriya who reviles a Brahman ought to be fined one hundred *panas;* a Vaishya one hundred and fifty or two hundred; but a Shudra ought to receive corporal punishment.

A Brahman should be fined fifty if he has thrown insult on a Kshatriya, but the fine should be a half of the fifty if on a Vaishya, and twelve if on a Shudra.

If one of the twice-born abuses a man of like caste, he should be fined twelve, but the fine should be twice this amount for words that ought never to be spoken.

If a man of one birth assaults one of the twice-born castes with virulent words, he ought to have his tongue cut, for he is of the lowest origin.

If he make mention in an insulting manner of their name and caste, a red-hot iron rod, ten fingers long, shall be thrust into his mouth.

If this man through insolence gives instruction to the priests in regard to their duty, the king should cause boiling-hot oil to be poured into his mouth and ear.

If one through insolence denies their learning, country, caste, or bodily ceremonies, he should be fined a fine of two hundred.

If he insults a one-eyed man, or a lame man, or any other person deformed in like manner, he should be fined a fine of at least one kārsāpana, even if he speaks the truth.

He who slanders his own mother, father, wife, brother, son, or spiritual teacher, should be fined one hundred, and also he who does not give the right of way to his spiritual teacher.

The fine to be imposed by a wise king on a Brahman and Kshatriya for mutual insults is the first in the case of the Brahman, and the medium fine in the case of the Kshatriya.

Exactly thus and in accordance with the caste of each should be the application of punishment in the case of a Vaishya and Shudra, except the cutting of the tongue: thus is the decision.

Thus has the rule of punishment in regard to verbal injuries been declared in accordance with truth. Now, furthermore, I will proclaim the law of corporal injuries.

If a man of the lowest birth should with any member injure one of the highest station, even that member of this man shall be cut off: this is an ordinance of Manu.

If he lift up his hand or his staff against him, he ought to have his hand cut off; and if he smite him with his foot in anger, he ought to have his foot cut off.

If a low-born man endeavours to sit down by the side of a high-born man, he should be banished after being branded on the hip, or the king may cause his backside to be cut off.

125 BHAGAVAD GITĀ: THE SEARCH FOR SALVATION

The *Bhagavad Gitā* has been popular in India through the ages because it answers the special questions posed by the doctrines of *karma*, transmigration, and *dharma*. The setting for the poem is the war between the Pāndavas and the Kurus, members of the same family but rivals for control of the Kuru kingdom. Arjuna, the leader of the Pāndavas, is dismayed at the thought of fighting against his own relatives, and he turns to his charioteer, Krishna, for help in his perplexity. Krishna is in fact an incarnation of the highest deity, and the answers he gives to Arjuna reveal his identity and at the same time help Arjuna make his difficult decision. To Hindus, the teachings of the *Gitā* are the profoundest statements of religious truth, and they have always looked to it for answers to their questions. During the struggle for Indian independence, for example, many leaders turned to it as a guide to social action. The *Gitā* is a never-failing source of information because it contains a wide spectrum of religious belief, including ideas that sometimes seem contradictory.

In the following selections from the *Gitā*, we find two ideas which have been especially important. One is that salvation comes from fulfilling the assigned duties of life—the *dharma* of one's class. It is not a call to service in the ordinary sense; one must act, but action consists simply of performing the function defined by one's *dharma*. This concept of "motiveless action" is extremely important in the Indian tradition, and its reinterpretation by Mahatma Gandhi was used to sanction "non-cooperation" and similar effective political techniques used in twentieth-century India.

Another predominant idea in the *Gitā* is the importance of devotion to Krishna as a means of salvation. Here the emphasis is on Krishna as the supreme god who accepts the devotion of men and responds to it with loving grace. In western religion the concepts of salvation by works or grace represent polar positions, but in the *Gitā* no great conflict arises between a religion of law and one of grace. It is symbolic of the special genius of the Indian religious tradition that two extremes could be comprehended within a single religious document.

Arjuna spake:—

"As I look, O Krishna, upon these kinsfolk meeting for battle,
my limbs fail and my face withers.
Trembling comes upon my body, and upstanding of the hair;
Gāṇḍiva falls from my hand, and my skin burns. I cannot stand in my place; my mind is as if awhirl.

Contrary are the omens that I behold, O Long-Haired One. I see no blessing from slaying of kinsfolk in strife;

I desire not victory, O Krishna, nor kingship, nor delights. What shall avail me kingship, O Lord of the Herds, or pleasures, or life?

They for whose sake I desired kingship, pleasures, and delights stand here in battle-array, offering up their lives and substance—

teachers, fathers, sons, likewise grandsires, uncles, fathers-in-law, grandsons, brothers-in-law, kinsmen also.

These though they smite me I would not smite, O Madhu-Slayer, even for the sake of empire over the Three Worlds, much less for the sake of the earth.

What pleasure can there be to us, O Troubler of the Folk, from slaughter of Dhṛitarāshtra's folk? Guilt in sooth will lodge with us for doing these to death with armed hand.

Therefore it is not meet that we slay Dhṛitarāshtra's folk, our kinsmen; for if we do to death our own kith how can we walk in joy, O Lord of Madhu?

Albeit they, whose wits are stopped by greed, mark not the guilt of destroying a stock and the sin of treason to friends,

yet how, O Troubler of the Folk, shall not we with clear sight see the sin of destroying a stock, so that we be stayed from this guilt?

In the destruction of a stock perish the ancient Laws of the stock; when Law perishes, Lawlessness falls upon the whole stock.

When Lawlessness comes upon it, O Krishna, the women of the stock fall to sin; and from the women's sinning, O thou of Vṛishṇi's race, castes become confounded.

Text: Lionel D. Barnett (trans.), *The Bhagavad Gitā* (London: J. M. Dent & Sons, Ltd., 1905), pp. 84-91, 127-31 *passim*.

Confounding of caste brings to hell alike the stock's slayers and the stock; for their Fathers fall when the offerings of the cake and the water to them fail.

By this guilt of the destroyers of a stock, which makes castes to be confounded, the everlasting Laws of race and Laws of stock are overthrown.

For men the Laws of whose stock are overthrown, O Troubler of the Folk, a dwelling is ordained in hell; thus have we heard.

Ah me! a heavy sin have we resolved to do, that we strive to slay our kin from lust after the sweets of kingship!

It were more comfortable to me if Dhritarāshtra's folk with armed hand should slay me in the strife unresisting and weaponless."

Sanjaya spake:—

So spake Arjuna, and sate down on the seat of his chariot in the field of war; and he let fall his bow and arrows, for his heart was heavy with sorrow.

Sanjaya spake:—

So was he stricken by compassion and despair, with clouded eyes full of tears; and the Slayer of Madhu spake to him this word.

The Lord spake:—

"Wherefore, O Arjuna, hath come upon thee in thy straits this defilement, such as is felt by the ignoble, making not for heaven, begetting dishonour?

Fall not into unmanliness, O Prithā's son; it is unmeet for thee. Cease from this base faintness of heart and rise up, O affrighter of the foe!"

Arjuna spake:—

"O Madhu's Slayer, how shall I contend in the strife with my arrows against Bhīshma and Drona, who are meet for honour, O smiter of foes?

Verily it were more blest to eat even the food of beggary in this world, without slaughter of noble masters; were I to slay my masters, I should enjoy here but wealth and loves—delights sullied with blood.

We know not which is the better for us, whether we should overcome them or they overcome us; before us stand arrayed Dhritarāshtra's folk, whom if we slay we shall have no wish for life.

My soul stricken with the stain of unmanliness, my mind all unsure of the Law, I ask thee—tell me clearly what will be the more blest way. I am thy disciple; teach me, who am come to thee for refuge.

I behold naught that can cast out the sorrow that makes my limbs to wither, though I win to wide lordship without rival on earth and even to empire over the gods."

So spake to the High-Haired One the Wearer of the Hair-Knot, affrighter of foes; "I will not war," he said to the Lord of the Herds, and made an end of speaking.

And as he sate despairing between the two hosts, O thou of Bharata's race, the High-Haired One with seeming smile spake to him this word.

The Lord spake:—

"Thou hast grieved over them for whom grief is unmeet, though thou speakest words of understanding. The learned grieve not for them whose lives are fled nor for them whose lives are not fled.

Never have I not been, never hast thou and never have these princes of men not been; and never shall time yet come when we shall not all be.

As the Body's Tenant goes through childhood and manhood and old age in this body, so does it pass to other bodies; the wise man is not confounded therein.

It is the touchings of the senses' instruments, O Kuntī's son, that beget cold and heat, pleasure and pain; it is they that come and go, that abide not; bear with them, O thou of Bharata's race.

Verily the man whom these disturb not, indifferent alike to pain and to pleasure, and wise, is meet for immortality, O chief of men.

Of what is not there cannot be being; of what is there cannot be aught but being. The bounds of these twain have been beheld by them that behold the Verity.

But know that That which pervades this universe is imperishable; there is none can make to perish that changeless being.

It is these bodies of the everlasting, unperishing, incomprehensible Body-Dweller that have an end, as it is said. Therefore fight, O thou of Bharata's race.

He who deems This to be a slayer, and he who thinks This to be slain, are alike without discernment; This slays not, neither is it slain.

This never is born, and never dies, nor may it after being come again to be not; this unborn, everlasting, abiding Ancient is not slain when the body is slain.

Knowing This to be imperishable, everlasting, unborn, changeless, O son of Prithā, how and whom can a man make to be slain, or slay?

As a man lays aside outworn garments and takes others that are new, so the Body-Dweller puts away outworn bodies and goes to others that are new.

Weapons cleave not This, fire burns not This, waters wet not This, wind dries it not.

Not to be cleft is This, not to be burned, nor to be wetted, nor likewise to be dried; everlasting is This, dwelling in all things, firm, motionless, ancient of days.

Unshown is This called, unthinkable This, unalterable This; therefore, knowing it in this wise, thou dost not well to grieve.

So though thou deemest it everlastingly to pass through births and everlastingly through deaths, nevertheless, O strong of arm, thou shouldst not grieve thus.

For to the born sure is death, to the dead sure is birth; so for an issue that may not be escaped thou dost not well to sorrow.

Born beings have for their beginning the unshown state, for their midway the shown, O thou of Bharata's race, and for their ending the unshown; what lament is there for this?

As a marvel one looks upon This; as a marvel another tells thereof; and as a marvel another hears of it; but though he hear of This none knows it.

This Body's Tenant for all time may not be wounded, O thou of Bharata's stock, in the bodies of any beings. Therefore thou dost not well to sorrow for any born beings.

Looking likewise on thine own Law, thou shouldst not be dismayed; for to a knight there is no thing more blest than a lawful strife.

Happy the knights, O son of Pritha, who find such a strife coming unsought to them as an open door to Paradise.

But if thou wilt not wage this lawful battle, then wilt thou fail thine own Law and thine honour, and get sin.

Also born beings will tell of thee a tale of unchanging dishonour; and to a man of repute dishonour is more than death.

The lords of great chariots will deem thee to have held back from the strife through fear; and thou wilt come to be lightly esteemed of those by whom thou wert erstwhile deemed of much worth.

They that seek thy hurt will say many words of ill speech, crying out upon thee for thy faintness; now what is more grievous than this?

If thou be slain, thou wilt win Paradise; if thou conquer, thou wilt have the joys of the earth; therefore rise up resolute for the fray, O son of Kuntī.

Holding in indifference alike pleasure and pain, gain and loss, conquest and defeat, so make thyself ready for the fight; thus shalt thou get no sin. . . .

Into a godlike nature, O son of Pritha, enter great-hearted men who worship Me with undivided mind, knowing Me to be the Beginning of born beings, the unchanging;

Ever singing My praises, labouring firm in their vows, devoutly doing homage, everlastingly under the Rule, men wait on Me.

Others again there are that wait on Me, offering the Sacrifice of Knowledge, according to My unity, or My severalty, or My manifold aspects that face all ways.

The sacrifice am I, the offering am I, the Fathers' oblation am I, the herb am I, the spell am I, the butter-libation am I, the fire am I, the rite of oblation am I;

father of this universe am I, mother, ordainer, grandsire, the thing that is known and the being that makes clean, the word *Om,* the Ṛik, the Sāma, and the Yajus;

the way, the supporter, the lord, the witness, the dwelling, the refuge, the friend, the origin, the dissolution, the abiding-place, the house of ward, the changeless seed.

I give heat; I arrest and let loose the rain; I am likewise power of immortality and death, Being and No-Being, O Arjuna.

Men of the Threefold Lore that drink the *soma* and are cleansed of sin, worshipping me with sacrifices, pray for the way to paradise; winning as meed of righteousness the world of the Lord of Gods, they taste in heaven the heavenly delights of the gods.

When they have enjoyed that wide world of paradise and their wage of righteousness is spent, they enter into the world of mortals; thus the lovers of loves who follow the Law of the Three Books win but a going and a coming.

But to the men everlastingly under the Rule, who in undivided service think and wait on Me, I bring power to win and to maintain.

They also who worship other gods and make offering to them with faith, O son of Kuntī, do verily make offering to Me, though not according to ordinance.

For I am He that has enjoyment and lordship of all sacrifices; but they recognise Me not in verity, and therefore they fall.

They whose vows are to the gods go to the gods, they whose vows are to the Fathers go to the Fathers; they who offer to ghosts go to ghosts; but they that offer to Me go to Me.

If one of earnest spirit set before Me with devotion a leaf, a flower, fruit, or water, I enjoy this offering of devotion.

Whatever be thy work, thine eating, thy sacrifice, thy gift, thy mortification, make thou of it an offering to Me, O son of Kuntī.

Thus shalt thou be released from the bonds of Works, fair or foul of fruit; thy spirit inspired by casting-off of Works and following the Rule, thou shalt be delivered and come unto Me.

I am indifferent to all born beings; there is none whom I hate, none whom I love. But they that worship Me with devotion dwell in Me, and I in them.

Even though he should be a doer of exceeding evil that worships Me with undivided worship, he shall be deemed good; for he is of right purpose.

Speedily he becomes righteous of soul, and comes to lasting peace. O son of Kuntī, be assured that none who is devoted to Me is lost.

For even they that be born of sin, O son of Pritha,—women, traffickers, and serfs,—if they turn to Me, come to the supreme path;

how much more then shall righteous Brahmans and devout kingly sages? As thou has come into this unstable and joyless world, worship Me.

Have thy mind on Me, thy devotion toward Me, thy sacrifice to Me, do homage to Me. Thus guiding thyself, given over to Me, so to Me shalt thou come."

The Lord spake:—

"Again, O strong-armed one, hearken to My sublime tale, which in desire for thy weal I will recite to thy delighted ear.

The ranks of the gods and the saints know not My origin; for I am altogether the Beginning of gods and saints.

He who unbewildered knows Me to be the unborn, the one without beginning, great lord of worlds, is released from all sins amidst mortals.

Understanding, knowledge, unconfounded vision, patience, truth, restraint of sense and spirit, joy and sorrow, origination and not-being, fear and fearlessness,

harmlessness, indifference, delight, mortification, almsgiving, fame, and infamy—these are the forms of born beings' existence severally dispensed by Me.

The seven Great Saints, the four Ancients, and the Manus had their spirit of Me, and were born of My mind; of them are these living creatures in the world.

He that knows in verity My power and rule is assuredly ruled by unwavering Rule.

I am the origin of the All; from Me the All proceeds; with this belief the enlightened, possessed of the spirit, pay worship to Me.

126   *VISHNU PURĀNA:* THE WORSHIP OF GOD IN MANY FORMS

When the monotheistic, idol-hating Muslims conquered India, they were horrified, as were Christians at a later time, by the incredible number and variety of gods worshiped by the Hindus. There was, for example, the fierce Kālī, goddess of destruction, garlanded with skulls, dancing on the prostrate bodies of her foes. In contrast, there was the noble Rāma, symbol of all manly virtues, and Sītā, his gentle consort. In addition to the many major gods and goddesses there were hosts of local deities. To the knowledgeable Hindu, however, these many forms represented not different gods, but expressions of the infinite richness and diversity of reality. This multiple faith found literary expression in a vast literature known as the *Purānas*. A selection from one of these, the *Vishnu Purāna*, is given here; as the title indicates, the theme of this work is the god Vishnu, with special attention being given to his incarnation in the form of Krishna. Vishnu, like the other gods, has been incarnated in earthly forms many times. As a result, all of India is regarded as holy land, for there are few spots where some divinity has not revealed himself to his devotees. This is particularly true of Krishna, and the identification of his great deeds with well-known locations has had a powerful effect on the Indian imagination.

The Krishna of the *Bhagavad Gītā* (see Document 125) is a very different figure from that of the *Vishnu Purāna*, where he appears as a gay, light-hearted, amorous youth. It is thought by scholars that Krishna as he finally appears in Indian religion represents the fusion of a number of gods. It is possible that Krishna in the *Gītā* preserves the memory of some actual warrior hero who was deified. This deity came to be identified with a cowherd god and, later, with other traditional hero-gods. It is the youthful Krishna of the *Purāna* that has appeared most frequently in Indian art and literature; the account given here of his relations with the milkmaids, the *gopīs*, is a familiar theme in many paintings and poems. The story is interpreted from a religious point of view to mean that Krishna's expansive love for the many milkmaids symbolizes the god's gracious love for all men. As the story opens, Krishna has just saved the cowherds and their cattle from being destroyed by a deluge sent by the jealous god Indra. Krishna did this by uprooting a mountain and holding it over their heads as an umbrella.

After Śakra had departed, the cowherds said to Krishńa, whom they had seen holding up Govardhana: "We have been preserved, together with our cattle, from a great peril, by your supporting the mountain (above us). But this is very astonishing child's play, unsuitable to the condition of a herdsman; and all thy actions are those of a god. Tell us what is the meaning of all this. Káliya has been conquered in the lake; Pralamba has been killed; Govardhana has been lifted up: our minds are filled with amazement. Assuredly, we repose at the feet of Hari, O thou of unbounded might. For, having witnessed thy power, we cannot believe thee to be a man. Thy affection, Keśava, for our women and children, and for Vraja; the deeds that thou hast wrought, which all the gods would have attempted in vain; thy boyhood, and thy prowess; thy humiliating birth amongst us,—are contradictions that fill us with doubt, whenever we think of them. Yet, reverence be to thee, whether thou be a god, or a demon, or a Yaksha, or a Gandharva, or whatever we may deem thee; for thou art our friend." When they had ended, Krishńa remained silent, for some time, as if hurt and offended, and then replied to them: "Herdsmen, if you are not ashamed of my relationship; if I have merited your praise; what occasion is there for you to engage in any discussion (concerning me)? If you have (any) regard for me; if I have deserved your praise; then be satisfied to know that I am your kinsman. I am neither god nor Yaksha, nor Gandharva, nor Dánava. I have been born your relative; and you must not think differently of me." Upon receiving this answer, the Gopas held their peace, and went into the woods, leaving Krishńa apparently displeased.

But Krishńa, observing the clear sky bright with the autumnal moon, and the air perfumed with the fragrance of the wild water-lily, in whose buds the clustering bees were murmuring their songs, felt inclined to join with the Gopís in sport. Accordingly, he and Ráma commenced singing sweet low strains, in various measures, such as the women loved; and they, as soon as they heard the melody, quitted their homes, and hastened to meet the foe of Madhu. One damsel gently sang an accompaniment to his song; another attentively listened to his melody. One, calling out upon his name, then shrunk abashed; whilst another, more bold, and instigated by affection, pressed close to his side. One, as she sallied forth, beheld some of the seniors (of the family), and dared not venture, contenting herself with meditating on Krishńa, with closed eyes, and entire devotion, by which, immediately, all acts of merit were effaced by rapture, and all sin was expiated by regret at not beholding him; and others, again, reflecting upon the cause of the world, in the form of the supreme Brahma, obtained, by their sighing, final emancipation. Thus surrounded by the Gopís, Krishńa thought the lovely moonlight night of autumn propitious to the Rása-dance. Many of the Gopís imitated the different actions of Krishńa, and, in his absence wandered through Vrindávana, (representing his person). "I am Krishńa," cries one. "Behold the elegance of my movements." "I am Krishńa," exclaims another. "Listen to my song." "Vile Káliya, stay! For I am Krishńa," is repeated by a third, slapping her arms in defiance. A fourth calls out: "Herdsmen, fear nothing; be steady: the danger of the storm is over. For, lo! I lift up Govardhana, for your shelter." And a fifth proclaims: "Now let the herds graze where they will: for I have destroyed Dhenuka." Thus, in various actions of Krishńa, the Gopís imitated him, whilst away, and beguiled their sorrow by mimicking his sports. Looking down upon the ground, one damsel calls to her friend, as the light down upon her body stands erect (with joy), and the lotoses of her eyes expand: "See, here are the marks of Krishńa's feet as he has gone along sportively, and left the impressions of the banner, the thunderbolt, and the goad. What lovely maiden has been his companion, inebriate with passion, as her irregular footmarks testify? Here Dámodara has gathered flowers from on high; for we see alone the impressions of the tips of his feet. Here a nymph has sat down with him, ornamented with flowers, fortunate in having propitiated Vishńu in a prior existence. Having left her in an arrogant mood, because he had offered her flowers, the son of Nanda has gone by this road; for, see, unable to follow him with equal steps, his associate has here tripped along upon her toes, and, holding his hand, the damsel has passed, as is evident from the uneven and intermingled footsteps. But the rogue has merely taken her hand, and left her neglected; for here the paces indicate the path of a person in despair. Undoubtedly, he promised that he would quickly come again; for here are his own footsteps returning with speed. Here he has entered the thick forest, impervious to the rays of the moon; and his steps can be traced no further." Hopeless, then, of beholding Krishńa, the Gopís returned, and repaired to the banks of the Yamuná, where they sang his songs; and presently they beheld the preserver of the three worlds, with a smiling aspect, hastening towards them.

Text: Horace Hayman Wilson, *Works* (London: Trübner & Co., 1868), IX, 322-31.

On which, one exclaimed "Krishńa! Krishńa!" unable to articulate anything else; another affected to contract her forehead with frowns, as drinking, with the bees of her eyes, the lotos of the face of Hari; another, closing her eyelids, contemplated, internally his form, as if engaged in an act of devotion. Then Mádhava, coming amongst them, conciliated some with soft speeches, some, with gentle looks; and some he took by the hand: and the illustrious deity sported with them in the stations of the dance. As each of the Gopís, however, attempted to keep in one place, close to the side of Krishńa, the circle of the dance could not be constructed; and he, therefore, took each by the hand, and, when their eyelids were shut by the effects of such touch, the circle was formed. Then proceeded the dance, to the music of their clashing bracelets, and songs that celebrated, in suitable strain, the charms of the autumnal season. Krishńa sang the moon of autumn,—a mine of gentle radiance; but the nymphs repeated the praises of Krishńa alone. At times, one of them, wearied by the revolving dance, threw her arms, ornamented with tinkling bracelets, round the neck of the destroyer of Madhu; another, skilled in the art of singing his praises, embraced him. The drops of perspiration from the arms of Hari were like fertilizing rain, which produced a crop of down upon the temples of the Gopís. Krishńa sang the strain that was appropriate to the dance. The Gopís repeatedly exclaimed "Bravo, Krishńa!" to his song. When leading, they followed him; when returning, they encountered him; and, whether he went forwards or backwards, they ever attended on his steps. Whilst frolicking thus with the Gopís, they considered every instant, without him, a myriad of years; and, prohibited (in vain) by husbands, fathers, brothers, they went forth, at night, to sport with Krishńa, the object of their affection. Thus, the illimitable being, the benevolent remover of all imperfections, assumed the character of a youth amongst the females of the herdsmen of Vraja; pervading their natures, and that of their lords, by his own essence, all-diffusive like the wind. For, even as, in all creatures, the elements of ether, fire, earth, water, and air are comprehended, so, also, is he everywhere present, and in all.

127 RĀMĀYANA: THE IDEAL OF FAMILY LIFE

Within the Indian social system, the family rather than the individual has been the object of ethical concern, and questions concerning moral rights and responsibilities have traditionally been discussed in relation to the preservation of the family. Furthermore, the family was not only the usual group of parents and children, but included a complex array of relatives comprising what is known as a "joint" family. The importance of relatives is suggested by the fact that Indian languages have special terms for each degree of consanguinity; there are, for example, words to indicate whether a grandfather is on the maternal or paternal side.

The results for the social order of family-oriented ethics have been significant. All really important decisions, such as the choice of a marriage partner or of a career, were matters to be decided by the head of the family, not the individual immediately concerned. The ideal of this social structure was loving obedience by children to their parents and wives to their husbands, since both forms of obedience looked to the same figure of authority, the father. (It should be noted that among some Indians, matriarchal, not patriarchal, authority existed, but this was localized.)

The most famous story of India, the *Rāmāyana*, pictures the ideal relationship of child to father and of wife to husband. Rāma, Prince of Ayodhya, willingly goes into exile because of a promise his father had made to one of his queens to give her anything she wanted. The queen requested that Rāma, the heir apparent, should be banished and that her own son should rule in his stead. Rāma's wife Sītā followed him into exile, and the story of their journey and of the perils they encountered have become part of the Indian heritage. For at least two thousand years, all Indian people have learned in common the story of Rāma and Sītā.

. . . "O Sita, my honoured father has commanded me to go into exile. O Princess, born of an illustrious family, acquainted with the law of dharma and eminent in virtue, hear, while I tell thee what has befallen me. Long ago my father, a lover of truth, granted two boons to my mother Kaikeyi. Beholding the preparations for my coro-

Text: H. P. Shastri (trans.), *The Rāmāyana of Vālmīki* (London: Shanti Sadan, 1952), I, 220-21, 226-28.

nation, Kaikeyi demanded the fulfilment of her boons and has now gained ascendency over his mind. In accordance with the two boons granted to her, it is mine to pass fourteen years in the Dandaka forest and Prince Bharata to be installed as regent. I am now going into exile and have come to bid thee farewell. Let no words in praise of me be repeated to Prince Bharata, lest he withhold his protection from thee. It is for thee to submit to his will for the sake of thy support. The king has conferred the regency on Prince Bharata forever. It behoves thee to act in such a way that he be not displeased with thee. O Wise One, now I go to the forest in obedience to my father's behest, remain here with a quiet heart. O Sinless One, when dressed as a hermit I leave for the forest, then do thou also cease to adorn thyself. Rising early, do thou worship the gods according to the prescribed rituals, then, approaching my father and mother, offer obeisance to them. My mother, Queen Kaushalya, having grown old, is afflicted on account of my departure, it becomes thee to serve her with respect. My other mothers should be honoured and served by thee like Queen Kaushalya, their hearts are also full of love towards me. Like my own mother Kaushalya, they have also cherished me, therefore I deem them worthy of the same honour. My brothers Bharata and Shatrughna should be regarded by thee as thy brothers or thy sons. It behoves thee never to provoke Prince Bharata, from now ruler of the kingdom and chief of the family. Served with sincerity, a king is pleased, but if provoked, he becomes full of wrath. A monarch renounces his own offspring if they oppose him and receives even strangers, as friends, who have promoted his welfare. O Kalyani, obeying King Bharata, remain here, seeking his good. O Dear One, I shall enter the great forest, it behoves thee to remain here; I charge thee to act in such a manner that no one will be displeased."

The sweet-speaking Sita, worthy of Rama's love, thus being instructed to remain in Ayodhya, though filled with affection, indignantly replied: "O Offspring of a great king, O Rama, how canst thou speak in such wise? O Prince, thy words evoke laughter. O Chief of Men, father, mother, son and daughter-in-law live according to their merit and dependent on it, but a wife enjoys the fortune of her husband since she is a part of himself. I am therefore entitled to share thy father's command and also go into exile.

"The happiness of a woman depends on her husband, neither father, mother, son, relative or companion avail her at death; in this world and in the other world, the husband alone is her all-in-all. If thou to-day depart for the forest, I will precede thee on foot, clearing the thorns and kusha grass from thy path. O Hero, relinquishing anger and pride, take me with thee without hesitation. There is no fault in me that merits my remaining here, without thee. The joy experienced by lords of men whether dwelling in a palace or transported in an aerial chariot through the heavens or possessing the eightfold psychic powers, is far inferior to the joy of the wife in the service of her lord. My royal father has instructed me fully in the duties of a wife and, therefore, I have no need of further instruction in the matter. Assuredly I shall accompany thee to the forest, uninhabited by men, filled with savage beasts, such as bears and bulls. O My Hero, I will dwell in the forest as happily as in the palace of my father, having no anxiety in the three worlds save the service of my spouse. O Hero, I will wander with thee in the forest according to the ancient spiritual ordinance, free from desire for pleasure, traversing the honey-scented woodland. O Lord of my Life, since thou canst protect and support innumerable people, canst thou not more easily protect me? Without doubt to-day I shall enter the forest with thee, O Fortunate Prince, none can break my resolve. . . .

"O Rama, why dost thou desire to surrender me to Bharata, I, who, long resident with thee, thy youthful spouse, am solely devoted to thee? Whether living as an ascetic or hermit or residing in heaven, I will follow thee. Journeying in the forest will not weary me; by following thee, I shall experience the same delight as walking in the gardens or sporting with thee in the woods. O Rama, in thy company the thorny briars such as kusha, sarpat and shara will seem to me as soft as deer skin. The dust raised by the storm, covering my body, will be as sandalpaste to me. I shall share with thee the couch of grass with the same delight as a bed of silken down. Whatever leaves, roots or fruits thou dost bring for me will be as sweet and satisfying as ambrosia. Enjoying with thee, the fruits and flowers of every season, I shall not call to mind my mother, father and home. No anxiety will be caused to thee by my presence in the forest, neither shall my sustenance be a burden to thee. I tell thee the forest will be heaven in thy company, and without thee even the palace will be hell to me. Be pleased, therefore, to let me go to the forest with thee. I fear nought in the forest, but if thou still refuseth to take me with thee, then will I end my life by poison; never will I dwell among strangers. O My Lord, without thee nothing is left to me but death; abandoned by thee, it were better to die. I cannot endure the grief of thy separation even for an hour, how then shall I suffer it for fourteen years?"

Thus Sita, lamenting and embracing Shri Rama, wept aloud. From her eyes, like a she elephant wounded by poisoned arrows, long-restrained tears issued, as fire is kindled by the friction of wood. Crystal drops fell from her eyes as water slips from the petals of the lotus flowers. The face of the princess resembling the full moon, withered by the fire of intense grief, looked like a lotus withdrawn from water.

Shri Ramachandra, taking Sita, afflicted and fainting, in his arms, spoke to her in the following wise: "O Devi, I do not desire even to enter heaven if it causes thee pain! Nought do I fear! Like Brahma, I am wholly fearless! Though able to protect thee in every way, yet not fully knowing thy mind, I declined to let thee share my exile. Seeing thou art destined to share my exile, I do not desire to abandon thee, as a man of virtuous conduct determines not to sacrifice his good name. O Beautiful One, following the example of the good of yore, I shall act in the same manner; do thou follow me as Suvarchala follows the sun. O Daughter of King Janaka, I am not entering the forest by my own desire, but to obey the injunctions of my father. O Devi, it is the duty of a son to obey his parents, I could not endure life if I failed to observe my father's command. Fate is invisible, who can control it, but the parents and the spiritual preceptor are visible deities and their orders must be obeyed. What in the world is so sacred as the worship of that which grants dharma, prosperity and pleasure? By this worship, homage is paid to the three worlds. O Sita, observance of truth, charity and sacrifice accompanied by suitable offerings (dakshina) is of less avail in obtaining the spiritual realm than the service of parents and the Guru. Those who serve their parents and the spiritual preceptor obtain heaven, wealth, learning and progeny and nothing is impossible for them. Those who are devoted to their parents and their Guru obtain entrance to heaven and the regions of the devas, the gandharvas and Brahma. This is eternal righteousness—to obey the command of thy parents, fixed in the practice of truth. O Sita, not knowing thy mind, I advised thee not to accompany me, but now seeing thy fixed resolve I desire to take thee with me. O Princess, whose eyes sparkle like wine, thou art destined to be my companion, do thou assist me in the performance of my duty. It is well that thou didst desire to be with me in accordance with the custom of our forbears. O Sita, prepare to go into exile without delay; without thee, even heaven does not please me. Bestow thy jewels on the brahmins in charity and offer food to the poor; hasten, make no delay. Give to the brahmins, jewels, ornaments, rich apparel, whatever thou possessest or is employed for my entertainment, all that is mine and thine, couches, coverlets, and vehicles give in charity to the brahmins and what remains distribute among the servants."

Shri Sita, happy at the acquiescence of Prince Rama and knowing her departure to be fixed, began to distribute all her possessions. Free from anxiety, Sita bestowed on the pious brahmins her wealth and all her jewels.

THE COMING OF THE MUSLIM CONQUERORS

128 ZIĀ UD-DĪN BARNĪ, TĀRĪKH-I-FĪRŪZ SHĀHĪ: THE DILEMMA OF THE MUSLIM RULER IN INDIA

Although Islamic peoples had been raiding India since the eighth century, and Arabs had actually established themselves in the lower Indus Valley, the conquest of the country did not get under way in earnest until the last quarter of the twelfth century. By the middle of the fourteenth century Muslim power was reasonably secure, and although a unified empire had not yet been created, it was plain that political control had passed from the hands of the Hindu rulers.

The conditions that Islam met in India were quite different from those encountered elsewhere in its extraordinarily successful history. In North Africa, Asia Minor, and the Middle East, the conquered populations had accepted the religion of the victors either because of forced conversions or because of the attractiveness of the simple, dynamic creed. In India, however, the vastness of the population and the cohesiveness of the social structure prevented the widespread acceptance of a religion introduced by a handful of invaders. Despite considerable violence, devoted missionary work, and great social pressure, Islam remained a minority religion in India.

The existence of a large non-Muslim population presented a serious problem to the Muslim rulers. The Koran plainly stated that the duty of a ruler was to convert infidels.

According to the strictest interpretation, the only recourse a ruler had was to offer "unbelievers" the alternatives of submission to Islam or to the sword. An exception was made in the case of Christians and Jews, since they were people with a revealed Book. They were offered a legal, but inferior, status as *zimmīs* on the payment of a tax called *jizya*. The idol-worshiping Hindus, however, were especially offensive to the Muslims and many pious Muslims thought that no exception should be made for them. Yet, since every Muslim ruler was aware that the bulk of his revenue came from his Hindu subjects, he was disposed toward tolerating their existence; at the same time, he felt impelled to follow the dictates of his religion. It is this dilemma that the great historian Ziā ud-dīn Barnī (c. 1285-1357) is touching upon in the following account of an incident during the rule of Alā-ud-dīn Khaljī (1296-1316), one of the most successful and ruthless of the Muslim conquerors. Barnī's account shows that the sultan's motive for oppressing the Hindus was only nominally religious; his main concern was to prevent them from rebelling. After Alā-ud-dīn's death his very harsh regulations were abandoned, and, as Barnī complains, the Hindus "again found pleasure and happiness." While Alā-ud-dīn had lived, the Hindus were "so harassed by corporal punishment that they had not had time to scratch their heads," but once he was gone "they now put on fine apparel, rode on horseback and shot their arrows." They repaid the new sultan's indulgence, according to Barnī, with "disaffection and rebellion."

. . . [T]he Sultán requested the wise men to supply some rules and regulations for grinding down the Hindus, and for depriving them of that wealth and property which fosters disaffection and rebellion. There was to be one rule for the payment of tribute applicable to all . . . and the heaviest tribute was not to fall upon the poorest. The Hindu was to be so reduced as to be left unable to keep a horse to ride on, to carry arms, to wear fine clothes, or to enjoy any of the luxuries of life. To effect these important objects of government two regulations were made. The first was that all cultivation, whether on a small or large scale, was to be carried on by measurement at a certain rate for every *biswa*. Half (of the produce) was to be paid without any diminution, and this rule was to apply . . . without the slightest distinction. . . . The second related to buffaloes, goats, and other animals from which milk is obtained. A tax for pasturage, at a fixed rate, was to be levied, and was to be demanded for every inhabited house, so that no animal, however wretched, could escape the tax. Heavier burdens were not to be placed upon the poor, but the rules as to the payment of the tribute were to apply equally to rich and poor. Collectors, clerks, and other officers employed in revenue matters, who took bribes and acted dishonestly, were all dismissed. Sharaf Káí . . . an accomplished scribe and a most honest and intelligent man, who had no rival either in capacity or integrity, exerted himself strenuously for some years in enforcing these regulations in all the villages and towns. They were so strictly carried out that the . . . [local officials] were not able to ride on horseback, to find weapons, to get fine clothes, or to indulge in betel. The same rules for the collection of the tribute applied to all alike, and the people were brought to such a state of obedience that one revenue officer would string twenty . . . [local officials] together by the neck, and enforce payment by blows. No Hindu could hold up his head, and in their houses no sign of gold or silver . . . or of any superfluity was to be seen. These things, which nourish insubordination and rebellion, were no longer to be found. Driven by destitution, the wives of the . . . [officials] went and served for hire in the houses of the Musulmáns. Sharaf Káí, *náib-wazír*, so rigorously enforced his demands and exactions against the collectors and other revenue officers, and such investigations were made, that every single *jítal* against their names was ascertained from the books of the . . . village accountants. Blows, confinement in the stocks, imprisonment and chains were all employed to enforce payment. There was no chance of a single *tanka* being taken dishonestly, or as bribery, from any Hindu or Musulmán. The revenue collectors and officers were so coerced and checked that for five hundred or a thousand *tankas* they were imprisoned and kept in chains for years. Men looked upon revenue officers as something worse than fever. Clerkship was a great crime, and no man would give his daughter to a clerk. Death was deemed preferable to revenue employment. Ofttimes fiscal officers fell into prison, and had to endure blows and stripes.

'Aláu-d dín was a king who had no acquaintance with learning, and never associated with the learned. When he became king, he came to the conclusion that polity and government are one thing, and the rules and decrees of law are another. Royal commands belong to the king, legal

Text: Sir H. M. Elliot and John Dowson (eds. & trans.), *The History of India as Told by Its Own Historians* (London: Trübner & Co., 1871), III, 182-185.

decrees rest upon the judgment of *kázís* and *muftís* [Muslim judges and scholars]. In accordance with this opinion, whatever affair of state came before him, he only looked to the public good, without considering whether his mode of dealing with it was lawful or unlawful. He never asked for legal opinions about political matters, and very few learned men visited him. Kází Mughísu-d dín, of Bayánah, used to go to court and sit down in private audience with the *amírs*. One day, when the efforts were being made for the increase of the tribute and of the fines and imposts, the Sultán told the *Kází* that he had several questions to ask him, and desired him to speak the plain truth. The *Kází* replied, "The angel of my destiny seems to be close at hand, since your Majesty wishes to question me on matters of religion; if I speak the truth you will be angry and kill me." The Sultán said he would not kill him, and commanded him to answer his questions truly and candidly. The *Kází* then promised to answer in accordance with what he had read in books. The Sultán then asked, "How are Hindus designated in the law, as payers of tribute or givers of tribute?" The *Kází* replied, "They are called payers of tribute, and when the revenue officer demands silver from them, they should, without question and with all humility and respect, tender gold. If the officer throws dirt into their mouths, they must without reluctance open their mouths wide to receive it. By doing so they show their respect for the officer. The due subordination of the *zimmí* (tribute-payer) is exhibited in this humble payment and by this throwing of dirt into their mouths. The glorification of Islám is a duty, and contempt of the Religion is vain. God holds them in contempt, for he says, 'Keep them under in subjection.' To keep the Hindus in abasement is especially a religious duty, because they are the most inveterate enemies of the Prophet, and because the Prophet has commanded us to slay them, plunder them, and make them captive, saying, 'Convert them to Islám or kill them, enslave them and spoil their wealth and property.' No doctor but the great doctor (Hanífa), to whose school we belong, has assented to the imposition of the *jizya* (poll tax) on Hindus. Doctors of other schools allow no other alternative but 'Death or Islám.'"

The Sultán smiled at this answer of the *Kází's*, and said, "I do not understand any of the statements thou hast made; but this I have discovered, that the . . . [Hindu officials] ride upon fine horses, wear fine clothes, shoot with Persian bows, make war upon each other, and go out hunting; but of the . . . tribute, . . . poll tax, . . . house tax, and . . . pasture tax, they do not pay one *jítal*. They levy separately the . . . land-owner's share from the villages, give parties and drink wine, and many of them pay no revenue at all, either upon demand or without demand. Neither do they show any respect for my officers. This has excited my anger, and I have said to myself, 'Thou hast an ambition to conquer other lands, but thou hast hundreds of leagues of country under thy rule where proper obedience is not paid to thy authority. How, then, wilt thou make other lands submissive?' I have, therefore, taken my measures, and have made my subjects obedient, so that at my command they are ready to creep into holes like mice. Now you tell me that it is all in accordance with law that the Hindus should be reduced to the most abject obedience." Then the Sultán said, "Oh, doctor, thou art a learned man, but thou hast had no experience; I am an unlettered man, but I have seen a great deal; be assured then that the Hindus will never become submissive and obedient till they are reduced to poverty. I have, therefore, given orders that just sufficient shall be left to them from year to year, of corn, milk, and curds, but that they shall not be allowed to accumulate hoards and property."

INTERPRETATION OF INDIA

129

A. L. BASHAM, *THE INDIAN SUB-CONTINENT IN HISTORICAL PERSPECTIVE:* **INDIAN CIVILIZATION IN HISTORICAL PERSPECTIVE**

Attempts to make generalizations concerning the history of any great civilization are dangerous, but special circumstances compound the difficulties in the case of India. The continuity of development in that culture leads us almost inevitably to confuse existing institutional structures with ones in the past that may have had only a superficial resemblance. This is true in discussions of caste in modern India. Another difficulty is that present aspects of the culture which appear to be genuine survivals from the past may have been consciously revived in recent times. Moreover, the many sources available for the study of the civilization present their own distortions, for they are mainly the product of one class. Another source of difficulty is that the rulers of India have for long periods been alien in race, religion, and culture—as was the case with the Muslims and British. A result has been that those in power have often given their authority to versions of Indian history that justified their own conquests. Indian historians complain, for example, that British writers have overstressed the disunity of India in order to throw into sharper contrast the advantages of unifying British rule. It is not surprising, then, that many of the generalizations made in the past about Indian civilization are currently being questioned. One of the most interesting examinations of some of these assumptions was made by Professor A. L. Basham of the University of London in a lecture given on his inauguration as Professor of the History of South Asia. His criticism provides a useful guide for reviewing the ideas presented in this section.

. . . I propose to consider three well-known generalizations on the history of the Indian subcontinent, which for the sake of brevity I shall henceforth generally refer to as India.

The first of these is the proposition that an all-Indian empire cannot last more than a few generations, a statement which was widely heard around the time of the transfer of power and partition of 1947. It is certainly the case that hitherto none of the greater empires of India has remained intact for more than a century and a half, as against the 400 years of the Roman Empire and the two millenniums of China. On this basis it is tempting to deduce a general law from the five or six historical instances, and to suggest that the inevitable process of disintegration began once more with the transfer of power.

To test the accuracy of this view we must briefly survey the course of Indian history. We find in the earliest period a highly developed unitary city civilization emerging from a congeries of chalcolithic village cultures—that was a common enough process in the history of the ancient world. But the course of Indian history was different from that of the history of Mesopotamia, Egypt, or China, for the city civilization was submerged by barbarians, who developed a quasi-feudal order in the valley of the Gaṅgā. This in turn slowly gave way to a more centralized system of government, with the reappearance of what seem to be elements of the earlier city civilization. This phase began in what a modern German philosopher calls the *Achsenzeit*, the axial period in the history of the ancient world, around the time of the Buddha, and culminated in the great empire of the Mauryas, in the third century B.C. That empire broke up, and Mauryan bureaucracy gave way to quasi-feudalism once more. The typical state system of Hindu India was one in which a king loosely controlled a number of powerful vassals, who in turn were masters of lesser lords, in a descending scale down to petty village chieftains. With minor changes in its character, and with only occasional and temporarily successful efforts at establishing more centralized control, this system continued down to the days of the East India Company, and indeed it did not entirely vanish until after the great events of 1947.

Thus India failed to establish a single centralized government on a permanent basis, while China succeeded in doing so. I have heard several reasons suggested for this—among them the enervating character of the Indian climate, difficulties of communication, the fact that India had no sense of history, and the very other-worldly nature of the Indian character, which is said to concentrate on the things of the spirit and to care little or nothing for the things of practical everyday life. None of these explanations satisfies me. The Indian climate was not sufficiently enervating to prevent many centuries of constant internecine warfare. Communications were no more difficult than in the Roman and early Chinese empires. The absence of a strong sense of history might be as likely to encourage as to inhibit the development of a permanent imperial system, since the inhabitants of the various regions of the empire would have but vague and faint traditions of their earlier autonomy. Moreover, this generalization does not apply to the Muslims, who were little more successful in building empires in India than the Hindus, but who had a well-developed sense of history. And I believe the other-worldly character of India to be a further fallacious generalization, which I shall consider later. If there is any reason for the impermanence of empires in India it is certainly not that her rulers were so intoxicated with the things of the spirit that they had no time for empire-building. Indeed Hinduism, if not Islām, actually encouraged their imperial ambitions.

Long before the first great Indian empire, that of the Mauryas, kings were inspired to enlarge their frontiers by such institutions as the horse-

Text: A. L. Basham, *The Indian Sub-Continent in Historical Perspective* (London: School of Oriental and African Studies, University of London, 1958), pp. 6-12, 18-22.

sacrifice. In later times they were constantly reminded of the legendary *digvijayins*, who were said to have conquered the whole sub-continent from the Himalayas to Ceylon. It became a conventional hyperbole of royal panegyrics to claim that a powerful king had actually carried his arms to the very bounds of Bhāratavarṣa in all four directions. Thus we read of a sixth-century ruler of western India:

> From the lands where the Brahmaputra flows,
> from the flanks of the southern hills, thick with
>   groves of palms,
> from the snowy mountain whose peak the
>   Gaṅgā clasps,
> and from the ocean of the West,
> come vassals, bowing at his feet,
> their pride brought low by his mighty arm,
> and his palace court is a-glitter
> with the bright jewels of their turbans.

Similar passages may be found in many medieval inscriptions and in much panegyric literature. Thus throughout the history of Hindu India, though the land was broken into many kingdoms, the inspiration of the *digvijaya* was always present, and the ideal of a single hand controlling the whole of the sub-continent was never forgotten. It seems to have been inherited by the Muslims. The first Muslim ruler to invade the Deccan, 'Alā ud-dīn Khaljī, followed an internal policy which reminds one of that of the *Arthaśāstra* ascribed to Kauṭilya, the great minister of Candragupta Maurya; his chief general, Malik Kāfūr, was a converted Hindu, and it is reasonable to suggest that he had heard something of the Hindu traditions of government. The efforts of Delhi and Agra to gain and maintain control of the Deccan may be looked on as a continuation of similar efforts on the part of earlier rulers of Hindu India, and Muḥammad bin Tughluq's transfer of his capital to Daulatābād must surely be explained as part of a long-term plan to build a consolidated empire over the whole of the sub-continent. It is more than likely that Akbar's Hindu friends told him of the *digvijaya* tradition, while Aurangzeb's intense but fruitless efforts to hold his southern possessions are quite in keeping with the old Hindu ideals. The Muslim sultans and pādshāhs had much the same ambitions as their Hindu predecessors, and were generally quite as unsuccessful in fulfilling them.

I believe that the main reason for the failure of Hindu and Muslim alike was that no Indian ruler or dynasty was capable of providing administrative machinery adequate to control a really large state. About 320 B.C. Candragupta Maurya established the first great Indian empire; less than a hundred years later Ch'in Shih Hwang Ti did the same in China. In China one dynasty succeeded another, but generally the empire survived—if it was temporarily divided it was ultimately reunited, and if provinces slipped from the control of the centre they were soon brought back. In India, on the other hand, the Mauryan empire began to break up within a century of its foundation, and had vanished within a century and a half. Its rulers appear to have developed a sounder governmental machine than any that existed in India until the days of the East India Company, but yet the empire failed to survive. I believe that this was chiefly due to the fact that even the Mauryan administration, though more efficient than the administrations of succeeding dynasties, was inadequate to its task.

In both India and China civil servants were selected by examination, but the examination system of ancient India was merely the testing of the honesty and loyalty of the servant of the state by means of spies and *agents provocateurs*. The textbooks on polity regularly advise that all bureaucrats should be continually watched by spies. In such circumstances an atmosphere of suspicion and mistrust must have prevailed throughout the civil service of the ancient Indian kingdom, and led to inefficiency and lack of initiative. In Hindu literature kings are frequently described as righteous and benevolent, and high ministers as faithful to the death of their masters. But rarely if ever do we meet a lesser official of the state who is benevolent and conscientious. The *Arthaśāstra* warns the king to be on his guard against the peculations of his underlings, which are impossible to prevent, but which must be kept within reasonable limits. Aśoka inveighs against the local officials who do not carry out his orders or put his new policy into effect. Kalhaṇa, the chronicler of Kashmir, tells of many conscientious and loyal ministers, but invariably describes the lesser officials, the *kāyasthas* and *diviras*, as oppressive and corrupt.

It would seem that the Indian bureaucrat, even under the Mauryas, never achieved the comparatively high standards of efficiency and probity reached by the Chinese mandarin, trained in the political ethics of Confucius. Moreover, even the Mauryan system of administration, inadequate as it was, never really took root in India. The officials of the lesser states which succeeded the Mauryas seem to have been often loosely controlled, and to have held their positions rather by right of birth than by merit. At a distance from the capital the medieval Indian civil servant merged imperceptibly into the quasi-feudal baron.

In China the hierarchy of mandarins, though some of its members were certainly inefficient or oppressive, could often lessen the evil effects of an incompetent emperor and maintain the machinery of government in working order against serious strain. In India there were no mandarins, but only a group of high officials who owed their loyalty rather to the king's person than to the state, and a horde of extortionate petty chiefs, scribes, and accountants. None but the strongest and most efficient of rulers could maintain a large empire intact by such inadequate means.

A further reason for the failure of Indian empires to survive may have been a corollary of the first. Without the tradition of an efficient bureaucracy the direct control of a large empire was almost impossible. Hence Indian theorists made a virtue of necessity. It was legitimate, indeed praiseworthy, for a king to attack and defeat his neighbour. To depose the conquered king and annex his territory was a breach of the *dharma* of kings, and a great sin. The Mauryas cared little for such precepts, and for a while the Guptas seem to have paid scant attention to them, but few if any rulers after the Guptas even aspired to build up a large centralized empire. Their ambition was rather to establish a circle of vassal states linked in quasi-feudal relationship to their overlord. The empires of the great conquerors of tradition were believed to have been of this type, and this was the only form of empire consistent with *dharma*. Though superficially somewhat different the Indian Muslim concept of empire rarely departed from these quasi-feudal ideas, except under 'Alā ud-dīn Khaljī, Muḥammed bin Tughluq, Sher Shāh, and the greater Mughals. The Maratha system was little different from that which went before—a small centrally governed kernel, surrounded by a circle of subordinate states which from the point of view of the overlord were little more than sources of glory and tribute.

The British conquerors imported a system of government which made an all-Indian empire once more possible, and they produced a bureaucracy more efficient and better organized than anything seen in India since the days of the Mauryas. The introduction of telegraphs and railways doubly ensured the unity of the sub-continent, and made it possible for central control to be extended to regions which had never previously been governed from India. . . .

Two further generalizations about India, which I believe to be very inaccurate, I propose to treat at less length. Both of these refer to Hindu India, and to cultural rather than political history.

There is a widespread view that Hindu culture has always had a uniquely spiritual and otherworldly character. This generalization is still sedulously propagated by some Indians, and is often to be found in European writings on India, especially those written before the transfer of power. To my mind it is no more true of India than of medieval Europe and many other earlier cultures. It is impossible to measure the intensity of religious faith or spirituality, but I am inclined to believe that the level of religious earnestness in India was at no time higher than in the nineteenth and twentieth centuries. Hinduism has never been static, and in recent years it appears to have undergone a revitalization, which has made it somewhat different from what it was in the past, and led to a great access of strength.

Like Roman Catholicism, traditional Hinduism had a double or even multiple standard of conduct. There was one norm for the *sannyāsī* or ascetic, and another for the layman, the latter varying much according to caste, region, and period. The chief feature of the lay ethics of classical Hinduism was the *Trivarga,* the three aims of life—piety, profit, and pleasure. These were all recognized as legitimate, though it was held that when the claims of one conflicted with those of another the former should always be given precedence. Buddhism, as far as the layman was concerned, was equally considerate of material interests. Thus in one of the oldest and most respected sections of the Pāli canon we find the following very practical advice to the ambitious and acquisitive business man. The verses are attributed to the Buddha himself:

> The wise and moral man
>   shines like a fire on a hilltop,
> making money like the bee
>   which does not hurt the flower.
> Such a man makes his pile
>   as an anthill, gradually.
> The man grown wealthy thus
>   can help his family
> and firmly bind his friends
>   to himself. He should divide
> his money in four parts;
>   on one part he should live,
> with two expand his trade,
>   and the fourth he should save
> against a rainy day.

It would be possible to marshal much evidence such as this, even from sacred literature, to show that, allowing for differences of time and culture, early Indian society was as acquisitive as are the societies of present-day Europe and America. And every student of Sanskrit literature is well aware that ancient India devoted much of its attention to the third aim of life, the pleasures of the senses. I believe in fact that those who try to establish the intense spirituality of early Indian social life are guilty of falsely projecting the present upon the past. From the time of the medieval popular hymnodists it has been the tendency of Hindu religious leaders to encourage their lay followers to adopt as far as possible the ascetic way of life of the *sannyāsī*. This tendency has been much strengthened in the last fifty years and at no time in the long history of Hinduism have so many ordinary Hindu layfolk been roused to such intense spiritual and moral fervour as under the influence of Mahātmā Gandhi and Vinoba Bhave.

In fact there are features in modern Hinduism which seem to have little in common with the comparatively easy-going lay ethics of earlier times. Thus at no period in ancient or medieval Hindu India would the head of a great state have lived in almost ascetic simplicity, as does the President of the Indian Republic today. At no time in the past would lay Hindus of high caste have devoted themselves in large numbers to raising the standards of their humbler compatriots, as they are doing nowadays through the inspiration of Gandhi and Vinoba. And this great growth of socially minded religious activity is not confined to Hinduism, but has influenced Muslims, Christians, and Parsis. Work for the social uplift of the Muslims of the sub-continent is as old as Sir Sayyid Aḥmad, and the Buddhists of Ceylon are by no means unaffected by the new spirit of religious earnestness and religiously guided social service. Critics may point to the fact that unbelief is growing in India and many educated Hindus seem to have lost their faith. This is true; but the unbelievers must still compose only a minute fraction of the whole population of India, and their existence does not invalidate my claim that the intensity of earnest religious feeling in the Indian sub-continent has probably never been higher than it is today. This tremendous development of social activity in a religious spirit is yet another feature of the contemporary situation which could not have been foreseen in the last century, though it was already beginning at that time.

This brings me to a brief discussion of the last misleading generalization. At one time, especially in the last century, it was often said that the essential character of Indian civilization was quite unchanging, that the social and religious conditions seen by Megasthenes 300 years before Christ were not appreciably different from those of the nineteenth century, and that for all the many invasions of India Hinduism had remained essentially the same. These propositions are not much to be heard nowadays from responsible sources, but they have tended to give place to a kindred view, that Hindu India has a remarkable absorptive capacity, and is able to accept and adapt to its own pattern elements of almost every kind in an almost infinite quantity. This, in my opinion, is no more true of India than of several other civilizations and cultures. Admittedly most of the many invaders of India have lost their identity in the broad unity of Hindu civilization. But much the same may be said of other regions of the world. Thus Mesopotamia down to the early Christian centuries and China down to the present day both enjoyed over 3,000 years of civilization, suffered numerous invasions of peoples with differing cultures, and made many contacts of a more peaceful character; yet in both cases the essential continuity of culture was maintained. Taking Europe as a single cultural unit the same may be said of our own civilization, for even in the Dark Ages the continuity of the traditions inherited from the ancient world was not wholly broken. Moreover, we have seen that the absorptive capacity of Hinduism has not been altogether unlimited, for it has been unable to absorb Islām, though Islām has had some influence on certain aspects of Hindu life and thought, especially in northern India. In fact none of the feats of absorption which Hindu India has achieved in the past is to my mind as spectacular as that which she is performing at the present time.

Though the process is by no means fully achieved, and though new factors may slow it down or alter its direction somewhat, Hindu society appears to be in the course of changing from a closely compartmentalized hierarchy of classes and castes to an equalitarian order, yet without losing its essential character or its continuity with the past. New ideas, largely originating in the West, are being rapidly assimilated, and in the process are taking on an individual character, so that they seem to be of purely Indian origin. Yet there is nothing really exceptional in this phenomenon, impressive as it is, for much the same is happening in other parts of Asia, and indeed the process has been going on in Japan for nearly a century.

This remarkable development in Hindu civilization is something which could scarcely have been predicted in the light of previous history. In the last century it was widely thought that, though Hinduism might be long in dying, it would give way within a few generations either to Christianity or to unbelief. Instead it has displayed surprising vitality, and, whatever the future of some of its more effete aspects, as a distinct religious system and way of life it shows no signs of disappearing. Hinduism of the new type provided both the main ideology of the national movement which led the way to India's independence and the unique method by which that independence was achieved. With its capacity to adapt itself to new circumstances and to face new problems it gives no evidence of decay.

By these few examples I have tried to show that most historical generalizations about India are inadequate and unreliable, and that the causes of historical change in India have been numerous, varied, and obscure. . . .

China

CONCERN FOR THE RIGHT ORDERING OF SOCIETY

130 CONFUCIUS, ANALECTS: GOVERNMENT BY GOODNESS

One of the characteristic concerns of Chinese civilization has been a desire to define the relationships that should exist between rulers and the people. The discussion of this problem has involved consideration of such questions as the fundamental nature of man and his relation to the universe. The predominant source used in providing satisfying answers and in molding the social attitudes of the Chinese people has been the teachings of Confucius (c. 551-479 B.C.). To an extent perhaps unparalleled by any single individual in any of the other great ancient cultures, Confucius has furnished the background for the social and political life of his people.

In spite of his great fame, very little is known about the life of Confucius. He lived at a time when China was torn by wars between a number of small states, and the once-great Chou Dynasty was unable to restore unity. His great ambition was to find a ruler who would employ him and allow him to put his theories of government into practice. "If only someone were to make use of me for a single year," he once said, "I could do a great deal; in three years I could finish the whole work." He found no one who was interested, however, and he was finally forced to retire to a life of teaching. He hoped that his pupils would fulfill his belief that with right men in control, the turmoil of the times would end. "Only if the right sort of men had charge of a country for a hundred years," he said, "would it become really possible to stop cruelty and do away with slaughter."

Superficially, Confucius' idea of a good government was simple: a just and durable social order evolved when a virtuous ruler set an example of good conduct for the people. But the decision as to what is meant by "virtuous" and "good conduct" is far from simple, and it is the definition of these terms that constitutes the heart of Confucian doctrine. Like many reformers, Confucius maintained that what he wanted was a return to the past, an acceptance of the way of life that had made China great during the days of the mythical "sage-kings." He advocated the maintaining and transmitting of the values of the past through the use of rituals that formalized wisdom and history. The aim of life was to become virtuous—which implied the possession of such attributes as benevolence, humaneness, and moderation. If man was not capable of achieving perfection, at least he could live a balanced and harmonious life. The ideal ruler was a "gentleman," but this was an expression of character, not of birth. "By nature men are much alike," he said; "it is learning and practice that set them apart." What he hoped to create, then, was an elite capable of ruling the people by setting an example of virtue. This emphasis on a learned elite eventually found expression in a civil service based on examinations, one of the greatest and most enduring of Chinese institutions. Confucius relied on the moral rectitude and integrity of the statesman, rather than on force, to control the people.

The *Analects* give the substance of Confucius' teachings as handed down by his pupils, but they do not by any means represent a systematic statement of political philosophy. The meaning of the short aphorisms is often not clear, and it is possible to interpret the more enigmatic sayings in a variety of ways. No doubt their ambiguity helped to preserve the *Analects'* vitality through changing times.

Book II

1. The Master said, He who rules by moral force (*tê*) is like the pole-star, which remains in its place while all the lesser stars do homage to it.

2. The Master said, If out of the three hundred *Songs* I had to take one phrase to cover all my teaching, I would say 'Let there be no evil in your thoughts.'

3. The Master said, Govern the people by regulations, keep order among them by chastisements, and they will flee from you, and lose all self-respect. Govern them by moral force, keep order among them by ritual and they will keep their self-respect and come to you of their own accord.

4. The Master said, At fifteen I set my heart upon learning. At thirty, I had planted my feet firm upon the ground. At forty, I no longer suffered from perplexities. At fifty, I knew what were the biddings of Heaven. At sixty, I heard them with docile ear. At seventy, I could follow the dictates of my own heart; for what I desired no longer overstepped the boundaries of right.

5. Mêng I Tzu asked about the treatment of parents. The Master said, Never disobey! When Fan Ch'ih was driving his carriage for him, the Master said, Mêng asked me about the treatment of parents and I said, Never disobey! Fan Ch'ih said, In what sense did you mean it? The Master said, While they are alive, serve them according to ritual. When they die, bury them according to ritual and sacrifice to them according to ritual.

6. Mêng Wu Po asked about the treatment of parents. The Master said, Behave in such a way that your father and mother have no anxiety about you, except concerning your health.

7. Tzu-yu asked about the treatment of parents. The Master said, 'Filial sons' nowadays are people who see to it that their parents get enough to eat. But even dogs and horses are cared for to that extent. If there is no feeling of respect, wherein lies the difference?

8. Tzu-hsia asked about the treatment of parents. The Master said, It is the demeanour that is difficult. Filial piety does not consist merely in young people undertaking the hard work, when anything has to be done, or serving their elders first with wine and food. It is something much more than that. . . .

. . . 18. The Master said, Hear much, but maintain silence as regards doubtful points and be cautious in speaking of the rest; then you will seldom get into trouble. See much, but ignore what it is dangerous to have seen, and be cautious in acting upon the rest; then you will seldom want to undo your acts. He who seldom gets into trouble about what he has said and seldom does anything that he afterwards wishes he had not done, will be sure incidentally to get his reward.

19. Duke Ai asked, What can I do in order to get the support of the common people? Master K'ung replied, If you 'raise up the straight and set them on top of the crooked,' the commoners will support you. But if you raise the crooked and set them on top of the straight, the commoners will not support you.

20. Chi K'ang-tzu asked whether there were any form of encouragement by which he could induce the common people to be respectful and loyal. The Master said, Approach them with dignity, and they will respect you. Show piety towards your parents and kindness towards your children, and they will be loyal to you. Promote those who are worthy, train those who are incompetent; that is the best form of encouragement.

21. Someone, when talking to Master K'ung, said, How is it that you are not in the public service? The Master said, The Book says: 'Be filial, only be filial and friendly towards your brothers, and you will be contributing to government.' There are other sorts of service quite different from what you mean by 'service.'

22. The Master said, I do not see what use a man can be put to, whose word cannot be trusted. How can a waggon be made to go if it has no yoke-bar or a carriage, if it has no collar-bar?

23. Tzu-chang asked whether the state of things ten generations hence could be foretold. The Master said, We know in what ways the Yin modified ritual when they followed upon the Hsia. We know in what ways the Chou modified ritual when they followed upon the Yin. And hence we can foretell what the successors of Chou will be like, even supposing they do not appear till a hundred generations from now.

24. The Master said, Just as to sacrifice to ancestors other than one's own is presumption, so to see what is right and not do it is cowardice.

Text: From *The Analects of Confucius*, trans. Arthur Waley. Copyright 1939 by The Macmillan Company and reprinted by their permission and the permission of George Allen & Unwin Ltd. Pp. 88-89, 92-93, 102-03, 168-69 *passim*.

Book IV

1. The Master said, It is Goodness that gives to a neighbourhood its beauty. One who is free to choose, yet does not prefer to dwell among the Good—how can he be accorded the name of wise?

    2. The Master said, Without Goodness a man
    Cannot for long endure adversity,
    Cannot for long enjoy prosperity.

The Good Man rests content with Goodness; he that is merely wise pursues Goodness in the belief that it pays to do so.

3, 4. Of the adage 'Only a Good Man knows how to like people, knows how to dislike them,' the Master said, He whose heart is in the smallest degree set upon Goodness will dislike no one.

5. Wealth and rank are what every man desires; but if they can only be retained to the detriment of the Way he professes, he must relinquish them. Poverty and obscurity are what every man detests; but if they can only be avoided to the detriment of the Way he professes, he must accept them. The gentleman who ever parts company with Goodness does not fulfil that name. Never for a moment does a gentleman quit the way of Goodness. He is never so harried but that he cleaves to this; never so tottering but that he cleaves to this.

6. The Master said, I for my part have never yet seen one who really cared for Goodness, nor one who really abhorred wickedness. One who really cared for Goodness would never let any other consideration come first. One who abhorred wickedness would be so constantly doing Good•that wickedness would never have a chance to get at him. Has anyone ever managed to do Good with his whole might even as long as the space of a single day? I think not. Yet I for my part have never seen anyone give up such an attempt because he had not the *strength* to go on. It may well have happened, but I for my part have never seen it.

7. The Master said, Every man's faults belong to a set. If one looks out for faults it is only as a means of recognizing Goodness.

8. The Master said, In the morning, hear the Way; in the evening, die content!

Book XII

. . . 19. Chi K'ang-tzu asked Master K'ung about government, saying, Suppose I were to slay those who have not the Way in order to help on those who have the Way, what would you think of it? Master K'ung replied saying, You are there to rule, not to slay. If you desire what is good, the people will at once be good. The essence of the gentleman is that of wind; the essence of small people is that of grass. And when a wind passes over the grass, it cannot choose but bend.

20. Tzu-chang asked what a knight must be like if he is to be called 'influential.' The Master said, That depends on what you mean by 'influential.' Tzu-chang replied saying, If employed by the State, certain to win fame, if employed by a Ruling Family, certain to win fame. The Master said, That describes being famous; it does not describe being influential. In order to be influential a man must be by nature straightforward and a lover of right. He must examine men's works and observe their expressions, and bear in mind the necessity of deferring to others. Such a one, whether employed by the State or by a Ruling Family, will certainly be 'influential'; whereas the man who wins fame may merely have obtained, by his outward airs, a reputation for Goodness which his conduct quite belies. Anyone who makes his claims with sufficient self-assurance is certain to win fame in a State, certain to win fame in a Family.

21. Once when Fan Ch'ih was taking a walk with the Master under the trees at the Rain Dance altars, he said, May I venture to ask about 'piling up moral force,' 'repairing shortcomings' and 'deciding when in two minds'? The Master said, An excellent question. 'The work first; the reward afterwards'; is not that piling up moral force? 'Attack the evil that is within yourself; do not attack the evil that is in others.' Is not this 'repairing shortcomings'?

'Because of a morning's blind rage
To forget one's own safety
And even endanger one's kith and kin'

is that not a case of 'divided mind'?

22. Fan Ch'ih asked about the Good (ruler). The Master said, He loves men. He asked about the wise (ruler). The Master said, He knows men. Fan Ch'ih did not quite understand. The Master said, By raising the straight and putting them on top of the crooked, he can make the crooked straight. Fan Ch'ih withdrew, and meeting Tzu-hsia said to him, Just now I was with the Master and asked him about the wise (ruler). He said, By raising the straight and putting them on top of the crooked he can make the crooked straight. What did he mean?

Tzu-hsia said, Oh, what a wealth of instruction is in those words! When Shun had all that is under Heaven, choosing from among the multitude he raised up Kao Yao, and straightway Wickedness disappeared. . . .

131 MO TZU: EGALITARIANISM AND UNIFORMITY

Another answer to the problems inherent in man's relations with the social order was given by Mo Tzu, or Motse, (c. 470-390 B.C.). While his teachings have never been as influential as those of Confucius (see Document 130), he was regarded by the Confucianists as their principal rival. Although he agreed with Confucius that rulers must be virtuous, he differed from him in his emphasis on the need for man to conform his will to that of the divine and to express this through universal love for all mankind. Over against the Confucian demand that filial piety be the central expression of one's virtue, Mo Tzu insisted that all men should be loved equally. The Confucian practices of observing rituals, of listening to music, of paying attention to food and clothing, seemed hindrances to universal human welfare to Mo Tzu. He argued for enforced uniformity within the state so that all energy could be concentrated on bringing about desirable social ends. His equation of the useful and the good suggests how he thought people might be brought to practice universal love: the good ruler would endeavor to make the people realize that it was in their own interest to do what was right. But although Mo Tzu argued that the good ruler would be rewarded by the trust and obedience of his people, he did not depend upon persuasion alone. He advocated a thoroughly disciplined state where the subjects unquestioningly followed the example of the ruler—"What the superior approves all must approve; what the superior condemns all must condemn." Mo Tzu's theory of universal love could easily be transformed into a defense of the totalitarian state.

Motse said: The interest of the wise (ruler) lies in carrying out what makes for order among the people and avoiding what makes for confusion.

But what is it that makes for order among the people?

When the administration of the ruler answers to the desires of the people there will be order, otherwise there will be confusion.

How do we know it is so?

When the administration of the ruler answers to the desires of the subjects, it manifests an understanding of the approvals and disapprovals of the people. When there is such an understanding, the good will be discovered and rewarded and the bad will be discovered and punished, and the country will surely have order. When the administration of the ruler does not answer to the desires of the subjects, it shows a lack of understanding of the approvals and disapprovals of the subjects. When there is no such understanding then the good will not be discovered and rewarded and the bad will not be discovered and punished. With the good unrewarded and evil unpunished, such a government will surely put the country into disorder. Therefore when rewards and punishments do not answer to the desires of the people, the matter has to be carefully looked into.

But how can the desires of the people (being so many and various) be met?

Therefore Motse said: It can be done only by adopting the principle of Identification with the Superior in government.

How do we know the principle of Identification with the Superior can govern the empire?

Why not then examine the administration and the theory of government of the ancient times? In the beginning there was no ruler and everybody was independent. Since every one was independent, there would be one purpose when there was one man, ten purposes when there were ten men, a hundred purposes when there were a hundred men, a thousand purposes when there were a thousand men and so on until the number of men became innumerable and the number of different purposes became innumerable with it. And all of them approved their own ideas and disapproved those of others. And there was strife among the strong and struggle among the weak.

Thereupon Heaven wished to unify the standards in the world. The virtuous was selected and made emperor. Conscious of the insufficiency of his power alone to govern the empire, the emperor chose the next best (in virtue and wisdom) and honoured them to be the three ministers. Conscious of the insufficiency of their powers alone to assist the emperor, the three ministers in turn divided the empire into feudal states and assigned them to feudal lords. Conscious of the insufficiency of his power alone to govern all that were within his four borders, the feudal lord in turn selected his next best and commissioned

Text: Y. P. Mei (trans. and ed.), *The Ethical and Practical Works of Motse* (London: Arthur Probsthain, 1929), I, 70-73, 87-91.

them ministers and secretaries. Conscious of the insufficiency of their power alone to assist their feudal lord, the ministers and secretaries again selected their next best and appointed them district heads and clan patriarchs. Therefore, in appointing the three ministers, the feudal lords, the ministers and secretaries, and the district heads and clan patriarchs, the emperor was not selecting them for wealth and honour, leisure and ease. It was to employ them to help in administration and jurisdiction. Hence, when Heaven established the empire and located the capital and commissioned the sovereign, kings, lords, and dukes, and appointed secretaries, scholars, professors, and elders—it was not to give them ease, but only to divide up the task and let them help carry out the light of Heaven.

Why are the superiors now unable to govern their subordinates, and the subordinates unwilling to serve their superiors? It is because of a mutual disregard.

What is the reason for this? The reason is a difference in standards. Whenever standards differ there will be opposition. The ruler may think a man good and reward him. The man, though rewarded by the ruler, yet by the same act provokes the condemnation of the people. Therefore those who do good are not necessarily encouraged by rewards. The ruler may think a man evil and punish him. This man, though punished by the ruler, yet at the same time receives the approval of the people. Therefore those who do evil are not necessarily obstructed by punishments. Thus reward and honour from the ruler cannot encourage the good and his denunciation and punishment cannot prevent the evil. What is the reason for this? The reason is a difference in standards.

But how can the standards in the world be unified?

Motse said: Why not let each member of the clan organize his purposes and identify them with those of the patriarch? And let the patriarch give laws and proclaim to the clan: "Whoever discovers a benefactor to the clan shall report it; whoever discovers a malefactor to the clan shall report it. Whoever reports the benefactor of the clan upon seeing one is equivalent to benefiting the clan himself. Knowing him the superior will reward him, hearing of him the group will praise him. Whoever fails to report a malefactor of the clan upon seeing one is equivalent to doing evil to the clan himself. Knowing him the superior will punish him, hearing of him the group will condemn him." Thereupon all the members of the clan wish to obtain reward and honour and avoid denunciation and punishment from their superior.

Seeing the good they will report; seeing the evil they will report. And the patriarch can reward the good and punish the evil. With the good rewarded and the evil punished, the clan will surely have order. Now, why is it that the clan becomes orderly? Just because the administration is based on the principle of Identification with the Superior....

Motse said: The purpose of the magnanimous lies in procuring benefits for the world and eliminating its calamities. Now among all the current calamities, which are the most important? The attack on the small states by the large ones, disturbances of the small houses by the large ones, oppression of the weak by the strong, misuse of the few by the many, deception of the simple by the cunning, disdain towards the humble by the honoured—these are the misfortunes in the empire. Again, the lack of grace on the part of the ruler, the lack of loyalty on the part of the ruled, the lack of affection on the part of the father, the lack of filial piety on the part of the son—these are further calamities in the empire. Also, the mutual injury and harm which the unscrupulous do to one another with weapons, poison, water, and fire is still another calamity in the empire.

When we come to think about the cause of all these calamities, how have they arisen? Have they arisen out of love of others and benefiting others? Of course we should say no. We should say they have arisen out of hate of others and injuring others. If we should classify one by one all those who hate others and injure others, should we find them to be universal in love or partial? Of course we should say they are partial. Now, since partiality against one another is the cause of the major calamities in the empire, then partiality is wrong.

Motse continued: Whoever criticizes others must have something to replace them. Criticism without suggestion is like trying to stop flood with flood and put out fire with fire. It will surely be without worth.

Motse said: Partiality is to be replaced by universality. But how is it that partiality can be replaced by universality? Now, when every one regards the states of others as he regards his own, who would attack the others' states? Others are regarded like self. When every one regards the capitals of others as he regards his own, who would seize the others' capitals? Others are regarded like self. When every one regards the houses of others as he regards his own, who would disturb the others' houses? Others are regarded like self. Now, when the states and cities do not attack and seize each other and when the clans and individuals do not disturb and harm one another—is this a calamity or a benefit to the world? Of course it is a benefit. When we come to think about the several benefits in regard to their cause, how have they arisen? Have they arisen out of hate of others and injuring others? Of course we should say no. We should say they have arisen out of love of others and benefiting others. If we should classify one by one all those who love others and benefit others, should we find them to be partial or universal? Of course we should say they are universal. Now, since universal love is the cause of the major benefits in the world, therefore Motse proclaims universal love is right.

And, as has already been said, the interest of the magnanimous lies in procuring benefits for the world and eliminating its calamities. Now that we have found out the consequences of universal love to be the major benefits of the world and the consequences of partiality to be the major calamities in the world; this is the reason why Motse said partiality is wrong and universality is right. When we try to develop and procure benefits for the world with universal love as our standard, then attentive ears and keen eyes will respond in service to one another, then limbs will be strengthened to work for one another, and those who know the Tao will untiringly instruct others. Thus the old and those who have neither wife nor children will have the support and supply to spend their old age with, and the young and weak and orphans will have the care and admonition to grow up in. When universal love is adopted as the standard, then such are the consequent benefits. It is incomprehensible, then, why people should object to universal love when they hear it.

Yet the objection is not all exhausted. It is asked: "It may be a good thing, but can it be of any use?"

Motse replied: If it were not useful then even I would disapprove of it. But how can there be anything that is good but not useful? Let us consider the matter from both sides. Suppose there are two men. Let one of them hold to partiality and the other to universality. Then the advocate of partiality would say to himself, how can I take care of my friend as I do of myself, how can I take care of his parents as my own? Therefore when he finds his friend hungry he would not feed him, and when he finds him cold he would not clothe him. In his illness he would not minister to him, and when he is dead he would not bury him. Such is the word and such is the deed of the advocate of partiality. The advocate of universality is quite unlike this both in word and in deed. He would say to himself, I have heard that to be a superior man one should take care of his friend as he does of himself, and take care of his friend's parents as his own. Therefore when he finds his friend hungry he would feed him, and when he finds him cold he would clothe him. In his sickness he would serve him, and when he is dead he would bury him. Such is the word and such is the deed of the advocate of universality.

These two persons then are opposed to each other in word and also in deed. Suppose they are sincere in word and decisive in deed so that their word and deed are made to agree like the two parts of a tally, and that there is no word but what is realized in deed, then let us consider further: Suppose a war is on, and one is in armour and helmet ready to join the force, life and death are not predictable. Or suppose one is commissioned a deputy by the ruler to such far countries like Pa, Yüeh, Ch'i, and Ching, and the arrival and return are quite uncertain. Now (under such circumstances) let us inquire upon whom would one lay the trust of one's family and parents. Would it be upon the universal friend or upon the partial friend? It seems to me, on occasions like these, there are no fools in the world. Even if he is a person who objects to universal love, he will lay the trust upon the universal friend all the same. This is verbal objection to the principle but actual selection by it—this is self-contradiction between one's word and deed. It is incomprehensible, then, why people should object to universal love when they hear it.

Yet the objection is not all exhausted. It is objected: Maybe it is a good criterion to choose among ordinary men, but it may not apply to the rulers.

Let us again consider the matter from both sides. Suppose there are two rulers. Let one of them hold partiality and the other universality. Then the partial ruler would say to himself, how can I take care of the people as I do of myself? This would be quite contrary to common sense. A man's life on earth is of short duration, it is like a galloping horse passing by. Therefore when he finds his people hungry he would not feed them, and when he finds them cold he would not clothe them. When they are sick he would not minister to them, and upon their death he would not bury them. Such is the word and such is the deed of the partial ruler. The universal ruler is quite unlike this both in word and in deed. He would say to himself, I have heard that to be an upright ruler of the world one should first attend to his people and then to himself. Therefore when he finds his people hungry he would feed them, and when he finds them cold he would clothe them. In their sickness he would minister to them, and upon their death he would bury them. Such is the word and such is the deed of the universal ruler.

132 LAO TZU: MYSTICISM AND ANARCHY

Confucianism represented an extremely influential phase of Chinese civilization with its emphasis on serious attention to the duties of life, its demand for attention to the past, its call for responsible action, and its belief in the need for profound study (see Document 130). Yet there was another, scarcely less vital, aspect of Chinese tradition which replaced the common sense of Confucius with outrageous paradox and proposed to substitute anarchy for a rational, ordered system of government. This was Taoism, a school of thought that held that there was a great unifying principle *(tao)* in the universe—without form or personality, undefinable, and ultimately unknowable. Man's end in life was identification with the *tao*. A belief in Taoism implied that all political and social institutions were false, and that all attempts to create a stable social system were doomed to failure. Truth was discovered not by conscious striving after knowledge but by unconscious intuition.

The teaching of Taoism, with its emphasis on man's oneness with nature, has profoundly influenced Chinese artists. The Taoist's love for unfettered speculation was also significant; as a by-product of Taoist alchemy—the aim of which was an elixir for immortality—valuable discoveries in chemistry and medicine were made.

The following selections are from the book known as the *Tao Te Ching*, which was compiled from the teachings of the Taoist philosopher Lao Tzu. Filled with paradoxes and seeming absurdities, Lao Tzu's writings forced men to examine their preconceptions regarding man's place in nature. His political philosophy is summed up in the saying, "Ruling a large kingdom is like cooking [a] small fish"—meaning that the less it is handled, the better it will be. His profound pessimism concerning the results of governmental activity probably was caused by the conditions he saw around him.

1

Tao can be talked about, but not the Eternal Tao.
Names can be named, but not the Eternal Name.

As the origin of heaven-and-earth, it is nameless:
As "the Mother" of all things, it is nameable.

So, as ever hidden, we should look at its inner essence:
As always manifest, we should look at its outer aspects.

These two flow from the same source, though differently named;
And both are called mysteries.

The Mystery of mysteries is the Door of all essence.

2

When all the world recognizes beauty as beauty, this in itself is ugliness.
When all the world recognizes good as good, this in itself is evil.

Text: From Asian Institute Translations, No. 1 *Lao Tzu/Tao Teh Ching*, copyright 1961, St. John's University, New York.

Indeed, the hidden and the manifest give birth to each other.
Difficult and easy complement each other.
Long and short exhibit each other.
High and low set measure to each other.
Voice and sound harmonize each other.
Back and front follow each other.

Therefore, the Sage manages his affairs without ado,
And spreads his teaching without talking.
He denies nothing to the teeming things.
He rears them, but lays no claim to them.
He does his work, but sets no store by it.
He accomplishes his task, but does not dwell upon it.

And yet it is just because he does not dwell on it
That nobody can ever take it away from him.

3

By not exalting the talented you will cause the people to cease from rivalry and contention.
By not prizing goods hard to get, you will cause the people to cease from robbing and stealing.
By not displaying what is desirable, you will cause the people's hearts to remain undisturbed.

Therefore, the Sage's way of governing begins by

> Emptying the heart of desires,
> Filling the belly with food,
> Weakening the ambitions,
> Toughening the bones.

In this way he will cause the people to remain without knowledge and without desire, and prevent the knowing ones from any ado.
Practice Non-Ado, and everything will be in order.

4

The Tao is like an empty bowl,
Which in being used can never be filled up.
Fathomless, it seems to be the origin of all things.
It blunts all sharp edges,
It unties all tangles,
It harmonizes all lights,
It unites the world into one whole.
Hidden in the deeps,
Yet it seems to exist for ever.
I do not know whose child it is;
It seems to be the common ancestor of all, the father of things.

5

Heaven-and-Earth is not sentimental;
It treats all things as straw-dogs.
The Sage is not sentimental;
He treats all his people as straw-dogs.

Between Heaven and Earth,
There seems to be a Bellows:
It is empty, and yet it is inexhaustible;
The more it works, the more comes out of it.
No amount of words can fathom it:
Better look for it within you.

17

. . . The highest type of ruler is one of whose existence the people are barely aware.
Next comes one whom they love and praise.
Next comes one whom they fear.
Next comes one whom they despise and defy.

When you are lacking in faith,
Others will be unfaithful to you.

The Sage is self-effacing and scanty of words.
When his task is accomplished and things have been completed,
All the people say, "We ourselves have achieved it!"

18

When the Great Tao was abandoned,
There appeared humanity and justice.
When intelligence and wit arose,
There appeared great hypocrites.
When the six relations lost their harmony,
There appeared filial piety and paternal kindness.
When darkness and disorder began to reign in a kingdom,
There appeared the loyal ministers.

19

Drop wisdom, abandon cleverness,
And the people will be benefited a hundredfold.

Drop humanity, abandon justice,
And the people will return to their natural affections.

Drop shrewdness, abandon sharpness,
And robbers and thieves will cease to be.

133 LORD SHANG: TOTALITARIANISM

A theory of the state was formulated in the fourth and third centuries B.C. that differed sharply from the ideas expressed in previous statements (see Documents 130-132). A number of able political thinkers, known as the Legalists, turned away from the old belief in the need for virtuous and humane rulers, arguing that what the times demanded was absolute monarchy. Confucius had upheld the ruler who guided political life by example of his virtue, but the Legalists said that the wise ruler was one who commanded obedience by force, rather than by ethical appeal. The Legalists' ideas found practical application when the small state of Ch'in rose rapidly to power and destroyed the old central dynasty. The leading part in the creation of the powerful new state was played by its chief minister, Shang Yang, in the middle of the fourth century B.C.

The selections which follow are taken from *The Book of Lord Shang*, supposedly written by Shang Yang to record the methods he used in developing the state of Ch'in. While there is considerable doubt as to its authorship, the book expresses attitudes that became of great consequence in Chinese history. The problems discussed in *The Book of Lord Shang* were similar to those confronting western political thinkers in the sixteenth century: how can power be centralized? What steps should a king take to destroy the pretensions and political ambitions of great families? How can a government be made rich enough to free it from dependence upon wealthy subjects? Lord Shang's answers provide an interesting comparison with those of Machiavelli in Europe or Kauṭilya in India. The Legalists put their faith in rewards and punishments, in laws supported by force, and in the use of war as an instrument of policy. Since maintenance of the state's stability was the goal of all political action, ruthlessness in the exercise of power was justifiable; in fact, the scrupulous or indulgent ruler was regarded as a menace to social order.

Sophistry and cleverness are an aid to lawlessness; rites and music are symptoms of dissipations and licence; kindness and benevolence are the foster-mother of transgressions; employment and promotion are opportunities for the rapacity of the wicked. If lawlessness is aided, it becomes current; if there are symptoms of dissipation and licence, they will become the practice; if there is a foster-mother for transgressions, they will arise; if there are opportunities for the rapacity of the wicked, they will never cease. If these eight things come together the people will be stronger than the government; but if these eight things are non-existent in a state, the government will be stronger than the people. If the people are stronger than the government, the state is weak; if the government is stronger than the people, the army is strong. For if these eight things exist, the ruler has no one to use for defence and war, with the result that the state will be dismembered and will come to ruin; but if there are not these eight things, the ruler has the wherewithal for defence and war, with the result that the state will flourish and attain supremacy.

If virtuous officials are employed, the people will love their own relatives, but if wicked officials are employed, the people will love the statutes. To agree with, and to respond to, others is what the virtuous do; to differ from, and to spy upon, others is what the wicked do. If the virtuous are placed in positions of evidence, transgressions will remain hidden; but if the wicked are employed, crimes will be punished. In the former case the people will be stronger than the law; in the latter, the law will be stronger than the people. If the people are stronger than the law, there is lawlessness in the state, but if the law is stronger than the people, the army will be strong. Therefore is it said: "Governing through good people leads to lawlessness and dismemberment; governing through wicked people leads to order and strength." A country which attacks with what is difficult will gain ten points for every one that it undertakes; a country which attacks with what is easy will lose a hundred men for every ten that it marches out. A country that loves force, is said to attack with what is difficult; a country that loves words is said to attack with what is easy. People find it easy to talk, but difficult to serve. A state where, when the laws of the country are applied, conditions for people are hard and by military service those conditions are eased, so that it attacks with force, will gain ten points for every one it undertakes; but a state where, when the laws of the country are applied, conditions for the people are easy, and by military service those conditions are made hard, so that it attacks with words, will lose a hundred men for every ten that it marches out.

The fact that penalties are heavy makes rank the more honourable, and the fact that rewards are light makes punishments the more awe-inspiring. If rank is honoured, the ruler loves the people, and if punishments are so awe-inspiring, the people will die for their ruler. Therefore, in a prosperous country, the people profit by the application of penalties, and by the distribution of rewards, the ruler will gain credit.

If the law goes into details, the punishments will be multitudinous; if the laws are multitudinous, punishments will be scarce.

If, from a condition of rule and order, the people become lawless, and if one tries to rule this lawlessness, it will only increase; therefore, it should be ruled while it is still in a state of rule and order, then there will be true rule and order;

Text: J. J. L. Duyvendak (trans.), *The Book of Lord Shang* (London: Arthur Probsthain, 1928), pp. 206-09, 286-87.

if it is ruled, while it is in a state of lawlessness, lawlessness will remain.

It is the nature of the people to be orderly, but it is circumstances that cause disorder. Therefore, in the application of punishments, light offences should be regarded as serious; if light offences do not occur, serious ones have no chance of coming. This is said to be "ruling the people while in a state of law and order".

If in the application of punishments, serious offences are regarded as serious, and light offences as light, light offences will not cease and in consequence, there will be no means of stopping the serious ones. This is said to be "ruling the people while in a state of lawlessness". So, if light offences are regarded as serious, punishments will be abolished, affairs will succeed and the country will be strong; but if serious offences are regarded as serious and light ones as light, then punishments will appear; moreover, trouble will arise and the country will be dismembered.

. . . What is the cause of one's reputation becoming respected and one's territory wide, so that one attains sovereignty? (It is because one conquers in war.) What is the cause of one's reputation becoming debased and one's territory diminished, so that one comes to ruin? It is because one is worn out by war. From antiquity to the present time, it has never happened that one attained supremacy without conquest, or that one came to ruin without defeat. If the people are brave, one conquers in war, but if they are not brave, one is defeated in war. If one can unify the people for war, they are brave, but if one cannot unify the people for war, they are not brave. A sage-king obtains the kingship through the efforts of his soldiers. Therefore, he rouses the country and charges it with the obligation of military service. If one enters a state and sees its administration, it is strong if its people are of use. How does one know that the people are of use? If they, on perceiving war, behave like hungry wolves on seeing meat, then they are of use. Generally, war is a thing that people hate; he who succeeds in making people delight in war, attains supremacy. With the people of a strong state, the father, in making a parting bequest to his son, the elder brother to his younger brother, the wife to her husband, all say: "Do not return unless you win." And further they say: "If you incur death by failing in obedience to the law or by transgressing orders, we too shall die." If in the villages they are governed in an orderly manner, then deserters from the ranks will have no resort and stragglers will have nowhere to go. By the order in the ranks they should be organized into bands of five; they should be distinguished by badges and controlled by mandates, so that there would be no place for bungling and no danger that exhaustion would arise. Thus the multitudes of the three armies obeyed the mandates like running water, and in danger of death, they did not turn on their heels.

If a state is in disorder, it is not because the law is disorderly, but because its law is not applied. All states have laws, but there are no laws that guarantee that the laws are practised. All states have laws that prohibit crime and wickedness, and that punish thieves and robbers, but there are no laws that guarantee that criminals and wicked people, thieves and robbers, are caught. If those who commit crimes and wickedness, theft and robbery, are punished with death, and if, in spite of this, crime and wickedness, theft and robbery do not cease, then is it because they are not always caught. If they are always caught, and if, in spite of this, there still remain criminals, wicked people, thieves and robbers, then it is because punishments are too light.

THE CREATION OF AN IMPERIAL STRUCTURE

134 LI SSU, MEMORIAL TO THE EMPEROR: THE ABOLITION OF FEUDALISM

After the conquest of the whole of China by the Ch'in state (see Document 133), the Ch'in ministers set out to unify the vast territory that had been brought under control. The previous dynasty, the Chou, had administered the country through a large number of territorial magnates who were bound in allegiance to the emperor and sent him a share of the taxes they collected. This feudal system had brought order and stability to China, but as in Europe, it checked the power of the king and tended in times of stress to lead to disunity and internal strife. One of the first acts of the Ch'in Dynasty was the abolition of the old feudal states in favor of centralized administration. This was largely accomplished through the work of Li Ssu (c. 280-208 B.C.), the able chief minister of the first Ch'in emperor. In addition to nullifying the power of the magnates through the creation of new administrative districts controlled by officials appointed by the central government, Li Ssu promoted unification through standardization of weights and measures, the use of a common script for writing, and the building of roads. He also ordered the burning of all books that might lead to criticism of the regime. "Anyone referring to the past to criticize the present," he declared, "should, together with all his family, be put to death." It is difficult to believe that such ferocious and all-encompassing orders could have been carried out systematically, but at least they were a powerful means of frightening the opposition. Although the Ch'in Dynasty was overthrown in 207 B.C., the administrative reorganization worked out by Li Ssu endured, substantially unchanged, until the twentieth century.

"The Grand Councillor, (Wang) Kuan, and others said: 'The feudal lords now for the first time have been destroyed. The territories of Yen, Ch'i and Ching (i.e., Ch'u) are far removed, and if kings are not established for them, there will be no means of keeping them in order. We beg that the sons of the imperial family be established in these positions. May it but please Your Majesty to give his consent.'

"Shih-huang handed over this proposal to his ministers, all of whom considered it to be advantageous. But the Minister of Justice, Li Ssŭ, criticized it, saying: 'The fiefs given by (Kings) Wen and Wu of the Chou to their sons, younger brothers, and the members of their family, were extremely numerous. But as time passed these near relatives became divided and estranged; they attacked each other [as] if they were enemies. More and more the feudal lords killed and warred with one another, without the Son of Heaven of Chou being able to prevent them. Now, owing to the divine power of Your Majesty, everything within the seas is bound into one unit, and all has been laid out into commanderies and prefectures. The sons of the imperial family and the meritorious ministers have been amply rewarded by being given the title of Duke and by receiving an income from the taxes. This greatly facilitates easy government. Let there be no varying opinions concerning it in the empire. This is the way . . . to have peace and tranquility. The establishment of feudal lords would not be advantageous.'

"Shih-huang said: 'If the whole world has suffered from unceasing warfare, this comes from there having been feudal lords and kings. Thanks to the aid of my ancestors, the empire has now for the first time been pacified, and for me to restore (feudal) states would be to implant warfare. How difficult then to seek for peace and repose! The advice of the Minister of Justice is right.'

"(Ch'in Shih-huang then) divided the empire into thirty-six commanderies, and in these commanderies he established Administrators, Military Governors and Overseers. He gave to the people the new name of 'black headed ones'. At a great banquet he received all the weapons in the empire, and had them brought together at Hsien-yang. There they were melted into bells and bell supports, and made into twelve metal human figures, each weighing one thousand *tan*, these being placed within the imperial palace. The laws and rules and weights and measures were unified; carts were all made of equal gauge; and the characters used in writing were made uniform. . . The powerful and rich people of the empire, amounting to one hundred and twenty thousand families, were moved to Hsien-yang. . . Each time that Ch'in had destroyed a feudal lord, it copied the plan of his palace and had it rebuilt at Hsien-yang."

Text: Derk Bodde, *China's First Unifier* (Leiden: E. J. Brill, 1938), pp. 77-78.

135 THE MINISTERS' MEMORIAL: THE CONCEPT OF EMPIRE

A significant part of creating the long-enduring Chinese Empire was the development of a theory explaining the role of the emperor. A memorial addressed to the first Ch'in emperor by his ministers in 221 B.C. suggests how the problem was solved at that time. As the ruler of a great empire, the emperor wanted a title that would indicate the extent of his power as well as the sanctions by which he claimed the right to rule. As already noted (see Part One), the nature of kingship had been a matter of great import in the ancient Near East since antiquity. The Ch'in emperor, however, did not attempt to define his status by claiming a divine origin, as did many of the kings of the Near East. The title he chose, translated here as "Sovereign Emperor," emphasizes the human greatness of the king but, seemingly, does not imply divinity. Later the emperor was thought to occupy a special place in the universal order and was given the title "Son of Heaven," but this did not link the ruler with the powers of the universe as did similar titles of ancient Egyptian kings. He ruled by the "mandate of heaven," one of the most interesting of Chinese political concepts. Possession of the mandate by a dynasty was indicated by its success in maintaining control; failure was a sign that the mandate had been withdrawn.

"Of old, the territory of the Five Emperors constituted a square of one thousand *li*. Beyond this were the domains of the feudal lords and of the barbarians. Some of the feudal lords came to court to do homage, and some did not; the Son of Heaven was unable to keep control over them. But now Your Majesty has raised his armies of righteousness and put to death oppressors and brigands. He has pacified the world and has laid out all within the seas into commanderies and prefectures. Laws and ordinances emanate from one center. Such a thing has never existed from high antiquity until now; it is something the Five Emperors did not attain to. We, your ministers, having carefully deliberated with the scholars of wide learning, would say: Of old there were the Celestial Sovereign, the Terrestrial Sovereign, and the Great Sovereign. The Great Sovereign was the most honorable. We, your ministers, at the risk of death (for our words), would propose as an honorable appellation that the King be called the Great Sovereign, that his mandates be called decrees . . . , and his ordinances be called edicts. . . . And let the Son of Heaven term himself in his speech as *chen* ['we']."

"The King said: 'I reject *Great*; I adopt *Sovereign*. From high antiquity I choose the title of *Emperor*. My title will be *Sovereign Emperor*. As for the rest, let it be as you deliberated.' A decree declared the approval."

Text: Derk Bodde, *China's First Unifier* (Leiden: E. J. Brill, 1938), pp. 77-78.

136 EDICTS OF KAO-TSU AND HSAIO-WEN: THE CREATION OF THE BUREAUCRACY

In the year 165 B.C. an imperial edict was issued in China ordering "the vassal kings, the ministers, and the commandery administrators to present to the emperor those who were capable and good, and could speak frankly and admonish their superiors unflinchingly." The emperor himself examined those who were nominated by presenting a literary exercise in which they "set forth in written words their ideas for adoption." This is our earliest account of the examination system for the Chinese civil service, the institution that made possible the continuance of efficient administration even when dynasties were overthrown by foreign invaders. (See Document 129 for A. L. Bashdm's comparison of the Chinese and Indian experience in this area.) Even before the edict of 165 B.C., the emperor had issued another order, aimed at finding and training the best possible men to work as government servants. This command is preserved in the writings of Pan Ku, a member of a famous family of historians of the first century A.D. The following passage shows how Chinese historians used carefully preserved state archives in writing history. As a result, the recorded political history of ancient China is far more precise than that of India.

[The edict] also said, "Verily [We] have heard that no [true] king was greater than [King] Wen of the Chou [dynasty] and no Lord Protector was greater than [Duke] Huan of Ch'i—both needed capable men in order to make a name for themselves. At present in the world there are capable men who are wise and able; why should only men of ancient times [be capable]? The trouble is that the ruler of men does not meet them. By what means could a gentleman have access [to me]? Now I, by the spiritual power of Heaven, [and by my] capable gentlemen and high officials have subjugated and possess the empire

Text: Pan Ku, *The History of the Former Han Dynasty*, trans. Homer H. Dubs (New York: American Council of Learned Societies, 1938), I, 130-32.

and have made it one family. I wish it to be enduring, that generation after generation should worship at my ancestral temple without cessation. Capable persons have already shared with me in its pacification. Should it be that [any capable persons] are not to share together with me in its comfort and its benefits? If there are any capable gentlemen or sirs who are willing to follow and be friends with me, I can make them honorable and illustrious. Let [the foregoing] be published to [all] the world, to make plain Our intention. Let the Grandee Secretary [Chao] Yao transmit it to the Chancellor of State; let the Chancellor of State [Hsiao Ho], the Marquis of Tso, transmit it to the vassal kings; the Palace Secretary for Administrating the Laws shall transmit it to the Commandery Administrators. If any [among their people] have an excellent reputation and manifest virtue, [the officials] must personally urge [them to come], provide them with a quadriga, and send them to go to the courts of the Chancellor of State to have written down their accomplishments, their appearance, and their age. If there are [such ones] and [any official] does not report them, when [this fact] becomes known, he shall be dismissed. Those who are aged, infirm, or ill should not be sent."

137 WANG MANG, EDICTS ON TAXATION AND MONOPOLY: THE IMPERIAL CONCERN FOR A SOUND ECONOMY

The Chinese emperors and their advisers realized that, along with a centrally controlled administrative structure, a sound economy was necessary for a stable and powerful kingdom. An edict of 178 B.C. pointed out, "Agriculture is the great foundation of the world; it is what the people depend upon for their very life." Although the political power of the great property-holders had been destroyed by the Ch'in Dynasty, the land was now in the hands of landlords who ruthlessly exploited the farmers renting from them. Humanitarians had long been aware of the injustices and inequalities suffered by the peasants, and the government itself complained that it was not receiving a fair share of the produce of the land. "How is it," asked the emperor in 163 B.C., "that the people's food is scarce and lacking? Is there some fault in our way of government . . . or is it that salaries of officials are perhaps too lavish, or that useless activities are too many?"

For over a century the country's unsteady economy had caused concern, but the first serious attempt to remedy matters was made by Wang Mang, an official who overthrew the Former Han Dynasty in 9 A.D., and made himself emperor. Wang Mang carried out one of the most radical agrarian reforms in the history of China by nationalizing the land and then portioning it out to the cultivators. He maintained his hold on the rest of the economy by tightening governmental control on existing state monopolies such as salt, iron, and wine. He also made one of history's most sweeping currency reforms, which involved the turning in of all gold coins to the treasury. The widespread effect of this measure led to the drain of gold from the West to the East, creating financial problems for the Romans in the first century A.D. Wang Mang's reforms were opposed not only by the landowners but also by the peasants, who resented change, and by the civil service. He was killed in an uprising in 23 A.D., but his ideas lived on to inspire later reformers.

[Wang Mang] also [ordered], "In accordance with the [system of] taxing the common people in the *Chou Offices*, all fields that are not plowed are 'unproductive [fields,'] hence] shall pay taxes for three heads of households; residences inside the inner or outer city walls that are not planted [with fruit-trees] or cultivated [for garden produce] are 'denuded of vegetation,' and shall pay the hemp-cloth [tax] for three heads of households; common people who wander about and have no occupation must pay [the tax of] one roll of hemp-cloth for a head of a household. Those who are not able to pay the hemp-cloth [tax] shall work at incidental occupations for the imperial government and shall be clothed and fed by it.

"Those who collect articles of any kind, birds, beasts, fish, turtles, or the various insects from the mountains, forests, streams, or marshes, to-

Text: Pan Ku, *The History of the Former Han Dynasty*, trans. Homer H. Dubs (New York: American Council of Learned Societies, 1955), III, 495-503.

gether with those who rear or care for domestic animals, women who collect mulberry leaves, rear silkworms, weave, spin, or sew, laborers, artisans, physicians, shamans, diviners, invokers, together with [people who have] other recipes or skills, peddlers, traders, merchants who sit down and spread out [their wares] or who arrange them at stopping-places, or who visit houses, shall all and each themselves, at the places where they are, testify to the imperial government what they do, exclude their principal, calculate their [net] profit, divide off from it one-tenth, and use this one-[tenth] as their tribute. Those who presume not to testify themselves, or who themselves in testifying do not accord with the facts shall have all that they have collected or taken confiscated and paid [to the government] and shall work for the imperial government for one year.

"The [Masters] in Charge of Markets shall regularly, in the second month of [each of] the four seasons, determine the true [prices] of the articles that they take care of and make high, middle, and low prices [for the respective grades of these goods]. Each [Master] shall himself use [these prices] at his own market to equalize [prices there] and shall not restrict himself [by the prices] at other places. When the mass of common people have sold and bought the five [kinds of] grains or articles of hempen-cloth, silk cloth, silk thread, or silk wadding, which are used everywhere among the common people, whenever any has not been sold, and the office for equalization has examined and inspected the reality of that [fact, the office] shall take those [articles] at their cost price, so as not to cause [the people] to lose a cash. When [any of] the myriad things rise [in price and become] expensive, so that they surpass by one cash [the prices at which they have been] equalized, then [the accumulated stock] shall be sold to the common people in accordance with the price at which they have been equalized. If the price goes down and becomes cheap, below [the price at which it is to be] equalized, the common people shall be permitted to sell [goods] amongst each other at the market-place, in order to prevent any from storing [goods] up [for the purpose of keeping them until they become] expensive.

"If any of the common people wish to sacrifice or perform funeral and mourning ceremonies, and have not the means, the Office for Money shall give to them on credit, without requiring interest, whatever laborers or merchants have paid in as tribute, [in the case of] sacrifices, for not more than ten days, [and in the case of] mourning ceremonies, for not more than three months. If any of the common people are lacking and have no [means] or wish to borrow on interest in order to establish a productive occupation, [the money] shall be impartially given to them, and, after their expenses have been deducted, they shall calculate what [profit] they have made, and shall pay interest [to the amount of] not more than one-tenth [of his income] per year."

The Hsi-and-Ho, Lu K'uang, said, "The controls of the famous mountains and great marshes, salt and iron, cash and spade-money currency, the five equalizations, selling on credit and lending on interest, are in [the hands of] the imperial government. Only the selling of fermented drinks alone is not yet monopolized. Fermented drink is the most beautiful happiness from Heaven, whereby the lords and kings have nourished the country. Meetings for offering sacrifices, for praying for blessings, for succoring the decrepit, for caring for the sick, and all the rites, cannot be carried on without fermented drink.

"Hence the *Book of Odes* says,

'If I have no fermented drink, I buy it, do I,' but the *Analects* says, '[Confucius] would not drink purchased fermented drink.' These two are not contradictory.

"Verily, the ode refers to [a time when] peaceful reigns succeeded [each other, when] the fermented drink purchased at a [government] office was harmonious, agreeable, and suited to people, so that it could be offered [to others]. [In the time of] the *Analects*, Confucius [lived] in [the period when] the Chou [dynasty] was decaying and in disorder, so that the sale of fermented drink was in [the hands of] the common people, [and hence] was of poor quality, bad, and not free from adulteration. For this reason [Confucius] suspected it and would not drink it.

"If now the empire's fermented drink is cut off, then there will be no means of performing the rites or of cherishing others. If permission is given [to anyone to make it] and no limit is set [to its manufacture], then it will consume wealth and injure the common people. [Hence] I beg that you will imitate ancient [practises] and order the [government] offices to make fermented drink, taking 2500 piculs as one standard [unit] and accordingly open one shop to sell [this quantity]. If the selling of fifty fermentations is taken as one standard [unit]; one fermentation requires two *hu* of coarse grain and one *hu* of yeast, [from which] is obtained six *hu* six *tou* of finished fermented drink. If for each [fermentation] one counts up together the price of the three *hu* of grain and yeast, according to [the price at] the market-place on the first day of the month, divide it by three, and take one part as the average for one *hu* of [material for] fermented drink, if one deducts the original price of the grain and yeast and counts up the profit, then seven parts in ten will be paid to the government. The three [other parts], together with the lees, vinegar, ashes, and charcoal may be given to the workmen for the expense of the utensils and firewood."

The Hsi-and-Ho, [Lu K'uang], established [officials, ranking as] Mandated Officers, to supervise the five equalizations and the six monopolies. [In each] commandery there were several [such] men. Everywhere he employed rich merchants, [such as] Nieh Tzu-chung and Chang Ch'ang-shu from Lo-yang, Hsin Wei from Lin-tzu, and others. [Traveling] in riding quadrigae, they sought for profit and made numerous contacts [all over] the empire, and, availing [themselves of their opportunities], they communicated their wickedness to the commanderies and prefectures, and made many false accountings. The yamens and storehouses were not filled, and the people suffered all the more.

[Wang] Mang knew that the common people suffered from these [measures, so he] again issued an imperial edict, which said, "Verily, salt is the greatest of foods; fermented drink is the chief of all medicines and the best feature of auspicious assemblies; iron is the fundamental [thing] in [the cultivation of] fields and in agriculture; the famous mountains and the great marshes are storehouses of abundance; the five equalizations and [the system of] selling on credit and lending on interest [are means by which] the people may receive the equalization of high [prices], in order to give assistance [to the people against profiteers]; cash and spade-money, and the casting of copper make wealth circulate and furnish [what is needed] for the common people's use. These six [matters] are not [things that] the enrolled households of equal common people are able to make in their homes, so that, if [the prices of these goods] are high in the market-place, although [these things] may be several times as expensive [as usual, the people] inevitably have no alternative but to purchase them, [hence] eminent common people and wealthy merchants can thereupon coerce the poor and weak. The ancient sages knew that it would be so, hence they made controls (monopolies) of these [matters]."

For each control (monopoly) he established rules and precepts to interdict and prohibit [violations of the monopoly]; the penalties for violation extended to capital [punishment]. Wicked officials and cunning common people both at the same time encroached upon the mass of people, so that every [person] was disquieted with life.

The fifth year after, in [the period] T'ien-feng, the first year, [Wang Mang] again sent down [a message], increasing and decreasing considerably the price and value of gold, silver, tortoise-[shell], and cowry currency, and abolishing the large and small cash. Instead he made "currency spade-money (*huo-pu*)," two inches five *fen* in length and one inch in width, with their heads eight *fen* and a fraction long and eight *fen* wide, their circular holes two *fen* and a half in diameter, their feet eight *fen* long, their opening [between the feet] two *fen* wide, their legend, on the right reading, "Currency (*huo*)" and on the left reading, "Spade-money (*pu*)." Their weight was twenty-five *shu*, and they were worth twenty-five of the currency cash. The currency cash (*huo-ch'üan*) were one inch in diameter, and weighed five *shu*. Their legend on the right reads "Currency (*huo*)" and on the left reads "Cash (*ch'üan*)." One [such] was worth one [cash]; it and the currency spade-money [formed] two denominations, which circulated concurrently.

Moreover, because the large cash had circulated for a long time, [Wang Mang] abolished them, fearing that the common people would keep them and not stop [using them]. So he ordered that the common people should only temporarily circulate the large cash, and that one [such large cash] should be worth one of the new currency cash, that their concurrent circulation should be ended in the sixth year, and that [people] should not [then] be any more allowed to possess the large cash.

Each time that the money was changed, the common people were thereby ruined financially and fell into serious punishment. Because so many were those who violated the laws and [whoever] privately cast cash had to die and [whoever] criticized or put obstacles [in the circulation of] the valuable currency should be thrown out to the four borders, with the result that [their sentences] could not be entirely carried out, [Wang] Mang therefore changed and lightened these laws: those who privately cast or made cash or spade-money were confiscated with their wives and children and became government slaves or slave-women. Officials and the group of five [families, of which the culprit was a member], who knew of [the crime] and did not bring it forward or denounce it, [were tried] with [the culprit as having committed] a like crime. As to those who criticized or put obstacles [in the circulation of] the valuable currency: common people were to be punished [by being made] to work for one year and officials were to be dismissed from their offices. When violations became the more numerous and [the people in the group of] five [families who were held responsible] were sentenced together with them and all were confiscated to [the government penal service], the commanderies and kingdoms, with accompanying [guards], sent them in carts and cages, with iron locks [about their necks], to the Office for Coinage at Ch'ang-an. Six or seven out of [every] ten [of these people] died from the hardships and suffering.

The sixth year after the currency spade-money had been issued, the Huns made great incursions and robberies, [hence Wang] Mang made a great solicitation of the empire's prisoners, convicts, and people's slaves, naming them, "Boar braves who are porcupines rushing out." He temporarily taxed the officials and common people, taking one-thirtieth of their property. He also ordered that the ministers and those of lower [rank, down] to the officials in the commanderies and counties who wore yellow sealcords, should all guarantee the rearing of horses for the army, and the officials all in turn gave [these horses to] the common people [to care for them]. Whenever the common people moved their hands, they ran upon a prohibition. They could not plow or cultivate silkworms, for the corvée service was troublesome and distressing, and withering droughts and [plagues of] insects and locusts followed each other.

THE FLOWERING OF CHINESE CIVILIZATION

138 WEI SHOU: THE ASCENDANCY OF BUDDHISM

One of the most remarkable movements in Chinese history was the popular acceptance of Buddhism in the first century A.D. The actual date of the arrival of Buddhism in China is obscure, as is its means of propagation, but it is thought that missionaries and traders brought its message from India. By the time Buddhism reached China it was greatly changed from the days of its founding; the *Mahayana*, or "Great Vehicle," form that came to be accepted in China had much to offer the religious man. Buddhism had become in the course of centuries a religion for all men: it promised eternal life to those who followed its teachings; it had ways of salvation that appealed to both the educated and the untaught; its emphasis was not on the virtue of the devotee, as in much Chinese philosophy, but on the free grace bestowed by Buddha. The Indian doctrine of *karma* explained life's injustices and inequalities and at the same time made it possible for a man to work out his own salvation. The immense pantheon of gods that had been added to Buddhism since its agnostic beginnings, the beautiful liturgy of its worship, the marvelous literature it had produced in India, proved irresistible to many Chinese.

Buddhism's rapid expansion was not achieved without creating problems for rulers. An insight into some of these problems is provided by the historian Wei Shou (506-572), who was writing at a time when Buddhism was well established. The fifth and sixth centuries were a time of troubles for China—political disunity, invasions from without, and natural disasters combined to destroy the prosperity of the nation. Buddhism provided a refuge for its believers: the rich gave their lands to monasteries to avoid taxation, and the disillusioned and those wanted by the law fled from the confusion of life to the safety of monasticism. In the first part of the following selection, Wei Shou is quoting from an official's report on possible reforms. In the second part, Wei Shou's own account, the "disaster" referred to is one typical of the age. A usurper had seized the government of the Wei Dynasty of northern China and, having killed the child emperor, he put to death two hundred members of the former ruling party.

"Let us respectfully reflect upon Kao-tsu [471–499]. . . . Planning and devising everything, his regulations set in harmony heaven and man. Creating his institutions, and breaking in two the tablets of investiture, he has transmitted them to our descendants forever. Accordingly, the regulations for the capital read: 'Within the city it is decided that there shall be only the one site for the Yung-ning monastery, and within the first suburb there is to be only one nunnery. All the rest shall be outside the city and the first suburb.'

Text: J. R. Ware, "Wei Shou on Buddhism," in *T'oung Pao*, ed. Paul Pelliot (Leiden: E. J. Brill, 1933), XXX, pp. 168-71, 176-77.

It was his desire that we should long follow this regulation, and that none should dare infringe upon the precedent.

"In the beginning of the period Ching-ming [500—503] there were slight infringements of this prohibition. Shih-tsung [499—515], therefore, respectfully renewing his predecessor's desires, issued a clear decree that within the city there should not be built and erected stūpas and monasteries for the monks and nuns — he wanted to check their hopes and desires. Is it that the two emperors [Kao-tsu Hsiao-]wên [471—499] and [Shih-tsung Hsüan-]wu [499—515] did not like and esteem Buddhism? Because the religious and laity have different goals, they arranged that the two should not be confused. Nevertheless, the laity have been dazzled by the empty glory [of building,] and the monks have been greedy for rich favors. Altho there was a clear prohibition, they have taken upon themselves to build.

"In the third year [506] of the period Chêng-shih, the Chief of the Śramaṇas Hui-shên, there being some violations of the prohibitions of the period Ching-ming [500—503], said: 'As for the monasteries which have been completed, we cannot bear that they should be removed and destroyed. It is requested that from today on it be no longer permitted to build [within the proscribed limits].' The previous edicts being relaxed, and the laws being suppressed upon request, the formerly issued proclamations were rolled up again and not executed. Later there ensued everywhere a hurly-burly of visits on private business.

"In the second year [509] of the period Yung-p'ing [Hui-]shên and the others again set up regulations. Their circular read: 'From today on, when one wants to build a monastery, if the monks are limited to fifty or more and a report is made, permission will be granted to build. If anyone build on his own accord, [he shall be punished] like a layman guilty of violating an imperial edict. The monks of this monastery will be exiled to the provinces.

"For the last ten years the building [of monasteries] on one's own accord has increased, but punishments and exiles have not been heard of. Is it not that, altho the court's regulations are clear, all do wrong while putting their trust in merit? The regulations for the Samgha merely stand there, and out of regard for profit none follow them. It is peculiar neither to the laity nor to the religious, [this] bending of one's energies to break the law. But can the insatiableness of man know no limit?

"Now their teachings are most profound, and are not the things which a frivolous intellect would understand. The vastnesses and silences of the Mystic Sect can they be discussed in a few words? But a pure dwelling free from the world is what the religious prefer. The doctrine of merit is obscure and profound, and lays no value upon sham and dissimulation. If they can sincerely believe that a child who builds [at play] a stūpa of sand can attain the bodhimaṇḍala, the place where Buddha attained enlightenment . . . what necessity is there to give free rein to their thefts in order to build monasteries? This is a case where 'when the people entrust themselves much to luck there is no prosperity.'

"Of late, however, private construction has surpassed a hundred. [People] go to request public land in order to strengthen their own merit, or, succeeding in building a monastery by permission, they extend the laws beyond their limits. Such deceptions and wrongs amount to no small figure.

"Your minister with his poor talents truly disgraces the position which he holds. But respectfully following established customs, as Chief of the Boards of Works, he has opened up and examined the old decrees, and pondered upon their plans and provisions. Of his own accord he has sent a subordinate to his secretary . . . into the capital and first suburb to inspect the monasteries. Their number surpasses five hundred, not including the vacant ground, the mast of chattra, and the stūpas which are not yet completed. This is the result of the people's not revering the law. During the more than two periods of twelve years since the removal of the capital, the monasteries have usurped a third of the people's dwelling [-land].

"When Kao-tsu set up his regulations, not only did he want to differentiate the paths of the religious and laity, but he also regulated the minutest details and laid deep plans. Shih-tsung followed in his [Kao-tsu's] foot-steps, and also did not stop or forbid [building]. There was merit for building at that time, and crowding had not yet begun. But the present-day monasteries — no spot is without one. Either side by side they fill the center of the city, or close upon one another they spread over the meat and wine markets. Three or five young monks together form one monastery; sanskrit chants and the cries of butchers unite their echoes under contiguous eaves. The statues and stūpas are wrapped in odors of meat; man's nature and the spiritual powers are submerged in lust and desire. Truth and falsehood dwell together in disorder; relations are pell-mell and confused. The lower officials acquiesce in [these] practises and do not blame [them]; the monks are face to face with the regulations, but do not inquire about [them. However,] when wrong taints the true practises, when the world soils trained monks, and when fragrance and stench share the same utensils, is it not excessive?

"According to the decree [issued] in the first month of this year [519] it is requested that the future builders be judged according to the Saṃgha's regulations or according to the provisions of the law.

"In cases where the monks do not number fifty, since they receive one another everywhere, let the small group go to the larger ones that they may be sure to fulfil the requirements [of number]. The land, let it be sold or returned [to the state] as in the above examples.

"After today, when there is a desire to build a monastery in the outer provinces and the monks number fifty or more, let them have the province in question explain the matter in a petition. . . . After examination, if the report is approved, the building may be done. In cases of infraction let everything be done in conformity with the previous regulations. As for the provinces and prefectures on down which out of indulgence do not prohibit [unlawful building], their wrong-doing is similar to the violation of an imperial decree.

"It is hoped that [the people] will honor and follow the imperishable works of our former emperors, and will respectfully execute the kind, compassionate orders of the present edict. Then the rules and regulations will remain whole, and the Way of our rulers will not fail."

The report was approved.

Shortly afterwards the empire was thrown into confusion. Because of the disaster at Ho-yin and the death of the capital officials, their families for the most part abandoned their homes as gifts to the monks and nuns, and the better homes of the capital became, on the whole, monasteries. The former restrictions and orders were not practised again.

In the autumn of the first year [538] of the period Yüan-hsiang a decree read: "The brahmavihāra is subtle and obscure; its concept belongs to peaceful solitudes. The monastery is a Pure Land; its principle is a variance with the noise and dust [of the world]. In the capital of our predecessor [the monasteries] were formerly under restrictions. Since our later removal to Yeh all has been in accord with the old regulations, but, when the princes and common people first came to the capital, a new city outside the old one also offered a home to all. In an instant there was everywhere a pretense of mature deliberation, but a moment later there was no permanency [to the decision].

"According to the reports men have in many cases obtained land in two places, or, abandoning the homes which the old city loaned, they have taken upon themselves to turn them into monasteries. Knowing that it was not their own [that they were giving away], there are pretending all this renown [of being the builder of a monastery]. Finally, fearing that the practise may spread widely and damage greatly the constant norm, it is fitting to charge the officers to apply the regulations zealously. . . . Let the newly erected monasteries be destroyed—all of them."

139 CHU HSI: THE CONFUCIAN REVIVAL

Although Buddhism dominated Chinese life for eight or nine centuries, the Confucianists' influence continued to be felt. (The examination system for the civil service, for example, continued to be based on a knowledge of the Confucian classics.) And under the Sung Dynasty (960-1279) a great revival of Confucian thought was begun. Many believed that Buddhism's powerful impression on Chinese life was due to the fact that its ideas were more suited to changing conditions than were those of the classics. To preserve the best of both philosophies, a more or less conscious effort was made to create a synthesis from the two sources. One of the greatest of the Neo-Confucian thinkers was Chu Hsi (1130-1200), whose role in the historical development of a Confucian orthodoxy is somewhat similar to that of Thomas Aquinas in the West a few generations later. J. P. Bruce, Chu Hsi's translator, sums up his contribution by saying that "his teachings have done more than almost any other to mould the thought of the Chinese race."

Chu Hsi's central philosophy was that there is an immutable principle of ultimate (called *li*) which underlies all the universe; in addition, there is "substance" or matter, (called *ch'i*), which gives differentiation and physical form to things. Man's spiritual nature is fundamentally good, he taught, because it is part of the ultimate, but evil enters when this original nature is obscured by matter. "Heaven, Earth, and Man have the same *li*," he said, indicating that there is a fundamental harmony in the universe.

The aim of man, then, is the achievement of this original state. This is to be accomplished through rigorous examination and study—in the familiar Confucian phrase, through "the investigation of things." What was meant was the study of the classics and the elaboration of the ideas found there. For this reason the Neo-Confucian synthesis, which was intended as a liberating force for men's minds, became an orthodoxy that aimed at preventing change. Nevertheless, the synthesis played an important part in making China what it became in the twelfth century—the home of the most brilliant and advanced culture of the time.

In the passage from his writings given here, Chu Hsi is arguing against the Taoists and Buddhists, especially against the meaning they had given to the word *tao*, or *way*. The "Master" referred to is Confucius. Chu Hsi's teaching is often cast in the form of a dialogue, with the question sometimes containing the point that he wants to make. This is the case here, for his reply to the questioner was, "Your communication accords with my own mind in all respects. It shows your fine ability."

Is it maintained that Tao is lofty and distant, inscrutable and mysterious, and beyond the possibility of human study? Then I answer that Tao derives its very name from the fact that it is the principle of right conduct in everyday life for all men, that it is like a road which should be travelled upon by the countless myriads of people within the four seas and nine continents. It is not what the Taoist and Buddhist describe as Tao, empty, formless, still, non-existent, and having no connexion with men. Is it maintained that Tao is far removed from us, so vast as to be out of touch with our needs, and that we are not called upon to study it? Then I say that Tao, present as it is in all the world in the relation between sovereign and minister and between father and son, in down-sitting and uprising and in activity and rest, has everywhere its unchangeable clear law, which cannot fail for a single instant. For this reason the saints and sages exerted themselves and gave us their instruction so as clearly and perfectly to manifest its meaning, both in its vastness and minuteness, in its fineness of detail and broad outlines; and the student of their books must not be satisfied with examining the letter only, for the mere pleasure of analysis and synthesis, he must discuss their teachings intelligently, and examine them exhaustively, in order to remember them, practise them, and manifest them in the business of life; only thus can he fulfil his mission and take his place in the universe. He must not examine the letter only for the mere pleasure of tracing out and compiling. When, therefore, Tzǔ Yu quoted the Master as saying: "When the man of high station is a disciple of Moral Law he loves men; when the man of low station is a disciple of Moral Law he is easily ruled," the Master endorsed his words. How different is "the study of Moral Law", as presented to us here, from the teaching of the scholars of this age! . . .

You regard the heretical doctrine of Tao as useless, and therefore go on to make the Tao itself a useless thing. Can that be right? On the contrary, while the word "Love" refers directly to the mystery pertaining to man's Mind, the word "Tao" is the comprehensive term for the moral nature common to all. Therefore, although the description of it combines both the individual and the transcendental, there are not really two entities, the *Doctrine of the Mean* says, "Moral Law is cultivated by Love." Hu Tzǔ also says, "If a man has not Love, the essence of Moral Law is gone," which conveys the same idea. . . .

Question. There is only one Law of Heaven and Man. The root and fruit are identical. When the Moral Law of man's Nature is perfected, the Moral Law of Heaven is also perfected. The realization of the fruit does not mean separation from the root. Even those whom we regard as saints spoke only of perfecting the relationships of human life. The Buddhists discard man and discourse on Heaven, and thus separate the fruit from the root, as if they were two horns of a dilemma of which you must choose one and reject the other. The presence of the Four Terminals and the Five Cardinal Virtues in man's nature they regard as masking the Nature. The indispensable relationships between father and son, sovereign and minister, husband and wife, senior and junior, they regard as accidental. They even go so far as to regard Heaven and Earth, the Two Modes of Matter, men and other creatures, as phantasmal transformations. They have never so much as inquired into their reality, but simply assert the Nature of the Great Void. Now there are no two laws in the universe; how then can they take Heaven and Man, the root and fruit, summarily asserting the one and denying the other, and yet call this Tao? When their perceptions are so partial, so small and incomplete,

Text: Chu Hsi, *The Philosophy of Human Nature,* trans. J. P. Bruce (London: Arthur Probsthain, 1922), pp. 278-83.

what possibility is there of the familiar doctrine of a perfect union between the transcendental and the lowly? Those who follow the sacred Confucian school, on the other hand, "from the study of the lowly understand high things"; they advance from the humble accomplishments of "sprinkling and sweeping, answering and replying, advancing and receding". Whether in food and drink or in the relation between the sexes, they were never lacking in seriousness. For "the Moral Law which the noble man follows after is far-reaching and yet mystical". Far-reaching, it embraces the whole of his daily life; mystical, it is Divine Law. With this Divine Law, then, in daily life—in the relation between sovereign and minister, father and son, husband and wife, senior and junior, or when engaged in the toasting and pledging of social intercourse, or when eating, resting, seeing, and hearing—there is not one sphere of activity which is not under the guidance of Law, and not one that can be confused; for wherever there is confusion Divine Law has perished. "Therefore the noble man is never lacking in seriousness." By this means the Mind is held fast with firmness, the practice of good is mature, and so the hidden and manifest are blended, the outward and inward are united; and Moral Law dwells within me! What is there in Buddhism adequate to express this! What Buddhists call "Intelligence" is no more than a glance at the connecting thread. The reality and unchangeableness of Divine Law and man's Mind they have not apprehended. What they call "culture", also, is nothing more than control of the Mind and sitting in silence. Discarding human relationships, destroying the Divine Law, they reap no good that can be perceived. As you, sir, said: after all, they fail even to get near a solution of the problem. "Before the stirrings of pleasure, anger, grief, and joy," is the condition when "the Nature is still and without movement". Here we have the Mind of Heaven and Earth, the Source of the universe. There are not two sources in the universe; therefore the transformations of Ch'ien and K'un, and the classification of species, all proceed from this one source. Every form, produced and reproduced, has each the Nature of Heaven. This is the reason for the inseparableness of the creature from its source. Receiving its spiritual essence we become man, and within the confines of the four cardinal principles it resides, inscrutable, formless, still, and, it would seem, unnameable. Tzŭ Ssŭ, having regard to the absence in it of any leaning to one side or the other, called it The Mean. Mencius, having regard to its perfect purity called it Good. The Master having regard to its life-producing substance called it Love. The terms differ but the thing named is the same, and is not separable from everyday life. This is why you said that its meaning is manifest without our seeking it. Formerly I read many books from different points of view, but failed to grasp their main drift; I studied vaguely such subjects as Heaven and Earth, the Two Modes, man and other creatures, good and evil spirits, but did not find any principle of unity. With the truth near me, I was seeking it afar off, suffering probably from the mistake of over-eagerness in my search. I also heard that in the discourses of the Master Kuei Shan it is said: "Before we speak of perfecting the Mind, we must understand what the Mind is; after we have realized this clearly and distinctly, we may proceed to discuss the idea of perfecting it"; and my former explanation accorded with this exactly. But "Moral Law cannot be left for a single instant". In everyday life it is brightly shining; why should there be any waiting to search for it? This is what you, sir, have enjoined and taught, and I could not venture to do other than respectfully receive your teaching. . . .

140   WANG AN SHIH, "DISCUSSION OF CURRENT AFFAIRS": THE REFORM OF THE BUREAUCRACY

The most energetic attempt to institute reform during the Sung Dynasty (960-1279) was made by Prime Minister Wang An Shih (1021-1086). Wang An Shih called for a radical overhaul of the fiscal system of the empire, claiming to base his policies on the example of the past. His main proposals included the introduction of a graduated tax on incomes, instead of the hated forced labor, to accomplish public works; the prohibition of high rates of interest on agricultural loans; the establishment of a state monopoly of commerce to ensure the most profitable sale of produce given for taxes; and a reassessment of the taxes on cultivated land. Wang An Shih realized that only an honest, efficient bureaucracy could carry out this kind of program, knowing how corrupt the civil service had become and how ruthlessly its members exploited the people. The document given here is part of the memorandum he presented to the emperor when he was seeking support for his schemes. It is easy to see why officials were bitterly opposed to his plans. The forces against him were firmly entrenched in their privileged positions, and many of his reforms failed because the officials who were supposed to carry them out refused to do so.

"I, your Majesty's ignorant and incapable servant, have been honoured with your commission to take a part in the administration of one of the circuits. I feel it to be my duty, now that I am called to Court to report on conditions in my district, to bring to your attention certain matters affecting the Government. I presume to do this on the ground of the experience gained during my period of official service, and regardless of my own inability. I shall consider it most fortunate if my suggestions receive your careful attention, and if you can see your way to adopt such as seem in your opinion to be of a reasonable character.

"Your Majesty is well-known to be of a careful and economical disposition, endowed with great knowledge and wisdom, devoted and energetic in the discharge of your routine duties, and to be entirely averse to licentious and time-wasting pleasures. Your love for the people is cherished by all. Your method of selecting those whom people desire to be in the highest offices of the State, in a public manner, and your appointment of them regardless of the opposition of slanderous and speciously clever folk, has never been surpassed, not even by the rulers of the Golden Age.

"When one bears these things in mind, it might naturally be expected that poverty would be unknown in any homestead, and that the Empire as a whole would be gloriously prosperous.

"Such, however, is not the case. One cannot ignore the fact that the internal state of the country calls for most anxious thought, and that the pressure of hostile forces on the borders is a constant menace to our peace. The resources of the Empire are rapidly approaching exhaustion, and the public life is getting more and more decadent. Loyal and courageous hearts are becoming increasingly apprehensive as to the outcome of this unsatisfactory state of affairs.

"My own opinion is that all this is the result of the prevailing ignorance of a proper method of government. I realize that against this may be urged the fact that the Imperial laws are being strictly enforced, and that the regulations for the administration of affairs are quite adequate. My meaning, however, is not that we have no laws and regulations, but that the present system of administration is not in accordance with the principles and ideas of the ancient rulers.

"We read in Mencius, 'When a ruler is sincerely loving, and generally known to be so, but the effects of his benevolent disposition are not realized by the people in any adequate way, it must be because the method of government is not moulded after the pattern of the ancient rulers.' We need look no further than this quotation to discover the reason for the defective character of the extant administration.

"I am not arguing that we should revive the ancient system of government in every detail. The most ignorant can see that a great interval of time separates us from those days, and our country has passed through so many vicissitudes since then that present conditions differ greatly. So a complete revival is practically impossible. I suggest that we should just follow the main ideas and general principles of these ancient rulers.

"Let us recall the fact that we are separated from the rule of these great men by over a thousand years of history: that they had their periods of progress and decline: that their difficulties and circumstances differed greatly. But although the measures they devised and adopted to meet their various circumstances varied in character they were at one in the motives which actuated them, and in their observance of the relative importance of affairs.

"Therefore I contend that we need only to follow their principles. I believe that if that could be done, the changes and reforms that would ensue would not unduly alarm the people, or excite undue opposition, but would in the end bring the government of our day into line with that of the Golden Age.

"Though that is true, I am bound to admit that the present state of affairs is of such a character that even though your Majesty should desire to reform the administration it would be practically impossible to do so. It may be urged that as your Majesty is of such a careful and restrained disposition, your intelligence and wisdom, and your loving consideration for the people, are all that is necessary to success, provided that you devote yourself sincerely to the task. My reason for saying that the realization of your object is impossible is that there is an insufficient

Text: H. R. Williamson, *Wang An Shih* (London: Arthur Probsthain, 1935), I, 48-51, 54-60.

number of capable men to help you. Without these it is not feasible to reform the government so that it may conform to the pattern of that set up by the ancient rulers.

"My observation leads me to suggest that there never has been such a scarcity of capable men as exists to-day in the service of the State. Should it be urged that these men do exist, but that they are hidden away in the country districts, I would say that although I have prosecuted my search with diligence, I have found very few indeed.

"Does not this indicate that the method of producing such men is faulty? I may be permitted to quote my own experience of official life, for it adds weight to my impression that capable men are too scarce. In my travels through my Circuit, extending over 300 miles, I have found extremely few officials who are able to carry out government orders in any satisfactory way, or who have the capacity to lead their people to fulfil their obligations to the State. On the contrary those who are incapable, negligent, avaricious and mean, are innumerable. In some prefectures there is absolutely no one who is capable of applying the ideas of the ancient rulers to current conditions, or of even explaining how such might be done. The result is that no matter how fine and complete the regulations and orders of the Court might be, the possible benefit of these is never realized by the people because of the incapacity of the local officials. Not only is that true, but the subordinates in the districts are able to take advantage of these orders to carry on corrupt practices and induce disturbances.

"Seeing that there is this scarcity of capable men in the provincial positions, even though you should have some amongst your Court Ministers who are capable of appreciating your intention to reform the administration, and even though they themselves be desirous to carry it out, it would still fail of realization. For when you take into account the immense size of the Empire, how can one or two such men ensure that all the people will derive the benefit of such ideas? . . .

". . . [T]he number of capable men available depends upon the ruler taking such a course as shall develop . . . [useful] gifts in the people, and on making it possible for such to bring their natural gifts to fruition. By this I mean that a proper method should be devised whereby such men can be trained, maintained, selected and appointed.

"Firstly, what is the proper method of instructing these?

"The ancient rulers had a graded system of schools ranging from the National University to the district and village schools. For the control and development of these, a considerable number of educational officers and teachers were appointed, who had been selected with the greatest care. The conduct of Court ceremonies, music, and Government administration were all part of the recognized Curriculum. So that the model held up before the student, and in which he gradually became well versed, was the example, precept, and fundamental principles of government observed by the ancient rulers. The students trained under this system were found to be of such ability and character as the Government required and could use. No student was received into the schools who had not shown promise of developing such a capacity. But all who demonstrated that they possessed this potentiality were without exception received.

"This I consider to be the right method of training these men.

"Secondly, what is the proper method of maintaining them?

"In a word, they should be given adequate financial provision; they should be taught the restraints of propriety, and controlled by adequate laws and regulations.

"With regard to providing them with adequate financial resources, I would say that it is only natural for a man who is dissatisfied in this matter of financial provision, to proceed to all manner of loose and corrupt practices.

"The ancient rulers were fully cognizant of this fact, and drew up their regulations governing salaries, beginning with those who were allocated a share in the public services, although not on the recognized official roll, ensuring that they received sufficient to make up for what they had lost by being called upon for public work, necessitating absence from their agricultural or other pursuits. In increasing scale the salaries advanced, assuring each official of whatever grade sufficient to keep him honest, self-respecting, and free from corruption. They then made further provision for the sons and grandchildren of officials by their system of maintenance grants. In these ways the ancient rulers ensured that the officials they employed had no undue anxieties during their own lifetime about the support of their families, or about exceptional expenditure such as was caused by weddings, funerals, and the entertainment of guests. They also so arranged matters that after their death their descendants should have no cause to grieve over an insufficiency of the means of life.

"Then as regards the necessity of inculcating in them the restraints of propriety, I would say that once you have satisfied a man's natural desire for sufficient financial resources, it is essential that he should be restrained by the ordinances of propriety, otherwise he will proceed to a reckless extravagance in everything.

"The ancient rulers were cognizant of this fact, and drew up a series of regulations regarding weddings, funerals, sacrifices, support of the aged, banquets, presents, dress, food, utensils, etc., etc. Expenditure on these things was to be regulated according to the rank and grade of official. The aim was to adjust their financial outlay in an equitable manner, having due regard to their varying circumstances. A man might have a certain rank, which, if that alone was considered, would demand the expenditure of considerable sums on such things. But he might not possess the means to do the thing in the style which his rank required. The regulations provided for this contingency and he was not expected to conduct such matters in the lavish way that his rank alone would call for. But supposing a man had the means to meet all the requirements of high official rank on such occasions, but lacked the necessary rank which entitled him to make such a display, the regulations forbade him to do so, prohibiting the addition of the smallest fraction to the standard he was entitled to observe under them.

"Further as regards the measures to be devised for controlling the officials.

"The ancient rulers gave the officials moral instruction, as well as seeking to make them accomplished in the Arts. That having been done, those who failed to act up to the instruction they had received were banished to distant outposts, and were deprived of their official status for the whole of their life. They were also instructed in the restraints of Propriety. If they transgressed the rules in this sphere, the penalty exacted was banishment or even death.

"We read in the . . . Book of Rites, that if there was any delinquency committed in the matter of the proper clothing to be worn, that the prince of the State concerned should be banished.

"In the Book of History . . . we read, 'Should information come to you that drinking is going on, you should . . . proceed to arrest the drinkers, and bring them to the capital for execution.'

"It may be urged that such matters as wearing the wrong clothes or getting drunk are very light crimes, and that banishment or execution for the miscreants were altogether out of proportion. The fact that the ancient rulers permitted such heavy penalties was with a view to unifying the customs of the country, and thus accomplishing the true aim of all government.

"By this imposition of the restraints of Propriety and the penalties of the Law, they sought to bring all alike into subservience and submission. But they not only relied upon the power of prohibition and inspection, they afforded in their own person an example of sincere and sympathetic conduct. In this way all those officials of high rank who had direct access to the presence of the ruler, were induced to carry out his wishes in a loyal manner. It was agreed that punishment should be inflicted upon the one who failed to do so. The ruler gave a sincere example of living out his precepts, and those of high rank learned to avoid doing the things of which he disapproved. The idea was that thus the majority of the people at large would need no penalties to keep them from unworthy practices.

"The above is the right method of maintaining the officials.

"Thirdly, what is the correct method of selecting officials?

"The method adopted by the ancient rulers was to permit the country folk and students in the village or district schools to recommend those whom they thought had the requisite character and ability for appointment by the throne. Investigation was then made as to the real character and ability of such men, and each was then given a period of probation in some position suited to his capacity.

"It should be emphasized that in this investigation into the merits and ability of any candidate, personal observation or information from others were not the only factors on which the ruler depended. He never depended upon the judgment of any single individual either. A man's character was adjudicated by his conduct and his ability was tested by enquiry as to his views on current affairs. These having been ensured, he was actually tested out in some office for a time. As a matter of fact the meaning of the term 'investigation' was just this period of probation in actual employment. Yao's appointment of Shun was of this type. We can legitimately infer that this would be the procedure stringently followed in regard to other appointments.

"Now when we consider the vast extent of the Empire, and the enormous number of positions that have to be filled, one gets some idea of the large number of men that are required. We must acknowledge also that the Emperor cannot possibly investigate the character and ability of each and every one individually. Neither can he lay this responsibility on any individual, or expect him in a day or two to conduct such enquiry as would enable him to adjudicate the merit or demerit of any.

"So I propose that those whom you have already found by experience to be of good character and great ability, and to whom you have committed important responsibilities, should be entrusted with the task of selecting men of like qualifications. Also that these should be given an adequate period of probation in official life, after which they too should be allowed to make recommendations to the throne. When this has been done, and when the men recommended have been found to be worthy, rank, emoluments, and promotion should be conferred by way of reward.

"Fourthly, what is the right method to be adopted regarding the appointment of officials?

"The ancient rulers were cognizant of the fact that men differ in character, and their ability for actual work. They recognized that they were specially suited for certain definite tasks, and could not be reasonably expected to take up any and every kind of work indiscriminately.

"So they appointed those who had special qualifications for the work of Agriculture to the Ministry of Agriculture. Those who were skilled in engineering they appointed to the Ministry of Works. The chief positions were reserved for those who had the finest character and greatest ability, those of lesser gifts and qualifications being appointed to subordinate posts.

"They further recognized the fact that it is only after a prolonged period in any one appointment, allowing one's superior sufficient time to learn of his real capacity and attainments, and for the people under him to become truly subservient and happy under his control, that the really worthy have the chance to display their worth, and on the other hand that the evil-minded may have their wickedness exposed.

"Hence they made provision for a prolonged period of probation, as the best method of testing the appointees. This being ensured, those of real character and ability realized that they would be afforded a full chance to carry their projects to a successful issue, and were not distressed by the prospect that possibly they could not carry out their ideas properly, or that they would be deprived of their just reward. On the other hand, idlers and negligent fellows, who have become inured to thinking that they might maintain their good name and position for a short time, would be stimulated to a more worthy view of their responsibilities, as they would be made aware of the certainty of degradation and disgrace which would ensue on a prolonged period of service, unless they reformed. Those who knew they possessed no ability for a certain post would refrain from assuming such on the same grounds.

"After a prolonged period of probation in any one appointment, one's incapacity or unworthiness to occupy it, would certainly be manifest. This we have seen would deter unworthy or incapable men from embarking upon an official career. Still less would fawning and flattering folk find any inducement to compete for official position with this system functioning.

"So we see that due caution was paid to the selection of officials in those days, that they were given appointments for which they were deemed qualified, that they were kept in office for a sufficiently lengthy period, that they were regulated and rewarded in a careful manner, and ... were afforded a full opportunity for the carrying out of their duties."

INTERPRETATION OF CHINA

141 J. K. FAIRBANK, *THE UNITED STATES AND CHINA*: THE INFLUENCE OF THE CONFUCIAN PATTERN ON CHINESE SOCIETY

"China has been a problem," writes Professor J. K. Fairbank of Harvard University, "because she was a different type of society, outside the Western scheme of things, a mature state organized on fundamentally different principles." It is with this understanding that Professor Fairbank analyzes the value system accepted by the Chinese for over two millennia. Greater knowledge of other civilizations, it is often argued, would show that despite surface differences we are essentially one, but Professor Fairbank suggests that this is a false—and dangerous—way to approach Chinese society. The Chinese concept of the role of the individual, for example, differs greatly from that of the West, and while we may think ours preferable, "we cannot show how our view can ever be realized within the crowded circumstances of Chinese life." His discussion of Confucian thought patterns and their role in shaping Chinese history illustrates this argument.

The principles of Confucian government, which still lie somewhere below the surface of Chinese politics, were worked out before the time of Christ. Modifications made in later centuries, though extensive, have not been fundamental.

First of all, from the beginning of Chinese history in the Shang and Chou periods (from prehistoric times before 1400 B.C. to the third century B.C.) there was a marked stratification into the classes of the officials and nobility on the one hand, and common people on the other. Thus the term "hundred names" (*pai-hsing*) referred originally to the clans of the officials who were in a category quite different from the common people (*min*). It was not until much later that the modern term "old hundred names" (*lao-pai-hsing*) became transferred to the populace. This difference between the ancient ruling class and the common people gave rise to a particular type of aristocratic tradition which has been preserved and transmitted through Confucianism down to the present. The Confucian aristocrat has been the scholar-official.

In the second place, Confucianism has been the ideology of the bureaucrat. The bureaucratic ruling class came into its own after the decentralized feudalism of ancient China gave way to an imperial government. The unification of 221 B.C., in which one of the warring states (Ch'in) swallowed the others, required violent dictatorial methods and a philosophy of absolutism (that of the so-called "Legalist" philosophers). But after the short-lived Ch'in dynasty was succeeded by the Han in 202 B.C., a less tyrannical system of administration evolved. The Emperors came to rely upon a new class of administrators who superintended the great public works—dikes and ditches, walls, palaces, and granaries—and who drafted peasant labor and collected the land tax to support them. These administrators supplanted the hereditary nobility of feudal times and became the backbone of the imperial regime.

In the two centuries before Christ the early Han rulers firmly established certain principles. First, that the political authority in the state was centralized in the one man at the top who ruled as Emperor. Second, the Emperor's authority in the conduct of the administration was exercised on his behalf by his chief ministers, who stood at the top of a graded bureaucracy and who were responsible to him for the success or failure of their administration. Third, this bureaucracy was centralized in the vast palace at the capital where the Emperor exercised the power of appointment to office. His chief task became the selection of civil servants, with an eye to the maintenance of his power and his dynasty. For this reason the appointment of relatives, particularly from the maternal side, became an early practice. (Maternal relatives were the one group of persons completely dependent upon the ruler's favor as well as tied to him by family bonds, in contrast to paternal relatives who might compete for the succession.) Fourth, the early Han rulers developed the institution of inspection which later became the censorate, whereby an official in the provinces was checked upon by another official of lower rank, who was sent independently and was not responsible for the acts of his superior. In this and in many other ways the central problem of the imperial administration became that of selecting and controlling bureaucrats. It was here that Confucianism played its central role.

This ideology did not, of course, begin with Confucius (551-479? B.C.). The interesting concept of the Mandate of Heaven, for example, went back to the early Chou period (*c.* 1000-771 B.C.). According to the classic *Book of History*, the wickedness of the last ruler of the preceding dynasty of Shang, who was a tyrant, caused Heaven to give a mandate to the Chou to destroy him and supplant his dynasty, inasmuch as the Shang people themselves had failed to overthrow the tyrant. As later amplified this ancient idea became the famous "right of rebellion," the last resort of the populace against tyrannical government. It emphasized the good conduct or virtue of the ruler as the ethical sanction for preserving his dynasty. Bad conduct on his part destroyed the sanction, Heaven withdrew its Mandate, and the people were justified in deposing the dynasty, if they could. Consequently any successful rebellion was justified and a new rule sanctioned, by the very fact of its success. "Heaven decides as the people decide." The Chinese literati have censored bad government and rebels have risen against it in terms of this theory. It has also reinforced the belief that the ruler should be advised by learned men in order to ensure his right conduct.

Government by Moral Prestige. Confucius and his fellow philosophers achieved their position by being teachers who advised rulers as to their right conduct, in an age when feudal princes were competing for hegemony. Confucius was an aristocrat and maintained at his home a school for the elucidation and transmission of the moral principles of conduct and princely rule. Here he taught the upper class how to behave. He emphasized court etiquette, state ceremonies, and proper con-

Text: Reprinted by permission of the publishers from John King Fairbank, *The United States and China* (Cambridge, Mass.: Harvard University Press). Copyright 1948 by The President and Fellows of Harvard College. Pp. 54-58.

duct towards one's ancestors and in the famous five degrees of relationship. One of the central principles of this code was expressed in the idea of "proper behavior according to status" (*li*). The Confucian gentleman or *chün-tzu* ("the superior man," "the princely man") was guided by *li*, the precepts of which were written in the classics.

It is important to note that this code which came to guide the conduct of the scholar-official did not originally apply to the common people, whose conduct was to be regulated by rewards and punishments rather than moral principles.

This complex system of abstruse rules which the Confucians became experts at applying stemmed from the relationship of Chinese man to nature, which has already been mentioned. This relation had early been expressed in a primitive animism in which the spirits of land, wind, and water were thought to play an active part in human affairs. The idea is still prevalent in the practice of Chinese geomancy or *feng-shui* (lit., "wind and water"), which sees to it that buildings in China are properly placed in their natural surroundings. Temples, for example, commonly face south with protecting hills behind them and a water course nearby. In its more rationalized form this idea of the close relation between human and natural phenomena led to the conception that human conduct is reflected in acts of nature. To put it another way, man is so much a part of the natural order that improper conduct on his part will throw the whole of nature out of joint. Therefore man's conduct must be made to harmonize with the unseen forces of nature, lest calamity ensue.

This was the rationale of the Confucian emphasis on right conduct on the part of the ruler, for the ruler was thought to intervene between mankind and the forces of nature. As the Son of Heaven he stood between Heaven above and the people below. He maintained the universal harmony of man and nature by doing the right thing at the right time. It was, therefore, logical to assume that when natural calamity came, it was the ruler's fault. It was for this reason that the Confucian scholar became so important. Only he, by his knowledge of the rules of right conduct, could properly advise the ruler in his cosmic role.

The main point of this theory of "government by goodness," by which Confucianism achieved an emphasis so different from anything in the West, was the idea of the virtue which was attached to right conduct. To conduct oneself according to the rules of propriety or *li* in itself gave one a moral status or prestige. This moral prestige in turn gave one influence over the people. "The people (are) like grass, the ruler like the wind"; as the wind blew, so the grass was inclined. Right conduct gave the ruler power.

On this basis the Confucian scholars established themselves as an essential part of the government, specially competent to maintain its moral nature and so retain the Mandate of Heaven. Where the Legalist philosophers of the Ch'in unification had had ruthlessly efficient methods of government but no moral justification for them, the Confucianists offered an ideological basis. They finally eclipsed the many other ancient schools of philosophy. As interpreters of the *li*, they became technical experts, whose explanations of natural portents and calamities and of the implications of the rulers' actions could be denied or rejected only on the basis of the classical doctrines of which they were themselves the masters. This gave them a strategic position from which to influence government policy. In return they provided the regime with a rational and ethical sanction for the exercise of its authority, at a time when most rulers of empires relied mainly upon religious sanctions. This was a great political invention.

Japan

THE FOUNDATIONS OF SOCIETY

142 PRINCE SHOTOKU'S CONSTITUTION: THE INTRODUCTION OF NEW IDEALS OF GOVERNMENT

The crucial event in the history of Japanese civilization was the introduction of Chinese influences about the fifth century A.D. By that time Japan had come under the rule of one tribe, the Yamato, who gained enough dominance over the traditional warring groups to assert the paramountcy of their chief. This leadership was eventually to develop into the office of emperor.

China made three main contributions to Japan: a script for written language, the Buddhist religion, and Confucian thought. One of the leaders in introducing these aspects of Chinese civilization was Prince Shotoku, regent for the empress from about 593 to 622 A.D. He sent agents to China to study the political system and the political and religious ideas upon which it was based. The result was Japan's "Constitution," as it is usually called, although it is a code rather than a constitution, issued in 604. (Some scholars think that the code was written some years later, after Prince Shotoku's death, and that it was ascribed to him to gain prestige for the document.) This paper formulated for the first time in Japan a view of the state based on a comprehensive ethical and philosophical foundation. The code places great emphasis on due obedience to superiors, but includes an insistent reminder that those who govern are under obligation to care for the welfare of the people. Perhaps the most interesting aspect of the code is the assertion that the emperor is supreme and that his authority is exercised through officials whom he appoints. While this ideal of a centralized state controlled by the emperor was not realized for a long time, it remained the goal of Japanese political life. During these formative years in Japanese history it is possible to watch the unique spectacle of a ruling class consciously seeking to transform its mode of government by modeling it on a pattern which had proven stable elsewhere.

Summer, 4th month, 3rd day [604 A.D.]. The Prince Imperial in person prepared for the first time laws. There were seventeen clauses, as follows:

I. Harmony is to be valued, and an avoidance of wanton opposition to be honoured. All men are influenced by class-feelings, and there are few who are intelligent. Hence there are some who disobey their lords and fathers, or who maintain feuds with the neighbouring villages. But when those above are harmonious and those below are friendly, and there is concord in the discussion of business, right views of things spontaneously gain acceptance. Then what is there which cannot be accomplished!

II. Sincerely reverence the three treasures. The three treasures, viz. Buddha, the Law and the Priesthood, are the final refuge of the four generated beings, and are the supreme objects of faith in all countries. What man in what age can fail to reverence this law? Few men are utterly bad. They may be taught to follow it. But if they do not betake them to the three treasures, wherewithal shall their crookedness be made straight?

III. When you receive the Imperial commands, fail not scrupulously to obey them. The lord is Heaven, the vassal is Earth. Heaven overspreads, and Earth upbears. When this is so, the four seasons follow their due course, and the powers of Nature obtain their efficacy. If the Earth attempted to overspread, Heaven would simply fall in ruin. Therefore is it that when the lord speaks, the vassal listens; when the superior acts, the inferior yields compliance. Consequently when you receive the Imperial commands, fail not to carry them out scrupulously. Let there be a want of care in this matter, and ruin is the natural consequence.

IV. The Ministers and functionaries should make decorous behaviour their leading principle, for the leading principle of the government of the people consists in decorous behaviour. If the superiors do not behave with decorum, the inferiors are disorderly; if inferiors are wanting in proper behaviour, there must necessarily be offences. Therefore it is that when lord and vassal behave with propriety, the distinctions of rank are not confused: when the people behave with propriety, the Government of the Commonwealth proceeds of itself.

V. Ceasing from gluttony and abandoning covetous desires, deal impartially with the suits which are submitted to you. Of complaints brought by the people there are a thousand in one day. If in one day there are so many, how many will there be in a series of years? If the man who is to decide suits at law makes gain his ordinary motive, and hears causes with a view to receiving bribes, then will the suits of the rich man be like a stone flung into water, while the plaints of the poor will resemble water cast upon a stone. Under these circumstances the poor man will not know whither to betake himself. Here too there is a deficiency in the duty of the Minister.

VI. Chastise that which is evil and encourage that which is good. This was the excellent rule of antiquity. Conceal not, therefore, the good qualities of others, and fail not to correct that which is wrong when you see it. Flatterers and deceivers

Text: W. G. Aston (trans.), *Nihongi, Chronicles of Japan from the Earliest Times to A.D. 697*, Transactions and Proceedings of the Japan Society, London, Supplement I (London: Kegan Paul, Trench, Trübner & Co., 1896), I, 128-133 *passim.*

are a sharp weapon for the overthrow of the State, and a pointed sword for the destruction of the people. Sycophants are also fond, when they meet, of dilating to their superiors on the errors of their inferiors; to their inferiors, they censure the faults of their superiors. Men of this kind are all wanting in fidelity to their lord, and in benevolence towards the people. From such an origin great civil disturbances arise.

VII. Let every man have his own charge, and let not the spheres of duty be confused. When wise men are entrusted with office, the sound of praise arises. If unprincipled men hold office, disasters and tumults are multiplied. In this world, few are born with knowledge: wisdom is the product of earnest meditation. In all things, whether great or small, find the right man, and they will surely be well managed: on all occasions, be they urgent or the reverse, meet but with a wise man, and they will of themselves be amenable. In this way will the State be lasting and the Temples of the Earth and of Grain will be free from danger. Therefore did the wise sovereigns of antiquity seek the man to fill the office, and not the office for the sake of the man.

VIII. Let the ministers and functionaries attend the Court early in the morning, and retire late. The business of the State does not admit of remissness, and the whole day is hardly enough for its accomplishment. If, therefore, the attendance at Court is late, emergencies cannot be met: if officials retire soon, the work cannot be completed.

IX. Good faith is the foundation of right. In everything let there be good faith, for in it there surely consists the good and the bad, success and failure. If the lord and the vassal observe good faith one with another, what is there which cannot be accomplished? If the lord and the vassal do not observe good faith towards one another, everything without exception ends in failure.

X. Let us cease from wrath, and refrain from angry looks. Nor let us be resentful when others differ from us. For all men have hearts, and each heart has its own leanings. Their right is our wrong, and our right is their wrong. We are not unquestionably sages, nor are they unquestionably fools. Both of us are simply ordinary men. How can any one lay down a rule by which to distinguish right from wrong? For we are all, one with another, wise and foolish, like a ring which has no end. Therefore, although others give way to anger, let us on the contrary dread our own faults, and though we alone may be in the right, let us follow the multitude and act like them.

XI. Give clear appreciation to merit and demerit, and deal out to each its sure reward or punishment. In these days, reward does not attend upon merit, nor punishment upon crime. Ye high functionaries who have charge of public affairs, let it be your task to make clear rewards and punishments.

XII. Let not the provincial authorities or the Kuni no Miyakko levy exactions on the people. In a country there are not two lords; the people have not two masters. The sovereign is the master of the people of the whole country. The officials to whom he gives charge are all his vassals. How can they, as well as the Government, presume to levy taxes on the people?

XIII. Let all persons entrusted with office attend equally to their functions. Owing to their illness or to their being sent on missions, their work may sometimes be neglected. But whenever they become able to attend to business, let them be as accommodating as if they had had cognizance of it from before, and not hinder public affairs on the score of their not having had to do with them.

XIV. Ye ministers and functionaries! Be not envious. For if we envy others, they in turn will envy us. The evils of envy know no limit. If others excel us in intelligence, it gives us no pleasure; if they surpass us in ability, we are envious. Therefore it is not until after a lapse of five hundred years that we at last meet with a wise man, and even in a thousand years we hardly obtain one sage. But if we do not find wise men and sages, wherewithal shall the country be governed?

XV. To turn away from that which is private, and to set our faces towards that which is public—this is the path of a Minister. Now if a man is influenced by private motives, he will assuredly feel resentments, and if he is influenced by resentful feelings, he will assuredly fail to act harmoniously with others. If he fails to act harmoniously with others, he will assuredly sacrifice the public interests to his private feelings. When resentment arises, it interferes with order, and is subversive of law. Therefore in the first clause it was said, that superiors and inferiors should agree together. The purport is the same as this.

XVI. Let the people be employed (in forced labour) at seasonable times. This is an ancient and excellent rule. Let them be employed, therefore, in the winter months, when they are at leisure. But from Spring to Autumn, when they are engaged in agriculture or with the mulberry trees, the people should not be so employed. For if they do not attend to agriculture, what will they have to eat? if they do not attend to the mulberry trees, what will they do for clothing?

XVII. Decisions on important matters should not be made by one person alone. They should be discussed with many. But small matters are of less consequence. It is unnecessary to consult a number of people. It is only in the case of the discussion of weighty affairs, when there is a suspicion that they may miscarry, that one should arrange matters in concert with others, so as to arrive at the right conclusion.

143 DOCUMENT ON BUDDHISM: THE ARRIVAL OF BUDDHISM IN JAPAN

The introduction of Buddhism into Japan was closely associated with the political upheavals of the fourth and fifth centuries A.D. In the struggle for power, one faction stood for the old religions and native traditions, while the other, the "progressives," believed that a new order in government would benefit from the religious ideology as well as the political thought of the Chinese. The triumph of the progressives meant the widespread promulgation of Buddhism, and Japan thus became heir to two great eastern traditions, since Buddhism brought with it a wealth of Indian literature and ideas (considerably modified by transmission through China). The culture that resulted from this entrance of alien thought was, interestingly enough, thoroughly Japanese in character, bringing about a renaissance of exquisite Japanese architecture, painting, sculpture, and literature. However, it should be noted that while Buddhism brought great advantages to Japan, it was not long before the nation suffered from the same abuses that had appeared in China: hordes of men abandoned their vocations for monasticism; priests began interfering in politics; and great gifts given to the temples resulted in losses in taxes for the treasury.

The documents presented here are from the ancient history, *The Chronicles of Japan*, and give the traditional account of Buddhism's introduction. In the background it is possible to see the animosity of two contending factions, one standing for the old ways, the other anxious to share in the advantages of the higher civilization on the mainland. Many of the contacts with Chinese civilization were made through Pèkché, Koguryo, and Silla, kingdoms in what is now Korea. The King of Pèkché was seeking an alliance with the Japanese ruler against his rival, Silla, at the time—hence the overtures to the emperor. In the first selection below, Iname is the "Oho-omi," or "Chief of Chieftains"; in the second selection, Iname's son, Mŭmako, has succeeded to his father's office. A period of about thirty years separates the two incidents.

5th month, 8th day [552 A.D.]. Pèkché, Kara, and Ara sent the Tŏk-sol of the Middle Division, Mok-hyöp-keum-ton, and Asăpita, of the Kahachi Be, to make representation to the Emperor, saying:—"Koryö and Silla, having established friendly relations and joined their powers, design to overthrow thy servants' countries, together with Imna. Therefore we humbly request an auxiliary force, so that we may first attack them unawares. The number of the troops is left to the Emperor's decision."

The Emperor commanded, saying:—"We have now heard all that the King of Pèkché, the King of Ara, the King of Kara, and the Omi of the Japanese Government have conjointly by their envoys represented to Us with regard to the state of affairs. Let them continue, along with Imna, to unite their hearts and strength as heretofore, and they will be undoubtedly blessed with the protection of High Heaven, and can, moreover, place their trust in the spirits of the August Emperors."

Winter, 10th month. King Syöng-myöng of Pèkché [also called King Syöng] sent Kwi-si of the Western Division, and the Tal-sol, Nu-ri Sa-chhi-hyé, with a present to the Emperor of an image of Shaka Butsu in gold and copper, several flags and umbrellas, and a number of volumes of "Sutras." Separately he presented a memorial in which he lauded the merit of diffusing abroad religious worship, saying:—"This doctrine is amongst all doctrines the most excellent. But it is hard to explain, and hard to comprehend. Even the Duke of Chow and Confucius had not attained to a knowledge of it. This doctrine can create religious merit and retribution without measure and without bounds, and so lead on to a full appreciation of the highest wisdom. Imagine a man in possession of treasures to his heart's content, so that he might satisfy all his wishes in proportion as he used them. Thus it is with the treasure of this wonderful doctrine. Every prayer is fulfilled and naught is wanting. Moreover, from

Text: W. G. Aston (trans.), *Nihongi, Chronicles of Japan from the Earliest Times to A.D. 697*, Transactions and Proceedings of the Japan Society, London, Supplement I (London: Kegan Paul, Trench, Trübner & Co., 1896), II, 65-67, 101-102.

distant India it has extended hither to the three Han, where there are none who do not receive it with reverence as it is preached to them.

Thy servant, therefore, Myŏng, King of Pèkché, has humbly despatched his retainer, Nu-ri Sachhi, to transmit it to the Imperial Country, and to diffuse it abroad throughout the home provinces, so as to fulfil the recorded saying of Buddha: 'My law shall spread to the East.' "

This day the Emperor, having heard to the end, leaped for joy, and gave command to the Envoys, saying:—"Never from former days until now have we had the opportunity of listening to so wonderful a doctrine. We are unable, however, to decide of ourselves." Accordingly he inquired of his Ministers one after another, saying:—"The countenance of this Buddha which has been presented by the Western frontier State is of a severe dignity, such as we have never at all seen before. Ought it to be worshipped or not?" Soga no Oho-omi, Iname no Sukune, addressed the Emperor, saying:—"All the Western frontier lands without exception do it worship. Shall Akitsu Yamato alone refuse to do so?" Okoshi, Mononobe no Ohomuraji, and Kamako, Nakatomi no Muraji, addressed the Emperor jointly, saying:— "Those who have ruled the Empire in this our State have always made it their care to worship in Spring, Summer, Autumn and Winter the 180 Gods of Heaven and Earth, and the Gods of the Land and of the Grain. If just at this time we were to worship in their stead foreign Deities, it may be feared that we should incur the wrath of our National Gods".

The Emperor said:—"Let it be given to Iname no Sukune, who has shown his willingness to take it, and, as an experiment, make him to worship it."

The Oho-omi knelt down and received it with joy. He enthroned it in his house at Oharida, where he diligently carried out the rites of retirement from the world, and on that score purified his house at Muku-hara and made it a Temple. After this a pestilence was rife in the Land, from which the people died prematurely. As time went on it became worse and worse, and there was no remedy. Okoshi, Mononobe no Ohomuraji, and Kamako, Nakatomi no Muraji, addressed the Emperor jointly, saying:—"It was because thy servants' advice on a former day was not approved that the people are dying thus of disease. If thou dost now retrace thy steps before matters have gone too far, joy will surely be the result! It will be well promptly to fling it away, and diligently to seek happiness in the future."

The Emperor said:—"Let it be done as you advise." Accordingly officials took the image of Buddha and abandoned it to the current of the Canal of Naniha. They also set fire to the Temple, and burnt it so that nothing was left. Hereupon, there being in the Heavens neither clouds nor wind, a sudden conflagration consumed the Great Hall (of the Palace). . . .

Autumn, 9th month [584 A.D.]. Kafuka no Omi, who had come from Pèkché, had a stone image of Miroku, and Saheki no Muraji an image of Buddha. This year Soga no Mŭmako no Sukune, having asked for these two Buddhist images, sent Shiba Tattō, Kurabe no Sukuri, and Hida, Ikenobe no Atahe, in all directions to search out persons who practised (Buddhism). Upon this he only found in the province of Harima a man named Hyé-phyön of Koryö, who from a Buddhist priest had become a layman again. So the Oho-omi made him teacher, and caused him to receive Shima, the daughter of Shiba Tattō, into religion. She took the name of Nun Zen-shin. Moreover he received into religion two pupils of the Nun Zen-shin. One was Toyome, the daughter of Ayabito no Yaho. She took the name of Nun Sen-zō. The other was Ishime, daughter of Nishikori Tsubu. She took the name of Nun Kei-zen. Mŭmako no Sukune, still in accordance with the Law of Buddha, reverenced the three nuns, and gave them to Hida no Atahe and Tattō, with orders to provide them with food and clothing. He erected a Buddhist Temple on the east side of his dwelling, in which he enshrined the stone image of Miroku. He insisted on the three nuns holding a general meeting to partake of maigre fare. At this time Tatto found a Buddhist relic on the food of abstinence, and presented it to Mŭmako no Sukune. Mŭmako no Sukune, by way of experiment, took the relic, and placing it on the middle of a block of iron, beat it with an iron sledge-hammer, which he flourished aloft. The block and the sledge-hammer were shattered to atoms, but the relic could not be crushed. Then the relic was cast into water, when it floated on the water or sank as one desired. In consequence of this, Mŭmako no Sukune, Ikenobe no Hida, and Shiba Tattō held faith in Buddhism and practised it unremittingly. Mŭmako no Sukune built another Buddhist Temple at his house in Ishikaha. From this arose the beginning of Buddhism.

144 LADY MURASAKI, *THE TALE OF GENJI*: THE CULT OF BEAUTY

Any account of Japan's culture and civilization would be incomplete without reference to the Japanese cultivation of beauty. This aspect of society is vividly portrayed in Japan's most famous novel, *The Tale of Genji*. Written at the end of the tenth century—long before the novel, as a literary form, was developed in the West—by a woman at the court of a Heian emperor, the book recounts the adventures, mostly amorous, of Prince Genji, son of the emperor. The author does not concern herself with the struggles and deprivations of the lower classes at that time, nor is there much reflection on contemporary politics, even though the setting is the imperial court and Genji is a high official. What the novel does convey is the feeling of a social order which encouraged an extravagant appreciation of beauty and developed its tastes until only the most elegant manifestations of color, sound, and form could satisfy them. Professor Donald Keene, an outstanding interpreter of Japanese culture, has written that "a belief in intuitive experience, in the preferability of the emotions to cold logic, in the necessity of presenting thought and experience in an elegant and pleasing form, avoiding the harsh edges of more direct expression, has accounted for many of the finest things in Japanese arts and letters as well as some of their shortcomings." These values, he suggests, are illustrated to a remarkable degree in *The Tale of Genji*. In the following selections, Genji has just been exiled to a remote country place for his misdemeanors, and his reactions to the setting and to the people around him are illuminating.

At Suma autumn had set in with a vengeance. The little house stood some way back from the sea; but when in sudden gusts the wind came 'blowing through the gap' (the very wind of Yukihira's poem) it seemed as though the waves were at Genji's door. Night after night he lay listening to that melancholy sound and wondering whether in all the world there could be any place where the sadness of autumn was more overwhelming. The few attendants who shared the house with him had all gone to rest. Only Genji lay awake, propped high on his pillow, listening to the storm-winds which burst upon the house from every side. Louder and louder came the noise of the waves, till it seemed to him they must have mounted the fore-shore and be surging round the very bed on which he lay. Then he would take up his zithern and strike a few notes. But his tune echoed so forlornly through the house that he had not the heart to continue and, putting the zithern aside, he sang to himself the song:
"The wind that waked you,
Came it from where my Lady lies,
Waves of the shore, whose sighs
Echo my sobbing?"
At this his followers awoke with a start and listened to his singing with wonder and delight. But the words filled them with an unendurable sadness, and there were some whose lips trembled while they rose and dressed.

What (Genji asked himself) must they think of him? For his sake they had given up their homes, parents, brothers, friends from whom they had never been absent for a day; abandoned everything in life which they had held dear. The thought that these unfortunate gentlemen should be involved in the consequences of his indiscretion was very painful to him. He knew that his own moodiness and ill humour had greatly contributed to their depression. Next day he tried to cheer them with jokes and amusing stories; and to make the time pass less tediously he set them to work to join strips of variegated paper into a long roll and did some writing practice, while on a piece of very fine Chinese silk he made a number of rough ink sketches which when pasted on to a screen looked very well indeed. Here before his eyes were all those hills and shores of which he had so often dreamed since the day long ago when they had been shown to him from a far-off height. He now made good use of his opportunities and soon got together a collection of views which admirably illustrated the scenery of this beautiful coast-line. So delighted were his companions that they were anxious he should send for Chiyeda and Tsunenori and make them use his sketches as models for proper-coloured paintings. His new affability soon made them forget all their troubles, and the four or five retainers who habitually served him

Text: Lady Murasaki, *The Tale of Genji,* trans. Arthur Waley (New York: Houghton Mifflin Company; London: George Allen & Unwin, Ltd., 1926), II, 126-29, 134-36.

felt that the discomforts of exile were quite outweighed by the pleasure of waiting upon such a master.

The flowers which had been planted in front of the cottage were blooming with a wild profusion of colour. One particularly calm and delightful evening Genji came out on to the verandah which looked towards the bay. He was dressed in a soft coat of fine white silk with breeches of aster-colour. A cloak of some dark material hung loosely over his shoulders. After reciting the formula of submission ('Such a one, being a disciple of the Buddha Śākyamuni, does obeisance to him and craves that in the moonlit shelter of the Tree of Knowledge he may seek refuge from the clouds of sorrow and death') he began in a low voice to read a passage from the Scriptures. The sunset, the light from the sea, the towering hills cast so strange a radiance upon him as he stood reading from the book, that to those who watched he seemed like some visitant from another world. Out beyond the bay a line of boats was passing, the fishermen singing as they rowed. So far off were these boats that they looked like a convoy of small birds afloat upon the high seas. With the sound of oars was subtly blended the crying of wild-geese, each wanderer's lament swiftly matched by the voice of his close-following mate. How different his lot to theirs! And Genji raised his sleeve to brush away the tears that had begun to flow. As he did so the whiteness of his hand flashed against the black wooden beads of his rosary. Here indeed, thought those who were with him, was beauty enough to console them for the absence of the women whom they had left behind. . . .

The New Year had begun. The days were growing longer and already there was a faint show of blossom on the cherry-trees which Genji had planted in his garden at Suma. The weather was delightful, and sitting idly in the sunshine he recalled a thousand incidents that were linked in his mind with former springs. The twentieth day of the second month! It was just a year ago that he left the Capital. All those painful scenes of farewell came back vividly to his mind, bringing with them a new access of longing. The cherry-trees of the Southern Hall must now be in full bloom. He remembered the wonderful Flower Feast of six years ago, saw his father's face, the elegant figure of the young Crown Prince; and verses from the poems which he had himself made on that occasion floated back into his mind.

All this while Tō no Chūjō had been living at the Great Hall, with very little indeed to amuse him. He had been put down again into the Fourth Rank and was very much discouraged. It was essential to his prospects that he should not come under any further suspicion, but he was an affectionate creature and finding himself longing more and more for Genji's society, he determined, even at the cost of offending the Government, to set out at once for Suma. The complete unexpectedness of his visit made it all the more cheering and delightful. He was soon admiring Genji's rustic house, which seemed to him the most extraordinary place to be living in. He thought it more like some legendary hermit's hut in a Chinese book than a real cottage. Indeed the whole place might have come straight out of a picture, with its hedge of wattled bamboo, the steps of unhewn stone, the stout pine-wood pillars and general air of improvisation. Chūjō was enchanted by the strangeness of it all. Genji was dressed in peasant style with a grey hunting-cloak and outer breeches over a suit of russet-brown. The way in which he played up to this rustic costume struck Chūjō as highly absurd and at the same time delighted him. The furniture was all of the simplest kind and even Genji's seat was not divided off in any way from the rest of the room. Near it lay boards for the games of *go* and *sugoroku*, and chessmen, with other such gear as is met with in country houses. The meals, which were necessarily of a somewhat makeshift character, seemed to Chūjō positively exciting. One day some fishermen arrived with cockles to sell. Genji sent for them and inspected their catch. He questioned them about their trade and learned something of the life led year in and year out by those whose homes were on this shore. It was a story of painful unremitting toil, and though they told it in a jargon which he could only half understand, he realized with compassion that their feelings were, after all, very much like his own. He made them handsome presents from his wardrobe and they felt that these shells had indeed been life-giving.

145

KITABATAKE CHIKAFUSA, *RECORDS OF THE LEGITIMATE SUCCESSION OF THE DIVINE SOVEREIGNS*: THE POSITION OF THE EMPEROR IN SHINTO THOUGHT

The triumph of Buddhism did not signal the extinction of the native primitive religion of *Shinto*. Shintoism lived on, partly because many country people still turned to the nature gods identified with their particular localities, partly because the old gods were incorporated into Buddhism. Its survival was also due to its connection with the imperial family; most noble Japanese families traced their descent from various gods and the ancestor of the imperial house was the greatest of the nature deities, the sun goddess. This identification of the emperor with the most powerful figure of the indigenous religious tradition proved invaluable, as it gave him an unrivaled status in Japanese life. At times the divine origin of the emperor might be deëmphasized, but often, especially when the state was threatened either by internal or external dangers, it was an effective rallying cry.

An expression of this imperial divine status is found in a *Shinto* document of the early thirteenth century entitled, significantly, *The Records of the Legitimate Succession of the Divine Sovereigns*. The author, Kitabatake Chikafusa, was a partisan of the emperor at a time when his right to rule was in dispute. With its insistence on the uniqueness of both Japan and the emperor, Kitabatake's interpretation of history helped create a national consciousness which enabled the state to survive in the face of great turmoil. As the bearer of a tradition transmitted from "the Age of the Gods," Shintoism became the religious expression of nationalism in the nineteenth and twentieth centuries.

Japan is the divine country. The heavenly ancestor it was who first laid its foundations, and the Sun Goddess left her descendants to reign over it forever and ever. This is true only of our country, and nothing similar may be found in foreign lands. That is why it is called the divine country.

The Names of Japan

In the Age of the Gods, Japan was known as the "ever-fruitful land of reed-covered plains and luxuriant ricefields." This name has existed since the creation of heaven and earth. It appeared in the command given by the heavenly ancestor Kunitokotachi to the Male Deity and the Female Deity. Again, when the Great Goddess Amaterasu bequeathed the land to her grandchild, that name was used; it may thus be considered the primal name of Japan. It is also called the country of the great eight islands. This name was given because eight islands were produced when the Male Deity and the Female Deity begot Japan. It is also called Yamato, which is the name of the central part of the eight islands. The eighth offspring of the deities was the god Heavenly-August - Sky - Luxuriant - Dragon-fly - Lord - Youth [and the land he incarnated] was called Ō-yamato, Luxuriant-Dragon-fly-Island. It is now divided into forty-eight provinces. Besides being the central island, Yamato has been the site of the capital through all the ages since Jimmu's conquest of the east. That must be why the other seven islands are called Yamato. The same is true of China, where All-Under-Heaven was at one time called Chou because the dynasty had its origins in the state of Chou, and where All-Within-the-Seas was called Han when the dynasty arose in the territory of Han.

The word Yamato means "footprints on the mountain." Of old, when heaven and earth were divided, the soil was still muddy and not yet dry, and people passing back and forth over the mountains left many footprints; thus it was called Yama-to—"mountain footprint." Some say that in ancient Japanese *to* meant "dwelling" and that because people dwelt in the mountains, the country was known [as] Yama-to—"mountain dwelling."

In writing the name of the country, the Chinese characters Dai-Nippon and Dai-Wa have both been used. The reason is that, when Chinese writing was introduced to this country, the characters for Dai-Nippon were chosen to represent the name of the country, but they were pronounced as "Yamato." This choice may have been

---

Text: Kitabatake Chikafusa, *The Records of the Legitimate Succession of the Divine Sovereigns*, in *Sources of the Japanese Tradition*, ed. R. Tsunoda et al. (New York: Columbia University Press, 1958), pp. 274-75, 279.

guided by the fact that Japan is the Land of the Sun Goddess, or it may have thus been called because it is near the place where the sun rises. . . .

The beginnings of Japan in some ways resemble the Indian descriptions, telling as it does of the world's creation from the seed of the heavenly gods. However, whereas in our country the succession to the throne has followed a single undeviating line since the first divine ancestor, nothing of the kind has existed in India. After their first ruler, King People's Lord, had been chosen and raised to power by the populace, his dynasty succeeded, but in later times most of his descendants perished, and men of inferior genealogy who had powerful forces became the rulers, some of them even controlling the whole of India. China is also a country of notorious disorders. Even in ancient times, when life was simple and conduct was proper, the throne was offered to wise men, and no single lineage was established. Later, in times of disorder, men fought for control of the country. Thus some of the rulers rose from the ranks of the plebeians, and there were even some of barbarian origin who usurped power. Or, some families after generations of service as ministers surpassed their princes and eventually supplanted them. There have already been thirty-six changes of dynasty since Fu-hsi, and unspeakable disorders have occurred.

Only in our country has the succession remained inviolate, from the beginning of heaven and earth to the present. It has been maintained within a single lineage, and even when, as inevitably has happened, the succession has been transmitted collaterally, it has returned to the true line. This is due to the ever-renewed Divine Oath, and makes Japan unlike all other countries.

FEUDALISM AND THE SHOGUNATE

146 THE HOJO CODE: THE LEGAL AND ADMINISTRATIVE IDEALS OF FEUDALISM

The term *feudalism* can be applied rather accurately to the society which existed in Japan from the twelfth to the nineteenth centuries. In the twelfth century the centralized state gave way to warring factions; one of these factions, the Minamoto family, finally gained the upper hand in 1185. They established their headquarters in Kamakura and created a government based upon the allegiance of vassals who had received fiefs from them. The emperor was not deposed; he retained considerable prestige even though he was not allowed to exercise any real administrative control. As will be seen later (Part Ten), the deeply entrenched reverence for the imperial house endured a long eclipse of actual power to reassert itself as a force for national unity in the nineteenth century.

The Hojo code (1232) represented an attempt to codify the feudal relationships that had replaced the old order. Hojo was an army commander who had seized for himself the office of *shogun*, the title given to the military commander who exercised effective control over the country. His code, which has been called "the taproot of the whole subsequent growth of Japanese feudal law," sets forth general principles for the conduct of the administration. Feudalism is characterized by a hierarchical structure of duties and obligations, with a continued stress put upon fulfilling the duties of one's station. The code defines what may be called "the inequalities of life"; the heart of the Japanese feudal system was unswerving loyalty to one's lord—a duty assumed throughout the document. As in most ancient and medieval codes, the primary place of agriculture is recognized, and the feudal lords are enjoined to treat their peasants according to the prescribed laws. A contrast with contemporary European life is suggested by the high place given to women: apparently, they could hold fiefs on much the same conditions as men. In general, the code may be seen as an attempt by the feudal lords to adjust laws and customs to new conditions of life without destroying the value of the past. The *samurai* mentioned in the text are the warrior class, who constituted the backbone of the feudal system. The "military disturbance" and "the battle at the Capital" refer to attempts made by the emperor to regain power from Hojo in 1221.

... 2. (Buddhist) Temples and pagodas must be kept in repair and the Buddhist services diligently celebrated.

Although (Buddhist) temples are different from (Shinto) shrines, both are alike as regards worship and veneration. Therefore the merit of maintaining them both in good order and the duty of keeping up the established services, as provided in the foregoing article is the same in both cases. Let no one bring trouble on himself through negligence herein.

In case the incumbent does what he pleases with the income of the temple benefice or covetously misappropriates it, or if the duties of the clergy be not diligently fulfilled by him, the offender shall be promptly dismissed, and another incumbent appointed.

3. Of the duties devolving on Protectors in the Provinces.

In the time of the august Right General's House it was settled that those duties should be the calling out and despatching of the Grand Guard for service at the capital, the suppression of conspiracies and rebellion and the punishment of murder and violence (which included night attacks on houses, robbery, dacoity and piracy). Of late years, however, Official Substitutes have been taken on and distributed over the counties and townships and these have been imposing public burdens (corvée) on the villages. Not being Governors of the provinces they yet hinder the (Agricultural) work of the province: not being Land-Reeves they are yet greedy of the profits of the land. Such proceedings and schemes are utterly unprincipled.

Be it noted that no person, even if his family were for generations vassals of the August House (of the Minamoto) is competent to impress for military service unless he has an investiture of the present date.

On the other hand again, it is reported that inferior managers and village officials in various places make use of the name of vassals of the August House as a pretext for opposing the orders of the Governor of the provinces or of the lord of the Manor. Such persons, even if they are desirous of being taken into the service of the Protectors, must not under any circumstances be included in the enrolment for service in the Guards. In short, conformably to the precedents of the time of the August General's House, the Protectors must cease altogether from giving directions in matters outside of the hurrying-up of the Grand Guards and the suppression of plots, rebellion, murder and violence.

In the event of a Protector disobeying this article and intermeddling in other affairs than those herein named, if a complaint is instituted against him by the Governor of the Province or the lord of a Manor, or if the Land-Reeve or the folk aggrieved petition for redress, his downright lawlessness being thus brought to light, he shall be divested of his office and a person of gentle character appointed in his stead. Again, as regards Delegates not more than one is to be appointed by a Protector.

4. Of Protectors omitting to report cases of crime and confiscating the successions to fiefs, on account of offences.

When persons are found committing serious offences, the Protectors should make a detailed report of the case (to Kamakura) and follow such directions as may be given them in relation thereto; yet there are some who, without ascertaining the truth or falsehood of an accusation, or investigating whether the offence committed was serious or trifling, arbitrarily pronounce the escheat of the criminal's heriditaments, and selfishly cause them to be confiscated. Such unjust judgments are a nefarious artifice for the indulgence of license. Let a report be promptly made to us of the circumstances of each case and our decision upon the matter be respectfully asked for, any further persistence in transgressions of this kind will be dealt with criminally.

In the next place, with regard to a culprit's rice-fields and other fields, his dwelling-house, his wife and children, his utensils and other articles of property. In serious cases, the offenders are to be taken in charge by the Protector's office; but it is not necessary to take in charge their farms, houses, wives, children and miscellaneous gear along with them.

Furthermore, even if the criminal should in his statement implicate others as being accomplices or accessories, such are not to be included in the scope of the Protector's judgment, unless they are found in possession of the booty (or other substantial evidence of guilt be forthcoming).

5. Of Land-Reeves in the provinces detaining a part of the assessed amounts of the rice-tax.

If a plaint is instituted by the lord of the Manor alleging that a Land-Reeve is withholding the land-tax payable to him, a statement of account will be at once taken, and the plaintiff shall receive a certificate of the balance that may be found to be due to him. If the Land-Reeve be adjudged to be in default, and has no valid plea to urge in justification, he will be required to make compensation in full. If the amount is

---

Text: J. C. Hall, "The Hojo Code of Judicature," in *Transactions of the Asiatic Society of Japan*, XXXIV, 1906, 18-21, 24-27, 38-39.

small, judgment will be given for immediate payment. If the amount be greater than he is able to pay at once, he will be allowed three years within which to completely discharge his liability. Any Land-Reeve who, after such delay granted, shall make further delays and difficulties, contrary to the intention of this article, shall be deprived of his post. . . .

11. Whether in consequence of a husband's crime the estate of the wife is to be confiscated or not.

In cases of serious crime, treason, murder and maiming, also dacoity, piracy, night-attacks, robbery and the like, the guilt of the husband extends to the wife also. In cases of murder and maiming, cutting and wounding, arising out of a sudden dispute, however, she is not to be held responsible.

12. Of abusive language.

Quarrels and murders have their origin in abusive and insulting language. In grave cases the offender shall be sent into banishment, in minor cases, ordered into confinement. If during the course of a judicial hearing one of the parties gives vent to abuse or insults, the matter in dispute shall be decided in favour of the other party. If the other party however has not right on his side, some other fief of the offender shall be confiscated. If he has no fief, he shall be punished by being sent into banishment.

13. Of the offence of striking (or beating) a person.

In such cases the person who receives the beating is sure to want to kill or maim the other in order to wipe out the insult; so the offence of beating a person is by no means a trivial one. Accordingly, if the offender be a *Samurai*, his fief shall be confiscated; if he has no fief he shall be sent into banishment: persons of lower rank, servants, pages and under, shall be placed in confinement.

14. When a crime or offence is committed by Deputies, whether the principals are responsible.

When a Deputy is guilty of murder or any lesser one of the serious crimes, if his principal arrests and sends him on for trial, the master shall not be held responsible. But if the master in order to shield the Deputy reports that the latter is not to blame, and the truth is afterwards found out, incriminating him, the former cannot escape responsibility and accordingly his fief shall be confiscated. In such cases the Deputy shall be imprisoned (in order to be tried and dealt with).

Again, if a Deputy either detains the rice-tax payable to the lord of the Manor or contravenes the laws and precedents even though the action is that of the Deputy alone, his principal shall nevertheless be responsible.

Moreover, whenever, either in consequence of a suit instituted by the lord of a Manor, or in connection with matters of fact alleged in a plaintiff's petition, a Deputy receives a summons from the Kwanto or is sent for from Rokuhara, and instead of making up his mind to come at once, shilly-shallies and delays, his principal's investiture shall in like manner be revoked. Extenuating circumstances may, however, be taken into consideration.

15. Of the crime of forgery.

If a *Samurai* commits the above, his fief shall be confiscated; if he has no investiture he shall be sent into exile. If one of the lower class commits it, he shall be branded in the face by burning. The amanuensis shall receive the same punishment.

Next, in suits if it is persistently alleged that the title-deed in the defendant's possession is a forgery and when the document is opened and inspected, if it is found to be indeed a forgery then the punishment shall be as above provided; but if it be found to be without flaw, then a fine proportionate to his position shall be inflicted on the false accuser, to be paid into the fund for the repairing of Shrines and temples. If he have not means wherewith to pay the fine he shall be deported.

16. Of the lands which were confiscated at the time of the military disturbance of Shokyu (1219-1221).

In the case of some whose tenements were confiscated in consequence of their having been reported to us as having taken part against us in the battle at the Capital, it is now averred that, they were innocent of such misdoing. Where the proof in support of this plea is full and clear, other lands will be assigned to the present grantees of the confiscated estates, which will be restored to the original holders. By the term present grantees is meant those of them who have performed meritorious services.

In the next place, amongst those who took part against us in the battle at the Capital were some who had received the bounty of the Kwanto (i.e. had received grants of land from the *Shogun*). Their guilt was specially aggravated. Accordingly they were themselves put to death and their holdings were confiscated definitively. Of late years, however, it has come to our knowledge that some fellows of that class have, through force of circumstances, had the luck to escape punishment. Seeing that the time for severity has now gone by, in their case the utmost generosity will be exercised, and a slice only of their estates, amounting to one fifth, is to be confiscated. However, as regards Sub-Controllers and village officials, unless they were vassals of the *Shogun's* own House, it is to be understood that it is not now practicable to call them to account, even if it should come to be found out that they were guilty of siding with the Capital. The case of these men was discussed in the Council last year and settled in this sense; consequently no different principle is applicable.

Next as regards lands confiscated on the same occasion in respect of which suits may be brought by persons claiming to be owners. It was in consequence of the guilt of the then holders that those lands were confiscated, and were definitively assigned to those who rendered meritorious service. Although those who then held them were unworthy holders, there are many persons we hear who now petition that in accordance with the principle of heredity the lands may be allowed to revert to them by grant. But all the tenures that were confiscated at that time stand irreversibly disposed of. Is it possible for us to put aside the present holders and undertake to make enquiry into claims of a past age? Henceforth a stop must be put to disorderly expectations.

17. As regards the guilt of those who took part in the battle on the same occasion, a distinction is to be made between fathers and sons.

As regards cases in which although the father took the side of the Capital the son nevertheless took service with the Kwanto and likewise those in which although the son took the side of the Capital the father took service with the Kwanto, the question of reward or punishment has been decided already by the difference of treatment. Why should one generation be confounded with the other as regards guilt?

As regards cases of this kind occuring amongst residents in the Western provinces, if one went to the Capital, whether he were the father or the son, then the son or the father who remained at home in the province cannot be held blameless. Although he may not have accompanied his guilty kinsman he was his accomplice at heart. Nevertheless in cases where owing to their being separated by long distances or boundaries it was impossible for them to have had communication with one another or to be cognizant of the circumstances, they are not to be regarded as reciprocally involved in each other's guilt. . . .

40. Of Buddhist clergy within the Kamakura Domain striving at their own option to obtain ecclesiastical positions and rank.

Inasmuch as it leads to the deranging of the due subordination in the hierarchy, the practice of applying at will (to Kyoto) for preferment is in itself a source of confusion and furthermore entails undue multiplication of the higher ecclesiastical dignities: for clerics of mature age and ripe intelligence are overpassed by younger men of slight ability; whereby the formers' labour and expenses in following their calling are made of no avail and the principles of religion are at the same time contravened.

Henceforth if any one should in future apply for preferment without first having received our permission he shall, if he be the incumbent of a temple or shrine, be deprived of his benefice. Even if he belong to the clergy specially attached to the chaplaincies of the *Shogun* he shall nevertheless be dismissed.

Should, however, one of the Zen Sect make such an application, an influential member of the same sect will be directed to administer a gentle admonition.

41. Of Slaves and unclassed persons.

(In cases of dispute respecting the ownership of such persons) the precedent established by the late *Shogun's* House must be adhered to; that is to say, if more than ten years have elapsed without the former owner having asserted his claim, there shall be no discussion as to the merits of the case and the possession of the present owner is not to be interfered with.

42. Of inflicting loss and ruin on absconding farmers under the pretext of smashing runaways.

When people living in the provinces run away and escape, the lord of the fief and others, proclaiming that runaways must be smashed up, detain their wives and children, and confiscate their property. Such a mode of procedure is quite the reverse of benevolent government. Henceforth such must be referred (to Kamakura) for adjudication, and if it is found that the farmer is in arrear as regards payment of his land-tax and levies, he shall be compelled to make good the deficiency. If he is found not to be so in arrear, the property seized from him shall be forthwith restored to him. And it shall be entirely at the option of the farmer himself whether he shall continue to live in the fief or go elsewhere.

147 DAI-Ō AND HŌNEN: ZEN, THE RELIGIOUS EXPRESSION OF FEUDALISM, AND AMIDA, THE RELIGION OF THE MASSES

The Japanese feudal warriors found in Zen Buddhism a doctrine admirably suited to their emotional and intellectual needs. One of the many Buddhist sects that had developed through the years, Zen emphasized meditation and the grasping of truth through an intuitional experience rather than through the study of sacred texts. Zen stressed self-discipline and obedience to a master, and placed greater value on moral austerity than on intellectual achievement. Though such aspects as those mentioned reinforced traditional *samurai* attitudes, Zen was not, of course, confined to the feudal class—it influenced all forms of creativity, giving to the arts much of what has come to be thought of as characteristically Japanese.

Pure Land or Amida Buddhism was the religion of the masses, for whom Zen had little appeal. Hōnen, one of the founders of the Pure Land Sect, summed up the teaching of Buddhism in the formula *Namu Amida Butsu*, meaning that all that was necessary for salvation was to call on the name of Amida Buddha. To pronounce the name would mean eternal life in the Pure Land. The emphasis is on Buddha as a god of grace who is willing to save all those who cast themselves upon his mercy. The spread of this gospel in a time of turmoil and misery is easy to understand.

The first selection given here is by Dai-ō Kokushi (1235-1308), an exponent of the *Rinzai* school of Zen. The translation is by D. T. Suzuki, the author of many books interpreting Zen for western readers. The second selection is from Honen (1133-1212).

Dai-ō Kokushi "On Zen"

There is a reality even prior to heaven and earth;
Indeed, it has no form, much less a name;
Eyes fail to see it;
It has no voice for ears to detect;
To call it Mind or Buddha violates its nature,
For it then becomes like a visionary flower in the air;
It is not Mind, nor Buddha;
Absolutely quiet, and yet illuminating in a mysterious way,
It allows itself to be perceived only by the clear-eyed.
It is Dharma truly beyond form and sound;
It is Tao having nothing to do with words.

Wishing to entice the blind,
The Buddha has playfully let words escape his golden mouth;
Heaven and earth are ever since filled with entangling briars.

O my good worthy friends gathered here,
If you desire to listen to the thunderous voice of the Dharma,
Exhaust your words, empty your thoughts,
For then you may come to recognise this One Essence.
Says Hui the Brother, "The Buddha's Dharma
Is not to be given up to mere humanly sentiments."

Things Hōnen Was Always Saying

1. "A man who reads about the doctrines of the Jōdo without receiving oral instruction will miss the thing really necessary to the attainment of Ōjō. Men of high station such as Nāgārjuna and Vasubandhu, and on the other hand men of the lowest rank of common latter-day sinners guilty of the ten evil deeds and the five deadly sins, used to be the object of the Buddha Shaka's exhortations to enter the Land of Perfect Bliss. Now we common men of the lowest class, when we hear the Buddha exhorting good men, at once begin to depreciate ourselves, and to think that we cannot be born into the Pure Land, and so we actually by our doubts prevent ourselves from reaching that birth after death. The main thing, then, is that we clearly distinguish between the teaching intended for the good, and that applicable to the evil like ourselves. If we are so minded, our faith in the certainty of our own birth will become assured, and through the power of the Buddha's Original Vow we shall accomplish our birth into that land at death."

2. "There is no secret about calling upon the sacred name except that we put our heart into the

Text: From *Manual of Zen Buddhism* by Daisetz Teitaro Suzuki (New York: Grove Press, Inc., and London: Hutchinson & Co. Ltd., 1960), p. 145. Reprinted by permission of the publishers. All rights reserved.

act, in the conviction that we shall be born into the Land of Perfect Bliss."

3. "We must not think that the expression 'Namu Amida Butsu' (Sk. Namo'mitābhāya-buddhāya) means anything but simply 'Save me, oh! Amida Buddha.' So then let us pray in our hearts. 'Save me, oh Amida,' and say with our lips 'Namu Amida Butsu.'"

4. "While believing that even a man guilty of the ten evil deeds and the five deadly sins may be born into the Pure Land, let us, as far as we are concerned, not commit even the smallest sins. If this is true of the wicked, how much more of the good. We ought to continue the practice of the Nembutsu uninterruptedly, in the belief that ten repetitions, or even one, will not be in vain. If this is true of merely one repetition, how much more of many!"

5. "If a man says he can be born into the Pure Land by ten repetitions of the sacred name, or even one, and then begins to be careless about the practice, his faith will hinder his practice. On the other hand if a man says, as Zendō did, that he unceasingly repeats the Nembutsu, but in his heart has doubts about the certainty of Ōjō, in the case of one who only practises it once, then his practice will hinder his faith. So then, believe that you can attain Ōjō by one repetition, and yet go on practising it your whole life long. If you think there is uncertainty as to the efficacy of calling upon the sacred name once, then it means that there is doubt about it every time you call upon the sacred name. The Buddha's Vow was to give birth into the Pure Land to those who would call upon his name even once, and so there is efficacy in every repetition of the sacred name."

6. "Do not be worrying as to whether your evil passions are strong or otherwise, or whether your sins are light or heavy. Only invoke Amida's name with your lips, and let the conviction accompany the sound of your voice, that you will of a certainty be born into the Pure Land."

INTERPRETATIONS OF JAPAN

148 E. O. REISCHAUER, *JAPAN, PAST AND PRESENT*: GROWTH AND CHANGE IN MEDIEVAL JAPAN

The Kamakura period (1185-1333), which saw the establishment of feudal institutions in Japan, was a relatively peaceful time, even though the rivalry of the great families for power remained intense. But when the Kamakura shogunate was finally overthrown by the Ashikaga family, Japan began two and a half centuries of continuous warfare and strife. It is not surprising, then, that the Ashikaga shogunate (1338-1573) is often referred to as the Dark Ages of Japanese history. Despite the turmoil and strife, Japanese society remained remarkably vigorous and creative. Artistic production reached a high level, while trade and commerce expanded throughout the eastern seas. This period of growth and vitality is discussed in the following selection by Professor E. O. Reischauer of Harvard University.

As was to be expected in this turbulent age, the artists and men of letters usually were Buddhist priests and monks, and the great monasteries more than ever became the repositories of learning and the centers of creative art. The Zen monks in particular dominated the cultural life of the time. This was not so much because they received official patronage as because they were in much closer contact with China than any other group and were consequently the first to learn of new cultural trends on the continent. Actually, the predominantly Zen culture of the Ashikaga period was a rich blending of the native culture with many new cultural elements from the continent.

Despite their traditional anti-scholasticism, the Zen monks reintroduced the use of pure Chinese as an important literary medium, and at the same time they led in the development of Japan's first true dramatic form, the so-called Nō drama. The major purpose of Nō was to teach concepts of Buddhism. Since it had evolved originally from early religious dances, symbolic dances quite naturally remained one of its most important features. But perhaps the greatest merit of the Nō was the fine poetic recitations chanted by the actors and an accompanying chorus. The texts of the Nō drama still remain one of the great literary expressions of the Japanese people, and a small

Text: E. O. Reischauer, *Japan, Past and Present.* Copyright 1946, 1952 by Alfred A. Knopf, Inc., and reprinted by their permission. Pp. 70-76.

band of devotees even today keep the Nō alive as a highly formalized and completely outmoded dramatic form.

In the field of architecture, fresh influences from China made for significant new forms, but the Zen culture of the Ashikaga period found its fullest expression in painting. Zen monks, living simple lives close to nature, took with enthusiasm to the Chinese style of monochrome landscape painting, often rivaling the skill and depth of feeling of the Chinese masters. The richness of the artistic work of the time is seen in the fact that side by side with this Chinese school of painting existed a vigorous native school specializing in picture scrolls portraying the history of some temple or the incidents of a famous campaign, such as that against the Mongols.

The medieval Zen monks also brought from China three other arts which became so characteristic of Japanese culture that they are now considered to be typically Japanese. One was landscape gardening, which the Japanese developed to a perfection unexcelled in any other land. The second was flower arrangement, which started with the placing of floral offerings before representations of Buddhist deities but eventually became a fine art which is now part of the training of every well-bred Japanese girl. The third was the tea ceremony, an aesthetic spiritual ritual in which a beautiful but simple setting, a few fine pieces of old pottery, a slow, formalized, extremely graceful ritual for preparing and serving the tea, and a spirit of complete tranquillity all combine to express the love of beauty, the devotion to simplicity, and the search for spiritual calm which characterize the best in Zen.

Increased trade contacts with the continent, which had brought many new cultural impulses from China, also served as an impetus to an unprecedented and rapid expansion of Japanese trade and industry. Another impetus may have been the decline and disappearance of the estates. As long as these had existed, they tended to be self-contained economic units, but their going allowed a wider exchange of goods and greater specialization in production by localities or by groups within each locality. Because of the need for protection from the many restrictions and fees in a feudal society, this new economic specialization usually resulted in the formation of guilds of merchants dealing in certain commodities and guilds of manufacturers producing various types of wares.

Under the guilds, trade and manufacture expanded steadily, and centers of paper-making, metal-working, weaving, and the like grew up all over the land. Small market places developed into little trading towns. Kyoto remained the largest city of Japan, but gradually a rival city of purely commercial and industrial origin grew up at the eastern end of the Inland Sea. This town, later to be called Osaka, was until the late sixteenth century a type of free city outside the domains of the feudal lords, dominated only by the local merchants and the great temple-castle of the True Pure Land Sect.

The true measure of the economic growth of Japan during the feudal period is perhaps best seen in foreign trade. There had been some trade with the continent ever since Prince Shotoku sent the first official embassy to China, but overseas trade began to assume significant proportions only in the late twelfth century. From that time on, it grew steadily until by the fifteenth and sixteenth centuries it was a tremendous factor in the economic life of Japan.

The Japanese imported from the continent tropical products, which had originally come from Southeast Asia or even from India, and manufactured goods from China, such as silks, porcelains, books, manuscripts, paintings, and copper cash. The last loomed largest in bulk and value, because from the thirteenth century on, money increasingly replaced rice and cloth as the chief medium for exchange in Japan, and the Japanese depended almost entirely on China as the source for their currency.

In the early feudal period, Japanese exports were limited for the most part to raw goods, such as sulphur, lumber, gold, pearls, mercury, and mother of pearl. However, by the fifteenth and sixteenth centuries Japan itself was exporting large quantities of manufactured goods to China and the continent. Chief among these were swords and painted folding fans and screens. Folding fans and screens apparently were inventions of either the Koreans or the Japanese and were highly prized in China. The curved swords of medieval Japan, made of the finest laminated steel and unexcelled even by the famous blades of Damascus or Toledo, were in great demand throughout East Asia and were exported by the thousands.

In the early days, the Koreans were the chief mariners and traders in the waters between Japan and the continent, but slowly the Japanese themselves took to the sea. In the late eleventh century, Japanese traders were crossing to Korea; in the twelfth, some were venturing as far as China; and by the fourteenth and fifteenth centuries, they were beginning to dominate the shipping and commerce of the whole East China Sea.

Various groups in Japan participated in this lucrative trade with the continent. As mentioned previously, many Buddhist monasteries sponsored trading ventures in order to raise funds, as did various families of feudal lords, including the Ashikaga themselves. In fact, the Ashikaga, in order to secure some of the profits of this trade for their shaky regime, accepted the Chinese theory that international trade was simply the bringing of tribute to the Chinese court by barbarian peoples and the beneficent bestowal of gifts upon the barbarians by the court in return. To fit this pattern, some of the Ashikaga Shogun, with complete disregard of the theory of imperial rule, permitted themselves to be invested as "Kings of Japan" by the emperors of the Ming dynasty of China and then sold credentials to private Japanese traders, to give them legal and official status in their trading ventures in China.

Despite the interest in foreign trade on the part of the monasteries and the Shogun in central Japan, leadership in overseas trading was taken primarily by the small feudal lords, the ordinary warriors, and the merchants of western Japan, who merged to form a class of adventurous and hardy mariners. Like their counterparts in Europe, these men of the sea were primarily traders, but they were not averse to piracy when opportunity offered. Credentials from the Ashikaga or trading permits from the Chinese court meant little to them. Already in the thirteenth century piratical acts by Japanese warrior-merchants had become frequent in Korean waters, and during the fourteenth century, Japanese pirates became a menace to the very existence of the kingdom of Korea. Emboldened by their successes in Korean waters, they shifted their activities more and more to the coast of China. As the Ming dynasty declined in the sixteenth and early seventeenth centuries, Japanese pirates ravaged the great coastal cities of China almost at will, contributing greatly to the final collapse of the dynasty during the middle decades of the seventeenth century.

The so-called Japanese pirates of the sixteenth century were not always pirates, however, nor were they always Japanese. Many Chinese joined them in preying on the coastal trade and cities of China. One of the most important elements in this mixed group of Chinese and Japanese, who were both traders and pirates, was furnished by the natives of the Ryukyu Islands. Closely related to the Japanese and speaking a variant form of the language, they owed a dual allegiance in the seventeenth century to China and to the great Daimyo domain of Satsuma in southern Kyushu.

When the European merchant-adventurers rounded the Malay Peninsula and entered Far Eastern waters early in the sixteenth century, they found the seas dominated more by Japanese than by Chinese. In the course of the century, thousands of Japanese established themselves as traders and adventurers in the towns and colonies of Southeast Asia; and the Spanish and Portuguese, recognizing the martial traditions and fine fighting qualities of the Japanese, frequently employed them as mercenaries in their campaigns and wars in the Far East. In a typical colonial city like Manila, the Japanese community grew large and strong, and in the early seventeenth century, Japanese adventurers were influential enough at the Siamese capital to engineer a successful revolution there and to put a friendly faction in power.

During the "dark ages" of political confusion in Japan, the people had developed industrially to a point where they equalled or even excelled their Chinese teachers in many fields of manufacturing. Despite the feudal political framework, they had built up a far stronger commercial system than they had achieved in previous ages; and in a burst of new physical power and vitality, their warrior-traders had come to dominate the waters of East Asia. Japan entered the feudal period in the twelfth century, a small, weak, economically backward land on the fringes of the civilized world. It emerged in the sixteenth century from a prolonged period of feudal anarchy, an economically advanced nation, able in many ways to compete on terms of equality with the newly encountered peoples of Europe and even with the Chinese.

149 SIR GEORGE SANSOM, JAPAN, A SHORT CULTURAL HISTORY: THE NATURE OF JAPANESE FEUDALISM

In *Japan, A Short Cultural History*, Sir George Sansom carefully examines the manner in which a centralized, bureaucratic state modeled on the Chinese pattern was replaced by a feudal society. After describing how private warriors all over Japan took land for themselves during the disorder marking the end of the Heian period (794-1185), he shows how many of these warriors, who had as the principle sanction for their conquests the ability to maintain them by force of arms, entrusted their estates to the head of their clan in return for protection. These clan leaders in turn offered their allegiance to one of the great families who were struggling for control of the country. When the feudal dictator Yoritomo finally gained victory over his rivals in 1185, he consolidated his power by giving land to his followers—or increasing the possessions of those who had already won land for themselves—in return for loyalty. "Thus, scattered over all parts of Japan, thickly in the east, more thinly elsewhere, were land and armed forces which the Minamoto overlord controlled either directly or through his lieges." The organization of these fiefs into a workable system of government was the task of centuries, and resulted in the creation of a new way of life. In the following selection the nature of the society that evolved is discussed and its values analyzed. Sir George Sansom writes out of long experience as a British diplomat in Japan and as a university professor later in the United States.

The House Laws of the great families had much to do with shaping the development of Japanese institutions, and a study of them reveals the interesting fact that some of the distinguishing features of the feudalism evolved in Japan can be traced back to the early patriarchal system, while others show the influence of Chinese political theory. We have seen that, in spite of efforts to change the structure of society, clan feeling again and again asserted itself, and found expression in the rise, one after another, of powerful families tending to act as self-contained units. Even the imported codes, as adapted in Japan, allowed a considerable independence to nobles of high rank, providing for a regular hierarchy in their households of functionaries, guards and menials. As their lands grew they acquired an almost complete control over the persons and property of those inhabiting their estates, including the power to inflict punishment. Some forms of tenure even conferred freedom from the entry of public officers. As these autonomous units expanded, each developed customary rules governing the relations between its members. Such rules dealt with the duties of members of the clan, matters of marriage, succession and ancestral rites, and in general they formed and preserved a family tradition of conduct. It was under the influence of this habit that were built up the house laws of the military families; and thus the code which regulated, for example, the behaviour of a Minamoto warrior towards his clan leader was of the same type as the body of instructions which were observed by the Fujiwara and their dependents. Consequently the early feudal relation between lord and vassal in Japan can be said to owe something to the patriarchal system of pre-feudal and even of prehistoric times. The warfare which brought the fighting classes to the fore naturally emphasised the military aspect of the bond between the leader and his man, but it remained true for a long time after the establishment of the Bakufu that the relation between lord and vassal partook more of the nature of family loyalty than of a contractual obligation. As the Minamoto extended their powers and acquired supporters outside their own clan, they were, of course, obliged to offer their new vassals some material return; but even Yoritomo's former enemies were invited to become his "house-men," and so to establish with him a connection approaching kinship.

Though it would be foolish to suppose that the feudal régime subsisted upon abstract loyalty, without nourishment in the shape of concrete benefits, it can be said that, ideally, loyalty came first. In theory the vassal owed service to his lord simply because he was his lord, and he did not claim, though he might reasonably hope for, protection and reward. Thus Sasaki Sadatsuna, a partisan of the Minamoto, for whom he and his forbears had wrought valiantly and suffered, in his injunctions to his son spoke as follows: "It is the duty of a warrior to be like a monk observing a rule. It is his business to preserve the state by protecting the sovereign. Whether he holds but a pin's point of land or rules a thousand acres, his loyalty must be the same. He must not think of his life as his own, but as offered by him to his lord." The lord may grant favours to a vassal who has done him no service, or he may deny gifts to one who has given him aid; for the personal relationship exists, independently of reward, on a basis of mutual reliance and trust. This conception of a vassal's duty, ethical rather than practical, was naturally fostered by the feudal chieftains, who found in Confucian doctrine a very convenient warrant for promoting their own interest. True, the Chinese teaching was in origin and growth designed to stabilise a peaceful, bureaucratic order and, though it insisted in general terms upon the importance of loyalty, it had in view chiefly such civic virtues as filial piety and obedience to officials. But it was easy to naturalise this morality in a warlike society by giving special

Text: George B. Sansom, *Japan: A Short Cultural History.* Copyright, 1943, D. Appleton-Century Company, Inc. Reprinted by permission of the publishers, Appleton-Century-Crofts, Inc., New York, and Cresset Press, Ltd., London. Pp. 280-85.

eminence to one type of loyalty, that of a warrior to his overlord. So we find Tameyoshi, the grandfather of Yoritomo, when summoned to the court of a cloistered emperor, saying: "I come because I have been told to come by the head of my house. Otherwise not even an imperial edict could bring me to the palace, for we Minamoto do not serve two masters." Not only does the warrior serve only one master, but he owes him a loyalty which transcends all other loyalties. They are evanescent relations, but the bond of service belongs to past, present and future. The saying was, "Parent and child one generation, husband and wife two generations, lord and retainer three generations"; and the catharsis in classical Japanese tragedy is usually provided by the clash between duty to a superior and the natural affections. A mother substitutes her child for the infant of the chieftain, and reveals no emotion when her own offspring is slain before her eyes by the enemy whom she has tricked. A son sacrifices his parents on his war-lord's behalf, a husband sells his wife into harlotry to get funds for the defence of his own honour as a soldier.

Of such a kind was the ethical code of the military caste, described in early works not as *Bushido* (which is a word of recent currency) but as "the way of the horse and the bow," a term analogous to our word "chivalry." Yet the likeness is largely philological. The code of European knighthood grew up in an atmosphere of religious fervour, and centred round the duty of the strong towards the weak, which was expressed in the cult of deference to women. The Japanese feudal warrior, though he might worship the god of war and pray devoutly to Buddhist deities, was not inspired by crusading zeal. He did not go into battle wearing a holy relic, invoking the angels and the saints, but cried out in a loud voice his name and his pedigree. A Taira soldier, in a great sea-fight, boards a ship proclaiming, "I am he, known to the very children in the streets in these days as an ally of the Heike, the second son of Etchū Zenshi, Shimosa Akushichihyōe Kagekiyo!" In the lyric drama called "Benkei-in-the-Boat" even a wraith announces his ancestry, in these words: "This is I, offspring of the emperor Kwammu in the ninth generation, Taira no Tomomori, his ghost." In the life of intrigue and ceremony at the imperial court, feminine influence was strong, while women seem to have had a good deal to do with the practical management of feudal estates; but in Japan the knight of mediæval romance did not ride abroad to succour damsels in distress, and he would have been deeply shocked at the thought of tilting for some lady's favour. Though there are many tales, sad and heroic, of noble Japanese women of this age, they figure not as queenly beauties compelling homage and inspiring passion, but as devoted servants and companions.

Both the European and the Japanese codes subserved the interest of a special class, and both had grave shortcomings. The Japanese ideals, in their way and within their limited scope, helped to create a fine tradition of duty and self-sacrifice. Conduct, of course, fell far short of ideals, and even in the early feudal period, when military aspirations were fresh and before the code had been subjected to the strain of greed and the wear of time, there were many revolting examples of treachery. Yoritomo himself, the keystone of the arch of loyalty, was guilty of cruel and cowardly acts, and often a knight, who would go to fantastic lengths to keep his plighted word, would commit the basest and most unnatural crimes if they were not expressly forbidden by the unwritten law of his caste. Yet, for all that, the code fostered a certain power of resistance to moral and material hardship, and a high sense of obligation, which have been of much value to the nation.

Though these virtues, it is interesting to observe, are based upon a philosophy rather than a religious faith, it must not be supposed that the thoughts and the deeds of the military class were free from the influence of religion. The spread of the doctrines of the meditative Zen sect—perhaps the most remarkable development of Buddhism in Japan—had its beginnings in this age. Throughout the feudal period both lords and vassals frequently founded religious institutions, and attached to most great manors were Buddhist temples and Shintō shrines supported by the landholders and devoted to the worship of some patron deity or the performance of rites on behalf of the dead. A warrior past his active campaigning days would shave his head and enter religion, taking a Buddhist name; though this did not as a rule mean that he forsook the world and secular affairs. In oaths of fealty and in legal bonds the gods were called upon to punish a breach of faith. In times of peril all the Buddhist and Shintō deities were invoked, with prayer for strength or victory in battle. Sometimes a great soldier's spirit was deified and worshipped in a shrine erected by his posterity. In general the military class were liberal in their expenditure on ecclesiastical buildings and ceremonies, but —if a distinction can be made between their creed and European chivalry—the ideals which they cherished were not religious ideals, and religion was a subsidiary and not a primary motive of their conduct. Here we cannot speculate as to whether this difference arose from deep springs of racial instinct, or was caused by external conditions. But it is worth remembering that, in the middle ages, it fell to feudal warriors to protect Western Europe against the encroachment of heathen peoples, and it was as the defender of Christian territory that feudalism fought for the Christian church. In Japan there arose no such circumstances to identify feudal and religious interests. Buddhism had spread over the whole Far Eastern world, and even Khubilai Khan's Mongols had come under its influence when they invaded Japan; so that it would have been difficult for a Japanese Peter the Hermit to rouse the Minamoto vassals by crying that dangers assailed the faith.

ILLUSTRATIONS:

PART I   Temple at Luxor: Photo by Wim Swaan, from *Thebes of the Pharaohs,* Elek Books Ltd., London, 1965. Thanksgiving Scroll: Photo by Helene Bieberkraut, Fig. 16, from Sykenick, *Dead Sea Scrolls of the Hebrew University*. Courtesy of The Magnes Press, The Hebrew University, Jerusalem, 1955. Seal impression: Courtesy of the Staatliche Museen, Berlin. Hammurabi's Code: Hirmer Fotoarchiv, Munich.   PART II   Parthenon: Photo by W. Suschitzky, London. Bowl of Socias: Marburg-Art Reference Bureau. *Marcus Aurelius:* Alinari-Art Reference Bureau.
PART III   Hagia Sophia: Photo by Martin Hürlimann. Byzantine crucifix: Alinari-Art Bureau. Koran: Courtesy of the Freer Gallery of Art, Smithsonian Institution, Washington, D.C.
PART IV   Cologne Cathedral: Photo by Helga Schmidt-Glassner, Stuttgart. Miniature from the *Livre des propriétés des choses,* agricultural scenes, Flemish, 1482, Ms. Roy. 15. E II fol. 247v., Courtesy of the Trustees, The British Museum. Harlech Castle: Photo by Edwin Smith.
PART V   Botticelli's *Primavera* (detail): Alinari-Art Reference Bureau. Michelangelo's *Moses:* Courtesy of Braun & Cie., Paris-New York. Da Vinci's sketch of embryo: Royal Collection, Windsor Castle, reproduced by gracious permission of Her Majesty Queen Elizabeth II. Frontispiece and beginning of the Book of Genesis from Luther's translation of the Bible, 1534: From *Propylaen Weltgeschichte, Reformation und Gegenreformation,* p. 184, Chap. 12, H.E. 2B.
PART VI   Phoenix Hall, Uji, Japan: Bijutsu Shuppan-sha, Tokyo.

5 6 7 8 9 10 –GBC– 80 79 78 77 76 75

LISTEN TO RAP!

Exploring a Musical Genre

ANTHONY J. FONSECA

Exploring Musical Genres
James E. Perone, Series Editor

GREENWOOD

An Imprint of ABC-CLIO, LLC
Santa Barbara, California • Denver, Colorado

Copyright © 2019 by ABC-CLIO, LLC

All rights reserved. No part of this publication may be reproduced, stored in a retrieval system, or transmitted, in any form or by any means, electronic, mechanical, photocopying, recording, or otherwise, except for the inclusion of brief quotations in a review, without prior permission in writing from the publisher.

Library of Congress Cataloging-in-Publication Data

Names: Fonseca, Anthony J. author.
Title: Listen to rap! : exploring a musical genre / Anthony J. Fonseca.
Description: Santa Barbara, California : Greenwood, 2019. | Series: Exploring musical genres | Includes bibliographical references and index.
Identifiers: LCCN 2019020181 (print) | LCCN 2019021233 (ebook) | ISBN 9781440865671 (ebook) | ISBN 9781440865664 (hardcopy : alk. paper)
Subjects: LCSH: Rap (Music)—History and criticism.
Classification: LCC ML3531 (ebook) | LCC ML3531 .F65 2019 (print) | DDC 782.421649—dc23
LC record available at https://lccn.loc.gov/2019020181

ISBN: 978-1-4408-6566-4 (print)
      978-1-4408-6567-1 (ebook)

23 22 21 20 19   1 2 3 4 5

This book is also available as an eBook.

Greenwood
An Imprint of ABC-CLIO, LLC

ABC-CLIO, LLC
147 Castilian Drive
Santa Barbara, California 93117
www.abc-clio.com

This book is printed on acid-free paper ∞

Manufactured in the United States of America

Contents

Series Foreword	ix
Preface	xiii
Acknowledgments	xv
1 Background	1
2 Must-Hear Music	15
Beastie Boys	15
Big Daddy Kane and Doug E. Fresh and the Get Fresh Crew: "Smooth Operator" and "La Di Da Di"	19
Big Pun	22
Birdman, Drake, and Lil Wayne: "Money to Blow" and "4 My Town (Play Ball)"	26
Bone Thugs-N-Harmony: *The Art of War*	29
Bubba Sparxxx and Donatan: "Ugly" and "Country Folks"/"Słowiańska Krew" and "Nie Lubimy Robić"	33
Busta Rhymes and Tech N9ne: "Break Ya Neck" and "Worldwide Choppers"	38
Cardi B: "Bodak Yellow" and "Money"	41
Chance the Rapper: *Coloring Book*	45
C-Murder: *Bossalinie*	48

Coolio: "Gangsta's Paradise"	52
Cypress Hill	54
Da Brat, Foxy Brown, and Lil' Kim	57
De La Soul	62
DJ Jazzy Jeff & the Fresh Prince	65
Drake: *Scorpion*	68
Dr. Dre: *The Chronic*	72
Missy Elliott: *Miss E . . . So Addictive* and *Under Construction*	76
Eminem: *The Marshall Mathers LP*	80
Eric B. & Rakim	86
50 Cent: "How to Rob" and "Ghetto Qu'ran (Forgive Me)"	89
Geto Boys: *We Can't Be Stopped*	92
Grandmaster Flash and the Furious Five: "The Message"	96
Lauryn Hill: *The Miseducation of Lauryn Hill*	99
Insane Clown Posse: "Crop Circles" and "Off the Track"	103
Jay-Z and Danger Mouse: *The Black Album* and *The Grey Album*	107
Jean Grae: "My Story" and "Desperada"	112
KRS-One: "Outta Here" and "Sound of da Police"	115
Talib Kweli: *Eardrum*	118
Kendrick Lamar: "Humble."	124
LMFAO and Shaggy: "Party Rock Anthem" and "Sexy and I Know It"/"Angel" and "Don't Make Me Wait"	127
Macklemore & Ryan Lewis and Professor Elemental: "Thrift Shop" and "Fighting Trousers"	131
MC Hammer: *Please Hammer, Don't Hurt 'Em*	135
MC Lyte: *Bad as I Wanna B*	137
Nas and K'naan: "One Mic" and "Take a Minute"	141

Nicki Minaj: *Pink Friday* and *Pink Friday: Roman Reloaded*	145
The Notorious B.I.G.	150
N.W.A.: *Straight Outta Compton*	154
OutKast: *Stankonia*	158
Panjabi MC, Featuring Jay-Z, and Panjabi Hit Squad, Featuring Ms. Scandalous: "Beware of the Boys" ("Mundian To Bach Ke") and "Hai Hai"	162
Public Enemy: *Fear of a Black Planet*	165
Run-D.M.C.: *Raising Hell*	169
Salt-N-Pepa and Queen Latifah: "Ain't Nuthin' But a She Thing" and "U.N.I.T.Y."	173
Gil Scott-Heron and Aceyalone: "The Revolution Will Not Be Televised" and "The Guidelines"	177
Snoop Dogg	181
The Sugarhill Gang and Blondie: "Rapper's Delight" and "Rapture"	185
A Tribe Called Quest: *The Low End Theory*	188
Tupac Shakur: *All Eyez on Me*	191
The 2 Live Crew: *As Nasty as They Wanna Be*	196
Wu-Tang Clan: "Wu-Tang: 7th Chamber" (I and II) and "16th Chamber/O.D.B. Special"	200
3 Impact on Popular Culture	205
4 Legacy	217
Further Reading	231
Index	241

Series Foreword

Ask some music fans, and they will tell you that genre labels are rubbish and that imposing them on artists and pieces of music diminishes the diversity of the work of performers, songwriters, instrumental composers, and so on. Still, in the record stores of old, in descriptions of radio-station formats (on-air and Internet), and at various streaming audio and download sites today, we have seen and continue to see music categorized by genre. Indeed, some genre boundaries are at least somewhat artificial, and it is true that some artists and some pieces of music transcend boundaries. But categorizing music by genre is a convenient way of keeping track of the thousands upon thousands of musical works available for listeners' enjoyment; it's analogous to the difference between having all your documents on your computer's home screen versus organizing them into folders. So, Greenwood's Exploring Musical Genres series is a genre- and performance group–based collection of books and e-books. The publications in this series will provide listeners with background information on the genre; critical analysis of important examples of musical pieces, artists, and events from the genre; discussion of must-hear music from the genre; analysis of the genre's impact on the popular culture of its time and on later popular-culture trends; and analysis of the enduring legacy of the genre today and its impact on later musicians and their songs, instrumental works, and recordings. Each volume will also contain a bibliography of references for further reading.

We view the volumes in the Exploring Musical Genres series as a go-to resource for serious music fans, the more casual listener, and everyone in between. The authors in the series are scholars, who probe into the details of the genre and its practitioners: the singers, instrumentalists, composers, and lyricists of the pieces of music that we love. Although the authors' scholarship brings a high degree of insight and perceptive analysis to the reader's understanding of the various musical genres, the authors approach their subjects with the idea of appealing to the lay reader, the music nonspecialist. As a result, the authors may provide critical analysis using some high-level scholarly tools; however, they avoid any unnecessary and unexplained jargon or technical terms or concepts. These are scholarly volumes written for the enjoyment of virtually any music fan.

Every volume has its length parameters, and an author cannot include every piece of music from within a particular genre. Part of the challenge, but also part of the fun, is that readers might agree with some of the choices of "must-hear music" and disagree with others. So while your favorite example of, say, grunge music might not be included, the author's choices might help you to open up your ears to new, exciting, and ultimately intriguing possibilities.

By and large, these studies focus on music from the sound-recording era: roughly the 20th century through the present. American guitarist, composer, and singer-songwriter Frank Zappa once wrote:

> On a record, the overall timbre of the piece (determined by equalization of individual parts and their proportions in the mix) tells you, in a subtle way, *WHAT* the song is about. The orchestration provides *important information* about what the composition *IS* and, in some instances, assumes a greater importance than *the composition itself* (Zappa with Occhiogrosso 1989, 188; italics and capitalization from the original).

The gist of Zappa's argument is that *everything* that the listener experiences (to use Zappa's system of emphasizing words)—including the arrangement, recording mix and balance, lyrics, melodies, harmonies, instrumentation, and so on—makes up a musical composition. To put it another way, during the sound-recording era, and especially after the middle of the 20th century, we have tended to understand the idea of a piece of music—particularly in the realm of popular music—as being the same as the most definitive recording of that piece of music. And this is where Zappa's emphasis on the arrangement and recording's production comes into play. As a result, a writer delving into, say, new wave rock will examine and analyze the B-52's' version of "Rock Lobster" and not just the words, melodies, and chords that any band could sing and play and still label the result "Rock Lobster." To use Zappa's graphic way of highlighting particular words, the B-52's' recording *IS* the piece. Although they have expressed it in other ways, other writers such as Theodore Gracyk (1996, 18) and Albin J. Zak III (2001) concur with Zappa's equating of the piece with the studio recording of the piece.

In the case of musical genres not as susceptible to being tied to a particular recording—generally because of the fact that they are genres often experienced live, such as classical music or Broadway musicals—the authors will still make recommendations of particular recordings (we don't all have ready access to a live performance of Wolfgang Amadeus Mozart's *Symphony No. 40* any time we'd like to experience the piece), but they will focus their analyses on the more general, the notes-on-the-page, the expected general aural experience that one is likely to find in any good performance or recorded version.

Maybe you think that all you really want to do is just listen to the music. Won't reading about a genre decrease your enjoyment of it? My hope is that you'll find that reading this book opens up new possibilities for understanding your favorite musical genre and that by knowing a little more about it, you'll be able to listen with proverbial new ears and gain even more pleasure from your listening experience. Yes, the authors in the series will bring you biographical detail, the history of the genres, and critical analysis on various musical works that they consider to be the best, the most representative, and the most influential pieces in the genre. However, ultimately, the goal is to enhance the listening experience. That, by the way, is why these volumes have an exclamation mark in their titles. So please enjoy both reading and listening!

—*James E. Perone, Series Editor*

REFERENCES

Gracyk, Theodore. 1996. *Rhythm and Noise: An Aesthetics of Rock*. Durham, NC: Duke University Press.

Zak, Albin J., III. 2001. *The Poetics of Rock: Cutting Tracks, Making Records*. Berkeley: University of California Press.

Zappa, Frank, with Peter Occhiogrosso. 1989. *The Real Frank Zappa Book*. New York: Poseidon Press.

Preface

Rap music, a subset of hip hop, is as much a sociopolitical movement as it is a music style. Like Motown, it gave African American musicians, music studio entrepreneurs, producers (here meaning financiers), and even music engineers (the people responsible for most of a rap song's sound through mixing and mastering) a chance to make their mark in a predominantly white business. More importantly, it gave African Americans, and to a lesser extent Latino Americans/Chicanos, a chance to become multimillionaires. Ultimately, rap (and nonrap hip hop) redefined the music industry, replacing rock and roll as the top moneymaker; today, even *Rolling Stone*, an icon of rock music, devotes most of its pages to rappers and music engineers (often also called producers, though they are not always the financiers of a recording). Even the political nature of rap has had a big influence on music journalism, which has become more overtly and actively political.

Looking back, it seems a longshot that rap music has made the impact that it has. Most early labels got their start when rappers and producers used glorified home studios to record music CDs, which were then sold out of their car trunks. No Limit (New Orleans, Louisiana), one of the biggest early rap labels, got its start this way. Sugar Hill Records (Englewood, New Jersey) found its rappers in places like pizzerias, where they were working at the time. Ruthless Records (Compton, California, and later Los Angeles) found its rappers, music engineers, and executives selling drugs on street corners. Death Row Records (Los Angeles) strong-armed its rivals into breaking contracts so that it could hire rappers from other labels. Despite these humble and troubled beginnings, and despite attempts at censorship, rap caught on, and not just with the African American community. Today rap is a multibillion-dollar industry that has interests in music, fashion, and the performance arts, and it is a mainstream industry, with rappers now performing at the Kennedy Center and on Broadway and being inducted into the Rock & Roll Hall of Fame, the Smithsonian, and the Library of Congress.

Listen to Rap! Exploring a Musical Genre traces the origins, personalities, labels, and sociocultural contexts of rap music and provides a listening-oriented discussion of the creative output of artists, including soloists and rap crews (a.k.a. bands). In addition, it provides a close listening/reading of a diverse set of songs, albums, and artists. The entries on specific albums address those albums as a collection of songs meant to be experienced as a whole. Some entries pair albums together to highlight significant connections in style or treatment. The entries on artists and bands represent subgenres like gangsta, g-funk, snap, trap, mobb, alternative, and chopper (these could also simply be called styles, as they differ mainly in specific lyrical content, although slight differences in instrumentation, production, and vocal delivery/flow sometimes exist). Entries that focus on specific songs analyze and deconstruct musical elements, discuss the sound of the songs, give attention to production values (including sampling, which is a staple of rap), and provide historical and sociocultural context. These songs were selected for their influence and musical elements.

Acknowledgments

Being born in the early 1960s to a family that had Cajun French, Latino, and Caucasian roots, I did not grow up with rap music. However, I was the first person in my neighborhood (a dead-end street where everyone was related) and one of the few people in my high school who looked for music outside of rock and roll, having grown bored with its typical offerings. I discovered what was called new wave, then alternative, then indie, and finally rap. Having worked on an encyclopedia of global rap music, I further discovered the incredible variety in both rappers and instrumentation, gaining a huge amount of respect for how talented rap producers (here meaning music engineers) had to be to create the kind of music that made people take notice.

This book has been nothing short of a pleasure, an absolute party for the ears. Performing the kind of close listening needed to discuss the albums, artists, and songs in depth has taught me an appreciation for the intricacies of engineer-producers like Beats by the Pound, Dr. Dre, Danger Mouse, J Dilla, Just Blaze, the Bomb Squad, RZA, and Timbaland, as well as the lyrical and flow skills of rappers like Big Pun, Busta Rhymes, Chuck D, Missy Elliott, Jay-Z, MC Lyte, Nicki Minaj, Ol' Dirty Bastard, and Talib Kweli.

I am grateful to ABC-CLIO's acquisitions editor, Catherine M. Lafuente, for bringing this series to my attention, and to *Exploring a Musical Genre* series editor James E. Perone for his guidance. I wish to thank Melissa Ursula Dawn Goldsmith and Jim Gallant, two close friends also writing in the series, for never getting bored when we talked shop—and Melissa especially for being my sounding board when I needed a music theorist, since I, like most of the rappers and producers in this book, have no formal background in music other than

xvi Acknowledgments

I know what I like and why (based on my time recording and mixing). I owe a debt of gratitude to Goldsmith and fellow researchers Susannah Cleveland, Christine Lee Gengaro, Jessica Leah Getman, Lauron Jockwig Kehrer, Terry Klefstad, Katy Leonard, Bryan J. McCann, Celeste Roberts, Jennifer L. Roth-Burnette, Amanda Sewell, Scott Warfield, and Paige A. Willson for their contributions to *Hip Hop around the World* (Greenwood, 2018). Their expertise was a starting place for me on many entries for this book.

I am also grateful to friends like Amy Baker, Steve Berlin, Kathleen Chapman, Alaina Di'Giorgio, Marco Garcia, Valerie Lavender, Michael Smith, and especially Latisha Rocke (whose superior taste in music introduced me to Chance the Rapper) for their genuine interest in the book as it progressed. Finally, I would like to dedicate this book to my mother, Elta Leontine, who knew to put the radio in my crib at night to help me sleep, and who never stopped singing while doing her housework. I may not owe my musical taste to her (I can only imagine what she'd say if she were alive to know I am on my second rap music book), but I do owe her my love of music.

CHAPTER 1

Background

WHAT IS RAP?

Rap music is a style of hip hop known for its urban slang and its preference not for singing but rapping, a syncopated or rhythmic version of rhymed talking similar to talk singing or the patter song, both of which were used by singers in some stage and film musicals previous to rap's birth, as well as in some rock songs. While rap owes its vocalization theory to these two genres (i.e., musicals and rock), it owes its lyrical content and concerns to spoken-word jazz poetry (directly) and to the West African tradition of the griot (indirectly). Rappers refer to their vocals by various names, including rhyming, spitting, and emceeing (almost always represented as "MC'ing"). Rap can be performed a cappella, with a second person beatboxing, or against instrumentation, normally featuring a strong beat and samples of previously recorded songs (a practice called "sampling") or turntable scratching done by a DJ (also known as a "turntablist").

Rapping can be either scripted (a typical practice with recorded songs) or fully or partially improvised, a practice used in what are called "rap freestyle battles," where rappers compete head-to-head to determine who can extemporize best. Freestyle skill is judged by the rapper's mastery of rhymes, lyric content, and vocal delivery (i.e., flow). Rappers, both freestyle and recorded, are judged on their style, which can range from fast-paced and aggressive to laid-back and chant-like, as well as their flow, which can range from the sing-song rhythms of schoolyard chants, childhood taunts, jump rope rhymes, and clapping games to complex melodic lines with varying cadences and surprising enjambment. The ability to create complex rhymes within a rap song's typical 4/4 beat also factor into a rapper's skill; those who can incorporate multiple end rhymes and use interior rhymes (and near rhymes) are considered more skilled.

BEGINNINGS

The word "rap" was used to describe rhythmic talking on records as early as 1971 (on Isaac Hayes's song "Ike's Rap" from the album *Black Moses*). Rapping as a practice can be traced back to the aforementioned West African griot tradition, where poets would rhythmically talk while accompanied by drums and sparse instrumentation. American precursors include the patter song and talk-sung dialogue songs like Glenn Miller's "The Lady's in Love with You" and "The Little Man Who Wasn't There" (both from 1939). The most direct antecedent to rap music is jazz poetry, much like the type parodied to comic effect by boxer Muhammad Ali to "trash talk" his opponents. Serious, socially conscious jazz poetry was made famous by Gil Scott-Heron (1949–2011) in songs like his 1971 single "The Revolution Will Not Be Televised." Early MCs also cite the band the Last Poets (1968–) as an early rap influence.

Another influence on rap's development was the Jamaican deejay. His main function was delivering what were called "toasts," set to music. These toasts, done in a monotone flow with a microphone and set against a beat, could include tales of heroism, simple boasting (braggadocio), taunts aimed at specific people, and calls to an audience to engage in dancing. From the Jamaican deejay developed the MC, the hype man, and the rap DJ, who was more of a producer/mixer, sampler, and turntablist and served the purpose of engaging a crowd and supporting a group's MC (or MCs) vocally. Rap's quintessential hype man is Flavor Flav (William Jonathan Drayton Jr., 1959–) of Public Enemy (1982–). Toasting found its way into the United States in the 1970s when Jamaican immigrant DJ Kool Herc (Clive Campbell, 1955–) introduced not only the idea of short rap stanzas and toasts at his block parties but also elaborate sound systems and samples of previously released songs. Although it is impossible to determine who exactly was the first rapper, one possibility is Manhattan DJ Hollywood (Anthony Holloway, 1954–), who is considered the first radio DJ to syncopate with a music track (i.e., beginning each line on the downbeat) in order to create an extended flow of about a minute. Early rap, sometimes called old-school rap, typically followed the example of the party DJ, keeping the rhymes simple and dealing with themes like romance, sex, money, and partying.

Around the mid-1980s, rappers began experimenting more with rhyme and melodic line, and lyrics started dealing with sociopolitical issues like drugs, violence, activism, and police brutality. Rakim (William Michael Griffin Jr., 1968–), of Eric B. & Rakim (1986–93; 2016–), is credited with changing the sound of rap with his focus on less predictable flow. In addition, as gangsta rap (which both attacked and embraced the urban lifestyle choices of drugs, sex, and murder) emerged, lyrics started to emphasize urban crime issues; gangster life was also glamourized by some artists, so materialism—the accumulation of what was nicknamed "bling"—also became popular in songs.

LOCATION, LOCATION, LOCATION

Although it has become internationally popular, rap music is at its core a local phenomenon. When rap first became popular in the United States, it began on both the East and West Coasts, in several New York City boroughs and in South Central Los Angeles, and moved its way across the country only when major African American–owned labels emerged in New Orleans (with the No Limit, Ca$h Money, Young Money, and Bossalinie labels) and Atlanta (with the So So Def, Disturbing Tha Peace, and LaFace labels). African Americans began to create, maintain, and control label-associated rap scenes in urban cities like Oakland, California; Newark, New Jersey; Philadelphia, Pennsylvania; Miami, Florida; and Houston, Texas. These cities became rap meccas and could lay claim to virtually all rap music production and talent, with one major exception—Hampton, Virginia, a relatively small city of 137,000 people. Hampton was the home of Jodeci (1988–96; 2014–) ex-member and producer DeVante Swing (Donald Earle DeGrate Jr., 1969–), whose Swing Mob Collective, also known as Da Bassment Cru, included fellow native Virginians Missy Elliott (Melissa Arnette Elliott, Portsmouth, 1971–) and Timbaland (Timothy Zachery Mosley, Norfolk, 1972–), arguably two of the most influential forces in rap after 2003. Other Swing Mob members included multiplatinum rapper Ginuwine (Elgin Baylor Lumpkin, 1970–). As a rapper and producer duo, Missy Elliott and Timbaland countered the local quality of urban rap with the production of more universal songs, since Hampton, Portsmouth, and Norfolk would likely have not been good fodder for lyrics. Nonetheless, the two netted five consecutive platinum albums themselves, and both went on to produce for various musicians.

Other rappers, however, set their lyrics in their local environs, especially in areas like South Central Los Angeles, where West Coast rappers latched onto gangster-based urban themes and wrote about life on their streets, including problems faced by their black community with drugs and police violence. Even the local gang wars made their way into the music, with songs that featured the Bloods and Crips. Because rap was a local phenomenon, it became a point of pride to be the first crew to accomplish any new breakthrough, and this led to some of the first rap wars—which proved commercially lucrative. On the East Coast, for example, MC Shan's (Shawn Moltke, 1965–) "The Bridge" (off of *Down by Law*, 1986) claimed that rap started in Queens. This annoyed Boogie Down Productions (BDP, 1985–92), a South Bronx crew led by rapper KRS-One (Lawrence Parker, 1965–), which felt rap originated in the Bronx. BDP answered with the song "South Bronx" (1986), which led to MC Shan's answer "Kill That Noise" (1987), which in turn led to BDP's "The Bridge Is Over" (1987). Other rap diss-track (i.e., songs meant to attack others) battles included MC Shan's "Beat Biter," which called Long Island superstar LL Cool J (James Todd Smith, 1968–) a plagiarist.

GANGSTA RAP

MC Shan also claimed the origin of gangsta rap. Arguably, gangsta rap began in the Northeast, with Philadelphia's Schoolly D (Jesse Bonds Weaver Jr., 1962–), the Bronx's BDP, and Newark's Ice-T (Tracy Lauren Marrow, 1958–), who drew on gangsta themes. Nonetheless, the West Coast can lay a legitimate right to gangsta rap. The Compton, California-based crew N.W.A. (1986–91) made it popular because despite the band's urban and ethnic themes, mainstream America fell in love with the music. N.W.A. was led by rapper Eazy-E (Eric Lynn Wright, 1963–95), who cofounded Ruthless Records. N.W.A. and Ruthless became the driving force behind gangsta rap. N.W.A.'s platinum albums *Straight Outta Compton* (1988) and *Efil4zaggin* (1991) spawned the careers of various influential solo West Coast gangsta rappers: Eazy-E, Dr. Dre (Andre Romelle Young, 1965–), and Ice Cube (O'Shea Jackson, 1969–).

Five years after the launch of Ruthless, Death Row Records (1991–2008) was cofounded by Dr. Dre in Los Angeles, working with The D.O.C. (Tracy Lynn Curry, 1968–) and director of operations Suge Knight (Marion Hugh Knight Jr., 1965–). Dr. Dre, The D.O.C., and Michel'le (Michel'le Denise Toussaint, 1970–) left Ruthless to join Death Row, which then dominated the rap charts with Dr. Dre and other gangsta acts like Tupac Shakur (Lesane Parish Crooks, 1971–96) and Snoop Dogg (Calvin Cordozar Broadus Jr., 1971–). Gangsta rap became a music force to be reckoned with when it became the target of intense criticism by elected officials and law enforcement, leading to labeling, censorship, and ironically, higher sales. More West Coast gangsta rappers like Compton's Most Wanted (C.M.W., 1987–93, 2015–) found that public notoriety brought commercial success, and gangsta rap evolved into various styles, the most popular being g-funk (gangsta funk), which sampled funk albums of the 1970s and used a less aggressive tone both instrumentally and vocally, as it was informed by a laid–back ethos. Ultimately gangsta went mainstream, when Coolio (Artis Leon Ivey Jr., 1963–) saw his 1996 hit single "Gangsta's Paradise" sell 5 million units, rise to No. 1 in fifteen countries, and win a Grammy.

WEST COAST V. EAST COAST

Because it relied heavily on the local setting, the West Coast rap scene became known for its diversity. Los Angeles was home to rap poetry, electronic dance rap, Chicano rap, and experimental turntablism. Rapper and poet Aceyalone (Edwin Maximilian Hayes Jr., 1970–) recorded poetry and alternative trip hop, while Black Eyed Peas (1992–) launched the era of hip hop and electronica rap, which proliferated once will.i.am (William Adams, 1975–) and Fergie (Stacy Ferguson, 1975–) pursued solo careers, and will.i.am and apl.de.ap (Allan Pineda Lindo, 1974–) began producing other bands and soloists. Los Angeles–based Chicano rap combined Latin rhythms, hip-hop beats, and gangsta rap and was popularized by Kid Frost (Arturo Molina Jr., 1962–) in the 1990s, while Cypress Hill (1988–) became the first certified platinum Latino American hip hop group. West Los Angeles's Cut Chemist (Lucas MacFadden, 1972–) became known for his sample-based turntablism. Recent West Coast rap has become more socially conscious, as with the work of Compton-based Grammy winner Kendrick Lamar (Kendrick Lamar Duckworth, 1987–).

Northern California also contributed to rap's development, perhaps in the most important way possible, through diplomacy and aggressive marketing. The Oakland-based Hip Hop Coalition (1997–) promoted hip hop via a nationally syndicated radio host and radio show producer. Oakland also produced an early rap legend (although his status has lessened as of late), MC Hammer (Stanley Kirk Burrell, 1962–), the quintessential old-school rapper and dancer who achieved icon status, won three Grammys, and sold over 50 million albums. Like Los Angeles, Oakland produced experimental rap acts such as Michael Franti (1966–), the leader of the rap, funk, reggae, jazz, folk, and rock band Michael Franti & Spearhead (a.k.a. Spearhead, 1994–), as well as Del the Funky Homosapien (Teren Delvon Jones, 1972–), who formed hip hop collective Hieroglyphics (1991–) and the Hiero Imperium (1997–)

label. Oakland's Ant Banks's production technique, infusing rap songs with funk-influenced bass lines, caught on along the West Coast. Sacramento's Brotha Lynch Hung's (Kevin Danell Mann, 1969–) debut EP, *24 Deep* (1993), is considered a benchmark album in the rap style known as horrorcore. Turntablism also became important in Northern California; in San Francisco iconographic scratcher/producers DJ QBert (Richard Quitevis, 1969–) and Mix Master Mike (Michael Schwartz, 1970–) cofounded Invisibl Skratch Piklz (1995–2000; 2014–). Mix Master Mike went on to be a Grammy Award–winning turntablist for Beastie Boys (1981–2012) and was inducted into the Rock & Roll Hall of Fame with the band.

Between 1974 and 1978, New York City became home to the earliest b-boy (i.e., break dancing) crews, SalSoul and Rockwell Association, consisting almost entirely of New York–based Puerto Ricans. By 1978, the most influential rap dance crew in the United States (and arguably the world), the Rock Steady Crew, was being formed by iconic dancers Ken Swift (Kenneth Gabbert, 1966–), Crazy Legs (Richard Colón, 1966–), and Frosty Freeze (Wayne Frost, 1963–2008). Rapping made its way into funk and rock music with bands like the Fatback Band (1970–) and Blondie (1974–82; 1997–). Blondie's "Rapture" (1981) even hit No. 1 on the Billboard Hot 100. By this time, rap was becoming more common, and early rappers started to emerge: Barbados-born Doug E. Fresh (Douglas E. Davis, 1966–) became famous for his beatboxing and rapping during the 1980s, and LL Cool J released his first studio album, *Radio* (1985), inspired by the rap songs of the Treacherous Three (1978–84) and the Sugarhill Gang's (1979–85; 1994–) "Rapper's Delight" (1979). His second album, *Bigger and Deffer* (1987), went triple platinum. Beastie Boys became one of the great crossover successes (punk, guitar rock, and rap), coming into prominence after working with Def Jam Recordings' (1983–) Rick Rubin (Frederick Jay Rubin, 1963–). The band's first studio album went multiplatinum. Two duos emerged middecade: EPMD (1986–93) and Eric B. & Rakim, both considered integral to the early development of rap music.

Toward the end of the decade, New Rochelle–based Brand Nubian (1989–95; 1997–) became known for its association with Islam, and Yonkers-based DMX (Earl Simmons, 1970–) went from beatboxing to rapping, as his first album, *Flesh of My Flesh, Blood of My Blood* (1988), was released on Def Jam Recordings. Jungle Brothers (1987–) began fusing old-school hip hop with jazz, funk, electronica, dance, house music, R&B, and Afro beats and became core members of the New York City hip hop collective Native Tongues (1989–), which included A Tribe

Called Quest (1985–98; 2006–13; 2015–), De La Soul (1987–), and Black Sheep (1989–95; 2000–02; 2006–). As turntablism became more complex, DJs like Roc Raida (Anthony Williams, 1972–2009) and turntablist collaboratives like the X-Ecutioners (1989–) became popular. The 1980s transitioned into the 1990s with acts like Brooklyn-born Mos Def (Dante Terrell Smith, 1973–) and Staten Island–based Wu-Tang Clan (1992–). Mos Def later formed the duo Black Star (1997–) with Talib Kweli (Talib Kweli Greene, 1975–). Wu-Tang Clan led to the careers of Ol' Dirty Bastard (Russell Tyrone Jones, 1968–2004), Ghostface Killah (Dennis Coles, 1970–), Method Man (Clifford Smith, 1971–), and Raekwon (Corey Woods, 1970–). Collectively, members of the group have sold over 40 million records. More recent New York City–identified hip hop acts include Kanye West (Kanye Omari West, 1977–).

In the Bronx, Kingston, Jamaica–native Kool Herc became the first turntablist, and his experimental techniques and technology influenced Barbados-native turned New Yorker Grandmaster Flash (Joseph Saddler, 1958–), who created Grandmaster Flash and the Furious Five (1976–82) and introduced the beat box drum machine and custom-built instruments. Grandmaster Flash influenced Grand Wizzard Theodore (Theodore Livingston, 1963–), who is credited with developing turntable scratching.

Like on the West Coast, East Coast rap had a tendency to be local in its concerns and lyrics. Bronx-born KRS-One began recording in 1986 with BDP, while Afrika Bambaataa (Kevin Donovan, 1957–), Puerto Rican American rapper Big Pun (Christopher Lee Rios, 1971–2000), and London-born Slick Rick (Richard Martin Lloyd Walters, 1965–), who moved to New York and teamed up with beatboxer Doug E. Fresh to form the Get Fresh Crew (1985–2003) put the Bronx rap scene on the map. The turn of the century saw the formation of the Welfare Poets (1997–), who introduced the fusion of Afro-Caribbean *bomba y plena* and rumba, reggae, blues, jazz (bebop, cool, and Latin), and 1970s soul. Big Pun is routinely listed among the best MCs in history, as is Brooklyn's Big Daddy Kane (Antonio Hardy, 1968–), who started as a member of the rap collective the Juice Crew All-Stars (1983–91). In Brooklyn, in Queens, and on Long Island, rapping became popular early on due to Brooklyn rappers Busta Rhymes (Trevor George Smith Jr., 1972–), Jay-Z (Shawn Corey Carter, 1969–), and Nas (Nasir bin Olu Dara Jones, 1973–). Busta Rhymes became an eleven-time Grammy nominee and went on to found the record label Conglomerate/Flipmode Entertainment (1994–), and Jay-Z cofounded the independent label Roc-A-Fella Records (1996–2013). Nas produced seven RIAA-certified platinum albums with an impressive charting record—all have peaked in either the No. 1 or No. 2 position on Billboard's top R&B/Hip-Hop Albums chart. Meanwhile, duo Smif-N-Wessun (1993–) introduced a unique use of smooth jazz rhythm and Jamaican patois. Brooklyn also introduced an early successful female rapper, Lil' Kim (Kimberly Denise Jones, 1975–), known for her hypersexual performances; she was the only female member of Junior M.A.F.I.A. (1992–97), which was mentored and promoted by the Notorious B.I.G. (Christopher George Latore Wallace, 1972–). Fab 5 Freddy (Fred Brathwaite, 1959–), a graffiti artist, rapper, and filmmaker, also emerged from the Brooklyn scene.

Long Island is one of the locales that can lay claim to being the home of diss rap and rap wars; this is where Roxanne Shanté (Lolita Shanté Gooden, 1969–) launched the Roxanne Wars. Long Island's most iconic act, Public Enemy, introduced the Bomb Squad (1986–), the premiere American early–hip hop production group. Public Enemy's *It Takes a Nation of Millions to Hold Us Back* (1988) and *Fear of a Black Planet* (1990) became rap classics, and cofounders Chuck D (Carlton Douglas Ridenhour, 1960–) and Flavor Flav joined Def Jam. Long Island's De La Soul debuted with *3 Feet High and Rising* (1989), generally regarded one of the greatest hip hop albums of the 1980s, if not all time. Queens-based A Tribe Called Quest, the most commercially successful member of the Native Tongues posse, achieved critical acclaim, especially for its 1991 album *The Low End Theory*. Other early Queens hip hop acts included Run-D.M.C. (1981–2002), MC Lyte (Lana Michelle Moorer, 1971–), and Salt-N-Pepa (1985–2002; 2007–). Run-D.M.C. achieved rap firsts: the first multiplatinum record and the first Grammy nomination. MC Lyte was one of the first women rappers to challenge sexism and misogyny. Salt-N-Pepa became one of the first all-female rap groups to achieve both commercial and critical success with a debut album that went platinum. Recent Queens rappers include 50 Cent (Curtis James Jackson III, 1975–) and Nicki Minaj (Onika Tanya Maraj, 1982–). 50 Cent became a platinum-certified musician, and Nicki Minaj, originally from St. James, Trinidad and Tobago, became one of hip hop's most successful and critically acclaimed female acts after she signed with Young Money Entertainment.

Harlem (in the borough of Manhattan) also produced a few highly influential rap acts. The Last Poets became one of hip hop music's earliest influences, introducing rapping, MC'ing, and beatboxing to inner-city youth looking for a music to call their own. Spoonie Gee (Gabriel Jackson, 1963–), of the Treacherous Three, which featured Grammy Award–winner Kool Moe Dee (Mohandas Dewese, 1962–), gave the East Coast a face for gangsta rap. Meanwhile, Kurtis Blow (Kurtis Walker, 1959–) went in the other direction and worked toward mainstreaming rap music. In 1980, he had the first certified-gold rap single, "The Breaks," and he became the first rapper to appear on *Soul Train*. Kool Moe Dee made a name for himself as a solo act in 1987 using what would be called "old-school style," which is sing-song in its vocal melodic line and uses end rhyme almost exclusively, but then he made the successful transition in 1989 to a raw delivery, with extended lines, uneven rhythms, and more interior rhymes. At the turn of the decade, two rap icons, Puff Daddy (a.k.a. P. Diddy, Sean John Combs, 1969–) and Tupac Shakur emerged in Harlem, the former becoming a leading producer, performer, entrepreneur, celebrity, and founder of Bad Boy Records (1993–), and the latter tying social consciousness with the gangsta ethos and becoming the most notable victim of the East and West Coast rap wars. Harlem was also the home of an influential rap style called new jack swing, which fused hip hop elements with R&B, sometimes including funk and gospel.

OTHER NORTHEAST CITIES

Aside from New York, the Northeast's contributions to rap come mainly from Boston, Pittsburgh, and Philadelphia. In fact, some of the earliest rap successes came out of Philadelphia. DJ Jazzy Jeff (Jeffrey Allen Townes, 1965–), a world DJ champion, cofounded the rap duo DJ Jazzy Jeff & the Fresh Prince (1985–97) with Will Smith (Willard Carroll Smith, 1968–). The duo won two Grammy Awards, with the album *He's the DJ, I'm the Rapper* (1988) going triple platinum. Smith went on to have one of the most successful film careers in modern history. Philadelphia is also the home of the Roots (1987–) and Jill Scott (1972–). The Roots have released eleven studio albums and a handful of collaborative albums with musicians like John Legend (John Roger Stephens, 1978–) and Elvis Costello (Declan Patrick MacManus, 1954–), and they have been the house band for Jimmy Fallon since 2009. Scott, a prolific singer-songwriter, became a benchmark alternative–hip hop artist, fusing her beats with neo soul, R&B, jazz, and spoken word. The city of Boston was a latecomer to the rap scene, although its early successes included Bahamadia (Antonia Reed, 1976–), who began her career by working with Boston- and Brooklyn-based Gang Starr (1986–2006). A recent Massachusetts rap phenomenon is Worcester-based (fifty miles from Boston) Joyner Lucas (Gary Maurice Lucas Jr., 1988–), whose 2017 mixtape *508-507-2209* and dialogue-based singles such as "I'm Sorry" and "I'm Not Racist" had garnered over 226 million YouTube views by the end of 2018. North Dakota–native but Pittsburgh-based Wiz Khalifa (Cameron Jibril Thomaz, 1987–) has had two albums certified platinum.

Although New Jersey lost one of its native rappers when Ice-T moved to Los Angeles and helped establish gangsta rap, its rap scene emerged in the 1990s with Poor Righteous Teachers (1989–96), a Trenton trio known for Five-Percenter rap (named after the Islamic and Afrocentric Five Percenters movement founded in 1964). Queen Latifah (Dana Elaine Owens, 1970–), from Newark, is known as the First Lady of Hip Hop because of her varied career of Afrocentric and feminist rapper, sitcom actor, film actor, talk show host, and jazz vocalist. In 1995, she cofounded her own label and management company, Flavor Unit Entertainment. South Orange–native Lauryn Hill (Lauryn Noelle Hill, 1975–) eventually earned five Grammy awards for her solo album, *The Miseducation of Lauryn Hill* (1998), a collection of songs that bridge the gap between hip hop, soul, and R&B, but she became famous for her collaboration with the South Orange–based Fugees (1992–97), which included Haitian-born Wyclef Jean (Nel Ust Wyclef Jean, 1969–). New Jersey is also known as the home of brick city club, a house music popular from 1995 to 2000 that consisted of breakbeat music strung together, along with repetitive sound bites, to create high-energy dance rhythms.

THE SOUTH

The South was well represented by rappers and labels in cities like New Orleans, Houston, Miami, and Atlanta. New Orleans's 1990s contributions to rap are due largely in part to two record labels, No Limit Records, later revived as No Limit Forever Records, and Ca$h Money Records. No Limit was founded by Master P (Percy Robert Miller, 1970–), a New Orleans native who, along with his brothers, C-Murder (Corey Miller, 1971–) and Silkk the Shocker (Vyshonne King Miller, 1975–), created various rap crews and solo acts. In addition, Master P launched the career of his son, Lil' Romeo (Percy Romeo Miller, 1989–). Master P went on to found P. Miller Enterprises and Better Black Television (2008–). As a rapper, he has released solo albums, as well as albums with the groups TRU (1995–2002) and 504 Boyz (2000–05), the latter including Mystikal (Michael Lawrence Tyler, 1970–). In 1995, he moved No Limit from California to New Orleans and had breakthroughs with the albums *True* (1995), *Ice Cream Man* (1995), and *Ghetto D* (1997). C-Murder is currently incarcerated but has released various albums and has founded the label Bossalinie Records. Ca$h Money Records was cofounded by Birdman (Bryan Christopher Williams, 1969–), a rapper who produced Juvenile (Terius Gray, 1975–), Lil Wayne (Dwayne Michael Carter Jr., 1982–), Drake (Aubrey Drake Graham, 1986–), and Nicki Minaj. Lil Wayne went on to found his own imprint, Young Money Entertainment (2005–) and became one of the best-selling artists in any genre. New Orleans is also home to Big Boy Records and a music style called bounce, which recreates rap as dance party and regional music.

Houston's main contribution to rap was the popularization of hardcore rap and horrorcore. About the same time that the debut album of Detroit-based Esham (Rashaam Attica Smith, 1973–), *Boomin Words from Hell 1990* (1989), introduced horrorcore lyrics, Houston-based Ganksta N-I-P (Lewayne Williams, 1969–) released his debut album *The South Park Psycho* (1990), preparing rap fans for the Geto Boys (1987–2005), who proved to be influential on both horrorcore and Dirty South. Original Geto Boys members Bushwick Bill (Richard Stephen Shaw, 1966–), Scarface (Brad Terrence Jordan, 1970–), and Willie D (William James Dennis, 1966–) went on to have successful solo careers, and the single "Mind Playing Tricks on Me" (1991) became a genre classic.

Miami's contribution to rap music was a style called Miami bass, best represented by the band 2 Live Crew (1982–98) and its rapper/promoter Luke (a.k.a. Luke Skyywalker, Luther Roderick Campbell, 1960–), who created a heavy bass, synthesized melodic and drum sound. Another Miami bass practitioner, Cuban American Pitbull (Armando Christian Pérez, 1981–), has released ten albums since 2004 and has worked with Lil Jon (Jonathan Smith, 1971–).

Atlanta is best known for the subgenres crunkcore and trap, the former a hybrid subgenre of electronica/dance/pop, screamo, and crunk, and the latter an extreme version of urban rap concerned with gritty portrayals of urban street life. Atlanta's other contribution, the 1990s Dirty South fad, was a rap style associated with regional slang and speech patterns, danceable beats, and pronounced bass. Snap is another music style that came out of Atlanta. Snap is an early- to mid-2000s hip hop style derived from crunk. Popular snap artists included D4L (2003–06). Trap—related to crunk, mobb (an East Coast style that glamorized organized crime figures), and hardcore—took as its topic violence, drug deals, and the income gap. It spread from Atlanta to urban areas like Houston and Memphis, Tennessee. Its signature sound is the product of two Atlanta producers, Shawty Redd (Demetrius Lee Stewart, 1981–) and Lex Luger (Lexus Arnel Lewis, 1991–). Ludacris (Christopher Brian Bridges, 1977–), originally from Champaign, Illinois, moved to Atlanta as a teen and worked with Timbaland, guest rapping on *Tim's Bio:*

From the Motion Picture 'Life from da Bassment' (1998). He later cofounded Disturbing Tha Peace Records. His second album (with Def Jam), *Word of Mouf* (2001), is a benchmark Dirty South album.

Atlanta is also the home of three influential hip hop artists, Bronx-born Swizz Beatz (Kasseem Dean, 1978–), hip hop trio TLC (1991–2002; 2014–), and Dirty South duo OutKast (1991–2006; 2014–). Swizz Beatz has worked with rap mainstays such as Busta Rhymes, Eve (Eve Jihan Jeffers, 1978–), and Jay-Z. As a boy, he moved to Atlanta to live with two of his uncles who had established Ruff Ryders Entertainment, and in 2001 he created Full Surface Records. TLC included rapper Left Eye (Lisa Nicole Lopes, 1971–2002) and produced four Hot 100 No. 1 songs. RIAA diamond-certified OutKast (1991–2006; 2014–) fused hip hop with funk, psychedelic music, drum and bass, electronica, techno/industrial hip hop, R&B, and gospel. It included star rappers André 3000 (André Lauren Benjamin, 1975–) and Big Boi (Antwan André Patton, 1975–). Last but not least, Atlanta is home to one of hip hop's most sought after agents, Wendy Day (1962–).

THE MIDWEST

Although it has produced notable hip hop music and rappers, the Midwest has produced few influential rap movements or record labels. While Chicago is home to jazz and funk composer Herbie Hancock (Herbert Jeffrey Hancock, 1940–), spoken-word artist Gil Scott-Heron, female rapper Da Brat (Shawntae Harris, 1974–), and more recent popular rappers like Chance the Rapper (Chancellor Jonathan Bennett, 1993–) and Common (Lonnie Rashid Lynn Jr., 1972–), it has lagged behind other urban areas in its rap scene. Hancock's most famous connection to hip hop is his hit song "Rockit" (1983), which featured early turntablism. Scott-Heron, an influential jazz poet, is in many respects a rapper prototype. Da Brat had a certified platinum album and single. Common became known for his verbose and socially conscious lyricism, and Chance the Rapper broke music industry barriers with his multimillion-selling self-released mixtape *Coloring Book* (2016).

Other Midwest cities that contributed to hip hop were Indianapolis, St. Louis, Detroit, Cleveland, and Kansas City. Indianapolis-based Babyface (Kenneth Brian Edmonds, 1959–) is an eleven-time Grammy winner known for working with L.A. Reid (Antonio Marquis Reid, 1955–) and ultimately cofounding Edmonds Entertainment (a.k.a. Babyface Entertainment). Akon (Aliaune Badara Thiam, 1973–) is a Senegalese American from St. Louis whose album *Konvicted* (2006) was certified triple platinum. Detroit's claim to fame is that it is the adopted home of Eminem (Marshall Bruce Mathers III, 1972–) and his rap crew D12 (1996–). A native of St. Louis, Eminem began with D12 but went on to become one of the world's top-selling solo rappers, with six No. 1 solo studio albums on the Billboard 200. He is also the founder of New York's Shady Records (1999–). Detroit can also claim producer J Dilla (James Dewitt Yancey, 1974–2006), known for working with benchmark artists like A Tribe Called Quest, De La Soul, Busta Rhymes, Common, Erykah Badu (Erica Abi Wright, 1971–), the Roots, and the Pharcyde (1989–).

Arguably, however, the biggest contribution to rap from the Midwest was the chopper (i.e., rapid) style of delivery. It began in the 1980s in urban areas like Cleveland, Chicago, and Kansas City. By the early 1990s, it had spread to California with the Project Blowed movement (1994–), led by Aceyalone and his Freestyle Fellowship. Early practitioners included the Dayton Family (1993–) from Flint, Michigan, and Chicago's Twista (Carl Terrell Mitchell, 1973–), although Cleveland's Bone Thugs-N-Harmony (1991–) was by far the best known of the early practitioners of chopper. The style became even more popular when Kansas City underground rapper/songwriter Tech N9ne (Aaron Dontez Yates, 1971–) released a number of chopper-heavy collaborative singles.

CHAPTER 2

Must-Hear Music

ACEYALONE: "THE GUIDELINES"
(SEE GIL SCOTT-HERON AND ACEYALONE)

BEASTIE BOYS

Beastie Boys (1980–2012), the name being a backronym of Boys Entering Anarchic States Toward Internal Excellence, were a 1980s New York City rap and hard rock phenomenon. The band consisted of a trio of rapper musicians, drummer Mike D (Michael Diamond, 1965–), guitarist Ad-Rock (Adam Horovitz, 1966–), and bassist MCA (Adam Yauch, 1964–2012), as well as DJs Mix Master Mike (Michael Schwartz, 1970–) and Eric Bobo (Eric Correa, 1968–) occasionally. Beastie Boys became a crossover success, approaching iconographic status and leading to rap's being accepted by a wider (and white) audience. Like many successful East Coast rap acts, Beastie Boys worked with producer Rick Rubin at Def Jam Records. The trio's debut studio album *Licensed to Ill* (Def Jam, 1986) achieved diamond status, and subsequent albums (all on Capitol Records)—*Ill Communication* (1994), *Hello Nasty* (1998), and *To the 5 Boroughs* (2004)—went to No. 1 on the Billboard 200, all this despite only moderate singles success on the Billboard Hot 100 and the Hot R&B/Hip Hop Songs charts.

The Beastie Boys' music, like that of Public Enemy (1982–), differed from early rap in that it was informed by typical rock music instrumentation and aesthetics—the band started as a hardcore punk quartet. Beastie Boys' lyrics differed from other rap groups because the songs' kitschy humor and sophomoric lyrics were juxtaposed against worldly references and clever insights about the local scene. Generally, Beastie

16   Listen to Rap!

Boys rap about their specific environs—songs reference local (usually Brooklyn) establishments and New Yorker sensibilities.

The trio's early albums, *Licensed to Ill, Paul's Boutique* (Capitol, 1989), and *Check Your Head* (Capitol, 1992), established its thematic concerns and sound. *Licensed to Ill* opens with "Rhymin' & Stealin'," which uses piracy as a metaphor for rap music, at the time a new sound based on rhythmic spoken word and sampling. What is immediately noticeable is the band's unique sound: heavy bass kick drum rotated with snare, hard rock–style guitar, heavy electric bass, and three rappers with various vocal ranges, from baritone to tenor, raspy and throaty to nasally and boyish. The three didn't just take turns on verses. They harmonized on lines and chants, traded off lyrics in the middle of lines, and vocalized grunts and other sounds (usually in conjunction with a turntablist) for emphasis—not only on phrase endings but also in the middle of lines, creating unexpected points of interest. Although they were adapting rap to their own purposes, the trio did use typical elements such as turntablism, heard in the absurdist "The New Style." The album's breakouts were the party anthem "Fight for Your Right," the drinking song "Brass Monkey," and the sex song "She's Crafty." "Fight for Your Right," also known as "Fight for Your Right (to Party)," reached No. 7 on the Billboard Hot 100, becoming their most successful chart single. "Brass Monkey," with its offbeat sax ostinato, prefigured Macklemore and Professor Elemental. "She's Crafty" samples a guitar ostinato from Led Zeppelin's "The Ocean" and includes an extended outro that showcases Mike D's drumming.

Paul's Boutique produced only two singles, "Hey Ladies" and "Shadrach," while *Check Your Head* spawned "Pass the Mic," "So What'cha Want," "Jimmy James," "Gratitude," "Professor Booty," and "Something's Got to Give," with only "So What'cha Want" making it into the Hot 100. *Paul's Boutique* showed the band playing with a funkier, more danceable sound, as in "Shake Your Rump," "Johnny Ryall," "High Plains Drifter," and "Hey Ladies," with "Johnny Ryall" incorporating surf guitar and "Hey Ladies" incorporating Caribbean percussion. *Paul's Boutique* also includes the gimmick song "The Sounds of Science," whose first half is offbeat classic dancehall and second half is classic rock, using Beatles samples (among others) from "Back in the U.S.S.R.," "Sgt. Pepper's Lonely Hearts Club Band," and "When I'm Sixty-Four." *Check Your Head* begins with the funk-based "Jimmy James," which contains the trio's best pre–Mix Master Mike DJing. As a whole, the album returns to the hard rock origins of the trio, with songs like "Gratitude" (which includes a grinding prog-rock bass), "So What'cha Want" and

"Stand Together" (which both use distorted rock vocal effects), "Time for Livin'" (which contains punk elements), and "Pow" and "Namaste" (which are done jazz rock fusion style).

Artistically, the trio turned a corner with *Ill Communication*. The album begins with "Sure Shot," which contains a jazz flute intro, and its ostinato continues throughout the song, set against a snare and cymbal beat (eventually joined by turntable), more evidence that the trio was branching out musically during its heyday. More jazz flute (which would also be used prominently in "Song for Junior" and "Picture This" off of *Hello Nasty*, where it is paired with vibes and Brazilian-style singing, respectively) can be heard in "Flute Loop," and the instrumental "Eugene's Lament" contains dissonant violin (both bowed and plucked) and jazz guitar; jazz guitar also informs "Shambala." Other jazz and funk-infused songs include the bass-heavy braggadocio "Root Down" and the instrumental "Sabrosa" (which combines funk with a Latin beat). The album also includes guitar-heavy, punk-infused songs such as the satiric "Tough Guy," the aggressive declaration of war against critics, "Sabotage," and the hardcore punk "Heart Attack Man." Rock beats and rock-style vocal distortion can be heard in the aforementioned "Sabotage," the skills boast "B-Boys Makin' with the Freak Freak," and the sociopolitical, environmental statement "The Update." The album's gimmick/comic songs include "Get It Together," and Buddhist monk chanting can be heard in "Bodhisattva Vow."

For *Hello Nasty*, Beastie Boys had the services of Mix Master Mike on turntable and Eric Bobo on percussion. The album's opening song, the skills braggadocio "Super Disco Breakin'," uses a synthesizer ostinato set against a jazz drumbeat, with a peppering of 808 drums and sound effects such as sirens and crowd noises. The album's standout songs, "The Move," "Intergalactic," and "The Grasshopper Unit (Keep Movin')" feature turntablism, a bass kick and snare drum beat, sub-bass, vocalizations created with hiccups and reverb, vocal processing to create a robot voice, dramatic strings, guitar with wah pedal, harpsichord, and a Chicano pop sample in Spanish. "Body Movin'" is a drum and bass, danceable rhythm guitar–based (with wah pedal) party anthem that features a percussive vocal repetition (the phrase "Body movin', body movin'/A1 sound, and the sound's so soothing") used to contrast the heavy bass drum, creating part of the song's beat. The diss track "Just a Test" stands out for the trio's rapping, as they alternate at the phrase level and harmonize the end of phrases. As with *Ill Communication*, *Hello Nasty* contains rock-infused songs such as the absurdist "Remote Control," the cynical and melancholic "Song for the Man," "And Me,"

18 Listen to Rap!

and "I Don't Know" (which all feature singing rather than rapping and sound like the Stone Roses). Songs such as the skills braggadocio "Puttin' Shame in Your Game" feature jazz fusion instrumentation, in this case a grand piano ostinato, set against a bass kick beat and Mix Master Mike's scratching. The instrumental "Sneakin' out the Hospital" and the old-school rap "Three MC's and One DJ" showcase Mix Master Mike's beat-making and turntablism, and the philosophical "Flowin' Prose," lyrically the best song on the album, showcases MCA's rapping, delivered here as a backgrounded cross between rap, talk-singing, and chanting.

To the 5 Boroughs opens with the party anthem (and announcement that the trio has come out of retirement after a six-year hiatus), "Ch-Check It Out," a song that aggressively starts out with a synthesizer stinger, which is soon combined with a snare and bass kick beat in verses. Refrains feature guitars and a more rapid snare and tom drum beat. Skill bragging songs include "Rhyme the Rhyme Well," which is informed by power synth chords and a constant 808 drum beat; "Triple Trouble," which has Caribbean and Latin percussion set against a funk bass and funk drum beat and turntable (and the trio doing fake British accents); and "Oh Word?," which offers power synth chord stingers against bass kick, 808, a keyboard ostinato that sounds like an arp or sine wave, and vocals processed to sound like Alvin and the Chipmunks. Most of the album's songs are more rap than funk or rock influenced, with the notable exception of "An Open Letter to NYC" (rock) and "Crawlspace" (funk). Two of the trio's protest songs, "Right Right Now Now" and "Time to Build," contain harpsichord and chanting, a bass kick and snare, grand piano, synthesizer beats (including a tabla voice), 808 drums, vocal hiccups, and turntable. The former has a mellow beat against which the trio raps both individually and in harmony, while the latter has a frenetic energy that builds throughout the song. "That's It That's All" protests the George W. Bush White House. As with most of their albums, *To the 5 Boroughs* contains gimmick songs, "Hey F— You" and "Shazam." "Hey F— You" has a beat created by bass kick drum, 808, and thin-sounding plucked ukulele or four string guitar ostinato. The diss song "Shazam" has backgrounded vocals, with a beat created by turntable, 808 drum, sub-bass, and oddball vocalizations. Mix Master Mike is showcased on the bass-heavy "We Got The."

Beastie Boys influenced Eminem and Rage Against the Machine (1991–2000; 2007–11). The trio eventually started its own Capitol subsidiary label, Grand Royal (1992–2001), which produced two of its No. 1 albums, and it created a Los Angeles–based clothing line called

X-Large (1991–). In 2012, Beastie Boys (and Mix Master Mike) were inducted into the Rock & Roll Hall of Fame.

BIG DADDY KANE AND DOUG E. FRESH AND THE GET FRESH CREW: "SMOOTH OPERATOR" AND "LA DI DA DI" (*IT'S A BIG DADDY THING*, COLD CHILLIN', 1989, AND B-SIDE SINGLE, REALITY, 1985)

Among old-school rappers from the 1970s, two MCs stand out for both their lyrical abilities and their flow. Brooklyn's Big Daddy Kane (Antonio Hardy, 1968–), a rapper since the age of fourteen who was also a record producer, actor, and model, and London's Slick Rick (Richard Martin Lloyd Walters, 1965–), known for his storytelling raps, his use of multiple character voices, his narrative structures, and his quick wit. Big Daddy Kane started as a member of the rap collective the Juice Crew All-Stars (a.k.a. Juice Crew, 1983–91), along with rapper and beatboxer Biz Markie (Marcel Theo Hall, 1964–). He eventually earned the reputation as a skilled MC, one able to syncopate over faster hip hop beats to become a pioneer of fast rapping (which eventually led to chopper style). His style of rap is hard-edged, urban, but with a touch of dry wit, including clever wordplay, brilliant satire, unexpected and highly literate similes, and good-natured boasting. More than any other rapper, Big Daddy Kane shows the influence of James Brown's performance style, including the use of heavy funk rhythms (with liberal use of rhythm guitar), break beats (he dances in most of his videos), and metatextual lines. Slick Rick was known for his smooth, melodic sound, use of British English (from Received Pronunciation to vernacular), and story adventures. His initial success was as MC Ricky D in Barbadian-American beatboxer, rapper, and producer Doug E. Fresh's (Douglas E. Davis, 1966–) Get Fresh Crew (1985–2003).

Big Daddy Kane wrote for the Juice Crew, which included rap pioneers like Roxanne Shanté and Kurtis Blow. In 1987, he debuted with the underground hit single "Raw." His debut album *Long Live the Kane* (1988) featured the hit "Ain't No Half Steppin'." His second and most commercially successful album was *It's a Big Daddy Thing* (1989), which included Hot R&B/Hip Hop/Rap Songs and Hot Rap Songs chart crossover single hits like "I Get the Job Done" (Nos. 27 and 9), "Cause I Can Do It Right" (Nos. 22 and 4), and "Smooth Operator" (Nos. 11 and 1, as well as reaching No. 65 on the U.K. singles chart). "Smooth Operator," a skills braggadocio, begins with a mid-tempo 4/4 beat and the sound of a female voice, slightly harmonized with itself to sound sexy, talk-singing the phrase "I'm gonna give it to ya." Big Daddy Kane chimes in, his rap voice a booming baritone. Although he is technically an old-school rapper, within four lines it is apparent that he is experimenting with the style: he uses interior rhyme, enjambment, and multiple rhymes—skills associated with the second generation of rappers. The instrumentation against which he raps is minimal—a heavy bass and 4/4 simple drum beat, with brass and keyboard, and an occasional saxophone ostinato, introduced after thirty seconds, with vibes added in the song's final verse. Unlike most rap songs, "Smooth Operator" has an instrumental refrain, which gives the song a danceable groove.

The song's lyrics brag of Big Daddy Kane's rap skills, as well as his sexual prowess. Its first verse establishes Kane as a rap chameleon, capable of great variety and of changing a line on a dime. He packs each verse full of cleverly juxtaposed pop culture references that come at the listener so quickly that the song requires multiple hearings. Verse two takes on other rappers, who are characterized as being wild, indicating their rhymes are out of control and lack style. Big Daddy Kane also disses these rappers for "fronting," or pretending. The third verse is about his ability to seduce and subdue any woman with his style. The song's outro is the bass groove and the female voices heard in the intro leading to an old-school sign-off by Big Daddy Kane.

As part of Doug E. Fresh and the Get Fresh Crew, Slick Rick (as MC Ricky D) recorded "La Di Da Di" as the B-side to the crew's first single, "The Show" (1985), which achieved RIAA gold certification. "La Di Da Di" features both Slick Rick's storytelling in rhyme as well as Doug E. Fresh's beatboxing. The song—basically a freestyle narrative—gained cult popularity, went platinum, and caused Slick Rick to become one of the most sampled rappers in history. Part of the song's appeal was Slick Rick himself—at age eighteen months, he was blinded in the right eye by a flying piece of glass from a broken window, so he wore an eye patch, which along with his proper British accent, became his trademark. In "La Di Da Di," he combines his careful articulation of words with a nasal delivery, elongating words to emphasize them—this delivery style would later influence Humpty Hump (a.k.a. Shock G) of Digital Underground.

"La Di Da Di" begins sparsely, with only Doug E. Fresh's minimalist beatboxing while Slick Rick serves as master of ceremony, explaining to listeners, whom he addresses formally as ladies and gentlemen, what they are about to hear. In his extended intro (forty-seven seconds long), he then goes on to both diss other rappers and brag about the duo's skills, while Doug E. Fresh continues to slowly build up his beatboxing, now including three sounds—a plosive-based beat made with his mouth, a castanet sound he makes with his teeth, and a laser sound he makes by putting the mic up to his throat. He continues to combine these three as Slick Rick leads into the song, clearly pointing out where it begins in metatextual lyrics ("it goes a little something like this"). He cues Doug E. Fresh, at which point the beatboxing becomes more frenetic and aggressive, concentrating more on the plosives, which are now voiced at a deeper register to give the song a sense of bass; at this point and throughout the song, the beatboxing becomes more regular and predictable so that Slick Rick can rap against it. In a second brief intro, the absurdist phrase "la di da di" is repeated four times, with varying intonation on each syllable, finally leading to the verse, which begins Slick Rick's story about having two women, one much older than he, fight over him. Before he goes into the story, however, he establishes that he and Doug E. Fresh are innocuous, perhaps in a bid to soothe over early white rap audiences, who may have associated rap music with urban problems. He specifically points out that they are just two men who want to entertain on two microphones and, at worst, they enjoy partying.

The second verse begins the narration of the events that led up to the fight between two women. It is filled with images of the mundane, Slick Rick's waking up, preparing himself for his day in the bathroom (with comic moments such as talking conceitedly to his mirror and brushing his gold teeth), and a brief conversation with his mother as he walks out the door. He continues to use his highly articulated but nasal voice, often using a lilt to make the words sound more comical. His rap is straightforward old-school style, with end-rhymed lines, but he creates some variety through call-and-response with Doug E. Fresh and by breaking into song on two occasions, sampling A Taste of Honey's "Sukiyaki" (1981), as well as pretend crying at one point. The song ends with Slick Rick's breaking the hearts of both women, being particularly insulting toward the older one. This leads to a brief beatboxing outro by Doug E. Fresh.

Big Daddy Kane has appeared on tracks with R&B legends like Patti LaBelle and Quincy Jones. In 1990, he won the Grammy for Best Rap Performance by a Duo with Jones. He collaborated with Tupac Shakur and toured with Jay-Z, whom he had helped early in Jay-Z's (previously JZ) career by bringing him out to freestyle while he made wardrobe changes. His later albums, such as *Taste of Chocolate* (1990), *Prince of Darkness* (1991), *Looks Like a Job For. . .* (1993), *Daddy's Home* (1994), and *Veteranz Day* (1997), did not see commercial success. In the 2000s, he collaborated with A Tribe Called Quest, but this did little to revitalize his career. However, he did not give up touring. His hip hop dress style influenced a number of hip hop trends, such as high-top fades, velour suits, gold medallions, heavy chains, fedoras, and four-finger rings.

In 1988, Slick Rick released his solo debut studio album *The Great Adventures of Slick Rick* with Def Jam Recordings (1983–). The album peaked at No. 31 on the Billboard 200 and No. 1 on Billboard's R&B/Hip Hop Albums charts. Generally, his studio solo albums had varying success, due to various personal problems, a PCP addiction, being committed to a mental ward, a prison sentence resulting from a gunfight with his cousin, and immigration issues that led to threats of deportation. In 2008, New York governor David Paterson granted him a full and unconditional pardon, and in 2016 he was granted U.S. citizenship. *The Art of Storytelling*, his 1999 album, featured artists who had been inspired by him, such as Nas and Snoop Dogg.

BIG PUN

Big Pun (Christopher Lee Rios, 1971–2000), also known as Big Punisher, makes just about every rap fan's and hip hop scholar's list of top ten rappers, despite a very brief career cut short by his death due to heart failure. A Bronx-based Puerto Rican wordsmith known for his mastery of alliteration, rhyming (interior and exterior), wordplay, and pop culture references, he was unmatched for his breathless delivery, needing only minimal pauses to breathe, resulting in longer lyrical lines.

His 1998 solo debut album featured salsa beats, heavy drum, piano, and electric guitar–based tunes, achieving a variety not often seen in 1990s rap. His second solo album, *Yeeeah Baby* (Loud Records, 2000), had to be completed after his death. A posthumous compilation album, *Endangered Species* (Loud Records, 2001) features both hits and previously unreleased material, as well as remixes. It peaked at No. 7 on the Billboard 200. In 2000, Big Pun failed to make a scheduled performance on *Saturday Night Live* due to health issues. Two days later, he suffered a fatal heart attack. His biggest hit was a featured appearance on "From N.Y. to N.O." (1999), a song by New Orleans rapper Mr. Serv-On, which reached No. 20 on the Billboard Hot 100 and No. 3 on the Hot Rap Tracks chart. His biggest solo hit, "Still Not a Player," reached No. 13 on Billboard's Hot Rap chart and No. 24 on the Hot 100. His "I'm Not a Player" had reached No. 3 on the rap chart.

With his debut album, Grammy-nominated *Capital Punishment* (Loud Records, 1998), which reached No. 1 on the Top R&B/Hip Hop Albums chart and No. 5 on the Billboard 200, Big Pun became the first Latino solo rapper to have an album certified multiplatinum. It begins with a spoken-word dialogue by two young unidentified boys, one of whom proclaims that Big Pun is going to take down all other rappers. The first musical notes of track one, "Beware," produced by JuJu (Jerry Tineo, 1968–), are those of a guitar, with two notes played on one string (the second allowed to ring) to create a sparse treble texture, which is joined after a few measures by a heavy bass and synth. A voice reminds listeners they've been given a fair warning, and then Big Pun's rap explodes into the foreground, his first fifteen lines being rapped almost breathlessly in twenty-seven seconds (only four quick breaths are taken during this time), with little vocal processing other than a wet echo, and only occasional doubling to emphasize certain phrases. "Beware" sets the stage for Big Pun's assertion of dominance, as it is a braggadocio song featuring a dazzling array of pop culture references. For example, the first verse references the film *Carlito's Way*, James Brown's "Say It Loud—I'm Black and I'm Proud" (1968), *The Smurfs*, and rapper Freddie Foxxx. Such lyrical showmanship establishes his dominance as a lyricist, and he goes so far as to state that fans better believe the truth of this assertion as if it came from God. Big Pun's ability to deliver lengthy, breathless lines chopper style is later made even more clear in "Fast Money," the album's second-to-last track.

Similarly, the gangsta rap song "You Ain't a Killer" strings pop culture references together effortlessly, with allusions to Charles Manson, Anita Baker, Prince, and John Madden, to name a few. Other songs attest to the musical brilliance of the album as a whole. The funk-inspired bragging song "Super Lyrical," produced by Rockwilder (Dana Stinson, 1971–), kicks off with an ominous, deeply resonant drum (either a timpani or a bodhran), which is joined by a virtual instrument sub-bass voice, both set against a sparse guitar ostinato; these set the stage for a rap about Big Pun's "murderous rap verbal attack" that will break other rappers. Set against this instrumentation, Big Pun uses interior and exterior rhyme over a series of lines, at one point using difficult three-syllable rhymes. For example, the word "attack," introduced in line one, is rhymed for the next five lines, the sixth line introducing a playful double rhyme, with the words "madness" and "on," which are rhymed for three subsequent lines. Other bragging rights songs include "The Dream Shatterer," an aggressive, breathless rap that features a shawm (an Indian woodwind) ostinato and "Caribbean Connection," which features Wyclef Jean and fuses hip hop with Jamaican rhythms and Latin percussion, along with relentless punning and wordplay. Clever instrumentation and wordplay can also be heard in the bragging songs "You Came Up" and "Tres Leches (Triboro Trilogy)."

The album's skits, which are sparse, typically introduce songs. The spoken-word sex-themed "Taster's Choice" (about a threesome) introduces "Still Not a Player," which features Fat Joe (Joseph Antonio Cartagena, 1970–), Big Pun's Bronx-based mentor. This R&B combined urban rap hit uses humor to decry the life of the player (rolling with an entourage) while bragging that celebrity brings with it lots of money, fine cars, and free sex with a variety of high-class women. Like "I'm Not a Player" (which samples the O'Jays), the song establishes Big Pun's skills when it comes to sexually satisfying women. Though instrumentally predictable, in its outro the song introduces a clever twist in the form of drum sticks being played against one another in a tap dance shuffle rhythm. The theme of gangster glamour is also found in "Glamour Life," which features an orchestral string ostinato; the song is a standout for its use of interior rhyme.

In a similar vein, the skit "Pakinamac Pt. I," in which Big Pun rescues a teen from a drug lord, introduces the ultraviolent "You Ain't a Killer," followed by the second part of the Pakinamac skit, which concludes the violent trilogy comically with an a cappella–musical *Lone Ranger* mash-up. The gangsta rap standout on the album is "Capital Punishment," produced by Trauma (a.k.a. Mike Trauma D, Michael Dewar, n.d.) and Jugrnaut (Collin Dewar, n.d.), which features the same two-note ostinato as "Beware," this time played on a bell-like keyboard voice, giving the song an eerie quality. In contrast to "Glamour Life," here (and in "Boomerang"), Big Pun presents a desolate urban scene where a life of crime is the only way out. The closest thing to a love song on *Capital Punishment* is "Punish Me," which is actually a neo-soul breakup duet about an unfaithful woman.

His platinum follow-up, *Yeeeah Baby*, reached the top spot on the R&B chart and hit No. 3 on the Billboard 200. A sense of humor is much more prevalent here, in both skits and songs (for example, in "Wrong Ones," guest rapper Sunkiss says that Big Pun is "dead, and still killin' s—"). The album is also more concerned with Puerto Rican musical and thematic elements, and it prominently features Puerto Rican American R&B singer Tony Sunshine (Antonio Cruz, 1978–) on many tracks. Though Big Pun's flow is breathless, distinctly missing in some songs are the pronounced breaths that can be heard on *Capital Punishment*, indicating that some songs' lyrics likely had to be pieced together from various sessions due to his untimely death or that he was already showing signs of his heart condition and could not complete as many lines as previously on just one breath, so the lines had to be run together in postproduction. The album begins with an absurdist skit, "The Creation," a dialogue between a mad scientist and his assistant, as the former builds a rapper who combines Big Daddy Kane, Kool G Rap, Rakim the Master, Eddie Murphy, and Michael Jackson—the result being the Punisher, Big Pun, who begins walking heavily and makes a comic failed attempt at articulating "yeah baby" (a sound that also ends the album). This transitions into the bragging song "Watch Those," whose intro includes some metatextuality in the form of Big Pun's repetition of a level check against a heavy synth-based beat, which is soon joined by heavy electric guitar in the song's refrain. In fact, the entire album is full of instrumental surprises, such as a balalaika or mandolin in "We Don't Care" (featuring Cuban Link), a piccolo and virtual instrumentation that sounds like a glockenspiel or xylophone (which contrast heavy bass) in "100%" (which also has birdcalls in its outro), a picked electric bass set against a virtual ektara or tumbi (a single-string Indian instrument) in "Ms. Martin," a virtual accordion, oboe, and tuba (set against scratching) on "You Was Wrong," and the use of boy band and R&B instrumentation (and vocals) in "My D—," an absurdist sexual prowess and entourage loyalty song.

The album's standouts are "Off wit His Head," "It's So Hard," "New York Giants," and "Laughing at You." "Off wit His Head," produced by Just Blaze (Justin Smith, 1978–), begins with synthesized Spanish guitar strings set against a Gregorian chant and hip hop beat; its refrain juxtaposes lyrics about crew/entourage loyalty and images of gangsta violence, rapped against bowed and plucked strings, bells, and dramatic chanting. The outro consists of operatic chanting and singing (the same instrumentation and vocal choices used in the outro to "Wrong Ones"). Younglord (Richard Frierson, 1978–) produced "It's So Hard," a song about jealousy and betrayal (which includes many autobiographical elements such as weight issues and the Grammy Awards). "It's So Hard" is a veritable study of virtual and analog instrument interplay, using 808 drums and a drum kit beat set against a new age keyboard voice and piano bass chords that serve as occasional accents. "New York Giants" involves clever vocal interplay between Big Pun, M.O.P., Lil' Fame, and Billy Danzini over a steady, aggressive keyboard and drum beat, as well as flawless postproduction vocal processing (very likely multitracked), so that at any given time, a line can surprise with heavy echo, reverb, or hiccup effects. Produced by DJ Ogee (Gary S. Scott, n.d.), "Laughing at You," a bragging/revenge song, features elaborate vocal interplay between Big Pun and Tony Sunshine, as well as an extremely clever adaptation of Simple Minds' "Don't You Forget About Me" (1985).

Big Pun began writing rap songs as a teen and formed an underground rap group. He got his recording start with a guest appearance on the second album by Fat Joe, *Jealous One's Envy* (1995). In 1997, Big Pun signed with New York City's Loud Records (1991–). He also became a member of Fat Joe's Terror Squad (1998–2009), but Terror Squad released only one album. Coming from a turbulent childhood and homelessness, Big Pun struggled with depression and an eating disorder; by age twenty-one he weighed 300 pounds. He died of a heart attack at age twenty-nine, having produced only two albums but having appeared about a dozen times on other hip hop artists' recordings. At the time, he weighed 698 pounds. A tribute documentary film, *Big Pun: The Legacy*, was released in 2009.

BIRDMAN, DRAKE, AND LIL WAYNE: "MONEY TO BLOW" AND "4 MY TOWN (PLAY BALL)" (*PRICELE$$*, CASH MONEY, 2009)

Cash Money Records cofounder Birdman (Bryan Christopher Brooks, 1969–) released his eponymous debut album in 2002. Later albums included 2009's *Pricele$$*, which went to No. 33 on the Billboard 200 and hit the Top Ten on both the Top R&B/Hip Hop Albums (No. 6) and Top Rap Albums (No. 3) charts. A frequent collaborator with rappers such as Rick Ross, Mick Maine, and Lil Wayne, Birdman also sometimes collaborated with Drake, and *Pricele$$* includes two tracks, "Money to Blow" and its planned sequel, "4 My Town (Play Ball)," on which he worked with both Lil Wayne and Drake. Lil Wayne's diverse rap flow (from laid-back, slow, and measured to chopper style) allows him to complement other rappers, which is apparent on the two songs.

"Money to Blow" is a bling braggadocio track as well as an expression of record label pride. Its verses are a list of what Drake (verse one), Birdman (verse two), and Lil Wayne (verse three) can afford to buy now that they have taken the rap world by storm with their Cash Money and Young Money record labels. The song marks one of the few times that the three collaborate equally on a song (as opposed to being featured on each other's tracks). In his verse, Drake raps about getting free champagne at any nightclub and being able to buy expensive cars, adding that his haters need to leave him alone because his lyrics are full of catchy hooks and clever rhymes. Birdman brags about his label's RIAA certifications and drops upscale brand names like Gucci, Lamborghini, Bentley, Cartier, Ferrari, and Mercedes, cleverly referring to diamonds in the same verse that he brags about certifications. Lil Wayne brags about his ability to buy the best champagne and marijuana, adding that with money, he has also gained power.

Drake begins the song, and the intro features spoken word (Drake, using his deepest register and no auto-tuning) against the song's main keyboard chord-based ostinato, claps, and bass kick drum, with occasional metal-on-metal percussion. Once Drake begins singing, he moves into his highest register, and his voice is highly auto-tuned. As verse one begins, a second keyboard voice, which sounds slightly like an arp, is introduced. Because both keyboards play melodies in the treble range, the song has an airy or dreamlike quality, but the energy is raised in the middle of the verse, when a whirring synthesizer effect introduces an 808 drum, which plays against the bass kick. The whirring effect introduces the refrain, which Drake sings against all the keyboard and drum effects simultaneously, creating a barrage of sound that stands in contrast to the more minimalist and ethereal verses. Birdman, who has a deeper voice than Drake and a more pronounced Southern accent, raps in a more staccato style, his words less carefully articulated and his voice less auto-tuned than either Drake's or Lil Wayne's. Synthesizer power chords are introduced midway through his verse, and an auto-tuned (to sound bass baritone) speaking voice that serves as counterpoint to a few of his lines is also introduced, creating bass effects to complement the more trebly keyboard voices and Lil Wayne's backgrounded vocalizations, which appear near the end of the verse. The hook is repeated before Lil Wayne takes up his verse, his voice more raspy than Drake's or Birdman's and his rapping high-pitched and boyish sounding, as well as highly auto-tuned. The instrumentation against which he sings is a repetition of that in verse one. The hook then returns, this time with more spoken-word vocalizations (of the hype man type) that serve as counter to Drake's singing, and the refrain serves as the song's outro in the form of a slow fade-out. The track differs from many rap songs in that, it utilizes the typical "oh oh oh" vocalization of rock music in its sung sections, giving it a more pop feel.

"4 My Town (Play Ball)," which borrows a verse from a Drake track that uses baseball as its extended metaphor, is similar in theme to "Money to Blow" in that, it brags about both the rappers' skills and their money. In Lil Wayne's verse, he expresses pride in the Cash Money label, while in Drake's verse, pride is expressed in being part of a rap entourage, and in Birdman's verse it's in being part of a city like New Orleans. In the refrain and in his verse (the first one), Drake drops brand names such as Aston Martin, Ace of Spades (champagne), and Opus One (wine), and he brags about his stardom, noting that some of his fans express their love for him in almost religious terms. Birdman, who takes the second verse, brags about his money, adding that he has stayed humble because he knows finances can dry up any time, and he mentions Dom Perignon, Marc Jacobs (clothing), and Bentley as well as his ability to buy the best marijuana. In verse three, Lil Wayne brags about his sexual prowess and his thug status. In the song's hook, the ability the three have to make women do anything because they have money is noted.

The track begins with the sound of a bat hitting a ball, crowd noises, and an umpire yelling "play ball," followed by Birdman's spoken-word introduction, in which he counts his blessings, both material and nonmaterial. In contrast to "Money to Blow," synth-created bass power chords give the song a more solid and dramatic feel; these chords complement the main keyboard voice (likely an accordion or similar voice), playing a mid-range oscillating ostinato. The drum beat is snare-based, accompanied intermittently by a rapid-paced, almost rattling synth-produced 808 drum voice. Drake raps first in the song's hook. Using his deepest register (against the power chords and snare drum beat), he raps eight lines that revolve around the word "mound," which is rhymed in seven of the lines. His flow is a speedy auto-tuned monotone, double-tracked, creating a breathless quality between lines (lines begin as soon as previous lines end, with little discernible pause). He raps against the mid-range keyboard voice and drum beat. Against the same instrumentation, with a sudden foregrounding of the 808, Drake also raps the first verse, in his highest register, without auto-tuning, with vocalizations supplied by Birdman. With little pause between verses, Birdman takes up the rap in verse two as the drums disappear and the power chords return, his flow old-school (singsong). He continues this as drums are reintroduced, switching over to a staccato flow of multisyllabic words and phrases when the synthesizer disappears, leaving only his vocals and the drum beat. Toward the end of his verse, the synth power chords return, and an 808 drum is introduced. The hook returns, leading to Lil Wayne's verse, his voice boyish and not auto-tuned. The instrumentation mirrors that of the first verse, and his rap flow is breathless like Drake's but with pronounced pauses between lines. Midway through his verse, the song's energy picks up, and reverb is introduced into his vocals. As he nears the end of his verse, all instrumentation except the drum beat and a simple keyboard ostinato disappear, giving his last few lines an a cappella feel. This leads to the final instance of the hook/refrain, with more pronounced hype man vocalizations by Birdman, and then to a quick fade-out.

Besides his solo projects, Birdman also released albums as part of the duo Big Tymers (1993–2005) (with producer Mannie Fresh) and as part of the collaborative Rich Gang (2013–14). Birdman and Lil Wayne created Young Money Cash Money Billionaires (YMCMB) by combining their interests in Cash Money Records and Young Money Entertainment. Lil Wayne, who started as a teen in the duo the B.G.'z (1995–96) with fellow New Orleans rapper B.G./Lil Doogie (Christopher Noel Dorsey, 1980–) and later the rap crew Hot Boys (1997–2003), has gone on to become one of the best-selling musicians of all time, surpassing Elvis Presley's record for male artist with the most songs on the Billboard Hot 100. His album *Tha Carter IV* (2011) broke records for number of iTunes downloads, reached No. 1 on the Billboard 200, and was certified double platinum after just two months. In 2005, the same year he founded his own imprint, Young Money Entertainment, Lil Wayne was named the CEO of Cash Money Records, which under his leadership has released a number of commercially successful albums, including Drake's *Thank Me Later* (2010) and Nicki Minaj's *Pink Friday: Roman Reloaded* (2012).

BLONDIE: "RAPTURE" (SEE THE SUGARHILL GANG AND BLONDIE)

BONE THUGS-N-HARMONY: *THE ART OF WAR* (RUTHLESS RECORDS, 1995)

Cleveland, Ohio, home of the Rock & Roll Hall of Fame, is generally not known for its rap scene. However, it did produce one of the first rap bands of note in Bone Thugs-N-Harmony (BTNH), consisting of rappers Bizzy Bone (Bryon Anthony McCane II, 1976–), Wish Bone (Charles C. Scruggs Jr., 1974–), Krayzie Bone (Anthony Henderson, 1973–), and brothers Layzie Bone (Steven Howse, 1974–) and Flesh-n-Bone (Stanley Howse, 1973–). After a debut album (as B.O.N.E. Enterpri$e) on the Stoney Burke label, the rap crew was signed by Eazy-E (Eric Lynn Wright, 1964–95) to Ruthless Records in late 1993, producing in 1994 the gangsta rap EP *Creepin on ah Come Up*, which reached No. 12 on the Billboard 200 and was certified four times platinum. It was BTNH's first collaboration with newcomer producer DJ U-Neek (Tim Middleton, 1969–), who would go on to craft the sound of their next two albums, which featured typical gangsta-themed songs but also included a rap flow that was different from their peers: melodic, close harmonies and rap (usually at a breakneck pace) that bordered often on talk-singing and singing.

BTNH's next two studio albums, *E. 1999 Eternal* (1995) and *The Art of War* (1997), both on Ruthless Records, contained lyrics that revolved around the band members' neighborhood, the St. Clair Avenue and E. 99th Street corner in Cleveland. Both albums would reach No. 1 on the Billboard 200 and be certified multiplatinum as well, the former six-times platinum. The two albums produced two of the three Top Ten hits (and the only No. 1) that the band would land on the Billboard Hot 100, Grammy-winner "Tha Crossroads" (*E. 1999 Eternal*, No. 1) and "Look into My Eyes" (*The Art of War*, No. 4). The other Top Ten hit was "I Tried" (No. 6) from the 2007 album *Strength and Loyalty*. *E. 1999 Eternal*, named after a Cleveland eastside street and Eazy-E's compilation album *Eternal E.* (1995) as a show of respect after his death, included two singles that reached the Top Ten of the Hot Rap Tracks chart, "1st of tha Month" (No. 4) and "Tha Crossroads" (No. 1). DJ U-Neek based most of the tracks around rumbling piano chords, mellotron, and synthesizer-based strings.

The Art of War, produced by DJ U-Neek, focused more on spirituality and family. Despite its violent imagery, the album had an ambient, mellow sound. Two of its singles made it into the Top Ten of the Hot Rap Tracks chart, "Look into My Eyes" (No. 2) and "If I Could Teach the World" (No. 3). The album showcased each rapper's unique style. Bizzy Bone raps in his highest range, and effects were used to make his voice sound even higher, his flow so fast and breathless and full of enjambment that most lines are unintelligible. Krayzie Bone, his voice a baritone and his words carefully articulated, has a rap flow similar to that of Busta Rhymes as he speeds through the first three-fourths of a line but slows down for the final few words and pronounced phase endings. Layzie Bone has the most boyish of the rap crew's voices, his range slightly higher than Bizzy Bone's, with no effects needed to make him sound higher. While he articulates his lines carefully, his chopper flow is consistent but breathless, with lots of enjambment. He also at times sings using a funk delivery. Wish Bone both raps (in his highest range, a tenor) and uses funk-style singing (as a baritone), with very little vocal effects used other than multitracking.

The album's intro, "Retaliation," is a skills brag rap that challenges the group's critics, using the metaphor of war. Indicative of the oddball creativity introduced by DJ U-Neek into BTNH's songs, it begins with the sound of martial drums and soldiers marching and chanting. This is interrupted by DJ U-Neek's distorted voice (to sound robotic and bass) that announces the return of BTNH and then laughs manically as screams and gunshots are heard. The song's sung lyrics by DJ U-Neek and Layzie Bone are accompanied by a keyboard ostinato that references the *Halloween* theme song (a later keyboard voice references

"Tubular Bells"), along with heavy bass kick, and electric bass. "Handle the Vibe" continues the thematic concern with rappers who attempt to emulate BTNH's style, calling them out, threatening them, and using violent imagery. It features heavy bass and claps, snare, hi-hat, and ride cymbal (and later synthesizer voices, including strings and bells), and a sung hook by Krayzie Bone, whose voice is multitracked and harmonized. Verses are rapped by Bizzy, Krayzie, and Layzie Bone, with a sung final verse by Wish Bone. "Mind of a Souljah," which features only Layzie Bone as soloist, is the album's statement of purpose; in fact, it even asks the question of why the band is declaring war on critics, haters, and imitators—he comes to the conclusion that the need to fight is a combination of being born and raised thug, combined with being pushed to the limit by evil people.

Other tracks that fall into the braggadocio/threat category are "Look into My Eyes," "Body Rott," "It's All Mo' Thug," "Ready 4 War," "Wasteland Warriors," "Neighborhood Slang (Interlude)," "U Ain't Bone," "All Original," and "Mo' Thug Family Tree." "Wasteland Warriors" continues the thematic concern with rappers who attempt to emulate BTNH's style, calling them out especially if they do so and then diss BTNH; the track threatens imitators and haters, using violent warrior imagery such as swordplay. "Neighborhood Slang (Interlude)" attests to the street cred of BTNH, stating they are not pretenders. "U Ain't Bone" continues the thematic concern with rappers who attempt to emulate BTNH's style, calling them clones. "All Original" is a combination gangsta rap and commercial success brag, establishing that even though BTNH is a certified multiplatinum act, they are still thugs, even more so now that they can afford better guns. "Mo' Thug Family Tree" is a label entourage song. "Look into My Eyes" is a challenge to the group's haters as well as rappers who have tried to rip off its style, namely Twista (Carl Terrell Mitchell, 1973–) and Three 6 Mafia. "Ready 4 War" continues the threats of the earlier tracks, especially the threat of leaving the bodies of people who attack anyone in the BTNH entourage to rot. Here Bizzy Bone in the second verse portrays such violence in mythical terms, as part of preparation for fighting evil on Earth, a theme visited in a few of the album's tracks.

BTNH has only a few gangsta rap songs, strictly speaking, on the album, "Get Cha Thug On," "Body Rott," "It's All Mo' Thug," and "Thug Love." "Get Cha Thug On" is an unremarkable typical gangsta rap song. "Body Rott" is a typical gangsta rap song lyrically, leveling threats against both haters and cops, who should all be killed, their bodies left to rot. (The album's other anti–police harassment song is

"Let the Law End," which features direct threats to police officers that they will be shot dead if they try to harass these "thuggish ruggish" thugs). "It's All Mo' Thug" contains three verses, by Krayzie Bone, Bizzy Bone, and Wish Bone, that deal with philosophical issues such as the nature of good and evil, the idea of heaven, and the nature of life, rather than simply threatening violence against haters and imitators. "Thug Luv," featuring Tupac Shakur (as 2Pac), embraces the thug lifestyle. "Mo' Thug (Interlude)" is a throwaway interlude that tries to balance the band's thug image with its humility.

The album also contains a couple of socially conscious tracks, "Ain't Nothin Changed (Everyday Thang Part 2)" and "Clog Up Ya Mind." "Ain't Nothin Changed (Everyday Thang Part 2)" paints a dismal picture of urban life, with drugs and death, all in the pursuit of money. "Clog Up Ya Mind" continues the message of "Ain't Nothin Changed" with an emphasis on how money runs the hood and is the main cause of violence, the difference being that here BTNH explains why this makes its members into thugs.

The album's best songs, lyrically, are those that envision the world in mythological terms, portraying urban issues as signs of the end times. These include "It's All Real," "If I Could Teach the World," "Hatin' Nation," "Evil Paradise," and "7 Sign." "It's All Real," which features only Krayzie Bone on solo raps, makes similar threats to haters and imitators as do other tracks, but in this case the culprit is clear—a lack of respect. Here lyrics become surreal as Krayzie explains that he has demons in him that make him violent toward haters. His rap contains a wonderful image of his getting high and passing out on his Ouija board, where he meets these demons. "If I Could Teach the World" establishes that the war BTNH envisions is a mythical one, a final battle between good and evil. Layzie, Krayzie, and Bizzy Bone rap about the world going to hell in a handbasket and defend marijuana usage as one method of staying in touch with one's true self during dark times, as well as a method of achieving harmony. (The album contains one other marijuana track, an interlude titled "Blaze It"). "Hatin' Nation" attacks "playa hatas," described in the terms of disingenuous friends who use people—the profligate behavior of these haters is a sign of the Apocalypse. "Evil Paradise" takes a mythological/religious approach to the problems of the world, which BTNH sees as near the end times. The weakest of the tracks, "7 Sign," is a myth-informed skills braggadocio vehicle for featured rapper Maje$ty (Roderick Wiggins, n.d.) of Da King & I (1992–93).

Among the album's more personable (and more approachable) tracks are "Hard Times (Interlude)," "Family Tree," "How Many of Us Have

Them," and "Whom Die They Lie." "Hard Times (Interlude)" takes the form of a prayer, wherein Krayzie wonders if he will ever escape the hell of life unscathed enough to have his soul ascend to heaven. "Family Tree" looks at different definitions of family, from the literal (Layzie Bone raps about losing his son) to the figurative (Bizzy and Wish Bone rap about taking care of their entourage and community). Layzie's verse is BTNH's most spiritual/religious statement on the album. "How Many of Us Have Them" (a new take on the 1985 Whodini song "Friends") is a track whose purpose is to differentiate between true and false friends, as well as true lovers and hoes. "Whom Die They Lie" ties all of the band's themes (haters, posers, imitators, police, other gangstas) together in one long threat track.

In 2000, the band released *BTNHRESURRECTION*, which achieved platinum status in one month. *Thug World Order* (2002) would be the band's only other album to be certified at least gold. Other albums included *Bone 4 Life* (2005), *Thug Stories* (2006) and *Art of War: WWIII* (2013). Band members have also released solo albums, such as Flesh-n-Bone's (who never signed with Ruthless) *T.H.U.G.S: Trues Humbly United Gatherin' Souls* (Def Jam, 1996), Bizzy Bone's *Heaven'z Movie* (1998), *Hell'z Movie* (1999), and *The Gift* (2001), Layzie Bone's (as L-Burna) *Thug by Nature* (2000), and Krayzie Bone's *Thug on da Line* (2001), *Gemini: Good vs. Evil* (2005), and *Fixtape* series (2007–11). Conflicts led to the temporary departure of Krayzie Bone and Wish Bone in 2011 to work with their independent label, The Life Entertainment. In June 2018, BTNH reunited for shows in Massachusetts, Missouri, and California, which led to an official 2018–19 tour.

BUBBA SPARXXX AND DONATAN: "UGLY" AND "COUNTRY FOLKS"/"SŁOWIAŃSKA KREW" AND "NIE LUBIMY ROBIĆ" (*DARK DAYS, BRIGHT NIGHTS*, BEATCLUB RECORDS, 2001, *PAIN MANAGEMENT*, BACKROAD RECORDS, 2013/*RÓWNONOC: SŁOWIAŃSKA DUSZA*, URBAN REC, 2012)

Rap music is usually an urban phenomenon, but this convention did not stop a style that can best be described as country rap from producing engaging music. From LaGrange, Georgia, in the United States, Bubba Sparxxx (Warren Anderson Mathis, 1977–) combined rap and new country to create songs that express pride in his rural upbringing without sugarcoating that reality—he plays into rural Southern stereotypes to parody and deconstruct them, with the result of granting what he called "country folk" the dignity they deserve. Similarly, Donatan (Witold Czamara, 1984–) from Kraków, Poland, uses traditional Slavic instruments (the main one being the accordion) to create songs about Polish pride and to counter the stereotypical view of Poles as being rural and simple—instead he introduces a Poland that is full of fast cars, lots of alcohol, and beautiful (and in his videos, well-endowed) Slavic women.

Bubba Sparxxx has had a seesaw career, mainly due to issues with substance abuse and weight gain. Early on, his brand of country rap caught fire, propelling some of his early singles onto the Billboard Hot 100. His debut album, *Dark Days, Bright Nights* (Beatclub, 2001) was RIAA certified gold, and it got as high as No. 3 on the Top R&B/Hip Hop Albums chart, as well as on the Billboard 200, and his next two albums, *Deliverance* (Interscope, 2003) and *The Charm* (Virgin, 2005), went to Nos. 10 and 9 on the Billboard 200, respectively. *Dark Days, Bright Nights*' lead single, "Ugly" (featuring Timbaland), got into the Hot 100 Top Ten, peaking at No. 15, and made it into the Top Ten of both the Top R&B and Hot Rap Songs chart. Bubba Sparxxx had a second big hit with the more mainstream dance song "Ms. New Booty" (off of *The Charm*), which featured Ying Yang Twins and Mr. Collipark and made it to No. 7 on the Hot 100 (and was certified gold). His personal issues then led to a seven-year hiatus, during which he beat his addictions and began a new life. He failed to chart again on mainstream or rap charts (for either albums or singles), but his first album back, *Pain Management* (Backroad, 2013), became his first to hit the Hot Country Songs chart (peaking at No. 40). Its lead single, "Country Folks," featuring singer-rappers Danny Boone (Daniel Alexander, n.d.) of Rehab (1998–) and Colt Ford (Jason Farris Brown, 1970–), did not chart but became a fan favorite, garnering 26 million YouTube views as of 2019.

"Ugly," which charted not only in the United States but also in the United Kingdom (Top Ten), the Netherlands, and Norway, is unique in that it featured guest vocals from producer Timbaland (Timothy Zachery Mosley, 1972–), who seldom does vocals. The song starts out as a braggadocio rap, with Bubba Sparxxx owning the fact that he wants commercial success despite the fact that his lyrics contain some disturbing images—and he brags of his ability to skillfully create ugly rhymes (his rhyme schemes incorporate exterior and interior rhymes, with a high number of near rhymes) with lyrics that include Southern colloquialisms. By the song's end, it morphs into a defense of rural Southern culture. The beat to "Ugly" is similar to the sped-up tumbi ostinato that establishes the beat to Missy Elliott's "Get Ur Freak On" (which the song also samples). Specifically, the tumbi ostinato in "Ugly" is in the same range as the secondary, higher pitched tumbi voice that appears midway in the third verse of Elliott's single as a countermelody to the iconic tumbi voice that creates the song's beat. "Ugly" begins with a high-energy bass kick and synthesized bass beat, with the sped up tumbi voice ostinato in the treble range and comic vocalizations (e.g., mouthing a turntable scratch). As the song progresses, other synth voices in the bass range (distorted strings) are heard, with the addition of male vocalizations in the form of extremely aggressive chants and yells (a la 2 Live Crew) appearing in the refrain. In the final instance of the hook, gospel-style singing as a countermelody to the chanting and yelling is introduced. Bubba Sparxxx raps mid-tempo, his voice a bass baritone and slightly deeper than that of most rappers. His style is one that involves articulating some lines carefully while almost slurring others (particularly lines heavy with rural Southern colloquialisms) with pronounced pauses between lines.

"Country Folks" is a stronger statement about rural Southern culture, defending its people for being genuine and true to themselves with lyrics that express that Bubba Sparxxx embraces his Southern roots as part of who he is despite adopting a musical style that seems at odds with those roots. He characterizes his generation as one that loves Hank Williams Jr. and Tupac Shakur, and Colt Ford (in his rapped verse) characterizes it as one that loves George Straight and OutKast. The song begins with its hook, sung by Danny Boone, with a heavily pronounced country music lilt, against slide guitar ostinato and guitar chord progressions played on two acoustic guitars (one in a Southern rock style), with very light percussion as a beat (possibly drumsticks being lightly hit together or light clapping; in later instances of the hook a bass kick drum, snare, and cymbal beat is added). Bubba Sparxxx is first heard in a vocalization ("come on"), which signals the song to kick into a higher gear, with claps now becoming much more pronounced. While Bubba Sparxxx and Colt Ford rap verses, a bass kick becomes prominent and is set against the secondary acoustic guitar melody (the main acoustic melody is saved for sung refrains) and a fiddle. In verses one and three, Bubba Sparxxx uses his usual rap flow, with pronounced pauses after each line; his voice is doubled (harmonized) on the second half of each line to create a sense of building energy. Colt Ford, who provides hype man vocalizations in Bubba Sparxxx's verses, raps the second verse, with Bubba Sparxxx providing similar hype man vocalizations. Ford's vocals are defined by the same flow/pauses and voice doubling effect, his voice a higher baritone and his rural Georgia accent much more prominent. The song's outro is a fiddle melody, played against a bass kick drum.

More a DJ and beat maker than a rapper (similar to Timbaland), Donatan cofounded RafPak with Teka (Tomasz Kucharski, 1982–), an R&B and Dirty South–influenced DJ and producer who went on to found the label Diginoiz. Donatan, who went on to become a much sought-after producer himself, began his musical career at age eighteen and quickly ruffled feathers in Russia (he is part Russian and part Polish, and he lived seven years in Russia) for allegedly preaching paganism and Satanism and for allegedly being pro–Red Army and communism. After returning to Poland, he released his first solo album, *Równonoc: Słowiańska Dusza* (roughly translated, *Equinox: Slavic Soul*), on the Urban Rec label in 2012, wherein he combined traditional Slavic music and instrumentation with hip hop beats. The album and its lead single, "Słowiańska Krew" (a.k.a. "Słowiańska Dusza"; in English "Slavic Blood" or "Slavic Soul"), both hit No. 1 on the OLiS (Oficjalna Lista Sprzedaży), Poland's official music sales chart. The album's third single, "Nie Lubimy Robić" (literally "We Don't Like Doing") has had 37.6 million YouTube views as of 2019.

"Nie Lubimy Robić," which features Polish rapper and music producer Borixon (Tomasz Borycki, 1977–) and Polish rapper Kajman (Michał Radzian, 1981–), employs sarcasm and irony to poke fun at Polish stereotypes (backward, rural, behind-the-times all farmers) in what the refrain's lyrics call a hymn for all Slavic peoples. The song's intro is a spoken-word dialogue (with farm animal noises in the background) between an older woman and a young man as she is asking him if he has completed all his chores. He continually expresses disdain for the farm work, finally stating he wants to go for a ride in an expensive, fast car. When the music begins, the first instrument heard is an accordion, which is joined by a bass kick drum after two measures, which is soon joined by a simple down-tempo (and based on the E string) electric bass walk. A drum kit snare, bass, and cymbal beat then takes over as a highly autotuned (harmonized and reverbed) female voice chimes in to sing-chant the refrain, which introduces the first verse, rapped by Borixon. His rap style is laid-back in tone but rapped quickly, with lines run together through enjambment. The refrain returns, followed by a rapped verse by Kajman, whose softer voice uses the same flow as Borixon, laid-back but speed-rapped lines—the main difference being he uses vocalizations and repetition more for emphasis. The refrain returns after his verse, followed by a lengthy outro that features accordion and electric bass playing the song's main melody together. As the bass finishes, the accordion takes up a new melody that is set against vocalizations that are clipped, distorted, and repeated in quick succession to give a hiccup effect.

"Słowiańska Krew" looks at Polish history with pride, paying homage to past warriors and soldiers while expressing the need to continually fight evil to save the Slavic soul. Featuring Polish rappers Sheller (a.k.a. Shellerini, Sebastian Warzecha, 1983–), Gural (Piotr Górny, 1980–), Kaczor (Dominik Kaczmarek, 1979–), RY23 (a.k.a. Ramona 23, Łukasz Wrzalik, 1981–), and Rafi (a.k.a. Degustator, Rafał Lochman, 1976–), the song begins with the sound of someone blowing a warrior horn (a long curved horn made from a hollowed-out tusk) as men's voices are heard talking and then chanting the song's hook about life, death, and honor. They chant (with Gural's guttural voice taking lead) against a heavy bass kick drum, clapping, and an accordion, as a higher (possibly female) voice sings a countermelody. Sheller then raps the first verse against the female countermelody introduced in the intro. The melody is accordion-heavy, with bass kick drum and claps, and Sheller's voice is in the lower tenor range, but gravelly and throaty, and his flow incorporates both hard stopped lines and enjambment. After a repeat of the hook, Kaczor raps the second verse against the same music and countermelody, his voice gravelly as well, but deeper, a bass baritone, and his flow enjambment-filled with speed-rapped lines that bleed together. Toward the end of Kaczor's verse, a synthesizer-based oscillated note signals a second blowing of the warrior horn, which bridges to the refrain. RY23 raps verse three, his voice a high tenor (boyish) and his flow staccato, giving the lines a hiccupped (almost percussive) feel. After the hook repeats, Rafi (baritone) raps the final verse, his delivery the most laid-back (similar to that of Snoop Dogg) of the five rappers, his lyrics almost mumbled, his flow a mix between staccato lines and extended, run-on lines. The song's outro is the sound of two female voices, chant-singing "Slavic blood is in me."

In addition to his albums, Bubba Sparxxx has released a mixtape with DJ Burn One titled *Survive Till Ya Thrive* (2007). In 2016, he left eOne (a subsidiary of Death Row), which had produced his 2014 album *Made on McCosh Mill Road*, and signed with Slumerican to record the EP *The Bubba Mathis*. His last release was the streaming album *Rapper from the Country* (2018).

In 2013, Donatan, along with his sometime musical partner, Polish singer Cleo (Joanna Klepko, 1983–),was nominated for Best Polish Act at the MTV Europe Music Awards, and both were chosen to represent Poland at the 2014 Eurovision Song Contest with their duet "My Słowianie" (literally "We Are Slavic"), which reached No. 2 in 2013. The song was a parody of Polish stereotypes, and it had 69 million views on YouTube as of 2019. The two collaborated to produce the album *Hiper/Chimera*

(2014). Since then, Donatan has limited himself to producing for the labels Universal Music Polska, Proximite, and Step Records.

BUSTA RHYMES AND TECH N9NE: "BREAK YA NECK" AND "WORLDWIDE CHOPPERS" (*GENESIS*, J RECORDS, 2001, AND *ALL 6'S AND 7'S*, STRANGE MUSIC, 2011)

Chopper style (a.k.a. chopping or speed rap) is a rap flow that originated in the Midwestern United States. Its practitioners use a pace of rhyming that is so fast that it was nicknamed chopper because when lines included a lot of plosives, the rapper sounded like he was imitating an AK-47 assault rifle or a rotating helicopter blade. The best-known choppers—rappers like Twista, Tech N9ne, Twisted Insane (Michael Johnson, 1982–), Busta Rhymes, Rebel XD, Krizz Kaliko, Mr. Shadow, Dyablo, Mr. Sancho, and Snow Tha Product—pride themselves on being both articulate and fast. The rap group Bone Thugs-N-Harmony includes three of the best choppers in rap—Layzie Bone, Krayzie Bone, and Bizzy Bone, who were so skilled they could rap lines that contained bars of twice or three times as many syllables as normal, all the while incorporating sophisticated rhyme schemes. Chopper music has a faster tempo, ranging from 90 to 180 bpm. The first group to speed rap was the Treacherous Three ("The New Rap Language," 1980), but it wasn't until the 1990s that chopper became a distinct style via the music of Twista and Tech N9ne, who are, besides Bone Thugs-N-Harmony, the best known choppers.

In songs such as the metatextual "Break Ya Neck" (2001), eleven-time Grammy nominee Busta Rhymes (Trevor George Smith Jr., 1972–), combined his outlandish style and intricate rhyming (including internal rhyme and half rhyme) with speed rapping. Busta Rhymes, an ex-member of Leaders of the New School (1989–94) and founder of a production crew (The Conglomerate, a.k.a. Flipmode Squad), saw his first five albums go platinum. "Break Ya Neck," produced by Dr. Dre and Scott Storch (1973–), was included in the fifth of those studio albums, *Genesis*. The song uses the central image of head-bobbing to rap to establish that Busta Rhymes can brag that his flow is so fast and his lyrics so hot (and authentic, showing his street cred) that fans will bob their heads (and dance) to it so hard they may break their necks (willingly). The song also challenges other labels to gather their crews and "soldiers" to challenge his and Dr. Dre's skills, to no avail since they won't be able to compete.

Busta Rhymes's flow here is an interesting combination of chopper style and mid-tempo articulated rapping, depending on where he is in a lyrical line. His tendency is to begin every phrase with almost mumbled speed rapping, which he will carry for two or three lines, ending each phrase by suddenly switching from chopper to mid-tempo, usually for two or three words. In some instances, he will do so in back-to-back lines. His rhyming is both interior and exterior, and he uses lots of assonance and repetition to make speed even more possible. Musically, the song is almost comical. Its main melody is an arp-sounding keyboard riff that gives the song a bouncy feel. It is balanced by a secondary synth voice, similar to a bassoon or oboe, and an electric bass, snare drum, clap, and 808 beat. The song's beat is consistent, with only one time stop, cleverly used after the command "stop!" in the second verse. Verses are rapped by Busta Rhymes, with some breaking into song, while refrains are both sung (staccato funk style, with emphasis on every word) and rapped; vocalizations occur throughout the song. Some auto-tuning is used on the track's sung parts, but while Busta Rhymes's rapping is not auto-tuned, generally his voice is doubled (sometimes accompanied by his speaking voice, creating an eerie effect) with slight reverb added, which makes it come across as even more raspy and throaty.

With songs such as his iconic hit "Worldwide Choppers" (2011), Kansas City, Missouri–native Tech N9ne (Aaron Dontez Yates, 1971–) earned the stage name (based on the TEC-9 semiautomatic handgun) given him by fellow rapper Black Walt, due to his chopper-style rapping. He began his rapping career in 1991 with Black Mafia (1991–93), Nnutthowze (1991), and 57th Street Rogue Dog Villains (1998–2007), finally joining Yukmouth with the Regime (1997–). In 1999, he and business partner Travis O'Guin founded the record label Strange Music. "Worldwide Choppers," from the album *All 6's and 7's* (Strange Music, 2011), is literally what its title suggests, a forum for chopper-style rappers from around the world (more specifically Turkey, Denmark, and the United States) to display their skills. The track features lyrics in English, Danish, and Turkish, with rappers such as Ceza (Bilgin Özçalkan, 1976–), U$O (Ausamah Saed, 1981–), Yelawolf (Michael Wayne Atha, 1979–), Twista, Twisted Insane, and Busta Rhymes, among others. Tech N9ne, who raps the first verse, references Top of the Pops, Edgar Allan Poe, and Picasso in a braggadocio rap that establishes his unique skills, despite the fact that chopper-style rappers can be found worldwide. In an interesting twist, Yelawolf, in his verse, challenges other rappers to go toe to toe not with himself but with Tech N9ne and Busta Rhymes. Other verses involve guest rappers establishing their chopper skills dominance.

"Worldwide Choppers" begins with an a cappella vocalization of nonsense "weemah weh" syllables in a minor key, creating a sense of foreboding that is realized immediately when a female voice announces "Turkey," at which point sparse instrumentation in the form of a drum (a distorted tom crash, at the beginning of each line) kicks in, accompanied by the same vocalizations as in what turns out to be the first section of a trifurcated intro. As Ceza begins chopper rapping in Turkish, his voice high and boyish, his lyrics centered around hard plosives, the drum crashes become more frequent, hinting that the song's dynamics are about to change. Here the song subverts expectations—Ceza's brief rap turns out to be a second section of the intro—as the drum disappears, leaving only the vocalizations and an unidentified male vocalist (using a high level of distortion) loudly hyping the upcoming song in the intro's third section (about the internationalization of the chopper style), as it leads to the song's first verse, by Tech N9ne.

After the female voice announces "Kansas City," Tech N9ne's baritone comes in just as the tom crash returns, now accompanied by a keyboard ostinato (in the higher range) and claps created by an 808 drum, which, just as Tech N9ne is taking his first breath, creates a foregrounded drum hiccup. As he finishes his first eight lines, distorted guitars and a drum kit are introduced (the 808 claps continue), and his flow switches from elongated lines to short lines, which slowly build back up in length. Generally, Tech N9ne's flow is very smooth, concerned not with variation as much as with speed, continuity, and keeping to the beat. Interspersed throughout his verse are gruff bass baritone vocalizations of the word "chop" or simply the "ch" sound. His verse leads to the refrain, a heavy metal–influenced (heavy guitars and arena-style vocals) sung braggadocio hook in which Tech N9ne's voice is multitracked.

JL (Jason Varnes, n.d.) takes up the next verse after the female voice announces Kansas City, his tenor voice a counter to Tech N9ne's. Here the music gets louder as a secondary keyboard voice is introduced. JL's flow is much different, as he pauses briefly in the middle of and at the end of each line, giving his flow a sense of being a series of chopper phrases rather than a breathless rapping of two or three lines. The female voice returns, announcing "Denmark." U$O's rap is breathless as he rattles off, in his boyish voice, six consecutive lines. The female voice chimes in with "Alabama," at which point Yelawolf begins his verse. His voice is the highest of all the song's rappers (second tenor), and he speed raps through his lines, briefly pausing at the end of each one, with only a few exceptions where he runs together two lines. As his verse ends, the 808 drum introduces a new hiccup, which leads into the second iteration of the hook.

Twista, the fastest of the chopper rappers on the track, jumps in so quickly on his verse that he drowns out the female announcement of "Chicago." His flow varies between a speed rap that is not concerned with keeping the beat and a strict chopper style based on assonance and multisyllabic words (he actually does sound like chopper blades on a few lines). During the first part of his verse, all instrumentation disappears except for the distorted electric guitars (chords being hit in 4/4 time) and the 808 hiccup, which complements some of his faster lines; the keyboard ostinato and 808 claps are reintroduced as his verse continues.

The hook occurs a third time, introducing Busta Rhymes, who, like Twista, jumps in so quickly that he drowns out the female announcement of his hometown, New York. His voice is a raspy baritone, and his chopper flow is an interesting combination of lines that begin with words run together (his words are almost unintelligible) and carefully articulated line endings, usually the last two words of a line. He varies his flow more than the others on the song—as his verse continues, he ceases to slow down and pause at the end of lines and begins running them together despite the use of couplet end rhymes in his lines, and he switches from long, smoothly flowing lines to staccato phrasing. (At this point all instruments except the 808 clap disappear, making his section more dramatic). The end of his verse reintroduces the hook. The song ends with two short verses by D-Loc (Dustin Miller, 1977–), announced as Kansas City, and Twisted Insane, announced as California. Both have higher, boyish voices, the former using a flow that gives his words a hiccup feel, and the latter showing off a smooth mastery of speed, flowing words together so organically that he achieves the helicopter blade effect. On Twisted Insane's last two words (he raps "I'm a worldwide" and a distorted deep voice adds "chopper"), the song comes to an abrupt end.

CARDI B: "BODAK YELLOW" AND "MONEY" (BOTH DIGITAL RELEASES, ATLANTIC, 2017 AND 2018)

What started out as viral Internet celebrity from Vine and Instagram eventually became record-breaking chart performance for Cardi B (Belcalis Marlenis Almánzar, 1992–), a Dominican and Afro-Trinidadian Bronx native whose two mixtapes, *Gangsta B—Music, Vol. 1* (2016) and *Gangsta B—Music, Vol. 2* (2017) launched a career that has to this point resulted in three Billboard Hot 100 chart toppers, "Bodak Yellow," "I Like It," and "Girls Like You" (a Maroon 5 collaboration on which she was featured). Cardi B became only the second female rapper to top the Billboard Hot 100 with a solo track (Lauryn Hill being the first in 1998). As of 2019, she holds the overall record for No. 1 hits by a female rapper (featured or guest) with three.

Her debut studio album with Atlantic, *Invasion of Privacy* (2018, RIAA certified double platinum), debuted at No. 1 on the Billboard 200 and earned a Grammy Award for Best Rap Album. With her collaborations on "No Limit" (with G-Eazy and A$AP Rocky) and "MotorSport" (with Migos and Nicki Minaj), she became the first female rapper to reach the Top Ten with her first three song entries. In 2018, she became the first woman to have five Top Ten singles simultaneously on the Hot R&B/Hip Hop chart. Her debut studio single, "Bodak Yellow," was released through digital distribution, and when the track topped the Billboard Hot 100, it made her the first person of Dominican descent to reach No. 1. The song was eventually certified seven-times platinum; it won Single of the Year at the 2017 BET Hip Hop Awards.

With an infectious beat by Dallas, Texas, producer J. White Did It (Anthony Germaine White or Anthony Jermaine White, 1984–), who also coproduced "I Like It" and the later Cardi B hit "Money," "Bodak Yellow" is a reinterpretation of Kodak Black's "No Flockin" (self-released in 2014; also a hidden track on the 2014 album *Heart of the Projects*), which peaked at No. 95 on the Billboard Hot 100. For "Bodak Yellow," Cardi B (in her heavy Washington Heights accent) copies faithfully Kodak Black's melodic rap structure (his flow), down to the emphasis on the final two words of each line for each Section A (verses are bifurcated), followed by speed rapping with less accentuation on the final words of lines for each Section B. Instrumentally, J. White Did It copies only the idea of the minor key–based piano ostinato of Kodak Black's original, which creates an ominous atmosphere. Lyrically the song falls into the category of braggadocio and threat song, but it is aimed specifically at women. In it Cardi B references her ability to make millions of dollars, as both an exotic dancer (a job she held while in college) and as a rapper and fashion icon. Unlike most bragging raps, which concentrate on the lyrical skills of the rapper, here the emphasis is on Cardi B as a brand (or media personality). She references her ability to afford Christian Louboutin designer shoes, BAPE street wear, Saint Laurent designer clothes, Ferraris, Rolls-Royces, and a Rolex. The attitude of the song is summed up in the lines where she proclaims she is a "boss," while her detractors are "workers," and she explains she has gone from using money moves (as a dancer) to now making money move (as a consumer and investor).

"Bodak Yellow" begins with the minor-key synth-produced ostinato being played with the sparse accompaniment of a 4/4 eighth note–based snare beat (synth-produced as well). This creates an eerie atmospheric beat that immediately introduces a male whisper, adding to the atmospherics. As the beat continues, a backgrounded and highly reverbed to the point of echoing female voice calls out "Cardi," which then reverberates against the music, soon replaced by the echoing words "if they wanted to," which later become part of the first verse. An 808 hiccup, heavy on bass, introduces the first verse. Cardi B's chant-rap is deep and resonant, multitracked to sound fuller. During the verse, the instrumentation remains sparse: keyboard ostinato, snare, and occasional 808-produced bass kick for emphasis. As the refrain kicks in, the ostinato continues, albeit with a key change (becoming deeper), and a second keyboard voice (bell-like) is added, but used sparingly, usually mirroring the first note of the main ostinato.

As mentioned, verse one contains both an A and a B section, the former chant-rapped slowly and deliberately, the latter speed rapped breathlessly. The B section repeats the instrumentation of the A section, but the snare speeds up to sixteenth notes, giving the song a sense of urgency at this point. As the verse continues, vocalizations (female) are added at the end of each line, alternately making a whooping sound, grunting, hissing, rolling r's (e.g., "brrrah" or "burrrrrr"), or repeating the last word rapped by Cardi B. During the B section, Cardi B switches to speed rapping, as the 808 bass drum becomes more prominent and speeds up. Vocalizations occur more frequently, adding texture to the otherwise sparse music. The refrain is then repeated, followed by verse two—which mirrors verse one instrumentally and vocally in both its A and B sections—and then followed by the refrain one final time, with Cardi B's final word echoed off into a bounce effect. The song's outro mirrors its intro, with only the keyboard ostinato and snare sound, as backgrounded echoed words (unintelligible) can be heard in both left and right speakers, giving them a sense of buzzing by the listener.

With "Money," which is planned as the first single off of her next album (likely 2019), Cardi B visits the same theme. The song, which peaked at No. 13 on the Billboard Hot 100 and was certified platinum, is even more overt in its declaration that success can be measured mainly by buying power while staying "real" ("street"). Where it differs from "Bodak Yellow" is in its approach—here Cardi B threatens her detractors (some claimed she sold out for mainstream pop) through more physical means, a conventional trope of rap music. However, the bulk of the song is about her success, as the song's hook establishes.

She posits her lifestyle as not only a mark of success but also something she was born for, and her money is something that both she and her infant daughter (Kulture Kiari Cephus) will need. Musically the song shows the influence of Missy Elliott and Timbaland's experimentation with cartoons and vocalizations, as well as Dizzee Rascal's weird female and impossibly high-pitched break vocalizations (particularly notable in the song "I Don't Need a Reason" from the 2013 album *The Fifth*, on Dirtee Stank Recordings).

"Money" opens with power chords on a grand piano voice (left speaker), accentuated by a highly reverbed secondary synth voice (right speaker), which gives the effect of allowing the piano chord to reverberate and oscillate with a percussive effect. This minimalist instrumentation continues throughout the first verse and first instance of its B section, with only Cardi B's chant-rapping, multitracked to sound fuller and slightly reverbed to sound wetter, as accompaniment. At times a slight delay on her secondary vocal tracks creates an echo effect (especially in the song's final verse). This minimalist opening of course puts a great deal of pressure on Cardi B to carry the song vocally for the first thirty seconds, which she does admirably. At this point, the grand piano voice is joined by a new piano voice in a higher key, which mirror the chords, as well as an 808 drum and claps/snaps, suddenly increasing the song's dynamics (to coincide with the first line that uses the vocalization refrain "money" and to lead into the song's hook). As verse two begins, a bass kick and synth-produced sub-bass are added to the previous instrumentation, creating a sense that the song's volume is increasing, which leads naturally to the song's first sound effect, a gunshot that coincides with Cardi B's promise to eliminate her rivals (here she references "hammer time"). The section B repetition and hook that ensue use the same instrumentation as before, as does verse three, where again Cardi B speeds her rap flow to coincide with a speeding up of the 808 drums. The song's outro emphasizes the sub-bass, which counters a repetition of the earlier high-pitched break vocalization of the word "money." The two play against one another until the song ends on the sub-bass.

With "Bodak Yellow," Cardi B joined Lauryn Hill as woman rappers of iconic status. "I Like It" and "Girls Like You" solidified this reputation that began in 2015, when Cardi B joined the cast of the VH1's reality television series *Love & Hip Hop: New York*. By 2017, she had become a rising star, garnering nine nominations at the 2017 BET Awards, tying her with DJ Khaled and Kendrick Lamar. The next year she had twelve nominations, tying her with Drake for the record. In 2018, *Time* named her one of the one hundred most influential people in the world.

CHANCE THE RAPPER: *COLORING BOOK* (SELF-RELEASED MIXTAPE, 2016)

Coloring Book, the third mixtape by Chicago MC Chance the Rapper, is a concept album that defied all odds and surpassed all expectations. Although it was distributed on the Internet as a freely streamed mixtape, it made him the most successful independent rap artist in history. His two previous efforts, *10 Day* and *Acid Rap*, received critical acclaim, but *Coloring Book* was both a critical and a financial success. In 2017, it became the first Grammy Award–winning streaming-only album, earning three awards—Best Rap Album, Best New Artist, and Best Rap Performance. Based on number of streams alone, *Coloring Book* was also the first streaming album to chart on the Billboard 200, peaking at No. 8.

Chance the Rapper is a tenor, and both his singing and rapping voices are smooth and soft, sometimes breaking or sounding tentative, betraying a boyish charm and sense of humility. The gospel-influenced *Coloring Book* begins with an overture of sorts, "All We Got," a clever braggadocio track featuring Kanye West (Kanye Omari West, 1977–) that claims to be not an intro but an entrée. It jumps right out at the listener with a soprano brass horn section heavy on trumpet that introduces strings in a bass range, which in turn lead to the album's first vocals, Chance the Rapper's soft voice repeating of the phrase "we back." Once the drum beat is introduced, the horns become ornamental; the strings take over the beat, and a gospel choir is introduced, ushering in more foregrounded lead vocals that are auto-tuned and aggressive this time. The song is sonically complex and full of clever metaphors—its message is that music is the only certainty in the world, and therefore a song should be a work of art (and should be commercially successful), leaving nothing to chance.

"No Problem," a clever take on the diss track, features 2 Chainz (Tauheed Epps, 1977–) and begins with a heavy funk beat that turns into an aggressive challenge to major record labels that try to stop independent musicians, informing them (the labels) that the last thing they want to do is create a problem for Chance by trying to stop him from collaborating with their artists. The song disses rappers who sold out to major labels, with various grunts and angry masculine vocalizations to drive the point home; these vocalizations also accent the lead rap and sung vocals, the latter being Jamaican-influenced. This track and "All We Got" include complex backing vocals, which is a pitch-altered (to sound higher) feminine choir. The third track, the nostalgic snap-based "Summer Friends," begins with an a cappella masculine R&B choir made to sound as if it is in a cavernous room, until a snare-based beat is introduced. Chance the Rapper raps in his softest register (which is slightly auto-tuned) against both the choir and the beat, until bass strings signal the song's end, wherein he reminds his childhood friends (at least the male ones) that he has not forgotten them despite his success.

The album's shortest song, "D.R.A.M. Sings Special" (at 1:42), features D.R.A.M. (Shelley Marshaun Massenburg-Smith, 1988–) singing a love song that begins with a keyboard voice that invokes new age music (at one point, waves can even be heard). As the song reaches its outro, it introduces a feminine choir and ends with a surprise Hammond organ—making it a clever offering rather than a throwaway track. The other seeming throwaway tracks, "All Night" and "Smoke Break," occur later on the album. "All Night" is a drinking song, but it transcends its subject matter through a clever keyboard, bass, and percussion (shakers and claves) beat. "Smoke Break" is a marijuana song that laments the fast pace of the recording and touring life that seldom offers time for a smoke break. It uses down-tempo 808 drums, strings, and new age keyboard voices juxtaposed against Chance's Jamaican-style speed rapping and a laid-back sung refrain.

The fifth and twelfth tracks, "Blessings" and "How Great," are down-tempo R&B-styled gospel songs that praise God and Jesus Christ, something Chance the Rapper promised himself he would do more often in his songs. The former includes spoken-word (rather than rapped) verses. "Blessings" renews Chance's attack on the music industry, which has standardized music, made it about money, and made it impossible for any musician to establish and hone musical talent. In the second refrain, Chance sings countermelody to the gospel choir, which is juxtaposed against bright brass instrumentation (mainly trumpets) and adds vocal complexity to what is otherwise a simple song. "How Great" uses gospel choir and spoken word and talk-singing to express the idea that Chance creates rap music for God's glory, to "spit a Spotify to qualify a spot on His side."

The album's standout track, "Same Drugs," is also gospel influenced, though it begins very quietly with Chance singing against a retro synth voice, giving the song a 1970s feel, with a gospel-style solo by featured singer Eryn Allen Kane (n.d.) in the third refrain. The song laments the drifting apart of two friends who "don't do the same drugs no more," cleverly invoking the Peter Pan syndrome as it is sung to a Wendy, who has aged despite the singer's belief that she (and by extension he) would never grow up or forget how to fly. The lyrics support a secondary interpretation with a play on the nickname for Chicago, "the windy city," indicating that Chance as a songwriter may be lamenting watching his neighborhood change—the song ends with references to bleeding out and weeds (dandelions) set against a vocal, string, and piano outro. The album revisits nostalgia in the ninth track, "Juke Jam," featuring Justin Bieber. It is a mellow recollection of on-again, off-again friendship, childhood parties at the local skating rink, and the encroachment of young adulthood.

The album immediately changes directions with "Mixtape," another lamentation song, which begins with an expletive and features Young Thug (Jeffery Lamar Williams, 1991–) and borrows elements from Jamaican toast–based hip hop. Exasperated because music has become too commercial, Chance half sings, half raps here against a minimalist beat created by a simple synth voice and 808 drums, allowing his singing voice to constantly break when he wonders if he is the last rapper to care about mixtapes, which represent artistic freedom and the prioritization of the rap audience. The lyrics cleverly use stream of consciousness to weave between music, baseball, basketball, and sexual imagery, though the song fails on some levels because its meaning becomes obfuscated. The next track, "Angels," continues the aggressiveness of "Mixtape." An up-tempo beat is established immediately that the song will not be a lament, and Chance the Rapper switches back into braggadocio mode, but rather than brag about his musician and rapping skills, he promises to be one of Chicago's saviors (through music) since he is establishing himself as a man who is protected by angels (again here, he plays with a double meaning, angels being both the Christian messengers of God and the city's youth). The song is notable for its clever local allusions, which Chance rattles off effortlessly.

"Finish Line/Drown," which features T-Pain (Faheem Rasheed Najm, 1985–), echoes the "we back" repetition of the album's opening, bringing the album full circle. Another nostalgia song, its first section, "Finish Line" is an upbeat chronicle of Chance's career, from a K–12 education that failed him (he admits he didn't give it a chance) to a Xanax addiction that almost cost him his music career and from an aborted attempt at a rap career in Los Angeles to his eventual local (Chicago) success, turning rap music into a calling and a way to support his family (his girlfriend, now pregnant, is a character in many of the album's songs). The song's second part, the pensive gospel-influenced "Drown," is a reminder that no matter what life brings, defeat is not an option ("never drown"). The album ends with a reprise of "Blessings," which uses spoken stream of consciousness to tie the album's themes of nostalgia, family, spirituality, grace (including an openness to blessings), self-reliance, and self-actualization together, replacing the dandelions of "Same Drugs" with "endless fields of daffodils and chamomile." The album ends on a note of self-definition: Chance promises he will remain a modest human being, despite being a rapper.

In addition to performing as a vocalist, Chance the Rapper is a multi-instrumentalist (though his instrument of choice is the keyboard or piano), songwriter, composer, and producer, and he has recently become a philanthropist. His lyrics are created through erudite language and intelligent metaphor, and his rapping style includes highly skilled internal rhyme and a constant juxtaposition of pathos and humor. Musically his compositions combine the rhythms and beats of hip hop with eclectic samples as well as musical elements of gospel and R&B. His themes include relationships and love, dance, and above all, pride for his home city, Chicago. His fame began with the release of *Acid Rap* when he began touring with Macklemore & Ryan Lewis. Meanwhile, he was a member of the band Savemoney (2014–), a Chicago hip hop collective, as well as a lead vocalist for the band The Social Experiment (2014–). In 2015, Social Experiment released its own critically acclaimed hip hop, R&B, and neo-soul album, *Surf*. Between 2013 and 2017, he collaborated on singles and EPs with hip hop, electronic, R&B, soul and dubstep singer-songwriter-producers like James Blake and John Legend, as well as rapper Action Bronson and rapper-turntablist-producer DJ Khaled.

C-MURDER: *BOSSALINIE*
(*BOSSALINIE*, NO LIMIT RECORDS, 1999)

When Master P (Percy Robert Miller, 1970–) founded No Limit Records in New Orleans, Louisiana, in 1990, he had no idea that what started as a venture to sell CDs out of the trunk of his car would lead to an influential label and ultimately a $350 million enterprise (by 2013) with offshoots such as P. Miller Enterprises and Better Black Television. No Limit launched the careers of Master P, TRU (a.k.a. The Real Untouchables, 1995–2002), 504 Boyz (2000–05), Louie V Mob (2013), and Money Mafia (2015), as well as the solo careers of Master P's brothers and son: rapper and producer C-Murder (Corey Miller, 1971–), rapper Silkk the Shocker (Vyshonne King Miller, 1975–), and rapper-actor Lil' Romeo (Percy Romeo Miller Jr., 1989–). In 1995, the same year that Master P moved No Limit from Richmond, California, to New Orleans to create a team of Southern-style rappers, TRU had its breakthrough with *True*, which peaked at No. 25 on the Top R&B/Hip Hop Albums chart. Armed with an in-house production team, Beats by the Pound, No

Limit released Master P's *Ice Cream Man* (1995) and *Ghetto D* (1997), which went platinum, as well as TRU's *Tru 2 da Game* (1997), a daring double CD by a little-known (at the time) group. *Tru 2 da Game* is today considered a benchmark recording in gangsta rap (referred to as thug rap by No Limit).

C-Murder initially gained fame in the mid-1990s as a member of TRU, and he went on to release several solo albums of his own, including the certified platinum debut *Life or Death* (No Limit, 1998), which reached No. 3 on the Billboard 200. Between 1999 and 2001, he released the platinum album *Bossalinie* (No Limit, 1999), which reached No. 2 on the Billboard 200 and spawned the singles "Like a Jungle" and "Gangsta Walk," featuring Snoop Dogg. *Trapped in Crime* (No Limit, 2000), a No. 8 charting album, contained his biggest single, "Down for My N's," which also featured Snoop Dogg. *C-P-3.com* (2001) was his final record with No Limit.

Bossalinie, produced by Beats by the Pound, entered the Billboard 200 at No. 2 and stayed on the chart for eleven weeks. Two of its songs, "Ghetto Boy" and "Street Keep Callin'," challenge the idea that money and bling can change someone from the ghetto who is used to the violence and despair of the streets. The former, which features a keyboard ostinato, set against a drum kit and 808 beat, heavy bass, and percussive vocal chanting, contains comic, hyperbolic verses that show that being ghetto is both a curse—it includes living in poverty, urban decay, a lack of education, and grime—and a badge of honor. Those who survive the urban environment are heroic, especially since the ghetto stays with them their entire lives. "Street Keep Callin'" is a down-tempo, jazz-influenced, R&B-infused song that takes a serious tone to express C-Murder's fatalistic view of life. Containing soulful sung refrains that establish a sense of despair, the song is as much a heavily reverbed spoken-word track (against a minimal beat) as it is a rap. Similar in theme, the soul-infused "Like a Jungle" and the danceable "Gangsta Walk" are both about being streetwise and tough. The intro to "Like a Jungle" references Grandmaster Flash and the Furious Five's iconic hit "The Message" (1982) in its refrain, giving it a sense of gravitas, as opposed to the absurdity of "Ghetto Boy" or the braggadocio of "Gangsta Walk." "Ghetto Boy" offers a minimal bass and snare beat (using brushes and sticks) against a highly reverbed rap (which creates a sense of vocal doubling). C-Murder's baritone vocal register is used for both spoken word and rap. The darkly comic "Gangsta Walk" includes clever pop culture references and percussive points of interest, with instruments such as vibraslap and crash cymbal set against the percussive chant of the words "gang" and "walk" being used throughout. In these songs, the streets are mean, death is everywhere, murder is a harsh reality, and an impending sense of doom colors all. In "Like a Jungle," the ghetto makes C-Murder into something he can no longer recognize, encapsulated in the line "f— the man in the mirror, I don't trust him." Still, being "street" is equated to being black and real, which translates into being heroic and memorable.

"Ghetto Millionaire," "Murder and Daz," and "Where We Wanna," which feature Snoop Dogg, Nate Dogg (Nathaniel Dwayne Hale, 1969–2011), Daz Dillinger (Delmar Drew Arnaud, 1973–), and Goodie Mob (including CeeLo Green), are entourage songs that exalt C-Murder's Third Ward New Orleans environment and No Limit soldiers for taking control of their neighborhoods through violence when necessary—in other words, for being real gangsta. "Ghetto Millionaire" features a dramatic keyboard scale-based ostinato played against vocalizations, heavy bass played low on the E string, and a snare beat played with brushes. The upbeat "Still Makin' Moves," featuring Mo B. Dick and Master P, is also an entourage song, but its narrative is as much about escaping the streets through music as it is about ruling the streets through violence. It features keyboard power chords, an 808 and snare drum beat, and neo-soul singing, as well as the best group rapping and chanting on the album. The toy piano voice, cajon, and conga–based "Can't Hold Me Back" attacks those who would diss No Limit Records and its rappers. "On My Enemies," which features organ set against a snare and 808 drum beat and bass played low on the E string (and begins and ends with a tribute to Tupac Shakur), is C-Murder's diss track concerned with enacting violence against his enemies and the enemies of all No Limit soldiers. The standout entourage song is the synth-based (against an 808 drum and grand piano) "Ride on Dem Bustas," which has an interesting percussive opening wherein a helicopter blade sound is replaced by the chant-like repetition of "real n—," which prefigures the chant-like quality of the song's rapping (similar to the chant-rapping style of Three 6 Mafia), as well as its chopper-style rapping in the third verse, rapped by New Orleans local Mr. Serv-On.

Another standout is the Latin and Western Art Music–flavored "Livin' Legend," which features Master P. The song is a shout-out to African American heroes from C-Murder, who calls himself a lost soul who used to think he could transcend his upbringing. These heroes include the streetwise dealers, the rappers who escaped the streets, and basketball players who escaped the streets. Here he bemoans the fact that all he wants to do is succeed financially with his music, but haters in his community are holding him back. Other songs about the recording industry include "Money Talks" and "Freedom." The funk-based "Money Talks" features the album's most memorable bass line and the vocals of Silkk the Shocker; it is a shout-out to the various No Limit rapping crews, reminding them that C-Murder was able to exchange trying to make money on the streets for multiplatinum success as a rapper. "Freedom," which features the sound effect of dripping water as part of its beat, is a 1970s soul–infused track that attacks both record companies and the prison system, juxtaposing both to give the sense that signing with a large record company is like being incarcerated. In his most chant-like, monotone (but effective, when played against a female gospel choir singing the phrase "I want my freedom") flow on the album, C-Murder explains his decision to stay with No Limit because it allows its rappers their freedom to be true to themselves.

Beside the typical fare for a rap album, *Bossalinie* includes many thoughtful songs about the sadness of the ghetto. "Lord Help Us," which begins with a 1970s-style soul refrain, is a talk-sung sociopolitical statement about the poverty C-Murder witnessed in the Third Ward. What it offers as answers are spiritual in nature, love and faith, although in some verses it questions the efficacy of both, at one point questioning if Jesus was crucified for naught. The most powerful song on the album, "Lil N—," dedicated to a friend who was killed in gang fighting, features resonant church bells playing a scale, and a Gregorian-style chant, both set against a snare beat and occasional strings for dramatic effect. The lyrics bemoan the fate of African American youth who don't make it out of the urban ghetto. The more typical rap song "Closin' Down Shop" uses heavy funk bass, a 1980s keyboard voice, and rhythm guitar to tell the story of giving up drug dealing for various reasons, although mainly because it has become too dangerous. The R&B-infused, bass-heavy "I Remember" is a nostalgia song about growing up poor but happy, although the memories in its second verse are about street life and dealing drugs before deciding to straighten out.

The album includes only two relationship songs, which stand out for eschewing the typical b— and hoes theme heard in most rap songs. The Ennio Morricone–influenced music of "Nasty Chick" is set against a narrative rap about gold diggers who have used C-Murder just for his money. Although the song has undertones of misogyny, the lyrics hint that the anger felt by C-Murder is actually his response to having his heart broken by one such woman. "Don't Wanna Be Alone" is a melodramatic romance song about an originally unrequited love that tried C-Murder's patience, but which finally led to a relationship with his love interest that prevents both people from being alone in a harsh world where jealousy tries to tear lovers apart. Musically, the song is a typical pop song, featuring synth, piano, bass kick, snare, and string voices.

In 2002, C-Murder was arrested for a nightclub murder, and he was sentenced to life in prison in 2009. He is currently serving his sentence in the Louisiana State Penitentiary, although issues with witnesses recanting statements occurred in 2018. Before and after his incarceration, he has consistently released new albums, mostly on TRU Records: *The Truest S— I Ever Said* (2005), *Screamin' 4 Vengeance* (2008), *Calliope Click Volume 1* (2009), *Tomorrow* (2010), *Ain't No Heaven in the Pen* (2015), and *Penitentiary Chances* (2016). In 2000, he founded Bossalinie Records. He has written three novels.

COOLIO: "GANGSTA'S PARADISE" (*GANGSTA'S PARADISE*, TOMMY BOY, 1995)

Compton's Coolio (Artis Leon Ivey Jr., 1963–) was a respected gangsta rap, g-funk, and West Coast singer and rapper who began recording in 1987, but his albums *It Takes a Thief* (1994), *Gangsta's Paradise* (1995), and *My Soul* (1997) made him a mainstream star (the Tommy Boy label was known for its mainstreaming of hip hop). Doug Rasheed (n.d.) produced "Gangsta's Paradise," which featured singer L.V. (Larry Sanders, n.d.), was the winner of the 1996 Grammy Award for Best Rap Solo Performance as well as the winner of two MTV Video Music Awards (Best Rap Video and Best Video from a Film) and a Billboard Music Award. It sold five million copies in the United States and went to No. 1 on the Billboard Hot 100 as well as on the charts in Australia, Austria, Denmark, France, Germany, Ireland, Italy, the Netherlands, Norway, New Zealand, Sweden, Switzerland, and the United Kingdom. It was Billboard's biggest selling single of 1995.

The song's theme is the hopelessness of the gangsta lifestyle, created by the hopelessness of an urban environment. Here both a violent environment and a damaged relationship with his mother has drained all hope from the song's narrator, who starts out with philosophical introspection but soon finds himself falling into his old ways—his thoughtfulness is interrupted by his need to threaten any who would stand against him, including rival gangs. He feels trapped by his environment despite his understanding of the fact that he could be killed at any time. "Gangsta's Paradise" samples the chorus and instrumentation of Stevie Wonder's "Pastime Paradise" (1976) and begins with a quote from Psalm 23:4, "As I walk through the valley of the shadow of death," but it breaks off there to relate that the narrator examined his life and realized that there was "nothin' left." The song's refrain includes a countermelody created by a full choir, which is actually L.V.'s multitracked various vocal ranges, from soprano to tenor to bass. After L.V. recorded all the sung parts, Coolio was brought in to rap.

"Gangsta's Paradise" begins with a low rumble that sounds like the interior of a train, possibly a subway train, as it's moving. A heartbeat is introduced and then the sound of a baby crying (which give the low rumble a possible new meaning, that of the sound of the womb). After a beat, a long exhale is heard, which introduces the song's main musical theme, high-pitched strings playing a dramatic ostinato that begins with a downward bowing motion—this immediately introduces melodrama and tension. Other instrumentation is quickly introduced: percussion (shakers), a bass kick (on the upbeat to cap off phrases), claps, a drum kit (heavy on kick and tom), and a grinding bass that approaches sub-bass level pitches. Vocals then begin with a woman's (identified as his mother in the next few lines) speaking voice, asking the song's narrator what is wrong. The first verse starts with introspection as the rap indicates life is not worth living anymore. Lyrics then establish that the urban ghetto has made the narrator hard and sardonic, and even somewhat insane; however, a pattern is introduced here that occurs throughout the song, where introspection gives way to threats of violence (and vice versa). The verse devolves into threats that are rationalized with the explanation that the narrator's victims deserved their fates, as well as some gangsta braggadocio (he is the gangsta everyone wants to emulate). The verse returns to introspection and despair, with the narrator on his knees, praying in the streets. The refrain is sung by L.V. against a choir countermelody, with higher pitches in the vocals emphasized to create a sense of a heavenly chorus.

Verse two identifies two new culprits, the environment and the media. Urban living has made the narrator a survivalist, and surviving involves a life of crime and violence. Media representations of the American dream have disillusioned him while instilling in him a need for consumerism and materialism (bling). This verse also ends with threats to others not to arouse his anger. As in verse one, anger is mixed with introspection, in this case about life and death—he realizes his life is "do or die" and fatalistically wonders if he will live out the year. This is followed by a middle eight where L.V., using vocal processing, sings as the voice of reason, asking why urban youth are blind to the pain and suffering they cause and to the possibility of a better life. The refrain follows. For both the middle eight and its refrain, strings and bass are heard, but the drums become quieter, while the sub-bass, bass kick, and claps disappear, giving the song a quiet, pensive moment.

Verse three is about money and power. Again the narrator blames his environment, specifically people who fail to reach him because they can't understand him. He accuses these people of "fronting," or putting up a disingenuous front of genuine concern. Vocals here are tense and emotional as he comes to the realization that his world approaches chaos and he is out of luck. This returns the song to the refrain, followed by a repetition of the middle eight, but this time against full instrumentation and the choir (as countermelody). As "Gangsta's Paradise" fades out, we hear the choir performing a cappella, with more emphasis on L.V.'s deeper vocal registers.

The video for "Gangsta's Paradise" was directed by Antoine Fuqua, who went on to direct various films, including *Training Day* (2001). The video featured Michelle Pfeiffer, who reprised her earlier role in *Dangerous Minds* (1995), as the song was written for the film. The song's success allowed Coolio to go on to become a record producer, actor, and professional chef, hosting his own web series. Known for his raspy baritone and an over-articulated delivery, as well as his unique hairstyles, Coolio differed from most gangsta rappers in that he emphasized positive messages and the ability to change one's life, lessons he himself lived out. His cooking show, *Cookin' with Coolio* (2014–), which followed from his writing a popular soul food and special diet cookbook, *Cookin' with Coolio: 5 Star Meals at a 1 Star Price* (2009), was created to help people who grew up in poverty, like himself, eat healthy and well. "Gangsta's Paradise" reached the top spot on the Billboard Hot 100 for three weeks, and its follow-up album, *Gangsta's Paradise*, was certified double platinum and produced the Top Ten hit "1, 2, 3, 4 (Sumpin' New)." "Gangsta's Paradise" was also included on the *Dangerous Minds* soundtrack. The album *I Am L.V.* (1996) included "L.V.'s Version," which is mostly sung. Several parodies of the song exist, including "Amish Paradise" (1996) by Weird Al Yankovic.

CYPRESS HILL

Cypress Hill (1988–), a West Coast rap trio from Los Angeles (South Gate), has sold eighteen million albums internationally. Consisting of Cuban American rapper Sen Dog (Senen Reyes, 1965–), rapper B-Real (Louis Mario Freese, 1970–), and turntablist DJ Muggs (Lawrence Muggerud, 1968–), the band also spawned the solo career of Sen Dog's brother, Mellow Man Ace (Ulpiano Sergio Reyes, 1967–). Important because it was the first certified platinum and multiplatinum Latino

American hip hop recording group, Cypress Hill produced four platinum studio albums, all on Ruffhouse Records: *Cypress Hill* (1991), *Black Sunday* (1993), *III: Temples of Boom* (1995), and *Skull & Bones* (2000). Two of its songs, "How I Could Just Kill a Man" (1991) and "Insane in the Brain" (1993), reached No. 1 on the Hot Rap Songs chart. Cypress Hill also became the first rap group to have two albums simultaneously in the Top Ten.

Its sound is defined by its use of funk, hardcore rock, and metal conventions; of offbeat sampling; and of childlike, playfully melodic motifs, as well as B-Real's idiosyncratic vocals. The music is defined by a heavy bass and unusual sound effects (digital and analog, including animal sounds), which are looped throughout each song. B-Real is known specifically for his exaggerated, high-pitched, nasally but smooth vocal delivery that makes the band's sound unique, especially when contrasted with Sen Dog's deep, gravelly (and sometimes processed, with harmonizing) vocals, which are generally used to punctuate phrases. The band was also unique (in early rap) for its bilingual approach to lyrics.

Cypress Hill introduces itself quickly in its debut album as a streetwise half-Latino (Chicano), half–African American band through the intro to the album's first song, "Pigs," a parody of "This Little Piggy." The lyrics excoriate the LAPD for its harassment and killing of minorities in urban neighborhoods, and the song ends with a celebration of what happens to crooked police officers once they are imprisoned. B-Real's nasal, lilting, almost comic delivery is front and center, set against offbeat instrumentation—heavy McCartney-esque melodic rock bass, snare drum, and an electric guitar octave-based ostinato with tremolo effects. The album's second song, "How I Could Just Kill a Man," which has a quirky beat created by funk bass, vocalizations, tambourine, a repetitive piano effect (the same chord over and over on the first beat), and jazz rock drum kit, has lyrics that clearly establish Cypress Hill as both pro gangsta and pro ganja—both themes get equal treatment throughout. Other quirks on the album include a hiccupped, repeated sample of Gene Chandler's 1962 No. 1 hit "Duke of Earl," offbeat instrumentation and synth voices, refrains that borrow from children's taunts, and randomly absurd lyrics. Interspersed throughout are staples of rap: funk-based drumming, looped funk bass, sub-bass, scratching, guitars (funk and rock) used to complement drum beats, and synthesizer-produced ostinatos and stingers. The album's standouts include "Light Another" and "The Phuncky Feel One," both funky, danceable songs that include funk guitar, heavy bass, funk drumming, brass, claps, and B-Real's using some of his higher registers, which make his voice seem even more quirky.

The more funk-based *Black Sunday* continued the quirky brilliance of Cypress Hill's debut, becoming the band's only No. 1 album and producing it's only Top 40 hit, "Insane in the Brain," which reached No. 19 on the Billboard Hot 100. The album opens with an idiosyncratic synthesizer-oscillating stinger that is repeated until a bass and drum kit introduce the funk beat of "I Wanna Get High," a gimmicky song that would be at home on any Dr. Demento radio show. Standouts include "I Ain't Going Out Like That," "Insane in the Brain," and "Lick a Shot." The first two songs use heavy bass juxtaposed against snare and a high-pitched, oscillating synth voice. "Insane in the Brain" even features a calliope in its third verse. "Lick a Shot" has a frenetic bass and drum beat set against various synth voices, including a high-pitched shawm. *Black Sunday*'s lyrics, like those of its predecessor, alternate between gangsta violence and drug use and show an evolution toward a greater use of comic vocalizations, pop culture allusion, clever wordplay, and image juxtaposition; vocal processing for effect is also more prominent. The band's third album, *Temples of Boom*, introduced a greater use of skits (as song intros), including one in Spanish ("Killa Hill N—") and immediately established a move toward the more laid-back g-funk sound. The album's major theme is championing marijuana use as a way of opening up the mind's creative possibilities, as in "Spark Another Owl." Album standouts include the entourage song "Throw Your Set in the Air," which features rock bass, snare and hi-hat/ride drumming, metal percussion, and two disparate synth voices, one which sounds like a cross between a harpsichord and organ, and the other a high-pitched two-chord oscillating ostinato. Oddball instrumentation abounds on the album: "Stoned Raiders" includes tubular bells and sine waves; "Illusions" features sitar and a synth-based vibraphone ostinato, the latter also heard on the gangsta song "Boom Biddy Bye Bye"; "Make a Move," another gangsta threat song, has an intro that includes a musical saw, and the entire song is based on a three-note, two-measure bass ostinato (with the same note on beats one and three, and octave on beats two and four). On *Temples of Boom*, B-Real's flow is taken to a new level, becoming more percussive through his use of fricatives, a staccato delivery, and choppy pauses (which sound like musical hiccups).

Cypress Hill IV, produced by DJ Muggs, immediately announces itself as a darker album with the antihero song "Looking through the Eye of a Pig." The song, which laments that moment when an individual realizes his own corrupt nature, comes across as harder, with bass and drum moved to the forefront and vocals backgrounded, with more reverb to make them sound more ethereal and disturbed. Aside from the hit "Tequila Sunrise" and the marijuana-friendly "Dr. Greenthumb," standouts include the frenetic "Checkmate," a punk-based, extremely aggressive drum and bass song that allows B-Real and Sen Dog to interact vocally (comparable to vocals associated with Beastie Boys), and the quirky "Audio X," which features an odd ostinato created by a distorted shawm or clarinet synthesizer voice. Other songs show the band's diversity: "From the Window of My Room" features dramatic strings, while the violent "Prelude to a Come Up," which features MC Eiht (Aaron Tyler, 1971–), is classic g-funk. It and "Riot Starter" would comfortably fit on N.W.A.'s *Straight Outta Compton* (1988).

Skull & Bones, also produced by DJ Muggs, continues the experimentation of *Cypress Hill IV* with its first two tracks, "Intro" and "Another Victory," continuing the previous album's wall-of-sound feel, with heavy melodramatic synthesizer beats that use keyboard and string voices, with vocals slightly backgrounded; the album also features a greater use of media samples than previously. Standouts include the Eminem-influenced "Rap Superstar" and "Highlife," the first of which features Eminem's guest rapping against drum kit, bass, and string voices and toy piano ostinatos. "What U Want from Me" features plucked strings and full orchestration. The album's gangsta songs, such as "Cuban Necktie," are in the more violent mobb rap style, with lyrics that reference mafia-based films like *Scarface* (1983) and *Goodfellas* (1990). In songs like "Stank Ass Hoe," the band returns to its earlier, more gimmicky sound, with sine waves (produced by a synthesized musical saw voice) and other offbeat synth voices. "Can I Get a Hit" exhibits a return to some of the band's early humor as the song laments having friends who bogart (smoke all of the band's weed). The band continues its experimentation with songs such as "We Live This S—," which has a beat created by bass drum (or timpani) set against an ostinato created by piccolo and violin strings.

The band's popularity began to wane around 2000, and its final three albums, *Stoned Raiders* (Columbia, 2001), *Till Death Do Us Part* (Columbia, 2004), and *Rise Up* (Capitol, 2010), all had disappointing sales. In 2012, Cypress Hill teamed up with dubstep artist Rusko (Christopher William Mercer, 1985–) to produce *Cypress X Rusko,* an EP of five songs that bridged electronica (dubstep) with hip hop. Over the course of its career, Cypress Hill has had three Grammy nominations. The band has also been the official spokesperson for NORML (the National Organization for the Reform of Marijuana Laws).

DA BRAT, FOXY BROWN, AND LIL' KIM

Rap music began as a male phenomenon, with record label crews usually consisting of a handful of men and one woman. Considering the hypermasculine stance of early rappers that glamorized strength, violence, and competition for competition's sake (everyone or every rap crew had to be the best, which he/it accomplished by dissing others through battle raps), it came as no surprise that the status of women in rap was to be a "b—," a "ho," or a "vixen." Videos for sex rap songs were filled with video vixens, scantily clad women who danced for men and admired their bling while they (the men) rapped. Few women challenged this, with the earliest example being Queens rapper Roxanne Shanté (Lolita Shanté Gooden, 1969–), a member of the Juice Crew, who launched "The Roxanne Wars," a series of rap diss songs between herself and two Brooklyn-based acts: the all-male rap crew U.T.F.O. (Untouchable Force Organization) and the Real Roxanne (Adelaida Martinez, 1963–), a rapper hired by U.T.F.O. to respond to Roxanne Shanté.

It would take nearly a decade before three women helped opened the door for female rappers by both embracing the vixen image and countering it with the idea of the strong woman who was both more aggressive professionally (no longer willing to dance in the background) and more actively sexual (rather than passively sexualized). Chicago's Da Brat (Shawntae Harris, 1974–), along with two Brooklyn female rappers, Lil' Kim (Kimberly Denise Jones, 1975–) and Foxy Brown (Inga DeCarlo Fung Marchand, 1978–), followed in the footsteps of Roxanne Shanté and female rap pioneer MC Lyte. Foxy Brown, Lil' Kim, and Da Brat appeared together only once, on Total's 1996 song "No One Else"; since Foxy Brown later had diss wars with many rappers, including Lil' Kim.

Da Brat debuted with her first So So Def album, *Funkdafied* (1994), a certified platinum record that spawned the No. 1 rap single "Funkdafied," which reached No. 6 on the Billboard Hot 100, along with two other Top 40 hits, "Fa All Y'all" (No. 37) and "Give It 2 You" (No. 26). She became the first solo female rap artist to have an RIAA certified platinum album and single. A trained drummer, she created music that incorporated elements of gangsta rap, funk, and pop, and her popularity led to appearances in movies such as *Kazaam* (1996) and *Glitter* (2001) and roles on television, in such shows as *The Parent 'Hood* (1997–98) and, most recently, *Empire* (2015). Da Brat's other So So Def output includes *Anuthatantrum* (1996), *Unrestricted* (2000, certified platinum and her best charter, reaching No. 5 on the Billboard 200), and *Limelite, Luv and Niteclubz* (2003). She is also well known for her collaborations with and appearances on albums of high-profile artists, including the Notorious B.I.G., Mariah Carey, Missy Elliott, Lil' Kim, Left Eye Lopes, and Ludacris. In the early years of her career, Da Brat positioned herself as a female version of Snoop Dogg, not only emulating the rapper's relaxed rhyming tempo and g-funk musical style but also appearing in baggy clothes.

Funkdafied features songs that, like the album's name implies, are funk-infused, such as "Funkdafied" and "Fa All Y'all," both produced by Jermaine Dupri (Jermaine Dupri Mauldin, 1972–) of the So So Def label. The main melodic line in "Funkdafied" is created with a 1980s-style funk keyboard voice set against a simple 4/4 snare beat (with occasional brush effects), turntable, synth bass, and vibraslap. Here Da Brat (who has a girlish voice) and Dupri sing and rap. Da Brat's flow varies between laid-back, carefully measured, articulated lines and breathless speed rapping, with some chopper vocalizations (like stutters). "Fa All Y'all" combines George Clinton–style synth-funk with gangsta rap elements (references to violence) and synth bass, programmed drums, reverbed claps, and funk-style singing in the hook/refrain. Da Brat's rap flow is more breathless and aggressive here, with lots of interior rhyme and enjambment to prevent lines from being singsong (as in old-school rap). On *Anuthatantrum*, Dupri ups the funk game with singles like "Sittin on Top of the World," a braggadocio and diss rap that features a melodramatic keyboard ostinato intro. The track showcases Da Brat's speed rapping in its verses (she actually flirts with chopper style), along with funk slap bass, a piano melody, and a snare and tom beat. Its refrain is sung funk style, with male harmonies, with Da Brat's rapping used as a countermelody. Despite keeping her girlish voice, by *Unrestricted*, Da Brat's raps become more adult-oriented and complex, as in the sex song "Wha'chu Like," which is produced by Dupri and features Tyrese (Tyrese Gibson, 1978–). The track is informed not by funk but by Caribbean rhythms instead. To complement and bookend Tyrese's sung hook, Da Brat's rap flow evolves. Here it is more complex as she is able to rap both on and off the beat, which allows for surprising lyrical pauses (for subtle humor) and makes it possible for her to rap against a complex beat. By *Limelite, Luv and Niteclubz*, which she produced herself along with L. T. Hutton (Lenton Terrell Hutton, 1974–) of Death Row and Ruthless Records, Da Brat had evolved from rapping about entourages, lyrical skills, and gangsta issues to rapping about romance and sex. Throughout her career, she stayed with the So So Def label.

Lil' Kim is best known for her sexually explicit lyrics and provocative dress. In the early 1990s she was the only female member of Junior M.A.F.I.A. (1992–), whose debut album, *Conspiracy* (Big Beat, 1995), was certified gold. She established her hypersexual reputation early on with her debut, *Hard Core* (Big Beat-Undeas, 1996), which contained hardcore rap and sexually explicit lyrics. The album's lyrics were noteworthy for their raunchiness; for example, in her opening verse for "Big Momma Thang," she uses explicit slang to express that she has gotten over her fear of male genitalia and anal intercourse, unusual lyrics for female rappers at the time. *Hard Core* peaked at No. 11 on the Billboard 200 and was certified double platinum, with singles charting on the Billboard 100: "No Time" (No. 18) and "Not Tonight (Ladies Night Remix)" (No. 6). "No Time" reached the top spot on the Hot Rap Songs chart; "Not Tonight" peaked at No. 2. Her second album, *The Notorious K.I.M.* (2000), on her own Queen Bee label, was certified platinum after just four weeks. Many hip hop fans viewed Lil' Kim's explicit performances as an empowered approach to and expression of female sexuality, but civil rights activist C. Delores Tucker objected to Lil' Kim's lyrics, calling her music "gangsta porno rap." Despite a three-year prison sentence, Lil' Kim produced two more studio albums—*La Bella Mafia* (2003, platinum) and *The Naked Truth* (2005)—and four mixtapes, and in 1999 she created Queen Bee (renamed International Rock Star Records).

Her debut sound on *Hard Core* can best be described as graphic sex rap (its intro is a skit about masturbating in a porn theater) meets neo soul and down-tempo funk, as exemplified in the singles "No Time" and "Crush on You." "No Time," produced by Puff Daddy (Sean John Combs, 1969–) and Stevie J (Steven Aaron Jordan, 1971–) and featuring Puff Daddy and the Notorious B.I.G., is a laid-back rap track (of the type that would be made popular by Snoop Dogg), despite its graphic sex rap. Instrumentation consists of piano, keyboard, synth string voices, a snare drum beat, and down-tempo male vocals and vocalizations, around which Lil' Kim raps. "Crush on You," produced by Andreao Heard (n.d.) and with a guest appearance by a laid-back Notorious B.I.G., is a mid-tempo funk-soul track, with keyboard, a simple snare and hi-hat beat with tom flourishes, and electric funk bass. By the production of *La Bella Mafia*, the rapper had evolved from sex rap to gangsta/bling and braggadocio rap and had embraced the g-funk, mobb, and snap styles, heard even in its intro, which features the Notorious B.I.G. "Hold It Now" and the single "Magic Stick," produced by Sha Money XL (Michael Clervoix, 1976–) and Fantom of the Beat (Carlos Evans, 1971–) exemplify this sound. "Hold It Now" features g-funk's typical kick bass and distorted snare to sound like claps or snaps, along with an occasional synthesizer stinger. Lil' Kim's vocals here are more highly processed to sound harmonized and chant-like. "Doing It Way Big," produced by Jay Garfield, features synth-produced world instrument voices, such as tabla, monkey drum, and chimta. "The Jump Off" is high-energy dance music that has a hook reminiscent to that of Missy Elliott's "Get Ur Freak On."

Foxy Brown is known for both her solo work and her brief stint as part of the short-lived hip hop group The Firm (*The Album* was released in 1997 on the Aftermath label). Her Def Jam albums include *Ill Na Na* (1996), *Chyna Doll* (1999), and the Grammy-nominated *Broken Silence* (2001), her productivity being affected by an extensive arrest record (usually for physical altercations), incarceration time, addiction problems, and hearing-loss issues. Foxy Brown started out with guest appearances on songs by LL Cool J, Toni Braxton, and Jay-Z, leading to her being signed by Def Jam Records at the age of seventeen. *Ill Na Na* debuted at No. 7 on the Billboard 200 and went on to go platinum. In 1996–97, Foxy Brown joined Nas, AZ, and Nature to form The Firm, which recorded one album, coproduced by Dr. Dre. That album reached No. 1 on the Billboard 200, as did her second solo album, *Chyna Doll*. *Broken Silence* debuted at No. 5 and was certified gold. Foxy Brown has made a comeback of late: in 2018 she made her first guest appearance since 2009 on Nicki Minaj's "Coco Chanel" (from *Queen*), and she is currently working on a fourth studio album, *King Soon Come*.

Ill Na Na, a g-funk meets thug (reminiscent of the early albums of C-Murder) production managed to produce one Top Ten hit, "I'll Be," which samples "I'll Be Good" (1985) by René and Angela and features Jay-Z. Though she is more auto-tuned (harmonized), Foxy Brown's flow is more varied and complex than those of Da Brat or Lil' Kim. Her raps are clearly more gangsta-oriented as well. This is evident in the first music track on *Ill Na Na*, the Trackmasters-produced "(Holy Matrimony) Letter to the Firm," whose lyrics make it clear that the gangsta life is a lifetime commitment. The song's instrumentation is complex, a melodic piano set against a snare, kick, and hi-hat beat, with a brief baritone guitar ostinato used as an occasional tag (a hiccup to bridge between verses). "I'll Be," also produced by Trackmasters, combines sex bragging with skills bragging. It is a danceable rap, with a synth bass and snare beat accompanied by a keyboard scale (on beat one in the odd-numbered phrases and on all four beats in the even-numbered phrases, with occasional variation by way of rests).

A heavier funk sound informs *Chyna Doll*, which begins with a graphic skit that chronicles the birth of Foxy Brown as well as her mother's advice to be gangsta. The album's single, "Hot Spot," produced by Lil Rob (Roberto L. Flores, 1975–) and Irv Gotti (Irving Domingo Lorenzo Jr., 1970–), is a 1970s funk–infused programmed drum, 808, synth bass, and keyboard ostinato dance track against which Foxy Brown creates an entourage and brag rap. By *Broken Silence*'s "Candy," produced by the Neptunes, Foxy Brown's sound becomes more pop-influenced. "Candy" is a sex brag dance song that includes a pop refrain by Kelis (Kelis

Rogers, 1979–), against which verses are rapped mid-tempo but aggressively by Foxy Brown. Overall, *Broken Silence* shows the influence of various styles (pop singing, dance, Jamaican toasting, and Latin rhythm, to name a few) more than any Foxy Brown album as it has seventeen different producers.

DANGER MOUSE: *THE GREY ALBUM* (SEE JAY-Z AND DANGER MOUSE)

DE LA SOUL

De La Soul (1987–) is one of those bands that can best be described as indescribable. Like its Long Island counterpart Public Enemy, this trio boasts an album that is widely considered one of the best hip hop albums ever—*3 Feet High and Rising* (1989)—though a rap fan would be hard-pressed to think of an album more different from Public Enemy's iconic *Fear of a Black Planet* (1990). Despite its experimental nature, *3 Feet High and Rising* reached No. 24 on the Billboard 200, No. 1 on the Top R&B/Hip Hop Albums chart, and was the band's only RIAA certified platinum album. Although the trio never had a Top Ten hit on the billboard Hot 100, it did appear on Gorillaz's biggest hit, "Feel Good Inc.," which almost managed that feat, peaking at No 14.

Individual tracks on *3 Feet High and Rising* were linked with a fictional game show in which each member of the group and producer Prince Paul (Paul Edward Huston, 1967–) is asked questions about life, the universe, shredded wheat, and Batman. One of the album's standouts, "Cool Breeze on the Rocks," is a collage of dozens of different sung and spoken samples from various musicians and historical figures. "The Magic Number" references Bob Dorough's music from *Schoolhouse Rock*, while creating a heavy bass song about the nature of life. "Eye Know" uses rock guitar samples set against laid-back rapping about romance. The short piece "A Little Bit of Soap" uses the bass riff from "Stand by Me" and the idea of the 1961 Jarmels hit "A Little Bit of Soap" to offer advice on personal hygiene. The album also featured the trio's only Top 40 hit, "Me, Myself, and I."

Debuting on the more mainstream Tommy Boy label (1981–) with members Trugoy the Dove (a.k.a. Dave, David Jolicoeur, 1968–), Maseo (Vincent Mason Jr., 1970–), and Posdnuos (a.k.a. Pos; Kelvin Mercer, 1969–), the trio De La Soul worked with producer Prince Paul to define its trademark features early on. These included quirky lyrics, eclectic sampling (including from French language instruction records), and offbeat skits, all set against a varied array of beats and instrumentation from funk, soul, and blue-eyed soul. Sampled artists ranged from Hall & Oates, the Turtles, and Johnny Cash to Michael Jackson, Flavor Flav, and MC Lyte; even comedian Richard Pryor is sampled. However, after a copyright lawsuit was settled out of court for an undisclosed sum, the members of De La Soul became cautious about sample clearance, and by 1993's *Buhloone Mindstate* (the band's third studio album) they began featuring new performances—some by legendary funk musicians such as trombonist Fred Wesley (1943–) and saxophonist Maceo Parker (1943–). Concurrently, the trio's lyrics began to take on darker subjects. On its second album, *De La Soul Is Dead* (1991), songs began dealing with issues like child abuse and crack addiction ("Millie Pulled a Pistol on Santa" and "My Brother's a Basehead," respectively). *Buhloone Mindstate* included "Patti Dooke," which satirizes mainstream efforts to control the messages and style of black music.

De La Soul Is Dead, which features many female guest vocalists who rap, sing, and provide chatter for skits and songs, is structured as a macabre children's story of a found mixtape (found in the garbage), *The Adventure of De La Soul Is Dead*. Unlike its predecessor, it contains not absurdist questioning but foul language and childish insults. The album's first song, "Oodles of O's," juxtaposes heavy funk bass and drum against keyboards and guitars that are high treble; vocals are old-school, sing-song rap. The funk beats continue through the romance song "Talkin' Bout Hey Love" and the updated traditional "Pease Porridge," both of which include spoken-word dialogue and singing, the latter juxtaposing a constant clacking sound of bones (likely a sample from Brother Bones, made to sound like tap dancing) and a sampling of Harrell and Sharron Lucky, as well as Kermit the Frog, against a heavy bass and drum funk rhythm section. It also samples Brother Bones's B-Side to "Sweet Georgia Brown," "Black Eyed Susan Brown" (date unknown). The dance tune "A Rollerskating Jam Named 'Saturdays'" features scratching and old-school rapping as well as diva (house music) singing. The album's standout, "Millie Pulled a Pistol on Santa," uses a funk beat to tell the story of a young girl who is raped by her father, narrated by a friend of the father (he at first does not believe Millie, thinking his friend is incapable of rape). The song ends abruptly, with Millie's shooting her father while he plays department store Santa at Macy's.

Buhloone Mindstate found the trio moving away from funk and the idea of the frame device, experimenting with trance and smooth jazz, exemplified in tracks such as "I Am, I Be" and "I Be Blowin'," the latter including an extended saxophone solo. In contrast, "Ego Trippin' Part 2" is old-school hip hop with a funk-infused rhythm juxtaposed against

Middle Eastern traditional instrument sampling (the shawm). "Patti Dooke" features a male-female dialogue, set against a heavy trance beat and clarinet samples. "Stone Age" is a dialogue, with beatboxing, among the three members set against a heavy bass and drum beat for the purpose of "making London bridges fall" and bringing it "back to the beat box" to attract women.

The band's highest charting album (reaching No. 9 on the Billboard 200), *Art Official Intelligence: Mosaic Thump* (2000) saw De La Soul's moving away from old-school rapping and toward a raw, aggressive rapping style, which is juxtaposed against R&B and neo soul–style singing. Guest performers included Busta Rhymes and Redman (Reginald Noble, 1970–). "My Writes" is a braggadocio rap that includes violent reactions to disingenuous rappers who misrepresent themselves and know little about the issues of black and urban communities. Although it is also about urban issues, "Thru Ya City" is classic De La Soul, sampling the Lovin' Spoonful hit "Summer in the City" (1966) for its refrain and sung against rapped verses set to a steady bass-heavy beat. The album's standouts are the bragging song "I C Y'all," which features a heavy keyboard bass, plucked strings, and Busta Rhymes, and "Oooh," a down-tempo funk and Brick City party anthem featuring Redman (the song's video parodies *The Wizard of Oz* as a Brick City club scene).

The follow-up album, *AOI: Bionix* (2001), a self-proclaimed "second installment" of *Mosaic Thump*, begins with a computerized female voice that welcomes listeners using language associated with television's *The Six Million Dollar Man* (1973–78) and promises an album that is "better, stronger, faster"—a message of rap self-realization echoed in the first track, "Bionix," a funk-based tune that both thanks fans and promises more good music. It transitions smoothly into the bass-heavy "Baby Phat," an anti-body-shaming sex song. Both songs use the vibraphone to add a jazzy feel to the beat. "Simply," an upbeat club song about enjoying life, uses a retro 1970s beat and old-school rapping juxtaposed against an altered sampling of Paul McCartney's "Wonderful Christmastime" (1979). The album also includes urban rap, such as "Held Down," "Watch Out," and "Am I Worth You," the first being an R&B and gospel-infused, drum, bass, organ, and rhythm guitar song about beating the odds of an inner-city upbringing, which leads to one of the few interlude characters on the album, Reverend Do-Good; he appears in three segments, the latter two being smooth jazz–influenced (including a vibraphone) bragging songs that establish De La Soul's New York City street cred. Romance songs include "Special," a bass-heavy song that features new age keyboard voices and strings.

The trio's most recent album on the band's AOI label, *And the Anonymous Nobody* (2016), features Jill Scott (1972–) in a spoken-word album introduction titled "Genesis," Yukimi Nagano (1982–) of the Swedish electronic band Little Dragon, and Snoop Dogg. "Royalty Capes" is the album's standout, a diss and braggadocio track that dismisses android MCs who create iPhone rap (the song is heavy on wordplay). Here rap is set against a fanfare of brass, woodwinds, plucked strings, and rumbling bass. "Pain" is a 1970s funk–infused song (in the Earth, Wind, and Fire vein) about surviving adversity. "Property of Spitkicker.com" is a minimalist, self-reflective, metatextual song that creates an imagistic tapestry of personal, pop cultural, and historical allusions to tell the story of the trio's long history. The album also includes a love song, "Memory of . . . (Us)." The album's midsection includes experimental sociopolitical crossover tracks, including its longest song, clocking in at over seven minutes, the rock and metal–infused "Lord Intended," which features Justin Hawkins (1975–) of the British rock band The Darkness; the catchy alternative, multisection song "Snoopies," which features David Byrne (1952–); and the laid-back alternative rap and neo-soul song "Greyhounds," a commentary on disillusioned urban youth, which features refrain singing by Usher (Usher Raymond IV, 1978–). The genuinely sad "Greyhounds," which begins a trio of songs (the sequels being "Sexy B—" and "Trainwreck") is the album's finest moment.

De La Soul released albums every three or four years until 2004, after which it did not release another album until the 2012 collaboration *Plug 1 and Plug 2 Present . . . First Serve*. They remained active in the interim, however, working with groups such as Gorillaz, Yo La Tengo, and LA Symphony. The trio won its first Grammy Award in 2006 for its collaboration with Gorillaz on the single "Feel Good Inc." Overall, De La Soul's lyrics espoused its concept of the D.A.I.S.Y. Age (an acronym for "da inner sound, y'all"), a catchall concept for harmony and peace. The trio came to be associated with the New York–based Native Tongues collective, which included the Jungle Brothers (1987–) as well as Queens-based groups Black Sheep and A Tribe Called Quest. The music of Native Tongues groups generally promoted Afrocentric lyrics and featured jazz-based samples, quirky or unusual sampling, and an overall sense of positivity.

DJ JAZZY JEFF & THE FRESH PRINCE

Philadelphia's DJ Jazzy Jeff (Jeffrey Allen Townes, 1965–) and the Fresh Prince (Willard Carroll Smith Jr., 1968–) were an early old-school rap duo. Both were multitalented: Jazzy Jeff went on to become an R&B DJ, record producer, actor, and world DJ champion (1986). Will Smith (the Fresh Prince) became a television star and one of the most popular and sought-after actors of the last two decades, having been nominated for two Academy Awards and five Golden Globe awards. As a trio that also included beatboxer Ready Rock C (Clarence Holmes, 1968–), DJ Jazzy Jeff & the Fresh Prince signed with Word Records, soon renamed Word Up, but then switched over to Jive Records as a duo since Ready Rock C was preparing to depart (and would do so in 1990); he would later unsuccessfully sue Smith. With Jive, the duo produced the triple platinum album *He's the DJ, I'm the Rapper* (1988). Although it had only one Top Ten hit on the Billboard Hot 100, "Summertime," which reached No. 4 and was its first platinum single, the duo won two Grammy Awards. The 1988 song "Parents Just Don't Understand," which reached No. 12 on the Hot 100, became an MTV standard, won the first ever Grammy Award for Best Rap Performance, and led to Smith's acting career with the television series *The Fresh Prince of Bel-Air*. When DJ Jazzy Jeff & the Fresh Prince disbanded, the duo did so with two platinum albums, *He's the DJ, I'm the Rapper* and *Homebase* (1991).

The band's debut, *Rock the House* (1987), contains its first minor hit, "Girl's Ain't Nothing but Trouble," which made it into the Hot 100, peaking at No. 57. It's an old-school story rap that sampled the theme from *I Dream of Jeannie* and subsequently led to a lawsuit. The album's standout is "The Magnificent Jazzy Jeff," a song designed to showcase Jazzy Jeff's turntablism. "Just One of Those Days" is another story rap; it samples Irving Berlin's "Puttin' on the Ritz" (1927). Both songs are simply constructed of beats, turntable, sample, and old-school rap. "Rock the House," a live performance, is notable in that it features Ready Rock C's beatboxing.

He's the DJ, I'm the Rapper was the first double-disc hip hop release on vinyl. It spawned three singles, "Brand New Funk," "Parents Just Don't Understand," and "A Nightmare on My Street," the last two reaching the Billboard Hot 100 at Nos. 12 and 15, respectively. The comic "A Nightmare on My Street," which led to a lawsuit for copyright against the band, is indistinguishable from funk-based 1980s rock in instrumentation—synthesizer bass and drum. Smith's rapping is unique for its singsong quality, with little to no variety in line length, as well as for his boyish sounding, high vocal register. "Parents Just Don't Understand" is similar in tone and structure, and both are narrative raps (stories told chronologically). Other old-school style songs include the braggadocio "As We Go." In contrast, "Brand New Funk," which samples James Brown, is notable for its use of rumbling electric bass against snare and ride cymbal (and at times hi-hat), as well as Jazzy Jeff's turntable solo. Smith's rapping, which contains lines of varied length, prefigures chopper style in sections. Similar in style are the turntable and rock bass–heavy "Charlie Mack." The album also contains the mostly instrumental tracks "DJ on Wheels," "Hip Hop Dancer's Theme," and "Jazzy's in the House," as well as the spoken word and rap "He's the DJ, I'm the Rapper" and "Rhythm Trax." These allow for Jazzy Jeff to show off his skills, the latter being the best song on the album as it also shows Smith at his best, improvising a rap based on constant flow changes. "My Buddy" is the only example of Ready Rock C's beatboxing on the album.

Homebase, a collection of dance rap songs, includes the duo's most successful song, "Summertime." It is a funk-based dance song in which Smith uses his deepest register and loses his old-school rap singsong flow, going as far as using enjambment on many lines. The song also uses a female guest singer to give it more of an R&B feel, but what is lost is Jazzy Jeff's turntablism. Other songs, such as "The Things That U Do" and "Caught in the Middle (Love & Life)," also show the duo moving away from pure rap and toward danceable funk, soul, and R&B, with rapping included. "Caught in the Middle" stands out as containing some of Smith's most aggressive rapping; it also shows Smith moving toward the new-school style of rap, where flow varies, and interior rhyme becomes as prominent as exterior rhyme. The album's stand out song is the braggadocio "I'm All That," a bass-heavy and 808 drum–based song about Smith's rapping ability, which is on full display through extremely clever lyrics, as is Jazzy Jeff's scratching, which fills an extended outro.

DJ Jazzy Jeff & the Fresh Prince's final album, *Code Red* (1993), is a continuation of the duo's evolution toward dance rap. It starts with "Somethin' Like Dis," a party anthem that includes a chanting male chorus; a snare, ride, and bass beat; synthesizer-produced brass; and a liberal use of turntablism. It stands out for its inclusion of Jazzy Jeff's rapping, in dialogue with Smith, who here diversifies his flow and includes a masterful chopper-style verse. Along with "Boom, Shake the Room" and "Twinkle, Twinkle (I'm Not a Star)," it stands out as one of the best songs on the album. "Boom, Shake the Room," an aggressively rapped party anthem where Smith uses his deepest register, at points even grunting (an unusual vocalization practice for him), reached No. 13 on the Hot 100. Jazzy Jeff is limited to beat making on the song, but he excels at creating a funk-based, bass-heavy beat, with a gimmick keyboard voice (sounding something like an arp) adding interest points in the refrain. "Twinkle, Twinkle" is a down-tempo anti-braggadocio gimmick-infused song, featuring various voices in dialogue with Smith's rapping, creating a sound similar to early De La Soul. Typical romance songs include "I'm Looking for the One (To Be with Me)" and "Can't Wait to Be with You." The former uses neo-soul elements and features sung refrains (using vocal processing); its lyrics are interesting for their challenging of the prominence of gangsta rap, arguing that music should soothe, a theme featured in "Just Kickin' It" as well. The latter is more R&B and soul–infused and features soul singer Christopher Williams (Troy Christopher Williams, 1967–), the cousin of Al B. Sure! and nephew of Ella Fitzgerald. Though forgettable songs musically, the Cypress Hill–like "Code Red" and "I Wanna Rock" are notable for small elements. The former includes some of Smith's best vocal delivery, as most verses end with an aside or linguistic undercutting of the lyric content that breaks the flow in a humorous and clever way; the latter showcases Jazzy Jeff's turntablism.

In 1990, Jazzy Jeff, well known for the diversity of his sampling and his unique turntable techniques such as the "Transformer" and "Chirp" scratches, founded A Touch of Jazz, Inc., a stable of producers working on rap and R&B projects in Philadelphia. He also played the character Jazz on *The Fresh Prince of Bel-Air*. As a solo act, Jazzy Jeff has released two albums, *The Magnificent* (2002) and *The Return of the Magnificent* (2007). He also collaborated with Smith on his solo album *Willennium* (1999). Smith's acting and personality made him popular with mainstream audiences, especially with white Americans. Since the mid-1990s, he has starred in some of the highest-grossing films of all time. His most successful commercial solo album was *Big Willie Style* (1997).

DONATAN: "SŁOWIAŃSKA KREW" AND "NIE LUBIMY ROBIĆ" (SEE BUBBA SPARXXX AND DONATAN)

DOUG E. FRESH AND THE GET FRESH CREW: "LA DI DA DI" (SEE BIG DADDY KANE AND DOUG E. FRESH AND THE GET FRESH CREW)

DRAKE: "MONEY TO BLOW" AND "4 MY TOWN (PLAY BALL)" (SEE BIRDMAN, DRAKE, AND LIL WAYNE)

DRAKE: *SCORPION* (CASH MONEY RECORDS-YOUNG MONEY ENTERTAINMENT, 2018)

Drake is a Canadian rapper, songwriter, producer, and actor who has four No. 1 certified platinum albums on the Canadian and Billboard 200 album charts, two certified platinum mixtapes, twenty Top Ten singles in the Hot 100, sixteen No. 1 singles on the U.S. R&B/Hip Hop Songs chart (a record), and seventeen No. 1 singles on the Hot Rap chart. He also released a chart-topping album, *More Life* (2017), as a playlist. Because he split his childhood between suburban and affluent Toronto neighborhoods (with his mother) and urban Memphis, Tennessee, (with his father), his raps portray both urban ("hood") and middle-class existence. He began as Drizzy Drake with three self-released mixtapes (2006, 2007, 2009), two on his October's Very Own (a.k.a. OVO Sound, 2007–) label. His third mixtape, *So Far Gone* (2009), produced "Best I Ever Had," a No. 2 hit on the Billboard 100 and Grammy nominee. In 2009, he signed with Cash Money Records and its imprint, Young Money Entertainment. His debut album, *Thank Me Later* (2010), hit No. 1 on the Hot 200, the R&B/Hip Hop, and the Hot Rap charts. His second studio album, *Take Care* (2011), won a Grammy Award. His third, *Nothing Was the Same* (2013), was followed by two Cash Money mixtapes in 2015, *If You're Reading This It's Too Late* and *What a Time to Be Alive*, all certified platinum. Drake's fourth studio album, *Views* (2016), like his previous albums, reached No. 1 in the United States and Canada, as well as in Australia, the United Kingdom, and New Zealand. The album won two Grammy Awards.

Scorpion, his fifth studio album, was released in June 2018. *Scorpion* is autobiographical, including details about Drake's paternity saga with adult film star Sophie Brussaux. The album starts with "Survival," a laid-back braggadocio song that uses mostly end rhymes. It recounts Drake's trials as a superstar rapper, emphasizing that although he has been dissed by fellow rappers and called irrelevant by music critics, he continues to survive and, in fact, lives "on the charts." The song's lyrics border on introspection as Drake admits that some of the criticism he has faced, combined with problems he has encountered (namely fathering a child), have him rethinking his choices. The song ends abruptly with the statement that it is only an intro. It flows well into a second autobiographical bragging song, "Nonstop," the title referring to his hit-making abilities. Here, with sub-bass played against a snare drum beat and an 808, Drake brags about his popularity, his celebrity status, his street cred, and his lack of using gimmicks to cover a fear of rapping over a g-funk sound.

Truly, the song (and most of the album's A side) is gimmickless. Drake's rapping is generally monotone, reminiscent of the rapping of Three 6 Mafia, interspersed with a second voice, a husky whisper. The song's beat is also consistent, to the point where it pushes monotony, with hardly any new instrumentation introduced at any point. A similar g-funk sound informs "Elevate," perhaps the most lyrically weak song on the album. The song can be described as basically a beat with a backgrounded synthesized piano voice. Here Drake's rapping is even more of a monotone than usual, with slight auto-tuning. The song's saving grace is a slight peppering of rhythmic change and secondary (multitracked) voices (vocalizations and media samples) that emphasize the end of lines and join in on some refrains. Drake's voice is more raspy here, almost croaky.

The album's standout rap songs are "Mob Ties," "I'm Upset," and "Can't Take a Joke." The gangsta rap song "Mob Ties" starts with a guitar playing arpeggiated chords, combined with an 808 drum, sub-bass/bass kick (played together), grinding electric bass, rhythm sticks, claps, and a synthesizer voice playing the most melodic ostinato on the album. Taking a page from Timbaland's book, the song includes lots of vocalizations and media samples, as well as some female singing. Drake's rapping here is the most interesting on the album, though it is highly auto-tuned (similar to the vocal production values of Childish Gambino). Here Drake raps in his highest register (including using falsetto for singing parts) and uses his most varied flow on the album; he switches between a staccato, slow delivery, and speed rapping, with backing vocalizations usually accentuating the end of lines. The song's outro is a nice combination of synthesizer and drum beat. "I'm Upset" begins with atmospheric keyboard, which continues throughout and is aided by an 808 drum and a bass kick. Drake's vocals are less auto-tuned than usual, less of a monotone, and more on the beat. Here he doesn't rap so much as he uses rhythmic talk-singing, similar to what is heard in Jamaican toasting. Vocalizations are peppered throughout the song, usually to accentuate random words and mostly at the end of phrases. These vocalizations differ from those in other songs as they vary, creating more points of interest. Toward the song's end, a new synthesizer voice is introduced, a grinding trebly sound, giving the impression of new age music. "Can't Take a Joke," also a rap about surviving and thriving in the face of adversity and disrespect, features an oscillating synthesizer beat with a rhythmic bass kick drum. Drake's rapping is slightly auto-tuned, and production effects make his vocal delivery sound dryer than usual—he spits lines that are breathless and longer than others on the album. His rapping is a combination of old-school end rhyme and new-school varied flow, by far his most skilled rapping on the album. Though his voice is again monotonous, it is intriguingly so, set against vocalizations and sound samples (such as car screeching).

The remainder of the album's side A includes "Emotionless," "God's Plan," "8 Out of 10," and "Sandra's Rose." "Emotionless," which features

Mariah Carey (1969–), begins with gospel singing that becomes backgrounded as a bass kick/sub-bass beat takes over, accentuated by a phrase-ending hiccup created by dry metallic percussion (which sounds like a metal scraper run over a cheese grater), along with a synthesizer piano voice. Drake's rapping here is off the beat, although it is rhythmically consistent—the hiccup allows his rapping to get back on beat near the end of verses. "God's Plan" begins with a synthesizer voice playing a four-chord ostinato. Here Drake's rapping is singsong; in fact, he almost breaks into speech-song at times, though his voice is a monotone and highly auto-tuned. Drumming includes bass kick and hi-hat. A second keyboard voice plays a countermelody. In the outro, a bass is introduced, but only very briefly. "8 Out of 10" begins (its intro) as an a cappella piece, a singsong, old-school-style rap. The rapping is later joined with a new age–sounding synthesizer voice and a ride cymbal that is accentuated by an 808 hiccup. Here a female voice sings and vocalizes. Full orchestral strings are introduced as the song progresses, eventually joined by bass guitar, making the song more soul than funk. Drake uses an old-school rapping style throughout, with all end rhymes, his voice only slightly auto-tuned. Here his flow is similar to that of Jay-Z. "Sandra's Rose" stands out for being more R&B-oriented than other songs. Featuring female sung vocals, its beat is created by a drum kit (bass/snare) and a high-pitched synthesizer organ voice. Drake's rapping, in his deepest register, is highly foregrounded for emphasis, more than on *Scorpion*'s other songs. The song can best be described as old-school gangsta rap, with all end rhymes. In fact, the song's lines have monotonous lengths. Side A's final two songs, "Talk Up," and "Is There More," add little to the album.

Scorpion was a double album consisting of twenty-five tracks. Its A side contains twelve rap songs, while its B side contains thirteen R&B and pop songs. The album, which uses thirty-two producers for twenty-five songs, featured guest appearances from Jay-Z and Ty Dolla Sign (Tyrone William Griffin Jr., 1985–), posthumous appearances from Michael Jackson (1958–2009) and Static Major (Stephen Ellis Garrett, 1974–2008), and additional vocals by a variety of other artists. It was supported by the prereleased singles "God's Plan," "Nice for What," and "I'm Upset" and singles "Don't Matter to Me," "In My Feelings," and "Nonstop," which all reached the Top Ten on the Billboard Hot 100, plus "God's Plan," "Nice for What," and "In My Feelings" reaching No. 1. On the July 14, 2018, Hot 100 chart, all twenty-five songs were listed, a record. In its first day of release, it broke Spotify's one-day global record for album streams with 132.45 million, as well as Apple

Music's single-day record with 170 million streams. In the United States, it debuted at No. 1, selling 732,000 album-equivalent units in its first week. With *Scorpion*, Drake became the first musician to simultaneously debut four Top Ten songs on the Hot 100.

DR. DRE: *THE CHRONIC* (DEATH ROW RECORDS, 1992)

Compton-born DJ and rapper Dr. Dre (Andre Romelle Young, 1965–) is arguably the top producer and music engineer in the rap music industry. As both a rapper/DJ and record executive, he helped define and promote the West Coast sound and is one of two people, along with fellow Ruthless Records rapper Cold 187um (Gregory Fernan Hutchinson, 1967–), who can be credited with the creation of the g-funk (gangsta-funk) style, featuring Parliament-Funkadelic-style beats. Dr. Dre developed his interest in music at a popular upscale dance club in Compton, Eve After Dark, where he first appeared under the stage name Dr. J, after his favorite basketball player. The club had a modest recording studio in a back room, and there, working with DJ Yella (Antoine Carraby, 1967–), Dr. Dre recorded and produced his first song, "Surgery" (1984), a local hit.

He soon joined the rap band World Class Wreckin' Cru (1983–88), and he and DJ Yella also appeared on KDAY, a radio station serving South Central Los Angeles; he quickly emerged as a local music celebrity. In the late 1980s, Dr. Dre began to work primarily as a producer for Eazy-E's recording label, Ruthless Records. There he collaborated with Ice Cube (O'Shea Jackson, 1969–) to create much of the material that Dr. Dre, Eazy-E, Ice Cube and a few others would record as the group N.W.A. (1986–91) on their albums *Straight Outta Compton* (1988) and *Efil-4zaggin* (1991), the latter marking a move from aggressive gangsta rap to g-funk. In 1991, Dr. Dre agreed to join with the D.O.C. (Tracy Lynn Curry, 1968–) and Suge Knight (Marion Hugh Knight Jr., 1965–) to form a new label, Death Row Records, and a year later he issued his debut solo album, *The Chronic*, which reached No. 3 on the Billboard 200 and was certified triple platinum, earned a Grammy, and ignited a craze for g-funk.

The Chronic, which was produced almost entirely by Dr. Dre, features many appearances by Snoop Dogg (as Snoop Doggy Dogg)) and guest spots that included RBX (Eric Dwayne Collins, 1968–), Kurupt (Ricardo Emmanuel Brown, 1972–), Bushwick Bill (Richard Stephen Shaw, 1966–), and the Lady of Rage (Robin Yvette Allen, 1970–). Lyrics included both subtle and direct diss tracks aimed at Ruthless Records, Eazy-E, and Tim Dog (Timothy Blair, 1967–2013), among others. The album's sound was informed by 1970s-funk beats, a keyboard or synth ostinato played sometimes against chords, and occasional rhythm guitar. It spawned three Hot 100 singles: "Nuthin' but a 'G' Thang" (No. 2), "F— Wit Dre Day (and Everybody's Celebratin')" (No. 8), and "Let Me Ride" (No. 34). The album's success established Death Row Records as a dominant force in rap. Its intro, "The Chronic (Intro)," jumps out at listeners with Dr. Dre's signature sound: heavy bass (in this case playing a simple walk), an accompanying keyboard ostinato set high in the treble range, occasional turntable for accentuation, and toasting (in this case by Snoop Dogg delivering one of the earliest appearances of his "izzo" style). The track sets the stage thematically by dissing Ruthless Records—the general theme of "F— Wit Dre Day (And Everybody's Celebratin')," a diss track that attacks Tim Dog, Eazy-E and Jerry Heller of Ruthless, as well as Luke Skyywalker of the 2 Live Crew. Listeners get a lot of bass again here, in fact some sub-bass (synth-created, resulting in a down-tempo funk sound) as well, set against a single keyboard ostinato (this keyboard becomes more prominent in Snoop Dogg's verse, which references George Clinton's 1982 hit "Atomic Dog"), a secondary keyboard voice set high in the treble range, and at times a piano voice playing a countermelody. Here Dr. Dre's flow is meticulous and his style down-tempo, featuring lots of pauses, and carefully articulated lines.

The album's standouts are its gangsta activity (threat) songs, most of which are placed near the end of the album. The first two of these, "The Day the N— Took Over" and "Lil' Ghetto Boy," both reference the 1992 riots caused by the Rodney King verdict. The former features lyrics that explain the rioting and looting (and some lyrics refer to the shooting of police officers) as necessary forms of protest. The track's intro is a media sample (an interview with one of the angry rioters) set against an extended synthesizer note, with a four-note synth bass (octave-based) ostinato introduced midway through. Throughout the track, media footage of reporters can be heard, usually accompanied by a heavier funk bass and a high-pitched, dissonant keyboard voice. The main beat is a bass ostinato, two keyboard voices, and a snare and ride cymbal beat, with occasional 808 drum, and the song comes across not as much a rap as a collage of sounds and voices with rap interspersed (mid-tempo but aggressive, with occasional speeding up and voice breaking at alarming points, such as the appearance of police helicopters). Like much of the album, the song features Jamaican patois.

"Lil' Ghetto Boy" presents the argument that African Americans need to defend and fend for themselves, especially economically (by owning businesses), while also making the case that the urban ghetto is a dog-eat-dog environment and the streets make a person hard (and smart) by teaching him/her that weapons are a necessity (the streets aren't a fistfight). The song has a bifurcated intro, its first part a media file and its second introducing a flute voice set against down-tempo bass (both of which have similarities in their harmonic progressions to the bass and guitar of the Animals 1964 hit "The House of the Rising Sun"). Its main beat is composed of the first two notes of the established bass progression, followed by an improvisation based on those two notes, accompanied by an air loop tape, a snare and hi-hat beat, more flute voice, and occasional sound effects (e.g., gunshots) and vocalizations. The rap is mid-tempo: Snoop Dogg's is laid-back, while Dr. Dre's is aggressive. The refrain/hook is a bluesy soul-funk one, reminiscent of Gil Scott-Heron's jazz-funk work with Brian Jackson.

Similar themes inform standouts "A N— Witta Gun" and "Rat-Tat-Tat-Tat," produced by Daz Dillinger. The former samples "F— Wit Dre Day" in its intro, played in the background during a media file of an argument. Its bass line is one the best of the album—a heavy eight-note ostinato using the hammer on/off technique to create the sound of bent notes set against a snare hit hard on beats two and four (with a synth stinger on beat one and an occasional turntable on beat four). An oscillating keyboard voice is added in some verses, which are foregrounded and rapped aggressively. "Rat-Tat-Tat-Tat," a gangsta threat song, has a more typical g-funk sound. It begins with the sound of gunshots that lead into a low-fi intro (flute and acoustic guitar). The intro, a call for peace, is interrupted suddenly by a turntable, which introduces a heavy bass beat (which mirrors a soon-to-be introduced baritone guitar); the baritone guitar ostinato melody is ended by a discordant keyboard stinger and a synth voice that sounds like distorted strums across the guitar bridge. A snare beat on the treble end complements the bass, and discordant sound effects (e.g., screams) occur throughout, with vocals that showcase a foregrounded and aggressive rap flow (seemingly multitracked to sound fuller). The song's hook is rapped and chanted by various male voices in harmony.

The album's other two gangsta activity tracks, "Lyrical Gangbang" and "Stranded on Death Row," use gangsta prowess as a metaphor for lyrical ability. "Lyrical Gangbang" is a braggadocio track that begins with a media file intro. It boasts the album's heaviest drum beat (bass kick and tom with snare) and sounds like a Beastie Boys or Rage Against the Machine effort, with a distorted electric guitar ostinato, turntablism, a synth oscillator in the bridge and a treble-heavy keyboard ostinato in the last verse. Rapped verses by the Lady of Rage (her rap mentions

Bushwick Bill), Kurupt, and RBX are aggressive (and seemingly slightly distorted to emphasize anger). "Stranded on Death Row" begins with a Bushwick Bill toast (highly reverbed) that references the radio drama *The Shadow*. Aggressive, slightly reverbed rapped verses by Bushwick Bill, Kurupt, the Lady of Rage, and Snoop Dogg are set against heavy funk bass, a bass kick and snare beat, and distorted guitar chords and bridge strums (made to sound like horror movie noises). Snoop Dogg sings and raps the final verse, which flows into the outro, another reverbed toast by Bushwick Bill.

Other notable songs include "Let Me Ride," "Nuthin' but a 'G' Thang," and "B— Ain't S—." "Let Me Ride," a generic diss track and driving song (not with an entourage but alone), is a g-funk treat that begins with an intro in Jamaican patois. Its bass is played funk style (slap bass), and its keyboard (a recorder or penny whistle voice) is set high in the treble range as contrast. The song has a snare and kick bass beat with turntable in its bridge (after refrains, which are sung R&B style), which marks a stop time into the ensuing verse. Raps are mid-tempo, with a varied flow and mainly exterior rhyme (some lines have interior rhyme and alliteration/assonance). "Nuthin' but a 'G' Thang" is also a threat song (with a sub-theme about "b—" and "hoes"). A highly influential beat, it contains samples of Leon Haywood, Congress Alley, Kid Dynamite, Ronnie Hudson and the Street People, and Public Enemy. Its original music includes rhythm guitar, kick bass, a keyboard ostinato, vibraslap, occasional turntablism, and a four-note funk bass ostinato (with variation on each fourth phrase). Vocals include vocalizations (a female voice making an "ah" sound, as if a thirst were quenched), a laid-back rap (especially by Snoop Dogg), some call-response, and chanting in the refrain. "B— Ain't S—," which is introduced by a sex skit called "The Doctor's Office," is the album's sole sex song (women are good for only sex, and the double standard, women cannot be unfaithful but men can be). Some verses take pot shots at Eazy-E and Jerry Heller. The song begins with a drum vamp, which introduces a rock-infused funk bass line, a kick and snare beat, and synth sounds of various types (including a keyboard four-note octave ostinato and what sounds like a faithful recording of a copy machine or scanner—giving the effect of a midi sweep). The song's rapping is laid-back and mid-tempo.

The weakest spots on the album are the drug-related and joke songs and skits: "Deeez Nuuuts," "The $20 Sack Pyramid," "High Powered," and "The Roach (The Chronic Outro)." "Deeez Nuuuts," a street brag about being too real to be "faded," begins with two skits, sex jokes (one a phone call gag) that trick women into embarrassing statements.

Musically, the track contains sub-bass, a snare and ride beat, and a simple keyboard ostinato that gives way to a second oscillated distorted synth guitar voice. The rap is up-tempo, with some funk singing, talk-singing, and chanting. "The $20 Sack Pyramid" is an absurd comic skit filled with inside jokes based on the American television show *Pyramid*. It does offer a clever moment, a subtle exchange that references the intro to the Sweet's "The Ballroom Blitz" (1973) and The The's "Armageddon Days Are Here (Again)" (1989). "High Powered" is a chronic (slang for marijuana) spoken-word track with funk bass and a snare and hi-hat beat, as well as a thin-sounding keyboard ostinato high in the treble. The use of background female vocalizations by the Lady of Rage is the song's high point. "The Roach (The Chronic Outro)" begins with RBX's talking against a laid-back beat: bass, kick bass, hi-hat, and horns with a later keyboard in the treble range and additional distorted synth guitar voices. The song is a psychedelic funk piece, with a chorus of male voices, a mainly sung countermelody and refrain, and some spoken-word dialogue in the verses.

Dr. Dre has gone on to become the founder of several successful record companies, including Aftermath Entertainment (1996–), a boutique label that stressed quality over quantity and has produced seventeen platinum albums; his business acumen has made him one of the wealthiest entertainment executives in the world. He was responsible for Eminem's major-label debut, *The Slim Shady LP* (1999), and his landmark *The Marshall Mathers LP* (2000), which would become the highest selling hip hop album in history. Beyond recording and producing music, Dr. Dre has appeared on screen in a handful of minor roles, and his music has been licensed for well over one hundred motion pictures, television shows, and video games. He has also directed a few music videos and produced films, most notably the N.W.A. biopic *Straight Outta Compton* (2015). His most significant non–music business venture has been the development and marketing of a line of headphones, Beats by Dr. Dre, which have sold well primarily as fashion accessories. The purchase of the Beats brand by Apple in 2014 reportedly made Dr. Dre the richest hip hop associated act in the world.

MISSY ELLIOTT: *MISS E... SO ADDICTIVE* AND *UNDER CONSTRUCTION* (ELEKTRA, 2001 AND 2002)

With the release of *Miss E . . . So Addictive* and *Under Construction*, Missy Elliott (Melissa Arnette Elliott, 1971–) served notice that she was evolving from being Misdemeanor Elliott to becoming a top lyricist, singer, rapper, and producer in her own right—becoming Miss E, someone who commands respect (and her own label, the Goldmind). In fact, her success was somewhat unexpected considering that she hailed not from New York, Los Angeles, Houston, or New Orleans, the urban areas responsible for virtually all first and second wave rappers, but from Portsmouth, Virginia. In a series of fortunate events, this talented female producer, who has perhaps the best ear in all of hip hop, surrounded herself with equally talented and visionary male artists: Norfolk producer, music mixer, and rapper Timbaland and Hampton record executive, producer, singer, and former Jodeci member DeVante Swing (Donald Earle DeGrate Jr., 1969–). With Timbaland, she became a member of the Swing Mob Collective (a.k.a. Da Bassment Cru), a group of artists working with DeVante Swing in New York.

Ultimately, her musical partnership with Timbaland netted five consecutive platinum and multiplatinum albums, and among those were her breakout albums *Miss E . . . So Addictive* and *Under Construction*. The two albums spawned Top Ten singles on the Hot 100: "Get Ur Freak On" (No. 7), "Work It" (No. 2), and "Gossip Folks" (No. 8), as well as the hit "One Minute Man" (No. 15). "Get Ur Freak On," "Work It," and "Scream (a.k.a. Itchin')," earned her a Grammy for Best Female Rap Solo Performance (Elliott has been nominated for twenty-one and has won five Grammys). More importantly, the albums charted in Australia, Belgium, Germany, Ireland, the Netherlands, New Zealand, Sweden, Switzerland, and the United Kingdom, and Elliott became a music video fixture. In addition, the two albums established Elliott and Timbaland as hip hop pioneers as they experimented with synthesizer voices, sampled sounds, vocals, beats, and quirky effects, making the "cartoon" (an offbeat, unexpected moment created by vocals, vocalizations, or altered samples) a mainstay of hip hop music.

In *Da Real World*, she and Timbaland experimented with a harsher, urban sound that had more sexual energy. The album and its individual songs included her trademark song intros, which usually include ad-libbed talking and erotic vocalizations. *Da Real World*'s hits, "Hot Boyz" and "She's a B—," prefigure the sound she would perfect in *Miss E . . . So Addictive* and *Under Construction*. In fact, "She's a B—" marks one of Elliott's earliest uses of nonsense rhymes and cartoons juxtaposed against a driving beat and syncopated rhythms created between synthesizer and drum, techniques which inform many of the songs on her next albums. Her rapping style also became more breathless and included much more profanity, often for comic effect.

Miss E . . . So Addictive begins with a humorous R&B profanity-laden intro ballad that establishes immediately that the album is going to deliver not smooth R&B but danceable music unlike anything ever heard before, so good in fact that listeners will get high on it. The album intro morphs seamlessly into the heavy funk-infused club beat of "Dog in Heat," which features Method Man (Clifford Smith, 1971–) and Redman. The remainder of the album is predominantly similar funk-infused rap music intended for club dancing mixed with humorous interludes and songs filled with comic innuendo—as in "One Minute Man," which begins with a neo-soul female trio who decry minute men (both men who do not stick around and men who do not last during sex), transitioning into a funky synth hip hop beat that features an innuendo-laced sex rap by Ludacris (Christopher Brian Bridges, 1977–), who boasts of his sexual prowess. The next two songs, "Lick Shots" and "Get Ur Freak On," exemplify Elliott and Timbaland at their best, with simple beats and complex vocalizations juxtaposed against hard-edged urban rapping by Elliott. "Lick Shots" is straightforward braggadocio wherein Elliott warns that she is "about to turn it up." With a spoken intro in Japanese, "Get Ur Freak On" continues the bragging theme, but it borrows from Eastern music by using a synthesized, sped-up tumbi voice to create its beat. It also showcases Elliott's use of musical cartoon surprises, in this case vocalizations to fill space and create comic moments (such as an operatic voice singing the words "motherf—" and "n—" and the sound of someone spitting to play on the phrase "spitting rhymes").

The single "4 My People," which features Eve (Eve Jihan Jeffers, 1978–), and "Watcha Gonna Do" feature breathing, screams, growls, howls, and grunts that help establish the beat early and then become part of the instrumentation. In comparison to her earlier albums, Elliott's rapping becomes faster and her voice more sultry, using deeper vocal registers in the club songs "Scream (a.k.a. Itchin)" and "Watcha Gonna Do." "Scream" is the first song on the album to feature Timbaland's baritone, gravelly voice. "Watcha Gonna Do" is the closest thing Timbaland personally has to a bragging song, as he raps about his beat-making prowess. Peppered among the club songs are hip hop–infused R&B romance songs, such as "Old School Joint" and "X-Tasy," and neo-soul songs like "Take Away" and "I've Changed." The oddest beat on the album can be found on "Slap! Slap! Slap!," a down-tempo song with a drum, bassoon, and pitch-altered guitar–created beat that are juxtaposed against an unexpected aggressive message (*Under Construction*'s "Funky Fresh Dressed," "Hot," and "Slide" have a similar offbeat minimalist feel, the last using a pitch-altered cello).

Miss E . . . So Addictive's lyrics tell of her musical dominance. A similar theme and many of the same techniques, especially the use of spoken intros, appear on *Under Construction*. A spoken-word intro opens the album; it references East Coast versus West Coast feuding, her friend and fellow singer Aaliyah's (Aaliyah Dana Haughton, 1979–2001) untimely death, and self-actualization. The album intro morphs into a club beat that establishes Elliott is a hard-working rap star and ends with the phrase "let the show begin," which introduces "Go to the Floor," a self-referential bragging song about beat making. Method Man and Ludacris return for "Bring the Pain" and "Work It." "Bring the Pain" is a heavy funk sex song where Timbaland again creates beats through instrumentation and vocalizations (gasps, grunts, and howls). The duo experiment with sine waves, bass kicks, and lyrics in reverse in "Work It" (and in another self-referential moment, the reversed lyrics occur right after Elliott raps that she will flip and reverse as part of her twerking and later during sex). "Work It" is a sex song that boasts some of the cleverest innuendo—both vocal and instrumental—in rap music. The album's standout song, "Gossip Folks," uses adult dialogue and children's voices as part of the beat, and Elliott experiments with consecutive harshly delivered (her voice breaks on occasion) short lines that all rise vocally (and sound somewhat like a screech). The song also samples Frankie Smith's "Double Dutch Bus" (1981), and is, in many ways, an homage to it.

Like *Miss E . . . So Addictive*, *Under Construction* contains peppered moments of hip hop–flavored R&B songs such as "Back in the Day," "Pussycat," and "Play that Beat." The album also includes two gospel-infused tracks, "Nothing Out There for Me," which features Beyoncé (Beyoncé Giselle Knowles, 1981–), and "Can You Hear Me," featuring TLC (1990–). Many of the songs begin with the reverberated phrase "this is a Missy Elliott exclusive." *Under Construction* influenced Elliott's next two albums, *This Is Not a Test!* (Elektra, 2003) and *The Cookbook* (Atlantic, 2005). The latter shows even more experimentation with beats, as in "Lose Control," which contains synthesized video game sounds in an ascending scale combined with frenetic vocal layering. The album also reintroduces old-style hip hop techniques, such as scratching and the use of R&B.

In 2004, Elliott costarred in a Gap commercial with Madonna and performed with her, Britney Spears, and Christina Aguilera at the 2003 MTV Video Music Awards. *The Cookbook,* her first solo album not entirely produced by Timbaland (she worked with fourteen producers and production teams), received five Grammy nominations, and the video for "Lose Control" won a Grammy. She won Best Female Hip Hop Artist at the 2005 American Music Awards and was nominated for Best International Female Artist at the 2006 BRIT Awards. After *The Cookbook,* Elliott went on hiatus, concentrating on writing and production. In 2016, she released the single "WTF (Where They From)" with the promise of an upcoming album (which as of 2019 has not been released). Elliott has had six songs reach the Top Ten of the Billboard Hot 100 chart, and she was featured on six other Top Ten songs by various artists. Overall, she has had seventeen solo singles and twenty-five singles where she is a featured guest rapper hit the Hot 100. She is also known for a shyness that is uncharacteristic of hip hop and rap performers, although she possesses a great camera presence and a willingness to don oddball costumes and makeup for performances and videos. In 2019, she became the first female rapper to be inducted into the Songwriters Hall of Fame.

EMINEM: *THE MARSHALL MATHERS LP* (AFTERMATH ENTERTAINMENT, 2000)

The odds of a white high-school dropout from St. Joseph, Missouri, becoming one of the most respected and commercially successful rappers in history are pretty low, but this did not stop Eminem (Marshall Bruce Mathers III, 1972–), who had been held back several times in ninth grade, from ultimately producing eight RIAA certified platinum (including two diamond) studio albums, topping the Billboard 200 ten times, and developing a transatlantic following. His studio albums have reached No. 1 in Australia, Belgium, France, Germany, Japan, New Zealand, Switzerland, and the United Kingdom—a staggering total of fifty times. Now based in Detroit, he is a rapper, record producer, and actor, and he has become central in the public conversation on the negotiation of race in rap as well as issues like homophobia, misogyny, and violence (due to his lyrics). His second studio album, *The Slim Shady LP* (1999), launched a successful career of fifteen Grammy Awards (six for Best Rap Album).

Eminem's lyrics tend toward the extremely violent, misogynistic, and homophobic, although his friendship and artistic partnership with Elton John has silenced some critics, especially since his lyrics and interviews show a complex and high degree of self-awareness. He claimed, for example, that the lyrics to *The Slim Shady LP*'s "Guilty Conscience," which unambiguously encouraged men to kill their wives if they cheat, was performed as his alter ego, Slim Shady, and in 2000, he acknowledged through the lyrics to "Stan" (released on his EP of the same name) that his music could have a negative influence on fans. His "Love the

Way You Lie" (from *Recovery*, 2010) presents the destructive cycle of domestic abuse. It has been embraced by some as addressing the complexities of domestic violence. And while white rappers have a difficult time breaking into the industry, he has been embraced by it because of his quest for personal authenticity, without attempting to sound or act black. In 2017, he was greeted with both accolades and criticism when he dissed president Donald Trump in one of his live performances.

The Marshall Mathers LP, his third studio album, was produced mostly by Dr. Dre, Mel-Man (Melvin Charles Bradford, n.d.), Bass Brothers (1984–), and Eminem himself. The songs are generally concerned with Eminem's relationship with his fans, his attempts to deal with fame, his relationships with his wife and his mother (both depicted negatively), and whether he has a social responsibility as a lyricist. The album sold almost 1.8 million copies in the United States in its first week alone, becoming the fastest-selling studio album by any American solo artist at that time. In 2001, the album won the Grammy Award for Best Rap Album and was nominated for Album of the Year. It has sold over thirty-five million copies worldwide, at least eleven million in the United States, and spent eight weeks at No. 1 on the Billboard 200. There is a censored version of *The Marshall Mathers LP* that often either omits swear words completely or obscures them with added sound effects. References to violence and weapons were also significantly altered, titles were altered, and the album's most controversial song, "Kim," is absent.

The album begins with an intro, "Public Service Announcement 2000," in which producer Jeff Bass (of the Bass Brothers, Eminem's early production team), imitating a newscaster's voice, announces that Slim Shady is not worried about what the public thinks. The message is that since fans purchased *The Slim Shady LP* and will purchase *The Marshall Mathers LP*, thereby making Eminem wealthy, they don't have the moral authority to complain about the violent lyrics of either. This leads into one of the album's standouts, "Kill You," a track that serves as a diss message to anyone who fell for the Slim Shady character as being anything but a character. The over-the-top descriptions of violence in its lyrics serve as a metaphor for Eminem's relationship with his audience (who he refers to as b—, whether male or female): he doesn't have to shoot them; he can just hold out a bullet (his album) and they'll walk right toward it. The lyrics also constantly point out that he did not invent violence, and they criticize the media for posting images of him everywhere because of the controversy that surrounded *The Slim Shady LP*. The song's secondary theme is that his current mental state is a product of his upbringing by a drug-addicted, insane mother. Both of these themes reoccur throughout the album. Here Eminem's flow is fast-paced, and his tone is aggressive, but his delivery is clever, with surprising pauses and intentional stream of consciousness slip-ups (a technique nicknamed slip-hop). This is juxtaposed against music that is laid-back: a stop time beat created by a distorted arpeggiated guitar ostinato set against a bass and snare beat, with a synth music box voice and sound effects (e.g., chainsaws) added later. Here, and throughout most of the album, Eminem's vocals are processed to have a slight dry echo effect, multitracked in places to give a fuller vocal sound, especially when he talk-sings or sings.

This is followed by various songs and skits that deal with the Slim Shady versus Marshall Mathers issue, the use of violent lyrics to make a point, and the problems incurred with newfound fame. The skit "Paul," a fake phone call from manager Paul Rosenberg about how the new album is too controversial (in fact, Paul is rendered speechless), is followed by "Who Knew," which attacks the critics of violent lyrics as being duped into believing they can be the cause of real violence while pointing out the hypocrisy of parents, teachers, and the media (particularly film media) who expose kids to violence and foul language. At the same time, some of the track's lyrics question Eminem's culpability as a role model. Here music is more funk-based: electric funk bass, snare and metal percussion beat, with string voices in the hook/refrain (which features harmonized chants). Vocals in the verses are a combination of rapping and talk-singing.

"Who Knew" leads into "Stan," one of the album's hits despite its being one of its few weak tracks. "Stan" samples Dido's "Thank You" from her 1999 album *No Angel*, a song about needing a specific person to get you through the rough times, to paint a portrait of an obsessed and disturbed Slim Shady fan who commits murder-suicide because his letters to the star aren't answered quickly enough. While the lyrics are clever (Eminem voices the parts of Stan and himself), especially when they reference Phil Collins' "In the Air Tonight" (1981) in a context that has to do with whether lyrics can be taken at face value (the name of Collins' album), the song's vision is flawed and somewhat trite. At the end of Stan's third verse, he realizes right before he drowns himself and his pregnant girlfriend by driving off a bridge that now he can't send his last audiotaped letter to Slim Shady, who in the next verse is finally getting around to writing him back, only to realize what Stan had done. "Stan" has a down-tempo beat that is snare and bass heavy, along with constant pen-scratching sounds in the background to indicate correspondence. As Stan, Eminem raps in a higher register, with a laid-back flow that slowly gets faster as the character spirals into madness (vocals are not processed, so they sound thinner, until the third verse, where multitracking is used to make Stan's voice fuller). As Eminem/Slim Shady, his flow is mid-tempo but his tone aggressive and stream of consciousness–based (and the vocals are dry-echo processed).

The next skit, "Steve Berman," is a fictional meeting with Berman, the president of sales at Interscope Records. Berman invites Eminem to his office to confront him about his lyrical content, believing the new album will be a commercial disaster because of its language and thematic concerns (an ironic skit, since the album was wildly successful). This leads into the standout "The Way I Am," which opens with an echo of the last lines of the Berman skit. The track is an unapologetic refusal to be nice to fans or the media, the former for invading his privacy and the latter for blaming him for violence, and both for asking dumb questions. He also attacks the media for blaming the likes of Marilyn Manson for the Columbine High School massacre instead of focusing on bad parenting. The song's beat is created by metal percussion and set against electric bass, with church bells that become more dramatic in the hook. Throughout, the rapping is aggressive, a brilliant modification of old-school rap's singsong style, with clipped phrases that are run together breathlessly. The same themes are examined in "B— Please II," which features Dr. Dre, Snoop Dogg, Nate Dogg, and Xzibit (Alvin Nathaniel Joiner, 1974–), with secondary themes being that Eminem is accepted as legitimate by black rappers and that fans and critics need to take him for what he is, not what they want him to be. The song has elements of rock and g-funk, as well as R&B (Nate Dogg's singing in the refrain), with a down-tempo funk bass, an organ voice, and a high-pitched keyboard voice, all set against a simple snare and kick drum beat. Rapping varies depending on the rapper, with everything from laid-back and smooth to mid-tempo to aggressive and throaty.

The album's best song is its biggest hit, the braggadocio rap "The Real Slim Shady," which reached No. 4 on the Billboard Hot 100 (and has a brilliantly clever video). Its lyrics poke fun at pop culture icons such as Britney Spears, Christina Aguilera, and Will Smith, pointing out their lack of talent while establishing that even though his raps are a bit disturbing, there are lots of people like him, angry and ready to tell the world off—and he is their voice because he is the best at rapping the message (the lyrics include an interesting pro–gay marriage line). The song's beat is synth-based with a keyboard ostinato and synth bass and a simple 4/4 snare and cymbal beat, against which Eminem speed raps in an aggressive tone but with comic pauses right before absurd images, as well as comic voices and accents. These make it clear that the song is ironic in tone, even though the anger and frustration are real.

Other songs that deal with similar thematic concerns are "Remember Me?" and "I'm Back." The former, which includes the most autobiographical verse on the album, features rappers RBX and Sticky Fingaz (Kirk Jones, 1973–). One of the album's most clever moments occurs with the song's metatextuality, when Eminem promises to not say "f—in" for six minutes (a promise on which he delivers). The music is an aggressive version of g-funk with heavy bass set against a bass kick, snare, and tom beat (with sounds of a spray-paint can being shaken in the intro). RBX's rap is a highly reverbed, Jamaican toast style, while Sticky Fingaz's is dry but fast paced and throaty, extremely aggressive, with lots of plosives; Eminem's is aggressive, his voice doubled to sound more like he is spiraling out of control as his delivery gets faster and faster until his words run together almost incomprehensibly. "I'm Back," which contains a line of animal cruelty, is a song about his rise to fame as Slim Shady. Here he disses people who think he was successful and liked by MTV only because he is white while questioning how demented people interpret his lyrics, which are already demented. The song has a funk-based beat with lots of turntable, kick drum, and snare, against which a synth bass plays an ostinato that is mirrored by vocals in the refrain (which adds an oscillated synth voice). Verses include vocalizations (reverbed screams) and sound effects, set against a speed rap containing lots of violent imagery but rapped nonaggressively and in a matter-of-fact tone.

Other strong songs on the album include "Marshall Mathers," "Drug Ballad," and "Under the Influence." "Marshall Mathers" includes vocals that mock the chorus of LFO's 1999 hit "Summer Girls" to make fun of boy and girl bands. Basically the song is a diss track aimed at pop artists such as NSYNC, Ricky Martin, the Backstreet Boys, and Britney Spears, as well as fans who have tried to use Eminem for his fame and unskilled rappers who try to imitate legends like the Notorious B.I.G. It also takes a pot shot at gold-digging groupies. The music here is sparse, a minimalist production featuring acoustic guitar. It is followed by the skit "Ken Kaniff" (a recurring fictional gay friend), which takes a shot at the members of Insane Clown Posse, with whom Eminem was feuding. "Drug Ballad" features Dina Rae (n.d.) singing backup in its refrain and details the struggles and misadventures caused by Eminem's drug addiction (which includes snorting glue as a child as well as alcohol, marijuana, and ecstasy). Its music is reminiscent of funk a la Michael Jackson, with elements of R&B: heavy bass, a snare and hi-hat beat, and sixteenth note cymbal hits on the downbeat of every other phrase, against which a keyboard scale-based ostinato is played as Eminem speed raps breathlessly, with vocals processed for three different effects (dry, wet, and heavily harmonized).

"Under the Influence" features D12 (1996–) and details similar escapades as "Drug Ballad" but with the added wrinkle that here Eminem admits he sometimes writes under the influence, adding that fans can just deal with it. Its beat is a down-tempo version of the vocal hook from the tune of D12's 2004 hit "My Band," with an additional simple 4/4 kick drum and snare beat as well as some sound effects of violence (e.g., gunshots, screams). The refrain's vocals mirror the down-tempo beat, while the rapped verses vary depending on rapper, from speed rapping, to aggressive and angry, to down-tempo, to laid-back.

The album's weakest song is its most controversial, "Kim," a prequel to "'97 Bonnie and Clyde" from *The Slim Shady LP*. It amounts to a chaotic murder dialogue where Eminem plays both himself and the voice of his wife Kim. In it, he kills her new lover, that man's son, and his wife, chronicling this through vocals that are enraged. The song begins innocently with a music box and Eminem talking to his infant daughter, but this is followed by a piano ostinato that suddenly becomes louder (and is accompanied by a heavy bass and a snare, tom, and cymbal down-tempo rock beat). Here the vocals become shrill as he becomes angry over her infidelity, and they are later accompanied by disturbing sound effects. Although he literally shrieks during the verses, Eminem sings the refrain (vocals are processed to sound like a radio, with a buzzing sound in the background).

Fortunately "Kim" is bookended by two decent violence-for-violence's-sake tracks, "Amityville" and "Criminal." "Amityville," which features Bizarre (Rufus Arthur Johnson, 1976–), is an extremely violent track about living in Detroit, the murder capital of the United States. It is bass-heavy and has the heaviest bass kick drum sound on the album (along with snare) and intermittent horn voices. Although the vocalizations in the intro are down-tempo, its rapped verses are aggressive and the vocals kept thin and dry to balance the multitracked, fuller-sounding vocals in the refrain. Vocalizations and screams are peppered throughout. "Criminal," which features production from F.B.T. (the Funky Bass Brothers), has a simple message: don't take Eminem's rhymes seriously—the violent imagery is just a staple of rap (though he admits he has a criminal mind and plays these scenarios out in his head and may have done some in his past). The intro is spoken word by Eminem, accompanied by church organ and an air loop tape, and this gives way to a bass and snare beat, accompanied by a keyboard scale, two notes per phrase, with a flourish on each eighth phrase. The rap vocals are dry but doubled-tracked, especially on the throaty repetition of the word "criminal" in verses, as well as a spoken-word countermelody in the hook. The outro is a skit in which Eminem robs a bank and shoots the teller.

In 1999, Eminem created his own record label, New York City–based Shady Records, and has since produced records for 50 Cent and D12 (a.k.a. the Dirty Dozen, Eminem's side band). As an actor, he gave a critically acclaimed performance in *8 Mile* (2002). He also won an Academy Award for Best Original Song for the single he wrote for this movie ("Lose Yourself"), the first hip hop track to earn this distinction. His further albums, all on the Aftermath and Shady labels, *The Eminem Show* (2002), *Relapse* (2009), *Recovery*, *The Marshall Mathers LP2* (2013), *Revival* (2017), and *Kamikaze* (2018), have sold over seventy million copies. He has also earned four Grammy Awards for Best Rap Solo Performance for the songs "My Name Is" (1999), "The Real Slim Shady" (2000), "Lose Yourself" (2002), and "Not Afraid" (2010), and he won (for "Lose Yourself") Best Male Rap Solo Performance. Despite the controversies that surround his music, Eminem has been wildly successful as a performer and producer, and Billboard lists him as one of the best-selling artists of the first decade of the 21st century.

ERIC B. & RAKIM

Eric B. & Rakim are a legendary American hip hop duo consisting of turntablist Eric B. (Louis Eric Barrier, 1965–) and Rakim (a.k.a. MC Rakim Rakim, the God MC, Kid Wizard, Rakim Allah, William Michael Griffin Jr., 1968–). The duo is considered integral to the early development of rap music, heavily influencing the next wave of artists, especially during the latter half of the 1980s. Eric B. grew up as a musician, playing trumpet, drums, and turntables; Rakim was a jazz saxophone player and a member of the Nation of Gods and Earths (a.k.a. the Five Percent Nation) who had been writing raps. His brother worked at a plant where bootleg albums were pressed, so the duo had access to the fresh, new music it needed to DJ at parties. The two also sought a mentor, the legendary Marley Marl (Marlon Williams, 1962–), whom Eric B. hired to engineer the duo's first single, "Eric B. Is President" (1986). After Def Jam Recordings founder Russell Simmons (1957–) heard the single, he signed Eric B. & Rakim to Island Records.

The duo's debut album, *Paid in Full* (1987), was characterized by Eric B.'s solid beats (heavy on the tom and kick bass), his sampled funk loops, and his liberal use of reverb and hiccups (the album contained three instrumentals) as well as Rakim's even and methodical vocal delivery and freestyle handling of rhythm. Rakim introduced the idea of eschewing old-school rap and doing away with the singsong, overly rhythmic rapping; rather, he opted for a flow that could be independent of musical phrasing and use enjambment to create a highly intricate delivery. The album made it into the Top Ten on Billboard's Top R&B/Hip Hop Albums chart, peaking at No. 8. The duo then signed with MCA Records, for whom it released two albums, *Follow the Leader* (1988) and *Let the Rhythm Hit 'Em* (1990), which showed the evolution away from minimalism. Both albums were well received. A later guest appearance on Jody Watley's "Friends" (1989) resulted in Eric B. & Rakim's first Billboard Hot 100 Top Ten. Overall, the duo's albums did not do well commercially, but each one's talent for innovation and improvisation, as well as an encyclopedic knowledge of jazz and funk, did not go unnoticed by critics. Their next album, *Don't Sweat the Technique* (1992), included two singles that were used in the 1991 comedy *House Party 2*.

Paid in Full opens with the braggadocio battle rap "I Ain't No Joke," a mid-tempo track with a heavy kick drum beat, tom and mirrored claps, turntable, and a jazz-style horn ostinato, against which Rakim raps, his voice a relaxed baritone and his flow a varied combination of staccato lines and enjambed, breathless lines. His lyrics include interior and exterior rhymes as well as multisyllabic rhymes (usually involving a clever combination of words). "My Melody" and "I Know You Got Soul" are also skills bragging raps: "My Melody" comes in cleverly with vibes, piccolo, heavy bass kick and turntable, and vocal reverb (in Rakim's rap, which is carefully articulated and laid-back), and "I Know You Got Soul" is a driving jazz/funk-influenced snare, kick, and hi-hat track, with slap bass and horns in the refrain/hook. Among the weaker braggadocio songs are "Move the Crowd," "As the Rhyme Goes On," and "Eric B. Is President," all old-school raps. Instrumentals include "Eric B. is on the Cut," a raucous track with both distorted and undistorted turntable, a heavy tom beat with a bass kick, and electric bass; "Chinese Arithmetic," a turntable scratching virtuosity track that features water as one of its main sounds; and "Extended Beat," a jazz-funk instrumental that showcases Eric B.'s sampling abilities.

Follow the Leader and *Let the Rhythm Hit 'Em* show the duo adapting to a new style of rap, although its lyrical themes are still fixated on battle raps. The former's opening braggadocio track, "Follow the Leader," introduces synthesizer into Eric B.'s repertoire and showcases a more breathless rap flow for Rakim. "Microphone Fiend" showcases Eric B.'s funk abilities with more funk bass and rhythm guitar combined with sleigh bell percussion and turntable scratching, while "Lyrics of Fury" incorporates conga drums, ride cymbal, and distorted electric guitar set against an aggressive, fast-paced Rakim rap flow. *Follow the Leader* also includes Eric B. instrumentals, such as "Eric B. Never Scared" and "Just a Beat," the former showcasing the DJ's beat-making abilities and turntablism, and the latter his ability to create synth-based voices (strings and a distorted hi-hat, where the delay is cut off). "Put Your Hands Together," like "Chinese Arithmetic," shows Eric B.'s mastery of Oriental scales, this time using a piano voice in an intro to an old-school rap by Rakim.

Let the Rhythm Hit 'Em opens with its titular song, a standout industrial beat track featuring a heavy snare, kick, and hi-hat jazz-infused beat, set against a frenetic electric bass ostinato, rhythm guitar, turntable, and various stinger voices and distorted crowd noise vocalizations, against which Rakim raps without a pause, in a breathless but carefully articulated style reminiscent of jazz improvisation. The album's second track, "No Omega," shows the duo moving toward Five Percenter rap in its thematic concerns in a turntable-heavy track featuring muted horns, a jazz drum beat, rhythm guitar, and a breathless rap flow filled with multiple interior and exterior rhymes. "Step Back," another Five Percenter rap, is soul and funk–infused, and features some of Rakim's best lyrics (metaphors based on the Earth's mass). The album also features the duo's first social consciousness songs, such as "In the Ghetto," a 1970s-funk and soul-infused track (bordering on g-funk) that features some of Rakim's best down-tempo rapping (which almost sounds like talk-singing). The album also features Eric B. instrumentals, such as "Eric B. Made My Day," which showcase the DJ's turntablism and his media file sampling.

Don't Sweat the Technique opens with "What's On Your Mind," one of the duo's few romance tracks. It is a mid-tempo song centered around a bass kick, snare, and tom beat, accompanied by claps and a 1980s keyboard voice. Here Rakim raps mid-tempo, as opposed to his breathless style on the previous album, and sampled countermelodies sung R&B style are introduced into the duo's repertoire. Rakim's rap also includes more stream of consciousness (seemingly freestyle) lines. The duo also includes more social consciousness raps, such as "Teach the Children," a jazz-infused track (with additional melodic guitar and strums along the guitar bridge, as well as R&B-style countermelodies) that exposes the problems of urban living. The album includes braggadocio songs, such as the frenetic "Pass the Hand Grenade," which includes lead guitar and horn voices set against a timbale, hi-hat, and ride cymbal beat and accompanied by horns and rhythm guitar. Rakim's rap is fast-paced and breathless, though carefully articulated. More funk-infused tracks such as "Casualties of War" and "Keep the Beat" make the album a fan favorite. "Casualties of War" features more rhythm guitar and jazz-infused drumming (as well as Hammond organ) as well as Rakim's angrier rap flow, including repeated lines and calls for action. "Keep the Beat" is a romance song that has a laid-back funk-infused rap that is heavy on electric bass (set against a piano voice in the high treble range). It includes female-sung refrains/hooks, rare in Eric B. & Rakim songs.

The personality differences that had worked well for the duo began to work against them, which led to a breakup and both members' solo careers. In 1992, Eric B. had taken precautionary legal steps that tied Rakim's hands, forcing him to keep a low profile and limiting him to only one notable musical appearance in 1993. Eric B. went on to produce his solo album *Eric B.* (1995), and Rakim later released *The 18th Letter* (1997, which reached No. 4 on the Billboard 200 and was certified gold) and *The Master* (1999). Rakim signed with Dr. Dre's Aftermath Entertainment record label from 2000 to 2003, and then he went into semiretirement but retained the masters he had made with Dr. Dre. In 2009, he released *The Seventh Seal* (three years after his originally planned launch date). The album spawned two singles, "Holy Are You" and "Walk These Streets." As time has passed, Rakim has become widely acknowledged as one of the best—if not the best—rap lyricists of all time, and he is regarded as one of the most skilled MCs. Since 2016, rumors of a reunion have been announced on the duo's website, but as of 2019, no details have emerged.

50 CENT: "HOW TO ROB" AND "GHETTO QU'RAN (FORGIVE ME)" (*POWER OF THE DOLLAR*, BOOTLEGGED, 1999)

Despite (or perhaps because of) his involvement with drugs, brushes with the law, being shot, and frequent feuds with other rappers, 50 Cent (Curtis James Jackson III, 1975–) has been incredibly popular with rap fans, becoming in time one of hip hop culture's wealthiest individuals. What makes his success even more astounding is the fact that he never had much of a chance. His mother was a teenaged cocaine dealer; she was murdered when he was eight, and he was raised by his grandparents in Queens, New York. As a teen, he sold drugs and was arrested several times before he was twenty years old. His fate turned when he opted for six months in a boot camp, during which time he earned his GED. He also adopted the nickname 50 Cent, from a 1980s Brooklyn thief who would steal from anyone, as a reminder that through rap music he could make money legally. Jam Master Jay of Run-D.M.C. took an interest in his potential and mentored him on songwriting and flow.

His first appearances on rap tracks were uncredited while he worked on his first album. His debut single, off the album *Power of the Dollar* (1999), was "How to Rob" (1999). The album was originally meant to be released as his debut studio album, but it was cancelled after 50 Cent was shot nine times (his involvement in the shooting or why it occurred was never clarified) two months before the release date; *Power of the Dollar* can now be found as a bootlegged digital download. His debut album ended up being 2003's *Get Rich or Die Tryin'* (Shady Records), which went to No. 1 on the Billboard 200, was RIAA certified six times platinum, and sold fourteen million copies worldwide.

"How to Rob" (released as part of an EP by Columbia) is an absurdist track featuring tha Madd Rapper, the comic alter ego of Bad Boy producer D-Dot (Deric Michael Angelettie, 1968–), known for his 1997 appearances on the Notorious B.I.G.'s *Life After Death*, Puff Daddy's *No Way Out*, Mase's *Harlem World*, and his own comic album *Tell 'Em Why You Madd* (2000). The lyrics amount to brief (usually two lines) caricatures of rappers and singers such as Puff Daddy, Bobby Brown, Whitney Houston, Brian McKnight, Keith Sweat, Mase, Ol' Dirty Bastard, Foxy Brown, Kurupt, Jay-Z, Tone Loc, Slick Rick, Big Pun, Master P, Silkk the Shocker, Timbaland, Da Brat, DMX, and members of the Wu Tang Clan, among others. Within these parameters, 50 Cent raps about stealing from and/or shooting them, all in all over forty R&B and rap musicians. Most references to a fellow musician take the form of subtle ribbing, usually through quoted or reimagined lines from their songs or references to their personal lives; most of the jokes are benign and ridiculous, though a few are mean-spirited, such as a jab at Missy Elliott for her weight. However, despite the song's refrain stating specifically that the lyrics are meant to be taken tongue-in-cheek, not all fans and targets of the satire got or appreciated the joke—response to the song was therefore mixed.

In 50 Cent's defense, the song's structure makes pretty clear that it is not to be taken seriously. Its intro clues listeners in to the satire immediately, with tha Madd Rapper acting as hype man, doing a decent Flavor Flav impersonation as he introduces the song and its central conceit. He begins a cappella, with the typical hype greeting of "yo, yo," but on his second line a heavy funk bass intro on the E string introduces the bass riff—a call and response that begins with a grinding two- or three-note E string ostinato that is answered by a three-note, high-pitched, hammered on and off ostinato. This is complemented by a three-note funk-jazz style drumming in the form of a repetition of bass-tom-snare (that matches the bass's low to high and back again theme) and a metal-on-metal percussion sound that alternates between eighth and sixteenth notes. This rhythm section interplay informs the song as a whole, giving it an offbeat, down-tempo, almost g-funk sound. Verses are rapped by 50 Cent using a varied flow that ranges from staccato, singsong phrases to elongated lines that at times threaten to go off the beat (50 Cent manages to adjust constantly and get his vocals back on the beat). During the verses, an occasional turntable supplies a hiccup, at times marking a stop time in the beat by either introducing it or bridging between it and the beat's reintroduction. The refrain/hook is talk-sung in a slightly off-key falsetto by tha Madd Rapper with 50 Cent supplying vocalizations. The song's outro brings back tha Madd Rapper, who warns other rappers that they are not safe from being robbed by himself and 50 Cent. The song ends abruptly on tha Madd Rapper's last line, "we gonna get you whether you like it or not."

"Ghetto Qu'ran (Forgive Me)" is a detailed account of the Queens and Brooklyn crime scenes, with a particular emphasis on Queens' drug dealer and record label (Murder Inc. Records, founded by Irv and Chris Gotti) associate Kenneth "Supreme" McGriff (1960–), leader of the crack distribution ring called the Supreme Team. Authorities later believed McGriff was involved in the attempted murder of 50 Cent—rumored to be in retaliation for the song's outing his criminal activity and for making him sound less menacing than his nephew, who served as his strongman—and this led to the murder of Run-D.M.C.'s Jam Master Jay, who had continued to work with 50 Cent after being told not to. The song's lyrics, which were intended ostensibly as an object lesson about the harshness of urban street life (hence the "Qu'ran" of the title), chronicle the fates of various crime family members who were involved with the Supreme Team and the drug trade; lyrics include information gleaned from news stories and widely circulated rumors. The secondary purpose of the song's lyrics is to establish 50 Cent's street cred, establishing that he is authentic because he has been associated with drug trafficking since he was young; hence the song amounts to name-dropping.

Musically it differs greatly from "How to Rob" in that it is neo soul and R&B–infused, featuring 50 Cent's singing during the refrain/hook. It begins with a turntable hiccup, which introduces a melodic keyboard ostinato, using a 1980s keyboard voice. Down-tempo but heavy rock bass, snare drum (made to sound like claps), and percussion (likely synth-produced shaker sounds) are added to create the song's melody, which is consistent throughout, with the exception of occasional turntable hiccups to bridge refrains and verses. The song begins with its hook, 50 Cent singing about forgiveness for his sins, while background singers punctuate his lines using a gospel-infused soul singing style (akin to sweet soul). Verses are rapped in a highly articulated, melodic flow created by the use of staccato lines of the same length, with longer lines occurring toward the end of verses. In the second verse, backgrounded synthesizer strings are introduced and mirror the keyboard ostinato. The third refrain introduces more reverb and echo into the vocals. The third and final verse showcases 50 Cent's mastery of longer lines, which he delivers breathlessly while staying on the beat. The outro is a non-sung version of the refrain, with only the backing vocals against the song's instrumentation, which slowly fades out.

Despite his high-profile debut, it would take a few years before 50 Cent would enjoy mainstream success. *Get Rich or Die Tryin'* spawned 50 Cent's first Billboard Hot 100 No. 1 single, "In da Club." He would later hit No. 1 twice, with "51 Questions" (2003) and "Candy Shop" (2005). His follow-up album, *The Massacre* (Aftermath and Shady Records, 2005), sold over one million copies in its first four days and earned five Grammy Award nominations. In 2003, he was given his own label, G-Unit Records (2003–). His studio albums since have included Aftermath's *Curtis* (2007) and *Before I Self Destruct* (2009), and G-Unit's *Animal Ambition: An Untamed Desire to Win* (2014). In 2010, he won a Grammy Award for Best Rap Performance by a Duo or Group for "Crack a Bottle" with Eminem and Dr. Dre. He also became an entrepreneur, selling beverages, fragrances, condoms, luxury clothing, and headphones. His latest investments include boxing promotion. However, a 2015 court loss and its associated legal fees led to his filing for bankruptcy.

FOXY BROWN (SEE DA BRAT, FOXY BROWN, AND LIL' KIM)

GETO BOYS: *WE CAN'T BE STOPPED* (RAP-A-LOT RECORDS, 1991)

The album cover is graphic—rapper Bushwick Bill in the hospital, his eye shot out (from an argument with his then girlfriend). His bandmates, rappers Scarface (Brad Terrence Jordan, 1970–) and Willie D (William James Dennis, 1966–), are on either side of his hospital bed, which had been wheeled out into the hallway for the photo op. The resulting image, as disturbing as many of the lyrics for which Geto Boys were known, had been commissioned by the trio's management as a way to market its third studio album, *We Can't Be Stopped* (1991). More than anything, the cover accurately represented the urban reality of Geto Boys (1987–2005), a Houston-based rap group with varying membership, the stabilizing influence being J Prince (a.k.a. Lil' J, James Prince, James A. Smith, 1964–), producer and owner of Rap-A-Lot Records (1986–). He had conceived of a rap group that could dramatize the problems of Houston's impoverished Fifth Ward.

Through nine albums, Geto Boys became influential for Southern rap, also known as the Dirty South sound. By the first album, *Making Trouble* (1988), the group's lineup consisted of Sire Jukebox (Keith Rogers, n.d.), DJ Ready Red (Collins Leysath, n.d.), Prince Johnny C (n.d.), and Little Billy, a Jamaican rapper/dancer dwarf who soon became famous as Bushwick Bill. The most successful incarnation of the band, which appears on *We Can't Be Stopped*, included Scarface, Willie D, and Bushwick Bill. The band's earlier albums, *Grip It! On That Other Level* (1989) and *The Geto Boys* (1990), addressed pressure from the Parents Music Resource Center (PMRC) and the onset of Parental Advisory labels, which prompted Geffen Records to balk as distributor because of the album's violent content (misogyny, gore, psychotic experiences, and necrophilia), forcing Rap-A-Lot to change its distributor for *The Geto Boys* to Rick Rubin's Def American Recordings (now American Recordings) and to later use Priority Records.

Regardless of lineup changes, the band's sound is consistent. It prioritizes raps over instrumentation, which is usually backgrounded (so that vocals stand out) and keeps a constant 4/4 rhythm. All members of the band take turns rapping, so the foregrounding of vocals emphasizes each rapper's unique vocal quality and style, as well as each one's lyrical contribution. Faster songs sample funk, while slower songs usually sample R&B loops, typically keyboard or jazz guitar riffs, which add to the laid-back quality of the down-tempo drum loops. In slower songs, Geto Boys vocalists use a quiet, almost understated method of rapping juxtaposed against little background or harmonized singing. In angrier songs, typically songs about killers and protest songs like "We Can't Be Stopped" and "Crooked Officer," rappers use more immediate and breathless rapping styles in a higher range, and these vocals in later albums may be juxtaposed against Jamaican rhythms and/or accompanied and complemented by background singing.

We Can't Be Stopped (1991), whose title was a criticism of the group's intended distributor, Geffen, after the label refused to distribute

The Geto Boys, took only a few weeks to record. The album is notable for its anger and desperation, usually on a personal level, although the Bushwick Bill solo "F— a War" had political overtones: war is just a trick to get African Americans, whom the country holds back economically, killed, so that the rich can get richer. The album produced the iconic hit "Mind Playing Tricks on Me," which peaked at No. 23 on the Billboard Hot 100. Overall, the album contains three solo tracks by each member of the group, with all three rappers performing vocals on three tracks. DJ Ready Red, who left the group during the recording, can be heard on the title track only.

The album opens with "Rebel Rap Family," an intro challenge to other rebel rap families that establishes Geto Boys as "a band of musical assassins" ready to take over the rap scene. Besides war, Geto Boys protest poverty and discrimination in music. "Ain't With Being Broke" is a socioeconomic protest song that challenges the practice of keeping black Americans poor and economically oppressed. Although it is a typical gangsta song in that it argues that if selling drugs and prostitution allow a person to make more money than a legal, minimum wage job, people will chose to break the law, it is a more thought-provoking take on the issue because the song's lyrics emphasize the sadness of ghetto life and poverty rather than the lure of money and bling. Bushwick Bill's verse is unique, as it is rapped from the point of view of a disappointed child at Christmas. "Trophy" is Willie D's diss song about the music industry, specifically the Grammy Awards, which, despite its finally having a category for rap music, have become a popularity contest at best, and at worst a tainted awards show that rewards musicians who pay to play. The song ends with Willie D's rapping joke awards, such as B— Killa of the Year, which he gives to Ice Cube, the Nasty Group Award, which he gives to 2 Live Crew, the High Roller of the Industry, awarded to Ice-T, and the Pro-Black G, awarded to Public Enemy—as well as a Lip-Sync Grammy to Milli Vanilli, as Willie D dismisses the duo angrily as the type of fake music the Grammy Awards love.

Standout tracks include "We Can't Be Stopped," "Mind Playing Tricks on Me," and "Gotta Let Your N— Hang." "We Can't Be Stopped" chronicles the band's previous albums as attempts on breaking into the music industry by knocking at its door—it portrays the album as the trio finally just deciding to kick the door in with raw lyrics about the real ghetto, Houston's Fifth Ward. The song names Geffen executives as hypocrites, willing to distribute violent lyrics by white rock and roll bands but not black rap bands. Although it is about violence, "Mind Playing Tricks on Me" is a pensive song, as it deconstructs the accepted insanity of tracks such as "Another N— in the Morgue" and "Chuckie" to question what is lost when a gangsta loses his humanity. Scarface begins the song with a verse that considers his current loneliness. He has developed insomnia and hallucinates, becoming paranoid and overly aggressive, and the lyrics make it clear that he has become his own worst enemy, the person he has to fear most in the world. In the third verse, Scarface adds that he has become suicidal. Willie D takes the second verse, which continues the paranoia of the first, as he images that he is being followed, possibly by gangsters bent on revenge. Bushwick Bill finishes the track with a verse about a fateful Halloween night of stealing candy from children—the verse ends with his narrating how he and his crew jumped a police officer and beat him to death, but then Bushwick Bill comes out of a daze and realizes he has been beating his fist against a concrete sidewalk. "Gotta Let Your N— Hang" is an anti-police and anti-authority song. Scarface raps about how police ruin his drug business, pointing out the hypocrisy in the fact that elected officials, such as ex–Washington, DC, mayor Marion Barry, have been caught doing drugs. The song is interesting for its businessman's approach to drug dealing, with lyrics that decry practices such as price cutting to knock out the competition. It also marks the group's admission that women are fair victims if they are in the drug-dealing game.

Set next to each other on the album "Another N— in the Morgue" and "Chuckie" are informed by ultraviolence, horror imagery, and gore. "Another N— in the Morgue" begins metatextually, with Scarface calling for more drums so that he can rap to a beat about the number of people he has killed (usually because they have brought it on themselves by threatening him). "Chuckie" introduces the idea that even children are fair game during gang-related violence, as Bushwick Bill threatens to cut into "88 pieces" (a clever reference to music composition via keyboard) his enemy's children and relatives, ostensibly with an axe or butcher knife. Both songs establish clearly that the members of Geto Boys are insane and will kill for fun. The anti-diss song "Homie Don't Play That" attacks the band's critics, pointing out that talk is cheap, and these critics (who are "fronting") are afraid to back up their words; the song threatens physical violence as retribution, while offering an olive branch—if those that would diss the band would simply be quiet, nothing need happen.

The album also contains sex and male-female relationship songs. Willie D raps "I'm Not a Gentleman," a misogynistic song that attacks women for expecting men to be gentlemen; the track unapologetically revels in bad male behavior. "Quickie" is a sex song monologue by Scarface, with its opening verse rapped as a phone call to a woman he is interested in meeting for a casual sexual encounter. The song then becomes a graphic description of their sex, admitting that the woman was left disappointed because she wanted more than a quickie. "The Other Level" is a Bushwick Bill sex song that details a threesome between him, his girlfriend, and one of her friends. Like "Quickie," it is graphic and revels in minutia in its description of sex. "Punk-B—Game" is a call and response party anthem with a twist: it pits men against women in a game of who gets to be called a "punk b—" based on how badly they get "played" by the opposite sex.

Willie D eventually left the group for a solo career, so Scarface and Bushwick Bill were joined by Big Mike (Michael Barnett, 1971–) for the album *Till Death Do Us Part* (Rap-A-Lot, 1993), which was certified gold and spawned the hit "Six Feet Deep" (No. 40 on the Billboard Hot 100). Willie D returned to record *The Resurrection* (1996) and *Da Good Da Bad and Da Ugly* (1998), both on Rap-A-Lot. Scarface remained with the group while releasing a series of solo albums; he also created his own label, Face II Face Records in 1993, and was coordinator and president of Def Jam South in New York; he was influential in signing and popularizing Ludacris.

GRANDMASTER FLASH AND THE FURIOUS FIVE: "THE MESSAGE" (*THE MESSAGE*, SUGAR HILL RECORDS, 1982)

Bridgetown, Barbados–native Grandmaster Flash (Joseph Saddler, 1958–) is best known for his association with Bronx-based The Furious Five (1976–82), who were inducted into the Rock & Roll Hall of Fame (2007) as well as honored in the Grammy Hall of Fame (2011). Modeling his sound system and style after pioneering hip hop artist DJ Kool Herc (Clive Campbell, 1955–) and Grandmaster Flowers (Jonathon Cameron Flowers, n.d.), he took the DJ idea one step further, from being a celebrated party presence to creating music for rappers, in his case Kurtis Blow (Kurtis Walker, 1959–) and Lovebug Starski (Kevin Smith, 1960–2018). He took his knowledge of music and expertise in electronics to create the technology and techniques that would allow him to both remix preexisting music and create his own beats, introducing the electronic beat box and turntablism (scratching); pioneering the Quick Mix Method, which incorporated cutting, backspin, and double-back; and using the turntables in innovative ways, such as a counterpoint to vocals.

Greatness tends to attract more greatness, so he ended up working with Grand Wizzard Theodore (Theodore Livingston, 1963–), who is credited with developing turntable scratching, and Melle Mel (Melvin Glover, 1961–), who can single-handedly be credited with changing the landscape of rap music with his lead vocals on the recording of "The Message" (1982), released under the Grandmaster Flash and the Furious Five name. Released on the Sugar Hill label, "The Message" (from the album *The Message*) was the first militant, aggressive, socially conscious rap song. Melle Mel had recorded a similar song earlier with "New York, New York" (1982) and would do so again with the limited edition release of "White Lines (Don't Don't Do It)" (1988), creating songs that popularized what would be called message rap, or rap music that had as its goal a serious discussion of social and political issues. The narrative of "The Message," delivered in Melle Mel's gritty, powerful style, focused on endemic poverty, violence, a lack of positive role models, and the evils of the prison system, all which ruined the lives of many African American youth. Though Melle Mel rapped the entire recorded version, live performances often featured all five rappers of the Furious Five taking a verse.

Although the song is revered mainly for its refrain, it has a memorable beat created by Grandmaster Flash, a mid-tempo, slow buildup of tension that never reaches its release point. It begins with a heavy bass kick drum beat, which is replaced by a steady tom and snare interchange (which sometimes gives the impression of clapping). These are set against a playful keyboard ostinato and a funk and slap bass. The drums, keyboard, and bass are joined intermittently by conga drums and varying keyboard gestures—with the drum and bass becoming the song's relentless beat against which Melle Mel raps. Interspersed in spots are sound effects, such as glass breaking or an overheard incident of police brutality. Melle Mel's rap flow is, for the most part, old-school style with lots of end rhyme and, like the beat, mid-tempo. At times he speeds up a verse line, especially when there is unexpected interior rhyme. At the end of the refrain, his rapping devolves into a parody of laughter, which comes across as both sardonic and sarcastic. In the song's refrain, Melle Mel uses his deepest, most measured voice; however, in each verse, he alternates between his highest register, almost yelling and creating a sense of desperation and anger, and his measured, deeper register, which gives a sense of thoughtfulness to some lines. For example, he uses the more measured vocal style when considering his son's future but the higher register when describing the degradation of his neighborhood and the black community.

Unlike many songs, which begin with an intro that is never referred to again in the text, "The Message" begins with an introductory four lines that make up the second half of the refrain. These lines compare living in the black community to trying to survive in a jungle and express the narrator's despair about being metaphorically drowned in such an environment. When used as part of the refrain, the aforementioned lines serve as a tag that completes the song's most memorable lines: "don't push me cuz I'm close to the edge/I'm trying not to lose my head."

The verses introduce various problems within the inner-city ghetto. Verse one is about the physical environment, full of broken glass, urine stains and smells, noise pollution, rats, and roaches. Its lyrics move from the ugliness of the community to its danger—a drugged out junkie waiting with a baseball bat. Each of the first three verses ends with the realization that escape is impossible: Verse one ends with the narrator's being stuck because his transportation has been repossessed. Verse two ends with a young girl who takes the bus out of the ghetto but fails to make it on her own, returning as a prostitute. Verse three ends with the narrator's losing his job because of a transit strike.

The second and third verses continue to enumerate the despair of the black community by introducing some of its beaten down characters. Verse two tells of an insane bag lady who has been reduced to eating out of garbage cans and of the aforementioned young woman, a "zircon princess" who had tried to escape all the creepy men at the strip bars by moving to the city, only to fail and end up on the streets. Verse three introduces the narrator's family. Having fallen on hard times, his brother has stolen their mother's television (all his mother ever does is watch TV, mainly programs with nothing but white people in them). His wife lives in constant fear that the next phone call will be a collection agency. Looking back at his situation, he realizes that he is a product of both bad choices and forces beyond his control—a subpar education, double-digit inflation, chronic back pain, and migraines. By the end of the verse, he questions his sanity.

Verse four introduces his son via the recollection of a troubling dialogue. The son is giving up on education, blaming his teacher for making his lessons irrelevant. He is also beginning to bend to peer pressure—all his friends are smoking marijuana. These forces have the boy thinking that he would be better off taking a menial job (a street sweeper), busking for money (as a dancer), or becoming a con man, or possibly a drug dealer, since the only thing that matters is having money. The son gives his father an education in grifting, telling stories of people who jumped in front of trains or suffered stab wounds so they could sue for damages. The verse ends with the narrator's needing a walk to clear his head but lamenting that he can no longer do so without a gun.

The fifth and final verse takes the form of a didactic slippery slope speech given by the narrator, possibly to his son, possibly to any and all youth in the community. He reminds the young that they were born innocent and that although they are children of God, they will face tough times and live the existence of second-class citizens. This will produce a deep hatred in their hearts for both their community and their environment, which will cause them to want to live like the criminals (bookies, gangsters, petty thieves, pimps, drug dealers, gamblers, and con men) they encounter—but such a future would include a lack of education, unemployment, and ultimately prison, where they may be abused, possibly raped or killed, or become suicidal.

"The Message" became bigger than any of the band members' expectations. It reached No. 4 on the Hot R&B/Hip Hop Songs chart (it also reached No. 2 on New Zealand's Recorded Music RZ chart) before going platinum, and both *Village Voice* and *Rolling Stone* named it single of the year. In 2002, the Library of Congress chose it for the National Recording Registry, becoming the first hip hop recording to receive this honor. Melle Mel was one of three rappers who began with Grandmaster Flash, along with the Kidd Creole (Nathaniel Glover, n.d.). The addition of Scorpio (Edward Morris, n.d.) and Rahiem (Guy Todd Williams, n.d.) created the Furious Five, which signed with Enjoy Records to release "Superappin" (1979) and then Sugar Hill Records to release "Freedom" (1980). However, only Melle Mel achieved icon status, and namely for "The Message."

LAURYN HILL: *THE MISEDUCATION OF LAURYN HILL* (RUFFHOUSE RECORDS, 1998)

Lauryn Hill (Lauryn Noelle Hill, 1975–) came into prominence for her work with hip hop and neo-soul group Fugees (1992–97), a South Orange (New Jersey) trio with Haitian singer-rapper Wyclef Jean (Nel Ust Wyclef Jean, 1969–) and American rapper-songwriter-producer Pras (Prakazrel Samuel Michél, 1972–). The trio was known for the album *The Score* (1996)— which hit No. 1 on the Billboard 200, was certified sextuple platinum, and won a Grammy for Best Rap Album—as well as its hip hop rendition of Roberta Flack's "Killing Me Softly (with His Song)" (1971), with Hill on lead vocals. The song went to No. 2 on the Billboard Hot 100 and won a Grammy Award for Best R&B Performance by a Duo or Group with Vocals. The album also featured a rendition of Bob Marley and the Wailers' reggae classic "No Woman No Cry" (1974) and the Delfonics' R&B and soul song "Ready or Not

Here I Come (Can't Hide from Love)" (1968). Despite success, Fugees disbanded, and Hill began to pursue her successful solo career.

Her debut, *The Miseducation of Lauryn Hill* (1998), went to No. 1 on the Billboard 200, was certified eight times platinum, and made Hill the first female artist to win five Grammys in one night. The album's lyrics touched on her strained relationship with Jean, a turbulent romance that ended with his infidelity. It also explored a lack of support from Jean and Pras for her solo endeavor and outside factors like the stress of performance schedules and handling notoriety. The inspiration for the album's title came from the book *The Mis-Education of the Negro* (1933) by Carter G. Woodson. The first single, "Doo Wop (That Thing)," became a Billboard Hot 100 No. 1, while "Ex-Factor" and "Everything Is Everything" peaked at Nos. 21 and 35, respectively.

Best described as a concept album about the nature of love, *The Miseducation of Lauryn Hill* begins with a classroom skit. In it, a teacher calls roll, and all students except for Hill respond present—the first four songs are bracketed by three such classroom skits; the message that slowly emerges is that Hill missed that lesson and therefore never learned about love and betrayal. "Lost Ones" is the first song to interrupt the skits. It begins explosively, with a kick drum beat, which then merges into a steady keyboard and bass drum and snare beat, which is kept simple to foreground Hill's rap. Her vocals have a distinct Jamaican reggae flavor, including a great deal of reverb, especially in the refrain, which builds musically (a new element being added with each iteration). Featuring triple and double syllable end rhymes, the song is basically a diss rap to Wyclef Jean, calling him out on his abusiveness and infidelity. As such, "Lost Ones" serves as an excellent starting point for the airing of dirty laundry. The album's tenth track, the reggae-infused neo soul "Forgive Them Father," is the clearest articulation that one of the issues between Hill and her fellow Fugees was that they purposefully held her back, seeing her success as somehow a detriment to their own. It features the Jamaican-styled rap vocal of Shelly Thunder (Michelle Harrison-Timol, n.d.), which is the song's standout element.

A skit about love also introduces the more R&B and neo-soul flavored "Ex-Factor," which is, in essence, a deconstruction of her dysfunctional relationship with Jean. Tracks eight and nine, the bass-heavy neo-soul songs "When It Hurts So Bad" and "I Used to Love Him," the latter featuring Mary J. Blige (1971–), also look at Hill and Jean's dysfunctional relationship, though in a more impressionistic fashion, examining the nature of love and Hill's own complicity, rather than any specific betrayal. In "Ex-Factor," Hill sings in her highest register (which comes across as a challenge for her), but the song's strength is in its doubling of her vocals and its backing vocals, which use gospel elements. Its downtempo beat and use of simple instrumentation offers the opportunity for experimentation in the form of a surprise rock-style electric guitar solo in the outro, which serves to introduce the albums fourth track and standout song, "To Zion," a song that begins with Carlos Santana (1947–) on Spanish guitar set against a spoken-word intro by Hill. Here Hill sings (against Santana's playing) in her deepest register, where she seems more comfortable. The lyrics tell about her pregnancy (not by Jean) and decision to give birth and raise a son, whom she named Zion. Addressed to her son, the song explains that one day he will understand what she went through. The song, which ends dramatically with battle drums, a gospel choir, a showcase of Santana's guitar chops, and one of the singers hitting a sustained high note, is appropriately followed by a classroom skit on love, which challenges the notion that young boys are incapable of falling in love and responding to a person's inner glow. The twelfth track, the neo soul down-tempo "Nothing Even Matters," which features D'Angelo (Michael Eugene Archer, 1974–), is the most positive love song on the album—it examines this idea of love's being about that glow.

The album's hit, "Doo Wop (That Thing)," addresses both the issue of sex (women being used by men, specifically) and how black women and men are portrayed in hip hop culture. It stresses to women that they need to stop allowing themselves to be sexualized and to men that they need to eschew the gangsta lifestyle, which includes objectifying women. It begins with Hill's spoken-word set against harmonizing vocalists, soon joined by a keyboard (playing scales) and heavy bass and kick drum beat. Hill's speed rapping, when addressed to women, takes a gospel-style call-response structure, with backing vocalists responding through vocalizations of assent (e.g., stylized "yeah," "uh huh," and "girlfriend"). In the last verse, addressed to men, there are no backing vocals, indicating (by omission) that men may not even be listening, an interpretation bolstered by the fact that the song's outro is a warning to women only. The song's refrain introduces a brass section and Hill's sung vocals (and in later iterations, a male singer vocalizing bass notes).

After a brief skit about youth and love, the neo-soul sixth track, "Superstar," continues the commentary on music begun in "Doo Wop (That Thing)," except here Hill disses commercialized hip hop (including Jean) and its concern only with charting rather than attempting to inspire. The song begins with a children's song–styled ostinato played on keyboards, which is set against a heavy funk bass and snare beat, accompanied by children's percussions, while Hill sings in her deep register accompanied by gospel-style backing vocals. In later verses, Hill switches to speed rapping, and the backing vocals become response vocalizations. The third consecutive song about her music, the down-tempo and funky "Final Hour," begins with a guitar ostinato and repetitive drum beat that recalls the Beatles' "Rocky Raccoon" (1968) and is accompanied by a flute that is reminiscent of the style used by Brian Jackson when working with Gil Scott-Heron on his spoken-word albums. Her rap vocals are heavily reverbed and slightly backgrounded, with the guitar, drum, bass, flute, and an occasional keyboard taking foreground.

"Every Ghetto, Every City," the most funk-influenced song on the album, is bookended by a return to the schoolroom skits, in this case the teacher briefly talking to a male student about why he needs love and what love is specifically. The opening skit transitions into the slap bass and hand claps (and in its outro, beatboxing) of "Every Ghetto, Every City," the most fully autobiographical song on the album. In a vocal delivery reminiscent of a young Michael Jackson, Hill sings of how ghettos she visits remind her of childhood in South Orange, New Jersey, with fond memories like popsicles, cartoons, cocoa bread, childhood chase games, and bicycle riding. The song, which features Hill's best vocals on the album, includes a reference to her mother's support of her desire to be a singer. Hill carries this positivity into "Nothing Even Matters" and "Everything Is Everything," both of which posit that love conquers all and that what is meant to be, will be. The latter, a new jack swing–infused, gospel-influenced sing-along with various voices, describes the cycle of life as working toward perfection. Again, here Hill's vocals are self-assured and strong, and the vocal interplay between singers (and Hill's occasional rapping) makes the song a standout. A cover of Frankie Valli's "Can't Take My Eyes Off of You" (1967) and the Hill-written "Tell Him" continue the theme of love, self-acceptance, and self-actualization. "The Miseducation of Lauryn Hill" is the most retro song, with Hill singing an overtly gospel song against only a thin 1980s keyboard voice, bass, and strings (with occasional organ). "Tell Him" is the perfect ending to the album. A neo soul, R&B (girl band) song, it uses a steady snare beat, bass, acoustic guitar, and kick drum to create a down-tempo expression of a willingness to love again; it also portrays Hill as someone who has learned about her own weaknesses when it comes to love and relationships—she now has wisdom and knowledge; her education is complete.

Hill has also performed and collaborated on various projects, including the Grammy-nominated track "So High (Cloud 9 Remix)" (2005) with John Legend. Wyclef Jean and Pras also continued with solo endeavors. The former's debut album *The Carnival* (Ruffhouse Records, 1997) was certified double platinum, and he became politically active, filing for candidacy in the 2010 Haitian presidential election. Pras's first solo studio album, *Ghetto Supastar* (Ruffhouse Records, 1998), peaked at No. 55 on the Billboard 200. An unsuccessful attempt at a Fugees reunion took place between 2004 and 2006.

INSANE CLOWN POSSE: "CROP CIRCLES" AND "OFF THE TRACK" (PSYCHOPATHIC RECORDS, 2005)

No rap group has as dedicated a fan base as Insane Clown Posse (a.k.a. ICP), a rap duo that consists of Violent J (Joseph Bruce, 1972–) and Shaggy 2 Dope (a.k.a. 2 Dope; Joseph Utsler, 1974–), rappers and producers who cofounded the label Psychopathic Records in 1991 just two years after the two united as a band; the label signed local rap band Twiztid from 1997 to 2012. The duo's fans, called Juggalos, not only strongly defend ICP's skills as rappers and lyricists, but also adopt a lifestyle, complete with its own language and festival (The Gathering, an annual festival that ranges between ten to twenty thousand face-painted, Faygo-drinking, and Faygo-spraying fans). ICP, known for its elaborate live performances, is usually categorized as either hardcore rap or horrorcore.

Each of ICP's first three albums, Psychopathic's *Carnival of Carnage* (1992) and *Ringmaster* (1994), and Battery Records' *Riddlebox* (1995), sold over 500,000 units despite failing to chart in the Billboard 200. Its fourth and fifth studio albums, *The Great Milenko* (Hollywood Records, 1997) and *The Amazing Jeckel Brothers* (Island, 1999), were both RIAA certified platinum, the latter breaking the Billboard 200 Top Ten, peaking at No. 4 (the duo's next eight albums would all reach the Top 20). During this string of successful sales, the duo released its best-performing EP, *The Calm* (2005), its first completely self-produced work. *The Calm*, a prelude to the band's album *The Tempest* (also on Psychopathic, 2007), reached No. 32 on the Billboard 200, No. 5 on the Top Rap Albums chart, and No. 1 on the Independent Albums chart.

ICP's songs in general are concerned with the nature of extreme human evil (e.g., cannibalism, murder, and necrophilia), with the Dark Carnival (a purgatory-like liminal state), and with the Dark Carnival–associated series of stories called Joker's Cards (which form a central mythology, with a concept similar to the Christian heaven, referred to as Shangri-La). Despite the similarity to Christianity, the duo insists they are not a Christian rap band. ICP's themes are often sociopolitical and concerned with the problems of the Detroit ghetto, such as racism, domestic violence, and child abuse. Influenced by Detroit horrorcore rapper Esham (Rashaam Attica Smith, 1973–), Insane Clown Posse (originally billed as Inner City Posse) decided to adopt an acid rap style, using horror tropes to get its message across. Early on, the duo's sound was minimalist rap, but more rock music instrumentation and beats were added in time. Despite problems such as an eight-year feud with Eminem that ended in 2005, critics not taking the band seriously, and constant legal and personal problems while on tour to promote *The Great Milenko*, ICP was very successful and had received national recognition.

The Calm is the first ICP work following its Jokers Card Saga. Although the EP begins with the typical rap braggadocio song "Rolling Over" and contains a couple of tracks that are informed by conventional rap themes such as positivity ("We'll Be Alright" and "Like It Like That") and seductresses and unfaithful women ("Rosemary" and "Deadbeat Moms," which features Esham), it includes two tracks that stand out because of their idiosyncratic concerns with, of all things, crop circles and their significance as a sign of the apocalypse. These two tracks, "Crop Circles" and "Off the Track," both produced by ICP, are also the two best songs on the EP. Lyrically, they stand out for a complexity that is uncharacteristic of the EP as a whole, and musically, they are the most well-structured and creative.

"Crop Circles" is, as its title suggests, about the mysterious formation of crops, usually flattened to create a pattern. As a phenomenon, they fall into the category of either man-made hoax or unexplained events (usually attributed to alien origins), depending on the inclinations of the person studying them (a cereologist). The song begins with a general history of crop circles, with an emphasis on their mysterious nature and how people have tried to interpret them. In verse one, the lyrics take a turn when Shaggy 2 Dope raps that when he gets near them, he gets a nosebleed and that he instinctively understands that they are important to his life. He relates them to other supernatural beliefs, such as ghosts and time portals. The verse ends on an environmental note—that human abuse of nature is going to come back to haunt us. The song's hook is a simple statement that the circles are created to convey a message. In verse two, Violent J takes up the environmental theme, as he personifies Earth as an avenging giant. Like Shaggy 2 Dope, he expresses an affinity with the circles, which he tried to understand by laying in fields at night. He muses that either aliens or animistic spirits are responsible. After the second iteration of the refrain, the two take turns with short four-line raps that take different approaches to the phenomena: historical, numerological, and supernatural. The track ends with the warning to stay away from them, with a last second twist by Violent J that turns the song into a brag track—the message being that only ICP is brave enough to try.

"Off the Track" begins with a strange Violent J verse vision, that he is battling samurais and "falling through the future," which allows him to see an apocalyptic vision. The song's hook simply states that the human race has lost its direction and is free-falling toward a dark destiny. The second verse by Shaggy 2 Dope, which takes the form of a different kind of vision (a long drive while freestyle rapping) begins with references to natural and supernatural end-times phenomena—nuclear war, Marfa lights, and the aforementioned crop circles. Like Violent J, Shaggy 2 Dope raps of a futuristic vision that is dark. However, he adds a touch of comedy, rapping that ICP will keep it real (in this case "Juggalo," rather than "street") and enjoy the Dark Carnival (the verse has a great absurdist line, stating they will be found eating Lucky Charms off the Milky Way). After the second refrain, the break reiterates that for ICP, the ride will be like a roller coaster. In the third verse, Violent J invites fans to come along for the wild ride (marijuana and opium being part of the journey) of the Dark Carnival wagons. The song ends with a refrain-break-refrain structure, followed by Violent J's outro, in which he states that despite these dark visions, ICP will never stop making music.

Musically, both "Crop Circles" and "Off the Track" are informed by the aesthetics of psychedelia—down-tempo beats, lots of reverb, offbeat instrumental choices, and laid-back vocals. Each song is built around an unconventional instrument for rap music: "Crop Circles" uses a baritone guitar (or synth-created guitar voice), which is backgrounded and reverbed, sounding reminiscent of the guitar sound made famous by Ennio Morricone in Sergio Leone's spaghetti westerns, while "Off the Track" uses a synth-voice that is set to reverb and echo so that it sounds as if it has a sympathetic string, the effect being similar to that of a sitar.

"Crop Circles" begins with an off-kilter, down-tempo synthetic drum beat (mostly bass kick and tom, with rests placed in what come across as seemingly random places), joined by reverbed claps, the baritone guitar voice and an eerie-sounding four-note keyboard riff (the voice sounds like a circus piano, albeit higher pitched) that is reminiscent of a carnival theme. In the first verse, the drum becomes snare-based and plays a simple 4/4 beat (which continues throughout, as it is easier to rap against than the offbeat intro drum beat), and a synthesizer-produced vibe voice is added, as a foregrounded countermelody instrument to the guitar (the eerie piano now backgrounded). In the refrain, the instrumentation is stripped down to the drum and guitar, and backgrounded vocalizations and backing vocals processed to sound like monastery chanting act as a countermelody to the sung vocals. The instrumentation remains constant throughout all verses and refrains. The song ends on the refrain, with an abrupt cutoff after the instrumentation is manipulated to sound as if it is sped up into an incoherent buzz.

"Off the Track" likewise begins with an off-kilter synth drum kick and snare-heavy beat (likely an 808, as it hiccups) that has seemingly random rests. This switches to a more consistent 4/4 beat as verse one begins. In the intro and throughout verses, two synth voices are played against this beat, the first sounding like a 1980s Roland voice, the second being the pseudo-sitar voice. They are played call-and-response style, respectively. Rapping against this is laid-back and carefully articulated. Hiccups created by the 808 drum (tapped off with a cymbal crash) are placed at the end of lines, which conclude full thoughts. During the refrains, a third keyboard voice is added, this one having the range of the 1980s voice but the reverb and echo of the pseudo-sitar (it brilliantly links the two keyboard voices). As the second verse comes to an end, Violent J harmonizes briefly with Shaggy 2 Dope, who starts rapping slightly faster, and a new synth voice, a high-pitched, funky sixteenth note keyboard voice, appears out of nowhere and changes the song's dynamic, taking it from the down-tempo, relaxed atmosphere to an immediate, almost threatening one; this is capped off by a turntable scratch, which returns the instrumentation to its previous, down-tempo state.

During the break, the beat breaks down and instrumentation becomes muddled, almost discordant, with the only clearly discernible sounds being that of the sixteenth note keyboard voice and an electric bass, the notes sliding up and down almost randomly; against this the two rappers sing, their lines staccato but laid-back. The verse music then returns for the final verse, but in the ensuing refrain strings are added to the keyboard voices. The song ends with a break-refrain-outro structure. The break uses the same discordant instrumentation as previously, while the refrain uses the instrumentation of the previous refrain (strings added). The outro uses the instrumentation associated with verse two, including the sixteenth note keyboard voice—all instrument voices but this one end abruptly (on the line "never stop b—"), and it fades out over the song's last three seconds.

In 2007, ICP released *The Tempest*, which debuted at No. 20 on the Billboard 200. Its eleventh studio album, *Bang! Pow! Boom!* (2009), debuted at No. 4. ICP's later albums included *The Mighty Death Pop!* (2012), *The Marvelous Missing Link: Lost* (2015), and *The Marvelous Missing Link: Found* (2015). After 2000, all of ICP's albums were released on Psychopathic. In 2010, Psychopathic Records signed a contract with Universal Music Group's Fontana Distribution. The duo took to film, starring in *Big Money Rustlas* (2010), a Western spoof. The duo is also known for its brief foray into professional wrestling: in various independent promotions in Michigan (1990–97), in Extreme Championship Wrestling (ECW, 1997), in the World Wrestling Federation (WWF, 1998), and as members of World Championship Wrestling (WCW, 1999–2000). The duo continue to wrestle in Juggalo Championship Wrestling, where they created the stable called the Juggalo World Order.

JAY-Z AND DANGER MOUSE: *THE BLACK ALBUM* AND *THE GREY ALBUM* (ROC-A-FELLA RECORDS, 2003, AND DIGITALLY SELF-RELEASED, 2004)

Brooklyn's Jay-Z (Shawn Corey Carter, 1969–) is one of the most successful rap artists of all time, having released an impressive number of critically praised and commercially successful albums. As a musician and businessman, he has amassed a fortune that he has used to build a financial empire—his forays into entrepreneurship include fashion, entertainment, and sports management, making him one of hip hop's wealthiest figures. After he released the official version of *The Black Album* on his Roc-A-Fella label, he exhibited his marketing skills, releasing an a cappella version, intended for music engineers and producers to remix and create new albums of their own.

At least a dozen remix producers did so, but the most noteworthy of these was White Plains, New York–native Danger Mouse (Brian Joseph Burton, 1977–). His self-released *The Grey Album*, an experimental project intended for a limited three thousand copy release in February 2004, combined Jay-Z's rapping with samples taken from various Beatles songs from the 1968 *White Album* (a.k.a. *The Beatles*). A follow-up, "The Grey Video," was created by Swiss directing team Ramon & Pedro to promote Danger Mouse's "Encore," which mixes fragments of the Beatles' "Glass Onion" and "Savoy Truffle" with the Jay-Z original; it features mashed up footage of *A Hard Day's Night* with live Jay-Z footage, using CGI to have black female dancers interact with John Lennon, and body doubles to make it seem that Lennon break-dances into a head spin and Ringo Starr DJs (behind a turntablist console labeled "Danger Mouse").

The Black Album chronicles Jay-Z's rise from a childhood in Brooklyn's Bedford-Stuyvesant neighborhood, a family death due to murder, an absent father, and drug deals—his only escape being music. Jay-Z had started by selling his first recordings out of his own car, eventually founding Roc-A-Fella Records (1996–2013). His debut album, *Reasonable Doubt* (1996), rose to No. 23 on Billboard's Top 200 and eventually reached platinum status. His second solo album, *In My Lifetime, Vol. 1* (1997), debuted at No. 3 and reached an even bigger audience, in part due to a Roc-A-Fella distribution deal with Def Jam Recordings. *Vol. 2 . . . Hard Knock Life* (1998) debuted at No. 1 on the Billboard 200. Over the next several years Jay-Z delivered a remarkably consistent string of hit albums, hitting his stride with *The Black Album*, which would sell over three million units.

The Black Album begins with "Interlude," a brief introduction (spoken word to incidental music) by producer Just Blaze, who also produces a later track, the organ-based, hard rock "Public Service Announcement." The introduction likens Jay-Z to a tree that will spread its seeds so more may grow, and "Public Service Announcement" serves as an intermission (even though it is track ten of fourteen), as well as an ending—it promises that this will be Jay-Z's final album, the second such promise on the album itself. "December 4th," the second track, offers instrumental (synthesized strings, woodwinds, brass, and choir voices) fanfare and features spoken-word interludes by Jay-Z's mother (Gloria Carter) as she recounts his childhood in brutally honest terms, the defining moment being when his father left. The song's rapped lyrics are both apologetic (for the problems he has caused) and straightforward (his acceptance of who he was and has become). These same issues resurface in "Moment of Clarity," produced by Eminem and Luis Resto (1961–), which begins with an ominous keyboard, sub-bass, and snare drum beat, with dramatic strings throughout. Here Jay-Z raps (Eminem joins him on the refrain) in detail about his father's and uncle's deaths and gives a genuinely straightforward explanation of why he made a conscious decision to make his music more commercial and less esoteric, like the raps of Talib Kweli and Common (a.k.a. Common Sense), stating that he can't help the poor if he is poor himself. The album's final and best song, "My First Song," a blues-infused snap song, offers a further explanation of his musical choices over his career; it features sound bites from an interview with the Notorious BIG (a.k.a. Biggie Smalls), to whom Jay-Z pays homage at the song's end.

"What More Can I Say?" follows "December 4th," and it has an aggressive intro that samples the film *Gladiator* (2000) and asks, "Are you not entertained?" It features sonic highs (drums, bass, synth-based orchestra) and lows (a single keyboard voice with snare drum), includes an R&B-influenced sung refrain, and ends with Jay-Z's rapping himself breathless, a cappella. The lyrics are about his music career, calling out his critics, other rappers, and groupies as he establishes that he has always been true to his craft and himself. "Encore" begins with a brass section ostinato that is set against dry-sounding percussion and Jay-Z's speed rapping (which slows toward the song's end), with vocal doubling in the refrain. Produced by Kanye West, it includes an opera-style vocal, cheering crowd noise, and grand piano in its outro. By contrast, "Change Clothes" has a down-tempo R&B instrumentation, combined with an idiosyncratic use of metal surface drumming (e.g., a fire extinguisher or scuba tank, other flat metal surfaces, and mic stands), and features Pharrell (Pharrell Lanscilo Williams, 1973–) as guest singer. Bordering on neo soul, its lyrics are half concerned with sex and half with bragging on Jay-Z's rap style, with a final message that rappers do not have to always act tough in their raps, that sometimes style makes a statement. Pharrell appears on the string-heavy "Allure," an uplifting gangsta song based on the film *Scarface* (1983), about enjoying life's violent moments; it has interesting interplay being maudlin string orchestration and gunfire sounds used as percussion.

The album's standouts are "Dirt off Your Shoulder," "Threat," and "99 Problems." The Timbaland-produced "Dirt off Your Shoulder" features a synth-produced beat (a thin keyboard voice set against a kick drum) with sound effects peppered throughout and a countermelody keyboard voice added later. Jay-Z uses a staccato rap style that emphasizes the ends of lines, which usually fall on the bass kick. About two-thirds in, the song suddenly switches to a heavy organ-based 1970s funk sound, returning in the outro to the original keyboard. "Threat," a basic gangsta rap song (the others being the more predictable "Justify My Thug" and "Lucifer," the former using disco-style keyboard bass and the latter using a wood block percussion) was produced by 9th Wonder (Patrick Denard Douthit, 1975–) and begins with a spoken-word gangsta intro by Cedric the Entertainer (Cedric Antonio Kyles, 1964–), who appears throughout. This gives way to a steady drum kit beat and piano, with an interspersed 808 drum as Jay-Z raps about his past (and possibly future) reliance on violence, when pushed. Its lyrics are extremely clever, as Jay-Z weaves a tapestry of pop culture references and wordplay (e.g., Bill O'Reilly is riling him up, and the phrase "I Sinatra shot ya"). Produced by Rick Rubin, the cofounder of Def Jam Recordings, "99 Problems" is a hard rock rap song, with turntables and a surprise triangle, cowbell, and guiro. Lyrics that chronicle the problems faced by Jay-Z (indicative of the black community), such as poverty and police brutality, are set against a Beastie Boys sound—it is even written for various voices, achieved by Rubin with vocal postproduction effects. The song ends on a clever metatextual moment when Jay-Z outs Rubin for being crazy for producing the song.

Danger Mouse, an American music producer and multi-instrumentalist, took up Jay-Z's challenge to remix *The Black Album*, the result being *The Grey Album* (a.k.a. *The Gray Album*), a self-released digital download. It highlighted his career as a member of Gnarls Barkley (1999–) with CeeLo Green and then as a solo act, a stint as a member of the short-lived project band DANGERDOOM in 2005, and a stint as a member of Broken Bells, which released two Top Ten albums. Danger Mouse later produced albums for dozens of different artists and won several Grammy Awards. *The Grey Album* was a noncommercial project in which Danger Mouse combined distorted and remixed samples from *The White Album* with the a cappella copy of *The Black Album*. It features a dizzying array of sampling, mixing, and remixing seconds-long fragments from Beatles songs and combining these with original hip hop beats.

The Grey Album begins with *The Black Album*'s tenth track, "Public Service Announcement," in which Danger Mouse samples "Long, Long, Long." Here he adds vocal processing that makes Just Blaze's intro sound like backgrounded archived news footage, the result being that the first foregrounded voice heard is Jay-Z's, which raps against kick drums, synth-produced flute voices, and percussion. Rather than *The Black Album*'s second track, "December 4th," Danger Mouse follows with "What More Can I Say?" sampling "While My Guitar Gently Weeps." His version dumps the Gladiator sample and Jay-Z's intro, jumping right into Jay-Z's rap, set against the famous Beatles piano ostinato, bass, and cymbal crash—Danger Mouse slows down the piano and replaces cymbal with snare. To this he adds 808 drums, a kick drum and tom routine, and the occasional George Harrison guitar ostinato. "Encore" is next, and it features "Glass Onion" and "Savoy Truffle." The song's beat is taken from the former's refrain, featuring the rhythm guitar strike, Lennon's "oh yeah," Ringo's drumming, and the background strings, which are foregrounded here. Danger Mouse makes great use of stop-start instrumental hiccups, which match Jay-Z's rapping. When Jay-Z begins verse two, the sample switches to the organ and lead guitar interplay of the "Savoy Truffle" refrain, with the guitar voice being replaced by synthesized bass or baritone guitar voice. The inclusion of "December 4th" (which samples "Mother Nature's Son") as the next song serves the purpose of keeping three of the first four tracks of the *Black Album* grouped together, albeit in a new order. Danger Mouse replaces the synthesized fanfare of Jay-Z's recording with the acoustic guitar and French horn from the refrain of the Beatles song, but he sharpens it and raises its volume, pitting it against a foregrounded 808 drum to turn the gentle ostinato from "Mother Nature's Son" into a percussive beat to set spoken word and rap against. Gloria Carter's first spoken section is omitted, but those between verses are kept, with the final line to each coinciding with a switch from the aforementioned percussive beat to the plucked strings (with a slightly changed pitch) of the intro.

The next four songs, "99 Problems," "Dirt off Your Shoulder," "Moment of Clarity," and "Change Clothes" are the album's standouts. Sampling "Helter Skelter," "99 Problems" has the same high energy and hard rock feel as the original song. Rather than sample any specific guitar ostinato, Danger Mouse here manipulates minute elements from the "Helter Skelter" refrain: the song's high register "ah" chorus, part of Paul McCartney's bass, the guitar tag, and Ringo Starr's snare flourish (with some added snare), with Ringo's cymbal crashes held off for later verses. Danger Mouse cleverly mixes and matches these into various combinations and varies the volumes of all voices to create sonic diversity (although usually the volume increases on the "ah" chorus). "Dirt off Your Shoulder," which samples "Julia," reproduces the high/low dynamic of Timbaland's production, pitting Lennon's gentle acoustic guitar against a hiccupping 808 drum (with lots of bass kick), with a clapping tag. Lennon's vocals are reduced to syllables that feature a long "u" and short "a" sound. Like the drums, the guitar and Lennon's vocals are hiccuped throughout, the result being an off-kilter beat that always leaves the listener guessing. Here Danger Mouse keeps all lyrics from the original song, including spoken-word segments. "Moment of Clarity" uses the gently played guitar ostinato from the opening of "Happiness Is a Warm Gun," which has also been broken into chords and recombined into two new patterns, mixed and matched in continuous phrases throughout; these are played both separately and together, against an 808 drum adjusted for a longer decay (giving the drumming a slapping sound). The arrangement of the guitar snippets is such that its melodic structure cleverly approximates the dramatic string melody of Jay-Z's original. "Change Clothes" samples "Piggies," giving it a decidedly different feel than Jay-Z's R&B song. Here it is more up-tempo, with a beat created by the Beatles' main harpsichord melody that is sampled from two sections of "Piggies" to create an 8-bar phrase that is repeated and set against the cello from "Piggies," which is manipulated to sound like jug blowing. The beat is created by a drum kit and an 808 drum hiccup.

The album's four final songs are "Allure," "Justify My Thug," "Lucifer 9," and "My First Song." "Allure" samples the guitar ostinato from "Dear Prudence" in its outro, uses a keyboard ostinato of ringing chords (with a cymbal crash tag), claps, and bass kick interplay to create a playful rhythm. "Justify My Thug," which samples the bass/guitar interplay (sped up), bass walk, and harmonica ostinato of "Rocky Raccoon," uses a hiccupping 808 drum with cymbal crash tags, making it at times engaging and at times muddled in its overmixing. "Lucifer 9," which samples the enigmatic "Revolution 9" and bluesy "I'm So Tired," is for the most part an experimental piece. It uses chords and vocal snippets from "I'm So Tired" as well as offbeat synth and tape-produced elements of "Revolution 9," combined with a bass guitar, snare, and 808 drum (hiccupped) beat, peppered with moments of a grand piano. "My First Song," which samples "Cry Baby Cry" throughout, set against an 808 drum, a snare and tambourine interplay, and synthesized saxophone sound, also samples guitars from "Savoy Truffle" and "Helter Skelter" in the last third of the song's outro. It comes across as muddled and overproduced but has interesting moments.

After the album's release, Danger Mouse received a cease-and-desist letter from EMI, the copyright holder of the Beatles' music. EMI's actions sparked an online protest, leading to music industry activist group Downhill Battle's response: the coordination of the Grey Tuesday protest (February 24, 2004), when over one hundred participating websites made the album available, and estimates of 100,000 to one million copies were downloaded (the exact number is still debatable). The album sparked conversations about the relationship of copyright and creative expression, and a number of critics named the *Grey Album* as one of the best albums of the year.

JEAN GRAE: "MY STORY" AND "DESPERADA" (*JEANIUS*, BLACKSMITH MUSIC, 2008)

The daughter of South African jazz musicians, Cape Town's Jean Grae (Tsidi Ibrahim, 1976–) rose to prominence in New York's underground rap scene (she had been raised in New York City, where her parents relocated). Recording under the name Ground Zero, she worked with producer George Rithm Martinez (George Martinez, 1974–) in 1995 to produce a critically acclaimed demo. She later joined Natural Resource, which in 1996 released a pair of 12-inch singles but broke up in 1998. Over time she changed her stage name from What? What? to Jean Grae and released her first album on the underground Third Earth Music label, *Attack of the Attacking Things . . . The Dirty Mixes* (2002). In 2005, she self-released *Hurricane Jean: The Jeanius Strikes Again*, which featured Talib Kweli on the song "Black Girl Pain" (the track was also released on Talib Kweli's 2004 *The Beautiful Struggle*).

In 2004, she began work on the album *Jeanius*, which was eventually released in 2008 on Talib Kweli's Blacksmith Music label, working with producer 9th Wonder (a.k.a. 9thmatic), who began his career as the main producer for the North Carolina rap crew Little Brother. His production style, infused by 1970s soul such as that of Al Green and Curtis Mayfield, got attention when he remixed Nas's *God's Son* (2002) as *God's Stepson* (2003) and produced the track "Threat" from Jay-Z's *The Black Album* (2003) and three tracks on Destiny's Child's *Destiny Fulfilled* (2004) album: "Girl," "Is She the Reason," and "Game Over." *Jeanius*, Jean Grae's third studio album, contains two standout tracks; "My Story" and "Desperada" are both brutally honest attempts to deal with a pain-filled past, making them stand out lyrically. Instrumentally, they exemplify 9th Wonder's laid-back style, which can best be described as a cross between 1970s soul and trip hop.

"My Story" tells the story of a woman who has had two abortions due to unplanned pregnancies and abandonment by the fathers, and she later suffers a miscarriage when she tries to carry to term. How much of the song is autobiographical is uncertain, but speculation is that most of it is since it is told from the point of view of someone who has suffered through the events, feels extremely guilty about them, and continues to live the trauma. Jean Grae has indicated in interviews that the song does help her deal with her past, which also lends credence to an autobiographical reading. Other clues include lines (in the song's hook) that indicate that rapping the story is too painful for her—she hints twice that she cannot continue the song because of its effect on her emotionally. And, of course, the track is titled "My Story." This is not to say that the song does not contain fictionalized elements, as many autobiographical works of art do for various reasons.

Instrumentally, "My Story" is reminiscent of some of the Brian Jackson and Gil Scott-Heron spoken-word jazz tracks of the 1970s. Its drum beat, bass, and flute come directly from a sample of "I Have a Dream" (1979, off of *Invitation*) by Norman Connors, an American jazz drummer, composer, arranger, and producer known for his love ballads such as "You Are My Starship" (1976). Connors's drum beat is down-tempo jazz-funk (with some 808 hiccups added for effect, usually to bridge sections). Unlike "I Have a Dream," which foregrounds the flugelhorn and theremin-like vocals, 9th Wonder foregrounds the original's funk bass, centered on the octave, as well as its flute melodies, and he backgrounds rhythm guitars (throughout) and horns (used occasionally), keeping the latter muffled. Taken altogether, the instrumentation of the manipulated sample gives the track a downbeat jazzy feel that borders on trip hop. While this would present difficulties for most rappers (finding an organic flow that works against the trancelike music), Jean Grae handles it deftly because she is a master of flow variation, switching between old-school rap lines (fixed length and rhythm, creating a singsong effect) and modernized use of pauses and enjambment to vary delivery and stay on the beat. In addition, her rapping is carefully articulated and her lyrics highly articulate. Her rapping vocals are multitracked to make them sound wetter and fuller. She sings the hooks, her vocals processed to be multitracked and slightly auto-tuned for harmonies. Verse two stands out for its instrumental representation of being under anesthesia—the music is processed to sound as if it is coming from an old radio in the distance, while rapping gets foregrounded. This disconnected music-vocal combination is used again in the bridge after verse two and at the beginning of verse three, in the scenes about the miscarriage. In that bridge and in the song's outro, highly reverbed vocalizations (less theremin-like and more evocative of avant-garde opera) are added to the mix, giving the music an even more ethereal sense and adding a sense of drama.

"Desperada" is a shorter, prayer-like track that also takes a look back at Jean Grae's painful history but in a much more abstract, big picture way. The lyrics express a need to both lock the past into a closet or safe box and deal with it, presumably when the time is right. Whereas "My Story" is about grief and crippling guilt, "Desperada" is about overcoming grief; while the hook in "My Story" is one of self-damnation, "Desperada" has a hook of self-realization and contentment, celebrating what has been overcome and the personal strength that was realized in the process. The song fixates not on the journey but the journey's end, the understanding that the route taken has resulted in many positive, self-affirming experiences, including realizing the ability to face new problems, solve them, and evolve as a person.

The song opens with a looped and distorted guitar, against which Jean Grae repeats the word "wait" (the "wait" sounds are looped as well, and likely both sounds were looped together, possibly indicating the inclusion of a studio accident). This intro establishes that she is not quite ready yet, in the context of the song perhaps not yet prepared to begin the prayer that leads to both painful memories and realizations. The music behind the rapping of the first verse consists of a downbeat funk-jazz drum beat, rhythm guitar, synthesizer, and funk-rock bass.

Jean Grae's rapping is new school—there is no sign of the old-school singsong couplet of "My Story." On a couple of occasions, 9th Wonder uses stop time to allow the rapping to go on a cappella for a line or two, making the rapped lines foregrounded and more powerful in their effect. R&B and soul–influenced vocalizations are interspersed throughout both the verses and the hooks. Refrains are chant sung, with refrain vocals processed similarly to "My Story" and dry claps added. The outro is a sung version of the prayer "Now I Lay Me Down to Sleep," with the vocals less processed and not multitracked. The overall effect is that of trip hop, a dreamlike atmosphere better suited for contemplation than dance or partying.

After taking a hiatus from the recording industry, in 2011 Jean Grae released a free mixtape entitled *Cookies or Comas* on the underground Gangsta Grillz label, followed by the self-released ten-track *Dust Ruffle* (2012) featuring unreleased songs from between 2004 and 2010. Between October and November of 2013 she released a series of EPs on the indie KAGD label entitled *Gotham Down Cycle 1: Love in Infinity* (2013), *Gotham Down Cycle 3: The Artemis Epoch* (2013), and *Gotham Down Cycle II: Leviathan* (2016). In late 2017, she got engaged to fellow rapper and producer Quelle Chris (Gavin Christopher Tennille, n.d.), collaborating with him on *Everything's Fine* (2018) with Mello Music Group (MMG), an American independent hip hop label. The album is a satirical jazz and pop-infused album whose tracks feature comedians Hannibal Buress, Nick Offerman, Michael Che, and John Hodgman, among others.

K'NAAN: "TAKE A MINUTE" (SEE NAS AND K'NAAN)

KRS-ONE: "OUTTA HERE" AND "SOUND OF DA POLICE" (*RETURN OF THE BOOM BAP*, JIVE, 1993)

KRS-One (Lawrence Parker, 1965–), who later went by the stage name Teacha, is one of the most notable pioneers of hip hop music. A rapper, turntablist, record producer, and social activist, he began recording in 1986 as part of the hip hop group Boogie Down Productions (BDP, 1985–92), which he formed with DJ Scott La Rock (Scott Monroe Sterling, 1962–87) and beatboxer D-Nice (Derrick Jones, 1970–) in South Bronx, New York, after his and La Rock's first band, Celebrity Three, broke up. BDP's debut album, *Criminal Minded* (B-Boy Records, 1987), sold over 200,000 copies and ushered in the era of gangsta and diss rap; the album cover depicted the band wearing ammunition and brandishing guns and featured two early diss tracks called "South Bronx" and "The Bridge Is Over," songs considered part of the so-called Bridge Wars. BDP is also credited with helping to introduce rock music sampling and Jamaican rhythms into rap music; however, DJ Scott La Rock was shot and killed while attempting to intervene in a fight, causing KRS-One to retool the group and resulting in a series of solo projects until 1993, when he began releasing records as KRS-One.

Without Scott La Rock, KRS-One released the second Boogie Down Productions album, *By All Means Necessary* (Jive, 1988). With its next releases, BDP began to exhibit the didactic and political stances for which it would become known. Future Jive albums such as *Ghetto Music: The Blueprint of Hip Hop* (1989), *Edutainment* (1990), *Live Hardcore Worldwide* (1991), and *Sex and Violence* (1992) made it clear that BDP was mainly KRS-One as its music reflected his concerns with identity politics and social issues. Each of the four albums charted in the Billboard 200, at Nos. 75, 36, 32, and 42, respectively, and *Ghetto Music* and *Edutainment* both broke into the Hot R&B/Hip Hop Songs chart Top Ten. *Ghetto Music* produced two Top Ten singles on the Hot Rap Singles chart: "Jack of Spades" (No. 3) and "Why Is That?" (No. 5). His second and third solo albums, both with Jive, *KRS-One* (1995) and *I Got Next* (1997), both hit No. 2 on the R&B chart, with the latter breaking into the Billboard 200's Top Ten, peaking at No. 3. His first solo album was *Return of the Boom Bap* (Jive, 1993), which peaked at No. 35 on the Billboard 200 and No. 3 on the Hot R&B chart. It spawned his debut and highest-charting solo single on the Hot Rap Songs chart, "Outta Here," which reached No. 5. It also produced his first Billboard Hot 100 charter, "Sound of da Police," which hit No. 89 but also charted on the Hot Rap Songs chart (No. 17) and the Hot R&B/Hip Hop Songs chart (No. 79), making it his first song to place on all three charts.

"Outta Here," a song about the early history of rap music in Queens, conforms to the typical intro, three verses, and refrain structure of most rap songs. Its intro establishes that BDP is a force in rap music and the band is not a joke or a one-hit wonder. The song's verses faithfully chronicle KRS-One's experiences with rap music, from attending concerts—sometimes block parties and sometimes outdoor park events by early hip hop musicians and rappers such as Whodini and Jimmy Spicer (a.k.a. Super Rhymes)—to meeting Scott La Rock at a homeless shelter and from cofounding BDP and engaging in the Bridge Wars to hanging out with rappers like Eric B. and watching Public Enemy introduce socially conscious rap music. The song's refrain challenges rappers to remain true to the art and to remain in their local communities rather than take the first opportunity to sell out and get out. Musically, "Outta Here" is old-school rap: a solid 4/4 bass kick, snare, and ride cymbal drum beat set against a heavy synth-produced octave-based bass beat. Its verses foreground the bass and drum beat so that KRS-One can vary his flow between old-school singsong rap lines and free-flowing phrases that run words together or incorporate dramatic pauses. The refrains use terrace dynamics (the sounds get louder in calculated steps, with the introduction of crowd noises, distorted guitar sounds, and turntable). This limits the rapping in the refrain to basic old-school style, which KRS-One offsets by raising his voice into almost an angry yell as he accuses the newer rap crews of selling out (and relying on nonfunk samples) and creating songs solely for commercial success, which then leads to an opulent lifestyle that takes them out of the ghetto, the true home of rap.

"Sound of da Police," produced by Showbiz (Rodney Lemay, n.d.), samples Sly and the Family Stone, Grand Funk Railroad, and BDP. Generally speaking, it criticizes police brutality and systematic and historical racism. The lyric's central conceit is that the word "officer" is similar to "overseer," that is, the man whose job it was to oversee slaves on a plantation and keep them in line. Just as overseers were known for their cruelty (e.g., making slaves into examples through public punishment for small infractions), the police here are represented as cruel, using harassment techniques on a daily basis to intimidate the African American community. The song also offers a subtle threat to police officers—that if they continue to harass the community, they will rile it up and become the catalyst for anti-police violence. In the third verse, KRS-One also offers some historical perspective: generation after generation on his father's side has had to deal with abuse from the police, a cycle that has to end for there to be peace between police and the community. The song begins with KRS-One's "whooping" (twice quickly, and reverbed and echoed to imitate the sound of a siren), followed by a short pause and two lines that both state this is the sound of the police and the sound of the biblical beast, an implicit equation of the two. This becomes part of the refrain, a reminder that people in his community have to deal with this sound constantly—it becomes a part of their lives.

On the third iteration of the intro, the song begins and is introduced with the recurring phrase "yes indeed." A 4/4 bass and snare drum beat accompanied by heavy bass (a sample loop of Grand Funk Railroad's "Inside-Looking Out") adds both energy and tension; by the first verse, which is introduced by a brief synth-created buzzing sound, distorted horns appear on the fourth beat, making the music chaotic and seemingly dissonant (and in the official video, footage of police brutality accompanies this part of the verse). The drum, bass, and horn–produced beat continues through the rest of the song as KRS-One raps almost in a yell, using a Jamaican patois, his voice highly reverbed, producing mainly short, staccato lines that play up the anger and frustration of the situation. His flow in the verses varies between these staccato lines and longer, breathless lines that at times are used in a feat of linguistic cleverness, usually to emphasize a point, such as the similarity between the words "officer" and "overseer." The song's outro is a repetition of its bridge (which occurs between the second verse and the refrain) and a reintroduction of the buzz effect synth sound (which recalls buzzing bees and adds to the chaos as KRS-One repeats "yes indeed").

In the 2000s, KRS-One founded the Temple of Hip Hop Ministry, Archive, School, and Society (M.A.S.S.) to maintain and promote hip hop culture, and he recorded *Kristyles* on Koch Records(2003). He then switched to Grit and Antagonist Records, respectively, for *Keep Right* (2003) and *Life* (2006). Only *Kristyles* managed to break into the R&B Top Ten. He collaborated with Marley Marl on *Hip Hop Lives* (Koch, 2007) and has since released eleven albums as a solo act and as a collaborator, with only one solo project, *Adventures in Emceein* (Echo-Vista, 2008), breaking into the Billboard 200. He has also appeared on several songs with other artists, ultimately earning nine gold and seven platinum records. Aside from his music, KRS-One is known for his political activism, including cofounding the Stop the Violence Movement after the death of La Rock and producing the 1991 EP *H.E.A.L.* (*Human Education Against Lies*). In 1999, KRS-One became vice president of artists and repertoire at Reprise Records, which is now Warner Bros. Records. He has written four books, *The Science of Rap* (1996), *Ruminations* (2003), *The Gospel of Hip Hop* (2009), and *Knowledge Reigns Supreme* (2009), as well as a comic book, *Break the Chain* (1994); he has also been invited to lecture at Yale and Harvard Universities.

TALIB KWELI: *EARDRUM* (BLACKSMITH MUSIC, 2007)

Eardrum, the third solo album by Brooklyn's Talib Kweli (Talib Kweli Greene, 1975–), could well be the most artistic and complex rap album ever made. Recorded after a three-year hiatus following the release of *The Beautiful Struggle* (Rawkus Records, 2004), which hit No. 14 on the Billboard 200, *Eardrum* debuted at No. 2 on the Billboard 200, selling sixty thousand copies in its first week. Many fans considered it the album they always wanted from the rapper, songwriter, entrepreneur, social activist, and label owner (Blacksmith Music and Javotti Media).

Kweli was known for collaborating with some of the most recognizable names in rap, including Kanye West and Pharrell. *Eardrum* was no exception, as it featured Jean Grae, UGK (a.k.a. Underground Kingz, 1987–2007), Kanye West, Norah Jones (Geethali Norah Jones Shankar, 1979–), will.i.am, KRS-One, and Justin Timberlake (1981–). The songs showcased his tenor or second tenor vocal range, as well as his boyish rapping voice, both being rare for rap (with notable exceptions in comic rap), which normally features men with baritone and bass voices. Like his other albums, the rap lyrics here contain references not only to popular culture, but also to literature and philosophy, usually delivered as quickly rapped, clever lines filled with wordplay and unexpected multisyllabic rhyme and near rhyme. As a soloist, his music varied during his career as he evolved from hardcore rap beats to neo soul, R&B, and funk–influenced beats, often using chill-out rhythms; he then returned to hardcore urban beats. *Eardrum*, a collection of intellectual, spiritual, and philosophical questions being worked out in rhyme and rap, marked the combination of these styles.

The album begins with the braggadocio track "Everything Man," a song produced by Madlib (Otis Jackson Jr., 1973–). It introduces Kweli as a legend in the making, whose purpose is not merely to entertain but to be a rapper historian and a catalyst for self-actualization and change—a man who can be everything to every listener. Unlike those of most rap lyricists, his lyrics here are imagistic and poetic, with very little concern for the mundane. The song's instrumentation includes *tabla* (Indian drums) and thunder sound effects (in its spoken-word intro), which give way to a 1980s keyboard voice for its groove, set against a solid kick drum and snare beat, electric bass, and a synthesizer gurgling sound effect (to create a hiccup feel). With an overall easy listening R&B feel, the song employs female neo-soul lead singer Sonia Sanchez (n.d.), with soul/R&B backup harmonies by Res (Shareese Renée Ballard, n.d.) in its refrain. Media files (people speaking about their love for Talib Kweli's music) make up the outro. Whereas "Everything Man" is about the rapper, the skills bragging track "NY Weather Report," produced by Nick Speed (Nicholas Marcell Speed, 1980–), takes into account the importance of his fans, who have made Kweli's rap journey one worth taking—especially since they have encouraged him to move beyond gangsta rap toward something more philosophical and spiritual. Lyrically the song is extremely clever, with many puns and inside jokes, interior and exterior rhyme, and multiple rhymes (in one verse, he rhymes eight consecutive lines). Talib Kweli both speaks carefully (in the intro) and raps breathlessly (throughout the song), and the song's music begins with a synthesizer fanfare, which gives way to a funk-based kick and snare with an octave-based electric bass riff (one of the album's best), set against claps, rhythm guitar, and string synthesizer voices, with turntable added in the refrain.

The album's most brilliant songs are "More or Less" and "Listen!!!" "More or Less," produced by Hi-Tek (Tony Cottrell, 1976–), uses oppositions in its refrain (what we need more of, what we need less of) to point out the problems in the world, calling for more reflection as the solution. It's intro begins with what sounds like a tambourine shaken frenetically to accompany a traditional Greek chorus of vocalizations ("la" sung on a scale), which gives way to the song's hook, consisting of sung lines, alternating between high and low pitches on every syllable and accompanied only by bass kick, claps, and crash cymbal (at the end of every phrase). This is juxtaposed against the traditional Greek scale singing. The scale singing continues through the rapped verses, occurring intermittently, set against an aggressive rap and melodic keyboard riff, (which mirrors the sung scale). The outro continues the scale, again set against tambourine, with heavy electric guitar added, playing the same scale. "Listen!!!," produced by Kwamé (Kwamé Holland, 1973–), is the album's anthem, as its lyrics make clear that it was produced to be a message for the rap community, which needs resuscitation and rapper leaders. The song begins with a synth flute ostinato (made to sound like a shawm at first), which turns into a jazz flute ostinato once verse one begins. Kick drum, sub-bass, and claps create the beat with a soaring keyboard ostinato as the flute continues, all of which is set against a mid-tempo rap and a diva-style (house music) countermelody.

Along with "The Perfect Beat" and "Oh My Stars," "Listen!!!" is part of *Eardrum*'s consecutively occurring rap skills brag trilogy. "The Perfect Beat" features KRS-One and samples Bob Marley and the Wailers. It is a braggadocio rap that disses less-skilled rappers who don't understand a search for the perfect beat or the skilled use of metaphors and similes, making fans doubt their abilities. The song starts with a bossa nova–style intro featuring male vocalizations and female vocals, which comes to a time stop before continuing with Talib Kweli's introductory rap (which serves as a second intro, the first being fake). Rapping by KRS-One then takes over, set against claps, kick drum, keyboard, and the bossa nova vocalizations. KRS-One turns the mic over to Talib Kweli in the second verse, and he raps against the same music as verse one. The two then take turns trading lines, with quick trade-offs and rap harmonies, leading to a Jamaican-style toasting and turntable outro.

"Oh My Stars," produced by DJ Khalil (Khalil Abdul-Rahman, 1973–), doubles as a message to Talib Kweli's children, the message being that he loves them, that they are stars in his eyes, and that they are a part of him. The song's intro includes children rapping against claps, which gives way to Talib Kweli's singing the song's neo-soul hook. Verses are speed-rapped against funk bass, 1980s keyboard, claps, and light bells. Eventually the hook becomes a countermelody to the rapped verses as new male singing voices are added. The song's outro is a fade of Kweli's singing against a countermelody by Musiq Soulchild (a.k.a. Musiq, Taalib Johnson, 1977–).

The album's other standout tracks are its third, "Hostile Gospel, Pt. 1 (Deliver Us)" produced by Just Blaze, and its nineteenth and second-to-last, "Hostile Gospel Pt. 2 (Deliver Me)" produced by DJ Khalil. Both songs serve as warnings to the hip hop community, that it is helping unfriendly forces (such as police and governmental censorship entities) to destroy it; "Pt. 2 (Deliver Me)" is Kweli's more personal take and his prayer for individual guidance. Both tracks' rhymes are extremely clever, and the lyrics are filled with references to pop culture, politics, philosophy, and the arts. One of the album's most powerful statements, "Hostile Gospel, Pt. 1," begins with a gospel choir singing "deliver us," elongating the short "i" (in the second syllable) by holding the note, with a piano chord being struck on each downbeat for dramatic effect and turning into a melodic piano line toward the end of the intro. Kweli comes in on the third iteration of "deliver us," at first rapping staccato, with brief phrases that decry "what the people want," a dark version of commercialism that is destroying communities. As he transitions into section B, he switches to speed rapping, almost chopper style, and piano chords are hammered more heavily, while a bass kick and snare (played hard with brushes) create a complex juxtaposition of bass and treble. The beat and speed rapping stay consistent during verse two, but the piano becomes more melodic, playing a jazzy countermelody against the rapped lyrics. The song's refrain (which occurs regularly between verses) harks back to its intro, with the choir voice running counter to Talib Kweli's staccato rapping. In the third verse, more strings are introduced. The song's lengthy outro begins with a solo sung as a counterpart to the choir, and the two blend as the song works toward the instrumental part of its outro, which is a fifty-second-long cello and violin duet that serves to emphasize its sadness and gravitas.

"Hostile Gospel, Pt. 2" is a soft-funk and R&B song, with Jamaican undercurrents in its sung harmonies by Sizzla (Miguel Orlando Collins, 1976–). Sung sections include a calypso version of the phrase "deliver me oh my Father," sung by Kweli and Sizzla. Its instrumentation is mainly synthesizer and rhythm guitar with heavy electric bass. Kweli's rapping is breathless and fast in the verses, and the refrain includes highly reverbed Jamaican toasting and talk-singing. The song is sonically the opposite of "Hostile Gospel, Pt. 1" in that its instrumentation and vocals are kept simpler and sonically quieter—it comes across as a private prayer, rather than the church service of Part 1. It stands out for its production values—the perfect mixing of its three distinct parts in various combinations, and a masterful use of reverb and echo.

"The Nature," featuring and produced by Justin Timberlake, ends the album as an answer to the two "Hostile Gospel" tracks. It offers advice on how to survive the world by getting back to our essential nature, which is divine, and getting back to our quest, which is an intellectual and philosophical spirituality. It starts with a simple beat created by claps, bass kick, and vocalizations (grunts), which are joined by synthesizer (sub-bass and a melodic synth vibe voice). The refrain is a neo-soul duet between Timberlake and Kweli, and its B section is a highly reverbed talk-sung chant by the two.

Other well-constructed, memorable songs include "Say Something," "Give 'Em Hell," "Country Cousins," and "Hot Thing." "Say Something," which features Jean Grae and is produced by will.i.am, is a skills bragging song that showcases Kweli's control of lyrics, with an extremely clever stream-of-consciousness idea flow, in one verse jumping from references (usually as part of a simile) of cheap alcohol, to bloggers, to opera, to *The Godfather* (film), to gobstoppers (a candy), to *chakras*, to frying fish, to Islam, and to Reaganomics—all within a handful of lines. The song begins with a fanfare (horns) that introduce Kweli as rap's savior. Instrumentation consists of a heavy African drum beat, turntable, synth horn sounds, and Tijuana brass–style trumpet (also used in the song's intro). Both Kweli and Jean Grae rap aggressively against the simple but heavy beat and percussive vocalizations (hiccups, grunts, and "ahs"). "Give 'Em Hell," produced by DJ Battlecat (Kevin Gilliam, 1968–) and Terrace Martin (1978–), challenges preachers and supposed religious churchgoers who misrepresent God and Christianity, instead advocating for a personal relationship with God and Christ. Its lyrics (especially its refrain) lament that religion is being used to sow hatred and corrupt the world, which is headed for inevitable destruction. One of the more experimental songs on the album, it is informed by a keyboard ostinato that sounds almost like a whistle combined with a glass bell version of "Tubular Bells" (Mike Oldfield, 1973), set against a funk bass riff and claps (for verses), with a drum kit introduced only in the refrains, giving the song a low-loud-low sonic flow.

"Country Cousins," produced by A Kid Called Roots (Patrick Lawrence, n.d.) and Sha-la Shakier (anonymous), like "Holy Moly," produced by Pete Rock (Peter O. Philips, 1970–), is an autobiographical account. "Country Cousins" tells how Kweli became more streetwise and eventually discovered an affinity for West Coast and Southern Rap, with musicians he terms his country cousins. It lists many of his influences, such as Rakim, Run-D.M.C., EPMD, Public Enemy, N.W.A., MC Eiht, OutKast, Geto Boys, NIP, and UGK. "Holy Moly" tells of Kweli's father's musical influence on him. Its lyrics consist of clever and surprising similes that liken his negative experiences as a rapper, such as critical disrespect and lack of sales despite his skill, to pop culture events. One of the album's softer songs, it borders on soft funk/jazz rock (a la Earth, Wind, and Fire), neo soul, and soft R&B, with mainly claps, kick drum, electric bass (funk), and synth horn voices, but the rap is chopper style—an interesting juxtaposition. Singing (refrains and as countermelody to the rapping) is done in a soft funk/jazz rock style, with falsetto and baritone ranges harmonized.

"Hot Thing," featuring and produced by will.i.am, is as close to a love song as the album gets; it compares a woman to the sun and contains lines that indicate that she is everything to both rappers. The track flows into "Space Fruit (Interlude)," produced by Sa-Ra, which is slightly more sexual. It is sub-bass (possibly an electric bass plucked hard low on the E string) and bass kick heavy, which is juxtaposed against a cymbal beat (for treble), with an occasional keyboard ostinato—although its refrain introduces brass.

The album has only two weak songs, "Soon the New Day" and "Hush." The diss song "Hush," featuring Jean Grae and produced by Chad Beat (Chad Dexter Burnette, n.d.), comes across as a B side due to its simplistic beat (bass kick and snare) set against a toy piano voice. "Soon the New Day," a sex song featuring Norah Jones (singing a forgettable refrain) and produced by Madlib, comes across as a throwaway neo-soul song, with a softer, old-school rapping style set against a 1980s keyboard. A similar sound informs "Stay Around," produced by Pete Rock, but a trumpet versus muted trumpet outro, as well as Kweli's rap, saves what is otherwise an unremarkable track. The lyrics are an answer to Kweli's (mostly male) critics who diss his voice, choice of producers, flow, and decision to avoid gangsta rap, noting that female fans love him.

The album's remaining songs include "Eat to Live" and "In the Mood." "Eat to Live," produced by Madlib, is a "ghetto prayer" for the poor and hungry children of the ghetto, starving for both sustenance and hope—the latter which can be supplied by Kweli's raps. The track is jazz rock and R&B–influenced, with heavy electric bass, snare (reverbed to sound like claps) and ride cymbal, and a synth vibe voice, against which sung R&B vocals run counter to Kweli's rapping, which is mid-tempo but breathless, with few breaks despite an emphasis at the end of lines. The song's refrain is a heavily reverbed talk-sung chant by Kweli. "In the Mood," produced by Kanye West, is a rap skills brag masquerading as a sex song. It draws a comparison between artificiality in music and female beauty. The track has lux-influenced, time-stop-heavy rhythm (giving it a sense of hiccupping), with a simple kick and snare beat against constant vocal harmonies (slightly auto-tuned) and distorted female vocalizations ("ooohs"), as well as vibes, synth flute, and horn voices.

Talib Kweli will be remembered as an anomaly in the rap music world. He was born the son of an English professor and a university administrator, and his brother went on to become a Yale graduate, Supreme Court clerk, and professor of constitutional law. But like many of his less fortunate contemporaries, he was more interested in music, and like many of them, he had to work his way up in the industry—starting out with a guest appearance on the Cincinnati, Ohio–based rap group Mood's (a.k.a. Three Below Zero, 1993–) album *Doom* (1997). His big break came when he joined with fellow Brooklyn rapper Mos Def (Dante Terrell Smith, 1973–) to form the duo Black Star (1997–), and the two recorded for Rawkus Records, using friend and Cincinnati-based collaborator Hi-Tek to produce. The duo's album *Mos Def and Talib Kweli Are Black Star* (Rawkus, 1998) has now earned the reputation as a classic. But he always wanted to push the boundaries of hip hop, so his 2002 Rawkus debut as a solo rapper, *Quality*, became influential as an example of how well neo soul and R&B could be incorporated into rap. Following *Eardrum*, he collaborated with Hi-Tek for *Revolutions per Minute* (Warner Bros., 2010). His subsequent self-released (on his Javotti label) solo studio albums, *Gutter Rainbows* (2011), *Prisoner of Conscious* (2012), *Gravitas* (2014), and *F— the Money* (2015), all prove that his influence on rap culture would be his long-standing crusade to make rap less materialistic and violent, and more eloquent and activist.

KENDRICK LAMAR: "HUMBLE"
(*DAMN*, AFTERMATH ENTERTAINMENT, 2017)

Compton's Kendrick Lamar (Kendrick Lamar Duckworth, 1987–) is a West Coast rapper known for his socially conscious rap. He is both critically acclaimed and commercially successful. His songs, with musical influences in spoken word, funk, and jazz, address issues such as institutionalized racism, gang culture, addiction, and depression. In 2012, Lamar made his major label debut, releasing on Aftermath Entertainment (distributed by Interscope Records) *good kid, m.A.A.d City*, a concept album about addiction, gangs, love, and religion set in the Compton neighborhood of his youth during the summer of 2004. The album was certified platinum. Kendrick Lamar's success continued as he released the critically acclaimed *To Pimp a Butterfly* album in 2015, winning a Grammy for Best Rap Album.

"Humble," a fairly short song at 2:57, was prereleased in 2016 and as part of the 2017 album *DAMN*, released jointly on Top Dawg and Aftermath. It became Kendrick Lamar's first No. 1 single on the Billboard Hot 100 (as lead artist) and achieved platinum status; it also reached No. 1 in New Zealand. It was produced by Mike Will Made It (Michael Len Williams II, 1989–), known for his work with Southern rap and trap artists. The accompanying music video, which won MTV's Video of the Year, was released in 2017. It contrasted images of Lamar dressed all in white and all in black and alluded to Leonardo da Vinci's *The Last Supper* for the purpose of juxtaposing the gangsta lifestyle (including throwing money around as if it were nothing) with the more pensive, philosophical, and spiritual side of Lamar's personality.

The song's intro starts with a scratch sound that gives the impression of a needle being dragged across a record or a car coming to a screeching halt. This is followed by a heavy synthesizer bass beat that is combined with synth-produced short tones that sound like a telegraph sending a message, creating a two-instrument ostinato that references the intro to Queen's "We Will Rock You" (1977): two short beats followed by one elongated beat. It plays as Kendrick Lamar's voice can be heard stating that he does not need prayers (in one version) and that he is wicked (in the other). Both versions end with an elongated yell of the word "way" (e.g., "waaaay"), followed by a staccato vocalization (the word "yeah" repeated twice, quickly, seemingly cross-faded to clip the last consonant). The effect is a rhythmic percussive sound of one long beat followed by two shorts beats that is the opposite of the opening ostinato.

Verses are informed by yet a third ostinato created by neighboring tones played on the low end of a keyboard or piano, where the lowest note is hit hard to create an echo. This is played twice, with a slight variation in the second iteration, and complemented by what sounds like reverbed hand claps or snaps created by an 808 drum hiccup. Kendrick Lamar's tenor (almost boyish) rapping is breathless, with a monotonous vocal delivery, but unlike Drake's similar monochromatic delivery,

Lamar features both interior and exterior rhymes, making the song more lyrically dramatic. This delivery is continued for twelve consecutive lyrical lines, with the effect being a sense of a buildup that culminates in a quick, unexpected pause followed by a sudden sonic change, where Lamar suddenly switches to a higher register and yells out a line about going viral, which is followed by three lines that transition slowly from his higher register back to the register used during the verses.

Verse one begins with memories of his childhood in a poverty-stricken household, which he contrasts to his current status: he now has an accountant, can buy women if he wants to, and can buy a Mercedes. The verse ends on his bragging about his sexual prowess. The song's refrain is a reminder that he has to stay humble, no matter his success. The music here returns to the keyboard/piano ostinato with the same claps or snaps as before. Verse two is about being true to oneself, "keeping it real" as it were. Here he challenges artists who put up a front by referencing photoshopped images and following up with asking to be shown natural images—here he covertly attacks rap music that is too artificial or too dependent on gimmicks, while also advocating for a sense of natural blackness (such as an Afro). Bragging on his own abilities, he points out that he doesn't have to fabricate (while others are fake) to succeed and achieve fame, all the while remaining modest and allowing his soul to speak. The song then returns to the refrain, its music becoming the song's outro, which gives the impression it will fade out, but then it comes to a dead stop.

The song's success was enhanced by its video, directed by Dave Meyers and the Little Homies. Lamar first appears in what looks like Vatican cardinal robes, his head down as if in prayer or a realization of humility. He robotically alternates between this stance of humility and raising his head high as he raps the song's intro. The video's scenes similarly alternate between scenes of humility and consumeristic worldliness. Kendrick Lamar is seen lying on a table throwing money while surrounded by women in their underwear; sitting in a salon under a hair dryer, surrounded by women; and hitting golf balls while standing atop a car in a reservoir. These images are contrasted with images of simplicity, such as Lamar's riding his bicycle in the streets, and images of religious spirituality, such as the Last Supper (with Lamar as Christ). His white clothing stands in contrast to that of those who surround him, who are all black-clad and look exactly alike. In several scenes he stands in the center of this crowd of conformity (all bobbing their heads to the same rhythm), and he's also clad in black, but the camera makes sure that even if he finds himself in the middle, he is always the focal point. The video also includes strikingly dark historical imagery, such as a group of black men with lynching ropes completely covering their heads/faces; the ropes are on fire. It ends with the rapper, dressed in a white suit, surrounded by well-dressed (but all in black) African American men. As he finished his message, they all walk off—the prophet sending his converts out to do good works.

Early on, Kendrick Lamar released four mixtapes on the independent Top Dawg label under the moniker K-Dot: *Youngest N— in Charge* (a.k.a. *Y.N.I.C.*, 2005), *Training Day* (2005), *No Sleep Till NYC* (2007), and *C4* (2009). His fifth mixtape, *O(verly) D(edicated)* (2010), was his first under the name Kendrick Lamar, released under Top Dawg. Also with Top Dawg he released his first full studio album, *Section.80*, in 2011. Kendrick Lamar is a member of and frequent collaborator with the collective Black Hippy (2009–). He is also a frequent guest on songs by both rap and pop artists such as A$AP Rocky and Big Sean. He has won Grammys for Best Rap Song, Best Rap Performance, and Best Rap/Sung Collaboration.

LIL' KIM (SEE DA BRAT, FOXY BROWN, AND LIL' KIM)

LIL WAYNE: "MONEY TO BLOW" AND "4 MY TOWN (PLAY BALL)" (SEE BIRDMAN, DRAKE, AND LIL WAYNE)

LMFAO AND SHAGGY: "PARTY ROCK ANTHEM" AND "SEXY AND I KNOW IT"/"ANGEL" AND "DON'T MAKE ME WAIT" (*SORRY FOR PARTY ROCKING*, WILL.I.AM MUSIC GROUP-CHERRYTREE RECORDS, 2011/ *HOT SHOT*, MCA RECORDS, 2000, AND *44/876*, A&M-CHERRYTREE RECORDS, 2018)

Electronic dance rap was popularized by the Black Eyed Peas with their 2005 album *Monkey Business*, but it existed before its four members released their 2009 string of No. 1 hits ("Boom Boom Pow," "I Gotta Feeling," and "Imma Be"). Kingston, Jamaica's Shaggy (Orville Richard Burrell, 1968–), who raps as well as toasts, previously had hit albums and singles that fused dance music, reggae, alternative rock, pop, R&B, dancehall, dubstep, and hip hop. *Boombastic* (Virgin, 1995), his most critically acclaimed album, stayed at No. 1 on the Reggae Albums chart for thirty consecutive weeks and won a Grammy Award for Best Reggae

Album. It peaked at No. 34 on the Billboard 200 and was certified platinum. The album spawned a No. 3 Hot 100 single with "Boombastic." *Hot Shot* (MCA, 2000), Shaggy's best commercial success, was RIAA certified six-times platinum and topped the Billboard 200. From that album came one of Shaggy's biggest hits, "Angel." It would take him eighteen years to produce another in the form of "Don't Make Me Wait," from his collaborative album with Sting (Gordon Matthew Thomas Sumner, 1951–) of The Police, titled *44/876* (A&M, 2018). Although the album got no higher than No. 40 on the Billboard 200, it topped the Reggae Albums chart, and "Don't Make Me Wait" has garnered 18.4 million views on YouTube as of 2019.

After the Black Eyed Peas went on hiatus, the electronic dance rap baton was handed to a good friend of will.i.am's, Redfoo (Stefan Kendal Gordy, 1975–) of the Los Angeles electronic dance duo LMFAO, which consists of Redfoo and his nephew Sky Blu (Skyler Austen Gordy, 1986–). The duo, DJs and rappers who are the son and grandson of Motown Records founder Berry Gordy Jr., formed LMFAO in 2006, getting a fair bit of local airplay as part of the electro house scene. In 2009, LMFAO released its debut studio album on will.i.am's label, *Party Rock*, which peaked at No. 33 on the Billboard 200 and included the double platinum single "Shots." The duo's second big break came in 2010, when it was featured (along with Fergie of the Black Eyed Peas) on French house music producer David Guetta's "Gettin' Over You," which reached No. 31 on the Billboard Hot 100 and hit No. 1 in France and the United Kingdom. In 2011, LMFAO's second will.i.am Music Group studio album, *Sorry for Party Rocking*, charted in the Top Ten of the Billboard 200 and produced two No. 1 singles on the Billboard Hot 100, "Party Rock Anthem" and "Sexy and I Know It," the former reaching No. 1 also in Australia, Austria, Belgium, Brazil, Canada, Denmark, France, Germany, Ireland, New Zealand, Switzerland, and the United Kingdom.

"Party Rock Anthem" was released as *Sorry for Party Rocking*'s lead single. The song can best be described as 4:23 (3:52 for the radio edit) of pure dance energy (its tempo is 130 beats per minute), with both rapping and electronically manipulated (auto-tuned to sound robotic) chanting and singing. Produced by GoonRock (David Jamahl Listenbee, 1975–) and Redfoo and featuring singer and model Lauren Bennett (1989–), the song became the third best-selling digital song in U.S. history, and its official video, a dance video set to an apocalyptic setting (a loose parody of the 2002 film *28 Days Later*), had almost 1.6 billion YouTube views as of 2019. "Party Rock Anthem," which has been used in several

TV series, begins with an intro dance beat—programmed drums and a simple synthesizer percussive sound, which give way to a programmed bass kick beat (with an occasional distorted snare hit high in the treble range). The addition of a treble-heavy synth ostinato creates a sound similar to house music and electronic dance music (EDM). The hook/refrain kicks in as a catchy, highly auto-tuned (robotic) eight-line sung section (with end line vocalizations) that introduces a breakneck-speed programmed snare drum beat (which is distorted to sound like claps) about midway through. The song uses various instances of stop time, the first of which occurs before the first verse. Sky Blu raps the first verse against the song's most sparse music, a simple 4/4 beat and mid-range keyboard ostinato; his rapping is old-school style with singsong lines and lots of end rhyme, although his eight-line verse uses repeated rhyme (short and long "o") throughout, a rhyme scheme that Redfoo takes up for the first two of his talk-sung lines (four longer lines that end the verse) before ending with a couplet that uses a different rhyme. The refrain then returns, followed by another stop time moment that leads to the B section, which is talk-sung by LMFAO (with a guest chant song by Bennett) as the music builds up more speed with a whirling synth sound, followed by a brief stop time pause, which takes the song back to the hook, though this time with Bennett's vocals as a countermelody. The song ends where it begun, with talk-sung a cappella lines. "Party Rock Anthem" has a structure that begs for play in dance clubs, with constant stop time for dance freezes (and rests) from the high energy dance music and a repetitive arrangement that lends itself to back-to-back play.

"Sexy and I Know It" (124 beats per minute) the album's third single, is just about as danceable, but it exposes one of the major weaknesses of LMFAO's music, which is the duo's tendency to write beats that are so similar as to be almost indistinguishable, something for which critics have taken it to task. Conversely, it exemplifies the duo's greatest strength, which is combining electronic dance and rap in a way that is more engaging than such attempts by the Black Eyed Peas. The song begins with a Giorgio Moroder–style disco synthesizer beat, accompanied by a programmed drum (which gives the impression of claps). The rapped verses (by Redfoo) are simple: each has eight rhymed lines of varying lengths, rapped/talk-sung so that line lengths seem to vary (because of carefully placed pauses), which introduces the first refrain, an auto-tuned (to sound robotic) chanted repetition (by Sky Blu) of "girl look at that body." A bridge leads to the second verse, which introduces the second hook, which leads to the second verse, which follows the same pattern as the first (with call-response added). The first refrain, bridge, and second refrain follow, and then the high-energy music takes over. As the song progresses, synth voices—an arp voice, a repeated note, and an oscillated keyboard voice—are added to the mix. Vocalizations and chants set against the high-energy beat lead to the song's abrupt end, on the repeated keyboard note.

"Angel," a reggae fusion love song that samples Chip Taylor's "Angel of the Morning" (1968) and Steve Miller's "The Joker" (1973) and features Barbadian singer Rayvon (Bruce Alexander Michael Brewster, 1968–), was the follow-up to Shaggy's first No. 1 hit, "It Wasn't Me" (2000). Reaching the top spot of the Billboard Hot 100, it also topped the charts in Australia, Germany, Ireland, and the United Kingdom. A study in artistic simplicity, the song begins with a brief drum intro, then a snare and electric bass beat ("The Joker"), along with electric guitar and a synth-based theremin voice that combine to play the tune of "Angel of the Morning," as Shaggy toasts and Rayvon scats. As the refrain kicks in, Rayvon sings against a simple 4/4 snare and kick drum beat; Shaggy adds vocalizations to punctuate phrases. Two acoustic guitars kick in, playing against the bass sample. The guitars disappear by Shaggy's verse, which he talk-sings (Jamaican Sing-J–style rapping/singing) against bass, drum beat, and occasional vibraslap, with additional vocalizations by Rayvon to punctuate phrases. This is followed by a second sung refrain, with the same instrumental accompaniment, and a second verse that mirrors the first in structure and instrumentation. A third refrain follows (a repetition of the first verse), followed by a middle eight section, where Shaggy and Rayvon duet, talk-singing and singing. A final verse by Shaggy and an extended recurrence of the hook round the song out.

Like "Angel," "Don't Make Me Wait," a love song about fear of commitment, uses Jamaican-style rap (talk-singing) as well as toasting, but the bulk of the song is sung (by Sting, mainly reggae fashion during the hook/refrain, although in the second verse he sings rock ballad style, a la the Police's down-tempo songs). The music is a typical down-tempo reggae rhythm, made famous by Bob Marley and the Wailers. Instrumentation includes acoustic guitar, rhythm guitar, a brushed snare drum beat with brushed cymbal, a repetitive bass line that mirrors the acoustic guitar, with a mellow keyboard voice added in the refrain. The song's structure includes an instrumental and vocal (sung) introduction (part of what will become the refrain), accompanied by Shaggy's toasting. This is followed by the first iteration of the refrain, which leads to Shaggy's rapped (talk-sung) verse. He showcases his now famous tenor voice and style—his lines stay very close to a tonal center, but he modulates to a higher pitch on unexpected words (usually monosyllabic words like adjectives), returning within a few notes to the tonal center. He rhymes lines using both interior and exterior rhyme, and he freely uses enjambment, which allows for a freer flow (and thus his tonal shifts). The refrain returns, then Sting's verse, then a half verse by Shaggy, then the refrain and an outro, in which Sting sings both reggae and rock style.

In early 2012, LMFAO performed the Super Bowl XLVI's halftime show with Madonna, doing a medley of Madonna's "Music" and their "Party Rock Anthem" and "Sexy and I Know It." That same year, Redfoo was sued for breach of contract. In September 2012, LMFAO announced an indefinite hiatus. After *Hot Shots*, Shaggy released other albums (on various labels) including *Clothes Drop* (2005), *Intoxication* (2007), *Shaggy and Friends* (2011), *Summer in Kingston* (2011), *Rise* (2012), and *Out of Many, One Music* (2013), but none would equal his earlier success.

MACKLEMORE & RYAN LEWIS AND PROFESSOR ELEMENTAL: "THRIFT SHOP" AND "FIGHTING TROUSERS" (*THE HEIST,* NOT ON LABEL, 2012, AND *THE INDIFFERENCE ENGINE,* TEA SEA RECORDS, 2010)

Rap and hip hop beats are normally created by electric bass, bass kick drum, snare drum, or synthesizer-based drum voices. Rarely are they created by horns (woodwinds and brass), and even more rarely do gimmicky comic beats find their way into a hit song, so when they do, the song becomes a standout for its originality, catchiness, and overall novel appeal. Two such songs that did make it big, and in doing so made rap fans take notice, launched the careers of Macklemore & Ryan Lewis in the United States ("Thrift Shop," 2012) and Professor Elemental in the United Kingdom ("Fighting Trousers," 2010).

The Seattle- and Spokane-based duo consisting of rapper and lyricist Macklemore (Benjamin Hammond Haggerty, 1983–) and producer, music engineer, and mixer Lewis (1988–) is known for its narrative rapping informed by various elements of storytelling, with an emphasis on character and setting as events unfold chronologically over the course of a song. Though most of Macklemore's lyrics are about his experiences with addiction and with the music industry, he has also been known to create humorous scenarios that combine satire, good-natured parody, and elements of the diss track. Adding to the humor through instrumentation and postproduction, Lewis, an American DJ, videographer, graphic designer, and photographer, produced "Thrift Shop," as well as both of the duo's albums, including the highly successful full-length album, *The Heist* (2012), which followed *The VS. EP* (2009). *The Heist* sold 1.5 million units, earned four Grammy Awards, and spawned two Billboard Hot 100 No. 1 hits: "Can't Hold Us" and "Thrift Shop." "Thrift Shop" also topped the charts in France, the United Kingdom, Canada, and Australia. *The Heist* debuted at No. 1 on iTunes and No. 2 on the Billboard 200, an impressive feat for an independently self-produced, self-recorded, and self-released album. An unlikely hit, the quirky "Thrift Shop" was the fourth single released off the album, but it won two Grammy Awards in 2014 for Best Rap Performance and Best Rap Song, paving the way for Macklemore and Lewis's Grammys for Best New Artist and Best Rap Album.

"Thrift Shop" begins with a voice chanting the rhythmic phrase "what, what, what, what," which is then repeated to become the song's intro beat, especially when it is joined by the recurrence of the rhythmic vocalization "bada, bada, bada, de-da," vocalized roughly a perfect fifth higher. The two voices create an a cappella beat until an offbeat saxophone ostinato takes over (introduced by a third voice yelling "ho"). The voices and saxophone continue into the first occurrence of the refrain, with the sax suddenly becoming foregrounded (the vocalizations soon fade out) and an 808 drum, claps, and synthesizer-produced sound effects are introduced. Guest artist Wanz (Michael Wansley, 1961–), who has a bass voice, sings the refrain, which praises the idea of thrift store shopping as a way to better one's style and earn coolness points (here called a "come up"), even with only $20 to spend, concluding that the experience is "f— awesome."

Macklemore's rapped verses (which are peppered with Wanz's spoken-word asides), are accompanied by the sax, 808, reverbed clapping, scratching, and occasional instances of the repeated "ho" vocalization. The first verse makes clear the comic intention of the song, which becomes a list of the idiosyncratic and bizarre items that can be purchased. Macklemore enters the store dressed in pink, with green alligator shoes and a leopard mink, which he then realizes smells like urine (the song here takes a jab at R. Kelly), all bought at an earlier thrift store run. The verse lists items he passes on, like smelly moccasins. He addresses a woman in the store who looks at him askance (giving him a side eye) by teasing her—he threatens to buy her grandfather's clothes, which he identifies as a velour jumpsuit, house slippers, and a leather jacket. He even buys a broken keyboard. This is followed by Wanz's second refrain, which adds the detail that he is bargain hunting, a metaphor that Macklemore takes up in the second verse when he finds himself digging through old luggage, finding a plaid button-up shirt, and musing on finding women's flannel zebra onesies, which he will pass off as stylish and expensive. Wanz then takes up the bridge (introduced by a synthesized bass rift and pitch-altered female vocals and accompanied by Macklemore's counter vocals), which reiterates that used "grandpa" clothes can make someone look cool. This is followed by a final refrain and then a brief moment of dialogue with a female child who laughs and asks if Macklemore is wearing his grandmother's coat. Overall, "Thrift Shop" is clever, catchy, and aggressive, taking an in-your-face attitude toward people who look down on oddball fashion styles and used clothing.

Recorded two years earlier than Macklemore & Ryan Lewis's hit, "Fighting Trousers" by Norwich, England's Professor Elemental (Paul Alborough, 1975–) helped internationalize both chap hop and steampunk rap. Best known for his affiliation with the steampunk movement and for his 2010 feud with fellow chap hop artist Mr. B the Gentleman Rhymer, Professor Elemental performs in costume, his rap persona evoking the science fiction of Jules Verne as he frequently sports a pith helmet while in cargo shorts (caravan wear) and refers to himself as a mad scientist. He is accompanied by an orangutan butler named Geoffrey, with whom he conducts scientific experiments. He regularly appears at steampunk events and has been the headlining act at the Steampunk World's Fair, a convention held in the United States annually since 2010, and Waltz on the Wye, a steampunk festival held since 2011 in Chepstow, a town on the border of England and Wales. In addition, visual aspects of steampunk humor appear throughout his videos.

He began developing a local fan base with the track "Cup of Brown Joy" (2010) from his debut album *Rebel without Applause* (billed as Elemental & Tom Caruana, Tea Sea Records, 2009). The song is an ode to tea (more precisely, to black tea, not to herbal ones) and was remixed on his subsequent Tea Sea album, *The Indifference Engine* (2010). The album combines hip hop, swing jazz, and elements of musical exoticism and animal sound effects. Also from the album, "Fighting Trousers" begins by grounding itself squarely in the steampunk ethos, as its intro is comprised of a shawm playing what is easily identifiable as a traditional Indian ostinato (or at least, a British colonialist's impression of traditional Indian music). This introduces the song's beat, created by a quirky bassoon ostinato, which is joined briefly by a Middle Eastern–sounding string instrument. As the song continues, the beat is created by the interplay of the bassoon and a muted trumpet, the latter being used as a response instrument; this interplay is set against a steady snare drum beat and hand claps that accent every other phrase.

The first vocals heard are Professor Elemental's spoken directions to Geoffrey, who he instructs to get his "fighting trousers" (which in the song's video are khaki jungle safari knee-length shorts). The opening verse calls out (in proper British style, with "Dear Sir") Mr.B the Gentleman Rhymer, accusing him of cashing in on Professor Elemental's success—he tells him to "shelve this Professor impersonation." The song then becomes a diss track, making fun of his rival's reliance on parody chap hop (comic hip hop informed by RCP, or Received Pronunciation, also called BBC English), referring to Mr.B's "Chap Hop History" (2008), a song which samples various famous American raps. He challenges Mr.B to do some actual rapping, hinting he should write his own lyrics and warning Mr.B that if he doesn't put down his ukulele (Mr.B plays a banjolele), he'll tell him where to stick it.

"Fighting Trousers'" refrain, which features the drum, claps, and a trumpet riff (descending chromatic scale), disses Mr.B's trademark tweed jacket and challenges him to a rap battle, with Professor Elemental declaring victory even before the event. He explains the reasons in the next verse: he has super producers and a solid youthful fan base, as opposed to Mr.B, who sports a handlebar mustache and is a George Formby clone or the Piers Morgan of rap. He further declares that he is willing to match his wit (rapping skill) against Mr.B's, or if necessary, fight him with a big stick (probably an allusion to Mr.B's ubiquitous cricket bat). Verse three accuses Mr.B of being a sell-out, having sold his soul to Coca Cola. The song ends as properly (and cleverly) as it began, with Professor Elemental's signing off with "yours, et cetera, et cetera, sincerely, and so forth, Professor Elemental." The refrain follows, as well as an outro featuring a comic dialogue between Professor Elemental and Geoffrey, who has decided to play a jazz drum solo (actually Geoffrey begins playing an African rhythm on what sounds like a djembe, which the Professor mistakenly calls a jazz solo, perhaps parodying the racist stereotyping of colonialism).

Like Mr.B the Gentleman Rhymer, Professor Elemental raps in Received Pronunciation. He wrote and performed "Fighting Trousers" to create a comic diss feud between himself and Mr.B. In response, Mr.B released "Like a Chap" (2012). Since then, the two have performed together both live and in recordings as guests on each other's songs. When live, they often engage in what they have termed a chap-off.

MC HAMMER: *PLEASE HAMMER, DON'T HURT 'EM* (CAPITOL RECORDS, 1990)

Oakland's MC Hammer (a.k.a. Hammer, Stanley Kirk Burrell, 1962–), the quintessential face of old-school rap and hip hop dance, is best known for his quick string of Billboard Hot 100 Top Ten hits: "U Can't Touch This" (1990, No. 8), "Have You Seen Her" (1990, No. 4), "Pray" (1990, No. 2), "Too Legit to Quit" (1991, No. 5), and "Addams Groove" (1991, No. 7). He is also remembered for his catch phrase, "Hammer time." Some of his dance moves and flashy clothing, including his trademark parachute pants, helped him achieve icon status; his influence on the world of fashion was far-reaching in the 1980s and early 1990s. His athletic dance moves and extremely high-energy moves have made him a mainstay in music video history.

His third and fourth studio albums, the RIAA certified diamond *Please Hammer, Don't Hurt 'Em* (1990) and three-times platinum *Too Legit to Quit* (under the name Hammer, 1991) were both released on the Capitol Records label, making them two of the first hip hop albums on a major label. *Please Hammer* went to No. 1 on the R&B/Hip Hop Albums chart. It also topped the Billboard 200, holding that position for twenty-one weeks and popularizing rap music with a new audience.

Please Hammer is a study in diverse sampling. The album spawned the single "U Can't Touch This," which sampled Rick James's 1981 funk hit "Super Freak (Part I)" (No. 16 on the Billboard Hot 100), unfortunately leading to a lawsuit. "Pray" also included a sample from Prince and the Revolution's new wave pop-funk "When Doves Cry" (1984, No. 1) and Faith No More's indie punk "We Care a Lot" (1987, did not chart). *Please Hammer* also sampled R&B and soul acts such as the Jackson 5 and Marvin Gaye and contained the successful cover of the Chi-Lites' "Have You Seen Her" (1971, No. 3). The album begins with two skills bragging tracks, "Here Comes the Hammer" and "U Can't Touch This." The former is an aggressive, high-energy, danceable rap song that borrows from house music. A skills bragging track, its verses are rapped with male grunts interspersed, but its refrains are simply vocalizations—the repetition of "uh oh" chanted on a scale. Its instrumentation includes heavy use of drums and percussion, accompanied by synthesizer (the song's bass is a synth bass). "U Can't Touch This," the album's iconic megahit, juxtaposes "Super Freak" (its main melody) against a kick drum and 808 beat; MC Hammer raps and talks (which results in an interesting variety in flow) in his deepest register. Both "U Can't Touch This" and "Here Comes the Hammer" jump out at the listener. The same high-energy production values can be heard in the straightforward dance song "Dancin' Machine," which samples the Jackson 5. The song stands out as one of the earliest dance rap songs, as its lyrics are specifically about moves MC Hammer is performing in the video, and invites listeners to perform.

MC Hammer's cover of "Have You Seen Her" is a mixture of spoken word and singing (in the same vein as the original), but the lyrics are updated to replace walking in the park with a California night drive, looking for a "fly" girl. It also replaces the breakup of the Chi-Lites' original lyrics with a search for the perfect lover who hasn't been met yet, and interspersed among the song's lyrics of longing are comical shout-outs to sitcom stars, soul singers, and rappers, asking if they have seen the theoretical perfect woman. Musically, the song follows the structure and style of the original—a down-tempo sweet soul beat with four-part harmony.

"Help the Children" is an R&B-style track concerned with the problems MC Hammer sees in the African American community—absentee fathers, drugs, and violence. Although the lyrics prefigure later rap (especially gangsta), they do not focus on painting a picture of despair or shocking listeners with graphic images (which MC Hammer does in "Crime Story"); rather, the lyrics take the form of advice given to listeners. The song's instrumentation is that of adult contemporary music: down-tempo congas and timbales, flute voices, and a tinkling piano, along with a sample of Marvin Gaye's 1971 hit "Mercy Mercy Me (The Ecology)." Against this groove MC Hammer whispers and raps/talk-sings in his deepest baritone register. The same sentiments can be heard in three dance tracks: "Pray," "On Your Face," and "Let's Go Deeper."

"Pray" is both an autobiographical statement in music and a sociopolitical examination of the problems facing urban communities. Against a heavy beat and a sample of "When Doves Cry," MC Hammer talk-sings, joined by a sung funk-style harmonized countermelody (female voices) and an aggressive, percussive chant (male voices). At times, all three melodies play against each other, leading to a complex, full sound. "On Your Face" is a Motown-influenced didactic rap song that teaches being positive about life, smiling no matter what comes your way. Against a dance beat (programmed drum beat, Latin percussion, soaring keyboards, horn voices, and bass), MC Hammer crosses rap with talk-singing, and refrains are sung R&B-style with Charles Salter (n.d.) sounding a bit like a cross between The Temptations and Michael Jackson. "Let's Go Deeper" is an Afrocentric statement about realizing potential and power despite the sociological forces of oppression. It borrows from house music, featuring synth bass (almost sub-bass) against timbales and a programmed dance beat (mainly snare), and it stands out as the album's angriest song.

"Crime Story" and "She's Soft and Wet" are the album's anomalies. Borrowing from the newly emerging gangsta rap style, the lyrics in "Crime Story" tell four stories from the first person point of view about criminals (drug dealers, pimps, gangbangers) who either kill or are killed, with the final verse being the song's moral—a life of crime is no life at all. Unfortunately, the seriousness of the song's subject matter is undercut by its dance rhythm: Latin percussions, a rock drum kit beat, soaring keyboard voices, and funk bass. Sound effects play a prominent role in the song, but its old-school feel makes it sound disingenuous, a criticism often made against MC Hammer. "She's Soft and Wet" is funk-based and a typical rap sex song, albeit a very tame one. Musically in the vein of 2 Live Crew, it is based on the heavy beat associated with Miami Bass, although here it is done with tom and snare rather than bass kick.

MC Hammer's entertainment career began modestly in 1973 when he served as a dancer, batboy, and play-by-play analyst for Major League Baseball's Oakland Athletics, and his music career began in 1985 after a three-year stint in the military and a brief stint with a Christian rap group (the Holy Ghost Boys). He released the album *Feel My Power* in 1987 on his independent label, Bustin' Records, selling sixty thousand copies, an inauspicious start to an iconic career. Overall, MC Hammer has won three Grammys, and his albums have sold over fifty million copies worldwide despite a limited number of hit singles. Unfortunately, his influence on the hip hop genre is limited because his legacy has been that of a commercially successful entertainer and choreographed dancer, rather than a serious musician or songwriter. After 2006, he basically retired from music, becoming a Christian preacher from 1999 to 2006 on *Praise the Lord* (1973–), a voice actor for the Saturday morning cartoon *Hammerman* (1991), and producer of a reality show called *Hammertime* (2009).

MC LYTE: *BAD AS I WANNA B* (EASTWEST RECORDS, 1996)

Hailing from Queens, New York, arguably the home of rap music, MC Lyte (Lana Michele Moorer, 1971–) was one of the first woman rappers to challenge sexism and misogyny in rap music. She began rapping at the age of twelve, releasing her first album, *Lyte as a Rock* (1988), on the Brooklyn-based First Priority Music label (the label's second release) five years later. *Lyte as a Rock* has the honor of being the first LP released by a solo female MC. She followed up in 1989 with *Eyes on This*, her most successful album commercially, which produced the single "Cha Cha Cha," which went to No. 1 on the Billboard Hot Rap Singles chart. Two other singles from that album, "Cappucino" and "Stop, Look, Listen," made it into the Top Ten. Her third album, the new jack swing–oriented *Act Like You Know* (1991), was less successful but included two singles, "When in Love" and "Poor Georgie." In 1993, MC Lyte released her fourth album with First Priority, *Ain't No Other*, and "Ruffneck," its single, became the first single by a solo female rapper to achieve RIAA gold certification and earn a Grammy nomination.

An old-school rapper of the 1980s, MC Lyte is best known for her lyricism and distinctive flow, as well as her proving that female rappers could write and rap just as well as male MCs. Her vocal range is very similar to Queen Latifah's: her voice is resonant and sultry, and it is usually processed to be harmonized with itself so that it sounds even fuller. Her raps are complex and clever, with flows that vary to match a diverse set of beats, ranging from down-tempo (a smooth groove) to g-funk and from dance to new jack swing. And although she did not shy away from the braggadocio rap battle aesthetic, she has generally collaborated with and advocated for woman rappers and other female artists.

In 1996, MC Lyte released her first album after moving to EastWest Records, *Bad as I Wanna B*, produced by Jermaine Dupri and R. Kelly (Robert Sylvester Kelly, 1967–). It reached No. 11 on Hot R&B/Hip Hop Albums chart and No. 59 on the Billboard 200, becoming her highest mainstream charting album. It also spawned two certified gold singles, "Keep On, Keepin' On" and "Cold Rock a Party," the latter featuring an early performance by Missy Elliott. The album featured only eleven songs, including two remixes, with no original song clocking in over 4:32 (the time of its longest song and opening track, "Keep On, Keepin' On"). "Keep On, Keepin' On," which features vocal group Xscape (1992–98; 2017–), is a sex song that turns the tables on the typical male rapper sex song, as it places MC Lyte in power—she can be as choosy as she wishes in finding partners, can rank them based on their sexual skills, and can dismiss any who use her as a way to try to become rich or famous. The instrumentation has a funky R&B feel, with heavy bass, a down-tempo snare beat that accentuates the end of phrases, a vibe voice that plays an ostinato as well as an occasional flourish, and a synthesizer-created choir voice that oscillates the same note throughout.

MC Lyte's rap is mid-tempo but aggressive (lots of plosives) and carefully articulated, with emphasis on end rhymes. Male vocalizations are peppered throughout. The song's female-sung refrain is a combination of house style and R&B vocals, with harmonized voices to add a higher register.

The same thematic concerns inform "Everyday," which establishes a detailed routine—sexual and chore-based—that a man has to follow in order to become one of her lovers. Here instrumentation is similar, with the addition of a 1980s keyboard voice that gives the song a neo-soul feel. MC Lyte's rap is mid-tempo, with clever pauses when a surprise detail is dropped in her list of chores and foreplay acts. Backing vocals include female call-response vocalizations (e.g., "that's right," "uh huh," "yeah") and female harmonies in the sung refrain. Also a sex song, "One on One" has a specific male target: a male rapper whose song she admires. It is a mid-tempo song that features the album's heaviest funk bass line (played on the low end of the E string), set against a snare and kick beat, with an oscillating keyboard ostinato. All of this is joined by a highly processed male vocalization (the word "one" distorted to various pitches). Like "One on One," "Two Seater" is a sex song, but it masquerades as a road trip rap (it is filled with high-performance auto-based metaphor). Like the other sex songs on the album, it establishes strict criteria for men—in this case, they cannot be high or stoned if they want to enjoy the good life (or sex) with MC Lyte. The music is highly experimental, an oscillating keyboard scale with a secondary keyboard ostinato, heavy funk bass, and a bass kick and snare drum beat, creating an offbeat groove against which MC Lyte raps, while other female voices processed to sound ethereal serve as harmonies, vocalizations, and call-response voices.

The album's sole breakup song, "Druglord Superstar," is an angry dismissal of a relationship with a man who became too involved with gangsta activity, to the point where his violent lifestyle had begun to affect her domestic life. For the angriest song on the album, it has the most relaxed beat: bass, bass kick drum, snare, and claps against an easy-going keyboard ostinato (a flute voice), along with a vibe voice distorted to sound like glass. It prominently features Da Brat as a harmonizing rap voice, as well as the call-response voice of reason in the refrain and outro.

The standout "Have U Ever" is arguably one of the best rap braggadocio songs ever recorded, with lyrics that liken MC Lyte's music skills to sexual prowess in one verse and to natural forces of destruction in another, ending on the threatening lines, "The clock is ticking, time is up, before the world destructs . . . I'ma be the one to lights this motherf— up."

The track's instrumentation borrows from orientalism (its main synth ostinato invokes Japanese musical scales) and is set against a slow funk bass line and a treble-heavy snare beat with rhythm guitar. The entire song is rapped, with male voices and vocalizations provided by producer Jermaine Dupri to emphasize the last words of phrases. Its instrumental outro is the same bass-heavy groove, with a hiccup introduced into the beat. The album's other standout, "TRG (The Rap Game)," is a fascinating take on the rap music industry, wherein MC Lyte explains that rappers have to constantly change their flow and style (even down to their fashion), or they end up in the dustbin of music history (at the bottom of dusty crates). However, the song does not brag about her skills or ability to escape this fate—rather it takes a fatalistic attitude: at some point in her career, she will have to know when to give up rapping. The song features her voice heavily harmonized with itself to make the vocals sound thicker and has a heavy kick drum beat set against a simple bass ostinato and 1980s keyboard voice, with an occasional vocalization (a highly distorted scream, made to sound almost like a bird scream), usually at the end of phrases. One of her best raps, the lyrics feature heavy internal, repeated rhyme, varied flow from line to line, and an excellent half-chanted, half-rapped refrain.

The most danceable track on the album, "Cold Rock a Party," which samples the Mary Jane Girls and Audio Two and covers the refrain of Diana Ross's "Upside Down" (1980), is part skills brag, part diss rap that attacks other MCs who try to keep pace with MC Lyte. Her rapping is set against a dance beat that is reminiscent of those popularized by Ross in "Upside Down" and Scritti Politti on its album *Cupid & Psyche '85* (1985). Instrumentation includes a disco-based guitar riff and a keyboard-based rhythm, with syncopation on the second and fourth beats. This creates a heavy sense of swing. MC Lyte raps and chants, her voice made more resonant via postproduction harmonizing effects. Also extremely danceable despite its ominous atmosphere, "Zodiac" is literally a rap about the signs of the zodiac and their associated personality traits, including propensity for love, professional success, and creativity. Its music, which has an experimental g-funk feel, starts with a synth-produced distorted guitar voice and time-stop-based intro. This motive continues throughout the song, working against a snare beat, with a power-chord, synth-produced horn voice ostinato peppered throughout. The rap is breathless and stream of consciousness–oriented with a varied flow that allows MC Lyte to work within the constant time-stopping.

In 1998, she released her third and final EastWest album, *Seven and Seven*, which did not chart on the Billboard 200. Her last two studio albums, *The Undaground Heat Vol. 1* (2003) and *Legend* (2015), did not chart either. Aside from rapping, MC Lyte has also worked as an actor, appearing on TV shows such as *New York Undercover*, *In the House*, and *The District*, and she played (from 2004 to 2006) the recurring character Kai Owens on *Half and Half*. She has also done films, including *Fly By Night* (1992), *Train Ride* (2000), and *Playas Ball* (2003).

NAS AND K'NAAN: "ONE MIC" AND "TAKE A MINUTE" (*STILLMATIC*, COLUMBIA, 2002, AND *TROUBADOUR*, A&M OCTONE RECORDS, 2009)

Brooklyn's Nas (Nasir bin Olu Dara Jones, 1973–), the son of a jazz cornetist, guitarist, and singer, grew up in the Queensbridge Houses, the largest housing project in North America and once home to pioneering American hip hop artists like producer Marley Marl and several Juice Crew rappers. By the late 1980s, he met hip hop producer Large Professor (William Paul Mitchell, 1972–), who gave him studio access. Beginning with *Illmatic* (Columbia, 1994), Nas established his style: hardcore lyrical content informed by a mastery of internal rhymes, first-person urban storytelling, and the imagistic juxtaposition of poverty, crime, and police brutality with gangsta conventions such as braggadocio, bling, and street authenticity. After a feud with Puff Daddy and Jay-Z tarnished his reputation, Nas had a comeback in 2002 with *Stillmatic* (Columbia, 2001), and in 2002 Columbia Records released *The Lost Tapes*, containing Nas's unreleased earlier songs.

Nas is for many fans the face of not only rap fusion but also socially conscious rap lyrics, although arguably he could share that honor with Somalia-born Canadian singer and rapper K'naan (Keinan Abdi Warsame or Keynaan Cabdi Warsame, 1978–). K'naan's "Wavin' Flag" (2009), originally written for the Somalian people to inspire their fight for freedom (the 2009 version reached No. 2 on the Canadian Hot 100), was rereleased twice in 2010—by Young Artists for Haiti and as a remix recorded for use as Coca-Cola's promotional anthem for the 2010 FIFA World Cup, hosted by South Africa. Nas went on to become a producer, film and television actor, entrepreneur, and philanthropist. K'naan, whose texts favor English but who also raps in Somali, has achieved international fame not only as a singer/rapper but also as a songwriter, poet, multi-instrumentalist, and philanthropist who fuses hip hop with indie, R&B, neo soul, Ethiopian jazz, traditional Somali music, and Afro beats. His warm singing style and use of positive message rap is comparable to that of Chance the Rapper. His four studio albums are *My Life Is a Movie* (released on his Track and Field label, 2004), *The Dusty Foot Philosopher* (Sony BMG, 2005), *Troubadour* (A&M Octone, 2009), and *Country, God, or the Girl* (A&M Octone, 2012). *Troubadour* charted internationally, peaking at No. 32 on the Billboard 200 and No. 7 on the Canadian Albums Chart. *Country, God, or the Girl* peaked at No. 129 on the Billboard 200.

Nas's "One Mic," produced by himself and Chucky Thompson (Carl E. Thompson, n.d.) and sampling Phil Collins's "In the Air Tonight" (1981), was the third single released from *Stillmatic*. Whereas Collins's song builds slowly toward an intense sense of anger and frustration, Nas's builds in dynamics and flow speed in each verse then returns to its original quiet groove, informed by the brooding keyboard melody of "In the Air Tonight," only to build up again. Despite its experimental structure, "One Mic" was a commercial success—it reached No. 43 on the Billboard Hot 100, and Nos. 10 and 7 on the Hot Rap Singles and Hot Rap Tracks charts. The song chronicles a desire for simplicity, juxtaposed against the hurdles that people in the African American community face (racism being foremost), which make simplicity next to impossible. It begins with a sustained keyboard power chord that introduces the slower drum rhythm from "In the Air Tonight," with the sound of backgrounded church bells that lead to the song's first verse. The verse is marked by the introduction of the Collins keyboard melody, which joins the still slow-paced drum beat to create a sense of melancholy and thoughtfulness, edging toward despair. Nas's baritone voice lends itself well to this atmosphere as he raps in a quiet, evenly paced flow about his desire for simplicity, since simplicity leads to understanding and inner peace.

The lyrics are somewhat metatextual, referring to one mic with one beat, which fairly accurately describes what is going on musically. However, the song avoids becoming cliché or maudlin because among the items that need to be simplified are one gun, one "hater," and one "crib" (an indication of bling). This indelicate balance is accurately captured in the image of one "cup of virgin blood, mixed with 151" (which is also a wonderful verbal jest, since 151 begins with the word "one"). Nas's flow then speeds up as he starts to think about the gangsta lifestyle, bullets with names on them, plotting crimes, and "hood politics." As his delivery builds in intensity, he incorporates more internal and repeated rhyme as he narrates a story about narrowly escaping death in a police shootout after a profiling stop.

Unlike many rap songs that overuse sound effects (gunshots, sirens), "One Mic" only briefly alludes to split-second sound effects, which sets up the final third of the first verse, where a continuous police siren actually becomes part of the quickening beat against which Nas raps about his responsibility to the community as messenger—delivering a message of doom if changes aren't made. The verse ends with his proclamation of immediacy, and on the word "now," the song's dynamics return to a brooding pace for the refrain, which is about the need for one mic. Verse two parallels verse one in that it uses biblical imagery to return to a gangsta theme of gang-related killings; it's a standout verse for its complexity of thought (going from the age of Jesus at crucifixion to the number of bullets involved in the murder of a gang member, with his hope that the victim's funeral will not be the site of more violence). Lyrics and flow build in intensity as the drumming become heavier, a second keyboard voice is introduced, and an 808 drum adds speed to the beat; Nas invites his enemies to end his pain, with the word "now" again marking the verse's end and a return to the song's brooding music. Verse three, a diss verse that instrumentally mirrors the final verse of "In the Air Tonight," is aimed at his detractors and doubters. It begins with Collins's intense rhythm but works slowly toward quiet as Nas narrates "movin' with a change of pace." The song ends on its refrain, which slowly fades out to the lone keyboard voice.

Like Nas, K'naan came from a musical family, as his aunt was a traditional Somali singer known for patriotic songs during the Ethiopian-Somali War (a.k.a. the Ogaden War, 1977–78), and she sang to him, becoming his earliest exposure to poetry and lyric writing. However, the Somali Civil War (1986–) led to the suppression of music and the exile of musicians. By age thirteen, in 1991, most of K'naan's immediate family had moved to New York City and Toronto, Ontario, Canada. To help himself learn English, K'naan memorized rap lyrics and studied patterns of internal and end rhymes. He began writing and rapping while growing up in one of Toronto's toughest neighborhoods, focusing not only on his experiences during the Somali Civil War but also as a Somali immigrant often exposed to his new home's street violence. His texts and musical choices were strongly influenced by Nas, who tied autobiographical storytelling to message in versatile ways. From his album *Troubadour*, "Wavin' Flag (Celebration Mix)" and "Is Anybody Out There?" were both Music Canada certified platinum and made him the most famous Somali rapper in the world. However, his most representative song is "Take a Minute," which features song, rap, and spoken word and ties his social consciousness with his personal life—lessons taught him by his mother.

Released as a promotional single for *Troubadour* (but never as an actual single), "Take a Minute" begins with K'naan's gentle, nasally tenor singing voice, accompanied by piano, with organ added after two lines to give the intro (which becomes the song's refrain/hook) more intensity. The message of the refrain is a simple one: with knowledge comes the understanding that we know less than we think, and we don't understand pain at all, which requires that we "take a minute" to think about acceptance and the point of life. For the first verse, the organ disappears, but the piano is joined by sub-bass and a snare and tom drum beat, as K'naan half raps, half talk-sings about pain, suffering, and survival. He considers the plights of great leaders like Mandela and Gandhi, which leads him to think about his mother and how much she suffered from racism and war, at one point requiring hospitalization—she beat death, forgave her attackers, and returned to raise K'naan and teach him about giving and forgiveness. Toward the end of the first verse, a synth horn voice and backing vocals are introduced, creating the bridge to the refrain, which includes the same instrumentation and backing vocals, with the organ returning. Verse two parallels the first verse instrumentally, with one exception—an arpeggiated keyboard voice replaces the piano chords, giving the verse a bouncier feel as K'naan raps about Somalia. While the first verse cited political heroes, this verse calls out K'naan's musical hero, Akon, whom he notes is now winning awards. Like Nas in "One Mic," K'naan comes to the realization that he needs to be a messenger, in his case making sense out of and finding beauty in heinous situations, that (as he talk-sings in lieu of a third verse) "nothing is perfect man, that's what the world is." After a reverbed vocalization, the song returns to its hook, which is followed by an outro where new backing vocals are introduced against K'naan's talking and singing the hook.

Nas is considered a rap legend because of his output: the highly successful and influential Columbia albums *Illmatic*, *It Was Written* (1996), *I Am . . .* (1999), *Nastradamus* (1999), *Stillmatic*, *God's Son* (2002), and *Street's Disciple* (2004), and the Def Jam releases *Hip Hop Is Dead* (2006), *Untitled* (2008), and *Life Is Good* (2012). In 2018, he released the EP *Nasir* and a reissue of *Illmatic* recorded with the National Symphony Orchestra. He has had seven albums RIAA certified platinum and three gold. His albums also have an impressive charting record. *It Was Written*, *I Am . . .*, *Hip Hop Is Dead*, *Untitled*, and *Life Is Good* all reached No. 1 on the Billboard 200. He also helped his younger brother Jungle (Jabari Jones, n.d.), a member of the Queensbridge hip hop group Bravehearts (1998–), release the group's debut studio album, *Bravehearted* (2003). In 2011, K'naan visited Somalia and wrote an opinion piece in the *New York Times* Sunday Review. His latest album, *Country, God, or the Girl*, took on a different, more commercially oriented sound that included pop. However, since its 2012 release, K'naan has not recorded an album. In 2016, HBO picked up his pilot for *Mogadishu, Minnesota*, which he wrote and directed. As of 2019, he plans to return to recording.

NICKI MINAJ: *PINK FRIDAY* AND *PINK FRIDAY: ROMAN RELOADED* (CASH MONEY RECORDS, 2010, 2012)

No rapper knows that sex sells more than Nicki Minaj. When Onika Tanya Maraj (1982–) moved to join her immigrant parents in Queens, New York, no one could have known that this artistically gifted child who successfully auditioned for the prestigious Fiorello H. LaGuardia High School of Music & Art and Performing Arts as an acting major would grow up to release sexually graphic mixtapes that launched her career as video vixen and rapper Nicki Minaj. A native of Port of Spain, Trinidad and Tobago, she would become one of rap's most successful and critically acclaimed female acts. Her rapid-fire flow filled with wordplay and clever, humorous, and sometimes hypersexualized imagery (used for songs about sex, for bragging rights, and for diss tracks), combined with her electrifying videos full of colorful costumes (including multicolored dyed hair and wigs), have earned her a large fan base and popularity both as a soloist and featured rapper.

She began her rap career with the release of mixtapes *Playtime Is Over* (Dirty Money Records, 2007), *Sucka Free* (with Lil Wayne, Young Money, 2008), and *Beam Me Up Scotty* (Self-released, 2009), the last featuring the single "I Get Crazy," which peaked at No. 20 on Billboard's Hot Rap Tracks and No. 37 on Billboard's Hot R&B/Hip Hop Songs. Her 2010 decision to record fewer sex songs did little to hurt her marketability. Following the release of her solo album *Pink Friday* (2010), she gained exposure through a five-day promotional tour and by opening for Britney Spears during Spears's Femme Fatale Tour (in 2011). This helped her market *Pink Friday*, which became RIAA certified three-times platinum and spawned the Billboard Hot 100 No. 3 hit "Super Bass." The song also hit No. 2 on the Hot Rap Songs chart and was certified eight times platinum, her biggest commercial single. The tour also helped Nicki Minaj promote her upcoming second studio album, *Pink Friday: Roman Reloaded* (2012).

Pink Friday: Roman Reloaded and its follow-up, *The Pinkprint* (2014), were both certified double platinum. The former produced her second Top Ten single, "Starships," which reached No. 5 on the Hot 100.

The Pinkprint featured "Anaconda," her breakthrough No. 2 hit whose hypersexualized, fetish-heavy video reached nearly twenty million views in its first day (872 million views as of July 2019). Two songs from *The Pinkprint*, "Anaconda" and "Only," reached No. 1 on both the Hot Rap Songs and the Hot R&B/Hip Hop Songs charts. Also helping her marketability was her acting background and the fact that she is video-oriented, two traits that allow her to slip into different characters, such as the hyper-feminine, passive Harajuku Barbie and the aggressive, masculine Roman Zolanski (she does so in interviews as well), thereby keeping her image fresh and engaging. In her music, these translate more into lyrical themes than different voices, although she will use accents and subtle comic voice modulations during her character-based raps (Roman has a bad, lilting British accent).

Generally speaking, her rap flow varies between chanting, carefully pronounced mid-tempo rapping, and speed rapping, at times approaching chopper style. Her lyrical concerns include braggadocio (skills bragging and diss tracks about other rappers), sex/romance, and ethnic minority and feminist issues. Stylistically, her raps are based on clever wordplay and the sometimes use of internal rhymes and near rhymes, although she relies heavily on old-school style rapping in her mid-tempo raps (singsong lines, lots of end rhyme, and lots of repetition on the ends of lines). She can best be described as a cross between Yolandi Vi$$er (of Die Antwoord) and Missy Elliott, but she consciously eschews the androgyny of Vi$$er and the subtlety of Elliott. Like Vi$$er and Elliott, Nicki Minaj is an aggressive, in-your-face rapper who pulls no punches lyrically. She is also similar to Elliott in the diversity of sound per each of her albums, which is exemplified in *Pink Friday* and *Pink Friday: Roman Reloaded*, two albums that couldn't possibly be more different musically.

Pink Friday can best be described as bubblegum rap (perhaps the nickname "bubble rap" is appropriate). A hotly anticipated album by a cult fan base (based on her mixtapes), it featured guest vocals from some of the top names in rap and hip hop music: Eminem, Rihanna (Robyn Rihanna Fenty, 1988–), Drake, will.i.am (William Adams, 1975–), and Kanye West. Although the criticism that it is more pop than rap is deserved, the album does have its high points. Its standout tracks include "Did It On 'Em," "Right Thru Me," "Dear Old Nicki," "Your Love," and "Last Chance." "Did It On 'Em" can best be described as hardcore rap dubstep. It is a diss track that attacks Nicki Minaj's critics (mainly the female ones). It features chanting in the hook/refrain, and a Nicki Minaj rap that is slow and measured, consisting of end rhymes. Instrumentally, the song is mainly synthesizer (power chords), part of a sparse beat that also features 808 drums against a programmed drum beat. The overall effect is a slightly offbeat rhythm. "Right Thru Me," a love song that begins with a keyboard ostinato, followed by a big, almost orchestrated sound with plucked strings against a drum kit beat (bass kick, hi-hat, and ride cymbal), is structured on descending fifths (e.g., Pachelbel's "Canon in D"). Nicki Minaj's rap flow is staccato, based on end rhymes, but her delivery is breathless. The song features a neo-soul sung (auto-tuned) hook, but it works because of its catchy melodic structure.

The album's best song, "Dear Old Nicki," is a wonderfully clever twist on the breakup song—here the broken relationship is Minaj and what she considers to be her old self. The song features the most compelling keyboard melody on the album, as well as its best production values, with synth string voices, claps, and a house music feel, against which Nicki Minaj talk-sings. Although the line lengths are predictable lines, she uses interesting pauses to create variety. "Your Love," a mid-tempo snap song with an auto-tuned chorus and a sampling of the hit "No More I Love You's" (*The Lover Speaks*, 1986), with additional bass, drum-loops, and hip hop backbeats, is a love song that almost rivals "Dear Old Nicki." Unfortunately, it has a too-highly auto-tuned sung hook. Nicki Minaj's rapping is slow and measured and well executed. Instrumentally, the album's most interesting song is "Last Chance," a braggadocio track about beating the odds. It features synth string voices against distorted guitar, set against an 808 beat. Minaj here uses a speed rap style, with interesting flow changes at the end of some phrases. Unfortunately the song's effect is lessened by its sung hook, which is bubblegum pop–flavored.

Other songs on *Pink Friday* that deserve attention are "Check It Out," "I'm the Best," "Roman's Revenge," and "Moment for Life." The skills bragging and diss track "Check It Out" heavily samples the piano and vocal hook from the Buggles' "Video Killed the Radio Star" (1979). It has points of interest, such as where Nicki Minaj's auto-tuned talk-singing to the tune of the original Buggles song is set against a counter-melody by will.i.am (who raps the second verse). "I'm the Best," an autobiographical song about her rise to fame and fortune, features high energy house music, synth-based programmed drums, and Minaj's most girlish voice, her rapping a combination of old-school and modern rap styles. "Roman's Revenge," produced by Swizz Beatz (Kasseem Dean, 1978–), references the Roman Zolanski alter ego and features Eminem's alter ego Slim Shady. This aggressive and angry brag rap is a lesson in speed rapping and absurdist vocalizations. The rapping is set against a plethora of sci-fi synth sounds and orchestral synth voices, postproduction vocal hiccups, and diverse types of voices, some comical. "Moment for Life," which features Drake, is about beating the odds. Here a synth intro—a simple ostinato—is joined by a programmed drum; then a kick and hi-hat beat is played against a measured and articulated rapping and speech-singing, which turns into breathless speed rapping with flow varied between staccato lines and longer enjambed lines.

The album does features some weak songs, "Fly," "Save Me," "Blazin," "Here I Am," and the hit "Super Bass." "Fly" features Rihanna but is generally a pop song with a simple old-school singsong rap, with too much end rhyme and repetition in the place of rhyme. "Save Me" is a simple pop song about being flawed, with a down-tempo beat that flirts with a change to high energy but stays slow and too melodramatic. "Blazin," featuring Kanye West, is a house music–based melodramatic pop tune with predictable rhymes. "Here I Am" is bubblegum. "Super Bass," a romance and sex club song, is also too mired in pop to be interesting, but its masterful speed rapping almost overcomes its auto-tuned melodramatic hook, sung with harmonies (vocalizations on a scale).

In contrast to the bubblegum pop nature of *Pink Friday*, *Pink Friday: Roman Reloaded* can best be described as electronic post-punk rap with a nasty attitude. Moreover, it just plain rocks where *Pink Friday* swayed. Its standouts, "Roman Holiday," "Come on a Cone," "I Am Your Leader," "Starships," and "Stupid Hoe," would be standouts on any rap album. "Roman Holiday" is expertly produced by BlackOut Movement (Winston Thomas, n.d.). The song is a combination of self-study and advice for dealing with haters ("take your medication Roman/ take a short vacation Roman") and diss rap (when Roman takes over her body) against other female rappers and "haters." Its music is high energy, a creative and complex mix of instrumentation (which early on mirrors refrain vocals) and production—its hook is a synth ostinato reminiscent of a fanfare, with a sine wave, a whirring synth voice that builds up, and an 808 drum, against which Nicki Minaj sings with a pronounced lilt. Its rapped verses showcase various styles and voices, set against timbale and conga with synth power chords, and the song's B section is a wonderful parody of "O Come All Ye Faithful." The bragging and diss track "Come on a Cone," produced by Hit-Boy (Chauncey Hollis Jr., 1987–), is Missy Elliott and Timbaland–inspired. It features a whirring synth voice (evocative of "Flight of the Bumblebee"), Nicki Minaj's weird vocalizations, bongos, timbale, and synth stingers—against a speed rap where she lets her voice break (as the song kicks into high gear). Its rhymes are brilliant, with lots of wordplay humor.

"I Am Your Leader," produced by Fernando Garibay (n.d.) and Hit-Boy, is an aggressive braggadocio and diss track featuring Rick Ross (William Leonard Roberts II, 1976–) and Cam'ron (a.k.a. Killa Cam, Cameron Ezike Giles, 1976–). Instrumentation includes an oscillating synth-based multioctave ostinato, with snaps that later become reverbed claps and bass kick. Set against this in Minaj's mid-tempo, highly articulated rap that includes lots of references to pop culture—leading to a hook done up as a stage musical (a highly stylized chant song) and set against an 808. "Starships" and "Pound the Alarm" are club and dance songs that celebrate success. The better of the two, "Starships," opens with a distorted acoustic guitar, later juxtaposed against rave music. Its rap is up-tempo and done in comic voices, and its hook is sung house style (with a synth and programmed drum beat). The track highlights Minaj's best sung vocals on the album, as well as lots of comic vocalizations and Missy Elliott–style cartoons. "Stupid Hoe" is the album's most creative song instrumentally and vocally. Produced by DJ Diamond Kuts (Karlis Griffin, n.d.), this diss song against haters features a "whoop" sound (synth-produced) and a heavy eighth note kick and snare drum beat (that transforms into a kick, bass, sub-bass, Brazilian whistle, 808, and synth-produced sound effects beat), and against all this Minaj speed raps with lots of comic effects (such as a wonderfully elongated comic vocal note).

Other excellent songs include "Beez in the Trap," a snap song with two synth beats making a high-pitched popping sound (like a submarine depth gauge) that travel left to right and are sometimes heard in both speakers, as well as bass kick (verse two), with an old-school rap. "Roman Reloaded" features 808 drum and gunshot sound effects (which occur at time-stop moments at the end of verses), as well as bass kick, and timpani, and a later synth buildup (a whirring Doppler effect).

The album's weaker songs are its most pop-oriented. "HOV Lane" has a heavy synth and 808 beat with reverbed claps added later and a fast-tempo rap, which unfortunately has overly simple staccato lines, with some male and female vocalizations in the hook. "Champion" features Drake, Young Jeezy (Jay Wayne Jenkins, 1977–), and Nas, each on a verse. The track has a melodramatic and powerful synth opening with a martial drum beat in its intro (that gets taken over by a kick drum, 808, claps, and later timbale), but overall the beat becomes too monotonous. Drake and Young Jeezy's raps are weak (although the latter's voice is a point of interest). Nas's rap stands out but cannot save the song. "Sex in the Lounge" is a typical pop song with heavy auto-tuning, a forgettable slow staccato, and all end-rhyme old-school rap. "Whip It" is a slightly better sex and club song (rave-influenced with some references to calypso and some of Nicki Minaj's best rap voice switches), but only slightly. The album also contains nonrapped, completely sung dance songs: "Automatic," "Beautiful Sinner," "Fire Burns," and "Right by My Side." Nonetheless, some completely sung songs, such as "Marilyn Monroe," "Young Forever," and "Gun Shot," featuring Beenie Man (Anthony Moses Davis, 1973–), are quite good.

In 2013, Nicki Minaj took a recording hiatus and appeared as a judge on *American Idol*. Recently, she has built her acting resume, appearing in the films *The Other Woman* (2014) and *Barbershop: The Next Cut* (2016). In 2016, ABC Family cut the television series *Nicki* during its planning stage. The show would have been about her early years in Queens. In 2017, she surpassed Aretha Franklin for having more songs chart on the Billboard Hot 100 than any other female artist. She has also turned her attention to philanthropy. Through Twitter, she offered to pay tuition, fees, or loans for thirty of her fans; she has also given donations for hurricane relief efforts after Hurricane Harvey hit Houston, and she has supported the development of small villages in India. She has recently released five singles in support of her fourth studio album, *Queen* (2018), which reached No. 2 on the Billboard 200 and was RIAA certified platinum.

THE NOTORIOUS B.I.G.

The Notorious B.I.G. (Christopher George Latore Wallace, 1972–97), known also as Biggie Smalls, was one of the leading East Coast rappers of the mid-1990s. A high profile murder victim during the East Coast-West Coast rap wars, he lived just long enough to see the release of one album, the fatalistic *Ready to Die* (1994). His second, *Life after Death* (1997), was released posthumously. Despite his limited output, his skill with rhyming and delivery are considered iconic—he is considered among the most talented rappers of all time, often discussed in the same breath as his rival Tupac Shakur. Both rappers were murdered, and the murders are to this day considered related, with the Notorious B.I.G.'s murder being possibly a retaliation killing.

Born to Jamaican immigrants living in Brooklyn and raised by a single mother, Biggie Smalls began rapping as a street entertainer in the Bedford-Stuyvesant neighborhood, facing perpetual trouble with the law for drugs, guns, and probation violations. A demo tape he made in the early 1990s made its way to Puff Daddy, who signed him with Uptown Records, and he followed Puff Daddy to his Bad Boy Records label (a.k.a. Bad Boy Entertainment) a few months later. He had early mainstream chart success, hitting the Billboard Hot 100 with "Juicy" (No. 27), "Big Poppa" (No. 6), "One More Chance" (No. 2), "Sky's the Limit" (No. 26), and two No. 1 hits, "Hypnotize" and "Mo Money Mo Problems." He also had five songs hit the top spot on the Hot Rap Songs chart, as well as four songs on which he was featured hit the top spot.

By 1994, the Notorious B.I.G. had completed his first studio album, the quadruple platinum *Ready to Die*; it featured production by Puff Daddy. (In 2006, Bridgeport Music and Westbound Records won a federal lawsuit against Bad Boy Records for copyright infringement, with a jury deciding that three of the album's songs used illegal samples; all versions of the album released since the lawsuit's lost appeal are without the disputed samples). Many of the album's tracks were freestyle raps, with some improvised in performance (e.g., "Unbelievable," reportedly improvised at 3:00 a.m.). The album, a Junior M.A.F.I.A. production, features guest appearances by Method Man, Total (Bad Boy's girl group, 1994–2000; 2014–), and Diana King (1970–). *Ready to Die* begins with a brief skit ("Intro") but unlike many rap albums of the time, it does not include a large number of skits. Most of the songs can best be characterized as g-funk, gangsta rap with a more laid-back feel and a beat typically created by the interplay of electric bass guitar (sometimes slap bass) and snare drum. The album's instrumentation is sparse, with prioritization given to the Notorious B.I.G.'s rapping; he raps both as a baritone and as a tenor, depending on the song, uses both ranges (for different characters in dialogue raps) and flows that vary.

The album's musical standouts are "Warning" and "Respect." "Warning" is much more R&B-oriented than the album's other songs, though it does use a funk bass. Here the Notorious B.I.G.'s delivery is slow, soft-spoken, and measured, with the song taking the form of a phone call dialogue between Biggie and Pop (both roles rapped by the Notorious B.I.G.). Postproduction phone-call effects make it sound as though Pop is actually on a phone. The story is that he has called Biggie at 6:00 a.m. to warn him that another crew is planning to rob and kill him. Biggie responds by bragging about his arsenal and willingness to kill. The song ends comically when Biggie steps outside with his Doberman to investigate a noise and sees red dots on his and his Doberman's head, right before two gunshots are heard. The autobiographical story-based "Respect" has the album's most aggressive beat and is one of the few songs that includes guitar (as well as the usual bass and drum). Here the kick drum is prominent, giving the song a sense of urgency, and reggae elements and Jamaican toasting (by King) complement the song's rapping. "Gimme the Loot," a more funk-oriented gangsta rap track, is also memorable. It features heavier bass and more turntable (in the refrain) than other songs. Again the Notorious B.I.G. raps in two roles, as both his younger self and his adult self (using his higher and lower registers) as they engage in a dialogue about the need to be a criminal when you live in a criminal environment filled with the lure of money. The album's songs are mostly gangsta-related, packed with violent imagery and overt threats to other crews, haters, and rappers who diss the Notorious B.I.G.

Despite this, the album begins innocently with "Things Done Changed," with lyrics about urban life "back in the day" (before crime and drugs). The song immediately establishes that the music will be R&B and funk-infused, with a peppering of neo soul. Instrumentation includes brass sections that are set against the song's heavy keyboard-based bass and snare beat; in certain verses, strings and harp imply the trip down memory lane. As with all the album's songs, here the rhymes are predominantly end rhymes (though he uses interior rhyme—usually in threes—in a few tracks), and the rap flow varies to prevent an overuse of the sing-song sound of old-school rap. "Machine Gun Funk" shows off the rapper's comic side as he brags about retaining his street cred even though he has given up dealing drugs for making music. The song, produced by Darnell Scott (n.d.), also shows off production values that prioritize experimental instrumentation (pitch modified horns made to sound dissonant), semi-comic sound bites, and offbeat vocal processing.

Produced by Easy Mo Bee (Osten Harvey Jr., 1965–), "Ready to Die" starts with a church organ that then transitions into a funk-infused rap where the Notorious B.I.G. explains why he is not afraid to die, even though he will put up a fight. Similar thematic concerns inform "Suicidal Thoughts" and "Everyday Struggle." Both songs stand out for their lyrics, an honest expression of the despair that urban stress can cause, the latter featuring its refrain "I don't wanna live no more" and a synthesized flute voice set against jazz-rock drumming, the former taking the form of a last phone call to a friend; it ends in Biggie's suicide. "One More Chance," "Me and My B—," and "Friend of Mine" are the album's relationship songs. The first has the album's longest intro (women call to yell at Biggie because he is using them only for sex) and an R&B sung refrain that references the Jackson 5's "I Want You Back" (1969). "Me and My B—" ends with a brief skit: an interview with the Notorious B.I.G. "Friend of Mine," also produced by Easy Mo Bee, features interesting vocal cacophony and instrumental percussion. The lyrics position women as the enemy, as gold diggers at worst and disloyal at best. "Juicy," produced by Poke (Jean-Claude Olivier, n.d.) of Trackmasters and Puff Daddy, is a true marriage of funk and R&B/soul. The track is the outlier on the album, containing programmed drums, treble percussions to contrast heavy slap bass, and refrain singing by Total.

Life after Death is a double album (four CDs) about urban street culture glamour and grit; it is one of the few rap albums to have reached RIAA certified diamond status. Featuring guest appearances by Jadakiss (Jason Terrance Phillips, 1975–), R. Kelly, Puff Daddy (as P. Diddy), Jay-Z, and Lil' Kim, as well as samples of Martin Lawrence, the album contains standout songs, including the musically engaging "What's Beef" and "Mo Money Mo Problems" and the lyrically brilliant "Sky's the Limit." "What's Beef," produced by Carlos Broady (n.d.) and Nashiem Myrick (n.d.), is synthetic string-heavy revenge rap (against rappers who diss Biggie) that features sub-bass, hi-hats, rides, and an 808 drum, rare in the rapper's repertoire, while "Mo Money Mo Problems" samples heavily Diana Ross's "I'm Coming Out" (1980). "Sky's the Limit," a continuation (thematically) of the autobiographical "Respect," is an imagined scene between Biggie and his mother, who in earlier songs like "Suicidal Thoughts" is represented as regretting his birth. Here she is supportive of her son and loving as he recounts his rags to riches story.

Like on *Ready to Die*, here most of the songs have gangsta themes and are filled with violent imagery. For example, the album's first track, "Somebody's Gotta Die," produced by 6 July, Myrick, and Puff Daddy, is a revenge song that spouts an eye for an eye mentality following the murder of a crew member. Listeners are immediately treated to complex production values—for example, the song uses an atmospheric synthesizer voice, and overall it marks a bigger commitment to the g-funk sound. "Last Day," produced by D-Dot and Havoc (Kejuan Muchita, 1974–), is a gangsta song that features Jadakiss prominently, and in contrast to many of the album's songs, it is frenetic and dissonant; unfortunately for fans, the Notorious B.I.G. raps only the fourth verse. "Hypnotize," produced by Amen-Ra (Ron Lawrence, n.d.), D-Dot, and Puff Daddy, is a funk-heavy song that also serves as a rap brag. It features funk bass, snare, claps, and synthesized guitar, as well as response vocalizations and a sung refrain. "Kick in the Door," produced by DJ Premier (Christopher Edward Martin, 1966–), is one of the Notorious B.I.G.'s few strict braggadocio raps; it features a synthesizer, snare, and bass beat set against percussive bells and a synth oscillator. The track begins with an interview with tha Madd Rapper, a character created by D-Dot and used later on *Tell 'Em Why U Madd* (2000). In a fit of jealousy, tha

Madd Rapper disses the Notorious B.I.G. because he achieved success too quickly, which tha Madd Rapper equates with his losing his authenticity. He is interrupted by scratching and a rap that establishes Biggie's dominance as "the King" of New York City. "F— You Tonight," produced by Daron Jones (1976–) and Puff Daddy, is a neo soul and '80s keyboard–heavy laid-back sex rap that features singing by R. Kelly in the refrain. The R&B-infused bling rap "I Love the Dough" splits verses between Jay-Z and Biggie. "Another," a relationship song, is unique in that it features Biggie's and fellow Junior M.A.F.I.A. member Lil' Kim's singing in the refrain.

The Notorious B.I.G. was originally friends with Tupac Shakur—until he and Puff Daddy were accused of robbing and shooting Tupac Shakur in 1994, charges which both denied. In 1995, the Notorious B.I.G. released "Who Shot Ya," which was taken as a diss track, beginning a diss track war that ended with Tupac Shakur's murder. In 1997, the Notorious B.I.G. traveled to Los Angeles to promote the impending release of his second album—it was there he was gunned down.

N.W.A.: *STRAIGHT OUTTA COMPTON* (RUTHLESS RECORDS, 1988)

Straight Outta Compton (1988) took both black and white America by storm. Despite its having no tour and little to no radio airplay, it went platinum and in 1989 reached No. 37 on the Billboard 200, peaking at No. 9 on Billboard's Top R&B/Hip Hop Albums chart. It also reached the Top Ten on Australia and Ireland's album charts. By 2015, it had sold over three million copies, outpacing N.W.A.'s follow-up, *Efil4zaggin* (1991), which was certified double platinum by the RIAA. Due to the release of the 2015 biopic film on N.W.A., also called *Straight Outta Compton*, the album reentered the Billboard 200 at No. 173, a full twenty-seven years after its release—a couple of weeks later it rose to No. 4.

More importantly, the album launched the careers of N.W.A. members Dr. Dre, MC Ren (Lorenzo Jerald Patterson, 1969–), Eazy-E, and Ice Cube, and it put Los Angeles–based Ruthless Records (1987–2010), cofounded by Eazy-E and Jerry Heller (Gerald Elliot Heller, 1940–2016), on the map (which indirectly led to the formation of its rival label, the iconic Death Row Records). Because of its use of extreme profanity and images of violence, it popularized gangsta rap and hinted at the emergence of g-funk, which became the most commercially viable rap music subgenre. As an album, it is notable as the only N.W.A. work to feature

Ice Cube, as he left the group soon afterwards. In essence, the album launched rap and hip hop as we know it today, adding a complexity to old-school music and lyrics and determining the subject matter for most rap music to come, so much so that rap musicians to this day are judged by whether they have what N.W.A. could boast, "street cred."

Ice Cube and MC Ren wrote most of the album's songs—with studio writer D.O.C. (Tracy Lynn Curry, 1968–) contributing on a few and Arabian Prince (Kim Renard Nazel, 1965–) writing one—while DJ Yella and Dr. Dre produced virtually all of the tracks. Featured rapping is usually done by Ice Cube, MC Ren, and Eazy-E with skits featuring Dr. Dre. Sampled artists include an array of Motown, funk, and rap acts: Average White Band, Beastie Boys, James Brown, Big Daddy Kane, Boogie Down Productions, Davy DMX, Doug E. Fresh and Slick Rick, Funkadelic, Marvin Gaye, Kool & the Gang, Kool Moe Dee, the Isley Brothers, Ohio Players, Wilson Pickett, Pointer Sisters, Richard Pryor, Public Enemy, Steve Miller Band, and N.W.A. itself, as well as Eazy-E.

The album's first three songs are about police brutality, gangster life, and violence, and its opening track, "Straight Outta Compton," features three rapped sections, by Ice Cube, MC Ren, and Eazy-E, and includes a sampling of Brown's "Funky Drummer," one of the most sampled funk songs in all of rap. Dr. Dre introduces two of the three sections of the song, with the middle section introduced by a brief dialogue between Eazy-E and MC Ren. "Straight Outta Compton" jumps right out at the listener as a series of police sirens are set against heavy bass and snare, and Dr. Dre reminds everyone that the police do nothing when black people are killed. Ice Cube and MC Ren's raps both reference AK-47s, and Ice Cube's rapping is aggressive as he almost yells into the mic while set against keyboard power chords and carefully placed reverbed vocals to accentuate important lines. MC Ren, who raps smoothly though aggressively, blatantly states that his lyrics will offend certain women. Eazy-E's section is rapped in his typical high-pitched, boyish voice, and its tone has an uncharacteristic anger; his lyrics are mainly about his sexual prowess and his ability to outthink the police, with his violent imagery kept indirect. The song's outro features unexpected sirens and gunshots, which flow without pause into the second track, the most controversial song on the album.

At 5:45, "F— tha Police" is the album's longest song. It features a sample from Eazy-E's "Ruthless Villain" (from the "Street Side" of his *Eazy-Duz-It* EP) and starts out as a mock trial set against horns and scratching, with Judge Dre presiding in the case of N.W.A. versus the police department (the LAPD is not referenced specifically). Ice Cube raps the first verse, pointing out that cops have "the authority to kill a minority," use profiling, and mistreat black prisoners, including strip-searching them. The song offers humor in parts, such as when Ice Cube's rap questions the sexuality of police who take too much pleasure in strip searches. Included in the song are small skits, such as the one that follows Ice Cube's rap: Dr. Dre and MC Ren spoof being pulled over. MC Ren's verse offers as many threats to police officers as did Ice Cube's, but it becomes more overt with references to shooting police as a sniper. A second skit has Eazy-E being arrested without cause. This is followed by Eazy-E's section, where he continues the theme of police officers being reduced to targets once they take off their uniforms and badges, the only real power they possess. The song ends with the verdict—the police department is found guilty of being too white and too redneck. The song's chorus and skits are memorable for its use of vocal modulation, scratching, and a modulated sampling of the *Twilight Zone* theme. The third track, "Gangsta Gangsta," prefigures some gangsta rap as it introduces the concept of the gangster lifestyle as being necessary to survival (reality) rather than simply a means to money ("it's not about a salary"). The song's lyrics aren't without humor, including some metatextual references to the song's instrumentation and a sly reference to Ruthless Records.

After these first three tracks, the theme switches to one of swagger or braggadocio about the band's skills in laying down beats and creating memorable rap through intense vocal delivery. Featuring a self-referential sample of "Straight Outta Compton," the fourth track, "If It Ain't Ruff," is one of the few solo tracks on the album, written and rapped by MC Ren, whose lyrics reference freestyling, associated with battle rapping. Creating an interesting juxtaposition to the song's clever and polished verse is the chorus, in which MC Ren claims that he must be "ruff" to be himself and that he identifies with being gangsta. Likewise, "Parental Discretion Iz Advised," which follows, takes as its subject N.W.A.'s song production, establishing that N.W.A. is unbeatable as a rap crew and its members intend to shock with imagery and language. "Something Like That," which follows, features Dr. Dre on vocals, and his solo verse stands out for its clever rhymes and his referencing something funky, foreshadowing his pioneering efforts into g-funk. "Compton's N the House (Remix)" self-samples the song "Something Like That," originally from the five-song *Gangsta Gangsta* EP. Rapped by MC Ren and Dr. Dre, it amounts to five minutes of calling out what Run-D.M.C. would popularize as "sucker MCs." N.W.A. challenges copycat rappers to a rap fight, saying it will use guerilla warfare, thus making it known that N.W.A. cannot be duplicated or challenged for music skill or street cred. MC Ren revisits this theme again in "Quiet On tha Set." Easily the cleverest of the bragging songs in its rhymes and word use, it is also the most self-referential, mentioning, among other plans, that future songs will have more percussion and will be even more danceable. Also a battle song, "Express Yourself" is about being true to one's character (in lyric writing) as it mentions that some MCs who use profane language at home cannot bring themselves to do so on the mic, which makes them untrue to themselves.

The album's drug songs begin with "8 Ball (Remix)," written by Ice Cube and featuring a solo rap by Eazy-E. It includes liberal sampling and a xylophone-inspired beat to tell the story of a night of being drunk and high (on cocaine). "Dopeman (Remix)," written and rapped by Ice Cube, also features Eazy-E on vocals. Despite its images of drug dealing leading to riches, the song is obviously anti–crack cocaine, as it calls out both men and women who get hooked, reminding them that they will eventually turn to attacking their own friends and giving away sexual favors just to get high. The song's outro, in fact, threatens the "dopeman" (drug dealer) with murder if he hooks any of the rappers' sisters. "Dopeman (Remix)" is also interesting in that it contains unique street slang terms like "gank" (to trick someone out of money) and "strawberry" (a strung out woman who will have sex with anyone and everyone, even participating in gangbangs).

"I Ain't tha 1," written and rapped by Ice Cube, is the album's first song about women who try to game him so that they can get his money. Ironically, he calls these women out while admitting that the only reason he pursues a relationship is for sex, dismissing his behavior as typically male. The album ends with "Something 2 Dance 2," a relatively short song written by Arabian Prince that includes raps by himself, DJ Yella, Dr. Dre, and Eazy-E. The song doesn't pretend to be anything more than what its title suggests, which is a beat with simple rapping, something to dance to.

Topical even thirty years after its initial release, *Straight Outta Compton* has been reimagined and rereleased various times, first as a tribute album (1998) featuring rap acts like MC Eiht, Bone Thugs-N-Harmony, Snoop Dogg, C-Murder, Ant Banks, Silkk the Shocker, Big Pun, Fat Joe, and N.W.A. The original album was reissued in 2002 as a remastered version containing bonus tracks, "Express Yourself (Extended Mix)," "Bonus Beats," "Straight Outta Compton (Extended Mix)," and "A B— Iz a B—." It was reissued again in 2007 in honor of the original release's twentieth anniversary, and in 2015 the Universal Music Group reissued it on a limited edition red cassette as part of their Respect the Classics series. It has been included in *Rolling Stone*'s list of the five hundred greatest albums of all time. In 2017, the Library of Congress selected it for preservation in the National Recording Registry. It also got the attention of governmental organizations like the LAPD, the FBI, and the U.S. Senate, which attempted to censor its lyrics, particularly due to "F— tha Police," which did not appear on the censored version of the album. In 2016, *Straight Outta Compton* was the first hip hop album inducted into the Grammy Hall of Fame.

OUTKAST: *STANKONIA* (LAFACE RECORDS, 2000)

OutKast (1991–2006; 2014–) can be credited with popularizing the Dirty South style of rap music and with putting LaFace Records on the hip hop map. The Atlanta duo, composed of two rapper-producers, André 3000 (a.k.a. André, André Lauren Benjamin, 1975–) and Big Boi (Antwan André Patton, 1975), combined dance-based electronic hip hop with funk, psychedelic music, rock, jazz, drum and bass, and R&B. Before its breakup, OutKast produced five studio albums, four of which were RIAA certified multiplatinum and one of which was certified diamond. Three of the five reached No. 2 on the Billboard 200, and one, the double album *Speakerboxxx/The Love Below,* reached No. 1. *Southernplayalisticadillacmuzik* (1994), OutKast's first album, had a breakout single, "Players Ball," which topped Billboard's Hot Rap Songs chart. The album's success paved the way for OutKast's original sound: André 3000 was known for his flow and funk-styled singing and quirky lyrics that contrasted well with Big Boi's chopper-style rap. The duo's second and third albums, *ATLiens* (1996) and *Aquemini* (1998), exemplified its move toward beats that owed more to progressive jazz or jazz funk than to hip hop.

The duo's fourth album, Grammy-winning *Stankonia* (2000), is the culmination of these disparate styles, including neo soul, exemplified in the Grammy-winning single "Ms. Jackson," OutKast's first Billboard Hot 100 No. 1 hit. Because it was recorded in the duo's recently purchased Atlanta recording facility Stankonia Studios, there were fewer time and recording constraints faced by the production teams Earthtone III, consisting of OutKast and Mr. DJ (David Sheats, n.d.), and Organized Noize (1992–). The final product was an experimental album featuring uncharacteristic high energy (extremely rapid beat per minute rhythm tracks).

Songs fused elements of various styles, including Latin, funk, drum and bass, rave, psychedelia, gospel, jazz, rock, and jazz fusion—with all informed by the Dirty South aesthetic. André 3000 experimented with not only rap but also singing and talk-singing. The album debuted at No. 2 on the Billboard 200 and produced three singles: "B.O.B.," "Ms. Jackson," and "So Fresh, So Clean."

Throughout the album, extremely clever skits are strategically placed to allow for mood changes in the music; they become break points for listeners (in fact, the skits end with André 3000's and Big Boi's clapping and yelling "break" before the ensuing song, a reference to breaking a sports huddle before executing a called play). The first of these occurs at the album's onset: "Intro" is a space-age-music–inspired piece that introduces the concepts of "Stankonia," or a land of funk, and "bounce," a sort of *je ne sais quoi* in a rapper's or rap band's style that indicates progressiveness, coolness, and swagger. It introduces the album's standout, "Gasoline Dreams," a Public Enemy meets funk indictment of American politicians who make uneasy alliances based on oil needs—but the lyrics go beyond that, pointing out that the American dream, like apple pie (an American icon), is not to everyone's taste because the dream is fake, as expressed in the line "the highway up to Heaven got a crook on the toll." The song's instrumentation epitomizes its anger—harsh, treble-heavy guitars, a fast-paced jazzy snare and crash cymbal drum beat, a funky bass walk, lots of whistles and high-pitched bells, and discordant Latin percussion. Rap vocals (verses) and chanted/talk-sung vocals (hooks), mixed in the treble range, are foregrounded and aggressive, with lyrics that require many plosives.

The anger and energy of "Gasoline Dreams" is soothed with the skit "I'm Cool," a parody of the Snowden scene from the 1970 anti-war film *Catch-22*. It transitions into a down-tempo Prince-style funk (sometimes called p-funk) piece, "So Fresh, So Clean," a bling braggadocio that establishes that the duo is "dope." The song combines sung funk hooks (with a doubled voice to create harmony in the deep register) with alternated rapped verses and a 1970s funk bridge that showcases André 3000's ability to sing in the funk style. This is followed by the highly personal and genuinely apologetic (for breaking off a relationship) "Ms. Jackson," which begins with a keyboard riff (played in a style usually associated with alternative music), set against piano, and a snare and kick beat. Bass and sound effects are introduced during the first rapped voice, which is done chopper style by Big Boi. Like "So Fresh, So Clean," "Ms. Jackson" includes a funk bridge that showcases André 3000's singing. An inherently weak song because of its content, it is saved by irony: a satiric moment where the Wedding March is played with a comic synth voice, which sounds like a cross between guitar and kazoo.

The album's experimental standouts follow, "Snappin' & Trappin'" and "Spaghetti Junction," with the skills brag skit "D.F." inserted between them. "Snappin' & Trappin'" features an oddball synth voice, horror stingers (oscillating sine waves), Jamaican toasting, snare, and an 808 drum mixed to sound high in the treble range. The beat is one big hiccup, which challenges both rappers, causing some moments of nonsynchronized rapping, but overall the song works because it challenges the listener with new sounds. The trap-themed "Spaghetti Junction" (a term that refers to Atlanta's turnpike) introduces the duo's jazz-funk rap sound, with music that features a snare and hi-hat beat, heavy bass played on the E string, synthesizer stingers, and synth-created horns. The song is a warning to Atlanta's youth to avoid the path of drugs and alcohol, which would get them lost so badly they would never find their way back home. The comic, gossipy phone call skit "Kim & Cookie" breaks the tragic feel of "Spaghetti Junction" by introducing the theme of the next song, the experimentally funky "I'll Call Before I Come," which is men's ability to please women sexually rather than worrying about their own gratification. The song, featuring Gangsta Boo (Lola Mitchell, 1979–) and Eco (Marcello Pacheco, n.d.), is a battle of the sexes comic rap with a plot twist—it turns out that both members of the duo are unknowingly having sex with the same woman.

The album's most masterfully constructed song, "B.O.B." (an acronym for "Bombs Over Baghdad"), is an extremely clever braggadocio (skills bragging) and advice (for African American youth) rave rap that contains the most autobiographical and local community references on the album. It starts out quietly, with a synth voice reminiscent of a music box, over which André 3000 does a countdown (which Big Boi will later echo, though in Spanish), at which point the music explodes into a frenetic rave beat, heavy on kick and tom and set against a keyboard harpsichord voice and sound effects (reverbed rhythm sticks). The refrain/hook features heavy funk bass, both electric and keyboard produced, after which 808 drum and electric guitar are added to the mix, followed by synth-based arp and organ voices. The song ends on a lengthy outro that features a guitar solo and turntable, chanted lyrics that reference the rag top (a popular footwork-intense Atlanta hip hop dance), and a call for an electric revival. The same rave–inspired aesthetic is featured a few songs later in the Latin funk "Humble Mumble," a song about humility that features Erykah Badu (Erica Abi Wright, 1971–) and contains the album's best sung hook and turntablism.

Among the album's weaker songs (although each has its high point) is the diss song "Xplosion," which attacks wannabe rappers who don't measure up to OutKast. It features B-Real of Cypress Hill and begins with a harpsichord and organ voice along with synth funk bass and a snare and hi-hat beat. It does have excellent moments, such as when it showcases André 3000's funk rap style, which stands out for its intonation and flow. B-Real holds his own with his chopper-style verses. The skit "Good Hair" serves as an interlude between "Xplosion" and the semi-comic "We Luv Deez Hoez," a sex song that features Big Boi's best rapping on the album. The skits "Drinkin' Again" and a frenetic rap interlude about black-on-black crime lead into the turntable-heavy diss song "Red Velvet," a rap against the duo's critics. The interlude "Cruisin' in the ATL" introduces "Gangsta S—," a g-funk and trap rap track.

The album unfortunately ends on three extremely weak songs—all of which take themselves too seriously, both lyrically and musically: "Toilet Tisha," "Slum Beautiful," and "Stankonia (Stanklove)." The three eschew the irony and musical experimentation of the rest of the album, sounding instead like down-tempo Prince songs. "Toilet Tisha" includes buzzed guitar and falsetto funk vocals, and "Slum Beautiful," which features rapping by CeeLo, features a synth and guitar funk ostinato set against vocals that are slightly out of synch with the song's beat. The comic skit "Pre-Nump" leads to the synth funk–infused "Stankonia (Stanklove)," the album's sole love song.

The duo's final studio nonsoundtrack album, *Speakerboxxx/The Love Below* (Arista, 2003), indicated a near future split in that it was a double album: *The Love Below* featured mainly André 3000, and *Speakerboxxx* featured Big Boi. Both rappers reached the top spot on the Billboard Hot 100, however: Big Boi with "The Way You Move" and André 3000 with "Hey Ya!" The album won the 2004 Grammy Award for Album of the Year. OutKast's final album, *Idlewild* (La Face, 2006), was the soundtrack to its Great Depression–era film of the same name. After the duo's breakup, Big Boi went on to release three solo albums, including 2017's *Boomiverse*, with Epic Records. André 3000, who now goes by André Benjamin, released one and became an entrepreneur, creating the Benjamin Bixby clothing line and creating *Class of 3000*, a short-lived animated television series.

PANJABI HIT SQUAD, FEATURING MS. SCANDALOUS (SEE PANJABI MC, FEATURING JAY-Z AND PANJABI HIT SQUAD)

PANJABI MC, FEATURING JAY-Z, AND PANJABI HIT SQUAD, FEATURING MS. SCANDALOUS: "BEWARE OF THE BOYS" ("MUNDIAN TO BACH KE") AND "HAI HAI" (*BEWARE*, SEQUENCE RECORDS AND MINISTRY OF SOUND, 2003, AND RELEASED AS A SINGLE, VARIOUS LABELS, 2003, 2004, 2006)

Many classical and popular Indian musicians have had a longtime fascination with African American music, initially modeling their solo work after the improvisations of jazz. By the mid-1980s, with access to American break-dancing motion pictures like *Wild Style* (1983) and *Beat Street* (1984), Indian youth started to create rap music in India's major urban cities, Mumbai, Delhi, and Chennai. American and British rapping styles and slang were emulated before Indian hip hop artists turned to using their own languages for rap songs in the 1990s.

From the Punjab (a.k.a. Panjab) region of India and Pakistan, a new music called bhangra-beat (a.k.a. urban desi) emerged—a hybrid genre that has much in common with hip hop and rap, as well as the folk dance and the traditional work songs of Punjabi farmers. Like rap music, bhangra-beat embraces remix culture, and it shares with hip hop the influence of reggae and trance music, creating an East-West hybridization that also incorporates older, classical and/or traditional Indian and Pakistani music. Bhangra-beat is related to, but vastly different from, Bollywood-influenced dance music, which is more influenced by house music. A second-generation music, bhangra-beat is more tradition-influenced than earlier Indian hip hop (which mimicked American rap), incorporating both the traditional vocals in Punjabi and the traditional drum and string instrumentation of Punjabi folk music (e.g., the dhol and the ektara), juxtaposed against Western hip hop rhythms and rap.

By 1997, the sound was popular in the underground dance club circuit, but in the United States, the cross-borrowing between Indian, American, and British hip hop musicians took flight in 2002 when Jay-Z decided to remix the megahit "Mundian To Bach Ke" by Panjabi MC (Rajinder Singh Rai, 1973–)." The result was retitled "Beware of the Boys," and it is a benchmark text in that the song departs from previous instances of rap's sampling phrases and/or ostinatos from Bollywood music that usually resulted in songs where the Indian composer was left anonymous. Instead, "Beware of the Boys" is a true collaboration. Initiated by

Jay-Z after he heard a popular version of the song in a Swiss nightclub, the song is structured so that hip hop and bhangra musical elements get equal time, and more importantly, it was released by Panjabi MC with Jay-Z billed as a featured guest.

From the point of view of Panjabi MC, the song was a breakthrough in commercial marketing because it sold 100,000 singles in two days and became MTV's "Dance Hit of the Year," despite the fact that it appeared on his label only. Informed by a prominent drum and dhol sound, and vocals by Bollywood singer Labh Janjua (n.d.–2015), "Beware of the Boys" marked the beginning of American hip hop's infatuation with the bhangra-beat form. The original song, in Punjabi, is basically an overly long warning to teenage women to be careful not to show off their bodies (or even their eyes) too much and to preserve their youth and innocence by being wary of what boys are really like. The Jay-Z remix is just Jay-Z's rapping over instrumentation and vocal breaks (and in some places simultaneously with the Punjabi vocals).

The song's beat is created by a tumbi (or ektara), joined by dhol, electric bass, and tabla. The lyrics begin with the typical self-referential call of rap music, wherein Jay-Z identifies members of his entourage. He also establishes that the song is an American product, coming to listeners from Brooklyn. These lines, rapped in rhymed couplets, are equally interspersed and alternated with Punjabi lyrics. Generally speaking, Jay-Z's song text is split. The first half is concerned with the male tendency to objectify, sexualize, and seduce. It also establishes Jay-Z's crew's dominance in the sexual arena, as they will steal women from other men's arms. While in the Punjabi version women are warned, here other men in the club are warned—to beware of Jay-Z's boys, who want nothing other than to use their women sexually. The bhangra-beat is punctuated with vocalizations, in this case gasps, which are sexually suggestive, especially when combined with Jay-Z's repetition of the word "bounce," a staple of dance-oriented hip hop.

After the entrance of the accompanying Hindi song in the refrain, Jay-Z employs a softer style of rapping that comes closer to resembling singing. These vocalizations result in a breathy sound that also evokes a sexier and more lyrical mood than in the first part of the song. Ironically, the second half of the song is a protest against George W. Bush's invasion of Iraq and the subsequent Iraq War, as well as the policies of Ronald Reagan before him, which is compared to Bin Laden's 9/11 attack for the amount of damage it did to America. Here Jay-Z's rap makes it clear that his crew is not protesting soldiers, as he wishes them all a safe return, but the idea that war is the only solution to fight anti-American sentiments of hatred. The second half of the song posits that only love conquers hate. As the verse ends, Jay-Z brings the theme back to dancing to club music, saying that further concerns are for another day.

Compared to "Hai Hai," "Beware of the Boys" employs more sensuality through sound, but its beat is not clearly as dance-driven. The original self-released "Hai Hai" was a fast-paced dhol, tabla, dholki, shawm, harmonium, and whistle *giddha* (a Punjabi region folk dance) song sung by Satwinder Bitti (n.d.–). In the remix, the four-man mix crew Panjabi Hit Squad (PHS, 2002–) samples only Bitti's vocals, which are added to a danceable club beat and rapping by Ms. Scandalous (Savita Vaid, 1985–), a newcomer whom PHS discovered. Released on the compilation albums *Desi Beats, Volume 1* (2003), *Vibe Asian/Bhangra Beats & Garage Grooves* (2004), and *The Asian Club Night* (2006), PHS's remixed "Hai Hai," a YouTube phenomenon, launched the career of Ms. Scandalous, one of the London, England, female MCs in late 1990s who began to produce rap and hip hop hits and move beyond the role of the video vixen and featured musical guest in Bollywood hip hop songs. Her rapping, which shows a clear British accent, is fast and expertly rhymed (here she uses eight-line verses, with at least four consecutive lines rhymed in every verse).

Instrumentally, "Hai Hai" is complex and clever, as opposed to "Beware of the Boys," which uses only one rhythmic tumbi and either dhol or electric bass beat and introduces variety only through vocalizations in the form of male gasps or a male-chorus monosyllabic party/dance chant (with sparse scratching in the outro). "Hai Hai" begins with a thin-sounding intro—a synth-manipulated guitar made to sound like a tumbi (or ektara), which is doubled by an air loop or slider for eight iterations, with only one hiccup midway through; this transitions into an aggressive 808 drum hiccup that brings in an energetic, loud 808 drum manipulated to sound like a tabla, which is juxtaposed against a heavy-snare rock beat (the manipulated guitar continues its ostinato). The song's first section is Bitti's sampled Punjabi singing against the beat.

Eighty seconds in, Ms. Scandalous announces her first rapped verse with "you ready for this?" The rapping of verse one is processed to sound as if it is being broadcast via a radio mic. It is set against the thinner-sounding guitar/air loop. But as the verse ends, again an 808 hiccup signals a sonic shift—in the second verse, the aggressive, louder 808 and snare beat plays against Ms. Scandalous, with her rap now more foregrounded. As verses continue against this beat, a grinding sub-bass is added until the last two verses, when only the guitar-air loop returns, now played against the more aggressive, foregrounded rap vocals. A club song, "Hai Hai" has lyrics that are mainly concerned with dancing and looking fashionable. However, half of the lyrics are braggadocio in nature, extoling the skills of both Panjabi Hit Squad and Ms. Scandalous. The song serves as a warning to MCs that London rappers will knock them out—in the song's official video, the first image is that of a lone mic, waiting for an MC, the second shot showing Ms. Scandalous walking in slow motion toward the camera, like a prizefighter, ostensibly to take the mic (which she does). In her spoken-word intro, she asks again, "Can you handle this?"

In the less well-known "Garage Mix" version of "Hai Hai," Ms. Scandalous usurps the role of men in "Beware of the Boys," warning other women that she will steal their men, as in verse one where she warns women in her rap that she will outshine them, characterizing herself as a lady of fashion, dressed in designer brands that include Versace, Armani, and Gucci. Her message, however, is aimed mainly at men, advising them that if they want to approach and captivate women like her, they must know how to arouse female curiosity, which includes whispering softly, touching gently, kissing gently and with care, and dancing seductively.

PROFESSOR ELEMENTAL: "FIGHTING TROUSERS" (SEE MACKLEMORE & RYAN LEWIS AND PROFESSOR ELEMENTAL)

PUBLIC ENEMY: *FEAR OF A BLACK PLANET* (DEF JAM RECORDINGS, 1990)

One of the defining moments of rap music history occurs in the Spike Lee film *Do the Right Thing* (1989): the character Radio Raheem carries a boom box that blares Public Enemy's "Fight the Power." The now iconic song from this Long Island rap crew is the final track on the RIAA certified platinum album *Fear of a Black Planet*. Led by political rapper Chuck D (Carlton Douglas Ridenhour, 1960–) and surrealistic, absurdist hype man (and sometimes Mad Hatter) Flavor Flav (William Jonathan Drayton Jr., 1959–), and consisting at the time of Professor Griff (Richard Griffin, 1960–) and Terminator X (Norman Rogers, 1966–), Public Enemy was one of the most important early rap groups because of the militant nature of its socially conscious music. Set against the aggressive production of the Bomb Squad (1986–), Chuck D's delivery is explosive, with vocals that often feature a complex flow of varying rhythms.

Public Enemy was more than just a couple of MCs rapping against electric guitars and heavy keyboard, drum, and bass; it was an organization consisting of a Minister of Information (Professor Griff), a "media assassin" or PR expert (Harry Allen, 1964–), and a legendary producer (Rick Rubin of Def Jam Recordings). Following the band's Def Jam albums *Yo! Bum Rush the Show* (1987) and *It Takes a Nation of Millions to Hold Us Back* (1988), *Fear of a Black Planet* (whose artwork shows two planets, an unnamed black planet and Earth, eclipsing) has the force of the Black Power movement, encouraging listeners to be socially aware ("woke") and to educate themselves. These albums led to a peak in Public Enemy's popularity, which led to four No. 1 songs on the Hot Rap chart in 1990 and 1991.

Conceived by Chuck D and the Bomb Squad as a musical version of Dr. Frances Cress Welsing's theory of color-confrontation and racism (white supremacy) and consisting of deep and complex songs that lent themselves to live performance, *Fear of a Black Planet* would be ahead of its time even today. It created a media storm when it was released by Def Jam and Columbia Records in April 1990. The album is sixty-three minutes and twenty-one seconds of militant hardcore rap against elaborate sound collages and samples, varying rhythms, media sound bites, and eccentric loops. It spawned five singles, "Fight the Power," "911 Is a Joke," "Welcome to the Terrordome," "Brothers Gonna Work It Out," and "Can't Do Nuttin' for Ya Man," which all hit the Hot Rap chart, the first two going to No. 1.

Like N.W.A. in *Straight Outta Compton*, Public Enemy samples freely, including from its own previously recorded songs. A list of artists sampled is impressive in its eclecticism: Afrika Bambaataa (1957–) and the Soulsonic Force, Average White Band, the Bar-Kays, the Beatles, Big Daddy Kane, Biz Markie, Kurtis Blow, Boogie Down Productions, Brothers Johnson, James Brown, George Clinton, the Commodores, Diana Ross & the Supremes, DJ Grand Wizard Theodore, Funkadelic, Grandmaster Flash and the Furious Five, Hall & Oates, Isaac Hayes, the J.B.s, Jackson 5, Michael Jackson, Rick James, Kool & the Gang, Malcolm McLaren, Bob Marley, the Meters, Eddie Murphy, Musical Youth, Parliament, Prince, Richard Pryor, Run-D.M.C., Schoolly D, the Soup Dragons, the Spinners, Sly & the Family Stone, Spoonie Gee, the Temptations, the Time, and Uriah Heep. The opening track, "Contract on the World Love Jam" is a funk-based, tension-building, sonically energetic collage of approximately fifty samples, scratch cuts (small, quick scratches), and media (especially radio) sound bites backed by heavy bass and drums, with the word "controversy" emphasized through repetition. The song eases in and builds with backgrounded sound bites that eventually become juxtaposed against foregrounded aggressive vocalizations by Chuck D, ending on the phrase "public enemy." This is followed by Chuck D and Flavor Flav's rapping about black empowerment and unity in the black community in the optimistic "Brothers Gonna Work It Out," which comes in with a turntable hiccup effect and features cacophony created through pitch-manipulated guitar sounds run against a heavy funk beat. Chuck D raps it with toasts, harmonies, and additional vocals (that occasionally start and end phrases) by Flavor Flav. Track three, "911 Is a Joke," is rapped old-school style (singsong) by Flavor Flav; it jumps out sonically at listeners with even more sound bite cacophony (voices, laughter, manipulated rhythm guitars, and horns) against a funk beat, juxtaposed in turn against foregrounded vocals that criticize the inadequacy of the 911 emergency system and police response.

"Incident at 66.6 FM" is an instrumental collage of sound bites from a radio call-in show interview of Chuck D where the rapper was confronted with the fact that many called the band's music rabble-rousing. It parodies critics who had told the band to go back to Africa and features a quick toast by Terminator X. "Incident" segues into horns, turntables, and more sound collage of voices as the introspective but angry "Welcome to the Terrordome" opens. Here Chuck D uses quick-paced, internal rhymes and clever wordplay (e.g., "Check the record and reckon an intentional wreck/played off as some intellect") to create verses that establish his skill at rapping and exhort the Bomb Squad's production skills. The lyrics transition in verse three to mention the assassinations of activists Malcolm X and Huey Newton by members of the black community, and in verse four to reference Yusef Hawkins, a sixteen-year-old who was murdered by a gang of white youth, as well as the 1989 Greekfest Riots in Virginia Beach. Verses are introduced by sound bites and Flavor Flav's deejaying, which sets the tone for each. "Welcome to the Terrordome" is followed by a brief song about AIDS, "Meet the G That Killed Me," which caught some flack because it satirizes and blames homosexuality for the epidemic.

"Pollywanacraka" has a more laid-back sound with less sampling (its main sampled sound bite is a series of domestic arguments) and comes across more as a spoken-word track than a rap, with Chuck D using his deepest register. It concerns interracial relationships, although it takes a dim view of them if they lead people to deride and leave the black community. It segues into "Anti-N— Machine," which has a long intro consisting of sound bites and a funk beat. Its theme is much the same as "Welcome to the Terrordome," although it goes more into the reasons for Chuck D's frustration and anger with America. It references a California rally led by Louis Farrakhan following the 1990 murder by police deputies of Oliver Beasley, a Nation of Islam peace activist who died as a result of a traffic violation stop. Track nine, "Burn Hollywood Burn," which features Ice Cube and Big Daddy Kane, satirizes black movie stereotypes and certain blaxploitation films, as well as films like *Driving Miss Daisy* (1989), which cast black actors in servile roles; it expresses a need for more Spike Lee–type films or films with black casts. Even blaxploitation mafia films like *Black Caesar* (1973) would be considered an improvement. Likewise, "Who Stole the Soul?" condemns the treatment of black musicians by the recording industry. Another empowerment song, "Power to the People," is an up-tempo, Miami bass–influenced electronic dance song.

The title track is placed twelfth on the album. Using media sound clips and samples of pitch-altered vocals (which are almost cartoonish), it looks at white fear and racist beliefs about interracial relationships while asserting that humanity descended from black people and there is nothing wrong with adding color to one's family tree (the reasoning being that any interracial relationship technically leads to a black child). "Revolutionary Generation" samples new jack swing and references Aretha Franklin's 1967 Grammy Award–winning hit "Respect" (written in 1965 by Otis Redding and released with changes on her album *I Never Loved a Man the Way that I Love You*). The song decries sexism and misogyny in the black community and in hip hop, arguing that it takes a strong woman to make a man stronger. The black women Chuck D references in the song's lyrics have gained their strength from surviving attacks, both physical and on their character, by white men in America. The next track, "Can't Do Nuttin' for Ya Man," is an energetic, bass-heavy song rapped by Flavor Flav. It denounces black men who create their own marital problems, get into trouble with criminals, or fall back on welfare dependence, implying that each man has to fend for himself because all men have problems of their own (Flavor Flav references his own problems, for example).

The next track, "Reggie Jax," uses a slow, even pace to create an ominous musical tapestry for Chuck D's braggadocio lyrics about "PE Funk," which he states is better than the other, drug-related rap music available for consumption, as it allows fans to get "low" instead of high. This is followed by an instrumental with lyrical borrowings (including the Tom Tom Club), "Leave This Off Your F— Charts," and then "B Side Wins Again," which brags about the danceable rhythms created by Terminator X while simultaneously criticizing the music industry for relegating such music to B-side status. The song boasts the most adventurous vocal processing on the album, with postproduction techniques to create drier vocal effects for Chuck D, as well as vocal hiccups, pitch-modified doubling, and lots of reverb. "War at 33 1/3" references Chuck D's attendance at Farrakhan's California rally, noting that it was the event that "woke" him and caused him to challenge current political discourse. Positioned between this and "Fight the Power" is the brief instrumental interlude, "Final Count of the Collision between Us and the Damned," which segues into "Fight the Power," a call to subversive action through unity. Chuck D's updating of the Isley Brothers' 1975 song of the same name, "Fight the Power" begins with media samples of Martin Luther King Jr., which then transitions into a bass-heavy funk beat wherein Chuck D advocates for awareness, knowledge, and freedom of speech, the only tools that can fight the powers of government-authorized racism that have kept the black community down for four hundred years.

Both "Fight the Power" and *Fear of a Black Planet* were nominated for a Grammy Award. *Fear of a Black Planet* reached No. 10 on the Billboard 200 and was ranked number 300 on *Rolling Stone*'s list of the five hundred greatest albums. *NME* (New Musical Express) named it the ninety-sixth best record ever, and the Library of Congress has added it to the National Recording Registry for its cultural significance. *Fear of a Black Planet*'s success with critics and consumers (especially white audiences) was a significant factor to hip hop's mainstream emergence, and black consciousness became the prevalent theme of rap. Public Enemy has continued to record albums into the 21st century, working closely with the Bomb Squad while increasing the use of rock-based and acoustic instruments. In 2016, Chuck D announced that he and other members of Public Enemy would be teaming up with members of Rage Against the Machine and Cypress Hill to form a hip hop supergroup called Prophets of Rage, a name based on a single from Public Enemy's *It Takes a Nation of Millions to Hold Us Back*.

QUEEN LATIFAH: "U.N.I.T.Y." (SEE SALT-N-PEPA AND QUEEN LATIFAH)

RUN-D.M.C.: *RAISING HELL* (PROFILE RECORDS, 1986)

Run-D.M.C. (1981–2002), a trio consisting of rapper Run (Joseph Simmons, 1964–), childhood friend D.M.C. (Darryl Matthews McDaniel, 1964–), and legendary turntablist Jam Master Jay (Jason William Mizell, 1965–2002), was an extremely successful early Queens-based (from the

Hollis neighborhood) rap group. The trio achieved many hip hop and rap firsts: the first gold record, the first platinum record, the first multiplatinum record, the first Grammy nomination, the first hip hop group to have its music videos played on MTV, and the first to have its image appear on the cover of *Rolling Stone*. Following Bronx-based pioneer rap group Grandmaster Flash and the Furious Five (1976–88), Run-D.M.C. is the second rap group to be inducted into the Rock & Roll Hall of Fame.

Run-D.M.C.'s first single, "It's Like That (Sucker MCs)," was released in 1983 on Profile Records and reached No. 15 on the R&B/Hip Hop Songs chart. The trio released a self-titled debut album on the same label in 1984 and achieved modest success, with singles including "Rock Box" and "Jam Master Jay." Its next two Profile albums, *King of Rock* (1985) and *Raising Hell* (1986) both went platinum. The triple-platinum *Raising Hell* was produced by Def Jam Recording's Rick Rubin and Russell Simmons. Run was the younger brother of Simmons. The album reached No. 3 on the Billboard 200 and No. 1 on the Top R&B/Hip Hop Albums chart. Four of its singles hit the Hot R&B/Hip Hop/Rap Songs chart: "My Adidas" (No. 5), "Walk This Way" (No. 8), "You Be Illin'" (No. 12), and "It's Tricky" (No. 21). "Walk This Way" hit the Billboard Hot 100 Top Ten, peaking at No. 4, while "You Be Illin'" and "It's Tricky" also charted on the Billboard Hot 100.

Run-D.M.C.'s style can best be described as socially conscious lyrics set against a hard rock–infused beat and Jam Master Jay's trademark sound—sampled and manipulated guitar riffs. It is exemplified on *Raising Hell*, which was distributed by Def Jam; the album marked the trio's breakthrough into the mainstream. On a larger scale, it redefined the possibility of commercial success for rap groups (some rap albums were already being considered critical successes). "Walk This Way," a rap version of the Aerosmith song, featured Aerosmith lead singer Steven Tyler (Steven Victor Tallarico, 1948–) and lead guitarist Joe Perry (Anthony Joseph Perry, 1950–) and was the first rap song to crack the Top Five of the Billboard Hot 100. In 2018, it was selected for preservation in the National Recording Registry by the Library of Congress for its cultural, historical, and/or artistic significance.

Raising Hell begins modestly with the semi-comic skills braggadocio "Peter Piper." The song begins as an a cappella tongue twister nursery rhyme rap interchange between Run and D.M.C. As the rap transitions from lines out of "Peter Piper," "Humpty Dumpty," and "Jack Be Nimble" to those of "Little Bo Peep," turntable and metallic Latin percussion enter into the mix, accompanied by a bass kick—and subsequent nursery rhymes are revised to compare their characters (and creators) to Jam

Master Jay, whose creative output dwarfs theirs. After the first verse, an extended instrumental interlude that includes distorted guitar sounds and distorted sound bites showcases Jam Master Jay's technique. The second through fourth verses continue the trio's brag: They are going to rock the house, courtesy of Jam Master Jay's brilliance.

The next three songs make up three of the four album's hits. The rock-oriented "It's Tricky" (a song about such perils of hip hop fame such as groupies following the band everywhere, a complete lack of privacy, women being gold diggers, and people mistaking the band for drug dealers) begins with a cabasa and shaker beat and accentuated booming electric bass notes, creating an intro that foreshadows what is to come—a heavy drum kit (emphasis on the snare), more booming bass, and a distorted electric guitar melody, reminiscent of the Knack's 1979 hit "My Sharona." Some phrases end with the bass and guitar tag from the Knack hit. Against this hard rock instrumentation Run and D.M.C. rap to a modified melodic version of Toni Basil's 1982 hit "Mickey." The lyrics are concerned with the difficulties of rapping, showcasing the two MCs' skill at handing off lines and phrases to one another while staying on beat. "My Adidas" is an old-school pseudo-entourage rap, with the shoes serving the purpose of the usual entourage. Its rapping—Run and D.M.C. alternating verses—is set against heavy bass kick, snare, guitar, electric bass, and synthesizer power chord stingers (some of which sound like a distorted brass voice). The song's lyrics chronicle all of the adventures that Run and D.M.C. have had, from tours (Live Aid) to bar fights, travels in different countries, playing basketball, feeling at home in an upscale part of California, and planning a movie career. The shoes are merely a vehicle through which to tell the trio's story.

"Walk This Way," the album's second longest song at 5:11 ("Raising Hell" comes in at 5:31), begins with Aerosmith's original ride cymbal, snare, and tom intro, which Jam Master Jay extends and turns into a bass kick, snare, and ride cymbal beat to make it more dramatic and danceable (he also seems to have raised the EQ [Equalization] limiter to increase each instrumentation's loudness and clarity). The first verse of the song is a faithful cover of Aerosmith (with some added cymbal), with Run and D.M.C. rapping lines. The refrain brings in Aerosmith's Tyler, who simply recreates the refrain of the original song. Verse two, though still a cover, takes the instrumentation in a new direction—toward a typical rap beat, featuring turntable, snare, ride cymbal, bass kick, and occasional guitar, as Run, D.M.C., and Tyler all rap. Verse three returns the song into the realm of rock, with all three now singing. The refrain then returns, with Tyler's singing against original Aerosmith instrumentation, which has seemingly been remastered. The song's outro is Perry's faithful rendition of the original guitar riff, though he is eventually joined briefly by Jam Master Jay's distorted guitars.

The album's other skills-bragging songs include "Is It Live," "Perfection," and "Hit It Run." "Is It Live" features both Run and D.M.C. rapping simultaneously in its intro. The first verse, rapped by Run, has a good bit of interior rhyme, which is atypical of early old-school rap. The song stands out for its Latin percussion (timbales with cowbell) and synthesizer stingers. "Perfection" sounds very much like a Beastie Boys song, as it involves both rappers rapping against a heavy kick, snare, and ride cymbal beat, often taking turns with lines and phrases and accentuating each other's lines with vocal tags. "Hit It Run," which makes an implied claim that rap music is a subgenre of rock (Run refers to himself as the "king of rock" and to the band's music as "gangsta hard rock nonstop hip hop"), features stop time between verses for dramatic buildup, vocal reverb (extremely heavy in the intro), synthesizer power chords, and a heavy kick and snare beat, as well as Jam Master Jay's turntablism and beatboxing (heard only here and in the thirty-second interlude track, "Son of Byford"). "Raising Hell" features the album's best alliteration usage in its lyrics, which play on the idea of hell, heat, and smoke to establish that Run-D.M.C. is hot. Serving as the band's introduction song (the rap identified each member, like a band callout during a live concert), the song features not only turntablism but Jam Master Jay–produced heavy metal guitars, including guitar solos (similar to Beastie Boys and AC/DC) set against a kick and snare beat with occasional cymbal crashes.

The album's most comic song is "You Be Illin'." Placed toward the end of the album, its lyrics narrate four stories of people so stoned or drunk that they do ridiculous things, and it samples Kurtis Blow and Run-D.M.C. Although its beat is less interesting than those of other songs on the album, its use of turntablism, horns, distorted piano chords, and crowd noises add points of interest, turning what seems like a throwaway track into a bona fide potential hit. It stands in contrast to the album's other comic song (and the album's weakest), "Dumb Girl," a diss song about gold diggers and "hoes" (alternately), women who uses sex to either get close to men with money or because they have no self-control. Instrumentation features a monotonous kick and snare beat (with sub-bass). The album's final track, "Proud to Be Black," is its sole sociopolitical track—and by far its angriest song. Against a simple kick and snare beat set against synthesizer stingers (with occasional turntablism and 808 drum), Run and D.M.C. rap about the problems of racism and discrimination while referencing African American heroes like Harriet Tubman, Martin Luther King Jr., Malcolm X, George Washington Carver, Jesse Owens, and Muhammad Ali.

For Run-D.M.C.'s fourth album, *Tougher than Leather* (Profile, 1988), Jam Master Jay introduced a greater variety of sample sources, including funk and soul; more skills-based internal and polysyllabic rhymes were added to the raps. The 1990 new jack swing–influenced album on Profile, *Back from Hell*, did not do well, indicating that the trio might be in decline. The next album, *Down with the King* (Profile, 1993), returned to the earlier sounds of *Tougher than Leather*, and some of the album's lyrics subtly reflected the newfound religious values that both of the group's rappers had adopted. The band's final studio album, *Crown Royal* (Arista, 2001), featured D.M.C. on only three of its tracks as he was in the process of leaving the band. Run-D.M.C. was considering dissolving entirely when Jam Master Jay was murdered at his recording studio in Queens in 2002. This prompted Run and D.M.C. to formally disband the group and retire its name.

SALT-N-PEPA AND QUEEN LATIFAH: "AIN'T NUTHIN' BUT A SHE THING" AND "U.N.I.T.Y." (SINGLE RELEASE ONLY, LONDON RECORDS, 1995, AND *BLACK REIGN*, MOTOWN, 1993)

Like the music industry in general, rap music has traditionally been a male phenomenon, open usually to women who choose to become video vixens, using sexuality and body image to sell their music. The two notable early exceptions to this rule were Salt-N-Pepa (1985–2002; 2007–) and Queen Latifah (Dana Elaine Owens, 1970–), female-powered rap acts out of Queens, New York City, and Newark, New Jersey, respectively. A trio, Salt-N-Pepa was composed of rappers Salt (Cheryl James, 1964–) and Pepa (Sandra Denton, 1964–) and DJ Spinderella (Deidra Muriel Roper, 1971–). The three became the first all-female rap group to achieve both commercial and critical success.

Salt-N-Pepa enjoyed only moderate success until San Francisco radio DJ and music engineer Cameron Paul remixed "Push It" (1987). The remix was the trio's breakthrough song, even though it was originally released as a B-side to "Tramp" (1987). It reached No. 19 on the Billboard Hot 100 and was later added to new pressings of Salt-N-Pepa's debut album, *Hot, Cool, Vicious* (Next Plateau Records, 1986). The single's success helped *Hot, Cool, Vicious* sell over one million copies—making it the first album by a female rap artist (solo or group) to achieve both RIAA certified gold and platinum status. Although it did not have the same commercial success, reaching only No. 38 on the Billboard Hot 100, the trio's best expression of feminism was "Ain't Nuthin' but a She Thing" (perhaps a play on Dr. Dre's "Nuthin' but a 'G' Thang"), released in 1995 as a non-album single.

"Ain't Nuthin' but a She Thing" challenges the notion of "a man's world," threatening that women will unify and do away with the sugar and spice expectations that patriarchy has imposed. The song begins with a call and response section that establishes the song's feminist overtones via chanted lines that threaten to turn patriarchy upside down, with the response of "you go girl" establishing the idea of unity among women—this leads to the song's chorus/hook, which uses talk-singing rather than rap. The hook is an empowering statement that a woman (especially a minority woman) can be anything she wants to be (which includes being sexy, as the song's official video makes clear) and her strength comes from within. Instrumentation includes a rock-based dance drum beat, electric bass played mainly on the E string near the first and third frets (giving it almost a sub-bass sound), and a synthesized, highly reverbed siku (pan flute) sound.

The song's rapped sections, by both Salt (verses one and three) and Pepa (verses two and four), satirize various clichés to argue that a woman can have interests that are both traditionally feminine and masculine: she can enjoy cooking, pleasing a man sexually, and keeping a good household, but she can also be professional, hardworking, and goal-oriented. The verses also challenge the hurdles placed before professional women: lack of respect, lack of equal pay, not being recognized for their intellects, and hitting the glass ceiling when it comes to advancement. The lyrics also decry the ideas that women are sex objects and that aggressive and assertive women are referred to as "b—" and "witches." Lyrics in the first verse also note that although men call women the weaker sex, women handle painful experiences like childbirth, which no man would survive. The second verse argues that women can be both sensitive and rough, wise and intelligent, family-oriented yet self-sufficient—in a word, complicated. They can not only dream but also they can realize their dreams. The third verse is a shout-out to strong women who take control of their lives, righting wrongs in the process; it is aimed particularly at mothers, pointing out that they determine the future of the nation. The fourth and final verse is the song's strongest statement of feminism. It stops just short of stating that women have advantages over men due to their biological makeup, but it does remind women in no uncertain terms that they are as capable as men and, as a group, have come a long way over the course of history; they must keep moving forward so that future generations can benefit from feminism. The rapped lines are accentuated by either the call and response chanters, who reference James Brown's "Say It Loud (I'm Black and I'm Proud"), or by singing.

Also a feminist statement, Queen Latifah's "U.N.I.T.Y" challenges both African American men and women to rethink how language (name-calling) is an element of misogyny. Queen Latifah, an early Afrocentric and feminist rapper, successfully transitioned to acting, modeling, and producing, ultimately making her name a household word. Her first album, *All Hail the Queen* (BCM Records, 1989) showed that she, unlike early female rappers such as Lil' Kim and Roxanne Shanté, would not allow herself to be used as a sexual object. Rather than short skirts and tight shorts or g-strings, she wore athletic or sophisticated professional-looking clothing, and she insisted on maintaining artistic and financial control of her music. Ultimately, she founded her own label and management company, Flavor Unit Entertainment, in 1995.

Queen Latifah is known for her clear contralto or first alto range vocals, as well as her enunciation and intonation. Her songs are R&B influenced, often with liberal use of brass. *All Hail the Queen* produced three Hot Rap chart hits, "Dance for Me," "Ladies First," and "Come into My House," and she was to repeat this feat with the Motown-released album *Black Reign* (1993), with the songs "Just Another Day," "Blackhand Side," and "U.N.I.T.Y." The last became her biggest hit, reaching No. 23 on the Billboard Hot 100 and No. 2 on the Hot Rap chart. It won the 1995 Grammy for Best Rap Solo Performance. The song attacked the disrespect of women through harassment and domestic violence, as well as through name-calling and misogynist slurs in hip hop culture. Radio and TV stations decided not to censor it, despite the words "b—" and "ho." The song, which includes an immediately introduced Jamaican-style refrain/hook, begins with Queen Latifah's singing (with conventional Jamaican effects such as a Rastafarian accent and vocal reverb) the letters that spell the word "unity" and expressing the need for love and respect between black men and black women, which includes the need for men to stop referring to black women as b— or hoes. Although the song's rapped sections are angry and at times threatening, the music is down-tempo R&B and soul-inspired, with its main instrumentation being cool jazz–inspired saxophone, set against a soulful electric bass riff, along with a simple rock-based drum beat that consists mostly of snare, hi-hat, and ride cymbal.

The song's rapped lyrics establish early the reason for the juxtaposition of its angry lyrics against the laid-back music: whenever Queen Latifah hears a man use misogynistic slurs to describe a woman, instinct kicks in, and her blood boils because she understands that men use such slurs to wear down women's self-esteem and self-respect. The song instructs such men that their behavior has to change—unless name-calling is done in a playful manner where both participants understand and accept that they are joking with one another. Otherwise name-calling will incur her wrath. She then tells a story of how she was physically accosted on the street by a stranger simply because she was wearing shorts on a hot day; she ends up giving him a black eye. The next verse begins with her expressing some regret for turning violent, but she does add that next time a man tries to touch her without her permission, she will have him arrested. The narrative then switches to an abusive relationship she endured because of a lack of self-esteem, which she ended when she realized that her children would witness both the verbal and physical abuse. Verse three is addressed to young women who allow themselves to become the b— and hoes of local gangs, thinking that they will build themselves up by being tough and mean. She calls them wannabes, pointing out that all they are inviting is inevitable violence against themselves.

Salt-N-Pepa released four more albums, *A Salt with a Deadly Pepa* (Next Plateau-FFRR, 1988), *Blacks' Magic* (Next Plateau, 1990), *Very Necessary* (FFRR, 1993), and *Brand New* (London Records-Red Ant, 1997), with *Very Necessary* producing the Hot 100 Top Ten hits "Shoop" and "Whatta Man," as well as the Grammy-winning "None of Your Business" (making Salt-N-Pepa the first female hip hop artists ever to win a Grammy). *Brand New* was released on the trio's own Red Ant imprint. Salt-N-Pepa also starred in its own reality television show, *The Salt-N-Pepa Show* (2007–08). The trio formally disbanded in 2002, but they have continued to perform together since 2007 at live events, such as the 2008 BET Hip Hop Awards and in 2012 when they opened for Public Enemy during the Martin Luther King Jr. Concert Series. Queen Latifah's later albums, *Order in the Court* (Motown, 1998), *The Dana Owens Album* (A&M Records, 2004), and *Trav'lin' Light* (Verve, 2007), ranged from rap to pop and jazz standards, and she established herself as a serious actor in both television and film. For her role as Matron Mama Morton in *Chicago* (2002), she was nominated for an Oscar as Best Actress in a Supporting Role. In 2006, she became the first hip hop artist to be awarded a star on the Hollywood Walk of Fame.

GIL SCOTT-HERON AND ACEYALONE: "THE REVOLUTION WILL NOT BE TELEVISED" AND "THE GUIDELINES" (*THE REVOLUTION WILL NOT BE TELEVISED*, FLYING DUTCHMAN, 1974, AND *A BOOK OF HUMAN LANGUAGE*, PROJECT BLOWED, 1997, 1998)

Los Angeles–based spoken-word artist, poet, and rapper Aceyalone (Edwin Maximilian Hayes Jr., 1970–) and Chicago native Gil Scott-Heron (Gilbert Scott-Heron, 1949–2011) are both known for their alternative/experimental rap music, as well as their use of variant forms of music, most notably jazz. Scott-Heron, nicknamed the "godfather of rap" and the "Black Bob Dylan," was an influential jazz-poet, spoken-word recording artist, and proto-rapper best known for his spoken-word recordings of the 1970s and 1980s. Scott-Heron is the precursor of jazz and alternative rappers and of socially conscious rap, which fuses sociopolitical and self-actualization lyrical concerns with percussive beats, jazz, soul, and blues. Aceyalone was influential in the 1990s alternative-rap scene, which positioned itself against the more popular West Coast gangsta rap scene. Opting for intimate venues like cafés, workshops, and sidewalks, his live performances focused on lyrics of aspiration and philosophy, his songs approaching the nerdcore style, as in "The Guidelines" (*A Book of Human Language*, 1998) or "Five Feet" (*Accepted Eclectic*, 2001), both on the Project Blowed label and both of which use scientific metaphors and are cleverly self-referential.

Scott-Heron grew up in the Bronx until his parents' separation when he was a teen, at which time he was sent to live with his maternal grandmother in Jackson, Tennessee (his autobiography informs his final studio album before his death, *I'm New Here* [XL Recordings, 2010]). Scott-Heron attended Lincoln University in Pennsylvania, where he met flutist and keyboardist Brian Jackson (1952–), with whom he began a lifelong musical collaboration, first forming their own band, Black and Blues, modeled after the Last Poets. The duo's later track, "The Revolution Will Not Be Televised," achieved iconographic status and was released by the Flying Dutchman label on *Small Talk at 125th and Lenox* (1970), an album on which Scott-Heron was billed as "a new black poet" (in this version he read against sparse accompaniment on conga and percussion). It was reissued on other Flying Dutman recordings, *Pieces of Man* (1971) and on *The Revolution Will Not Be Televised* (1974). With these two versions, produced by Bob Thiele (1922–96), the spoken word against funk and jazz instrumentation laid further groundwork for rap music. In addition, Scott-Heron's albums *The Revolution Will Not Be*

Televised and *Winter in America-Summer in Europe* (Pickwick, 2004) inspired socially conscious rappers such as Chuck D, KRS-One, and Talib Kweli.

"The Revolution Will Not Be Televised" is three minutes of fast-paced references to the differences between white culture, which is represented by the media, and black culture, which is represented as victimized by white culture and the media. Thiele, a jazz producer whose claim to fame was cowriting Louis Armstrong's "What a Wonderful World" (1967) with George David Weiss, went for a jazzy, upbeat atmosphere musically, which acts as a nice juxtaposition for the lyrical references to discrimination and racism. Throughout the track, Scott-Heron enumerates mainstays of white culture, such as people (Richard Nixon, John Mitchell, Spiro Agnew, Natalie Wood, Steve McQueen, Jackie Onassis, Francis Scott Key, Glen Campbell, Tom Jones, Johnny Cash, and Engelbert Humperdinck), products (Dove soap and Coca-Cola), and television series (*Green Acres*, *The Beverly Hillbillies*, *Petticoat Junction*, and *Search for Tomorrow*). At one point he undercuts this ubiquitousness of whiteness when he says, "The revolution will not be right back after a message about a white tornado, white lightning, or white people." The whitewashing of culture is contrast to images of black culture—it is a culture that has been appropriated by whites for economic gain (e.g., hog maws "confiscated" from Harlem and Willie Mays starring in a dumb TV commercial). It is also a culture of disenfranchisement, with Whitney Young and Roy Wilkins being run out of Harlem and being made ridiculous, respectively. The point of the track is to move the black community to see that the white community does not have its back, and to therefore actively protest and revolt.

In the full band version, the song begins with a jazz-funk drum beat. A tom-based vamp introduces a heavy funk octave-based bass four-note ostinato and then the main drum beat, a jazzy snare, hi-hat, and ride cymbal 4/4 beat that accompanies the bass, and a jazz flute melody. As the verses progress, the flute fades in and out, often accentuating the end of lyrical lines with either a single note, a flurry of a few notes, or a phrase from the main flute melody. The first vocal heard is Scott-Heron's raised voice declaring to the black community "you will not" (followed by everyday events it will not be able to partake in because it will be disrupted by the revolution). This is the first of various repetitive phrases that Scott-Heron uses throughout the spoken-word poem to give it a beat poetry feel, a la Allen Ginsberg. In the second verse, the bass moves to a different key (the root note now on a lower string), now deeper and more resonant—this pattern continues into verse three as the drum kit beat and flute melody remain constant. On the fourth verse, the bass suddenly does a flourish and changes its ostinato, becoming more complex—this is the verse that mentions Willie Mays's "sell-out" to commercial TV; the verse ends on a bass flourish that leads back into the complex bass ostinato, but with slight variations (based in the original four-note ostinato) for the fourth and fifth verses. Here the lyrics for the first time mention violence, and although the drums and flute remain consistent, the bass begins to improvise into four, five, six, and seven-note ostinatos, giving the song a sense of entropy, as if it can fall apart at any time. As the song progresses, the bass changes its root note to higher pitches, lower pitches, and again higher pitches. As the song ends, both the drum and bass flourish and crescendo as the energy builds into the final line, "the revolution will be live."

Aceyalone grew up with future rapper and producer Myka 9 (Michael Troy, 1969–). While in high school in the late 1980s, the two formed the short-lived MC Aces with rapper Self Jupiter (Ornette Glenn, 1970–); the ensemble was a precursor to their Freestyle Fellowship at open-mic nights at the Good Life Café, a health-food store and restaurant in South Central Los Angeles. Freestyle Fellowship added former high school friend, rapper, and musician P.E.A.C.E. (Mtulazaji Davis, n.d.). The band rapped over jazz, sometimes incorporated R&B and funk, and honed its skills at double-time rapping—rhyming to a slower beat to accommodate multisyllabic words and/or longer lines. In 1994, Aceyalone and rapper Abstract Rude (Aaron Pointer, n.d.) began the open-mic workshop Project Blowed and its related hip hop collective as an alternative to gang and drug activity. Aceyalone had a concurrent prolific solo recording career with his studio albums.

Although "The Guidelines" (also released as an EP: "Faces"/"Guidelines 94"/"Fortitude") is a skills braggadocio, it begins with an offering of peace, "Asalaam Alaikum" (Aceyalone is a Five Percenter). Unlike many brag raps, the lyrics never threaten others with bodily injury or annihilation; rather, they simply establish that Aceyalone's skills are going to redefine rap music and save it from the commercialization that has turned too many rappers into rats running through a maze. Aceyalone's verbal skills are indeed impressive: he manages a stream of consciousness flow filled with interior rhyme, assonance, alliteration, and free association of ideas, as well as wordplay and puns (such as telling would-be imitators they "can try-any-angle," but he'll be "octa-gone in the wind").

Like the entirety of *A Book of Human Language*, "The Guidelines" was produced by Mumbles (Matthew Fowler, 1975–), a producer who would become Aceyalone's working partner for the entire album. In 1994, Mumbles met Aceyalone, and they recorded three tracks for the album *All Balls Don't Bounce* (Capitol, 1995), which led to their full album collaboration. Mumbles came from a jazz family, as his father Steve Fowler and his uncles Bruce, Tom, Walt, and Ed had formed the Fowler Brothers in the 1970s, a band that would go on to play with Frank Zappa and the Mothers of Invention, Bobby McFerrin, Ray Charles, and others. The familial effect on Mumbles's sense of production is a complexity of rhythm, melody, and harmony.

"The Guidelines" begins with a bass walk based on major thirds, accompanied only by a shaker. When Aceyalone's vocals appear, a conga and timbale beat is added. Midway through the first verse, a keyboard voice with a definite 1980s feel appears—it plays a glissando and ostinato combination that continues as he raps, with an ethereal female backing vocal soon adding a couple of notes to the end of the keyboard combination. This continues briefly, with the keyboard and backing vocals disappearing after a few phrases, leaving just the beat, until a distorted synth-based horn voice is introduced, offering a different counterpoint to the percussion-bass and/or just percussion beat. The keyboard-backing vocal combo appears briefly again, replacing the horn voice; it disappears and reappears as the song progresses. This instrumentation continues throughout the remainder of the song, even after the vocals end, with a brief time-stop fake ending. The song instead ends abruptly with a spoken one-sentence outro.

While in college, Scott-Heron took a hiatus to write two novels. Although he would never complete his bachelor's degree at Lincoln, he earned a creative writing master's degree from Johns Hopkins University in 1972. Scott-Heron's studio album *The Mind of Gil Scott-Heron* (1978) marked his move from Flying Dutchman to Arista Records. He eventually released several recordings that addressed the United States' role in apartheid in South Africa, criticizing how the United States was lacking in its handling of racial issues. His song "Message to the Messengers" mentors rappers on becoming teachers through music. In 2002, he appeared on West Coast alternative-rap group Blackalicious's (1994–) album *Blazing Arrow*, with MCA Records. Between 2001 and 2007, he was in and out of prison for drug possession. As of 2018, Scott-Heron's spoken-word recordings and songs have been sampled over three hundred times.

Most of Aceyalone's recordings have received critical acclaim. His solo albums *Accepted Eclectic* (2001), *Love and Hate* (2003), and *Magnificent City* (2006), all with Project Blowed, charted on Billboard's

Independent Albums at Nos. 36, 31, and 43, respectively. As part of the Freestyle Fellowship, which typically rapped over jazz, R&B, and funk, he was featured on the studio albums *To Whom It May Concern* (Sun Music, 1991) and *Innercity Griots* (4th and Broadway, 1993). The group continues to record as of 2018. Aceyalone's Project Blowed workshop hosts rap battle and open-mic events, freestyle rapping, slam poetry, alternative hip hop, and spoken-word art. Two compilation albums, *Project Blowed* (Afterlife Music, 1995) and *Project Blowed: 10th Anniversary* (Decon, 2005), resulted from these workshops.

SHAGGY: "ANGEL" AND "DON'T MAKE ME WAIT" (SEE LMFAO AND SHAGGY)

SNOOP DOGG

Whether he is known as Snoop Dogg, Snoop Doggy Dogg, or Snoop Lion, Calvin Cordozar Broadus Jr. (1971–) of Long Beach, California, is arguably one of the few performers who could be called the poster child of rap music. He is not only a prolific lyricist, but also he is a highly influential rap pioneer, later becoming a producer, actor, television personality, and entrepreneur. His output includes fifteen studio albums and twenty mixtapes. His albums have all charted on the Billboard 200, including the Top Ten Priority released *No Limit Top Dogg* (1999), *Paid tha Cost to Be da Boss* (2002), and *Doggumentary* (2011), as well as Geffen released *R&G (Rhythm & Gangsta): The Masterpiece* (2004), *Tha Blue Carpet Treatment* (2006), and *Ego Trippin'* (2008). He has also had three No. 1 albums: *Doggystyle* (Death Row, 1993), *Tha Doggfather* (Death Row, 1996), and *Da Game Is to Be Sold* (No Limit, 1998). Seven of his albums reached platinum or multiplatinum status. Some of Snoop Dogg's singles have crossed over into mainstream popularity, namely "What's My Name?" and "Gin and Juice" (both 1993), "Still a G Thang" (1998), "Beautiful" (2003), "Drop It Like It's Hot" (2004), and "Sexual Eruption" (2007). He also formed the trio 213 (1990–2011) with his cousin Nate Dogg and his best friend, producer Warren G (Warren Griffin III, 1970–).

Despite his penchant for hypersexualized lyrics and his reputation for supporting pornographic content, Snoop Dogg is by most standards a mild-mannered rapper, and his post-rap career as a media personality is nothing short of family friendly (e.g., he did comic skits for the National Hockey League in 2018–19). His interest in music began when he sang and played piano in church. Unfortunately, he also got involved in the

Eastside Rollin' 20 Crips, and he served time for cocaine possession in the early 1990s. Once out, his freestyle skills caught the attention of Dr. Dre and Death Row Records, which he signed with in 1992. He showed great potential in rhyming, lyrics, and flow, his delivery being a smooth, laid-back vocal style that always bordered on singing in his low tenor range. Dr. Dre and the D.O.C. (a.k.a. Doc T) worked with then Snoop Doggy Dogg on lyrical and musical structure, forming hooks and choruses, and creating theme-based verses. Snoop Dogg became one of the pioneers of West Coast g-funk, creating Tha Dogg Pound (1992–2002; 2005–), which included Kurupt and Daz N— Daz (a.k.a. Daz Dillinger).

His debut album, *Doggystyle*, often considered a companion album to Dr. Dre's *The Chronic* (1992), is a West Coast g-funk classic that sold 806,000 copies in its first week alone and eventually sold over eleven million copies worldwide. Featuring Tha Dogg Pound, RBX, the Lady of Rage, and Nanci Fletcher (n.d.), the album is famous for its extreme lyrics about gang violence, black-on-black crime, marijuana, sex, and the lure of the gangsta life, as well as the marks of Dr. Dre's producing: an amalgamation of background singers and rappers, quirky samples, and horror-themed keyboard progressions. Its opening skit establishes Snoop's character immediately, a laid-back drug dealer—albeit one who is considering calling it quits—enjoying a hot tub with a sexy woman. The album's songs are funk-heavy, with various guest rappers whose aggressive deliveries complement Snoop Doggy Dogg's relaxed, nasal vocals, filled with idiosyncratic pauses. Album standouts include "Gin and Juice," which features neo-soul-sung refrains and creative autotuning; "Lodi Dodi," a revision/homage/parody of Doug E. Fresh and the Get Fresh Crew's "La Di Da Di" (1985) that replaces original lyrics with drug references and features sampling of A Taste of Honey's "Sukiyaki" (1980), as well as keyboard-based sine waves, vibraslap, and funk bass; and the 1970s R&B–based and George Clinton–influenced p-funk upbeat anthem "Who Am I (What's My Name)?" The instrumental standout is "Serial Killa," which features wonderful instrumentation: bass, snare drum, organ, and a sine wave voice synth ostinato, all set against four different types of laid-back and aggressive vocal modification.

Toward the end of recording *Doggystyle*, Snoop Doggy Dogg—who underwent his first name change to Snoop Dogg—was arrested in 1993 for his connection to the murder of a rival gang member. Defended by Johnnie Cochran, he was acquitted. Dr. Dre and Snoop Dogg eventually left Death Row because of Suge Knight's public feuding with hip hop artists like Luke and Puff Daddy, and Snoop signed with No Limit Records, which ultimately enabled him to launch his own label, Doggy

Style Records, in 1995. Meanwhile, Death Row continued to release some of Snoop Dogg's previously unreleased work into the 2000s (in 2012 Snoop Dogg, a member of the Nation of Islam, announced a name change to Snoop Lion and a new career as a reggae artist after a trip to Jamaica).

Upon its release in 1996, *Tha Doggfather* debuted at No. 1. It did not involve Dr. Dre, but was an attempt at keeping the g-funk sound, and it was the debut of Snoop Dogg as a producer, with the track "(O.J.) Wake Up." The album's lyrics are much less violent and controversial, as Snoop Dogg was trying to create a more positive image for himself. Most of his raps are about his lyrical skill. It stands in sharp contrast to *Doggystyle* instrumentally, opening with strings set against media sound bites concerned with Snoop's murder trial. Its opening song, "Tha Doggfather," uses electronic drums (in a high treble range) and two different synthesizer voices (one playing a sine wave pattern). His mixing foregrounds the beat, rather than vocals, which throughout the album are more processed than on *Doggystyle*. Other production differences include less p-funk but more looped beats, industrial sounds, backing vocalizations, and use of baritone and electric guitar, arp, and whistles. Overall, it is more polished than *Doggystyle*, though it lacks its ingenuity.

Snoop's first No Limit recording, *Da Game Is to Be Sold* (1998), features instrumentation such as flute, rock bass, toy piano keyboard voices, 808 drum hiccups, power chords, congas and other Latin percussions, scratching, chopper rapping (from guest rappers), vocalizations that prefigure Missy Elliott and Timbaland's cartoon sounds, and vocals that are backgrounded and heavily processed for echo, delay, and reverb effects. Unfortunately, one side effect is that Snoop Dogg's smooth rapping voice is lost in all the experimental production. His mid-career effort, *Tha Blue Carpet Treatment* (on major label Geffen Records), featured Dr. Dre, the Neptunes, and Timbaland, among others, and it resurrected his early g-funk days, with better (and likely more expensive) production values. He returned to his laid-back delivery, with elongated pauses and sexual and drug (marijuana) themes, adding more skilled rhyming techniques such as interior rhyme and repeated rhymes (sometimes four or five words consecutively). He also returned to more sung refrains and interludes, which reintroduced a neo-soul sound into his music. New instrumentation included experimental percussion, a liberal use of strings, interspersed classical guitar, drum kits with a heavier bass kick, accordion and bell-like keyboard voices, and R&B sung vocals.

In his later recordings, he changed his sound when he became Snoop Lion. His 2013 album *Reincarnated* (on the Berhane Sound System label) showed a new side, as philosophical considerations on death, impermanence, and societal responsibility found their way into his lyrics, and reggae and Jamaican toast influences found their way into his songs. Here his vocal style is even more laid-back, with heavy doubling and reverb. The album's opening song, "Rebel Way," which features sung refrains, snaps, and heavy electric guitar, is one of his best tracks. "Get Away" stands out for its use of pentatonic scale-based ostinato (an Oriental melody) on keyboard and taiko drums. The album also contains liberal use of children's vocals. His 2015 album, *Bush*, featured guest appearances by Kendrick Lamar, Stevie Wonder, Charlie Wilson, Gwen Stefani, T.I., and Rick Ross. Produced by the Neptunes (1992–) and released on his label, Doggystyle Records, it returned to Snoop's days of neo-soul-inspired hip hop. Here he experiments with snap ("California Roll"), disco funk ("This City" and "Awake"), 1970s R&B funk ("R U a Freak"), p-funk ("Peaches N Cream"), jazz-influenced Dirty South ("Edibles"), and the rock musical–inspired "Run Away" (featuring Gwen Stefani). His Doggystyle 2017 album *Neva Left*, which featured guest vocalists Redman, Method Man, B-Real, KRS-One, Charlie Wilson, and Wiz Khalifa, was his challenge to critics who stated that he had lost his street cred and edge. It shows a return to g-funk, albeit with high production values and instrumentation that includes grand piano, brass, synthesized snaps and reverberated claps, and jazz drumming, as in "Neva Left" and "Moment I Feared." Heavy kick drum and sub-bass set against ride cymbals inform the polyrhythmic "Bacc in da Days," which has an energetic Dirty South feel, while 808 drums, synthetic bass, and cowbell make "Promise You This" stand out as one of the album's most engaging songs. Others include "Big Mouth," which features drums and percussion—and an aggressive refrain—that just about jump out at the listener, and "420 (Blaze Up)," which invokes the music of De La Soul, featuring psychedelic synthesized guitar phrasing, down-tempo drumming, and backing vocals that use a swirl and/or delay effect.

Snoop Dogg often tours and supports other hip hop artists, such as Slick Rick, Pharrell, and Thaitanium. His concert appearances and recordings are a combination of previously written and memorized rap and freestyle lyrics. He works to form a rapport with his audience through simply talking and improvising, often incorporating audience members' involvement in performance. In 2009, Priority Records appointed Snoop Dogg as creative chairman of Priority Records. In 2007, he had been certified for medical marijuana and since has advocated its use, becoming an investor in the California-based medical marijuana delivery business Eaze in 2015.

THE SUGARHILL GANG AND BLONDIE: "RAPPER'S DELIGHT" AND "RAPTURE"
(*THE SUGARHILL GANG*, SUGAR HILL RECORDS, 1979, AND *AUTOAMERICAN*, CHRYSALIS, 1990)

When New Yorker Sylvia Robinson (née Vanderpool, 1936–2011) was recording under the name Little Sylvia and later as half of the R&B duo Mickey & Sylvia (1956–61), she could not possibly know that in 1979 she would change the face of popular music forever. But in that year she became co-owner and CEO of her second record label, Sugar Hill Records (following the dissipation of All Platinum, which was formed in 1967). Her vision of Sugar Hill was to make it the first recording label to specialize in hip hop music and the first label to produce a rap hit, which became "Rapper's Delight" (1979), a fifteen-minute-long (on the 12-inch recording) single, also released as a seven-minute radio version and a five-minute album version. She accomplished this feat by single-handedly creating the disco-flavored rap group the Sugarhill Gang (1979–85, 1994–), also known as the Original Sugarhill Gang. What began as a modest attempt to introduce rap to a mainstream niche audience became a single that made hip hop music popular worldwide and caused notable old-school hip hop pioneers such as Crash Crew (1977–), Funky 4 + 1 (1977–83), Grandmaster Flash and the Furious Five (1976–82), the Sequence (1979–85), Treacherous Three (1978–84), and the West Street Mob (1981–84) to sign to her label.

Robinson created the Sugarhill Gang after she heard Harlem World nightclub MC Lovebug Starski rapping during instrumental breaks. She immediately began searching for a rapper for the label, and that is when she heard pizzeria manager Big Bank Hank (Henry Jackson, 1958–2014) rapping over a PA system while working; she hired him and teamed him with a high school student known as Master Gee (Guy O'Brien, 1963–) and a flower salesman known as Wonder Mike (Michael Anthony Wright, 1956–). The trio's sound in "Rapper's Delight" can best be described as danceable funk-infused hip hop, featuring a heavy beat accentuated by claps and a heavy bass, with constant rapping alternated by the three MCs. Singing occurs sparingly and tends to be singsong when it does, coming across as a conscious parody of itself. Robinson played bass, and samples of Chic's "Good Times" and "Here Comes That Sound Again" (both 1979) by British disco group Love De-Luxe, were used. Radio stations ignored the song until WESL in St. Louis, Missouri, picked it up. The eventual result was an eight-times platinum single that peaked at No. 36 on the Billboard 100 and charted in Canada, the Netherlands,

Austria, France, Germany, Norway, Sweden, Switzerland, and the United Kingdom.

The song opens with a Latin percussive rhythm set against piano power chords, which gives way to the first beat, created by heavy bass, cymbal, and claps. In the middle of the first verse, a second beat, informed by a sample of "Good Times," appears. The rest of the song alternates between these two beats as the rappers take turns rapping, with little vocal interaction other than to introduce each other. The song's lyric structure is a simple but breathless rap by all three MCs, with call and response vocalizations by Robinson (such as a high pitched "say what?" during Big Bank Hank's verses). Overall, it is a simple braggadocio song with lyrics that boast about the trio's ability to rap, its financial success (an early version of the concern with bling), and its ability to move people to dance.

The song begins with the first version of its refrain/hook, rapped by Wonder Mike, an alliterative collection of words chosen more for their sound than meaning (the refrain is actually absurdist). Wonder Mike introduces the band and himself with a "hello," promising to entertain and make listeners dance. Following Wonder Mike's highly articulated style of rapping, Big Bank Hank chimes in with the second verse, his voice more expressive and immediate/dramatic. His verse is an early example of a braggadocio about sexual prowess, talent, and money. He follows this with a second version of the song's hook, which introduces Master Gee, who raps the third verse in a style similar to Wonder Mike's, alternating between articulating words carefully in a slightly higher register and playfully pseudo-scatting. His verse is about making people, especially women, dance provocatively. Wonder Mike then takes over for verses four and five, with the initial version of the refrain as a bridge between them, and then hands off to Big Bank Hank (who actually scats). His verse is a long bragging rap about his lyrical and sexual skills that includes a narrative about meeting and seducing a female reporter (it turns out to be Lois Lane, who leaves Superman for him). Unfortunately the verse includes unnecessary insults toward gay men. Master Gee then relates his own narrative about seducing a woman through his rap skills, and this is followed by verse eight, Wonder Mike's diss of bad rap, in the form of a litany of unfulfilling items and events. Verse nine is rapped by Big Bank Hank and is a diss of MCs who steal other rappers' rhymes, while verse ten, rapped by Master Gee, is a continuation of verse eight. The song ends with the hook and a boast that the Sugarhill Gang is America's best rap crew, East or West.

Two years later, New York–based punk and new wave band Blondie (1974–82; 1997–) released "Rapture," the first song to prominently include rap and reach No. 1 on the Billboard Hot 100. The band had previous commercial success in the 1970s with No. 1 hits "Heart of Glass" (1979), "Call Me" (1980), and "The Tide Is High" (1981), but unlike contemporary punk bands, Blondie incorporated elements of reggae in their music, which also featured disco, synth-pop, rock, and funk. "Rapture," as its name suggests, incorporated rap. The 7-inch single was included on the album *Autoamerican* (1981), as was a slightly longer 12-inch version. The song is overall a laid-back, alternative disco track—but its lengthy B section is a full on rap. While rap was at the time typically associated with male performers, here it is performed by lead singer Debbie Harry (Angela Tremble, 1945–), whose rapping voice is lower than her airy, muted soprano singing voice. "Rapture" was significant not only because it was rap's first Billboard Hot 100 No. 1 hit but also because it was rapped by a white woman who was part of an all-white band.

Despite issues of white appropriation of black music, "Rapture" was lauded for its collaboration between the early New York punk and hip hop scenes, including prominent graffiti artists like Fab 5 Freddy and Lee Quiñones, as well as Jean-Michel Basquiat. The song also led to the first hip hop video on MTV. Like "Rapper's Delight," "Rapture" includes a narrative that takes an absurd turn wherein the rap's main character, the Man from Mars, invades Earth, where he eats cars, people, and ultimately guitars (which cues a guitar solo). The text is old-school, stressing end rhymes, but more importantly, it was innocuous enough for mainstream radio.

"Rapture" begins with a 4/4 moderate tempo drum beat, which is joined by a funk/disco bass and the sound of church bells ringing to match the scale Debbie Harry sings in an ethereal voice that elongates syllables. A saxophone and electric guitar are soon introduced. The song begins with lyrics about a dance club: a two-verse montage tells of people slow dancing and holding one another tightly, and then dancing to a faster beat, snapping their fingers, and doing the bump. This leads to the song's B section, a rap (also two verses): the rap immediately references Fab 5 Freddy and an unnamed turntablist, both of whom are enjoying a dance scene with many "fly" (hip or cool) people. Here the saxophone begins a funky ostinato, and reverbed claps can be heard, as well as Latin percussion (metal drumming or a timbale). The lyrics switch to an absurd narrative that follows clubbers into the parking lot as they end their night of dancing with their drive home. At this point the lyrics become unquestionably absurd, even ridiculous: one driver has an extraterrestrial encounter with "the man from Mars," who kills and eats his/her head. At this point, the viewpoint switches to that of the eaten human, who now sees through the Martian's eyes, as it begins eating cars, then bars (a reference back to the song's dance club), and once it discovers that if it eats too many things there will be no television, guitars (they become its sole diet). This is followed by a guitar solo set against the song's beat and the sax's higher registers (to create drama). What stands out as one listens to the song is how innocuous its rap section is—it doesn't deal with sexual prowess, bling, violence, or bragging rights, concerns that are the staple of rap. Rather, it can best be described as gimmicky. Whether this explains why it was acceptable to mainstream radio listeners is unclear.

Financial and legal issues led to the end of Sugar Hill Records in 1985, and Sylvia Robinson subsequently had to deal with litigation issues against Wonder Mike and Master Gee, as well as MCA Records over a distribution deal. In 1994, Rhino Records purchased Sugar Hill Records' masters. In 2011, Sylvia Robinson died at age seventy-six, but she became the basis of the television character Cookie Lyon on the television series *Empire*. Overall, the Sugarhill Gang recorded five studio albums between 1979 and 1999, but they were not commercially successful. Big Bank Hank died of cancer in 2014, the same year that the band was inducted into the Grammy Hall of Fame for "Rapper's Delight." The song was named to the National Recording Registry of the Library of Congress in 2011. "Rapture" has been sampled by the Jungle Brothers, KRS-One, Foxy Brown, and Destiny's Child. In 2014, Blondie rerecorded the song for their compilation album *Greatest Hits Deluxe Redux*, which celebrated the band's fortieth anniversary.

TECH N9NE: "WORLDWIDE CHOPPERS" (SEE BUSTA RHYMES AND TECH N9NE)

A TRIBE CALLED QUEST: *THE LOW END THEORY* (JIVE, 1991)

Hailing from Queens, New York, A Tribe Called Quest (ATCQ, 1985–) is known for being the most commercially successful member of the Native Tongues (1989–), a collective or group of bands and soloists who collaborated on each other's songs. Native Tongues included rap pioneers such as De La Soul, Jungle Brothers, Queen Latifah, and Afrika Bambaataa. ATCQ was composed of rapper and producer Q-Tip (Kamaal Ibn John Fareed; 1970–), rapper Phife Dawg (a.k.a. Phife, Malik Izaak Taylor, 1970–2016), and DJ and producer Ali Shaheed Muhammad (1970–), although Jarobi White (1971–) appeared on the group's first album, *People's Instinctive Travels and the Paths of Rhythm* (1990). In 1989, the group had signed with Jive Records (1981–), producing music that promoted Afrocentric ideas and positivity, using jazz-based samples against a hip hop beat. ATCQ's second Jive album, *The Low End Theory*, with tracks produced mostly by the band's members, is informed by vocal interplay between Phife Dawg and Q-Tip, backed by a bass-heavy collection of down-tempo beats, which became the trio's signature sound; the album was a commercial and critical success, selling half a million copies within a year of its release. This set the stage for future Jive produced success, as with *Midnight Marauders* (1993) and *The Love Movement* (1998).

The Low End Theory opens with "Excursions," which has an intro consisting of a jazz-style double bass that plays for four measures and is then joined by Q-Tip's idiosyncratic rapping, which is characterized by his high-pitched voice (albeit in his lowest, most relaxed register), where he sounds like a teenager who carefully articulates each and every word. Bass and rap continue until the second verse, when a heavy snare-based drum beat is introduced. Cool jazz horns appear in the refrain, which is a spoken-word sample, a Last Poet's (1968–) poem about the nature of time. The song is basically a thinking person's braggadocio, which equates the trio's skill with its roots in jazz and in African music and culture, amounting to "knowledge being dropped over beats." Q-Tip's lyrics are pensive and philosophical, and his rhymes are both interior and exterior, with a liberal use of enjambment.

The album has other standouts, including the satirical "Show Business," "Check the Rhime," and "Jazz (We've Got)." "Show Business" is a funk-based, stop time–filled indictment of the music industry (full of snakes, fakes, and liars) that contains the best interplay of double bass, drum kit, rhythm guitar, horns, and synthesizer on the album. The song features verses rapped by Brand Nubian's Sadat X (Derek Murphy, 1968–) and Lord Jamar (Lorenzo Dechalus, 1968–), as well as Diggin' in the Crates Crew's Diamond D (Joseph Kirkland, 1968–). "Check the Rhime" uses horn samples in its intro, synthesizer, drum kit, and electric bass to challenge rappers and music industry executives and media personalities who would diss ATCQ, while pointing out the shadiness of the music industry. The song includes some autobiographical lyrics and some of the few instances of vocal interplay between Q-Tip and Phife Dawg. The down-tempo skills bragging song "Jazz (We Got)" sounds as much like a De La Soul track as it does an ATCQ one. It is jazzy with a metallic-sounding drum beat, jazz double bass, synthesized horn voices, and turntable. Here Q-Tip's lyrics stand out for their multisyllabic rhymes and varied flow.

"What?" features some of Q-Tip's most clever rapping and flow. Unlike most of his other tracks, it is a veritable catalog of pop culture references, both high and low, set against a funk-based rhythm guitar (processed through a wah pedal effect) and a drum kit and percussion Latin-infused beat. "Buggin' Out," whose lyrics vary between skills bragging and social commentary (about things that make the black community crazy), begins with a double bass, albeit with a more down-tempo feel—it is almost immediately joined by a jazz drum beat and aggressive rapping by Phife Dawg, whose vocal range is deeper than Q-Tip's but who raps in a much higher register, almost at the level of a shout. His lyrics are less philosophical but possess a different cleverness through constant pop culture references, although his rhymes are mostly simple end rhymes. Q-Tip's "Verses from the Abstract," which features jazz bassist Ron Carter and singer Vinia Mojica, is both a braggadocio and an answer to Phife Dawg's "Butter," the song that precedes it. "Butter" is an autobiographical rap about women that features synthesizer (playing a high/low call and response series of ostinatos), bass, and drum kit. The song plays with opposites, especially virginal women versus hoes and genuineness versus posing and artificiality. While "Butter" is about Phife Dawg's love life, "Verses from the Abstract" establishes that Q-Tip had to move beyond preoccupation with sex to create rhymes that deal with higher concepts and with social realities. It includes some of his best puns, such as the phrase "met her for" for "metaphor." The music is laid-back and funk-based, with bass, rhythm guitar, and drum kit (mainly snare), and the song contains instances of stop time, as well as shout-outs to rappers and musicians that Q-Tip admires. Other skills bragging songs include the psychedelic jazz-based "Vibes and Stuff," which features jazz guitar and both the abstract, philosophical rapping of Q-Tip and the more worldly, clever allusions of Phife Dawg.

"Rap Promoter" is a "letter" to promoters that explains the trio's demands: full payment, a nonhostile audience, and respect. Unlike the tracks that precede it, it begins with R&B rhythm guitar (with a modified wah pedal effect), which is joined by sub-bass and snare drum, with a peppering of turntable. Overall, it is upbeat. The rock and funk-based "Everything Is Fair" is one of the few narrative songs on the album; it tells the story of a woman named Elaine, whose heart has been hardened by the city, which has made her mercenary. It features a chorus sung by Phife Dawg, set against Q-Tip's highly articulated rapping against an up-tempo jazz-based rap beat. "Scenario," which features a Dirty South–style drum beat (heavy kick and tom with ride cymbal) set against a synthesizer ostinato and heavy electric bass, features Leaders of the New School, including Busta Rhymes. It is a threat and diss song that challenges critics who argue that ATCQ lacks musical skills.

The weakest songs lyrically on the album are "The Infamous Date Rape" and "Skypager." In the former, Q-Tip's verses warn men they need to walk away when a woman decides she doesn't want sex, but Phife Dawg's verse warns men that sometimes women claim rape even after consensual sex, especially with famous men; the latter sounds like a commercial for pagers but is salvageable because it has one of the best drum beats on the album.

After the release of *Midnight Marauders*, Q-Tip and Muhammad joined forces with producer J Dilla (James Dewitt Yancey, 1974–2006) to form a production collective called the Ummah, after an Arabic word for both community and brotherhood. In addition to its work with A Tribe Called Quest, the Ummah would later produce music for Q-Tip's 1999 solo album *Amplified* (with Arista) as well as for its own *Beats, Rhymes and Life* (Jive, 1996). A Tribe Called Quest officially disbanded following *The Love Movement*. Phife Dawg recorded a single solo album, *Ventilation: Da LP* (Groove Attack Productions, 2000), while Muhammad formed a hip hop supergroup called Lucy Pearl (1999–2002) with members of Tony! Toni! Toné! and En Vogue. He also released one solo album, *Shaheedullah and Stereotypes* (Penalty Recordings, 2004). Members reunited for live concert performances, but Phife Dawg passed away in 2016 of complications related to diabetes. In 2017, remaining members plus Busta Rhymes made an appearance on *Saturday Night Live* as the musical guests—in a show scheduled just after Donald Trump was elected president of the United States. ATCQ's performance expressed both sadness about and anger-fueled determination against Trump's political agenda.

TUPAC SHAKUR: *ALL EYEZ ON ME* (AS 2PAC, DEATH ROW RECORDS, 1995)

Forever remembered as the first music artist to perform as a hologram years after his death (at Coachella 2012), Tupac Shakur (a.k.a. Tupac, 2Pac, Lesane Parish Crooks, 1971–96), born in East Harlem, New York, was one of the most gifted and influential American rappers of the early 1990s, and possibly of all time. He honed his talents at a young age, rapping by the age of twelve and performing with the 127th Street Repertory Ensemble in Harlem (and later in the Baltimore School for the Arts), appearing in plays and dances and writing/reciting poetry. When he was nineteen and living in California, music promoter Atron Gregory got him a gig as dancer and hype man with Digital Underground (1987–2008), and he eventually guest rapped on "Same Song," the lead track on its second release. His first solo album, *2Pacalypse Now* (as 2Pac, Interscope Records, 1991), achieved gold status with songs that focused on the inner city's social problems—racism, poverty, crime, police brutality, and teenage pregnancy. His second album, *Strictly 4 My N.*.*.*.A.Z.* (as 2Pac, Interscope-TNT, 1993), debuted at No. 24 on Billboard Top 200 and achieved platinum status. As 2Pac, he followed this with the equally successful *Me against the World* (Interscope, 1995) and the double album *All Eyez on Me* (1996), the latter for Death Row Records after owner Suge Knight paid a $1.4 million bail bond to get him released from incarceration for his involvement in a robbery and shooting and Tupac's agreeing to record three albums.

Tupac Shakur's flow exhibited an exceptional control of language, and his lyrics exemplified his strong social consciousness within the gangsta ethos, perhaps influenced by his parents' membership in the Black Panther party. This is evident on *All Eyez on Me*, the last of his albums released before he was killed. The album charted at No. 1 on both the Billboard 200 and the Top R&B/Hip Hop Albums charts and was certified diamond in 2014. It spawned five singles, including two that went to No. 1 on the Billboard Hot 100, "How Do U Want It" and "California Love," both released as part of a four song EP (the latter was also released as a radio mix single).

The album, which is for the most part a gangsta rap celebration, features Dr. Dre, Snoop Dogg, Nate Dogg, George Clinton (1941–), Method Man, and Redman, among others, and most of the songs were produced by Johnny J (Johnny Lee Jackson, 1969–2008) and Daz Dillinger. The album begins with Tupac Shakur's chant-singing the intro to the g-funk-sounding "Ambitionz Az a Ridah," produced by Daz Dillinger. Apparent immediately is his control of the language. Lots of repeated interior rhyme (and near rhyme), assonance, and a natural sense of the rhythmic line can be heard as the rapper warns listeners that he is gangsta—that he has street cred. The song also establishes the complexity of his lyrics as it cannot be neatly categorized as braggadocio, gangsta, entourage, sex song, or gold digger criticism—it contains elements of all five, with clear evidence of deeper thought. The lyrics both question and dismiss gold diggers and express a need for female company, and while the song states that Tupac is a real gangsta and can be hard and invincible, it also has lyrics that point to a sense of uncertainty and a need for an almost maternal guidance. The instrumentation is also complex, with a keyboard ostinato set against string voices and delay-distorted snare drum voice (to give each mid-tempo 4/4 beat a longer delay and sense of echo), against which he raps using a staccato effect, giving the lines a hiccupped feel, which is emphasized by carefully placed background vocals (sometimes vocalizations, sometimes words). The overall effect, especially given the repeated interior rhyme and assonance, is that the end of lines are never clear, creating a breathlessness and constant flow, even as verses transition into refrains and vice versa. This works beautifully against what is an interesting but monotonous instrumental beat as vocals make up for the lack of instrumental variety.

Among the album's standouts are the Daz Dillinger–produced songs: "Skandalouz," "Got My Mind Made Up," "2 of Amerikaz Most Wanted" (featuring Snoop Dogg), and "I Ain't Mad at Cha." "Skandalouz," an R&B gold-digger song, begins with a metatextual intro by Tupac and Nate Dogg, who sings the refrains. Verses alternate between diss lines on women who play not only Tupac but also many of his "homies" and soul-searching about his own scandalous tendencies (women and alcohol especially), which leave him vulnerable. Instrumentation includes a heavy booming bass, rhythm guitar, a snare and hi-hat beat, and various keyboard voices and diverse, constant sound effects (shakers, clickers, bells, guiros, earth bells, and the like) that move between the left and right speakers. The neo soul and cool jazz–inspired skills-bragging song "Got My Mind Made Up" shows Tupac's lyricism at its best; as he extends interior and exterior rhymes for up to seven lines in his verse; it stands in contrast to the much less polished verses of the track's guest rappers, Daz Dillinger, Kurupt, Method Man, and Redman. Instrumentally the song is simple, but it features some of the best bass and drum interplay on the album, as well as a descending groove created by the bass and a vibe voice (that accentuates phrases through). The braggadocio and entourage g-funk track "2 of Amerikaz Most Wanted" is a celebration of Death Row's ability to attract the best rappers, although as its intro points out, this practice will draw the attention of authorities. The song's grinding bass, set against claps and a cymbal-heavy (both hi-hat and ride) beat, establishes one of the album's best grooves. The song showcases Daz Dillinger's engineering, as sounds move between left and right speakers, and verses move seamlessly between Tupac and Snoop Dogg, an effect that was likely created in postproduction.

Other notable songs include "How Do You Want It," "No More Pain," "Heartz of Men," "I Ain't Mad at Cha," "Holla at Me," "What'z Ya Phone #," "Can't C Me," "Shorty Wanna Be a Thug," "Check Out Time," "All Eyez on Me," "Ain't Hard 2 Find," "Heaven Ain't Hard 2 Find," and "Run Tha Streetz." The heavily funk-inspired sex bragging and anti-censorship song "How Do U Want It," produced by Johnny J, is interesting for its references to Parental Advisory labels. The song calls out C. Delores Tucker, Bill Clinton, and Bob Dole, all of whom are "too old to understand the way the game's told" and just get in the way of a poor musician's attempts to make money by giving fans what they want. The track features excellent rhythm guitar and grinding bass interplay, as well as some of the album's best guest vocal harmonies. An extremely complex song, "No More Pain," produced by DeVante Swing, is about sex, violence, bragging rights, rap skills, and the inevitability of death for a gangsta. Lyrically, it prefigures Tupac's murder as he raps about death as being an end to pain ("my only fear of death is reincarnation"), with one caveat—he must die as a living legend. The song has an old-school meets g-funk sound, with an experimental feel: a harmonically dissonant keyboard ostinato, eerie vocalizations (such as whispering and unexpected laughter in the left speaker), an odd-sounding "whomp-whomp-whomp" synth secondary ostinato, and an atmospheric feel created by a two-chord oscillated synthesizer voice.

"Heartz of Men," produced by DJ Quik (David Marvin Blake, 1970–), showcases bass and ride cymbal (with a simple funk-jazz drum beat) and is a funk-heavy misanthropic track that divides the world into two types of people: enemies and false friends, with the only notable exception being Death Row's entourage. Given this, it is no surprise that Tupac comes to the conclusion that the only response is the gangsta life, to live like a "G" until the day he dies. One of the most energetic songs on the album, it also has the best intro/hook, a danceable horn-based funk groove set against spoken-word media files, and the best intro lyrically, an extended conversion between Tupac and Suge Knight about the nature of people. "I Ain't Mad at Cha" and "Holla at Me" are both songs in which Tupac attempts to make peace with some of the seemingly disloyal homies mentioned in "Heartz of Men" and "Only God Can Judge Me." In the former, peace is harder to find with disloyal friends, including an ex-thug friend who has converted to Islam and traded a life of crime for a wife and family. In the latter, peace is impossible, leading to the song's final lines, that these ex-homies better hope the song's narrator doesn't find out where they live.

The sex song "What'z Ya Phone #" is a frenetic, danceable rave-infused, funk-influenced, breathless track that ends with a cacophonous, semicomical, but very graphic, phone sex skit. The skills, bling, sexual prowess, and gangsta bragging song "Can't C Me," which features George Clinton and is produced by Dr. Dre, is a bass-heavy, funk-infused angry, aggressive rap that contains some of Tupac's best humorous references and allusions. The catchy g-funk and experimental rap song "Shorty Wanna Be a Thug" is part celebration of the thug life and part warning about engaging in gangsta activities at too young an age (and ruining your life), featuring an engaging keyboard melody and synth countermelody, along with oddball instrumentation such as guiros and klezmer-style woodwinds.

The 1980s keyboard voice heard in both the party track "Check Out Time" and the sex song "Ratha Be Ya N—" is set in the former against a synthesizer flute voice and female-sung refrains and in the latter against a solid snare beat and female sung refrains juxtaposed against male-chanted countermelody refrains. Both tracks are musically interesting. Heavily influenced by funk beats, "All Eyez on Me" and "Ain't Hard 2 Find" celebrate the thug lifestyle while also acknowledging that it creates problems because it produces a lot of enemies as well as police surveillance. The funk and R&B romance song "Heaven Ain't Hard 2 Find" and the girl band g-funk relationship male-female duet "Run Tha Streetz" are songs that indicate that the gangsta lifestyle is not incompatible with a happy domestic relationship.

As is likely for any double album, throwaway songs are to be included. Among *All Eyez on Me*'s weakest songs are the neo-soul-flavored romance-centered "All Bout U" and ballad-like "Life Goes On," as well as "Only God Can Judge Me," "Tradin' War Stories," "California Love (Remix)," "Wonda Why They Call U B—," and three tracks on which Tupac appears only sparsely: "When We Ride," "Thug Passion," and "Picture Me Rollin'." "All Bout U" and "Wonda Why They Call U B—" express ambivalence toward women as being both dangerous (on a mission to take his money and use him) and alluring (the need for a sexual relationship). Instrumentally, "All Bout U" is uninteresting, with a 1980s synthesizer voice, electric bass, and snare-ride cymbal beat that never varies, all of which culminate in an uninspired Snoop Dogg spoken-word outro. "Wonda Why They Call U B—" has a more interesting beat, hook, and vocal melodic line created by synthesizer and drum machine, and it is more thoughtful lyrically, but it doesn't measure up to the rest of the album.

The neo soul "Life Goes On" is a softer track produced by Tupac and Johnny J. It shows Tupac's ambivalence toward the gangsta life, as he realizes that even though he embraces it, the lifestyle has killed two of his friends. The lyrics alternate between grief (including drinking oneself into a stupor) and determination, with the realization that life will go on. Informed by a keyboard melody of descending fifths (e.g., Pachelbel's "Canon in D"), the funk bass-heavy "Only God Can Judge Me" continues the misanthropy of "Heartz of Men," with lyrics that speak of betrayal, judgment, gang violence, black-on-black crime, and despair (one image is of a thug with tears in his eyes). The song uses a simple kick and snare drum beat set against various 1980s keyboard voices and sound effects, including highly auto-tuned background vocals. The R&B-infused, synthesizer-heavy "Tradin' War Stories" is a gangsta threat narrative and Death Row entourage song. "California Love (Remix)," produced by and featuring Dr. Dre, is a g-funk serenade to the streets of L.A., especially Compton, as well as the rest of the California West Coast rap scene. Unfortunately, the song is overproduced, with highly auto-tuned vocals. "When We Ride," a g-funk-based gangsta entourage and threat song; "Thug Passion," a highly auto-tuned R&B and 1980s-soul sex song; and "Picture Me Rollin'," a neo-soul-influenced song about Tupac's return from prison, barely feature Tupac. "Picture Me Rollin'" does have some interesting elements, however, such as the use of a groove created by electric bass, reverbed claps, kick drum, and triangle.

After *All Eyez on Me*, Tupac Shakur had further Death Row projects, including *The Don Killuminati: The 7 Day Theory* (1996), released shortly after his violent death in Las Vegas as part of the feud between East and West Coast rappers—an incident that served to amplify his legacy. In the decades since his death, his reputation as one of the greatest rap artists has grown, and his music continues to sell at a rate that many living performers can only envy. Critics, fans, and other rappers point to the exceptional quality of his work, which is highly admired.

THE 2 LIVE CREW: *AS NASTY AS THEY WANNA BE* (LUKE SKYYWALKER RECORDS, 1989)

When the 2 Live Crew (1982–98) put out its third album, *As Nasty as They Wanna Be* (1989), a man who at that time went by Luke Skyywalker (Luther Campbell, a.k.a. Luke, 1960–), put his hometown of Miami and styles called Southern rap and Miami bass on the hip hop and rap maps—the album was the first Southern-rap album to go platinum. *As Nasty as They Wanna Be* drew criticism both for its explicit sexual content and its problems with alleged copyright infringement, but it was a huge commercial success, became RIAA certified double platinum, and made it into the high-rotation playlists of just about every American dance club. Although the 2 Live Crew changed membership in its sixteen years of existence, the best-known lineup included DJ Mr. Mixx (David P. Hobbs, n.d.) and rappers Fresh Kid Ice (Chris Wong Won, 1964–2017), Brother Marquis (Mark D. Ross, 1967–), and Luke

Skyywalker, who also served as the band's promoter. The 2 Live Crew sound is best summed up as Miami bass, a rap subgenre characterized by heavy bass and synthesized melodic and drum sounds. Lyric concerns can pretty much be summed up in one word, sex, but in all its graphic glory. The crew's music was anything but serious; it sampled comedians such as Richard Pryor and Cheech & Chong.

The album's samples attest to the eclectic tastes of DJ Mr. Mixx and include lines from Stanley Kubrick's *Full Metal Jacket* (1987) and Eddie Murphy's *Which Way Is Up?* (1977), as well as song fragments from Nancy Sinatra, the Chakachas, Kraftwerk, Clarence Carter, Rob Base, Beastie Boys, Van Halen, Guns N' Roses, Jimi Hendrix, and the Beatles, as well as the aforementioned comic routines by Murphy, Pryor, Andrew Dice Clay, Cheech & Chong, and Laid Back. The oversexualization of lyrics is immediately apparent to the listener. The album kicks off with the danceable "Me So Horny," which begins with a skit wherein a hooker offers services, followed by sexual moaning and a media sample (a Vietnamese hooker saying "me so horny, me love you long time") from *Full Metal Jacket*, followed by a rap about sexualizing women. The song includes hard-rock guitars and drumming, juxtaposed against the ubiquitous heavy 4/4 bass kick with an occasional synthesizer riff. The next song, "Put Her in the Buck," an explicit song about rough sex, has an even heavier bass kick beat and rock drumming, combined with electric funk bass, conga drums, and funk synthesizer; the song ends with the sounds of a male and female having sex.

The album's standout is "Break It on Down," which has the heaviest bass on the album (approaching a sub-bass sound) set against a snare and Latin percussion rhythm section and scratching. Though it is the sixth track, it is the first non–sex song on the album. Best characterized as a skills braggadocio, it features the most skilled lyrics on the album and ends with a scratching exhibition by DJ Mr. Mixx. The album's better songs are "D— Almighty," "C'mon Babe," "I Ain't Bulls—," and "Mega Mixx III." Though lyrically insipid, the sexual braggadocio song "D— Almighty" stands out musically for its juxtaposition of an '80s new wave keyboard voice and scratching against heavy funk bass and high-pitched (possibly a wood block and/or timbale) 4/4 sixteenth-note Latin percussive drumming shuffle. DJ Mr. Mixx's skill is apparent in "C'mon Babe," where he mixes moans, vocal samples, kick bass, synthesizer riffs, and conga drums. The song begins simply with a skit of a woman moaning in sexual ecstasy, and then the music—a Latin-flavored drum and bass ostinato—jumps out. The song's rapping is interesting for its embrace of old-school rap aesthetics. "I Ain't Bulls—" begins with skilled scratching that leads to a heavy drum kit, funk bass, and spoken-word diss track. The comedic sexual-hygiene song, "The F— Shop," contains sampled metal and rock guitars throughout. However, its lyrics are some of the most explicitly degrading toward women on the album. "Mega Mixx III" is the album's high-energy dance song, where DJ Mr. Mixx shows off his scratching skills against a Latin beat. The song also shows off his skills with beat making (it has the best drumming on the album). However, it contains no rapping; rather, its vocals are sampled singing and spoken-word media files.

The comedic "Dirty Nursery Rhymes" begins with an 808 hiccup that gives way to a heavy bass kick, wood block, reverberated hand claps, and scratching, and the 808 hiccup is used again as a bridge between verses. The song includes a humorous outtake moment. "2 Live Blues" is a bass kick–heavy, synthesized power chord-infused parody of the 12-bar blues song that includes images that reference famous blues songs, as well as a turntable, arp, and synthesized/distorted blues guitar solo. Lyrics are the reaction to an unfaithful woman, and they quickly degenerate into an explicit sex song about the newfound sexual joy of being single. "Get Loose Now" is an R&B-flavored braggadocio (about freestyle rapping skills) and party dance song that features a rhythm guitar and bass kick beat, with occasional brass, as well as turntable solos; its final verse contains one of the few examples of nonexplicit sex lyrics on the album. "Bad Ass B—" begins with an electric bass, bass kick, and Latin percussion beat, set against vocalizations in the form of chatter—the chatter recurs throughout the song, adding points of interest to what is otherwise an old-school rap about gangbang sex with an older woman. "Coolin'" is the album's most innocuous song, narrating in old-school style a day at the beach as an entourage.

The album's weakest songs are all among its later tracks. These include "If You Believe in Having Sex," "My Seven Bizzos," "Get the F— out of My House," "Fraternity Record," and "Reggae Joint." "If You Believe in Having Sex" is a call and response party and sex song. The 2 Live Crew here uses toasting and spoken word instead of rap, with rhythmic chanting in the call-response sections, some of which are tongue-in-cheek parodies of television commercials. "Fraternity Record," which cleverly sets the Beatles "Day Tripper" sample against bass kick and snare and contains a masterful distorted guitar solo, is unfortunately the same song, with the call-response here being juvenile disses of various fraternities, in the form of "f— the (insert fraternity name)." "My Seven Bizzos" is an old-school rap (set to a heavy bass kick and snare funk beat, played against intermediate guitar and turntable) about having a different woman for each day of the week; though it has the least interesting beat on the album, it does feature some of the best scratching. The diss song (an attack on women who are b—) "Get the F— out of My House" is an extended mix dance song that has a Latin percussion shuffle beat that alternates with a disco beat, created mainly by an '80s new wave keyboard voice; its rap too often degenerates into silly vocalizations and off-the-beat rapping. "Reggae Joint" begins with Jamaican toasting and has a sub-bass with snare beat. Despite the interesting instrumentation, the song is weak because the rap is a bad imitation of a Jamaican accent. In fact, it is heavily distorted in an attempt to cover its weakness.

Although the group's first two albums on Luke's label, *The 2 Live Crew Is What We Are* (1986) and *Move Somethin'* (1988), both sold relatively well, *As Nasty as They Wanna Be* made it famous, with explicit songs such as "Me So Horny" and "The F— Shop." The 2 Live Crew followed with a tongue-in-cheek censored version (which contained a label warning that the album did not contain explicit lyrics), *As Clean as They Wanna Be*, which sold poorly and did not quiet any of objections to the original version, leading to a 1990 verdict that *As Nasty as They Wanna Be* was obscene and therefore could not be sold legally, making it the first album to be declared obscene in a court of law and leading to the arrest of three of the group's members. The verdict was overturned on appeal in 1992, and the three were released without incident. This did not solve the band's problem, however, as it was sued by Acuff-Rose Music for *As Clean as They Wanna Be*'s unauthorized parody of Roy Orbison's "Oh, Pretty Woman" (1964). The case Campbell v. Acuff-Rose Music went all the way to the United States Supreme Court, which held that the group's song was a commercial parody and therefore did not violate copyright.

During the 1990s, the group's personnel changed several times, and although Luke Skyywalker and company continued to release albums, none sold as well or achieved as much notoriety as *As Nasty as They Wanna Be*. Further, he was forced to change the name of his record label from Luke Skyywalker Records to simply Luke Records after a copyright infringement lawsuit filed by American filmmaker George Lucas, creator of the *Star Wars* franchise and the Luke Skywalker character. The band's next album, *Banned in the U.S.A.* (1990), billed as Luke featuring the 2 Live Crew, was one of the first albums to bear a Parental Advisory sticker from the RIAA, a label created to caution parents of explicit lyrics.

WU-TANG CLAN: "WU-TANG: 7TH CHAMBER" (I AND II) AND "16TH CHAMBER/O.D.B. SPECIAL" (*ENTER THE WU-TANG (36 CHAMBERS)*, RCA-LOUD RECORDS, 1993, AND *8 DIAGRAMS*, BODOG MUSIC, 2007, 2008)

With a mind-set and a band name taken from kung fu films, the Staten Island, New York–based Wu-Tang Clan creates music based on kung fu aesthetics: self-defense, personal identity, and honorable battle. The Wu-Tang Clan is unique for its consistency of mythology and stories/themes, so much so that one of its members, RZA (Robert Fitzgerald Diggs, 1969–), penned a guidebook, *The Wu-Tang Manual: Enter the 36 Chambers* (2004), as a method to explain its mysteries. The band evolved from the short-lived (1992) All in Together Now Crew, which included cousins RZA, GZA (Gary Grice, 1966–), and Ol' Dirty Bastard (a.k.a. O.D.B., Russell Tyrone Jones, 1968–2004). The addition of Ghostface Killah (Dennis Coles, 1970–), Method Man, Raekwon (Corey Woods, 1970–), U-God (Lamont Hawkins, 1970–), Inspectah Deck (Jason Hunter, 1970–), and Masta Killa (Elgin Turner, 1969–) led to the formation of the Wu-Tang Clan.

The group's first track was self-released, the single "Protect Ya Neck" (1993). It did not chart, but its B-side, "Method Man," peaked at No. 17 on the Hot Rap Songs chart. A successful tour led to a contract with Loud Records, which granted Wu-Tang Clan members the right to sign deals with other labels. Individual members have recorded for a variety of labels, with RZA producing or coproducing most releases. Collectively and as soloists, members of the group have earned six platinum albums and sold over forty million records. Their first release on Loud, *Enter the Wu-Tang (36 Chambers)* (1993) introduced the martial arts themes and metaphors that would pervade all of their music. It also introduced the theme of the thirty-six chambers in the tracks "Wu-Tang: 7th Chamber" and "Wu-Tang: 7th Chamber, Part II." After the incarceration of Ol' Dirty Bastard and a six-year hiatus from 2001 to 2007, Wu-Tang Clan reunited for *8 Diagrams* (Universal Motown, 2007). The 2007 and 2008 European releases of that album included the track "16th Chamber/O.D.B. Special."

"Wu-Tang: 7th Chamber" is likely a reference to the seven verses by seven different members. The track represents both the projects of New York and rap in general as a type of war. Producer RZA consciously decided to stay off the mic as much as possible and devote his time to beat making and sampling. The song was to be the first of the thirty-six chambers tracks that the band had envisioned. As of 2019, only four exist: the aforementioned "7th Chamber" and "16th Chamber" tracks, GZA's (as Genius/GZA) "4th Chamber" on *Liquid Swords* (1995), and Inspectah Deck's "9th Chamber" on *Uncontrolled Substance* (1999). "Wu-Tang: 7th Chamber" begins with martial arts fighting sounds, followed by a skit in which an argument between Method Man and Raekwon is interrupted by the entrance of U-God and Ghostface Killah, who have both just witnessed a homicide in Stapleton Houses, Staten Island's largest projects at the time and home to Ghostface, who grew up just six buildings away from the killing. The song itself is basically a braggadocio rap, using images of sexual prowess (Raekwon), urban street violence (Raekwon, Method Man, and Inspectah Deck), martial arts films (Method Man, RZA, O.D.B., and GZA), history (Inspectah Deck, Ghostface, and GZA), fast cars (Ghostface), literature/songwriting (RZA), and pop culture (GZA) to establish rap skills dominance.

RZA's production of "Wu-Tang: 7th Chamber," which samples "Spinning Wheel" (1970) by Lonnie O. Smith, "Down in the Valley" (1965) by Otis Redding, and "As Long As I've Got You" (1967) by the Charmels (which he had also used in the Wu-Tang track "C.R.E.A.M.") relies heavily on the drum beat, in this case an alternation of a tinny, very dry synth-produced snare voice with a sample of Smith's heavy bass kick, timed to coincide with the bass end of a turntable (which also gives the bass beat a hiccup). As these beats resolve into 4/4 time with the emphasis on the third beat, an off-kilter keyboard ostinato (that sounds as though it is being played on an out of tune piano) is juxtaposed against the drum track and Raekwon's aggressive rapping in his higher range. The only other instrumentation is a keyboard-produced string shriek (which sounds somewhat like a whale call) that occurs midway through Raekwon's verse and at the end. Verse two features the same instrumentation, with the exception of the string voice being added to every line, as Method Man's raspy but laid-back voice takes over. His rap is capped off by distorted media clips and sounds, creating a sense of discord in a song that has thus far been smooth. Like Raekwon, Inspectah Deck raps (verse three) in his highest range with the same sense of urgency. The music he raps against is a continuation of that found in verse two but with added turntable scratches. As Ghostface Killah's boyish voice takes over for verse four, the keyboard voices disappear briefly, and the isolated drum beat swings a bit more due to the addition of a guitar strike on the third beat (carried over from the last few lines of verse three), creating a funk-infused rap. After a few lines, the music switches back to the song's main theme before it returns to the isolated drum and guitar, with added turntable, as the verse ends. RZA, his voice deep, throaty, and gravelly (an excellent juxtaposition to Ghostface's voice), takes up the next verse, which is rapped against the main theme but with added vocalizations to accent lines. At this point, media file distortion is again introduced, which leads to O.D.B.'s verse. Rapping against the same music as the previous verse, his baritone voice nearly breaks into song—his flow much more playful (with pauses, lilts, and vocal effects) than that of the other clan members. As GZA takes over the final verse, the tinny snare beat from the intro is reintroduced and isolated, played against only the guitar strike. GZA, his voice comparable to that of Slick Rick, funk-raps against this new beat for a few lines, at which point the song's main theme returns and transitions into its outro, which has added guitar and drum flourishes (on the snare). This plays into a fade-out.

"Wu-Tang: 7th Chamber, Part II," the album's twelfth track, features the same rapped portions (from each Wu-Tang member) as the original song, but RZA remixes the beat. The intro is a brief sample from "Clan In Da Front," the album's third track. Once the song begins, RZA goes heavy on the sub-bass (played against the 4/4 drum beat of the original) and experiments with more distorted guitar sounds and a cappella rapping in verse one. He also adds background vocalizations (e.g., "oooh oooh oooh oooh") to make the song funkier and more danceable. By verse two, the sub-bass (on the octave) becomes the song's main beat and remains so throughout, with constant distorted guitar and horn sounds (the latter made to sound warped) as well as a handful of stop time instances added for points of interest. The outro features the background singing, sub-bass beat, and distorted guitars and resolves into a drum kit version of the sub-bass beat that plays until fade-out.

"16th Chamber/O.D.B. Special" is an entourage and threat song that borders on a skills bragging rap. With lengthy verses rapped by Method Man and O.D.B., it uses violent imagery to warn off all haters and dissers of the "clan" or anyone associated with it. One of the unique aspects of the song is that it is full of pop culture references, but almost all of them relate to white culture: Method Man mentions Mistic Iced Tea, Snapple, Popeye, and Harry S. Truman, while O.D.B. references Rick Dees, Ron Howard, *The Andy Griffith Show*, *Welcome Back Kotter*, and *Hong Kong Phooey*. These are juxtaposed with references to black athletes and rap culture phenomenon (such as fronting) as a means of "flipping the script" (an O.D.B. line). The intro is a heavy bass kick beat, against which Method Man speaks. As he begins rapping the first verse, the dynamics change completely, and the clear sound of the intro gives way to a highly backgrounded, somewhat muddled in the mix, funk-infused beat (the beat sounds as if it is on a distant radio, while the raps are foregrounded and clear). The beat is based on drum kit (bass-tom-snare-tom/ride, with emphasis on beat three), electric bass (a distorted slap at the end of every two phrases), and distorted guitar sounds. Even more guitar distortion occurs in the bridge, which also has backgrounded and distorted vocalizations (e.g., "nah nah nah nah") and ends in a funk horn break. The added distorted guitar sounds continue into verse two, rapped playfully by O.D.B., with unexpected pauses, repetitions, and wordplay.

After a platinum Method Man solo album, the group recorded *Wu-Tang Forever* (RCA-Loud, 1997), which was certified four-times platinum and became the group's biggest seller. Additional solo projects followed until 2000, with the release of *The W* on the Loud label. The next full album, *Iron Flag* (Loud, 2001), was recorded without Ol' Dirty Bastard. After *8 Diagrams*, the crew recorded *A Better Tomorrow* (Warner Bros., 2014) and self-released, the privately owned (auctioned off to a single buyer) *Once Upon a Time in Shaolin* (2015). During recordings, each member of the band would bring in his own stable of collaborators, granting them the brand of the Wu-Tang Clan and supporting their work. Controversial pharmaceutical CEO and entrepreneur Martin Shkreli won *Once Upon a Time in Shaolin* at auction for $2 million; upon learning who the buyer was, the band donated a significant amount of the proceeds to charity. The Wu-Tang Clan have managed its brand through Wu-Wear Clothing (1995), the comic book line *The Nine Rings of Wu-Tang* (2001), and a kung fu video game, *Wu-Tang: Shaolin Style* (1999).

CHAPTER 3

Impact on Popular Culture*

RAP'S IMPACT ON CULTURAL PHENOMENA

Rap is one element of hip hop culture, albeit its most lucrative, with only fashion being as financially rewarding. And hip hop as a whole is not just a culture but also an aesthetic that influences movements in everything from music (both rap and boy/girl bands) and dance to art and literature. From humble beginnings in the Bronx in the early 1970s to now influencing almost every aspect of daily life, rap has recreated many elements of what we could call "lifestyle." Included among these aspects are the aforementioned music (MC'ing, DJing, and beatboxing) and fashion (e.g., FUBU and Hilfiger) as well as dance (b-boying or b-girling), art (graffiti and gang tagging), language, activism, film, and literature. In fact, rap aesthetics have greatly influenced even gang culture. Although it is an urban-born phenomenon, hip hop (especially rap) has spread to suburban and rural communities not only in the United States but also internationally. Like earlier African and Latin American music styles (jazz, funk, calypso, and Latin rhythm), rap and boy/girl band–based hip hop have taken the world by storm because of their appeal to youth.

Where rap differs most greatly from the other form of hip hop music, boy/girl band (e.g., Destiny's Child, NSYNC, Tony! Toni! Toné!) is in its ties to street culture. As such, rap is informed by "street cred," or authenticity. No other music style requires that its musicians come from a particular type of background, which includes geographic area, familial structure, and lifestyle, having been either abused in a drug-addicted, dysfunctional family (Eminem), lived on the streets (Big Pun), been a

---

* Melissa U. D. Goldsmith and Paige A. Willson contributed to this chapter.

gang member (Snoop Dogg), or engaged in criminal activity (N.W.A.). Rappers can achieve success without this background, but those who do (e.g., Drake) are rare, and when they do, they spend their careers trying to establish their street cred. Woman rappers have to establish a similar authenticity: they have to adopt the "b—" persona (Foxy Brown, Nicki Minaj, Cardi B) and spend their careers engaging in diss battles with (mostly) other female rappers and "haters" (celebrity critics, including other rappers). It should come as no surprise then that one of the first phenomena rap influenced was competition, in the form of rap battling (in fact, according to some accounts, battling created rap, but this is a chicken-egg argument). Battling is a concept that has existed in both rap music and b-boying/b-girling since the early years of both. Rap battling, which employs a style of delivery called freestyle, is an improvisational method of rapping that can be accompanied by a basic instrumental beat, a sample, or beatboxing. A battle rap can even be delivered a cappella. Battles can take place informally on street corners or formally on a concert or battle stage and can be either freestyle or based on prepared lyrics—with the point being to challenge an opposing rapper's skills through clever lyrics and wordplay while establishing dominance. In order to prove that a freestyle is being made up on the spot, rappers will often refer to places and objects in their immediate setting or take suggestions on lyrics from the crowd.

Associated with battling is the concept of beatboxing (not to be confused with Grandmaster Flash's idea of the beat box, a manually-operated, custom-rigged synthesizer drum machine). Beatboxing is a way of creating a beat when no instrumentation is available, which is especially useful in informal street rap battling, as it allows for the creation of music (a consistent rhythmic beat that establishes musical time, against which a rapper can rap). Simply defined, beatboxing is the practice of making drum and synthesizer sounds using mainly the mouth and nose, although some very skilled beatboxers literally beat on body parts as well, or stomp. Master beatboxers like Doug E. Fresh—nicknamed the human beat box—created both a beat and a melodic line simultaneously, emulating the sounds of drum machines, tap dancing, various percussion instruments, and synthesizers. Incredibly, Doug E. Fresh did so using only his mouth, throat, and a microphone. Beatboxing can also be seen as an entry into rapping: Biz Markie began as a beatboxer, working closely with his friend Big Daddy Kane. Beatboxing battles survive today in a more formal atmosphere, currently held internationally (in Germany) every three years. Beatboxing champions as of 2018 are Mael

Gayaud of France and Kaila Mullady of the United States. The current crew (group) champion is Beatbox Collective out of England.

Rap also introduced another method of creating beats: turntablism (a.k.a. DJing). Turntablism and sampling involve skills that result in creating and modifying sounds through the use of two or more turntables; it also involves isolating sampled sounds (usually a musical phrase or two) from preexisting music, creating what is called a loop or hiccup. Also called scratching, turntablism techniques also involve moving an armed needle back and forth on one or two vinyl records, or picking the needle up and setting it back down to play only certain parts of songs. The turntablist, commonly called a DJ, can literally pick up the needle and place it back in its original place while the record is turning or shift it back lightly in a technique called rubbing. With two vinyl records, a DJ can shift quickly between two pieces of music by switching power from one turntable to another through a device called a crossfader (which can be a knob or a slider, or both). Turntablism can be traced back to DJ Kool Herc, who spun funk albums by the likes of James Brown, creating an uninterrupted dance experience using what he would later call break beats. He influenced Grandmaster Flash and Afrika Bambaataa, the latter purchasing a sound system and inviting people, including b-boys/b-girls, to join his Universal Zulu Nation. Grandmaster Flash came up with the quick-mix theory, sectioning off parts of albums on his turntables, creating what he called backspin and the double-back.

A mentee of Grandmaster Flash, Grand Wizzard Theodore, came up with the idea of scratching, or moving the record back and forth under the stylus. DJ Grand Mixer DXT furthered scratching by making it more rhythmic and using two turntables at different velocities to alter the pitch. He made scratching mainstream by using it on Herbie Hancock's hit song "Rockit" (1982). By the 1980s, scratching became a staple of rap as DJs increasingly provided music for rappers (a.k.a. MCs). MCs Run and D.M.C. made their DJ famous by emphasizing the skills of Jam Master Jay in their performances and recordings. However, the role of the DJ was quickly downplayed in rap because MCs became the focus of bands, and there was an increased use of computer software, tapes, and other studio techniques. One of the first rappers to use the title MC was MC Hammer; however, the practice itself goes back further to the Jamaican practice of toasting, when a master of ceremonies, or emcee (MC), working in the dance halls uses rhymed introductions and announcements to engage the crowd before and after a dancer or a band performs. Given the preference for the MCs and rappers, turntablism had to become more of an art form in its own right. DJs continue to show off their skills through crews such as Invisibl Skratch Piklz, World Famous Beat Junkies (which created its own DJ school, the Beat Junkie Institute of Sound), and the X-Ecutioners; DJ crews battle in national and international competitions.

RAP'S SOCIOPOLITICAL IMPACT

The Black Power Movement of the mid-1960s and early 1970s inspired songs that expressed black pride, such as James Brown's "Say It Loud (I'm Black and Proud)" (1969) and Gil Scott-Heron's spoken-word-to-jazz track "The Revolution Will Not Be Televised" (1971), and were influences on early political and socially conscious rap. Socially conscious rappers such as Public Enemy, Tupac Shakur, and Kendrick Lamar were inspired by Scott-Heron and the Last Poets, and they saw rap as a way to express dissatisfaction with injustice and disenfranchisement. You could say that rap was by nature a political music, partly by choice (rappers tend to be musical activists who argue against racism, discrimination, and related economic issues) and partly because rap was repeatedly attacked by politicians and therefore needed to defend itself. During the 1990s, rap music was censored for both its violent and sexual content, which politicians tried to argue was the cause of the destruction of American values. In fact, in 1990, Florida governor Bob Martinez and Nick Navarro, Broward County sheriff, brought obscenity charges against 2 Live Crew for its album *As Nasty As They Wanna Be* (1989), arguing that record store owners that sold the album might be prosecutable, and in 1992, U.S. vice president Dan Quayle called on Interscope Records to withdraw Tupac Shakur's *2Pacalypse Now* (1991). It took until 2008 for politicians to embrace the music—in 2008 Barack Obama referenced Jay-Z by doing his "brush the dirt off your shoulder" (from *The Black Album*, 2003) motion in a rally. Today, rap is de rigueur in politics and is actually actively used by the U.S. State Department in what is called hip hop diplomacy.

Hip hop diplomacy is the use of hip hop cultural practices to cultivate and encourage good will and diplomatic relationships between countries, especially between the United States and other nations. The State Department began to incorporate hip hop into its diplomacy programs beginning in the early 2000s. In 1961, the U.S. Congress passed the Fulbright-Hays Act, officially known as the Mutual Educational and Cultural Exchange Act, to create a cultural exchange between the United States and other countries, and in 2005 the State Department began sending groups of hip hop artists, including rappers, DJs, and dancers, to parts of Europe, Africa, Asia, and the Middle East in an attempt to combat the radicalization of Muslim youth in those areas. Hip hop was identified as a musical genre with which global youth, especially Muslim youth, could identify because of its roots as protest music in marginalized communities in the United States as well as its international popularity with minority immigrant communities. This is a recognition of the fact that Islam has always been an important aspect of rap, with followers of the Five-Percent Nation and the Nation of Islam achieving rap success, followers such as Rakim, Public Enemy, Poor Righteous Teachers, and Busta Rhymes. The State Department also began (in 2014) an arts-based exchange using multidisciplinary hip hop collaborations, sending groups of beat makers, DJs, break-dancers, and MCs to lead exchange programs that last from four to six weeks. Called Next Level, the project is designed to be a collaborative that engages youth and artists from various countries with interactive performances of local musicians, lecture demonstrations, workshops, and jam sessions.

Domestically, rap has served another important political function—the vehicle by which black nationalism was made popular. Black nationalism argues for a global black population as part of one coherent nation and that black people of African descent share fundamental common interests and should view their membership in the black global nation as their primary basis for cultural identification. Black nationalism began with the idea of an actual geographic nation state, an idea put forth after the "back to Africa" political theories of Martin Delany and Marcus Garvey, but in time it embraced unification in nongeographic terms (a nation as an idea could be traced to the theories of Frantz Fanon, Stokely Carmichael, Malcolm X, and Louis Farrakhan). Black nationalism has had a strong influence on rap, and vice versa. For example, Public Enemy's politically charged music and videos contained many elements of black nationalism; Afrika Bambaataa formed the Universal Zulu Nation, now found in France, Japan, South Africa, Australia, and South Korea; and the activist rap duo Dead Prez's self-identification with the nationalist Uhuru Movement and the International People's Democratic Uhuru Movement, led it to incorporate black nationalist colors into its album artwork and music videos.

The related Five-Percent Nation (a.k.a. Poor Righteous Teachers), an Islamic organization sometimes also referred to as the Nation of Gods (men) and Earths (women), was founded by a former member of the Nation of Islam, Clarence 13X, in the early 1960s and took its name from the belief that the world's population is divided into three categories and that five percent is comprised of those who know the truth and seek to educate and enlighten others. This five percent have a spiritual responsibility to teach others the doctrine of their faith, which posits that God and the universe can be understood through science and mathematics/numerology, each number having a symbolic meaning. Five Percenters have played an influential role in hip hop from its earliest days. Artists such as Rakim and Chuck D used Five Percent teachings in their music, as did Brand Nubian, Wu-Tang Clan, Poor Righteous Teachers, Big Daddy Kane, Nas, Mos Def, Gang Starr, the Roots, and Erykah Badu. In turn, their music inspires youth to look into Five Percenter organizations.

RAP'S IMPACT ON GANG CULTURE

Gang activity has been highly influenced by rap music. Early efforts by rappers were to prevent localized street and area gangs, such as the Bloods and the Crips of Los Angeles, from uniting youth in criminal activity and gang warfare against perceived enemies. Afrika Bambaataa, for example, wanted to emulate gang culture's ability to unite youth into a common cause, but without the violence. It is no accident that hip hop dance's origins in New York City during the late 1970s coincided with a significant peak in gang activity in poor and working-class minority areas. Early on, hip hop pioneers sought to draw young black men away from these gangs. Afrika Bambaataa did so through the Universal Zulu Nation as a replacement for the unification principal of gangs; however, he tried to make the common cause of youth not violence but the pursuit of common culture. Public Enemy rapped about organizing politically and independently of the gang scene. In 1990, several West Coast rappers, under the name West Coast Rap All-Stars, released the single "We're All in the Same Gang" to promote an antiviolence message. Missy Elliott also used her music to direct young people away from gangs.

Gangs and rap had a reciprocal relationship: Gang activity early on played a major role in rap, providing rappers with subject matter that led to the creation of thug (New Orleans), gangsta (Compton), mobb (New York), and horrorcore (Detroit and Houston) rap. Schoolly D and N.W.A. drew heavily on the gang scene for the stories they rapped and the stage personas they crafted in order to do so. In his lyrics, Snoop Dogg drew on a gang-affiliated past, and Geto Boys portrayed the violence of gang life in loving detail. In turn, rap music offered an alternative to the gangsta lifestyle, offering a longer expected lifespan and, more importantly, a method for African Americans to use capitalism in their favor, rather than become its economic victims.

RAP'S IMPACT ON DANCE

By the early 1970s, break dancing, originally called b-boying (for break boy) and later b-girling, was beginning to flourish in New York. In addition to his influence on early rapping, James Brown influenced dance, as recordings of his dancing while singing the funk song "Get on the Good Foot" (1972) inspired some early hip hop moves, such as the boogaloo and the camel walk, which influenced the moonwalk. The Lockers, a Los Angeles–based dance group established by dancers and choreographers Toni Basil and Don "Campbellock" Campbell, promoted street dance as an art form—they introduced some of the earliest hip hop dance styles, such as popping and locking. Popping and locking are American hip hop dance moves sometimes associated with a third move called dropping. Combined, the dance moves create the illusion of the body's motion being slowed or even reversed, as in dubstep dancing. Popping consists of various techniques that cause it to differ greatly from most break-dancing techniques; there is very little floor work (dance moves performed while lying down), positioning oneself upside down, or sitting down in popping. Popping best creates its illusions when the dancer is standing. Locking, today used extensively in hip hop, was originally a funk dance technique. Like popping, it is a dance technique designed to create a robotic illusion, achieved by starting with a fast, usually large-scale movement, and then immediately freezing and locking into a statuesque position. This freeze is typically held for a while, which makes locking different from popping, which is more consistently fluid. This influenced turntablism because when performers took turns with solos, there was a need for break beats (segments of looped music), to allow them to set up a move. The Zulu Nation created some of the earliest breakdance crews, which led to more professional crews like Rock Steady Crew and the Electric Boogaloos. Break-dancing battles allowed rival crews to compete.

Hip hop dance eventually evolved to include more floor work influenced by gymnastics, acrobatics, and martial arts moves that showcased balance and agility. Freezes became conventional, and competitions began to focus on freezing, breaking, and power moves. Styles like gangsta (e.g., the Crip Walk and the Blood Bounce), jookin, turfing, jerkin', clowning, and krumping became popular, and significant changes to freestyle form led to counts (choreographing dance moves to coincide with beats and musical phrases), a technique credited to Basil, whose work on 1980s videos introduced a new way of structuring hip hop dancing. Organizations like Hip Hop International have since created dance championships, competitions between all-male and all-female crews who battle and showcase power moves. American crews such as Jabbawockeez, Quest Crew, Poreotics, and Beat Freaks have competed internationally and influenced international crews, such as South Korea's Morning of Owl. Break-dancing battles can be solo or team-oriented and, like rap battles, can happen informally on street corners or at staged competitions. B-boy and b-girl battles are a combination of prepared material and improvisation (although less improvisation is used than with rap battling due to the nature of team dancing). These battles are social events, where teams interact with each other and with the judges and spectators, often incorporating humor in the form of subtle jabs at opposing teams' skills. The break beat continued to provide a rhythmic basis that let dancers display their improvisational skills within the duration of a break.

Rap music has also created dances, such as jerkin,' a Los Angeles–based young adult and teen street dance that began gaining popularity on both the East and West Coasts around 2009 after hip hop duo New Boyz released their single "You're a Jerk." The video featured the duo and its posse doing street dancing, using various versions of the jerk. That same year, another hip hop duo, Audio Push, released the single "Teach Me How to Jerk," which uses a similar hiccupped/repeated chorus as Cali Swag District's more famous Top 40 hit "Teach Me How to Dougie," also released in 2009. Jerking hip hop crews included The Rej3ctz, whose 2011 dance single "Cat Daddy" made it into the Billboard Hot 100.

RAP'S IMPACT ON ART AND FASHION

Graffiti art can be found in almost any urban environment, usually on buildings, train cars, and other means of public transportation. These spray-painted symbols, words, and images have a rich history and recently developed into an art form in many cities, with some graffiti art being commissioned by private companies and city leaders. Today's graffiti has multiple functions, from expressing the artist's individuality and prowess to protesting war or calling attention to significant political issues in America and abroad. It has ties not only to pop culture iconography but to gang symbols as well. Gang-related tagging can commonly be found on highway overpasses, train cars, public concrete walls, and government buildings and grounds. Additionally, large-scale murals are now a significant part of graffiti art.

American graffiti artist and rapper Fab 5 Freddy was known for having introduced elements of hip hop such as street art, dancing, and rapping to the art world. He is best known as the original host of MTV's (1981–) *Yo! MTV Raps* (1988–95). He also produced the classic American break-dancing film *Wild Style* (1983) and was referenced in Blondie's "Rapture," making an appearance in the song's official video. His earliest exposure to music was likely jazz, since his godfather was drummer, percussionist, and composer Max Roach; he and Roach were close friends. In the early 1980s, Fab 5 Freddy went on the first rap tour in Europe with Afrika Bambaataa, Grand Mixer D.ST (a.k.a. Grand Mixer DXT), and the Rock Steady Crew, among others. In 1991, he served as associate producer for *New Jack City*, and he directed hip hop videos for Queen Latifah, Snoop Dogg, and Nas.

Fashion is as big a part of hip hop culture as is it with mainstream culture in general; pop culture fashion movements since the 1960s have involved emulating the clothing worn by musicians. In the 1970s, dance crews like the Lockers (a.k.a. The Campbell Lockers) and the Electric Boogaloos wore costumes rather than clothing. These dance crews were easily identified by their large, colorful beret-style hats, colorful knickers, large suspenders, and striped socks, as well as black hats and white gloves, clothing that resembled those worn by artists who study mime. The predominant color combination was black and white. Such costuming influenced a lot of the West Coast funk fashion, as seen on television series such as *Soul Train* and *What's Happening!!* On the East Coast, break-dancers wore more athletic clothing—tracksuits were popular, along with the new name-brand tennis shoes, especially Nike, Adidas, and Keds, as well as Kangol hats. The most popular color combinations (into the early 1980s) were red and black, and dance crews wore leather jackets and punk accessories, such as zippers and chains. As the 1980s drew to a close, hair and accessories became more pronounced (more voluminous and bigger) as the popularity of hip hop and rap culture grew. Popular rap artists set a new trend called bling: oversized jewelry, chains especially, but also watches and rings. Gigantic hoop earrings made their way into women's fashion. Shirts and jackets incorporated the large shoulder and small waist look, and pants ranged from very tight leather to very baggy "harem" pants (parachute pants), the latter nicknamed "MC Hammer pants" since he popularized them in his videos.

In time, a new variant emerged as a cultural shift toward roots pride occurred, leading to the inclusion of traditional African prints and colors as well as Rastafarian accessories and hairstyles, such as dreadlocks.

Rap music's current influence on fashion began in the 1990s, when rappers and DJs started wearing clothing that emphasized a softer, baggier look and bright colors (including neon), popular with young rappers like the Fresh Prince. The trio TLC set the tone for many women's fashions. Rappers embraced designer clothing, namely Hilfiger and FUBU (originally an acronym for Four Urban Brothers United, it became For Us By Us in 1992). Designers who embraced hip hop culture started to employ rappers for their runway shows. Sports jerseys (sometimes described as throwback jerseys) and team hats continued to be prominent. The emphasis on large clothing earned a nickname, "balla," which included flashy gold and diamond jewelry and other expensive accessories. Some woman rappers, such as MC Lyte and Queen Latifah, embraced masculine fashion and wore the same clothing but with the added touch of makeup to feminize themselves. Rappers like Lil' Kim and Foxy Brown popularized a sexier look for women that accented the female silhouette. In addition, mainstream fashion began to adopt a hip hop and rap ethos, sometimes embracing a boxy look that resembled prison wear, limited to very achromatic variations of black, white, and gray; this color scheme was embraced by the hard core or gangsta rappers that were emerging in the 1990s as a way to preserve the street origins of hip hop.

Soon hip hop artists, rappers, and producers were branching into the fashion scene themselves with labels and designs of their own. In 1998, Puff Daddy began his award-winning clothing line, Sean John, which was especially known for its tailored dress jackets. That same year, Def Jam Recordings cofounder Russell Simmons created Phat Farm and followed up a year later with a children's hip hop clothing line, Baby Phat. In 2002, OutKast started their own clothing line, OutKast Clothing (which soon folded). With less success than earlier, Simmons created new clothing lines in the 21st century: Argyleculture (2008) and Tantris (2012). For the most part, labels started by musicians have folded because the trends change so quickly it is hard for one clothing line to keep pace.

RAP'S IMPACT ON FILM

Filmmaking, both in the United States and around the globe, has been greatly influenced by rap music and hip hop culture—from soundtrack choices to story content, character development, and cinematic style.

An example of the latter is Darren Aronofsky's film π (a.k.a. Pi, 1998), in which he adopted a form of audiovisual editing he called "hip hop montage," which featured visual and sonic ruptures, fractures, and repetitions inspired by the backspinning, punch phrasing, and scratching of turntablism. The origins of rap-influenced filmmaking are usually associated with the hip hop musicals of the early 1980s and the related tradition of Hollywood-style gangsta films of the 1990s.

The 1980s saw the popularization of American films such as *Wild Style* (1983), *Beat Street* (1984), and *Krush Groove* (1985), all of which got international attention because of their emphasis on b-boying and b-girling. In addition, New Jack Cinema produced classics such as *New Jack City* (1991). These early 1980s films featured celebrities, including rappers, playing themselves. For example, *Krush Groove* featured Run-D.M.C., LL Cool J, and the Beastie Boys. These films introduced key urban youth concerns and themes, including rap celebrity, graffiti art, b-boying and b-girling, and hip hop fashion—and urban areas, such as the Bronx, became a meaningful locale. Spike Lee's *Do the Right Thing* (1989) explored racism in a single block of Brooklyn's Bed-Stuy (Bedford-Stuyvesant) neighborhood, and he used rap music, which showed other directors that the genre could be used to depict a wide array of emotions and perspectives.

Films such as *Do the Right Thing* provided a model for the burgeoning New Jack Cinema (new black realism), named after the highly successful *New Jack City*. New Jack Cinema focused on young black men in the inner city of Brooklyn or Los Angeles, typically would-be and burgeoning gangstas deeply involved in drug culture. These films tend to be violent and visually realistic, and they demonstrate that innocent women, children, and the elderly are often the victims of such conflicts. Films such as *Boyz n the Hood* (1991), *Straight out of Brooklyn* (1991), *Menace II Society* (1993), and *Above the Rim* (1994) portrayed real anxieties over rising unemployment in black communities and its role in turning young black men into criminals. Rap was prominent in these works, down to its sometimes misogynistic lyrics. Hollywood rap has broadened in genre and style, resulting in films such as *Dead Presidents* (1995), *Eve's Bayou* (1997), and *Love and Basketball* (2000), as well as parodies such as *Don't Be a Menace to South Central While Drinking Your Juice in the Hood* (1996). Since the 2000s, diverse films about rap emerged, including opera adaptations (e.g., 2001's *Carmen: A Hip Hopera*). Documentary filming techniques have been employed more than ever in several popular rap musician biopics, as exemplified in *Straight Outta Compton* (2015) and *All Eyez on Me* (2017).

Early hip hop documentaries included *Right On!: Poetry on Film* (1971), which featured music by members of Harlem's The Last Poets. Director Tony Silver and hip hop photographer Henry Chalfant created the American documentary *Style Wars*. Often credited as the first hip hop documentary, *Style Wars* introduced audiences worldwide to hip hop culture, presenting graffiti as an art as opposed to vandalism. The film included interviews with prominent New York City graffiti artists and featured b-boys Crazy Legs and Frosty Freeze, as well as a soundtrack of mostly old-school rap songs, such as the Sugar Hill Gang's "8th Wonder" (1980), Grandmaster Flash and the Furious Five's "The Message" (1982), and Treacherous Three's "Feel the Heartbeat" (1981). The American documentary *Beat This: A Hip Hop History* was released in 1984. Later documentaries, such as *Wreckin' Shop from Brooklyn* (1992), focused on break dancing and influenced the British documentary *Electro Rock* (1985), which offered some of the earliest footage of non-American b-girls, including Bubbles. *Big Fun in the Big Town* (1986), filmed in New York City, focused on both proto-punk and the New York rap scene, with interviews and performances by the Last Poets, Grandmaster Flash, Roxanne Shanté, Doug E. Fresh, Run-D.M.C., LL Cool J, and Schoolly D. Rusty Cundieff's *Fear of a Black Hat* (1993) offered parody in the form of a mockumentary, which parodies real hip hop artists like the members of Public Enemy and N.W.A. Behind-the-scenes concert preparations and reunions continue in documentaries like *Rock the Bells* (2006), about Wu-Tang Clan's intended final concert performance, as well as *Notorious B.I.G.: Bigger Than Life* (2007), *2 Turntables and a Microphone: The Life and Death of Jam Master Jay* (2008), *The Wonder Year* (2011), and *Ruthless Memories: Preserving the Life and Legend of Eric (Eazy E) Wright* (2012). Other rap topics in documentaries include beatboxing, as in *Beatboxing: The Fifth Element of Hip Hop* (2011); b-boying, as in *Bomb It*, *Bomb It 2*, and *Bouncing Cats* (2010); and the British film *Turn It Loose!* (2009).

CHAPTER 4

Legacy

Rap's legacy has outpaced its humble origins of freestyle battling and outlasted the continual controversies with censorship, violence, and misogyny in the media. Its legacy has survived the East Coast-West Coast rivalry and the murders of Tupac Shakur and the Notorious B.I.G. This is because rap was born of a solid origin—the hip hop culture of young urban African Americans and Latino Americans—and its roots were set solidly in the African oral tradition (such as that of the griot), as passed down through jazz poetry and spoken word. What began as the voice of marginalized and disenfranchised youth has been adopted (because of its commercial success) by the music industry as a whole. Like many other music genres, rap started out as a scapegoat for all that Americans found wrong in youth culture, including minority-on-minority crime, ultimately to be appropriated as a commodity.

Rappers themselves have become urban heroes, having survived the poverty, drugs, and meanness of the inner city. For example, people with disabilities have begun to use rap music to address the disabled experience for the purposes of activism and education. Like much rap, disability hip hop tracks are often protests against social and political conditions—in this case problems such as lack of access, affordability of care, and discrimination. African American poet, writer, activist and cerebral palsy sufferer Leroy F. Moore Jr. created the Krip-Hop Nation, which highlighted deaf rappers like Wawa, who uses sign language as a way to bridge hearing audience members into the deaf world and give the message that it is important to keep a sense of humor and stay positive. Rappers, like rap music, have influenced culture: fashion, movies, television, marketing, and American English. But more than anything else, rap's legacy can be seen in the music industry, both in the United States and internationally.

AMERICAN MUSIC

Rap's legacy can best be seen in how it has infiltrated various styles of music to create crossover or hybrid subgenres. This has led to the emergence of Chicano rap, trip hop, Christian hip hop, hip house, glitch hop, and other new types of rap music. These new music styles differ from rap not only in message and thematic concerns but also in instrumentation, vocalization, sampling, and flow.

Chicano music can be traced back to Tucson, Arizona–native Lalo Guerrero, who wrote big band and swing songs in the 1930s. He influenced the Chicano rock artists of the 1950s–1970s, such as Ritchie Valens, Carlos Santana, and Linda Ronstadt, and later Chicano pop stars like Selena. These artists mixed Mexican, Tejano, and American elements to one degree or another in their music, which became popular among southwestern and midwestern Mexican Americans who often self-identified as Chicano (a.k.a. Chicana, Xicano, or Xicana). It was inevitable that the Latin rhythms and rock beats would be combined with hip hop beats and dance or gangsta rap lyrics to create Chicano rap, made popular by the likes of Mellow Man Ace, Kid Frost (a.k.a. Frost), A.L.T. (and the project band Latin Alliance), Jonny Z, Cypress Hill, and its lead MC B-Real. A Chicano version of N.W.A., named Brownside, was created by Eazy-E in 1993.

Trip hop, which came into prominence in the early 1990s in Bristol, England, thanks to the efforts of Massive Attack, Portishead, and Tricky, was a combination of many of the musical foundations of psychedelic rock and hip hop/rap. It borrowed from rap such musical practices as looped samples, scratches, and sequencing, which it added to its atmospheric melodic instrumentation and ethereal lead singing. In trip hop, rapping became secondary (with the exception of the band Massive Attack) because artists suspected that the British accent might not be marketable in the United States on rap tracks. Against either sung or rapped vocals, trip hop artists created an atmospheric sound with laid-back tempos and an artful multilayering of instruments, samples that had been elaborately changed, especially in relation to tempo, and backgrounded voices. Unfortunately, trip hop is highly influenced by technology, resulting in a studio (synthesizer and computer hookup) sound that was difficult to reproduce live. Trip hop did evolve to include greater clarity of instrumental sound, less vocal distortion, and acoustic instruments—unfortunately, the bands who made these changes, such as Morcheeba, Sneaker Pimps, Lamb, Goldfrapp, and Thievery Corporation, moved away from rap and hip hop and toward psychedelia.

Rap was combined with Christian music to create CHH (a.k.a. Christian hip hop), old-school-style rap concerned with Christian values and biblical verses. CHH emerged in 1985 with Stephen Wiley's four-song EP *Bible Break*, released just six years after "Rapper's Delight" by the Sugarhill Gang. Like many of his contemporaries in the early CHH scene, Wiley was an African American youth minister who used rap to teach his students. In 1987, Michael Peace released his highly influential *RRRock It Right*, widely recognized as the first full-length commercially released CHH album. Other early CHH MCs and groups include D-Boy Rodriguez, Dynamic Twins, LPG (a.k.a. Living Proof of Grace), P.I.D. (a.k.a. Preachers in Disguise or Preachas), and S.F.C. (a.k.a. Soldiers for Christ). Gangsta rap fully hit the CHH scene in the early 1990s with Christian groups such as Gospel Gangstaz. Other prominent CHH groups include the Cross Movement, KJ-52, Lecrae, Mase, the New Breed (a.k.a. Israel Houghton & New Breed), and T-Bone. Though CHH was largely dominated by African American male performers, female rappers such as Elle R.O.C. and Sister Souljah emerged after 1992. The success of RedCloud ushered in the representation of Native Americans and Hispanic Americans in CHH. Since the 1990s, several labels, including Reach Records and Cross Movement Records, have been devoted solely to CHH.

Industrial hip hop fuses hip hop beats and/or rap vocals with industrial music, which is typically experimental electronic music that draws on harsh, discordant, metallic-sounding beats, noise, and power chords. The two are an excellent fit since both rap and industrial music generally are both transgressive and provocative lyrically, and because industrial music is related to some styles of trip hop, dubstep, and digital hardcore. Early influences included Bristol, England, vocalist Mark Stewart, London keyboardist and producer Adrian Sherwood, and New York City–based bassist and producer Bill Laswell. Guitarist, rapper-songwriter, and spoken-word artist Michael Franti cofounded the Beatnigs, a band that combined hardcore punk, industrial, jazz, and rap on the West Coast. Meanwhile, Sherwood cofounded the band Tackhead, working with Sugar Hill Records musicians. These pioneers paved the way for early industrial rap bands such as Meat Beat Manifesto, Franti's the Disposable Heroes of Hiphoprisy, and MC 900 Ft. Jesus. Second generation industrial rap acts included Antipop Consortium, Death Grips, and Dälek.

A related music style, hip house (a.k.a. rap house or house rap), is a combination of house music, normally associated with dance-oriented nightclubs, and hip hop beats. It became popular in the late 1980s, appearing first in large urban areas such as New York and Chicago. One of the earliest bands to popularize hip house was the Beatmasters, who, working with the pop crossover female rap duo Cookie Crew, released the hit "Rok Da House" (1987). Other early recordings included that of Tyree and Kool Rock Steady, whose "Turn up the Bass" was released in 1988, and Vitamin C's 1990 club hit "The Chicago Way." However, the two songs that made hip house ubiquitous with clubbing were by jazz and hip hop trio Jungle Brothers and the duo of Rob Base and DJ E-Z Rock, with "I'll House You" and "It Takes Two," respectively. Hip house since 2000 has evolved into a sound called electro hop—which is hip house combined with electropop, a style of synth-pop featuring a harder sound—and it has influenced iconic pop performers such as Lady Gaga. Artists who have adopted electro hop include LMFAO, Black Eyed Peas, Pitbull, Flo Rida, Azealia Banks, and Diplo.

Another style of hip house, Brick City club, became popular from 1995 to 2000 in the Newark, New Jersey, area. Here DJs created tracks that bordered on house music but consisted of break beats and strung-together, repetitive sound bites (short looped vocal excerpts similar to those in trap and bounce) with musical phrases that emphasized high energy over lyrical content or musical complexity. Generally, Brick City had its own stable of beats that DJs could use different techniques to mix, but no matter the DJ, Brick City used a pronounced bass kick in the programmed drum tracking, and samples are short (or "chopped"). Brick City also favors synthesizer over the brass associated with funk-infused rap or hip hop. The style was renamed Jersey club when DJs outside Newark became more involved with its production and popularity. Though it was influenced by rap, the style has in turn influenced rap artists like Missy Elliott and Timbaland, particularly on the album *Miss E . . . So Addictive* (2001).

Rap merged with R&B, as well as funk and gospel, to create new jack swing, named in 1987 by writer Barry Michael Cooper in a *Village Voice* article. R&B and hip hop singer Teddy Riley introduced the sound at nightclubs in Harlem, but Babyface, Bernard Belle, Jimmy Jam, Terry Lewis, and L.A. Reid took the sound national. In addition, Quincy Jones read Cooper's article and asked Riley to work on the screenplay for the American crime thriller film *New Jack City* (1991), which guaranteed the music would catch on with mainstream audiences. Notable early new jack examples included Janet Jackson's "Nasty" (1986), Club Nouveau's "Lean on Me" (1986), Keith Sweat's "I Want Her" (1987), and Bobby Brown's "Don't Be Cruel" (1988). New jack swing employs typical rap music instrumentation—drum machines, synthesizers, and turntables—along with a funky bass line played by either a synthesizer or bass guitar and sampled beats sometimes produced by a Roland TR-808 (a.k.a. 808 drum). Looped beats are used, usually with kick drum on the first and third beats, as well as snare drum on the second and fourth beats for a syncopated swing sound. Sixteenth-note percussion on the first beats produces a shuffle effect, as in Paula Abdul's "Straight Up" (1988). Other well-known new jack swing artists include Bell Biv DeVoe, Boyz II Men, and Tony! Toni! Toné!

Rap even found its way into laptop music with glitch hop, a subgenre of both electronica and rap. Glitch hop blends break beats, hip hop bass grooves, and rap samples with the sounds, techniques, and looping practices of glitch music, which is music that deliberately incorporates errors or glitches, such as audio malfunctions—skips, hums, distortion, noise, and even incorrect bit rate use. Glitch and hip hop merged in the late 1990s with Push Button Objects. Its EP *Cash* (1997) was heavily influenced by hip hop, relied on a drum machine to create break beats using the machine's looping and layering functions, and sampled preexisting sounds and vocal passages, usually transforming them digitally to mimic scratching effects created on turntables. This approach is also found in the first album by Prefuse 73, *Vocal Studies + Uprock Narratives* (2001). Glitch hop can lean more toward electronic dance music (EDM) than rap, but this is not always the case. It is popular internationally, with the majority of artists originating from the United States, the United Kingdom, Australia, New Zealand, and Japan. New jack swing as well went international, with songs charting in Australia, Canada, New Zealand, Sweden, and the United Kingdom. The French group Tribal Jam recorded several new jack swing songs in French.

INTERNATIONAL MUSIC

Hip hop and rap may have begun in the United States, but during the formative years, exchanges between artists from the United States and artists who were either in other countries or part of the American immigrant experience resulted in the emergence of hip hop culture's basic elements—beat making, b-boying and b-girling, graffiti production, fashion, literature, education, filmmaking, and rapping. For example, Harlem's The Last Poets, one of rap music's earliest influences, engaged in hip hop activities that were an exchange among African American, West African, and Puerto Rican cultures and music, as well as among members who were strongly involved in black and Puerto Rican nationalist movements. By the early 1970s on the West Coast, a hip hop dance crew known as the Lockers had been founded by African American and Italian American choreographers Don Campbell and Toni Basil, and near the end of that decade, break-dancing crews such as Rock Steady Crew had emerged in the Bronx, also revealing an exchange between African American and Puerto Rican artists. Meanwhile, deejaying and turntablism developed, emerging first with DJ Kool Herc, whose family emigrated from Kingston, Jamaica, to the Bronx.

Hip hop quickly extended its global reach to countries where Americans could bring artifacts like sound recordings, films, or music and were allowed to teach break dancing. Puerto Rico and countries in the Caribbean, such as Jamaica, are just a few examples of places where American hip hop became popular close to the same time as its emergence in the United States, as are American Samoa, Samoa, and New Zealand as well. A second and much larger fertile ground for hip hop's reception was a set of countries that already had a music industry and were active in a global exchange of music, especially with hits. For example, the first commercial release of a rap song, the Sugarhill Gang's "Rapper's Delight" (1979), not only charted on the Billboard Hot 100 but charted also in Austria, Belgium, Canada, France, Germany, Israel, the Netherlands, Norway, South Africa, Sweden, Switzerland, and the United Kingdom. Its parent album, which went double platinum in the United States, attained platinum status in Canada, gold in Spain, and silver in the United Kingdom. In addition, Blondie's "Rapture" (1980) reached the Top 40 in every country where "Rapper's Delight" charted. MTV, which began in 1981 in the United States, was aired in most of the same countries where these songs were hits. By at least a year, the music videos for "Rapture" and "Buffalo Gals" predated the releases and international distribution of the first American full-length motion pictures featuring hip hop culture: *Wild Style* (1983), *Flashdance* (1983), *Beat Street* (1984), *Breakin'* (1984), and *Breakin' 2: Electric Boogaloo* (1984). Like audiocassettes, videocassettes were artifacts of hip hop that could be shipped, exchanged, bootlegged, pirated, and sold. The popularity of these films also helped hip hop spread to more countries in Africa, East Asia, India, Southeast Asia, and South America.

The spread of American hip hop and cultural exchanges are just part of the story of global hip hop. Some countries' artists responded by using American vernacular and adapting previously composed beats in their music as well as by learning American break-dancing footwork and moves. Examples of this activity could be found by the mid to late 1980s in countries such as Botswana, Brazil, Bulgaria, Ghana, Greece,

India, Jamaica, Pakistan, South Africa, Vietnam, and former Yugoslavia. As influential as early American hip hop was to artists, the need to make the music local—using the home language of a nation or tribe—grew. Likewise, fusing rap with native music or other kinds of local popular music allowed artists to give hip hop an authentic, local feel. In places like Puerto Rico, France, and Portugal, the need to make hip hop local and part of an authentic cultural identity tied to regional dialect was strong. For this reason, French hip hop (in French) focused more on political and socially conscious lyrical content than did early American rap, which was more dance and party based. French rap therefore became more influential than American rap in French-speaking countries worldwide, many of which were dealing with volatile social issues. By 1983 French rap became popular in countries like Belgium, Cameroon, Canada, Congo, Gabon, Guadeloupe, Lebanon, Martinique, the Netherlands, Nigeria, Senegal, and Vietnam. Likewise, Portuguese hip hop, known as hip hop tuga, became popular in Angola, Brazil, Cape Verde, Guinea-Bissau, and Mozambique, where Portuguese is the official language or a common language.

Of course, using a native language is not the only way countries make rap local. Many countries began to fuse hip hop beats with traditional or indigenous music using authentic instrumentation. For example, Ghanaian hip hop used American-inspired rap music beats but had a softer sound because of its fusion of reggae. By the early 1990s, Ghanaian hip hop acts had started to combine elements of rap with modernized Ghanaian highlife, an acoustic guitar musical style with roots tracing back to the 1920s. Highlife was itself a fusion of American swing jazz and rock with Jamaican ska and Congolese soukous. The result was called hiplife. Reggae's influence on hip hop has been especially strong in the Caribbean, Africa, parts of South America, and Oceania.

The need to make rap local was felt especially in marginalized areas, particularly those consisting of immigrants and indigenous populations. For example, rap culture quickly became popular among urban indigenous populations living in Australia (in the urban areas of Melbourne and Sydney), where indigenous peoples self-identified with urban African American youth and embraced rap's blackness. Rap became for them a tool for political discourse, a way for disenfranchised youth to criticize local living conditions and discrimination as well as confront social and economic inequality. Since the 1980s, indigenous hip hop—consisting of both indigenous music and indigenous-related lyrical content—has had a strong presence in Australia and New Zealand as well as Bolivia, Canada, Colombia, Ecuador, Finland, Mexico, Mongolia, and the

United States. Rap acts that employ indigenous musical elements often use instrumentation and traditional performance practice to give their sound an identity, as in Algeria, Burkina Faso, Cameroon, Congo, Costa Rica, Egypt, El Salvador, the Gambia, Iceland, India, Ireland, Israel, Ivory Coast, Morocco, and Senegal.

In immigrant communities, rap music appealed to youth because it offered a history and sociology lesson, enabling them to dialogue with native youth in their new home countries. Immigrants also found ways to make hip hop their own; for example, the immigrant communities in Stockholm, Sweden, took an early interest in recreating hip hop music as a unique, immigrant-based experience. By the early 1990s, Swedish rappers rapped in both Swedish and Rinkeby, a local pidgin dialect with American English, Arabic, Kurdish, Italian, Persian, Spanish, and Turkish slang. The Latin Kings, which had members of Chilean or Venezuelan descent, used this dialect. Germany is the home to most Turkish hip hop acts (and most early German rappers were Turkish immigrants), while Belgium is home to many Congolese hip hop acts, and Portugal is home to many Angolan hip hop acts. Romani hip hop acts can be found in Austria, the Czech Republic, Denmark, and Hungary. In short, contemporary hip hop is informed by global exchanges, and the incorporation of traditional music instruments in instrumentation creates a fusion of diverse world music styles in rap.

The nations that have embraced rap most fully are Canada, the United Kingdom, India, Nigeria, and Ghana. The first commercially successful Canadian rapper was Maestro Fresh Wes, an old-school rapper comparable to the American rapper Big Daddy Kane. Toronto-based, Jamaican-born radio DJ Ron Nelson helped to popularize hip hop music in Canada by promoting early acts such as Main Source, Dream Warriors, Dan-e-o, Devon, and female rapper/actor Michie Mee. "Northern Touch" (1998), a rap collective song, served as the Canadian hip hop mission statement, and this brought Vancouver-based rap group Rascalz, whose 1998 Juno Award protest led to rap awards being held on stage, rather than off camera, into the public eye. Rap found its way into the mainstream in 2001 when radio station CFXJ (93.5) became the country's first urban music station. A second generation of Canadian hip hop artists, including Kardinal Offishall, Drake, and Somali Canadian K'naan emerged. Drake went on to rewrite the American Billboard Hot 100 record books in various categories.

As of 2019, producer, singer, and actor Yo Yo Honey Singh (a.k.a. Honey Singh) is the most popular rap artist in India. Like many countries, India was introduced to rap in the mid-1980s, and Indian youth started to create a hip hop culture that became extremely popular in India's major urban cities such as Mumbai, Delhi, Chennai, Bangalore, and Kolkata. Kolkata was striking in that it was host to many aboveground hip hop dance workshops and academies that emerged by the late 1980s. In contrast, rap developed in the open in Mumbai, Delhi, Bangalore, and Chennai. Baba Sehgal was India's first rapper, releasing his debut and second albums *Dilruba* and *Alibaba* in 1991. However, it was the Tamil film *Kadhalan* (1994) that caused hip hop to catch on, as it produced a hit song, "Pettai Rap," in a scene that featured a colorful, androgynous character who emulated Flavor Flav in his comic dress style and vocal choices. In addition, bhangra-beat, a hybrid music genre that combines hip hop and rap with the folk dance and music of Punjabi farmers, became popular first in Pakistan and India and then in the United States and Canada.

Nigeria saw reggae and hip hop emerge in the 1980s. By 2014 Nigeria had become Africa's largest economy, and it has one of the largest youth populations in the world, making it fertile ground for a proliferation of rap music infused with traditional folk and popular sounds, highly influenced by the country's various ethnic regions. Traditional instrumentation tends toward diversity, with the most common instruments being xylophones (balafons), marimbas, bells, scrapers (similar to guiros), shakers, drums, brass instruments, and woodwinds. Nigerian hip hop is named Naija hip hop, and Sound on Sound's *From Africa from Scratch* (1988) was an early Nigerian example of hip house (the band has connections to Sugar Hill Records). By the early 1990s, Nigerian youth were listening to not only American and French hip hop but also to African hip hop. In 1991, the trio Emphasis released *Big Deal!*, often considered the earliest Naija hip hop album. Other early acts included Junior & Pretty, Fela Kuti, Eedris Abdulkareem, eLDee, and Naeto C. Hip hop continued to gain popularity, and the founding of Kennis Music, eLDee's Trybe Records, Payback Tyme Records, and Dove Records officially established the rap recording industry. Recent notable acts include M.I., Jesse Jagz, Ice Prince, and Nikki Laoye, Nigeria's most popular female rapper.

In the 1980s, Ghanaian hip hop (a.k.a. GH rap) emerged in the capital city, Accra, shortly after the arrival of American hip hop. Most GH rap was in English with American vernacular, though pidgin English (combining English with Ghanaian dialects) was sometimes used. Ghana's first rap crew, Chief G and the Tribe, was started by a ten-year-old New York–born rapper and singer-songwriter, Jay Ghartey. Other pioneering artists such as Native Funk Lords, Talking Drums, and Nananom (Kings and Queens) began combining highlife (especially its heavy use of rhythm guitar) with American hip hop, creating hiplife. In 1993, Talking Drums released "Aden?," the first hiplife single. In 1999, Obrafour (a.k.a. the Executioner) had the best-selling hiplife album in Ghana, *Pae mu ka* (*To Proclaim the Truth*). Ghana's current most popular rapper is Sarkodie.

LIMITS TO RAP'S LEGACY

Despite rap's international appeal, it could not get a foothold in some countries for political, cultural, or economic reasons. For example, Afghanistan had no hip hop scene until 2002 as a result of the Taliban government's control of radio and the Internet, that is until the new government under President Hamid Karzai allowed an Afghan popular music scene to emerge. It took until 2013 for hip hop to become part of the global music curriculum at Afghanistan's National Institute of Music and for woman rappers, such as Sonita Alizadeh, to emerge. As of 2019, some governments continue to severely restrict hip hop activity to the extent that underground performance is forbidden, censored, and punished. Censorship and exile are practiced, and rappers may be sued, imprisoned, tortured, or killed. Some countries had earlier hip hop activity until new governments came into power. One gets a real sense of how controversial rap is and how geared it is toward activism by looking at a list of countries that limit rap activity (to various extents): Afghanistan, Albania, Algeria, Angola, Argentina, Armenia, Azerbaijan, Bahrain, Bangladesh, Belarus, Brunei, Burundi, Cambodia, Central African Republic, Chad, Chile, China, Comoros, Croatia, Cuba, Democratic Republic of the Congo, Djibouti, East Timor, Ecuador, Egypt, Equatorial Guinea, Eritrea, Ethiopia, the Gambia, Georgia, Guatemala, Guinea, Guinea-Bissau, Honduras, Indonesia, Iran, Iraq, Ivory Coast, Jordan, Kazakhstan, Kenya, Kyrgyzstan, Laos, Lebanon, Liberia, Libya, Malaysia, the Maldives, Mali, Morocco, Mozambique, Myanmar, North Korea, Oman, Pakistan, Palestine, Papua New Guinea, Paraguay, Peru, Qatar, Republic of Congo, Russia, Rwanda, Saudi Arabia, Singapore, Somalia, South Sudan, Sudan, Swaziland, Syria, Tajikistan, Thailand, Tibet, Togo, Tunisia, Turkey, Turkmenistan, Uganda, Ukraine, United Arab Emirates, Uzbekistan, Venezuela, Vietnam, Yemen, and Zimbabwe.

Examples of rap censorship abound in some African and European nations. In Algeria, rap, which actually dated back to 1988, was disrupted because of the Algerian Civil War and threats of imprisonment or death. Algerian rappers were forced into exile, typically in France. Angola was introduced to American rap, which it fused with African and

Caribbean beats using drum machines to create rap angolano, used for social activism and government criticism—until the Angolan Civil War caused many musicians to establish or continue careers in exile. Egypt was first exposed to hip hop in the 1990s, which eventually led to rap crews such as Arabian Knightz, which formed in 2005 despite a dictatorship that actively sought to quash underground protest music and flooded public spaces with pro-regime pop music. Arabian Knightz and other underground hip hop acts received frequent warnings from and were often censored by the Egyptian Ministry of Culture, though it was able to release some music on the Internet. After the January 2011 revolution that led to the ousting of President Hosni Mubarak, Arabian Knightz was able to release a long-awaited debut LP, *Uknighted State of Arabia* (2012).

Ethiopia's history is intertwined with the history of reggae and hip hop, with musical preferences favoring Ethiopian traditional music, American jazz, rock, and Jamaican reggae. A small hip hop scene exists in Ethiopia's capital city, Addis Ababa, but rappers have to record under aliases to protect themselves from threats and punishment. Woman rappers have yet to emerge aboveground in Ethiopia. In Belarus, a 2005 law mandated that 75 percent of all music broadcast must be national and that all lyrics would be carefully checked. For this reason, Basowiszcza, the biggest Belarusian music festival, is actually held in Poland (in the border town of Gródek). The dominant official Belarusian musical style is bubblegum pop sung in Russian, and many Belarusian rappers have moved to Poland or Russia—those who remain in Belarus are driven to the underground scene. Bosnia-Herzegovina has had trouble developing a hip hop scene because of constant political unrest, war, and ethnic cleansings through massacre and deportations. In 2000 (after the Kosovo War), a successful Bosnian hip hop crew emerged, Disciplinska Komisija (a.k.a. DK or the Disciplinary Commission), which fused old-school hip hop with reggae and rock, and suddenly free television, radio, and Internet introduced hip hop to more Bosnian-Herzegovinians.

Southeast Asian nations Brunei and Cambodia are simply too dangerous for rappers. In Brunei, a Sunni nation ruled by Sharia law, the government controls all media. Its rap scene was nonexistent until recently, when businesses globalized and started hiring from other countries. Cambodia has a history marred by the Vietnam War–related U.S. bombing of Cambodia, widespread genocide by the Khmer Rouge, and the Cambodian-Vietnamese War, events that stifled the country's musical growth. It had no hip hop culture until the late 1990s, when self-exiled Cambodians returned to their country. The Democratic Republic of the

Congo (a.k.a. the DRC) is one of the poorest and most dangerous countries in the world, plagued by the First and Second Congo Wars, the neighboring Rwandan Civil War, and its role in the Rwandan genocide. Limited media delayed access to hip hop.

In some cases, cultural preferences make it difficult for rap to gain a larger audience. Bermuda's rap scene, for example, influenced by American hip house, Jamaican reggae, dancehall, raga, Trinbagonian soca, and Puerto Rican reggaetón, gets overshadowed by American jazz, rock, and pop and Bahamian junkanoo (parade music). In the 2000s, a distinct Bermudian hip hop, performed mainly by youth, emerged in Bermuda's capital city, Hamilton, but it has yet to take serious hold. Chile's relative isolation has resulted in comparatively little development of a hip hop scene. What does exist is limited to its largest urban area, Santiago, and it's a slow growth that can be attributed in part to societal homogeneity as a result of the repressive censorship policies of the Augusto Pinochet dictatorship and its aftermath (nevertheless, one of South America's most successful female rap artists, Ana Tijoux, returned to Chile after being exiled in France).

Rap was brought to Argentina in the 1980s by American hip hop films like *Wild Style*, but generally speaking, very little rap is currently being produced in Argentina, with the exception of a small scene in Buenos Aires—as recently as 2013, rap artists had recorded only thirty albums in Buenos Aires. Guatemalans have a diverse sense of musical styles and an alternative, underground music movement since the 1990s, including a growing rap scene, even though most rap is imported from the United States. Iraq has a young hip hop scene because of the suppression of anything associated with Western culture during the reign of Saddam Hussein, which ended in 2003. Said to have sprung from influence of U.S. troops during its occupation of Iraq that began in 2003, Iraqi rap was heard on Voice of Youth, a radio station owned by Hussein's eldest son, Uday, and broadcast exclusively in English to pander to Iraqi youth. In addition, U.S. soldiers brought rap recordings and freestyle performance.

Ireland is known for its traditional music, which has managed to survive despite globalization. Due to cultural tastes that favor traditional and rock music, the country has not fully embraced rap, even though Irish hip hop acts have been known for the use of absurd and dark humor. The Ivory Coast has hosted an annual rap battle, Le Défi (The Challenge) since 1998 in its capital city, but Ivorian hip hop was successful only on the local level, and as of 2018, no Ivorian rappers have achieved popularity beyond that. Kazakhstan, an Islamic constitutional republic whose music is heavily influenced by Russia, with little

American influence, embraces music such as Q-pop (a.k.a. Qazaq pop, based on K-pop/Korean pop and J-pop/Japanese pop). The two most prolific rap acts are Rasiel and Post Mortem, which have produced only six albums total.

Some countries are simply too poor to support a thriving rap music scene. East Timor, a sovereign island nation of over one million people in Southeast Asia, had not seen a rap scene until 2013, when the Australian government began sending emissaries to teach East Timor youth break dancing and hip hop culture through workshops and makeshift music studios. As of 2019, East Timor is still suffering from ongoing terrorist attacks and third-world development issues, such as lack of access to clean running water and a disengaged youth culture that has resorted to rebellion and crime. Equatorial Guinea's capital city, Malabo, has hosted an International Hip Hop Festival since 2006 to promote tourism; however, the country, which is isolated geographically, rarely produces popular music, so musicians usually travel to neighboring Cameroon or to Europe to record. Haiti saw street rappers in the 1980s, but most of these musicians faded into obscurity, with the exception of the originator of Haitian hip hop music and culture, Master Dji, known for his 1982 rap song "Vakans." Recent popular hip hop acts mainly come from Port-au-Prince: Barikad Crew, RockFam Lame-a, Dug G, and Jimmy O (one of the rappers killed during the 2010 Haitian earthquake).

Further Reading

Adler, Bill. (2002). *Tougher than Leather: The Rise of Run-D.M.C.* Los Angeles: Consafos.
Aidi, Hisham D. (2014). *Rebel Music: Race, Empire, and the New Muslim Youth Culture.* New York: Pantheon Books.
Asante, Molefi K. (2008). *It's Bigger than Hip Hop: The Rise of the Post-Hip-Hop Generation.* New York: St. Martin's Press.
Bailey, Julius, ed. (2011). *Jay-Z: Essays on Hip Hop's Philosopher King.* Jefferson City, NC: MacFarland.
Bailey, Moya. (2011). "'The Illest': Disability as Metaphor in Hip Hop Music." In *Blackness and Disability: Critical Examinations and Cultural Interventions*, edited by Christopher M. Bell, 141–48. East Lansing: Michigan State University Press.
Baker, Houston A. (1993). *Black Studies, Rap, and the Academy.* Chicago: University of Chicago Press.
Baram, Marcus. (2014). *Gil Scott-Heron: Pieces of Man.* New York: St. Martin's Press.
Basu, Dipannita, and Sidney J. Lemelle, eds. (2006). *The Vinyl Ain't Final: Hip Hop and the Globalization of Black Popular Culture.* Ann Arbor, MI: Pluto Press.
Blanco, Alvin. (2011). *The Wu-Tang Clan and RZA: A Trip through Hip Hop's 36 Chambers.* Santa Barbara, CA: Praeger.
Borgmeyer, John, and Holly Lang. (2007). *Dr. Dre: A Biography.* Westport, CT: Greenwood Press.
Bradley, Adam. (2009). *Book of Rhymes: The Poetics of Hip Hop.* New York: Basic Civitas Books.
Bradley, Adam, and Andrew DuBois, eds. (2010). *The Anthology of Rap.* New Haven, CT: Yale University Press.
Braiker, Brian. (2007). "Geeksta Rap Rising." *Newsweek*, February 5, 2007.
Brewster, Bill, and Frank Broughton. (2010). *The Record Players: DJ Revolutionaries.* New York: Black Cat.

Bua, Justin. (2011). *The Legends of Hip Hop*. New York: Harper Design.
Bynoe, Yvonne. (2006). *Encyclopedia of Rap and Hip-Hop Culture*. Westport, CT: Greenwood Press.
Cepeda, Raquel. (2004). *And It Don't Stop: The Best American Hip-Hop Journalism of the Last 25 Years*. New York: Faber and Faber.
Chang, Jeff. (2005). *Can't Stop Won't Stop: A History of the Hip-Hop Generation*. New York: Picador.
Charnas, Dan. (2010). *The Big Payback: The History of the Business of Hip-Hop*. New York: New American Library.
Charry, Eric, ed. (2012). *Hip Hop Africa: New African Music in a Globalizing World*. Bloomington: Indiana University Press.
Choi, Seokhun. (2017). "The Marionette: Intermedial Presence and B-Boy Culture in South Korea." *Theatre Research International* 42, no. 2 (July): 132–45.
Christensen, Miyase, and Tindra Thor. (2017). "The Reciprocal City: Performing Solidarity—Mediating Space through Street Art and Graffiti." *International Communication Gazette* 79, no. 6–7 (October–November): 584–612.
Coker, Cheo Hodari. (2003). *Unbelievable: The Life, Death, and Afterlife of the Notorious B.I.G.* New York: Three Rivers Press.
Coleman, Brian. (2007). *Check the Technique: Liner Notes for Hip-Hop Junkies*. New York: Villard.
Collins, Karen. (2005). "Dead Channel Surfing: The Commonalities between Cyberpunk Literature and Industrial Music." *Popular Music* 24, no. 2 (May): 165–78.
Corrigan, Jim. (2007). *Will Smith*. Philadelphia: Mason Crest Publishers.
Cullen, Shaun. (2016). "The Innocent and the Runaway: Kanye West, Taylor Swift, and the Cultural Politics of Racial Melodrama." *Journal of Popular Music Studies* 28, no. 1 (March): 33–50.
Davidson, Sandra, and Betty Houchin Winfield, eds. (1999). *Bleep! Censoring Rock and Rap Music*. Westport, CT: Greenwood Press.
Davis, Mike. (2006). *City of Quartz: Excavating the Future in Los Angeles*. London: Verso.
DeRogatis, Jim. (2003). *Turn On Your Mind: Four Decades of Great Psychedelic Rock*. Milwaukee, WI: Hal Leonard.
Diethrich, Gregory. (2000). "Desi Music Vibes: The Performance of Indian Youth Culture in Chicago." *Asian Music* 31, no. 1 (Autumn 1999–Winter 2000): 35–61.
Durand, Alain-Philippe, ed. (2002). *Black, Blanc, Beur: Rap Music and Hip-Hop Culture in the Francophone World*. Lanham, MD: Scarecrow Press.
Dyson, Michael Eric. (2003). *Holler If You Hear Me: Searching for Tupac Shakur*. New York: Basic Civitas Books.
Dyson, Michael Eric, and Sohail Daulatzai, eds. (2010). *Born to Use Mics: Reading Nas's* Illmatic. New York: Basic Civitas Books.

Dyson, Michael Eric, Jay-Z, and Nas. (2007). *Know What I Mean: Reflections on Hip Hop.* New York: Basic Civitas Books.

Edwards, Paul. (2009). *How to Rap: The Art and Science of the Hip-Hop MC.* Chicago: Chicago Review Press.

Edwards, Paul. (2013). *How to Rap 2: Advanced Flow and Delivery Techniques.* Chicago: Chicago Review Press.

Eminem, and Sacha Jenkins. (2008). *The Way I Am.* New York: Dutton.

Fab 5 Freddy. (2011). "Fab 5 Freddy: A Jazz Upbringing at the Roots of Hip Hop." Interview by Willard Jenkins. *JazzTimes,* May 19, 2011.

Fernandes, Sujatha. (2011). *The Edge: In Search of the Global Hip Hop Generation.* London: Verso.

50 Cent. (2004). *From Pieces to Weight: Once upon a Time in Southside Queens.* London: MTV Books.

Forman, Murray. (2002). *The 'Hood Comes First: Race, Space, and Place in Rap and Hip-Hop.* Middletown, CT: Wesleyan University Press.

Forman, Murray, and Mark Anthony Neal, eds. (2012). *That's the Joint!: The Hip-Hop Studies Reader.* 2nd ed. New York: Routledge.

Frane, Andrew V. (2017). "Swing Rhythm in Classic Drum Breaks from Hip-Hop's Breakbeat Canon." *Music Perception* 34, no. 3 (February): 291–302.

French, Kenneth. (2017). "Geography of American Rap: Rap Diffusion and Rap Centers." *GeoJournal* 82, no. 2 (April): 259–72.

Fricke, Jim, and Charlie Ahearn. (2002). *Yes Yes Y'all: The Experience Music Project Oral History of Hip-Hop's First Decade.* Cambridge, MA: Da Capo Press.

Gaunt, Kyra Danielle. (2006). *The Games Black Girls Play: Learning the Ropes from Double-Dutch to Hip-Hop.* New York: New York University Press.

George, Nelson. (1998). *Hip Hop America.* New York: Viking Press.

Goldsmith, Melissa Ursula Dawn, and Anthony J. Fonseca. (2013). "Bhangra-Beat and Hip-Hop: Hyphenated Musical Cultures, Hybridized Music." In *Crossing Traditions: American Popular Music in Local and Global Contexts,* edited by Babacar M'Baye and Alexander Charles Oliver Hall, 157–74. Lanham, MD: Scarecrow Press.

Goldsmith, Melissa Ursula Dawn, and Anthony J. Fonseca, eds. (2018). *Hip Hop around the World: An Encyclopedia.* 2 vols. Santa Barbara, CA: ABC-CLIO.

Goldsmith, Melissa Ursula Dawn, Paige A. Willson, and Anthony J. Fonseca, eds. (2016). *The Encyclopedia of Musicians and Bands on Film.* Lanham, MD: Rowman & Littlefield.

Gopal, Sangita, and Sujata Moorti. (2008). *Global Bollywood: Travels of Hindi Song and Dance.* Minneapolis: University of Minnesota Press.

Gopinath, Gayatri. (1995). "'Bombay, UK, Yuba City': Bhangra Music and the Engendering of Diaspora." *Diaspora: A Journal of Transnational Studies* 4, no. 3 (Winter): 303–21.

Further Reading

Gosa, Travis L., and Erik Nielson, eds. (2015). *Hip Hop and Obama Reader.* New York: Oxford University Press.

Graham, Natalie. (2016). "Cracks in the Concrete: Policing Lil Wayne's Masculinity and the Feminizing Metaphor." *Journal of Popular Culture* 49, no. 4 (August): 799–817.

Green, Tony. (2003). "OutKast: *Southernplayalisticadillacmuzik*; *ATLiens*; *Aquemini*; *Stankonia*." In *Classical Material: The Hip-Hop Album Guide*, edited by Oliver Wang, 131–34. Toronto: ECW Press.

Greenburg, Zack O'Malley. (2015). *Empire State of Mind: How Jay-Z Went from Street Corner to Corner Office.* Rev. ed. New York: Portfolio/Penguin Press.

Gucci Mane, and Neil Martinez-Belkin. (2017). *The Autobiography of Gucci Mane.* New York: Simon & Schuster.

Guzman-Sanchez, Thomas. (2012). *Underground Dance Masters: Final History of a Forgotten Era.* Santa Barbara, CA: Praeger.

Hanson, Carter F. (2014). "Pop Goes Utopia: An Examination of Utopianism in Recent Electronic Dance Pop." *Utopian Studies* 25 (2): 384–413.

Hess, Mickey, ed. (2007). *Icons of Hip Hop: An Encyclopedia of the Movement, Music, and Culture.* 2 vols. Westport, CT: Greenwood Press.

Hess, Mickey, ed. (2010). *Hip Hop in America: A Regional Guide.* 2 vols. Santa Barbara, CA: Greenwood Press.

Hill Collins, Patricia. (2006). *From Black Power to Hip Hop: Racism, Nationalism, and Feminism.* Philadelphia: Temple University Press.

Howe, Blake, Stephanie Jensen-Moulton, Neil Lerner, and Joseph Straus, eds. (2016). *The Oxford Handbook of Music and Disability Studies.* New York: Oxford University Press.

Jackson, Lauren Michele. (2017). "The Rapper Laughs, Herself: Nicki Minaj's Sonic Disturbances." *Feminist Media Studies* 17, no. 1 (February): 126–29.

Jay-Z. (2010). *Decoded.* New York: Spiegel & Grau.

Kajikawa, Loren. (2009). "Eminem's 'My Name Is': Signifying Whiteness, Rearticulating Race." *Journal of the Society for American Music* 3, no. 3 (August): 341–63.

Kajikawa, Loren. (2015). *Sounding Race in Rap Songs.* Oakland: University of California Press.

Katz, Mark. (2010). *Capturing Sound: How Technology Has Changed Music.* Berkeley: University of California Press.

Katz, Mark. (2012). *Groove Music: The Art and Culture of the Hip-Hop DJ.* Oxford: Oxford University Press.

Keyes, Cheryl Lynette. (2002). *Rap Music and Street Consciousness.* Urbana: University of Illinois Press.

Kitwana, Bakari. (2002). *The Hip Hop Generation: Young Blacks and the Crisis in African American Culture.* New York: Basic Civitas Books.

Kitwana, Bakari. (2005). *Why White Kids Love Hip-Hop: Wankstas, Wiggers, Wannabes, and the New Reality of Race in America.* New York: Basic Civitas Books.

Kojima, Rie, Teruo Nomura, and Noriyuki Kida. (2016). "Expressing Joy through Hip-Hop Dance Steps: Focus on New Jack Swing." *Journal of Music and Dance* 6 (1): 1–11.

Krims, Adam. (2000). *Rap Music and the Poetics of Identity*. Cambridge: Cambridge University Press.

KRS-One and Michael Lipscomb. (1992). "Can the Teacher Be Taught?" *Transition* (57): 168–89.

Lang, Holly. (2007). *The Notorious B.I.G.: A Biography*. Westport, CT: Greenwood Press.

Lemmens, MaryJo. (2008). *Cypress Hill*. Broomall, PA: Mason Crest.

Lena, Jennifer C. (2006). "Social Context and Musical Content of Rap Music, 1979–95." Social Forces 85 (1): 479–83, 486–87, 489–95.

Light, Alan, ed. (1999). *The Vibe History of Hip Hop*. New York: Three Rivers Press.

Lipsitz, George. (2006). "Breaking the Silence: The Fugees and the Score." *Journal of Haitian Studies* 12 (1): 4–23.

Locilento, Micah. (2002). *Shaggy: Dogamuffin Style*. Toronto: ECW Press.

Lynne, Douglas. (2013). *Kanye West: Grammy-Winning Hip-Hop Artist & Producer*. North Mankato, MN: ABDO Publishing.

Maire, Sunaina. (1998). "Desis Reprazent: Bhangra Remix and Hip Hop in New York City." *Postcolonial Studies* 1 (3): 357–70.

Manero, J. K. (2009). *Bust a Move: Six Decades of Dance Crazes*. New York: It Books.

Massood, Paula J. (2003). *Black City Cinema: African American Urban Experiences in Film*. Philadelphia: Temple University Press.

McFarland, Pancho. (2006). "Chicano Rap Roots: Black–Brown Cultural Exchange and the Making of a Genre." *Callaloo* 29 (3): 939–55.

McFarland, Pancho. (2008). *Chicano Rap: Gender and Violence in the Postindustrial Barrio*. Austin: University of Texas Press.

McQuillar, Tayannah, and Fred L. Johnson. (2010). *Tupac Shakur: The Life and Times of an American Icon*. Cambridge, MA: Da Capo Press.

Merrill, Samuel. (2015). "Keeping It Real? Subcultural Graffiti, Street Art, Heritage and Authenticity." *International Journal of Heritage Studies* 21 (4): 369–89.

Miller, Matt. (2012). *Bounce: Rap Music and Local Identity in New Orleans*. Amherst: University of Massachusetts Press.

Miller, Paul (DJ Spooky), ed. (2008). *Sound Unbound: Sampling Digital Music and Culture*. Cambridge, MA: MIT Press.

Miszczynski, Milosz, and Adriana Helbig, eds. (2017). *Hip Hop at Europe's Edge: Music, Agency, and Social Change*. Bloomington: Indiana University Press.

Mitchell, Tony, ed. (2001). *Global Noise: Rap and Hip-Hop outside the U.S.A.* Middletown, CT: Wesleyan University Press.

Miyakawa, Felicia M. (2005). *Five Percenter Rap: God Hop's Music, Message, and Black Muslim Mission*. Bloomington: Indiana University Press.

Miyakawa, Felicia M. (2007). "Turntablature: Notation, Legitization, and the Art of the Hip-Hop DJ." *American Music* 25 (1): 81–105.

Monteyne, Kimberley. (2013). *Hip Hop on Film: Performance, Culture, Urban Space, and Genre Transformation in the 1980s*. Jackson: University Press of Mississippi.

Neal, Mark Anthony, and Murray Forman. (2004). *That's the Joint: The Hip-Hop Studies Reader*. New York: Routledge.

Ntarangwi, Mwenda. (2009). *East African Hip Hop: Youth Culture and Globalization*. Urbana: University of Illinois Press.

Ogbar, Jeffrey Ogbonna Green. (2007). *Hip-Hop Revolution: The Culture and Politics of Rap*. Lawrence: University Press of Kansas.

Oliver, Richard, and Tim Leffel. (2006). *Hip-Hop, Inc.: Success Strategies of the Rap Moguls*. New York: Thunder's Mouth Press.

Palmer, Lorrie. (2011). "Black Man/White Machine: Will Smith Crosses Over." *Velvet Light Trap: A Critical Journal of Film and Television* 67 (Spring): 28–40.

Pate, Alexs D. (2010). *In the Heart of the Beat: The Poetry of Rap*. Lanham, MD: Scarecrow Press.

Perkins, William Eric. (1996). *Droppin' Science: Critical Essays on Rap Music and Hip-Hop Culture*. Philadelphia: Temple University Press.

Perry, Imani. (2004). *Prophets of the Hood: Politics and Poetics in Hip Hop*. Durham, NC: Duke University Press.

Pinn, Anthony B., ed. (2003). *Noise and Spirit: The Religious and Spiritual Sensibilities of Rap Music*. New York: New York University Press.

Price, Emmett George. (2006). *Hip Hop Culture*. Santa Barbara, CA: ABC-CLIO.

Prickett, Stacey. (2013). "Hip-Hop Dance Theatre in London: Legitimising an Art Form." *Dance Research* 31 (2): 174–90.

Proctor, Michael, Erik Bresch, Dani Byrd, Krishna Nayak, and Shrikanth Narayanan. (2013). "Paralinguistic Mechanisms of Production in Human 'Beatboxing': A Real-Time Magnetic Resonance Imaging Study." *Journal of the Acoustical Society of America* 133 (2): 1043–54.

Questlove, and Ben Greenman. (2013). *Mo' Meta Blues: The World According to Questlove*. New York: Grand Central Publishing.

Quinn, Eithne. (2005). *Nuthin' but a "G" Thang: The Culture and Commerce of Gangsta Rap*. New York: Columbia University Press.

Rajakumar, Mohanalakshmi. (2012). *Hip Hop Dance*. Santa Barbara, CA: Greenwood Press.

Rambsy, Howard, II. (2013). "Beyond Keeping It Real: OutKast, the Funk Connection, and Afrofuturism." *American Studies* 52 (4): 205–16.

Rausch, Andrew J. (2011). *I Am Hip Hop: Conversations on the Music and Culture*. Lanham, MD: Scarecrow Press.

Reeves, Marcus. (2008). *Somebody Scream! Rap Music's Rise to Prominence in the Aftershock of Black Power*. New York: Faber and Faber.

Reynolds, Simon. (2012). *Energy Flash: A Journey through Rave Music and Dance Culture*. Berkeley: Soft Skull Press.

Richardson, Elaine. (2006). *Hiphop Literacies*. Abingdon, England: Routledge.
Rivera, Raquel Z. (2003). *New York Ricans from the Hip Hop Zone*. New York: Palgrave Macmillan.
Ro, Ronin. (2005). *Raising Hell: The Reign, Ruin, and Redemption of Run-D.M.C. and Jam Master Jay*. New York: Amistad.
Ro, Ronin. (2007). *Dr. Dre: The Biography*. New York: Thunder's Mouth Press.
Romero, Elena. (2012). *Free Stylin': How Hip Hop Changed the Fashion Industry*. Santa Barbara: Praeger.
Rose, Tricia. (1994). *Black Noise: Rap Music and Black Culture in Contemporary America*. Middletown, CT: Wesleyan University Press.
Rose, Tricia. (2008). *The Hip Hop Wars: What We Talk about When We Talk about Hip Hop—and Why It Matters*. New York: Basic Civitas Books.
RZA, and Chris Norris. (2005). *The Wu-Tang Manual*. New York: Riverhead.
RZA, and Chris Norris. (2009). *The Tao of Wu*. New York: Riverhead.
Samy Alim, H., Jooyoung Lee, and Lauren Mason Carris. (2011). "Moving the Crowd, 'Crowding' the Emcee: The Coproduction and Contestation of Black Normativity in Freestyle Rap Battles." *Discourse & Society* 22 (4): 422–39.
Sarig, Roni. (2007). *Third Coast: OutKast, Timbaland, and How Hip-Hop Became a Southern Thing*. Cambridge, MA: Da Capo Press.
Scarface and Benjamin Meadows Ingram. (2015). *Diary of a Madman: The Geto Boys, Life, Death, and the Roots of Southern Rap*. New York: HarperCollins.
Schloss, Joseph G. (2004). *Making Beats: The Art of Sample-Based Hip-Hop*. Middletown, CT: Wesleyan University Press.
Schloss, Joseph G. (2009). *Foundation: B-Boys, B-Girls, and Hip-Hop Culture in New York*. Oxford: Oxford University Press.
Scott, Cathy. (2000). *The Murder of Biggie Smalls*. New York: St. Martin's Press.
Scott, Cathy. (2014). *The Killing of Tupac Shakur*. Las Vegas: Huntington Press.
Scott-Heron, Gil. (2012). *The Last Holiday: A Memoir*. New York: Grove Press.
Serrano, Shea, and Arturo Torres. (2015). *The Rap Year Book: The Most Important Rap Song from Every Year since 1979, Discussed, Debated, and Deconstructed*. New York: Abrams Image.
Sewell, Amanda. (2014). "How Copyright Affected the Musical Style and Critical Reception of Sample-Based Hip-Hop." *Journal of Popular Music Studies* 26 (2–3): 295–320.
Sewell, Amanda. (2015). "Nerdcore Hip-Hop." In *The Cambridge Companion to Hip-Hop*, edited by Justin Williams, 223–31. Cambridge: Cambridge University Press.
Shanks, David. (2010). "Uptown, Baby! Hip Hop in Harlem and Upper Manhattan." In *Hip Hop in America: A Regional Guide*, Vol. 1, edited by Mickey Hess, 31–46. Santa Barbara, CA: ABC-CLIO.
Small, Michael W. (1992). *Break It Down: The Inside Story from the New Leaders of Rap*. New York: Carol Pub.

Soojin Park, Judy. (2015). "Searching for a Cultural Home: Asian American Youth in the EDM Festival Scene." *Dancecult: Journal of Electronic Dance Music Culture* 7 (1): 15–34.

Spady, James G. (2006). "The Fluoroscope of Brooklyn Hip Hop: Talib Kweli in Conversation." *Callaloo* 29 (3): 993–1011.

Spady, James G., H. Samy Alim, and Samir Meghelli. (2006). *The Global Cipha: Hip Hop Culture and Consciousness*. Philadelphia: Black History Museum Publishers.

Spencer, Zoe, and Molefi Kete Asante. (2011). *Murda', Misogyny, and Mayhem: Hip-Hop and the Culture of Abnormality in the Urban Community*. Lanham, MD: University Press of America.

Stewart, James B. (2005). "Message in the Music: Political Commentary in Black Popular Music from Rhythm and Blues to Early Hip Hop." *Journal of African American History* 90 (3): 196–225.

Tanz, Jason. (2007). *Other People's Property: A Shadow History of Hip-Hop in White America*. New York: Bloomsbury.

Terkourafi, Marina, ed. (2010). *The Languages of Global Hip-Hop*. London: Continuum.

Thaller, Jonel, and Jill Theresa Messing. (2014). "(Mis)Perceptions around Intimate Partner Violence in the Music Video and Lyrics for 'Love the Way You Lie.'" *Feminist Media Studies* 14 (4): 623–39.

Vanhanen, Janne. (2003). "Virtual Sound: Examining Glitch and Production." *Contemporary Music Review* 22 (4): 45–52.

Walter, Carla Stalling. (2007). *Hip Hop Dance: Meanings and Messages*. Jefferson, NC: McFarland.

Wang, Oliver, ed. (2003). *Classic Material: The Hip-Hop Album Guide*. Toronto: ECW Press.

Wang, Oliver. (2015). *Legions of Boom: Filipino American Mobile DJ Crews in the San Francisco Bay Area*. Durham, NC: Duke University Press.

Ware, Tony. (2012). "Idle Warship Rapper Talib Kweli and Singer Res Discuss Defying Musical Definitions, and the Ten-Year Collaboration that Culminated in Habits of the Heart." *Electronic Musician* 28 (7): 32–40.

Warwick, Jacqueline. (2000). "'Make Way for the Indian': Bhangra Music and South Asian Presence in Toronto." *Popular Music and Society* 24 (2): 25–44.

Watkins, S. Craig. (2005). *Hip Hop Matters: Politics, Pop Culture, and the Struggle for the Soul of a Movement*. Boston: Beacon Press.

Webber, Stephen. (2008). *DJ Skills: The Essential Guide to Mixing and Scratching*. Burlington, MA: Focal Press.

Westhoff, Ben. (2011). *Dirty South: OutKast, Lil Wayne, Soulja Boy, and the Southern Rappers Who Reinvented Hip-Hop*. Chicago: Chicago Review Press.

Westhoff, Ben. (2016). *Original Gangstas: The Untold Story of Dr. Dre, Eazy-E, Ice Cube, Tupac Shakur, and the Birth of West Coast Rap*. New York: Hachette Books.

White, Theresa Renée. (2013). "Missy 'Misdemeanor' Elliott and Nicki Minaj: Fashionistin' Black Female Sexuality in Hip-Hop Culture—Girl Power or Overpowered?" *Journal of Black Studies* 44 (6): 607–26.

Williams, Justin. (2013). *Rhymin' and Stealin': Musical Borrowing in Hip-Hop Music*. Ann Arbor: University of Michigan Press.

Williams, Justin, ed. (2015). *The Cambridge Companion to Hip-Hop*. Cambridge: Cambridge University Press.

Woodstra, Chris, John Bush, and Stephen Thomas Erlewine. (2008). *Old School Rap and Hip-Hop*. New York: Backbeat Books.

Wragg, Jeff. (2016). "Just Don't Call It Trip Hop: Reconciling the Bristol Sound Style with the Trip Hop Genre." *Organised Sound* 21 (1): 40–50.

Zanfagna, Christina. (2012). "Kingdom Business: Holy Hip Hop's Evangelical Hustle." *Journal of Popular Music Studies* 24 (2): 196–216.

Index

Aceyalone, 177, 179–180, 181
Aerosmith. *See* "Walk This Way"
Afrika Bambaataa, 210
"Ain't Nuthin' But a She Thing," 173, 174–175
"Ain't With Being Broke," 94
All Eyez on Me, 191, 192–196
All Hail the Queen, 175
"All We Got," 45
"Ambitionz Az a Ridah," 192–193
"Amityville," 85
And the Anonymous Nobody, 65
"Angel," 127, 130
"Angels," 47
"Another N— in the Morgue," 95
"Anti-N— Machine," 167–168
AOI: Bionix, 64
The Art of War, 29–33
Art Official Intelligence: Mosaic Thump, 64
As Clean as They Wanna Be, 199
As Nasty as They Wanna Be, 196–199
Atlanta, Georgia, 11–12

"B.O.B," 160–161
Bad as I Wanna B, 137, 138–141
"B— Ain't S—," 75
Bass Brothers, 81, 85
Battling, 206–207. *See also* Freestyle

B-boying. *See* Breakdancing
Beastie Boys, 15–19
Beatboxing, 20–21, 206–207
The Beatles, 107, 110–112. *See also The Grey Album*
Bennett, Lauren, 128–129
"Beware," 23
"Beware of the Boys," 162–164
B-girling. *See* Breakdancing
Bhangra-beat, 162
Big Daddy Kane, 19–20, 21–22
Big Pun, 22–26
Biggie Smalls. *See* The Notorious B.I.G.
Birdman, 26–29
Biz Markie, 19, 166, 206
The Black Album, 107–110. *See also The Grey Album*
Black Eyed Peas, 127
Black nationalism, 209
Black Sunday, 56
"Blessings," 46
Blondie, 185, 187–188
Bloods. *See* Gangs
Tha Blue Carpet Treatment, 183
"Bodak Yellow," 41, 42–43
Bone Thugs-N-Harmony, 29–33
Boogie Down Productions, 115–116
"Boom, Shake the Room," 67
Borixon, 36

Bossalinie, 48, 49–52
"B— Please II," 83
"Break It on Down," 197
"Break Ya Neck," 38–39
Breakdancing, 6, 211–212. *See also* Fashion
Brick City club, 220
Broken Silence, 61–62
The Bronx, New York, 7
Brooklyn, New York, 7
"Brothers Gonna Work It Out," 167
Bubba Sparxxx, 33–35, 37
"Buggin' Out," 190
Buhloone Mindstate, 63–64
"Burn Hollywood Burn," 168
Bush, 184
Busta Rhymes, 38–41
"Butter," 190

The Calm, 103–104
Campbell, Luther. *See* Luke
"Can't Take a Joke," 70
Capital Punishment, 22–24
Cardi B, 41–44
Cash Money (Ca$h Money), 10–11, 26
Ceza, 39, 40
"Champion," 149
Chance the Rapper, 45–48
"Change Clothes," 109, 111
Chap hop, 133
"Check the Rhime," 189
Check Your Head, 16–17
Chicago, Illinois, 12
Chopper, 13, 38–41
Christian hip hop, 219
The Chronic, 72–76
Chuck D. *See* Public Enemy
"Chuckie," 95
Chyna Doll, 61
"C'mon Babe," 197–198
C-Murder, 48, 49–52
Code Red, 67–68
"Cold Rock a Party," 140

Collins, Phil, 142–143. *See also* Nas; "One Mic"
Coloring Book, 46–48
Colt Ford, 35
"Come on a Cone," 148
"Compton's N the House (Remix)," 156–157
"Contract on the World Love Jam," 166–167
Coolio, 52–54
"Country Cousins," 123
"Country Folks," 33, 34, 35
Country rap, 33–34
"Crime Story," 137
"Criminal," 85
Crips. *See* Gangs
"Crop Circles," 103, 104–106
Cypress Hill, 54–57
Cypress Hill IV, 55–56

"D.R.A.M. Sings Special," 46
Da Bassment Cru. *See* Swing Mob Collective
Da Brat, 57, 58–59
Da Game Is to Be Sold, 183
Da Real World, 77
Danger Mouse, 107, 110–112
Danny Boone, 35
The Dark Carnival, 103, 105
"The Day the N— Took Over," 73
Daz Dillinger, 192, 193
De La Soul, 62–65
De La Soul Is Dead, 63
"Dear Old Nicki," 147
Death Row Records, 4, 72–73, 182, 183, 192, 193, 196
"December 4th," 108, 110
"Deeez Nuuuts," 75
"Desperada," 112, 114–115
DeVante Swing, 77
"Did It On 'Em," 146–147
"Dirt off Your Shoulder," 109, 111
Disability hip hop, 217–218
Diss-track, 4

Index

DJ Jazzy Jeff, 65–68
DJ Jazzy Jeff & the Fresh Prince, 65–68
DJ Mr. Mixx, 196, 197–198
DJ Scott La Rock, 115–116
DJ U-Neek, 29
DJing. *See* Scratching; Turntablism
D-Loc, 41
Documentaries, 215–216. *See also* Film
Tha Doggfather, 183
Doggystyle, 182–183
Donatan, 33, 36–38
"Don't Make Me Wait," 127, 130–131
Don't Sweat the Technique, 88–89
"Doo Wop (That Thing)," 101
"Dopeman (Remix)," 157
Doug E. Fresh, 19, 20–21
Dr. Dre, 72–76, 182. *See also* N.W.A.
Drake, 26–28, 68–72
"Drug Ballad," 84–85
"Druglord Superstar," 139
"Duke of Earl," 55

Eardrum, 118, 119–124
East Coast rap, 7
"Eat to Live," 123–124
Eazy-E. *See* N.W.A.
"8 Ball (Remix)," 157
"8 Out of 10," 71
"Elevate," 70
Elliott, Missy, 76–80
Eminem, 80–86
"Emotionless," 70–71
"Encore," 109, 110
Eric B. & Rakim, 86–89
"Every Ghetto, Every City," 102
"Everyday," 139
"Everything Is Everything," 102
"Everything Man," 119
"Excursions," 189
"Ex-Factor," 100–101

"Fa All Y'all," 59
Fab 5 Freddy, 213. *See also* Graffiti
Fashion, 213–214
Fear of a Black Planet, 166, 167–169
50 Cent, 89–92
"Fight the Power," 165, 169
"Fighting Trousers," 131, 133–134
Film, 214–215. *See also* Documentaries
"Final Hour," 102
"Finish Line/Drown," 47
The Firm, 61
Five-Percent Nation, 209
Flavor Flav. *See* Public Enemy
Follow the Leader, 87–88
"Forgive Them Father," 100
"4 My Town (Play Ball)," 27–28
Foxy Brown, 57, 61–62
"Freedom," 51
Freestyle, 1–2. *See also* Battling
The Fresh Prince, 65–68
"F— tha Police," 155–156
Fugees, 99, 103
"Funkdafied," 59
Funkdafied, 59
"F— Wit Dre Day," 73

Gangs, 210
"Gangsta Gangsta," 156
Gangsta rap, 4
"Gangsta's Paradise," 52–54
"Gasoline Dreams," 159
"Get Ur Freak On," 78
Geto Boys, 92–96
"Ghetto Boy," 49–50
"Ghetto Qu'ran (Forgive Me)," 89, 91
Ghostface Killah. *See* Wu-Tang Clan
"Gimme the Loot," 152
"Give 'Em Hell," 122
Glitch hop, 221
"God's Plan," 71
"Gossip Folks," 79
"Got My Mind Made Up," 193

"Gotta Let Your N— Hang," 95
Graffiti, 212–213. *See also* Fab 5 Freddy
Grandmaster Flash and the Furious Five, 96–99
The Grey Album, 107, 110–112. *See also The Black Album*
Grey Tuesday, 112
"The Guidelines," 177, 179–180
Gural, 37
GZA. *See* Wu-Tang Clan

"Hai Hai," 162, 164–165
"Handle the Vibe," 31
Hard Core, 59–60
Harlem, New York, 8–9
"Have U Ever," 139–140
"Have You Seen Her," 136
"Heartz of Men," 194
The Heist, 132
"Held Down," 64
Hello Nasty, 17–18
"Help the Children," 136
"Here Comes the Hammer," 135
He's the DJ, I'm the Rapper, 66–67
Hill, Lauryn, 99–103
Hip hop diplomacy, 208–209
Hip house, 219–220
Hi-Tek, 124
"Hit It Run," 172
"Hold It Now," 60
"Holy Moly," 123
"Hostile Gospel, Pt. 1," 121–122
"Hostile Gospel, Pt. 2," 121
Houston, Texas, 11
"How Do U Want It," 193–194
"How I Could Just Kill a Man," 55
"How to Rob," 89, 90–91
"Humble," 124, 125–127
"Humble" (video), 126–127

"I Ain't No Joke," 87
"I Am Your Leader," 149
"If I Could Teach the World," 32
"If It Ain't Ruff," 156

Ill Communication, 17
Ill Na Na, 61
"I'm Back," 84
"I'm Upset," 70
"In the Air Tonight," 142–143. *See also* Nas; "One Mic"
"In the Mood," 124
"Incident at 66.6 FM," 167
The Indifference Engine, 133
Industrial hip hop, 219
Insane Clown Posse, 103–107
Inspectah Deck. *See* Wu-Tang Clan
International rap, 221–229
"It's All Real," 32
"It's Tricky," 171

J. White Did It, 42–44
Jackson, Brian, 177–178
Jam Master Jay. *See* Run-D.M.C.
Jay-Z, 107–110, 162–164
Jean Grae, 112–115, 122
Jeanius, 112–113
Jersey club. *See* Brick City club
JL, 40
Johnny J, 192, 193–194, 195
Just Blaze, 108

Kaczor, 37
Kajman, 36
K-Dot. *See* Lamar, Kendrick
"Keep On, Keepin' On," 138–139
"Kick in the Door," 153
"Kill You," 81–82
"Kim," 85
K'naan, 141, 143–145
KRS-One, 115–118, 120
Kweli, Talib, 113, 118–124

"La Di Da Di," 20–21
Lamar, Kendrick, 124–127
"Last Chance," 147
"Let Me Ride," 75
Let the Rhythm Hit 'Em, 87–88
"Let's Go Deeper," 136–137
Licensed to Ill, 16

Life after Death, 153–154
"Life Goes On," 195
"Lil' Ghetto Boy," 73–74
Lil' Kim, 57, 59–60
"Lil N—," 51
Lil Wayne, 26–28
"Livin' Legend," 50–51
"Listen!!!," 120
LMFAO, 127–131
Long Island, New York, 8
"Lord Help Us," 51
"Lost Ones," 100
The Low End Theory, 188, 189–191
Luke, 196–197
L.V., 52–54
"Lyrical Gangbang," 74–75

"Machine Gun Funk," 152
Macklemore & Ryan Lewis, 131–133
Tha Madd Rapper, 153–154
Marley Marl, 86
"Marshall Mathers," 84
The Marshall Mathers LP, 80, 81–86
Master P, 48–49
MC Hammer, 135–137
MC Lyte, 137–141
"Me So Horny," 197
Melle Mel, 97–99
"The Message," 96–99
"Millie Pulled a Pistol on Santa," 63
"Mind Playing Tricks on Me," 94–95
The Miseducation of Lauryn Hill, 99–103
Miss E . . . So Addictive, 76, 77–78
Mix Master Mike, 17–18
"Mixtape," 47
"Mob Ties," 70
"Moment of Clarity," 108, 111
"Money," 41, 43–44
"Money to Blow," 26–27
"More or Less," 120
Mr. B the Gentleman Rhymer, 133–134
"Ms. Jackson," 159–160

Ms. Scandalous, 162, 164–165. *See also* Panjabi Hit Squad
Mumbles, 179–180
"Mundian To Bach Ke." *See* "Beware of the Boys"; Jay-Z
"My Adidas," 171
"My First Song," 108
"My Story," 112, 113–114

N.W.A., 154–158
Nas, 141, 142–143, 144
Nation of Gods and Earths. *See* Five-Percent Nation
"The Nature," 122
Neva Left, 184
New Jack Cinema, 215
New jack swing, 220–221
New Orleans, Louisiana, 10
New York City. *See* The Bronx; Brooklyn; Harlem; Long Island
Nicki Minaj, 145–150
"Nie Lubimy Robić," 33, 36
"911 Is a Joke," 167
9th Wonder, 113, 115
"99 Problems," 109–110, 111
No Limit, 10, 48–49
"No More Pain," 194
"No Problem," 45
"No Time," 60
"Nonstop," 69
The Notorious B.I.G., 150–154
"Nuthin' but a 'G' Thang," 75
"A N— Witta Gun," 74
"NY Weather Report," 119–120

"Off the Track," 103, 105–106
"Off wit His Head," 25
"Oh My Stars," 121
Ol' Dirty Bastard. *See* Wu-Tang Clan
"On Your Face," 136
"One Mic," 141, 142–143
"One Minute Man," 78
"One on One," 139
"Only God Can Judge Me," 195–196
"The Other Level," 96

OutKast, 158–161
"Outta Here," 116–117

Paid in Full, 86–87
Panjabi Hit Squad, 162, 164–165
Panjabi MC, 162–163
"Party Rock Anthem," 127, 128–129
"Pass the Hand Grenade," 88–89
Patter song, 1
Paul's Boutique, 16
"The Perfect Beat," 120
"Peter Piper," 170–171
Pharrell, 109
Philadelphia, Pennsylvania, 9
"Pigs," 55
Pink Friday, 145, 146–148
Pink Friday: Roman Reloaded, 145–146, 148–150
Please Hammer Don't Hurt 'Em, 135–137
Politics, 208–209. See also Hip hop diplomacy
"Pray," 136
Pricele$$, 26
Prince Paul, 62
Professor Elemental, 131, 133–134
Project Blowed, 177, 179, 180–181
"Proud to Be Black," 172–173
Public Enemy, 166–169
Puff Daddy, 150–151
"Push It," 173

Queen Latifah, 173, 175–176
Queens, 8
"Quickie," 95–96

Raekwon. See Wu-Tang Clan
Rafi, 37
Raising Hell, 169, 170–173
Rap-A-Lot Records, 92–93
"Rapper's Delight," 185–186
Rapping, 1–2
"Rapture," 185, 187–188
"Rat-Tat-Tat-Tat," 74

Rayvon, 130
Ready Rock C, 66, 67
Ready to Die, 151–153
"The Real Slim Shady," 83–84
Reincarnated, 183–184
"Remember Me?," 84
"Respect," 151–152
"Retaliation," 30–31
Return of the Boom Bap, 116
"The Revolution Will Not Be Televised," 177–179
"Revolutionary Generation," 168
"Right Thru Me," 147
Robinson, Sylvia, 185–186, 188
Rock the House, 66
"Roman Holiday," 148
"Roman's Revenge," 147–148
Roxanne Shanté, 58
Run-D.M.C., 169–173
Ruthless Records, 4, 72–73
RY23, 37
RZA. See Wu-Tang Clan

Salt-N-Pepa, 173–175, 176
"Same Drugs," 46–47
"Sandra's Rose," 71
Santana, Carlos, 101
"Say Something," 122
Scorpion, 68, 69–72
Scott-Heron, Gil, 177–179, 180
Scratching, 207–208. See also Turntablism
"Sexy and I Know It," 127, 129–130
Shaggy, 127, 130–131
Sheller, 37
"Show Business," 189
"Sittin on Top of the World," 59
"16th Chamber/O.D.B. Special," 200, 202–203
"Skandalouz," 193
Skull & Bones, 57
"Slap! Slap! Slap!," 78
Slick Rick, 19, 20–22
The Slim Shady LP, 80, 81

Index **247**

"Słowiańska Krew," 33, 37
"Smooth Operator," 19–20
"Snappin' & Trappin'," 160
Snoop Dogg, 72–73, 181–184
"So Fresh, So Clean," 159
"Somebody's Gotta Die," 153
"Sound of da Police," 117–118
"Spaghetti Junction," 160
"Stan," 82–83
Stankonia, 158–161
"Starships," 149
Steampunk, 133
"Steve Berman," 83
"Still Makin' Moves," 50
Sting, 130–131
"Straight Outta Compton," 155
Straight Outta Compton, 154, 155–158
"Stranded on Death Row," 75
"Street Keep Callin'," 49
"Stupid Hoe," 149
The Sugarhill Gang, 185–187, 188
"Summer Friends," 45–46
"Summertime," 67
"Super Lyrical," 23
"Superstar," 101–102
"Survival," 69
Swing Mob Collective, 3

"Take a Minute," 143–144
Tech N9ne, 38–41
"Tell Him," 102
Temples of Boom, 56
Thiele, Bob, 177–178
"Things Done Changed," 152
"Threat," 109
3 Feet High and Rising, 62–63
"Thrift Shop," 131, 132–133
Timbaland, 34, 77–78
Timberlake, Justin, 122
To the 5 Boroughs, 18
"To Zion," 101
Toasting, 2
"TRG (The Rap Game)," 140

A Tribe Called Quest, 188–191
Trip hop, 218–219
"Trophy," 94
Tupac Shakur, 191–196
Turntablism, 207. *See also* Scratching
Twista, 39, 41
Twisted Insane, 39, 41
"2 Live Blues," 198
The 2 Live Crew, 196–199
"2 of Amerikaz Most Wanted," 193
2Pac. *See* Tupac Shakur
"Two Seater," 139

"U Can't Touch This," 135–136
U-God. *See* Wu-Tang Clan
"U.N.I.T.Y.," 173, 175–176
U.T.F.O., 58
"Ugly," 33, 34–35
Under Construction, 76, 78–79
"Under the Influence," 85
Universal Zulu Nation, 210
U$O, 39, 40

"Verses from the Abstract," 190

"Walk This Way," 170, 171–172
Wanz, 132–133
"Warning," 151
"The Way I Am," 83
"We Can't Be Stopped," 94
We Can't Be Stopped, 92, 93–96
"Welcome to the Terrordome," 167
West Coast rap, 5
"Wha'chu Like," 59
"What More Can I Say," 108–109, 110
"What's on Your Mind," 88
The White Album, 107, 110–112. *See also The Grey Album*
"Who Knew," 82
will.i.am, 128
"Work It," 79
"Worldwide Choppers," 39–41
Wu-Tang Clan, 200–203

248 Index

"Wu-Tang: 7th Chamber," 200–202
"Wu-Tang: 7th Chamber, Part II," 200, 202
Wyclef Jean, 99, 100, 102

"Xplosion," 161

Yeeeah Baby, 24–25
Yelawolf, 39, 40
"You Be Illin'," 172
"Your Love," 147

"Zodiac," 140

About the Author

ANTHONY J. FONSECA is library director and adjunct associate professor of humanities at Elms College in Massachusetts, where he teaches rock-and-roll history, rap music and rap lyrics as text, first year seminar, and serves as the college's interim archivist and rare books librarian. He is originally from Southeast Louisiana and currently resides in Western Massachusetts. Apparently, his interest in music began at a young age, when his mother had to place a radio in his crib so he would sleep at night. As a composer, songwriter, music engineer, and multi-instrumentalist for Dapper Kitty Music in Northampton, Massachusetts, he coproduces indie, progressive, hard rock, electronica, jazz, traditional covers, incidental music, spoken word, and poetry with music sound recordings.

As a scholar, Fonseca specializes in popular music (vampire-related music and hip hop) and film music (horror film). His books on music include *Hip Hop around the World: An Encyclopedia* (ABC-CLIO, 2018), coauthored and edited with Melissa Ursula Dawn Goldsmith, and *The Encyclopedia of Musicians and Bands on Film* (2016), coauthored with Paige A. Willson and Goldsmith. He has also written books on horror with June Michele Pulliam—*Ghosts in Popular Culture and Legend* (ABC-CLIO, 2016), *Richard Matheson's Monsters: Gender in the Stories, Scripts, Novels, and Twilight Zone Episodes* (2016), *Encyclopedia of the Zombie* (ABC-CLIO, 2014), *Hooked on Horror: A Guide to Reading Interests in Horror Fiction* (Libraries Unlimited, 2009, 2003, 1999), and *Read On . . . Horror* (Libraries Unlimited, 2006)—and one book on librarianship, *Proactive Marketing for the New and Experienced Library Director* (2014).

His book chapters on music have appeared in *Dracula's Daughters: The Female Vampire on Film* (2014), *Crossing Traditions: American Popular Music in Local and Global Contexts* (2013), and *The Fantastic Vampire: Studies in the Children of the Night* (Greenwood Press, 2002), and his reviews have appeared in *Screening the Past*, *Dead Reckonings: A Review of Horror Literature*, *The Journal of Film Music*, and *The Los Angeles Review of Books*. His works on horror have appeared in the book *Ramsey Campbell: Critical Essays on the Modern Master of Horror* (2013) and in the online journals *Aickman Studies* and *Dissections: The Journal of Contemporary Horror*. His works on librarianship have appeared in the book *Informed Transitions: Libraries Supporting the High School to College Transition* (ABC-CLIO, 2013), as well as in the journals *Technical Services Quarterly*, *Codex: The Journal of the Louisiana Chapter of the ACRL*, *Portal: Libraries and the Academy*, *Collaborative Librarianship*, *Louisiana Libraries*, and *Computers in Libraries*.